U.S. Health
Policy and Politics

U.S. Health Policy and Politics: A Documentary History

Kevin Hillstrom

Los Angeles | London | New Delhi
Singapore | Washington DC

Los Angeles | London | New Delhi
Singapore | Washington DC

FOR INFORMATION:

CQ Press
An Imprint of SAGE Publications, Inc.
2455 Teller Road
Thousand Oaks, California 91320
E-mail: order@sagepub.com

SAGE Publications Ltd.
1 Oliver's Yard
55 City Road
London, EC1Y 1SP
United Kingdom

SAGE Publications India Pvt. Ltd.
B 1/I 1 Mohan Cooperative Industrial Area
Mathura Road, New Delhi 110 044
India

SAGE Publications Asia-Pacific Pte. Ltd.
33 Pekin Street #02-01
Far East Square
Singapore 048763

Development Editor: Andrew Boney
Production Editor: Laura Stewart
Copy Editor: Colleen McGuiness
Typesetter: C&M Digitals, ltd.
Proofreader: Ellen Howard
Indexer: Gloria Tierney
Cover Designer: Naylor Design, Inc., Washington, DC
Marketing Manager: Ben Krasney

Printed in the United States of America

Library of Congress Cataloging-in-Publication Data

Hillstrom, Kevin, 1963-

U.S. health policy and politics : a documentary history / Kevin Hillstrom.

p. cm.
Includes bibliographical references and index.

ISBN 978-1-60871-026-3 (alk. paper)

1. Medical policy—United States—History. 2. Medical laws and legislation—United States—History. I. Title.

[DNLM: 1. Health Policy—history—United States. 2. Delivery of Health Care—history—United States. 3. Health Policy—legislation & jurisprudence—United States. 4. History, Modern 1601—United States. 5. Politics—United States. WA 11 AA1]

RA395.A3H555 2011

362.10973—dc23   2011019493

This book is printed on acid-free paper.

12 13 14 15 16 10 9 8 7 6 5 4 3 2

Contents

Documents

4. HEALTH CARE IN THE PROGRESSIVE ERA, 1890–1920   133

Documents

6.   PARTISAN JOUSTING OVER HEALTH CARE IN THE POSTWAR ERA, 1940–1960

Documents

Documents

Thematic Table of Contents

Documents

END-OF-LIFE ISSUES

ENVIRONMENTAL ISSUES AND FOOD SAFETY

HEALTH CARE REFORM EFFORTS
UNDER BARACK OBAMA

HEALTH CARE REFORM
EFFORTS UNDER BILL CLINTON

HEALTH INSURANCE, HEALTH
CARE REFORM, AND MEDICAL COSTS

HEALTH PROFESSIONALS AND MEDICAL EDUCATION

HEALTH SERVICES FOR SPECIAL GROUPS

HIV AND AIDS

HOSPITALS

MEDICAL RESEARCH

MEDICARE AND MEDICAID

MENTAL HEALTH

PHARMACEUTICALS AND VACCINES

SOCIAL SECURITY

TOBACCO

Preface

U.S. Health Policy and Politics: A Documentary History is part of CQ Press's new retrospective and topical documentary history series. These volumes are based on the same formula that has made CQ Press's acclaimed *Historic Documents* series a mainstay of public, university, and high school library collections across the country: carefully selected primary sources supplemented with authoritative original writing that provides vital context for featured documents.

Unlike the original *Historic Documents* series, which uses primary documents to chronicle worldwide events in politics, economics, popular culture, health, and other areas in a single calendar year, these new volumes are devoted to providing users with detailed information on a single major aspect of American history from the colonial era to the twenty-first century.

Overview of Coverage

As with every volume of the series, *U.S. Health Policy and Politics* provides a broad cross section of essential and illuminating—and some hard-to-find—primary source documents from various eras in American history. The approximately 150 documents featured in this book are necessary to any meaningful study of America's evolving attitudes and policies toward health care and health insurance. They provide fascinating insights into the perspectives of health care professionals, lawmakers, advocacy organizations, health industry players, and ordinary Americans on health care issues and controversies.

The book consists of a variety of document types from both governmental and nongovernmental sources. Legislative acts, presidential addresses, Senate floor speeches, court decisions, agency reports, and congressional testimony provide students with thorough documentation of government regulation and political debate. Examples of these primary sources range from early milestones such as An Act for the Relief of Sick and Disabled Seamen (1798) and Theodore Roosevelt's call for universal health insurance (1912) to materials that explain landmark events in the creation of the modern welfare state such as the Social Security Act (1935), the establishment of Medicare and Medicaid (1965), and the Patient Protection and Affordable Care Act (2010). Examples of nongovernmental sources range from an insurance executive's broadside against "government-run" health insurance (1920) to the triumphant reaction of disability activist Justin Dart when the Americans with Disabilities Act became law (1990).

In addition to these essential resources, *U.S. Health Policy and Politics* features numerous lesser-known documents that illuminate America's historical efforts to provide its citizens with competent and affordable health care and address pressing public health issues while still remaining true to the ideals of a capitalistic and individualistic society. Examples of these documents include Dorothea Dix's 1845 report on squalid conditions in American mental health facilities, the surgeon general's landmark 1964 report on smoking, and the U.S. Supreme Court's 1973 *Roe v. Wade* decision legalizing abortion. These and other works reveal long-standing disputes about whether access to health care constitutes a basic American right, as well as profound disagreements about the essential character and wisdom of government-run health care programs, systems, and regulations.

Together, this collection of primary documents constitutes a unique, unparalleled resource for the study of American attitudes and policymaking on health care from the colonial era to the present day. The wide breadth of coverage enables readers to explore the many ways in which past policy decisions and political attitudes have shaped modern health care policymaking and to understand why some political battles have recurred time and again over the past two centuries.

Organization of the Book

One of the chief goals of the topical documentary histories is to show how every featured primary document fits into the larger story of America's historical development. To meet this mandate of explaining how each primary source document is a response—in one way or another—to America's ever-evolving political, cultural, and demographic landscape, the authors place great emphasis on providing a historical context for understanding.

To that end, this volume is organized into thematic chapters. Most of the documents in these chapters are organized in chronological order, although a few are arranged by subject matter. Each chapter opens with an introductory overview that puts the primary documents in a larger social, political, economic, and scientific context. This informative chapter overview introduces the main players, events, and themes that are fleshed out in the documents. An authoritative headnote provides historical background about the document that follows. This introductory note provides details (who, what, where, when, why) about the circumstances under which the featured document was created. Together, these narratives provide users with a full understanding of the myriad forces that converged in the making of each document. Many of the documents have been excerpted to focus on their essential portions. In all cases, a full citation to the original is at the end of the document. The book also contains a chronology of major health care laws and events in U.S. history, a bibliography of sources used in the production of the book, and a subject index.

Acknowledgments

Many archivists, researchers, historians, and librarians were of enormous help to me during the course of this project. I received especially valuable and timely assistance from Geraldine Strey and Harry Miller at the Wisconsin Historical Society, Julia Proctor at the University of Michigan's Harlan Hatcher Graduate Library, Daniel Hope of the George J. Mitchell Department of Special Collections and Archives at Bowdoin College, Larry DeWitt at the Social Security Administration, Cindy Lachin in the Food and Drug Administration's History Office, and Russell L. Riley of the Presidential Oral History Program at the University of Virginia's Miller Center for Public Affairs.

I would like to extend my thanks to the entire staff at the Brighton District Library in Brighton, Michigan, for their friendly professionalism. I relied on the staff early and often in the production of this work. I am also deeply indebted to Doug Goldenberg-Hart, Andrew Boney, Laura Stewart, Josh Benjamin, and Andrea Bradley at CQ Press for their hard work in guiding this book to completion. Thanks also to copyeditor Colleen McGuiness for her help in polishing the manuscript.

Introduction

Health care politics and policymaking have undergone many permutations in the United States over the last two hundred–plus years. Back in the earliest days of the republic—and even before then, when European colonists carved out their earliest footholds in the New World—regulation of medicine was practically nonexistent. Early American lawmakers occasionally crafted quarantine measures and other legislation to address threats to the health of the wider community. Meanwhile, the generally poor quality of health care available from medical practitioners kept prices of health care goods and services within the reach of people of even very modest means.

This state of affairs remained in place for much of the nineteenth century. The questionable efficacy of medical treatment, combined with America's affinity for individual liberty and free market economics, kept state and federal regulation over the private health care industry to a minimum through the 1850s. The Civil War spurred the creation of a variety of new health care institutions and agencies to care for wounded soldiers. Later in the century, increased scientific knowledge and improved methods of medical treatment brought greater acceptance of public health programs, as well as medical licensing and other forms of regulatory oversight.

The pivotal era in the history of American health care—and American health care politics—came in the 1910s and 1920s. These years encompassed the end of the Progressive Era, when many Americans came to feel that state and federal authorities had the right, and even the obligation, to take up arms against poverty, corruption, and other social ills. Simultaneously, biomedical advances ushered in revolutionary breakthroughs in medical practice that suddenly made health care a genuinely valuable commodity. And as demand for the services provided by American hospitals, physicians, and other health care institutions rose, the price of those services steadily rose. Health care—a commodity unlike other, more elective, items in the American marketplace—promptly soared out of the financial reach of a growing percentage of American households at the very same time that it became worth having. This development, which took place with disorienting speed for lawmakers, health care practitioners, and especially patients, gave rise to private "sickness" insurance and, in the 1930s and 1940s, various schemes of government-subsidized health insurance (known as "socialized medicine" to its detractors).

In the post–World War II era, health care politics in America became even more complex. A steady succession of medical discoveries and innovations enabled people with access to health care to live longer and healthier lives than ever before. But millions of poor and working-class Americans remained unable to afford the new drugs and treatments. The extension of health care benefits and financial aid to these populations thus became a growing preoccupation of liberal reformers and a rising source of alarm to fiscal conservatives. In addition, health issues that had previously been nascent (tobacco use, abortion, disability rights, air and water pollution) or nonexistent (acquired immune deficiency syndrome or AIDS, physician-assisted suicide) emerged as major hot-button topics with significant economic, cultural, and moral implications.

In the 1960s state involvement in health care reached its zenith with the advent of Medicare and Medicaid. These ambitious entitlement programs, which were crafted to extend health care services to the elderly and the poor, respectively, were of enormous benefit to tens of millions of Americans. But the cost of these programs was also immense, and the fiscal scaffoldings of Medicare and Medicaid quickly emerged as two of the more explosive flashpoints in the ongoing debates over health policy in America.

Since then, the financial stakes of health care regulation and policymaking seemed to grow exponentially higher with each passing decade. By the late 1990s health care spending accounted for nearly 15 percent of the American economy, and all of the king-doms within the industry guarded their income streams with cunning and tenacity. The various industry stakeholders—doctors and other professional medical practitioners, hospitals and other care facilities, pharmaceutical companies, medical product manufac-turers, commercial insurance companies, medical education institutions—have become adept at using their tremendous economic resources to reshape health care policymaking to their liking. The presence of all this money has made the jockeying for political posi-tioning and legislative victory more intense than ever.

Ultimately, American lawmakers, health care industry titans, and consumers are still warring over the same two fundamental questions that came to the fore back in the 1920s, when access to health care became an important facet of American life: What is the appropriate role of state and federal governments in the protection of public health and the provision of health care for the poor, children, senior citizens, people with disabilities, and other vulnerable constituencies? How should the nation respond to the ever-spiraling cost of U.S. style health care and its attendant economic drain on American families and businesses?

As a review of the following pages shows, these distinct but deeply intertwined issues—opposing sides of the same golden coin—have shaped the character of every major piece of health care legislation that has passed or failed to pass in the last one hun-dred years, including Franklin D. Roosevelt's 1935 Social Security Act, Lyndon B. John-son's Medicare and Medicaid programs, the failed national health insurance initiatives of Harry S. Truman, Richard M. Nixon, and Bill Clinton, and Barack Obama's 2010 Patient Protection and Affordable Care Act.

CHAPTER 1

Health Care and Medical Practice in the New World

1600–1800

When European settlers arrived in the New World in the seventeenth and eighteenth centuries, their daily battles for survival against disease and illness were waged with crude medicines and treatments that betrayed ignorance of basic tenets of biology and germ theory. Despite these impediments, the early colonists survived and in some cases even prospered. As the early colonies grew out of the North American wilderness—one that was peopled by numerous indigenous tribes—medical practice and care in frontier homesteads and early cities evolved into an amalgam of traditional folk remedies, European therapies of learned medicine imported from the Old World, and reliance on indigenous plants and practices that were curative staples of Native American tribes.

Still, medical care remained sorely lacking in large cities and small hamlets alike. During the 1700s, this problem was further exacerbated by incompetent or unscrupulous quacks, who rushed to meet the soaring market demand for relief from pain and illness. But medical education advanced only fitfully in the colonies, and occasional calls to impose some legal parameters on the activities of physicks (physicians), chirurgeons (surgeons), and apothecaries failed to gain traction in a colonial environment that excoriated government tyranny, praised individual initiative on economic matters, and held to a fatalistic faith in providential design on many matters of life and death. As a result, few proposals to regulate medical schooling, licensing, and the daily practice of medicine and surgery were successful. The only meaningful exceptions to this generally hostile attitude toward regulation came in the areas of disease prevention and national defense, two realms in which regulatory intervention could be robustly defended as vital to the common good.

MEDICAL CARE IN THE EARLY COLONIAL SETTLEMENTS

The earliest British colonies in America attracted few doctors, so the small number of physicians who did decide to chart new lives for themselves in the New World were spread few and far between among the settlements. Most educated physicians in Europe were already content with their lives of privilege and comfort. They saw no reason to uproot themselves and their families for an uncertain existence on the other side of the cold Atlantic. The main exception to this rule was the minister-physician who was motivated to emigrate from Europe to escape religious or political persecution.

These individuals were generally men of God first and physicians second, but they nonetheless possessed far greater knowledge of basic anatomy and medical practice than their less-educated pilgrim peers. These clergymen played dominant roles in both the practice and the academic study of medicine in the early colonies. Minister-physicians such as Samuel Fuller, one of the founders of the Plymouth Colony, not only became pillars of the colonial communities in which they lived, but also emerged as their foremost health authorities.

As the colonies expanded in size and territory, the medical work of these elite minister-physicians was supplemented by contributions from a steadily expanding assortment of midwives, bonesetters, apprentice-trained physicians, and entrepreneurial dispensers of folk remedies. The growth in these practitioners' numbers stemmed in part from the continued absence of formally trained health professionals in most rural outposts and villages. But even larger towns experienced severe shortages of trained practitioners.

This dynamic became more problematic as colonial populations grew, for the colonies of the seventeenth century had neither the resources nor the inclination to develop the necessary infrastructure—whether in the form of medical colleges or physicians' guilds—to produce home-grown physicians, surgeons, and apothecaries. Besides, the relatively few trained doctors who did ply their trade in the colonies generally practiced heroic medicine, a system of treatment that emphasized vomiting, bloodletting, blistering, high doses of toxic drugs such as calomel, and other horrific and counterproductive prescriptions for restoring patients' humors to their proper balance and thus "curing" them. Practitioners of heroic medicine "could neither prevent nor cure most of the disorders troubling patients," wrote medical historian John Duffy. Given that grim reality, concluded Duffy, "it is not surprising that the public turned to anyone who could promise relief."[1]

The other main source of medical assistance in seventeenth-century colonial towns and farmhouses came from local Indian tribespeople who knew how to unlock the healing properties of indigenous plants found in the surrounding woodlands, marshes, and meadows. Some colonists, hamstrung by deep-seated prejudices, could not bring themselves to accept medical help from what they considered a heathen source (although they often embraced this knowledge when it came to them via a more circuitous route; some white herbalists in the colonies came to rely on sales of remedies appropriated from local Indians for much of their business). Other early settlers, however, eagerly cultivated the medical knowledge of Indian healers, whom they praised as "Incomparable Physicians" and possessors of "extraordinary Skill and Success." As one Englishman commented after traveling through the Carolina colonies in 1701, Indian healers routinely performed "admirable Cures . . . which would puzzle a great many graduate Practitioners."[2] One North Carolinian even suggested in 1714 that intermarriage with local tribespeople should be encouraged in part because it would help colonists obtain "a true Knowledge of all the Indian's Skill in Medicine and Surgery."[3]

Unfortunately, Native American knowledge of the medicinal benefits of local plants provided little defense against the deadly pathogens that European explorers and colonists brought with them to the New World. These infectious diseases (smallpox, measles, typhus, diphtheria, and others) were soon supplemented by yellow fever, hookworm, and other public health menaces introduced via the African slave trade. These virulent diseases spread like wildfire among the Indian tribes. Bereft of any immunological defenses against the diseases, many native populations suffered horrific outbreaks without ever laying eyes on a white man.

Some early colonists expressed regret about this grim phenomenon. In 1617, for instance, Plymouth Colony governor William Bradford delivered a stark account of the toll of disease on coastal Indians who had engaged in trade with whites: "Thousands of them dyed, they not being able to burie one another; their sculs and bones were found in many places lying still above ground, where their houses & dwellings had been; a very sad spectacle to behold."[4] Less than two decades later, a Massachusetts Bay colonist reported that "whole towns" of local Indians had been "swept away [by smallpox], in some not so much as one soul escaping Destruction."[5] As disputes of land ownership and resource use intensified with westward settlement, the Indians' vulnerability to European diseases became a key factor in white land acquisition efforts. In numerous instances, white settlers and soldiers moving deeper into the interior found that epidemics of deadly disease had already preceded them, severely eroding the capacity of resident tribes to stave off the incursions.

Smallpox and other deadly diseases among the tribes were usually the unintentional result of social interactions between and among Indian tribes and white communities. In a few notorious cases, however, whites knowingly employed what amounted to germ warfare in their efforts to remove "troublesome" Indians who insisted on clinging to traditional territories in the face of white advances. In 1763, for example, British troops consciously doled out blankets from the smallpox hospital in the Ohio River Valley's Fort Pitt to visiting Indians in hopes of sparking an epidemic. As one British officer darkly wrote in his journal, "Out of our regard to them, we gave them two blankets and an handkerchief out of the Small Pox Hospital. I hope it will have the desired effect." His hopes were fulfilled, as smallpox erupted among the tribes of the Ohio Valley a short time after the bestowal of this "gift."[6]

QUARANTINES AND OTHER EARLY PUBLIC HEALTH LAWS

The white residents of the British colonies also suffered greatly from periodic epidemics of infectious diseases. As one historian summarized, epidemics struck the colonies "with relentless regularity, leaving a train of death and debility in their wake."[7] These events did not reach the holocaust-like dimensions of the outbreaks that swept through Indian encampments and tribal groups, but fearsome epidemics of highly communicable diseases such as smallpox, measles, and yellow fever ripped through Boston, Charleston, New Orleans, Philadelphia, and other cities on a recurring basis in the seventeenth and eighteenth centuries. Some of these outbreaks claimed the lives of as much as 10 percent of the local population.

Colonial officials and humble farmers alike recognized that communicable diseases cast a pall over everyday life in British America, to say nothing of its economic, cultural, and territorial development. Consequently, municipal officials and colonial governors gradually approved an assortment of regulatory measures to address this threat. These generally modest regulations—the earliest public health laws in America—took a variety of forms. Primitive sanitation practices, such as disposal of sewage, trash, and livestock waste, were codified into law by officials acting on a vague but accurate recognition that disease often blossomed in areas of filth and decay. The first of these public sanitation regulations was passed in Virginia Colony in 1610 (**See Document 1.1**), but other colonial communities quickly followed suit.

Overcrowded and polluted conditions in fast-growing cities became a particular spur to the implementation of these regulations. In 1634, for example, the city of Boston passed a law prohibiting the dumping of fish or other garbage near common landings. In 1644 the Dutch city fathers of New Amsterdam passed an ordinance prohibiting the deposition of filth and other trash in the harbor, then followed up thirteen years later with a law that prohibited dumping of garbage in the streets. In Charleston, legislation was passed in

1698 giving officials the authority to fill up offensive privies and shut down livestock yards and slaughterhouses deemed to be a "nuisance." In 1721 the Philadelphia assembly passed a law that expressly prohibited the slaughter of any animals within city limits.

By the early eighteenth century, municipal and provincial authorities introduced numerous public health regulations. These ordinances were especially popular in the burgeoning population centers of the Northeast: New York, Boston, and Philadelphia. By 1700, in fact, these towns had passed ordinances governing everything from the disposal of trash and animal carcasses and the placement, construction, and maintenance of privies and sewage systems to the imposition of business zones for slaughterhouse operations, tanneries, and other high-polluting industries.

These limited measures, however, did nothing to address the primary vectors of disease to the New World: the ships that brought colonists, slaves, livestock, and rats to America from European, African, and Caribbean ports. To respond to the specter of shipborne plague, city authorities and assemblymen up and down the Atlantic coastline imposed a variety of naval quarantine measures. Inspections of incoming ships for suspected contagions, as well as measures to arrange for the quarantine of mariners and cargo in positive cases, were introduced as early as 1629 in the Massachusetts Bay Colony, but historians identify a measure adopted by the General Assembly of Pennsylvania in 1700 as the first full-fledged quarantine act in colonial history.[8] This act, titled "An act to prevent sickly vessels coming into this Government," imposed a penalty of one hundred pounds on any infected vessel that landed at any port in Pennsylvania province **(See Document 1.4)**. Other quarantine acts of similar scope and intent soon followed in Massachusetts (1701), South Carolina (1712), Virginia (1722), and Delaware (1726). By the beginning of the Revolutionary War in 1775, most of the colonies had an assortment of naval quarantine regulations on their books (the first federal quarantine act, designed to supplement instead of supplant state laws, was adopted by Congress in 1799).[9]

In addition to ship quarantines, city leaders and provincial lawmakers introduced laws designed to isolate disease carriers who were already in the general population. Authorities in the colonies used public funds to construct pesthouses to sequester residents and sailors who fell victim to infectious disease, while other towns kept sick people locked up in their own residences. The specific isolation methods employed by these locales varied somewhat. In Virginia, for instance, sentinels were deployed outside homes with outbreaks to keep visitors away, and ordinances passed in Massachusetts and South Carolina required infected households to post warnings outside their doors.[10] In some instances, entire towns suffering from outbreaks of smallpox, measles, or other infectious diseases were "cut off from all communication with the rest of the country," in the words of one Frenchman passing through eighteenth-century Virginia.[11] These sorts of precautions were by no means sufficient to eliminate the threat of deadly epidemics at busy seaports and surrounding environs, especially because business interests dependent on maritime trade often worked against the establishment and enforcement of quarantine regulations. Nonetheless, the more stringent and tightly enforced acts may have forestalled or reduced the severity of some outbreaks.

State Support for Early Colonial Hospitals

Although the Spanish were the first American colonizers to establish hospitals in the New World—by the close of the 1600s they had erected more than 150 hospitals for poor Spanish and indigenous patients across New Spain—the British colonial hospital model would ultimately prove more influential and durable.[12] The first hospital built in the British colonies was located in Virginia, but it was lost to an Indian uprising in 1622, a mere ten years after it opened. Most of the health care institutions that arose during the remainder of the colonial era were almshouses, which were built and operated more with an eye toward charity and social welfare than medical science and profit.

The colonial-era almshouse was created by local authorities who recognized that they had to make some sort of provision for the care of indigent community members and passing strangers who were stricken with severe illness or other disability. In addition, many communities placed orphans, the insane, the senile, and the crippled in these institutions. Finally, colonial officials used almshouses as mechanisms for social control, depositing public nuisances—a designation that could encompass epileptics, beggars, and other disturbers of community tranquility—within almshouse walls. By the close of the seventeenth century, almshouses were widely recognized as the homes of people, young and old, who simply had nowhere else to go. All other colonists (those with functional shelter, financial resources, and family support systems) continued to receive health care treatment and undergo convalescence in their own homes.

The funding and operation of colonial almshouses was usually the joint responsibility of local government and area churches. Townships raised money for the care and sustenance of almshouse residents through a poor tax levied on community members, while churches used poor boxes and other means to raise money for the institutions. In some cases, municipal and church officials also used these funds to pay for in-home care, by compensating colonists who took care of seriously infirm neighbors, for instance. But this general policy of benevolence, borne out of a combination of communal identity and religion-based conceptions of brotherhood and mercy, was extended more grudgingly to transients needing care. In Virginia, for example, assemblymen in 1727 passed a statute that mandated the return of a sick transient to the parish of his or her origin. If the illness or disability was too severe to make this a reasonable option, the community from which the traveler hailed was legally responsible to reimburse the caregiving community for all services. Similar statutes were passed in subsequent decades in Plymouth Colony **(See Document 1.2)** and other places.

The publicly funded almshouse did not begin its metamorphosis into the modern diagnosis and treatment-oriented hospital that is known today until the mid-eighteenth century. In 1752 Philadelphia's Pennsylvania Hospital, established through the combined support of the provincial legislature and wealthy private sponsors, became the first permanent general hospital in America built specifically to care for the sick instead of the indigent. By the close of the eighteenth century, a handful of other hospitals—some springing directly from existing almshouses—had also been established in the fast-growing port cities of Boston, New Orleans, and New York. In addition, philanthropic medicine dispensaries, which provided free outpatient care to the poor and served as a valuable training ground for medical students, were opened in Philadelphia (1786) and New York City (1791).

THE BOSTON SMALLPOX EPIDEMIC OF 1721

Although widespread agreement existed in most colonial communities about the necessity of providing basic care and sustenance for the sick and poor, reaching consensus on virtually any other aspect of public health or the practice of medicine remained a considerably more difficult task. Riven by competing economic interests and clashing beliefs about science, medicine, capitalism, and religious practice, towns and cities frequently had

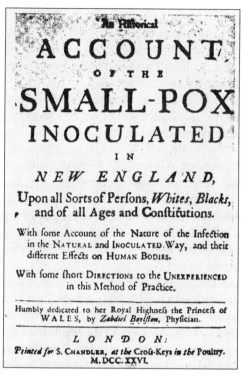

At the height of the smallpox inoculation debate, pro-variolation advocate Dr. Zabdiel Boylston released a comparative study of fatality rates between smallpox victims who underwent variolation and those who did not.

difficulty attaining unity when confronting epidemics, sources of water pollution, and other threats to the general health of the community.

This fact was brought home in particularly vivid detail during the Boston smallpox epidemic of 1721, which cleaved that town's medical and religious elite into two bitter factions. The smallpox outbreak began in April 1721. By the time it ran its course in December, nearly six thousand Bostonians had contracted the disease and 844 had died of it, which accounted for about 75 percent of the city's total deaths that year.[13] When smallpox first began ravaging the city, some prominent Bostonians, including the Reverend Cotton Mather (who had earlier lost his wife and three children to a measles epidemic) and the Reverend Benjamin Colman, urged citywide variolation, that is, smallpox inoculation. They pointed out that the practice had long been successfully employed in Africa, China, and Europe, insisted that variolation would save the lives of countless Bostonians, and argued that the very *capacity* to inoculate against smallpox was a gift from God **(See Document 1.6)**. The only Boston physician who was persuaded by their arguments, however, was Zabdiel Boylston, who launched a voluntary variolation program that eventually inoculated about 180 city residents.

The unresponsiveness of the rest of Boston's physician community to the entreaties of Mather and Colman was due in large part to a formidable antivariolation campaign led by William Douglass, the city's only university-trained doctor. Douglass and his supporters argued that variolation might worsen the epidemic. This fear that had some basis in fact, for primitive inoculation did cause fatalities in a few cases. They also argued that smallpox inoculation amounted to interference with God's divine plan **(See Document 1.7)**. Tensions steadily rose between the camps, and at one point opponents of variolation bombed Mather's home.

After the crisis passed, Mather and Boylston sponsored a comparative analysis study to defend their viewpoint. They reported that the fatality rate for Bostonians who contracted the disease naturally was 14 percent, while those who underwent variolation had only a 2 percent fatality rate. These data did not assuage the Douglass camp. When Boylston launched a second program of voluntary variolation in the spring of 1722, Boston officials immediately quarantined recipients and forbade the physician from undertaking further inoculations "without the knowledge & approbation of the Authority of the Town." Douglass rejoiced at this development, declaring that the "Serpent" of inoculation had been "effectually crushed in the Bud, by the *Justices, Select-Men*, and the *unanimous Vote* of a general Town-Meeting."[14]

Douglass's gloating was premature, however. To be sure, resistance to inoculation remained strong in some places. Virginia, for example, passed punitive legislation against physicians practicing variolation as late as 1769 **(See Document 1.10)**.[15] The success of the variolation program championed by Mather, Colman, and Boylston, along with the deadly impact of subsequent smallpox outbreaks in the 1750s and 1760s, spurred gradual growth in public support for inoculation programs across much of the British colonies. The Continental Army's successful smallpox inoculation program during the Revolutionary War further increased public comfort with the practice. By the close of the 1700s, when physicians Edward Jenner and Benjamin Waterhouse carried out pioneering work in variolation, immunology was regarded as a legitimate and valuable weapon in combating epidemic disease.

An Unregulated Marketplace for Health Care Practitioners

Domestic and maritime quarantine regulations were generally regarded as appropriate responses to smallpox, measles, yellow fever, and other fearsome, shadowy threats to the collective well-being of the community. In addition, many legislators and public officials showed no hesitation about wading into controversies over inoculation and other public health matters. The British colonies, however, showed no corresponding appetite for overseeing the private practice of medicine, even as the number of such practitioners exploded in various population centers (physician shortages remained acute in rural communities). For much of the seventeenth century, colonial authorities were generally uncomfortable with doing anything beyond passing vague appeals to medical practitioners to carry out their duties in a moral manner **(See Document 1.3)**. As a result, the health care marketplace in colonial America metastasized into a riot of competing factions by the early eighteenth century, with every camp boasting batteries of intensive treatments, strange ointments, and overheated rhetoric to attract sick patients.

So-called "regular physicians" operated from a fairly attractive, though by no means unassailable, vantage point in this feverish scramble for business. Many of these practitioners, the beneficiaries of training in European medical schools, possessed considerable advantages in social station, political connections, access to information about cutting-edge scientific research, and financial resources for the acquisition of new pharmaceutical treatments and medical equipment. These physicians cultivated a self-consciously elite and exclusive place for themselves within the wider egalitarian culture of the colonies, and the best of them "provided satisfactory medical care and were highly regarded in their communities," as historian John Duffy noted.[16]

Even so, medical care at the hands of a regular physician was hardly a surefire path to wellness. Many subscribed to monism, a belief that all disease stemmed from one cause, and even the most highly trained physician had very limited scientific and medical knowledge by twenty-first-century standards. "For example, because of the absence of any knowledge of infection, even the best trained physicians could unknowingly transmit puerperal fever to their obstetrical cases," wrote historian William G. Rothstein. "An outstanding Boston physician of the period wrote: 'In general the physical practice in our colonies is so perniciously bad that, excepting in surgery and some very acute cases, it is better to let nature, under a proper regimen, take her course than to trust to the honesty and sagacity of the practitioner. . . . Frequently there is more danger from the physician than from the distemper.'"[17] The professional practitioner's continued allegiance to heroic medicine was responsible for many of these regrettable outcomes. As Duffy observed,

> [C]olonial records abound with complaints of patients dying from excessive purging and vomiting. The prescription for a patient suffering from rheumatism in 1720 illustrates this point all too well. On the first day the patient was to be purged twice. On the second day he or she was to be bled twelve to fourteen ounces of blood, preferably from the foot. A day or so later the patient was to be purged twice more. On the days when purging or bleeding was not carried out, the patient was to be given various powders and herbal concoctions. If nothing else, this treatment must at least have had the merit of distracting the patient's attention from the pains of rheumatism.[18]

Another broad group of medical practitioners consisted of occupational specialists: bonesetters, midwives, surgeons, and apothecaries who provided a relatively narrow range of services to patients. Skilled and experienced midwives were especially prized in colonial settlements, for they provided a potent mix of obstetrical, pediatric, and nursing services to families.

Colonists suffering from health disorders also had the option of seeking the services of a physician whose medical knowledge came not from a European university, but rather from apprenticeship with an already established physician. Formally trained physicians were dismissive of these "country doctors." One practitioner in Virginia offered a representative sentiment of his professional class when he proposed that such physicians advertise their services with a coat of arms ornamented with three duck heads and the motto, "Quack, Quack, Quack."[19] Nonetheless, apprenticeship was the leading form of medical training throughout the later colonial period. Moreover, the relatively small ranks of the regulars received valuable replenishment during the latter half of the 1700s from striving apprentices who went on to seek formal education in London, England, Edinburgh, Scotland, and other centers of medical instruction. "The ones who returned home," explained historian Paul Starr, "brought back with them the ambition to create in America a profession with the standards and dignity that physicians in Europe possessed."[20]

The small frontier communities that dotted the colonies did not generate enough business for formally trained physicians, so health care was often provided in these hamlets through empirics, untrained folk medicine practitioners who purveyed to their clients a distinctive blend of superstition and commonsense remedies gleaned from years of practical experience. These types of practices became popular in many population centers as well, to the considerable dismay of regulars.

Finally, many colonial families sought no outside assistance whatsoever for their health problems. Unable to afford professional care or distrustful of its possible impact on their loved ones, these early Americans relied instead on domestic medicine, which blended the healing traditions of family or clan with medical advice culled from early almanacs, newspapers, physician-penned pamphlets, and book-length guides to domestic practice, such as John Wesley's *Primitive Physick* (1747) and William Buchan's *Domestic Medicine* (1771). "Any individual who could read could treat," summarized scholar Oscar Reiss.[21]

In the best cases, these resources served as repositories of useful information about disease outbreaks or provided helpful assistance to laymen in identifying illnesses or producing their own domestic herbal medicines. But a good deal of the health and treatment information contained in this literature was erroneous and, thus, destructive in that it ushered many readers down false paths of healing. Some of these resources openly blended medicine with astrology, with one book instructing readers to "take a vomit when the moon is in Aries, Taurus, or Capricorn."[22]

Most notably, colonial newspapers became the preferred method of advertising patent medicines (also known as nostrums) to members of the public. "The development of newspapers and patent medicines went hand in hand," wrote historian James Harvey Young. "Without the advertising columns, nostrum makers reached only a small portion of the public. Without the revenue from patent medicine advertising, newspapers would have been deprived of an important source of income. Such advertising had its origin in the *Boston News-Letter* in 1704. Benjamin Franklin set ads for Seneca Rattlesnake Root and Dr. Bateman's Pectoral Drops."[23]

CHARLATANS, QUACKS, AND THE PATENT MEDICINE TRADE

Eighteenth-century colonial America offered an exceedingly hospitable environment for the rise of medical charlatans and quacks. The citizens of towns and villages remained generally uneducated, but they were increasingly affluent and thus able to pay for treatment. Moreover, public health and sanitation regulations remained in their infancy, effective practices of preventive health had yet to be incorporated into daily life, existing health care options failed to inspire confidence, and the rugged nature of daily colonial existence frequently resulted in injuries. Finally, the devastating impact that long-term disability or sickness could have on one's economic fortunes in colonial America made seeking medical help an imperative in many cases. Citizens, however, were left in a state of bewilderment by the cacophony of imprecations that regular and irregular practitioners leveled at one another. "Reputable doctors waged violent pamphlet warfare contesting the merits of their respective monisms," observed Young. "With regular medicine in such a state, quackery was bound to flourish. . . . Amidst the babel of appeals, whom was the average citizen to believe?"[24]

The quack doctors and nostrum promoters who stepped into this breach were not all malicious and greedy hucksters. Some genuinely believed that their treatments and elixirs could help people in their struggles with asthma, diarrhea, gout, syphilis, nearsightedness, scurvy, halitosis, fever, arthritis, and other afflictions. But many others were charlatans who knowingly trafficked in fraudulent claims about the curative powers of their services and products to reap financial gain. And because the colonies imposed no meaningful restrictions on the practice of medicine, both frauds and skilled midwives, bonesetters, and other practitioners were free to set up shop wherever they liked. "Quacks abound like locusts in Egypt," wrote William A. Smith, a famous historian of eighteenth-century New York City. "This is the less to be wondered at, as the profession is under no kind of regulation. Loud as the call is, to our shame be it remembered, we have no law to protect the lives of the king's subjects, from the malpractice of pretenders. Any man, at his pleasure, sets up for physician, apothecary, and chirurgeon. No candidates are either examined or licensed, or even sworn to fair practice."[25]

The first patent medicines were introduced to America from England, where they were initially manufactured. The term "patent medicine" was in actuality a misnomer. The manufacturers refused to divulge the contents of their nostrums, so their products were not legally patented in the literal sense (though bottle designs, labels, and explanatory pamphlets for nostrums could be patented). Instead, they became linked in the popular imagination with "patents of royal favor"—legally sanctioned monopolies, essentially—that kings of England and British Parliaments had bestowed on some medicine makers in the seventeenth century.

As these nostrums filtered into the colonies, customers initially put great stock in ensuring that the potions originated in England. Advertisers took pains to list the name of the vessel that carried the medicines to America from the Old Country until the Revolutionary War and the attendant cessation of trade with England. When that pipeline was cut off, home-grown nostrums were quickly developed and gained widespread acceptance, in large part because of continued public dissatisfaction with the services offered by physicians.[26] This enthusiasm for patent medicines, many of which were heavily garnished with alcohol or narcotics, became an even greater public health threat in the 1800s.

COLONIAL EFFORTS TO REGULATE HEALTH CARE SERVICES

During the eighteenth century, the continued dismal state of medicine in the British colonies finally prompted disillusioned legislators, fearful citizens, and frustrated regular physicians to call for some measure of regulatory intervention by the state. Up to this point, the only forays of this nature had been extremely limited. In addition to the aforementioned smattering of ethics codes for practitioners, a handful of colonies imposed loose ordinances protecting patients from excessive medical service fees in the seventeenth and early eighteenth centuries. The most stringent and influential of these early laws was probably the one passed by Virginia legislators in 1736 (**See Document 1.8**). Occasional efforts to codify the duties of midwives and other practitioners, both to their patients and the larger society, also appeared during the first half of the eighteenth century (**See Document 1.5**). Finally, some Southern colonies imposed draconian laws to ensure that black slaves would not prepare or administer medicine. One such mid-eighteenth-century law called for the execution, without the presence of clergy, of slaves found to have practiced medicine without the express consent of their master (in cases in which the slave's health care efforts did not have a detrimental effect on the patient, the architects of the bill magnanimously allowed for a sentence of death with clergy).[27]

Not until the 1750s and 1760s, however, did the professional class of regular physicians mount a sustained, and partially successful, drive to improve the state of health care through the establishment of meaningful medical licensing laws. (In the 1600s it was not uncommon for legislatures to bestow honorific licenses on individual physicians who had been of special service to the colony.) To be sure, this campaign was not an entirely, or even primarily, altruistic one. Economic self-interest lay at the root of much of the regular physicians' support for licensing, for the simple reason that it would cull the herd of competitors swirling around them. Nonetheless, the calls for licensing of medical practitioners were received sympathetically by a number of state legislatures.

The push for medical licensing of physicians, apothecaries, surgeons, and other health caregivers owed much to the mid-eighteenth-century founding and development of two important medical institutions. Eager to promote their professional bona fides and distinguish themselves from irregular practitioners, regular physicians at this time organized numerous local and state medical societies that bore more than a passing resemblance to the medical guilds that had long been powerful influences on medicine and law back in England. The first American medical schools were also established around this period, starting with the University of Pennsylvania in 1765 and King's College in New York City in 1767.[28]

The emergence of domestic medical schools and professional medical societies gave physicians and surgeons important vehicles through which they could amplify their calls for licensing regulations. Faculty staff and societies energetically petitioned city governments and state legislatures to step in and impose licensing requirements that would weed out the quacks, charlatans, and frauds gumming up the medical trade. These efforts had only a limited impact, and legions of quacks continued to ply their trade. But in some places, such as Maryland and South Carolina, medical societies not only successfully pressed for licensing legislation, but also managed to have the responsibility for examination and licensing placed in the hands of the societies themselves. In other places, they contented themselves with state or municipal oversight of the licensing process. In 1760, for example, New York City passed an ordinance forbidding anyone from working as a surgeon or physician until he secured formal approval from an examining board of distinguished laymen that included a state supreme court judge, the state attorney general, and the city's mayor **(See Document 1.9)**. Twelve years later, New Jersey followed suit with a similar law that "placed responsibility for granting licenses exclusively in the hands of laymen (political and judicial officeholders) who were empowered to solicit the advice of physicians. Here, too, it was believed that intelligent laymen were quite competent to evaluate the ability of physicians."[29]

Not all lawmakers were swayed by these campaigns. Leery of monopolies or sympathetically disposed to irregular medical practitioners, legislators in Pennsylvania and Virginia rejected medical society licensing drives in the late 1700s. And some of the licensing laws that were proposed or enacted were so modest that they elicited expressions of disdain from well-established regular physicians. In 1799 correspondence to another physician, for example, New York doctor S. L. Mitchell wrote: "There is an act of the Legislature relative to the practice of Physick and Surgery, but it is a poor stupid thing, and I believe few pay any attention to it."[30]

Despite these setbacks, the general trend toward professionalism and licensing in the field of health care continued apace. The leadership of elite physicians in America's successful bid for independence from Great Britain was an important element in this regard. Twenty-six physicians were members of the Continental Congress, and four doctors—Josiah Bartlett, Lyman Hall, Benjamin Rush, and Matthew Thornton—were among the signatories to the Declaration of Independence.[31] After the Revolution, the opinions of these distinguished regular physicians carried even more weight in their respective communities. Moreover, the licensing cause was aided by explosive growth in the regular physician fraternity from expanding apprenticeship programs and the new medical colleges. This same growth drove the establishment of new medical societies and guilds as well. During the 1780s and 1790s, in fact, several states passed bills that established medical societies and imposed licensing regulations in one fell swoop. Such bills were passed into law in Massachusetts (1781), New Hampshire (1791), Connecticut (1792), Maryland (1799), and Rhode Island (1812).[32]

SHIFTING ATTITUDES ABOUT GOVERNMENT'S ROLE IN PUBLIC HEALTH

The Revolutionary War also provided the first rumblings of a tectonic shift in attitude toward governmental responsibility for public health. The war had come about as a direct result of colonial unhappiness with the abuses and overreaching of monarchical central authority, and the U.S. Constitution ratified in 1787 did not explicitly frame community health as a federal or state responsibility. Nonetheless, wartime experiences convinced many Americans that at least some measure of government direction was necessary in the realm of health. This belief stemmed in large part from the experiences of Continental Army troops during the War for Independence.

When the Revolutionary War broke out in 1775, a handful of colonies—most notably Massachusetts—took decisive steps to provide quality medical care for their troops, from reviewing the qualifications of regimental surgeons to arranging for the purchase of adequate medical supplies and the establishment of military hospitals. But other provincial legislatures were slow to follow suit. In addition, the Army Medical Hospital created by the Second Continental Congress in July 1775 to oversee the Continental Army's health affairs performed indifferently for much of the war due to shortages of supplies and qualified doctors, as well as bureaucratic inefficiencies. The primitive state of battlefield surgery and ignorance of basic sanitation measures among militia members also took a heavy toll, although the distribution of Benjamin Rush's 1777 pamphlet *Directions for Preserving the Health of Soldiers* and other primers on basic military hygiene to Continental Army officers helped somewhat **(See Document 1.11)**.

The greatest triumph of the Continental Army in the sphere of soldier health care, by contrast, was almost certainly General George Washington's successful implementation of a comprehensive smallpox inoculation program for new army enlistees in the late 1770s **(See Document 1.12)**.[33] "Washington removed a major threat to the health of his soldiers and protected the overall strength and reliability of the Continental Army by systematically inoculating his troops," summarized historian Anne M. Becker. "Once citizens and soldiers recovered from the milder inoculated smallpox and acquired immunity, they were permanently 'freed of the apprehensions of that fatal distemper.' From a public health perspective, compulsory army inoculations also helped encourage the civilian population to use this preventive procedure."[34]

A good number of Americans emerged from the Revolutionary War armed with the distinct—and accurate—impression that intervention by the national government in the health and hygiene of its military and civilian populations had been a net positive during some pivotal points in the conflict. This belief made it easier for them to accept subsequent government interventions in the realm of public health as both legitimate and potentiallybeneficial. It also eased the passage of a variety of municipal and state public health measures designed to combat urban pollution, disease, and squalor, including notable new sanitation laws in Boston (1786), New York State (1796), Massachusetts (1797), and New York City (1798).

The most notable development in American health care at the close of the eighteenth century came in 1798. That year, the U.S. Congress enacted a milestone law, An Act for the Relief of Sick and Disabled Seamen, that established civilian health care as a legitimate area of policymaking for the federal government **(See Document 1.13)**. Maritime commerce was the lifeblood of the young nation's economy, and Congress was determined to maintain the labor force upon which this commerce rested. The legislation was fairly modest in scope. It imposed a 200 cents per month tax on seamen's wages to pay for their medical care in the event that they were felled by illness or injury, and it also put mechanisms in place for the construction and operation of what came to be known as Merchant Marine hospitals. But the precedent that this legislation set would have major repercussions on American health care policymaking in the decades and centuries to come.

NOTES

1. John Duffy, *From Humors to Medical Science: A History of American Medicine,* 2nd ed. (Urbana: University of Illinois Press, 1993), 19.
2. Quoted in Colin G. Calloway, *New Worlds for All: Indians, Europeans, and the Remaking of Early America* (Baltimore: Johns Hopkins University Press, 1997), 26.
3. Quoted in Virgil J. Vogel, *American Indian Medicine* (Norman: University of Oklahoma Press, 1970), 52.
4. Quoted in Calloway, *New Worlds for All,* 35.
5. Quoted in John Duffy, "Smallpox and the Indians in the American Colonies," *Bulletin of the History of Medicine* 25 (July–August 1951): 327.
6. Barbara Alice Mann, *The Tainted Gift: The Disease Method of Frontier Expansion* (Santa Barbara, CA: Praeger/ABC-CLIO, 2009), 12.
7. Suzanne M. Schultz, "Epidemics in Colonial Philadelphia from 1699 to 1799 and the Risk of Dying," *Early America Review* (Winter/Spring 2007), www.earlyamerica.com/review/2007_winter_spring /epidemics.html#endnotes.
8. Oscar Reiss, *Medicine in Colonial America* (Lanham, MD: University Press of America, 2000), 99.
9. *Medical Record: A Weekly Journal of Medicine and Surgery,* Vol. 61: January 5–June 28, 1902 (New York: William Wood, 1902), 926.
10. Elizabeth Anne Fenn, *Pox Americana: The Great Smallpox Epidemic of 1775–82* (New York: Macmillan, 2001), 30.
11. Fenn, *Pox Americana,* 30.
12. Calloway, *New Worlds for All,* 40.
13. "The Boston Smallpox Epidemic, 1721," *Contagion: Historical Views of Diseases and Epidemics: Harvard University Library Open Collections Program,* http://ocp.hul.harvard.edu/contagion /smallpox.html.
14. Quoted in John Blake, *Public Health in the Town of Boston, 1630–1822* (Cambridge, MA: Harvard University Press, 1959), 62.
15. Reiss, *Medicine in Colonial America,* 104.
16. Duffy, *From Humors to Medical Science,* 18.
17. William G. Rothstein, *American Physicians in the Nineteenth Century: From Sects to Science* (Baltimore: Johns Hopkins University Press, 1985), 36–37.
18. Duffy, *From Humors to Medical Science,* 15.
19. Rothstein, *American Physicians in the Nineteenth Century,* 36.
20. Paul Starr, *The Social Transformation of American Medicine* (New York: Basic Books, 1982), 39.
21. Reiss, *Medicine in Colonial America,* 80.
22. Quoted in Reiss, *Medicine in Colonial America,* 90.
23. James Harvey Young, "Patent Medicines: The Early Post-Frontier Phase," *Journal of the Illinois State Historical Society* 46, no. 3 (Autumn 1953): 257.
24. Young, "Patent Medicines," 255.
25. William A. Smith, *The History of the Province of New York* (New York: Thomas Wilcox, 1757), 212.
26. Reiss, *Medicine in Colonial America,* 77.
27. Reiss, *Medicine in Colonial America,* 111.

28. John Harley Warner and Janet A. Tighe, eds., *Major Problems in the History of American Medicine and Public Health* (Boston: Houghton Mifflin, 2001), 55.

29. Rothstein, *American Physicians in the Nineteenth Century*, 38.

30. S. L. Mitchell, "Letter to Lyman Spalding, October 31, 1799," in *Dr. Lyman Spalding*, ed. James Spalding (Boston: W. M. Leonard, 1916), 20.

31. Starr, *The Social Transformation of American Medicine*, 83.

32. Rothstein, *American Physicians in the Nineteenth Century*, 74.

33. Mary V. Thompson, "More to Dread . . . Than from the Sword of the Enemy," *Mount Vernon Annual Report* (2000), www.mountvernon.org/visit/plan/index.cfm/pid/237/.

34. Anne M. Becker, "Inoculation in Washington's Army: The Battle against Smallpox," in *Science in Uniform, Uniforms in Science: Historical Studies of American Military and Scientific Interactions*, ed. Margaret Vining and Barton C. Hacker (Lanham, MD: Scarecrow Press, 2007), 24–25.

| DOCUMENT 1.1 | Virginia Colony Imposes the First Public Health Law in the New World |

Virginia Colony Imposes the First Public Health Law in the New World

"Upon Paine of Whipping and Further Punishment"

1610

As the early colonists labored to carve out sustainable ways of living in the New World, they quickly came to realize that poor sanitation practices posed a threat to both individual health and community prosperity. To this end, some colonies introduced regulations designed to limit the impact of human and livestock waste and other refuse on public health and community aesthetics. The first of these public sanitation regulations, reprinted here, was passed in Virginia Colony in 1610.

There shall no man or woman, Launderer or Launderesse, dare to wash unclean Linne, driue bucks, or throw out the water or suds of fowle cloathes, in the open streete, within the Pallizadoes, or within forty foote of the same, nor renche, and make cleane, any kettle, pot, or pan, or such like vessell within twenty foote of the olde well, or new Pumpe: nor shall any one aforesaid, within less than a quarter of one mile from the Pallizadoes, dare to doe the necesseties of nature, since by these unmanly, slothful, and loathsome immodesties, the whole Fort may bee choaked, and poisoned with ill aires, and so corrupt (as in all reason cannot but much infect the same) and this shall they take notice of, and avoid, upon paine of whipping and further punishment, as shall be thought meete, by the censure of a martiall Court.

Every man shall have an especiall and due care, to keepe his house sweete and cleane, as also so much of the streete, as lieth before his door, and especially he shall so provide and set his bedstead whereon he lieth, that it may stand three foote at least from the ground, as he will answere the contrarie at a martiall Court.

Source: Smillie, Wilson George. *Public Health: Its Promise for the Future.* New York: Macmillan, 1955. Reprint: New York: Arno Press, 1976, pp. 61–62.

Plymouth Colony Assigns Responsibility for Health Care Expenses

"They Shalbe Releeved and Mayntained by the Towneships Whence They Came"

1642

As the British colonies developed, many communities created almshouses—the forerunner to the modern hospital—to take care of sick, poor, and disabled individuals who did not possess the financial or human resources (friends or family) to take care of themselves. Most of the people who took up residence in the almshouse were locals, but transients who fell victim to injury or illness were also treated in these facilities.

Funding for colonial almshouses was usually provided for via a combination of poor taxes on community members and financial contributions from churches, and the use of these monies to care for longtime community residents was not a significant source of controversy. But some townships became leery that other communities might foist their sick and poor on them to reduce their financial outlays in this regard. To discourage such unscrupulous behavior, several colonies passed statutes that mandated the return of a sick transient to the parish of his or her origin for long-term care or required the home parish to reimburse the caregiving community for all services it provided. In addition, townships and colonies passed measures to ensure that financial responsibility for sick servants and apprentices brought over from England would remain with their masters. One such set of statutes, reprinted here, was passed by Plymouth Colony in 1642 as part of a series of laws designed to provide public assistance to the poor.

RECEIVING PERSONS INTO A TOWNE, WHO ARE LIKE TO BE CHARGABLE.

If hereafter any Inhabitant or Inhabitants of any Towne within this Governt shall receive or bring in any person or persons as is apparently likely to be chargeable to the Towne-ship against whom just exception is made at the tyme of his comeing or within a month after without the consent & assent of the Townesmen in a lawfull generall publicke towne meeting the partie or parties that so received or brought them shall discharge the Towne of them.

If any person or persons comeing out of England or els where bring any person or persons who by reason of impotency disease or otherwise is apparently likely to be char-gable to the place where hee shall come to inhabite the person or persons so bringing in any such person or persons shall discharge the Township of them during the tyme of the diseaseds abode there. But in case any Inh'ite within this Colony shall bring over from England or els where or procure to be sent unto them any servant or servants which by Gods Providence shall fall diseased lame or impotent by the way or after they come here, they shalbe mayntayned and provided for by their said masters &c. during the terme of their service & covenants, although their said masters release them out of their said service, & afterwards to be releeved by the Towneship where hee is.

PERSONS FOR NURTURE OR PHYSICKE

If any children or elder persons shalbe sent or come from one Towne to another to be nursed schooled or otherwise educated or to a Phisician or Chirurgeon to be cured of any disease or wound [and] . . . they come to stand in need of releafe they shalbe releeved and mayntained by the Townships whence they came or were sent from and not by that Towneship where they are so nursed educated or at cure, and in case they come or be sent from any Towne or place out of this Colony then if the nurse educator physicõn or Chirurgeon take not sufficient securyty of the person to be nursed educated or cured to discharge the Towneship of and from all cost and charge which shall or may come and befall the said Towneship in which hee or they is so to be nursed educated or cured. Then they the said nurse educator phisicõn or Chirurgeon as neglects the same shall discharge the said Towneship of them themselves.

Source: Brigham, William, comp. *The Compact with the Charter and Laws of the Colony of New Plymouth.* Boston: Dutton and Wentworth, 1836, pp. 72–73.

Massachusetts Colony Passes an Act of Instruction for Medical Caregivers

DOCUMENT 1.3

"To Encourage and Direct Them in the Right Use of [Their Skill]"

1649

Massachusetts was an early leader in crafting medical laws and regulations in the British colonies. In 1649, for example, legislators in Massachusetts passed a law of instruction for medical caregivers, reprinted here, that became a model for similar legislation in New York and New Jersey. Such efforts to codify standards of professional behavior among physicians, surgeons, and midwives reflected a conviction, widespread in the colonies, that medicine's "rules of art" were well within the ken of laymen.

AN ACT RESPECTING CHIRURGIONS, MIDWIVES AND PHYSICIANS.

Forasmuch as the law of God allows no man to impair the life, or limbs of any person, but in a judicial way:

It is therefore ordered, that no person or persons whatsoever, employed at any time about the bodies of men, women or children, for preservation of life or health; as chirurgions, midwives, physicians, or others, presume to exercise, or put forth any act contrary to the known approved rules of art, in each mystery and occupation, nor exercise any force, violence or cruelty upon, or towards the body of any, whether young or old, (no not in the most difficult and desperate cases) without the advice and consent of such as are skilful in the same art, (if such may be had) or at least of some of the wisest and gravest then present, and consent of the patient or patients if they be mentis compotes [of sound mind], much less contrary to such advice and consent; upon such severe punishment as the nature of the fact may deserve, which law nevertheless, is not intended to discourage any from all lawful use of their skill, but rather to encourage and direct them in the right use thereof, and inhibit and restrain the presumptuous arrogancy of such as through prefidence of their own skill, or any other sinister respects, dare boldly attempt to exercise any violence upon or towards the bodies of young or old, one or other, to the prejudice or hazard of the life or limb of man, woman, or child.

Source: An Act Respecting Chirurgions, Midwives, and Physicians. *The Charters and General Laws of the Colony and Province of Massachusetts Bay.* Published by order of the General Court. Boston: T. R. Wait, 1814, pp. 76–77.

DOCUMENT 1.4

The First Naval Quarantine Act in British America

"An Act to Prevent Sickly Vessels Coming into this Government"

1700

Confronted by recurring waves of epidemic disease, authorities in the colonies embraced a variety of naval quarantine measures. These regulations reflected a recognition that smallpox, measles, and other dread communicable diseases were entering the Americas via passenger vessels and cargo ships and finding fertile conditions for growth in the crowded and unsanitary port cities.

Inspections of incoming vessels for suspected ship-borne illnesses were first implemented in the 1620s and 1630s, but the first truly comprehensive system of regulations for naval quarantine was not passed until 1700, when the General Assembly of Pennsylvania passed "An act to prevent sickly vessels coming into this Government," reprinted here. This act was passed at the instigation of William Penn, founder of the Pennsylvania Colony. Returning to Philadelphia in 1699 after a long stint in England, Penn was confronted by an outbreak of yellow fever traced to a ship that had recently arrived in port from Barbados. Greatly troubled by the outbreak's impact on the colony's people and economy, Penn believed that public health regulation was the best way of reducing Pennsylvania's vulnerability to future plagues.

Whereas, It hath been found, by sad experience, that the coming and arriving of unhealthy vessels at the ports and towns of this province and territories, and the landing of their passengers and goods, before they have lain some time to be purified, have proved very detrimental to the health of the inhabitants of this province: *Be it therefore enacted, by the authority aforesaid,* That, from and after the publication hereof, no unhealthy or sickly vessels, coming from any unhealthy or sickly place whatsoever, shall come nearer than one mile to any of the towns or ports of this province or territories without bills of health; nor shall presume to bring to shore such vessels, nor to land such passengers or their goods at any of the said ports or places, until such time as they shall obtain a license for their landing at Philadelphia, from the Governor and Council, or from any two justices of the peace of any other port or county of this province or territories, under the penalty of

ONE HUNDRED POUNDS for every such unhealthy vessel so landing, as aforesaid, to the use of the Proprietary and Governor; and that suitable provision be ordered by the Governor and Council for their reception, if they be permitted to land or come on shore."

Source: *Proceedings and Debates of the Third National Quarantine and Sanitary Convention, Held in the City of New York, April 27th, 28th, 29th, and 30th, 1859.* New York: E. Jones, 1859, pp. 279–80.

DOCUMENT
1.5

A Law for Regulating Midwives in New York City

"You Shall Not For Sake or Leave the Poor Woman to Go to the Rich"

1716

One of the first meaningful attempts to regulate medical practice in the colonies via licensing took place in New York City in 1716. Spurred on by numerous stories of deplorable and incompetent medical care, city officials imposed a licensing requirement on all midwives. Ironically, incompetent midwifery was much less of a health problem in the colonies than the inept performance of surgeons, physicians, apothecaries, and other professions dominated at the time by men. Midwives, though, were part of the fabric of societal stability in a way that the other professions were not. They were seen by church and state alike, for example, as important—even authoritative—sources of information on bastardy, infanticide, and other childbirth issues deemed worthy of investigation. The license requirements imposed by New York City on midwives provided further confirmation of this status. As historians Richard W. Wertz and Dorothy C. Wertz observed, "such licenses in effect placed the midwife in the role of servant of the state, a keeper of social and civil order."[1]

A Law For Regulating Mid Wives Within The City Of New York

BE IT ORDAINED by the Mayor Recorder Aldermen and Assistants of the City of New York Convened in Common Council and it is hereby Ordained by the Authority of the same that No Woman whatsoever within this Corporation of the City of New York Shall be Capable of, or in any manner whatsoever Use or Exercise the Office or Imploy of A Mid Wife within the said Corporation untill She Shall before the Mayor Recorder and Aldermen of the said Corporation for the time being or any One of them take the Oath of a Midwife hereafter Mentioned which Oath they or any one of them have hereby power to Administer in the Words following.

    You Shall swear, first that you Shall be Dilligent and faithfull And Ready to help Every Woman Labouring of Child As well the poor as the Rich; And that in time of Necessity you shall not for sake or Leave the poor Woman to go to the Rich ITEM you Shall Neither Cause nor suffer any Woman to Name or put any other father to the Child, but only him which is the Very true father thereof Indeed According to the Uttmost of your power. ITEM You shall not Suffer any Woman to Pretend feign or surmise her self to be

Delivered of A Child who is not Indeed, Neither to Claim any other Womans Child for her own. ITEM You Shall not suffer any Womans Child to be Murthered Maimed or Otherwise hurt as much as you may And so often as you shall perceive any perill or Jeopardy Either in the Woman or in the Child in any such wise as you Shall be in Doubt what shall Chance thereof you shall thenceforth in Due time send for other Midwifes and Expert Women in that faculty and use their Advice Councel and Assistance in that behalf. ITEM You Shall not Give any Counsel or Administer any Herb Medicine or Potion or any other thing to any Woman being with Child whereby She Should Destroy or Miscarry of that she goeth withall before her time ITEM You Shall not Enforce any Woman being with Child by any pain or by any UnGodly Ways or Means to give you any more for your pains or labour in bringing her A Bed than they would Otherwise Do. ITEM You shall not Consent Agree Give or Keep Counsel that any Woman be Delivered secretly of that which she goeth with but in the presence of Two or three Witnesses ready ITEM You shall be secret and not Open any matter Appertaining to your Office in the presence of any Man unless Nessessity or Great Urgent Cause do Constrain you so to do. ITEM. If you shall know any MidWife using or doing any thing Contrary to any of the premisses or in any otherwise then shall be seemly or Convenient You shall forthwith Detect and Openly shew the same to the Mayor Recorder and Aldermen of the City of New York for the time being or one of them. ITEM you shall use yourself in honest behaviour unto the Woman being Lawfully Admitted to the Room and Office of A Mid Wife in all things Accordingly. ITEM You Shall not make or Assign any Deputy or Deputies to Exercise or Occupy under you in your Absence the Office or Room of a Mid Wife but such as you shall perfectly know to be of Right honest and Discreet behaviour as also Apt Able and having sufficient knowledge and Experience to Exercise the said Room and Office. ITEM if any Woman in Labour under your Care Shall Desire the Advise or Assistance of any other Mid Wife or Mid Wifes you Shall Readily Consent to the Same and use their Advice Counsell and Assistance in that behalf if in your Conscience you think it for the Benifitt of such Woman in Labour. ITEM You shall not Conceal the Birth of any Bastard Child within the Corporation of the City of New York but Shall forthwith upon Understanding thereof Give Knowledge of the same to the Mayor Recorder and Aldermen of the City of New York for the time being or any one of them or to the Alderman or Chief Magistrate of the Ward where such Bastard Child Shall be born All which Articles and Charge you Shall faithfully Observe & keep So help you God. AND be it Ordained by the Authority Aforesaid that the Mayor Recorder & Aldermen of the City of New York for the time being or any one of them before whom such Oath Shall be taken Shall Certifie the taking of such Oath to the Mayors Next Court there to be Recorded AND be it Ordained by the Authority Aforesaid that if any Woman within the said Corporation of the City of New York Shall after the third Day of August Next Ensueing the Date hereof Use Occupy or Exersize the Office of A Mid Wife within the said Corporation of the City of New York before the Oath before Mentioned hath been Duely Administred unto her by the Mayor Recorder and Aldermen of the said City of New York for the time being or one of them that then And in such Case such Woman so useing Occupying or Exersizeing the Office of A Mid-Wife within the said Corporation of the City of New York for Every Default shall forfeit and pay the sum of forty shillings of Lawfull Money of the province of New York to be Recovered before the Mayor Recorder and Aldermen of the said City of New York for the time being or any one of them by A summary proceeding which forfeiture shall be Levyed by Distress and sale of the Goods and Chattells of such Offender against the Tenor of this Law by Warrant under the hand & seal of the said Mayor Recorder and Aldermen of the City of New York for the time being or any one of them and shall be Disposed of in manner following that is to say one half of the said forfeiture to the Treasurer of the City of New York for the time being for the use of the Corporation of the said City of New York And the Other half to the person or persons who Shall sue for or prosecute the same And in Case such Offender against the Tenor of this Law shall not have sufficient goods and Chattells to be found within the said Corporation to satisfie the said forfeiture then and in such Case It shall And may be Lawfull for the Mayor Recorder and Aldermen of the City of New York for the time being or any one of them by Warrant under hand and seal to Committ such Offender to the Common Goal of the Said City there to Remain without Bail or Mainprize for the Space of Thirty Days After the Date of such Warrant Unless the said forfeiture be in the Mean time paid and satisfyed. . . .

Source: A Law for Regulating Mid Wives within the City of New York. *Minutes of the Common Council of the City of New York, 1675–1776.* Vol. 3. New York: Dodd, Mead, 1905, pp. 121–23.

NOTE

1. Richard W. Wertz and Dorothy C. Wertz, *Lying-in: A History of Childbirth in America* (New Haven, CT: Yale University Press, 1989), 7–8.

DOCUMENT 1.6

Supporting Inoculation in Boston during a Smallpox Epidemic

"The Inoculated . . . Are in as Good a State of Health as Ever They Enjoy'd"

1721

When Boston was besieged by a smallpox epidemic in the spring of 1721, the prominent minister Cotton Mather urged a citywide variolation campaign against the disease. Mather had learned about the procedure from the Philosophical Transactions of the Royal Society and from one of his slaves, and he believed that inoculation would greatly reduce the death toll from the dreaded disease. Mather was joined in this campaign by several other influential Boston clergy, including the respected Congregationalist minister Benjamin Colman. The pro-variolation camp in Boston was strongly opposed by a coalition of local physicians and clergymen who argued that variolation was not only unacceptably dangerous, but also an affront to God's will. Mather and Colman strongly objected to this characterization of smallpox inoculation, as seen in the following letter penned by Colman to John Leverett, the president of Harvard College, at the height of the controversy.

Resistance to the variolation proposals advanced by Mather, Colman, and their allies blunted public acceptance of inoculation, and in the end only about three hundred Bostonians were inoculated against the disease. After the crisis was over, statistical analysis revealed that inoculated people fared much better against the disease than those who caught the disease naturally. All told, Boston's 1721 smallpox inoculation campaign greatly advanced the cause of immunology in America, and though it admittedly "enraged the town and called forth a bitter newspaper and pamphlet war," in the words of historian John B. Blake, it also ranked as "the earliest important experiment in preventive medicine in America."[1]

To the Reverend Learned, Mr. *John Leverett*, President of *Harvard College*, in *Cambridge*, in New–England, letter of November 23, 1721

When I first had the Account of this common Practice in the *Levant,* and of the wonderful Success of it there, given by *Gentlemen of Learning* to such a Body as that of the *Royal Society in London*, I could not but give Credit to their *Testimony,* in a Matter of fact whereof they were Eye-Witnesses. Immediately the *little Phylosophy* I am Master of led me into the *apparent Reasons* of the thing. The more readily & easily *these* occurr'd to me, the more I was affected with the Goodness of GOD *Almighty* therein to a Miserable World. I immediately tho't with myself, and said to some *Superior Persons* in the Town, (who possibly may remember it) What An astonishing Mercy to Us in this Land, this Discovery of a *Gracious Providence* might prove. The more I mus'd upon the thing, and discours'd upon it, the more light I had, or seem'd to my self to have. It appear'd to me as rational as it was surprising, and gave me great pleasure in the prospect of so great a Benefit to Mankind. For I had not forgot the terrors of the *Small-Pox* when it was here the two last times, Nineteen and near Thirty Years since; tho' it was nothing so Mortal either time as it had been before, (1678.) and has been now again. Besides it being now nineteen Years since the *Small-Pox* had been in the Town, it gave us a very dreadful prospect of Distress and Deaths, whenever is should come among us; all the Children and all the Young People born in the Town, or come into it from the Country, within that long term of time having it before them. Now in proportion to the distress sore seen and expected by us, my Joy naturally rose upon the Discovery of such a Way of Relief as seem'd Opening before us, by the favour of GOD to us. In this simplicity of heart (I speak before GOD who searches it) I gave into a kind of Opinion of this *New Method;* My Affection to my *Country* and the saving the *Lives* of my People being the Sole Motive to me, under the *Glory* that should thence redound unto the Name of GOD. I freely spake my Tho'ts in Company and on Occasions as it seem'd proper to me, and when some pubilckly demanded of us "*Whether People could trust in GOD in using this Means of Self-preservation?* I openly answer'd (among my *Brethren*) in the *Affirmative,* that I judg'd they might. This was after that Dr. *Boylstone* had begun the practice which I never put him upon, nor had I light to disswade [sic.] him from it. According to my hope and Expectation it succeeded; altho' the first Experiment was the most discouraging; for Mrs. *Boylstone* being in the Country and the *Doctor* taken up abroad among his Patients, the Children were too much exposed & neglected, and from my house (which faces into the Doctors yard) One of them was seen three or four days after their being Inoculated dabling in the cold water under the Pump. This or the like disorders in the first Inoculated *Child* threw him, as well they might, into a high and threatning fever. The cause was apparent to the Dr. and so did not discourage him, nor at all disgrace the practice with us that saw it. It was a pleasure however to see that the Small-Pox might be communicated, as the *Gentlemen* from the *Levant* had informed us. The next Experiments were made with more care, and accordingly more answered the Accounts, which they had given us of a very *light fever* and *few pustles.* By this time the *Town* was full of the Sickness, and the Deaths that began to multiply led a few more into this *Means of Safety;* as they hop'd by the favour of GOD to find it. The Blessing of GOD went along with it; they found *ease* and *sweetness,* and lay praising GOD on their Beds, or rather sat up in their Chairs doing so. Their friends stood smiling about them. Their tongues were filled with laughter, and ours with Thanksgiving on their account when we went to see 'em. We saw them recover fast; the communicated Distemper working uniformly upon them, and as one would desire. We saw this with wonder and Joy at what GOD had wro't for us. We saw *Scores* thus recover, even as many as went into the happy practice, and it appear'd to us more and more to be *the Lord's Doing and marvellous in our eyes.* They were as discreet and religious a number of People, and Persons of as good sense and understanding, and of as much caution and fear as their Nei'bours, who made these Experiments; and they did it with meekness and humility, patience and silence, and many prayers, under much provocation from too many. Only *one Gentlewoman* has yet died out of an *hundred*, who have now passed thro' the Operation. But as you must needs suppose in a Town so full of Infection as this has been, some ten or twelve of this number appear'd to have taken the Infection in the common way; (among whom the Person deceas'd was evidently one) and accordingly they had it of the *Confluent* Kind, or in a fulness of the *distinct* sort, not known among the Inoculated in the *Levant.* This will by so far from seeming strange to you, that indeed it would be next to a *Miracle* had it been otherwise. At the same time it must be allowed, that a good number of those that passed so favourably thro' the Inoculation, would probably have had it very favourably in the common way. But that so many should pass so favourably and *easily*, as well as *safely*, thro' the Inoculation; while their Nei'bours had so many in every hundred that suffer'd so much, as well as *died*, is a sufficient Distinction put by Providence on the Method which we praise GOD for. . . .

I come now to say, *What I have seen in the Chambers of the Inoculated*; for I have made it my Business to visit some of them, and *to observe the Work of GOD to his praise*; And what I blame in others is, that they have not visited them, and without prejudice or passion, or regard to any private Interest or pique, informed themselves as they might easily have done of this great Thing which GOD has brought to light is our Day; and if I may serve to set it in any true light before others, I shall account myself honoured of GOD therein. . . .

It is now some Months, four or five, since many of the Inoculated are come abroad, and they find neither boil nor sore upon them; but are in as good a state of health as ever they enjoy'd in their Life: Nay some have found a much better Complexion and Stomach than ever they had before; and particularly my own *Child* has found so thro' the favour of GOD. . . .

Upon the whole, I do not think that I . . . go out of my *Line* in the present Essay. The plain intent of it is to serve unto the preserving of Life, and to minister unto the comfort of Families. This is a Care beseeming me, or any one else, if it be manag'd with modesty & decency. My care to do it so, is I think visible eno' in the present writing. I have avoided any appearance of seeming learned in *Physick.* I am not: Nor shall I matter it at all, if I have betray'd my Ignorance therein. I write with another design, & if that be answer'd I have all my desire; or if it be rejected with scorn and revil'd I shall be satisfyed in *this,* That I have again endeavoured the Good of this People.

FINIS

Source: Colman, Benjamin. *Some Observations on the New Method of Receiving the Small Pox by Ingrafting or Inoculating.* Boston: B. Green, 1721.

NOTE

1. John B. Blake, "The Inoculation Controversy in Boston: 1721–1722," *New England Quarterly* 25 (1952): 489.

DOCUMENT 1.7

A Prominent Boston Physician Campaigns against Smallpox Inoculations

"The Promoters Thereof [Shall Be] Stigmatized as Murderers"

1721

When the city of Boston was hit by a terrible smallpox epidemic in the spring of 1721, a rhetorical firefight quickly broke out between advocates and opponents of variolation, or smallpox inoculation. The leading critic of the variolation program proposed by ministers Cotton Mather and Benjamin Colman, and ultimately carried out on a limited basis by Dr. Daniel Boylston, was the distinguished physician William Douglass. A graduate of the prestigious medical school in Edinburgh, Douglass was by far the city's most respected doctor.

In the pamphlet excerpted here, Douglass lays out his religious objections to the variolation program , but he also attacks it on medical grounds. "[Douglass] argued that Mather's inoculations undermined legitimate medical authority and contended that inoculation without regulated quarantine of the inoculated afterwards would only make the epidemic worse. Given that Mather was neither carrying out his inoculations in an organized manner nor isolating newly inoculated patients appropriately, Douglass's criticism was legitimate."[1]

In the aftermath of the epidemic, Mather and his allies trumpeted statistics and anecdotal evidence showing that their inoculation program had been beneficial in reducing the severity of the outbreak. Douglass remained unconvinced, but by the close of the eighteenth century, the usefulness of carefully administered inoculation programs in combating smallpox and other public health threats was well established.

. . . Their Seventh *Reason* [for urging inoculation], (which is the only Argument they ought to use and rely on) is its Success. I need not tell them that there is Successful *Wickedness* for a time; or as [Boston minister] *John Williams* says, GOD *permitted* Pharoah's *Magicians*, to imitate his own Judgments, even to the hardening of the People's Hearts.

Their History of its Success is shortly this. At first they gave out, That it was a Method not infecting, procuring only a small quantity of Eruptions, but never Death, nor any bad consequence, and was an infallible Security against ever having the Small Pox. . . . [But] we soon found it infecting; many have dy'd of the Infection received from the Inoculated, whose Deaths in a great measure lies at the Inoculators Doors. . . .

What has been said in favour of it by way of *Cant*, &c. does not deserve mentioning; as the calling of it a *discriminating Mark* of the Good from the Ungodly, the Saints from the Wicked; their throwing the Odium of *Party* on the *Anti-Inoculators:* They who continue in an even steedy Course, as before, are said to form a *Party;* not they who are active, and endeavour to introduce new and *dubious Practices* and Customs. O BRASS! If it be a *Party Business*, it is of their own making; for we may generally observe, the Inoculated are generally the *Devotees* of some *Inoculating Parson:* At first it was *Congregational*, being almost confined to Mr. W—b's Heaters; then it spread among the *Devotees* of Dr. *M.* and Mr. *C.*; and lately many being buzz'd in the Ear with the great *Losses* sustain'd in the Natural Way, have as it were in *Despair* come into it. . . .

My humble Opinion of *Inoculation* is as of all bold Experiments of Consequence in the *Practice of Physick*. That whatever the Success or Consequences may be, (and the more Tryals the more Light) they may be of a publick Advantage, tho' at the *Risque* of the first patients. If it answer, after Generations will reap the Benefit of it; if otherways, the miserable Sufferers will be recorded as bold, rash, infatuated *Fools,* the Practice for ever after abhor'd, and the Promoters thereof stigmatized as *Murderers.*

All solid and sound *Phylosophy,* that is *Natural History,* is founded on *Observations* made, and *Experiments* taken of the various Actions and Influences of *Natural Bodys* on one another. I was always fond of this kind of Knowledge, especially as it related to *Humane Bodies* in a *Healthy* or *Morbid* state; and if these two dear Characters of a Good *Citizen* and a Good *Christian* could be dispensed with, I should have been pleased to see some Thousands inoculated with several other Distempers as well as the *Small Pox;* but for the following *Reasons* I could not at present comply with this novel . . . and *dubious* Practice.

1. *Poysoning and spreading infection, are by the penal Law of* England *Felony.* Inoculation falls in with the first without any Contradiction, and if a Person of so *weak a Constitution,* that any the least Illness may prove fatal to him, should be inoculated, and suffer but the tenth part of what several of the *Inoculated* have done, he must unavoidably perish, and his *Inoculator* deem'd guilty of willful *Poysoning.* This is the Reason I suppose, why the Practitioners of *Boston* thought themselves not *safe* to venture on a Thing of such Consequence. Supposing only One in a Thousand should die of this Method, it cannot with Safety to the *Inoculator* be practis'd, without an *Act of Parliament,* exempting *Inoculation* by a sworn Practitioner from the Penaltys of *poisoning and spreading Infection.* . . .

Instead of contriving Methods to secure the *Inoculated* from taking the Infection the common Way, and their Neighbours from being infected by them, they inoculate indifferently in all Corners, and set the Town all in a Flame in one Moment as it were; *many perish* who had the Infection from the Inoculated, whose Deaths perhaps *in foro divino* they may be found guilty of. Their Authors *Timonius* and *Pylarinus* tell them, The Person who collects the Matter, ought not to apply it, least a *double Infection* ensue; and that the Advantage of this Practice is, that a *suitable Season* and a *well prepared Body* may be had to rencounter the Infection; but these things, as trivial, they neglect, and run headlong as if push'd on by Some *Fury.* . . .

If the Inoculators had designed a publick Good, why did they run headlong into it, without observing the *Circumstances* and *Cautions* which might have made it useful; to begin in the Heart of the Town, where was no Infection; to inoculate all *Ages* and *Constitutions* from the very Beginning, without being first assur'd of it's Success on the *Young and Healthy.* Why did they not *petition the Government,* that none should be inoculated till his Name was recorded, that for the publick Good *in times to come,* it might be known who dy'd, and what *state of Health* they afterwards enjoy'd who surviv'd; say also have contriv'd some Method, that none might take the Infection from the *Inoculated;* This Neglect has occasioned the Death of many. . . .

We have learnt from our 5 or 6 Mo[nths of] Experience of Inoculation, *1. That the* Small Pox *may sometimes be communicated by Inoculation.* I cannot say always, because some have been Inoculated more than once before it wrought, and many have from thence had only a sort of *eruptive Fever,* but no genuine Small Pox, so far as I am able to judge. *2. That the* Small Pox *so acquired, is frequently more favourable than in the common way of Infection, and not altogether so mortal:* What the dismal Consequences may be, I shall not pretend to determine; but Reason and the Testimonies of some Gentlemen from the *Levant,* give us ground to *suspect. 3 That not one of the inoculated during the space of five or six Months has had the* Small Pox *in the natural way,* so far as we know; for the Inoculators in every thing that makes against them, by LYES and EQUIVOCATIONS endeavour to keep us in the dark. It is then a *palliative Prevention* of the Small Pox for some time, and not *very mortal;* and consequently may be of great Use to the *Guinea Traders,* when the Small Pox gets among their Slaves aboard to inoculate the whole Cargo, and patch them up for a *Market.* . . .

Source: Douglass, William. *Inoculation of the Small Pox as Practised in Boston, Consider'd in a Letter to A—S—M.D. & F.R.S. in London.* Boston: J. Franklin, 1722, pp. 11, 12–14, 16, 19–20.

NOTE

1. "The Boston Smallpox Epidemic, 1721," *Contagion: Historical Views of Diseases and Epidemics: Harvard University Library Open Collections Program,* http://ocp.hul.harvard.edu/contagion/smallpox.html.

DOCUMENT
1.8

Virginia Regulates the Fees of Physicians and Apothecaries

"No Practicer in Physic Shall Recover More than the Rates Hereafter Mentioned"

1736

One of the first serious efforts to regulate the practice of medicine in the British colonies came from Virginia legislators who, in 1736, passed a law setting a fee scale for health care services provided by university-trained physicians as well as surgeons and apothecaries trained through apprenticeships. According to this fee scale, surgeons and apothecaries could charge a rate of five shillings a visit when practicing "physic" within five miles of their resident township and ten shillings when practicing within ten miles. Physicians who had earned a medical degree from a European medical school (the only option, because medical schools did not yet exist in America) were allowed to charge double these rates according to the terms of this bill, which is reprinted here. This same law also required physicians to specify the drugs prescribed on their bills, a requirement that led medical historian John Duffy to call the Virginia bill America's first "truth-in-advertising law."[1]

AN ACT FOR REGULATING THE FEES AND ACCOUNTS FOR PRACTICERS OF PHYSIC.

Passed August, 1736.

I. *Whereas,* the practice of physic in this colony, is most commonly taken up and followed, by surgeons, apothecaries, or such as have only served apprenticeships to those trades, who often prove very unskilful in the art of a physician; and yet demand excessive fees, and expect unreasonable prices for the medicines which they administer, and as too often, for the sake of making up long and expensive bills, load their patients with greater quantities thereof, than are necessary or useful, concealing all their compositions, as well to prevent the discovery of their practice, as of the true value of what they administer; which is become a grievance, dangerous and intolerable, as well to the former sort of people, as others, and doth require the most effectual remedy that the nature of the thing will admit:

II. *Be it therefore enacted,* by the Lieutenant Governor, Council, and Burgesses, of this present General Assembly, and it is hereby enacted, by the authority of the same, That from and after the pasting of this act, no practicer in physic, in any action or suit whatsoever, hereafter to be commenced in any court of record in this colony, shall recover, for visiting my sick person, more than the rates hereafter mentioned: that is to say,

Surgeons and apothecaries, who have served an apprenticeship to those trades, shall be allowed:

	£. s. d.
For every visit and prescription, in town or within five miles	00 5 00
For every mile, above five, and under ten.	00 1 00
For every visit, of ten miles.	00 10 00
And for every mile, above ten,	
With an allowance for all ferriages in their journeys.	00 00 06
To surgeons, for a simple fracture, and the cure thereof.	02 00 00
For a compound fracture and the cure thereof	04 00 00

Bat those persons who have studied physic in any University, and taken any degree therein, shall be allowed:

	£. s. d.
For every visit, and prescription, in any town, or within five miles	00 10 00
If above five miles, for every mile more, under ten	00 1 00
For a visit, if not above ten miles	1 00 00
And for every mile, above ten,	
With an allowance of ferriages, as before.	00 1 00

III. And to the end the true value of the medicines administered by any practicer in physic, may be better known, and judged of. *Be it further enacted by the authority aforesaid,* That whenever any pills, bolus, portion, draught, electuary, decoction, or any medicines, in any form whatsoever, shall be administered to any sick person, the person administering the same shall, at the same time, deliver in his bill, expressing every particular thing made up therein; or if the medicine administered, be a simple, or compound, directed in the dispensatories, the true name thereof shall be expressed in the same bill, together with the quantities and prices, in both cases. And In failure thereof, such practicer, or any apothecary, making up the prescription of another, shall be non-suited, in any action or suit hereafter commenced, which shall be grounded upon such bill or bills; nor shall any book, or account, of any practicer in physic, or any apothecary, be permitted to be given in evidence, before a court; unless the article therein contained, be charged according to the directions of this act.

IV. *And be it further enacted,* by the authority aforesaid, That this act shall continue and be in force for and during two years, next after the passing thereof, and from thence to the end of the next session of Assembly.

Source: An Act for Regulating the Fees and Accounts for Practicers of Physic. *Hening's Statutes at Large of Virginia. Vol. 4: 1711–1736.* Richmond, VA: 1820, p. 509. Reprinted in *Transactions of the Medical Society of the State of New York.* New York: Medical Society of the State of New York, 1850, p. 97.

NOTE

1. John Duffy, *From Humors to Medical Science: A History of American Medicine,* 2nd ed. (Urbana: University of Illinois Press, 1993), 40.

DOCUMENT
1.9

New York City Issues Regulations for "The Practice of Physick and Surgery"

"Many Ignorant and Unskilful Persons . . . Do Take Upon Themselves to Administer Physick"

1760

State regulation of medical practice in the British colonies took a major step forward in 1760, when New York City passed the first law in America that vested the government—a lay panel of high-profile municipal officials, in this case—with the legal authority to examine and license prospective doctors. This law also gave the city the power to impose fines on unlicensed health care practitioners. In 1792 this pioneering law, reprinted here, was reenacted, and five years after that its provisions were extended to health practitioners across the entire state of New York.

AN ACT TO REGULATE THE PRACTICE OF PHYSICK AND SURGERY IN THE CITY OF NEW-YORK, PASSED THE 10TH OF JUNE, 1760.

Whereas, many ignorant and unskilful Persons in Physick and Surgery in order to gain a subsistence, do take upon themselves to administer Physick, and practice Surgery in the City of New York, to the endangering of the Lives and Limbs of their Patients; and many poor and ignorant Persons inhabiting the said City, who have been persuaded to become their Patients, have been great sufferers thereby: For preventing such Abuses for the Future:

I. *Be it Enacted* by his Honor the Lieutenant Governor, the Council, and the General Assembly, and it is hereby *Enacted* by the Authority of the same, That, from and after the publication of this Act, no Person whatsoever shall practice as a Physician or Surgeon in the said City of New-York, before he shall first have been examined in Physick or Surgery, and approved of and admitted by one of his Majesty's Council, the Judges of the Supreme Court, the King's Attorney-General, and the Mayor of the City of New-York, for the time being, or by any three or more of them, taking to their assistance for such examination, such proper Person or Persons as they in their discretion shall see fit. And if any candidate after due examination of his Learning, and skill in Physick and Surgery as aforesaid, shall be approved and admitted to practice as a Physician and Surgeon or both, the said Examiners, or any three or more of them, shall give, under their hands and Seals to the person so admitted as aforesaid, a Testimonial of his Examination and Admission, and in the form following, to wit: To all to whom these Presents shall come, or may concern:

> *Know Ye* That we whose names are hereunto subscribed, in pursuance of an Act of the Lieutenant Governor, and Council and General Assembly, made and published at New-York, the ....Day of ....in

the year of our Lord, one thousand seven hundred and ...., entitled, An Act, To Regulate the Practice of Physick and Surgery in the City of New-York, have duly examined ...., Physician (or) Surgeon, (or) Physician and Surgeon (as the case may be), and having approved of his skill, have admitted him as a Physician (or) Surgeon, (or) Physician and Surgeon, to practice in the said Faculty or Faculties throughout this Province of New-York.

In testimony whereof, we have subscribed our names and affixed our Seals to this Instrument, at *New-York,* this ....day of .... Anno Domini, ... One thousand ....

II. *And Be It Further Enacted,* by the authority aforesaid, That if any Person shall practice in the City of New-York, as a Physician or Surgeon, or both as Physician and Surgeon, without such testimonial as aforesaid, he shall for every such offence forfeit the sum of Five Pounds; one-half thereof to the use of the Person or Persons who shall sue for the same, and the other Moiety to the Church Wardens and Vestrymen of the said City for the use of the Poor thereof; the said Forfeiture to be recovered without costs, before the Mayor, Recorder, or any one of the Aldermen of the said City, who are hereby empowered in a summary way, to hear, try and determine any suit brought for such Forfeiture, and to give Judgment and to award Execution thereupon.

Provided, That this act shall not extend to any person or persons administering Physick, or Practicing Surgery within the said City before the publication hereof; or to any Person having his Majesty's Commission, and employed in his Service as a Physician or Surgeon.

Source: Walsh, James Joseph. *History of the Medical Society of the State of New York.* New York: Medical Society of the State of New York, 1907, pp. 14–16.

DOCUMENT
1.10

Virginia Legislators Move to Punish Smallpox Inoculators

"Shall Forfeit and Pay the Sum of One Thousand Pounds"

1769

As smallpox epidemics ravaged the British colonies repeatedly in the eighteenth century, many colonists willingly underwent variolation, or smallpox inoculation. They reasoned that because smallpox outbreaks were so frequent, especially in port cities and other urban population centers, it was much better to get the less severe, induced version of the disease instead of the natural one. Resistance to variolation, though, remained formidable in many parts of the country. This resistance stemmed from legitimate fears about the safety of the practice—people who were inoculated did occasionally die from the disease or transmit it to others—as well as concerns that medical intercession amounted to interfering with God's divine will. Distrust of inoculation resulted in laws such as a 1769 measure, reprinted here, passed by Virginia legislators. The law did not outright forbid variolation in all instances, but it imposed strict limits on where, how, and when it could be employed, and its language is suffused with skepticism about the wisdom and efficacy of the practice.

I. WHEREAS the wanton introduction of the Small-Pox into this colony by inoculation, when the same was not necessary, hath, of late years, proved a nuisance to several neighbourhoods, by disturbing the peace and quietness of many of his majesty's subjects, and exposing their lives to the infection of that mortal distemper, which, from the situation and circumstances of the colony, they would otherwise have little reason to dread: To prevent which for the future, *Be it enacted, by the Governor, Council, and Burgesses, of this present General Assembly, and it is hereby enacted, by the authority of the same,* That if any person or persons whatsoever, shall wilfully, or designedly, after the first day of September next ensuing, presume to import or bring into this colony, from any country or place whatever, the small-pox, or any variolous or infectious matter of the said distemper, with a purpose to inoculate any person or persons whatever, or by any means whatever, to propagate the said distemper within this colony, he or she, so offending, shall forfeit and pay the sum of one thousand pounds, for every offence so committed; one moiety whereof shall be to the informer, and the other moiety to the churchwardens of the parish where the offence shall be committed, for the use of the poor of the said parish; to be recovered, with costs, by action of debt, bill, plaint, or information, in any court of record within this dominion.

II. But forasmuch as the inoculation of the smallpox may, under peculiar circumstances, be not only a prudent but necessary means of securing those who are unavoidably exposed to the danger of taking the distemper in the natural way, and for this reason it is judged proper to tolerate it, under reasonable restrictions and regulations:

III. *Be it therefore enacted, by the authority aforesaid,* That from and after the said first day of September next, if any person shall think him or herself, his or her family, exposed to the immediate danger of catching the said distemper, such person may give notice thereof to the sheriff of any county, or to the mayor or chief magistrate of any city or corporation, and the said sheriff, mayor, or chief magistrate, shall, immediately, and without loss of time, summon all the acting magistrates of the said county, city, or borough, to meet at the most convenient time and place in the said county, city, or borough, and the said magistrates, or such of them as shall be present, being assembled, shall consider whether, upon the whole circumstances of the case, inoculation may be prudent or necessary, or dangerous to the health and safety of the neighbourhood, and thereupon either grant a licence for such inoculation, under such restrictions and regulations as they shall judge necessary and proper, or prohibit the same, as to them, or a majority of them, shall seem expedient.

IV. *And be it further enacted, by the authority aforesaid,* That if any person or persons shall inoculate, or procure inoculation of the small-pox to be performed within this colony, without obtaining a licence in the manner before directed, or shall not conform to the rules and regulations prescribed by such justices, he, she, or they, shall forfeit and pay respectively, for every such offence, the sum of one hundred pounds; one moiety whereof shall be to the informer, and the other moiety to the churchwardens of the parish wherein such offence shall be committed, for the use of the poor of the said parish; to be recovered, with costs, by action of debt, bill, plaint, or information, in any court of record within this dominion. And moreover it shall and may be lawful for any justice of the peace, upon information given to him, upon oath, to issue his warrant against any person so offending, and upon sufficient proof, before him made, to cause such offender to give security, in such reasonable penalty as such justice shall think fit, for his or her good behaviour, and upon failure to give such security, to commit him or her to the gaol of his county, there to be confined until such security is given.

V. And whereas checking of the progress of the said distemper, where it may accidentally break out, or the regulations which may be established for carrying on inoculation, may be attended with some expence: *Be it therefore enacted, by the authority aforesaid,* That it shall and may be lawful for the justices of the court of every county, at the time of laying their levy, and for the mayor, recorder, aldermen, and common council, of any city or borough, at such time as they shall judge most convenient, to levy on the tithable persons in their said county, city, or borough, so much tobacco or money as will be sufficient to defray the expences necessarily incurred for the purposes aforesaid, in any such county, city, or borough.

VI. *And be it further enacted, by the authority aforesaid,* That if any sheriff, mayor, or chief magistrate, shall, upon application to him made, in manner aforesaid, refuse, or unreasonably delay, to summon the magistrates of any county, city, or borough, for the purpose aforesaid, or if any magistrate so summoned, shall refuse or neglect to attend according to such summon, every such sheriff, mayor, or chief magistrate, shall forfeit the sum of one hundred pounds, upon his refusing or neglecting to give such notice, without reasonable excuse; and every other magistrate so refusing or neglecting, without reasonable excuse, shall forfeit and pay the sum of five pounds, to the person aggrieved; to be recovered, with costs, by action of debt, in any court of record within this dominion.

Source: An act to regulate the inoculation of the Small-Pox within this colony. *The Statutes at Large: Being a Collection of All the Laws of Virginia.* Edited by William Waller Hening. New York: R&W&G Barton, 1821, pp. 371–74.

DOCUMENT
1.11

Benjamin Rush Gives Directions for Preserving the Health of Soldiers

"Your Duty Requires That You Should Attend to the Health of Your Men"

1777

Few public figures in America during the second half of the eighteenth century were as influential as Benjamin Rush. A hugely important figure in early American medicine and psychiatry, Rush was a signatory to the Declaration of Independence, helped establish the Philadelphia Dispensary for medical relief of the poor (the first institution of its kind in America), and cofounded Philadelphia's first medical college as well as several other institutions of higher learning.

Rush's brand of heroic medicine, with its attendant reliance on aggressive bleeding, purging, and other treatments, has long since been discredited. But his studies of mental illness were pioneering, and he made important early contributions in the field of public health. Specifically, in 1777 he wrote and published a work called "Directions for Preserving the Health of Soldiers" in his capacity as surgeon general of the Middle Department of the Continental Army. This text, which was first published in the Pennsylvania Packet *newspaper in 1777 and then distributed in pamphlet form a year later by order of the Board of War, was an early landmark in military hygiene, preventive medicine, and public health governance. General George Washington implemented many of the sanitary and health recommendations contained in Rush's work during the course of the Revolutionary War, and the pamphlet became an oft-consulted standard reference for the military medical service during the War of 1812. Half a century later, the text, which is excerpted here, was even reprinted by the Massachusetts Temperance Alliance in Boston for distribution to Union soldiers.*

Fatal experience has taught the people of America that a greater proportion of men have perished with sickness in our armies than have fallen by the sword. The two last campaigns produced melancholy proofs of this assertion. But we ought to consider upon this occasion, not only the mere loss of those worthy citizens who perished in this manner. The complicated distress, which accompanied their sickness and death, should never be forgotten. The gallant youth who had torn himself from the arms of his parents, or the partner of his joys, who had plighted his life to his country in the field, and who perhaps, in the enthusiasm of his military ardor, has courted death from a musket or a cannon ball, was often forced from the scene of action and glory by the attack of a fever, and obliged to languish for days or weeks in a hospital; and, at last, to close his eyes, deprived of the sweet consolation of a dying soldier, the thoughts of ending his life in the arms of victory, or in an act of just resentment against the enemies of the liberties of his country.

The munificence of the congress has made the most ample provision for lessening the calamities of war from sickness in their armies, and, if possible, to prevent it altogether; for I maintain that the mortality from sickness in camps is not necessarily connected with a soldier's life: It was unknown to the armies of ancient Greece and Rome. Their armies had no diseases peculiar to themselves; nor were the diseases, to which their soldiers were subject, attended with any peculiar symptoms. But the munificence of the congress, and the skill of physicians and surgeons, will avail but little in preventing mortality from sickness among our soldiers, without the concurrence of the officers of the army. Your authority, gentlemen, is absolutely necessary to enforce the most salutary plan, and precepts for preserving the health of the soldiers. Your own personal safety is concerned in concurring in the plan adopted by the congress. But if this were not the case, I am persuaded humanity and patriotism would not plead in vain in favour of those brave men, whose lives are committed to your care by the suffrages of your country.

The art of preserving the health of a soldier consists in attending to the following particulars: 1 *Dress.* 2 *Diet.* 3 *Cleanliness.* 4 *Encampments.* And, 5 *Exercise.*

1. The *Dress* of a soldier has a great influence upon his health. It is to be lamented, that the peculiar situation of our country, from the infancy of our foreign trade and domestic manufactures, has obliged us to clothe our soldiers chiefly in linen. It is a well known fact, that the perspiration of the body, by attaching itself to linen, and afterwards, by mixing with rain, is disposed to form miasmata, which produce fevers. Upon this account I could wish the rifle shirt was banished from our army. Besides accumulating putrid miasmata, it conceals filth, and prevents a due regard being paid to cleanliness. . . . I have known several instances where the yearly visits of the intermitting fever have been checked in the state of Pennsylvania, in places most subject to that disease, by nothing else but the use of flannel shirts.

The hair, by being long uncombed, is apt to accumulate the perspiration of the head, which by becoming putrid sometimes produces diseases. There are two methods of guarding against this evil: the first is by combing and dressing the hair every day; the second is by wearing it thin and short in the neck. The former is attended with delays often incompatible with the duty of a soldier; and therefore the latter is to be preferred to it. . . .

2. The *Diet* of soldiers should consist *chiefly* of vegetables. The nature of their duty, as well as their former habits of life, require it. If every tree on the continent of America produced Jesuit's bark, it would not be sufficient to preserve or to restore the health of soldiers who eat one or two pounds of flesh in a day. Their vegetables should be well cooked. It is of the last consequence that damaged flour should not be used in the camp. It is the seed of many diseases. It is of equal consequence that good flour should not be rendered unwholesome by an error in making it into bread. Perhaps it was the danger to which flour was always exposed of being damaged in a camp, or being rendered unwholesome from the manner of baking it, that led the Roman generals to use wheat instead of flour, for the daily food of their soldiers. Caesar fed his troops with wheat only, in his expedition into Gaul. It was prepared by being husked and well boiled; and was eaten with spoons in the room of bread. If a little sugar or molasses is added to wheat prepared in this manner, it forms not only a wholesome food, but a most agreeable repast.

What shall I say to the custom of drinking spirituous liquors, which prevails so generally in our army? I am aware of the prejudices in favour of it. It requires an arm more powerful than mine; the arm of a Hercules to encounter it. The common apology for the use of rum in our army is, that it is necessary to guard against the effects of heat and cold. But I maintain, that in no case whatever, does rum abate the effects of either of them upon the constitution. On the contrary I believe it always increases them. The temporary elevation of spirits in summer, and the temporary generation of warmth in winter, produced by rum, always leave the body languid, and more liable to be affected with heat and cold afterwards. Happy would it be for our soldiers, if the evil ended here! The use of rum, by gradually wearing away the powers of the system, lays the foundation of fevers, fluxes, jaundices, and the most of diseases which occur in military hospitals. It is a vulgar error to suppose that the fatigue arising from violent exercise or hard labour is relieved by the use of spirituous liquors. The principles of animal life are the same in a horse as in a man; and horses, we find undergo the severest labour with no other liquor than cool water. There are many instances where even reapers have been forced to acknowledge that plentiful draughts of milk and water have enabled them to go through the fatigues of harvest with more pleasure and fewer inconveniences to their health, then ever they experienced from the use of a mixture of rum and water. . . .

3. Too much cannot be said in favour of *Cleanliness*. If soldiers grew as speedily and spontaneously as blades of grass on the continent of America, the want of cleanliness would reduce them in two or three campaigns to a handful of men. It should extend, 1. To the *body* of a soldier. He should be obliged to wash his hands and face at least once every day, and his whole body two or three times a week, especially in summer. The cold bath was part of the military discipline of the Roman soldiers, and contributed much to preserve their health. 2. It should extend to the *clothes* of a soldier. Frequent changes of linen are indispensably necessary; and unless a strict regard is paid to these articles, all our pains to preserve the health of our soldiers, will be to no purpose, 3. It should extend to the *food* of a soldier. Great care should be taken that the vessels in which he cooks his victuals should be carefully washed after each time of their being used.

Too many soldiers should not be allowed on any pretence whatever to crowd into the same tent or quarter. The gaol fever is the offspring of the perspiration and respiration of human bodies brought into a compass too narrow to be diluted, and rendered inert by a mixture with the atmosphere. . . .

The commanding officer should take the utmost care never to suffer a soldier to sleep, or even to sit down in his tent with wet clothes, nor to lie down in a wet blanket or upon damp straw. The utmost vigilance will be necessary to guard against this fruitful source of diseases among soldiers.

The environs of each tent, and of the camp in general, should be kept perfectly clean of the offals of animals and of filth of all kinds. They should be buried or carefully removed every day beyond the neighbourhood of the camp.

4. The formation of an *Encampment* is of the utmost importance to the health of an army. It is to no purpose to seek for security from an enemy in the wisest disposition of troops in a country where marshes and mill-ponds let loose intermitting fevers upon them. Sometimes it may be necessary to encamp an army upon the side of a river. Previously to this step, it is the duty of the quarter master to inquire from what quarter the winds come at the season of his encampment. If they pass across the river before they reach his army, they will probably bring with them the seeds of bilious and intermitting fevers, and this will more especially be the case in the fall of the year. The British troops at Pensacola, by shifting their quarters every year, so as to avoid the winds that come over a river in the neighbourhood of the town, at a certain season, have preserved their health in a manner scarcely so [sic] be paralelled in so warm a climate.

Frequently changing the spot of an encampment has been found to contribute greatly to the health of an army. It effectually guards the men against the effects of those offal matters which are so small, or so concealed, as to elude the vigilance of an officer. . . .

5. Idleness is the bane of a soldier. It exposes him to temptations not only to every kind of military vice, but to every species of military disorder. But his exercise should be *regular,* and performed at *stated* periods; nor should it be suspended during his recess from the toils of war in his winter quarters. "We remark (says Montesquieu in his excellent treatise on the rise and fall of the Roman greatness) in modern times, that our soldiers perish from *immoderate* fatigue, notwithstanding it was by immense labour the Romans preserved their armies. The reason I believe was, their labour was *constant,* whereas among us our soldiers pass from the extremes of labour to the extremes of idleness, than which nothing can be more destructive to the lives of men."

The fire and smoke of wood, as also the burning of sulphur, and the explosion of gunpowder, have a singular efficacy in preserving and restoring the purity of the air. There was an instance in the last war between Britain and France, of a ship in sir Edward Hawke's fleet, that had above a hundred men on board ill with a low fever. This ship was obliged to bear her part in the well known battle between sir Edward and Monsieur Conflans. A few days after the engagement, every man on board this ship recovered, and an entire stop was put to the progress of the disease. This extraordinary event was thought to be occasioned by the explosion and effluvia of the gunpowder.

I shall conclude these directions by suggesting a few hints which appear to be worthy of the attention of the gentlemen of the army.

Consider in the first place, that the principle study of an officer, in the time of war, should be to save the blood of his men. An heroic exploit is admired most when it has been performed with the loss of a few lives. But if it be meritorious to save the lives of soldiers by skill and attention in the field, why should it be thought less so to preserve them by skill and attention of another kind in a march, or an encampment? And on the contrary, if it be criminal in an officer to sacrifice the lives of thousands by his temerity in a battle, why should it be thought less so to sacrifice twice their number in a hospital, by his negligence? . . .

Consider that your country and posterity look up to you for the preservation of the only means of establishing the liberties of America. The wisdom and eloquence of writers and orators have long since yielded to the more powerful oratory of our sword. All our hopes, therefore, are in our army. But if any thing can be added to these motives, consider further, that there is scarcely a soldier under your command who has not a mother, a wife, a sister, or a child. These helpless members of society made great sacrifices to their country when they urged the beloved objects of their affection to follow the recruiting drum to the camp. Whenever, therefore, your duty requires that you should attend to the health of your men, imagine you see *one* or perhaps *all* of their female and helpless connexions standing at the door of your tents or quarters, and beseeching you by the remembrance of the pleasures you have enjoyed, and by the prospect of the pleasures you expect, in those connexions, to repair immediately to the tents or huts of your men, and to attend to every thing which reason and conscience tell you are necessary for the preservation of their health and lives.

Source: Rush, Benjamin. *Directions for Preserving the Health of Soldiers: Addressed to the Officers of the Army of the United States. Pennsylvania Packet,* 1777. Reprint: Philadelphia: Thomas Dobson, Fry, and Kammerer, 1808.

DOCUMENT
1.12

Washington Orders Compulsory Smallpox Inoculation of the Continental Army

"Necessity Not Only Authorizes But Seems to Require the Measure"

1777

The scourge of smallpox darkened the thoughts of the commanders of both the Continental and British Armies during the Revolutionary War. Severe outbreaks of the dread disease flared in Boston and other parts of the continent throughout the conflict, and military leaders plotted many of their troop movements with an eye toward avoiding the latest conflagration. General George Washington of the Continental Army, who was himself a survivor of a 1751 battle with smallpox, was keenly aware of this threat. In July 1775, for example, he informed the Continental Congress that "I have been particularly attentive to the least symptom of smallpox: and hitherto we have been so fortunate as to have every person removed, so soon as noting, to prevent any communication, but I am apprehensive it may gain in the camps. We shall continue the utmost vigilance against this most dangerous enemy."[1]

Washington knew that his own army's vulnerability to smallpox was greater than that of the British troops, many of whom had already gained immunity due to previous inoculation or childhood bouts with the disease. And as the conflict deepened, he became increasingly concerned—for good reason, according to historians—that the British were maneuvering smallpox carriers into the path of colonial troops for the express purpose of igniting a crippling outbreak.[2] By the close of 1776, repeated, barely suppressed outbreaks of smallpox within the Continental Army convinced Washington that a program of mandatory inoculation had to be implemented quickly. On January 6, 1777, he issued a directive to this effect to William Shippen, the surgeon general of the Continental Army. This directive is reprinted here.

The colonial variolation program emphasized inoculation of new inductees so as to mitigate its impact on the army's military operations, but special military smallpox hospitals were also established to inoculate veterans who had never had the disease. In the end, Washington's successful smallpox inoculation program has been cited by scholars as one of the pivotal events in the Revolutionary War. Not only did it give Washington more strategic options in prosecuting the war, but it also neutralized an enemy that was potentially far more deadly to the Continental Army than any assemblage of Redcoats.

To DOCTOR WILLIAM SHIPPEN, JUNIOR

Head Quarters, Morristown, January 6, 1777.

Dear Sir: Finding the small pox to be spreading much and fearing that no precaution can prevent it from running thro' the whole of our Army, I have determined that the Troops shall be inoculated. This Expedient may be attended with some inconveniences and some disadvantages, but yet I trust, in its consequences will have the most happy effects. Necessity not only authorizes but seems to require the measure, for should the disorder infect the Army, in the natural way, and rage with its usual Virulence, we should have more to dread from it, than from the Sword of the Enemy. Under these Circumstances, I have directed Doctr. [Nathaniel] Bond, to prepare immediately for inoculating in this Quarter, keeping the matter as secret as possible, and request, that you will without delay inoculate all the Continental Troops that are in Philadelphia and those that shall come in, as fast as they arrive. You will spare no pains to carry them thro' the disorder with the utmost expedition, and to have them cleansed from the infection when recovered, that they may proceed to Camp, with as little injury as possible, to the Country thro' which they pass. If the business is immediately begun and favoured with the common success, I would fain hope they will be soon fit for duty, and that in a short space of time we shall have an Army not subject to this, the greatest of all calamities that can befall it, when taken in the natural way.

Source: Washington, George. Letter of January 6, 1777, to Doctor William Shippen. *The Writings of George Washington.* Vol. 6. Edited by John C. Fitzpatrick. New York: G. P. Putnam, pp. 473–74.

Notes

1. Quoted in Donald R. Hopkins, *The Greatest Killer: Smallpox in History* (Chicago: University of Chicago Press, 2002), 258.
2. Elizabeth Anne Fenn, *Pox Americana: The Great Smallpox Epidemic of 1775–82* (New York: Macmillan, 200); and Jonathan B. Tucker, *Scourge: The Once and Future Threat of Smallpox* (New York: Grove Press, 2001).

Congress Passes An Act for the Relief of Sick and Disabled Seamen

"The Said Directors Shall Hold Their Offices during the Pleasure of the President"

1798

In 1798 the U.S. Congress passed a law—An Act for the Relief of Sick and Disabled Seamen—that had significant repercussions for the republic's subsequent approach to issues of public and environmental health. Prior to this law, legislative provisions to combat disease and address the needs of the poor and destitute had been local in nature. But the 1798 act placed the responsibility for the health care of U.S. merchant seamen, a vital cog in the nation's growing economic machinery, squarely on the shoulders of the federal government. Moreover, its principal funding mechanism—a modest tax on the wages of mariners—paved the way for the U.S. government to get into the hospital-building business. Within a few decades of the passage of this bill, which is reprinted here, U.S. Marine Hospitals were sprouting in port cities up and down the Atlantic seaboard. In addition, the marine hospital tax contained in the bill was in many ways a forerunner of the payroll tax. "The gentlemen attorneys and merchants who wrote this legislation did not trust mariners to personally pay hospital taxes," explained scholar Gautham Rao. "Rather ship captains garnished the wages and paid them directly to federal customs officials."[1]

Section 1. *Be it enacted by the Senate and House of Representatives of the United States of America in Congress assembled,* That from and after the first day of September next, the master or owner of every ship or vessel of the United States, arriving from a foreign port into any port of the United States, shall, before such ship or vessel shall be admitted to an entry, render to the collector a true account of the number of seamen, that shall have been employed on board such vessel since she was last entered at any port in the United States,—and shall pay to the said collector, at the rate of twenty cents per month for every seaman so employed; which sum he is hereby authorized to retain out of the wages of such seamen.

Sec. 2. *And be it further enacted,* That from and after the first day of September next, no collector shall grant to any ship or vessel whose enrolment or license for carrying on the coasting trade has expired, a new enrolment or license before the master of such ship or vessel shall first render a true account to the collector, of the number of seamen, and the time they have severally been employed on board such ship or vessel, during the continuance of the license which has so expired, and pay to such collector twenty cents per month for every month such seamen have been severally employed, as aforesaid; which sum the said master is hereby authorized to retain out of the wages of such seamen. And if any such master shall render a false account of the number of men, and the length of time they have severally been employed, as is herein required, he shall forfeit and pay one hundred dollars.

Sec. 3. *And be it further enacted,* That it shall be the duty of the several collectors to make a quarterly return of the sums collected by them, respectively, by virtue of this act, to the Secretary of the Treasury; and the President of the United States is hereby autho-rized, out of the same, to provide for the temporary relief and maintenance of sick or disabled seamen, in the hospitals or other proper institutions now established in the sev-eral ports of the United States, or, in ports where no such institutions exist, then in such other manner as he shall direct: *Provided,* that the monies collected in any one district, shall be expended within the same.

Sec. 4. *And be it further enacted,* That if any surplus shall remain of the monies to be collected by virtue of this act, after defraying the expense of such temporary relief and support, that the same, together with such private donations as may be made for that purpose (which the President is hereby authorized to receive) shall be invested in the stock of the United States, under the direction of the President; and when, in his opinion, a sufficient fund shall be accumulated, he is hereby authorized to purchase or receive ces-sions or donations of ground or buildings, in the name of the United States, and to cause buildings, when necessary, to be erected as hospitals for the accommodation of sick and disabled seamen.

Sec. 5. *And be it further enacted,* That the President of the United States be, and he is hereby authorized to nominate and appoint, in such ports of the United States, as he may think proper, one or more persons, to be called directors of the marine hospital of the United States, whose duty it shall be to direct the expenditure of the fund assigned for their respective ports, according to the third section of this act; to provide for the accom-modation of sick and disabled seamen, under such general instructions as shall be given by the President of the United States, for that purpose, and also subject to the like general instructions, to direct and govern such hospitals as the President may direct to be built in the respective ports: and that the said directors shall hold their offices during the pleasure of the President, who is authorized to fill up all vacancies that may be occasioned by the death or removal of any of the persons so to be appointed. And the said directors shall render an account of the monies received and expended by them, once in every quarter of a year, to the Secretary of the Treasury, or such other person as the President shall direct; but no other allowance or compensation shall be made to the said directors, except the payment of such expenses as they may incur in the actual discharge of the duties required by this act.

Approved, July 16, 1798.

Source: An Act for the Relief of Sick and Disabled Seamen. Fifth Congress, 1798, pp. 695–696, http://history.nih.gov/research/downloads/1StatL605.pdf.

NOTE

1. Gautham Rao, "Sailors' Health and National Wealth: Marine Hospitals in the Early Republic," *Common-Place* 9, no. 1 (October 2008), www.historycooperative.org/journals/cp/vol-09/no-01/rao/.

CHAPTER 2

Health Care and Regulation in Antebellum America

1800–1860

When the United States emerged from the Revolutionary War, it marched into the nineteenth century on unsteady legs. True, the fledgling nation boasted several major commercial ports, a stunning wealth of timber, coal, rich soil, and other natural resources, an ambitious and hardy population of about four million people (including 700,000 slaves), and a deep stable of remarkable political talent. These assets were not inconsequential. As George Washington remarked after the signing of the Treaty of Paris in 1783, Americans had not only made themselves "the sole Lords and Proprietors of a vast Tract of Continent . . . abounding with all the necessaries and conveniences of life," but also established themselves as "Actors on a most conspicuous Theatre, which seems to be peculiarly designed by Providence for the display of human greatness and felicity."[1]

Still, Washington and the nation's other Founders recognized that the newborn republic was a fragile thing. Its political institutions were untested, its financial scaffolding was no longer supported by the British Crown, and its political environment was supercharged. Other formidable obstacles to growth included epidemics of deadly disease, deep cultural divisions within the new republic, and Indian tribes that had become restive and angry about proliferating intrusions into their traditional homelands.

Little wonder, then, that health care politics and policies came to be marked by contradiction and confusion in antebellum America. On the one hand, the United States government and individual states claimed and exercised authority in some important public health realms, as concerns about the community welfare and national good trumped apprehension about state and federal authority over individual liberties. The expansion of America's nascent hospital system, reforms in the treatment of the mentally ill, and increased rates of vaccination for smallpox all came about as a direct result of regulatory intervention by the state during this era. On the other hand, efforts to impose some measure of order on the practices of physicians, surgeons, apothecaries, and manufacturers of patent medicines—the bedrock elements of private medical care in America—continued to run aground on the shoals of individual liberty concerns. These difficulties were further amplified by continued unhappiness with the performance of regular physicians and the overall anti-intellectual tenor of Jacksonian America.

EARLY OUTLINES OF A GOVERNMENT-SUPPORTED HOSPITAL SYSTEM TAKE SHAPE

During the first half of the nineteenth century, hospitals remained a rare sight across most of America. The most visible hospitals were those that were opened and operated by the U.S. Marine Service in the aftermath of congressional passage of the 1798 Act for the Relief of Sick and Disabled Seamen. This legislation, which aimed to provide health and disability assistance to merchant seamen, is frequently described as the first federal health care initiative in the United States. By the mid-1800s, the federal government had expanded its Marine Hospital System from its origins in the bustling port cities of the Atlantic seaboard to important trade centers on the Mississippi and Ohio Rivers and other inland waterways of the western frontier. Territorial legislatures and merchants petitioned the federal government for their own marine hospitals throughout the opening decades of the nineteenth century. This demand fed steady growth. From 1818 to 1858 the Marine Hospital System expanded from twenty-six to ninety-five facilities (although most facilities were leased spaces within private hospitals and boardinghouses, not new buildings). In addition, annual admissions into the system jumped during this same span of time from the low hundreds to ten thousand a year.[2]

Inadequate federal funding for these hospitals was a perennial issue, as was overcrowding and understaffing. When the U.S. Navy raised the possibility of incorporating its own modest health care system into the larger Marine Hospital System, Congress authorized an 1849 review of the Marine hospitals with an eye toward assessing the feasibility of the Navy proposal. The resulting report, delivered two years later, indicated that most of the facilities were in serious disrepair due to years of miserly funding and inattention from Congress. The authors of the report also charged that it was a "system" in name only, as "neither in form nor character has any uniformity in their arrangement been observed."[3] The merger idea was quickly shelved, but Congress still failed to act decisively to shore up the ailing Marine hospitals. Increasingly distracted by the sectional conflict over slavery, Congress continued to neglect the system through the Civil War, when both armies used Marine hospital facilities in their territories as infirmaries.[4]

In the meantime, a growing number of hospitals under private control, though funded from a mix of public and private sources, were opening their doors across America to care for the sick poor. These facilities did not supplant the almshouse. To the contrary, almshouses, which had been the only source of institutional health care for paupers in colonial times, grew in prominence in the first half of the nineteenth century. This was especially true after 1828, when states stripped away the modest funding they had previously provided for home relief to the sick poor. "By making the almshouse the only source of governmental aid to the poor, legislatures hoped to restrict expenditures for public assistance," explained historian Paul Starr. "Often squalid and overcrowded, a place of shame and indignity, the almshouse offered a minimum level of support—its function as a deterrent to poverty and public assistance ruled out any amenities."[5]

By contrast, early American hospitals enjoyed far greater amounts of public support. Following the example of cities such as New York and Philadelphia, both of which had in the eighteenth century provided public funds to breathe life into America's earliest hospitals, city and state governments bestowed state funds on new hospitals in Boston, Chicago, New Orleans, and New York.[6]

SECOND U. S. MARINE HOSPITAL, PORT OF BOSTON, MASS. OCCUPIED 1827-1860.
(Still standing in Chelsea.)

An Act for the Relief of Sick and Disabled Seamen (1798) was a federal initiative to provide health care for all merchant seamen. After its passage, a system of Marine hospitals was created to carry out this landmark legislation. The pictured Marine hospital in Boston, Massachusetts, was the second one established in the United States.

The willingness of state legislatures to assist with the operating expenses of these and other new hospitals through grants, auction and court fees, taxes on certain business establishments **(See Document 2.2)**, lotteries, and other means showcased the competitive spirit that animated early legislatures, but other factors were also at work. Hospitals were a manifestation of Christian beliefs about the need to minister to the poor, and they were touted as a training ground for young physicians. Finally, the affluent private citizens who served as trustees, sponsors, and administrators of these early hospitals accrued personal benefits from these roles. As Starr observed, "the sponsorship of hospitals gave legitimacy to the wealth and position of the donors, just as the association with prominent citizens gave legitimacy to the hospital and its physicians. Hospital philanthropy, like other kinds of charity, was a way to convert wealth into status and influence."[7]

Despite their growing popularity, hospitals remained concentrated only in the young nation's largest cities for the first three-quarters of the nineteenth century. In fact, most Americans—and American health care providers—of this period lived their entire lives without ever setting foot in a hospital ward. "The hospital was little more than an embryo in the era of [John] Adams and [Thomas] Jefferson," declared historian Charles E. Rosenberg. "And though hospitals increased in scale and numbers with the growth of America's urban population, they remained and were to remain insignificant in the provision of medical care in antebellum America. Yet to that handful of elite urban physicians who staffed them and those philanthropists who supported and administered them, these pioneer hospitals were significant indeed."[8]

REFORMS IN THE TREATMENT OF THE MENTALLY ILL

Government authorities of the antebellum era also enacted significant reforms in the treatment and care of the mentally ill. These changes were due in part to the late-nineteenth-century assimilation of Enlightenment thought in America, with its attendant emphasis on reason, empiricism, scientific research, social welfare, and individual rights. But it also was spurred to a considerable degree by the efforts of a few individuals. The first of these difference makers was Benjamin Rush, the famous Philadelphia physician and signatory to the Declaration of Independence. During the first years of America's existence, Rush used his prominent public station to advance his belief that mental illness was not a hopeless curse, as earlier generations had held, but rather a disorder that could be cured with sensitive and diligent care, not unlike other afflictions. Influential European physicians such as Philippe Piniel of France and William Tuke of England offered similar assessments of mental illness, further altering long-held conventional wisdoms about how society's "lunatics" and "maniacs" should be treated.

Out of these forces was born a fundamental shift in American attitudes toward those suffering from mental illness. A more humane system of care known as the moral treatment came to the fore in the early nineteenth century, gathering adherents left and right. It involved placing mental patients, who had previously been consigned to dank basements or other horrific quarters, in small, cheerfully appointed asylums in the countryside, where they could receive light outdoor exercise, regular exposure to music and other arts, friendly but professional staff attention, light and nutritious diet, and an overall "system of humane vigilance," as one New York clinician put it in 1811.[9]

Moral treatment was not universally embraced. Many institutions for the mentally ill remained exceedingly grim places. But moral treatment programs were implemented in some of America's leading institutions during the first half of the nineteenth century, including the Connecticut Retreat for the Insane, now commonly referred to as the Hartford Retreat, in Connecticut, Bloomingdale Insane Asylum in New York, and the Pennsylvania Hospital in Philadelphia. Positive early reports from these and other institutions had an impact in numerous statehouses where legislators were considering bills to establish new state insane asylums. But an even bigger factor in the ultimate passage of many of these bills was the indomitable Dorothea Dix, a Massachusetts schoolteacher who carried out a hugely successful one-woman crusade for better treatment of the indigent insane in the 1840s **(See Document 2.7)**.

More humane treatment of the mentally ill can be credited to the lobbying of Dr. Benjamin Rush, a Philadelphia physician and signer of the Declaration of Independence. Rush was the first prominent American figure to denounce immoral treatment of the mentally ill. He refused to accept that mental illness was unlike any other disorder, both curable and treatable.

Schoolteacher Dorothea Dix, a Massachusetts native, was extremely successful in lobbying state legislatures to build moral treatment insane asylums for the mentally ill. She took a special interest in poverty-stricken patients.

Compulsory Vaccination and Other Public Health Issues

Antebellum America also saw an overall increase in state and federal involvement in public health issues. But this increase was haphazard and halting, with some policy areas receiving much more attention than others. Regarding disease prevention, for example, municipalities, state officials, and federal departments all displayed a steadfast conviction that imposing and carrying out quarantine measures and compulsory vaccination programs were duties well within their authority. But in the realm of urban sanitation, government agencies at all levels—and especially the federal one—remained mostly on the sidelines, to the great consternation of midcentury sanitary reformers alarmed by the squalor and pollution afflicting the nation's fast-growing cities.

Vaccination campaigns in the Western world in the nineteenth century were a direct result of the 1798 announcement by British physician Edward Jenner that infecting people with cowpox, a disease of cattle that produced only mild symptoms in humans, could give them immunity against the related disease of smallpox. Within a matter of a few years, vaccination had eclipsed inoculation—an older, more primitive method of inducing immunity that sometimes triggered full onset of the disease itself—as the plague-fighter of choice in America. In 1809 Massachusetts enacted the nation's first mandatory vaccination law in the name of public safety and the common welfare. Other cities and states followed suit, and in 1813 the U.S. Congress passed a federal act to encourage smallpox vaccination **(See Document 2.1)**. By 1820 compulsory vaccination had joined naval quarantines and pesthouses as essential weapons in the battle against smallpox outbreaks.

Most citizens willingly complied with these vaccination efforts and accepted the authority of public officials to execute them. Vaccination initiatives did encounter pockets of resistance, however. In 1820, for example, residents of a small town in Vermont approved a new tax to pay for community-wide vaccination, only to have one local farmer refuse to pay the tax. His assertion that the township had no authority to levy such a tax was met stonily by the town's leadership, which confiscated his cow and sold it for payment. The outraged farmer sued, but the state Supreme Court eventually upheld the confiscation as well as the authority of municipalities to use public funds for vaccination purposes.[10] A far more contentious element of America's early public vaccination programs was whether the state could compel citizens to undergo the procedure. This became particularly problematic in the second half of the century, by which time smallpox outbreaks had become far less frequent.

Sanitary reformers urged city, state, and federal officials to adopt a similarly proactive stance in combating mounting squalor and filth in the nation's fast-growing cities and towns **(See Document 2.8)**. They asserted that the voluntary measures and private funds being used in these population centers to address leaking privies, faulty sewers, and overcrowded tenements that were incubators of sickness and disease were completely inadequate given the scale of these problems. Advocates of increased sanitary regulation also observed that ample precedent existed for lawmakers and government officials to take action. "I can see no good reason," fumed a New York City reformer in the mid-1840s,

> why a State and City that have *legislated so immensely*, and sacrificed so much public and private property to establish and execute Quarantine Laws, (many of them of more than doubtful utility,) to prevent the importation of Yellow Fever, Cholera, and the Plague, into our populous city, should by any means judge it absurd or unnecessary, to enact

a few laws, and appoint a few officers to inspect certain persons and places within the city, (with power to remove) where and by whom all those infectious and contagious maladies may be *manufactured,* and of such a quality, too, as to be perhaps more dangerous than those of foreign growth.[11]

Public health advances were most evident in the area of public water supply. City planners and managers recognized the importance of potable water, and in the first half of the nineteenth century many major cities invested in municipal waterworks systems. The arrival of these engineering marvels improved water quality in some urban areas, as did regulations approved in the wake of British scientist John Snow's 1854 discovery that a contaminated water pump had sparked a London cholera outbreak.

In most other realms, reformer calls for regulatory intervention were frustrated until midcentury, when a steady drumbeat of warnings about linkages between urban conditions and poor public health finally began to be heeded by some lawmakers, public administrators, and concerned private citizens. This progress was due in large part to the efforts of two sanitarians, John Griscom and Lemuel Shattuck, who produced ground-breaking sanitary studies of New York City and Massachusetts, respectively. Griscom's contribution was *The Sanitary Condition of the Laboring Population of New York*, which was first released in 1842 and subsequently published in pamphlet form in 1845 (**See Document 2.6**). Like other sanitary studies produced earlier in the century in both America and Europe, Griscom's study made a convincing case for the "elimination of common nuisances, regulation of noxious industries, cleaning of streets, and introduction of clean water and sewers."[12] But Griscom augmented these observations about the city's public spaces with an extensive examination of the unhealthy conditions that prevailed inside the tenement houses of New York City. He urged new public regulations for the "correction of interior conditions of tenements, when dangerous to health and life. The latter should be regarded by the legislator and executive with as much solicitude as the prosperity of citizens."[13]

Shattuck's contribution to the public health reform crusade, carried out under the banner of the Massachusetts Sanitary Commission, was the 1850 *Report of a General Plan for the Promotion of Public and Personal Health* (**See Document 2.10**). Making extensive use of statistical analysis of state morbidity and mortality rates and other data, Shattuck laid out a long slate of regulatory recommendations to tackle the sanitary problems facing America's fast-growing cities. Most notably, he issued a visionary call for the development of local and state mechanisms for the collection and processing of health data that would help policymakers reach informed decisions about public health.

Neither of these reports had an immediate impact on health policy in America, and little effort was made by lawmakers or public health officials to utilize the authors' evident public health expertise.[14] But the reform proposals laid out by Griscom and Shattuck were revisited after the Civil War, and in the late 1860s and 1870s local and state boards of public health that proliferated in the postwar era implemented many of their ideas.

THE REGULAR PROFESSION IN DISARRAY

Private health practitioners in antebellum America, meanwhile, operated in a virtually regulation-free environment. In many cases, in fact, the smattering of modest licensing laws and other regulations that had been passed during the colonial and post-Revolutionary eras to govern the practice of health care were struck down during the first half of the nineteenth century.

This decline in already meager state oversight of medical practice stemmed from several factors, each of which was deeply intertwined and mutually reinforcing. One important element was widespread public dissatisfaction with the quality of medical care dispensed by regular physicians in early nineteenth-century American communities. Many orthodox practitioners remained wedded to heroic depletive therapies such as purging, vomiting, and bloodletting that were actually injurious to patients. This faith in heroic medicine went largely unshaken—despite rising excoriation and ridicule from nontraditional healers and patients—until the 1830s and 1840s, when discerning physicians such as Boston's Jacob Bigelow confessed to serious doubts about its efficacy. "We should not allow [the patient] to be tormented with useless and annoying applications, in a disease of settled destiny," he told fellow regulars in an 1835 issue of the *Boston Medical and Surgical Journal*. "It should be remembered that all cases are susceptible of errors of commission, as well as of omission, and that by an excessive application of the means of art, we may frustrate the intentions of nature, when they are salutary, or embitter the approach of death when it is inevitable."[15]

Orthodox physicians also regularly engaged in unseemly public disputes with one another over the root causes of sickness and disease outbreaks, including horrible, recurring outbreaks of cholera and yellow fever. Their inability to reach consensus on the causes of these deadly epidemics, or the best treatments and preventive measures for combating the outbreaks, seriously eroded public faith in the competency of regular physicians. Members of the regular fraternity were keenly aware of this slippage, but the very nature of these impasses made compromise impossible. As a result, they pursued fruitless strategies to minimize the damage to their profession. In 1822, for example, a New York physician commenting on a proposed board of health for the city emphasized that its membership should be composed primarily of laymen, for "[if the board was] exclusively made up of medical gentlemen there is too much reason to fear that their different opinions might lead, as too often happens, to interminable disputes, and to most disastrous consequences."[16]

Finally, the fraternity of regular physicians suffered from a tremendous influx of charlatans and poorly trained practitioners into their midst during the early decades of the nineteenth century. Many people seeking medical care in this mostly regulation-free environment found it impossible to differentiate between competent, trained physicians and those who had only cursory training—or no training at all. Even a medical diploma provided little guarantee of skill or knowledge, because many medical colleges that sprouted during this period were of poor quality. Given this state of affairs, increased public skepticism of the abilities of all members of the profession was inevitable **(See Document 2.4)**.

ALTERNATIVE HEALING CHOICES IN THE MARKETPLACE

With regular physicians set back on their heels, America's health care marketplace was quickly overrun by purveyors of a wide variety of alternative healing therapies and philosophies of treatment. The most famous trailblazer in this regard was New England native Samuel Thomson, whose *New Guide to Health: or Botanic Family Physician* (1822) ranks as the most influential health care text of the era **(See Document 2.3)**. Thomson was a self-taught physician who developed and patented a system of commonsense botanic medicine that was embraced by huge numbers of Americans, especially in rural areas. Eschewing the need for formal medical knowledge, Thomson asserted that citizens who followed his basic rules could effectively address their health needs. This egalitarianism was a key element of Thomson's popularity, for his Jacksonian audience was enormously receptive to rhetorical flourishes about corrupt "elites" and their claimed "exclusivity of knowledge." Before long, battalions of Thomsonians who bought rights to this system (at $20 a pop) were marching across the countryside extolling its many virtues to carpenters, farmers, and shopkeepers.

The so-called Thomsonian movement enjoyed tremendous success throughout the 1820s and much of the 1830s, but it was in growing disarray by 1840. "Individuals and companies seized on Thomson's name and cashed in on it," explained John Duffy. "Even more ironic, his later disciples organized medical schools and began institutionalizing Thomsonian medicine, a development contrary to one of the fundamental principles of Thomsonianism."[17] The movement fragmented into two

A self-taught physician and founder of the Thomsonian medicine movement, Samuel Thomson achieved financial success and widespread popularity with his 1822 book, New Guide to Health: or Botanic Family Physician. *Thomson denounced the need for any formal medical education and instead advocated commonsense botanic methods of healing.*

separate societies, but neither lasted for long. The camp loyal to Thomson disintegrated soon after his death in 1843, while the other was gradually absorbed into another botanicals-based system known as eclecticism.

Eclectic practitioners cut against the grain of the Jacksonian self-help ethos by emphasizing the importance of specialized, professional knowledge. By midcentury, several eclectic schools of medicine were churning out graduates well versed in herbal remedies. Similar degree-granting medical schools were also opened to train physicians in other alternative healing systems such as hydropathy (also known as water cure), which flourished in the 1840s and 1850s.

The most notable of the other health sects to emerge in antebellum America was homeopathy. Developed by a university-trained German doctor named Samuel Hahnemann and introduced to America by physician Hans Gram in the 1820s, homeopathy emphasized the healing powers of nature over the usage of heroic therapies or medicinal drugs in anything but highly diluted form. Numerous regular physicians adopted broad planks of homeopathy for their own use, in large measure because victims of midcentury outbreaks of Asiatic cholera and yellow fever responded far better to the homeopathic method—which essentially amounted to extended bed rest and sympathetic attention from caregivers—than to bloodletting and other grueling orthodox treatments. In 1844 homeopaths formed the first national medical association, the American Institute of Homeopathy, and four years later it opened its first medical school, the Homeopathic Medical College of Pennsylvania. Other homeopathic institutions opened as well, including a major homeopathic medical school in New York City that was supported by poet, abolitionist, and editor William Cullen Bryant and other prominent citizens **(See Document 2.11)**.

Despite making inroads with a considerable number of open-minded regulars, homeopathy was violently opposed by orthodox practitioners as a group. Some critics, such as Oliver Wendell Holmes in his 1842 "Homeopathy and Its Kindred Delusions," attacked basic tenets of homeopathic science and methodology. Most opponents, however, focused on condemning the sect's acceptance of women as students and colleagues (a receptivity that other sectarian groups also displayed) or arguing, in often wounded tones, that homeopathic criticisms of regular physicians betrayed a level of unprofessional conduct that simply could not be countenanced. In 1852, for example, the Connecticut Medical Society publicized a report that characterized homeopaths as radical and implacable enemies of the regular profession: "Very different would have been the [regular] profession's attitude toward homeopathy if it had aimed, like other doctrines advanced by physicians, to gain a foothold among medical men alone or chiefly, instead of making its appeal to the popular favor and against the profession."[18] Angered and unnerved by homeopathy's rise, institutions dominated by regulars, from hospitals and the army corps to the American Medical Association (AMA), actively blackballed or otherwise shunned homeopaths from 1850 through the close of the century. Despite this stance, homeopathy remained popular in large northern cities and small southern communities alike.

Finally, the health care cacophony featured numerous peddlers of patent medicines and dispensers of folk remedies. Of the two, producers and sellers of patent medicines constituted a much greater threat to public health. Whereas the best folk medicine was based on generations of European and Native America experience with herbs and other natural materials, patent medicines had little to recommend them. In fact, these nostrums frequently included ingredients ranging from urine, dung, and wood lice—all included in response to the popular belief that the worse a medicine tasted, the greater its curative powers—to cocaine, opium, and morphine. These nostrums were decried by regular physicians, trained apothecaries, and sectarian groups, but their popularity soared in the nineteenth century due in large measure to newspaper and magazine advertising. The problem of adulterated drugs was further exacerbated by widespread difficulties with the adulteration of legitimate medicinal drugs due to a lack of regulation of the manufacturing process. In 1848 proliferating tales of permanent disability or death from the imbibing of dangerous nostrums and contaminated drugs finally convinced the U.S. Congress to take action with a law that forbade the importation of "adulterated and spurious drugs and medicines." But this law was a paper tiger in that it applied only to imported drugs at a time when the great majority of these substances was being produced by domestic manufacturers **(See Document 2.9)**.

JACKSONIAN DEMOCRACY AND HEALTH CARE

Policymakers proved utterly ill equipped to impose any order on the "anything goes" atmosphere of the health care industry in antebellum America. This ineffectual performance was in part a classic case of political gridlock, for the policymakers themselves cleaved into camps allegiant to the various healing systems emerging across the health care landscape. Regular practitioners, homeopaths, Thomsonians, and other sectarians all had their champions in city halls, state assemblies, and the U.S. Congress. Some of these legislators and officials acted out of genuine personal convictions about the superiority of one medical system over another. Others were motivated primarily by a wish to woo constituents and political sponsors in their ward or district.

The retreat of policymakers from any meaningful regulation and oversight of the health care industry was also a clear manifestation of the antielitist, antiprofessional underpinnings of Jacksonian democracy—an era of American history that began in the 1820s, reached its zenith with Andrew Jackson's presidency in 1828, and continued through midcentury. As scholar Paul Starr put it, "the Thomsonian movement and other developments in medicine were a relatively minor expression of a much larger cultural and political upheaval."[19]

Jacksonian democracy was marked, among other things, by a fervent belief that aristocratic professionals and other elites had come to exercise monopolies over U.S. government and business and that this system needed to be torn down and replaced by a more democratic and egalitarian model. The headstrong Jackson and his supporters subsequently spearheaded democratic initiatives that included extending voting rights from white male landowners to all white male citizens, selecting judges by ballot instead of relying on political appointment, and eliminating regulatory obstacles to entrance in medicine, law, and other professions.

Some salutary aspects to this crusade were meant to empower the "common man." As historian Craig James Hazen noted, the pungent blend of democratic and antielitist ideas floating around in Jacksonian America galvanized and excited ordinary citizens and made them much more likely to "discuss, debate, create, synthesize, modify, demonize or embrace religious, scientific, and philosophical ideas" on their own.[20] But these same stirrings too often resulted in blanket condemnations of "book learning" as an affectation or even as a likely sign of moral turpitude. By the early 1830s, observed historian Regina Markell Morantz-Sanchez, "hostility to all professional distinctions [had become] a featured aspect of American political rhetoric."[21]

A REGULATORY REGIME IN RETREAT

Jacksonians, Thomsonians, and other sectarians took full advantage of this political environment to demolish various barriers to entry in professions that had long been dominated by the affluent and university-trained. From the 1820s through midcentury, licensing statutes were repealed in numerous states and territories, especially in the areas of law and medicine. The number of states and territories mandating professional study to practice law, for instance, fell from three-quarters at the beginning of the century to a third by 1830.[22] Attacks on medical licensure were even more intense and successful, due to the political muscle of Thomsonians and other irregular sectarians.

Keenly aware that repeal of licensing regulations would produce a flood of new competitors in the marketplace, orthodox practitioners tried to beat back the deregulatory crusades by framing the licensing statute as a vital tool in helping the public differentiate between science (personified in regular professionals) and quackery (sectarians and untrained practitioners). The irregulars responded by noting that, in many states and territories, licensing authority had been placed in the hands of regular medical societies, the membership of which had a direct financial stake in keeping the playing field clear of sectarian competitors. Sectarians cited these arrangements—with some justification—as evidence that the entire medical licensing process was tainted, corrupt, and expressly designed to lock them out of the marketplace, regardless of the merits of their healing systems. Thomsonians, homeopaths, and other irregulars thus framed their struggle against licensing as one of free enterprise and individual liberty against pernicious special interests, and their arguments ultimately carried the day.

Medical licensing regulations fell like dominoes across the young republic. In Alabama, medical licensing laws that had been passed in 1823 were amended nine years later to exempt any person "practicing medicine on the botanical system of Dr. Samuel Thomson." In New York, state legislators in 1830 repealed a three-year-old law that had made the unlicensed practice of medicine a misdemeanor subject to fine and imprisonment. Fourteen years later, a sustained campaign from Thomsonians convinced state legislators to toss out its entire slate of medical licensing laws (**See Document 2.5**). In Georgia and Michigan, state lawmakers repealed all their medical licensing laws in 1839 and 1851, respectively. Maine, Maryland and Vermont struck down various licensing regulations in the late 1830s. Other states, including Kentucky, Missouri, Pennsylvania, and Virginia, proudly kept their decks clear of any medical licensing regulations throughout this tumultuous period.

By 1845 ten states had repealed their licensure statutes. Another eight states and territories, mostly in the West, never put any licensing regulations on the books in the first place.[23] The last holdouts to the licensure repeal crusades—Louisiana and New Jersey—fell in the 1850s and early 1860s. By the end of the Civil War, not a single state in the restored Union was making any attempt to regulate the practice of medicine.[24]

MEDICAL SCHOOL FREE-FOR-ALL

State oversight of medical education also was virtually nonexistent in the antebellum period, despite the fact that medical colleges sprouted like mad during this time. At the beginning of the nineteenth century, only four small medical colleges were operating in the United States. The number of educational institutions devoted to health and medicine soared as the century wore on, swollen by the immigrant-driven expansion in America's population as well as the continued absence of regulation regarding the establishment and operation of medical schools. By 1850 more than forty medical schools were operating in the United States, whereas all of France supported only three.[25]

Some of these institutions were founded and supported by regular physicians genuinely dedicated to upgrading the quality of medical care in the United States. These physicians also believed that an emphasis on formal education and training would give professionals a leg up over sectarian options in the marketplace. But these hopes were shaken, if not dashed entirely, by an influx of for-profit ventures that diluted the quality of instruction all across the board. These proprietary medical schools instituted a range of policies designed primarily to attract tuition-paying students (providing sound training was of secondary importance). Such policies included low tuition fees, short academic terms of instruction, and low standards, both for admittance and for graduation. Not surprisingly, these conditions made it difficult for colleges to attract top staff. This race to the bottom sucked in even some of the finest medical schools, which reluctantly reduced their academic years and relaxed their graduation requirements to keep their doors open in the hypercompetitive environment.

The rise of medical school diploma mills brought a corresponding increase in the number of poorly trained physicians in the marketplace, which further eroded public trust in regular medicine. This was a source of considerable distress to more reputable physicians such as New York's Nathan Smith Davis, who lamented in 1845 that only one out of a hundred physicians were truly worthy of the term:

But far otherwise is it with the great mass. With no *practical* knowledge of chemistry and botany; with but a smattering of anatomy and physiology, hastily caught during a sixteen weeks' attendance on the anatomical theatre of a medical college; with still less of real pathology; they enter the profession having mastered just enough of the details of practice to give them the requisite *self-assurance* for commanding the confidence of the public; but without either an adequate fund of knowledge or that degree of mental discipline, and habits of patient study which will enable them ever to supply their defects. Hence they plod on through life, with a fixed routine of practice, consisting of calomel, antimony, opium, and the lancet, almost as empirically applied as is cayenne pepper, lobelia, and steam, by another class of men.[26]

But the proliferation of medical schools in antebellum America did have some silver linings. Most important, the absence of regulation greatly facilitated women's access to the medical profession. A small number of women infiltrated the ranks of the male-dominated medical schools in the 1840s, and in 1850 the Female Medical College of Pennsylvania became the world's first all-woman doctor of medicine (MD)–granting medical school. This milestone paved the way for the opening of several other institutions that offered regular or homeopathic medical degrees to women.[27] In addition, elite physicians became increasingly supportive of hospitals, which gained a growing reputation as the best place for clinical training. The existence of diploma mills also did not wholly obscure the fact that some of the medical schools that operated in the antebellum era did provide a higher level of training for physicians, pharmacists, and surgeons than had ever been available before in America. The graduates of these programs would become a key element of the nation's health care advances in the post–Civil War era.

BIRTH OF THE AMERICAN MEDICAL ASSOCIATION

The American Medical Association, the leading physicians' organization in the United States today, was borne out of the furor that surrounded the rise of the medical school diploma mills. In the 1840s the antielitist ideology of Jacksonian democracy was still strong, but it was ebbing in some parts of the country. Sensing opportunity—and increasingly desperate to staunch the flow of inadequately trained practitioners into their ranks—leaders of regular medical societies in New England, New York, and Ohio lobbied their legislatures for laws that would raise the standards of medical schools.

These efforts were not successful, but the experience convinced the New York Medical Society, which had been perhaps the most unrelenting advocate for licensing and standard regulation, that a new approach was needed. Led by the reforming physician Nathan Smith Davis, the society's membership decided that a national organization was necessary. Such an organization could not only press for medical school and health industry reforms, but also fill the void left by state inaction by implementing its own standards of professionalism and practice. The AMA was thus founded in 1847, and at its very first meeting in Philadelphia it adopted the nation's first formal code of medical ethics, as well as the country's first national standards for preliminary medical education and MD degrees. The AMA's influence was at first limited. In its early years, it was perhaps best known for encouraging its membership to maintain a hostile attitude toward homeopathic practitioners and other sectarians. In the twentieth century, however, it would grow into one of the nation's most powerful players in the realms of health care politics and policymaking.

NOTES

1. George Washington, *Writings*, ed. John Rhodehamel (New York: Library of America, 1997), 517.

2. Gautham Rao, "Sailors' Health and National Wealth: Marine Hospitals in the Early Republic," *Common-Place* 9, no. 1 (October 2008), www.historycooperative.org/journals/cp/vol-09/no-01/rao/.

3. Quoted in Fitzhugh Mullan, *Plagues and Politics: The Story of the United States Public Health Service* (New York: Basic Books, 1989), 19.

4. Jesse L. Steinfeld, "The U.S. Public Health Service," in Department of Health, Education, and Welfare, Public Health Service, *U.S. Health in America, 1776–1976* (Washington, DC: Government Printing Office, 1977), 66–88.

5. Paul Starr, *The Social Transformation of American Medicine* (New York: Basic Books, 1982), 150.

6. Charles E. Rosenberg, *The Care of Strangers: The Rise of America's Hospital System* (New York: Basic Books, 1987), 106.

7. Starr, *The Social Transformation of American Medicine*, 153.

8. Rosenberg, *The Care of Strangers*, 18–19.

9. Quoted in Albert Deutsch, *The Mentally Ill in America: A History of Their Care and Treatment from Colonial Times* (New York: Doubleday, Doran and Co., 1937), 92.

10. James Colgrove, "Immunity for the People: The Challenge of Achieving High Vaccine Coverage in American History," *Public Health Reports* 122, no. 2 (March–April 2007): 248–57.

11. Quoted in John Hoskins Griscom, *The Sanitary Condition of the Laboring Population of New York* (New York: Harper, 1845), 29.

12. Elizabeth Blackmar, "Accountability for Public Health: Regulating the Housing Market in Nineteenth-Century New York City," in *Hives of Sickness: Public Health and Epidemics in New York City*, ed. David Rosner (Brunswick, NJ: Rutgers University Press, 1995), 54.

13. Quoted in *New York Journal of Medicine*, Vol. 1 (New York: Langley, 1843), 94.

14. Richard A. Meckel, *Save the Babies: American Public Health Reform and the Prevention of Infant Mortality, 1850–1929* (Baltimore: Johns Hopkins University Press, 1990), 17

15. Quoted in William G. Rothstein, *American Physicians in the Nineteenth Century: From Sects to Science* (Baltimore: Johns Hopkins University Press, 1985), 187.

16. Quoted in John Duffy, *From Humors to Medical Science: A History of American Medicine*, 2nd ed. (Urbana: University of Illinois Press, 1993), 148.

17. Duffy, *From Humors to Medical Science*, 82.

18. Quoted in Starr, *The Social Transformation of American Medicine*, 98.

19. Starr, *The Social Transformation of American Medicine*, 57.

20. Craig James Hazen, *The Village Enlightenment in America: Popular Religion and Science in the Nineteenth Century* (Urbana: University of Illinois Press, 2000), 3.

21. Regina Markell Morantz-Sanchez, "Science, Health, Reform, and the Woman Physician," in *Major Problems in the History of American Medicine and Public Health*, ed. John Harley Warner and Janet A. Tighe (Boston: Houghton Mifflin, 2001), 150.

22. Starr, *The Social Transformation of American Medicine*, 57.

23. Rothstein, *American Physicians in the Nineteenth Century*, 77, 145, 332–39; and Duffy, *From Humors to Medical Science*, 140.

24. Richard H. Shryock, *Medical Licensing in America, 1650–1965* (Baltimore: Johns Hopkins University Press, 1967), 30–31.

25. Starr, *The Social Transformation of American Medicine*, 42.

26. Quoted in Rothstein, *American Physicians in the Nineteenth Century,* 127.

27. John Harley Warner and Janet A. Tighe, eds., *Major Problems in the History of American Medicine and Public Health* (Boston: Houghton Mifflin, 2001), 126.

Congress Passes a Federal Vaccination Act

"To Furnish [Genuine Vaccine Matter] to Any Citizen"

1813

Antebellum-era policymakers at both the state and federal level were generally reluctant to involve themselves in health care regulation and public health issues, with the notable exception of disease control. In this area, authorities displayed a willingness to impose naval quarantines on disease-tainted ships, forcibly isolate diagnosed or suspected individual carriers of disease in pesthouses and other facilities, and pass compulsory smallpox vaccination laws. The first statewide mandatory vaccination law was passed by Massachusetts in 1809, and in 1813 the U.S. Congress signaled its approbation for this and similar measures by passing An Act to Encourage Vaccination, which is reprinted here. This act created one of the first public health programs in American history.

This federal act was welcomed by vaccination proponents who recognized its potential for increasing public acceptance of the practice. Consequently, they were sorely disappointed when the law was repealed nine years later, on May 4, 1822. The stated rationale for the repeal was that the 1813 act constituted excessive federal intrusion into state affairs and individual liberties. But repeal was primarily a response to an unfortunate incident in North Carolina in November 1821, when the federal agent responsible for the vaccination program inadvertently sent an envelope of live smallpox scabs, instead of vaccine, to a doctor in the town of Tarboro. When a small but deadly outbreak of smallpox erupted in the town, Congress decided to distance itself from the smallpox vaccination issue.

An Act to encourage Vaccination.

Be it enacted by the Senate and House of Representatives of the United States of America in Congress assembled, That the President of the United States be, and he is hereby authorized to appoint an agent to preserve the genuine vaccine matter, and to furnish the same to any citizen of the United States, whenever it may be applied for, through the medium of the post-office; and such agent shall, previous to his entering upon the execution of the duties assigned to him by this act, and before he shall be entitled to the privilege of franking any letter or package as herein allowed, take and subscribe the following oath or affirmation, before some magistrate, and cause a certificate thereof to be filed in the general post-office: "I, A. B. do swear (or affirm, as the case may be) that I will faithfully use my best exertions to preserve the genuine vaccine matter, and to furnish the same to the citizens of the United States; and also, that I will abstain from every thing prohibited in relation to the establishment of the post-office of the United States." And it shall be the duty of the said agent to transmit to the several postmasters in the United States a copy of this act: and he shall also forward to them a public notice, directing how and where all application shall be made to him for vaccine matter.

Sec. 2. *And be it further enacted,* That all letters or packages not exceeding half an ounce in weight, containing vaccine matter, or relating to the subject of vaccination, and that alone, shall be carried by the United States' mail free of any postage, either to or from the agent who may be appointed to carry the provisions of this act into effect: *Provided always,* that the said agent before he delivers any letter for transmission by the mail, shall in his own proper handwriting, on the outside thereof, endorse the word "Vaccination," and thereto subscribe his name, and shall previously furnish the postmaster of the office where he shall deposit the same with a specimen of his signature; and if said agent shall frank any letter or package, in which shall be contained any thing relative to any subject other than vaccination, he shall, on conviction of every such offence, forfeit and pay a fine of fifty dollars, to be recovered in the same manner as other fines or violations of law establishing the post-office: *Provided also,* that the discharge of any agent, and the appointment of another in his stead, be at the discretion of the President of the United States.

Approved, February 27, 1813.

Source: An Act to Encourage Vaccination. *The Public Statutes at Large of the United States of America.* Vol. 2. Boston: Little and Brown, 1850, p. 806.

DOCUMENT
2.2

State Funding Mechanisms for Charity Hospital in New Orleans

"From Every Circus One Hundred and Fifty Dollars"

1814, 1837, 1838

One of the major developments in the realm of American health care during the late eighteenth and early nineteenth centuries was the gradual emergence of medical hospitals in large population centers. These early institutions, the forerunners of today's state-of-the-art research and care facilities, were given vital financial support in their earliest stages of development by a mix of private and public benefactors. In many cases, wealthy individuals and groups of physicians provided the seed money for these institutions, but public funding became a crucial factor in their growth and long-term success.

This was certainly the case in New Orleans, where Charity Hospital emerged as one of the nation's finest hospitals during the antebellum era. Founded with private donations, Charity Hospital opened its doors in 1785. In 1811 Louisiana's territorial legislature placed the administration of the facility under the control of New Orleans. Three years later, it passed the first of several measures expressly designed to set aside public monies for hospital operations. Following here are three different acts passed by

Louisiana legislators—in 1814, 1837, and 1838—that provided vital financial support for Charity Hospital.

An Act to regulate the administration of the Charity Hospital of the city of New Orleans, approved March 7, 1814.

Sec. IX. All directors, managers or any other person or persons, intrusted with the administration of a theatre open to the public of New Orleans, shall be bound to give four representations per annum for the benefit of said hospital, at such periods as will be designated by the said council of administration, which shall appoint commissaries for the reception of the proceeds of said representations and the delivery of the same into the hands of the treasurer of the hospital.

Sec. XII. And whereas the funds belonging to the charity hospital of the city of New Orleans, and the state of the public treasury, do not allow to give immediately to that establishment all the extent required by the situation of this city, to which great numbers of our fellow citizens, inhabitants of the States and Territories bordering on the Mississippi, the Ohio, and the several waters that fall into those rivers, annually require: Be it further enacted, that the governor be, and he is hereby required to write to the legislature of the several States to propose to them a subscription for the benefit of the said establishment, and that the amount of the said subscription be especially destined to give to the buildings an extent which may enable them to receive a greater number of sick and to participate to them the relief of the charity.

An Act to provide permanently for the support of the Charity Hospital, approved March 11, 1837.

22. Sec. I. That from and after the passage of this act the treasurer of the State be, and he is hereby authorized and required to pay, upon the warrant or warrants of the president of the board of administrators of the charity hospital, to the order of the treasurer thereof, quarter annually, the nett [sic] proceeds of all sums of money which may be collected and paid over into the treasury of the State, arising from the recovery of forfeited bonds and recognizances and fines, which may be assessed in criminal cases, and for contempt of courts: Provided, that not more than forty thousand dollars shall be paid in any one year.

An Act for the relief of the Charity Hospital, approved March 12, 1838.

Sec. I. That the State bonds to the amount of one hundred thousand dollars is hereby authorized to be issued in favor of the treasurer of the administration of the charity hospital of the city of New-Orleans, signed by the governor of the State and countersigned by the treasurer of the State, and bearing interest at five per centum, payable semi annually, redeemable in twenty years; said bonds to be delivered to the said administrators.

Sec IV. That section ninth of an act to regulate the administration of the charity hospital, approved March seventh, eighteen hundred and fourteen, be so amended, that instead of exacting from the managers of theatres, four representations annually as set forth in said act, five hundred dollars be exacted from each, from every circus one hundred and fifty dollars, from every menagerie fifty dollars, and every show, twenty five dollars; and it shall be the duty of the mayor of the city of New-Orleans in authorizing any of the exhibitions, previously to require the receipt of the payment of said sums respectively, from the treasurer of said hospital.

Source: Bullard, Henry A., comp. *A New Digest of the Statute Laws of the State of Louisiana.* Vol. 1. New Orleans: E. Johns and Co., 1842, pp. 83, 86–87.

DOCUMENT 2.3

Samuel Thomson Reflects on His Medical System and Regular Physicians

"Hundreds Who Have Been Relieved from Sickness and Distress through My Means"

1822

New Hampshire native Samuel Thomson's entrance into the world of herbal medicine was profoundly shaped by his own family's medical experiences. Convinced that orthodox medical treatments had killed his mother (and nearly killed his wife until she was rescued by local herbalists), Thomson developed an alternative system of medical treatment in the opening decade of the nineteenth century that disowned depletive heroic therapies in favor of heat-oriented therapy. Specifically, Thomson argued that cold was the source of all disease, and that heat—in the form of steam and hot baths, "hot" botanicals such as cayenne pepper, and obstruction-clearing laxatives and emetics that would restore a body's "natural heat"—was the remedy.

In 1812 Thomson began issuing pamphlets explaining his methods, while taking out patents on many of the laxatives and emetics he developed. In 1822 he published a complete book on his healing system called New Guide to Health: Or Botanic Family Physician. *This work turned Thomsonianism into a full-blown phenomenon, especially in rural parts of America where self-treatment for health problems was often a necessity. Thomson reaped considerable financial benefits from selling the rights to his system, which he diligently guarded against patent infringement. But the movement he spawned fractured in the 1830s, when adherents led by Alva Curtis called for the creation of Thomsonian medical schools. Thomson opposed such professionalizing institutions as counter to the egalitarian principles upon which his system was founded, but his objections merely prompted his former acolytes to strike out on their own. This latter faction eventually became part of the wider eclectic health movement, while Thomson's purer brand of Thomsonian went into swift decline after his death in 1843.*

In this excerpt from New Guide to Health, *Thomson relates some of the incidents that drove the early development of his system and provides a succinct explanation of his faith in heat therapy.*

I was in the habit at this time of gathering and preserving in the proper season, all kinds of medical herbs and roots that I was acquainted with, in order to be able at all times to prevent as well as to cure disease; for I found by experience, that one ounce of prevention was better than a pound of cure. Only the simple article of mayweed, when a person has taken a bad cold, by taking a strong cup of the tea when going to bed, will prevent more disease in one night, with one cent's expense, than would be cured by the doctor in one month, and one hundred dollars expense in their charges, apothecaries' drugs, and nurses.

I had not the most distant idea at this time of ever engaging in the practice of medicine, more than to assist my own family; and little did I think what those severe trials and sufferings I experienced in the cases that have been mentioned, and which I was drove to by necessity, were to bring about. It seemed as a judgment upon me, that either myself or family, or some one living with me, were sick most of the time the doctor lived on my farm, which was about seven years. Since I have had more experience, and become better acquainted with the subject, I am satisfied in my own mind of the cause. Whenever any of the family took a cold, the doctor was sent for, who would always either bleed or give physic. Taking away the blood reduces the heat, and gives power to the cold they had taken, which increases the disorder, and the coldness of the stomach causes canker; the physic drives all the determining powers from the surface inwardly, and scatters the canker through the stomach and bowels, which holds the cold inside, and drives the heat on the outside. The consequence is, that perspiration ceases, because internal heat is the sole cause of this important evacuation; and a settled fever takes place, which will continue as long a the cold keeps the upper hand. My experience has taught me that by giving hot medicine, the internal heat was increased, and by applying the steam externally, the natural perspiration was restored; and by giving medicine to clear the stomach and bowels from canker, till the cold is driven out and the heat returns, which is the turn of the fever, they will recover the digestive powers, so that food will keep the heat where it naturally belongs, which is the fuel that continues the fire or life of man. . . .

Whenever any of my family were sick, I had no difficulty in restoring them to health by such means as were within my own knowledge. As fast as my children arrived at years of discretion, I instructed them how to relieve themselves, and they have all enjoyed good health ever since. If parents would adopt the same plan, and depend more upon themselves, and less upon the doctors, they would avoid much sickness in their families, as well as save the expense attending the employment of one of the regular physicians, whenever any trifling sickness occurs, whose extravagant charges is a grievous and heavy burthen upon the people. I shall endeavor to instruct them all in my power, by giving a plain and clear view of the experience I have had, that they may benefit by it. If they do not, the fault will not be mine, for I shall have done my duty. I am certain of the fact, that there is medicine enough in the country, within the reach of every one, to cure all the disease incident to it, if timely and properly administered.

At the birth of our third son, my wife was again given over by the midwife. Soon after the child was born, she was taken with ague fits and cramp in the stomach; she was in great pain, and we were much alarmed at her situation. I proposed giving her some medicines, but the midwife was much opposed to it; she said she wished to have a doctor, and the sooner the better. I immediately sent for one, and tried to persuade her to give something which I thought would relieve my wife until the doctor could come; but she objected to it, saying that her case was a very difficult one, and would not allow to be trifled with; she said she was sensible of the dangerous situation my wife was in, for not one out of twenty lived through it, and probably she would not be alive in twenty-four hours from that time. We were thus kept in suspense until the man returned and the doctor could not be found, and there was no other within six miles. I then came to the determination of hearing to no one's advice any longer, but to pursue my own plan. I told my wife, that as the midwife said she could not live more than twenty-four hours, her life could not be cut short more than that time, therefore there would be no hazard in trying what I could do to relieve her. I gave her some warm medicine to raise the inward heat, and then applied the steam, which was very much opposed by the midwife; but I persisted in it according to the best of my judgment, and relieved her in about one hour, after she had laid in that situation above four hours, without any thing being done. The midwife expressed a great deal of astonishment at the success I had met with, and said that I had saved her life, for she was certain that without the means I had used, she could not have lived. She continued to do well, and soon recovered. This makes the fifth time I had applied to the mother of invention for assistance, and in all of them was completely successful.

These things began to be taken some notice of about this time, and caused much conversation in the neighborhood. My assistance was called for by some of the neighbors, and I attended several cases with good success. I had previous to this time, paid some attention to the farrier business, and had been useful in that line. This, however, gave occasion for the ignorant and credulous to ridicule me and laugh at those whom I attended; but these things had little weight with me, for I had no other object in view but to be serviceable to my fellow creatures. . . .

The last sickness of my wife, I think took place in the year 1799, and about two years after she had another son and did well, making five sons that she had in succession; she afterwards had another daughter, which was the last, making eight children in the whole that she was the mother of; five sons and three daughters. I mention these particulars, in order that the reader may the better understand many things that took place in my family, which will give some idea of the experience and trouble I had to encounter in bringing up so large a family, especially with the many trials I had to go through in the various cases of sickness and troubles, which are naturally attendant on all families, and of which I had a very large share. The knowledge and experience, however, which I gained by these trying scenes, I have reason to be satisfied with, as it has proved to be a blessing, not only to me, but many hundreds who have been relieved from sickness and distress through my means; and I hope and trust that it will eventually be the cause of throwing off the veil of ignorance from the eyes of the good people of this country, and do away the blind confidence they are so much in the habit of placing in those who call themselves physicians, who fare sumptuously every day; living in splendor and magnificence, supported by the impositions they practise upon a deluded and credulous people; for they have much more regard for their own interest than they have for the health and happiness of those who are so unfortunate as to have any thing to do with them. If this was the worst side of the picture, it might be borne with more patience; but their practice is altogether experimental, to try the effect of their poisons upon the constitutions of their patients, and if they happen to give more than nature can bear, they either die or become miserable invalids the rest of their lives, and their friends console themselves with the idea that it is the will of God, and it is their duty to submit; the doctor gets well paid for his services, and that is an end of the tragedy. It may be thought by some that this is a highly colored picture, and that I am uncharitable to apply it to all who practise as physicians; but the truth of the statements, as respects what are called regular physicians, or those who get diplomas from the medical society, will not be doubted by any who are acquainted with the subject, and will throw aside prejudice and reflect seriously upon it—those whom the coat fits I am willing should wear it. There are, however, many physicians within my knowledge, who do not follow the fashionable mode of practice of the day, but are governed by their own judgments, and make use of the vegetable medicine of our own country, with the mode of treatment most consistent with nature; and what is the conduct of those who have undertaken to dictate to the people how and by whom they shall be attended when sick, towards them? Why, means that would disgrace the lowest dregs of society, that savages would not be guilty of, are resorted to for the purpose of injuring them, and destroying their credit with the public. I have had a pretty large share of this kind of treatment from the faculty, the particulars of which, and the sufferings I have undergone, will be given in detail in the course of this narrative. . . .

Soon after my family had got well of the measles, I was sent for to see a woman by the name of Redding, in the neighborhood. She had been for many years afflicted with the cholic, and could get no relief from the doctors. I attended her and found the disorder was caused by canker, and pursued the plan that my former experience had taught me, which relieved her from the pain, and so far removed the cause that she never had another attack of the disease. In this case the cure was so simply and easily performed, that it became a subject of ridicule, for when she was asked about it, she was ashamed to say that I cured her. The popular practice of the physicians had so much influence on the minds of the people, that they thought nothing could be right but what was done by them. I attended in this family for several years, and always answered the desired purpose; but my practice was so simple, that it was not worthy of notice, and being dissatisfied with the treatment I received, I refused to do any thing more for them. After this they employed the more fashionable practitioners, who were ready enough to make the most of a job, and they had sickness and expense enough to satisfy them, for one of the sons was soon after taken sick and was given over by the doctor, who left him to die; but after he left off giving him medicine he got well of himself, and the doctor not only had the credit of it, but for this job and one other similar, his charges amounted to over one hundred dollars. This satisfied me of the foolishness of the people, whose prejudices are always in favor of any thing that is fashionable, or that is done by those who profess great learning; and prefer long sickness and great expense, if done in this way, to a simple and natural relief, with a trifling expense.

Source: Thomson, Samuel. *New Guide to Health: Or Botanic Family Physician.* 1822. Boston: J. Q. Adams, 1835, pp. 31–35, 36–37.

DOCUMENT 2.4

John Gunn Attacks Regular Physicians in *Domestic Medicine*

"Big Words and High-Sounding Phrases Are Not Superior Wisdom"

1830

In 1830 a Tennessee physician named John Gunn published a treatise on domestic health care called Gunn's Domestic Medicine, or Poor Man's Friend, In the Hours of Affliction, Pain, and Sickness. *Following in the footsteps of earlier popular self-help manuals such as William Buchan's* Domestic Medicine *(first published in the United States in 1771) and Henry Wilkins's* The Family Advisor (Particularly of American Diseases) *(1801), Gunn's tome sought to provide readers with commonsense health remedies and therapies that regular physicians were either ignoring or hoarding for their own financial benefit. A regularly trained physician, Gunn offered a fairly positive appraisal of intrusive heroic therapies such as purging, blistering, and bloodletting, unlike many other critics of orthodox medical practice in antebellum America. But Gunn enthusiastically attacked the orthodox gatekeepers of medical knowledge for hypocrisy and arrogance. "When we take*

*from the learned sciences all their technical and bombastic language, they immediately
become plain common sense, very easily to be understood by all ranks of men," he declared.
Gunn's rhetoric struck a tremendous chord with Americans who were, at the time,
marinating in the antielitist, antiregulation ideology of Jacksonian democracy. Within ten
years of its initial publication,* Gunn's Domestic Medicine, *which is excerpted here, had
undergone nineteen printings and become a trusted health care resource in numerous
American households.*

REMARKS, PRELIMINARY TO THE MEDICAL PORTION OF THIS WORK.

I have now done with the passions most material to be thought of in a work like this. I
think I have spoken of them as they deserve; and as being the real causes of very many
and obstinate diseases; and I also think, without any sort of vanity on the subject, that I
have taken views of them which are not only new, but such as will be satisfactory to men
who are pleased with *common sense,* and *matter-of-fact* disclosures, instead of visionary
theories, and old doctrines that have been worn thread-bare by repetition. Where I have
found the *essences* of the passions beyond the reach of investigation, I have freely confessed the truth; being determined not to veil my ignorance of what is most likely hidden
from us by divine wisdom, by long sounding words which when explained would make
men of common sense laugh at medical quackery, and by technical language which
means next to nothing. I have spoken of the passions as I have seen and witnessed their
effects on the human system, and on the peace and happiness of society generally; and
particularly as regards intemperance, or rather excess in fear—joy—anger—jealousy—
love—grief—religion—gluttony and drunkenness, I have ventured to go as far into some
of the remote and constitutional causes of them, as I possibly could without running into
mere theories, not supported by the experience of mankind. In treating of them I have
been limited much by want of space; and have therefore in some instances, been compelled to comprise as much information as possible in a few words: and I must also
observe here, that on intemperance, religion, love, jealousy and anger, I have extended
my remarks further than on the rest of the passions; because I consider them of vastly
more importance to the *health* and *happiness,* and to the *diseases* and *miseries* of mankind, than all the rest of the passions put together. I have classed religion and intemperance under the head of the passions, because all our desires and aversions become
passions, when they become too strong to be controlled and moderated by moral sense
and reason; and if even these were not the facts, mere names are nothing but blinds,
frequently placed by the learned between the reader and the realities of things, to conceal
the naked poverty and barrenness of the sciences, as professed by literary men. If our
education consisted more in a knowledge of things, and less in a knowledge of mere
words than it does, and if the great mass of the people knew how much pains were taken
by scientific men, to throw dust in their eyes by the use of ridiculous and high-sounding
terms, which mean very little if any thing, the learned professors of science would soon
lose much of their mock dignity, and mankind would soon be undeceived, as to the little
difference that really exists between themselves and the *very learned* portion of the community. I am the more particular on this subject, not because I wish to lower the public
opinion respecting the real value of medical knowledge, but because the time has arrived
when the *hypocrisy* which has attached itself to *religion,* the pettifogging *dissimulation*
which has crept into the practice and science of *law,* and the *quackeries* which have so
long disgraced the practice and science of *medicine,* are about to be scattered to the four

winds of heaven, by the progress of real knowledge, and the general diffusion of useful intelligence. The great body of the people are beginning to find out as I remarked in substance in my dedication—that when we take from the learned sciences all their technical and bombastic language, they immediately become plain *common sense*, very easily to be understood by all ranks of men. I have also said in that same dedication, and I now repeat it, that the really valuable materials in medicine, and those which are the most powerful in the cure of diseases, are few and simple, and very easily to be procured in all countries; and on this subject I will say something more which may probably be considered new. I not only believe, that every country produces, or can be made to produce, whatever is necessary to the wants of its inhabitants—but also whatever is essential to the cure of diseases incidental to each country; it is by no means probable, that an all-wise creator would create man with wants he could not supply, and subject him to diseases for which there were no remedies to be found in nature, and in all the different countries and climates of which he is an inhabitant. If such were not the facts, how miserable would be the condition of the human species; eternally harrassed by the calls of wants which could not be satisfied, and afflicted with diseases for which they could find neither the means of alleviation nor cure! How did the Indian nations of this country become so populous and powerful, unless from finding the means of supplying their wants, and of mitigating and curing their diseases, on the soil and in the countries which gave them birth? The fact is, that this country, like all other countries, produces spontaneously, or can be made to produce by the genius and industry of its inhabitants, all that is required by the wants of the people, and all that is essential in medical science; and the sooner we set about finding out, and fully exploring the resources of our own country, the sooner will we be clear of the abuses and countless impositions in the adulteration of medical drugs; and the sooner will we be exempted from individual and national *dependence* on other nations. There are many drugs that come from abroad, that are made good for nothing, by adulterations or mixture before they reach us, or lose their virtues by long standing and exposure; and any professed druggist if he will tell you the truth, will tell you the same; and these among many others, are the reasons why I mean to be very particular in showing you, as respects the plants and roots, &c. of this country, not only how great are our resources, but how easily we can evade roguery and imposition, and obtain pure and unadulterated materials in medicine, if we will be industrious in developing the real resources of this country. The science of botany, like many others I could name, has dwindled into mere mummery and hard sounding names of plants, &c. I can find you, indeed you can easily find them yourselves, very many individuals profoundly learned in botany, who can tell you all about the *genus* and *species* of plants and herbs, and can call them individually by their long Latin names, who can tell you nothing whatever about their use to mankind, or whether they are poisonous or otherwise; and I want to know whether such information, or rather such want of information, is not mere learning without wisdom, and science without knowledge. But why need I speak of the science of botany alone, as having sunk into frivolity and superficial nonsense; the same may be said of many other of the sciences, which were in their origin and early progress useful to mankind. Real knowledge consists in understanding both what is *useful* and what is *injurious* to mankind; and true wisdom amounts to nothing more than appropriating to our use whatever is beneficial, and avoiding whatever is injurious to our enjoyments and happiness: this is the true distinction between *common sense* and *nonsense;* or if you will have the same idea in finer language, between *wisdom* and *folly*. For the common and useful purposes of mankind, the refined fripperies and hair-drawn theories of mere science, are of no use whatever; indeed they never have had much other effect, than to excite a stupid admiration for men who pretended to know more than the mass of mankind: and it is this stupid admiration, this willingness to be duped by the impudent pretensions of science and quackery combined, that has led to impositions and barefaced frauds upon society, without number. Wherever *artifice* is used, it is either to cover defects, or to perpetuate impositions and frauds; and if you wish to know how much of this artifice is in vogue in the science and practice of medicine, ask some physician of eminence to give you in plain common English, the meaning of those mysterious and high-sounding names you see plastered on bottles, glass jars, gallipots and drawers in a drug store, or doctor's shop. . . .

[T]he reader will easily distinguish, if he will look one foot beyond his nose, not only that big words and high-sounding phrases are not superior wisdom, but that three fourths of the whole science of physic, as now practiced and imposed upon the common people, amounts to nothing but fudge and mummery. In fact it has always seemed to me, whenever I have reflected seriously on this subject, that all these hard names of common and daily objects of contemplation, were originally made use of to *astonish the people*; and to aid what the world calls learned men, in deceptions and fraud. The more nearly we can place men on a level in point of *knowledge*, the happier we would become in society with each other, and the less danger there would be of *tyranny* on the one hand, and *submission* to the degradations of personal slavery on the other: nor are these all the benefits that would certainly arise from a more equal distribution of useful information among the people. We all know perfectly well, and if we do not we ought to do so, that there are two ways of acquiring a greater name than common among men. One is by putting on affected airs of superior wisdom, and the concealment of weakness and ignorance, to which all men arc subject: and the other is, by exhibiting to the world, great and useful energies of mind and character, of which nothing can be a more decisive proof, than success in our undertakings. But this is not all; the *less* we know of the weaknesses and imperfections of what the world calls *great men*, the more we are disposed to overrate their merits and wisdom, and to become their humble followers, admirers, and slaves. This is the reason why I wish to impress upon your minds, the simple and important truth, that there is not so great a difference between men as there appears to be; and that you are always to find out in the characters of men, the difference between *impudent presumption*, which seeks to blind you to defects, and modest and *unassuming merit*, which is above hypocrisy and deception. . . .

With these remarks, in which I have been as plain as possible in point of language: in order that you might the better understand my meaning, I will now go on to describe to you, in as plain language as can be made use of, all the diseases we are most liable to in this country, and all the best remedies for those which are brought to us from other countries. I intend also to describe particularly all the roots, and plants, and so on, which we have about us in our gardens, barn-yards, fields and woods, which are useful in the cure of diseases. These will be important considerations, because I am convinced we have many things the most common about us, that as medicines are as good as any in the world, and the knowledge of which by the people themselves, will enable them to cure their own diseases in many instances, and avoid many and great expenses. The language I will make use of, as I said before, will be extremely plain, the object of the work being, not so much to instruct the learned as the unlearned; nor will I regard in the slightest degree, any of those petty critical remarks, which may be made on such language, provided I succeed in adopting language which can be understood by those for whom this work is intended. . . .

Source: Gunn, John. *Gunn's Domestic Medicine, or Poor Man's Friend, In the Hours of Affliction, Pain, and Sickness.* 4th ed. Springfield, OH: Gallagher, 1835, pp. 131–35, 137–40.

DOCUMENT 2.5

New York Lawmakers Consider Thomsonian Licensing Petitions

"Their System Should Be Left to Stand or Fall on Its Own Merits"

1841

During the 1830s and 1840s, the twin forces of Jacksonian democracy and Thomsonianism generated an intense backlash against government regulation in numerous fields, including medicine. In New York State, for example, leaders of the Thomsonian movement organized a full-scale assault on state licensing laws that were keeping their practitioners out of the marketplace. The first major blow against these regulations came in 1840, when the Thomsonians presented the state legislature with citizen petitions calling for their repeal. Many of the thirty-six thousand signatures contained in these petitions were of questionable validity. Nonetheless, the impressive heft of the petitions caught the attention of the legislature, which promptly organized a legislative committee to study the Thomsonian demand for equal legal footing with regular physicians.

In 1841 this committee reported back to the full legislature with a unanimous recommendation that the state remove regulatory obstacles to Thomsonian practice. The committee members even suggested legislative language that would accomplish this goal. Their report, excerpted here, dramatically strengthened the political hand of the antiregulatory Thomsonians. In 1844, the full legislature decided that instead of passing a bill that would merely sanction Thomsonian practice, it would just repeal medical licensing laws altogether.

REPORT OF THE SELECT COMMITTEE ON PETITIONS OF NUMEROUS CITIZENS OF THE STATE PRAYING FOR THE PASSAGE OF A LAW AUTHORIZING THOMSONIAN PHYSICIANS TO COLLECT PAY FOR THEIR SERVICES. IN ASSEMBLY, JANUARY 30, 1841.

The committee have had the subject matter of these petitions under consideration. That the subject is one of a deep and abiding interest to a very numerous and respectable class of citizens of the State of New York, is clearly evinced by the long continued, persevering and earnest importunities with which the petitioners have pressed their case before the Legislature. They seem to have been neither dismayed at defeat or disheartened by rebuke. Their untiring perseverance seems to put the impress of *honesty* upon their designs and object.

They complain that their system of medical practice is, by the statute of this State, under legislative condemnation; while a system, antagonistic to theirs, having in *their opinion* less of merit than their own, has endorsed upon it a legislative sanction and recommendation.

Ten years and more have elapsed since the Revised Statutes went into effect containing provisions in relation to "the practice of physic and surgery," so at war with the rights and privileges of individuals that subsequent legislation has blotted some of the most odious features of those provisions from the statute book.

By the Revised Statutes it was made both a penal and criminal offense to practice physic or surgery in this State without being authorized by law. The authority required by law was a license or diploma from some medical society or institution recognized by the laws of this State. The offender was subjected to a fine of $25, to be sued for and recovered by the overseers of the poor; and, in addition to that, was liable to be indicted and punished for a misdemeanor; to be fined or imprisoned, or both. The people rose up and remonstrated against this latter provision. In 1830 it was stricken out, retaining the penal part. A modification of the penal part was subsequently procured, exempting from its operation "a person using the roots, barks and herbs, the growth or produce of the United States."

But another provision, and the one of which the petitioners now complain as unjust, oppressive and invidious, is left standing upon the statute. It is that clause which prevents a "physician, not authorized by law, from collecting pay for his services." The operation of this provision is to compel any one wishing to practice physic to go through with a course of study prescribed by the medical schools, pass examination by a board of censors, receive a license or diploma, and thereby compelled, *nolens volens,* to adopt and endorse the system. Or the other alternative is to be debarred the right of enforcing his claim in law for the services rendered.

Of this the petitioners complain.

Your committee, being none of them of the medical profession, and none of them practical Thomsonians, are not prepared or qualified to go into and discuss the comparative merits of the two systems; nor, if competent, would they feel called on to do so. Each of the two systems has its friends and supporters; each its untiring assailants.

The committee are not disposed to make inroads and innovations upon long established systems and theories, especially when those systems seem founded in truth and supported by fact and scientific experience. But the healing art, like all others, has been for ages undergoing changes and improvements, some of them of a fundamental character. And it would be strange indeed if this system, an exception to all others, should stand out alone as having attained the ne plus ultra of human perfection, The publishers think the "*regular system,*" so called, susceptible of great improvement, and most earnestly contend, (whether successfully or unsuccessfully the committee will not say,) that the "*Thomsonian system,*" so called, is a decided improvement and simplification of the former. It is a circumstance of no small moment, and one which the committee cannot disregard, that from 30,000 to 40,000 citizens of this State have pressed this subject upon the consideration of the Legislature; that they have knocked at the doors of legislative justice asking that only even handed justice maybe done in the premises. And while this boon has been denied them, they allege their numbers, and friends, and advocates, have been yearly increasing. Like the Israelites of old, the more they were oppressed the more they multiplied and grew. Even the intelligent of their enemies, the more candid of the "*regular profession,*" admit that the legislative enactments so far from effectually suppressing the

Thomsonian practice, has created a public sympathy altogether conducive to its support and perpetuity. Men cannot be legislated out of one religion and into another; nor can the Legislature thrust calomel and mercury down a man's throat while he wills to take only *cayenne* or *lobelia*.

The public mind has been sorely fretted by the legal enactments on this subject, and the more so as each revolving year has but increased the advocates of the new system, and, in the estimation of the petitioners, has brought out new facts and new proof in favor of their system. And if the Legislature will profit by the experience and observation of the five past years, it will be satisfied that our existing laws will no sooner put down the advocates of the Thomsonian system than Canada thistles can be exterminated in June by cutting down the stalk, having ten prolific branches to the root. . . .

[Thomsonians] contend that their system of practice is founded on the immutable laws of nature; they believe it to be a philosophical mode of treating disease; they appeal with great confidence to the success which has attended that mode of treatment. They adduce, as evidence of this success, the fact that there are now in this State 200 permanently located practitioners, obtaining a competent support in spite of the organized opposition and legislative proscription under which they have been compelled to labor. They claim that their system, so far as the practice of *medicine* is concerned, is a complete system; that one skilled in it will in *no* case have to borrow of the "regular faculty." . . .

They contend that their term of preparatory study is properly shorter and less complicated than the old system, because of the improved and simplified process of their practice; they maintain they are not obnoxious to the charge of "quackery and empiricism;" that a "quack is one who pretends to know what he does not," and they profess themselves happy in the reflection, that "quacks" are not exclusively confined to the Thomsonian creed, but may often be seen with their diplomas in their hand, and dignified with the title of M. D.

They adduce, as further evidence in favor of their improved system, the fact that many eminent physicians of the regular school, men of high attainments and professional skill, have abandoned the old and adopted the new system, and that these too have come in for their share of epithets of "quacks and empirics;" and these men themselves, who have left the old school ranks and gone to the new, notwithstanding their admitted qualifications to practice successfully in the former, have conceded that those who have prepared themselves, for practice by a simple compliance with Thomsonian rules, are equally skillful with themselves, and equally well qualified to practice on that system; from which they infer, the old course of preparation is not indispensable to a successful practice in the new.

They complain of another greivious imposition: that is, that students who conscientiously believe in the superiority of the Thomsonian system, cannot obtain diplomas from the *regular school*, even though they have passed the ordeal of examination; that however well qualified, they cannot obtain license to practice from the medical societies now organized by law, unless he renounces his "heretical notions" in medicine; and in support of this complaint, they allude to the expulsion of a Montgomery, Hearsay, Saunders, Roullon, Griffin and others, for having avowed their belief in the superiority of the Thomsonian system. They hence contend that they are compelled to sacrifice an honest conviction, or stand proscribed by the enactment of the Legislature.

In addition to all this, the petitioners adduce some high and distinguished authorities from the regular school, in support of their theory and practice. At the head of these authorities stands the learned Doctor Benjamin Waterhouse, late professor of theory and practice of medicine, Harvard University. He was professor twenty-five years.

Doctor Waterhouse, as early as 1834, expressed his confidence in the Thomsonian system; honored its founder, Doctor Samuel Thomson with the title of Reformer; warmly commended the use of lobelia and the vapor bath; pronounced the use of them, in sagacious hands, an improvement *valuable* in practice; bore testimony, that like Hippocrates of old, the author of this system had wisely studied the *book of nature*. Another authority from the regular school is Doctor Montgomery, an eminent physician in South Carolina, who attended the lectures of Drs. Rush, Woodhouse and Barton, at Philadelphia, and was a graduate of one of our colleges. After a trial of both systems, he frankly gave in his adhesion to the latter, and renounced the former. . . .

Messrs. Edgerton, Metcalf and Dimick, of the New York Legislature, in 1828, took occasion to investigate and learn, from personal observation, the nature of this system of practice and its result. Some of them visited the patients of Dr. Thomson, and witnessed the mode of treatment and the effect, and all were satisfied of its merit and efficacy. Also, Messrs. Elridge and Soper, of the Assembly, in 1829, and Messrs. Hammond and Buckman, members in 1830, were satisfied, from a personal inquiry of those who had been subjects to this mode of treatment, of its success. . . .

The committee are admonished that some legislative action is called for in this State, from the march of public sentiment abroad. Other States have taken the lead in this matter. Maryland, in 1838, abolished these restrictions. It is believed that Georgia did the same in 1840. Rhode Island and Pennsylvania have no such restrictions; and Vermont and Maine have blotted them from their statute books, one in 1838, and the other in 1839.

From all these facts and indications, your committee think that *justice* should be done to the petitioners; that these prohibitions should be removed; that their system should be left to stand or fall on its own merits, unaided by any "special legislation," and unfettered by any special legislative restraint.

Your committee believe this, and this only, will allay the irritation of the public mind on this subject. Professor Eaton, of Troy, who is one of the petitioners, and who has been some years professor in a regular medical institution, and whose professional standing and reputation entitle his opinions to great weight, is in favor of the legislation asked; his recommendation is to let them make their trial, collect their pay, believing that experience is better than theory.

It is due to the petitioners to state, that while they ask these legislative restrictions removed, they do not ask to be exempted from responsibility, civil and criminal, for malpractice. They wish to stand, in this respect, on a level with other physicians.

Your committee, therefore, without seeking to endorse the one or condemn the other of these systems, choose to rest the legislation asked for on the broad ground of justice and absolute right to the petitioners, and as measure of public policy. They have, therefore, come to a unanimous conclusion in favor of the prayer of the petitioners, and directed their chairman to ask leave to introduce a bill.

AN ACT to amend certain parts of the Revised Statutes relative to the practice of Physic and Surgery.

The People of the State of New York, represented in Senate and Assembly, do enact as follows:

Sec. 1. Section twenty-four of title seven, chapter fourteen, part first, of the Revised Statutes, shall be amended so that said section shall read as follows:

Every person not authorized by law, who shall for any fee or reward, practice physic or surgery within this State, shall be incapable of recovering by suit any debt arising from such practice; but the provisions of this section shall not apply to any person, using and applying for the benefit of the sick any roots, barks or herbs, the growth or produce of the United State, provided such person shall have received a diploma or license from the State Thomsonian Medical Society; but such person so practicing shall be liable for mal-practice to the same extent, and in the same manner as other physicians.

Source: *Transactions of the Medical Society of the State of New York, 1840-1-2 and 3.* Albany, NY: Van Benthuysen and Sons, 1868, pp. 263–69.

DOCUMENT 2.6 — John Griscom Urges Sanitary Reforms in New York City

"These Physical Evils . . . Should Arouse the Government"

1845

America's sanitary reform movement first stirred in the 1840s in the wake of several groundbreaking studies of sanitary conditions in major population centers. One of the first of these works was The Sanitary Condition of the Laboring Population of New York, *which was first released in 1842 and published in pamphlet form three years later. This work was produced by John Griscom, a Quaker educator, scientist, and social reformer who also spent time as an inspector for New York City's Board of Health. The following is an excerpt from Griscom's introduction to this landmark public health document.*

No duty can engage the attention of the magistracy of a city or state, more dignified in itself, more beneficial to the present generation, or more likely to prove useful to their descendants, than that of procuring and maintaining a sound state of the public health.

Of the three objects contemplated in the Declaration of Independence as necessary to be secured by government, the first named is "Life." Higher purposes cannot be conceived for which governments should be instituted.

As upon the condition of health of an individual are based his physical and mental strength, his ability for self-maintenance, his personal happiness, and that of others dependent on him, and also his usefulness to his family, to the community and his country ; and as the community depends for its prosperity upon the performances of its members, individually and collectively, in the measure of influence committed to them respectively, so does the health of the people affect the capacity and interests of the state.

As upon the individual, when sick, falls an increased pecuniary burden, with (in general) a suspension of income, so upon the state or city, must rest, not only the expenses of removing an unsound condition of public health, but also, from the attendant loss of character, a diminution of its resources.

When individuals of the pauper class are ill, their entire support, and perchance that of the whole family, falls upon the community. From a low state of general health, whether in an individual or in numbers, proceed diminished energy of body and of mind, and a vitiated moral perception, the frequent precursor of habits and deeds, which give employment to the officers of police, and the ministers of justice.

These, among other considerations, together with the recent expression by the chief magistrate of the city of his interest in the sanitary condition of his constituency, by the recommendation to the Common Council of a measure of no ordinary importance to their welfare and comfort [public baths], induce me to urge attention to a measure of improvement which has long impressed my mind, as one, above all others, demanding the action of the City Government.

When it was my pleasure, as it was my duty, in 1842 and '43, to devote my small energies to the sanitary improvement of my native city, stimulated by the consciousness of being engaged in a work heretofore untried in any systematic form, and promising results of the highest and most enduring interests to my fellow citizens, I seized the occasion to recommend to the Common Council the adoption of a measure of Health Police, which I thought of serious necessity. It was the last effort I was enabled to make upon the subject, before I was again consigned to the private ranks, by removal from office. I then hoped to see the small beginning 1 had made, grow into shape and usefulness under the fostering hands of whoever might be my successors. But, in common with all who had the subject so much at heart, I have been disappointed; for not only was it untouched, but the seeds which I had planted were neglected, and suffered to rot in the ground. Another political revolution brought with it the hope, strengthened by loud professions of municipal reform, that at last the day was certain and at hand, when this subject would be no longer allowed to slumber, but would be regarded as one of the most urgent, and among the first, of the objects of attention by the new Common Council. The expectations of the public could not be mistaken; but an erroneous appreciation, or an entire misconception, in some quarter, of the duties and requisite qualifications of an officer of health, has deferred the hopes entertained of the further prosecution of this interesting, and vitally important, sanitary reform.

The desire which stimulated me in former days was, however, not suffered to sleep in my bosom; a year's reflection, and daily and more extended observation, have not only confirmed my confidence in the feasibility, but increased the conviction of the necessity, of the measure I had proposed, and they have enabled me to modify, enlarge, and illustrate the plan, while the determination displayed by the new chief magistrate to do his share of the reforms promised, has inspired me afresh with the hope that the present might be a favourable time for a renewed presentation of my favourite design.

It is a measure of SANITARY REFORM. It is designed to relieve the city of a part of the heavy burden of sickness and mortality, which now oppresses its population, more especially that portion least able to relieve themselves, and most requiring the interposition and protection of Law. It will be seen to be a measure of humanity, of justice to the poor, of safety to the whole people, and of economy to the public treasury.

The objects of this communication, briefly stated, are these;—1st, to show that there is an immense amount of sickness, physical disability, and premature mortality, among the poorer classes;—2d, that these are, to a large extent, unnecessary, being in a great degree the results of causes which are removeable;—3d, that these physical evils are productive of moral evils of great magnitude and number, and which, if considered only in a pecuniary point of view, should arouse the government and individuals to a consideration of the best means for their relief and prevention; and 4th, to suggest the means of alleviating these evils and preventing their recurrence to so great an extent. . . .

While there is scarcely a disease which may not at times become epidemic or endemic, there are some more strikingly and uniformly so; ex. gr.: Fevers of various kinds, as Yellow, Typhus, Intermittent, and likewise Small Pox, Scarlatina, Cholera, Measles, &c.

Summer is the season generally deemed most prolific in diseases; the cause usually assigned for this is the heat of the weather acting upon animal and vegetable matter, producing more extensive and rapid decomposition, the gases from which are generally imagined to be so destructive to health and life. It is true that certain diseases prevail mostly during the hot months—these are Yellow Fever, Cholera Infantum, and the like, while Typhoid and Bilious diseases are frequent in autumn, the latter also attributable to the same causes. The quantity of these offensive vegetable and animal materials is, therefore, among other things, supposed to be, in a considerable degree, the generator, and regulator of the intensity, of these diseases. But this is not by any means the whole of this subject. By a reference to some of the Annual Mortality Reports, it will be seen that sometimes as great a number of deaths occurs during the cold months as during the hot. These are mostly of those affections attributable to the influence of cold and of increased moisture, principally diseases of the Lungs. To a certain degree this view of causes is correct, but in both cases, a well-directed inquiry into the condition in which people live, the position and arrangement of their working and lodging rooms, the character of their food, their habits of dress and cleanliness, the well or ill ventilated rooms they occupy by day and by night, would, in this city, as it has done in other places, develope [sic] an amount of ignorance and inattention to the laws of life which would astound the most credulous, and fully account for the great and premature mortality of our citizens.

At all seasons of the year, there is an amount of sickness and death in this, as in all large cities, far beyond those of less densely peopled, more airy and open places, such as country residences. Even in villages of small size, there is an observable difference over the isolated country dwelling, in the proportionate amount of disease prevailing; proving conclusively that the congregation of animal and vegetable matters, with their constant effluvia, which has less chance of escape from the premises, in proportion to the absence of free circulation of air, is detrimental to the health of the inhabitants.

These circumstances have never yet been investigated in this city, as they should be. Our people, especially the more destitute, have been allowed to live out their brief lives in tainted and unwholesome atmospheres, and be subject to the silent and invisible encroachments of destructive agencies from every direction, without one warning voice being raised to point to them their danger, and without an effort to rescue them from their impending fate. Fathers are taken from their children, husbands from their wives, "ere they have lived out half their days,"—the widows and orphans are thrown upon public or private charity for support, and the money which is expended to save them from starvation, to educate them in the public schools, or, perchance, to maintain them in the work-house or the prison, if judiciously spent in improving the sanitary arrangements of the city, and instilling into the population a knowledge of the means by which their health might be protected, and their lives prolonged and made happy, would have been not only saved, but returned to the treasury in the increased health of the population, a much better state of public morals, and, by consequence, a more easily governed and respectable community.

It is of course among the poorer labouring classes that such knowledge is most wanted. The rich, though they may be equally ignorant of the laws of life, and of the best means of its preservation, live in larger houses, with freer ventilation, and upon food better adapted to support health and life. Their means of obtaining greater comforts and more luxuries, are to them, though perhaps unconsciously, the very reason of their prolonged lives. Besides this, they are less harassed by the fears and uncertainty of obtaining for themselves and families a sufficiency of food and clothing. They are thus relieved of some of the most depressing influences, which tend to reduce the energy of mind and body in the poor, and render the latter more susceptible to the inroads of disease.

Sanitary regulations affect the pauper class of the population more directly than any other, because they live in situations and circumstances which expose them more to attacks of disease. They are more crowded, they live more in cellars, their apartments are less ventilated, and more exposed to vapours and other emanations, &c, hence, ventilation, sewerage, and all other sanitary regulations, are more necessary for them, and would produce a greater comparative change in their condition. The influence of drainage upon the health and lives of the population, is too well known to require, at this day, any argument. Almost every one has heard of the effects of marshy soil, in country situations, producing Intermittent Fever, or Fever and Ague, and of the entire disappearance of the disease, simply by draining off the water, and permitting the ground to become dry. Its results in populous cities are equally well marked. The last instance which has come to my knowledge is one stated by Professor Buckland, that in St. Margaret, Leicester, England, containing 22,000 inhabitants, it appeared that one portion of it was effectually drained, some parts but partially so, and others not at all. In the latter, the average duration of life is *thirteen years and a half*, while in the same parish, where the drainage is better, though only partial, the average is *twenty-two years and a half;* showing the frightful effects of a bad atmosphere. It were easy to quote several instances, some important ones, from London statistics, but it is unnecessary, as I presume the fact will not be disputed, that sewerage and its kindred measures, exert a striking influence over the condition and duration of human life. The investigations to which I have briefly alluded, as so necessary and desirable for this city, have been carried on in other countries, with a degree of enthusiasm, sustained by talent and learning, which does honour to Philanthropy. No one can rise from the perusal of the works of Edwin Chadwick of London, or of Parent Du Chatelet of Paris, or of many others who have laboured in this field of humanity, without feeling a portion of the ardor which inspires them, and wishing he had been thrown into the same pursuit, that some of the leaves of the same laurel might encircle his own brow. It is the cause of Humanity, of the poor, the destitute, the degraded, of the virtuous made vicious by the force of circumstances, which they are now investigating, and exposing to the knowledge of others. . . . These operations constitute a highly important part of the great work of melioration and improvement, in the condition of mankind, now going on, in nearly all civilized countries, and which characterize the present age.

If not on a par, in importance, with the improvement in education, which has of late made such rapid strides, it certainly is second only to it, and indeed it may well be questioned, whether improvement in the physical condition of the lower stratum of society, is not a necessary precedent, in order that education of the mind may exercise its full and proper influence over the general well-being. Teach them how to live, so as to avoid diseases and be more comfortable, and then their school education will have a redoubled effect, in mending their morals, and rendering them intelligent and happy. But without sound bodies, when surrounded with dirt, foul air, and all manner of filthy associations, it is vain to expect even the child of education, to be better than his ignorant companions, if indeed you do not, by educating him, give him an additional weapon, by which he may prey more successfully upon his fellows.

This country, and especially this city, it is hoped, will not much longer be behind others in this cause of the suffering poor and depressed humanity. Some movements, promoting this investigation, have recently been commenced, but much is yet to be done. The path has been pointed out to us by pioneers across the Atlantic; there is abundant disposition to pursue the object, which only requires to be sought out, and put to work by the authorities, to procure all the desirable results of such labours.

Source: Griscom, John Hoskins. *The Sanitary Condition of the Laboring Population of New York.* New York: Harper, 1845, pp. 1–6.

Dorothea Dix Lobbies State Legislators for a Hospital for the Insane

DOCUMENT 2.7

"The Provision for the Poor and Indigent Insane of Your State Is . . . Unworthy of a Civilized and Christian People"

1845

Treatment and care of Americans suffering from severe mental illness improved dramatically in the mid-nineteenth century, in great measure because of the Herculean advocacy efforts of Dorothea Dix, a New England schoolteacher. Dix's interest in improving the lives of the insane, and especially indigent sufferers whose families did not have the financial resources to arrange care, flared to life during an extended stay in England in the late 1830s. During this time she was influenced not only by the general belief in social reform activism held by Quaker friends, but also by a wider movement of "lunatic asylum" reform.

When Dix returned to her home in Boston in January 1841, she immediately set about investigating the conditions in area insane asylums and prisons (where many mentally ill persons also were held). The abysmal conditions she encountered prompted her to widen her investigation, and over the next few years she traveled to asylums in numerous states. Time after time, she found wretched living conditions and witnessed brutal treatment of the indigent insane in these facilities, which were woefully underfunded and almost completely unregulated by the states in which they operated. Dix documented her findings in a series of reports and that she delivered, usually in conjunction with testimony, to state assemblies in Illinois, Massachusetts, North Carolina, Pennsylvania, and elsewhere. These efforts were essential in changing practices and policies toward the insane poor in many parts of the country.

Following is an excerpt from a report that Dix delivered to the Pennsylvania legislature in Harrisburg on February 3, 1845. In this report, like many others, she blends grim accounts of the deplorable conditions she found with a rousing endorsement of the benefits of so-called humane treatment. Dix's advocacy efforts in Pennsylvania have been cited as a central factor in the state's eventual decision to create Harrisburg State Hospital, the first public mental hospital in the state.

To the Honorable, the Senate and the House of Representatives of the Commonwealth of Pennsylvania:

Gentlemen:

I come to represent to you the condition of a numerous and unhappy class of sufferers, who fill the cells and dungeons of the poor houses, and the prisons of your state. I refer to the pauper and indigent insane, epileptics, and idiots of Pennsylvania. I come to urge their claims upon the commonwealth for protection and support, such protection and support as is only to be found in a well conducted Lunatic Asylum.

I do not solicit you to be generous; this is an occasion rather for the dispensation of *justice.* These most unfortunate beings have claims, those *claims* which bitter misery and adversity creates, and which it is your solemn obligation as citizens and legislators to cancel. To this end, as the advocate of those who are disqualified by a terrible malady, from pleading their own cause, I ask you to provide for the immediate establishment of a State Hospital for the Insane.

If this shall appear to some of you an untimely demand on the State Treasury; and a too hastily, too importunately urged suit, I must ask all such to go forth, as I have done, and traversing the state in its length and breadth, examine with patient care the condition of this suffering, dependent multitude, which are gathered to your alms-houses and your *prisons,* and scattered under adverse circumstances in indigent families; *weigh the iron chains, and shackles, and balls, and ring-bolts, and bars, and manacles; breathe the foul atmosphere of those cells and dens, which too slowly poisons the springs of life; examine the furniture of these dreary abodes; some for abed have the luxury of a truss of straw; and some have the cheaper couch, which the hard, rough plank supplies! Examine their apparel. The air of heaven is their only vesture. Are you disquieted and pained to learn these facts? There are worse realities yet to be revealed under your vigilant investigations. The revolting exposure of men; the infinitely more revolting and shocking exposure of women; with combinations of miseries and horrors that will not bear recital. Do you start and shrink; from the grossness of this recital? What then is it to witness the appalling reality?* Do your startled perceptions refuse to admit these truths? They exist still; the proof and *the condition* alike; *neither have passed away.* The idiot mother; the naked women in the packing boxes; but yet for these last, perhaps, the legal measures resorted to for their relief have been availing. Perhaps both judge and jury have interposed for those, some merciful change. This relief may be but temporary, and may disappear with the first indignant excitement which procured it; for the effectual, permanent remedy and alleviation of all these troubles and miseries, this appeal is now made to the Legislature of Pennsylvania; and, gentlemen, you perceive that it is *just, not generous* action, I ask at your hands. . . .

[Dix then goes on to provide an exhaustive summary of conditions at various penitentiaries and almshouses around the state that house impoverished or indigent citizens suffering from mental illness.]

If idleness is the nurse of vice and crime, it would seem consistent with the purest political economy, to provide employment for all who are able to labor in the almshouse. If education is important to the youthful mind, especially moral culture, then a more careful attention to the school would be a public as well as individual good. If benevolent institutions for the protection of the friendless, and the recovery of the sick and disabled, to health and usefulness, are recognized as important and necessary in crowded cities, and a densely inhabited country, then it is well that these should be so established as to procure for the recipients of charity, all the benefits which they can be made capable of securing.

The exciting causes of insanity in large cities, are numerous. The poor and indigent are also numerous. If an extensive alms-house is necessary to receive the crowds, the thousands of sane paupers, surely a hospital, on a curative foundation, is also necessary, and to be preferred to a mere receptacle. In the one case, the maniac may be restored to reason and usefulness; in the other, there is a possibility, but it rests upon slight probability. It may be argued by some, that many who are sent to this hospital, are the victims of their own vices and indiscretions, and are undeserving the special care solicited. Many of them are unworthy; in all probability the majority may have abused their privileges, wasted property, and impaired their health by indulgences and excesses, which must be condemned. But shall not these find mercy, and pity, and succour? You do not abandon the criminal in the jail; the juvenile offender finds a "Refuge;" and the halls of your penitentiary echo to the voices of those who, by earnest counsels and instruction, strive to reclaim the convict from perverse and criminal habits, to rectitude and duty. Let not the erring, perhaps once vicious insane, alone be abandoned.

One of your own citizens has not long since said publicly, what none have attempted to disprove: "That unless means are taken to discover the real condition of the insane in the alms-house hospital, the people of this community will justly incur the infamy of sustaining a moral nuisance, an establishment disgraceful to humanity, and a libel upon the present state of our knowledge of the proper treatment of mental disease."

The city and county of Philadelphia needs its own hospital and asylum for the treatment and protection of the insane; as the cities of New York and Boston, sensible of the necessity of such provision for this class of their poor, have theirs. All large cities, as witness those just referred to, and not less Philadelphia and Baltimore, need for their own dependent citizens, a well established hospital.

It is but few years since the Alms-house of Suffolk county, Boston, revealed scenes of horror and abomination rarely exhibited, and such as we trust are now, in *the mass* at least, no where to be found in the United States. These mad-men and mad-women were the most hopeless cases, of long standing, and their malady was confirmed by the grossest mismanagement.

The citizens at length were roused to the enormity of these abuses; to the monstrous injustice of herding these maniacs in a building filled with cages, behind the bars of which, all loathsome and utterly offensive, they howled, and gibbered, and shrieked day and night, like wild beasts raving in their dens. They knew neither decency nor quiet, nor uttered any thing but blasphemous imprecations, foul language, and heart-piercing groans. The most sanguine friends of the hospital plan, hoped no more for these wretched beings than to procure for them greater decency and comfort; recovery of the mental faculties for these was not expected. The new establishment was opened, and organized as a curative hospital. The insane were gradually removed, disencumbered of their chains, and freed from the foul remnants of garments that failed to secure decent covering. They were bathed, clothed, and placed in comfortable apartments, under the management of Dr. Butler, now superintendent of the Retreat, at Hartford. In a few months behold the result: recovering health, order, general quiet, and measured employment. Visit the hospital when you please, at "no set time or season," but at any hour of any day, you will find these patients decently clothed, comfortably lodged, and carefully attended. They exercise in companies or singly, in the spacious halls; they may be seen assembled reading the papers of the day; or books loaned from the library; some labor in the yards and about the grounds; some busy themselves in the vegetable, and some in the flower-garden; some are employed within doors, in the laundry, in the kitchen, in the ironing-room, in the sewing-room. In every part of the house a portion of the patients find happiness and physical health, by well-chosen, well-directed employment. Care is had that this does not fatigue, that it is not mistimed; and the visitor sees, amidst this company of busy ones, some of the incurables who so long inhabited the cages, and wore away life for years in anguish, encompassed by indescribable horrors. And though, of this once most miserable company, less than one-sixth were restored to the right use of their reasoning faculties, with but few exceptions, they are capable of receiving pleasure, of engaging in some sort of employment, and of being taken to the chapel for religious services, where they are orderly and serious. Such, to the insane paupers of Suffolk county, Boston, have been, and continue to be, the benefits of the hospital treatment. Than theirs, no condition could be worse before removal from the old building; now none can be better for creatures of broken health and impaired faculties, incompetent to guide and govern themselves, but yielding to gentle influences and watchful care.

Gentlemen, I have endeavored to show you in the preceding pages,—*First,* that the provision for the poor and indigent insane of your state, is inappropriate, insufficient, and unworthy of a civilized and christian people: *Second,* that it is *unjust* and *unjustifiable* to convict as criminals and incarcerate those in prisons, who, bereft of reason, are incapable of that self-direction and action, by which a man is made responsible for the deeds he may commit: *Third,* I have, in the description of your alms-houses, adding the opinion of the most intelligent men of your state, shown that these are, in all essential respects, unfit for the insane; and that while they may, with uncommon care and devotedness on the part of the superintendents, and other official persons, be made decent *receptacles,* they cannot be made curative hospitals nor asylums, for affording adequate protection for the insane: *Fourth,* still less can these ends be accomplished in private families, even where pecuniary prosperity affords the means of supplying many wants. But in those where this calamitous malady is united with poverty and pinching want, it is barely within the bounds of probability that the patient should recover. There is then but one alternative—condemn your needy citizens to become the life-long victims of a terrible disease, or provide remedial care in a State Hospital. Let this be established on a comfortable, but strictly economical foundation. Expend not one dollar on tasteful architectural decorations. In this establishment, let nothing be for ornament, but every thing for use. Choose your location where the most good can be accomplished effectually, at the least cost. Let economy only not degenerate into meanness. Every dollar indiscreetly applied, is a robbery of the poor and needy, and adds a darker shade to the vice of extravagance, in misappropriation of the public funds.

Choose a healthful situation where you can command at least one hundred acres, and better if a larger tract, of productive land, mostly capable of cultivation. Let the supply and access to pure water, be ample and convenient: also consider the cost of fuel, which is a large item in the annual expenses. Furnish your establishment by means chiefly of convict labor, from your two state penitentiaries, with mattresses, bed-cloth-ing, chairs, &c. &c. You thus secure a sale for *their* work, and get good articles at reason-able cost for your own use. You will recollect that at some future time other hospitals will be needed and demanded, but let the location of the *first* have reference to sparing as far as possible to the poor at large, the heavy charge of travelling expenses. A substan-tial brick, or unhewn stone building, not more than three-stories high with the base-ment, to save labor, and the consequent multiplying of attendants, having the officers' apartments in the centre, and those of the male and female patients in the two wings respectively, will be found most commodious. Numerous minor considerations will, at a suitable time, receive a share of attention. But one thing should not be overlooked in a hospital designed to benefit *the people at large.* In this state it must be recollected that the medical superintendent, the governing, resident physician, who alone can be head of such an institution, and also his assistant, must have practical acquaintance with both the German and English languages, which are spoken in this commonwealth. Nearly half the insane of the lower classes, east of the mountains, are Germans, and cannot, in general, utter a sentence of English; and the medical adviser would find no little embar-rassment in directing the moral training and treatment of his patients, except he could speak their language fluently, and was familiar, by residence and practice, with some of their peculiarities and local customs. I have perceived the importance and value of this, from being frequently accompanied to the poor-house hospitals by the attending physi-cians; and as they have mixed with the inmates, addressing one in one language, one in another, I have seen that in a State Hospital for the Insane in Pennsylvania, it is abso-lutely necessary to possess these qualifications in order to be really successful. . . .

Gentlemen, of the Legislature of Pennsylvania, I appeal to your hearts and your understanding; to your moral and to your intellectual perceptions; I appeal to you as legislators and as citizens; I appeal to you as men, and as fathers, sons, and brothers; spare, I pray you, by wise and merciful legislation now, those many, who if you deny the means of curative treatment and recovery to health, will *by your decisions, and on your responsi-bility,* be condemned to irrecoverable, irremediable insanity: to worse than uselessness and grinding dependence; to pain and misery, and abject, brutalizing conditions, too ter-rible to contemplate; too horrible to relate!

Grant to the exceeding urgency of their case, what you would rightly refuse to expe-diency alone. Benevolent citizens of your commonwealth were the first of civilized people to establish a society for alleviating the miseries of prisons; shall Pennsylvanians be last and least in manifesting sensibility to the wants of the poverty-stricken maniac? Is the claim of the Lunatic less than that of the Criminal? Are the spiritual and physical wants of the guilty to be more humanely ministered to, than the bodily and mental necessities of the insane? You pause long, and hesitate to condemn to death the blood-stained mur-derer; will you less relentlessly condemn to a *living-death,* the unoffending victims of a dreadful malady?

The wise and illustrious Founder of Pennsylvania, laid broad the basis of her gov-ernment in justice and integrity: now—while her sons with recovering strength, are replacing the shaken *Keystone of the* ARCH, may they, as in the beginning, find *their Salvation,—Truth, and their Palladium,—*RIGHTEOUSNESS!

Source: Dix, Dorothea. *Memorial Soliciting a State for the Insane: Submitted to the Legislature of Pennsylvania, February 3, 1845.* Harrisburg, PA: J. M. C. Lescure, 1845, pp. 3–4, 51–54.

A Sanitary Commission Complains about the Lack of Public Health Regulation in America

"A Country in Which No Legislative Enactments Exist Regulating Its Sanitary Condition"

1848

As concerns about the links between urban sanitation shortcomings and public health problems deepened in the mid-nineteenth century, the few studies that were funded or otherwise sanctioned by state legislatures were supplemented with education and outreach efforts from reform institutions and groups. Two such organizations were the Washington, D.C.-based National Institute and the fledgling American Medical Association (AMA), both of which took on sanitary reform as a cause.

In 1848 a National Institute Committee on Hygiene headed by James Wynne (who later went on to become the first Committee of Public Hygiene chair for the AMA) sent a communication to the leadership of the American Medical Association about the state of public health in America. The correspondence, excerpted here, paints a dismal picture not only of the polluted and diseased innards of American cities, but also of a nation of policymakers and physicians who seem to feel no sense of urgency to tackle the problem.

[Notes have been removed.]

COMMUNICATION ON HYGIENE, FROM THE MEDICAL DEPARTMENT OF THE NATIONAL INSTITUTE

The Medical Department of the National Institute, at a sitting held May 1845, appointed a committee to inquire into the sanitary condition of the United States, with very extensive powers. The committee, when organized, consisted of:—

Dr. JAMES WYNNE, *Chairman.*

Dr. THOMAS SEWALL, Prof. of Medicine in the National Medical College, and Chairman of the Medical Department.

Dr. J. M. THOMAS, Prof. of Institutes of Medicine in the National Medical College, and Vice-Chairman of Medical Department.

Dr. BAILE, of Washington, *Surgeon U.S. Navy,* and Dr. MARCUS BUCK, *Secretary.*

The committee thus appointed, from time to time issued circulars to members of the medical profession, and others in different parts of the United States, soliciting information on the various causes supposed to exercise a prejudicial influence on health, and requested aid in the development of this important inquiry. Numerous replies have been received, and much valuable information obtained by the committee; but, notwithstanding its most strenuous endeavours, it has, up to the present moment, failed to collect such a minute, and at the same time, extended series of observations, as to enable it to make an accurate report based on such authority as it deemed due to so vital an inquiry.

Among others, two prominent causes tended greatly at the commencement of its labours, to retard its progress: 1st. The general apathy existing even in the minds of medical men on the subject of hygiene; and 2d. The favourable opinions entertained by almost every one addressed by the committee, of the healthiness of his own particular locality. The committee, and the department which created it, have had the gratification to witness the first of these causes yielding to an exceeding solicitude on the part of the members of the medical profession to discuss and develop this question, so that at the present hour there is scarcely a medical journal, society, or well educated man, who is not fully aroused to its importance. For much of this newly inspired zeal, they are doubtless indebted to the preliminary efforts of the American Medical Association, which has thus exhibited in its very inception, the great advantages which are likely to flow from its continuance, and the department indulges the hope that under its auspices the sanitary condition of the union may be fully developed, human life prolonged, and the desolations of disease curtailed.

Before, however, any considerable advances can be made, it will be necessary to make medical men aware of the operations of the injurious agencies constantly affecting human life, even in the most favoured localities, because until they are prepared to admit the existence of these evils, they will not be in a state of mind to detect and scrutinize them with sufficient accuracy to render their observations of any practical utility. The simultaneous movement in England, which has been attended with developments of the most extraordinary character has, in some degree, prepared the way for these admissions; but the department has reason to know that the medical profession in this country, as a general rule, has many preconceived prejudices to overcome, in order to prepare it to enter into the inquiry with that spirit of philosophic research, which can alone make its deductions practically useful.

The department would not presume to dictate to this highly honorable body, but as the pioneer in this sanitary movement, it is exceedingly desirous of interchanging sentiments with an association, which is destined hereafter to play so important a part in the development of a question in which they both take so deep an interest,—a question second in importance to none other which can occupy the deliberations of either.

The United States may be considered as a country in which no legislative enactments exist, regulating its sanitary condition, for which the exception of some municipal regulations, forced from the necessity of circumstances upon the large cities, and a few of the first steps of legislation in one or two of the States of the Union, each individual is permitted to exercise his own free will in regard to hygienic measures, too frequently either from ignorance of its laws, or cupidity, at the expense of great sacrifices of human life.

Society, whilst it possesses advantages, is likewise attended with evils, the most prominent of which is, the generation of causes detrimental to health, and destructive to life; and the more compact society becomes, *cœteris paribus,* the more manifestly these causes develop themselves; hence densely populated cities present the greatest complication of these evils, and those most difficult of eradication. The main question, however, which presents itself to the inquirer into the subject of human health, is not what state of society is most favourable to its continuance, but what measures may be resorted to for the purposes of mitigating the evils which its existing state induces.

Many of these causes operating directly on the human body, inducing disease and excessive mortality, are sufficiently obvious. No one will pretend to deny that deficient ventilation, improper drainage, accumulation of filth, and a scanty supply of water, are all in themselves powerful predisposing causes of disease, and that when conjoined, they cannot fail to produce a high rate of mortality. This is the theory; but is the practice in accordance with this theory? The department would appeal to the experience of every member of this association in justification of the position that it is not, and that there is not a populous town in this country, placed under such sanitary regulations as to insure the inhabitants against the operation of these causes. Dr. T. Southwood Smith, in his examination before the Committee of the House of Commons, declared, that "in every district in which fever returns frequently, and prevails extensively, there is uniformly bad sewerage, a bad supply of water, a bad supply of scavengers, and a consequent accumulation of filth, and I have observed this to be so uniformly and generally the case, that I have been accustomed to express the fact in this way. If you trace down the fever districts on a map, and then compare that map with the map of the commissioner of sewers, you will find that wherever the commissioners of sewers have not been, there fever is prevalent; and, on the contrary, wherever they have been, there fever is comparatively absent. "And again," he adds, "every day's experience convinced me that a very large proportion of these evils is capable of being removed; that if proper attention were paid to sanitary measures, the mortality of these districts would be most materially diminished; perhaps in some places one-third; in others, one-half." . . .

The testimony of these two gentlemen, who stand deservedly high in their different branches of the profession, is here adduced, in order to show that two of the most alarming and fatal scourges of humanity, typhus and puerperal fevers, are intimately connected with, and in a great degree dependent upon, accumulations of filth, and impure atmosphere, and that their ravages are immediately under the control of sanitary measures, and may be checked by a faithful compliance with proper legislative enactments.

But these powerful elements of disease do not always present themselves to the consideration of the medical man in forms thus concentrated and fatal. They may occur singly or in subtle forms, requiring great nicety of discrimination, and laboured research to detect them, and under these circumstances, it is impossible for the physician who has not fully acquainted himself with the subject, either to discover or apply the means necessary for their removal. The merest tyro in his profession is enabled to decide upon a strongly marked case of disease, exhibiting decided symptoms, but it requires the master of his art to discover through complications which mark the ailment, the true causes of aberration from health. If this be true in relation to the manifestations of disease in the human body, with how much greater force may it not be applied to the discrimination of those subtle agents, which, like the winged messenger of death, float unseen around us, and only manifest themselves in their effects.

It would be taking an exceedingly narrow view of this subject to confine the operation of these pernicious agents to the production of the two forms of fever already mentioned, or indeed all forms of fever, for there is scarcely a type of disease to which the human body is liable, that may not be directly induced, or at least sustained by them, and perhaps the evil influences exerted by the indirect action of these deleterious causes, are more to be dreaded than those more direct and fatal. When not sufficiently concentrated to produce fever, they may act by deranging the function of one or another of the organs of the body, and thus destroy its power to resist disease from other sources. Disorders of the digestive organs sufficiently numerous in themselves, occasioned by these causes, by enfeebling the body, render it susceptible to alternations of temperature, and thus death occurs from inflammation of the air-tubes, consumption, and kindred causes. It is scarcely possible to estimate the amount of mortality thus induced by the indirect action of these poisonous agencies.

In view of the immense and growing importance of this subject, the Medical Department of the National Institute would recommend to the American Medical Association—

1st. The establishment of a permanent committee on hygiene.

2d. A recommendation to the various State Legislatures to establish throughout the Union uniform systems for the registration of births, deaths, and marriages.

JAMES WYNNE, M.D.,

JOHN M. THOMAS, M.D.,

Delegates from the Medical Department of the National Institute to the American Medical Association

Source: "Communication on Hygiene, from the Medical Department of the National Institute." *The Transactions of the American Medical Association. Instituted 1847.* Vol. 1. Philadelphia: T. K. and P. G. Collins, 1848, pp. 305–10.

DOCUMENT 2.9

United States Begins Federal Inspections of Imported Drugs

"In Reference to Their Quality, Purity, and Fitness for Medical Purposes"

1848

By the 1840s the American marketplace was awash in a bewildering array of patent medicines and drugs that were touted by manufacturers and sellers as the solution to everything from baldness to syphilis. Many of these nostrums were worthless—or even damaging to the health of those who imbibed them—but calls for government intervention to at least reduce this flow were largely neutralized by the political influence of the newspapers that profited from medicine advertising and the general antiregulatory tenor of the times. The one exception to this inertia came in the area of imported drugs. In 1846 the U.S. Congress heard testimony from a New York customs inspector who described the United States as "the world's dumping ground for counterfeit, contaminated, diluted, and decomposed drug materials."[1] This dire assessment roused Congress sufficiently to pass a law in 1848 that turned off the spigot of "adulterated and spurious drugs and medicines" flowing into America from abroad. But because most of the medicines being bought and sold were of domestic origin, the law had only a modest overall impact.

An Act to prevent the Importation of adulterated and spurious Drugs and Medicines.

Be it enacted by the Senate and House of Representatives of the United States of America in Congress assembled, That from and after the passage of this act, all drugs, medicines, medicinal preparations, including medicinal essential oils, and chemical preparations used wholly or in part as medicine, imported into the United States from abroad, shall, before passing the custom-house, be examined and appraised, as well in reference to their quality, purity, and fitness for medical purposes, as to their value and identity specified in the invoice.

Sec. 2. *And be it further enacted,* That all medicinal preparations, whether chemical or otherwise, usually imported with the name of the manufacturer, shall have the true name of the manufacturer, and the place where they are prepared, permanently and legibly affixed to each parcel, by stamp, label, or otherwise; and all medicinal preparations imported without such names affixed as aforesaid, shall be adjudged to be forfeited.

Sec. 3. *And be it further enacted,* That if, on examination, any drugs, medicines, medicinal preparations, whether chemical or otherwise, including medicinal essential oils, are found, in the opinion of the examiner, to be so far adulterated, or in any manner deteriorated, as to render them inferior in strength and purity to the standard established by the United States, Edinburgh, London, French, and German pharmacopoeias and dispensatories, and thereby improper, unsafe, or dangerous to be used for medicinal purposes, a return to that effect shall be made upon the invoice, and the articles so noted shall not pass the custom-house, unless, on a reexamination of a strictly analytical character, called for by the owner or consignee, the return of the examiner shall be found erroneous; and it shall be declared as the result of such analysis, that the said articles may properly, safely, and without danger, be used for medicinal purposes.

Sec. 4. *And be it further enacted,* That the owner or consignee shall at all times, when dissatisfied with the examiner's return, have the privilege of calling, at his own expense, for a reexamination; and on depositing with the collector such sum as the latter may deem sufficient to defray such expense, it shall be the duty of that officer to procure some competent analytical chemist possessing the confidence of the medical profession, as well as of the colleges of medicine and pharmacy, if any such institutions exist in the State in which the collection district is situated, a careful analysis of the articles included in said return, and a report upon the same under oath; and in case the report, which shall be final, shall declare the return of the examiner to be erroneous, and the said articles to be of the requisite strength and purity, according to the standards referred to in the next preceding section of this act, the entire invoice shall be passed without reservation, on payment of the customary duties; but, in case the examiner's return shall be sustained by the analysis and report, the said articles shall remain in charge of the collector, and the owner or consignee, on payment of the charges of storage, and other expenses necessarily incurred by the United States, and on giving a bond with sureties satisfactory to the collector to land said articles out of the limits of the United States, shall have the privilege of reexporting them at any time within the period of six months after the report of the analysis; but if the said articles shall not be sent out of the United States within the time specified, it shall be the duty of the collector, at the expiration of said time, to cause the same to be destroyed, holding the owner or consignee responsible to the United States for the payment of all charges, in the same manner as if said articles had been reexported.

Sec. 5. *And be it further enacted,* That, in order to carry into effect the provisions of this act, the Secretary of the Treasury is hereby authorized and required to appoint suitably qualified persons as special examiners of drugs, medicines, chemicals, &c., namely: one examiner in each of the ports of New York, Boston, Philadelphia, Baltimore, Charleston, and New Orleans, with the following salaries, viz.: at New York, sixteen hundred dollars per annum; and at each of the other ports above named, one thousand dollars per annum; which said salaries shall be paid each year, quarterly, out of any moneys in the treasury not otherwise appropriated; and it shall be the duty of the said secretary to give such instructions to the collectors of the customs in the other collection districts, as he may deem necessary to prevent the importation of adulterated and spurious drugs and medicines.

Sec. 6. *And be it further enacted,* That the special examiners to be appointed under this act shall, before entering on the discharge of their duties, take and subscribe the oath or affirmation required by the ninth section of the act of the thirtieth of July, eighteen hundred and forty-six, entitled "An Act reducing the duty on imports, and for other purposes."

Sec. 7. *And be it further enacted,* That the special examiners to be appointed by the fifth section of this act shall, if suitably qualified persons can be found, be taken from the officers now employed in the respective collection districts; and if new appointments shall be necessary for want of such persons, then, as soon as it can be done consistently with the efficiency of the service, the officers in said districts shall be reduced, so that the present number of said officers shall not be permanently increased by reason of such new appointments.

Approved, June 26, 1848.

Source: An Act to prevent the Importation of adulterated and spurious Drugs and Medicines. *The Statutes at Large and Treaties of the United States of America.* Vol. 9. Boston: Little, Brown, 1862, pp. 237–239.

NOTE

1. Quoted in Robert I. Field, *Health Care Regulation in America: Complexity, Confrontation, and Compromise* (New York: Oxford University Press, 2007), 116.

Lemuel Shattuck Issues Recommendations for New Public Health Regulations

DOCUMENT 2.10

"Active Causes of Disease Have Increased Faster Than the Appliances for Their Prevention"

1850

The single most influential study of public health and sanitary conditions in American cities in the nineteenth century was carried out by a little-known statistician named Lemuel Shattuck on behalf of the Massachusetts Sanitary Commission. This 1850 work, titled Report of a General Plan for the Promotion of Public and Personal Health, *used detailed statistical analysis to buttress his call for new public health and sanitation laws and policies across the state. The so-called* Shattuck Report *did not make an immediate splash with legislators, most of whom were spending the bulk of their time and attention watching sectional tensions between North and South escalate. After the Civil War concluded and urban public health concerns came back into their field of vision, legislators returned to Shattuck's pioneering work. His public health recommendations became the foundation for important new policies and public health agencies in Massachusetts and many other states during the latter 1800s. This excerpt from Shattuck's report details several of the statistician's public health recommendations.*

The following are some of the many important conclusions to which the facts thus far disclosed lead us:

1. *It is proved* that there is a great difference, in this State, in the longevity of people living in different places and under different circumstances. . . .

2. *It is proved* that causes exist in Massachusetts, as in England, to produce premature and preventable deaths, and hence unnecessary and preventable sickness; and that these causes are active in all the agricultural towns, but press most heavily upon cities and populous villages.

3. *It is proved* that measures,—legislative, social and personal,—do not at present exist, or are not so fully applied, as they might be, by the people, for the prevention, mitigation, or removal, of the causes of disease and death.

4. *It is proved* that the people of this State are constantly liable to typhus, cholera, dysentery, scarlatina, small-pox, and the other great epidemics; and to consumption, and the other fatal diseases, which destroy so many of the human race in other parts of the world.

5. *It is proved* that the active causes of disease and death are increasing among us, and that the average duration of life is not as great now as it was forty or fifty years ago.

We are fully aware that the general opinion does not coincide with this fact, and that a directly opposite one has been expressed. It has been frequently said, that, owing to the different modes of living, the increased medical skill, and other causes, diseases have been ameliorated, and the average length of human life has been extended; and particularly within the last fifty years. We have long thought differently, especially in regard to the more recent periods of our history. Those who make this assertion seem to rely upon imperfect or uncertain data to support their opinion. Statistical observations of the living and the dead, gathered in ancient times, should be taken with great caution as comparative tests. Ten years since, it was said that "the average value of life is not as great as it was twenty years ago; that it was at its maximum in 1810 to 1820; and that it has since decreased." Subsequent investigations have fully established the correctness of this statement. . . .

It is undoubtedly true, that in many things society has improved; that medical skill in the cure of disease has greatly increased; and that some diseases are not as fatal as formerly, or are now better understood and controlled. But while all this may be true, it is no less true that the active causes of disease have increased faster than the appliances for their prevention and cure; that new diseases, or old ones in a new and modified form, equally fatal and uncontrollable, have appeared; and that sickness and death advance more rapidly than the improvements devised to arrest them.

State and Municipal Measures Recommended

Under this class of recommendations are to be included such measures as require, for their sanction, regulation, and control, the legislative authority of the State, or the municipal authority of cities and towns. They may be called the legal measures—the Sanitary Police of the State.

WE RECOMMEND that the laws of the State relating to Public Health be thoroughly revised, and that a new and improved act be passed in their stead. . . .

WE RECOMMEND that a GENERAL BOARD OF HEALTH be established, which shall be charged with the general execution of the laws of the State, relating to the enumeration, the vital statistics, and the public health of the inhabitants. . . .

WE RECOMMEND that a LOCAL BOARD OF HEALTH be appointed in every city and town, who shall be charged with the particular execution of the laws of the State, and the municipal ordinances and regulations, relating to public health, within their respective jurisdictions. . . .

WE RECOMMEND that local Boards of Health endeavor to ascertain, with as much exactness as possible, the circumstances of the cities and towns, and of the inhabitants under their jurisdictions; and that they issue such local sanitary orders and make such regulations as are best adapted to these circumstances. . . .

WE RECOMMEND that, in laying out new towns and villages, and in extending those already laid out, ample provision be made for a supply, in purity and abundance, of light, air, and water; for drainage and sewerage; for paving and for cleanliness. . . .

WE RECOMMEND that, as far as practicable, there be used in all sanitary investigations and regulations, a uniform nomenclature for the causes of death, and for the causes of disease. . . .

WE RECOMMEND that, before erecting any new dwelling-house, manufactury, or other building, for personal accommodation, either as a lodging-house or place of business, the owner or builder be required to give notice to the local Board of Health, of his intention and of the sanitary arrangements he proposes to adopt. . . .

WE RECOMMEND that local Boards of Health endeavor to prevent or mitigate the sanitary evils arising from overcrowded lodging-houses and cellar-dwellings. . . .

WE RECOMMEND that open spaces be reserved, in cities and villages for public walks; that wide streets be laid out; and that both be ornamented with trees. . . .

WE RECOMMEND that local Boards of Health, and other persons interested, endeavor to ascertain, by exact observation, the effect of millponds, and other collections or streams of water, and of their rise and fall, upon the health of the neighboring inhabitants. . . .

WE RECOMMEND that the local Boards of Health provide for periodical house-to-house visitation, for the prevention of epidemic diseases, and for other sanitary purposes. . . .

WE RECOMMEND that measures be taken to ascertain the amount of sickness suffered in different localities; and among persons of different classes, professions, and occupations. . . .

WE RECOMMEND that nuisances endangering human life or health, be prevented, destroyed, or mitigated. . . .

WE RECOMMEND that measures be taken to prevent or mitigate the sanitary evils arising from the use of intoxicating drinks, and from haunts of dissipation. . .

WE RECOMMEND that measures be taken to preserve the lives and the health of passengers at sea, and of seamen engaged in the merchant service. . . .

WE RECOMMEND that the authority to make regulations for the quarantine of vessels be intrusted to the local Boards of Health. . . .

WE RECOMMEND that measures be adopted for preventing or mitigating the sanitary evils arising from foreign emigration. . . .

Social And Personal Measures Recommended

Most of these recommendations may be carried into effect without any special legislative authority, State or municipal.

WE RECOMMEND that tenements for the better accommodation of the poor, be erected in cities and villages. . . .

WE RECOMMEND that persons be especially educated in sanitary science, as preventive advisors as well as curative advisors. . . .

WE RECOMMEND that, whenever practicable, the refuse and sewage of cities and towns be collected, and applied to the purposes of agriculture. . .

WE RECOMMEND that measures be taken to prevent, as far as practicable, the smoke nuisance. . . .

WE RECOMMEND that the sanitary effects of patent medicines and other nostrums, and secret remedies, be observed; that physicians in their prescriptions and names of medicines, and apothecaries in their compounds, use great caution and care; and that medical compounds advertised for sale be avoided, unless the material of which they are composed be known, or unless manufactured and sold by a person of known honesty and integrity. . . .

WE RECOMMEND that local Boards of Health, and other interested, endeavor to prevent the sale and use of unwholesome, spurious, and adulterated articles, dangerous to the public health designed for food, drink, or medicine.

Source: Shattuck, Lemuel, and the Sanitary Commission of Massachusetts. *Report of a General Plan for the Promotion of Public and Personal Health.* Boston: Dutton and Wentworth, 1850, pp. 102–5, 109, 111, 115, 121, 135, 149, 153, 164, 166, 168, 171, 183, 198, 200, 207, 208, 209, 212, 218, 220.

New York State Incorporates Its First Homeopathic Medical College

"For the Purpose of Instruction in the Various Departments of Medical Science"

1860

Homeopathy's rapid growth in popularity in antebellum America both drove and was fueled by the development of formal institutions—physicians' groups, hospitals, and colleges—dedicated to defending and disseminating its tenets. Notable landmarks in this vein included the 1835 establishment of the Allentown Academy, the 1844 formation of the American Institute of Homeopathy, the 1848 opening of the Homeopathic Medical College of Pennsylvania, and the 1855 arrival of the Hahnemann Medical College of Chicago (named after homeopathy's founder, Samuel Hahnemann). Another unmistakable sign of homeopathy's arrival as a major factor in American medicine came in 1860, when the New York legislature passed an act, reprinted here, incorporating a major homeopathic medical school in New York City, America's most populous metropolis. This school, located in the heart of Manhattan, became one of the discipline's leading centers of instruction. In 1863 a separate but related homeopathic school for women, New York Medical College for Women, was established under the direction of Dr. Clemence Sophia Lozier.

AN ACT to incorporate "The Homeopathic Medical College of the State of New York, in New York city."

Passed April 12, 1860.

The People of the State of New York, represented in Senate and Assembly, do enact as follows:

SECTION 1. Hollis White, A. Oakey Hall, Daniel F. Tiemann, Cyrus W. Field, Benjamin F. Pinckney, James M. Smith, junior, Abram B. Conger, Henry Nicoll, Horace H. Day, Francis A Hall, Gordon W. Burnham, Charles L. Frost, David Austin, jr., William Barton, John Haggerty, Charles E. Milner, Lot C. Clark, Frederick L. Talcott, James F. Hall, John P. Brown, J. M. Cooper, H. L. Van Wyck, P. M. Suydam, and their associates, are hereby constituted a body corporate, by the name of "The Homeopathic Medical College of the State of New York, in New York city," to be located in the city of New York, for the purpose of instruction in the various departments of medical science, professed and taught by said college.

§ 2. The said corporation may hold and possess real and personal estate to the amount of one hundred thousand dollars, and the funds or property thereof shall not be used for any other purpose than those declared in the preceding section. The said corporation may also hold such collection of books and of the productions of nature and of art, as may be necessary for purposes of medical and clinical instruction; and it may mortgage, from time to time, its property or any part thereof, by its bonds and mortgages, and may sell its property by its conveyances; and the same to be executed, under the common seal of said corporation, and acknowledged by the president, and may divide its property into shares of stock, transferable as personal property.

§ 3. The persons severally named in the first section of this act are hereby appointed trustees of the said corporation, with power to fill any vacancy in their board.

§ 4. The trustees, for the time being, shall have power to grant and confer the degree of doctor of homeopathic medicine, upon the recommendation of the board of professors of said college; but no person shall receive a diploma conferring such degree unless he shall be of the age of twenty-one years and upwards, and shall have pursued the study of medical science for at least three years after the age of sixteen, with some physician and surgeon, duly authorized by law to practice his profession, and shall also, after that age, have attended two complete courses of all the lectures delivered in some incorporated medical college, the last of which courses shall have been delivered by the professors of said college.

§ 5. The said college shall be subject to the visitation of the regents of the university, and shall annually report to them.

§ 6. The corporation hereby created shall possess the powers and be subject to the provisions of the eighteenth chapter of the first part of the Revised Statutes, entitled "of incorporations."

§ 7. The legislature may at any time alter, modify or repeal this act.

§ 8. This act shall take effect immediately.

Source: An Act to incorporate "The Homeopathic Medical College of the State of New York, in New York city." *Laws of the State of New York Passed at the Eighty-Third Session of the Legislature,* Albany, NY: Weed, Parsons, 1860, pp. 560–561.

CHAPTER 3

The Professionalization
of American Medicine

1860-1890

The second half of the nineteenth century was marked by heady industrial expansion, a spectacular tidal wave of new immigrants, and extravagant displays of wealth and opulence from railroad magnates, financiers, and others who sat at the head of the table of American capitalism. The Gilded Age, which extended roughly from the end of the Civil War in 1865 to the close of the nineteenth century, brought about major changes in the nation's orientation toward public and private health care. On the public health front, advances in biological knowledge, general hygiene, preventive treatment, and organizational efficiency spurred greater acceptance of federal, state, and local institutions concerned with disease prevention and other health issues. In the realm of private health care, increased medical knowledge and improved methods of health treatment engendered a turn away from Jacksonian deregulation and a cautious return to medical licensing and other forms of regulatory oversight. By 1890, well-educated and licensed physicians could legitimately assert that a bona fide medical profession worthy of public trust was coming into being.

THE CIVIL WAR AND PUBLIC HEALTH

Prior to the Civil War, the nation's paucity of public health care institutions had not been a source of widespread concern. Private citizens and public officials alike were generally accepting of maritime quarantines and similar measures to prevent outbreaks of cholera, yellow fever, and other fearsome diseases. Beyond that, Americans were largely unmoved by the small number of reformers who urged a greater government role in curbing urban pollution, educating the public on matters of hygiene, and monitoring the activities of physicians, surgeons, pharmaceutical manufacturers, medical schools, and other participants in the health care industry.

The Civil War, however, fully exposed the myriad shortcomings of America's public health infrastructure. When the conflict began, the North, which enjoyed a huge advantage in industrial capacity and development, and the South were forced to confront the fact that they had virtually no hospital or ambulance facilities for the millions of sick and wounded soldiers who would soon tumble off the battlefield. All they had were a scattering of Marine Service hospitals, most of which were small, understaffed, and modestly equipped. The U.S. Army Medical Corps consisted of a paltry 115 medical officers when hostilities erupted, and 27 of these men promptly resigned when the war began in 1861 because they were of Southern birth or otherwise sympathetic to the Confederate cause. Finally, neither Union nor Confederate units operated under any health or hygiene regulations in the opening months of the conflict, a state of affairs that resulted in explosions of dysentery, typhoid, and other bacterial infections in the filthy camps.

In the North, this void in medical care infrastructure and sanitation oversight was filled through an oft-tense but ultimately successful collaboration between federal and private institutions. The federal government provided the financial and manpower resources to build up ambulance services, expand hospital capacity, and recruit skilled physicians, surgeons, nurses, and interns to the bedsides of sick and wounded soldiers. By the last year of the war, the North had erected a sprawling system of two hundred hospitals that included more than 135,000 beds.[1] But these physical improvements to the Army's health care system were also greatly augmented by the efforts of a volunteer organization known as the U.S. Sanitary Commission (USSC).

The commission was the brainchild of members of the Women's Central Association of Relief and an assortment of affluent New York citizens, including clergyman Henry Whitney Bellows and Central Park architect Frederick Law Olmsted. Inspired by the Crimean War exploits of the volunteer British Sanitary Commission, which provided vital medical aid to British troops in that conflict, the founders of the USSC saw their group as one that could provide similar assistance to Union troops in wartime. President Abraham Lincoln was initially wary about approving the proposed venture. Opposition from a turf-conscious War Department led him to worry that the commission might become the "fifth wheel to the coach." On June 13, 1861, however, Lincoln gave his seal of approval and, thus, inaugurated a new era of public health policy in America **(See Document 3.1)**.

Over the next four years, the USSC undertook a wide array of activities in support of Union troops. Commission members carried out ambitious health education campaigns that were credited with dramatically improving hygiene in army camps, and they did much to disseminate the lessons of British nurse Florence Nightingale, who had revolutionized the nursing profession during the Crimean War. In this they were joined by Dorothea Dix, who in April 1861 had been appointed superintendent to the United

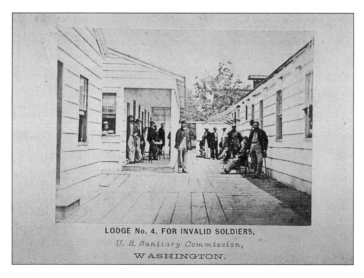

LODGE No. 4, FOR INVALID SOLDIERS,
U. S. Sanitary Commission,
WASHINGTON.

During the Civil War, the United States Sanitary Commission (USSC) was an extremely active volunteer organization for the Union. Its purpose was to improve sanitary conditions on the battlefield and in hospitals, as well as provide medical care to wounded troops. This USSC "Lodge for Invalid Soldiers" was located in Washington, D.C.

States Army Nurses. As a result, nursing became "a key weapon in the hygiene war—a nurse could do more good than a physician. Dirt caused disease, sickness was a warning, cleanliness a panacea, and nurses were ministers of hygiene."[2]

Volunteers with the U.S. Sanitary Commission and the allied Women's Central Association of Relief (the membership of the two groups overlapped considerably) also collected badly needed medical supplies by enlisting the support of thousands of ladies' aid societies, organized major drives to collect fresh meat and vegetables for soldiers, threw sanitary fairs to raise money for relief efforts, assisted sick and wounded soldiers in securing back pay and discharge papers, ran hospital ships, and worked as sanitary agents monitoring conditions in field camps and hospitals. Finally, the commission acted as an unapologetic gadfly toward civilian and military authorities in Washington, D.C. It continually pressed the Army to improve sanitation practices, successfully agitated for increased funding for medical care for soldiers, and even convinced Congress to pass legislation that reorganized the Army's Medical Department to better meet the needs of sick and wounded soldiers. This activism ruffled feathers in Washington, but the commission never wavered from its outspoken dedication to the Union soldiers' health and welfare **(See Document 3.2)**. "By the end of military action," summarized historian John Duffy, "the sanitary commission had affected the lives of millions of Americans and had given a strong impetus to the movement for sanitary reform."[3]

Postwar Changes to Public Health

By the time the Civil War concluded in 1865, the nation, battered and bruised as it was in many respects, had materially strengthened its public health institutions. The country emerged from war with a far more extensive—and extensively supplied—network of hospitals than it had supported a mere decade earlier, and the U.S. Sanitary Commission had greatly heightened public awareness about the importance of hygienic practices on both the micro level (such as washing hands before eating) and macro level (preserving community drinking water from contamination from sewage systems). Moreover, the federal government had emerged from the crucible of war with new stature and authority.

Baltimore, Maryland's Johns Hopkins Hospital is one of the oldest hospitals in the United States that is still standing today. It was the first hospital to administer a residency program for students enrolled in medical school, one of the many medical education reforms aimed at creating higher admission standards for those seeking to join the medical profession.

The national government moved quickly to build on this momentum. The Marine Hospitals Services Act of 1870 overhauled the operations of the Marine Hospital Service (MHS) and funneled responsibility for its operations into a central headquarters in Washington, D.C. **(See Document 3.5)**. One year later, John Maynard Woodworth took the reins of the MHS, which eventually evolved into the U.S. Public Health Service. As the MHS's first supervising surgeon (a title that was changed a few years later to supervising surgeon general), Woodworth moved quickly to place his imprint on the department. He adopted a military-style organizational structure for the agency, beefed up entrance standards for medical officers, and plied Congress with reports and other publications that urged a greater role for MHS in combating cholera, yellow fever, and other diseases. This assiduous campaign helped lay the groundwork for enactment of the National Quarantine Act of 1878, which expanded the authority of the service well beyond its original mandate of caring for sick and disabled seamen. This act extended MHS authority to medical inspections of ships and individual immigrants, as well as supervision of quarantine actions carried out in individual ports **(See Document 3.7)**. By the 1880s, for example, MHS inspections for trachoma, a highly contagious disease of the eye, were mandatory for the millions of immigrants arriving at gateways to America each year, including Ellis Island, which opened in 1892.

Quarantine was a crucial weapon in the arsenal of late-nineteenth-century public health efforts to curb foreign-born disease threats, as this illustration shows. Shadowy figures representing cholera, yellow fever, and smallpox stand behind a quarantine barricade with the New York skyline in the background.

Numerous states also shored up their public health institutions in the post–Civil War era. In 1866, for example, New York legislators passed "An Act to *create a metropolitan sanitary district* and board of health therein for the preservation of life and health, and to prevent the spread of disease." The agency created by this act became a trailblazer in crafting and enforcing public health regulations in the United States, and by 1900 the New York Metropolitan Board of Health was commonly employed as a measuring stick in gauging the strength and effectiveness of other municipal public health agencies **(See Document 3.4)**. Other health departments wielding real authority were created in the late 1860s and 1870s in Massachusetts and other places as well. These agencies devoted considerable energy to educating the public about health and sanitation issues, and their message resonated in many American communities. "By the end of the nineteenth century," wrote historian Regina Markell Morantz-Sanchez, "reform ideas about personal cleanliness, public health, and family hygiene had become familiar axioms of middle-class American culture—a badge of distinction by which members could set themselves off from 'illegitimate' immigrant groups, many of whom retained distinctly premodern daily habits and attitudes toward disease."[4] The agencies were also greatly aided by the

New York was a trailblazer in the post–Civil War era in establishing effective boards of health. This 1882 illustration shows New York Board of Health inspectors scrutinizing milk canisters.

settlement house movement led by social reformers such as Jane Addams and Lillian Wald. Their facilities helped inner-city immigrants assimilate by providing instruction in English, day care services, and assistance in finding employment. They also worked to educate new arrivals about the basics of disease prevention, such as by protecting the quality of drinking water.

The primary role of the public health agencies was to enforce a slowly growing number of ordinances governing the disposal of sewage, garbage, industrial effluents, and other potential threats to public health. By 1890 every state in the restored union had established a board of health, and hundreds of municipalities had formed local boards as well. These agencies assumed supervision responsibilities for everything from vaccination, garbage collection, and sewage disposal to milk pasteurization and school inspections.[5] They also worked with city engineers to bolster protections of municipal water supplies, which scientists had identified as key vectors of bacteriological diseases. The development of the germ theory of disease during the 1860s and 1870s by scientists such as Louis Pasteur in France and Robert Koch in Germany came just as many cities were making massive investments in water and waste distribution systems. By the late nineteenth century, "the sanitary revolution in America was in full swing, and health and sanitation were virtually synonymous," wrote historian John Duffy. "Possibly the key factor in all this was a rising standard of living, without which municipalities could not have afforded the enormous capital costs of the sewer and water systems nor the steadily increasing operating costs of health and sanitary programs."[6]

Not all state and local boards were created equal, however. Some never received the necessary funding to make a difference, others never received clear statutory guidelines for their operation, and others remained largely embryonic due to political opposition. In 1879, for example, the prominent New Orleans, Louisiana, physician Stanford E. Chaillé flatly told the Louisiana State Medical Society that "Louisiana has legislated on *paper* a State Board of Health and Vital Statistics; but in reality we have no state, merely a city board of health, organized under laws which nobody except politicians (and a designing or an ignorant class of these) can possibly approve."[7]

In other parts of the South, medical departments established after the war by the Freedmen's Bureau withered away after Reconstruction. And those limited public health services that did remain in place in the post–Reconstruction era were largely withheld from the region's African American population. The Freedmen's Bureau, explained scholar Todd L. Savitt, "developed no basic programs of self-help upon which freed people could build, mounted no health education campaigns among blacks or whites, and trained no black or white physicians or medical assistants. There was no overall plan, no blueprint. . . . Once the bureau was gone . . . freed people had no system of health care upon which to rely. Hospitals and dispensaries were left in the hands of white officials and white doctors. Freed people remained as dependent on the largess of whites as they had been as slaves before the Civil War."[8]

THE TRANSFORMATION OF ALMSHOUSES AND HOSPITALS

Other changes, but of a more beneficial nature, also took place within America's health care institutions during this time. Many almshouses, which had stood as virtually the sole source of government aid to the sickly poor since colonial times, underwent significant changes in operation in response to critical assessments from health and social reformers. These activists condemned almshouses as forgotten outposts of despair and squalor that shamelessly mixed young orphans, elderly invalids, and the mentally ill together without regard for their specific needs **(See Document 3.6)**.

Some legislators enacted almshouse reforms in response to these entreaties. Other almshouses evolved into early public hospitals. A number of these institutions, including New York's Bellevue Hospital and Philadelphia's General Hospital, even became leading institutions in the health care industry of the late nineteenth century.

These transformations exemplified the wider metamorphosis of American hospitals from 1870 through the close of the century. The mission, character, and capabilities of the modern hospital first began to come into focus during these decades. And as hospitals began this evolution "from places of dreaded impurity and exiled human wreckage into awesome citadels of science and bureaucratic order," in the words of historian Paul Starr, "they acquired a new moral identity, as well as new purposes and patients of higher status."[9]

To be sure, this evolution began under a cloud of uncertainty, and not all hospitals survived the journey. Operating at a time when most affluent people still paid for home-based care and health insurance was virtually nonexistent, most hospitals of the post–Civil War era found themselves engaged in a perpetual scramble to keep their doors open. Using a combination of community fund-raising that targeted wealthy citizens, allocations from local government, endowment revenue, and (to a much lesser degree) patient fees, many of these facilities managed to scrape together the necessary money to pay physicians, nurses, and other employees; pay for electricity, heating fuel, and other basic operational costs; and purchase equipment ranging from beds, desks, telephones, and linens to exciting new surgical and diagnostic equipment. But the line between success and failure was so thin that hospitals frequently welcomed assistance from women's associations and other local reform-minded groups that undertook fund-raising campaigns on their behalf. Another strategy for underwriting patient care that gradually grew in popularity was prepayment. "One form was indirect," observed scholar Charles E. Rosenberg. "Benevolent societies might negotiate reduced fees for members. Other hospitals, especially ethnic institutions and surgical hospitals in timber and mining areas, organized schemes through which individual workers could prepay medical care by subscribing small sums each week or month."[10]

Some cash-strapped hospitals had no choice but to engage in painful operational belt-tightening, especially because the rapidly rising general population was triggering steady growth in the numbers of dependent patients coming through their doors. In many cases, desperate administrators pressed medical staff to cycle inpatients through more quickly and be conservative in their use of drugs, surgical dressings, and other expensive items. Even these painful cost-cutting measures were insufficient in some cases, and especially in urban public hospitals that received a high percentage of patients— recent immigrants, poorly paid industrial workers, and the like—who could not pay for their medical treatment.

MEDICAL ADVANCES RESCUE AMERICAN HOSPITALS

In the end America's hospitals were rescued from this seemingly inexorable financial tailspin by a great and sustained wave of scientific breakthroughs and medical advances. Development and dissemination of the germ theory of disease turned American hospitals into important players in battles against bacteriological terrors such as cholera, diphtheria, gonorrhea, tuberculosis, and typhoid fever, for the institutional capabilities and controlled environments of hospitals made them natural centers for vaccination campaigns.

The emerging field of bacteriology had its greatest and most immediate impact on hospital operations by revolutionizing the practice of surgery. In the mid-nineteenth century, dentist William T. G. Morton had shown how ether could be used as a general anesthesia in surgical procedures. But the threat of infection kept surgical procedures extremely limited. Many hospitals thus seized on Joseph Lister's development of antiseptic surgery to greatly expand their surgical offerings from the late 1870s through the 1890s. The introduction of antiseptic surgery increased the success rate of operations and enabled surgeons to greatly expand their repertoire of major surgical procedures. From 1889 to 1892, for example, William Mayo and Charles Mayo, who later founded the famed Mayo Clinic in Minnesota, reported that they performed a total of fifty-four abdominal surgeries. By 1905, they were performing more than two thousand such operations a year.[11] Initially, these revolutionary changes were a source of considerable fiscal stress on medical institutions. For many institutions, any purchase of new surgical equipment required administrators to make painful cuts in daily operational areas or mothball plans for badly needed capital improvements (such as a new roof or ward). These technology investments eventually enabled hospitals to implement new business models that delivered them from the edge of the financial abyss, for they brought about a sea change in the social background of the people they treated. Hospitals across the land experienced an upsurge in middle-class and upper-class clientele—people who could afford to pay for surgical treatment and acute care, unlike the earlier poor and indigent folk who had traditionally been the primary focus of institutional care.

As hospitals experienced an increase in financial vitality and health, new investments in medical equipment, vaccines and other drugs, capital improvements (such as construction of wings of private rooms for affluent patients), and staff quickly followed. New hospital construction proliferated as well, as businessmen and investors came to realize the profit potential of hospitals as business enterprises.

Hospitals old and new also benefited enormously from a parallel development: the professionalization of nursing. Pointing to the myriad ways in which high-quality nursing had benefited sick and wounded troops during the Civil War, public health reformers and far-sighted doctors campaigned for much greater use of trained nurses in the nation's growing hospitals in the 1870s and 1880s. Some orthodox doctors were squeamish about the idea because they feared that educated nurses would question their authority, but these objections fell to the wayside as the new nurses proved their worth. And as hospitals grew in physical size and operational scope, student nurses and professional nurses became ever more integral to their care and treatment offerings. By the close of the century there were more than 430 nurse training schools in the United States, 427 more than there had been less than three decades earlier.[12]

All of these changes, coupled with a steady succession of new breakthroughs in medical understanding and innovations in treatment, further fueled the hospital's emerging status as society's central nexus of science and medicine. And the hospital industry's mission orientation changed accordingly, from one of faith-driven charity and long-term custodial care to one of intensive professional treatment of injury and disease in return for financial compensation. These changes brought about a corresponding shift in the balance of power between hospital trustees and major donors, who had once enjoyed near complete control over institutional affairs, and the staff surgeons, specialists, and other physicians, who came to exert much greater decision-making authority over admissions, releases, and other daily operations than ever before.

Ongoing Battles within the Medical Profession

The growing prominence of hospitals in the medical industry further deepened long-standing antagonisms between regular or allopathic physicians and various sectarian practitioners, the most prominent of which were homeopaths. Regulars held the reins at most of these institutions, and they devoted a great deal of time and effort to preventing irregulars from securing hospital appointments, or even the right to visit their own patients when they were admitted into hospital facilities. Regular physicians at Chicago's Cook County Hospital, New York's Bellevue Hospital, and Boston City Hospital, for example, all beat back attempts by homeopaths to gain facility access or staff positions in the late 1850s and early 1860s, despite considerable levels of popular support for homeopathic medicine in all of these cities.

Homeopathic practitioners suffered other setbacks and insults as well. State and local chapters of the American Medical Association (AMA) remained adamantly opposed to extending membership to homeopaths. Regulars also managed to keep homeopaths out of the Army Medical Corps during the Civil War, and in April 1865 a considerable number of them even denounced Army surgeon general Joseph K. Barnes for working at the side of a homeopathic physician to save the life of Secretary of State William Seward after an assassination attempt **(See Document 3.3)**. This response, hysterical though it might have been, accurately reflected the degree to which, among regulars, "the avoidance of contact with homeopaths took on all the gravity of a pollution taboo."[13]

Despite this implacable hostility, homeopathy managed to survive and even hold its own, especially in America's larger cities. Homeopaths established their own professional societies and medical colleges, and although they did not get any credit from orthodox physicians for doing so, they incorporated much of the new medical and scientific knowledge of the late nineteenth century into their practices.

Homeopathy and lesser sectarian practices were able to weather the orthodox storm in part because of their relative openness to having women physicians in their ranks. Although women accounted for less than 5 percent of all physicians in the United States in the late nineteenth century, they constituted a considerably higher percentage of homeopathic physicians.[14] During the last two decades of the nineteenth century, women accounted for 15 percent of all homeopathic medical school graduates, and they were integral parts of many sectarian institutions and organizations.[15]

The differences in attitude between the sectarian and orthodox medical camps toward women physicians were often stark. Many regular physicians scoffed at the very idea, asserting as one medical professor did that the "history, physiology, and the general judgment of society unite in the negative of woman's fitness for the medical office."[16] These negative judgments—whether based on Victorian sensibilities about gender roles, sexist convictions about the intellectual and moral capacities of women, or the prospect of losing women patients (obstetrics was a major source of income for many physicians)—presented monumental difficulties for prospective women physicians hoping to open an orthodox practice, for they closed off most avenues of formal medical education and membership in professional societies. By contrast, in 1871 the American Institute of Homeopathy (AIH) opened its membership to women, who promptly "became active participants in the organization, presenting papers and case reports at annual meetings, chairing committees, and contributing to decisions on institutional policy."[17]

Gradually, women physicians were able to knock down many of the barriers erected by orthodox practitioners. These barriers, whether membership in professional societies or access to elite educational institutions, were zealously guarded by some bastions of the old guard (**See Document 3.9**). But in the end, their objections to women physicians were swept aside by more powerful societal forces, including the reform and reorganization of American medical education.

Medical Education after the Civil War

Avenues for women hoping to establish careers for themselves in orthodox medicine did not begin opening up until the last quarter of the nineteenth century, when growing numbers of regular medical schools began accepting female students. Up to that point, intrepid women physicians such as Elizabeth Blackwell, the first American woman to graduate with a medical degree (from New York's Geneva College in 1849), had been regarded as curiosities, not trailblazers. Similarly, medical degrees earned from all-women schools were viewed condescendingly by male physicians (although this condescension became more muted as the high quality of instruction in some women's colleges became evident). The rise of coeducational medical institutions placed the accomplishments of Blackwell and other early women practitioners in an entirely new and historic light.

The entrance of women into previously all-male bastions of medical education took place against a turbulent backdrop of upheaval, both within medical schools and in the wider field of medicine. When America emerged from the smoke and ash of the Civil War, it did so under the burden of a profoundly dysfunctional health care industry. The Jacksonian retreat from regulation of physicians, combined with an attendant explosion in commercial medical schools, had flooded the marketplace with unqualified and poorly trained doctors who tainted the entire profession with their bungling. As an 1869 editorial in the *Medical Record* lamented, "In all our American colleges, medicine has ever been and is now, the most despised of all the professions which liberally-educated men are expected to enter."[18]

During the 1860s and 1870s, medical education in America cleaved down two distinct tracks of development. One track was occupied by the for-profit commercial medical colleges, most of which continued to disgorge graduates who had no business practicing medicine. On the other track stood a notable core of American universities that became synonymous with medical education—and the reform thereof.

The foundations for the eventual implementation of many of these reforms were laid with the 1862 passage of the Morrill Act. This legislation bestowed federal lands on each state, which could in turn sell the land to fund the creation, development, and ongoing operations of public universities. Financially secure and politically connected, the land grant colleges that emerged from this act would soon become the home of many of the nation's leading nursing and medicine programs. Even before these colleges evolved, however, the presidents of a handful of private institutions were spurring important education reforms in the medical field. These educators, led by Daniel Coit Gilman of Johns Hopkins University and Charles Eliot of Harvard University, were genuinely outraged by the sad state of medical education in America. "The ignorance and general incompetency of the average graduate of American Medical Schools at the time when he receives the degree which turns him loose upon the community, is something horrible to contemplate," wrote Eliot in the early 1870s. "The whole system of medical education in this country needs thorough reformation."[19]

Acting upon their convictions, educators such as Eliot and Gilman relentlessly pushed for higher admission standards, increased clinical training (including residencies, which were first introduced at Johns Hopkins), and heightened graduation requirements. Their efforts were supplemented by a wide array of supporters issuing new demands for professional competence, including staff-seeking hospital administrators, endowment-bestowing business magnates, and long-suffering members of the American public. And slowly but surely, as higher standards came to be seen as a reputation-enhancer, other leading institutions of medical learning began to follow suit.

Other changes took place as well in this general environment of reform and change. The doors of many elite medical schools and affiliated professional societies were opened to women who had previously been consigned to women-only institutions, and the percentage of women doctors in America jumped nationally from 2.8 percent in 1880 to 5.6 percent in 1900.[20] Meanwhile, American medical schools that had long lagged behind Germany and other European countries in the realm of medical research finally established their own laboratories and research facilities. In sum, the broad outlines of the modern American medical school were finally becoming discernable by 1890.

STATES PRESS FOR MEDICAL LICENSING REGULATIONS

These education reforms drove other changes in the health care industry, including a renewed interest in state regulation of medical practices. And while the latter drive was spearheaded by physicians instead of crusading educators, the two reform goals were nonetheless closely interwoven. "While the leading medical schools were reforming admission standards and curricula, the state medical societies were beginning to appreciate the potential strength of licensing boards," explained scholar Rosemary Stevens. "If state examining boards were established, a degree alone would no longer be regarded as a license, and teaching would finally be separated from licensure. Graduates of poor schools would not pass the license examinations; thus the boards would provide leverage in reforming the schools."[21]

Many advocates of peer-controlled (that is, licensing by state medical societies) or state-controlled licensing within the medical arts were also motivated by self-interest. Culling the vast herd of doctors and physicians across America would reduce competition for patients. But proponents of new licensing regulations, whether they were physicians or social reformers, were also spurred to action by the outright despair that many Americans were expressing about the state of private health care in their cities and towns. Many people in need of medical care simply did not know where to turn, because they had no sure way of determining whether physicians—orthodox or homeopathic, urban or rural, specialist or general practitioner—were competent in their declared vocation. "In the Healing Art our country is flooded with advisers from those of science, judgment and skill, to swarms of quacks, who know as much of physiology, pathology, anatomy and physics as a pet cat does about the Battle of Waterloo," wrote one disgusted citizen in 1875. "We have many of this class of advisers whose self-assurance, backed by some patent nostrum, gives them a passport among the credulous, and sometimes makes them leave in the distance a man of science, merit and worth, but too modest and unassuming for the times. Blustering impudence and foaming braggadocio have performed astonishing feats in our country within several years."[22]

The heightened interest in licensing was not limited to the medical field. Reformers were also calling for licensing of plumbers, embalmers, and an assortment of other professions that had become tainted by tales of fraud, incompetence, and general malfeasance under America's brawling, largely unregulated free market system of industrial capitalism. But the push to resurrect medical licensing was particularly notable because of its direct impact on the health of millions of Americans.

The licensing movement also paved the way for a rapprochement of sorts between sectarians and regular physicians. By the 1880s, some of the more reasonable orthodox physicians were openly acknowledging that sectarian acceptance of new breakthroughs in medical science and therapeutic treatment had bridged some of the differences between the two groups. They also acknowledged that some sectarian treatments and philosophical perspectives on caregiving had been integrated into orthodox practice, to the latter's benefit. But it was the licensing issue that facilitated the beginnings of a lasting convergence between the competing camps. Regular physicians from elite medical schools joined forces with homeopaths and other sectarians to lobby legislators for new licensing laws that would sweep the most unprincipled, untrained, and incompetent physicians out of their field.[23]

Some parts of the country pursued licensing reforms more energetically than others. In Mississippi, for example, the state's pro-regulation medical society lamented, with more than a little incredulity, that public indifference posed a significant obstacle to reform. "It would be difficult to have any law enforced which would deprive the people of the inestimable privilege of being poisoned in their own chosen way," the society remarked. "Until the necessity for such legislation shall be appreciated by the masses of the people, the passage of any such laws will be premature, and they will remain dead letters on the statute books."[24]

But this inertia was the exception rather than the rule. A wide array of medical licensing bills made their way through various state and territorial legislatures in the 1870s and 1880s. Defenders of the status quo (most notably doctors who had obtained their schooling through the commercial diploma mills) roused themselves against this threat, but to no avail. The momentum for reform had become hard for legislators to resist, and some states pursued the goal of licensing with the zeal of the newly converted. In 1877, for example, Illinois passed a sweeping law that gave state-appointed medical examiners the authority to reject medical diplomas from substandard schools and force those diploma holders to take state medical examinations to prove their competence. Within a decade of the passage of this bill, an estimated three thousand Illinois physicians were reported to have closed their doors.[25] Other states used the Illinois act as a model, and by the end of the century more than half of the states had passed medical licensing laws that required practitioners to hold a diploma from a reputable school and pass medical exams carried out by the states themselves. Virtually all of these licensing acts were challenged in court. But state courts sided firmly with the pro-licensure reformers, and in 1888 the US Supreme Court put its seal of approval on state regulation of medical licensing with its judgment in *Dent v. West Virginia* **(See Document 3.12)**.

THE RISE AND FALL OF THE NATIONAL BOARD OF HEALTH

At the same time that regular and sectarian physicians found common cause regarding the issue of medical licensing, the national government became mired in its first major inter-agency dispute over the management and protection of public health. This row pitted the venerable Marine Hospital Service against the upstart National Board of Health (NBH), a public health agency that was established by Congress in 1879 **(See Document 3.8)**.

The NBH was a bold federal initiative to bolster disease prevention and public health efforts across the country. Calls for such an agency had been germinating for the better part of a century, and they intensified with each new disease epidemic. But this quest took on new urgency after the Civil War, when both lawmakers and reformers saw the benefits of robust federal oversight of sanitation and hygiene practices. In addition, advocates of a larger federal role in public health gradually learned to frame their desires as an issue of national security and economic necessity. "The first and largest interest of the State lies in this great agency of human power—the health of the people," declared the famed Massachusetts sanitarian Edward Jarvis in 1874. "This creates and manages all its wealth, and the chief responsibility of government is to protect it, and if possible, to enlarge it and make it more productive."[26]

The final impetus for creation of a National Board of Health came in 1878, when cholera and yellow fever outbreaks convinced Congress of the need for such a department. But Congress spurned bills that would have increased the powers of the Marine Hospital Service or Army Medical Bureau in favor of a bill, sponsored by the American Public Health Association, that created a new federal agency and transferred to that agency the quarantine powers that had previously belonged to the MHS. This sudden reversal of fortune stunned the MHS and its surgeon general, John Maynard Woodworth, who collapsed and died a few days after the National Board of Health was born.

In June 1879, three months after its formal establishment, the NBH received expanded authority from Congress to coordinate maritime quarantines, monitor public health on behalf of the entire federal government, and assist state and local health authorities with other disease prevention programs. But this act included a fateful sunset provision, a stipulation that the NBH would enjoy these new powers for only four years. If Congress did not approve a continuation before that four-year authorization expired, then the agency's authority would automatically revert back to the MHS and state and local health boards.

The four-year clause gave new MHS surgeon general John Hamilton and various state officials considerable incentive to sabotage the NBH, and they did so with zeal. Within a matter of months, state officials across the former Confederacy had dusted off states' rights rhetoric and begun using it as a cudgel against the board. The worst offender in this regard was Louisiana. Under the leadership of New Orleans physician (and decorated Confederate officer) Joseph Jones, Louisiana's state board of health obstinately refused to cooperate with the National Board of Health on any matter of consequence **(See Document 3.10)**. By the summer of 1882, NBH inspector Stanford E. Chaillé, who was the agency's pointman in negotiations with Jones, was moved to write that "I shall hope never again to occupy such unpleasant and detrimental circumstances as my office has brought me during the past two years."[27]

In the meantime, as historian Wilson G. Smillie wrote, "a much more dangerous foe within the shadow of the National Capital was quietly plotting [the NBH's] destruction."[28] From 1879 to 1883 MHS surgeon general Hamilton carried out a low-key but ruthless campaign to erode congressional support for reauthorization of the NBH. His efforts contributed mightily to Congress's decision to abandon the agency over the protestations of the American Public Health Association and numerous state and regional departments of health. When the reauthorization deadline came and went on June 2, 1883, without any action by Congress, the National Board of Health was stripped of most of its powers and its maritime quarantine functions returned to MHS, which was still headed by Hamilton. As expected, various opponents of the NBH rejoiced at its downfall. But many champions of public health reform saw the evisceration of the agency as an injury to the American people, and they vowed to press Congress for "national legislation" that would provide meaningful and lasting protection to the public health **(See Document 3.11)**.

NOTES

1. Charles E. Rosenberg, *The Care of Strangers: The Rise of America's Hospital System* (New York: Basic Books, 1987), 97.

2. Roy Porter, *The Greatest Benefit to Mankind: A Medical History of Humanity* (New York: Norton, 1999), 378.

3. John Duffy, *The Sanitarians: A History of American Public Health* (Urbana: University of Illinois Press, 1992), 113.

4. Regina Markell Morantz-Sanchez, "Science, Health Reform, and the Woman Physician," in *Major Problems in the History of American Medicine and Public Health*, ed. John Harley Warner and Janet A. Tighe (Boston: Houghton Mifflin, 2001), 151.

5. James T. Bennett and Thomas J. DiLorenzo, *From Pathology to Politics: Public Health in America* (New Brunswick, NJ: Transaction Publishers, 2000), 7.

6. Duffy, *The Sanitarians*, 139.

7. Wilson G. Smillie, *Public Health: Its Promise for the Future* (New York: Macmillan, 1955), 315.

8. Todd L. Savitt, *Race and Medicine in Nineteenth- and Early-Twentieth-Century America* (Kent, OH: Kent State University Press, 2007), 117.

9. Paul, Starr, *The Social Transformation of American Medicine* (New York: Basic Books, 1982), 145.

10. Rosenberg, *The Care of Strangers*, 241.

11. Helen Clapesattle, *The Doctors Mayo* (Minneapolis: University of Minnesota Press, 1941), 323.

12. Jo Ann Ashley, *Hospitals, Paternalism, and the Role of the Nurse* (New York: Teachers College Press, 1976), 20.

13. Starr, *The Social Transformation of American Medicine*, 98.

14. Regina Markell Morantz-Sanchez, *Sympathy and Science: Women Physicians in American Medicine* (New York: Oxford University Press, 1985), 244.

15. Anne Taylor Kirschmann, *A Vital Force: Women in American Homeopathy* (New Brunswick, N.J.: Rutgers University Press, 2004), 7.

16. Quoted in Mary Putnam Jacobi, *Woman's Work in America* (New York: Henry Holt, 1891), 143.

17 Kirschmann, *A Vital Force*, 76.

18. "American versus European Medical Science," *Medical Record* (May 15, 1869): 133.

19. Quoted in Starr, *The Social Transformation of American Medicine.* 113.

20. Mary R. Walsh, *Doctors Wanted: No Women Need Apply* (New Haven, CT: Yale University Press, 1977), 176.

21. Rosemary Stevens, *American Medicine and the Public Interest* (New Haven, CT: Yale University Press, 1971); rev. ed. (Berkeley: University of California Press, 1998), 42.

22. "No. 45," letter to the editors, *Monthly Journal,* May 13, 1875, in *Locomotive Engineers Journal* 9 (1875): 308.

23. Starr, *The Social Transformation of American Medicine,* 102.

24. Quoted in Felix J. Underwood and R. N. Whitfield, *Public Health and Medical Licensure in the State of Mississippi, 1798–1937,* Vol. 1 (Jackson, MS: Tucker, 1938), 141.

25. Starr, *The Social Transformation of American Medicine,* 104.

26. Quoted in Smillie, *Public Health,* 311.

27. Quoted in Smillie, *Public Health,* 334.

28. Smillie, *Public Health,* 337.

DOCUMENT
3.1

The Lincoln Administration Approves the U.S. Sanitary Commission

"The Commission Will Direct Its Inquiries to . . . Preserving and Restoring the Health of Troops"

1861

In 1861 President Abraham Lincoln approved the creation of a volunteer U.S. Sanitary Commission to augment the health care and sanitary work of the Army Medical Corps. This decision, which came by way of the June announcement reprinted here, had a momentous and salutary impact on the lives of numerous Union soldiers. Headed by a talented and dedicated core of reformers, the commission used public pressure to force major sanitation improvements in army camps, hospitals, and other facilities from civilian and military authorities. In addition, it conducted ambitious sanitary education campaigns that convinced enlisted men as well as officers of the need to improve personal and camp hygiene. By war's end, the commission's efforts had helped turn public health and sanitary reform into much more high-profile policy issues than they had ever been in antebellum America.

ORDER OF THE SECRETARY OF WAR, APPROVED BY THE PRESIDENT, APPOINTING THE SANITARY COMMISSION.

WAR DEPARTMENT, Washington, June 9, 1861.

The Secretary of War has learned, with great satisfaction, that at the instance and in pursuance of the suggestion of the Medical Bureau, in a communication to this office, dated May 22, 1861, Henry W. Bellows, D. D., Prof. A. D. Bache, LL.D., Prof. Jeffries Wyman, M.D., Prof. Wolcott Gibbs, M.D., W. H. Van Buren, M.D., Samnel G. Howe, M.D., R. C. Wood, Surgeon U. S. A., G. W. Cullum, U. S. A., Alexander E. Shiras, U. S. A., have mostly consented, in connection with such others as they may choose to associate with them, to act as "A Commission of Inquiry and Advice in respect of the Sanitary Interests of the United States Forces," and without remuneration from the Government. The Secretary has submitted their patriotic proposal to the consideration of the President, who directs the acceptance of the services thus generously offered [sic].

The Commission, in connection with a Surgeon of the U. S. A., to be designated by the Secretary, will direct its inquiries to the principles and practices connected with the inspection of recruits and enlisted men; the sanitary condition of the volunteers; to the means of preserving and restoring the health, and of securing the general comfort and efficiency of troops; to the proper provision of cooks, nurses, and hospitals; and to other subjects of like nature.

The Commission will frame such rules and regulations, in respect of the objects and modes of its inquiry, as may seem best adapted to the purpose of its constitution, which, when approved by the Secretary, will be established as general guides of its investigations and action.

A room with necessary conveniences will be provided in the City of Washington for the use of the Commission, and the members will meet when and at such places as may be convenient to them for consultation, and for the determination of such questions as may come properly before the Commission.

In the progress of its inquiries, the Commission will correspond freely with the Department and with the Medical Bureau, and will communicate to each, from time to time, such observations and results as it may deem expedient and important.

The Commission will exist until the Secretary of War shall otherwise direct, unless sooner dissolved by its own action.

SIMON CAMERON,
Secretary of War.
I approve the above.
A. LINCOLN.
June 13, 1861.

Source: United States Sanitary Commission and Charles Janeway Stillé. *History of the United States Sanitary Commission: Being the General Report of Its Work during the War of the Rebellion*. New York: Lippincott, 1866, pp. 532–33.

DOCUMENT
3.2

U.S. Sanitary Commission Campaign to Reorganize the Medical Bureau

"It Was Difficult to Make Congress Understand the Importance of the Subject"

1862

As the Civil War raged across America in the early 1860s, volunteer reformers within the Sanitary Commission launched a sustained campaign to remake the U.S. Army Medical Bureau into a more efficient, professional, and responsive organization for the care of sick and wounded soldiers. The commission did this by bombarding the Army's overwhelmed and poorly organized medical department with proposals for operational changes both large and small. In addition, it badgered Congress to pass legislation that would reorganize and bolster the medical offices of the Army. Its efforts paid off in April 1862 with the passage of "An Act to reorganize and increase the efficiency of the Medical Department of the Army."

The zeal with which the commission pursued these and other public health efforts during the war was a source of some exasperation and resentment within the Army and Congress. United States Sanitary Commission member Charles J. Stillé acknowledges as much in the following excerpt from a history of the commission's work, which was published in 1868. But Stillé argues that "the great reforms in the Medical service of the Army, the value of which can only be measured by the wants of suffering men in future wars, would never have originated in official quarters."

While the Commission did not neglect its duty of providing for the wants of . . . distant expeditions [by Union forces in early 1862], its chief attention was fixed upon plans for the general improvement of the military administration, so far as it related to the hygienic and sanitary interests of the army. . . .

The great work of the Commission, without the accomplishment of which it was felt, that all else it might do, would prove but of partial temporary benefit, was the RE-ORGANIZATION OF THE MEDICAL DEPARTMENT OF THE ARMY. Its members were convinced, that while the existing system continued with its utter inadequacy of means to the end, and especially with the positive indisposition shown on all occasions by its higher officers so to modify its arrangements as properly to provide for all the needs of the new condition, there could be no permanent improvement in the care of the sick and wounded. They determined, therefore, to strike at the root of the evil, and to insist upon a thorough reform, to be effected through the legislation of Congress. There were many considerations which induced them to undertake the task of urging Congress to pass such a bill,—a task always arduous and distasteful in its nature, even when the dearest interests of humanity are involved in the success of such an effort.

Aside from their convictions of the absolute necessity of the measure itself, perhaps one of the strongest motives which influenced them, was a hope that they might be thus relieved from their own painful and thankless functions. They felt that their work would be in a great measure completed as soon as the needed reform was accomplished by legislation, and when some portion of that life and energy and effectiveness which was then beginning to be observed in some of the other important branches of the military service had been infused into the Medical Bureau. Experience had taught them the folly of attacking evils in detail, while the principle of the evil still existed in full force in the system itself. If the particular evil was abated by their agency, yet other evils not before conspicuous soon forced themselves, hydra-headed, upon their observation, until they seemed to be engaged in a task not only wearisome and endless, but utterly barren of results at all commensurate with the labor required for the radical reform of abuses. They hoped then to embody in a measure to be sanctioned by Congress, provisions which would force the Medical Department to do through its regular official channels the work which the Commission had hitherto done so partially and so unsatisfactorily. If they could succeed in this way in securing the appointment of a Surgeon-General who should have some adequate conception of the real wants of the Army, and capacity and energy enough to carry into execution such a liberal system of providing for those wants as Congress might be induced to prescribe, and particularly if a thorough system of inspection could be established and enforced by official authority, they felt that vast progress would have been made in accomplishing the very purposes which it was the object of their appointment to secure. Their struggles with the War Department and the Medical Bureau had been unceasing; their suggestions of reform were often unheeded; their warnings of certain impending danger had induced no proper precautions; they had tired out everybody in authority with their importunity for the remedy of abuses, and they now determined to make an effort to give that practical effect to their plans by force of law, which they had tried so long, and in vain to do by argument and persuasion. If they could succeed in this object they would gladly return to the Government the imperfect and inadequate powers which had been conferred upon them, and with entire confidence retire from the field, placing the responsibility for the humane and proper care of the sick and wounded upon that department of the Government, where they had always contended it rightfully belonged. . . .

The history of the Medical Department previous to the war, is that of a Bureau whose operations were confined to the wants of fifteen thousand men on a peace establishment. Its *personnel* consisted at the outbreak of the Rebellion of a Surgeon-General, twenty-six Surgeons, and eighty Assistant Surgeons. Of the Surgeons many were incapacitated for all duty, and one-half were unfitted for service in the field. The average length of service of the first thirteen on the list was thirty-two years, and that of the remaining, twenty-three years. By an act passed in 1834 a rigid examination of candidates for the post of Assistant-Surgeon in the Army was made necessary, and many young men of promise were thus introduced into the medical staff. These officers were scattered at isolated points on the frontier, without access to books, having no contact with their professional brethren in civil life, and with very little opportunity while their duties confined them to the medical care of a single company of soldiers, of improving themselves in a knowledge of that science which is perhaps of all others the most progressive. At these remote garrisons they were kept for at least five years, and the consequence was, that unless, in rare and exceptional cases, their professional ambition became deadened from the simple want of a stimulus to preserve it in proper activity. . . . The progress of the war proved that many of these Surgeons, particularly the younger among them, removed to a wider sphere of action, and permitted to carry out a more liberal system, recovered from the pressure, by which their energies during years of the mechanical performance of mere routine duties had become impaired. Some of them indeed during the war gained great and deserved distinction by the executive ability which they displayed in the administration of some of the higher offices of the medical staff. Still the tendency of the condition of things by which the Surgeons of the army were surrounded before the war, was necessarily towards complete stagnation in respect of everything which could stimulate a true professional zeal. . . .

The operations of the Bureau before the war, were on a scale, and conducted upon a system, which may be inferred from the limited number of the members of the staff, and the dispersion of the Army in small detachments, in garrisons along our extensive frontier. The arrangements existing in European armies for the care of the sick and wounded, which had improved with the increasing knowledge of medical science, and the more general diffusion of humane principles, were considered inapplicable to our limited establishment. Our Medical authorities therefore, as they had no occasion to imitate them, concerned themselves little about such improvements. It seems incredible, upon any other supposition, that deficiencies, such as were supplied during the war, could have existed at its commencement. It is perhaps still more extraordinary that any one who was at all familiar with the subject, could have supposed it possible that the old machinery, however modified, could have been made to perform the new work demanded of it.

Before the war no such establishment as a General Hospital existed in the army; the military hospitals were all Post Hospitals, that at Fort Leavenworth, the largest, containing but forty beds. It was necessary, therefore, to create in the midst of the crisis the entire system by which these establishments, so indispensable to the operations of a large army in the field, are governed. There were at that time no suitable buildings, no trained, efficient and numerous medical staff; no well-instructed nurses, no regulations or arrangements for a suitable diet for the sick, or provision for their clothing; no properly understood relations between General Hospitals and Regimental Hospitals; no means for supplying promptly proper medicines, and no arrangements for the humane and careful transportation of the sick and wounded. As we have before said, patients were crowded in the early part of the war into buildings wholly unsuited for their successful treatment. The agony and suffering which were endured by them during the first nine months of its continuance, owing to the delay in the construction of proper General Hospitals, can never be accurately known, but it is not easy to over-estimate it. The vivid recollection of the horrors of these miscalled Hospitals, which were apparent at that time to the most careless observer, is all that is necessary now to justify the strenuous efforts which were made by humane men throughout the country, to effect a radical change in the whole system. Previous to the war, there was no organized system of Inspection of Camps and Hospitals, as a means of enabling the Medical Department to perform its duties intelligently and thoroughly. . . .

The practical administration of the affairs of the Bureau was also much impeded, by its strangely complicated relations with the Quartermaster's and Subsistence Departments of the Army. To the first of these belonged by law, exclusively the construction of Hospitals and their equipment, the vital matter of the transportation of the sick and wounded, and the performance of a number of other duties, seriously affecting the sanitary condition of the troops. To the other, the supply of their food, which in any large view of the question, as affecting their suitable alimentation, was a medical or at least a hygienic matter of the very first practical importance. The Medical Bureau was wholly powerless to control the action of either of these Departments and so to shape their policy, towards those who were sick, or towards those who being well, were in danger from neglect of proper precaution of becoming sick, that they might receive the benefit of the vast modern improvements, which have been made, in this direction. . . .

These were some of the more obvious evils of the system, which existed at the commencement of the Rebellion, evils which soon made themselves felt, in the confusion, embarrassment, and inefficiency of the whole service of caring for the sick and wounded. These evils were apparent to any one who took the trouble to examine into the practical workings of the system. They became more and more painfully impressed upon the Sanitary Commission every day, for scarcely a day passed in which some shocking instance of inhumanity and neglect was not brought to its notice, which was fairly attributable to them. It was determined that its duty could only be properly performed, not by attempting to fix the responsibility of this condition of things on the officials who had been trained under the existing system, but by an effort to uproot the system itself, as wholly worthless for the purpose in view. It was proposed to substitute a new organization founded upon some proper appreciation of the real wants of the case. Representing the popular benevolence of the country towards the Army, and with a full view of all the facts, the Sanitary Commission was satisfied that nothing less than such a complete re-organization would cure the difficulty. It commenced, therefore, a movement to effect it, as we have said, by Congressional legislation.

It asked for certain specific objects in the proposed change. It desired, in the first place, that the principle of promotion by seniority, among the higher officers of the staff, should be abandoned. It wished to see at the head of the Bureau a young man of active and vigorous habits, and decided character, with professional ability and practical experience, which would enable him to grapple with the difficulties of the situation, who, while introducing all the improvements of modern science, in the humane and skilful care of the sick and wounded, would have energy enough to enforce their universal adoption in practice. It urged also that a complete and thorough system of Inspection should be established, and that a special corps of Inspectors should be appointed, through whose agency the reform of evils should be faithfully carried out. It asked that General Hospitals should be erected, wherever needed, upon plans recognized as best by universal European experience, and that the construction of these Hospitals should be superintended by officers who had some knowledge of the requirements of such buildings, and who would exhibit some zeal and energy in executing the plans. It wished that the transportation service of the sick and wounded should be transferred from the Quartermaster's to the Medical Department, and that an enlarged Ambulance system, under the special control of that Department, should be created. It was anxious that a large accumulation of medicines and Hospital supplies should be constantly maintained in the depots of the Medical Purveyors, so that the evil consequences, which had arisen from the long delays in furnishing such supplies, should not again occur. It wished also that some arrangements should be made, by which men who were languishing in Hospitals from diseases which rendered them incapable of further military service, should be discharged and sent home, and that those who remained under treatment should be provided with Hospital clothing and a proper diet.

In bringing this subject before Congress, in order to secure the proper legislation by which the objects we have enumerated should be accomplished, the Sanitary Commission was, as we have said, only the exponent of the anxious desire of the American people, who demanded the best possible care for the suffering of the Army. Its efforts were aided, of course, by the influence of many professional and benevolent men throughout the country, and no less effectually, though perhaps more quietly, by some of the junior members of the Medical Staff itself, who were perfectly aware of the deficiencies of the system, and welcomed gladly the prospect of the enactment of any law likely to add to the reputation of the corps for efficiency. . . .

It was difficult to make Congress understand, in the midst of all its preoccupations, the importance of the subject. Considerations of mere humanity seemed to have but little influence. It was generally admitted, that the evils complained of existed, but it was said that their importance and their consequences were exaggerated. To correct these false impressions, the Commission resolutely set itself to work. After all the usual means of influence with members of Congress had been resorted to, consisting in personal appeals, the earnest recommendation of the project by persons of position throughout the country, visits of influential deputations to Washington, discussions in the newspapers, and the like, the Commission was at last rewarded on the 18th of April, 1862, by the passage of a bill entitled, "An Act to reorganize and increase the efficiency of the Medical Department of the Army."

This Bill, although omitting some important features which had been proposed, still substantially created a system for the future operations of the Medical Department, which the Commission had striven so long to secure. By this most important law, the appointment of the Surgeon-General and of the higher officers of the staff, was to be made from the most competent officers of the whole corps, thus ignoring the usage of promotion by seniority. This was a most important step in the right direction, for if the Surgeon-General could be really appointed on the ground of qualification only, as the Bill directed, an efficient head of the whole system was secured, and vast progress towards a satisfactory result was made. Eight Medical Inspectors were also provided for by the Bill, and it may be here said in passing, that far larger powers of remedying evils were supposed to have been conferred upon them by it than they ever actually exercised in practice. Provisions were embodied in the Bill in reference to the transportation of the sick and wounded, and to the General Hospital administration, which experience had shown to be so much needed, and which those who were interested in the subject had striven so long and so wholly in vain to introduce under the old system. The law, of course, presented a mere outline or general sketch of the principles of the re-organiza-tion of a Medical Bureau such as Congress desired to establish, for in an administrative service of this kind, it is impossible, in a general measure, to provide for all the details which clothe the skeleton, and give life and vigor to the whole body. . . .

It will be seen, we trust, on a review of the work of the Commission, as we have presented it in this volume, that the Sanitary Commission accomplished substantially the object it proposed by the means which it had first suggested, as proper to be employed for such a purpose. The great end of its appointment was, as we have seen to aid the Government. If we consider some of the evil consequences which might have resulted to the country and the Army had the great power intrusted to it been abused or unwisely administered, the impression of the purity and sincerity of the motives of those who conducted it will be strongly confirmed. The great objection in this country to an extra-governmental organization like this, aside from the danger of its interfer-ence with the ordinary routine of Army discipline, was the fear, lest with its immense resources, and with the powerful support of a large body of influential men throughout the country, it might become in time, perhaps almost unconsciously, an instrument to subserve partisan ends. The power which it wielded during the war was vast, and did not fail to attract the attention of politicians. Its officers might easily and plausibly have indicated their preference for this or that General, or their approval or disapproval of a particular line of policy, and thus have become a cause of serious embarrassment to the Government. But the Commission steadily refrained from any such interference, and we shall look in vain, not only to its official acts, but to the most confidential reports of its Agents for any expression of unkind criticism, (except where the sanitary interests of the Army seemed to require it,) upon any act of the Government or its officers. Its Agents were strictly instructed to avoid all discussions of military or political questions in their intercourse with the officers of the Army, and they were forbidden by one of its rules from corresponding with newspapers. The great effort of the Commission at all times was to identify its work thoroughly with the success of the National cause in the widest sense. . . .

While the success of its methods had thus inspired the public with a confidence which grew as the war went on, the attitude of the Government towards it was not so satisfactory. . . . Deriving . . . its existence and all its power from the special appointment of the Government, and working wholly in aid of its service, it was natural to expect at all times from its officers, support, encouragement, and sympathy. As has been fully shown in the narrative of its work, military officers of high rank who had had the best opportunities of observing its practical usefulness never withheld that support and sympathy. It is a noteworthy fact that every General in command of an Army during the war, has placed on record an expression of his appreciation of the value of the Commission's services to his troops, while very many of them actively aided and encouraged its operations by all the means at their disposal. While such were its relations with those with whom its Agents were brought into daily contact, and whose natural prejudices against any extra governmental interference in the Army had been overcome by the evidence of its value, it must be confessed that there was a want of cordial cooperation with its plans on the part of those in the higher regions of official authority, which was on every account much to be regretted. The attitude of the War Department especially, towards it was never that of open hostility, but rather of neglect and indifference. It was never regarded by that Department as it should have been, as one of the great glories of the war, and as the most .comprehensive and successful method of mitigating its horrors known in history. While the evidence abounded in the reports of its own officers of the vast improvement which had been made in the condition of the troops through its instrumentality direct and indirect, no word of official approval of a work which was exciting the wonder, admiration, and gratitude of all humane and intelligent observers at home and abroad, was ever vouchsafed by the Government whose Agent it was. Although this want of appreciation of their labors existed in the quarter where they had the right to look most confidently for aid and encouragement, the members of the Commission were not disheartened. Carefully abstaining from asking favors at Headquarters, it was found that practically their work suffered little, so long as it enjoyed, as it did during the whole war, the confidence of the commanding Generals, and the cooperation of the various staff departments of the Army.

It would be very unprofitable to discuss all the causes which might be assigned for this want of cordiality towards the Commission on the part of the Government, and particularly of the War Department. One thing is certain, that during its whole existence no complaint was ever made to that Department, that the Commission had exceeded its authority, or neglected its duties. When it is remembered how intimate and delicate its relations with the Army officials were, how large, at all times, was its corps of Agents, and how embarrassing and difficult their position must often have been, this fact in itself is no small evidence of the wisdom of its policy, and the character of those employed to give it a practical shape. The simple, natural, explanation of the difficulty lies far deeper, however, than any mere suspicion that the Commission was not doing its duty, or even than that personal antipathy which was said to have existed between certain high officials of the Government, and its own, and which has sometimes been assigned as its chief cause. The truth is, the continued existence of the Sanitary Commission was a standing criticism upon certain of the methods employed by the Government, and a protest against the insufficiency of others. This was the great grievance. . . .

There can be as little doubt that any credit due the country for an improved care of its soldiers should be ascribed to the irresistible force of popular organizations outside of the Government agencies. If we examine the facts, nothing can be clearer than that the great reforms in the Medical service of the Army, the value of which can only be measured by the wants of suffering men in future wars, would never have originated in official quarters. If there had been no enlightened public opinion in regard to the real wants of the sick and wounded, and no Sanitary Commission to direct it aright, we should probably never have heard of the re-organization of the Medical Department, of improved Hospital buildings and administration, of a system of thorough inspection, of humane methods of transporting the suffering, or of the numerous other methods of mitigating the horrors of war, of which we have set the example in history.

Source: Stillé, Charles J. *History of the United States Sanitary Commission: Being the General Report of Its Work during the War of the Rebellion.* New York: Hurd and Houghton, 1868, pp. 110, 111–13, 114–15, 116–19, 120–26, 507–13.

DOCUMENT
3.3

An Assassination Attempt Renews Allopath-Homeopath Hostilities

"It Would Have Been More 'Professional' to Let the Secretary and His Son Die"

1865

On April 14, 1865, President Abraham Lincoln was shot by John Wilkes Booth in Washington, D.C. That same night, another fanatical Confederate sympathizer named Lewis Paine (also known as Lewis Powell) tried to kill Secretary of State William Seward, who was convalescing from a carriage accident in his Washington home. Seward and one of his sons suffered severe injuries from the attack, but Paine's assassination attempt failed. After Paine fled the scene (he was eventually captured and executed), several doctors arrived at Seward's home and worked together to care for the secretary of state and other victims. One of the physicians was Tullio Verdi, a homeopathic practitioner who was Seward's personal doctor. Another was Army surgeon general Joseph K. Barnes.

A few days later, Verdi distributed a letter meant to convey his appreciation for the professionalism and skills of Barnes and the other allopathic regular doctors who had assisted him on that tragic night in American history. He expressed particular gratitude about their willingness to set aside allopathic-homeopathic differences and work together. "I must say to their honor, that their energies were united with mine only to save and relieve the victims, and not one descended to that petty professional pique or ill-conceived pride of many practitioners in reference to associating with a medical gentleman of a different school of therapeutics. . . . We met on the same field, inspired by the same ambition to work together for the same end."[1]

Ironically, Verdi's note triggered an uproar among practitioners of conventional medicine, some of whom were scandalized that Barnes had evidently worked side by side with a homeopath. A number of allopathic doctors even broached the subject of censuring Barnes for this transgression, including members of the Ohio chapter of the American Medical Association. As seen in the following excerpt from an account of their June 21, 1865, meeting, a censuring resolution was tabled only after the physicians decided that Verdi was an unreliable witness.

The entire episode was treated with incredulity by homeopathic practitioners, especially after Barnes, sensing political danger, firmly denied the "allegations."

The second document featured here is an excerpt from a publication of the Homeopathic Medical Society of the State of New York that ridicules the "bigotry" of the regulars.

EXCERPT FROM MINUTES OF JUNE 21, 1865, MEETING OF THE MEDICAL SOCIETY OF THE STATE OF OHIO

. . . A resolution was offered by Dr. MUSSEY, censuring Surgeon-General BARNES, U. S. A., for consulting with VERDI, the homœopathist, in the treatment of Secretary SEWARD.

Dr. M. indulged in some remarks by no means complimentary to the Chief of the Medical Bureau of the army. He regarded the publication of VERDI, and his testimony in court, as conclusive evidence of the Surgeon-General's guilt.

The resolution was favored by several members, who thought if the Surgeon-General was innocent of the charge, he would not have suffered the published statement of VERDI, to be circulated throughout the land without a public contradiction.

The resolution was opposed by Surgeon McDERMOTT, who hoped the Society would have too much self respect to entertain so grave a charge against a distinguished member of the profession, when that charge had no foundation except the testimony of a homœopathist. For himself he would not harbor a suspicion against the humblest member of the profession on such testimony.

He thought the gentleman who offered the resolution ought to be censured for treating the statement of a homoeopathist with so much consideration. VERDI was a traitor to the profession—a quack. And therefore unworthy of credence in any issue between himself and Surgeon-General BARNES. Dr. McD. did not believe that the Surgeon-General had ever consulted with a homœopathist. And he had good reason to believe that VERDI was not known to him, much less participated with him in the treatment of Mr. SEWARD.

The resolution of censure was laid on the table. Subsequently a motion was carried instructing the President of the Society to appoint a committee to address a respectful inquiry to the Surgeon-General, in order to get the facts in the case.

INTOLERANCE OF THE ALLOPATHIC SCHOOL—AMERICAN MEDICAL ASSOCIATION.

"Our readers will remember that at the time of the attempt to assassinate Mr. Seward, he was suffering from injuries received from being thrown from his carriage. His medical attendant was Dr. T. S. Verdi, a homoeopathic physician, under whose care his recovery was progressing rapidly; and who, when the excitement at Washington was great and when every item was read with eagerness, wrote an account of his patient's illness, which was read before several homoeopathic societies and published in some of our Journals. In this account Dr. Barnes, the Surgeon-General, was mentioned as one of those called in consultation, probably on account of his position. Hence the following telegram to the associated press of New York, published in the daily papers of June 28th:

Vindication of the United States Surgeon-General.—Boston, Tuesday, June 27. "At the late session of the American Medical Association, it was charged that Surgeon-General Barnes had been guilty of unprofessional conduct, by consulting with an irregular practitioner in the case of the Sewards. It is officially announced by D. R. H. Stover, of this city, one of the Secretaries of the Association, that the charge was dismissed in consequence of

its emphatic and unequivocal denial by Dr. Barnes. The publication of this fact is important, as it had been omitted in the newspaper reports."

The following is from the New York Evening Post June 28th, 1865:

Medical Bigotry.—"At the late session of the American Medical Association at Boston, it was charged that Dr. Barnes, Surgeon-General of the United States army, had been
guilty of unprofessional conduct, by consulting with an 'irregular' practitioner while in
attendance upon Secretary Seward and his son. The allegation was promptly denied, but
as the reporters present omitted to make a note of denial, it has been considered necessary
to telegraph it to the newspapers.

"We infer from the language of the denial that, in the opinion of the Association, it
would have been more 'professional' to let the Secretary and his son die from want of
proper surgical advice than for Dr. Barnes to give his skill to a patient at whose bedside
he would have to meet a practitioner, no matter how skillful, who did not happen to be
'regular.' Similar bigotry has been displayed all through this war. A persistent effort was
made in a majority of the loyal States to exclude homoeopathic physicians and eclectics,
without regard to merit and scholarship, from the service. Occasionally a Governor was
found, like Morton, of Indiana, who would not permit this middle age intolerance to
control his surgical appointments.

"The people happily have outgrown this infantile condition, and will not suffer a
few men to prescribe what shall be considered 'regular' in medicine, or orthodox in religion. The despatch to which we have alluded might have answered for an encyclical letter
a century or two ago, but will hardly receive much respect at this period of the world's
civilization."

Source: Kynett, Harold Havelott, et al., eds. "Correspondence: Domestic: Medical Society of the State of
Ohio." *Medical and Surgical Reporter* 13. 1865, pp. 29–30. Homeopathic Medical Society of the State of
New York. *Transactions* 3. 1865, pp. 383–85.

NOTE

1. Quoted in Homeopathic Medical Society of the State of New York, *Transactions* 3 (1865): 383–385.

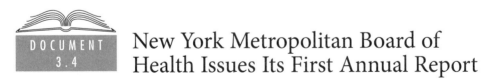

DOCUMENT
3.4

New York Metropolitan Board of Health Issues Its First Annual Report

"The Sanitary Inspectors . . . Have Doubtless Saved Many Lives"

1867

*After the Civil War came to a close in 1865, leaders of the U.S. Sanitary Commission
sought to extend the sanitary and public hygiene regulations they had instituted in the
U.S. Army to America's great population centers. One commission veteran was Stephen
Smith, who also served as the editor of the* New York Journal of Medicine. *Building
on the work of earlier urban sanitary reformers such as John Griscom and Lemuel
Shattuck, Smith led fellow reformers in a full-scale public relations blitz designed to*

convince state legislators of the need for sweeping new public health measures in New York City. The crowning piece of this effort was an April 1865 survey of health and sanitary conditions in the city that, in the words of historian Gert H. Brieger, "aroused indignation and wonderment" and "had emotional appeal beyond its intellectual content."[1]

In 1866 lawmakers passed the New York Metropolitan Health Act of 1866, formally known as "An Act to create a metropolitan sanitary district and board of health therein for the preservation of life and health, and to prevent the spread of disease." The municipal health department that was established in New York City as a result of this legislation constituted a major breakthrough in U.S. public health. Armed with genuine authority to build up and enforce meaningful public health regulations, the New York Metropolitan Board of Health became a model for other cities across the country.

The following excerpt from the board's first annual report provides an overview of the factors that led to the department's creation, as well as a proud account of its performance during its earliest months of existence, when a cholera outbreak threatened the city.

To The Governor Of The State Of New York:

The Board of Health of the Metropolitan Sanitary District of the State of New York, composed of the counties of New York, Kings, Westchester, and Richmond, and of the towns of Newtown, Flushing, and Jamaica, in the county of Queens, in accordance with the 19th section of chapter 74 of the Laws of 1866, respectfully transmits its Annual Report for the year 1866. This is its first report, and includes a general review of its proceedings from March 5th, 1866, the day of its organization, to the 1st of November, a period of nearly eight months.

Sanitary science has attracted considerable attention during the past eighty years, but it is only recently that an earnest interest in the subject has been manifested. This is a remarkable fact, considering the antiquity of the Mosaic Code, the greatest collection of health laws ever published, and the numerous examples of sanitary intelligence furnished by ancient Greece, Rome and Carthage. . . .

Greece and Rome built aqueducts, gymnasia, baths and sewers—some of which still remain—and enacted laws relating to food, which were calculated to produce a hardy race of soldiers.

The world fell back into barbarism, and all sanitary measures were neglected. The plague prevailed annually in Europe, and, as is supposed, carried off fully one-third of the inhabitants.

The great fire of London, in the year 1665, followed the great plague. "It destroyed thirteen thousand houses and eighty churches, in four hundred streets. After this the city was rebuilt, with more roomy houses and broader streets, and the plague never returned again. The imperfect drainage still exposed the city to fevers and dysenteries, and from the former cause alone the annual mortality was between one and two thousand." The great fire was an impressive lesson as to the value of sanitary measures, and London, by gradual improvements, has become one of the largest and healthiest of cities, and has reduced its mortality from one in twenty to one in forty-five of its inhabitants. . . .

Everything conspires to make hygienic measures the great question of the age; enlightened self-interest, the good of mankind, economic considerations, public and private, the wealth and power of the state, and religious obligations unite to urge this knowledge and observance upon every member of the community. In order to succeed, we need the co-operation of the majority of the citizens, and then we can compel ignorance and selfishness to cease their opposition. It is not the day to despair, for the future is full of promise.

Sanitary Condition of the Metropolitan District.

It would naturally be supposed that New York, situated upon a narrow island surrounded by rivers, supplied with pure air from the ocean or from the highlands of the Hudson, with its broad streets and avenues, its liberal supply of pure drinking water and its facilities for drainage, would be one of the healthiest cities in the world. The city of Brooklyn is also admirably situated, is well supplied with pure air and water, and covers more ground than New York in proportion to its population. The peculiar sanitary advantages of the two cities, have, probably, saved them from numerous destructive epidemics; but a reliance upon these advantages has produced an indifference to the growth of the destructive nuisances which now cause so fearful a mortality in their filthy and crowded districts. New York is the great commercial city of the country and the entrepôt of three hundred thousand immigrants yearly. Many arrive with broken constitutions, and soon sicken or die; many, especially of the Irish and Germans, become permanent residents in the city and vicinity. An entire change takes place in their habits, their previous lives having been spent in agricultural pursuits and in the open air. They crowd the filthy and ill-ventilated tenements, which are rendered pestilential by a hot sun in summer, or by artificial heat in winter. Meats and spirituous liquors abound to which they have not been accustomed, and they use them to excess. Sunstroke, which is rare among the native population, is common among immigrants, and a certain amount of acclimation seems necessary to secure their safety. These causes considerably increase the death-rate in New York and Brooklyn, while the smaller towns of the district, being less densely crowded, suffer only occasionally and in a more limited degree.

When the Metropolitan Board of Health commenced its labors, the cities of New York and Brooklyn were filled with nuisances, many of them of years' duration. The streets were uncleaned; manure heaps, containing thousands of tons, occupied piers and vacant lots; sewers were obstructed; houses were crowded, and badly ventilated, and lighted; privies were unconnected with the sewers, and overflowing; stables and yards were filled with stagnant water, and many dark and damp cellars were inhabited. The streets were obstructed, and the wharves and piers were filthy and dangerous from dilapidation; cattle were driven through the streets at all hours of the day in large numbers, and endangered the lives of the people; slaughter-houses were open to the streets, and were offensive from accumulated offal and blood, or filled the sewers with decomposing animal substances. Gas companies, shellburners, and fat-boilers, pursued their occupations without regard to the public health or comfort, and filled the air with disgusting odors. When complained of, they asserted that their private rights were invaded, and that their pursuits were not prejudicial to the public health. They virtually claimed that the fumes of sulphuretted hydrogen, carbonic acid or carbonic oxide did not vitiate the pure atmosphere, which had been made with its exact proportions of oxygen and nitrogen, for the purpose of securing physical and mental vigor.

The Health Laws of New York.

Immediately preceding and following the year 1800, most of the Health Laws were properly Quarantine Laws, and were intended rather to shut out disease from New York than to prevent its originating within the city limits. Most of the Health Laws passed since that period were valuable in many respects, but were not sufficiently comprehensive in their character, or properly enforced. For several years, the physicians of New York have endeavored to obtain the necessary legislative enactments and the establishment of a Board of Health, with full power to correct the many existing abuses and to prevent the great mortality that prevailed, but they were uniformly unsuccessful in their efforts.

Two years ago, the Citizens' Association, in connection with several eminent physicians, commenced a sanitary inspection of the city. Medical men were appointed as Inspectors to ascertain the nature of the soil and the character of the drainage, to survey and describe the crowded tenementhouses, to locate upon maps the places where fevers and diarrhœa abounded, and to examine, as far as possible, into all the causes which affected the public health. The result of their labors was published, and is a work of great value, not only to the present generation, but as a book of reference by which to judge of the future sanitary progress and condition of New York. The enterprise and energy of these gentlemen are worthy of all honor, and their influence and efforts were largely instrumental in securing the passage, on the 26th of February, 1866, of the Act "to create a Metropolitan Sanitary District, and Board of Health therein, for the preservation of life and health, and to prevent the spread of disease."

ORGANIZATION OF THE METROPOLITAN BOARD OF HEALTH.

The Sanitary Commissioners, appointed by the Governor, by and with the consent of the Senate, under the act above referred to, met at the office of the Secretary of State at Albany, on the first day of March, and proceeded, under his direction, to determine, by lot, which of them should hold for the respective terms of one, two, three, and four years, the said office of Sanitary Commissioner. . . .

The Board of Metropolitan Police was requested to execute and enforce the orders of the Metropolitan Board of Health, relating to cleanliness and the preservation of life and health; also, to ascertain and report to the Metropolitan Board of Health, once in each week, the streets and parts of streets, wharves, bulkheads, and piers, not cleaned in the cities of New York and Brooklyn, in pursuance of contracts for street cleaning in the respective cities. The Board of Metropolitan Police having tendered the use of that part of its large and commodious building fronting on Mott street, the office of the Metropolitan Board of Health was established at No. 301 Mott street. Dr. Edward B. Dalton was elected Sanitary Superintendent, and D. B. Eaton was elected Counsel, and George Bliss, Jr., Attorney to the Board. . . .

Eight Sanitary Inspectors were appointed for the city of New York, and six for the city of Brooklyn, and were subsequently assigned by the Sanitary Superintendent to the several districts into which the cities had been divided. . . . The Board of Metropolitan Police was directed to enforce all laws and ordinances of the cities of New York and Brooklyn relating to the preservation of life and health and the prevention of disease, and to serve all notices and execute all orders issued by this Board. "Complaint books" were ordered to be placed in the station-houses of all the Police Precincts, and citizens were publicly invited to enter therein their complaints against existing nuisances.

At a meeting held on the 30th of March, the Sanitary Committee recommended that, on account of the condition of the city and the impending danger from cholera, thirty clerks, to act as Assistant Inspectors, should be appointed for a period of two months, and be detailed for duty in various parts of the District. At the same meeting, clerks or Assistant Inspectors were appointed for Yonkers and Morrisania, and subsequently, upon application of the local authorities, clerks or Assistant Inspectors were appointed for nearly all the rural towns in the Metropolitan Sanitary District. These clerks or Assistant Inspectors continued in the service of the Board until the disappearance of the cholera from the District, when they were honorably discharged, with the thanks of the Board for their promptness and fidelity. . . .

The following report of the Sanitary Committee, upon the duties of Sanitary Inspectors, was approved by the Board, and the Sanitary Superintendent was directed to furnish each Inspector with a copy:

"1. The Inspectors will keep constantly in mind the great good to society and the scientific value of the knowledge expected to be gained by the present system of Health Police. It is desirable that they should take especial interest in all sanitary questions, and keep themselves informed of what is being done at home and abroad relative to the causes which affect health or disease. Thus they will contribute their full share to the accumulation of knowledge which is destined to prolong human life, and establish the science of medicine on the most permanent of foundations.

"2. So much depends upon the conscientiousness, intelligence and industry of the Inspectors, that they will be held to a strict accountability. They will be subject to the immediate control of the Superintendent, or his Deputy, and obey orders with promptness, and relinquish the demands of private business, in order the better to observe the obligations imposed upon them by their office.

"3. They shall present themselves at the office of the Superintendent, or his Deputy in Brooklyn, as often as is required by them, to receive orders and to make reports. . . . They are to watch over all cases of fever or small-pox, and if the patients are removed, to follow them with their supervision.

"4. Any perversion of the truth, from fear or interest, or any disrespect to the Board or its officers, on the part of the Inspectors, will justify the Superintendent or his Deputy in suspending them from office, without pay, until action is taken by the Board, when the delinquents shall be censured or dismissed.

"5. All the forms for making reports must be filled up legibly and minutely, and any information added that will throw light on the subject under investigation,

"6. They shall wear their badges prominently displayed when engaged in their official duties. On entering any house or premises, they must announce their authority and the object of their visit, and while endeavoring to avoid giving offence, must make their investigations minutely.

"7. If resistance is offered to the performance of their duties, they are to report the fact to the nearest Police Station. They will likewise report all who violate the Health Laws, in order that offenders may be summarily dealt with.

"8. All questions of doubtful authority must be referred to the Superintendent or his Deputy for decision."

The Sanitary Inspectors.

Although the law does not require that all the Sanitary Inspectors shall be physicians, the Board has appointed none but thoroughly educated medical men to these responsible positions. Their peculiar duties require intelligence, a knowledge of chemistry, physiology, and hygienic laws, and a familiarity with the causes of preventable disease, and with the symptoms and treatment of typhoid fever, small-pox, and cholera. They were selected chiefly from among the active young men who had graduated at the medical schools and hospitals of the city. It was originally intended by the Board that the Inspectors and their Assistants should make a complete and thorough sanitary survey of the built-up portions of the District, in order to discover the existence of any nuisances detrimental to the public health, and maps were to be made which should show each building, the purpose for which it was occupied, the number of tenants, and its sanitary condition in detail. The advent of cholera, and the consequent necessity of immediate attention to the particular districts in which it appeared, and to the parties attacked by the disease, interfered, to some extent, with the plans of the Board; but nearly every house in the District, especially in the filthy and crowded portions of it, has been visited by the Inspectors during the season, and the immense amount of valuable labor which has been performed by these officers can hardly be estimated. All complaints by citizens have been referred to them for examination and report, and when such complaints were well founded the nuisances have been promptly abated.

When the cholera appeared, the Inspectors, in addition to their other duties, were required to investigate every case reported to the Sanitary Superintendent in New York, or the Assistant Sanitary Superintendent in Brooklyn. Physicians and all others being compelled by law to report all cases to this Board, and the police telegraph being freely used for that purpose, the Inspectors were enabled to visit promptly the sick, and use the proper remedial measures. If the patient was already under medical treatment, the Inspector did not interfere, except to direct the use of such disinfectants as seemed necessary; but if the patient was destitute and uncared for, the Inspector caused his immediate removal to the hospital, and directed the disinfecting corps to cleanse or destroy the soiled bedding and clothing, and to disinfect the entire premises. As the cholera increased, additional Inspectors were detailed to the headquarters in New York and Brooklyn, and were on duty both night and day, to answer immediately all calls for their services. The cholera hospitals established by the Board were also under the immediate charge of the Inspectors and Assistant Inspectors. For more full details as to their services, you are respectfully referred to the report of the Sanitary Superintendent. The Sanitary Inspectors and their Assistants deserve the public gratitude. Always on duty, prompt to obey orders, exposed to many dangers, often acting both as nurses and physicians, they have doubtless saved many lives, and have been instrumental in preventing the spread of disease. It is a gratifying fact that, although some of them have been temporarily ill in consequence of their fatiguing and dangerous duties, none of their valuable lives have been lost from any cause during the epidemic. . . .

Source: *Annual Report of the Metropolitan Board of Health, 1866.* New York: C. S. Westcott, 1867, pp. 7–8, 12–18.

Note

1. Gert H. Brieger, "Sanitary Reform in New York City: Stephen Smith and the Passage of the Metropolitan Health Bill," *Bulletin of the History of Medicine,* no. 40 (1966): 407.

Marine Hospitals Services Act

"All Moneys . . . Are Hereby Appropriated for the . . . Marine Hospital Service"

1870

In 1870 the U.S. Congress passed the Marine Hospitals Services Act, which aimed to address several perennial shortcomings in the Marine Hospital Service (MHS), the forerunner to the U.S. Public Health Service. First, the law reorganized the MHS from a loosely affiliated collection of locally controlled hospitals to a centrally controlled network with dedicated administration, staff, and headquarters in Washington, D.C. Second, the law established a system of taxation on mariners' wages to provide for their health care needs in the event of sickness or disability. This tax provided a badly needed infusion of funding for the cash-starved service. Third, the law established the position of supervising surgeon of the MHS, which would evolve into the position of surgeon general. All of these elements gave the MHS a much-needed boost, and the agency grew quickly in size and influence over the last decades of the nineteenth century.

AN ACT TO REORGANIZE THE MARINE HOSPITAL SERVICE, AND TO PROVIDE FOR THE RELIEF OF SICK AND DISABLED SEAMEN.

Be it enacted, etc., That from and after the first day of August, eighteen hundred and seventy, there shall be assessed and collected by the collectors of customs at the ports of the United States, from the masters or owners of every vessel of the United States arriving from a foreign port, or of registered vessels employed in the coasting trade, the sum of forty cents per month for each and every seaman who shall have been employed on said vessel since she was last entered at any port of the United States, which sum said master or owner is hereby authorized to collect and retain from the wages of said employees.

Sec. 2. *And be it further enacted,* That from and after the first day of August no collector shall grant to any vessel whose enrollment or license for carrying on the coasting trade has expired a new enrollment or license, unless the master of such vessel shall have first rendered a true account to the collector of the number of seamen and the time they have been employed on such vessel during the continuance of the license which has so expired, and shall have paid to such collector forty cents per month for every such seaman who shall have been employed as aforesaid, which sum the said master is hereby authorized to retain out of the wages of such seaman; and if the master of any registered, enrolled, or licensed vessel of the United States shall render a false account of the number of seamen so employed, or of the length of time they have severally been employed, as is herein required, he shall forfeit and pay fifty dollars, which shall be applied to and shall make a part of, the general fund created by this act, and all needful regulations for the mode of collecting the sums hereinbefore mentioned shall be prepared under the direction of the Secretary of the Treasury, by such person as by him may be designated.

Sec. 3. *And be it further enacted,* That it shall be the duty of the several collectors to deposit the sums collected by them respectively under the provisions of this act, in the nearest United States depository, to the credit of "the fund for the relief of sick and disabled seamen"; making returns of the same with proper vouchers monthly, on forms to be furnished by the Secretary of the Treasury.

Sec. 4. *And be it further enacted,* That all moneys received or collected by virtue of this act shall be paid into the Treasury like other public moneys, without abatement or reduction; and all moneys so received are hereby appropriated for the expenses of the Marine Hospital Service, and shall be credited to the marine hospital fund, of which separate accounts shall be kept.

Sec. 5. *And be it further enacted,* That the fund thus obtained shall be employed, under the direction of the Secretary of the Treasury, for the care and relief of sick and disabled seamen employed in registered, enrolled, and licensed vessels of the United States.

Sec. 6. *And be it further enacted,* That the Secretary of the Treasury is hereby authorized to appoint a surgeon to act as supervising surgeon of Marine-Hospital Service, whose duty it shall be, under the direction of the Secretary, to supervise all matters connected with the Marine-Hospital Service and with the disbursement of the fund provided by this act, at a salary not exceeding the rate of two thousand dollars per annum and his necessary traveling expenses, who shall be required to make monthly reports to the Secretary of the Treasury.

Sec. 7. *And be it further enacted,* That, for the purposes of this act, the term "vessel" herein used shall be held to include every description of water craft, raft, vehicle, and contrivance used, or capable of being used, as a means or auxiliary of transportation on or by water. And all acts and parts of acts inconsistent or in conflict with the provisions of this act be, and the same are hereby, repealed.

Source: Marine Hospitals Services Act of 1870. Act of June 29, 1870. *United States Statutes at Large.* Vol. 16, pp. 169–70. Reprinted in *Regulations for the Government of the United States Public Health Service.* Washington, DC: Government Printing Office, 1913, pp. 143–44.

| DOCUMENT 3.6 | Reform Recommendations for Almshouses in Pennsylvania |

"These Wrongs Demand Prompt Redress"

1871

Health care reformers of the post–Civil War era took particular aim at almshouses, which had shouldered the burden of caring for sick and indigent members of the community since colonial times. Most almshouses of this era had become grim and squalid institutions that indiscriminately lumped diseased, homeless, orphaned, and insane individuals together under one roof. These conditions, created by a toxic combination of government neglect and public inattention, prompted some reformers to devote their time and energy to the nourishment of charity hospitals and other caregiving alternatives. Others, such as the

Pennsylvania health care reformers who prepared the report excerpted below, called for fundamental changes in the environments and treatments that almshouses offered and for much greater separation of almshouse populations by age and affliction.

COUNTY ALMSHOUSES.

The General Agent has visited almost all the almshouses in the State; and has, in many instances, been accompanied by one of the Commissioners. His report will give his impression of them individually; and will expose, to some extent, their deficiencies. He has reserved a more full and comprehensive exposition until all have been visited, for which the law allows two years.

The Board desire to call attention to some of their obvious defects; frequently involving not only deprivation of health and comfort, but contamination of the morals of the inmates.

1. *Ventilation.*—This "necessary thing" seems, with few exceptions, not to have been at all considered. Generally the buildings have not been constructed with any consciousness of its importance, and often where the appliances exist, they are not regarded. We have witnessed the propagation of disease to a large extent in consequence of defective ventilation.

2. *Nursing.*—The care of the sick and the insane is usually unsuitable and inadequate. It is mostly entrusted to paupers, whose dulled sensibilities, infirm principles and indolent disposition unfit them for any responsible or delicate service. There is no better economy in bad nursing than in bad medicines. Protracted sickness is the result in both cases, increasing the cost of cure and detaining from productive labor the enfeebled patient.

3. *Water-Closets.*—Neither these, nor close-stools in case of sickness, are common. The aged and infirm are obliged to seek conveniences out of doors, in the most inclement weather. Not unfrequently the sexes have them in common; and they are, in other respects, also, kept too much in community. It is an unquestionable fact that children are sometimes begotten and born in these places, and in one of them we saw an insane woman with her infant, whose paternity belonged in the institution.

4. *Employment.*—The picture of an almshouse scene is patent to every mind and every eye. Listless idleness seems fastened upon every living thing. Regular and continuous occupation should be furnished to every inmate, who is able-bodied; and all who are capable of earning their support should be required to do so. The helpless and decrepit should enjoy the consciousness of their exceptional immunity from labor, and the rest should not he further degraded by unremitted idleness.

5. *Instruction.*—The children who have their abode there should be instructed, and competent paid teachers should be employed for this purpose. Where this is the case, the whole bearing and demeanor of the children become changed; and they are better and happier. This is rarely attended to in almshouses. As a consequence, the young and mature mingle together to the injury of the former; the children are "in the way," and are often unjustly punished for their childish plays. We saw a boy of 7 years old, shrinking in the corner of the cell of an ill-visaged maniac, whose couch had been the floor of the madhouse, for the offence of romping with a playmate.

More especially do we wish to denounce the cruel wrongs which the insane suffer, who are inmates of almshouses. These institutions are generally wholly unsuitable for their care or even detention; or, if suitable, are presided over by persons who are entirely ignorant of the needs of this class of the sick and infirm, and whose administration is based upon the crudest ideas of mental disease: it is limited to the discovery of the most available methods of preventing them from harming anything or any person but themselves. We could instance the most glaring abuses; not, as we believe, intentionally inflicted, but the results of incapacity and ignorance. The time has gone by when a disturbed imagination or a disordered intellect should be held to have converted its human victim into a distempered brute; whose home should be akin to the sty or the stable; and whose lightest restraint should be perpetual incarceration within the limits of a cell. These wrongs demand prompt redress. No hospital for the insane should remain without the constant supervision of a medical superintendent. The stewards of almshouses are never selected from any consideration of the needs of the insane.

We would recommend that no recent case of insanity be received into an almshouse; that all curable cases be provided for in State hospitals for the insane, and that these institutions be adequately extended. With respect to the township poor, we need to make further investigation. We know that the system is not approved by many excellent men in the districts where it prevails; and we have observed instances of insufficient provision for this class. We do not doubt that their comfort, as a general rule, would be promoted by the adoption by these districts of the county poor house.

Source: *Annual Report of the Board of Commissioners of Public Charities of the State of Pennsylvania.* Transmitted to the legislature, March 1, 1871. Vol. 1. Harrisburg, PA: Singerley, 1871, pp. xlvi–xlviii.

DOCUMENT
3.7

National Quarantine Act

"To Prevent the Introduction of Contagious or Infectious Diseases"

1878

As the United States entered the last quarter of the nineteenth century, communicable disease remained one of its most implacable enemies. The scourges of cholera and yellow fever were particularly feared, and in the mid-1870s Surgeon General John Maynard Woodworth, who headed the Marine Hospital Service (MHS), carried out a sustained lobbying campaign to convince Congress to expand MHS powers to combat these threats. Woodworth was particularly vocal about the need to federalize ship quarantine practices, which had long operated under a patchwork of state regulations.

In early 1878, reports from the Caribbean about high incidences of yellow fever lent special urgency to Woodworth's crusade, and on April 26, 1878, President Rutherford B. Hayes signed the National Quarantine Act into law. Under this law, quarantine authority and functions were transferred from individual states to the federal Marine Hospital

Service. The transfer failed to head off the looming yellow fever epidemic. The dreaded disease claimed more than twenty thousand lives in the Mississippi Valley, including thousands of victims in both New Orleans, Louisiana, and Memphis, Tennessee. But the legislation, which is reprinted here, enabled Woodworth and the MHS to step squarely into the field of public health for the first time. This development in turn paved the way for the MHS's gradual metamorphosis into the U.S. Public Health Service.

AN ACT To prevent the introduction of contagious or infectious diseases into the United States.

Be it enacted by the Senate and House of Representatives of the United States of America in Congress assembled, That no vessel or vehicle coming from any foreign port or country where any contagious or infectious disease may exist, and no vessel or vehicle conveying any person or persons, merchandise or animals, affected with any infectious or contagious disease, shall enter any port of the United States or pass the boundary line between the United States and any foreign country, contrary to the quarantine laws of any one of said United States, into or through the jurisdiction of which said vessel or vehicle may pass, or to which it is destined, or except in the manner and subject to the regulations to be prescribed as hereinafter provided.

Sec. 2. That whenever any infectious or contagious disease shall appear in any foreign port or country, and whenever any vessel shall leave any infected foreign port, or, having on board goods or passengers coming from any place or district infected with cholera or yellow fever, shall leave any foreign port, bound for any port in the United States, the consular officer, or other representative of the United States at or nearest such foreign port shall immediately give information thereof to the Supervising Surgeon-General of the Marine Hospital Service, and shall report to him the name, the date of departure, and the port of destination of such vessel; and shall also make the same report to the health officer of the port of destination in the United States, and the consular officers of the United States shall make weekly reports to him of the sanitary condition of the ports at which they are respectively stationed; and the said Surgeon-General of the Marine-Hospital Service shall, under the direction of the Secretary of the Treasury, be charged with the execution of the provisions of this act, and shall frame all needful rules and regulations for that purpose, which rules and regulations, shall be subject to the approval of the President, but such rules and regulations shall not conflict with or impair any sanitary or quarantine laws or regulations of any State or municipal authorities now existing or which may hereafter be enacted.

Sec. 3. That it shall be the duty of the medical officers of the Marine-Hospital Service and of customs-officers to aid in the enforcement of the national quarantine rules and regulations established under the preceding section; but no additional compensation shall be allowed said officers by reason of such services as they may be required to perform under this act, except actual and necessary traveling expenses.

Sec. 4. That the Surgeon General of the Marine-Hospital Service shall, upon receipt of information of the departure of any vessel, goods, or passengers from infected places to any port in the United States, immediately notify the proper State or municipal and United States officer or officers at the threatened port of destination of the vessel, and shall prepare and transmit to the medical officers of the Marine Hospital Service, to collectors of customs, and to the State and municipal health authorities in the United States, weekly abstracts of the consular sanitary reports and other pertinent information received by him.

Sec. 5. That wherever, at any port of the United States, any State or municipal quarantine system may now, or may hereafter exist, the officers or agents of such system shall, upon the application of the respective State or municipal authorities, be authorized and empowered to act as officers or agents of the national quarantine system, and shall be clothed with all the powers of United States officers for quarantine purposes, but shall receive no pay or emoluments from the United States. At all other ports where, in the opinion of the Secretary of the Treasury, it shall be deemed necessary to establish quarantine, the medical officers or other agents of the Marine-Hospital Service shall perform such duties in the enforcement of the quarantine rules and regulations as may be assigned them by the Surgeon-General of that service under this act: *Provided,* That there shall be no interference in any manner with any quarantine laws or regulations as they now exist or may hereafter be adopted under State laws.

Sec. 6. That all acts or parts of acts inconsistent with this act be, and the same are hereby, repealed.

Source: National Quarantine Act of 1878. Act of April 29, 1878. *United States Statutes at Large.* Vol. 20, p. 37. Reprinted in *Regulations for the Government of the United States Public Health Service.* Washington, DC: Government Printing Office, 1913, pp. 144–46.

<table>
<tr><td>DOCUMENT
3.8</td></tr>
</table>

Congress Expands the Powers of the National Board of Health

"To Prevent the Introduction of Contagious or Infectious Diseases into the United States"

1879

One of the key milestones in the federalization of public health regulation in the United States took place on March 3, 1879, when Congress authorized the establishment of a National Board of Health within the Department of the Treasury. The powers and duties of this board were greatly expanded less than three months later with the passage of the supplementary "Act to Prevent the Introduction of Contagious and Infectious Diseases into the United States," which is reprinted here. This act, which became law on June 2, gave the National Board of Health explicit authority to impose and enforce federal rules and regulations for maritime quarantine. It also authorized the board to provide public health assistance to state and municipal boards of health.

ACT TO PREVENT THE INTRODUCTION OF CONTAGIOUS AND INFECTIOUS DISEASES INTO THE UNITED STATES.

Be it enacted by the Senate and House of Representatives of the United States of America in Congress assembled, That it shall be unlawful for any merchant ship or vessel from any foreign port where any contagious or infectious disease exists to enter any port of the United States except in accordance with the provisions of this act, and all rules and regulations of State Boards of Health, and all rules and regulations made in pursuance of this act; and any such vessel which shall enter, or attempt to enter, a port of the United States in violation thereof shall forfeit to the United States a sum, to be awarded in the discretion of the court, not exceeding $1,000, which shall be a lien upon said vessel, to be recovered by proceedings in the proper District Court of the United States. And in all such proceedings the United States District Attorney for such district shall appear on behalf of the United States, and all such proceedings shall be conducted in accordance with the rules and laws governing cases of seizure of vessels for violation of the revenue laws of the United States.

Sec. 2. All such vessels shall be required to obtain from the consul, vice-consul, or other consular officer of the United States at the port of departure, or from the medical officer, where such officer has been detailed by the President for that purpose, a certificate in duplicate setting forth the sanitary history of said vessel, and that it has in all respects complied with the rules and regulations in such cases prescribed for securing the best sanitary condition of the said vessel, its cargo, passengers, and crew; and said consular or medical officer is required, before granting such certificate, to be satisfied the matters and things therein stated are true; and for his services in that behalf he shall be entitled to demand and receive such fees as shall by lawful regulation be allowed, to be accounted for as is required in other cases.

That upon the request of the National Board of Health the President is authorized to detail a medical officer to serve in the office of the Consul at any foreign port for the purpose of making the inspection and giving the certificates hereinbefore mentioned: *Provided,* That the number of officers so detailed shall not exceed at any one time six: *Provided further,* That any vessel sailing from any such port without such certificate of said medical officer, entering any port of the United States, shall forfeit to the United States the sum of $500, which shall be a lien on the same, to be recovered by proceedings in the proper District Court of the United States. And in all such proceedings the United States District Attorney for such district shall appear on behalf of the United States, and all such proceedings shall be conducted in accordance with the rules and laws governing cases of seizure of vessels for violation of the revenue laws of the United States.

Sec. 3. That the National Board of Health shall cooperate with and, so far as it lawfully may, aid State and Municipal Boards of Health in the execution and enforcement of the rules and regulations of such Boards to prevent the introduction of contagious or infectious diseases into the United States from foreign countries, and into one State from another; and at such ports and places within the United States as have no quarantine regulations under State authority where such regulations are, in the opinion of the National Board of Health, necessary to prevent the introduction of contagious or infectious diseases into the United States from foreign countries, or into one State from another; and at such ports and places within the United States where quarantine regulations exist under the authority of the State, which, in the opinion of the National Board of Health, are not sufficient to prevent the introduction of such diseases into the United States, or into one State from another, the National Board of Health shall report the facts to the President of the United States, who shall, if, in his judgment, it is necessary and proper, order said Board of Health to make such additional rules and regulations as are necessary to prevent the introduction of such diseases into the United States from foreign countries, or into one State from another, which, when so made and approved by the President, shall be promulgated by the National Board of Health and enforced by the sanitary authorities of the States, where the State authorities will undertake to execute and enforce them; but if the State authorities shall fail or refuse to enforce said rules and regulations, the President may detail an officer or appoint a proper person for that purpose.

The Boards of Health shall make such rules and regulations as are authorized by the laws of the United States and necessary to be observed by vessels at the port of departure, and on the voyage where such vessels sail from any foreign port or place at which contagious or infectious disease exists to any port or place in the United States, to secure the best sanitary condition of such vessel, her cargo, passengers, and crew; and when said rules and regulations have been approved by the President, they shall be published and communicated to, and enforced by, the consular officers of the United States: *Provided,* That none of the penalties herein imposed shall attach to any vessel, or any owner or officer thereof, till the act and the rules and regulations made in pursuance thereof shall have been officially promulgated for at least ten days in the port from which said vessel sailed.

Sec. 4. It shall be the duty of the National Board of Health to obtain information of the sanitary condition of foreign ports and places from which contagious or infectious diseases are, or may be, imported into the United States; and to this end the consular officers of the United States, at such ports and places as shall be designated by the National Board of Health, shall make to said Board of Health weekly reports of the sanitary condition of the ports and places at which they are respectively stationed, according to such forms as said Board of Health may prescribe; and the Board of Health shall also obtain, through all sources accessible, including State and municipal sanitary authorities throughout the United States, weekly reports of the sanitary condition of ports and places within the United States; and shall prepare, publish, and transmit to the medical officers of the Marine Hospital Service, to collectors of customs, and to State and municipal health officers and authorities, weekly abstracts of the consular sanitary reports and other pertinent information received by said Board; and shall also, as far as it may be able, by means of the voluntary co-operation of State and municipal authorities, of public associations, and private persons, procure information relating to the climatic and other conditions affecting the public health; and shall make to the Secretary of the Treasury an annual report of its operations, for transmission to Congress, with such recommendations as it may deem important to the public interests; and said report, if ordered to be printed by Congress, shall be done under the direction of the Board.

Sec. 5. That the National Board of Health shall from time to time issue to the consular officers of the United States, and to the medical officers serving at any foreign port, and otherwise make publicly known, the rules and regulations made by it, and approved by the President, to be used and complied with by vessels in foreign ports for securing the best sanitary condition of such vessels, their cargoes, passengers, and crews, before their departure for any port in the United States, and in the course of the voyage; and all such other rules and regulations as shall be observed in the inspection of the same on the arrival thereof at any quarantine station at the port of destination, and for the disinfection and isolation of the same, and the treatment of cargo and persons on board, so as to prevent the introduction of cholera, yellow-fever, or other contagious or infectious diseases; and it shall not be lawful for any vessel to enter said port to discharge its cargo or land its passengers, except upon a certificate of the health officer at such quarantine station certifying that said rules and regulations have in all respects been observed and complied with, as well on his part as on the part of the said vessel and its master, in respect to the same and to its cargo, passengers, and crew; and the master of every such vessel shall produce and deliver to the collector of customs at said port of entry, together with the other papers of the vessel, the said certificates required to be obtained at the port of departure, and the certificate herein required to be obtained from the health officer at the port of entry.

Sec. 6. That to pay the necessary expenses of placing vessels in proper sanitary condition, to be incurred under the provisions of this act, the Secretary of the Treasury be, and he hereby is, authorized and required to make the necessary rules and regulations fixing the amount of fees to be paid by vessels for such service, and the manner of collecting the same.

Sec. 7. That the President is authorized, when requested by the National Board of Health, and when the same can be done without prejudice to the public service, to detail officers from the several departments of the Government, for temporary duty, to act under the direction of said Board, to carry out the provisions of this act; and such officers shall receive no additional compensation except for actual and necessary expenses incurred in the performance of such duties.

Sec. 8. That to meet the expenses to be incurred in carrying out the provisions of this act, the sum of $500,000, or so much thereof as may be necessary, is hereby appropriated, to be disbursed under the direction of the Secretary of the Treasury on estimates to be made by the National Board of Health, and to be approved by him. Said National Board of Health shall, as often as quarterly, make a full statement of its operations and expenditures under this act to the Secretary of the Treasury, who shall report the same to Congress.

Sec. 9. That so much of the act entitled "An act to prevent the introduction of contagious or infectious diseases into the United States," approved April 29th, 1878, as requires consular officers or other representatives of the United States at foreign ports to report the sanitary condition of and the departure of vessels from such ports to the Supervising Surgeon-General of the Marine Hospital Service; and so much of said act as requires the Surgeon-General of the Marine Hospital Service to frame rules and regulations, and to execute said act, and to give notice to Federal and State officers of the approach of infected vessels, and furnish said officers with weekly abstracts of consular sanitary reports, and all other acts and parts of acts inconsistent with the provisions of this act, be, and the same are hereby, repealed.

Sec. 10. This act shall not continue in force for a longer period than four years from the date of its approval.

Source: Medico-Legal Society. *The Sanitarian: A Monthly Magazine.* Vol. 7. Edited by Agrippa Nelson Bell. New York: Bell, 1879, pp. 357–60.

DOCUMENT
3.9

A Boston Medical Journal Mourns the Gains of Women Physicians

"To Descend from That High Pedestal upon Which We Men Have Always Placed Her"

1879

Women made inroads into the profession ranks of medicine throughout the second half of the nineteenth century. Although their emergence from the traditional confines of midwifery and into the full array of medical offices seems almost inevitable in retrospect, it was by no means certain. The ranks of regular physicians were divided on the issue (practitioners of alternative medicine were much more open to the idea of female doctors and surgeons), with some opponents assailing coeducational medical instruction and other indicators of female advancement in the medical profession as virtual signs of the apocalypse. "If I were to plan with malicious hate the greatest curse I could conceive for women," fumed one 1869 editorial in the Buffalo Medical Journal, "if I would estrange them from the protection of women, and make them as far as possible loathsome and disgusting to man, I would favor the so-called reform which proposed to make doctors of them."[1]

Similar sentiments were expressed in the wake of a decision by the Massachusetts Medical Society to admit women physicians to its august ranks in 1879. The society's decision stemmed in part from pressure from state authorities who had begun bestowing medical diplomas and licenses on women doctors, but it also reflected shifting sentiments within the professional ranks. When the 1,343 male members of the society were polled on the advisability of admitting qualified women to the organization in 1875, more than 700 responded favorably. These poll results made it much easier for proponents of female membership to make their case. The first woman to be accepted into the Massachusetts Medical Society was Dr. Emma Call, a graduate of the University of Michigan, and by 1889 eleven women physicians had became members in good standing.[2]

Still, the opening of the gates of the society to women was greeted with dismay by many men in the medical profession. A common lament of these critics was that the mere idea of a female physician constituted an affront to Victorian ideals of morality and decorum. These complaints sit front and center in the following document, an editorial that was published in the Boston Medical and Surgical Journal a week after the society voted to admit women.

THE ADMISSION OF WOMEN TO THE STATE SOCIETY.

We regret to be obliged to announce that at a meeting of the councilors held on October 1st, it was voted to admit women to the Massachusetts Medical Society. The report of the committee to whom was intrusted the investigation of this question was unfavorable to their admission as members, but a minority report was offered and substituted for it. The final vote was passed by a small majority, a large number voting in the affirmative, not because they believed in the desirability of female practitioners, but rather from a disinclination to oppose the movement. The arguments in favor of it seem to have been based upon a misconception of the nature of the objections influencing the minds of the opposition. Some of the speakers were at great pains to point out that the number of women who are now in active practice is so great, and their standing in the profession such, that we are no longer justified in withholding from them the advantages of membership. These arguments are freely used as convincing proof that a change is desirable, and all opposition is stigmatized as based upon narrow-mindedness and jealousy.

The real point at issue is systematically ignored. In this progressive age *we* are expected to overlook any little scruples of decency or morality which the etiquette of a by-gone time has thought necessary as a restraint to the sexes in their social intercourse. Enshrouded in her mantle of science, woman is supposed to be endowed with power to descend from that high pedestal upon which *we* men have always placed her, and to mingle with us unscathed in scenes from which her own modesty and the esteem of the other sex has hitherto protected her. *We* do not believe it possible that she can frequent our public meetings or lecture rooms when certain topics are discussed without breaking through barriers which decency has built up, and which it is for the interest of every lady and gentleman to preserve.

The action of the councilors will doubtless exert but little influence on the present condition of the body which they represent, but unless this whole movement die out, and the action prove virtually *nil,* the society will have taken a long step downward from the dignified attitude which it has hitherto assumed as a scientific body, and its moral tone will have been perceptibly lowered. It will gain temporary applause, but the reaction will be a loss of influence among a certain portion of the profession whose support it cannot afford to do without.

Source: "The Admission of Women to the State Society." Editorial. *Boston Medical and Surgical Journal,* October 9, 1879. Volume CI, July–December 1879. Boston: Houghton, Osgood and Company, 1879, pp. 527–28.

NOTES

1. Quoted in Mary Putnam Jacobi, *Woman's Work in America* (New York: Holt, 1891), 191, http://asp6new.alexanderstreet.com/wasm/wasmrestricted/doctext/S10010028-D0008.htm.

2. Helen Campbell, *Prisoners of Poverty: Women Wage-Workers, Their Trades, and Their Lives* (Boston: Little, Brown, 1900), 187–88.

DOCUMENT
3.10

Louisiana Politics Bedevil Federal Health Inspectors

"This Proposition is a Cause of Surprise and Regret to Us"

1881

After Congress created the National Board of Health in 1879, board administrators moved quickly to shore up quarantine measures across the country. Many state and port city officials cooperated with these efforts, but some took issue with the heightened federal involvement in their internal affairs. Hostility to the National Board of Health was particularly strong in the Deep South, where memories of Civil War defeat at the hands of federal troops still burned in the hearts of many whites. The most notorious resisters to quarantine policies and directives of the National Board of Health were found in the state of Louisiana. Health officials in Louisiana couched their intransigence regarding federal quarantine proposals in thickets of rhetoric about their economic impact on shipping, their insurance implications, and their overall legality. These objections were further garnished with pronouncements about state government's "sacred" role in governing the affairs of its citizens. Officials with the National Board of Health tried to assuage these fears and redirect the attention of Louisiana officials to the paramount issue of public health, but with limited success.

The following two excerpts provide a glimpse into the tensions that existed between Louisiana and federal health officials in the early 1880s. The first excerpted document is an 1881 report authored by Felix Formento, a prominent New Orleans physician and leading official in the state's health department. This report, which was prepared in response to a set of federal quarantine and public health instructions received by the state in May 1881, was unanimously approved by the Louisiana State Board of Health. Formento raised objections to many aspects of these instructions, but he reserved his strongest pushback for a National Board of Health proposal to establish a new ship quarantine system in the Gulf of Mexico. The second excerpted document is a response to Formento's complaints penned by Stanford E. Chaillé, supervising inspector of the National Board of Health.

EXCERPT FROM THE FORMENTO REPORT:

We now come to the fifth and most important proposition or request made by the National Board to the State board of health, viz: "It is considered highly desirable by the National Board that infected ships should be, as far as possible, excluded from the Mississippi River, and the inspector will endeavor to secure the cooperation of the Louisiana board toward obtaining this result, by having said board pass an ordinance similar to the resolution passed by the sanitary council of the Mississippi Valley at its last meeting, to the effect that all vessels from ports in which yellow fever is prevailing, or from ports where contagious or infectious diseases are reported to exist, shall be inspected at Port Eads, and if any such be found to be infected, or to furnish reasonable ground for suspicion of infection, such vessel shall not be allowed to pass Eadsport northwise, except upon presentation of a certificate from the inspector of the National Board of Health at the Ship Island quarantine station, setting forth that the vessel has been subjected to proper treatment and is not liable to convey contagion."

With all deference and respect for the National Board, and in spite of our most earnest desire to establish friendly relations and promote our cordial co-operation in order to accomplish our most cherished object, our ambition to protect our city and State, as well as the States of the Mississippi Valley, from the introduction of foreign pestilence, of yellow fever more particularly, we must acknowledge that this proposition is a cause of surprise and regret to us, for it is entirely inadmissible and impossible that we could for a moment consent to it.

Ship Island is a sand bank situated on the coast of the State of Mississippi, 100 miles from the mouth of the Mississippi River, entirely out of the course of any vessels coming to this port from any of the ports most likely to be infected, such as Rio Janeiro, Havana, and Vera Cruz. Admitting that Ship Island was the safest and the best equipped quarantine establishment in the world, that the said island presented all the sanitary advantages, with all imaginable facilities for loading and unloading vessels, for provisions, &c.; admitting that it was surrounded by deep water, permitting ships of heavy draught to load at the piers or wharves of said establishment; admitting all this, and everybody knows that the actual facts are quite the reverse, we say that this State board of health has no power conferred upon it by any of the several acts of the legislature creating said board and establishing quarantine for the protection of the State of Louisiana to order vessels out of the waters of Louisiana to any foreign or domestic port, or to any quarantine station under the jurisdiction of the United States or any State of the Union. To assume such power would simply be an abuse of authority on the part of the State board, which would not be tolerated by our State authorities nor any foreign power. Admitting that we should have the power to prevent admission in the Mississippi River of a vessel of a friendly power, doing legitimate business with our port, we have no right to force her out of her way; to be submitted to a thousand vexatious annoyances and trouble; to oblige her to procure a certificate from the inspector of the National Board of Health at the Ship Island quarantine station.

The distance from Ship Island to the mouth of the Mississippi River is 100 miles; a sailing ship during bad weather and unfavorable wind might be several days on the way.

Supposing that a vessel, after obtaining this certificate, which is to open to her the gates of the Mississippi River, should have cases of yellow fever, or other infectious diseases, to declare themselves on board of her on her way back from Ship Island station to Eadsport, an occurrence likely to take place under this latitude during the months of August and September, what then should be done with such a vessel? Should she be sent back a second time to the national station to undergo a second quarantine?

The proper place, the only one we recognize for vessels from foreign ports bound for New Orleans, to be stopped, inspected, and submitted to quarantine, established by the laws of the State of Louisiana, is our State Mississippi River quarantine station. It is admirably situated for that purpose, at a sufficient distance from our city to protect us from the neighborhood of infected ships, and yet near enough to procure provisions, supplies, acclimated laborers, physicians, nurses, &c., in case of necessity. It offers a safe and deep anchorage to immense fleets. This establishment has, under the administration of the present board of health, been put in thorough repair at a cost of nearly $7,000. It represents a value of $60,000, with large warehouses for storing cargoes; also, facilities for loading or unloading at the wharf. It has telegraph communications [with] all parts of the world. It is the best equipped and organized quarantine station outside of New York.

The rules and regulations governing our quarantine station are sufficiently strict to procure complete protection from foreign pestilence with as little detention and obstruction to commerce as possible.

Should we accept the proposition to inspect vessels at Eadsport and not allow them to pass northwise, except upon the presentation of a certificate of the inspector of the National Board of Health at Ship Island; in other words, should we force (if we had such power) the Ship Island quarantine upon foreign or domestic commerce, we should at once, to be consistent, abolish our State board with its well-equipped and costly quarantine establishments in the Mississippi River; we should at once abandon the power and authority conferred upon us by law; we should abandon the fulfillment of our sworn and sacred duties, that of protecting ourselves, the lives of our people, the interests of our commerce, not confiding to others, however great and powerful they may be, that sacred obligation.

Commerce once destroyed, as it would surely be by the enforcement of this strange and unnatural quarantine which is sought to be imposed upon us, we might as well abandon all our rights, powers, and duties, for Louisiana would no longer need any protection. It would be entirely ruined, and would soon disappear from the family of States. For all these reasons, and many others which we could add to these, we respectfully refuse to indorse the fifth and last proposition submitted to us by the supervising inspector of the National Board of Health.

Excerpt from Chaille's response:

The National Board long since declared that it had no desire to "abolish the State board," nor to usurp "the power and authority conferred upon it by law," nor cause you "to abandon the fulfillment of your sworn and sacred duties," nor to impair the resources of your board. On the contrary, the National Board would rejoice to see your power and resources increased; for, disregarding less selfish consideration, is it not evident that, since it is a paramount duty of the National Board to aid and cooperate with local boards, the greater the influence of these the greater must be its own?

The National Board has requested you to co-operate with it in providing New Orleans with what, it is believed, would prove an additional protection to the public health, and urges this for the sake, not only of this city, but also of many adjacent communities who firmly believe themselves in constant danger whenever New Orleans becomes infected. Would the Ship Island quarantine, as a station of refuge for infected vessels, furnish any additional protection? Stripping the disagreement between the two boards of all misapprehensions and false issues, this, in my opinion, is the sole question for consideration.

On May 8 I inspected your Mississippi River quarantine station, and testify, with pleasure, that I found it better than I had expected, and that I detected nothing to indicate that the officers in charge were not discharging their duty to the best of their ability, and as efficiently as the circumstances and the means at their disposal permitted. But I think that our future protection demands that these circumstances and means should be fully appreciated, for thus only can our legislature be induced to give you the liberal aid required, and thus only can we secure from others needed sympathy and aid.

You report that Louisiana has on the Mississippi River "the best equipped and organized quarantine station outside of New York." As I have not inspected all of the others I cannot add my testimony to yours, but I do know that no place in the United States has proved itself as liable to yellow fever as has New Orleans, and, therefore, that our quarantines should be second to none in efficiency. Dispensing with minor criticisms, I found two very great defects at the chief one of our three quarantine stations.

First. If there be any police force it is inadequate to prevent communication between the quarantine grounds and the neighborhood; it is inadequate to prevent the passengers and crews of infected vessels from communicating with uninfected vessels and with the residents below, above, and over the river opposite to the station; it is inadequate to prevent such passengers and crews from occasionally avoiding at Eadsport or elsewhere your quarantine and in reaching this city by tow boats or otherwise; and it is inadequate for the protection of Eadsport itself, as testified by Capt. James B. Eads in his letter published this day in the Democrat. Unless more amply provided with funds I do not believe it in your power to remedy this defect.

Second. Sanitation demands the thorough cleansing of an infected vessel, and this necessitates the discharge of its cargo, while commerce demands that these things shall be done promptly and economically, and these demands require an abundant supply of cheap labor. When inspecting the Mississippi River quarantine station I found one vessel paying $6 a day to every laborer, and the number secured by importation from New Orleans was inadequate, even at this price, to insure the thorough and prompt unloading, cleansing, and reloading requisite for the conjoint interests of sanitation and commerce. This grave defect is also out of your power to rectify. Nevertheless, however powerless you may be respecting the two defects cited, sanitarians and merchants, or both, will remain dissatisfied until some remedy for them is found.

The first defect is so inseparable from quarantine stations on the mainland that sanitarians unite in demanding their location on islands. Beside this inestimable advantage, I have been assured that an ample supply of laborers can be obtained at Ship Island for $35 a month. Further, I have much more confidence in the ability and will of the

United States to make its station at this island as perfect as is practicable than I have in your gaining either from the legislature of this impoverished State or from the council of this impoverished city the aid necessary to perfect our three quarantine stations—an end which must be accomplished, unless we are to continue tampering with half-way measures. Appreciating fully our great misfortune that Louisiana has no island for a quarantine station at the month of our river, and that Ship Island is so distant therefrom, and conceding that the three reasons now given in favor of this station may not be considered conclusively satisfactory, I will advance an additional reason, which, combined with the others, has sufficed to convince me that good policy dictates concession to the request of the National Board. The health authorities of the adjacent States of th [sic] Mississippi Valley demand this concession as necessary to their protection, and declare that, if their demand is not heeded, they will be forced to interrupt our commerce with them on the least suspicion of danger. Yellow fever is a public enemy, and our neighbors have as much right to a voice in its exclusion from the Mississippi River as upon the exclusion therefrom of any other public enemy. Louisiana has not hesitated, when to its advantage, to vociferate that the Mississippi River is a national highway, and that all the States should contribute to its jetties and levees; now, when other States demand what they think essential for the protection of their health, shall Louisiana inconsistently reply that the mouth of this national highway is exclusively under its control, and shall be managed regardless of their wishes? . . .

Several additional considerations deserve attention. Should our hope of greatly increased prosperity be fulfilled, then it is certain that our unacclimated population will increase, and thereby our danger of infection and our need for additional protection. Further, our traveling facilities will also be notably increased; with this the danger of infecting our neighbors, and with this their demands for better protection. These anticipated conditions will, it is to be hoped, continue to strengthen the pressure both within and without this city to keep itself clean and uninfected, and to adopt every reasonable precaution to attain these ends. Hence, it is idle to expect the present issue will die out, and if it be not met fairly and generously, then, when disaster overtakes us, as it may in spite of all efforts and concessions, New Orleans will find itself a helpless victim to the indignant distrust and hostile action of its neighbors. In this matter the National Board represents not only a large number of your fellow-citizens, and, in my belief, the health authorities of adjacent States, but also the same generous country which overwhelmed this city in 1878 with millions of dollars of bounty. Is it fitting to refuse a concession urged by such applicants, and to attribute to a mean spirit of commercial jealousy their anxiety to shield timid communities, which are not hardened by habit to our dreadful scourge, nor protected as we, in large numbers, are by acclimation? They ask no more than an apparent sacrifice of an insignificant fraction of our foreign tropical trade in lieu of what they deem better security both for them and for us, and in lieu of annual jeopardy to our inestimably more valuable interstate commerce. For my part, I advocate proving to our neighbors that we love them as ourselves, and I therefore would concede to them a voice, though opposed to our own, in controlling the importation of yellow fever into the mouth of our great national highway.

Your concession would result, I am confident, in diminishing our risks of infection, and thereby would tend to promote our growing grain trade, our European imports, our home manufactures, and our languishing summer business. Your concession would certainly accomplish the very desirable end of giving notice—as apart from the consideration of an inspector at Eadsport, should, I think, be given by you—to all owners, agents, and captains that vessels certainly infected shall no longer be permitted even to enter our river, but must, when destined for the Mississippi, proceed directly to the refuge for such vessels at Ship Island. By such measure you would teach them a much-needed lesson, namely, to enforce that better sanitary construction and regulation of their vessels which has enabled some steamship lines to ply between Havana and New York for a decenniad without having had a single case of yellow fever on board. This good result alone weighs heavily in the balance against the slight temporary injury to our commerce, and would, by permanent advantages, ultimately more than compensate this commerce.

Further still, your concession would give you greater influence in eventually promoting measures most desirable for our commerce; such, for instance, as gaining the aid of the United States in establishing quarantine stations perfectly satisfactory both to adjacent States and to Louisiana; and such as the stationing of sanitary officers both at Rio and Vera Cruz, whereby our intercourse with these ports would be rendered much safer, and the interests of our coffee and other trades would be greatly promoted.

In conclusion, gentlemen, it is my conviction that this question merits your further consideration, your personal inspection of the Ship Island quarantine station, and of all the subjects pertaining thereto, and that you would give great satisfaction to many of your fellow-citizens, within and without this State, should you consent to reconsider your refusal, based on what I have now stated my reasons for believing, were misapprehensions of the position on this subject of the National Board.

Very respectfully, yours,

STANFORD E. CHAILLE, Supervising Inspector National Board of Health.

Source: *Annual Report of the National Board of Health, 1881.* Washington, DC: Government Printing Office, 1882, pp. 317–18, 320–22.

A Commentary on "The Present Condition of National Health Legislation"

DOCUMENT
3.11

"National Health Legislation Is Sadly in Need of Revision"

1885

When health reformers witnessed the birth of the National Board of Health (NBH) in 1879, they hailed the agency as a welcome harbinger of a new age of federal health regulation. But the NBH was treated by the Marine Hospital Service (MHS) as an interloper and mortal threat to its policy turf. MHS surgeon general John Hamilton, who took office in April 1879 after the death of his predecessor, John Maynard Woodworth, became an energetic and effective critic of the NBH. Fully aware that most of the NBH's powers would expire without congressional reauthorization in 1883, he harried the board and its leadership at every turn, pounding the department with accusations of incompetence and malfeasance. Hamilton's lobbying efforts seriously undercut political support for the National Board of Health, and in 1883 Congress declined to renew the NBH law. As a result, the NBH became a ghost of its former self, most maritime quarantine functions reverted back to state and local agencies, and MHS ascended once again to its role as the central public health agency in the federal government.

The fall of the NBH was a happy event in the view of Hamilton and various state health departments that had crossed policy swords with the board during its short existence. Other observers, however, saw the demise of the NBH as a tragedy. They asserted that the NBH had performed well and nobly in defending public health, and they further contended that the politically motivated evisceration of the agency jeopardized the health and welfare of the American people. One of the most prominent physicians to hold this view was George F. Shrady, founded and editor in chief of the Medical Record, *one of the leading medical journals of the day. Following is an excerpt from an 1885 Shrady editorial on the downfall of the National Board of Health and its potential impact on public health in America.*

Threatened as we are with an invasion of small-pox from the north, and of cholera from the east, no occasion would seem to be more opportune than the present for calling the attention both of the medical profession and the public, sharply, to the anomalous condition of national health legislation. We do not need to discuss at this time the need of national sanitary legislation. Whatever diversity of opinion there may be as to the form of such legislation, it may be safely affirmed that, in view of our increasing commercial intercourse with foreign powers, and the facilities afforded for inter-State communication, the necessity for national legislation, through which the sanitary service of the several States may be efficiently co-ordinated is universally recognized. Passing over, then, the agitation of public health questions, which resulted in the establishment of the National Board of Health, which has rendered incalculable service to the country, let us come at once to the present condition of affairs.

Under the Act of Congress approved March 3, 1879, the National Board of Health was established. In accordance with that law the Board is required "to make investigations into, and collect information on, all matters affecting the public health, and to advise the several departments of the Government, the executives of the several States, and the Commissioners of the District of Columbia, on all questions submitted by them, or whenever in the opinion of the Board such advice may tend to the preservation and improvement of the public health." On June 2, 1879, Congress passed an Act enlarging the powers of the Board, and charging it with the duty of aiding State and local boards of health in their efforts to prevent the introduction of contagious or infectious diseases from abroad and their spread from one State to another. It was under the provisions of this Act that the Board co-operated with the health authorities of the Mississippi Valley in stamping out the epidemic of yellow fever of 1879, which made its appearance within a month after the passage of the Act; and again in 1881-82, with the authorities of the North and West, in putting an end to the progress of small-pox, which was rapidly overrunning the country from the Atlantic coast to the Mississippi Valley.

The record of those years is written, and the success which attended the efforts of the authorities, State and National, working hand in hand, established beyond a question both the necessity for national aid in such emergencies, and the wisdom of Congress in providing the legislation by which such co-operation could be secured. From that day to the present State boards of health, local boards, medical societies and associations, have been unanimous in their approval of the work of the National Board and urgent in their appeals to Congress and the President to support and strengthen it in its efforts to improve the health of the people.

The Act of June 2, 1879, took the place of an Act approved April 29, 1878, by which authority in sanitary matters was centered in the Surgeon-General of the Marine Hospital Service, and after defining the duties and powers of the Board, proceeds as follows:

"SEC. 9. So much of the Act entitled 'An Act to prevent the introduction of contagious or infectious diseases into the United States,' approved April 29, 1878, as requires consular officers or other representatives of the United States at foreign ports to report the sanitary condition of and the departure of vessels from such ports to the Supervising Surgeon-General of the Marine Hospital Service; and so much of said Act as requires the Surgeon-General of the Marine Hospital Service to frame rules and regulations, and to execute said Act, and to give notice to Federal and State officers of the approach of infected vessels, and furnish such officers with weekly abstracts of consular sanitary reports, and all other acts and parts of acts inconsistent with the provisions of this Act, are hereby repealed.

"SEC. 10. This Act shall not continue in force for a longer period than four years from the date of its approval."

In consequence of the provisions of this last section the duties of the National Board, so far as they were set forth in the Act of June 2, 1879, ceased on June 2, 1883, and since that date the Board has continued its operations under the Act of March 3, 1879.

In regard to the Act of June 2, 1879, the late Hon. Charles J. Folger, then Secretary of the Treasury, in his Report to Congress for the year 1883, used the following language:

"On June 2d last the Act of June 2, 1879, to prevent the introduction of contagious or infectious diseases, expired by limitation. There is now no legislation immediately to the same end. Whether there be need of reenacting any or all of the provisions of the Act of June 2, 1879, it is for Congress to determine." The decision of Judge Folger was in accordance with SECTION 12, Revised Statutes, edition of 1878, which reads as follows:

"Whenever an act is repealed, which repealed a former act, such former act shall not thereby be revived, unless it shall be expressly so provided"

In the face of this provision of law, a circular has recently been issued from the Treasury Department, citing the law of April 29, 1878, and assuming it to be in force.

This circular emanates from the "Office of the Supervising Surgeon-General, U. S. Marine Hospital Service," is signed by that officer, and is approved by the Secretary of the Treasury and the President. A more flagrant instance of assumption of power and authority, under color of law, cannot well be conceived. Acting under the provisions of this *repealed* law, the Surgeon-General proceeds "to frame rules and regulations, and to execute said law," and the Secretary and President approve his acts. Meantime the National Board of Health, the only national health authority now recognized in law, is entirely ignored by the department which it is required to advise on sanitary questions.

In view of the preceding facts it is apparent that national health legislation is sadly in need of revision, and we trust that, at the approaching session of Congress, such definite action will be taken as will determine positively the kind of central organization which we shall have, and the exact nature and scope of its duties. The danger of leaving the great and all-important question of the prevention of epidemics, such as cholera and yellow fever, to the discretion of the President, has been demonstrated by the ridiculous efforts which were made under his direction to control yellow fever in Texas, and the feeble measures now in operation to protect the country against small-pox. Fortunately, neither cholera nor yellow fever has reached us this year, and time is once more given to set our house in order. No proper effort should now be spared by the American Public

Health Association, which is largely responsible for whatever national legislation we have, to secure its revision, and to remedy its manifest defects.

Source: Shrady, George F. "The Present Condition of National Health Legislation." *Medical Record: A Weekly Journal of Medicine and Surgery.* Vol. 28, July 4, 1885–December 31, 1886. New York: William Wood & Co., October 31, 1885, pp. 490–91.

DOCUMENT 3.12

U.S. Supreme Court Affirms State Authority over Medical Licensing

"No One Has a Right to Practice Medicine without Having the Necessary Qualifications"

1888

In 1882 Frank Dent, a West Virginia eclectic physician (one whose practice was based on botanical remedies, not regular medicine), was charged with violating a new state law that required all practicing physicians to hold a degree from a "reputable" medical college, pass a medical exam, or prove that they had been practicing in the state for at least ten years. The charges arose after the West Virginia Board of Health, composed mainly of anti-eclectic regular physicians, determined that Dent's degree, which he had earned from Cincinnati's American Medical Eclectic College, did not meet its standards. Dent appealed the decision, but in 1888 the U.S. Supreme Court issued a unanimous opinion upholding the West Virginia statute as a legitimate and reasonable measure to improve medical care in the state. The opinion, excerpted here, was delivered by Justice Stephen Field.

This Supreme Court decision provided an official cap to a gradual but important change in American orientation toward medical licensing (and other forms of professional licensing) over the course of half a century. Back in the 1820s and 1830s, Jacksonianism and Thomsonianism had pushed even the most threadbare medical licensing statutes off the books in virtually every state and territory. But medical advances and growing acceptance of state and professional authority gradually eroded the anti-intellectual underpinnings of these movements, and medical licensing acts blossomed across the country in the last quarter of the nineteenth century. The Dent v. West Virginia *decision, then, was in many ways the culmination of this broader shift in societal attitudes, as well as a signal triumph for the regular medical establishment. With the* Dent *decision, "society granted the medical profession one of its most cherished goals: the authority to exclude practitioners deemed unworthy," according to one analysis. "The fact that other professions won protective legislation at the same time suggests that the physicians' achievement resulted more from a change in social policy than from a recognition of the improved state of medical science, impressive though it may have been."[1]*

Few professions require more careful preparation by one who seeks to enter it than that of medicine. It has to deal with all those subtle and mysterious influences upon which life depends, and requires not only a knowledge of the property of vegetable and mineral substances, but of the human body in all its complicated parts, and their relation to each other, as well as their influence upon the mind. The physician must be able to detect readily the presence of disease, and prescribe appropriate remedies for its removal. Every one may have occasion to consult him, but comparatively few can judge of the qualifications of learning and skill which he possesses. Reliance must be placed upon the assurance given by his license, issued by an authority competent to judge in that respect, that he possesses the requisite qualifications. Due consideration, therefore, for the protection of society may well induce the state to exclude from practicing those who have not such a license, or who are found upon examination not to be fully qualified. The same reasons which control in imposing conditions, upon compliance with which the physician is allowed to practice in the first instance, may call for farther conditions as new modes of treating disease are discovered, or a more thorough acquaintance is obtained of the remedial properties of vegetable and mineral substances, or a more accurate know edge is acquired of the human system and of the agencies by which it is affected. It would not be deemed a matter for serious discussion that a knowledge of the new acquisitions of the profession, as it from time to time advances in its attainments for the relief of the sick and suffering, should be required for its continuance in its practice, but for the earnestness with which the plaintiff in error insists that by being compelled to obtain the certificate required, and prevented from continuing in his practice without it, he is deprived of his right and estate in his profession without due process of law. We perceive nothing in the statute which indicates an intention of the legislature to deprive one of any of his rights. No one has a right to practice medicine without having the necessary qualifications of learning and skill; and the statute only requires that whoever assumes, by offering to the community his services as a physician, that he possesses such learning and skill, shall present evidence of it by a certificate or license from a body designated by the state as competent to judge of his qualifications.

There is nothing of an arbitrary character in the provisions of the statute in question; it applies to all physicians except those who may be called for a special case from another state, it imposes no conditions which cannot be readily met, and it is made enforceable in the mode usual in kindred matters, that is by regular proceedings adapted to the case. It authorizes an examination of the applicant by the Board of Health as to his qualifications when he has no evidence of them in the diploma of a reputable medical college in the school of medicine to which he belongs, or has not practiced in the state a designated period before March 1881. If, in the proceedings under the statute, there should be any unfair or unjust action on the part of the Board in refusing him a certificate, we doubt not that a remedy would be found in the courts of the state. But no such imputation can be made, for the plaintiff in error did not submit himself to the examination of the Board after it had decided that the diploma he presented was insufficient.

Source: "Decision of the United States Supreme Court Affirming the Validity of the West Virginia Medical Practice Act and the Right of the Board to Determine the 'Reputability' of a Medical College." *Dent v. West Virginia,* 129 U.S. *Fifteenth Annual Report of Illinois State Board of Health.* Springfield, IL: H. W. Rokker, 1894, pp. 232–33.

NOTE

1. Ronald L. Numbers, "The Fall and Rise of the American Medical Profession," in *Sickness and Health in America: Readings in the History of Medicine and Public Health,* 2nd ed. rev., ed. Judith Walzer Leavitt and Ronald L. Numbers (Madison: University of Wisconsin Press, 1985), 229.

CHAPTER 4

Health Care in the Progressive Era

1890-1920

During the roughly three-decade period of American history commonly known as the Progressive Era, significant and lasting changes to public health policy were enacted. Important new laws governing food and drug safety, waste disposal, and other sanitation issues were enacted, and federal authorities became much more involved in monitoring and, in some cases, directing industrial activities that influenced public health. Momentous changes took place in the health care marketplace as well. The modern hospital system emerged; the professionalization of nurses, doctors, surgeons, and pharmacists proceeded apace; and state and federal legislators and bureaucrats implemented laws and regulations relating to medical education and licensing. However, the holy grail of progressive health reformers—a system of national health insurance—continued to hover just out of reach, its implementation thwarted by opposition from industrial interests and advocates of limited government.

A Revolution in Public Health Regulation

The Progressive Era was a time in which all manner of perceived social ills were addressed by lawmakers and public officials, from unsustainable consumption of timber and other natural resources to child labor to the monopolistic practices of corporate trusts in major industries. But few reforms had as great an impact on the daily lives of Americans as the ones that were instituted in the realm of public health. Many of these measures not only improved quality of life (especially in urban population centers) but also brought reductions in infant mortality and overall gains in life expectancy.

The impact of these new policies was greatly augmented by other changes taking place in American society at the same time. Advances in scientific understanding of the root causes of disease and breakthroughs in the medical treatment of scourges such as cholera, yellow fever, tuberculosis, diphtheria, smallpox, and dysentery were keys to improved health. Public health also benefited mightily from the introduction of sophisticated engineering systems for water and waste distribution, tenement house reforms, the green space–oriented City Beautiful Movement, and other efforts to clean up inner cities. "The sanitary revolution in America was in full swing, and health and sanitation were virtually synonymous," observed historian John Duffy. "Possibly the key factor in all this was a rising standard of living, without which municipalities could not have afforded the enormous capital costs of the sewer and water systems nor the steadily increasing operating costs of health and sanitary programs."[1]

Heightened public consciousness about public health dangers was sometimes exploited by political actors with different agendas, however. Nativists and other critics of the era's great waves of immigration routinely described the new arrivals to America's shores as filthy and disease-ridden in an effort to drum up support for new immigration restrictions **(See Document 4.5)**. Most of the pressure that was exerted on policymakers to bolster sanitation and hygiene regulations came from reform-oriented organizations and movements that were focused on environmental improvements. These ranged from the settlement house movement helmed by Jane Addams, which brought meaningful sanitary reforms to some of America's most squalid city slums, to the Child Health Organization of America, which successfully pushed legislation that made health and hygiene instruction a part of the public school curriculum. Displaying both gritty perseverance and a talent for tapping into public discontent with Gilded Age social inequities, these and other progressive trailblazers convinced the government to take a much more active role in safeguarding the nation's health.

Their ability to rouse municipal, state, and federal lawmakers was greatly eased by America's muckraking newspapers and periodicals, the mass media of the day. The voices of the great social reformers were amplified in the pages of daily papers from coast to coast, and the urgency of their crusades was underscored on a regular basis by muckraking articles that appeared in *McClure's, Everybody's, Cosmopolitan,* and scores of other magazines in the early twentieth century. Many of the exposés published in these magazines focused on political corruption and corporate chicanery, but numerous others investigated issues that had a significant public health component, such as inner-city poverty. In some cases, muckrakers played a pivotal role in the passage of new public health laws. The Pure Food and Drug Act of 1906, for example, was a direct response to the public uproar that accompanied two muckraking works: Upton Sinclair's *The Jungle,*

Swift and Co.'s Packing House was a major Chicago meat-packing company in the early 1900s. Across the American meatpacking industry, tasks such as removing shoulders and splitting ribs were routinely completed with little to no regard for cleanliness or safety. The Pure Food and Drug Act of 1906 was a direct response to Upton Sinclair's muckraking novel on the Chicago meatpacking industry, The Jungle.

which provided a harrowing account of filthy and unhealthy practices in the nation's meatpacking industry, and Samuel Hopkins Adams's "Great American Fraud" series, which documented how America was drowning in a sea of dangerous, unregulated patent medicines **(See Document 4.7)**.

ROOSEVELT CHARTS A NEW COURSE IN PUBLIC HEALTH ADMINISTRATION

The evolution in the federal government's orientation toward public health issues also owed much to President Theodore Roosevelt, regarded today by many historians as the virtual personification of the Progressive Movement. In the closing years of the nineteenth century, prominent reformers spoke out. For example, William Henry Welch of the Johns Hopkins Medical School openly "deplored" the federal government for having "had so little share in [the] movement in public hygiene."[2] Roosevelt agreed with this assessment, as he made abundantly clear within months of taking the oath of office on September 14, 1901, following the assassination of William McKinley. Acting with his usual blend of confidence and moral certainty, Roosevelt energetically set about reshaping the federal government so that it could take a more direct hand in addressing public health problems (as well as a host of other issues identified by the president as threats to American exceptionalism).

During his eight years (1901–1909) in the Oval Office, Roosevelt and fellow reformers in Congress modestly expanded both the duties of and the appropriations for the U.S. Public Health Service (PHS), though PHS inspectors remained best known for their efforts to control trachoma and other easily transmitted diseases at Ellis Island and other immigration points of entry **(See Document 4.4)**. They also empowered important new public health agencies such as the Food and Drug Administration (FDA) to enforce progressive laws, including the Pure Food and Drug Act, which aimed to reduce public vulnerability to dangerous foods and patent medicines.

Into the twentieth century, patent medicines came under increased scrutiny by the federal government, especially with the creation of the Food and Drug Administration.

In addition, Roosevelt welcomed the creation of national commissions such as the Committee of One Hundred on National Health, an organization formed by the American Association for the Advancement of Science (AAAS) in 1906 under the direction of

Upon arriving at Ellis Island, immigrants to the United States were subject to medical examinations and inspections. The reputed danger of immigrant health and hygiene was a topic routinely exploited by politicians looking for votes.

Yale University economist Irving Fisher. The Committee of One Hundred issued reports and surveys stuffed with ambitious proposals to enlist the national government in improving and safeguarding public health.

Roosevelt, who was convinced that America's economic and cultural foundations rested on the shoulders of a healthy and virile populace, embraced many of these propositions. "There is a constantly growing interest in this country in the question of the public health," he declared in his seventh annual message to Congress in December 1907.

> The public mind is awake to the fact that many diseases, notably tuber-culosis, are National scourges. The work of the State and city boards of health should be supplemented by a constantly increasing interest on the part of the National Government. The Congress has already provided a bureau of public health and has provided for a hygienic laboratory. There are other valuable laws relating to the public health connected with the various departments. This whole branch of the Government should be strengthened and aided in every way.[3]

Roosevelt's comments about the necessity of supporting state and local public health initiatives reflected a recognition that, in many respects, those agencies already stood at the vanguard of the public health movement. By the turn of the century, these boards and agencies were regularly executing sanitation and vaccination campaigns that dramatically reduced the risk of disease outbreaks in their areas of jurisdiction, even though their efforts were not always appreciated or understood **(See Document 4.2 and Document 4.6)**. Some of these pioneering programs, such as the one carried out by New York City health officials against diphtheria (with serum developed by its in-house research laboratory), were widely copied by other cities.[4] And once the Progressive Era kicked into gear in the early 1900s, city and state health departments all across America opened clinics and health centers (sometimes in collaboration with voluntary groups) to provide diagnostic and educational services to local citizens of limited financial means. The specialized clinics that arose during this time, such as ones that were formed to combat tuberculosis, venereal disease, and infant mortality, were particularly popular. The number of tuberculosis clinics operating in the United States, for example, jumped from an estimated twenty facilities in 1905 to more than five hundred by 1915.[5]

The services offered by these health centers and clinics were fairly limited, despite pressure to expand them. Most health departments were controlled by physicians who balked at the idea of establishing public health services that had the potential to divert large numbers of patients from their own practices. "They supported some kinds of government intervention, such as quarantines, inoculations, and health education," explained scholars James T. Bennett and Thomas J. DiLorenzo, "[but] were wary of any trends toward the incremental governmental takeover of the private practice of medicine."[6]

At one point, it appeared that Roosevelt's crusade for the conservation of America's human resources might result in the establishment of a cabinet-level health department. When the Committee of One Hundred issued its 1908 *Report on National Vitality: Its Wastes and Conservation,* the organization supplemented its widely expected calls for new sanitary legislation, increased support for preventive medicine, and the curbing of social evils such as alcoholism with a bold proposal for federal lawmakers' consideration: the establishment of a cabinet-level department that would encompass the Public Health and Marine Hospital Service and all other government health and sanitation activities.

Roosevelt was intrigued, as were many progressive U.S. representatives and senators. But existing cabinet agencies joined with PHS surgeon general Walter Wyman in resisting the expansion idea, and Roosevelt did not act on the proposal before leaving office in March 1909. The question thus passed on to his successor, William Howard Taft, who adopted a position of equivocation. The action subsequently shifted to the U.S. Congress, where Democratic Oklahoma senator Robert L. Owen in 1910 introduced a bill to create a national health department (**See Document 4.9**).

Prominent health reformers such as Irving Fisher, head of the Committee of One Hundred, testified in favor of Owen's bill. "I believe the science of health would be revolutionized by the passage of this bill," Fisher declared in one hearing. "With a department of health, in a few years the average duration of life in this country will be several years longer than it is now."[7] The leadership of the fast-growing American Medical Association (AMA) initially expressed support for the scheme. But the reorganization bill was torpedoed by lobbying pressure from groups such as the Anti-Compulsory Vaccination League and the National League for Medical Freedom, a coalition of patent medicine manufacturers, medical sects, and other commercial interests that feared increased federal oversight of their business operations. When congressional support for a national health agency declined, proponents glumly settled for 1912 legislation that broadened the authority of the Public Health Service to include investigations of water pollution and other man-made sources of disease. Committee of One Hundred members and other health reformers expressed disappointment with this turn of events, but historian George Rosen asserted that their efforts to explain the "[benefits of] coordination of federal health agencies and programs, the importance of health research, and the social implications of health" helped lay the groundwork for many later developments in national health policy.[8]

THE SPANISH FLU EPIDEMIC OF 1918

After the campaign to create a national department of health subsided in 1912, crestfallen health reformers diverted their energies to other crusades, from ending child labor to proposing a system of national health insurance. In 1918 the quality of America's federal public health system came surging back to the fore as a policy issue with the arrival of a deadly influenza pandemic. The Spanish flu that raged across the United States from September 1918 through June 1919 claimed the lives of an estimated 675,000 Americans. The global toll reached between twenty million and forty million people, making it the most disastrous pandemic since the Black Death raged across medieval Europe during the fourteenth century. The outbreak, summarized Dr. Victor Vaughan, a former president of the American Medical Association, "encircled the globe, visited the remotest corners, taking toll of the most robust, sparing neither soldier nor civilian, and flaunting its red flag in the face of science."[9]

The influenza outbreak first made its presence felt in the United States in the spring of 1918, but the blow was only a glancing one. Convinced that the danger had passed, a strangely sanguine Surgeon General Rupert Blue, head of the Public Health Service, vetoed proposals made that summer to divert more of the agency's resources to pneumonia research. In September, a second wave of influenza marauded across the country, taking an especially fierce toll on otherwise healthy young men and women. Some of the worst havoc was wreaked on America's military bases and shipyards, where large numbers of soldiers were concentrated for World War I military training and deployment. The flu eventually struck approximately four out of ten men in both the Army and the Navy, and it turned Boston, Philadelphia, San Francisco, Seattle, and other cities that housed navy yards and army bases into epicenters of tragedy. The total number of American soldiers and sailors who died from the flu (and pneumonia, which commonly accompanied the virus) reached fifty-seven thousand before the virus, which was impervious to all diagnostic and treatment efforts, ran its course.[10]

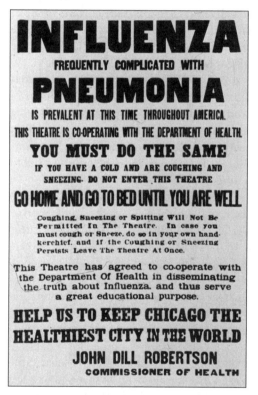

The 1918–1919 influenza pandemic killed more than 600,000 Americans and tens of millions worldwide. The epidemic severely tested the powers of both local and national public health authorities.

The public and official response to the outbreak was both belated and inadequate, reflecting a continued—and, in some cities, baffling—inability to confront the full scope of the crisis. Many Americans obeyed PHS and local orders to wear gauze masks in public (regulations that imposed fines or jail sentences on uncooperative "mask slackers" boosted cooperation in some cities). Similarly, many citizens heeded health officials' pleas for them to avoid large public gatherings. But millions of Americans flouted these and other efforts to halt the spread of the flu. Large crowds continued to gather for World War I–related rallies and parades, sporting events, religious services, and theatrical entertainment, and some attacked mask mandates and other flu-mitigation measures as outrageous infringements on individual liberty. "If the Board of Health can force people to wear masks," declared the *San Francisco Chronicle,* "then it can force them to submit to inoculations, or any experiment or indignity."[11]

The PHS response to the growing pandemic was sluggish, even after Congress hurriedly appropriated an additional $1 million in emergency funding for the agency in late September. Shortages of doctors and, especially, nurses hamstrung flu treatment efforts in many population centers and military bases, and the Public Health Service wasted precious time and resources researching specious war-fed rumors that the epidemic was an example of German biological warfare. PHS researchers even investigated claims that Bayer aspirin, manufactured domestically but under a German-held patent, was the source of the sickness.[12]

Meanwhile, Surgeon General Blue and the PHS were fairly effective in publicizing basic health measures that Americans could heed to ward off the flu. Working closely with the Red Cross and other volunteer agencies, the PHS distributed millions of flu-related circulars, pamphlets, and posters across the country **(See Document 4.13)**, and other state and local health departments followed suit with similar education campaigns. Historian Alfred Crosby wrote that "if influenza could have been smothered by paper, many lives would have been saved in 1918."[13]

In the aftermath of the Spanish flu devastation, Blue argued that the pandemic proved that the federal government needed to take a much stronger role in safeguarding public health. To this end, Blue proposed the development of a permanent organization within a dramatically expanded PHS that could better coordinate national, state, and local responses to future pandemics and other threats to public health. Remarkably, this call for increased investment in the national government's public health machinery was largely ignored by Congress, which declined to approve any major increases in appropriations for the PHS or meaningful expansion of government authority on public health issues. Instead, both Congress and the American public—which could have pressed Washington, D.C., for such changes if it had been so inclined—quickly forgot the horrors of the pandemic and embraced the "return to normalcy" that, they hoped, would follow the November 1918 end to the Great War.

The AMA Comes into Its Own

At the same time that public health policies were undergoing considerable change in the Progressive Era, so, too, was the private health care marketplace. And one of the primary architects of these alterations to America's health care system was the American Medical Association.

Prior to the twentieth century, the AMA had been a bit player in American health care policymaking and politics. Poorly organized and saddled with an ineffectual reputation, the AMA had only eight thousand members in 1900, fifty-three years after its founding.[14] In 1901, the AMA leadership approved a complete grassroots reorganization that spurred a dramatic rise in membership and a corresponding escalation of the group's political clout.

Under the 1901 reorganization, the association became a confederation of state medical societies that were, in turn, composed of county-level societies within the state. By making the local chapters (some of which previously had been independent county societies) the only gateway to state and national membership, the AMA managed to bolster the ranks of all strata of the organization in one fell swoop. By 1910 membership in the AMA had soared to seventy thousand physicians, about half of the total number of doctors in the entire nation, and "physicians began to achieve the unity and coherence that had so long eluded them."[15] The AMA's exceptional rate of growth was greatly aided by a decision on the part of regular practitioners and sectarians to lay down the rhetorical, legal, and political weaponry with which they had been clubbing each other for decades. The truce stemmed in part from the late-nineteenth-century resurgence of state licensing boards, which often included both regular physicians and sectarians. Such forced proximity not only helped humanize the opposition, but also increased awareness of the many similarities in medical treatment and scientific outlook between the two camps.

The relaxing of tensions was a gradual process. When the AMA's stunning rate of growth first became evident, for example, some sectarians issued apocalyptic forecasts about its meaning. "No kingdom or monarchy throughout the world has ever had such a cursed monster to exercise iron sway over the people [as the AMA]," fumed one critic. "It is the infamy of the infamous, It is the horror of this world—the 'Black Hand' of medical robbery and murder."[16] But when the AMA issued a revised code of ethics in 1903 that eschewed the organization's traditional condemnations of fraternizing with sectarians, much of the lingering sectarian distrust dissipated. Regular medical journals offered soothing reassurances to homeopaths and other sectarians. The new code of ethics, wrote one-time sectarian critic D. W. Cathell, "will everywhere promote and foster professional unity; and, far above all else, by putting an end to partisan agitations it will increase the good repute of every worthy medical man in America."[17]

Ironically, the removal of these long-standing barricades brought about a swift decline in the number of homeopathic and eclectic practices. Although movements such as Christian Science, chiropracty, and osteopathy emerged on the fringes of health care practice around this time, the much better established homeopathic and eclectic physicians became absorbed into regular practice after medical society membership and hospital privileges were opened to them. The number of institutions dedicated to these sects plummeted. From 1900 to 1918, for instance, the number of homeopathic medical schools operating in the United States fell from twenty-two to six, and those survivors eventually expired as well. "The turn of the century was both the point of acceptance [for homeopaths and eclectics]," summarized historian Paul Starr, "and the moment of incipient disintegration."[18]

REGULATING THE MEDICAL PROFESSION

American physicians made the most of their newfound organizational assets and professional contacts. AMA members relied on fellow doctors to provide friendly testimony in malpractice suits, used their collective buying power to secure low insurance rates, exchanged news and information on the latest medical advances and industry trends, and bolstered each others' businesses by handing out referrals and lobbying for beefed-up licensing requirements for newcomers into the profession. Those physicians who failed, or were unable, to take advantage of these myriad benefits operated at an increasingly steep competitive disadvantage.

The support of the American Medical Association also was tremendously helpful to progressives demanding greater regulation of the medical profession. Reformers wanted to enforce stringent licensing requirements for anyone who wanted to practice medicine in a given state. This regulatory trend, which had gathered momentum throughout the 1870s and 1880s, became even more evident in the Progressive Era, as state after state passed laws that required would-be doctors to pass medical examinations and possess diplomas from recognized educational institutions **(See Document 4.1)**.

As the tightening regulatory requirements for medical practice suggest, reformers were determined to implement greater standardization of medical education so as to reduce—and eventually eradicate—the population of poorly trained physicians who preyed on desperate or unsuspecting people. The AMA showed that this was a priority for the organization in 1904, when it formed a permanent Council of Medical Education that surveyed and rated the country's medical schools. "The catalyst for reform [of medical colleges and licensing boards] ultimately became the reorganized American Medical Association," wrote historian Rosemary Stevens. "AMA spokesmen increasingly linked the raising of medical school standards with the reduction in the number of doctors, a philosophy which was attractive not only to the leading educators, whose search for foundation money for the schools was predicated on educational reform, but also to the struggling practitioner competing for his living in an already crowded profession. . . . The interests of Eastern professors and Midwestern general practitioners were, for a crucial period, the same."[19]

By 1910 the number of medical schools operating in the United States had shrunk from 166 in the late nineteenth century to 126. That same year, the ongoing drive to reform the nation's medical education system was electrified by the release of Abraham Flexner's *Medical Education in the United States and Canada,* a muckraking survey of the best and worst medical colleges in North America. This comprehensive firsthand analysis, funded by the Carnegie Foundation and soon known to progressives, physicians, educators, and lawmakers as the Flexner Report, painted a damning portrait of a nation afflicted by dozens of scandalously incompetent medical schools **(See Document 4.8)**. The release of the Flexner Report further ratcheted up the pressure on city and state governments to shut down these outfits, and its recommendations for increased emphasis on clinical teaching and other curriculum improvements were widely implemented. By 1915 the number of medical schools in America had been reduced to ninety-six, and fifteen years later, the nation's physicians were being trained by seventy-six schools, less than half the number that had been in existence in the late 1800s.[20] Physicians and surgeons from the elite medical universities applauded these developments as a long overdue corrective that placed America squarely in the twentieth century. "The old fashioned family physician and general practitioner was a splendid figure and useful person in his day," wrote the prominent New York physician Charles L. Dana in 1913. "But he was badly trained, he was often ignorant, he made many mistakes, for one cannot by force of character and geniality of person make a diagnosis of appendicitis, or recognize streptococcus infection."[21]

The zeal with which physicians pursued and supported restrictive regulations and policies governing entrance into their ranks contrasted vividly with their attitude toward the professionalization of nursing. Some physicians and health administrators, including a number who occupied positions of leadership in leading hospitals, top medical universities, and medical fraternities, offered full-throated endorsements of state registration or licensing of nurses, usually through accreditation of nursing schools **(See Document 4.3)**. But many other doctors, surgeons, and officials in the health care marketplace opposed these policies, despite their seemingly obvious benefits to the health and welfare of patients. The specific objections varied. Many male physicians worried that the professionalization of nursing would create a new breed of insubordinate nurse with her own ideas about patient needs and courses of treatment. One concerned Philadelphia physician asserted that nurse regulation amounted to a "positive menace to the public good. . . . Isolated and individual opposition to the will of the physician may be over-looked, but *organized opposition,* with a show of legal authority to apparently justify it, must *command prompt and effective resistance!*[22] Administrators of small community hospitals, meanwhile, had more legitimate fears about what nursing reform might mean for them. Because community hospitals had limited facilities to provide nursing students with clinical training, they worried that new accreditation requirements would make it more difficult for them to attract student nurses, an important part of the staff of many small hospitals with limited budgets.[23] But the momentum for professionalization and regulation overwhelmed these concerns. Formal education and training requirements for nurses increased in state after state. But the number of hospitals and clinics requiring large nursing staffs was soaring as well, so the introduction of nursing education stan-dards did not shrink the number of participants in the profession. In fact, the number of nursing schools jumped from 432 in 1900 to 1,129 a decade later.[24]

EMERGENCE OF THE MODERN AMERICAN HOSPITAL

The growth of professional nursing was highly beneficial in improving health care in America's hospitals, but it was hardly the only force to transform these institutions during the Progressive Era. Other institutional trends that had first become evident in the latter decades of the nineteenth century also became more pronounced during these years. These trends included increased physician control over hospital operations; absorption of independently owned dispensaries into larger hospital operations; expansion of teaching internships and residencies (which were becoming core requirements for accreditation and licensing); and surging investment in clinical laboratories, surgical equipment, diag-nostic tools (such as x-rays), and new facilities.

These operational changes, acting in concert, also accelerated a demographic shift in patient identity. In earlier times, hospitals had cared almost exclusively for the impov-erished sick and chronically ill. But as the capacity of hospitals to fix health problems through surgery and other treatments increased around the turn of the century, middle- and upper-class clients poured into both private and public hospitals.

The sheer number of hospitals operating in the United States increased during this time as well. Some of these institutions were created by entrepreneurs and corporations that recognized the growth potential of the health care industry. Religious and ethnic groups added their hospital offerings, and these facilities became vital to the education and career growth of Catholic, Jewish, and black physicians and surgeons who were denied entrance to other hospitals. Still other hospitals were created by physicians and surgeons who believed that, by establishing their own proprietary models, they could enjoy a level of autonomy (or provide a level of care) that was absent in corporate- or trustee-directed facilities.

Physician-led facilities became particularly commonplace in rural and western parts of the country that previously had no hospital facilities of any kind, and many of them enjoyed heady levels of success. "By the first World War," explained historian Charles E. Rosenberg, "respectable Americans were beginning to find their way into hos-pitals—especially, but not exclusively, for surgery. This change was taking place not only in established urban institutions, but in a network of hospitals that had mushroomed in thousands of smaller communities—many in areas where such institutions were a novelty and where a hospital stay had never carried with it the stigma of indigence. The hospital was being integrated into medical care as it already had been into medical education and the structuring of elite careers."[25]

THE GROWING PROBLEM OF HEALTH CARE COSTS

The growing sophistication and capabilities of American hospitals, physician's offices, and other health care institutions fueled escalating demand for a wide range of medical services. But these valuable services were more expensive than those offered by hospitals and physicians of yesteryear. As a consequence, the percentage of people unable to afford badly needed medical care grew with each passing year. By the early 1900s the rising cost of health care was walling off many immigrants, unskilled laborers, and other impoverished and politically powerless people from the latest advances in medical treatment, as well as causing increased consternation among middle-class families who could not easily absorb the financial blow of a surgical procedure or extended hospital stay.

As this problem attracted growing levels of political attention, many American reformers turned to Europe for guidance. In 1883 German chancellor Otto von Bismarck had launched an ambitious program of social reform that included a nationwide system of compulsory sickness insurance. This program, which gave German workers and their families more financial security in the face of medical expenses than ever before, was cited by many progressives as a model to be emulated. And, they looked on enviously as other European nations followed Germany's lead and implemented health insurance programs from the late 1880s through the early 1910s, including Austria, Great Britain, Hungary, the Netherlands, Norway, Russia, and Serbia. Other nations, meanwhile, approved government subsidies to help employees' mutual benefit societies shoulder the financial burden of providing sickness insurance to their memberships. Denmark, France, Italy, Sweden, and Switzerland all followed this course of action. Some of these systems were more ambitious than others, but all reflected an official consensus that citizens needed help dealing with galloping health costs and that healthy economies depended on a healthy citizenry.

The U.S. government, by contrast, was slow to take up the issue of soaring health care costs. Lawmakers were exceedingly wary of wading into a policy area that had so many powerful stakeholders, and progressives were tackling so many other issues that sickness insurance frequently fell through the cracks. Moreover, a patchwork of sickness insurance programs had been developed by benevolent societies, fraternal orders, local trade unions, municipal governments, and early insurance companies in the 1880s and 1890s. These programs masked the scope of the problem to some degree, but they still left millions of Americans exposed to financial ruin from medical expenses. And while the best of these programs provided workmen's compensation to members in the event of industrial accidents or illness, many others were industrial life insurance policies that only paid for funeral expenses and provided modest lump-sum payments to survivors. These types of policies became the financial lifeblood of early insurance giants such as Prudential and Metropolitan Life of New York by generating revenues far in excess of their financial outlays. "Subscribers received in benefits only about 40 percent of what they paid in premiums," wrote historian Paul Starr. "The rest went to the agents and the companies. Yet the fear of a pauper burial was so great that Americans bought $183 million of such insurance in 1911—about as much as Germany spent on its entire social insurance system."[26]

In the 1910s, the issue of national health insurance landed squarely in the laps of American policymakers. It was placed there by the American Association for Labor Legislation (AALL), an organization that had been founded in 1906 by liberal reformers dedicated to bringing compulsory health insurance to the United States. By 1913 the AALL and its indefatigable president, economist Irving Fisher, had overcome longtime political inertia and generated clear political momentum for the passage of a national insurance law. This progress was not solely due to the efforts of the AALL. The cause was given a much-needed measure of political legitimacy during the 1912 presidential campaign, when Theodore Roosevelt and his Progressive "Bull Moose" Party embraced the concept **(See Document 4.10)**. "It is abnormal to throw back upon the community the human wreckage due to its wear and tear," roared Roosevelt in his keynote speech to the Progressive Party Convention in Chicago that summer.

> The hazards of sickness, accident, invalidism, involuntary unemployment, and old age should be provided for through insurance. This should be made a charge in whole or in part upon the industries, the employer, the employee, and perhaps the people at large, to contribute severally in some degree. Wherever such standards are not met by given establishments, by given industries, are unprovided for by a legislature, or are balked by unenlightened courts, the workers are in jeopardy, the progressive employer is penalized, and the community pays a heavy cost in lessened efficiency and in misery. What Germany has done in the way of old age pensions or insurance should be studied by us, and the system adapted to our uses, with whatever modifications are rendered necessary by our different ways of life and habits of thought.[27]

The AALL crusade was also able to secure the endorsement of such disparate groups as the National Association of Manufacturers, the American Medical Association, and the Public Health Service **(See Document 4.11)**. Their cooperation enabled the reformers to blunt the opposition of influential political players such as American Federation of Labor (AFL) president Samuel Gompers and other labor leaders, who feared that unions would be weakened if government became a major provider of social benefits and economic security.

In 1913 the AMA created its own Committee on Social Insurance and appointed the AALL's Isaac M. Rubinow to serve as its executive director—a clear indication that the AMA was in AALL's camp on the national health insurance issue. Later that year, Rubinow published a landmark study of the issue, called *Social Insurance*, which became an unofficial bible for the pro–national insurance movement. Rubinow framed the crusade as one of basic social justice, and he asserted that government-run health insurance would bring a cascade of beneficial changes to American life: "Only a very small proportion of those who are in need of it are as yet provided with sick-insurance, and this is what might be termed the aristocracy of the working class," he wrote. "With very few exceptions the entire burden of the cost of sick-insurance falls upon the shoulders of the wage-workers, which is neither ethically just nor socially expedient. . . . The progressive social worker must learn to understand that a sickness insurance law, even in one state, can do more to eradicate poverty, and is, therefore, a greater social gain, than a dozen organizations for scientific philanthropy with their investigations, their sermons on thrift, and their constant feverish hunt for liberal contributions."[28]

"The Next Great Step in Social Legislation"

In 1915 Fisher and other AALL reformers drew up a model bill laying out the details for a compulsory health insurance program that could be adopted on a state-by-state basis. Under this bill, which the AALL and other supporters described as "the next great step in social legislation," state governments would establish compulsory health insurance programs for working-class citizens (and their dependents) who earned less than $1,200 annually. It covered all medical expenses (including hospital services), provided sick pay (at reduced wages), extended maternity benefits to insured women and the wives of insured men, and paid a death benefit of $50 for funeral expenses. The proposed system, which bore a clear resemblance to the long-touted German sickness insurance system, was to be funded by contributions from employees (40 percent of costs), employers (40 percent), and state governments (20 percent).[29]

Congress promptly took up debate on the bill, as did state legislatures from New York to California. Prominent health reform allies such as the AMA did their part to pressure policymakers and generate public support. High-powered AMA officials stoked the fires of reform. AMA leader Frederick A. Green, for example, declared that the bill was "exactly in line" with his own views, and AMA representatives penned supportive editorials for publication in the *Journal of the American Medical Association (JAMA)* and influential newspapers and mainstream magazines.[30] But the AALL still remained the leading voice of the health insurance movement. Buoyed by the tireless efforts of Rubinow, Fisher, and Executive Secretary John B. Andrews, the group lobbied for passage of the organization's model bill in all fifteen states where it had been introduced by the close of 1917 **(See Document 4.12)**.

For a brief window of time, it appeared that compulsory health insurance was going to become a reality in a number of those states. But the coalition of bill supporters began to unravel in late 1917, just as the measure was coming to crucial votes in bellwether states such as California (where a referendum on the measure had been prepared), Illinois (where it was being studied by the state health commission), and New York (where it was being considered by the state legislature). Corporate interests that had initially reacted mildly to the proposal began to express increased uneasiness with the financial obligations they would incur under the proposed law. Even more critically, the AMA abruptly distanced itself from the measure in response to mounting concerns from rank-and-file members that compulsory health insurance would supplant the lucrative fee-for-service payment system that they enjoyed with a less financially rewarding flat salary or capitation arrangement. Other physicians complained that government-run health insurance would subject practitioners to an unacceptable level of government oversight and regulation. The AMA subsequently closed down its Committee on Social Insurance, and in 1920 it formally repudiated "any plan embodying the system of compulsory contributory insurance against illness."[31]

The most powerful force to weigh in against compulsory health insurance was the insurance industry itself. Insurance giants such as Prudential and Metropolitan Life accurately interpreted the funeral benefit that the AALL had included in its bill as a direct threat to one of their major profit streams, so they mounted a fearsome and sustained attack on the legislation. This offensive, led by insurance executives including Frederick L. Hoffman and Lee K. Frankel, worked to portray national health insurance as a misguided example of overbearing governmental paternalism. Industry allies in government, such as New York State Assembly Speaker Thaddeus C. Sweet, chimed in by framing the AALL bill as "legislation so confiscatory and burdensome that business and industry will be abandoned."[32] In addition, the insurance giants joined with employers and doctors to establish and fund citizens' groups that demonized national health insurance. The most notorious of these outfits was the New York League for Americanism, which left no stone unturned in its efforts to poison public opinion against compulsory health insurance.

Opponents of national health reform took particular advantage of an April 1917 political gift: the United States' decision to declare war on Germany and enter World War I. With anti-German sentiment on the rise all across the country, Hoffman and other critics moved quickly to emphasize the strong parallels between the AALL proposal and the German health insurance program **(See Document 4.14)**. A few months later, health reform opponents capitalized on public anxiety about another overseas development, the Russian Revolution, insinuating that health reformers and Bolsheviks were cut from the same radical cloth.

These ruthless lines of attack outraged progressives such as John B. Andrews, who stated that "we are in the most serious situation, when thinking men and women do not propose reforms without having their patriotism attacked."[33] But the attacks, coming as they did at a time when other constituencies were mobilizing against compulsory health insurance, knocked the reformers on their heels, and they never really recovered **(See Document 4.15)**. "Without meaningful ties to the labor movement or the ability to match the political lobbying and pamphleteering of the insurance industry," wrote historian Colin Gordon, "the AALL could neither sustain political interest nor answer charges that its program was the product of Bolshevik social engineering rather than a response to the needs and demands of ordinary Americans."[34]

The compulsory health insurance bills under consideration across the country suffered accordingly. In California, where voters had been deluged with propaganda that equated health insurance reform with the "Prussianization of America," the public referendum went down to a crushing defeat in 1918, with nay votes outnumbering aye votes by a nearly three-to-one margin. In Illinois, the state commission voted down the AALL's health insurance proposal by a 7–2 count. The reformers made a last stand of sorts in New York, where they had managed to enlist significant levels of support from state labor unions. Although progressives were able to pass the bill through the state senate, it was bottled up by Sweet and his lieutenants in the state assembly. By the close of 1920, the bill was dead—and so was the progressive campaign for compulsory health insurance in America.

NOTES

1. John Duffy, *The Sanitarians: A History of American Public Health* (Chicago: University of Illinois Press, 1992), 139.

2. Quoted in Lister Hill, "Health Care in America: A Personal Perspective," in U.S. Department of Health, Education, and Welfare, U.S. Public Health Service, *Health in America: 1776–1976* (Washington, DC: Government Printing Office, 1976), 8.

3. Theodore Roosevelt, Seventh Annual Message to Congress, December 3, 1907, *The American Presidency Project,* www.presidency.ucsb.edu/ws/?pid=29548.

4. John Duffy, *A History of Public Health in New York City, 1866–1966* (New York: Russell Sage Foundation, 1968), 247.

5. Paul Starr, *The Social Transformation of American Medicine* (New York: Basic Books, 1982), 191–92.

6. James T. Bennett and Thomas J. DiLorenzo, *From Pathology to Politics: Public Health in America* (New Brunswick, NJ: Transaction Publishers, 2000), 12.

7. House Committee on Interstate and Foreign Commerce, Statement of Professor Irving Fisher, *Hearings on Health Activities of General Government,* 61st Cong., 2d sess., 1910, Part 1, 112.

8. George Rosen, "The Committee of One Hundred on National Health and the Campaign for a National Health Department, 1906–1912," *Public Health: Then and Now* (February 1972): 263.

9. Quoted in Gina Kolata, *Flu* (New York: Farrar, Straus and Giroux, 1999), 47.

10. Alfred W. Crosby, *America's Forgotten Pandemic* (Cambridge: Cambridge University Press, 1989), 205–6.

11. Quoted in Christine M. Kreiser, "The Enemy Within," *American History,* December 2006, 26.

12. Kreiser, "The Enemy Within," 28.

13. Crosby, *America's Forgotten Pandemic,* 49.

14. Starr, *The Social Transformation of American Medicine,* 109.

15. Starr, *The Social Transformation of American Medicine,* 110.

16. James C. Whorton, "From Cultism to Cam," in *The Politics of Healing: Histories of Alternative Medicine in Twentieth-Century North America,* ed. Robert D. Johnston (New York: Routledge, 2004), 292.

17. Quoted in William G. Rothstein, *American Physicians in the Nineteenth Century: From Sects to Science* (Baltimore: Johns Hopkins University Press, 1992), 332.

18. Starr, *The Social Transformation of American Medicine,* 107.

19. Rosemary Stevens, *American Medicine and the Public Interest* (New Haven, CT: Yale University Press, 1971); rev. ed. (Berkeley: University of California Press, 1998), 61–62.

20. Howard Berliner, "A Larger Perspective on the Flexner Report," *International Journal of Health Services* 5, no. 4 (1975): 573–92.

21 Charles L. Dana, "The Doctor's Future," *New York Medical Journal* 97 (1913): 3.

22. Quoted in Charles E. Rosenberg, *The Care of Strangers: The Rise of America's Hospital System* (New York: Basic Books, 1987), 233.

23. Rosenberg, *The Care of Strangers,* 233–34.

24. Jo Ann Ashley, *Hospitals, Paternalism, and the Role of the Nurse* (New York: Teachers College Press, 1976), 20.

25. Rosenberg, *The Care of Strangers,* 237.

26. Starr, *The Social Transformation of American Medicine,* 242–43.

27. Theodore Roosevelt, "My Confession of Faith," in *The Birth of the New Party: or, Progressive Democracy,* ed. George Henry Payne (Naperville, IL: J. L. Nichols, 1912), 249.

28. Isaac Max Rubinow, *Social Insurance, With Special Reference to American Conditions* (New York: Holt, 1916), 297.

29. Ronald Numbers, *Almost Persuaded: American Physicians and Compulsory Health Insurance, 1912–1920* (Baltimore: Johns Hopkins University Press, 1978), 52–59.

30. Wendy Moore, "Uninsured in America? Blame the First World War," *BMJ* (August 12, 2009), www.bmj.com/cgi/content/full/bmj.b3269?ijkey=c1TUAtz4jRvU3jj&keytype=ref.

31 Harry A. Sultz and Kristina M. Young, *Health Care USA: Understanding Its Organization and Delivery* (Sudbury, MA: Jones and Bartlett, 2008), 37

32. Quoted in Beatrix Hoffman, *The Wages of Sickness: The Politics of Health Insurance in Progressive America* (Chapel Hill: University of North Carolina Press, 2001), 163.

33. Quoted in Hoffman, *The Wages of Sickness,* 177.

34. Colin Gordon, *Dead on Arrival: The Politics of Health Care in Twentieth-Century America* (Princeton, NJ: Princeton University Press, 2003), 262.

A Wisconsin Physician Urges State Regulation of Medical Practices

"To Prevent Quacks and Ignoramuses from Obtaining Legal Recognition"

1892

The first great wave of progressive legislation targeting public health and the private health care industry was carried out at the state level. This focus reflected the United States' traditional, to that point, preference for local and state regulation over federal oversight. This orientation also stemmed from the fact that, in the late nineteenth century, state-level societies or chapters of health care professionals, who took a leading role in agitating for reform, were frequently better organized and more active than their national counterparts. These same state-level groups were also better equipped to identify and respond rapidly to the objections of reform opponents than were national groups. This capability is in evidence in the following editorial, written in 1892 by Dr. Julius Noer of Stoughton, Wisconsin. In this note, written on behalf of the Special Committee on Legislation of the Medical Society of Wisconsin, Noer defends proposed new state regulations on the practice of medicine against criticisms from several of the state's most prominent newspapers.

In view of the fact that the press of this state, the moulder and the director of public opinion, has taken every opportunity not only to ridicule the efforts of this Society to secure the passage of a law having for its object the elevation of the standard of medical education, but to actually question the right of the people to pass any such law, it would not appear to be inappropriate to attempt to make a dispassionate reply to some of the specious arguments advanced—arguments that have had no little influence in preventing legislation.

It may be well, in entering upon the discussion of a theme upon which not a little difference of opinion may be anticipated, to quote a few passages touching the subject from authorities, whose clear and explicit statements can not be disregarded on the ground of being visionary or irrational.

Says Prof. William Osler, dean of the Johns Hopkins University Medical School:

> "The right to regulate the practice of medicine rests with the State, and I believe it is everywhere acknowledged that the right comes within that general public power which extends protection to the lives and limbs of the citizen. It is universally conceded that the basis of this legislation is the necessity of protecting the people against the depredations of ignorant graduates and of quacks. The aim is to provide a minimum standard of qualification to be required of all persons who desire to follow the calling of physician and surgeon."

George F. Shrady, of the New York *Medical Record*, is not less emphatic in commendation of these laws. He says:

"The statement that laws regulating medical education and practice have done no good, and had no part in securing our present progress, is quite erroneous, and shows much ignorance of the history of medical education in this country."

"A State examining board will not secure a medical millennium, but it may prevent the development of bogus and purely business medical colleges, which turn out dishonest and ignorant men, who fail or do not seek to pass at reputable institutions."—*Medical Record,* Dec. 14, 1889.

Finally Ex-Governor John M. Hamilton, of Illinois, whom we must consider a reasonably impartial judge, says in reference to the Medical Practice Act in force in that state:

"The Medical Practice Act was primarily a police regulation. Incidentally it was educational. Primarily the purpose of the law was to rid the State of incompetent, ignorant, and dangerous mountebanks and quacks, who were carrying on a fraudulent and nefarious business by all manner of deceit in a pretended practice of medicine among the people. It was to protect the lives, the health, the morals, and the property of the people of the State from the shameless depredations of swindlers and adventurers, who, by all manner of false representations and deceptive promises, were taking advantage of the misfortunes of the people in sickness and ailments of all kinds, to still further injure their health, endanger their lives and rob them of their money.

"Incidentally the law was designed to require a reasonable amount of education to fit one for the practice of medicine before he should be allowed to enter that profession, so directly and intimately connected with the lives, the health and the happiness of the people. Both of these purposes come clearly within the police powers of the State in affording such protection to its citizens."

A long line of supreme court decisions, upholding the right of the State to regulate medical practice could be cited, but it is needless to give further proof to sustain a proposition that has been established beyond the possibility of doubt.

The opposition to the proposed Medical Practice Act, the principal aim of which is to prevent quacks and ignoramuses from obtaining legal recognition as medical practitioners, comes mainly from two sources, namely: 1st, the quacks, and 2d, the public press.

These people are very solicitous about their personal rights and the liberty of the people, when any measure is proposed that bids fair to curtail the practice of the one and the advertising patronage of the other.

What is the need, they say, of a law to regulate medical practice?

Why not let physicians regulate their own practice?

We are already overburdened with regulative laws of all kinds, and our present laws are, so far as medicine is concerned, as perfect as they can be.

For the State to require medical practitioners to possess a moral character, and a certain degree of knowledge of anatomy, physiology, chemistry, sanitary science, materia medica, therapeutics, gynecology, obstetrics, pathology, and surgery, and to furnish evidence of some training in clinical medicine, is a needless interference with personal liberty.

To show the exact position of the opposition and to avoid the possibility of a misstatement of facts, a somewhat lengthy quotation, which is certainly a lucid gem of editorial wisdom, is herewith presented:

> "The objections in general to any further legislation for the regulation of the practice of medicine in Wisconsin have been presented at each session of the legislature for many years, and they have been effective, so far, in preventing the passage of the stereotype bill or any of its modifications. Legislators have not considered it desirable or to the advantage of the people that the State should give a certificate of professional efficiency to any doctor, since it is impossible that the State should be able to determine the qualifications of any practitioner. It has not been regarded as proper that the State, which is qualified to charter medical schools, should formally and directly issue diplomas through a state board when it can have no means to determine adequately the qualifications of applicants for a certificate that is practically a state indorsement and a diploma. It has been the deliberate conclusion of seven or eight legislatures in this State before which these medical bills have been urged, that the present law is as effective in the protection of the people as any law can be; that the mischief any of the proposed bills would work would not be counterbalanced by any public benefit; that the expense of the proposed board is a useless waste of public funds; that the mortality in Wisconsin is not as high as in other states where such laws are in operation; that there is no popular demand for the proposed legislation, which is urged by organized medical practitioners alone."—*Sentinel,* Feb'y 20, 1891.

If you should succeed in proving that the State has decided that it does possess the means by which "it can determine adequately the qualification of medical practitioners" they retort, that medicine is all humbug and hence entitled to no protection, as the following extract illustrates: "There is no evidence whatever that any accepted theory of the action of remedies is sound—and no conclusive evidence that the medical treatment of disease is less delusive than any other treatment—no evidence that the medical treatment of disease is not, what Carlyle calls it, 'a practice of fundamentally wrong principles.' As far as the State is concerned, it does not know, it cannot know, that a knowledge of what are called the fundamental branches of medicine is essential to the successful treatment of the sick, or that the absence of such knowledge disqualifies one for the successful treatment of the sick. Certainly the reality of cures by educated physicians rests on no better evidence than the reality of cures by Jim Lee, alias Gun Wa, by faith healers, by jim-jammie snapping doctors, by impossible high dilutions of homeopathic medicines."—*Sentinel,* March 2, 1891.

When this sort of buncomb is gravely propounded, as argument, by a man who wields an editorial pen on the staff of one of the largest papers in this state, it is small wonder that people lose faith in scientific medicine and go to the quack, who proclaims his wonderful discoveries and great virtues in the next column of the same paper. It is frankly admitted that it would be an impossible task to prove to the author of this diatribe, that medicine is a science, or has performed any service to humanity that would entitle it to legal recognition.

To him the services and the achievements of Harvey, of Jenner, of Pasteur, of Virchow, of Lister, or of J. Marion Sims, are of no significance, for "the reality of their cures is based upon no better evidence than the reality of cures by faith healers," and the frauds who "advertise in the newspapers."

To estimate the value of scientific medicine to the public by the cures performed, is a gross injustice.

The greatness and the glory of the science of medicine is its achievements in the prevention of disease, and not its cure. For a proof of this fact, it is sufficient to cite one single instance where medical science, represented by a body of men worthy of its name, was of the most singular benefit to our people, both from a commercial and humanitarian standpoint. I refer to the services of the "National Board of Health" during the recent memorable epidemic of yellow fever in the south.

The inefficiency of civil authorities and shot-gun quarantine, unaided by the strong hand of science, was thoroughly established before the National Board was organized and given the power necessary for the suppression of the demon.

The number of lives saved, and amount of suffering prevented, as well as the value of the services of this board to commerce, cannot be estimated in dollars and cents. Their services stand out, however, in bold relief, proving conclusively the great value of scientific medicine to humanity, when followed out to its logical conclusions by men of ability, and scientific learning.

It is for legal recognition of medicine as represented by men of this character that we are pleading, in asking the legislature of this commonwealth to dethrone ignorance and fraud, and place in their stead the votaries of science.

No one asks the passage of this bill on the sole ground that it is a benefit to the profession. It is in the interest and for the protection of humanity that we urge legislative action in this matter. In other words, we demand that the State require, that those to whose care is entrusted the life and the health of the community, shall be men who possess a high degree of intellectual and moral qualifications—a qualification commensurate in a degree with the duties and responsibilities involved.

We take upon ourselves the task of urging this reform, which is received with so much disfavor by our friends of the press, on the same broad and philanthropic principle upon which we have advocated the establishment of boards of health for the prevention of disease and suffering. The fact that boards of health seriously interfere with our practice, and our income, cannot be successfully contradicted. These organizations, which are of such signal benefit to the public, but so detrimental to our practice, are maintained almost entirely through the services of skilled and educated physicians. Their establishment and maintenance has at all times received the most enthusiastic support of the profession. Can any one point to an example of a more noble, a more unselfish, and a more heroic devotion to the cause of humanity?

Now, can it be possible, as is alleged by the press, that a profession with such a record can give its support to any measure from merely selfish and mercenary motives?

In proof of the fact that the State possesses ample means by which to test the educational and moral qualifications of medical practitioners, it is simply necessary to point to the solution of this problem in over thirty States of the Union, the Dominion of Canada, and every country upon the European Continent.

The statistics furnished by the various Boards of Medical Examiners in these different States and countries are conclusive evidence on this point.

Our own State has in fact admitted this by the enactment of similar laws requiring dentists, lawyers, and pharmacists to pass an educational and moral test before a State Board of Examiners.

It seems remarkable that the pharmacist who compounds your prescription should be required by the State to know something of the chemistry, therapeutics, and toxicology of the drugs you direct him to prepare, while you, who are the responsible party in the case, and the one to whom the patient looks for knowledge, become legally involved only after it can be demonstrated that your compound has killed or seriously injured the patient—a demonstration which in the nature of things is quite difficult. I protest that this post mortem responsibility is not favorable to the life and general welfare of the patient.

Legal prosecution, I must contend, is of little benefit to a dead man, or one whose health has been ruined. The legal remedy should, in the true spirit of modern preventive medicine, be applied to the character and the brains of the would-be prescriber, in such a way as to hinder him from obtaining an opportunity to either kill or jeopardize the life of the patient.

Source: Noer, Julius. "The Regulation of Medical Practice by the State." *Transactions of the State Medical Society of Wisconsin for the Year 1892.* Vol. 26. Madison, WI: Tracy, Gibbs & Co., 1892, pp. 323–29.

DOCUMENT 4.2

Political Warfare over Smallpox Treatment in Milwaukee

"Laws Are Not Enforced Because the Common Council Has Prevented Me"

1894

Although the years surrounding the close of the nineteenth century saw a considerable expansion in governmental regulation of public health and sanitation, this evolution did not always proceed smoothly. Resistance to expanded local, state, or federal powers was sometimes fierce, although the underlying reasons for this resistance varied from locale to locale.

In Milwaukee, Wisconsin, for example, an 1894 smallpox vaccination campaign carried out under the auspices of the city's health department imploded in spectacular fashion in a toxic cloud of political gamesmanship, ethnic tensions, and public ignorance of contagious disease vectors. As historian Judith Walzer Leavitt noted, the foundations of the debacle were laid in early 1894, when a local alderman representing city wards with a high percentage of residents of German origin expressed reservations about the city's new health commissioner, Walter Kempster, a recent arrival to Milwaukee and a man of English heritage. Kempster's relations with Milwaukee's Common Council further deteriorated when the commissioner tried to end the political patronage that had traditionally dictated employment in the health department, but they did not reach truly abysmal levels until the summer of 1894, when the city was hit by a smallpox outbreak.

Kempster responded promptly to the smallpox threat with a sensible and time-proven plan to contain the outbreak. He launched a citywide vaccination campaign, approved an education program to help the public understand the disease and its causes, and moved decisively to isolate smallpox sufferers, either by quarantining them in their homes or by moving them to Milwaukee's isolation hospital, which was located in the city's crowded South Side. Kempster was aided in the latter effort by existing city ordinances that gave him the authority to relocate smallpox patients to the hospital by force if necessary. But many city residents refused to cooperate, and the disease spread rapidly. Resistance to health department measures was particularly strong among South Siders, who blamed high neighborhood levels of smallpox on the pesthouse in their midst. By early August Kempster's foes on the city council were openly encouraging residents to defy the health department's vaccination and quarantine efforts. "Crowds of people took to the streets, seeking out health officials to harass," wrote Leavitt. "Quarantine officials watching guard over houses were frequently the object of the mob's attack. With thousands of people roaming the streets and entering houses infected with smallpox, the contagion was destined to spread throughout the district." As the unrest grew, some rioters even called for the execution of Kempster, who in the words of Leavitt, had come to symbolize "arbitrary governmental authority which was subverting immigrant culture and threatening personal liberty."

The turmoil paralyzed Kempster's health department, which was unable to carry out virtually any of its vaccination or quarantine duties. Sensing weakness, Kempster's political foes pounced, introducing a flurry of resolutions to strip the commissioner of his regulatory powers. "The laws are not enforced because the Common Council has prevented me," Kempster opined in a meeting with city doctors and businessmen. "Proposition after proposition has been made [by council members] to revise the laws as they now are. This has caused opposition among the people. We come to a house to remove a patient and are resisted. They tell us that their alderman informed them that next week the laws will be changed and they need not go. I have been tied hand and foot with investigations, injunctions and work that is never finished." [1]

The city remained mired in political warfare between pro- and anti-Kempster factions throughout the fall, even as the epidemic continued to rage. On November 26, 1894, the Common Council passed an ordinance, excerpted here, that made it impossible for the city health department to admit patients to the isolation hospital without their consent. At the same time that this legislation stripped Kempster of one of his most important epidemic-fighting powers, his political opponents engineered impeachment proceedings against him on the grounds of gross professional misconduct. During the course of this investigation, leading physicians from the Milwaukee Medical Society and the Wisconsin Board of Health strongly defended Kempster. By this time, however, the storm of politically inspired protests against him could not be tamed. In February 1895 the Common Council voted 22–14 to dismiss Kempster. This decision was excoriated in the city's English-language newspapers but was warmly received by the editors and writers of newspapers allegiant to Milwaukee's German immigrants. [2]

The mayor and common council of the city of Milwaukee, do ordain as follows:

Section 1. Section 3 of the ordinance entitled "An ordinance to amend section 199 of the general ordinances of the city of Milwaukee relating to the city hospital and the duties of the commissioner of health in connection therewith" is hereby amended so as to read as follows: "It shall be the duty of the commissioner of health to place in said hospital, under the care of competent nurses any person who may be found in the city of Milwaukee laboring under any of the following diseases, viz: Small-pox, diphtheria, scarlet fever, measles, typhus fever or any other dangerous, contagious or infectious diseases, when such person is a non-resident of this city, a traveler, a guest at a hotel, or has no residence of his own in this city where he can be taken care of. But the commissioner of health shall not remove to any Isolation Hospital in said city any child or person suffering from any such disease who can be nursed and cared for during such illness in his or her home during the continuance of the disease except upon the recommendation and advice of the said commissioner of health or one of the assistant commissioners of health, and the physician, if any, attending upon such child or person, not being a member of the health department of said city; and in case such commissioner, or assistant commissioner and such physician shall be unable to agree as to the advisability of removing such child or person, then they shall call in and appoint another physician not a member of the health department, and the decision of the majority of such physicians and commissioner or assistant commissioner shall be decisive of the question.

"The third physician called in, as above provided, shall not receive or be entitled to any fees from the city for consultation or service in the decision of the case submitted to such board of physicians." . . .

Any person suffering with small-pox who shall be removed to any Isolation Hospital in said city shall be conveyed there in an ambulance which shall be used for the purpose of removing persons suffering with small-pox only, and such persons shall not be taken to said hospital in any other vehicle or conveyance whatsoever. Whenever any person who may have recovered from any of said contagious diseases shall be dismissed from said hospital it shall be the duty of said commissioner of health to cause such person to be conveyed to his place of residence in said city of Milwankee [sic], in a proper vehicle to be kept and used, or hired for such purpose. The commissioner of health shall keep daily record of the condition of each patient confined in any Isolation Hospital in said city, and whenever he shall be requested thereto by any parent, guardian, relative or friend of such person, he shall furnish them with a copy of said report, verified by the signature of the secretary of the health department. Whenever any person who may have been removed to any Isolatiou [sic] Hospital in said city shall be so dangerously ill that his recovery is doubtful the commissioner of health shall at once notify the parents, guardians, relatives or friends of such person, and if any one of them shall desire to be admitted to said Isolation Hospital for the purpose of nursing and caring for said patient the commissioner of health shall give them a permit to enter and remain in said hospital for such purpose.

Source: "137—An Ordinance." *Milwaukee Common Council Proceedings, 1894–1895.* Ordinances Appendix, pp. 22–23.

NOTES

1. Quoted in Judith Walzer Leavitt, *The Healthiest City: Milwaukee and the Politics of Health Reform,* 2nd ed. (Madison: University of Wisconsin Press, 1996), 106.

2. Judith Walzer Leavitt, "Politics and Public Health: Smallpox in Milwaukee, 1894–1895," *Bulletin of the History of Medicine* 50, no. 4 (Winter 1976): 553–68.

A Famous Health Reformer Endorses State Registration of Nurses

"Trained Nursing Counts For as Much If Not More Than Any Scientific Discovery"

1903

Progressive reforms of the health care industry took myriad forms during the opening decades of the twentieth century. In addition to long-standing concerns with physicians' practices and training, reformers focused on such issues as registration of trained nurses, which was seen by proponents as vital to ensuring quality medical care in the nation's rapidly growing hospital system. In December 1903 the Johns Hopkins Nurses Alumnae Association gathered to discuss the issue. The meeting was chaired by M. Adelaid Nutting, longtime superintendent of nurses at Johns Hopkins Hospital and the first registered nurse in Maryland. It featured several guest speakers who offered full-throated endorsements of the nurses' proposed legislation, including Maryland judge Henry D. Harlan and physician, educator, and administrator William Henry Welch.

Welch's approval was no small matter, for he was one of the most famous medical men of the Progressive Era. Brilliant and energetic, Welch became the first dean of Johns Hopkins University's School of Medicine in 1894 and the first dean of its School of Hygiene and Public Health upon its founding in 1916. He also served at various times as president of such organizations as the Congress of American Physicians and Surgeons, American Association for the Advancement of Science, American Medical Association, and the National Academy of Sciences, and he sat at the helm of the Maryland State Board of Health from 1898 to 1922. The full text of Welch's remarks at the December 1903 meeting are reprinted here.

I knew nothing of this very interesting movement to secure state organization on your part, with special reference to securing legislation to guard your interests, until the other day when Miss Nutting told me about it, and, as soon as I heard the facts I was extremely interested and I deem it a privilege to be here and to express my interest in this movement. I feel confident that it will succeed because it is so manifestly right. Judge Harlan has said, it seems to me, all that can be said about this question. I am sure it requires no argument to convince you of the importance and the justness of its aim. Still Miss Nutting has suggested that a few words as to the efforts to secure similar recognition on the part of the medical profession may interest you, and even throw out a few hints to guide you.

In more stable countries of Europe with longer established civilization it has been recognized for centuries that the mere title of doctor of medicine conferred by a teaching body should not carry with it the license to practise medicine, the reason being manifestly that medical schools cannot be absolutely relied upon by the state to insure the capability of the candidate as regards requisite training and knowledge. Therefore in Germany, France and England one will find that there exist boards appointed or recognized by the state which must examine the candidate before he is given the right to practise his profession. The degree of doctor of medicine there does not carry with it a license to practise medicine and many practising physicians in Germany have no degree of doctor of medicine; they are simply licensed by the state, because to obtain the degree of doctor of medicine does not require so severe an examination as does the state examining board and it does not mean so much to the physician as a license from the state. It costs a little money and a great many do not take the trouble to procure the degree.

In the earlier days of America it was very important to secure a sufficient number of doctors to provide for the needs of the community and therefore no obstacles were put in the way of persons desiring to follow this profession, however imperfectly. Every effort was necessary to secure enough doctors so that when we endeavored to have state examining boards to confer a license to practise there existed large interests which were naturally opposed to any interference with the existing state of affairs. The lesson which you may possibly draw from this is that the longer you wait to secure state legislation the greater difficulty you will have; that it will be easier this year than it will be years ahead, so that the sooner you proceed in this matter the greater are the chances of success.

These licensing boards are, of course, matters of state legislation according to our form of government; they are of necessity matters of state legislation. We realize that it would be better, if it were possible, as it is not, to secure national control of this matter so that the qualifications should be alike throughout the country, but it has to be left to each state to prescribe what shall be the qualifications of the practising physician. It results in this, that the laws and the specified qualifications in the different states are so diverse that it is almost impracticable for one state setting up high standards to recognize a license which has been obtained in some other state with inferior qualifications and much lower standard. I hope, therefore, that in this state you will aim to secure such standards as are equal to the best. If that is not possible, get what you can, but, if possible, set up a standard that will be recognized not only here but in all the states of the country, so that a nurse who is a registered nurse in the state of Maryland shall by that very fact be recognized as qualified to practise her profession in any state of the union. I do not know that you will encounter the question that we have in the medical profession, that is, the great problem of reciprocity between the different states, but it is a matter for you to consider. The underlying difficulty has been just what I have stated, that the qualifications have been so little uniform in the different states that as a result a physician who has passed his examination and has been perhaps for a number of years practising in a given state finds great difficulty in changing his residence and engaging in practice in another state; he may no longer be able to pass the requisite examination.

Another matter, of course, was the granting of the most liberal recognition of all existing rights to practise under the original law and I take it that that will also be judiciously considered on your part. The great benefits of the law be in the future. Be therefore liberal, I should say, in the recognition of those who are already engaged in the profession. Of course none of those will be required to take the examination at all. Those who meet certain qualifications that you will decide upon will, of course, register, if this law is secured, as trained nurses, without submitting to any examination. The examination will pertain only to those who enter the profession after the law is in effect.

You are only endeavoring to secure for your profession what has already been secured for other professions. You are not therefore asking for anything that is novel, that is experimental, or the application of any new principles of legislation whatever. The conditions differ little as regards nurses than as regards physicians, or pharmacists, or dentists, or lawyers, all of whose professions are amply protected now by the law. It is not for the present and doubtless it will never be considered judicious to prescribe that those who do not meet your qualifications shall be hindered from the practice of nursing. . . . It is clear that such a purpose would encounter an overwhelming opposition. You ask for nothing of the kind. Everyone is permitted to practise the art of nursing. You simply ask that some definite meaning shall be attached to the term trained and registered nurse, that meaning implying that those qualified to register have had a certain definite training.

Now if all training schools in the country had high standards of education, similar periods of study and equal facilities or giving practical training, it might be questioned whether there was any urgent necessity for this registration of nurses. In the earlier days very likely such a need did not exist, but now the very fact that this movement has arisen and obtained in these three or four years since it began such momentum indicates that there is need for making clear in what the qualifications of a trained nurse really should consist.

The art of nursing, as Judge Harlan has stated, is a profession that is of the highest rank. It is one eminently fitted for women, it is one that requires a long period of training, one that requires special qualifications in the way of education on the part of the nurse, and I may say that I consider, although I am not a practitioner of medicine, that there is no improvement in modern medicine which outranks in importance, in its value in the prevention and cure of disease, the introduction of the system of trained nurses. One can put one's finger on great discoveries in medicine, the relation of bacteria, we will say, to the causation of disease, which is of the greatest interest in the progress of medicine, but so far as the treatment of disease is concerned the application of the system of trained nursing counts for as much, if not more than any scientific discovery in medicine. So important is it that it is the main factor in the treatment and management of a number of the important and prevalent diseases. The benefits, therefore, which will come from the passage of this law in a measure are to you as a body of trained nurses, but in larger measure to the medical profession and in still larger measure to the whole community, to the general public. Therefore it seems to me that all the enlightened forces of society should be interested in the furtherance of this great movement on your part.

The details of the law remain to be determined.

As I understand it you are here today to form a State Association of Trained Nurses. I suppose you will consider what shall be the qualifications for membership in that association. The organization of such an association seems to be an essential measure in providing for such a law. I have glanced over the laws which have been passed in New York and other states that have secured such legislation and find that in most of them the existence of such a state association was recognized.

An important feature of the law is an indication of the requisite preliminary training of the nurse. There may be some of you who will want to set that standard very high and others to set it much lower. I suppose that the minimum standard at present would be a two years' period of study; that anything shorter than that would be regarded as insufficient for the qualifications of a nurse to receive the state right to register.

The great advantage of this legislation will be for you, as it has been for the medical profession, an elevation of the standards of education of the trained nurse. It will not be interfering with the practice of nursing. It will not drive out, I think, the incompetent and untrained nurse, but the lines will be more sharply drawn than now between the unskilled, untrained nurse and the trained nurse, and the community can know whether the person claiming to be a trained nurse really is a thoroughly trained nurse. It will have an effect, of course, upon the inferior training schools, those which none of you here I am sure would for a moment vouch for; schools with only short terms. I understand that there are schools giving only two or three months training and graduating nurses at the end of that time; schools in small hospitals devoted to only one class or a few classes of disease. In that way it is impossible for a nurse to receive the sort of training which can be obtained only in a general hospital.

Also there will be as a result of this law some line drawn between the recognized training schools and those not recognized. They are perhaps better able to do that in the state of New York than in any other state in the Union. They can do that better for medical schools in New York in consequence of the existence of a Board of Regents as the guardian of higher education. Just how you can have a list of the so-called recognized training schools remains for you to consider. Of course you need not specify in your law the training schools recognized in New York, but in the practical working of the law doubtless you will be very much influenced by the New York recognition of such schools. The law should provide therefore that no one is eligible for registration without a specified preliminary training in a recognized training school,—one where the standards are sufficiently high. But you must not, at least at the beginning, make these standards too high, I think, or you will endanger the chances of securing the legislation. You must be liberal in that respect and consider what it is wise to require.

You have to consider exactly how to proceed to secure the state examining board. I noticed in several of the states that the law was almost imperilled by efforts to secure the presence of physicians upon these examining boards. Now I am quite sure that it is not the function of physicians to examine nurses. They have something to say in the training of the nurses; the nurse should not go forth without having come under the guidance of the physicians, but your profession is a skilled profession which requires special knowledge and a special knowledge that is possessed by the trained nurse and not by the physician. Akin as are the profession of medicine and of nursing, they are still distinct professions, and there is no necessity, in my opinion, and there are certain disadvantages, in the requirement that physicians should be members of the examining board. Most of these laws provide that the examining board shall consist of persons chosen, or at least nominated, by the state association, and that seems to me probably the wisest method.

These two features then are the ones which insure that the registered nurse has the requisite training and knowledge. They insure that she has been graduated from a recognized training school, one with proper standards as regards the period of study and practical training. The law further provides that after the nurse has given evidence that she possesses the preliminary training she must pass an examination, not by her own training school, where conditions come in that do not absolutely insure the necessary qualifications, but before a separate and distinct examining board. Those are the essential features of the law as I understand it—the existence in the first place of a State Association of Nurses, in the second place a provision in the law for a suitable preliminary training, and in the third place, passing the examination of a board of examiners, who have not of necessity been the candidate's own teachers.

What objection can possibly be raised against this desire on the part of the nurse's profession ? No real objection, but you are likely, I suppose, to encounter some opposition and I suppose that opposition will be based upon the idea that such a law sets up an unjustifiable distinction; that it sets apart a certain class from others. But the distinction is one eminently desirable, namely that the term "registered nurse" shall mean that here we have nurses who possess certain defined qualifications. . . . Perhaps the best argument is that of the benefit to the whole community, because the great majority of people at present have no way of determining who are the really qualified nurses, while the institution of the title of "registered nurse" would overcome this difficulty.

From every point of view that occurs to me your movement is one that should have the support and sympathy especially of the members of the legal profession, of the members of the medical profession and of all women who are interested in improving the opportunities for women of higher professional and practical work as indeed skilled nursing is a great field for women's activity. I wish you all success in your efforts, and shall be glad to be of any assistance to you in my power in securing the desired legislation.

Source: Welch, William Henry. "State Registration of Trained Nurses." Report of an Address Delivered before the Johns Hopkins Nurses Alumnae Association, 1903. *Papers and Addresses by William Henry Welch.* Vol. 3. Baltimore: Johns Hopkins Press, 1920, pp. 157–62.

DOCUMENT
4.4

Government Guidelines for the Medical Inspection of Immigrants

"It Is Usually Well to Commence at the Feet and Proceed Upward"

1903

In 1891 Congress passed a law requiring all immigrants entering the United States to undergo medical examination from federal health inspectors. This law, which took inspection responsibilities away from individual states and transformed Ellis Island (opened in 1892) into the largest public health operation in the nation's history, was the product of a variety of political and social forces. It reflected growing public concern with urban health and sanitation issues, organized labor's conviction that new immigrants posed a threat to job and wage security, and the xenophobic sentiments of nativists. But it also signified a belief, ascendant during the Progressive Era, that, through the careful application of medical knowledge and diligent screening, America had the capacity to separate diseased immigrant "chaff" from healthy immigrant "wheat." The following is an excerpt from a 1903 publication of the Public Health and Marine Hospital Service (the agency name was shortened to the PHS in 1912). These medical inspection guidelines detail some of the procedures that federal health inspectors were expected to follow when conducting physical examinations of new immigrant arrivals.

An act of Congress approved March 3, 1891, provides "That the following classes of aliens shall be excluded from admission into the United States, in accordance with the existing acts regulating immigration, other than those concerning Chinese laborers: all idiots, insane persons, paupers, or persons likely to become a public charge, persons suffering from a loathsome or a dangerous contagious disease," etc. Officers of this Service who have been detailed to make the medical inspection of arriving aliens, or physicians temporarily employed for that purpose, are directed to place in the possession of the Commissioner of Immigration, or other officer of the port under whose direction the inspection of the arriving aliens is being conducted, such information regarding the mental and physical condition of the aliens inspected as will enable the proper officials to determine whether any of them belong to one of the above-named excluded classes.

For the instruction and information of those charged with making the medical inspection of arriving aliens, attention is called to the following:

For the purpose of carrying out the provisions of the immigration law, diseased, abnormal, crippled, and deformed aliens may be regarded as divisible into two general classes—

Class A.—Those who are excluded from admission into the country by reason of the existence of a disease or abnormal condition of a character expressly declared by the law itself to constitute a ground for such exclusion.

Class B.—Those who present some disease or defect, physical or mental, which may be regarded as conclusive or contributory evidence to justify the exclusion, by the proper immigration officers, of the person in question as an alien "likely to become a public charge."

In accordance with the present law, aliens of Class A must fall within one of the four subdivisions of that class, viz:

(1) Persons suffering from dangerous contagious diseases.

(2) Persons suffering from loathsome diseases.

(3) Insane persons.

(4) Idiots.

Care should be taken to see that the form of the medical certificate in every case is such as to enable the immigration officers to see clearly to which class the alien in question belongs, and caution should be exercised especially in placing an alien in any of the subdivisions of Class A, because boards of special inquiry have no alternative but to exclude in such cases.

The medical examination should be made by daylight and never, except in an emergency, attempted in poorly lighted rooms or by artificial light. The preliminary line inspection should, be conducted on an even, level surface, so that the passengers may not be tempted to look where they are stepping. A basin containing a disinfecting solution should be placed near the examiner, so that he may disinfect his hands after handling cases of trachoma, favus, etc. Care should be taken to prevent crowding, to maintain a single file evenly spaced, with the individuals well separated (10 feet).

Whenever it can possibly be avoided, immigrants should not be permitted to take their baggage with them while undergoing inspection, because it interferes with the view of the examiner. There should be abundant light coming from behind the examiner. Direct sunshine or its reflection from the water directly in the faces of the approaching passengers must be avoided, as it causes them to squint or look down. Care should be taken to obviate the necessity of the passenger passing from a shadow into a light or vice versa. The file should make a right angle turn immediately in front of the examiner's position. This enables the examiner to observe both sides and the back of the passenger in the shortest possible time, besides bringing out lameness, defective eyesight (through passenger's efforts to adjust his vision to a new course), artificial eyes, conical opacities or roughened cornea (through light striking eye at changing angles of incidence as passenger turns). A clear view of the eyes may be secured by holding up a finger or some small object in front of the passenger just before he reaches the examiner. The examiner should not permit a passenger to approach nearer than 12 to 15 feet before beginning the scrutiny. In making this preliminary scrutiny it is well to follow a systematic plan. It is usually well to commence at the feet and proceed upward, reserving the matter of the eyes as the last feature to be inspected.

Cases turned aside for special examination, as well as any others to whom the attention of the examiner has been brought, should be subjected to a sufficiently thorough physical examination to determine whether there are other defects besides those which primarily attracted attention. The examiner should detain any alien or aliens as long as may be necessary to insure a correct diagnosis.

Source: *U.S. Book of Instructions for the Medical Inspection of Immigrants.* Washington, DC: Government Printing Office, 1903, pp. 5–6.

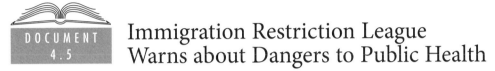

DOCUMENT 4.5 — Immigration Restriction League Warns about Dangers to Public Health

"We Do Not Want Any More of This Class of Immigrants"

1904

During the late nineteenth century, nativists, labor groups, and other immigration opponents integrated public health, which was emerging as a significant policy issue, into much of their anti-immigration rhetoric. They asserted that if lawmakers failed to curtail the flood of immigrants into America, feared diseases such as trachoma, syphilis, and tuberculosis would spread like wildfire, and the nation as a whole would become riddled with sickness. This line of argument was particularly favored by the Immigration Restriction League (IRL), the foremost of the many anti-immigration organizations that flourished around the turn of the century. Originally founded in 1894 by a handful of elite Bostonians alarmed by the growing political influence of Irish Americans in their city, the group quickly attracted adherents from across the country, including leading industrialists and members of Congress. The following IRL document excerpt begins by framing present immigration trends as an "astounding" drain on the federal Treasury, then moves on with a fairly representative sampling of public health concerns that the organization trumpeted as part of its efforts to shut down the stream of immigrants entering the United States.

COMPOSITION OF PRESENT IMMIGRATION.

Since 1880 there has been an average annual immigration of about 474,380 persons. The greatest number of persons who came in any one year was 857,046, in the fiscal year 1902-1903. Of this number 254,665, or nearly one-third, were destined to New York State, the Italians numbering 101,226, the Hebrews, 50,945, and the Poles, 16,018. There were in all about 195,000 from eastern and southern Europe, while the remainder were from western Europe. By eastern and southern Europe is meant Russia, Austria-Hungary, Italy, Turkey,

Bulgaria, Serbia, etc., and by western Europe, Great Britain, Scandinavia, Germany, France, Switzerland, Spain and Portugal.

The financial condition of those who came to New York may be estimated by referring to the report of the US Industrial Commission, page 284, from which it appears that south Italians brought on an average $8.84, Hebrews, $8.67, and Poles, $9.94 each. It must be conceded that this is not a large amount for a person to live on in New York while looking for work. Another very significant fact is that while of the total immigration last year, 71.3 per cent. came from eastern and southern Europe and 23.8 per cent, from western Europe, out of the total immigration destined to New York State nearly 80 per cent, was from eastern and southern Europe, while about 20 per cent, was from western Europe. This is unanswerable evidence that the former peoples tend to seek settled and, in many instances, overcrowded centres of population, while the latter class are more inclined to distribute themselves.

THE PRESENT LAWS INADEQUATE.

There are few, if any, who will not agree that we should rigorously exclude criminals, paupers and those who are physically incapacitated. Laws to that effect have been on the statute books for some time. In 1875, convicts and immoral women were prohibited; in 1882, lunatics, idiots and persons unable to care for themselves; in 1891, paupers and persons suffering from loathsome and contagious disease; and in 1903, epileptics, persons who have been insane within five years previous, professional beggars and anarchists were prohibited. It would therefore seem that there has for some time been no possibility of the admission of these three general classes of aliens, viz., criminals, paupers and those physically incapable. Yet what is the actual condition in this State? According to the *New York Press*, March 2, 1904, Dr. Petersen and Mr. Lockwood of the New York State Lunacy Commission appealed to the Secretary of the Department of Commerce and Labor for aid in keeping alien insane from becoming a burden to the State. These gentlemen are reported as stating that New York is expending the enormous sum of $10,000,000 *annually for the support of alien-born insane*; that 60 per cent. of the inmates of the insane asylums of the State were of alien birth, and that no less than 150 insane aliens who had been inmates of foreign insane asylums now awaited deportation. Is not this an astounding condition, and is it not sufficient ground of itself for a more severe scrutiny of incoming aliens than the present law directs? This tax of a dollar a year for each resident of New York State to maintain alien insane is by no means all of the burden. Dr. George F. Shrady writes:

> "Look at the constant stream of immigrants coining to this port. Two-thirds of the patients in our hospitals are foreigners."

There recently appeared a statement which has not been contradicted, to the effect that twenty of the principal New York City hospitals had an annual aggregate deficit of about $450,000, and various methods were suggested by which this deficit could be met. If Dr. Shrady's statement is a fact, and an inspection of the reports of several hospitals indicates that it is, would not the solution of this problem be in this very immigration question that we are considering? Is it not manifestly the proper thing to do to see that no more such aliens come? . . .

Thus it is evident that the aliens who are diseased and cared for in public and private institutions are an enormous tax upon the commonwealth.

Serious Danger from Diseased Immigrants.

Trachoma.

There are many immigrants, who, although they are not supported by others, constitute a menace to the communities in which they reside, because they are afflicted with disease in primary stages which does not interfere with their ability to do certain kinds of work. The most important of these diseases are trachoma, syphilis and tuberculosis. Take, for example, the present condition of persons afflicted with trachoma, of whom there are said to be 40,000 in this city alone, where practically none existed five years ago. The Board of Education and the Board of Health have found it necessary to examine the pupils in the public schools at frequent intervals in order to check the spread of trachoma among children. This disease has been introduced and extended almost entirely by aliens from southern and eastern Europe. The report of Special Inspector Marcus Braun, contained in the Report of the Commissioner-General of Immigration for 1903, contains the following:

> "In Hungary this disease [trachoma] has assumed such proportions that the government encounters great difficulty in some counties to muster the required men for military service, trachomatic people belonging to the class who are rejected for the army. To combat and, if possible, stamp out the disease, the Hungarian government maintains a special medical corps, consisting of fifty physicians who constantly travel to and fro, in certain respective districts to which they are assigned, it being the duty of every person to submit to an examination for such disease and, if found afflicted therewith, to present himself or herself for gratuitous treatment twice a week until cured. . . . Although this rule is strictly enforced, *people intending to emigrate rarely observe it* [italics are the writer's], and in order to be able to give the Department more definite information on this subject, I accompanied Dr. Simon Buchwald, one of the physicians appointed by the government of Hungary for the district of Lipto-Szt. Miklos, on one of his tours through the villages of his district, and was present at the examinations and treatment conducted by him. I succeeded in obtaining from Dr. Buchwald an extract of the official record of 35 persons of the age ranging from 17 to 42 years, *who had left the district for the United States and were afflicted with trachoma, had been treated by him, and at the time of their departure were not cured. Only four of these emigrants returned to their respective homes, having been refused at the medical examination regularly held at the control stations of the North German Lloyd and Hamburg American Lines at the Austro-Prussian border, upon the ground of this very affliction.* . . . [Italics are the writer's.] There are at least 60,000 persons in the Kingdom of Hungary suffering from trachoma. The worst conditions in this respect prevail in Russia, where at least 30 per cent. of the army are afflicted with this dread disease, who, after their discharge from the army, spread the affliction in all parts of the empire."

On page 6 of the report of the Commissioner-General it is stated that 572,726 aliens came from Austria-Hungary, Italy, and Russia, the very countries which Mr. Braun reports as being particularly affected by trachoma. The present law prohibits any person having this disease from landing. Of the number of persons deported last year, 748 were afflicted with trachoma. During the voyage from Europe these persons were in close association with their fellow passengers. How close that association is, only those who have visited the steerage quarters and seen 200 or more men, women and children in one open compartment, with no privacy, can realize. This contact is maintained from six to fifteen days, according to the time the vessel occupies on the voyage. From the nature of the case, no positive evidence can be submitted, but it is not unreasonable to say that each of the 748 innoculated at least one other person on the ship. Upon being inspected at Ellis Island, this would not be apparent because the period of incubation is not passed. As a result, probably 748 or more cases of trachoma were introduced into our midst last year, and we have no protection against it.

Tuberculosis.

Tuberculosis is a disease that is becoming more prevalent, especially in the overcrowded portions of New York City. At the Tuberculosis Exposition held in Baltimore last January it was stated that 30,000 persons were affected in New York City; that 8,500 died from its effects last year, and 13,000 new cases were reported to the Health Department during the same period. The following statement was made at that time by Dr. Herman N. Biggs, chief bacteriologist of the Health Department, according to the press reports:

> "The $500,000 expended by the municipality each year for the care and treatment of tuberculosis patients is estimated as only 2 per cent. of the actual loss to the city from this scourge. It kills or incapacitates the young and the most useful members of society and costs the city at least $25,000,000 each year."

In immigrants of low vitality we have the very class of people who, by reason of their physical condition and habits of crowding in unsanitary quarters are in a position to become easy victims of consumption. Dr. Henry L. Shively, of New York, says:

> "Infection from trachoma and favus is readily traced to immigrant sources; in tuberculosis the course of the disease is slow and insidious, and immediate sources of infection are less readily recognized. It is perhaps for this reason that the danger of the tuberculous immigrant to the health of the community has not been emphasized as it should be. . . . Their gregariousness causes them to herd together in thickly-populated urban communities of their own nationality, thereby lowering the standard of living among the city poor, and making their own education in the elementary principles of hygiene slow and difficult."

Here we see the professional man and the public official pointing out almost exactly the same objectionable class from totally different view points and entirely independent of one another. Having this testimony that many immigrants seek crowded quarters let us hear what the Church Association for the Improvement of Labor has to report on the actual conditions in these quarters. Referring to some of the tenement houses this report is made:

> "Under these conditions children work from early morning until late at night. Women work from morning to midnight, and on Sundays. The average wage is $3.00 per week. Trousers are finished for less than five

cents a pair and it takes two hours to make one pair. Not only 80 per cent. of the clothing sold in New York City but many other articles are made in tenement sweat shops. *One man was seen covering boxes with paper and using sputum to fasten it on. These boxes were for wedding cake.*"

Is there any language too strong to point out the danger resulting from this condition of living to which such numbers of immigrants flock? This Society goes on to state:

"Tuberculosis, diphtheria, smallpox, scarlet fever, measles, and affections of the eyes and skin are propagated in the rooms of the tenement house dweller, in which besides the family itself with an occasional lodger or two, assemble day by day, in defiance of law, as large a crowd of workers as can be packed into them. The atmosphere, already fetid enough by mere presence of those who fill it, is rendered still more oppressive and unwholesome by the heat of the stove and the irons required in the business, besides being highly seasoned by the malodorous preparations which enter into the cooking arrangements. Every piece of furniture, even the floor space, is utilized. If the children are in bed or in their cradles it makes no difference, the clothing, finished or unfinished, lies heaped up until it is taken back to the contractor. If the children have any contagious disorder it is of no consequence; the garments impregnated with disease germs go out all the same, carrying with them their seeds of sickness and death. It may be that candy or medicine boxes pass through the hands of the workers, some of whom may be afflicted with tuberculosis. It is all the same. The edges of the boxes are smeared with the germ-laden saliva and the boxes themselves are sent off to some candy or drug store, the bearers, possibly, of mortal disease to some unsuspecting victim."

. . . Is any further evidence necessary to prove that we do not want any more of this class of immigrants who are destined to the cities?

Source: Ainsworth, Frank H. *Burdens of Recent Immigration as Illustrated in the City of New York.* Publications of the Immigration Restriction League, no. 40, pp. 1–6.

U.S. Supreme Court Endorses Compulsory Vaccination in *Jacobson v. Massachusetts*

"A Community Has the Right to Protect Itself against an Outbreak of Disease"

1905

In 1905 the U.S. Supreme Court issued a landmark ruling that confirmed the state's authority to undertake mandatory vaccination campaigns and other activities that protected public health and the general welfare, even over the objections of individual citizens. This judgment had its roots in the mid-nineteenth century, when numerous states erecting public schools systems made smallpox vaccination a condition for enrollment. These requirements reflected a general public perception that although smallpox vaccination was not without risks—bacterial infections from vaccination were a particular problem in the pre-antiseptic age—it was a reasonable and necessary government intervention that helped shield communities from fearsome epidemics.

In the last decades of the nineteenth century, the opposition to compulsory vaccination actions became better organized and increasingly vocal. This cause gathered further momentum in the 1880s and 1890s, which were marked by only mild outbreaks of disease. Ironically, the reduced number of serious disease eruptions during this period has been widely credited to various public health reforms, from vaccination of children to sewage regulation. But the anti-vaccination camp framed the downturn as evidence that vaccination had outlived its usefulness, and they garnished this assertion with fierce denunciations of compulsory vaccination as an affront to American traditions of individual liberty and freedom. "Success bred complacency," summarized scholar James Colgrove. "Numerous anti-vaccination societies were established in the second half of the century, whose members distributed pamphlets and broadsides, lobbied legislatures for the repeal of compulsory laws, filed lawsuits, and sought to discourage the use of vaccination."[1]

By the turn of the century, America's courts were awash in legal challenges to vaccination statutes. Most of the subsequent rulings upheld the legitimacy of the laws, but the question of whether compulsory vaccination laws contravened the U.S. Constitution was not fully settled until the 1905 Supreme Court ruling in Jacobson v. Massachusetts. *In a 7–2 ruling, handed down on February 20, 1905, and excerpted here, the Court asserted that compulsory vaccination was a legitimate exercise of state governments' authority to safeguard the health, welfare, and safety of their citizenry. And it further held that the citizenry had no right to "defy the will of its constituted authorities, acting in good faith for all, under the legislative sanction of the State."*

[Case citations located in the original opinion have been removed.]

We come, then, to inquire whether any right given or secured by the Constitution is invaded by the statute as interpreted by the state court. The defendant insists that his liberty is invaded when the State subjects him to fine or imprisonment for neglecting or refusing to submit to vaccination; that a compulsory vaccination law is unreasonable, arbitrary and oppressive, and, therefore, hostile to the inherent right of every freeman to care for his own body and health in such way as to him seems best, and that the execution of such a law against one who objects to vaccination, no matter for what reason, is nothing short of an assault upon his person. But the liberty secured by the Constitution of the United States to every person within its jurisdiction does not import an absolute right in each person to be, at all times and in all circumstances, wholly freed from restraint. There are manifold restraints to which every person is necessarily subject for the common good. On any other basis, organized society could not exist with safety to its members. Society based on the rule that each one is a law unto himself would soon be confronted with disorder and anarchy. Real liberty for all could not exist under the operation of a principle which recognizes the right of each individual person to use his own, whether in respect of his person or his property, regardless of the injury that may be done to others. This court has more than once recognized it as a fundamental principle that

"persons and property are subjected to all kinds of restraints and burdens, in order to secure the general comfort, health, and prosperity of
the State, of the perfect right of the legislature to do which no question
ever was, or upon acknowledged general principles ever can be, made
so far as natural persons are concerned."

. . . In *Crowley v. Christensen*, we said:

"The possession and enjoyment of all rights are subject to such reasonable conditions as may be deemed by the governing authority of the
country essential to the safety, health, peace, good order and morals of
the community. Even liberty itself, the greatest of all rights, is not unre-
stricted license to act according to one's own will. It is only freedom
from restraint under conditions essential to the equal enjoyment of the
same right by others. It is then liberty regulated by law."

In the constitution of Massachusetts adopted in 1780, it was laid down as a fundamental principle of the social compact that the whole people covenants with each citizen,
and each citizen with the whole people, that all shall be governed by certain laws for "the
common good," and that government is instituted "for the common good, for the protection, safety, prosperity and happiness of the people, and not for the profit, honor or private interests of anyone man, family or class of men."

The good and welfare of the Commonwealth, of which the legislature is primarily
the judge, is the basis on which the police power rests in Massachusetts. Applying these
principles to the present case, it is to be observed that the legislature of Massachusetts
required the inhabitants of a city or town to be vaccinated only when, in the opinion of
the Board of Health, that was necessary for the public health or the public safety. The
authority to determine for all what ought to be done in such an emergency must have
been lodged somewhere or in some body, and surely it was appropriate for the legislature
to refer that question, in the first instance, to a Board of Health, composed of persons
residing in the locality affected and appointed, presumably, because of their fitness to
determine such questions. To invest such a body with authority over such matters was not
an unusual nor an unreasonable or arbitrary requirement. Upon the principle of self-
defense, of paramount necessity, a community has the right to protect itself against an
epidemic of disease which threatens the safety of its members. It is to be observed that,
when the regulation in question was adopted, smallpox, according to the recitals in the
regulation adopted by the Board of Health, was prevalent to some extent in the city of
Cambridge, and the disease was increasing. If such was the situation—and nothing is
asserted or appears in the record to the contrary—if we are to attach any value whatever
to the knowledge which, it is safe to affirm, is common to all civilized peoples touching
smallpox and the methods most usually employed to eradicate that disease, it cannot be
adjudged that the present regulation of the Board of Health was not necessary in order to
protect the public health and secure the public safety. Smallpox being prevalent and
increasing at Cambridge, the court would usurp the functions of another branch of government if it adjudged, as matter of law, that the mode adopted under the sanction of the
State, to protect the people at large was arbitrary and not justified by the necessities of the
case. We say necessities of the case because it might be that an acknowledged power of a
local community to protect itself against an epidemic threatening the safety of all, might

be exercised in particular circumstances and in reference to particular persons in such an arbitrary, unreasonable manner, or might go so far beyond what was reasonably required for the safety of the public, as to authorize or compel the courts to interfere for the protection of such persons. . . . In *Railroad Company v. Husen,* this court recognized the right of a State to pass sanitary laws, laws for the protection of life, liberty, health or property within its limits, laws to prevent persons and animals suffering under contagious or infectious diseases, or convicts, from coming within its borders. But as the laws there involved went beyond the necessity of the case and under the guise of exerting a police power invaded the domain of Federal authority, and violated rights secured by the Constitution, this court deemed it to be its duty to hold such laws invalid. If the mode adopted by the Commonwealth of Massachusetts for the protection of its local communities against smallpox proved to be distressing, inconvenient or objectionable to some—if nothing more could be reasonably affirmed of the statute in question—the answer is that it was the duty of the constituted authorities primarily to keep in view the welfare, comfort and safety of the many, and not permit the interests of the many to be subordinated to the wishes or convenience of the few. There is, of course, a sphere within which the individual may assert the supremacy of his own will and rightfully dispute the authority of any human government, especially of any free government existing under a written constitution, to interfere with the exercise of that will. But it is equally true that, in every well ordered society charged with the duty of conserving the safety of its members the rights of the individual in respect of his liberty may at times, under the pressure of great dangers, be subjected to such restraint, to be enforced by reasonable regulations, as the safety of the general public may demand. An American citizen, arriving at an American port on a vessel in which, during the voyage, there had been cases of yellow fever or Asiatic cholera, although apparently free from disease himself, may yet, in some circumstances, be held in quarantine against his will on board of such vessel or in a quarantine station until it be ascertained by inspection, conducted with due diligence, that the danger of the spread of the disease among the community at large has disappeared. The liberty secured by the Fourteenth Amendment, this court has said, consists, in part, in the right of a person "to live and work where he will," [*Allgeyer v. Louisiana*], and yet he may be compelled, by force if need be, against his will and without regard to his personal wishes or his pecuniary interests, or even his religious or political convictions, to take his place in the ranks of the army of his country and risk the chance of being shot down in its defense. It is not, therefore, true that the power of the public to guard itself against imminent danger depends in every case involving the control of one's body upon his willingness to submit to reasonable regulations established by the constituted authorities, under the sanction of the State, for the purpose of protecting the public collectively against such danger.

It is said, however, that the statute, as interpreted by the state court, although making an exception in favor of children certified by a registered physician to be unfit subjects for vaccination, makes no exception in the case of adults in like condition. But this cannot be deemed a denial of the equal protection of the laws to adults, for the statute is applicable equally to all in like condition, and there are obviously reasons why regulations may be appropriate for adults which could not be safely applied to persons of tender years.

Looking at the propositions embodied in the defendant's rejected offers of proof, it is clear that they are more formidable by their number than by their inherent value. Those offers, in the main, seem to have had no purpose except to state the general theory of those of the medical profession who attach little or no value to vaccination as a means of preventing the spread of smallpox, or who think that vaccination causes other diseases of the body. What everybody knows, the court must know, and therefore the state court judicially knew, as this court knows, that an opposite theory accords with the common belief and is maintained by high medical authority. We must assume that, when the statute in question was passed, the legislature of Massachusetts was not unaware of these opposing theories, and was compelled, of necessity, to choose between them. It was not compelled to commit a matter involving the public health and safety to the final decision of a court or jury. It is no part of the function of a court or a jury to determine which one of two modes was likely to be the most effective for the protection of the public against disease. That was for the legislative department to determine in the light of all the information it had or could obtain. It could not properly abdicate its function to guard the public health and safety. The state legislature proceeded upon the theory which recognized vaccination as at least an effective, if not the best, known way in which to meet and suppress the evils of a smallpox epidemic that imperiled an entire population. Upon what sound principles as to the relations existing between the different departments of government can the court review this action of the legislature? If there is any such power in the judiciary to review legislative action in respect of a matter affecting the general welfare, it can only be when that which the legislature has done comes within the rule that,

> "if a statute purporting to have been enacted to protect the public health, the public morals, or the public safety has no real or substantial relation to those objects, or is, beyond all question, a plain, palpable invasion of rights secured by the fundamental law, it is the duty of the courts to so adjudge, and thereby give effect to the Constitution."

Whatever may be thought of the expediency of this statute, it cannot be affirmed to be, beyond question, in palpable conflict with the Constitution. Nor, in view of the methods employed to stamp out the disease of smallpox, can anyone confidently assert that the means prescribed by the State to that end has no real or substantial relation to the protection of the public health and the public safety. Such an assertion would not be consistent with the experience of this and other countries whose authorities have dealt with the disease of smallpox. And the principle of vaccination as a means to prevent the spread of smallpox has been enforced in many States by statutes making the vaccination of children a condition of their right to enter or remain in public schools. . . .

Since, then, vaccination, as a means of protecting a community against smallpox, finds strong support in the experience of this and other countries, no court, much less a jury, is justified in disregarding the action of the legislature simply because, in its or their opinion, that particular method was—perhaps or possibly—not the best either for children or adults.

Did the offers of proof made by the defendant present a case which entitled him, while remaining in Cambridge, to claim exemption from the operation of the statute and of the regulation adopted by the Board of Health? We have already said that his rejected offers, in the main, only set forth the theory of those who had no faith in vaccination as a means of preventing the spread of smallpox, or who thought that vaccination, without benefiting the public, put in peril the health of the person vaccinated. But there were some offers which it is contended embodied distinct facts that might properly have been considered. Let us see how this is.

The defendant offered to prove that vaccination "quite often" caused serious and permanent injury to the health of the person vaccinated; that the operation "occasionally" resulted in death; that it was "impossible" to tell "in any particular case" what the results of vaccination would be or whether it would injure the health or result in death; that "quite often," one's blood is in a certain condition of impurity when it is not prudent or safe to vaccinate him; that there is no practical test by which to determine "with any degree of certainty" whether one's blood is in such condition of impurity as to render vaccination necessarily unsafe or dangerous; that vaccine matter is "quite often" impure and dangerous to be used, but whether impure or not cannot be ascertained by any known practical test; that the defendant refused to submit to vaccination for the reason that he had, "when a child," been caused great and extreme suffering for a long period by a disease produced by vaccination, and that he had witnessed a similar result of vaccination not only in the case of his son, but in the cases of others.

These offers, in effect, invited the court and jury to go over the whole ground gone over by the legislature when it enacted the statute in question. The legislature assumed that some children, by reason of their condition at the time, might not be fit subjects of vaccination, and it is suggested—and we will not say without reason—that such is the case with some adults. But the defendant did not offer to prove that, by reason of his then condition, he was, in fact, not a fit subject of vaccination at the time he was informed of the requirement of the regulation adopted by the Board of Health. It is entirely consistent with his offer of proof that, after reaching full age, he had become, so far as medical skill could discover, and, when informed of the regulation of the Board of Health, was, a fit subject of vaccination, and that the vaccine matter to be used in his case was such as any medical practitioner of good standing would regard as proper to be used. The matured opinions of medical men everywhere, and the experience of mankind, as all must know, negative the suggestion that it is not possible in any case to determine whether vaccination is safe. Was defendant exempted from the operation of the statute simply because of his dread of the same evil results experienced by him when a child and had observed in the cases of his son and other children? Could he reasonably claim such an exemption because, "quite often" or "occasionally," injury had resulted from vaccination, or because it was impossible, in the opinion of some, by any practical test, to determine with absolute certainty whether a particular person could be safely vaccinated?

It seems to the court that an affirmative answer to these questions would practically strip the legislative department of its function to care for the public health and the public safety when endangered by epidemics of disease. Such an answer would mean that compulsory vaccination could not, in any conceivable case, be legally enforced in a community, even at the command of the legislature, however widespread the epidemic of smallpox, and however deep and universal was the belief of the community and of its medical advisers, that a system of general vaccination was vital to the safety of all.

We are not prepared to hold that a minority, residing or remaining in any city or town where smallpox is prevalent, and enjoying the general protection afforded by an organized local government, may thus defy the will of its constituted authorities, acting in good faith for all, under the legislative sanction of the State. If such be the privilege of a minority, then a like privilege would belong to each individual of the community, and the spectacle would be presented of the welfare and safety of an entire population being subordinated to the notions of a single individual who chooses to remain a part of that population. We are unwilling to hold it to be an element in the liberty secured by the Constitution of the United States that one person, or a minority of persons, residing in any community and enjoying the benefits of its local government, should have the power thus to dominate the majority when supported in their action by the authority of the State.

While this court should guard with firmness every right appertaining to life, liberty or property as secured to the individual by the Supreme Law of the Land, it is of the last importance that it should not invade the domain of local authority except when it is plainly necessary to do so in order to enforce that law. The safety and the health of the people of Massachusetts are, in the first instance, for that Commonwealth to guard and protect. They are matters that do not ordinarily concern the National Government. So far as they can be reached by any government, they depend, primarily, upon such action as the State in its wisdom may take, and we do not perceive that this legislation has invaded any right secured by the Federal Constitution. . . .

Source: U.S. Supreme Court. Majority opinion in *Jacobson v. Massachusetts*, February 20, 1905. http:// supreme.justia.com/us/197/11/case.html.

NOTE

1. James Colgrove, "Immunity for the People: The Challenge of Achieving High Vaccine Coverage in American History," *Public Health Reports* 122, no. 2 (March–April 2007): 248–57, www.ncbi.nlm .nih.gov/pmc/articles/PMC1820430/.

A Muckraker Condemns America's Patent Medicine Industry

DOCUMENT
4.7

"The Drug in Question Is a Maker of Cocain Fiends"

1905

As progressive reformers embarked on their crusade to reengineer the health care landscape in the United States, one of their principal targets was the patent medicine industry. Armed with countless horror stories about the deadly impact of unregulated nostrums on American families, these reformers framed the passage of new laws that would outlaw dangerous drugs and regulate the manufacture and disbursement of other medicines as a moral imperative. Their efforts were greatly aided by the works of muckrakers such as Samuel Hopkins Adams, who published an eleven-part exposé of the patent medicine industry called "The Great American Fraud" in Collier's Weekly *in 1905. The first of these articles, titled "The Nostrum Evil" and originally published in October 1905, is excerpted here.*

The relentless progressive agitation for federal regulation of the pharmaceutical industry was rewarded in 1906 with the passage of the Pure Food and Drug Act. In addition to mandating federal inspection of meat products and slaughterhouse operations, this legislation placed significant restrictions on the manufacture, sale, and transportation of patent medicines.

Gullible America will spend this year some seventy-five millions of dollars in the purchase of patent medicines. In consideration of this sum it will swallow huge quantities of alcohol, an appalling amount of opiates and narcotics, a wide assortment of varied drugs ranging from powerful and dangerous heart depressants to insidious liver stimulants; and, far in excess of all other ingredients, undiluted fraud. For fraud, exploited by the skillfulest of advertising bunco men, is the basis of the trade. Should the newspapers, the magazines and the medical journals refuse their pages to this class of advertisements, the patent medicine business in five years would be as scandalously historic as the South Sea Bubble, and the nation would be the richer not only in lives and money, but in drunkards and drug fiends saved.

"Don't make the mistake of lumping all proprietary medicines in one indiscriminate denunciation," came warning from all sides when this series was announced. But the honest attempt to separate the sheep from the goats develops a lamentable lack of qualified candidates for the sheepfold. External remedies there may be which are at once honest in their claims and effective for their purposes; they are not to be found among the much-advertised ointments or applications which fill the public prints. Cuticura may be a useful preparation, but in extravagance of advertising it rivals the most clamorous cure-all. Pond's Extract, one would naturally suppose, could afford to restrict itself to decent methods, but in the recent epidemic scare in New York it traded on the public alarm by putting forth "display" advertisements headed, in heavy black type, "Meningitis," a disease in which witch-hazel is about as effective as molasses. This is fairly comparable to Peruna's ghoulish exploitation, for profit, of the yellow fever scourge in New Orleans, aided by various southern newspapers of standing, which published as *news* an "interview" with Dr. Hartman, president of the Peruna Company.

Drugs That Make Victims.

When one comes to the internal remedies, the proprietary medicines proper, they all belong to the tribe of Capricorn, under one of two heads, harmless frauds or deleterious drugs. For instance, the laxatives perform what they promise; but taken regularly, as thousands of people take them (and, indeed, as the advertisements urge), they become an increasingly baneful necessity. Acetanilid will undoubtedly relieve headache of certain kinds; but acetanilid, as the basis of headache powders, is prone to remove the cause of the symptoms permanently by putting a complete stop to the heart action. Invariably, when taken steadily, it produces constitutional disturbances of insidious development which result fatally if the drug be not discontinued, and often it enslaves the devotee to its use. Cocain and opium stop pain; but the narcotics are not the safest drugs to put into the hands of the ignorant, particularly when their presence is concealed in the "cough remedies," "soothing syrups," and "catarrhal powders" of which they are the basis. Few outside of the rabid temperance advocates will deny a place in medical practice to alcohol. But alcohol, fed daily and in increasing doses to women and children, makes not for health, but for drunkenness. Far better whiskey or gin unequivocally labeled than the alcohol-laden "bitters," "sarsaparillas" and "tonics" which exhilarate fatuous temperance advocates to the point of enthusiastic testimonials.

None of these "cures" really does cure any serious affection, although a majority of their users recover. But a majority, and a very large majority, of the sick recover, anyway. Were it not so—were one illness out of fifty fatal—this earth would soon be depopulated. . . .

The Magic "Red Clause."

With a few honorable exceptions the press of the United States is at the beck and call of the patent medicines. Not only do the newspapers modify news possibly affecting these interests, but they sometimes become their active agents. F. J. Cheney, proprietor of Hall's Catarrh Cure, devised some years ago a method of making the press do his fighting against legislation compelling makers of remedies to publish their formulae, or to print on the labels the dangerous drugs contained in the medicine—a constantly recurring bugaboo of the nostrum-dealer. This scheme he unfolded at a meeting of the Proprietary Association of America, of which he is now president. He explained that he printed in red letters on every advertising contract a clause providing that the contract should become void in the event of hostile legislation, and he boasted how he had used this as a club in a case where an Illinois legislator had, as he put it, attempted to hold him for three hundred dollars on a strike bill.

"I thought I had a better plan than this," said Mr. Cheney to his associates, "so I wrote to about forty papers and merely said: 'Please look at your contract with me and take note that if this law passes you and I must stop doing business.' The next week every one of them had an article and Mr. Man had to go."

So emphatically did this device recommend itself to the assemblage that many of the large firms took up the plan, and now the "red clause" is a familiar device in the trade. . . . Emboldened by this easy coercion of the press, certain firms have since used the newspapers as a weapon against "price-cutting," by forcing them to refuse advertising of the stores which reduce rates on patent medicines. Tyrannical masters, these heavy purchasers of advertising space. . . .

. . . It is disheartening to note that in the case of one important and high-class daily, the Pittsburg *Gazette,* a trial rejection of all patent medicine advertising received absolutely no support or encouragement from the public; so the paper reverted to its old policy.

One might expect from the medical press freedom from such influences. The control is as complete, though exercised by a class of nostrums somewhat differently exploited, but essentially the same. . . . There are to-day very few medical publications which do not carry advertisements conceived in the same spirit and making much the same exhaustive claims as the ordinary quack "ads" of the daily press, and still fewer that are free from promises to "cure" diseases which are incurable by any medicine. Thus the medical press is as strongly enmeshed by the "ethical" druggers as the lay press is by Paine, "Dr." Kilmer, Lydia Pinkham, Dr. Hartman, "Hall" of the "red clause," and the rest of the edifying band of life-savers, leaving no agency to refute the megaphone exploitation of the fraud. What opposition there is would naturally arise in the medical profession, but this is discounted by the proprietary interests.

The Doctors Are Investigating.

"You attack us because we cure your patients," is their charge. They assume always that the public has no grievance against them, or rather, they calmly ignore the public in the matter. In his address at the last convention of the Proprietary Association, the retiring president, W. A. Talbot of Piso's Consumption Cure, turning his guns on the medical profession, delivered this astonishing sentiment:

"No argument favoring the publication of our formulas was ever uttered which does not apply with equal force to your prescriptions. It is pardonable in you to want to know these formulas, for they are good. But you must not ask us to reveal these valuable secrets, to do what you would not do yourselves. The public and our law-makers do not want your secrets nor ours, *and it would be a damage to them to have them.*"

The physicians seem to have awakened, somewhat tardily, indeed, to counter-attack. The American Medical Association has organized a Council on Pharmacy and Chemistry to investigate and pass on the "ethical" preparations advertised to physicians, with a view to listing those which are found to be reputable and useful. That this is regarded as a direct assault on the proprietary interests is suggested by the protests, eloquent to the verge of frenzy in some cases, emanating from those organs which the manufacturers control. Already the council has issued some painfully frank reports on products of imposingly scientific nomenclature; and more are to follow.

What One Druggist Is Doing.

Largely for trade reasons a few druggists have been fighting the nostrums, but without any considerable effect. Indeed, it is surprising to see that people are so deeply impressed with the advertising claims put forth daily as to be impervious to warnings even from experts . . . .

Legislation is the most obvious remedy, pending the enlightenment of the general public or the awakening of the journalistic conscience. But legislation proceeds slowly and always against opposition, which may be measured in practical terms as $250,000,000 at stake on the other side. I note in the last report of the Proprietary Association's annual meeting the significant statement that "the heaviest expenses were incurred in legislative work." Most of the legislation must be done by states, and we have seen in the case of the Hall Catarrh cure contract how readily this may be controlled.

Two government agencies, at least, lend themselves to the purposes of the patent-medicine makers. The Patent Office issues to them trade-mark registration (generally speaking, the convenient term "patent medicine" is a misnomer, as very few are patented) without inquiry into the nature of the article thus safeguarded against imitation. The Post-Office Department permits them the use of the mails. Except one particular line, the disgraceful "Weak Manhood" remedies, where excellent work has been done in throwing them out of the mails for fraud, the department has done nothing in the matter of patent remedies, and has no present intention of doing anything; yet I believe that such action, powerful as would be the opposition developed, would be upheld by the courts on the same grounds that sustained the Post Office's position in the recent case of "Robusto."

A Post-Office Report.

That the advertising and circular statements circulated through the mails were materially and substantially false, with the result of cheating and defrauding those into whose hands the statements came;

That, while the remedies did possess medicinal properties, these were not such as to carry out the cures promised;

That the advertiser knew he was deceiving;

That in the sale and distribution of his medicines the complainant made no inquiry into the specific character of the disease in any individual case, but supplied the same remedies and prescribed the same mode of treatment to all alike.

Should the department apply these principles to the patent-medicine field generally, a number of conspicuous nostrums would cease to be patrons of Uncle Sam's mail service.

Some states have made a good start in the matter of legislation, among them Michigan, which does not, however, enforce its recent strong law. Massachusetts, which has done more, through the admirable work of its State Board of Health, than any other agency to educate the public on the patent-medicine question, is unable to get a law restricting this trade. In New Hampshire, too, the proprietary interests have proven too strong, and the Mallonee bill was destroyed by the almost united opposition of a "red-clause" press. North Dakota proved more independent. After Jan. 1, 1906, all medicines sold in that state, except on physician's prescriptions, which contain chloral, ergot, morphin, opium, cocain, bromin, iodin or any of their compounds or derivatives, or more than 5 per cent. of alcohol, must so state on the label. When this bill became a law, the Proprietary Association of America proceeded to blight the state by resolving that its members should offer no goods for sale there.

Boards of health in various parts of the country are doing valuable educational work, the North Dakota board having led in the legislation. The Massachusetts, Connecticut and North Carolina boards have been active. The New York State board has kept its hands off patent medicines, but the Board of Pharmacy has made a cautious but promising beginning by compelling all makers of powders containing cocain to put a poison label on their goods; and it proposes to extend this ruling gradually to other dangerous compositions.

Health Boards and Analyses.

It is somewhat surprising to find the Health Department of New York City, in many respects the foremost in the country, making no use of carefully and rather expensively acquired knowledge which would serve to protect the public. More than two years ago analyses were made by the chemists of the department which showed dangerous quantities of cocain in a number of catarrh powders. These analyses have never been printed. Even the general nature of the information has been withheld. Should any citizen of New York going to the Health Department, have asked: "My wife is taking Birney's Catarrh Powder; is it true that it's a bad thing?" the officials, with the knowledge at hand that the drug in question is a maker of cocain fiends, would have blandly emulated the Sphinx. Outside criticism of an overworked, undermanned and generally efficient department is liable to error through ignorance of the problems involved in its administration; yet one cannot but believe that some form of warning against what is wisely admittedly a public menace would have been a wiser form of procedure than that which has heretofore been discovered by the formula, "policy of the department."

Policies change and broaden under pressure of conditions. The Health Commissioner is now formulating a plan which, with the work of the chemists as a basis, shall check the trade in public poisons more or less concealed behind proprietary names.

It is impossible, even in a series of articles, to attempt more than an exemplary treatment of the patent-medicine frauds. The most degraded and degrading, the "lost vitality" and "blood disease" cures, reeking of terrorization and blackmail, can not from their very nature be treated of in a lay journal. Many dangerous and health-destroying compounds will escape through sheer inconspicuousness. I can touch on only a few of those which may be regarded as typical: the alcohol stimulators, as represented by Peruna, Paine's Celery Compound and Duffy's Pure Malt Whiskey (advertised as an exclusively medical preparation); the catarrh powders, which breed cocain slaves, and the opium-containing soothing syrups which stunt or kill helpless infants; the consumption cures, perhaps the most devilish of all, in that they destroy hope where hope is struggling against bitter odds for existence; the headache powders, which enslave so insidiously that the victim is ignorant of his own fate; the comparatively harmless fake as typified by that marvelous product of advertising effrontery, Liquozone; and, finally, the system of exploitation and testimonials on which the whole vast system of bunco rests, as on a flimsy but cunningly constructed foundation.

Source: Adams, Samuel Hopkins. "The Nostrum Evil." *Collier's Weekly*, October 7, 1905. Reprinted in *The Great American Fraud: Articles on the Nostrum Evil and Quackery Reprinted from Collier's.* Chicago: American Medical Association, 1912, pp. 3–12.

DOCUMENT
4.8

Flexner Report Demands Reforms of American Medical Education

"The Profession Has Been Diluted [by] Weak Schools with Low Ideals"

1910

One of the great and lasting triumphs of the Progressive Era in the realm of health care was the standardization of American medical education. This quest began in the years following the Civil War, when a variety of reformers joined with the American Medical Association (AMA) to urge greater regulation of the medical colleges that were sprouting across the country. Most of these entreaties were greeted with stony indifference by U.S. lawmakers—and even by many patients. As the medical educator John Shaw Billings stated in 1891, "the great mass of the public know little and care less about the details of professional education. . . . The popular feeling is that in a free country everyone should have the right to follow any occupation he likes, and employ for any purpose any one whom he selects, and that each party must take the consequences."[1]

By the turn of the century, the policymaking terrain had shifted considerably. Well-publicized advances in science-based medical practices and treatments during the last two decades of the nineteenth century convinced the public that doctors and surgeons needed to have a firm grounding in those areas. Moreover, this same period saw the rise of university-affiliated medical schools armed with ambitious training, treatment, and research agendas. When compared with these emerging citadels of learning, the rickety proprietary medical colleges that were still churning out poorly trained graduates by the score looked anemic.

This was the environment into which the so-called Flexner Report was released in 1910. This intensive survey of the state of medical education in the United States and Canada was spearheaded by educator Abraham Flexner at the behest of Henry S. Pritchett, president of the Carnegie Foundation. Flexner began his survey in 1908, and over the course of the ensuing eighteen months he personally inspected all 155 medical schools operating in the United States. He graded them on several criteria, including entrance requirements, faculty, endowment and tuition, laboratory and teaching facilities, and access to hands-on training at area hospitals.

Flexner's report harshly condemned most of the for-profit diploma mills operating in the country. He wrote that Tennessee's nine medical schools, if "treated on their merits, would speedily be reduced to one: The utterly wretched establishments at Chattanooga and Knoxville would be wiped out; the more showy, but quite mercenary concerns at Memphis, would be liquidated." Similarly, he stated that "the two Milwaukee schools [of medical education] are without a redeeming feature," and he opined that "the city of Chicago is in respect to medical education the plague spot of the country."² Flexner's solution for addressing these woeful schools was to insist on stringent new state regulations that would standardize medical education to the level of the nation's finest existing medical schools. "The point now to aim at," he said, "is the development of the requisite number of properly supported institutions and the speedy demise of all others."

The Flexner Report *had an electrifying effect on American medical education. Within months of its release, lawmakers and licensing boards across the country were citing its contents as they imposed new admission standards, hardier curriculum requirements, and other robust reforms. These changes vanquished the proprietary medical colleges and became the foundation for the research-based medical university model that Flexner championed. The following document is an excerpt from the introduction to the report, in which Pritchett summarizes Flexner's findings.*

The striking and significant facts which are here brought out are of enormous consequence not only to the medical practitioner, but to every citizen of the United States and Canada; for it is a singular fact that the organization of medical education in this country has hitherto been such as not only to commercialize the process of education itself, but also to obscure in the minds of the public any discrimination between the well trained physician and the physician who has had no adequate training whatsoever. As a rule, Americans, when they avail themselves of the services of a physician, make only the slightest inquiry as to what his previous training and preparation have been. One of the problems of the future is to educate the public itself to appreciate the fact that very seldom, under existing conditions, does a patient receive the best aid which it is possible to give him in the present state of medicine, and that this is due mainly to the fact that a vast army of men is admitted to the practice of medicine who are untrained in sciences fundamental to the profession and quite without a sufficient experience with disease. A right education of public opinion is one of the problems of future medical education.

The significant facts revealed by this study are these:

(1) For twenty-five years past there has been an enormous over-production of uneducated and ill trained medical practitioners. This has been in absolute disregard of the public welfare and without any serious thought of the interests of the public. Taking the United States as a whole, physicians are four or five times as numerous in proportion to population as in older countries like Germany.

(2) Over-production of ill trained men is due in the main to the existence of a very large number of commercial schools, sustained in many cases by advertising methods through which a mass of unprepared youth is drawn out of industrial occupations into the study of medicine.

(3) Until recently the conduct of a medical school was a profitable business, for the methods of instruction were mainly didactic. As the need for laboratories has become

more keenly felt, the expenses of an efficient medical school have been greatly increased. The inadequacy of many of these schools may be judged from the fact that nearly half of all our medical schools have incomes below $10,000, and these incomes determine the quality of instruction that they can and do offer.

Colleges and universities have in large measure failed in the past twenty-five years to appreciate the great advance in medical education and the increased cost of teaching it along modern lines. Many universities desirous of apparent educational completeness have annexed medical schools without making themselves responsible either for the standards of the professional schools or for their support.

(4) The existence of many of these unnecessary and inadequate medical schools has been defended by the argument that a poor medical school is justified in the interest of the poor boy. It is clear that the poor boy has no right to go into any profession for which he is not willing to obtain adequate preparation; but the facts set forth in this report make it evident that this argument is insincere, and that the excuse which has hitherto been put forward in the name of the poor boy is in reality an argument in behalf of the poor medical school.

(5) A hospital under complete educational control is as necessary to a medical school as is a laboratory of chemistry or pathology. High grade teaching within a hospital introduces a most wholesome and beneficial influence into its routine. Trustees of hospitals, public and private, should therefore go to the limit of their authority in opening hospital wards to teaching, provided only that the universities secure sufficient funds on their side to employ as teachers men who are devoted to clinical science.

In view of these facts, progress for the future would seem to require a very much smaller number of medical schools, better equipped and better conducted than our schools now as a rule are; and the needs of the public would equally require that we have fewer physicians graduated each year, but that these should be better educated and better trained. With this idea accepted, it necessarily follows that the medical school will, if rightly conducted, articulate not only with the university, but with the general system of education. Just what form that articulation must take will vary in the immediate future in different parts of the country. Throughout the eastern and central states the movement under which the medical school articulates with the second year of the college has already gained such impetus that it can be regarded as practically accepted. In the southern states for the present it would seem that articulation with the four-year high school would be a reasonable starting-point for the future. In time the development of secondary education in the south and the growth of the colleges will make it possible for southern medical schools to accept the two-year college basis of preparation. With reasonable prophecy the time is not far distant when, with fair respect for the interests of the public and the need for physicians, the articulation of the medical school with the university may be the same throughout the entire country. For in the future the college or the university which accepts a medical school must make itself responsible for university standards in the medical school and for adequate support for medical education. The day has gone by when any university can retain the respect of educated men, or when it can fulfil its duty to education, by retaining a low grade professional school for the sake of its own institutional completeness.

If these fundamental principles can be made clear to the people of the United States and of Canada, and to those who govern the colleges and the universities, we may confidently expect that the next ten years will see a very much smaller number of medical schools in this country, but a greatly increased efficiency in medical education, and that during the same period medical education will become rightly articulated with, and rightly related to, the general educational system of the whole country.

In the suggestions which are made in this report looking toward the future development of medicine, it ought to be pointed out that no visionary or impossible achievement is contemplated. It is not expected that a Johns Hopkins Medical School can be erected immediately in cities where public support of education has hitherto been meager. Nevertheless, it is quite true that there is a certain minimum of equipment and a minimum of educational requirement without which no attempt ought to be made to teach medicine. Hitherto not only proprietary medical schools, but colleges and universities, have paid scant attention to this fact. They have been ready to assume the responsibility of turning loose upon a helpless community men licensed to the practice of medicine without any serious thought as to whether they had received a fair training or not. To-day, under the methods pursued in modern medicine, we know with certainty that a medical school cannot be conducted without a certain minimum of expense and without a certain minimum of facilities. The institution which attempts to conduct a school below this plane is clearly injuring, not helping, civilization. In the suggestions which are made in this report as to what constitutes a reasonable minimum no visionary ideal has been pursued, but only such things have been insisted upon as in the present light of our American civilization every community has a right to demand of its medical school, if medicine is to be taught at all.

It seems desirable also in connection with both the medical school and the university or college to add one word further concerning the relation of financial support to efficiency and sincerity. Where any criticism is attempted of inadequate methods or inadequate facilities, no reply is more common than this: "Our institution cannot be judged from its financial support. It depends upon the enthusiasm and the devotion of its teachers and its supporters, and such devotion cannot be measured by financial standards."

Such an answer contains so fine a sentiment and so pregnant a truth that it oftentimes serves to turn aside the most just criticism. It is true that every college must ultimately depend upon the spirit and devotion of those who work in it, but behind this noble statement hides most of the insincerity, sham, and pretense not only of the American medical school, but of the American college. The answer quoted is commonly made by the so-called university that, with an income insufficient to support a decent college, is trying to cover the whole field of university education. It is the same answer that one receives from the medical school which, with wholly inadequate facilities, is turning out upon an innocent and long-suffering community men who must get their medical education after they get out of the institution. In many of these ill manned and poorly equipped institutions there is to be found a large measure of devotion, but the fact remains that such devotion is usually ill placed, and the individual who gives it loses sight of the interests of education and of the general public in his desire to keep alive an institution without reason or right to exist.

It will, however, be urged by weak schools that the fact that an institution is ill manned and poorly equipped is inconclusive; that in the time devoted to the examination of a single school it is impossible to do it justice. Objection of this kind is apt to come from schools of two types,—ineffective institutions in large cities, and schools attached to colleges in small towns in which clinical material is scarce. In my opinion the objection is without force. A trained observer of wide experience can go directly to the heart of a problem of this character. The spirit, ideals, and facilities of a professional or technical school can be quickly grasped. In every instance in which further inquiry has been made, the conclusions reached by the author of the report have been sustained.

The development which is here suggested for medical education is conditioned largely upon three factors: first, upon the creation of a public opinion which shall discriminate between the ill trained and the rightly trained physician, and which will also insist upon the enactment of such laws as will require all practitioners of medicine, whether they belong to one sect or another, to ground themselves in the fundamentals upon which medical science rests; secondly, upon the universities and their attitude towards medical standards and medical support; finally, upon the attitude of the members of the medical profession towards the standards of their own practice and upon their sense of honor with respect to their own profession.

These last two factors are moral rather than educational. They call for an educational patriotism on the part of the institutions of learning and a medical patriotism on the part of the physician.

By educational patriotism I mean this: a university has a mission greater than the formation of a large student body or the attainment of institutional completeness, namely, the duty of loyalty to the standards of common honesty, of intellectual sincerity, of scientific accuracy. A university with educational patriotism will not take up the work of medical education unless it can discharge its duty by it; or if, in the days of ignorance once winked at, a university became entangled in a medical school alliance, it will frankly and courageously deal with a situation which is no longer tenable. It will either demand of its medical school university ideals and give it university support, or else it will drop the effort to do what it can only do badly.

By professional patriotism amongst medical men I mean that sort of regard for the honor of the profession and that sense of responsibility for its efficiency which will enable a member of that profession to rise above the consideration of personal or of professional gain. As Bacon truly wrote, "Every man owes a duty to his profession," and in no profession is this obligation more clear than in that of the modern physician. Perhaps in no other of the great professions does one find greater discrepancies between the ideals of those who represent it. No members of the social order are more self-sacrificing than the true physicians and surgeons, and of this fine group none deserve so much of society as those who have taken upon their shoulders the burden of medical education. On the other hand, the profession has been diluted by the presence of a great number of men who have come from weak schools with low ideals both of education and of professional honor. If the medical education of our country is in the immediate future to go upon a plane of efficiency and of credit, those who represent the higher ideals of the medical profession must make a stand for that form of medical education which is calculated to advance the true interests of the whole people and to better the ideals of medicine itself. . . .

In the preparation of this report the Foundation has kept steadily in view the interests of two classes, which in the over-multiplication of medical schools have usually been forgotten,—first, the youths who are to study medicine and to become the future practitioners, and, secondly, the general public, which is to live and die under their ministrations.

No one can become familiar with this situation without acquiring a hearty sympathy for the American youth who, too often the prey of commercial advertising methods, is steered into the practice of medicine with almost no opportunity to learn the difference between an efficient medical school and a hopelessly inadequate one. A clerk who is receiving $50 a month in the country store gets an alluring brochure which paints the life of the physician as an easy road to wealth. He has no realization of the difference between medicine as a profession and medicine as a business, nor as a rule has he any adviser at hand to show him that the first requisite for the modern practitioner of medicine is a good general education. Such a boy falls an easy victim to the commercial medical school, whether operating under the name of a university or college, or alone.

The interests of the general public have been so generally lost sight of in this matter that the public has in large measure forgot that it has any interests to protect. And yet in no other way does education more closely touch the individual than in the quality of medical training which the institutions of the country provide. Not only the personal well-being of each citizen, but national, state, and municipal sanitation rests upon the quality of the training which the medical graduate has received. The interest of the public is to have well trained practitioners in sufficient number for the needs of society. The source whence these practitioners are to come is of far less consequence.

In view of this fact, the argument advanced for the retention of medical schools in places where good clinical instruction is impossible is directly against the public interest. If the argument were valid, it would mean that the sick man is better off in the hands of an incompetent home-grown practitioner than in those of one well trained in an outside school. Such an argument ought no longer to blind the eyes of intelligent men to the actual situation. Any state of the Union or any province of Canada is better off without a medical school than with one conducted in a commercial spirit and below a reasonable plane of efficiency. No state and no section of a state capable of supporting a good practitioner will suffer by following this policy. The state of Washington, which has no medical school within its borders, is doubtless supplied with as capable and well trained a body of medical practitioners as is Missouri with its eleven medical schools or Illinois with its fourteen. . . .

While the aim of the Foundation has throughout been constructive, its attitude towards the difficulties and problems of the situation is distinctly sympathetic. The report indeed turns the light upon conditions which, instead of being fruitful and inspiring, are in many instances commonplace, in other places bad, and in still others, scandalous. It is nevertheless true that no one set of men or no one school of medicine is responsible for what still remains in the form of commercial medical education. Our hope is that this report will make plain once for all that the day of the commercial medical school has passed. It will be observed that, except for a brief historical introduction, intended to show how present conditions have come about, no account is given of the past of any institution. The situation is described as it exists today in the hope that out of it, quite regardless of the past, a new order may be speedily developed. There is no need now of recriminations over what has been, or of apologies by way of defending a regime practically obsolete. Let us address ourselves resolutely to the task of reconstructing the American medical school on the lines of the highest modern ideals of efficiency and in accordance with the finest conceptions of public service. . . .

Source: Pritchett, Henry S. "Introduction." In Flexner, Abraham. *Medical Education in the United States and Canada: A Report to the Carnegie Foundation for the Advancement of Teaching.* Bulletin No. 4. New York: Carnegie Foundation, 1910, pp. x–xvi.

Notes

1. Josh Shaw Billings, "Ideals of Medical Education," *Science,* no. 18 (1891): 1–4.

2. Abraham Flexner, *Medical Education in the United States and Canada: A Report to the Carnegie Foundation for the Advancement of Teaching,* Bulletin No. 4 (New York: Carnegie Foundation, 1910), 216, 308, 319.

DOCUMENT 4.9

A Senator's Call for a Cabinet-Level Public Health Department

"This Is a Question of Vast National Importance"

1910

The authority and responsibilities of the Marine Hospital Service (MHS) to safeguard public health steadily expanded in the late nineteenth century, and by 1902, when its name was changed to the Public Health and Marine Hospital Service (PHMHS), the agency was universally recognized as the nation's frontline defense against communicable diseases, pollution, and other health threats. Still, many proponents of increased federal oversight of public health contended that the government's powers should be further augmented. The best way to do this, argued many reformers, was to create a cabinet-level department of public health.

One of the leaders in this effort was Democratic senator Robert L. Owen of Oklahoma. Following are excerpts from a March 24, 1910, speech that Owen delivered on the floor of the Senate urging support for a bill, crafted by the senator himself, that would establish a cabinet-level Department of Public Health in the executive branch of the U.S. government. Owen's efforts went unrewarded, but the activities and responsibilities of the U.S. Public Health Service (which shortened its name in 1912) continued to expand, and in 1944 it became the primary division of the cabinet-level agency today known as the Department of Health and Human Services.

For years I have deeply desired to see laws passed by the United States which would render efficient and co-ordinate its agencies for the preservation of the public health, and in this way promote the protection of our people against the preventable death and disease, which not only has greatly impaired the working efficiency of the American people, imposed hundreds of millions of dollars of unnecessary costs upon the Federal Treasury, but has prevented an increase in our population of many millions of people. All other bills and administration measures, however urgent are, in my opinion, of minor importance compared to this subject of gigantic national interest.

The President of the United States takes a deep concern in this matter. He has frequently declared his desire to have all health and sanitary agencies of the government brought together in one efficient body. He has expressed no objection to a department of public health, and I feel authorized to say so, but without committing himself to a department or a bureau, as preferring one to the other, he has vigorously expressed himself in favor of the concentration of all these health and sanitary agencies into one co-ordinate efficient body.

Mr. President, the people of the United States suffer a preventable loss of over 600,000 lives per annum, a daily senseless sacrifice of an army of over 1,700 human beings every day of the year, over one a minute from one year's end to another, and year after year. This terrible loss might be prevented by reasonable safeguards under the co-operation of the federal and State authorities, each within strict constitutional limits and with an expenditure that is utterly trivial in comparison with its benefits.

These preventable deaths are caused by polluted water, impure and adulterated food and drugs, epidemics, various preventable diseases—tuberculosis, typhoid and malarial fevers—unclean cities, and bad sanitation.

Measuring the money value of an American citizen at $1,700, this preventable loss by death alone is one thousand millions of dollars annually, equal to the gross income of the United States Government.

There are 3,000,000 people seriously sick all the time in the United States from preventable causes, of whom 1,000,000 are in the working period of life; about three-quarters of a million actual workers losing on an average of $700 per annum, an approximate loss from illness of five hundred millions, and adding a reasonable allowance for medicine, medical attendance, special food and care, a like sum of five hundred millions, these losses would make another thousand million dollars of preventable loss to the people of the United States.

Do you imagine that these figures are exaggerated or fanciful, Mr. President? They are confirmed to us by the report of the Committee of One Hundred on National Health in its Report on National Vitality. . . .

Mr. President, our pension roll of over $150,000,000 per annum is three-fourths of it due to illness and death from diseases that were preventable. Under a wise administration in the past the United States would to-day be saving an annual charge of over $100,000,000 on the pension list, and would have saved under this heading over $2,000,000,000 and much human misery and pain.

Will you fail to listen when your attention is called to the vast importance of this matter and to the high standing of those who vouch for the accuracy and reliability of this statement? Will you, as the representatives of the people of the United States, fail to investigate and to act in a matter of such consequence? . . .

I drew this bill (S. 6049) in the hope of cooperating with the administration in making effective the most important of all forms of conservation—the conservation of human life—and in the hope of making effective the expressed desires of the numerous associations and societies of the United States who stand for a department of public health.

Mr. President, since introducing this bill I have been receiving letters from the most distinguished men in the United States indorsing the principle of the bill and expressing the earnest opinion that the time has come for establishing a department of public health.

I quote here from an article in the Survey, of New York—formerly the Charities and Commons—published by the Sage Foundation, March 19, 1910, page 938:

> So, when Senator Owen introduces into the Senate of the United States the first really adequate bill to meet the problem of the conservation of our wasted national health—a bill for the establishment of a national department of health under a secretary who shall be clothed with the prestige and the authority of membership in the President's cabinet— when such a bill is presented to Congress, the old cry goes up from every quarter—the time is not ripe. But there are those who refuse to believe this, who know the time is overripe, some who even put it with Marcellus, that "something is rotten with the State."

The principle of the Owen bill is right. So says the American Medical Association, with its thousands of physicians; so says the Committee of One Hundred, with its thousands of men and women awake to the shortcomings of the multiplicity of government bureaus, each doing a little, some doing more, some doing less, and not all together doing a tithe of what needs to be done, and what co-ordination, consolidation, and unification in one great department could do. . . .

Mr. President, I believe in the conservation of our natural resources—of our coal fields, oil and gas fields, water powers, forests, and mines; the development of our natural resources in establishing good roads and improving our waterways.

The conservation of these great natural resources of our national wealth are of great importance, but the conservation of the life and efficiency of our people is of far greater importance, and should not be destroyed or impaired by unthinking commercialism. The conservation of the vitality and efficiency of our people is a problem of the first magnitude, demanding immediate intelligent attention.

Why conserve coal fields and not coal miners?

Why conserve plant life and not human life? Why conserve animal life and not child life?

We conserve our water powers and forests and forget our people.

We have a great department conserving animal life and plant life and no department conserving human life.

This cannot continue. . . .

Mr. President, I present this bill (S. 6409) to the Senate with no pride of authorship, because I deserve no credit in that respect, and am perfectly willing to assist a bill drawn by any other Senator which shall better accomplish the purposes which I have at heart.

I realize that my colleagues are intensely preoccupied with the multitude of demands upon their time and attention.

But this is a question of vast national importance. In eight years we have increased our expenditures over the average of preceding years by the huge sum of $1,072,000,000 for the army and navy, . . . and are spending 70 per cent of the national income to cover the obligations of past wars and the preparation for possible future war, or about seven hundred millions per annum for such purposes. But for war on preventable diseases, now costing us infinite treasure in life, efficiency, and commercial power and prestige, we spend practically nothing and do not even employ the agencies we have in an efficient manner.

In the name of the people of the United States, and of the great State of Oklahoma especially, and in the name of the American Medical Association, whose 80,000 associates and members are the faithful and self-sacrificing guardians of the health of our people, and in the name of the Committee of One Hundred of the American Federation of Labor, of the National Grange, and of the various health boards of the 46 States of the Union and of the great body of learned men who unanimously desire improved sanitation and the application of the improved agencies of preventing disease, disability, and death, I pray the Senate to establish a department of public health with a Cabinet officer at the head of it.

The principle of the bill meets the general approval of the public health societies and of the medical associations of the United States, and there should be no difficulty in perfecting this bill and in impressing upon the country the importance of organized effort to control the ravages of tuberculosis, typhoid and malarial diseases, which inflict such enormous injury upon the people of the United States, impose such vast, but needless, human misery and pain, with so great financial loss and loss of prestige and power. . . .

Thousands of people are ignorantly and needlessly exposed to the poison of the mosquito and fly, to bad water, bad air, bad food. We ought to have every school-teacher in the United States with bulletins in his hands, teaching the lessons of simple public health, the lessons that will protect the children from the infected mosquito, that will protect the country family from the infected fly that causes typhoid fever. We ought to save the lives of those people, and we cannot do it with a health bureau that has to ask the Secretary of the Treasury before the head of that bureau may make a comment on a public-health question.

It is unspeakably bad to have such a system of government. I think we ought to amend it; that we ought to amend it without delay, and that no pride of opinion ought to stand in the way.

Source: Owen, Robert L. "Speech of Senator Owen on the Bill to Establish a Department of Public Health." *Journal of the Medical Society of New Jersey* 6, 1910, pp. 641–43.

DOCUMENT 4.10

Roosevelt's "Bull Moose" Party Calls for Universal Health Insurance

"Protection of Home Life against the Hazards of Sickness"

1912

In August 1912 Theodore Roosevelt and the Progressive "Bull Moose" Party that coalesced around him in the wake of his break with the Republican Party held their preelection convention in Chicago. Convention speakers included many of the brightest stars in the era's progressive firmament, including Jane Addams of Hull House fame, who delivered the keynote address. On August 6, Roosevelt capped the convention with a stem-winder of a speech in which he highlighted his determination to secure universal health insurance for the American people. "It is abnormal for any industry to throw back upon the community the human wreckage due to its wear and tear," he declared, "and the hazards of sickness, accident, invalidism, involuntary unemployment, and old age should be provided for through insurance. This should be made a charge in whole or in part upon the industries, the employer, the employee, and perhaps the people at large contributing severally in some degree. Wherever such standards are not met by given establishments, by given industries, are unprovided for by a Legislature, or are balked by unenlightened courts, the workers are in jeopardy, the progressive employer is penalized, and the community pays a heavy cost in lessened efficiency and in misery."[1]

These sentiments reflected not only the Progressive Party's keen interest in health care policy, but also the conviction of Roosevelt and other party leaders that robust federal regulation of industry and social affairs was essential to the nation's future prosperity. These same beliefs suffused the Declaration of Principles, excerpted here, that party delegates approved in Chicago. The statement's ambitious list of policy goals included Roosevelt's unprecedented call for a "system of social insurance" that would protect American families "against the hazards of sickness, irregular employment and old age."

DECLARATION OF PRINCIPLES OF THE PROGRESSIVE PARTY

The conscience of the people, in a time of grave national problems, has called into being a new party, born of the nation's awakened sense of justice. We of the Progressive party here dedicate ourselves to the fulfilment of the duty laid upon us by our fathers to maintain the government of the people, by the people and for the people whose foundations they laid.

We hold with Thomas Jefferson and Abraham Lincoln that the people are the masters of their Constitution, to fulfill its purposes and to safeguard it from those who, by perversion of its intent, would convert it into an instrument of injustice. In accordance with the needs of each generation the people must use their sovereign powers to establish and maintain equal opportunity and industrial justice, to secure which this Government was founded and without which no republic can endure.

This country belongs to the people who inhabit it. Its resources, its business, its institutions and its laws should be utilized, maintained or altered in whatever manner will best promote the general interest.

It is time to set the public welfare in the first place.

THE OLD PARTIES

Political parties exist to secure responsible government and to execute the will of the people.

From these great tasks both of the old parties have turned aside. Instead of instruments to promote the general welfare, they have become the tools of corrupt interests which use them impartially to serve their selfish purposes. Behind the ostensible government sits enthroned an invisible government owing no allegiance and acknowledging no responsibility to the people.

To destroy this invisible government, to dissolve the unholy alliance between corrupt business and corrupt politics is the first task of the statesmanship of the day.

The deliberate betrayal of its trust by the Republican party, the fatal incapacity of the Democratic party to deal with the new issues of the new time, have compelled the people to forge a new instrument of government through which to give effect to their will in laws and institutions.

Unhampered by tradition, uncorrupted by power, undismayed by the magnitude of the task, the new party offers itself as the instrument of the people to sweep away old abuses, to build a new and nobler commonwealth.

A COVENANT WITH THE PEOPLE

This declaration is our covenant with the people, and we hereby bind the party and its candidates in State and Nation to the pledges made herein.

THE RULE OF THE PEOPLE

The National Progressive party, committed to the principles of government by a self-controlled democracy expressing its will through representatives of the people, pledges itself to secure such alterations in the fundam[en]tal law of the several States and of the United States as shall insure the representative character of the government.

In particular, the party declares for direct primaries for the nomination of State and National officers, for nation-wide preferential primaries for candidates for the presidency;

for the direct election of United States Senators by the people; and we urge on the States the policy of the short ballot, with responsibility to the people secured by the initiative, referendum and recall.

AMENDMENT OF CONSTITUTION

The Progressive party, believing that a free people should have the power from time to time to amend their fundamental law so as to adapt it progressively to the changing needs of the people, pledges itself to provide a more easy and expeditious method of amending the Federal Constitution.

NATION AND STATE

Up to the limit of the Constitution, and later by amendment of the Constitution, if found necessary, we advocate bringing under effective national jurisdiction those problems which have expanded beyond reach of the individual States.

It is as grotesque as it is intolerable that the several States should by unequal laws in matter of common concern become competing commercial agencies, barter the lives of their children, the health of their women and the safety and well being of their working people for the benefit of their financial interests.

The extreme insistence on States' rights by the Democratic party in the Baltimore platform demonstrates anew its inability to understand the world into which it has survived or to administer the affairs of a union of States which have in all essential respects become one people.

EQUAL SUFFRAGE

The Progressive party, believing that no people can justly claim to be a true democracy which denies political rights on account of sex, pledges itself to the task of securing equal suffrage to men and women alike.

CORRUPT PRACTICES

We pledge our party to legislation that will compel strict limitation of all campaign contributions and expenditures, and detailed publicity of both before as well as after primaries and elections.

PUBLICITY AND PUBLIC SERVICE

We pledge our party to legislation compelling the registration of lobbyists; publicity of committee hearings except on foreign affairs, and recording of all votes in committee; and forbidding federal appointees from holding office in State or National political organizations, or taking part as officers or delegates in political conventions for the nomination of elective State or National officials.

THE COURTS

The Progressive party demands such restriction of the power of the courts as shall leave to the people the ultimate authority to determine fundamental questions of social welfare and public policy. To secure this end, it pledges itself to provide:

1. That when an Act, passed under the police power of the State, is held unconstitutional under the State Constitution, by the courts, the people, after an ample interval for deliberation, shall have an opportunity to vote on the question whether they desire the Act to become law, notwithstanding such decision.

2. That every decision of the highest appellate court of a State declaring an Act of the Legislature unconstitutional on the ground of its violation of the Federal Constitution shall be subject to the same review by the Supreme Court of the United States as is now accorded to decisions sustaining such legislation. . . .

SOCIAL AND INDUSTRIAL JUSTICE

The supreme duty of the Nation is the conservation of human resources through an enlightened measure of social and industrial justice. We pledge ourselves to work unceasingly in State and Nation for:

Effective legislation looking to the prevention of industrial accidents, occupational diseases, overwork, involuntary unemployment, and other injurious effects incident to modern industry;

The fixing of minimum safety and health standards for the various occupations, and the exercise of the public authority of State and Nation, including the Federal Control over interstate commerce, and the taxing power, to maintain such standards;

The prohibition of child labor;

Minimum wage standards for working women, to provide a "living wage" in all industrial occupations;

The general prohibition of night work for women and the establishment of an eight-hour day for women and young persons;

One day's rest in seven for all wage workers;

The eight-hour day in continuous twenty-four-hour industries;

The abolition of the convict contract labor system; substituting a system of prison production for governmental consumption only; and the application of prisoners' earnings to the support of their dependent families;

Publicity as to wages, hours and conditions of labor; full reports upon industrial accidents and diseases, and the opening to public inspection of all tallies, weights, measures and check systems on labor products;

Standards of compensation for death by industrial accident and injury and trade disease which will transfer the burden of lost earnings from the families of working people to the industry, and thus to the community;

The protection of home life against the hazards of sickness, irregular employment and old age through the adoption of a system of social insurance adapted to American use;

The development of the creative labor power of America by lifting the last load of illiteracy from American youth and establishing continuation schools for industrial education under public control and encouraging agricultural education and demonstration in rural schools;

The establishment of industrial research laboratories to put the methods and discoveries of science at the service of American producers;

We favor the organization of the workers, men and women, as a means of protecting their interests and of promoting their progress. . . .

HEALTH

We favor the union of all the existing agencies of the Federal Government dealing with the public health into a single national health service without discrimination against or for any one set of therapeutic methods, school of medicine, or school of healing with such additional powers as may be necessary to enable it to perform efficiently such duties in the protection of the public from preventable diseases as may be properly undertaken by the Federal authorities, including the executing of existing laws regarding pure food, quarantine and cognate subjects, the promotion of vital statistics and the extension of the registration area of such s[t]atistics , and co-operation with the health activities of the various States and cities of the Nation. . . .

Source: "The Progressive Platform—An Appeal to the People's Conscience." In *The Birth of the New Party: or, Progressive Democracy,* edited by George Henry Payne. Naperville, IL: J. L. Nichols, 1912, pp. 303–8, 309–10.

NOTE

1. "Roosevelt's Own Creed Set Forth," *New York Times,* August 7, 1912, www.nytimes.com/packages /flash/health/HEALTHCARE_TIMELINE/1912_roosevelt.pdf.

DOCUMENT 4.11

Public Health Service Compares Health Insurance in America and Europe

"The Situation Is of Too Much Public Importance to Be Left to Commercial Organizations"

1913

By the opening days of the twentieth century, several European nations had established an array of compulsory and voluntary social insurance programs that provided government aid to sick and elderly citizens. The apparent success of many of these programs in providing a social and economic safety net for vulnerable people captured the imagination of American progressives, who devised a variety of schemes to import these government initiatives and Americanize them for domestic use. These efforts received enthusiastic support from the U.S. Public Health Service (PHS), which stood to reap new levels of authority (and corresponding growth in its budget) if such reforms came to pass. In the following PHS analysis from 1913 (footnotes removed), the agency frames its approbation of government-sponsored health insurance as a matter of both social justice and economic necessity.

GROWTH OF SOCIAL INSURANCE

The adaptability of the insurance method in the solution of modern economic problems is unmistakably shown in the spread of "social insurance" in countries whose governments embody widely different political ideals. As soon as certain economic risks have been recognized as menacing the wageworker and his family, the insurance method of meeting the risks has been used. These economic risks may be generally classified as those causing the death of the breadwinner in a family, the physical inability of the breadwinner to perform labor, and his inability to find employment. For a large proportion of the wage earners of any country those risks are too great to be provided for by individual effort and too little appreciated to be provided for even if the individual were able to do so. Hence, social provision through the distribution of loss has been found to be necessary. This kind of social provision has come to be known as "social insurance."

The recognition for the need of provisions of this character has been followed in every important modern industrial nation, with the exception of the United States, by various systems of social insurance. Even in this country accident insurance in the form of workmen's compensation is rapidly spreading. Accident insurance for workers has been established by governments throughout Europe and in many of the British colonies. Old-age insurance is established under governmental authority and is subsidized by the Governments of Italy, Belgium, Servia, and Spain, while old-age pension systems have been established by the Governments of Great Britain, Denmark, Iceland, France, Australia, and New Zealand. Unemployment insurance is a governmental system in Great Britain and is rapidly being adopted in many European cities. Health insurance is probably the most prevalent form of social insurance.

Growth of health insurance in Europe.—The extent to which European governments have encouraged and provided for health insurance is a fact which has not been fully appreciated in the United States. Voluntary health insurance systems have been subsidized by the Governments of France, Belgium, Denmark, Sweden, and Switzerland. But more significant as an evidence of the recognition of the efficacy of health insurance is the fact that compulsory systems have been established in Germany, Austria, Hungary, Norway, Great Britain, Servia, Russia, Luxemburg, Roumania, France (for miners, seamen, and railway employees), and Italy (for railway employees).

It is important to note that, while the growth of private and commercial health insurance plans, which preceded in nearly all instances the other systems, proved the great need of health insurance, subsidization by European governments not only further showed the need for health insurance, but was an admission that private systems had failed to meet the situation. According to the experience in other countries as well as in the United States, private and commercial health insurance has failed to afford the relief and lighten the burden in the case of workers who stand in the greatest need. Subsidized health insurance, experience has shown, has also failed to meet the situation, because its good results are not universal. Voluntary health insurance, whether subsidized or not, does not reach the low-paid workers, the very group who are in the greatest need of protection. State systems of health insurance which provide that all workers are entitled to benefits are the only systems which have reached all groups and provided universal protection.

Growth of health insurance in the United States.—In this country we are in the first stage in health insurance. No State, municipal, or other government in any way provides for or aids health insurance. There are, however, large numbers of private systems, such as mutual benefit associations and other societies which provide for health insurance, in addition to various employers' schemes which enable employees to have funds in times of sickness, trade union benefits, and commercial insurance companies with health insurance policies. These agencies may be classified as follows:

a. Trade unions: (1) National; (2) local.
b. Employers' organizations for benefit of employees: (1) railroad funds; (2) establishment funds.
c. Mutual societies: (1; Fraternal orders; (2) local lodges; (3) general benefit societies; (4) special sick benefit funds.
d. Commercial companies operating for profit or on the mutual principle: (1) Industrial insurance companies; (2) casualty companies doing industrial health insurance. . . .

[Recent trends in health insurance coverage in the United States] indicate two important facts:

First, that health insurance is more and more coming to be looked upon by employees and employers alike as a practicable method of dealing with the problem of the cost of sickness.

Second, that inasmuch as the cost of the insurance under the existing voluntary plans in the United States is paid almost altogether by the employees, only those who are able to afford to make the payments are in the position of receiving the advantages that accrue.

In other words, so far as they are able, wageworkers are rapidly adopting health insurance of their own accord. A constantly growing number of employers are inaugurating establishment funds which are largely supported by their employees. Commercial companies are finding their health policies more and more popular in spite of the relatively heavy cost to wage-earning holders. . . . What is worth emphasis here is the unmistakable tendency on the part of all concerned—the worker as well as the employer, the individual as well as the State—toward the adoption of the insurance principle as the most practicable and the most efficient method of attacking the problem of sickness. As Prof. [Joseph P.] Chamberlain has pointed out, health insurance is "already an accomplished fact in the United States, but is insufficient in amount and wrong in its methods and purposes. . . . Contribution of employers is already accepted in principle; cooperation of employer and employee is established and growing. The question of sickness insurance is therefore a problem of organization of existing forces and making use of existing resources and admitted principles, rather than the introduction of a dangerous novelty." Or, as Dr. [Isaac Max] Rubinow has said, "a sickness insurance law, even in one State, can do more to eradicate poverty, and is therefore a greater social gain, than a dozen organizations for scientific philanthropy with their investigations, their sermons on thrift, and their constant feverish hunt for liberal contributions."

V. Health Insurance: A Health Measure.

Any system of health insurance for the United States or any State should at its inception have prevention of sickness as one of its fundamental purposes. This country should profit by the experience of European countries where, after a long period of evolution, prevention is being recognized as the central idea necessary if health insurance is to attain its greatest success in improving the health and efficiency of the industrial population.

With the cooperative principle so generally recognized in industry and with the application of insurance as a method for the relief of sickness among wage earners so generally accepted in Europe and to some extent in America, the question naturally suggests itself: Can health insurance be so developed and coordinated with other agencies as to become an effective public-health measure without imposing a new policy on this country which is not in accord with its ideals and institutions?

Up to the present time, health insurance systems have not reached their highest development as public-health measures because they have been adopted more as methods for relief than for prevention of disease. It is true that in Germany many evidences are found where prevention is beginning to be considered the primary object. In Great Britain, with a few exceptions, health insurance is a relief measure. In fact, it has had very little connection and has been poorly coordinated with other health agencies. To obtain the highest degree of success in America, it would appear that health insurance systems should be very closely correlated with national, State, and local health agencies. If these agencies are at present inadequate, they should be enlarged and strengthened instead of attempting to create new and independent health agencies. . . .

The best-developed systems of health insurance provide for three kinds of benefits to insured persons:

1. Cash payments to insured persons for disability due to sickness, to nonindustrial accidents, and to childbearing by the beneficiary, for periods extending as long as six months.
2. Cash payments for deaths of insured persons due to sickness or nonindustrial accident sufficient in amount to cover funeral expenses.
3. Medical benefits to insured persons which include adequate medical and surgical care, medicines and appliances in home, hospital, sanatorium, or physician's office, beginning usually with the first day of disability, whether disability be due to sickness or nonindustrial accident or childbearing of insured person or wife of insured person, for a period of six months unless otherwise extended.

The benefits provided in existing plans in the United States, besides being more expensive to the insured than those under European systems, are more limited. There are practically no plans with cash and medical benefits combined, and maternity benefits are seldom provided. The duration of the benefits is in some cases limited to 13 weeks or less. The British National Insurance Act does not provide a death or funeral benefit, and the omission of this important provision resulted in the selling of death-benefit policies at exorbitant rates by commercial insurance companies which, under the act, had organized "approved societies" among their own policyholders for the purpose of conducting health insurance according to the provisions of the national system.

EXTENSION OF HEALTH INSURANCE TO ALL WAGE EARNERS.

In the governmental cooperative systems of Great Britain and Germany all workers in all industries and all occupations are insured and receive the benefits. In the United States, on the other hand, those who need financial assistance the most and who stand in the greatest need of better health conditions are seldom insured. The advantages of health insurance are out of the reach of practically all workers other than the highest paid, except in a comparatively few industrial establishments where membership in the so-called mutual sick-benefit funds is compulsory upon all employees and where oftentimes the workers are restive under an administration of the funds which they feel to be paternalistic. As a general rule only those workers in this country who are able to pay all of the cost of carrying insurance are able to obtain its advantages, and the cost of operation of health insurance, especially in commercial companies, necessitates a premium which contains a substantial profit to the company and which can be afforded only by the better-paid wage earner. The great mass of low-paid, unskilled workers are seldom found among those insured in union, establishment, mutual society, and commercial insurance company funds.

As constituted and practiced in the United States, therefore, health insurance practically leaves the problem of the health among low-paid wageworkers untouched. It is not going too far to say that the situation in the United States at present is not nearly so good as the situation in Great Britain prior to the passage of the National Insurance Act. Even in Great Britain, where the commercial and mutual health insurance organizations had probably reached a greater development than in any other country; less than half of the wage earners were benefited by them. This situation was described by Mr. David Lloyd-George, in his well-known speech in the House of Commons in 1911, in the following words:

> What is the explanation that only a portion of the working classes have made provision against sickness? Is it that they consider it not necessary? Quite the reverse. In fact those who stand most in need of it make up the bulk of the uninsured. Why? Because very few can afford to pay premiums continuously which enable a man to provide against these contingencies . . . . There are a multitude of the working classes who can not spare that, and who ought not to be asked to spare it, because it involves the deprivation of the children of the necessities of life.

Prior to the passage of the National Insurance Act, thousands of health-insurance policies lapsed every year in Great Britain among the wage-earning policyholders, thus occasioning a real loss to them because they found themselves unable to continue the policies until they received benefits. No one will deny that the same thing has occurred and is occurring every year in the United States. The reason for it is not hard to explain when it is remembered that a very large proportion of workingmen's families are living on a very narrow margin of subsistence; so narrow, in fact, that the continuous payment of commercial insurance premiums is plainly impossible. The situation, involved as it is in the entire question of disease prevention as well as of the care of the sick, is of too much public importance to be left to commercial organizations. It is essentially a public-health matter. Commercial companies have served a useful purpose in providing health insurance for the better-paid workers, but they have not reached and never can reach the lower-paid workers.

Distribution of Cost among Employees, Employers, and Public.

In European health insurance systems the principle has been thoroughly established that the cost of maintenance, or the total payments of premiums, is shared by employers and employees and to some extent by governments. Under the British National Insurance Act, employers pay three-ninths, employees four-ninths, and the Government two-ninths of the contributions to the health insurance fund for males. The proportion differs slightly for female insured persons. In the German system of sickness insurance, as a general rule, employers contribute one-third and employees two-thirds of the sickness insurance fund, while the Government bears the expense of governmental supervision. In some instances employers pay as much as one-half of the premiums of their employees.

In this country, on the other hand, the burden of the cost of health insurance is borne almost entirely by the wageworker. In consequence he is expected to bear the expense of meeting a responsibility which is not wholly his, but which should in part be shared by the public and the employer.

The employees' share.—It would be a serious error, however, for the cost of health insurance to be borne entirely by employers or by employers and the public. The employee should in no sense of the word be a ward. The expense of maintenance should be divided as nearly as possible according to the degree of responsibility, and it is but just that employees should pay the largest share, as they do in European countries, in view of the consideration that they receive the greatest direct benefits.

A governmental system of health insurance would hardly impose an additional burden upon the insured persons. On the contrary, it would probably materially reduce the amount they are now paying in medical bills and small life insurance premiums. It appears from budgetary studies that workingmen's families spend from 30 to 90 cents per week for health and small life insurance policies.

The experience in European countries in health insurance systems in which employers, employees, and the government are joint contributors, indicates that under a similar system in this country the expenditure by employees of the minimum amount (30 cents per week) stated above would provide not only adequate medical care and a small life insurance policy, but also a substantial cash payment during illness for a period not to exceed 26 weeks. A preliminary study of existing systems in the United States indicates that a governmental system could, at a weekly cost of 25 cents to the employee, 20 cents to the employer, and 5 cents to the Government, or a total of 50 cents per insured person, provide a minimum cash benefit for sickness of $7 a week for a maximum period of 26 weeks and a death benefit of $100 in addition to medical and hospital service. Thus the worker would have to pay only a small proportion of what he is now spending on insurance and health, and at the same time he would receive much greater benefits and obtain indirect results of an untold value from the cooperative action of all agencies in the prevention of disease.

The employers' share.—There can hardly be any doubt that the employer should bear a part of the expense of maintaining the health insurance fund of his employees, not only because he is responsible for many of the conditions that govern the health of his employees, but because he reaps some of the important results. It is an un-contradicted proposition that any measure that will maintain the health of the worker is a positive benefit to the employer. In fact, as already pointed out, there are some employers in the United States who have recognized the truth of this principle to such an extent that they pay for the entire cost of a sick fund for their employees. There are numbers of employers who contribute varying proportions of their establishment funds. In addition, many employers are paying considerable amounts in subscriptions to charities and to the maintenance of free clinics and hospitals, and the like. The establishment of a definite principle of sharing in the maintenance of the health insurance fund places all employers on an equal footing and compels all to meet their obligations in a businesslike and democratic manner, and not on a basis of charity or for the purposes of controlling or stabilizing their labor supply.

The public's share.—The responsibility of the public has already been emphasized, and its failure, under present conditions of public-health work, to discharge this responsibility toward the wage-earning population has been pointed out. The sharing by the Government in the cost of maintaining the health-insurance fund for wage earners will enable the public to meet its responsibility in a more definite and direct manner. Judging from the heavy burden the public already bears in its present inadequate efforts to meet its responsibilities, it is safe to say that the American public, as a contributor to health insurance funds, can perform its duties to wage earners at much lower financial expense to itself and with infinitely less loss of self-respect to the wage earner than at present. The public has the right to be a contributor on the ground that health insurance is a measure distinctly for its own welfare. One-third of the "public" are wage earners. The immense sums that are already being spent annually in public and private charities, in relief work, in caring for the victims of the conditions that cause ill health suggest the uneconomical and undemocratic nature of the methods now employed, as well as the fact, which the public has come to realize, that it does have a real and necessary responsibility to meet.

Source: U.S. Public Health Service. "Growth of Social Insurance." *Public Health Bulletin.* Issues 63–76. Washington, DC: Government Printing Office, 1913, pp. 48–55.

DOCUMENT 4.12   A Reformer Makes the Case for National Health Insurance

"The Power of Health Insurance toward Social Regeneration"

1916

In 1916 many observers believed that the United States was on the verge of instituting a federally directed program of national health insurance patterned after similar programs that had sprouted in Germany and other European nations around the turn of the century. Certainly, the leaders of pro–national health insurance organizations such as the American Association of Labor Legislation (AALL) and the American Medical Association (AMA) believed that they were poised at the precipice of a momentous policy victory that would forever change the nation for the better. Yale University economist and AALL president Irving Fisher was among these confident luminaries, as indicated by his remarks (excerpted here) at the tenth annual meeting of the AALL in Columbus, Ohio, in December 1916.

Fisher's optimism proved misplaced, however. Within a year of his upbeat address in Columbus, the campaign for universal health insurance in America was in full retreat, beleaguered by ruthless opposition from the insurance industry and the issue's suddenly damaging association with Germany, with which the United States had gone to war.

THE NEED FOR HEALTH INSURANCE

In the last six months, through the efforts of the American Association for Labor Legislation, a consciousness of the imperative need in this country for health insurance has dawned upon thinking Americans. Within another six months it will be a burning question in many states. As Dr. Blue, surgeon general of the United States Public Health Service, has said, it is the next great step in social legislation in this country.

At present the United States has the unenviable distinction of being the only great industrial nation without compulsory health insurance. For a generation the enlightened nations of Europe have one after another discussed the idea and followed discussion by adoption. It has constituted an important part of the policy and career of some of Europe's greatest statesmen, including Bismarck and Lloyd George. Germany showed the way in 1883 under the leadership of Bismarck. This act was the first step in her program of social legislation. Her wonderful industrial progress since that time, her comparative freedom from poverty, reduction in the death rate, advancement in hygiene, and the physical preparedness of her soldiery, are presumably due, in considerable measure, to health insurance.

Following the example of Germany, health insurance was adopted successively by Austria, Hungary, Luxemburg, Norway, Serbia, Great Britain, Russia, Rumania, and Holland. Other countries have adopted a subsidized voluntary system, namely, France, Belgium, Switzerland, Denmark, Sweden, and Iceland. Thus the only European countries which, like the United States, are without any general system are Italy, Spain, Portugal, Greece, Bulgaria, Albania, Montenegro, and Turkey.

Because we have a democratic form of government we have peacefully assumed that our civilization is more advanced than others, but while we have rested complacently on our oars, other nations have forged ahead of us. The war has at last startled us out of our Rip Van Winkle slumber, and we are now passing through a period of national self-examination.

There are special reasons to hope that health insurance may win favor rapidly. The war has made labor scarce and therefore dear. This fact will make not only for high wages, but also for the conservation of labor. Students of the history of slavery find that when slaves were abundant and cheap, masters worked them to death and replaced them when worn out. Consequently, cruelty was condoned and fashionable. On the other hand, when slaves were scarce and dear, the masters took good care of them and a humanitarian sentiment developed to correspond. I believe it to be a correct economic portent that the world is about to enter upon a period of life conservation. The war has for a time withdrawn much of the world's labor supply and destroyed and maimed a large part of that which it has withdrawn. The world will seek the greatest possible salvage out of the wreck. . . .

Fortunately we have already taken one step in a social insurance program. After a long and uphill fight, workmen's compensation has had a belated recognition in America. The American Association for Labor Legislation was foremost in this fight, and now at last it is ready for a similar fight to secure workmen's health insurance. For four years an able committee of this Association has been studying American conditions and foreign health insurance acts, and constructing a standard bill. This bill, with some variations, has been introduced into the state legislatures of Massachusetts, New York, and New Jersey, and commissions to consider the subject have been appointed in Massachusetts and California and are expected to report in January. It is significant that so large were the throngs which attended the public hearing of the Massachusetts commission on October 3 that the meeting place had to be twice changed during the hearing to larger quarters. During the ensuing year it is expected that the bill will be introduced in about twenty state legislatures.

The United States Public Health Service has issued a special study on *Health Insurance* by Dr. B. S. Warren and Edgar Sydenstricker. The American Medical Association has a working committee on health insurance of which Alexander Lambert is chairman and I. M. Rubinow secretary. This association has published a report on social insurance. Several medical societies, including the Pennsylvania State Medical Society and the State Medical Society of Wisconsin, and several public health associations, have endorsed the principle of health insurance. The American Association for the Study and Prevention of Tuberculosis and many of its affiliated organizations have, through public meetings and otherwise, helped the movement. A number of charitable organizations have also favored the idea and forty-five organizations of various natures, including the American Academy of Medicine, the International Association of Industrial Accident Boards, the National Conference of Charities and Correction, the New York Chamber of Commerce, and the American Public Health Association have appointed committees to study and report upon health insurance. . . .

Many trade unions have taken up the subject. Some have strongly favored the idea; a few leaders have vigorously opposed it, apparently because of a groundless fear that in some way the power of the labor unions would be lessened. Thus some oppose health insurance as they at one time opposed compulsory workmen's compensation. On the other hand several international unions, including the International Typographical Union, have definitely gone on record as favorable. State federations of labor in Ohio, New Jersey, Massachusetts, Missouri, Nebraska, and Wisconsin are favorable. A number of local trade unions have taken favorable action. Many individual labor leaders of prominence have definitely approved it; these include John Mitchell, Ignatius McNulty, Van Bittner, James H. Maurer, Andrew Furuseth, S. E. Heberling, John B. Lennon, James O'Connell, Austin B. Garretson, William Green, and James Duncan.

The cordial and almost unprecedented welcome which this movement has received in spite of the opposition of strong vested interests and their industrious and insidious efforts to misrepresent and injure the movement would seem to indicate that the time for health insurance in the United States is ripe.

The plan as put forth by the American Association for Labor Legislation is fully described in its draft of a standard bill and defended in its *Brief for Health Insurance*. The bill proposes the obligatory insurance of substantially all workingmen and women. In case of sickness the insured will receive medical or surgical service, medicines, and nursing, and a cash benefit amounting to two-thirds of the weekly wages of the insured for the period of illness up to six months. Maternity benefits are provided for childbirth, and funeral benefits for death.

Benefits are paid for at cost by the joint contributions of the insured employee, his employer, and the state. The cost to the employee will average about 1 ½ per cent of his wages. The cost to the employer will be an equal amount, while the state will pay half as much as either the employer or the employee. These are the main points covered in the standard bill. I am here concerned, however, not with the merits of this particular plan but with the need of some plan of universal health insurance for workmen.

The need for health insurance, like that for most other forms of insurance, is twofold. There is the need of indemnification against loss, and the need of diminishing the loss itself.

Indemnification is the essence of the insurance principle. It spreads the loss of each person in a group over them all. For each individual it converts large fluctuating haphazard losses into small regular and certain costs. Insurance aims to reduce fluctuations—to make the income stream more steady. It is more economical to pay a little premium for fire insurance each year than to suffer a big loss when the fire comes. This insurance principle is of the greatest importance in economics and in business. The well-to-do have long made use of it in fire insurance, marine insurance, life insurance, fidelity insurance, plate glass insurance, steam boiler insurance, and, to some extent, accident and health insurance. The capitalist has long endeavored to eliminate, or at least to reduce, every determinable risk. But the curious and melancholy fact is that outside of workmen's compensation the poor in this country have received, as yet, very little benefits from the application of the insurance principle. Yet it is the poor whose need of health insurance is greatest, and for two important reasons. One is that the worker is more likely to lose his health than the capitalist; for it is well known from several lines of research that the death rate, and therefore the sickness rate, prevailing among the poor is from two to three times that prevailing among the well-to-do. The other reason is that any loss from sickness is a far more vital matter to the poor than to the rich. The workman who loses his health loses his chief asset. That low-paid workingmen seldom insure against illness is undoubted.

. . . Certain it is that as yet the amount of voluntary health insurance in the United States such as that under fraternal societies, labor unions, establishment funds, and insurance companies, covers only a small fraction of workingmen and women. Judging from the tentative estimates of [Isaac Max] Rubinow, only about 5 per cent of our workmen needing insurance actually have it. The other 95 per cent have been deterred by the high cost of such insurance under the voluntary system, by their lack of appreciation of its benefits, by the inertia of custom, and by the sheer desperation of poverty. . . .

Certain interests which would be, or think they would be, adversely affected by health insurance have made the specious plea that it is an un-American interference with liberty. They forget that compulsory education, though at first opposed on these very grounds, is highly American and highly liberative, that prohibitory laws on various subjects such as habit-forming drugs and even alcohol have introduced liberative compulsions in many states in America, and that workmen's compensation acts have introduced liberative compulsion in this very field of workingmen's insurance. The truth is that the opponents of compulsory health insurance are in every case, as far as I can discover, subject to some special bias. They grasp at the slogan of liberty as a subterfuge only.

Oh liberty! liberty! How many crimes are committed in thy name!

According to the logic of those now shedding crocodile tears over health insurance we ought, in order to remain truly American and truly free, to retain the precious liberties of our people to be illiterate, to be drunk, and to suffer accidents without indemnification, as well as to be sick without indemnification. In fact, if compulsory health insurance is tyranny, all labor laws, all tenement laws, all health laws, all pure food laws, even *all* laws, are tyranny. In fact, all laws are an interference with some one's liberty, even laws against vice and crime. It is the nature of the Law to restrict. But it is by the compelling hand of the law that society secures liberation from the evils of crime, vice, ignorance, accidents, unemployment, invalidity, and disease. . . .

It is well known that the form of social insurance recently adopted in the United States, namely "workmen's compensation," has had the effect of greatly stimulating industrial methods in accident prevention. Out of workmen's compensation came the "Safety First!" slogan and the public movement which it represents. J. D. Beck, of the Wisconsin Industrial Commission, declared that more progress in accident prevention had been made in his state in one year under workmen's compensation than in any previous period of five years. . . .

Health insurance will afford a very powerful and pervasive stimulus to employers, employees, and public men to take fuller and speedier advantage of possible health saving devices. The standard bill of the Association is so drawn as to give any locality and any trade the benefit in lower contributions of any reduction in sickness rates which may be achieved, thus creating an immediate financial motive to reduce illness.

Just as employers have installed safeguards for dangerous machinery in order to reduce the cost of workmen's compensation, so in order to reduce the cost of health insurance they will supply, for instance, better sanitation, ventilation, and lighting, more physiological hours of labor, and fuller consideration for the special needs of employed women and children. In localities where the employer provides tenements for his workmen, he will be led to study and improve housing conditions. So-called welfare work will be made more effective and helpful. Employers will collect facts and statistics as to sickness, analyze them and apply such corrections as the facts discovered indicate. Dr. Rubinow states that a large corporation after introducing health insurance tried, for the first time, to discover its sickness rate and found it to be three times what is usual.

Further investigation showed that this excessive rate was due to bad conditions, not in the factory, but in the sanitation of the city. As a consequence an effort was made for the first time toward improving these conditions. It is especially to be expected that as soon as employers realize the nerve strain caused by over-long hours and consequent increase of illness and, therefore, the cost to themselves, they will acquaint themselves with the effects of long hours of labor and reduce them.

The employee, on the other hand, will be likewise stimulated to welcome and to utilize factory hygiene, and improve his own domestic hygiene and individual hygiene. If there could be any doubt as to the reality or strength of this impulse it would vanish after observing the experience in Connecticut of the employees' relief associations organized to combat tuberculosis. Each workman contributes at least 25 cents a year, and, as a consequence of that investment, takes a surprising interest in seeing that his money is wisely expended and that tuberculosis cases are promptly discovered and sent away for treatment. The possibilities of self-improvement through learning how to live are far beyond what any one who has not gone over the evidence realizes. The evils of bad air, bad food, imperfect teeth, wrong posture, improper clothing, constipation, self-drugging, alcoholism, etc., are now overlooked by ninety-nine workmen out of a hundred. Here is a wonderful opportunity for effective and intelligent leadership among committees of wage-earners. The employee will be more ready to apply to his own internal machinery a principle, long since applied by his employer to inanimate machinery, the principle of inspection and repairs. After health insurance has been adopted slight impairments to health will be remedied before they become serious.

At present we find the United States, in striking contrast to health insured Europe, is suffering from an increase of the death rate after middle life. The increase consists of an increase in degenerative or wear-and-tear diseases, and is due to the growing neglect of personal and other hygiene. The death rate from degenerative diseases in the United States registration area has increased 41 per cent in twenty years.

One important effect of such attention to the health of the workman will be the prolongation of his life and especially of its earning period. Fewer workingmen will be thrown on the scrap heap in their forties with all the tragic consequences involved to their families as well as to themselves.

Moreover, the cash benefit gives the workman a better chance for recovery as well as a more perfect recovery if attained; for, to the poor, the obstacles to recovery are largely economic—insufficient food or other necessaries, worry over making both ends meet, and the consequent necessity of a premature return to work while still half-sick. It is found that the longer the time given up to sickness, which means the more care given to get well, the lower the death rate. Critics of German insurance have pointed to the fact that the number of days' absence from work per person on account of illness has increased under health insurance, but as Dr. Rubinow points out, this increase is partly, if not wholly, due to improved and longer care of the sick. Only part, and probably a small part, can be charged up to malingering.

Again, under compulsory health insurance both employer and employee will cooperate with the general public in securing public water supply, better sewerage systems, better milk, meat, and food laws, better school hygiene, more playgrounds and parks, and proper regulation of liquor and other health destroying businesses.

Health insurance will also, as it did in Germany, help to meet the crying need for rural sanitation and bring adequate medical and housing care to American farmers and their families.

Health insurance will operate, as it did in Germany, to stimulate the general scientific study of disease prevention, the future possibilities of which though unknown are, we may be sure, enormous. . . .

Besides health insurance many other stimuli of course exist, but they need reenforcement [sic]. Moreover, nothing can equal health insurance as a stimulus to prevention among employers and employees.

But prevention of disease and disability is not the only prevention to be effected by health insurance. It will indirectly but powerfully tend to reduce poverty. In the first place the simple operation of the indemnity principle itself tends to reduce poverty. Poverty today is largely mischance. When a poor man becomes sick, unless he can tide the emergency over by insurance or otherwise, he runs the risk of getting "down and out," for he has little or no margin. Without health insurance a vast number sooner or later exhaust whatever margin they have and sink into poverty—a land from whose bourne few travellers return. Students of gambling condemn games of chance because sooner or later most gamblers must lose enough to throw them out of the game. At present the American workmen without health insurance are gambling with their livelihood and in millions of cases are sure to be thrown out of the game. It is not a question of *average* well-being but of the numbers diverging from the average. One opponent of health insurance says it is not needed in America because the "average" American workman is comfortably situated. Aside from the fact that the most comfortably situated workman needs health insurance, we must not forget that the majority of workmen have less than the average wages and that a large minority have more than the average sickness (of a little over a week) per year. It is true that American wages are, on the average, much higher than German wages, but poverty is, or was before the war, markedly less in Germany than in the United States. This is doubtless largely if not chiefly owing to health insurance. The German laborer has not been allowed to gamble with disease and let it often win away from him his little all. In America, where the workingman is not so protected, we see the results in the casual laborer. . . .

. . . [T]he Charity Organization Society of Buffalo reported in 1916 that "Last year in Buffalo less than 1 per cent of our poverty was due to lack of work, and more than 76 per cent to sickness." According to an officer of the United States Public Health Service, assigned to the Commission on Industrial Relations, sickness produces seven times as much destitution as industrial accidents. Dr. Devine found among 5,000 families known to the Charity Organization Society that in 75 per cent illness was a part cause of poverty. The report of the Immigration Commission of 1909 states that "The illness of the bread-winner or other members of the family was 'the apparent cause of need' in 38.3 per cent of the cases, while accidents were a factor in but 3.8 per cent of the total applications for aid." "At the New York legislative hearing on the health insurance bill in 1916 it was shown that 37 per cent of the families assisted by the New York Charity Organization Society are dependent because their wage-earners are disabled by sickness, while two-thirds to four-fifths of the expenditure of the New York Association for Improving the Condition of the Poor is for relief necessary because of illness." In the report of the New York Factory Investigating Commission (1915), one working woman gives it as her experience that "practically every week, in her factory, there is either a collection or raffle for the benefit of some worker who is sick, who has no resources, and who therefore is an object of the charity of her fellow employees." This custom, states the report, is really of considerable significance as an indication of how few are able to accumulate for times of emergency. It is also significant in showing how dire is the need of health insurance; for raffles and the like are a sort of stop-gap or make-shift for health insurance.

We see, then, that the claim that in America we do not need health insurance because the workman is so well-to-do is very evidently not in accord with the facts. As the *Brief for Health Insurance* of the American Association for Labor Legislation says, and as the above statistics would indicate, "America evidently presents no exception to the finding of Mr. and Mrs. Sidney Webb, that 'In all countries, at all ages, it is sickness to which the greatest bulk of destitution is immediately due.'" . . .

We conclude that health insurance is needed in the United States in order to tide the workers over the grave emergencies incident to illness as well as in order to reduce illness itself, lengthen life, abate poverty, improve working power, raise the wage level, and diminish the causes of industrial discontent. It is not a panacea. It will not bring the millennium. But there is no other measure now before the public which equals the power of health insurance toward social regeneration.

Source: Fisher, Irving. "The Need for Health Insurance." *American Labor Legislation Review*, March 1917. Published in *American Labor Legislation Review*. Vol. 7. New York: American Association for Labor Legislation, pp. 9–23.

DOCUMENT 4.13 — Educating Navy Personnel about a Deadly Influenza Epidemic

"Keep Well, and Do Not Get Hysterical over the Epidemic"

1918

As the 1918 Spanish flu epidemic swept across the United States, federal agencies, state governments, and municipal health departments all engaged in frantic rollouts of public education campaigns to minimize the impact of the influenza outbreak. Flyers such as this one, issued by the U.S. Navy's Division of Sanitation, were a key component of these education efforts. In this particular flyer, the Navy emphasizes the importance of fresh air, fluids, sleep, and minimizing contact with potential flu carriers in warding off the disease.

INFLUENZA

Influenza is "grippe." It is now spreading over the country in epidemic form. The last extensive epidemic occurred in 1889-90, and the disease was very prevalent for several years after.

The present epidemic disease is plain influenza. The term "Spanish influenza" has been applied because of its recent prevalence in Spain. Influenza occurs every year in the United States, but it is most contagious during an epidemic, and pneumonia is a more frequent complication.

Influenza is caused by a germ, the *influenza bacillus,* which lives but a short time outside of the body. Fresh air and sunshine kill the germ in a few minutes.

The disease is spread by the moist secretions from the noses and throats of infected persons.

Protect yourself from infection, keep well, and do not get hysterical over the epidemic.

Avoid being sprayed by the nose and throat secretions of others.

Beware of those who are coughing and sneezing.

Avoid crowded street cars—walk to the office if possible.

Keep out of crowds—avoid theaters, moving-picture shows, and other places of public assembly.

Do not travel by railroad unless absolutely necessary.

Do not drink from glasses or cups which have been used by others unless you are sure they have been thoroughly cleansed.

You can do much to lessen the danger to yourself by keeping in good physical condition.

Avoid close, stuffy, and poorly ventilated rooms—insist upon fresh air, but avoid disagreeable drafts.

Eat simple, nourishing food and drink plenty of water. Avoid constipation.

Secure at least seven hours sleep. Avoid physical fatigue.

Do not sleep or sit around in damp clothing.

Keep the feet dry.

Influenza usually has a sudden onset with chilliness, severe headache, and "aching all over." At times the disease begins with nausea, vomiting, and abdominal pain. Fever begins early. Frequently catarrhal symptoms do not appear until later. When they do they are the symptoms of a bad cold in the head with a raw throat and dry cough. Weakness and prostration out of proportion to the fever are common. Former epidemics have been characterized by marked mental depression. In the present epidemic many of the cases are having a gradual onset—more like a gradually increasing cold in the head.

Practically, the great danger from influenza is pneumonia, which tends to follow in a considerable percentage of the cases.

For the protection of others, if you are really sick stay at home and remain there until the fever is over. A day in bed at the very beginning may also save you from serious consequences later on.

If you are up and about, protect healthy persons from infection—don't spray others with the secretions from your nose and throat in coughing, sneezing, laughing, or talking. Cover the mouth with a handkerchief. Boil your handkerchiefs and other contaminated articles. Wash your hands frequently. Keep away from others as much as possible while you have a cough.

If you become ill don't try to keep on with your work. Fight the disease rationally and do not become unduly alarmed. In the average case recovery from acute symptoms follows in five or six days. To hasten recovery and lessen the danger of complications, go to bed at once and keep the body warm. There should be plenty of fresh air, but chilling is to be avoided. At the beginning of the disease a cathartic, such as 2 ½ or 3 grains of calomel, followed by a seidlitz powder or epsom salts, is useful. Aspirin in 5 grain doses is useful for pain, but do not take large doses of aspirin, phenacetin, or other medicines. Send for the doctor.

Source: U.S. Navy, Division of Sanitation. "Influenza." Circular No. 1, September 26, 1918. www.archives .gov/exhibits/influenza-epidemic/records-list.html.

An Insurance Executive Excoriates Government-Run Health Insurance

"An Arbitrary, Dictatorial Policy on the Part of the State"

1920

By 1920 the tide of public opinion had turned decisively against the kinds of government-based health insurance programs that were being propagated by progressive lawmakers and health reform groups such as the American Association for Labor Legislation (AALL). One of the key engineers of this reversal was Frederick L. Hoffman, an insurance executive who orchestrated a highly effective industry counterattack against the AALL and other national health insurance system enthusiasts. Hoffman bombarded his opponents with speeches and essays that cast public doubt on the rationality and trustworthiness of pro-reform "experts," emphasized national health insurance's roots in Germany (America's sworn enemy in World War I), and extolled the social benefits of private insurance. All of these themes can be found in the following excerpt from Hoffman's 1920 work, More Facts and Fallacies of Compulsory Health Insurance.*

Social Insurance in The United States

There is the utmost urgency for a rational utterance on the subject of compulsory health insurance, if ill-advised legislation is to be avoided. As observed by [mathematician Karl] Pearson, in his "Grammar of Science," "It is the want of impersonal judgment, of scientific method and of accurate insight into the facts, a want largely due to the nonscientific training which renders clear thinking so rare and random and irresponsible judgment so common in the mass of our citizens today."

There could be no better illustration of this want of strictly scientific judgment and freedom from bias than the fallacious arguments advanced in the annual address of the president of the American Association for Labor Legislation (at Richmond, Va., December 27, 1918). "Social insurance," he remarked, "simply means the application of the same principles" [of private insurance] "to matters in which there is an insurable interest on the part of the community, or society, or the State." In plain truth, social insurance is not insurance at all in the strict sense of the term, and its principles and practice vary fundamentally and essentially from those which have made private insurance a highly honored and satisfactory form of business enterprise throughout the civilized world. . . .

Arguments for health insurance are summarized in the statement that "Modern industry in America must assume more responsibility for the general welfare of its workers." Far-sighted labor leaders strenuously object to a policy in which industrial manhood assumes the viewpoint of the philanthropist and social worker in strict conformity to class distinctions, which, unfortunately, abroad stratify industrial society to the point of hopeless antagonism. Industry is not responsible for outbreaks of typhoid fever or smallpox, or for deaths from appendicitis, diabetes, etc. To burden industry wrongfully with a large portion of the cost of social insurance is merely to increase the cost of production and consequently needlessly so the high cost of living. To shift the responsibility for the highest attainable condition of health on the part of wage-earners and their dependents from the health administration, where it belongs, to the employer or the employing corporation is certain to lead to results possibly not far from disastrous. The object should be to strengthen the local health administration, providing it with more abundant resources, on the one hand, and holding it strictly accountable for results, on the other. It is absurd to say that "Physicians and medical societies know that the health conditions of many American working people are on the average not improving." Any one familiar with even elementary vital statistics well knows that there has been a very material and persistent lowering of the death rate, so much so that the lowest point on record was reached during the week of July 19, 1919. Faultfinders make much of the exaggerations of minor imperfections in health or physique, but they ignore, ignorantly or wilfully, the gratifying truth that the American people of today are probably and in every way physically superior to their ancestors of two or three generations ago. In consequence of a tremendous amount of public health education reaching to the very root of things, there has been a truly remarkable advance in physical well-being, which is reflected in a low and diminishing death rate, which would unquestionably be disclosed by an analysis of the rate of mortality, if comparable statistics for many years were available.

To argue that "Health insurance *probably* will cultivate the practice of the physical examination of prospective employees in many industries, and may easily develop a similar practice in all work where special physical fitness seems requisite," is mere conjecture, plainly contradicted by the facts of actual experience. There has been no such progress in physical or medical examination in Germany during the thirty years of compulsory health insurance, but there has been a very encouraging progress in this respect in the United States, and on a voluntary basis, during recent years. Merely to advance opinions without a proper regard to the facts of observed experience is not to make a contribution to scientific thought. Of course, any one can argue that "Health insurance, once accepted in principle and instituted in practice, becomes a continuous social force for the general betterment of the economic conditions of all working people," but no evidence that this is the case has been forthcoming, for strikes and labor-troubles otherwise have continued in Germany and Great Britain uninterruptedly since the initiation of social insurance and without any reference to its alleged efficacy in raising the level of social and economic well-being of the people. It is also pure guesswork to argue with reference to present objections to health insurance that they "will disappear within less than a generation of time. Such has been the history of the movement in all countries where tried." There is no evidence that such has been the history of the movement, and certainly not in Great Britain, where the act of 1911 was passed as an arbitrary measure, solely upon the prestige and personal initiative of Mr. Lloyd George. . . .

We do not need to go to Germany for information on insurance. No country in the world has made more extraordinary progress in the development of the theory and practice of insurance as conducted by private enterprise than the United States. So-called government insurance is a deception in that the term "insurance" is used as an equivalent of the arbitrary exercise of the taxing power. If the income of an insurance company is not sufficient to pay claims falling due, there is no alternative but a receivership. In so-called government insurance deficiencies are made good either by the imposition of additional burdens, whether specifically in the nature of taxes or not or by direct grants-in-aid or subsidies, such as have been the rule rather than the exception in Great Britain.

Nor do we need to go to superficially informed college professors who pretend to authority on social insurance. Professor Gurdon Ransom Miller is no exception to the large class of writers and speakers thoroughly unfamiliar with both insurance and questions or problems of public health. In his book on "Social Insurance in the United States," he remarks, for illustration, that the pioneer health insurance bill "was carefully drawn by professional men fully informed on all phases of European health legislation and administration." The writer was a member of the committee which for some months considered the bill in question, and no reference was ever made to health legislation or health administration, or, for that matter, to medical practice at home or abroad. Not one of the men most prominent in the furtherance of the propaganda for health insurance has ever in the slightest degree rendered effective help or assistance to voluntary health-promoting agencies. Not one has been instrumental in establishing a single movement for the betterment of health conditions. Not one is an authority on the prevention or control of tuberculosis, cancer, malaria, etc. It is a deliberate perversion of the facts, therefore, to say that the first health-insurance bill was drawn by men familiar with these aspects of compulsory health insurance.

The writer relies upon a fugitive item in the New York *Press*, of January 17, 1916, to the effect that "It is the belief of the United States Public Health Service that 35 per cent of the workers of the country must ask for public or private charity when disabled by disease or weakness." The United States Public Health Service has never made such an investigation to ascertain the relations of dependence or pauperism to illness or death. The percentage quoted is pure conjecture and unworthy of the source to which it is attributed. The United States Public Health Service is the highest authority on health questions in this country, and its reputation for accuracy, impartiality and fairness is placed in peril by such guess-work opinion used for partisan and propaganda purposes.

The only really true and conclusive statement in the work is a quotation from the *Insurance Advocate*, reading that "Ultimately the public pays the bill." The additional burdens resulting from compulsory health insurance will be enormous. A vast army of unnecessary officials will be created to perform artificial functions, all of which are in the nature of a curtailment of personal rights and privileges. The German experience in this respect is absolutely conclusive. The facts cannot be set aside by the president of the American Association for Labor Legislation, who, in his address as reprinted in the *Monthly Labor Review*, of the United States Bureau of Labor Statistics, for February, 1919, in the furtherance of its propaganda for compulsory health insurance, said that "Some recent silly twaddle about the failure of social insurance in Germany on the part of those whose patriotism needed advertising during the war, and on the part of misguided defenders and apologists for the crimes, errors, and mistakes of private insurance companies, has served to confuse the public mind." Being responsible for the statements made with reference to the failure of the German system, I cannot but take exception to this language, which is unworthy of a professor of Columbia University. It is not "silly twaddle" to present the facts and figures as derived from the official reports of practically all the German sickness-insurance institutions during January, 1917-18, secured with much difficulty on account of the war. There has been no confusion of the public mind in consequence other than such as has been brought about deliberately by the misstatement of facts in the utterance of fallacies by those who have, in season and out, been making propaganda for compulsory health insurance. A man is not less a patriot because he is opposed to German ideas of social reform. A man may be much less a patriot for giving furtherance to German ideas which, in the long run, must lead to the establishment of class distinctions, a permanent stratification of American industrial society, and the gradual destruction of all our ideals of Anglo-Saxon freedom and of safeguarded rights under the present order, against the menacing tendency towards the arrogance of an arbitrary, dictatorial policy on the part of the State.

The learned professor might read to advantage an article on "Social Insurance in Germany After the War," published in the *Monthly Labor Review* for April, 1919, being a translation of an article by Professor P. Moldenhauer, one of the foremost German authorities on insurance. This article confirms in every respect my discussion of "Facts and Fallacies of Compulsory Health Insurance" and the "Failure of German Compulsory Health Insurance—A War Revelation," pointing out for illustration that "The war has shifted the actuarial bases of social insurance to the disadvantage of the insurance carriers . . . .The mortality rates have risen. The successful combating of tuberculosis has been interfered with during the war, and the ravages of this disease have been increased by undernutrition. The unfavorable state of the health of ex-soldiers, especially of disabled soldiers, who sooner or later will file claims for pensions, must also be taken into account. . . . The average morbidity rate in fifty-one sick funds distributed over the whole Empire rose from 2.66 per cent. in 1915 to 3.03 per cent. in 1917. . . . Experience has, moreover, shown that claims for sick benefits are always more numerous during times of extensive unemployment. . . . The number of sick pensions has increased from 11,806 in 1913 to 79,834 in 1917." Invalidity pensions are referred to as "pitifully small;" "In the workmen's accident insurance system the unsound method has been adopted of computing the premiums in such a manner that they are just sufficient to cover the current annual expenditures. . . . The total expenditures of all trade-accident associations have increased from 10,500,000 marks ($2,499,000) in 1886 to 218,000,000 ($15,884,000) in 1916. . . . Thus the burden of the present generation is being lessened at the cost of the coming generation." Referring to a reduction in the contributions by the Building Trades Accident Association, it is pointed out that the loss in revenue had been made good "by withdrawals from the reserve fund." The war loans by social insurance institutions are said to have reached the colossal total of 2,000,000,000 marks ($476,000,000), representing more than half of the assets invested in bonds of the Empire and of the Federal States. Intimating the possibility of state bankruptcy it is said that this "would therefore also signify the bankruptcy of social insurance, at least of the invalidity, survivors', and salaried employees' insurance, while sickness and accident insurance would also be seriously upset by such a calamity." The question may properly be raised here whether these utterances by one of the foremost German authorities on social insurance, officially disseminated by the United States Bureau of Labor Statistics, are any more entitled to be called "twaddle" than the observations heretofore referred to and based upon the same official material. Public respect for educators and members of the teaching profession is not enhanced by such evidence of gross unfairness and incapacity to direct public opinion into channels which lead with certainty to the truth. It may not be out of place to quote in conclusion the remark of Professor Moldenhauer that "it can be said that social insurance cannot be preserved in its former extent if we waste our time with tiresome party squabbles, if we squander enormous sums on all kinds of overlapping administrative organizations, and if instead of working and producing real value we try socialistic experiments or chase after communistic Utopias." The same conclusion applies to the United States, in which private insurance is based upon the highest development of the altruistic instinct of self-denial to an extent not realized in any other country in the world. Where so much has been done on a voluntary basis it would seem a foregone conclusion that the field for further development is practically without limit. Labor-unions, fraternal organizations and the insurance companies can all aid towards the attainment of this ideal, which is strictly compatible with the highest idealism of independent life and labor in a modern democracy.

Source: Hoffman, Frederick L. *More Facts and Fallacies of Compulsory Health Insurance.* Newark, NJ: Prudential Press, 1920, pp. 129–35.

DOCUMENT
4.15

Progressives Assail Industry-Backed Opponents of Health Insurance Reform

"Special Interests Have Inaugurated a Regime of Pseudo-Patriotic Propaganda"

1920

As progressive dreams of health insurance reform began to slip away in the late 1910s, some reformers mounted a desperate, last-ditch attempt to resuscitate bills that were languishing in Washington, D.C., and various statehouses. In New York, for example, the New York State League of Women Voters released a hard-hitting pamphlet in the spring of 1920 that bluntly accused Speaker Thaddeus C. Sweet and his minions of being in thrall to Mark Daly, a lobbyist who represented the state's biggest association of manufacturers, insurers, and merchants opposed to health care reform. The League of Women Voters publication, reprinted here, also documented how the New York League for Americanism, a self-proclaimed patriotic organization opposed to workmen's compensation, state health insurance, and other reforms, was created and directed by some of New York's biggest corporate interests. In the end, the revelations contained in the pamphlet proved only embarrassing, rather than fatal, to Sweet, Daly, and other health reform foes targeted by the League of Women Voters. Thwarted at every turn by Sweet—and besieged by a steady drumbeat of smears from the camp of the New York League for Americanism—legislators in Albany who had long fought for health insurance reforms abandoned their efforts by the close of 1920.[1]

A REPORT TO THE GOVERNOR, LEGISLATURE AND PEOPLE OF THE STATE OF NEW YORK UPON THE DANGER CONFRONTING POPULAR GOVERNMENT IN THE LEGISLATURE AND PARTICULARLY IN THE ASSEMBLY OF THE STATE, ARISING OUT OF AN ORGANIZED LOBBY AND PROPAGANDA, KNOWN AS THE DALY LOBBY AND PROPAGANDA, BACKED BY THE ASSOCIATED MANUFACTURERS AND MERCHANTS ("THE ASSOCIATED INDUSTRIES OF NEW YORK STATE") AND PROMOTED BY THE SO-CALLED NEW YORK LEAGUE FOR AMERICANISM—THE COMBINATION BEING ONE THAT EXERTS AN INFLUENCE POWERFUL AND PERILOUS TO ORDERLY AND INTELLIGENT PUBLIC OPINION AT LARGE AND TO LEGISLATIVE OPINION AT ALBANY.

AN INVESTIGATION undertaken by the New York State League of Women Voters has disclosed a condition in the public affairs of New York State of which the State's responsible elected officers and the public generally should be informed. This condition has come to our attention through a report whose findings are of grave significance. After consideration of the evidence on which this report is based and after due deliberation, we have decided to make public our findings.

> Our investigation was undertaken not with the object of supporting any particular measures particularly in the Assembly, consideration impartially on their merits. To inform the public of the results of our investigation transcends in importance, we believe, any other service that the New York State League of Women Voters might render at this time.

We have found that there exists in New York State a dangerous subversion not only of legislative opinion, but of public opinion as well. We have found a condition by virtue of which it is evident that it has been made exceedingly difficult for any constructive social or industrial measure to get adequate and unbiassed consideration before either the public or the legislative opinion of the State, and we have found that the influences at work so far from being invisible, are flagrantly and cynically open and are rapidly becoming notorious.

We call the attention of our legislators and of the public generally to the fact that propagandism as created and financed by certain powerful, vested interests is assuming a highly potent, though unregulated, political and governmental function. Propagandism would seem, in fact, to be taking the place of political "bossism" such as ruled the State ten or twenty years ago. Since the people now have more or less direct control of party political machinery it has become impossible for one or two or three "bosses" at the top to command legislative action at will without regard for the possible resentment of the people. For the support of various little bosses, in or out of the Legislature, certain special interests have inaugurated a regime of pseudo-patriotic propaganda which has been used to confuse the people as a whole with regard to the real nature of such legislation as these particular interests may choose to consider "undesirable." Phases of this propaganda have even been used in a manner calculated to confuse the people as to what is and what is not reasonable and constitutional progress.

Concerning the Associated Manufacturers and Merchants, Their Aims and Methods.

THE DOMINANT obstructionist influence is an up state organization of some 1,600 members, the so-called up state Associated Manufacturers and Merchants, which has headquarters at Buffalo and which is just now changing its name to "The Associated Industries of New York State."

We are reliably informed that as early as last August this Association had raised a fund of between $100,000 and $200,000 for propaganda purposes and that this fund has been used for the support of the so-called New York League for Americanism, an organization which, though extremely active in "accelerating" public opinion, has, in fact, no patriotic nor constructive objects beyond the particular and selfish ends of its sponsors.

The propaganda of this so-called League for Americanism, conducted under the pretense of patriotism, has been calculated to arouse, by unscrupulously false and misleading statements, popular prejudice against and misunderstanding of such a measure as that providing for workmen's cooperative illness insurance as well as other measures of human welfare. In view of information obtained by us we believe that this has been done, not primarily because of impracticability in the measures themselves, but with the object of making the measure an "issue" and of furthering the primary object of certain up-State manufacturers to obstruct as long as possible any progressive industrial legislation in this

State and to establish a precedent at this time against such legislation—in a word, to make "horrible example" of such measures and their advocates.

It can scarcely be forgotten that leading members of this Manufacturers' Association vigorously opposed the Workmen's Compensation Law only a few years ago, though its members now subscribe to the measure in principle and admit that in operation it has bestowed benefits upon employers as well as upon injured workmen. It can scarcely be forgotten that in April of last year certain up-State employers protested at a joint committee hearing at the Capitol that the eight-hour law for women workers meant hardship, if not bankruptcy, for textile mills in the Utica district. They made a similar protest to Speaker Thaddeus C. Sweet at a conference at which they "commended him for refusing to let the eight-hour bill leave the Committee on Rules of which he was chairman." It was understood even then that the ruling legislative organization was undertaking to "protect" the textile industry of the State at the risk of alienating organized labor and the women voters; and since then it has been demonstrated that the claims upon which this demand for "protection" was based were false and groundless, for within a short time after inducing the legislative leaders "to take their view of textile industrial conditions, the employers voluntarily assume the handicap, as they called it, of a shorter workday, not merely for women workers, as the eight-hour bill provided, but for both men and women." . . .

Concerning Mark Daly, Lobbyist for the Associated Manufacturers and Merchants Whose Activities Are Increasingly Menacing to the Welfare of the State.

MARK A. DALY, lobbyist of the Associated Manufacturers and Merchants, backed by the funds and forces of obstruction and by his relations with certain influential members of the Legislature, aims to prevent the impartial consideration of such legislative measures as he sees fit to condemn. His methods are intended to defeat such measures before they even reach the floor of the Assembly.

Daly's influence and the influence of the Daly lobby are sustained by his misleading and inflammatory propaganda among manufacturers of the State and by the propaganda at large of his newly created and pseudo-patriotic ally, the so-called League for Americanism.

We do not question the right of the Associated Manufacturers and Merchants to be heard at Albany. They have the same right as any other group to offer fair criticism, suggestions and intelligent information regarding proposed legislation. We do not doubt that originally the Association may have been established for mutual, perhaps even for public service, but we know that the members of this Association are busy men. We would not be surprised to learn that almost unconsciously they have allowed certain of their responsibilities as citizens to slip away from them into the hands of a lobbyist whose domineering tactics are more dangerous than the members of this Manufacturers' Association have had time to realize. . . .

When it became apparent last year that Sweet and his associates would need "moral support" in getting the majority caucus to vote against letting the welfare bills out of committee, the machinery of the Associated Manufacturers and Merchants was set in motion at the instigation of the Daly lobby. Telegrams and letters were sent to manufacturers in and near Utica to prepare them for the work that was to be done. For the object desired, haste was necessary, and the work of gathering the signatures was accomplished in a few hours on a Monday morning and the result was sent to Speaker Sweet on the Empire State Express in time for his use in the caucus on Tuesday.

The so-called petitions came in every case from the officers of the various plants and in no case originated with the employees. On Monday morning, after Daly had deluged the manufacturers with telegrams and letters informing them of what was to be done, foremen and superintendents received instructions to go through the mills and get signatures from employees, and in this manner, we are informed, subtle methods of coercion were used. Many employees have been questioned as to the manner in which the so-called petitions were presented to them and as a result of this questioning we cite the following information:

No effort was made on the part of the signature collectors to give fair and unbiassed information concerning the proposed measures. Much false information was given workers who were asked to sign. Many employees were told that the State under the proposed measure would compel them to hire certain doctors. In one plant a foreman took the poll, stating to employees that he opposed the measure and hoped they would also. This foreman elaborated on the expense and did not inform employees that their wives were protected or that dentists' bills were included as well as payment for time lost through illness. Similar methods were employed in other plants. The canvass was everywhere taken by individuals who were prejudiced in advance against the proposed legislation. In one instance in a certain factory in Utica where a number of Englishmen are employed, the so-called petition was put before employees with the remark:

"Here, you don't want any of this damned Lloyd George insurance over here, do you?"

The so-called petition was circulated widely among the unorganized women in the textile mills, and the manner in which it was done, is clear from the statement made by one of them:

"They told me it would come out of my pay, and I signed because I didn't want to support some dago's wife every time she had a baby."

We are informed that it was a common argument in presenting the so-called petition that if the measure was enacted the employees would "have to support some dago's wife every time she had a baby." . . .

Concerning the So-called New York League for Americanism Which Was Created by and is Financed by an Inner Circle of Prominent Members of the Associated Manufacturers and Merchants. The Active Director and Promoter of this "League" is C. D. Babcock, a Professional Accelerator of Public Opinion, Whose Methods Are Fast Becoming Notorious.

THE PROPAGANDIST organization which was created by certain members of the Associated Manufacturers and Merchants and which has taken the deceptive name of the New York League for Americanism has headquarters at 471 South Salina Street, Syracuse, and branch offices in Buffalo and New York City.

The Secretary and active director of this organization is one Carleton D. Babcock, a man who has long been employed by certain insurance interests to wage propagandist warfare against any form of workmen's cooperative illness insurance and other measures of human welfare. The treasurer of the so-called League for Americanism is C. A. Chase of Syracuse, formerly a president and now a vice-president of the Associated Manufacturers and Merchants.

The so-called League for Americanism was founded by members of the upstate Manufacturers' Association with the object of "accelerating" public opinion against certain humanitarian legislative proposals. The reason for the adoption of its name is apparent. We are definitely informed that a certain upstate manufacturer who claims to have participated in the organization of the "League" has described the Americanism feature of it as a "catspaw."

There is no question but that Babcock, the "League's" promoter, has had long experience and is particularly skilled in the kind of propaganda sponsored by the so-called League for Americanism. He was brought to this State and hired to act as Secretary of the League after his fight in California on behalf of certain insurance interests against legislation similar to that proposed in New York State. He was brought to this State for propagandist warfare in spite of the fact that the methods he used in California resulted in protests and denunciation on the part of such citizens as had become innocently associated with him there. We are informed by affidavits on this subject that Babcock's methods in California resulted in a "wholesale repudiation" of Babcock and his so-called California Research Society, with much criticism of Babcock on the part of those whose names had been used to support his work. . . .

With regard to the methods of this Daly-Babcock "League" we cite another instance and in this matter, as in all others, have the evidence in our possession:

In 1919, Babcock sought to employ an investigator who should commit himself in advance to the false and tricky views of the "League" regarding illness insurance, to accept a commission to go to England and from there write for American newspapers, articles to influence the "rank and file" of the working-class against the measure proposed in this State. It was specifically stipulated by Babcock in writing that the investigator should be "in harmony with our views," and in view of the manner in which this mission was to have been performed, it appears that the newspapers of this State would have innocently given space to the deliberately prejudiced findings of the "League's" investigator without knowledge of the fact that he was a paid and biased emissary of this so-called League for Americanism. Babcock's attempt to get an investigator, qualified and disinterested, to prostitute himself to report adversely on the health insurance experience of England, was a failure.

It should be noted in passing that the same Frederick L. Hoffman of insurance connections, who assisted Babcock in California, later went to England and through the National Civic Federation and elsewhere is making adverse reports.

While it has been the custom of certain insurance interests to move Babcock from state to state to conduct his peculiarly insidious propaganda against any form of co-operative workmen's illness insurance and similar measures, we are informed that in this case, however, Babcock "has come to stay," and that he and the so-called "League" for Americanism are to be inflicted upon New York State permanently. We understand that certain of Babcock's sponsors are so well satisfied with the extent to which he has "accelerated " public opinion in this State that they plan to maintain the League permanently to wage its characteristic warfare against such legislative proposals as the League and its supporters may choose to consider "un-American."

What citizens of this State whose Americanism is not a cloak to cover some private purposes of their own may think of this proposal, is well indicated in an editorial that appeared on November 30 in the New York *World* under the title "UN-AMERICAN AMERICANISM:"

> "With headquarters in Syracuse, the New York League for Americanism calls for a 'million volunteers to fight un-Americanism wherever it appears.' In such a cause a million men may easily be enrolled if the

people are satisfied of the League's specific purposes. But its first task, we are told, is to fight—what? Bolshevism? Bomb-throwing? Mob rule? No! To fight compulsory health insurance! Thus this self-styled defender of American institutions begins by tooting its trumpet for the assault upon a measure praised by many Americans of the purest type, which can in no sense be called subversive or dangerous.

"A good American can advocate health insurance. Another good American can oppose it. A third may conclude that it might be advantageous if well administered, yet doubt if the state is up to the task. But any one of the three becomes un-American when he attempts to make this debatable issue a test of patriotism."

What may be expected of a "League" thus branded as un-American if it is made permanent? Using its tricky methods to the utmost, the "League" has already gone into one political campaign, and we are informed that in a recent interview Babcock boasted of the "League's" success in this sphere. The spite that animates this so-called League for Americanism is clear from the following statement which, we are informed, Babcock made to the lecturer formerly in the employ of the "League":

"You know we're killing off members of the Legislature who've been advocating the kind of legislation we're against."

We deplore the extent to which certain interests have come to rely on irrelevant and provocative propaganda for their specifically private and even selfish purposes. We particularly deplore the present tendency of such propagandist organizations to cloak themselves under the name of "Americanism." We know of no organization that uses more un-American methods than this Daly-Babcock "League," and we regard it as one of the chief obstacles in this State to any genuine Americanism.

It has misstated the effect and methods of operation of proposed industrial legislation. It has grossly exaggerated the cost. It has sought to lead industrial workers into believing that such measures would do them harm and deprive them of their individual rights, while, at the same time, it has devoted itself to rousing class antagonism by inciting among the farmers a belief that they would be heavily taxed for a measure that would benefit only industrial workers.

It has misled physicians and prevailed upon them to organize under the auspices of the "League" into so-called "Professional Guilds" by creating the impression that professional fees under the proposed workmen's co-operative illness insurance measure would be reduced as low as 50, 25, and even 6 cents, whereas it should be well known that the bill provides that professional fees shall be on a basis initiated by the various county medical societies.

The "League" has associated itself with and brought into its scheme of operation individuals who have been given to the most inflammatory and unfounded statements and innuendoes. In the form of so-called "boiler plate" it has repeatedly distributed to the numerous daily and weekly up-State newspapers propagandist material as false and misleading as any that could be devised.

The "League" has gained circulation for such statements not only through the press but through paid orators and has shown singular energy in hiring speakers to attack proposed industrial legislation on the basis of the League's own tricky assertions. It has particularly sought to create the impression that such legislation is of pro-German and Bolshevik origin, and this allegation, whether made by Babcock or by paid representatives of his "League," by members of the so-called professional guilds that operate under the auspices of his "League," or by certain Senators and Assemblymen who derive political support from his "League," we denounce as unjustifiable and un-American, both untruthful and cowardly.

Source: New York State League of Women Voters. "Report and Protest: To the Governor, the Legislature, and the People of the State of New York, by the New York State League of Women Voters." In *American Labor Legislation Review*. Vols. 10–11. New York: American Association for Labor Legislation, 1920, pp. 83–91, 94–95, 97–100.

NOTE

1. Beatrix Hoffman, *The Wages of Sickness: The Politics of Health Insurance in Progressive America* (Chapel Hill: University of North Carolina Press, 2001), 175–77.

CHAPTER 5

The Struggle over Health Insurance between the Wars

1920–1940

American medicine in the post–World War I era was revolutionized by spectacular advances in diagnosis and treatment, as well as by the heightened cultural authority and political power of physicians. As the healing capabilities of the medical profession and its institutions—most notably the hospital—continued to grow, the financial expense involved in obtaining health services escalated. When this problem further intensified during the Great Depression, making health care more accessible and affordable became a top priority of social reformers and New Dealers. Staunch opposition from the American Medical Association (AMA) and other foes stopped the most sweeping proposals to change the nation's health care system from coming to pass, even though President Franklin D. Roosevelt signed many other landmark social welfare bills into law during this same period.

AN AGE OF MEDICAL MARVELS AND SKYROCKETING MEDICAL EXPENSES

During the 1920s and 1930s scientists and physicians continued to make breathtaking gains in their ability to recognize and combat disease and other forms of sickness. These advances in medical science, the first wave of which had occurred in the decades immediately preceding and following the dawn of the twentieth century, brought about significant declines in outbreaks of infectious disease; increased reliance on both simple and complex surgical procedures; and unprecedented levels of public confidence in the drugs, therapies, and procedures that physicians prescribed for patients. Most doctors of this era remained general practitioners, but the steady flow of new medical knowledge and understanding also led doctors down various paths of medical specialization. Residency programs in various clinical specialties became commonplace in educational institutions across the country, and by 1940 formal certifying boards had been established in a wide range of areas, including obstetrics and gynecology (1927), pediatrics (1933), radiology (1934), orthopedic surgery (1934), urology (1935), psychiatry and neurology (1935), internal medicine (1936), and surgery (1937).

Not surprisingly, the financial fortunes, cultural influence, and political clout of the medical profession enjoyed a meteoric upward trajectory during this same period. Annual earnings surged for many physicians, surgeons, dentists, and other medical professionals, especially in the nation's fast-growing cities. The membership of the American Medical Association, which a half-century before had sustained only the faintest of voices in national conversations about health care, trumpeted its views on health care issues in the nation's leading newspapers and magazines, as well as within the pages of its own powerful *Journal of the American Medical Association (JAMA)*. The physicians' influence on public opinion, meanwhile, was rivaled by their sway over individual statehouses and Congress on various medical matters.

Evidence of the formidable political influence and professional authority of mainstream medical practitioners within their communities displayed itself in a variety of ways during the 1920s. Doctors, for example, pushed alternative healers to the margins of the competitive field like never before. Even midwives, the longtime default providers of prenatal and delivery care in countless American communities since colonial days, were shunted to the side by physicians who could provide obstetrical care in state-of-the-art hospitals. By the late 1930s midwifery was disappearing from all but the most rural parts of the country. Meanwhile, Morris Fishbein, the indefatigable editor of *JAMA* from 1940 to 1950, spearheaded a sustained and effective campaign against medical quacks, charlatans, and patent medicine purveyors who had long preyed on gullible or desperate members of the American public.

Physicians also ensconced themselves as arbiters of wider health and welfare issues within their communities. They posed a formidable obstacle, for example, to Margaret Sanger's efforts during the 1910s and 1920s to overturn the 1873 Comstock Act **(See Document 5.2)**. This law had indirectly outlawed contraception by banning the use of the U.S. mail system for distributing obscene literature or any materials intended to aid birth control or abortion. The Comstock Act enabled states with anti-contraception laws to close their borders against contraceptive information or devices, though a dangerous black market trade in birth control materials and abortion services flourished by the early twentieth century.

The rising power and prestige of physicians also fed the ongoing evolution of hospitals into America's primary repositories of medical technology and treatment. From 1920 to 1930 alone, the number of hospitals nationwide jumped from six thousand to seven thousand facilities. Most of this growth came in private sector hospitals of the nonprofit, voluntary variety. Many of these institutions, operated by religious associations or community groups, bristled with the latest diagnostic equipment and treatment innovations to combat heart disease, diabetes, cancer, and other diseases that became more commonplace with longer American life expectancies. Increasing numbers of these hospitals offered private rooms, nutritional and well-prepared food, and carefully tended grounds. They were able to offer these services because of payments from their increasingly middle-class and upper-class clientele, many of whom were admitted to the hospital by personal physicians who were also on staff.

Poor patients, meanwhile, were increasingly funneled into public hospitals at the municipal or county level, where they were frequently housed in large wards containing dozens of beds. As the percentage of charity cases at these government hospitals rose, administrators increasingly filled staff with faculty and interns from medical schools. Medical school affiliations boosted the level of care available at city- and county-operated hospitals but did not generate the necessary revenue for the same level of new investment in equipment, technology, and patient amenities that some private hospitals were making at the time. The absence of medical schools in more rural parts of the country added to the already significant economic challenges of establishing hospital facilities in the lightly populated countryside. Many rural communities were left behind in the general push of hospital building. By the close of the 1920s, a two-tiered hospitalization system demarcated by geographic location, economic class, and race was evident across the country.

THE ECONOMIC TOLL OF SICKNESS

Social reformers and public health advocates condemned the widening class-based chasm in access to quality health care. They charged that health care services were being priced out of reach of an ever-greater percentage of the public, to the detriment of working families and the industries that employed them. "It is only natural that illness should fall most heavily upon wage-earners, and especially upon industrial workers," wrote social insurance activist Abraham Epstein, who helped usher the Social Security Act into law in 1935. "Living in crowded and unhygienic quarters, eating poor and unsatisfying food, wearing inadequate clothing, working in unhealthy environments, and fatigued from prolonged mechanical labor, workers are naturally more susceptible to disease. Fearful of taking off a day, they permit their illnesses to become aggravated."[1] Noting that rising health care costs had been a problem in American communities since the turn of the century, Epstein and other reformers openly questioned how severe the situation would have to get before legislators and public officials intervened.

Their cries went unheeded for much of the 1920s, a historical period during which many Americans sought a respite from the social tumult of the Progressive Era and the carnage of World War I. Disquieting evidence of poor national health, such as the news that almost one-third of American men who enlisted for World War I were given deferrals because of various health defects, failed to arrest this retreat from health care politics. To be sure, such reports prompted periodic hand-wringing by newspapers and admonitions from public health officials. George Creel of the Committee on Public Information, for example, called the World War I rate of deferral both a "warning and a national disgrace."[2] But none of these calls for action made much of an impact. Virtually the only significant federal health care legislation that became law in the 1920s—the 1921 Sheppard-Towner Maternity and Infancy Protection Act, which contributed matching federal funds to states to establish and operate prenatal and child health care centers—survived for only six years before expiring from slashed funding **(See Document 5.1).**

The Great Depression was the galvanizing event that restored health policy to its Progressive Era–status as a pressing political issue. Specifically, the Depression greatly exacerbated the perils of rising health care costs, both for American families and for the hospitals, doctors, nurses, and administrators who treated them. As business fortunes crashed and unemployment soared across the nation, the percentage of families unable to pay for even modest levels of medical treatment, to say nothing of surgical procedures and other forms of more expensive hospital treatment, rose precipitously.

Public health services at the local, state, and federal level tried to fill the growing breach, but their resources were limited. Hospitals were thus confronted with a crushing load of patients who simply could not pay the medical bills they were incurring. One Iowa hospital administrator recalled that the struggle to "keep our doors open" during the early years of the Depression was an exceedingly grim one. "People brought chickens in and meat to pay their bills. They would paint or do work around the hospital of some kind. . . . Nurses would come in and beg us to give them a job without pay, for room and board, because they were starving."[3]

Members and analysts of the medical industry urged lawmakers to respond to the growing economic crisis facing hospitals or prepare for a massive wave of closures. "There is a crying need for the stabilization of hospital income," wrote Isidore S. Falk, one of the nation's leading scholars on public health and social insurance. "The hospital situation calls for the development of arrangements whereby the economic barrier shall be removed from the path of the individual who needs hospital care, without, at the same time, placing an impossible burden of charity service upon the hospital."[4]

Some observers cited expansion of sickness insurance as the most promising avenue by which the nation could both provide people with health care and at the same time stabilize the economic condition of the private practices and hospitals that were the cornerstones of the industry. "The American people have been attempting to apply the ordinary principles of sale and purchase to medical care, as if it were a commodity which could be purchased voluntarily, at the convenience of the patient, and in such quantities as suited his pocket book," stated insurance expert C. Rufus Rorem in a mid-thirties speech before the National Medical Association.

> But medical care is not an ordinary economic commodity. No one can
> tell when he will be sick or what his sickness will cost him. Sickness
> is a hazard, and the costs of medical care are economic hazards which
> can be removed only by substituting some certain and less burden-
> some expenditure [health insurance] for the possibility of a crushing
> load which might, and often does, prove impossible for the individual
> to carry.[5]

When the Depression struck, families with health insurance were the exception, not the rule. "It is not likely that more than a quarter of American wage-earners are now insured through the numerous institutions available," wrote social insurance scholar Harry A. Millis in 1937. "Voluntary sickness insurance remains the exception, non-insurance the rule, and most of it is substandard and inadequate. Moreover, those wage-earners most in need of sickness insurance particularly to compensate for wage losses when disabled are least likely to have it. Not only are there rejections of the bad or the less good risks, but it is chiefly those earning good wages who can pay the premiums when necessary."[6]

MANAGEMENT AND WORKER HEALTH
PROGRAMS IN THE EARLY DEPRESSION YEARS

The task of using insurance to address health costs and shore up the medical industry's sagging financial health was rife with challenges. For one thing, the United States entered the Depression awash in a welter of different sickness insurance systems, none of which was dominant but all of which were championed by interest groups with some measure of political influence.

By the late nineteenth century, a number of large employers had established modest health and welfare programs for workers. Among the first companies to pursue these plans, which generally amounted to minimal health services from area physicians under contract, were logging, rail, and mining corporations whose employees routinely engaged in dangerous and physically demanding work. This trend accelerated in the early twentieth century, as a number of states passed laws requiring employers to bear the medical costs incurred by employees as a result of industrial accidents. These laws, however, featured self-insurance clauses that gave Michigan copper mining companies, Washington timber companies, and West Virginia coal outfits the option to employ their own physicians and to make monthly deductions of wages to cover the health care services they were providing. In some cases, agreeing to these deductions was a compulsory condition of employment. By the early 1930s, similar paternalistic welfare plans with health care elements had been embraced in other industries by a variety of major players, including International Harvester, Goodyear Tire and Rubber, Endicott-Johnson, and U.S. Steel.

Workers' attitudes toward these programs were mixed. Some welcomed the increased access to health care services, and many employees in the more generous plans—such as the Endicott-Johnson program, which provided full medical care including hospital coverage to eighteen thousand workers and their families in exchange for small monthly wage deductions—viewed themselves as genuinely fortunate (coverage of dependents in other plans was spotty). But others distrusted the motivations behind early employee benefit plans. Organized labor, in particular, interpreted the programs as duplicitous campaigns designed to increase worker dependence on companies, weaken unionization efforts, and cover up problems with industrial workplace safety. Moreover, the American Federation of Labor had long preached a doctrine of worker self-reliance that rejected management- or government-sponsored social insurance programs.

Not surprisingly, then, some labor unions rejected management programs in favor of their own systems. The best of these programs featured old-age pensions, disability compensation, and limited coverage for treatment at union-affiliated medical facilities. Not incidentally, these programs were viewed as a way to bolster member loyalty to the union, a major consideration for labor leaders engaged in a perpetual battle to keep their organizations alive. Nonetheless, worker-sponsored programs remained spotty and extremely limited until New Deal labor policies of the mid-1930s dramatically strengthened the economic hand of the labor movement. In a comprehensive study of American trade unions in 1927–1928, the U.S. Bureau of Labor Statistics reported that while sixty-three unions paid death benefits to members, only fourteen provided benefits for disability and only eleven implemented sickness insurance programs to members.[7]

Some wage earners who could not obtain insurance against sickness through an employer or union turned to private accident and health insurance. About 175 life insurance companies had expanded their offerings to include individual accident and health insurance policies by the mid-1930s. But most of these policies only protected against accidents, and they were festooned with various limitations and exceptions to curtail the insurers' financial liability. These exceptions did not, in general, run afoul of the law. The main focus of the state regulations governing commercial health insurance during this period concerned insurer solvency in general and capitalization requirements in particular.

In addition, companies typically avoided selling even these policies to those who most needed them—workers employed in industries with hazardous or unsanitary working conditions. Finally, wage earners who did manage to secure voluntary private insurance policies typically paid very high monthly premiums. All of these factors kept individual health insurance policies from being a viable option for millions of American families engaged in an increasingly urgent quest to obtain at least some measure of financial protection against extended periods of illness or hospitalization.

Group Health Insurance and the Birth of Blue Cross

Another health insurance option, known as the group hospitalization plan, emerged during the late 1920s and early 1930s. Under these plans, individuals vulnerable to financial ruin in the event of unanticipated high medical expenses (such as extended hospitalization for treatment of disease or injury) banded together in groups that negotiated hospitalization plans with hospitals. Under group insurance plans, enrollees made payments, usually in the form of monthly installments of less than a dollar, in exchange for coverage of operating room and laboratory costs and other hospitalization expenses (physician fees not included) for a specified period, usually fifteen to thirty days. These insurance systems, with benefits of cash indemnities toward hospital bills, constituted a notable break from accident insurance plans of the day, which made only lump sum payments to blunt the impact of lost income.

By the early 1930s, prepaid group hospitalization plans were up and running in more than thirty towns and cities across the United States, with more than one hundred participating hospitals. They were popular not only with mainly middle-class subscribers, who welcomed the increased financial protection from otherwise ruinous health care bills, but also with hospitals that used the steady revenue from these plans to shore up their bottom lines.

Early trailblazers of particular note in the group insurance realm included Community Hospital of Grinnell, Iowa, and Brattleboro Memorial Hospital in Brattleboro, Vermont, both of which established financially viable plans in the mid-1920s. The best-known plan was implemented in Texas in 1929 by Baylor University Hospital in an agreement with Dallas schoolteachers. Unlike other group prepayment health plans emerging during this time, the Baylor scheme provided direct coverage for all services rendered during hospitalization, as opposed to cash reimbursements or payments to the policyholder.

This services benefit principle proved enormously popular, and within four years of the Baylor rollout, more than ten thousand subscribers had signed up. The Baylor prepaid plan, which guaranteed subscribers twenty-one days of hospital care for $6 per year, is recognized by scholars today as the first Blue Cross plan **(See Document 5.5)**. By 1935, fifteen hospital insurance plans had been established in eleven states, and by the close of 1936 more than 700,000 subscribers, the majority of them middle class, were enrolled in one plan or another. New Blue Cross plans continued to proliferate, and by 1939 they were present in twenty-seven states.

This rapid growth in group hospitalization plans was boosted by legislation that was passed in several states (starting with New York in 1934) that exempted Blue Cross plans from conventional insurance regulations.[8] The movement also benefited from the approval of labor leaders who recognized that they could negotiate more advantageous health care coverage for union members with the nonprofit Blues than they could with commercial insurance companies.

Expansion was also greatly aided by the inability of the medical profession to present a united front against the plans. Whereas the American Medical Association was able to rally the profession against most other forms of health insurance by branding them as incarnations of socialized medicine, prepaid hospitalization plans received the approbation of both the American Hospital Association (AHA, in 1933) and the American College of Surgeons (ACS, in 1934). This break reflected the fact that, when push came to shove, the administrators and surgical personnel who dominated the AHA and ACS determined that putting hospitals—the key to their own economic fortunes—on a sound financial footing was their highest priority.

As time passed, several of the emerging group hospitalization plans included important innovations, such as increased patient choice of hospitals and physicians, that were embraced by other programs. The American Hospital Association played a leading role in coordinating this growth, and in 1939 it adopted the Blue Cross symbol as a way to formally recognize prepaid hospitalization plans that met its standards. (In 1960 the AHA commission responsible for overseeing Blue Cross plans formally became the Blue Cross Association.)

DEBATING THE ROLE OF GOVERNMENT IN HEALTH CARE

During the 1920s and early 1930s, America's health insurance programs amounted to little more than a thin patchwork of plans available through commercial insurers, unions and fraternal societies, big employers, and (beginning in the 1930s) group insurance agreements with hospitals. In addition, medical expenses, though on the rise, had not yet reached the point where affluent Americans could not meet most of them through savings. This state of affairs left millions of poor Americans without any recourse. And it gave countless middle-class families without access to group insurance an unenviable choice between purchasing budget-busting commercial health insurance with exceedingly limited coverage and hoping that spouses and children avoided serious health problems ranging from childbirth complications to diseases such as polio, which frequently decimated family finances. (In the 1930s an iron lung for treatment of polio victims cost about $1,500, the average price of a home.)

As in the 1910s, many advocates of health care reform insisted that the best way to address the problem of inadequate access to medical care was for the federal government to intervene and enact major changes in the ways that health services were accessed and paid for, up to and perhaps including a national program for health insurance. Proponents of increased government involvement pointed out that the state's authority to lead on public health issues such as communicable disease outbreaks had been widely accepted since colonial times. Other more recent examples of federal engagement in public health issues were also trotted out, including the Chamberlain-Kahn Act of 1918, which bestowed federal grants for venereal disease control to states that agreed to provide matching funds, and the Sheppard-Towner Maternity and Infancy Protection Act of 1921, which featured a similar matching fund scheme to encourage state-level investment in prenatal and child health care centers. In 1930, passage of the Ramsdell Act reconstituted the small Hygienic Laboratory of the U.S. Public Health Service (PHS) into the National Institute of Health (NIH, later the National Institutes of Health) and authorized $750,000 for NIH research fellowships and construction of two buildings to house NIH offices. The NIH flourished from the outset, evolving into the nation's premier biomedical research institution.

Some reformers also emphasized that examples of compulsory insurance already existed in America, in the form of federal and state workmen's compensation laws that protected wage earners against loss from industrial accidents. Most reformers, however, opposed the idea of building a comprehensive health insurance system on the foundation of existing workers' compensation laws, because the regulations had been crafted to furnish cash benefits, not to ensure access to medical services. "Patching up old laws to meet new requirements is often a painful and ineffective procedure," declared Isidore S. Falk. "It would be far better to conceive compulsory insurance on the basis of its own needs, with full regard to former experiences."[9]

Public health professionals were among the most enthusiastic supporters of an expanded federal role in health care. During the 1920s organizations such as the American Public Health Association (APHA), the nation's leading society of public health professionals, boldly advocated a system of universal health care—essentially a government health system that would guarantee health insurance to all citizens. On the one hand, this position had an element of self-interest to it, as any system of national health insurance would inevitably increase the influence and profile of the various public health agencies to which APHA members belonged. On the other hand, leaders in the public health field such as Charles-Edward Amory Winslow, longtime president of the APHA, genuinely believed that national health insurance was the best solution to the United States' spiraling health care costs (**See Document 5.4**).

The perspective of the APHA was not shared by the AMA, to put it mildly. The AMA and other stakeholders with a vested interest in keeping the federal government from further expanding its health care role, such as commercial insurers, responded to proposals for compulsory national health insurance with apocalyptic rhetoric and formal condemnations of "state medicine" (**See Document 5.3**). Exquisitely sensitive to any outside threat to the status quo, which for many medical professionals was both lucrative and provided for a large measure of day-to-day autonomy, private physicians decried would-be health reformers as Socialist agents and utopian dreamers. Other conservative opponents of major health insurance reforms engaged in similar Red-baiting, explicitly portraying health reform advocates as enemies of American values and institutions. For example, when the 1921 Sheppard-Towner Act gave the Department of Labor's Children's Bureau authority to fund new prenatal and child health care programs at the state level, one conservative women's organization accused the architects and supporters of the law of "arousing women against men, wives against husbands [by] providing community care for children, legitimate and illegitimate."[10]

Concerned that legislation such as Sheppard-Towner and Chamberlain-Kahn amounted to precedent-setting expansions of government involvement in the health care industry, the American Medical Association lobbied Washington, D.C., relentlessly to quash these acts, either through repeal or by starving them of appropriations. By 1927 lawmakers in Congress had obediently taken the latter path to discontinue both programs. The AMA's victory was not complete, however. Many of the state public health agencies that had established maternity, child health, and venereal disease clinics with federal grants from these acts made budgetary adjustments to keep the doors of these facilities open after the federal assistance dried up.

The Committee on the Costs of Medical Care

By the mid-1920s, the AMA was well established as the nation's foremost opponent of health insurance reform. But its membership's seemingly monolithic opposition to reform was revealed to be an illusion in 1927, when a group of frustrated AMA delegates heeded a call from President Calvin Coolidge for a concerted research study into the "economic factors affecting the organization of medicine." This group, which quickly became known as the Committee on the Costs of Medical Care (CCMC), featured a number of nationally recognized names among its founding members, including Winford H. Smith, director of Johns Hopkins Hospital; Lewellys F. Barker, a member of the Johns Hopkins Medical School; Walton H. Hamilton, an economics professor at the Brookings Institution; Charles-Edward Amory Winslow, a Yale University public health professor and president of the APHA; and Michael M. Davis, a former director of the prestigious Boston Dispensary. These distinguished doctors and scholars also recruited Ray Lyman Wilber, a past president of the AMA and the sitting president of Stanford University, to take leadership of the committee.[11]

Over the next five years, the CCMC conducted an exhaustive survey of American health care economics. During that time, a wide array of physicians and dentists, public health officials, hospital administrators, economists, sociologists, and civic leaders joined the effort, which was funded by several private philanthropic foundations, including the Carnegie Corporation, the Russell Sage Foundation, the Milbank Memorial Fund, the Julius Rosenwald Foundation, the Josiah Macy Jr. Foundation, the New York Foundation, the Twentieth Century Fund, and the Rockefeller Foundation. The committee produced a number of detailed studies examining various aspects of American health care, thanks in no small part to Isidore S. Falk, who came on board in late 1928 to oversee the CCMC's research efforts. It was the CCMC's final report in 1932, however, that garnered all the attention from reformers, doctors and other health care professionals, and officials in Washington.

The CCMC's *Medical Care for the American People,* released during the worst depths of the Depression, called for significant changes in the way that Americans received and paid for medical care **(See Document 5.6)**. It urged a health delivery system overhaul that included reorganization of medical practices into physician groups (preferably organized around hospitals); implementation of national medical care coverage on a group payment basis through insurance, taxation, or a combination of the two; increased public health investment, including construction of new hospitals and other facilities in underserved areas of the country; higher educational standards for medical professionals; and expanded community coordination and oversight of medical care services. The overarching goal of these recommendations, stated the committee, was to reduce "widespread waste," streamline health care delivery processes in ways that benefited both industry stakeholders and the public, and extend basic health care to every American.

The committee framed its slate of proposed reforms as a necessary and measured response to escalating medical costs, inefficiencies in medical care provision, and larger societal changes.

> The predominant economic institution in medical practice today—private individual practice—dates back to ancient times. Under this system medical services are now so provided that many persons either cannot and do not receive the care they need, or are heavily burdened by its costs. At the same time, many of the practitioners and the agencies which provide medical service are inadequately occupied and poorly remunerated. A barrier—in large part economic—stands between practitioners, able and eager to serve, and patients who need the service but are unwilling or unable to pay for it.[12]

To bolster its case, the CCMC emphasized that total annual expenditures in the United States for medical care had reached $3.66 billion a year, approximately $30 per person, or about 4 percent of all personal income. But the report stressed that these averages, significant in their own right, masked the fact that thousands of unlucky American families from working-class or middle-class backgrounds incurred much greater costs than these when they were besieged by sickness or disease. The committee also asserted that its research had revealed ways for the nation to effectively address long-standing geographic and socioeconomic inequities in access to health care.

The CCMC thus heralded its recommendations as a pathway to a more healthy and vigorous nation, one that would no longer tolerate "preventable physical pain and mental anguish, needless deaths, economic inefficiency, and social waste."[13] As CCMC chairman Ray Lyman Wilbur summarized in his introduction to *Medical Care for the American People,* "today in American civilization, health occupies a high place among accepted social values. As we emerge from the present depression and build up a surplus of income not necessary for mere subsistence, we shall do well to realize that we can invest this surplus in no better way than in the preservation of health."[14]

A Political Battle Royal

The CCMC's political hand was weakened by the fact that it was unable to reach an internal consensus on its most controversial proposals: group health insurance (whether voluntary or compulsory) and group medical practice. Unwilling to countenance such "radical" solutions to America's health care troubles, a group of physicians within the committee issued the blistering "Minority Report Number One of the Committee on the Costs of Medical Care," which urged federal authorities to refrain from any further intrusions into the practice of private medicine. The authors of this minority report granted that the state had a legitimate public health role to play in the United States, but they insisted that the CCMC majority's "European-style" reforms would tear the existing doctor-patient relationship asunder and increase the cost of medical treatment (**See Document 5.7**).

The simultaneous release of the CCMC's majority and minority reports ("Minority Report Number One" was the most prominent of two minority reports published as part of *Medical Care for the American People*) mobilized stakeholders across the political spectrum. The many areas of widespread consensus that existed in the committee's report were lost amid the charges and countercharges that swirled around the majority's endorsement, vague though it was, of some kind of system of national health insurance. As expected, the American Medical Association took the lead in condemning the survey's proposed health insurance solutions. A representative AMA line of attack appeared in the December 1932 issue of *JAMA,* which denounced the majority's recommendations as "socialism and communism—inciting to revolution." The editorial also warned that if the CCMC's recommendations concerning group practice were implemented, physicians would become mere "hirelings" and sick people would be treated like "robots."[15]

Not all medical professionals were opposed to some system of group health insurance. Some AMA members bucked the organizational tide on that score, and in September 1933 the American Hospital Association endorsed the idea of periodic payment plans for the purchase of medical care. Nine months later the American College of Surgeons formally endorsed the idea of a national system of voluntary health insurance (to the considerable dismay of the AMA, which immediately adopted a resolution rebuking the ACS for its stance). In Washington, reaction to the CCMC broke down along the usual partisan lines, with free market conservatives excoriating the committee's work and liberal reformers defending it with equal vigor. And as the political symbolism of the report intensified, "the debate became a war of alliances rather than reason," wrote scholar Joseph S. Ross. "This is best evidenced by Dr. William J. Mayo, one of the founders of the Mayo Clinic, who declared his intention to support the AMA and Minority Recommendation No. 1, despite the fact that the Majority Recommendations almost exactly described the then current Mayo system."[16]

If the report had been released after Franklin D. Roosevelt's inauguration in March 1933, it might have met a different fate. But it was adopted and released during the final months of conservative Republican Herbert Hoover's presidency, which made it easier for opponents to keep it from gaining any traction. Frustrated and disillusioned by the furor over its work, the CCMC quietly disbanded without seeing any of its major recommendations taken up. In retrospect, the committee's efforts—and, in particular, its landmark report—spurred on the next wave of social reformers. And after Roosevelt took the oath of office, many of those reformers joined him in Washington.

Roosevelt and the New Dealers

From the outset of his presidency, Roosevelt signaled his bedrock conviction that the resources of government could and should be used extensively and without apology in providing relief to the millions of Americans suffering from the withering effects of the Depression. The most immediate and famous actions that Roosevelt took after surveying the wreckage he inherited from Hoover were aimed at shoring up the nation's financial infrastructure and chopping away at unemployment, which had reached staggering levels in many parts of the country (the national unemployment rate stood at 28 percent when he took office, with some cities registering rates of 40 percent or more). But another of Roosevelt's early priorities was to craft and roll out an ambitious set of agencies, programs, laws, and initiatives aimed at helping the United States' most vulnerable citizens— sick, homeless, and hungry Americans, many of them elderly, who had been pushed to the physical, emotional, and financial breaking point by the crisis.

Observers of Roosevelt's performance as governor of New York during the opening years of the Depression were not surprised by this approach. In New York he had pushed for guaranteed pensions for elderly citizens and created an innovative state relief agency called the Temporary Emergency Relief Administration (TERA). The flagship program of TERA was a matching fund initiative in which cities received two dollars from the state Treasury for every three dollars they spent on welfare and unemployment programs.

Once ensconced in the White House, Roosevelt's willingness to use the powers of the state to rescue or shield the populace from the Depression's most punishing aspects surprised even some of his most ardent admirers, as well as his most implacable critics. "[Roosevelt] dramatized the role of the federal government," wrote scholar James Mac-Gregor Burns, "so that people would see it not as a remote and passive power but as a force that could salvage them and shape the nation's economy."[17] A good deal of Roosevelt's interventions, rolled out with the assistance of huge Democratic majorities in both houses of Congress, consisted of short-term programs to provide immediate relief for the swelling ranks of hungry, homeless, and unemployed Americans. All the while, the president and his fellow New Dealers were constructing the scaffolding for a permanent safety net, not just a temporary edifice to be mothballed when the country returned to economic "normalcy."

A New Deal Push for Health Care Reform

In the opening months of Roosevelt's tenure, it appeared that health insurance might well become an integral component of that safety net. The president signaled his belief that a sound, government-sponsored health insurance program could increase public access to good, timely, and affordable medical care. In addition, New Deal–era agencies at the federal, state, and local levels began providing direct medical care to families on relief rolls, which was a clear indicator that the dire economic conditions were prompting reassessments of long-held assumptions about government's role in overseeing the nation's health. "The existence of millions of 'decent' unemployed, falling state and local revenues, and a growing conviction that individual financial status should not affect the quality of care received forced many states and localities to reexamine and change their system of providing medical care to the needy," wrote historian Daniel S. Hirshfield.[18]

At the federal level, the earliest and most visible effort to help struggling citizens obtain needed medical care came from the Federal Emergency Relief Administration (FERA). Initially created to manage and distribute federal funds to state and local governments for relief efforts, FERA operations changed when Director Harry Hopkins, one of the most stalwart and dedicated of all the New Dealers, determined that more direct intervention could provide a higher level of emergency medical relief to eligible recipients. Asserting that "the conservation and maintenance of the public health is a primary function of our government," Hopkins on September 10, 1933, unveiled *FERA Rules and Regulations No. 7 Governing Medical Care Provided in the Homes of the Recipients of Medical Care Relief.* FERA's new regulations directed state and local relief agencies to implement measures so that "indigent persons" would receive the same level of nursing, dental, and nonhospital medical care as would be rendered to a private patient. The policy lasted two years, until the Roosevelt administration stopped all direct relief grants in November 1935.

The AMA condemned FERA's more activist orientation, as well as other New Deal health care proposals simmering in various Washington agencies and reform-minded philanthropic foundations, as destructive to private medical practice and of a pernicious Socialist character. But unlike the administrations of Coolidge and Hoover, which were largely sympathetic to the AMA's position, the Roosevelt White House pushed back hard against these charges. One of its favorite strategies in this regard was to highlight the many ways in which municipal, state, and federal authorities already participated in the provision of medical care to the apparent satisfaction of a majority of Americans. Delegates at the annual meeting of the AMA in 1933, for example, received an earful from New York State commissioner of health Thomas Parran, who had served Roosevelt ably during his years as governor and who in 1936 would become the president's choice for surgeon general. "With two-thirds of the hospital beds in New York State owned by the public and supported through taxes; with 15 percent of the population receiving all the necessities of life from public funds, including medical care; with practically all cases of mental disease and a large proportion of tuberculosis being hospitalized at public expense; with one-half of the burden of syphilis treatment a public responsibility; with the care of crippled children an actual obligation, and the medical care of school children a legal obligation of the public; and with blanket authority existing for any city or county to construct and operate public general hospitals available to all citizens, it will be seen that, to a considerable extent, medical care already has become a matter of public participation," declared Parran, who added that "payment to physicians from public funds during the past year probably has meant the difference between solvency and insolvency for a great many doctors, particularly in rural areas."[19]

NATIONAL HEALTH INSURANCE AND THE COMMITTEE ON ECONOMIC SECURITY

The unfurling of Roosevelt's ambitious New Deal programs revived interest in the sort of government-run health insurance programs that the CCMC had pondered. Advocates came to believe—or at least found reasons to hope—that, with Roosevelt in the White

House and large Democratic majorities in both houses of Congress, a program of universal health insurance might become a reality.

Within months of Roosevelt's inauguration, evidence of momentum in this direction could be seen all across the country. Bills providing for the establishment of statewide compulsory health insurance systems were introduced in several state legislatures, most notably California and New York. The American College of Surgeons, the National Medical Association (an African American organization of physicians and surgeons), rebellious local chapters of the AMA, and some other health organizations signaled varying levels of receptivity to the concept of voluntary insurance. Eager to press their advantage, health care reformers delivered a new barrage of reports, editorials, studies, and speeches making the case for government-sponsored health insurance **(See Document 5.8)**.

Some of these advocates focused primarily on educating lawmakers and the general public about the alleged benefits of national health insurance. A growing number of them also ridiculed the insurance companies and medical professionals for cloaking their primary motivation for opposing national health insurance—diminished profits—behind a wall of pious rhetoric about the potential of such programs to destroy the "sanctity" of the patient-physician relationship and erode traditional American freedoms and values. In his classic 1934 work *The Quest for Security*, for example, social insurance theorist Isaac M. Rubinow wrote that

> [t]he generous display of altruism [from doctors and private insurers] can only be compared in its lavishness with the use of camouflage in the World War, when tanks were made to look like hillocks and storehouses of ammunition like Red Cross hospitals. Every representative of vested commercial interests insists upon shedding crocodile tears, but never for his own group; and all of them together develop a passionate concern for the preservation of the honor and moral stamina of the wage workers. Never did the wage workers have so many ardent disinterested friends. The holy traditions of American freedom, independence, initiative, the sanctity of the American wage worker's family, his love for his parents, his health and safety, his right of free choice of physician and above all his right to his entire pay envelope, all that is tenderly defended by his newly discovered friends. Humorous? It would be, if not for the amazing fact that so much of this brazen propaganda is so effective.[20]

The prospects for legislation that would usher in a program of national health insurance received another boost on June 8, 1934, when Roosevelt appeared before Congress and announced his support for a federal system of "social insurance" that would help shield citizens from the "hazards and vicissitudes of life" **(See Document 5.9)**. Three weeks later Roosevelt repeated this message in a radio address to the nation, and on June 29 he issued an executive order creating the Committee on Economic Security (CES) to craft a program of social insurance implementation.

The exact nature of the social insurance to which Roosevelt referred was purposely left vague. The White House wanted to give the CES flexibility to formulate policies in a wide range of areas beyond compulsory health insurance, including unemployment compensation, old-age pensions, maternity benefits, and workmen's compensation. The lineup of the Committee on Economic Security underscored the importance that the president was placing on the issue. The committee's executive board was composed of Labor secretary Frances Perkins, Agriculture secretary Henry A. Wallace, and FERA administrator Harry Hopkins—all dedicated New Dealers trusted by the president—along with Treasury secretary Henry Morgenthau Jr. and Attorney General Homer Cummings. Edwin E. Witte, a prominent expert on social insurance and longtime member of the reformist American Association for Labor Legislation, was tapped to serve as executive director. The CES also featured an advisory council of luminaries from the fields of labor, industry, social welfare, and local and state government, as well as assorted support personnel with expertise on hospital administration, child welfare, nursing, and other health care subjects.

The committee worked intensively for the next several months. For the most part it labored behind closed doors, but it organized a major conference in November 1934 that brought experts on social insurance from around the country to Washington. The most newsworthy event at this conference was a speech from Roosevelt himself that hinted at the direction of CES's internal deliberations. The president highlighted the importance of developing programs for unemployment insurance and old-age insurance that would be "self-maintaining," that is, the premiums paid into the systems would cover the outlays to beneficiaries. On the subject of national health insurance, Roosevelt was more circumspect, saying only that "whether we come to this form of insurance soon or later on, I am confident that we can devise a system which will enhance and not hinder the remarkable progress which has been made and is being made in practice of the professions of medicine and surgery in the United States."[21]

In January 1935 the Committee on Economic Security submitted its findings to Roosevelt **(See Document 5.10)**. As expected, the CES endorsed the creation of ambitious new unemployment and old-age insurance systems. But national health insurance was left out of the mix, with the CES committing only to a promise to give it further study. This decision did not mean that the CES felt that such a program did not have merit. To the contrary, many CES members thought that a system of national health insurance was highly desirable. But the committee ultimately made the political calculation that if it pushed for both national health insurance and old-age insurance, the latter of which was Roosevelt's higher priority, neither system might ever see the light of day. Witte, for example, determined that "it would probably be impossible to do anything about health insurance in a legislative way, due to the . . . strong opposition of the medical profession."[22] He added that "there is no way of appeasing that crowd."[23] Perkins concurred with this assessment, writing in the mid-1940s that "health insurance was then, as now, a difficult question. Powerful elements of the medical profession were up in arms over the idea of any kind of government-endorsed system."[24]

ROOSEVELT SIGNS THE SOCIAL SECURITY ACT

With the issue of national health insurance set aside for the time being, the Roosevelt administration focused on obtaining congressional passage of a "social security" bill that embodied the CES's old-age insurance recommendations. Nonetheless, AMA leaders reacted angrily to the fact that national health insurance was even referenced in the CES report. They also interpreted the report's call for additional study of the issue as an indication that they needed to keep their guard up. A special meeting of the AMA House of Delegates was subsequently convened in February 1935, at which time the organization reiterated its staunch opposition to compulsory health insurance systems imposed by either state or federal authorities. Mindful that a growing number of medical professionals were open to the idea of Blue Cross arrangements and other voluntary insurance schemes, the AMA did grudgingly endorse the idea of setting up voluntary plan experiments as long as they were managed by county and state medical associations. "This program was effectively calculated to unify the medical profession in opposition to compulsory health insurance," summarized Witte, and in that regard it was largely successful. "Time and again thereafter members of Congress received protests from medical associations and individual physicians against the economic security bill, all based on the assumption that this bill provided for health insurance," stated Witte. "These required many explanations on our part and invariably the members made it clear that they would have nothing to do with the bill if it contemplated [compulsory] health insurance."[25]

As Roosevelt's prized social security bill moved through Congress in the spring and summer of 1935, the CES's Medical Advisory Committee, led by Isidore S. Falk and Edgar Sydenstricker, made one last attempt to convince the president to include a national health insurance program in the legislation. But Roosevelt was wary of stirring up the AMA hornet's nest once again. He decided not to take any further action on health care reform until he had signed the Social Security Act into law. He did so on August 14, 1935, and in the process changed the American political landscape forever **(See Document 5.11)**.

The landmark Social Security Act of 1935 is best known for installing a system of pensions and other benefits to elderly American workers through a new federal government agency called the Social Security Board. The legislation also guaranteed benefits to victims of industrial accidents, unemployment insurance, aid for dependent mothers and children, the blind, and the physically handicapped. In addition, it contained appropriations and grants-in-aid to states for expanded family health programs and other public health services. Finally, the act permanently altered the framework of the state's relationship with the American people in that it gave formal sanction to the idea, long held in progressive circles, that government had both a right and an obligation to assist the most vulnerable members of the populace.

The Growing Governmental Role in Health Care

The precedent set by the Social Security Act was alarming to conservatives. They charged that the law was fiscally irresponsible and a repudiation of American traditions of self-reliance, limited government, and faith in free market principles. Republican presidential nominee Alf Landon even pledged to repeal the act if he was elected president in November 1936 **(See Document 5.12)**.

But progressive reformers remained undaunted by the anger from the right, especially after Landon was soundly thrashed at the ballot box by Roosevelt. In fact, the passage of the Social Security Act and Roosevelt's 1936 reelection convinced numerous New Dealers that they should return to the political battlefield, retrieve the battered but still breathing body of national health insurance, and drag it over the legislative finish line. Pro-insurance reformers such as Rubinow, John B. Andrews (American Association of Labor Legislation), Abraham Epstein (American Association for Social Security), Michael

M. Davis and C. Rufus Rorem (Julius Rosenwald Fund), and Paul Kellogg (Survey Associates), many of whom had held their tongues when national health insurance was shunted aside to get the Social Security Act through Congress, were even more outspoken about taking up health care reform again.

Proponents of such a strategy sought to reassure nervous members of Congress that such a move was less fraught with political peril than they feared. Besides Roosevelt's resounding victory, working-class and middle-class American voters had rewarded the Democratic Party, now inextricably tied to Roosevelt and his New Deal policies, with even more historic majorities than they had previously enjoyed. The election gave Democrats a huge 75–16 advantage over Republicans in the Senate and a mind-boggling 331–88 margin in the House. The results indicated that most Americans did not share the outrage expressed by political conservatives, big business, and the wealthy elite over the expansion of federal government power and influence taking place as a result of Roosevelt's New Deal policies.

Supporters of national health insurance also emphasized the many other areas in which government agencies were increasing their involvement in public health issues at the local, state, and federal levels, with relatively little controversy. The Social Security Act itself included assistance to the states for a wide range of public health work, including maternal and child health services as well as care for crippled children and the blind. Boosted by guidance from the American Public Health Association and new funding from the Public Health Service, the number of professionally staffed health departments in the United States was rapidly expanding as well. From 1935 to 1940 alone, the number of counties covered by full-time local public health services jumped from 762 to 1,577.[26] And in hard-hit agricultural states, the Farm Security Administration (FSA) implemented a group prepaid medical care program for struggling farmers. Under these cooperative plans, which by the early 1940s had popped up in eighty-eight counties across forty-three states, residents worked with FSA staff to negotiate annual care agreements with local medical societies in exchange for fixed payments.[27]

A doctor examines the fractured arm of a young girl at a Farm Security Administration (FSA) clinic. FSA provided prepaid medical care plans to people living in rural parts of the United States in the 1930s and 1940s.

Major bills expanding government's public health responsibilities continued to reach Roosevelt's desk. In 1937 Congress authorized the establishment of a National Cancer Institute under the auspices of the PHS **(See Document 5.14)**. One year later, it passed the Food, Drug, and Cosmetic Act, which mandated that medical drugs be proven safe through tests administered by the federal Food and Drug Administration before they could be marketed and distributed to the public. As scholar Paul M. Wax wrote, "the relationship between the government and the pharmaceutical manufacturers was profoundly changed by this event" **(See Document 5.15)**.[28]

Another significant piece of health care legislation passed in 1938 was the Venereal Disease Control Act, which authorized federal grants to states to combat the spread of sexually transmitted diseases. As a result of this legislation, the number of venereal disease clinics in the United States rose from about one hundred in 1936 to more than thirty-seven hundred by the end of 1944. Unfortunately, the government's zeal to find better venereal disease treatments also sparked a grim chapter in American public health history around this time. In 1932 the PHS quietly launched the Tuskegee Syphilis Study, in which government scientists treated four hundred African American men like human guinea pigs. This deplorable medical study lasted for four decades before it came to public light **(See Document 5.13)**.

Taking Up the Health Insurance Gauntlet Once Again

The renewed push for a system of national health care began in earnest in October 1936, when Roosevelt signed an executive order creating the Interdepartmental Committee to Coordinate Health and Welfare Activities. This gathering of representatives from various federal agencies was convened to study existing governmental health and welfare programs. Officially, they were directed only to make recommendations for better coordination of their various offerings, but everyone involved knew that the ultimate goal was a political one—to generate support for a federal health care program.

The interdepartmental committee subsequently appointed a Technical Committee on Medical Care chaired by Dr. Martha Eliot of the PHS Children's Bureau to shoulder the bulk of this work. In February 1938 the technical committee released a report, *The Need for a National Health Program,* which called for major changes in health care delivery across the United States **(See Document 5.16)**. Specifically, the committee urged the United States to use public health provisions contained in the Social Security Act to further expand public health, maternal, and child health services available through the government; extend federal grants to states for construction and operation of new hospitals; establish federal grants to states to fund medical care programs for citizens unable to afford medical care; provide federal support, in the form of subsidies and standard setting, for the implementation of state-level compulsory health insurance programs; and develop a federal program to compensate wage earners suffering from temporary or permanent medical disability.

In many ways, then, the committee's proposed National Health Program was a repackaging of policy goals espoused by the Committee on the Costs of Medical Care and the Committee on Economic Security earlier in the decade. But members relegated the most controversial component—the compulsory health insurance plank—to a lesser position of emphasis. They positioned it so that, if political circumstances made it necessary, it could be cut loose entirely. "Compulsory health insurance was thus seriously enfeebled by the time the Technical Committee finished its final report in February 1938," wrote historian Daniel S. Hirshfield. "It had been segregated and insulated from the other recommendations . . . and couched in the least specific terms. The efforts and hopes of the pro-insurance reformers were to no avail; the administration was apparently once again willing to sacrifice this reform on the grounds of political expediency."[29]

The Roosevelt administration organized a National Health Conference in July 1938 as a means to mobilize public support for the technical committee's recommendations. Much of the conference went as the Roosevelt White House hoped. The generally reform-minded invitees expressed general support for all elements of the National Health Program, and influential public health experts such as Charles-Edward Amory Winslow delivered impassioned speeches in support. Surgeon General Thomas Parran became so intoxicated by the pro-reform atmosphere that he was moved to declare that "it would appear to me . . . that people in general are beginning to take it for granted that an equal opportunity for health is a basic American right."[30]

As expected, representatives of the American Medical Association voiced strong opposition to the compulsory health insurance recommendation. They charged that it amounted to a Trojan horse for the eventual government control of all medical care, which would in turn unleash a host of burdensome bureaucratic intrusions into the provision of health care. The ultimate loser in such a sequence of events, argued speakers such as AMA secretary Olin West, would be the American public.[31]

Dr. Morris Fishbein, ten-year editor of the Journal of the American Medical Association, *was a relentless adversary of any and all schemes to establish universal health care in the United States.*

After the National Health Conference concluded, proponents of a national health care system worked to keep momentum alive. But private insurers, antiregulatory industry executives, and medical professionals labored mightily to sow public doubts about the wisdom of implementing such a "radical" new system **(See Document 5.17)**. At the same time, cries that the Roosevelt White House was pursuing socialized medicine echoed up and down the halls of Congress.

In 1939 Democratic Robert Wagner of New York, one of the progressive giants of the New Deal era in the Senate, introduced a National Health Bill (S. 1620) closely modeled on the National Health Program report of the Technical Committee on Medical Care. But the bill immediately ran into trouble from a coalition of Republicans and Southern Democrats, who had become increasingly anxious about the potential impact of government activism on segregationist practices in their home states. When the administration declined to intervene after Wagner's bill became hung up in the Senate Finance Committee, the chief government beneficiaries of the proposed legislation—the Public Health Service and its Children's Bureau—focused their lobbying energies on salvaging individual pieces of the National Health Program. These elements, which increased funding for various health care–related programs under their purview, were signed into law in August 1939 as amendments to the Social Security Act. But Wagner's bill—and the national health insurance proposal contained therein—quietly expired without ever passing out of committee, to the great dismay and frustration of reformers.

Notes

1. Abraham Epstein, *Insecurity: A Challenge to America: A Study of Social Insurance in the United States and Abroad* (New York: Smith and Haas, 1933), 407.

2. Quoted in Colin Gordon, *Dead on Arrival: The Politics of Health Care in Twentieth-Century America* (Princeton, NJ: Princeton University Press, 2003), 138.

3. Quoted in Robert Cunningham III and Robert M. Cunningham Jr., *The Blues: History of the Blue Cross and Blue Shield System* (DeKalb: Northern Illinois University Press, 1997), 11.

4. Isidore S. Falk, *Security against Sickness* (New York: Doubleday Doran, 1936), 27–28.

5. C. Rufus Rorem, "Medical Economics," *Journal of the National Medical Association* XXVIII, no. 2 (May 1936): 63–65.

6. Harry A. Millis, *Sickness Insurance: A Study of the Sickness Problem and Health Insurance* (Chicago: Chicago University Press, 1937), 28.

7. "Toward Health Insurance," *Editorial Research Reports,* March 6, 1937.

8. Gordon, *Dead on Arrival,* 56.

9. Falk, *Security against Sickness,* 319.

10. Quoted in Gordon, *Dead on Arrival,* 142–43.

11. Joseph S. Ross, "The Committee on the Costs of Medical Care and the History of Health Insurance in the United States," *Einstein Quarterly Journal of Biology and Medicine* 19, no. 3 (2002): 130.

12. Committee on the Costs of Medical Care, *Medical Care for the American People: Final Report of the Committee on the Costs of Medical Care* (Chicago: University of Chicago Press, 1932).

13. Committee on the Costs of Medical Care, *Medical Care for the American People,* 2.

14. Quoted in Committee on the Costs of Medical Care, *Medical Care for the American People,* x.

15. "Editorial," *Journal of the American Medical Association* 99, no. 23 (December 1932):1950–52.

16. Ross, "The Committee on the Costs of Medical Care and the History of Health Insurance in the United States," 132.

17. James MacGregor Burns, *Presidential Government: The Crucible of Leadership* (Boston: Houghton Mifflin, 1966), 200.

18. Daniel S. Hirshfield, *The Lost Reform: The Campaign for Compulsory Health Insurance in the United States from 1932–1943* (Cambridge, MA: Harvard University Press, 1970), 81.

19. Quoted in "Recovery and Relief," *The Survey* 69 (1933): 322.

20. Isaac M. Rubinow, *The Quest for Security* (New York: Henry Holt, 1934), 614.

21. Quoted in Jaap Kooijman, "Sooner or Later On: Franklin D. Roosevelt and National Health Insurance, 1933–1945" *Presidential Studies Quarterly* 29, no. 2 (June 1999): 360.

22. Edwin E. Witte, *The Development of the Social Security Act* (Madison: University of Wisconsin Press, 1963), 174.

23. Quoted in Jaap Kooijman, . . . *And the Pursuit of National Health: The Incremental Strategy toward National Health Insurance in the United States of America* (Amsterdam, The Netherlands: Rodopi, 1999), 56.

24. Frances Perkins, *The Roosevelt I Knew* (New York: Viking Press, 1946), 289.

25. Witte, *The Development of the Social Security Act,* 183–85.

26. William Shonick, *Government and Health Services: Government's Role in the Development of U.S. Health Services 1930–1980* (New York: Oxford University Press, 1995), 26.

27. Hirshfield, *The Lost Reform,* 86.

28. Paul M. Wax, "Elixirs, Diluents, and the Passage of the 1938 Food, Drug and Cosmetic Act," *Annals of Internal Medicine* 122, no. 6 (March 15, 1995): 456.

29. Hirshfield, *The Lost Reform,* 107–8.

30. Quoted in Alan Derickson, *Health Security for All: Dreams of Universal Health Care in America* (Baltimore: Johns Hopkins University Press, 2005), 82.

31. Hirshfield, *The Lost Reform,* 112–13.

DOCUMENT 5.1

Defending the Sheppard-Towner Maternity and Infancy Protection Act

"The Idea Is Not to Create a Great, Tyrannical Rule over the States"

1920

The Sheppard-Towner Maternity and Infancy Protection Act of 1921 was one of the only significant expansions of government involvement in public health to take place during the 1920s. Political support for the measure, which contributed matching federal funds to states to establish and run prenatal and child health care centers, was boosted greatly by women's suffrage. Members of Congress were fully aware that women's groups had been lobbying for this sort of social welfare program for years, and in 1918 Republican representative Jeannette Rankin of Montana—the first woman to serve in the U.S. House of Representatives—had introduced legislation to create such a program. When Democratic senator Morris Sheppard of Texas and Republican representative Horace M. Towner of Iowa joined with the Department of Labor's Children's Bureau to craft another such bill in 1921, mere months after American women received the franchise, lawmakers on both sides of the aisle were wary of crossing this new formidable voting constituency.

Still, some members of Congress did express concern about the expansion of federal authority implicit in the legislation, while others argued that administration of the program was better suited to the U.S. Public Health Service instead of the Children's Bureau, where the Sheppard-Towner Act placed administration of the program. These misgivings were evident when Children's Bureau chief Julia Lathrop appeared before a House committee in December 1920 to defend the proposed legislation. Following is an excerpt from the transcript of Lathrop's testimony, which featured questioning from Representatives Sam Rayburn (D-TX), Samuel E. Winslow (R-MA), John G. Cooper (R-OH), Edward E. Denison (R-IL), and Thetus W. Sims (D-TN).

The Sheppard-Towner bill eventually passed both houses of Congress by wide margins, and President Warren G. Harding signed it into law on November 23, 1921. The Children's Bureau operated the program for only a few years before it lost its funding. Nonetheless, the act is regarded as a landmark in the development of social welfare policies in the United States.

Miss Lathrop. I think I ought to say how this bill came into existence because I am well aware of the fact that it is not popular for bureaus to create new activities for themselves, nor ask for measures increasing their own powers.

The Children's Bureau was created in 1912, its object provided in the act being "to investigate and report upon all matters pertaining to the welfare of children and child life among all classes of our people, and especially to investigate the questions of infant mortality, the birth rate, orphanage, juvenile courts, desertion, dangerous occupations, accidents and diseases of children, employment, legislation affecting children in the several States and Territories."

This law directed governmental study in a new field, that of child welfare with the broadest definition, and it was hard to know where to begin. However, persons who had been active in urging the creation of the bureau had sent out letters before the bureau was under way, asking opinions as to what it ought first to undertake, and the replies were turned over to the bureau. So many of them urged preparation of information for everyday use of mothers that a series of popular bulletins on prenatal, infant, and child care was undertaken.

The bureau also began as promptly as possible field investigations—choosing for the first, the first subject mentioned in the law, infant mortality. Physicians and authorities in the social field have called public attention for years to the needless waste of infant life in foreign countries but the subject had awakened little popular attention in the United States. This subject was not approached as a medical problem. The plan was originated in the bureau and subjected to searching criticism in advance. In each city studied the history of every baby born in a given year was traced from birth through the first year of life or so long as the child survived in that year. The social, civic, family, and economic conditions surrounding the baby were noted with a view to learning what conditions accompanied varying infant mortality rates.

These investigations have been continued by the bureau since 1912 and have resulted in a body of facts showing the intimate coincidence of ignorance and poverty and civic neglect with high infant mortality rates. Studies of nearly 24,000 infants in 7 industrial cities show that an income earned by the father fairly guaranteeing the possibility of decent family life and permitting the mother to remain at home with her children, accompanies an infant death rate about three times as favorable as is the infant mortality rate in the lowest income group. In families in the lowest group, 1 baby in every 6 failed to survive its first year, while in families in the adequate income group but 1 baby in 17 died within the first year. . . .

The largest proportion of the total infant deaths occur in the first month of life and are apparently due to conditions preceding the birth of the child. Hence, authorities agree that prenatal instruction and care is of the highest importance, yet the bureau's studies in rural areas of six different States revealed the fact that 80 per cent of the mothers had received no advice or trained care during pregnancy. . . .

According to the most reliable obtainable data the United States has the highest maternal death rate in a list of 17 civilized countries, and the chances of a child surviving its first year in this country are worse than in 10 other countries.

We found, also, as we studied this matter, that every European country had made some sort of provision for the protection of maternity and infancy, provisions which would seem entirely inadequate, according to our standards; indeed, they were so meager that they had to be greatly increased when the war came on. But the public responsibility for protecting maternity and infancy was recognized, and as we considered the meaning of the reports and statistics secured in the bureau's investigations we felt that it was not for us to say that we had done enough when we had written pamphlets and had them printed and bound and sent them out to libraries for preservation, while the vast body of taxpayers never knew of their existence nor of the facts as to human life which they set forth in costly tabulations.

And therefore we are responsible for this measure which has been placed before you. Some of its provisions are necessarily experimental. We are confident, however, that if administered in good faith, with a sense of educational, social, and economic and hygienic values, enthusiasm and an interest can be created in the States which will make many of them go much further than duplicating the appropriations which we are suggesting from the Federal Government. . . .

The bill is designed to avoid an obnoxious governmental authority. It respects the rights and duties of the States and requires no rigid control of their appropriations. But experience shows that there should be a central source affording to the different States, when they make their plans, the best experience of all of the other States and of the world, and a central body competent to assure taxpayers and the special beneficiaries of the measure that its spirit is effectively carried out and that intelligent use is made of every dollar.

The actual public health nursing anticipated under the bill would be done by local employees, not by the Federal Government. The percentage of the appropriation that may be spent for administrative purposes by the Federal Government can not exceed 5 per cent, and at least 95 per cent must be allotted to the States.

The bill does not contemplate the creation of new machinery in the States. It is its purpose to have the work done in the States by State child-hygiene or child-welfare divisions, and 35 of the 48 States already have such divisions, most of them under the State boards of health. Necessarily, the bill provides for the creation of a suitable agency by States lacking such child-hygiene or child-welfare divisions. But there can be no danger of the creation of duplicating machinery in the States.

Mr. Rayburn. Will it interrupt you too much if I ask you a question at this point?

Miss Lathrop. No, sir.

Mr. Rayburn. Would you object to an amendment to this bill which would strike out this formation of a Federal board, and appropriate the same amount of money that you ask for in this bill, and put its distribution under the health authorities?

Miss Lathrop. Yes, sir.

Mr. Rayburn. You would object to that?

Miss Lathrop. I should. I object to it for this reason: It is because the entire activity for child welfare, and for the study of infant mortality, has been developed in the Central Government, by the Children's Bureau. When this bureau came into existence in 1912, this activity was nonexistent. Before beginning any investigations conferences were sought by me with the two bureaus touching the social field most closely, the Bureau of Education and the Public Health Service, because I wished to avoid any duplication. Especially was the Surgeon General of the Public Health Service consulted in regard to the infant-mortality inquiries. He stated that the plan was new and promised valuable results, and that the Public Health Service had no such studies in contemplation. No field work nor popular publication has ever been made by the bureau which duplicated or interfered with the work of any public or volunteer agency then in the same field.

Medical work is extremely important, and I fully recognize that, but it is only one item in the life of a family. The Children's Bureau is directed to investigate and report upon all matters affecting the welfare of children. I believe that the bureau which recognizes not only the medical, but the social and the economic and the family side, which recognizes that it is family entity and dignity which must be preserved and fostered in all social legislation, is a better body to administer and centralize the work suggested in this bill than is one which has purely the medical point of view.

The Children's Bureau has a child hygiene division with a competent woman physician as director. She does not know merely by printed reports what it means to live on those vast western prairies, and on the edges of the deserts. She has gone out to help make the reports where hotels are inaccessible and where she has slept at night on the ground in the open. She has seen for herself the brave, but sometimes hopeless, struggle of mothers in great remote homesteading sections. She knows the needs of mothers in industrial towns and has led in developing the public opinion which has now resulted in creating in 35 States divisions of child welfare, with which (whether in boards of education or health) the bureau is in constant communication.

The bill proposes an activity for the welfare of children requiring the coordinated use of various agencies, but it has a single purpose and forms a single unit and must have a single administrative direction. As the public health nurse must combine the functions of social worker, teacher, and health advisor, so the central administration must be a single administration but familiar with the social, educational, and hygienic aspects of this problem.

The fact that the bureau has hygiene, social service, industrial, publication, and statistical divisions furnishes an organization for coordinated effort which is essential to the best results and the most economical administration of the proposed measure.

Mr. Rayburn. Well, you would not contend, of course, that the Children's Bureau has done more for the health of the country than the United States Public Health Service?

Miss Lathrop. No, sir.

Mr. Rayburn. Well, it is one of the oldest and most distinguished services in the country.

Miss Lathrop. Yes, sir; I am not questioning that.

Mr. Rayburn. I think there is a little prejudice in the country against creating so many boards and commissions here in Washington; that is getting very irksome to the people of the country; they are getting rather tired of being told by some board here in Washington what they shall do about everything that comes up in their daily lives.

Miss Lathrop. There is a proposition to remove that board. I am willing to listen to that proposition. I should regret, and I believe the country would regret, changing the actual administration of this act, when it is new and untried, when it needs popularization and practical interpretation from the Children's Bureau, which has shown the need of the proposed act, to any service having a less comprehensive scope. . . .

Mr. Winslow. Would it cause any hindrance to the progress of your work if you were to be transferred to the United States Public Health Service?

Miss Lathrop. Well, Mr. Chairman, of course I should regard it as a fatal error to transfer a bureau whose business it is "to investigate and report upon all matters relating to the welfare of children and child life" to the sole supervision of physicians, earnestly as I may respect physicians. . . . We are aware that there are aspects of life which require the services of physicians, but they are a small part of child welfare and must be considered in relation to the social field.

Mr. Winslow. Granting that it means a social field, is this not specifically a medical proposition?

Miss Lathrop. I do not so regard it; and I am sure that anyone who had time to read the successive reports of the bureau upon infant mortality would not feel that this bill was primarily a medical proposition. I think it is a social and economic proposition, and we can not ignore those basic aspects of it without doing great violence to the value of whatever medical work is indicated.

Mr. Winslow. You would naturally look to the trained nurse as the field agent, would you not?

Miss Lathrop. I would certainly employ trained nurses.

Mr. Winslow. And then your next source of consultation might be the physicians of the neighborhood.

Miss Lathrop. Of course, both physicians and nurses would be necessary in the States. We must also, I think, have what has helped to give New Zealand the lowest infant death rate in the world, a rate about half that of our own country—namely, interest and wisdom to create hospitals and to create nursing services, and other necessary activities locally. It would be absurd for the Federal Government to undertake to control the medical authorities within the States, or to control local hospitals. This measure is permissive. No individual, no State, can be coerced under it. It offers services. It compels nothing. If a State accepts the money the bill offers, the Congress surely would not allow funds to be given out blindly without the Government's knowing or caring how they were spent or requiring any reports as to results secured by these expenditures. No subsidy or contribution in aid is prudent unless it carries responsibility for faithful, intelligent expenditure.

Mr. Winslow. Can you imagine the possibility, or can you prevent the possibility, in time, of conflict between you and the United States Public Health Service in working out a problem like this?

Miss Lathrop. No conflict if we both play fair.

Mr. Winslow. Well, that is a different question; that would clear up a good many difficulties of the Government if the different offices did that. . . .

Mr. Cooper. Do you find that the infant mortality is greater in the industrial congested centers of the country than it is outside of those centers?

Miss Lathrop. On the whole, yes. There are instances in cities of a very creditable reduction of infant mortality, because individuals, some of them doctors, some of them social welfare workers, some of them philanthropists, and some of them nurses, have taken hold of the problem jointly. They have taken an area and segregated it out as they have done in New York City, where the maternity centers have shown a very remarkable improvement in maternal mortality.

May I say this, that it is not solely a question of how many mothers and children die. The infant mortality rate, and the maternity mortality rate are an index of social well being; and every factor that lessens infant and maternal mortality tends to lift up living standards, and every advance in living standards automatically tends to lessen these death rates. It is really for this bigger reason that we ought to plead for this bill. . . .

Mr. Sims. I want to ask you this question. Miss Lathrop: Stress is put on the infant mortality, which is a matter of proper concern. But is it not also the fact that lack of proper education and lack of proper treatment in the maternity period are of vital importance? Is it not the fact that if the child and the mother may not die, but may live a life of more or less suffering due to this lack of knowledge? In other words, it is a kind of living death, which continues, perhaps, for a great number of years?

Miss Lathrop. Yes, sir.

Mr. Sims. I have not heard you emphasize that point.

Miss Lathrop. I do feel very strongly on that subject; I feel that you have stated the exact truth. . . .

Mr. Denison. What do you consider the most essential part of the bill; the appropriation of the money for the aid of the States or the creation of a bureau of the Federal Government to stimulate this kind of work?

Miss Lathrop. I think that it would be hard to divorce those two parts of the bill.

Mr. Denison. But if it should become necessary to divorce them, as a practical proposition, which do you think had better be retained, if either has to go?

Miss Lathrop. I do not know that I am quite willing to answer your question in that way, because, you see, if you made an appropriation there should be a board here in Washington to centralize information which can be put out to the States.

Mr. Denison. Right on that question, I do not know of any particular reason why there should be so much more intelligence here in Washington than might be in the State capitals. Why could not that intelligence be disseminated among the different States, instead of centralized here in Washington?

Miss Lathrop. I think it could be. I used to be a good deal in Springfield, and it would not become me to say that I am more intelligent in Washington than I was in Springfield.

Mr. Denison. Well, I was not speaking of any particular persons.

Miss Lathrop. But what I really mean to say is this: That in Washington we do bring 48 Springfields together; we do have the effect of the intercourse between all of these States; we can see what experiments work well in Illinois and what experiments work well in Texas. I think there should be a board here.

The women want this type of service, the correspondence of eight years shows it; they write that they are ignorant and helpless; they will accept services from the Federal Government and from the State governments if they can get them. I am sure that a network of activities in which the Federal Government and the State governments join, each doing its own part, would be more useful than if the Federal Government and the State governments worked alone.

Mr. Denison. Well, it occurs to me that what the States need is stimulation rather than a contribution of money from the Federal Government, and that the good purposes and benefits of this legislation might be obtained without the Federal Government making an appropriation. And then let the women's clubs and other women's organizations turn their attention to the States that are not doing anything along these lines, and they will soon get results; do you not think so?

Miss Lathrop. I really think you have to have somewhere some central repository of information, some central place from which you can stimulate, because, while some of these States may appear not to need this measure very much, others plainly need it urgently. Perhaps I overestimate the value of Washington, but I believe that scientific research which carries its own conclusions, translated into simple form, is the great innovation which the American Government has made in these scientific bureaus.

I believe that we can give something to every single State in the way of information, with constant research on the one side and constant popularization on the other; and that if they do not get this, the States will miss something. I think it is like that old fable about tying the sticks together and being unable to break them, and then unfastening the bundle and being able to break the sticks separately. The sticks are not weakened by being tied together.

I do want to say again that the idea is not to create a great, tyrannical rule over the States. Whatever is done by the Children's Bureau, and by the other scientific bureaus of the Government to serve the country is done by furnishing information and not by compulsion.

Source: House Committee on Interstate and Foreign Commerce. Statement of Miss Julia Lathrop, chief of the Children's Bureau, Department of Labor. *Public Protection of Maternity and Infancy: Hearings.* 66th Cong., 3d sess., December 1920, pp. 15–25.

Principles of the American Birth Control League

"Every Woman Must Possess the Power and Freedom to Prevent Conception"

1922

During the late nineteenth century, anti-abortion and anti–birth control statutes had become commonplace across the country. Physicians generally supported these statutes, and the American Medical Association adopted formal positions against contraception and other birth control measures. In the 1910s and 1920s, activist Margaret Sanger spearheaded a movement to strike down these laws and legalize various birth control practices.

America's physicians pushed back hard against Sanger's crusade. Doctors and surgeons, primarily white men of affluent background, asserted that birth control would jeopardize the sanctity of the family and erode sexual morality. Many of them also shared the concern, raised by conservative politicians, businessmen, and religious leaders, that encouraging birth control would further erode the position of families of western European descent in America's fast-growing "melting pot." "We who boast of our English, Irish, Scotch, and Irish-Celtic origin are going to be boasters after a while of ancient history and not of modern practice," warned Father Charles Coughlin. "It is our race, the Anglo-Saxon and Celtic . . . who are practicing birth control today. Negroes are not practicing it like we are; the Polish people are not practicing it as we are. The Italians are not practicing it as we are."[1]

Sanger and her allies rejected some of these complaints, which they said ignored women's rights and health considerations. But Sanger argued that rapid population growth among "unfit" peoples actually strengthened the case for the widespread adoption of birth control. In 1921 Sanger established the American Birth Control League (ABCL) as the primary vehicle for advancing the movement's legislative objectives and generating public support for its positions. Following is the ABCL's statement of principles from its founding convention.

Principles:

Many complex problems now confront America as the result of reckless population increase.

Too often we see incompetence and large families going hand in hand. Those least fit to carry on the race are increasing most rapidly. People who cannot support numerous offspring are encouraged and even aided to produce excessively large families. Many of the children thus begotten are subnormal or feeble-minded; many become criminals. The burden of supporting these undesirables has to be borne by the healthy elements of the nation. Funds that should be used to raise the standard of our civilization are diverted to the maintenance of those who lower it.

In addition to this great evil we witness the appalling waste of women's health and women's lives by too frequent pregnancies. These unwanted pregnancies often provoke the crime of abortion, or alternatively multiply the number of child workers and lower the standard of living.

To create a race of well-born children it is essential that the function of motherhood should be elevated to a position of dignity, and this is impossible so long as conception remains a matter of chance.

We hold that children should be

1. Conceived in love;
2. Born of the parents' conscious desire;
3. And only begotten under conditions which render possible the heritage of health.

Therefore we hold that every woman must possess the power and freedom to prevent conception except when these conditions can be satisfied.

Every mother must realize her basic position in human society. She must be conscious of her responsibility to the race in bringing children into the world.

Instead of being a blind and haphazard consequence of uncontrolled instinct, motherhood must be made the responsible and self-directed means of human expression and regeneration.

These purposes, which are of fundamental importance to the whole of our nation and to the future of mankind, can only be attained if women first receive practical scientific education in the means of Birth Control. That, therefore, is the first object to which the efforts of this League will be directed.

Aims:

THE AMERICAN BIRTH CONTROL LEAGUE, Inc., will endeavor to enlighten and educate all sections of the American public in the various aspects of the dangers of uncontrolled procreation and in the imperative necessity of a world program of Birth Control.

The League aims to correlate the findings of scientists, statisticians, investigators and social agencies in all phases of the population problem. To make this possible, it is necessary to organize various departments:

RESEARCH: To encourage the establishment and conduct of clinics, under capable medical direction, where Birth Control methods can be demonstrated, and data and records assembled, which shall make a firm and scientific foundation for contraceptive practice.

To stimulate scientific research into the relation between hap-hazard uncontrolled parentage and poverty, overcrowding, delinquency, defectiveness, child labor, infant mortality and international friction and war.

HYGIENE: Hygienic and Physiological instruction by the Medical Profession to mothers and potential mothers in harmless and reliable methods of Birth Control in answer to their requests for such knowledge.

EDUCATIONAL: The program of education includes: The enlightenment of the public-at-large, mainly through the education of leaders of thought and opinion—the teachers, ministers and writers—to the moral and scientific soundness of the principles of Birth Control and the imperative necessity of its adoption as the prerequisite to national and racial progress.

POLITICAL AND LEGISLATIVE: To enlist the support and co-operation of legal advisors, statesmen and legislators in effecting the removal of state and federal statutes which encourage dysgenic breeding, increase the sum total of disease, misery and poverty and prevent the establishment of a policy of national health and strength.

ORGANIZATION: To send into the various States of the Union field workers to enlist the support and arouse the interest of the masses to the importance of Birth Control so that laws may be changed and the establishment of clinics made possible in every State.

INTERNATIONAL: This department aims to co-operate with similar organizations in other countries to study Birth Control in its relations to the world population problem, food supplies, national and racial conflicts, and to urge upon all international bodies organized to promote world peace, the consideration of these aspects of international amity.

THE AMERICAN BIRTH CONTROL LEAGUE, Inc., proposed to publish in its official organ "The Birth Control Review," reports and studies on the relationship of controlled and uncontrolled populations to national and world populations.

THE AMERICAN BIRTH CONTROL LEAGUE, Inc., also proposes to hold annual conferences, to bring together from all aprts of the country those interested in the various phases of the subject, thus promoting the organization in every State of branches of the League which shall carry on the work of educating the public and pushing such legislation as is necessary to permit proper medical instruction in Birth Control.

Source: American Birth Control League, Inc. *What We Stand For: Principles and Aims of the American Birth Control League, Inc.* New York: American Birth Control League, 1922.

NOTE

1. Quoted in Eva R. Rubin, *The Abortion Controversy: A Documentary History* (Westport, CT: Greenwood Press, 1994), 30.

DOCUMENT
5.3

American Medical Association Formally Repudiates "State Medicine"

"Because of the Ultimate Harm That Would Come Thereby to the Public Weal"

1922

As the professional capacities, social stature, and financial earnings of early-twentieth-century physicians and surgeons steadily rose, many Americans looked to medical professionals for cues as to how to judge health policies—both existing and proposed—at the local, state, and national levels. As a result, the steadfast opposition of the American Medical Association (AMA) to government "incursions" into the health care industry posed a daunting obstacle to reformers who wanted to expand the state's role so as to ensure that all citizens had access to basic medical services. Little room for compromise existed in the AMA's position, as the following resolution, passed unanimously by the organization's House of Delegates in May 1922, makes clear.

The American Medical Association hereby declares its opposition to all forms of "state medicine," because of the ultimate harm that would come thereby to the public weal through such form of medical practice.

"State medicine" is hereby defined for the purpose of this resolution to be any form of medical treatment, provided, conducted, controlled or subsidized by the federal or any state government, or municipality, excepting such service as is provided by the Army, Navy or Public Health Service, and that which is necessary for the control of communicable diseases, the treatment of mental disease, the treatment of the indigent sick, and such other services as may be approved by and administered under the direction of or by a local county medical society, and are not disapproved by the state medical society of which it is a component part.

Source: *Supplementary Report of Reference Committee on Legislation and Public Relations.* Minutes of the Seventy-third Annual Session of the American Medical Association. St. Louis, Missouri, May 22–26, 1922, p. 44.

DOCUMENT 5.4

A Call for Expanded State Involvement in All Phases of Health Care

"Varied and Diverse Are the Movements Going On All about Us"

1926

Charles-Edward Amory Winslow was a renowned public health specialist who participated in many campaigns to increase authority and funding for public health programs, including the Committee on the Costs of Medical Care (CCMC). Upon being named to the presidency of the American Public Health Association (APHA) in 1926, Winslow wasted little time in using his position to call for better "organization" of medical service through new government programs and initiatives. In the following presidential address, delivered at APHA's fifty-fifth annual meeting in Buffalo, New York, on October 11, 1926, Winslow argues that local, state, and federal authorities need to expand their efforts to address the problem of inadequate medical care, especially in rural parts of America.

. . . It was quite obvious forty years ago that the individual sanitary engineer could not apply his resources effectively to the prevention of disease; and the same thing became clear thirty years ago as to the individual bacteriologist, and twenty years ago as to the individual public health nurse. Sanitary engineering and bacteriology and nursing have therefore been brought within the purview of the health program in such a way that their resources are available to every individual in any well-organized community. They have not been "socialized" in any arbitrary sense. There are still, and there always will be, sanitary engineers and bacteriologists and nurses, functioning in their private capacity; but we no longer rely chiefly on private expert service for the protection of water supplies, the laboratory diagnosis of disease or even for the nursing care of the sick in the home.

The major problem of health conservation, to-day, is the application on a scale of similar effectiveness of the resources of the science of medicine. It is on such an application that the control of heart disease and cancer depends and the issue is of such moment that in some fashion or other the desired end must surely be attained. Can it be reached in the normal course of events by the initiative of individual practicing physicians? Or must society through its official and voluntary agencies again take a hand and provide social machinery for facilitating its attainment?

LACK OR INADEQUACY OF MEDICAL CARE

I take it, from the criticisms one may hear on every hand, that the present organization of medical service in the United States has at least not yet reached a wholly ideal status. First of all, we are told that from the standpoint of the profession itself the conduct of medical practice on an extreme individualistic basis becomes increasingly unsatisfactory, since the growing complexity of medical science creates a corresponding necessity for laboratory tests and for consultation services, only to be met by some form of medical organization.

Second, from state after state comes the complaint of grave lack of medical service of any kind in rural districts and of efforts to meet this need by community grants to physicians who will consent to practice in such regions, an expedient duplicating a common experience of the New England settlements in colonial days. I doubt, however, whether financial reward is the chief determining factor in this problem, since there remains always the fact that a well-trained young doctor, unwilling to practice anything but good medicine, knows that he cannot practice good medicine in an isolated rural district without laboratory and hospital facilities and available consultation service. Nor can I accept the solution, propounded a year or so ago, of lowering the standards of medical education so as to produce physicians willing to practice in the country under existing conditions. I should prefer to keep our good doctors and through adequate organization enable them to do good work.

Third, we are told that the cost of adequate medical service has so risen that except for the very rich and the very poor such medical care is not actually available even in great cities and even in serious illness; and the surveys made by the Metropolitan Life Insurance Company make it clear that a large proportion of such illnesses do actually fail for one reason or another to receive the services of a physician.

Fourth, and of greatest importance in connection with the present discussion, is the problem of making medical service really preventive and not merely an attempted alleviation after the event. If disease is to be effectively controlled the doctor must generally be called in before the symptoms have become acute, and unless the characteristics of human nature shall be radically changed the average man will be slow to call in a physician for true preventive service if immediate and direct payment for the service rendered is thereby involved. It is this fundamental economic and psychological difficulty which has convinced so many that there must be some equally fundamental change in the system of compensation for medical service, some approximation to the ideal of annual payment or of payment through an insurance fund or through the tax levy, if medicine is to become truly preventive in its actual operation.

Organized Medical Service

Varied and diverse are the movements going on all about us which in greater or less measure are designed to meet one or more of the needs outlined above. . . . Group medicine solves the first of the four difficulties outlined above, and, as exemplified in such institutions as the Mayo Clinic, constitutes a very real contribution toward the organization of the profession. The development of hospital and dispensary services under public or semi-public auspices, as in the magnificent municipal hospital of the city of Buffalo, is one of the most potent forces in the progress of scientific medicine, as it was in Arabia six hundred years ago.

Industrial medicine has vast possibilities of usefulness and in this country has already perhaps accomplished more than any of the other tendencies which have yet been noted in bringing medical services to the individual at a stage when the most effective measure of prevention can be assured.

In Germany and England, National Health Insurance has been adopted as an official program and whatever doubts may exist as to the wisdom of combining cash benefit relief for disability due to illness with the medical care of such illness, a recent visit to England has convinced me that, thanks to the increasing supervision of the Ministry of Health, the plan is working better in that country than its unsympathetic critics (of whom I have been one) would have believed possible five years ago. . . .

Finally, there is a movement which in the United States seems to many of us to be the most important and most promising of all those here reviewed. I will call it, if I may, the Health Center Movement, meaning by that term the development with official funds, or with those contributed through voluntary agencies, of free public services for the examination of well persons or of persons who suspect the presence of disease, for their hygienic instruction and for the administration of preventive medical treatment or reference to private physicians or to institutions where such treatment can be secured. Prenatal clinics, infant welfare stations, school medical services, tuberculosis clinics, venereal disease clinics, mental hygiene clinics, heart clinics, cancer clinics are all undertakings of this class. They are rapidly on the increase and it is in regard to your attitude as health workers toward developments of this kind that a clear and convinced policy is of most immediate moment.

Criticisms and Catchwords

I am fully conscious of the criticisms which have been, and will be, made in regard to most and perhaps all of the projects for organizing medical service which have been outlined above. Some of these criticisms are sound and significant, others merely superficial and frivolous. The habit of condemning any attempt at intelligent community action by labelling it as "socialistic" and "bureaucratic" is for example unworthy of serious-minded men. Some things are better done by the individual, some better by the state; and catchwords will not help us to determine to which class a given activity belongs. I am often reminded, when I hear such alleged arguments, of a paragraph in an address by Dr. Royal Meeker, then United States Commissioner of Labor Statistics, who said:

> Many earnest people are afraid that social insurance will take away from the working man his independence, initiative, and self-reliance, which are so celebrated in song and story, and transform him into a

mere spoon-fed mollycoddle. This would be a cruel calamity. But if the worst comes to the worst, I, for my part, would rather see a race of sturdy, contented, healthful mollycoddles, carefully fed, medically examined, physically fit, nursed in illness and care for in old age and at death as a matter of course in recognition of services rendered or for injuries suffered in the performance of labor, than to see the most ferociously independent and self-reliant super-race of tubercular, rheumatic and malarial cripples, tottering unsocialistically along the socialized highways, reclining self-reliantly upon the communal benches of the public parks and staring belligerently at the communal trees, flowers and shrubbery, enjoying defiantly the social light of the great unsocialized sun, drinking individualistically the socialized water bubbling from the public fountain, in adversity even eating privately the communistic bread provided in the community almshouses, and, at last going expensively to rest, independently and self-reliantly in a socialized or mutualized graveyard full of little individualized slabs erected to the memory of the independent and self-reliant dead.

Nor do I believe that a more organized system of medical service will operate unfavorably upon the average income of the medical profession. It has not so operated in England and the profession in that country is now well satisfied with this particular aspect of the health insurance act.

On the other hand there are very real and very serious dangers in almost all plans for the better organization of medical service, which must be considered with the greatest care if we are really to attain the ideal results at which we aim. Even group practice by the medical profession itself is not without possibilities of commercialism. Industrial medicine may be twisted from its legitimate purpose and converted into a mere instrument for fighting compensation claims. The sale of salaried medical service to the public by non-medical profit-making organizations is in my judgment generally unsound. The administration of insurance plans and of health centers must be safeguarded with meticulous care if we are to avoid inadequate compensation for physicians, lowered standards of service, loss of independent initiative and the deadly blight of institutionalism. It will take the maximum of broad-minded statesmanship on the part of both health officials and the medical profession, if the good results of organized medicine are to be obtained without their possible attendant evils.

Tendency Toward Organization

Whether we like it or not, however, the tendency of the times makes it clear that some form, or forms, of organized community medical service are coming, as surely as the son will rise to-morrow. While we hesitate and consider, the thing is happening all about us. If we place our heads in the sand like the ostrich, or if we emulate King Canute and order back the tides the inevitable will still occur; but its form and its direction we can govern if we will. It is only through the leadership of the health officer as an agent of the public, solemnly charged with the duty of preventing disease and promoting health in every form, and through the thoughtful and broad-minded coöperation of the medical profession, that the legitimate demand for an organized preventive medical service can be wisely met.

Solution only through Cooperation

To avoid possible misunderstanding let me say here, with the utmost emphasis, that I am not arguing for group medicine, for state medicine, for health insurance or for any other panacea. The problem is one of the greatest delicacy and I have no easy answer to propound. The wise course must be found by the coöperative thinking and the coöperative experimentation of health officers and physicians during the next twenty years. . . .

Source: Winslow, Charles-Edward Amory. "Public Health at the Crossroads." *American Journal of Public Health* XVI, no. 11, November 1926, pp. 1080–85. (©) APHA. Used with permission. Used with permission.

| DOCUMENT |
| 5.5 |

Establishment of the First Blue Cross Plans

"An Idea Whose Time Had Come"

1930s

During the first quarter of the twentieth century, advances in scientific technology and medical knowledge made American hospitals much more effective at treating illness, injury, and disease than ever before. But these same advances also made hospital care prohibitively expensive for poor, working-class, and even middle-class patients. Voluntary prepaid group insurance plans emerged during the late 1920s and 1930s as a direct response to the challenge of obtaining affordable hospitalization coverage. In the following excerpts from interviews with Lewis E. Weeks, longtime hospitalization insurance experts C. Rufus Rorem and John R. Mannix recalled how these so-called Blue Cross policies, which covered 2.8 million Americans by 1938, came about.

ROREM: Hospital care insurance originated as a device by which an individual hospital would be guaranteed specified revenue and would in turn assume responsibility for specific services for groups of people who paid money to the institution. These people—beneficiaries—were eligible to receive specified care at that institution without having to pay any extra fees at the time of their illness and use of the hospital.

The most publicized of the early hospital insurance programs was the one initiated in Dallas, Texas, by the Baylor University Hospital.

Many individually sponsored insurance programs had been established before. Baylor, however, was probably the first to start a program of health service benefits, as opposed to one of cash indemnities toward the hospital bill. The services benefit principle is the feature, and probably the only distinctive characteristic, which explains the rapid growth of the insurance principle in paying for hospital care.

One weakness of the Baylor Hospital plan was that the benefits were available in only one hospital, a Baptist hospital. Therefore, the plan was not widely acceptable to people of other religious beliefs.

During the time that Baylor Hospital was expanding its coverage from approximately 1,600 to 6,000 beneficiaries in the city of Dallas, two other hospitals established similar and competing programs. One was a Catholic hospital, the other a Methodist institution. Both of these hospitals ultimately enrolled approximately 5,000 beneficiaries. These beneficiaries paid 75[¢] a month, through a promoter, for the same benefits as Baylor offered for 50¢ a month.

The hospitals received 50¢—of the total 75¢ monthly fee—for each person enrolled by the promoter. The enrollment in the Methodist and Catholic programs was not, however, deterred by the fact that their fee was $9.00 a year while the Baylor program was available at only $6.00 per year. Reluctance to participate, or at least what reluctance there was, arose from disbelief in these programs in their entirety, not from their price.

For example, I found out later, when interviewing business executives about enrollment of employees, that none of them objected on the grounds that family coverage was not worth, at that time, $24.00 a year. They doubted whether the contract was worth anything. They just did not believe in the program at all.

As originally organized, people were required to choose one hospital at the time they joined a group hospitalization plan. It soon became apparent that it was necessary to allow people to choose their hospital at the time of illness rather than at the time of enrollment. This meant, of course, that effective group insurance for hospital care should allow free choice among several alternative institutions. Interestingly, while being among the first to recognize the importance of group hospitalization, the state of Texas was among the last areas of the country to recognize and implement a free-choice, areawide plan. Ultimately, the single-hospital plans which had been formed in Dallas, Houston, and Fort Worth were merged into one plan, the Hospital Services Association of Texas.

The earliest plan to provide service benefits in several institutions appeared in New Orleans. There the Baptist Memorial Hospital joined with the Touro Infirmary to establish a citywide program with service benefits at the two institutions. Modest cash benefits were also provided for services in other hospitals.

The first full-blown, communitywide, free-choice, service benefit plan was developed in Newark, New Jersey. It was introduced in 1933 by Frank Van Dyk, who later moved to New York (1935) to become director of the New York City Plan. In Newark the areawide plan covered about 12 hospitals, each of which agreed to provide stated benefits for a stated amount expressed in terms of dollars per day.

Another important early citywide plan was developed in 1934 in St. Paul, Minnesota. Here Mr. E.A. van Steenwyk, a 29-year-old former real estate operator, conceived the idea of free-choice benefits among all the institutions in St. Paul. He also introduced for the first time the option of dependents' benefits. Up to that point, benefit coverage had emphasized just employed persons. No coverage was available for the wife or children of the employed individual. Van Steenwyk's idea was that, for an additional monthly premium charge, coverage could be purchased for that person's dependents.

As a footnote to van Steenwyk's idea, it's interesting to remember that initially it was the practice to charge an additional premium for each dependent who was covered. Within a few years, however, the data showed that it would be practicable, from a statistical point of view, to have a standard family rate, regardless of the size of the family. In other words, one rate for a one-person family, male or female, and one rate for a family of two or more persons, regardless of the number of dependents. So in time, pricing practices changed over to essentially what they are today. . . .

MANNIX: The Blue Cross plan in Cleveland was started in 1934 and has been very successful. An interesting aspect to me when I review the history of Blue Cross is that I have always thought of several plans starting at about the same time: one in Newark, New

Jersey; one in Washington, D.C.; the Cleveland plan; the St. Paul plan; and the plan at Sacramento, California. These plans were all started within about 18 months of each other. While I later got to know all of the individuals who took the leadership of these plans, none of us knew each other at that time. That was a perfect demonstration of an idea whose time had come.

I think the report of the Committee on the Costs of Medical Care accelerated this, but all of us were working on the idea without any particular knowledge of what the committee was doing or what they were likely to recommend. I do not believe that the people who were interested in developing these various initiatives had any more knowledge of the earlier history than I did. We all thought we had come up with a new, logical, and sound idea by independent actions in widely separated parts of the country.

Source: "C. Rufus Rorem, A First-Person Profile: Oral History," an interview with Lewis E. Weeks, 1984; and "John R. Mannix, A First-Person Profile: Oral History," an interview with Lewis E. Weeks, 1984. In *Shapers of American Health Care Policy: An Oral History,* edited by Lewis E. Weeks and Howard J. Berman. Ann Arbor, MI: Health Administration Press, 1985, pp. 139–42.

| DOCUMENT 5.6 | # Landmark Report from the Committee on the Costs of Medical Care |

"Human Life in the United States Is Being Wasted"

1932

In 1927 the Committee on the Costs of Medical Care (CCMC) was established to study escalating American health care costs and recommend ways to make medical care more affordable and, thus, increase the health, happiness, and productivity of the American people. The work of this committee, which included a wide array of prominent physicians, public health experts, and hospital administrators, was funded by a coalition of progressive philanthropic foundations. In 1932 the CCMC released its final report, called Medical Care for the American People, *in which it urged massive changes to the nation's system of medical care provision. Most of these changes, according to the CCMC, could best be accomplished through increased government involvement and investment in health care. In the following excerpts from this landmark report (footnotes removed), the committee examines the state of medical care in the United States, provides a summary of its principal reform recommendations (including widespread adoption of a system of group-based health insurance), and urges swift and decisive action on those recommendations.*

THE PRESENT STATUS OF MEDICAL CARE

The problem of providing satisfactory medical service to all the people of the Untied States at costs which they can meet is a pressing one. At the present time, many persons do not receive service which is adequate either in quantity or quality, and the costs of service are inequably distributed. The result is a tremendous amount of preventable physical pain and mental anguish, needless deaths, economic inefficiency, and social waste. Furthermore, these conditions are . . . largely unnecessary. The United States has the economic resources, the organizing ability, and the technical experience to solve this problem. . . .

As a profession, medicine has gone forward with strides during the last century and especially during the last 25 years. Its progress in understanding the human body and in perfecting techniques and instruments is almost unique in the history of civilization. Within the span of a single lifetime, the widespread utilization of anesthesia, aseptic surgery, bacteriology, physiology, and radiography has revolutionized the practice of medicine. . . . Physicians and other men of science have displayed an unparalleled generosity in making available to their colleagues and thus to mankind the results of their research and inventive genius.

As an economic activity, however, medicine has made much less phenomenal progress. The predominant economic institution in medical practice today—private individual practice—dates back to ancient times. Under this system medical services are now so provided that many persons either cannot and do not receive the care they need, or are heavily burdened by its costs. At the same time, many of the practitioners and the agencies which provide medical service are inadequately occupied and poorly remunerated. A barrier—in large part economic—stands between practitioners, able and eager to serve, and patients who need the service but are unwilling or unable to pay for it.

THE RECOMMENDATIONS OF THE COMMITTEE

Recommendation 1.—The Committee recommends that medical service, both preventive and therapeutic, should be furnished largely by organized groups of physicians, dentists, nurses, pharmacists, and other associated personnel. Such groups should be organized, preferably around a hospital, for rendering complete home, office, and hospital care. The form of organization should encourage the maintenance of high standards and the development or preservation of a personal relation between patient and physician. . . .

Recommendation 2.—The Committee recommends the extension of all basic public health services—whether provided by governmental or non-governmental agencies—so that they will be available to the entire population according to its needs. Primarily this extension requires increased financial support for official health departments and full-time trained health officers and members of their staffs whose tenure is dependent only upon professional and administrative competence. . . .

Recommendation 3.—The Committee recommends that the costs of medical care be placed on a group payment basis, through the use of insurance, through the use of taxation, or through the use of both these methods. This is not meant to preclude the continuation of medical service provided on an individual fee basis for those who prefer the present method. Cash benefits, *i.e.*, compensation for wage-loss due to illness, if and when provided, should be separate and distinct from medical services.

Except for some of the members signing the minority reports beginning on page 151, the Committee agrees to the principle of group payment for meeting the expenses of medical care. The methods of utilizing this principle, however, are numerous. They vary with the type of community, the social and economic groups to be served, and the scope of medical service to be provided. Hence, a number of specific steps are recommended. Some of these could be introduced promptly, as local experiments. Others, particularly the recommendation for required health insurance (3B), involve broad public policies and legislative action. Eight members endorse Recommendation 3B as a desirable and opportune step for certain states within the immediate future. The other members either do not consider it desirable in principle or believe that it should be approached only after adequate experience with other developments in group practice and group payment. . . .

3A. Voluntary Cooperative Health Insurance.—The Committee recommends that organized groups of consumers unite in paying into a common fund agreed annual sums, in weekly or monthly installments, and in arranging with organized groups of medical practitioners working as private group clinics, hospital medical staffs, or community medical centers, to furnish them and their families with virtually complete medical service. By "organized groups of consumers," the Committee means industrial, fraternal, educational, or other reasonably cohesive groups.

3B. Required Health Insurance for Low-Income Groups.—Some members of the Committee believe that the industrial states at least should immediately begin to plan for the adoption of legislation which will require all persons in certain income groups, certain occupations, or certain areas to subscribe for health insurance.

3C. Aid by Local Governments for Health Insurance.—If a community relies for the provision of medical service primarily upon the purchase by its people of voluntary health insurance, as described in Recommendation 3A, it will doubtless find that part of the people because of their low incomes cannot pay, even on a periodic basis, the full cost of complete service. Such communities may well use tax funds to the extent necessary to supplement the payments of these low-income families. Most members of the Committee believe that it is important for each individual or family which receives medical service to make, if possible, some definite personal payment for that service, according to its means, even though the payment may be considerably less than the full cost. When health insurance is required by law, it may also be necessary and desirable that a contribution be made from government funds.

3D. Salaried or Subsidized Physicians in Rural Areas.—The Committee recommends that rural areas or those of low economic resources, where suitable medical service is not now obtainable at a reasonable cost, should subsidize physicians or employ salaried physicians to furnish general medical service to residents of the area. Where the economic condition of the community permits, hospital service, public health nursing, dentistry, pharmacy, and occasional visits of specialists may be provided on the same financial basis and in coordination with the physicians' work. For the support of a local hospital, and, in certain instances, for other services, it will often be desirable, even necessary, for two or more counties of this type to join forces. Such a hospital may become a small medical center and should affiliate, if possible, with a large nearby general hospital or community medical center. Where only one physician is available in the area, he may also be the local health officer.

3E. State and Federal Aid.—For communities with such low per capita incomes that local tax funds are insufficient to supplement the payments of individuals and groups of patients, the Committee recommends state financial aid. In such cases the state should insist on the maintenance of reasonably high standards for the medical service.

In the less prosperous sections of the country, particularly those areas where pellagra, hookworm, malaria, typhoid fever, and tuberculosis raise the morbidity and mortality rates, and where the people have pitifully small money incomes, the Federal government should enable state and local governments to provide a basic minimum of good medical care.

In general, a majority of the Committee believe that it is wise never to rely on a larger unit when the cost can be borne by a smaller one. The community should not be called upon if the family can carry its own burden. The state should not be called upon if the community can meet the cost. The Federal government should not be asked to contribute if the state can pay its way. Where the smaller unit is economically unable to bear the entire burden, however, the larger unit must be ready to aid.

Recommendations for Supplementary or Temporary Use.—In addition to the foregoing five major recommendations, six others are presented.

3F. Voluntary Hospital Insurance.—The Committee recommends that, in the absence of a more comprehensive plan, general hospital service, not maintained by taxes or designed primarily for the wealthy, should be provided wholly or in part on a voluntary insurance basis, individuals or groups in the community paying agreed annual sums and receiving hospitalization when needed without further charge. Such plans will be of wider social benefit if they cover professional fees for hospitalized illness, as well as the charges for hospitalization itself. If there is more than one hospital in a community it will frequently be desirable for all the hospitals to enter a cooperative hospital insurance plan.

3G. Tax Funds for Local Hospital Service.—The Committee recommends that, where hospital facilities are lacking or inadequate, cities and counties use tax funds to provide hospital service, either through the construction of new hospitals or the extension of existing, well-managed institutions. Practitioners in such hospitals should be remunerated by the patients or by the community. In communities which are adequately supplied with hospital service, the Committee recommends that local and state tax funds be used to reimburse voluntary, non-profit hospitals which maintain good standards for all or part of the costs of service to patients who cannot meet their own expenses and who are not included in insured groups.

3H. Tax Funds for Medical Care of Indigent and Necessitous.—General medical care for those who are charges upon the community must be provided either by private charity, including the charitable services rendered by practitioners, or by public funds. The Committee believes that this burden should fall largely upon the latter and recommends that more adequate provision be made for meeting it. The service should include medical, dental, and nursing care, given in hospitals, clinics, or homes. Sound public policy demands that the practitioners as well as the agencies which provide such service be properly remunerated.

3I. Public Support for the Care of Chronic Diseases.—The Committee recommends adequate tax appropriations from local and state governments to insure hospitalization and other medical service for patients who are suffering from tuberculosis, mental disease, venereal disease, arthritis, and other chronic conditions, in so far as these patients are unable to provide suitable care from their own resources. The community payments may be used to support either governmental or non-governmental organizations. . . .

Recommendation 4.—The Committee recommends that the study, evaluation, and coordination of medical service be considered important functions for every state and local community, that agencies be forced to exercise these functions, and that the coordination of rural with urban services receive special attention. . . .

Recommendation 5.—The Committee makes the following recommendations in the field of professional education: (A) That the training of physicians give increasing emphasis to the teaching of health and the prevention of disease; that more effective efforts be made to provide trained health officers; that the social aspects of medical practice be given greater attention; that specialties be restricted to those specially qualified; and that postgraduate educational opportunities be increased; (B) that dental students be given a broader educational background; (C) that pharmaceutical education place more stress on the pharmacist's responsibilities and opportunities for public service; (D) that nursing education be thoroughly remoulded to provide well-educated and well-qualified registered nurses; (E) that less thoroughly trained but competent nursing aides or attendants be provided; (F) that adequate training for nurse-midwives be provided; and (G) that opportunities be offered for the systematic training of hospital and clinic administrators. . . .

THE CHALLENGE OF THE FUTURE

. . . As we survey the whole battle-field of the war between man and disease, we are struck by the fact that our victories have been attained only in certain sectors, while in others the enemy is holding his own or is even advancing. While reductions in the death rates from infant diseases, diphtheria, tuberculosis, typhoid fever, and other causes have resulted in an increase in the length of life, there remain many thousands of persons with uncorrected defects, a large proportion of illnesses that are uncared for, and a vast amount of preventable disease that is not prevented. Our failures result not only from insufficient scientific knowledge and from human weaknesses, but also from our failure to utilize existing knowledge, techniques, equipment, and personnel.

The successes of modern medicine have been achieved for the most part in those fields in which knowledge, techniques, equipment, and personnel have been organized under community leadership. Thus we have made concerted efforts to control infant mortality, tuberculosis, and the acute communicable diseases, and in large measure we have succeeded. Some disorders, on the other hand, have been left to the initiative of the private practitioner and the individual citizen with disappointing and sometimes negligible results. In our day it seems incredible that man studied the human body many thousands of years before he discovered what seems to us so obvious a phenomenon as the circulation of blood, but future ages may be equally astonished over our failure to utilize existing knowledge and facilities for a determined attack upon disease.

There is abundant evidence that the people of the United States are ready to enlist in such a warfare. Newspapers and magazines are contributing a vast amount of subject matter on the promotion of health. Commercial enterprises are exploiting the interest of the people in the improvement of their health. Women's clubs and business men's organizations have assumed leadership in the attack on various disease problems. As one result of their work, thousands of crippled children have been provided with corrective treatment. More particularly, hundreds of universities and industries have taken the initiative in providing organized medical services for a small proportion of the people.

The outstanding need is for effective leadership. . . . Whatever may be the nature of the group which the local community accepts for leadership, its effectiveness will depend largely upon an extensive knowledge and an unbiased attitude in regard to the existing situation. Obviously, there must be continued study of the diseases and conditions which are responsible for sickness and disability as well as a survey of all of the agencies, groups, and individuals which provide medical service. Private medical practice and public health work are so closely related that, in such a survey, it is folly to deal with them separately. If the community is to organize an effective attack on disease, all the facts must be systematically set forth in relation to all the other facts. . . .

In the various states, as in local communities, leadership may be assumed by a militant, state coordinating agency, by the state medical society, by the state department of health, or by some other agency. Here, also, the facts are essential as a basis for intelligent action. The state will not find a detailed program in the recommendations of the Committee, but must work out is own plan based on its own needs.

The cooperation of the professional groups in community or state leadership is essential. Their stake in these issues is very large; their interest is continuing. They should instigate as well as guide. The crucial point in the generalship of the forces at work is, perhaps, the development of a proper relation between the professional and the lay groups. The public should recognize the central place of the professional groups in determining standards and methods. The professions should recognize their ultimate responsibilities to the public. The control of undesirable commercial enterprises in this field will depend largely on the watchfulness of the professional bodies, on their ability to enlist lay cooperation, and on the development of sound and successfully operating non-commercial plans. . . .

Whatever means may be employed the time has come for action. European countries may not have proceeded with the greatest wisdom, but they have acted. Most of them have developed organized systems of medical care. We in the United States, above all other countries, are now in a position to go forward intelligently. With European experience available, and with the results of the five year program of study carried on by this Committee and collaborating agencies, a body of data is at hand which will enable each community and each state to take wise and adequate action.

Delay can no longer be tolerated. The death rates from cancer, diabetes, and appendicitis are rising threateningly. More babies are dying each year, many of them needlessly, than there were American soldiers killed in the World War. Every year tuberculosis kills its thousands and costs the country more than half a billion dollars. By early application of our knowledge we could double the cured cases of cancer. The venereal diseases still levy a heavy toll of blindness and mental disorders upon the nation. A great army of rheumatics remains untreated without hope of alleviation or cure. Many diabetics still remain without insulin or receive it too late. Human life in the United States is being wasted, as recklessly, as surely, in times of peace as in times of war. Thousands of people are sick and dying daily in this country because the knowledge and facilities that we have are inadequately applied. We must promptly put this knowledge and these facilities to work.

Source: Committee on the Costs of Medical Care. *Medical Care for the American People: Final Report of the Committee on the Costs of Medical Care.* Chicago: University of Chicago Press, 1932, pp. 2–3, 109, 118, 120–124, 146–150. Copyright (©) 1932 University of Chicago Press. Used with permission.

DOCUMENT
5.7

Minority Report of the Committee on the Costs of Medical Care

"There Are Great Dangers and Evils in Insurance Practice"

1932

When the Committee on the Costs of Medical Care (CCMC) published its long-awaited report, Medical Care for the American People, *in 1932, a long-simmering schism within the CCMC came into public view. Several physicians in the CCMC refused to sign on to the majority report because of objections to the committee's endorsements of group practice of medical services and some sort of system of group health insurance. The objections of these physicians were so great that they penned "Minority Report Number One of the Committee on the Costs of Medical Care," excerpted here, which laid out their rationale for opposing the proposed reforms. This report, which was signed by physicians A. C. Christie, George E. Follansbee, M. L. Harris, Kirby S. Howlett, A. C. Morgan, N. B. Van Etten, A. M. Schwitalla, Olin West, and Robert Wilson, was included in* Medical Care for the American People.

The minority group of the Committee whose names are subscribed to this report are in accord with the majority in many of their conclusions and recommendations. We find ourselves, however, in conflict with what we conceive to be the general tone or trend of the report and in certain instances in sharp disagreement with the recommendations for future action. . . . We regret the necessity for a minority report, but we are convinced that we would fail in our duty both to the public and to the medical profession if we did not point out as forcibly as possible what we conceive to be unwise recommendations or omissions in the majority report of this Committee.

We are in full and hearty accord with the majority in its recommendations for "The Strengthening of Public Health Services" and "Basic Educational Improvements," and we agree to some extent with the pronouncements of the Committee in respect to coordination of medical services. The first effect of "strengthening public health services" will be a considerable increase in the total cost of medical care, but we have the hope that eventually great savings will come from decrease in the incidence and duration of certain diseases. . . .

With regard to the majority Recommendations 1 and 3, dealing with "Organization of Medical Services" and "Group Payment for Medical Service," the convictions of this minority are so divergent from those of the majority that they must be discussed in detail.

ORGANIZATION OF MEDICAL SERVICES

The minority group recognizes the desirability of better correlation of the activities of the professions and it is in agreement with the majority upon some of the suggestions under the above heading. There is nothing, however, in the facts elicited by the Committee nor in the general experience of the medical professions to lead us to believe that "organization" can accomplish what is claimed for it in the majority report. On the contrary, it seems clear to us that many of the methods advocated will give rise to new and greater evils in the attempt to cure existing ones. . . .

1A. **Community Medical Centers.**—The emphasis placed upon this plan which is called "the Committee's most fundamental specific proposal" we believe to be far beyond any possibility of its ultimate value. It is admittedly an idealistic plan based almost solely upon theory. There is nothing in experience to show that it is a workable scheme or that it would not contain evil of its own which would be worse than those it is supposed to alleviate. Above all there is no evidence to prove that it would accomplish what ought to be the first object of this Committee, the lessening of the costs of medical care. The plan is suggestive of the great mergers in industry, the main medical center being in the nature of the parent holding company governing the activities of subsidiaries and branches. The idea that size and power are synonymous with excellence and efficiency has received some severe blows during the current economic depression, and opinions concerning it are undergoing revision. . . .

Among the many objections to the medical center plan which must occur to anyone familiar with the requirements of medical practice are the following: (1) It would establish a medical hierarchy in every community to dictate who might practice medicine there. This is inherent in the plan since any new member of the center must be chosen either by the chief or by a small staff. (2) It would be impossible to prevent competition among the many such centers necessary for large cities; cost would inevitably be increased by the organization necessary to assign patients to the various centers. This would add to the evils of medical dictatorship those of a new bureau in the local government with its attendant cost. (3) Continuous personal relationship of physician and patient would be difficult if not impossible under such conditions.

We look upon this plan as far-fetched and visionary. . . . It seems to us an illustration of what is almost an obsession with many people, namely that "organization" can cure most, if not all, human ills. . . .

[The Minority Report goes on to criticize other "organizational" proposals of the Committee majority, most notably industrial medical service and private group practice, before moving to the contentious subject of the health service payment policy proposals of the CCMC.]

Group Payment for Medical Service

The Committee on the Costs of Medical Care has been in existence for five years and during that time has collected at considerable expense a great body of data. Among these data are extensive comments on insurance medicine as it has developed and is now working out in various countries in Europe, and also in this country. In 1931 [A.M.] Simons and [Nathan] Sinai conducted a study of health insurance for the American Dental Association which the majority report of the Committee summarizes on page 99. One of the statements in their summary is as follows: "Every attempt to apply the principles of voluntary insurance on a large scale has proved to be only a longer or shorter bridge to a compulsory system. Every so-called 'voluntary' system is successful in just about the proportion that it contains compulsory features." Nothing has been made clearer than the fact that voluntary health insurance schemes have everywhere failed. In Europe they have been replaced by compulsory systems which are now under trial. Even in Denmark, where the system is nominally voluntary, there are indirect but very effective means of compulsion. In spite of these facts the majority of the Committee makes definite recommendations that this country adopt the thoroughly discredited method of voluntary insurance. It is admitted in the majority report on page 125 that there are many dangers inherent in the plan. The principal safeguard against these dangers offered by the majority is to tie the voluntary insurance system up with the visionary medical center plan which they have earlier offered as the "keystone" of all medical service. We have tried to show that such a medical center simply substitutes new and greater evils for old.

It seems clear that recommendations for further trial and expansion of voluntary insurance schemes in the United States are entirely inconsistent with the Committee's own findings. To recommend that our own country again experiment with discredited methods of voluntary insurance is simply to ignore all that has been learned by costly experience in many other countries as well as in our own.

Voluntary insurance systems are now in operation in many parts of the United States and are increasing in number and in size. In many places these schemes are being operated in accordance with the plan recommended by the majority of the Committee, that is, by making contracts with organized groups of the medical profession. That they are giving rise to all the evils inherent in contract practice is well known. Wherever they are established there is solicitation of patients, destructive competition among professional groups, inferior medical service, loss of personal relationship of patient and physician, and demoralization of the professions. It is clear that all such schemes are contrary to sound public policy and that the shortest road to the commercialization of the practice of medicine is through the supposedly rosy path of insurance. . . .

It seems clear, then, that if we must adopt in this country either of the methods tried out in Europe, the sensible and logical plan would be to adopt the method to which European countries have come through experience, that is, a compulsory plan under governmental control.

Before doing so, however, we should carefully examine this plan as it operates in Europe at present and face the objections to it. It should be remembered that compulsory systems of health insurance in European countries are still under trial. There is still no convincing proof that under these systems the costs of medical care have been reduced nor that the new evils to which they give rise are preferable to those which they are supposed to abate. The statement that most of the physicians in England prefer not to go back to the system under which they practiced before is not convincing because the system under which they practiced before was one of widespread voluntary insurance.

The objections to compulsory health insurance are almost as compelling to this minority group as are those to voluntary insurance. The operation of every form of insurance practice up to the present time has resulted in a vast amount of competitive effort on the part of practitioner groups, hospitals, and lay controlled organizations. Such competition tends to lower the standards of medical care, degrade the medical personnel, and make medical care a business rather than a profession. Proof of this is at hand in our own experience in this country with the only compulsory system with which we have yet had to deal, workmen's compensation insurance. The results named above are prevalent in many states. This is the rule to which there are a few notable exceptions. Under workmen's compensation, groups are soliciting contracts, often through paid lay promoters; laymen are organizing clinics and hiring doctors to do the work; standards of practice are being lowered; able physicians outside of the groups are being pushed to the wall; the patient is coerced by his employer to go to a certain clinic; and the physician is largely under the control of the insurance companies. These are not visionary fears of what may happen but a true picture of widespread evils attending insurance practice. We should need no better example of what must happen to medical care if compulsory insurance is extended to families.

There is one aspect of any system of insurance which should be kept in mind by all students of this question, namely, that the total cost of medical care is usually increased when it is paid for through insurance. There are two reasons for this. First, the cost of operation of the insurance plan must be added to the cost of medical care. . . . The second reason for the increased cost of medical care under insurance systems arises from a fact which has been thoroughly demonstrated, that is, the number of persons sick and the number of days sickness per capita always increase under any system of insurance. This is shown to be true for European countries by Simons and Sinai and has been demonstrated in relatively small health insurance projects in this country. . . .

We are not here attempting to marshal all of the facts or arguments that can be used against health insurance. Innumerable articles have been written on the subject. No absolute judgment is possible at the present time with regard to what place, if any, insurance should finally have in helping people to pay for medical care. We have tried only to show here that there are great dangers and evils in insurance practice which must be set over against the advantages of distributing the costs of medical care by this method and which, it seems to us, the majority report has minimized. The dangers are especially directed at the continued well-being and progress of the medical professions, which, after all, are the ones most concerned in maintaining a high grade of medical service. It ought to be remembered that compulsory insurance will necessarily be subject to political control and that such control will inevitably destroy professional morale and ideals in medicine. Since a qualified and untrammelled medical profession is the only agency through which scientific medicine can be applied for the benefit of the people, it follows that any plan which destroys professional morale will bring disaster to the public. One of the conclusions of Simons and Sinai is of especial significance in this connection. "While the statement might be disputed by insurance societies, a comparative study of many insurance systems seems to justify the conclusion that the evils of insurance decrease in proportion to the degree that responsibilities, with accompanying powers and duties, are intrusted to the medical professions." This statement is both a challenge to the medical profession and a warning to those who, without proper consideration of that profession, are willing to recommend the adoption of various new plans for the care of the sick.

It is our conviction that the Committee on the Costs of Medical care would have served its stated purposes and the cause of medical progress and the people's health much better if it had taken a strong stand against all of those methods of caring for the sick which have in them the dangers and evils of "contract practice." By doing so they would have come to the assistance of the medical profession in a battle against forces which threaten to destroy its ideals, disrupt its organizations and completely commercialize its practice, and which are at the same time opposed to the public welfare. The medical profession is now in many parts of the country extending and perfecting plans through which it can offer to the people in a more systematic way the services of *all* the physicians of each community at prices which all the people can afford. It is only by including *all* of the members of the medical profession of a community that the abuses under insurance systems may be avoided. . . .

Source: "Minority Report Number One of the Committee on the Costs of Medical Care." *Medical Care for the American People: Final Report of the Committee on the Costs of Medical Care.* Chicago: University of Chicago Press, 1932, pp. 152–55, 163–68. Copyright © 1932 University of Chicago Press. Used with permission.

DOCUMENT 5.8

I. M. Rubinow's Quest for Security

"Medical Aid Is a Service of a Peculiarly Urgent Character"

1934

Isaac M. Rubinow was one of the nation's leading specialists on social insurance in the first half of the twentieth century, as well as one of its most outspoken advocates of health care reform. His writings influenced the political thinking of multiple generations of lawmakers, reformers, and health administrators in both the public and private sectors. Rubinow's best-known work was the 1934 book The Quest for Security, *which was published two years before his death. In the following excerpt from this seminal work, Rubinow analyzes the impact of spiraling medical costs on the American people, ruminates on the meaning of "socialized medicine," and issues a blunt warning to medical professionals about their hostile attitude toward health insurance.*

. . . Medical aid is a service of a peculiarly urgent character. There is not much weighing or measuring of the quantity of service needed or desired. Normally the consumer does not want it at all. In fact, he does not even want to want it (if that does not sound too Irish); but when he wants it he wants it badly. He wants it at once. He wants as much of it as the situation may demand and more, and at the time he is willing to pay the highest possible price he can pay, whether he can afford it or not. If the demand is sufficiently strong, he is willing to sacrifice his savings of the past and mortgage his future. He is even willing sometimes to contract for a price which he knows he will never be able to pay. In other words, the conditions of price-making are quite different from the normal. Medical aid deals with health and life. When needed, it has an infinite use value. . . .

The question remains how these [medical] costs should be reduced. By cutting the physician's remuneration for his services? Is it simply a matter of battle between patient and doctor, between consumer and producer of medical services, a simple problem of control of price? Are the interests of patient and doctor diametrically opposite to each other? From the point of view of the nation's health, of which the medical profession is the natural guardian, that would be a very unfortunate situation. Is it not rather some fault of the very organization of the system of medical aid which may be contrary to the interest of both the patient and the doctor? A rising wave of both expert opinion and public feeling points at the latter as an answer. . . .

Source: Rubinow, I. M. *The Quest for Security.* New York: Henry Holt, 1934, pp. 195, 204.

DOCUMENT 5.9   Franklin D. Roosevelt Voices Support for National Social Insurance

"Security against the Hazards and Vicissitudes of Life"

1934

On June 8, 1934, President Franklin D. Roosevelt gladdened the hearts of health care reformers everywhere when he appeared before a joint session of Congress and delivered an unequivocal statement of support for the concept of national social insurance. This message, contained in a more wide-ranging address concerning the "broad objectives and accomplishments of the administration" since it had assumed the reins of power fifteen months earlier, made it clear that the president's focus was shifting from restoration of America's financial infrastructure to poverty, unemployment, and other pressing social welfare issues. Roosevelt's remarks are reprinted here.

A mere three weeks later, Roosevelt issued an executive order creating the Committee on Economic Security (CES), which was given a five-month deadline to submit "recommendations concerning proposals which in its judgment will promote greater economic security." Understandably, the health care reform movement regarded the CES's formation and mandate as an extremely auspicious development.

You are completing a work begun in March 1933, which will be regarded for a long time as a splendid justification of the vitality of representative government. I greet you and express once more my appreciation of the cooperation which has proved so effective.

Only a small number of the items of our program remain to be enacted and I am confident that you will pass on them before adjournment. Many other pending measures are sound in conception, but must, for lack of time or of adequate information, be deferred to the session of the next Congress. In the meantime, we can well seek to adjust many of these measures into certain larger plans of governmental policy for the future of the Nation.

You and I, as the responsible directors of these policies and actions, may, with good reason, look to the future with confidence, just as we may look to the past fifteen months with reasonable satisfaction.

On the side of relief we have extended material aid to millions of our fellow citizens.

On the side of recovery we have helped to lift agriculture and industry from a condition of utter Prostration.

But, in addition to these immediate tasks of relief and of recovery we have properly, necessarily and with overwhelming approval determined to safeguard these tasks by rebuilding many of the structures of our economic life and reorganizing it in order to prevent a recurrence of collapse.

It is childish to speak of recovery first and reconstruction afterward. In the very nature of the processes of recovery we must avoid the destructive influences of the past. We have shown the world that democracy has within it the elements necessary to its own salvation.

Less hopeful countries where the ways of democracy are very new may revert to the autocracy of yesterday. The American people can be trusted to decide wisely upon the measures taken by the Government to eliminate the abuses of the past and to proceed in the direction of the greater good for the greater number.

Our task of reconstruction does not require the creation of new and strange values. It is rather the finding of the way once more to known, but to some degree forgotten, ideals and values. If the means and details are in some instances new, the objectives are as permanent as human nature.

Among our objectives I place the security of the men, women and children of the Nation first.

This security for the individual and for the family concerns itself primarily with three factors. People want decent homes to live in; they want to locate them where they can engage in productive work; and they want some safeguard against misfortunes which cannot be wholly eliminated in this man-made world of ours.

In a simple and primitive civilization homes were to be had for the building. The bounties of nature in a new land provided crude but adequate food and shelter. When land failed, our ancestors moved on to better land. It was always possible to push back the frontier, but the frontier has now disappeared. Our task involves the making of a better living out of the lands that we have.

So, also, security was attained in the earlier days through the interdependence of members of families upon each other and of the families within a small community upon each other. The complexities of great communities and of organized industry make less real these simple means of security. Therefore, we are compelled to employ the active interest of the Nation as a whole through government in order to encourage a greater security for each individual who composes it.

With the full cooperation of the Congress we have already made a serious attack upon the problem of housing in our great cities. Millions of dollars have been appropriated for housing projects by Federal and local authorities, often with the generous assistance of private owners. The task thus begun must be pursued for many years to come. There is ample private money for sound housing projects; and the Congress, in a measure now before you, can stimulate the lending of money for the modernization of existing homes and the building of new homes. In pursuing this policy we are working toward the ultimate objective of making it possible for American families to live as Americans should.

In regard to the second factor, economic circumstances and the forces of nature themselves dictate the need of constant thought as the means by which a wise Government may help the necessary readjustment of the population. We cannot fail to act when hundreds of thousands of families live where there is no reasonable prospect of a living in the years to come. This is especially a national problem. Unlike most of the leading Nations of the world, we have so far failed to create a national policy for the development of our land and water resources and for their better use by those people who cannot make a living in their present positions. Only thus can we permanently eliminate many millions of people from the relief rolls on which their names are now found.

The extent of the usefulness of our great natural inheritance of land and water depends on our mastery of it. We are now so organized that science and invention have given us the means of more extensive and effective attacks upon the problems of nature than ever before. We have learned to utilize water power, to reclaim deserts, to recreate forests and to redirect the flow of population. Until recently we have proceeded almost at random, making mistakes.

These are many illustrations of the necessity for such planning. Some sections of the Northwest and Southwest which formerly existed as grazing land, were spread over with a fair crop of grass. On this land the water table lay a dozen or twenty feet below the surface, and newly arrived settlers put this land under the plow. Wheat was grown by dry farming methods. But in many of these places today the water table under the land has dropped to fifty or sixty feet below the surface and the top soil in dry seasons is blown away like driven snow. Falling rain, in the absence of grass roots, filters through the soil, runs off the surface, or is quickly reabsorbed into the atmosphere. Many million acres of such land must be restored to grass or trees if we are to prevent a new and man-made Sahara.

At the other extreme, there are regions originally arid, which have been generously irrigated by human engineering. But in some of these places the hungry soil has not only absorbed the water necessary to produce magnificent crops, but so much more water that the water table has now risen to the point of saturation, thereby threatening the future crops upon which many families depend.

Human knowledge is great enough today to give us assurance of success in carrying through the abandonment of many millions of acres for agricultural use and the replacing of these acres with others on which at least a living can be earned.

The rate of speed that we can usefully employ in this attack on impossible social and economic conditions must be determined by business-like procedure. It would be absurd to undertake too many projects at once or to do a patch of work here and another there without finishing the whole of an individual project. Obviously, the Government cannot undertake national projects in every one of the 435 Congressional districts, or even in every one of the 48 States. The magnificent conception of national realism and national needs that this Congress has built up has not only set an example of large vision for all time, but has almost consigned to oblivion our ancient habit of pork-barrel legislation; to that we cannot and must not revert. When the next Congress convenes I hope to be able to present to it a carefully considered national plan, covering the development and the human use of our natural resources of land and water over a long period of years.

In considering the cost of such a program it must be clear to all of us that for many years to come we shall be engaged in the task of rehabilitating many hundreds of thousands of our American families. In so doing we shall be decreasing future costs for the direct relief of destitution. I hope that it will be possible for the Government to adopt as a clear policy to be carried out over a long period, the appropriation of a large, definite, annual sum so that work may proceed year after year not under the urge of temporary expediency, but in pursuance of the well-considered rounded objective.

The third factor relates to security against the hazards and vicissitudes of life. Fear and worry based on unknown danger contribute to social unrest and economic demoralization. If, as our Constitution tells us, our Federal Government was established among other things, "to promote the general welfare," it is our plain duty to provide for that security upon which welfare depends.

Next winter we may well undertake the great task of furthering the security of the citizen and his family through social insurance.

This is not an untried experiment. Lessons of experience are available from States, from industries and from many Nations of the civilized world. The various types of social insurance are interrelated; and I think it is difficult to attempt to solve them piecemeal. Hence, I am looking for a sound means which I can recommend to provide at once security against several of the great disturbing factors in life—especially those which relate to unemployment and old age. I believe there should be a maximum of cooperation between States and the Federal Government. I believe that the funds necessary to provide this insurance should be raised by contribution rather than by an increase in general taxation. Above all, I am convinced that social insurance should be national in scope, although the several States should meet at least a large portion of the cost of management, leaving to the Federal Government the responsibility of investing, maintaining and safeguarding the funds constituting the necessary insurance reserves. I have commenced to make, with the greatest of care, the necessary actuarial and other studies for the formulation of plans for the consideration of the 74th Congress.

These three great objectives the security of the home, the security of livelihood, and the security of social insurance—are, it seems to me, a minimum of the promise that we can offer to the American people. They constitute a right which belongs to every individual and every family willing to work. They are the essential fulfillment of measures already taken toward relief, recovery and reconstruction.

This seeking for a greater measure of welfare and happiness does not indicate a change in values. It is rather a return to values lost in the course of our economic development and expansion.

Ample scope is left for the exercise of private initiative. In fact, in the process of recovery, I am greatly hoping that repeated promises of private investment and private initiative to relieve the Government in the immediate future of much of the burden it has assumed, will be fulfilled. We have not imposed undue restrictions upon business. We have not opposed the incentive of reasonable and legitimate private profit. We have sought rather to enable certain aspects of business to regain the confidence of the public. We have sought to put forward the rule of fair play in finance and industry.

It is true that there are a few among us who would still go back. These few offer no substitute for the gains already made, nor any hope for making future gains for human happiness. They loudly assert that individual liberty is being restricted by Government, but when they are asked what individual liberties they have lost, they are put to it to answer.

We must dedicate ourselves anew to a recovery of the old and sacred possessive rights for which mankind has constantly struggled homes, livelihood, and individual security. The road to these values is the way of progress. Neither you nor I will rest content until we have done our utmost to move further on that road.

Source: Roosevelt, Franklin D. Message to Congress Reviewing the Broad Objectives and Accomplishments of the Administration, June 8, 1934. "History: FDR's Statements on Social Security." Social Security Online. www.ssa.gov/history/fdrstmts.html#message1.

| DOCUMENT 5.10 | # Report of the Committee on Economic Security |

"We Are Not Prepared . . . to Make Recommendations for a System of Health Insurance"

1935

When the Committee on Economic Security (CES) was convened in mid-1934 to make the Roosevelt administration's case for new Depression-fighting social welfare programs, both supporters and critics of expanded social insurance expected medical care and health insurance to be major areas of CES focus. This expectation was borne out to some degree. The CES recommendations submitted to the president in January 1935 included a call for increased federal investment (in the form of grants-in-aid to states) in public health and maternal and child health services to go along with its attention-grabbing proposals for an old-age social security program and a system of unemployment compensation. But the CES refrained from giving its stamp of approval to a system of national health insurance, despite widespread support for the concept among committee members. Instead, it called for further study of the issue. This decision reflected considerable apprehension among Roosevelt and CES members that if they tried to get national health insurance through Congress, opposition might prove so strong that its other social insurance goals might be blocked. Excerpts from the CES report, including a summary of its chief recommendations, are reprinted here.

*In early 1935 a bill based on the CES social insurance recommendations began
making its way though Congress. At this point, a health insurance subcommittee of the
CES headed by Isidore S. Falk and Edgar L. Sydenstricker urged the Roosevelt
administration to amend the social security bill to include provisions for a national health
insurance program. But Roosevelt rejected this recommendation as politically unwise, and
a short time later the landmark Social Security Act passed Congress and was sent to the
White House for his signature. "The president did not intend to come out for health
insurance so long as the economic security bill was pending," wrote CES executive director
Edwin E. Witte. "No publicity whatsoever was given to the committee's report on health
insurance and the fact that such a report was made has never been publicized in the
newspapers."[1]*

NEED FOR SECURITY

The need of the people of this country for "some safeguard against misfortunes which
cannot be wholly eliminated in this man-made world of ours" is tragically apparent at this
time, when 18,000,000 people, including children and aged, are dependent upon emergency relief for their subsistence and approximately 10,000,000 workers have no employment other than relief work. Many millions more have lost their entire savings, and there
has occurred a very great decrease in earnings. The ravages of probably the worst depression of all time have been accentuated by greater urbanization, with the consequent total
dependence of a majority of our people on their earnings in industry.

As progress is made toward recovery, this insecurity will be lessened, but it is not
apparent that even in the "normal times" of the prosperous twenties, a large part of our
population had little security. From the best estimates which are obtainable, it appears
that in the years 1922 to 1929 there was an average unemployment of 8 percent among
our industrial workers. In the best year of this period, the number of the unemployed
averaged somewhat less than 1,500,000.

Unemployment is but one of many misfortunes which often result in destitution. In
the slack year of 1933, 14,500 persons were fatally injured in American industry and
55,000 sustained some permanent injury. Nonindustrial accidents exacted a much greater
toll. On the average, 2.25 percent of all industrial workers are at all times incapacitated
from work by reason of illness. Each year above one eighth of all workers suffer one or
more illnesses which disable them for a week, and the percentage of the families in which
some member is seriously ill is much greater. In urban families of low incomes, above
one-fifth each year have expenditures for medical and related care of above $100 and
many have sickness bills of above one-fourth and even one-half of their entire family
income. A relatively small but not insignificant number of workers are each year prematurely invalided, and 8 percent of all workers are physically handicapped.

At least one-third of all our people, upon reaching old age, are dependent upon others for support. Less than 10 percent leave an estate upon death of sufficient size to be
probated.

There is insecurity in every stage of life.

For the largest group, the people in middle years, who carry the burden of current
production from which all must live, the hazards with which they are confronted threaten
not only their own economic independence but the welfare of their dependents.

For those now old, insecurity is doubly tragic, because they are beyond the productive period. Old age comes to everyone who does not die prematurely and is a misfortune

only if there is insufficient income to provide for the remaining years of life. With a rapidly increasing number and percentage of the aged, and the impairment and loss of savings, this country faces, in the next decades, an even greater old-age security problem than that with which it is already confronted.

For those at the other end of the life cycle—the children—dependence is normal, and security is best provided through their families. That security is often lacking. Not only do the children under 16 constitute above 40 percent of all people now on relief, as compared to 28 percent in the entire population, but at all times there are several millions in need of special measures of protection. Some of these need individual attention to restore, as fully as may be, lives already impaired. More of them—those who have been deprived of a father's support—need only financial aid which will make it possible for their mothers to continue to give them normal family care.

Most of the hazards against which safeguards must be provided are similar in that they involve loss of earnings. When earnings cease, dependency is not far off for a large percentage of our people. In 1929, at the peak of the stock-market boom, the average per capita income of all salaried employees at work was only $1,475. Eighteen million gainfully employed persons, constituting 44 percent of all those gainfully occupied, exclusive of farmers, had annual earnings of less than $1,000; 28,000,000, or nearly 70 percent, earnings of less than $1,500. Many people lived in straitened circumstances at the height of prosperity; a considerable number live in chronic want. Throughout the twenties, the number of people dependent upon private and public charity steadily increased.

With the depression, the scant margin of safety of many others has disappeared. The average earnings of all wage earners at work dropped from $1,475 in 1929 to $1,199 in 1932. Since then, there has been considerable recovery, but even for many who are fully employed there is no margin for contingencies.

The one almost all-embracing measure of security is an assured income. A program of economic security, as we vision it, must have as its primary aim the assurance of an adequate income to each human being in childhood, youth, middle age, or old age—in sickness or in health. It must provide safeguards against all of the hazards leading to destitution and dependency.

A piecemeal approach is dictated by practical considerations, but the broad objectives should never be forgotten. Whatever measures are deemed immediately expedient should be so designed that they can be embodied in the complete program which we must have ere long.

To delay until it is opportune to set up a complete program will probably mean holding up action until it is too late to act. A substantial beginning should be made now in the development of the safeguards which are so manifestly needed for individual security. As stated in the message of June 8, these represent not "a change in values" but rather a "return to values lost in the course of our economic development and expansion." "The road to these values is the way to progress." We will not "rest content until we have done our utmost to move forward on that road."

Summary of Major Recommendations

In this report we discuss briefly all aspects of the problem of economic security for the individual. On many phases our studies enable us only to call attention to the importance of not neglecting these aspects of economic security and to give endorsement to measures and policies which have been or should be worked out in detail by other agencies of the Government.

Apart from these phases of a complete program for economic security with which we deal only sketchily, we present the following, major recommendations:

EMPLOYMENT ASSURANCE

Since most people must live by work, the first objective in a program of economic security must be maximum employment. As the major contribution of the Federal Government in providing a safeguard against unemployment we suggest employment assurance—the stimulation of private employment and the provision of public employment for those able-bodied workers whom industry cannot employ at a given time. Public-work programs are most necessary in periods of severe depression, but may be needed in normal times, as well, to help meet the problems of stranded communities and overmanned or declining industries. To avoid the evils of hastily planned emergency work, public employment should be planned in advance and coordinated with the construction and developmental policies of the Government and with the State and local public-works projects.

We regard work as preferable to other forms of relief where possible. While we favor unemployment compensation in cash, we believe that it should be provided for limited periods on a contractual basis and without governmental subsidies. Public funds should be devoted to providing work rather than to introduce a relief element into what should be strictly an insurance system.

UNEMPLOYMENT COMPENSATION

Unemployment compensation, as we conceive it, is a front line of defense, especially valuable for those who are ordinarily steadily employed, but very beneficial also in maintaining purchasing power. While it will not directly benefit those now unemployed until they are reabsorbed in industry, it should be instituted at the earliest possible date to increase the security of all who are employed.

We believe that the States should administer unemployment compensation, assisted and guided by the Federal Government. We recommend as essential the imposition of a uniform pay-roll tax against which credits shall be allowed to industries in States that shall have passed unemployment compensation laws. Through such a uniform pay-roll tax it will be possible to remove the unfair competitive advantage that employers operating in States which have failed to adopt a compensation system enjoy over employers operating in States which give such protection to their wage earners.

We believe also that it is essential that the Federal Government assume responsibility for safeguarding, investing, and liquidating all reserve funds, in order that these reserves may be utilized to promote economic stability and to avoid dangers inherent in their uncontrolled investment and liquidation. We believe, further, that the Federal act should require high administrative standards, but should leave wide latitude to the States in other respects, as we deem experience very necessary with particular provisions of unemployment compensation laws in order to conclude what types are most practicable in this country.

OLD-AGE SECURITY

To meet the problem of security for the aged we suggest as complementary measures non-contributory old-age pensions, compulsory contributory annuities, and voluntary contributory annuities, all to be applicable on retirement at age 65 or over.

Only non-contributory old-age pensions will meet the situation of those who are now old and have no means of support. Laws for the payment of old-age pensions on a needs basis are in force in more than half of all States and should be enacted every-where. Because most of the dependent aged are now on relief lists and derive their sup-port principally from the Federal Government and many of the States cannot assume the financial burden of pensions unaided, we recommend that the Federal Government pay one-half the cost of old-age pensions but not more than $15 per month for any individual.

The satisfactory way of providing for the old age of those now young is a contribu-tory system of old-age annuities. This will enable younger workers, with matching con-tributions from their employers, to build up a more adequate old-age protection than it is possible to achieve with non-contributory pensions based upon a means test. To launch such a system we deem it necessary that workers who are now middle-aged or older and who, therefore, cannot in the few remaining years of their industrial life accu-mulate a substantial reserve be, nevertheless, paid reasonably adequate annuities upon retirement.

These Government contributions to augment earned annuities may either take the form of assistance under old age pension laws on a more liberal basis than in the case of persons who have made no contributions or by a Government subsidy to the contributory annuity system itself. A portion of these particular annuities will come out of Govern-ment funds, but because receipts from contributions will in the early years greatly exceed annuity payments, it will not be necessary as a financial problem to have Government contributions until after the system has been in operation for 30 years. The combined contributory rate we recommend is 1 percent of pay roll to be divided equally between employers and employees, which is to be increased by 1 percent each 5 years, until the maximum of 5 percent is reached in 20 years.

There still remains, unprotected by either of the two above plans, professional and self-employed groups, many of whom face dependency in old age. Partially to meet their problem, we suggest the establishment of a voluntary Government annuity system, designed particularly for people of small incomes.

SECURITY FOR CHILDREN

A large group of the children at present maintained by relief will not be aided by employment or unemployment compensation. There are the fatherless and other "young" families without a breadwinner. To meet the problems of the children in these families, no less than 45 States have enacted children's aid laws, generally called "mothers' pension laws." However, due to the present financial difficulty in which many States find them-selves, far more of such children are on the relief lists than are in receipt of children's aid benefits. We are strongly of the opinion that these families should be differentiated from the permanent dependents and unemployables, and we believe that the children's aid plan is the method which will best care for their needs. We recommend Federal grants-in-aid on the basis of one-half the State and local expenditures for this purpose (one third the entire cost).

We recommend also that the Federal Government give assistance to States in pro-viding local services for the protection and care of homeless, neglected, and delinquent children and for child and maternal health services especially in rural areas. Special aid should be given toward meeting a part of the expenditures for transportation, hospitaliza-tion, and convalescent care of crippled and handicapped children, in order that those very necessary services may be extended for a large group of children whose only handicaps are physical.

RISKS ARISING OUT OF ILL HEALTH

As a first measure for meeting the very serious problem of sickness in families with low income we recommend a Nation-wide preventive public-health program. It should be largely financed by State and local governments and administered by State and local health departments, the Federal Government to contribute financial and technical aid. The program contemplates (1) grants in aid to be allocated through State departments of health to local areas unable to finance public-health programs from State and local resources, (2) direct aid to States in the development of State health services and the training of personnel for State and local health work, and (3) additional personnel in the United States Public Health Service to investigate health problems of interstate or national concern.

The second major step we believe to be the application of the principles of insurance to this problem. We are not prepared at this time to make recommendations for a system of health insurance. We have enlisted the cooperation of advisory groups representing the medical and dental professions and hospital management in the development of a plan for health insurance which will be beneficial alike to the public and the professions concerned. We have asked these groups to complete their work by March 1, 1935, and expect to make a further report on this subject at that time or shortly thereafter. Elsewhere in our report we state principles on which our study of health insurance is proceeding, which indicate clearly that we contemplate no action that will not be quite as much in the interests of the members of the professions concerned as of the families with low incomes.

RESIDUAL RELIEF

The measures we suggest all seek to segregate clearly distinguishable large groups among, those now on relief or on the verge of relief and to apply such differentiated treatment to each group as will give it the greatest practical degree of economic security. We believe that if these measures are adopted, the residual relief problem will have diminished to a point where it will be possible to return primary responsibility for the care of people who cannot work to the State and local governments.

To prevent such a step from resulting in less humane and less intelligent treatment of unfortunate fellow citizens, we strongly recommend that the States substitute for their ancient, out-moded poor laws modernized public-assistance laws, and replace their traditional poor-law administrations by unified and efficient State and local public welfare departments, such as exist in some States and for which there is a nucleus in all States in the Federal emergency relief organizations.

ADMINISTRATION

The creation of a social insurance board within the Department of Labor, to be appointed by the President and with terms to insure continuity of administration, is recommended to administer the Federal unemployment compensation act and the system of Federal contributory old-age annuities.

Full responsibility for the safeguarding and investment of all social insurance funds, we recommend, should be vested in the Secretary of the Treasury.

The Federal Emergency Relief Administration is recommended as the most appropriate existing agency for the administration of noncontributory old-age pensions and grants in aid to dependent children. If this agency should be abolished, the President should designate the distribution of its work. It is recommended that all social welfare activities of the Federal Government be coordinated and systematized.

Source: Committee on Economic Security. "Need for Security" and "Summary of Major Recommendations." *Report to the President of the Committee on Economic Security.* January 1935. www.ssa.gov /history/reports/ces/ces.html.

NOTE

1. Edwin E. Witte, *The Development of the Social Security Act* (Madison: University of Wisconsin Press, 1963), 188.

DOCUMENT 5.11 President Roosevelt Signs the Social Security Act

"A Law That Will Take Care of Human Needs"

1935

On August 14, 1935, President Franklin D. Roosevelt signed the Social Security Act into law. This was a truly momentous event in American politics. The measure not only delivered millions of elderly Americans from lives of destitution, but it also became the cornerstone of the modern social welfare state in the United States. Below are Roosevelt's remarks upon signing the act.

Today a hope of many years' standing is in large part fulfilled. The civilization of the past hundred years, with its startling industrial changes, has tended more and more to make life insecure. Young people have come to wonder what would be their lot when they came to old age. The man with a job has wondered how long the job would last.

This social security measure gives at least some protection to thirty millions of our citizens who will reap direct benefits through unemployment compensation, through old-age pensions and through increased services for the protection of children and the prevention of ill health.

We can never insure one hundred percent of the population against one hundred percent of the hazards and vicissitudes of life, but we have tried to frame a law which will give some measure of protection to the average citizen and to his family against the loss of a job and against poverty-ridden old age.

This law, too, represents a cornerstone in a structure which is being built but is by no means complete. It is a structure intended to lessen the force of possible future depressions. It will act as a protection to future Administrations against the necessity of going deeply into debt to furnish relief to the needy. The law will flatten out the peaks and valleys of deflation and of inflation. It is, in short, a law that will take care of human needs and at the same time provide the United States an economic structure of vastly greater soundness.

I congratulate all of you ladies and gentlemen, all of you in the Congress, in the executive departments and all of you who come from private life, and I thank you for your splendid efforts in behalf of this sound, needed and patriotic legislation.

If the Senate and the House of Representatives in this long and arduous session had done nothing more than pass this Bill, the session would be regarded as historic for all time.

Source: Roosevelt, Franklin D. Remarks on Signing the Social Security Act, August 14, 1935. Social Security Administration. www.ssa.gov/history/fdrstmts.html#signing.

DOCUMENT 5.12

Kansas Governor Landon Vows to Repeal Social Security If Elected President

"This Is the Largest Tax Bill in History"

1936

After Kansas governor Alf Landon won the Republican nomination for president in 1936, he made repeal of the Social Security Act a central plank in his campaign. Landon unveiled his intentions in a fiery September 26 speech in Milwaukee, Wisconsin, that characterized the act as fiscally irresponsible and contemptuous of Americans' capacity for taking care of their own needs. Following is the text of Landon's speech.

Most Republicans quickly fell in line behind Landon, both to show their support for the party standard-bearer and because they, too, felt that the Social Security Act was profoundly flawed. But there were a few exceptions, the most notable being former New Hampshire Republican governor John G. Winant, who had been appointed by Roosevelt to chair the newly created Social Security Board. A strong supporter of the program, Winant resigned his position on the board, which had been established as a nonpartisan entity, so that he could speak out against Landon's calls for repeal.

In the end, Landon's position failed to slow Roosevelt's march to a second term. The president crushed Landon in November in an election that was essentially a national referendum on the New Deal. Afterward, the Kansas governor conceded that his opposition to Social Security had probably not helped his cause. Roosevelt's lopsided victory gave his administration time and opportunity to further broaden the act's appeal to American voters. Amendments to the act were passed in 1939 that increased benefits, moved up the introduction of monthly benefit payments, shored up financing mechanisms, and expanded eligibility.

I am going to talk tonight about economic security—economic security for the men and women obliged to earn their daily bread through their own daily labor.

There is no question that is of deeper concern to us all. Even in good times there is ever present in the minds of workers the fear of unemployment. In periods of deep depression there is the fear of protracted idleness. And always, in prosperity and in depression, there is the ever-present dread of penniless old age.

From the standpoint of the individual, I know of no more intensely human problem than that of economic security. From the standpoint of the government there is no problem calling more for a sympathetic understanding and the best efforts of heart and mind.

But to solve the problem we must have more than a warm heart and a generous impulse. We must have the capacity and the determination to translate our feelings into a practical, workable program. Daydreams do not pay pensions.

Now in broad terms there are two ways to approach the development of a program of economic security. One is to assume that human beings are improvident—that it is necessary to have the stern management of a paternal government to force them to provide for themselves—that it is proper for the government to force them to save for their old age.

The other approach is to recognize that in an industrial nation some people are unable to provide for their old age—that it is a responsibility of society to take care of them.

The act passed by the present administration is based upon the first of these approaches. It assumes that Americans are irresponsible. It assumes that old-age pensions are necessary because Americans lack the foresight to provide for their old age. I refuse to accept any such judgment of my fellow-citizens.

I believe that, as a nation, we can afford old-age pensions—that in a highly industrialized country they are necessary. I believe in them as a matter of social justice.

Because of my firm belief in the justice, necessity and feasibility of old-age pensions, I am going to discuss the present act with the utmost frankness. It is a glaring example of the bungling and waste that have characterized this administration's attempts to fulfill its benevolent purposes. It endangers the whole cause of social security in this country.

In my own judgment—and I have examined it most carefully—this law is unjust, unworkable, stupidly drafted and wastefully financed.

Broadly speaking, the act is divided into three main sections. One deals with compulsory old-age insurance. It applies to about one-half of our working population. It excludes, among others, farmers and farm laborers and domestic servants.

Another part of the act attempts to force States to adopt unemployment insurance systems.

The third part of the act provides old-age pensions for those in need who do not come under the compulsory plan.

Now let us look at the so-called old-age insurance plan in more detail, and on a dollars and cents basis. In other words, let us see just how much the old people of this country are going to get, when they are going to get it and who is going to pay for it.

Here we are dealing not with opinions but with hard facts, with the provisions of the law.

Under the compulsory insurance plan of the present law, none of our old people will get any pension at all until 1942. If you happen to be one of those insured—and remember about half of our workers are not—you have to earn, on the average, $125 a month every single month for the next twenty years to get a monthly pension of $37.50. And you have to earn $125 a month for the next forty-five years to get a pension of $59.38 a month. Besides, these sums have to support both the worker and his wife.

But meanwhile, beginning Jan. 1 of next year, 26,000,000 working people begin paying taxes to provide these pensions. Beginning next January employers must start deducting these taxes from the pay envelopes of their employees and turn them over to the government.

Beginning next January employers must, in addition, begin paying taxes on the payrolls out of which your wages are to come. This is the largest tax bill in history. And to call it "social security" is a fraud on the working-man.

These taxes start at the rate of $2 in taxes for every $100 of wages. They increase until it is $6 in taxes for every $100 in wages.

We are told that this $6 will be equally divided between the employer and the employee. But this is not so, and for a very simple reason. The actual fact will be, in almost every case, that the whole tax will be borne either by the employee or by the consumer through higher prices. That is the history of all such taxes. This is because the tax is imposed in such a way that, if the employer is to stay in business, he must shift the tax to someone else.

Do not forget this: Such an excessive tax on payrolls is beyond question a tax on employment. In prosperous times it slows down the advance of wages and holds back re-employment. In bad times it increases unemployment, and unemployment breaks wage scales. The Republican party rejects any feature of any plan that hinders re-employment. . . .

One more sample of the injustice of this law is this: Some workers who come under this new Federal insurance plan are taxed more and get less than workers who come under the State laws already in force.

For instance, under the new law many workers now 50 years old must pay burdensome taxes for the next fifteen years in order to receive a pension when they are 65; whereas those of the same age who come under some State laws pay no taxes and yet actually get a larger pension when they reach the age of 65.

These are a few reasons why I called this law unjust and stupidly drafted.

There is a further important point in connection with the compulsory saving provided by the plan of the present administration. According to this plan, our workers are forced to save for a lifetime. What happens to their savings? The administration's theory is that they go into a reserve fund, that they will be invested at interest and that in due time this interest will help pay the pensions. The people who drew this law understand nothing of government finance.

Let us trace the process step by step.

The worker's cash comes into the Treasury. What is done with it? The law requires the Treasury to buy government bonds. What happens when the Treasury buys government bonds? Well, at present when there is a deficit, the Treasury gives some nice new bonds in exchange for the cash which the Treasury gives the Treasury. Now what happens to the cash which the Treasury gives the Treasury? The answer is painfully simple. We have good spenders at Washington, and they spend the cash that the Treasury gives the Treasury.

Now I know all this sounds silly, but it happens to be an accurate recital of what this administration has been foolish enough to enact into law.

Let me explain it in another way—in the simple terms of the family budget.

The father of the family is a kindly man, so kindly that he borrows all he can to add to the family's pleasure. At the same time he impresses upon his sons and daughters the necessity of saving for their old age.

Every month they bring 6 per cent of their wages to him so that he may act as trustee and invest their savings for their old age. The father decides that the best investment is his own I O U. So every month he puts aside in a box his I O U carefully executed, and, moreover, bearing interest at 3 per cent.

And every month he spends the money that his children bring him, partly in meeting his regular expenses, and the rest in various experiments that fascinate him.

Years pass, the children grow old, the day comes when they have to open their father's box. What do they find? Roll after roll of neatly executed I O U's.

I am not exaggerating the folly of this legislation. The saving it forces on our workers is a cruel hoax.

There is every probability that the cash they pay in will be used for current deficits and new extravagances. We are going to have trouble enough to carry out an economy program without having the Treasury flush with money drawn from the workers. . . .

With this social security money alone running into billions of dollars, all restraint on Congress will be off. Maybe some people want that, but I don't. . . .

To get a workable old-age pension plan we must repeal the present compulsory insurance plan. The Republican party is pledged to do this. The Republican party will have nothing to do with any plan that involves prying into the personal working records of 26,000,000 people. . . .

This brings us to the third main feature of the present act—the section dealing with pensions for the needy aged not covered by the compulsory insurance plan. This part of the present law can be made to serve as the foundation of a real old age pension plan. This, the Republican Party proposes to do. It proposes to overhaul this section and make of it a workable, common-sense plan—a plan to be administered by the States.

We propose through amendments to this section to provide for every American citizen over 65 the supplementary payment necessary to give a minimum income sufficient to protect him or her from want.

Frankly, I am not in a position to state with finality the total cost of this plan. . . . The plan which we propose will be much less expensive than the plan of the present administration because we will not create a needless reserve fund of $47,000,000,000.

Our plan will be on a pay-as-you-go basis, with the result that we will know year by year just what our pensions are costing us. That is sound, common-sense financing. . . .The precise method of taxation used will depend upon the decision of Congress working in cooperation with the Treasury. But there are three essential principles which should be complied with: The necessary funds should be raised by means of a special tax earmarked for this purpose so that the already difficult problem of budget-balancing may not be further complicated. The tax should be direct and visible. And the tax should be widely distributed. . . .

Let me repeat! I am a profound believer in the justice and necessity of old age pensions. My criticism of the present act is not that its purpose is bad. It is that this act will involve a cruel disappointment for those of our people least able to bear the shock of disappointment.

To these—our old people, our workers struggling for better conditions, our infirm—I will not promise the moon. I promise only what I know can be performed: economy, a living pension and such security as can be provided by a generous people.

Source: Associated Press. "Text of Gov. Landon's Milwaukee Address on Economic Security." *New York Times,* September 27, 1936, p. 31. Reprinted with permission from the YGS Group.

DOCUMENT 5.13

U.S. Public Health Service and the Tuskegee Syphilis Experiment

"A Considerable Portion of the Infected Negro Population Remained Untreated"

1936

In 1932 the U.S. Public Health Service (PHS) quietly launched one of the most notorious programs in the history of American public health policy. That year, PHS officials enrolled nearly four hundred poor black men afflicted with syphilis in a program designed to study the impact of the venereal disease when left untreated. The men, who hailed from poor black communities in Macon County, Alabama, were never informed that they were suffering from syphilis. Instead, scientists working on the project told them that they were being treated for "bad blood." The invitation to participate in the program and receive "special treatment," issued jointly by the PHS and Alabama state and county authorities, is reprinted here.

Over the next four decades, enrollees received free medical exams and free burial insurance, but they were not treated for the ravages of the disease—even after 1947, when researchers discovered that penicillin could be used to treat syphilis. Instead, public health officials and participating scientists monitored the progression of the disease in victim after victim. The Tuskegee Syphilis Study, as it came to be known, came crashing down in 1972, when a PHS researcher went to the press with the whole sordid story. The resulting media firestorm brought the study to a hasty end, but the entire episode, which essentially used American citizens as human guinea pigs, raised disquieting questions about medical ethics and government-sponsored racism. The revelations eventually led the U.S. government to approve financial restitution to the families of the abused men, as well as free health care for surviving enrollees and infected wives and children. But it was not until 1997 that the government issued a formal apology. "To the survivors, to the wives and family members, the children and the grandchildren, I say what you know: No power on Earth can give you back the lives lost, the pain suffered, the years of internal torment and anguish," stated President Bill Clinton. "What was done cannot be undone. But we can end the silence. We can stop turning our heads away. We can look at you in the eye and finally say, on behalf of the American people: what the United States government did was shameful."

Dear Sir:

Some time ago you were given a thorough examination and since that time we hope you have gotten a great deal of treatment for bad blood. You will now be given your last chance to get a second examination. This examination is a very special one and after it is finished you will be given a special treatment if it is believed you are in a condition to stand it.

If you want this special examination and treatment you must meet the nurse at

_____ on _____ at _____M. She will bring you

to The Tuskegee Institute Hospital for this free treatment. We will be very busy when these examinations and treatments are being given, and will have lots of people to wait on. You will remember that you had to wait for some time when you had your last good examination, and we wish to let you know that because we expect to be so busy it may be necessary for you to remain in the hospital over one night. If this is necessary you will be furnished your meals and a bed, as well [as] the examination and treatment without cost.

REMEMBER THIS IS YOUR LAST CHANCE FOR SPECIAL FREE TREATMENT. BE SURE TO MEET THE NURSE.

Macon County Health Department

Source: Tuskegee Study Group Letter. Macon County Health Department, Alabama State Board of Health, U.S. Public Health Service, and Tuskegee Institute, 1932.

DOCUMENT 5.14

National Cancer Institute Act

"To Conduct, Assist, and Foster Researches, Investigations, Experiments and Studies"

1937

Governmental expenditures on public health and medical research programs expanded significantly during the 1930s. Some of this increased investment came during the Hoover years—the National Institute of Health, for example, was established in 1930—but much of it was an outgrowth of the New Deal. In addition to providing grants to states and municipalities for new public health programs, the Roosevelt administration orchestrated the creation of major new medical research initiatives under the auspices of federal authorities. One such initiative was a 1937 bill passed by Congress that created the National Cancer Institute (NCI). Following is the full text of the act, which made the NCI the federal government's main agency for conducting research on the cause, diagnosis, and treatment of cancer.

An act to provide for, foster, and aid in coordinating research relating to cancer; to establish the National Cancer Institute; and for other purposes.

Be it enacted by the Senate and House of Representatives of the United States of America in Congress assembled, That for the purposes of conducting researches, investigations, experiments, and studies relating to the cause, diagnosis, and treatment of cancer; assisting and fostering similar research activities by other agencies, public and private; and promoting the coordination of all such researches and activities and the useful application of their results, with a view to the development and prompt widespread use of the most effective methods of prevention, diagnosis, and treatment of cancer, there is hereby established in the Public Health Service a division which shall be known as the National Cancer Institute (hereinafter referred to as the "Institute").

SEC. 2. The Surgeon General of the Public Health Service (hereinafter referred to as the "Surgeon General") is authorized and directed for the purposes of this Act and subject to its provisions, through the Institute and in cooperation with the National Cancer Advisory Council hereinafter established:

(a) To conduct, assist, and foster researches, investigations, experiments, and studies relating to the cause, prevention, and methods of diagnosis and treatment of cancer;

(b) To promote the coordination of researches conducted by the Institute and similar researches conducted by other agencies, organizations, and individuals;

(c) To procure, use, and lend radium as hereinafter provided;

(d) To provide training and instruction in technical matters relating to the diagnosis and treatment of cancer;

(e) To provide fellowships in the Institute from funds appropriated or donated for such purpose;

(f) To secure for the Institute consultation services and advice of cancer experts from the United States and abroad; and

(g) To cooperate with State health agencies in the prevention, control, and eradication of cancer.

SEC. 3. There is hereby created the National Advisory Cancer Council (herein referred to as the "Council"), to consist of six members to be appointed by the Surgeon General with the approval of the Secretary of the Treasury, and of the Surgeon General, who shall be chairman of the Council. The six appointed members shall be selected from leading medical or scientific authorities who are outstanding in the study, diagnosis, or treatment of cancer in the United States. Each appointed member shall hold office for a term of three years, except that (I) any member appointed to fill a vacancy occurring prior to the expiration of the term for which his predecessor was appointed shall be appointed for the remainder of such term, and (2) the terms of office of the members first taking office shall expire, as designated by the Surgeon General at the time of appointment, two at the end of the first year, two at the end of the second year, and two at the end of the third year after the date of the first meeting of the Council. No appointed member shall be eligible to serve continuously for more than three years but shall be eligible for reappointment if he has not served as a member of the Council at any time within twelve months immediately preceding his reappointment. Each appointed member shall receive compensation at the rate of $25 per day during the time spent in attending meetings of the Council and for the time devoted to official business of the Council under this Act, and actual and necessary traveling and subsistence expenses while away from his place of residence upon official business under this Act.

SEC. 4. The Council is authorized:

(a) To review research projects or programs submitted to or initiated by it relating to the study of the cause, prevention, or methods of diagnosis and treatment of cancer, and certify approval to the Surgeon General for prosecution under section 2 (a) hereof any such projects which it believes show promise of making valuable contributions to human knowledge with respect to the cause, prevention, or methods of diagnosis and treatment of cancer;

(b) To collect information as to studies which are being carried on in the United States or any other country as to the cause, prevention, and methods of diagnosis and treatment of cancer, by correspondence or by personal investigation of such studies, and with the approval of the Surgeon General make available such information through the appropriate publications for the benefit of health agencies and organizations (public or private), physicians, or any other scientists, and for the information of the general public;

(c) To review applications from any university, hospital, laboratory, or other institution, whether public or private, or from individuals, for grants-in-aid for research projects relating to cancer, and certify to the Surgeon General its approval of grants-in-aid in the cases of such projects which show promise of making valuable contributions to human knowledge with respect to the cause, prevention, or methods of diagnosis or treatment of cancer;

(d) To recommend to the Secretary of the Treasury for acceptance conditional gifts pursuant to section 6; and

(e) To make recommendations to the Surgeon General with respect to carrying out the provisions of this Act.

SEC. 5. In carrying out the provisions of section 2 the Surgeon General is authorized:

(a) With the approval of the Secretary of the Treasury, to purchase radium, from time to time, without regard to section 3709 of the Revised Statutes; to make such radium available for use in carrying out the purposes of this Act; and, for such consideration and subject to such conditions as the Secretary of the Treasury shall prescribe, to lend such radium to institutions, now existing or hereafter established in the United States for the study of the cause, prevention, or methods of diagnosis or treatment of cancer, or for the treatment of cancer;

(b) To provide the necessary facilities where training and instruction may be given in all technical matters relating to diagnosis and treatment of cancer to Service, in accordance with applicable law, such commissioned officers as may be necessary to aid in carrying out the provisions of this Act.

(c) This Act shall not be construed as superseding or limiting (1) the functions, under any other Act, of the Public Health Service or any other agency of the United States relating to the study of the prevention, diagnosis, and treatment of cancer; or (2) the expenditure of money therefor.

(d) The Surgeon General with the approval of the Secretary of the Treasury is authorized to make such rules and regulations as may be necessary to carry out the provisions of this Act.

(e) The Surgeon General shall include in his annual report for transmission to Congress a full report of the administration of this Act, including a detailed statement of receipts and disbursements.

(f) This Act shall take effect thirty days after the date of its enactment.

(g) This Act may be cited as the "National Cancer Institute Act."

Approved, August 5, 1937

Source: National Cancer Institute, Office of Government and Congressional Relations. "Legislative History: National Cancer Act of 1937." http://legislative.cancer.gov/history/1937.

DOCUMENT 5.15

Food, Drug, and Cosmetic Act

"The Following Acts and the Causing Thereof Are Hereby Prohibited"

1938

During the 1920s and 1930s, respected pharmaceutical companies and shady patent medicine manufacturers alike exploited loopholes in the 1906 Pure Food and Drug Act to introduce new products into the marketplace. Many of these drugs were unproven, and critics charged that some of them were dangerous to the health of consumers. But legislative efforts to provide more stringent regulation of the manufacture, distribution, and sale of these products languished in Congress until the fall of 1937, when a tragic event finally spurred passage. That year, a Tennessee-based drug company began marketing "elixir sulfanilamide" as a treatment for bacterial infections. The drug was distributed without any safety testing whatsoever and, when doctors began prescribing it, mass poisoning ensued. The chemical responsible for the disaster, which claimed 107 lives—many of which were children—was a toxic solvent similar to antifreeze.

The public outcry that followed this tragedy vaulted drug regulation to the top of the policy priority list in Washington, D.C. Reformers in Congress made effective use of the transformed political terrain to expand and strengthen the proposed bill. By the time President Franklin D. Roosevelt signed the Food, Drug, and Cosmetic Act into law on June 25, 1938, it included sweeping new regulations under which the drug, food, and cosmetics industries would have to operate. The act required safety testing of all new drugs before release, authorized government inspections of pharmaceutical factories, shored up drug labeling requirements, and dramatically increased state oversight of the production, marketing, and sale of foods, cosmetics, and therapeutic devices.

The following excerpt from the act, which remains the basis for many of the Food and Drug Administration's powers in the twenty-first century, provides a brief summary of the main thrust of the legislation's intent regarding drug, cosmetics, and food manufacturing operations. (Specific provisions mentioned below of particular note include Section 505, which explicated the premarket drug testing regulations under which pharmaceutical companies would be legally bound to obey, and Section 704, which provided Food and Drug Administration authorities with authorization to conduct factory inspections.)

Prohibited Acts

SEC. 301: The following acts and the causing thereof are hereby prohibited:

(a) The introduction or delivery for introduction into interstate commerce of any food, drug, device, or cosmetic that is adulterated or misbranded.

(b) The adulteration or misbranding of any food, drug, device, or cosmetic in interstate commerce.

(c) The receipt in interstate commerce of any food, drug, device, or cosmetic that is adulterated or misbranded, and the delivery or proffered delivery thereof for pay or otherwise.

(d) The introduction or delivery for introduction into interstate commerce of any article in violation of section 404 or 505.

(e) The refusal to permit access to or copying of any record as required by section 703.

(f) The refusal to permit entry or inspection as authorized by section 704.

(g) The manufacture within any Territory of any food, drug, device, or cosmetic that is adulterated or misbranded.

(h) The giving of a guaranty or undertaking referred to in section 303(c)(2), which guaranty or undertaking is false, except by a person who relied upon a guaranty or undertaking to the same effect signed by, and containing the name and address of, the person residing in the United States from whom he received in good faith the food, drug, device, or cosmetic; or the giving of a guaranty or undertaking referred to in section 303(c)(3), which guaranty or undertaking is false.

(i) Forging, counterfeiting, simulating, or falsely representing, or without proper authority using any mark, stamp, tag, label, or other identification device authorized or required by regulations promulgated under the provisions of section 404, 406(b), 504, or 604.

(j) The using by any person to his own advantage, or revealing, other than to the Secretary or officers or employees of the Department, or to the courts when relevant in any judicial proceeding under this Act, any information acquired under authority of section 404, 505, or 704 concerning any method or process which as a trade secret is entitled to protection.

(k) The alteration, mutilation, destruction, obliteration, or removal of the whole or any part of the labeling of, or the doing of any other act with respect to, a food, drug, device, or cosmetic, if such act is done while such article is held for sale after shipment in interstate commerce and results in such article being misbranded.

(l) The using, on the labeling of any drug or in any advertising relating to such drug, of any representation or suggestion that an application with respect to such drug is effective under section 505, or that such drug complies with the provisions of such section.

Source: Section 301: Prohibited Acts, Food, Drug, and Cosmetic Act of 1938. Food and Drug Administration History Office.

DOCUMENT
5.16

Report of the Technical Committee on Medical Care

"Disabling Sickness Hangs as an Ever-Present Threat over the Wage Earner"

1938

In 1936 President Franklin D. Roosevelt established the Interdepartmental Committee to Coordinate Health and Welfare Activities, which was designed to bring the best minds from various federal agencies together and make the case for a national health care program administered by state and federal authorities. The interdepartmental committee subsequently appointed a Technical Committee on Medical Care, which issued a major report, The Need for a National Health Program, *in early 1938. The report, which is excerpted here, contained an ambitious slate of proposals to remake the way in which American citizens received and paid for their health care needs. The committee's recommendations, not surprisingly, were hailed by progressive reformers and condemned by the more conservative medical establishment and other constituencies who believed that a national health program would be injurious to their business fortunes or America's political and cultural foundations.*

THE NEED FOR A NATIONAL HEALTH PROGRAM

I. Introductory Note

The cost of illness and premature death in this country amounts annually to about 10 billion dollars, including in this total the combined costs of health services and medical care, loss of wages through unemployment resulting from disability and the loss of potential future earnings through death. On an average day of the year, there are four million or more persons disabled by illness. Every year 70 million sick persons lose over one billion days from work or customary activities. Such fragmentary but specific estimates are indicative of the economic loss resulting from sickness and premature death, but they give no adequate indication of the incalculable social consequences of ill health.

We are not unmindful of the brilliant advances which have been made in scientific knowledge. Nor do we overlook notable improvements in medical, public health, dental and nursing education, or in the progress of research. Nor do we underestimate the contributions of individuals and associations, lay and professional, in raising the standards of professional service. All of these advances are written large on the credit side of the ledger of national progress and they count heavily in the measure of our national resources.

But it is not the task of this Committee merely to praise past performances and accomplishments. The Committee is charged with the duty to assess carefully the state of the nation's health, to relate what is being done against what can be done, to search out and define needs which are not being met through current practices, and to outline proposals through which the national health may be improved. Of necessity, therefore, this report deals primarily with the debit rather than with the credit side of the ledger—not by reason of any intent to give a distorted picture, but to discharge a specified task. Yet this limitation must be kept constantly in mind, lest otherwise the Committee be regarded as taking an unduly pessimistic view.

The Committee calls attention to the fact that illness precipitates large costs and enormous economic burdens, and that sickness is among the most important causes of economic and social insecurity. Sickness strikes at the basis of national vitality; the good health of the population is vital to national vigor and well-being. The accomplishments of the past in health conservation are therefore secondary to the needs of the present and of the future. While great advances have already been made, enormous needs still prevail. The amount of preventable sickness and disability which continues, the volume of unattended disease, the rate of premature mortality and the prevalence of avoidable economic burdens created by sickness-costs justify grave concern.

Do the methods of public health and medical sciences offer no hope of further reducing the national burdens of illness? On the contrary, the Committee finds that the essential lack consists not in inadequate knowledge but in inadequate funds. Indeed, at some points, the resources exceed the need, but they are used to less than capacity while people in need go without service. There are economic barriers between those in need of service and those prepared and equipped to furnish service. The essential inadequacy in respect to health services is not in our capacity to *produce* but in our capacity to *distribute*. The greater use of preventive and curative services which modern medicine has made available wait on the purchasing power rather than on the need of community or individual. The effective distribution and utilization of health and medical services requires a national plan for the economic application of our resources in maintaining and improving health. . . .

V. Income and Health Needs

In a representative sample of the urban population studied in the National Health Survey, 40 percent of the persons canvassed were found to be members of families with incomes of less than $1,000; 65 percent were in families with incomes under $1,500; and 80 percent in families with incomes of less than $2,000. About one-half of the group with incomes under $1,000 was in receipt of relief at some time during 1935. These figures are fundamental to any consideration of national health because they are basic to any contemplation of capacity to purchase not only food, shelter and clothing, but also medical care.

Rich and poor alike have benefited by the progress of public health and the medical sciences. Application of the newer knowledge has reduced to the vanishing point some of the plagues that once killed tens of thousands, and has led to great advances on other fronts where the accomplishments have been significant though partial. However, much of this progress has little significance for a large part of our population—the people who have small means. Community-wide services—so far as they exist—are, of course, available to them. Special services for the poor and the indigent are at their command. But the services they must buy with funds out of pocket are, in substantial measure, out of their reach when sickness strikes.

The advances in national health to which the Committee has directed attention have only limited significance for the poor. It is cause for grave concern, and for action, that the poor of our large cities experience sickness and mortality rates as high today as were the gross rates of 50 years ago.

In Massachusetts (where a long series of death records is available) 10 out of every 100 infants born alive in 1880 died during their first year; in that commonwealth today, the average loss is 4 deaths in every 100 infants born alive. Yet as recently as 1931, infants in Denver families with an annual income of less than $500, died at the same rate as average Massachusetts infants in 1880, while among Denver families with incomes of $3,000 or more there were only 3 infant deaths for each 100 live births. In Cleveland, in 1928, infants in the poorer districts died at the rate of 10 per 100 born alive, while infants in the better economic areas had a rate of 5 per 100.

In 1930, the tuberculosis death rate for unskilled laborers, in 10 States for which occupational mortality could be computed, was seven times that of professional men. In the general population, the death rate from this cause has been displaced from the leading cause of death to the rank of seventh place and this has been accompanied by a drastic reduction in the gross death rate: But among the industrial workers, among those exposed to special employment hazards, among Negroes and among other special groups, the rates remain much higher than for the population at large. There is danger in the complacent consideration of averages.

Death rates tell us of the annual loss of human lives, but we must keep in mind that death rates measure only a fraction of the toll which sickness exacts. For every death that occurs during a year, there are many illnesses. Indeed, if we count only severe disabling illnesses (i.e. those lasting for one week or longer), for each death there are 16 illnesses that mean loss of work for the family bread-winner, absence from school of the school child, or inability of the housewife to go about her normal duties.

The association of sickness with low income is illustrated by the following figures taken from a survey made among representative white families in many communities of the United States during the years 1928-1931; the figures relate to wage-earners of both sexes, ages 15 to 64, in the skilled, semi-skilled and unskilled occupations:

Family income	Annual days of disability per person
Under $1,200	8.9
1,200-2,000	5.7
2,000-3,000	5.0
3,000 and over	3.8

In the winter of 1935-1936, the Public Health Service canvassed three-quarters of a million families in 84 urban communities, and obtained information on illness and medical care in relation to family income and relief status. Preliminary results for 2,308,600 persons in 81 of these surveyed communities have brought out some pertinent facts. Disabling illness in the relief population occurred at an annual rate 47 percent higher for acute illness and 87 percent higher for chronic illness than the corresponding rate for families with incomes of $3,000 and over. The annual days of disability per capita in the relief group was found to be three times as great as among upper income families; the non-relief population with an income under $1,000 showed an amount of disability over twice that of the highest income group. One in every 20 family heads in the relief population was unable to work because of chronic disability, as contrasted with only one in 250 heads of families with incomes of $3,000 and over. Children of relief families experienced 30 percent greater loss of time from school and usual activities because of illness than did children in families in moderate and comfortable circumstances. . . .

Evidence on the association of sickness and poverty could be enumerated at great length. Perhaps these few citations will suffice. Every substantial study of sickness in the population, whether in urban or in rural communities, serves only to furnish additional proofs. And every careful inquiry, directed to the point, shows clearly that "environmental" factors are at least as certainly responsible as are "genetic" factors. Not the least of the "environmental" factors is economic status. Sickness rates are higher among the poor than among those who are in better economic circumstances. As a corollary, the poor need more health and sickness service than the well-to-do or the wealthy.

The poor have much sickness; sickness brings poverty. This circular relation brings anti-social results. The people who are involved in the vicious circle are trapped; they cannot raise themselves out of it by their bootstraps. Only society, which pays a heavy price for this continuing situation, can intervene and bring relief.

VI. Income and the Receipt of Health Service

The purchase of health services is still mainly a matter of private and individual action. Though government (Federal, State and local) spends considerable sums, and though organized groups pay an important share of the nation's bill for sickness, the individual patient still carries the lion's share through out-of-pocket payments. This may be illustrated by the breakdown of the national bill for all kinds of health and medical services, taking 1929 as illustrative of a prosperous pre-depression year, and 1936 as the most recent year for which comprehensive estimates are available:

	1929	1936
Total expenditures	$3,660,000,000	$3,210,000,000
Patients	2,890,000,000	2,560,000,000
Governments	510,000,000	520,000,000
Philanthropy	180,000,000	60,000,000
Industry	80,000,000	70,000,000

Although there are some important exceptions, medical care is, in the main, an "economic commodity" which is purchased and paid for directly by the individual who needs it. The fact that this "economic commodity" is chiefly a professional service does not alter the basic fact. It therefore results that the amount of medical care obtained by individuals differs with economic status; the well-to-do obtain more, the poor obtain less. This is so notwithstanding the fact that the poor have more sickness and more disability, and need more (not less) service. There are some notable exceptions to this generalization. In areas where extensive provision has been made for free hospital care for needy persons, the amount of hospital service received (per capita) by the poor is sometimes actually greater than the amount received by any except the very well-to-do. But this is only an exception proving the rule that the amount of medical care received (measured in number of services) varies with the person's ability to pay for it. . . .

Although there is more disabling sickness among the people in the low income groups than among those in the higher brackets, the proportion who went through a year of life without professional care was more than three times as high among the poorest as among the wealthiest families. This is summarized in the following figures:

Percentage of individuals in each family income group who received no medical, dental or eye care during a year

Family income	Percent
Under $1,200	47
1,200-2,000	42
2,000-3,000	37
3,000-5,000	33
5,000-10,000	24
10,000 and over	14

Without laboring the point, a few facts may be cited from the recently completed National Health Survey:

> No physicians' care was received in 30 percent of serious disabling illnesses among relief families and in 28 percent of such illnesses among families just above the relief level, as contrasted with a figure of 17 percent of illnesses receiving no care by a physician among families with incomes of $3,000 and more. 80 percent of the relief group were white and 20 percent were colored persons; unattended illnesses were

equally frequent in the two groups. Only 1 percent of disabling illnesses among relief families received bedside nursing care in the home, as compared with 12 percent in families with incomes of $3,000 and over.

The average child under 15 years of age in relief families received about one-half of the number of physicians' services and about one-twentieth the number of services from a private duty nurse that were received by children in families with incomes of $3,000 and over.

Only 5 percent of births were hospitalized among families on relief in southern cities of less than 25,000 as compared with 90 percent of births among families with incomes of $3,000 and over.

Nearly 13 percent of births among relief families in small southern cities were unattended by a physician or midwife as compared with 100 percent attendance by a physician either in hospital or home for the upper income class.

These findings are in accord with the facts revealed in numerous other surveys made in various parts of the country. Each study adds additional evidence that the receipt of medical care depends largely on income and that people of small means or none at all, though having the greatest need for care, receive the least service.

VII. Income and the Ability to Pay for Health Service

Although ignorance, indifference and other factors play a part, the main reason why persons in the lower income brackets do not receive proper medical care is that they are unable to pay for it. Surveys of family expenditures show that, by and large, families, tend to spend, on the average, 4 to 5 percent of income for medical care. The proportion of income spent for medical care is fairly constant, whatever the income, up to an annual family income of $5,000, beyond which it tends to decline slightly. A survey showed that in 1928-31, families with annual incomes under $1,200 spent $43 a year on the average for medical care; families with incomes between $1,200 and $2,000 spent $62 a year on the average; those with incomes between $2,000 and $3,000 spent $91; and families with incomes of $3,000 to $5,000 spent, on the average, $134 a year.

The present expenditures of families in the lower income brackets may be compared with the cost of adequate medical care. A number of estimates have been made of the per capita or per family cost of furnishing adequate medical care to a representative population group. Such estimates run from a minimum of $100 a year for a family of four, to more than double this amount. Even taking the lower figure, it is apparent that this cost is more than a sizable proportion of families can afford to spend for medical care. An examination of family budgets leads to the conclusion that families with incomes of $1,000 cannot afford to spend as much as $100 a year, on the average, for medical care. The same conclusion probably holds for families with annual incomes of $1,500. Yet, even in 1929, about 12 million families in this country, or more than 42 percent of all, had incomes of less than $1,500.

Although reductions in the cost of providing medical care are possible, and although education may induce people to divert a larger portion of income to the purchase of medical care, the fact nevertheless remains that a large proportion of the population—certainly one-third, and perhaps one-half—is too poor to afford the full cost of adequate medical care on any basis. This proportion of the population cannot purchase adequate medical care without depriving themselves of things which, in the long run, are just as necessary for decent healthy living as medical care. The one-third of the population which is ill-nourished, ill-housed, ill-clothed is also badly cared for in sickness and for the same reason: because income is too small.

The situation as regards the purchase of medical care, as thus outlined, is somewhat oversimplified by the fact that the analysis runs in terms of averages. In actuality, sickness comes to individual families in average amounts, as it were, only by chance. The individual family's need for medical care is uneven and unpredictable. In one year, little medical service or none whatsoever may be required; in another year, the family may suffer one or more severe illnesses among its members and medical service costing large amounts may be required; . . .

This situation has two results. One is that available income is not well harnassed to the purchase of medical care. The family spends its income from day to day and does not save against the day of serious sickness and large medical bills. As a consequence, many individuals who could pay for their medical care if they made regular provision therefor, either go without care when sickness comes or are forced to ask for charity. A second result of this situation is that families endeavoring to pay their own way are oftentimes confronted in severe illness with medical bills which they can pay only with hardship. The expense of proper medical treatment in certain illnesses has now become an economic hazard like unemployment or death, against which the average family requires protection.

The burden of sickness costs is mitigated in some measure by the arrangements whereby fees are adjusted to ability to pay. But the sliding scale operates only in limited ways and more particularly for specialists' than for other services. Though free and part-pay services and facilities have been extensively developed, especially in the large cities; though physicians give generously of their services; though hospitals are extensively equipped to care for the poor without direct charge to the patients and to give service at part pay; and though governments have greatly increased tax support for services furnished to the poor, the fact remains that large costs still fall on small purses. The poor still have fewer of their serious illnesses professionally attended and they purchase less adequate services than the well-to-do. The result is all the more serious because the poor have more sickness and more disability and need more—not less—services.

All evidence available to the Committee indicates that the problems raised by sickness costs present two clear-cut needs: (1) For people with incomes, ordinarily self-sustaining in respect to other essentials of living (food, shelter and clothing), health and sickness services must be made more extensively available through measures that will lighten the burdens of sickness costs. This requires appropriate arrangements to minimize the impact of these costs on individual families through distribution of the costs among groups of people and over periods of time. To what extent the result shall be attained through more extensive use of tax support and to what extent through social insurance, or through a combination of both, is not at issue. Each procedure is applicable to parts of the problem, and each may be more appropriate than the other for particular groups in the population and for particular areas. (2) Larger financial support is needed for services to be furnished to people who are without income, who are unable to obtain necessary care through their own resources.

Finally, it may be noted that what has been said regarding the unequal distribution of the costs of medical care applies also to the loss of wages suffered because of disability or permanent incapacity of the bread-winner. Disability wage-loss amounts, in the aggregate, to something like 2.5 percent of income. But it occurs among families variously in small and in large amounts. Disabling sickness hangs as an ever-present threat over the wage earner. He cannot budget individually against this risk. Provision through social insurance, or through systematic public assistance, or through both devices, is urgently needed to bring security of income against this common risk which threatens people of small and precarious earnings.

Source: Report of the Technical Committee on Medical Care. *The Need for a National Health Program.* Washington, DC: Interdepartmental Committee to Coordinate Health and Welfare Activities, 1938, pp. 1–2, 21–29. www.ssa.gov/history/reports/Interdepartmental.html.

DOCUMENT
5.17

Morris Fishbein Describes Health Insurance as a Threat to the Doctor-Patient Relationship

"Another Insidious Step toward the Breakdown of Democracy"

1939

The conclusions of the 1938 government study The Need for a National Health Program *were hotly disputed by a wide range of critics, the most influential of which were the American Medical Association, the commercial insurance industry, and conservative members of Congress philosophically inclined to limited government. These critics asserted that the members of the Technical Committee on Medical Care, who represented various federal agencies concerned with health care, commerce, and finance, had a vested interest in increased state oversight and administration of health care and health insurance issues. In addition, they charged that proponents of national health care programs minimized the problems that European countries had experienced with such system. Finally, they warned that the committee's zeal for imposing a "European-style" health system in America would do grave damage to the nation's social, political, and economic institutions.*

One of the leading spokesmen of this viewpoint was Morris Fishbein, the prominent editor of the Journal of the American Medical Association. *As the political battle raged in Washington, D.C., over the merits of the Technical Committee on Medical Care's report, Fishbein delivered a barrage of editorials and speeches that were aimed at undercutting support for its recommendations. Many of these broadsides, such as this 1939 editorial that appeared in the Rotary Club's monthly magazine, were squarely directed at middle-class American voters.*

"He who would surrender liberty for security," said George Washington in one of his important writings, "is likely to lose both." That warning is just as sound today as it was at the time of the Revolution. Then security meant the right of the individual to be free from unlawful search and seizure in his own home. Now, as we hear it discussed on every hand, it seems to mean the guaranty of food, fuel, clothing, and shelter, and freedom from the hazards of old age, unemployment, and illness.

Already the citizens of the United States are insured under a compulsory system against the hazards of old age and unemployment. Some would now extent that system to protect them against the hazards of sickness.

Now the chief opposition to compulsory sickness insurance rests squarely on the ground that it is compulsory, and thus represents another insidious step toward the breakdown of democracy. Consider existing conditions. In the event that a citizen finds himself unable to procure the necessities of life because of old age or unemployment, the Government returns to him the cash he has paid so that he may purchase these necessities. Bear in mind that it is always his own cash that is returned to him; social security does not create wealth—it merely redistributes money that workers earn.

The majority of the expense in such a system is paid by low-income workers. It is from their wages that the first deduction is made. The money paid by the employer in the form of tax is added by him to the price of the goods which are, in the vast majority of instances, purchased by the workers. Finally, only the workers pay income tax. The deduction from wages, already too small, of these costs tends to inhibit the ability of the worker to supply himself with the necessities of life, and thus may create more sickness than medical care can prevent or cure.

The opposition to compulsory health insurance rests also on the fact that it is not health insurance, but sickness insurance. The tendency of such plans is to provide little or nothing for preventive medicine. They attempt only to take care of those already sick. Immunization against disease is not provided by sickness insurance in any country. In no country in the world is periodic physical examination included as a part of the compulsory insurance system. Obviously, in no country could a really complete periodic physical examination be included, because the costs would be far beyond the reach of any such system.

In this connection it is important to realize that the death rates for such diseases as tuberculosis and diphtheria have declined more rapidly in this country than in those with compulsory sickness insurance systems. It should be pointed out that in the United States during 1938 the sickness and death rates were as low or lower than those of any other great country in the world.

American medicine opposes compulsory sickness insurance because it tends to break down that initiative and ambition which are the marks of a young country going ahead, and which disappear completely when civilization becomes too old and begins to decay. The young physician in the United States who has had a medical education involving four years of medical school and one or two years of internship, looks forward to beginning a career in which his progress will depend on his ability in taking care of the sick and the extent to which he is willing to give of his utmost for his patients. In contrast, the young physician in many another country steps into a salaried job or position at a fixed income, depending on the number of people assigned to him by the State, and then begins a mechanized routine type of service that is harmful not only to his patients, but also to his own character and advancement.

Compulsory sickness insurance encourages excessive attention to minor illnesses and complaints, and thus brings about deficiencies in the care of more serious conditions. The tendency of medical care under every compulsory sickness insurance system is to encourage a mechanical, unprofessional type of service, giving a low grade of medical service to more people, but at the same time lowering the standards of medical service for all the people.

In the United States the hospital system has developed beyond anything available in any other country. We have more than 6,200 acceptable hospitals, and the vast majority of medical care is given in these hospitals which are known as nonprofit, voluntary hospitals. These have been built out of that fundamental motive in every great religion which makes the care of the sick a high moral objective. The setting up of State compulsory sickness insurance systems would inevitably tend to throw the burden of serious illness on these hospitals. As in Great Britain, they would soon find themselves bankrupted by the State system. Moreover, the building of hospitals by the Federal Government and the equipment and maintenance of such hospitals, which would make even more difficult the work of the voluntary hospitals, would tend to destroy the voluntary system.

Compulsory sickness insurance exalts administration above the problems of the doctor and patient. The German system has for years employed more administrators than physicians. The reported costs of administration in different countries vary from 10 to 20 percent of the total income of the system. The bills for administration multiply while hospitals and laboratories deteriorate. The setting up of a State system introduces incompetent political control. Finally these systems throw such a burden of forms, blanks, and red tape on the doctor that he must spend anywhere from one to two hours of each day in satisfying the desires of the administrators for records.

Under the system of insurance against old age and unemployment, the worker receives cash to provide himself with what he needs. Under all systems, however, it is proposed to handle the problem of medical care not with cash, but with service. This question of payment in cash or in service is fundamental. Social-service workers oppose payment in cash because of the fear that either the worker will exploit the Government or the physician will exploit the Government. Somehow little has been said of the possibility that social-service workers may exploit the Government. Payment in service makes impossible any accurate, actuarial calculations as to the costs of the service.

Medical costs vary. With rapid progress the costs constantly increase. Under such circumstances the quality of the service is lowered to the patient, the medical profession and the hospital exploited, or modern methods neglected. If these conditions do not supervene, the system becomes bankrupt. There are excellent examples now available of this succession of events.

The 1938-1939 epidemic of influenza brought disaster to voluntary sickness insurance plans in existence in various parts of the United States, and threatens the financial status of hospitalization plans. Yet the epidemic of this year did not even approximate the scope or intensity of the influenza epidemic of 1918 or not a single insurance plan in existence in the country could have survived. Even the Government plan could hardly have survived under such circumstances.

Apparently it did not occur to the administrators to pass the increased cost along to the patients. The attempt is always made to balance the budget at the expense of either the hospitals or the doctors. The hospitals must get even by depreciating the quality or the amount of service rendered.

In the United States today, under our present system, we have reached a high degree of scientific advancement and a quality of medical service that is supreme. The chief difficulties are the inequalities in the availability of medical service of this high standard for great groups in the population. Nevertheless, the medical profession has not remained static in meeting this responsibility. Thousands of experiments are now being conducted in various parts of the country with the aid of the medical profession, leading to new methods of distribution and payment for medical service. These plans include 75 insurance hospitalization plans, 54 hospital insurance plans, 500 medical and hospital benefit organizations, 20 flat-rate hospital plans, 2,000 industrial medical-care plans, 24 sick-benefit union funds, 300 group medical-practice plans, 300 college health service plans, and 28 States in which the Farm Security Board has set up a system.

Much is heard of the three or four group plans which have been opposed by the medical profession. These plans are opposed, not primarily because they represent experiments with new forms of distribution of medical service, but because their operation has brought into the picture of medical practice business methods and commercialization which are fatal to medical science. Solicitation of patients, underbidding to secure contracts, and breaking down of the relationship between doctor and patient are three of the most serious aspects of such service. Opposition to all new plans is based wholly on the extent to which they deteriorate medical service, inhibit medical advancement, and break down confidence in the medical profession.

Every discussion of change in the nature of medical practice in the Untied States runs afoul of the habit of demanding an all-or-nothing policy in relationship to many human affairs. No scientific physician, and no established policy of the American Medical Association, has opposed social control where it represents the ideal method of dealing with medical problems. Already in New York some 35 percent of medical practice is State medicine or socialized medicine, most of it established with the encouragement of the medical profession. The work of the health departments in preventive medicine as applied to mankind in the mass, the sanitariums for the tuberculous, the institutions for the insane, and the clinics for the care of the indigent and those able to pay only a small part of the costs of medical service are examples of socialized medicine.

But these are far different from a system wherein every individual would be taxed under a State or Federal law for the setting up of a bureaucracy to administer complete medical service to every person in the State, or to the majority of the people who would be included under a less than $3,000 annual-income level or to one-half the people who might be included under a less-than-$2,000 income level. The forms of socialized medicine which take increasingly from the individual more and more of the responsibility for his own existence and which enter increasingly into the intimate affairs of human life must be opposed by all who treasure the life, liberty, and pursuit of happiness which mark the American democracy.

Source: Fishbein, Morris. "Maintain the Personal Doctor-Patient Relation." *The Rotarian.* September 1939, pp. 15, 57–59. © Rotary International. Reproduced with permission. All rights reserved.

CHAPTER 6

Partisan Jousting Over
Health Care in the Postwar Era

The fierce political battles that were waged over health care during the early years of the Franklin D. Roosevelt presidency subsided during World War II, only to be renewed with even greater fervor in the late 1940s and early 1950s. President Harry S. Truman raised the stakes for both Republicans and Democrats by making national health insurance one of his administration's top domestic priorities. He spent much of his nearly eight-year presidency locked in health policy deadlocks with Republicans and the American Medical Association (AMA), both of which relentlessly painted Truman's proposed reforms as "socialized medicine." This tactic, employed at a time when Cold War fears were cresting across much of America, effectively neutralized progressive efforts to rein in skyrocketing health care costs through new government programs and regulations. Proponents of sweeping health care reform despaired during the first years of the presidency of Republican Dwight D. Eisenhower, a steadfast champion of voluntary insurance and other market-based solutions to the nation's health care woes. By the end of his second term, however, economic and political trends were shifting once more—this time to the advantage of liberal advocates of federal health care legislation.

HEALTH CARE POLITICS DURING ROOSEVELT'S LAST YEARS

During the Roosevelt administration, the federal government had become an aggressive player in responding to a wide range of social and economic problems created or exacerbated by the Great Depression. But while landmark New Deal legislation such as the 1935 Social Security Act dramatically increased the economic security of elderly citizens and provided a social safety net for the unemployed, similarly bold proposals for government-administered programs of health care never reached Roosevelt's desk for his signature. Time after time, campaigns to pass national health insurance came up short, turned back by steadfast opposition from the powerful American Medical Association and the pragmatic political calculations of the administration. Reformers were forced to content themselves with incremental gains such as increased federal funding of state public relief programs that helped the indigent pay medical expenses, new health clinics for agricultural labor, and small pilot programs such as a prepaid medical care initiative administered by the Farm Security Administration (FSA).

The political environment became even more inhospitable to health care reform when the United States entered World War II in 1941, as the government and the general

In the summer of 1939, high-ranking members of the American Medical Association appeared at Senate committee hearings on the Wagner Health Bill. Dr. Edward H. Cary and Dr. R.G. Leland used numerous statistics and statements to argue that medical care in the United States was improving rapidly and that no need existed for a massive health bill.

public diverted much of their time, resources, and attention to the war effort. Roosevelt periodically indicated his support for a system of national health insurance. In his 1944 annual message to Congress, he even framed access to affordable and competent medical care as a basic right of citizenship. Rhetoric aside, he refrained from investing much political capital in health legislation. In 1943, for example, Democratic senators Robert Wagner (New York) and James Murray (Montana) and Democratic representative John D. Dingell (Michigan) unveiled a sweeping reform bill that would have established a national system of compulsory health insurance financed through payroll taxes. But Roosevelt declined to issue a formal endorsement of the so-called Wagner-Murray-Dingell (WMD) bill. Instead, he merely wished them "good luck with it."[1]

The president's stance was a significant blow to the bill, which was already under withering attack from the American Medical Association, commercial insurers, conservative farming organizations, and free market groups such as the U.S. Chamber of Commerce. Implacably opposed to any form of governmental interference with the health care, pharmaceutical, and insurance industries, this alliance of business interests joined with conservative allies in Congress and the news media to slam Wagner-Murray-Dingell as misguided at best and socialistic at worst. Indeed, the rhetoric employed by some opponents was incendiary. In one December 1943 speech, for example, Morris Fishbein, editor of the *Journal of the American Medical Association*, described Wagner-Murray-Dingell as "perhaps the most virulent scheme ever conjured out of the mind of man."[2] The bill's sponsors and supporters did their best to withstand this barrage, but the proposed legislation died in committee without ever coming to a floor vote.

Despite this highly publicized setback, proponents of health reform inside and outside of government continued to work behind the scenes, issuing a steady stream of reports and studies making the case for a national program of health insurance. This support, which came from administrators and experts within the National Resources Planning Board **(See Document 6.1)**, the U.S. Public Health Service (PHS), the Farm Security Administration, the Social Security Board, and other agencies helmed by New Deal veterans, was vital in keeping the idea of national health insurance alive. By 1944, leaders of these agencies were engaging in unabashed advocacy for such a system. Surgeon General (and PHS director) Thomas Parran declared that isolated advances in extending affordable health care to the American public "have not kept pace with accumulated needs and scientific discoveries. . . . A national health program, truly comprehensive in scope and extent, has been one of the American dreams, awaiting translation into reality, for more than a quarter of a century."[3] Similarly, the Social Security Board, which was led by dedicated reformers such as Arthur Altmeyer and Isidore S. Falk, openly called for the incorporation of a compulsory national health insurance program into the existing Social Security system. The board framed such a program as an economic imperative, given the pressure that rising health care costs were placing on American households. But at its heart, the board's support for federal intervention was based on social justice considerations. As it stated in its *Eighth Annual Report to Congress,* "sickness comes oftener and lasts longer, and death comes earlier, in the homes of the poor."[4]

Interest in national health insurance was also boosted by the December 1942 release of the Beveridge Report in Great Britain. This landmark publication, formally known as the *Report of the Inter-Departmental Committee on Social Insurance and Allied Services* but unofficially named for committee chairman William Beveridge, advocated a comprehensive social welfare system for postwar Britain, including a national health service. The Beveridge Report received a great deal of attention in the United States—in part because of a 1943 lecture tour across America conducted by Beveridge himself—and after the war it formed the basis for the creation of Britain's National Health Service, its system of national insurance, and other aspects of the country's expansive social welfare system. This series of events heartened American progressives who desperately wanted to believe that their own reform efforts might someday bear legislative fruit of similar size and scope.

Reformers were also fascinated by the success of medical care cooperatives organized by the Farm Security Administration in Depression-wracked rural states during the late 1930s and early 1940s. Enrollment in the FSA's voluntary prepaid medical care plans reached 650,000 poor rural farmers at its peak, and the agency experimented with statewide and countywide plans offering preventive and primary care services for people of all income levels. These experimental health care programs, which evolved out of the agency's wider rural rehabilitation efforts, elicited only sporadic protests from a distracted national AMA leadership—even after a 1938 *Saturday Evening Post* article charged the FSA with conducting a "gigantic rehearsal for state medicine."[5] The AMA shared this concern, but it treaded carefully because the FSA programs were popular with struggling rural physicians who had previously been providing free or heavily discounted medical care to their destitute patients. "I'm for the program 100 percent," declared one Arkansas physician in 1943. "Call it socialized medicine or what you will, it is helping a lot of farm families to get the best medical care they ever had, and that in the face of a wartime shortage of doctors. Every person ought to have access to the best medical care available, regardless of his ability to pay."[6]

Finally, the continued pursuit of national health insurance stemmed from a growing conviction that social welfare initiatives at the state level, regarded as a possible remedy only a few years prior, could not deliver the desired levels of reform. State-administered unemployment insurance plans were being pilloried by New Deal critics (and even some allies) for being inefficient and wasteful, which eroded support for placing additional social welfare responsibilities on the states. Moreover, few states evinced interest in passing state-level health insurance measures during the early 1940s, and the most visible effort to do so—undertaken by California governor Earl Warren—ended in a decisive defeat at the hands of commercial insurers, physicians, and other defenders of the status quo **(See Document 6.2)**.

TRUMAN TAKES UP THE CAUSE

In November 1945 President Truman made his position on national health insurance clear to both advocates and opponents. In a November 19 appearance before a joint session of Congress, he delivered an impassioned call for "health security for all, regardless of residence, station, or race—everywhere in the United States. We should resolve now that the health of this Nation is a national concern; that financial barriers in the way of attaining health shall be removed; that the health of all its citizens deserves the help of all the Nation" **(See Document 6.3)**. To accomplish this goal, Truman proposed a comprehensive federal health insurance program composed of five major planks: increased hospital construction, expanded public health services, new investments in medical education and research, cash payments for the disabled, and compulsory prepaid medical care. A bill (S. 1606) incorporating all of these proposals was introduced in Congress by Wagner, Murray, and Dingell, the three primary sponsors of the 1943 WMD bill. But instead of being referred to the Senate Finance Committee, where the 1943 bill had been killed by the committee's sizable contingent of conservative Southern Democrats, the new WMD was channeled to the Senate Education and Labor Committee, which was chaired by James Murray.

Republicans, conservative Democrats, and the medical profession were supportive to one degree or another of new investment in hospital construction and medical research, but they staunchly opposed Truman's proposed system of compulsory prepaid health insurance, which was to be financed through a 4 percent hike in the Social Security tax (poor people not eligible through Social Security would be covered by payments from general federal revenues). Predictably, this plank became the focus of virtually all the political warfare that swirled around the WMD bill when it came up for congressional debate in early 1946.

The Truman administration entered this battle with significant political resources. It enjoyed support from small but dedicated pro-reform physicians' groups such as the Physician's Forum, the Committee of Physicians for the Improvement of Medical Care, and the National Medical Association.[7] More important, the WMD bill was championed by a wide assortment of organizations and constituencies on the left, including a labor movement that had grown enormously in size and influence during the New Deal era. Not all unions looked favorably on national health insurance—John Lewis and the United Mine Workers (UMW) withdrew from the fray, for example, after they negotiated their own health benefits from mining companies—but groups such as the Congress of Industrial Organizations (CIO) provided vital support.

By 1946 this coalition had formally coalesced into the Committee for the Nation's Health (CNH), helmed by Michael M. Davis, the former medical director of the Julius Rosenwald Fund. The CNH provided supportive testimony in Senate hearings on the WMD bill, and many of its members invested heavily in public education campaigns. In addition, the bill was championed by high-profile administration officials such as PHS surgeon general Thomas Parran, Frederick Mott of the FSA, and Isidore Falk of the Social Security Administration (SSA; the Social Security Board was renamed the Social Security Administration in 1946). Lastly, the administration's proposed interventions in the health care sector seemed likely to attract the support of large numbers of poor and working-class voters anxious about rising health care costs. Ironically, support from these formidable demographic groups was muted somewhat by the 1944 passage of the Servicemen's Readjustment Act, better known as the GI Bill. The bill's generous social welfare benefits to World War II veterans included free medical care and disability pensions for soldiers and their dependents. Progressives lauded these provisions, but they came to realize after the war that mobilizing people who already had health benefits to support more expansive health care legislation was a formidable task.[8]

As expected, the powerful American Medical Association fought the bill's health insurance provisions with all its might, and because Americans of the 1940s viewed physicians as the single most trustworthy source of information on health matters, this opposition made passing WMD an enormously daunting challenge. AMA officials lambasted Truman's plan from the outset, but its offensive really geared up in February 1946, when hearings on WMD commenced. That month, the AMA House of Delegates released its own health insurance program, which insisted that government involvement in health care should be limited to financial support for local public health, maternity, and child care programs. Anything more than that, the delegates warned, amounted to perilous experimentation with "totalitarian" schemes that would sever sacred doctor-patient bonds and erode America's sense of liberty and individual responsibility. As scholar Michael R. Grey observed, this hard-line tack was applauded by most rank-and-file members who genuinely feared that national health insurance would "bureaucratize medicine and drive a wedge between doctors and their patients. . . . Many also believed that national health insurance represented an abdication of professional responsibility. . . . State and local medical societies as well as individual doctors commonly argued that the profession and the public alike would be better served if physicians cared for the medically indigent for free, rather than cede control to any third parties."[9]

The AMA also sought to thwart national health insurance by trumpeting the many fine qualities of voluntary prepayment systems—whether through Blue Cross, Blue Shield, or private commercial insurance policies—for hospital care and other medical care. This amounted to a startling shift in policy by the association. Only a decade earlier, the AMA had been denouncing voluntary prepayment schemes as both socialistic and unnecessary. But growing public interest in prepayment plans, and the specter of compulsory health insurance, was sufficient to convince the AMA to reverse its long-held position on the issue.

The AMA was able to marshal battalions of compulsory insurance opponents to its side as well. The Association of American Physicians, the Blue Cross Commission, the American Dental Association, the American Protestant Hospital Association, and the Catholic Hospital Association all opposed the bill and touted voluntary insurance as the preferred pathway for health care coverage. Wary of crossing the AMA, the American Hospital Association (AHA) came out against WMD as well. "A hospital administrator who gets the antagonism of his medical staff because he's an advocate of socialized medicine, will generally speaking, not carry the job in that hospital very long," explained Michael Davis. "The board of trustees, who has the ultimate control, will get rid of him if he's unpopular with the medical staff."[10] In addition, the pharmaceutical industry was roused to oppose the bill because of a WMD provision that would have allowed the federal government to set drug prices.[11] Other interest groups, including the American Bar Association, the National Grange, and the U.S. Chamber of Commerce, decried compulsory insurance as un-American and anathema to the nation's spirit of free enterprise.

Republicans in Congress lined up in opposition to the bill as well. Influential conservative senator Robert A. Taft of Ohio offered a representative GOP assessment of

WMD when he described it as "the most socialistic measure that this Congress has ever had before it." Conservatives supplemented this line of attack by linking Truman's bid for a national health insurance to the CIO and other labor unions that were championing the legislation. The strategy worked to their political advantage, for as historian Alan Derickson noted, "a spectacular national strike wave in 1945–1946 and growing public resentment against the perceived abuses of union power . . . made the close identification of health reform with organized labor an additional burden."[12]

Convinced that WMD was but the opening wedge in a liberal drive to obtain complete federal control over the nation's health care system, Republicans rallied behind alternate legislation proposed by Taft that preserved existing fee-for-service private practice and private health insurance. Taft's bill did include a provision that would have allowed for the issuance of federal grants to states for the care of indigent citizens, which was a tacit acknowledgement that professional health care services were well beyond the grasp of poor Americans. Progressives derided the provision as another example of a conservative mindset that viewed basic medical care as a charitable "favor" instead of a basic right, but this criticism was shrugged off by Republicans who affirmed that they did not see health care as a right.[13]

Finally, the push to pass WMD was hampered by federal agencies such as the Children's Bureau and the Veterans Administration (VA), which feared that the bill's passage might reduce their stature or otherwise cast uncertainty on their existing facilities and services. The anti-WMD stance of VA medical director Paul Hawley, who testified for the AMA that American medicine did not need "the government to tell it how to solve its problems," was a particular setback for Truman and his allies.[14] Such statements met with approbation by opponents of national health care inside and outside of Congress, Meanwhile, agencies that chose to enter the fray on the side of reform were savaged, none more so than the Farm Security Administration. The vocal support for national health insurance expressed by the idealistic but politically vulnerable agency made it a prime political target of Republicans and Southern Democrats, who were still seething about a 1942 policy enacted by the FSA that included payment of poll taxes in its rehabilitation loan packages to African American farmers in the South. By 1947 the FSA had been legislated out of existence, brought down by a succession of politically motivated appropriations cuts and hostile congressional inquiries.[15]

OUT OF THE ASHES

In the end, passage of S. 1606 proved to be a Sisyphean task for Truman and fellow advocates of compulsory insurance. Throughout the four months of hearings on the WMD bill, reformers patiently and repeatedly explained that a compulsory insurance program did not make doctors "employees of the government" but merely reimbursed physicians for services rendered in much the same way that they currently were compensated through private insurance. They further emphasized that a compulsory enrollment scheme that included (presently) young, healthy, and affluent Americans as well as more vulnerable groups was necessary to preserve the plan's actuarial soundness. Despite their best efforts, reformers could not erase the stigma of "socialized medicine" from the legislation.[16] Recognizing that they did not have the necessary votes for passage, supporters of S. 1606 never submitted the bill for a formal vote.

The defeat of WMD in 1946 prompted a tense debate among health care reformers. Prominent players such as the CNH and top officials of the Social Security Administration remained wedded to the idea of national health insurance, and they urged their allies to prepare for a new push after the 1946 midterm elections. Many others, however, began discussing a more incremental strategy, such as advancement of a bill that would provide universal coverage for hospitalization alone. The latter pragmatic approach won out in the short term, as Truman, Democratic leaders in Congress, and high-profile officials such as Parran decided to focus on elements of Truman's proposed health care overhaul that enjoyed bipartisan support.

With S. 1606 off the table, Democratic and Republican leaders worked together to craft two pieces of legislation that rank among the most consequential health care acts of the postwar era. The first of these bills was the National Mental Health Act, signed into law in July 1946, which was crafted in response to growing pressure from both health care professionals and the general public for fundamental changes in the way that America treated and cared for people suffering from mental illness. A truly transformative law, it provided grants to states for the establishment and renovation of mental health clinics and other facilities. It also led directly to the 1949 establishment of the National Institute of Mental Health (NIMH), which by the mid-1950s was the country's preeminent research institution on mental health issues (**See Document 6.4**).

The second act, signed by Truman just one month later in August 1946, was the Hospital Survey and Construction Act, better known as the Hill-Burton Act. Passed in response to a desperate need for new hospital facilities across much of the country—and especially in rural parts of the South, Midwest, and West—the Hill-Burton Act attracted broad and enthusiastic support from the AMA, the AHA, progressive reformers, construction industry executives, Republicans, and Democrats. The federal subsidies and loans generated by this legislation paved the way for the construction and rehabilitation of hundreds of hospitals that had suffered from inattention during the Depression and World War II. The act also made the aid conditional; it required recipients to guarantee that they would provide free or low-cost care to patients who did not have insurance or were otherwise unable to pay the medical costs they incurred (**See Document 6.5**). The legislation, combined with postwar revitalization of Veterans Administration hospitals (**See Document 6.6**), dramatically improved medical care for millions of Americans in the 1950s and beyond.

HEALTH CARE POLITICS AND THE COLD WAR

The 1946 midterm elections were widely interpreted as a referendum on the performance and priorities of Truman and his fellow Democrats, who had held the reins of Congress since 1933. The health care reforms pursued by Truman and liberal Democrats thus became a hot topic on the campaign trail. Democratic officeholders who had worked to pass Truman's ambitious legislation defended their positions, while Taft and other Republican luminaries countered with grim predictions that the Democrats intended to resurrect socialistic WMD legislation in 1947 if they retained power (**See Document 6.7**). These warnings dovetailed nicely with the wider Republican strategy of painting the Roosevelt and Truman presidencies as ones in which Reds—Communists and Socialists—had assumed virtual control over the federal government. House Republican leader Joe Martin pledged, for example, that if Republicans gained control of Congress, their highest priority would be to "[clean] out the Communists, their fellow travelers and parlor pinks from high positions in our Government."[17]

The Republican message resonated deeply with American voters who had become increasingly preoccupied with U.S.–Soviet Cold War tensions in the aftermath of World

War II. In November 1946 Republicans rode these anxieties to a wave of electoral victories that gave them control of both the Senate and House, and some political observers heralded the onset of a new age of political conservatism in America. Yet Truman and Democratic leaders in Congress did not abandon their quest for a national health insurance program, as widely expected. To the contrary, Truman highlighted proposed health insurance reforms in a special May 1947 address to Congress, his 1948 State of the Union address, and numerous other speeches. Meanwhile, liberal Democrats continued to introduce national health bills in Congress. These bills, and Truman's exhortations, were batted aside by Republican leaders and conservative Democrats, who had turned against the president over his liberal stance on civil rights issues. But the steady buzz of activity on the reformers' side showed that the battle over universal health insurance was still being waged.

The political prospects for health care reform changed once again as a result of the 1948 elections. Truman entered that year's presidential campaign saddled with anemic approval ratings and a threat from his left flank in Progressive Party candidate Henry A. Wallace, Roosevelt's secretary of agriculture. But Truman's continued embrace of national health insurance and other liberal policy planks kept Wallace's campaign from gaining any traction, and the president's feisty style of campaigning kept him within striking distance of Republican presidential candidate Thomas E. Dewey. On November 2 Truman achieved an astonishing come-from-behind victory over Dewey, defying legions of political pundits who had dismissed Roosevelt's vice president as nothing but a caretaker president. In addition, American voters gave control of both the Senate and the House back to the Democrats (the latter with a stunning gain of seventy-five seats).

Flush from these triumphs, and cognizant of promises made out on the campaign trail, Truman and the Democrats once again designated national health insurance a top domestic priority in early 1949 **(See Document 6.8)**. And once again, Republicans and their allies in the AMA and the business community mounted a desperate stand against this effort. Opponents intimated that Falk and other federal officials associated with health reform were treasonous agents or gullible dupes of the Kremlin. Critics also resurrected the charge that universal health insurance was the spear-point of a Communist plot to destroy the American way of life. In 1949, for example, the AMA organized a National Public Education Campaign to spread the "truth" about the perils of national health insurance and tout the benefits of private health insurance. By this time, the reputation of physicians as trusted experts on health care issues had been smudged somewhat by years of partisan political warfare. But public faith in the wisdom and morality of doctors was still fairly strong, and this cultural authority gave the AMA campaign formidable heft. Moreover, the National Public Education Campaign was crafted and carried out by Whitaker and Baxter, the same California political consulting firm that had torpedoed Governor Warren's health reform crusade in 1945. The agency (also known as Campaigns, Inc.) used the same strategic blueprint in 1949 that it had employed in that earlier skirmish. "All you have to do is give it a bad name, and have a Devil," recalled Whitaker, one of the agency's partners. "America's opposed to socialism so we're going to name national health insurance 'socialized medicine.'"[18]

Other organizations that were ideologically opposed to governmental involvement in the health care industry also rushed to the barricades. The U.S. Chamber of Commerce published and distributed a 1949 pamphlet, *You and Socialized Medicine,* that described the "compulsory insurance program of the Democrat planners" as a fateful step "toward further state socialism and the totalitarian welfare state prevailing in foreign lands."[19]

Commercial insurers weighed in as well, lobbying their representatives fiercely to ward off any new health insurance regulations that had the potential to reduce the flow of profits coming in from the postwar individual and group policies they were underwriting.

The Truman administration and its allies continued to plow forward with their proposals for national health insurance. They emphasized that millions of Americans remained unable to afford basic health care, despite the spread of voluntary insurance, and they argued that their reforms would not deprive any American of his or her liberty or freedom. Still, the charges that their proposed reforms were un-American or traitorous continued to resonate with middle America, and public support for national health insurance underwent a steady decline. These poll results convinced many reform supporters in Congress to quietly distance themselves from the legislation.

This state of affairs infuriated reformers such as Oscar Ewing, head of the Federal Security Agency, who stated in a 1949 speech to the American Federation of Labor (AFL) that opponents of national health insurance who talked about "liberty" had considerable nerve: "The rich man's son is free to enjoy good health, they say, and the poor man's son is free to be sick."[20] But such protests were to no avail, and as scholar Michael R. Grey related, the "coup de grace for the national health insurance movement was delivered, courtesy of the AMA, in the 1950 midterm elections. Assisted once again by a savvy public relations firm and a war chest swollen with mandatory contributions from its membership, the AMA mounted a highly effective political campaign and defeated nearly every congressional candidate who refused to swear off support for national health insurance. It is telling that after nearly two decades of emotionally charged national debate, Congress never took a formal floor vote for or against any of the national health insurance proposals."[21]

HEALTH INSURANCE COMES OF AGE

At the same time that Washington, D.C., was tying itself in knots over national health insurance, the massive wave of hospital construction that took place in the wake of Hill-Burton encouraged a significant jump in the purchase of private health and hospital insurance policies by individuals and groups. As new hospital beds and high-tech medical services became available, pent-up demand transformed many of even the most rural of facilities into beehives of health care activity. The increased acceptance of so-called voluntary insurance plans was fueled by several other factors as well, from the rising costs of hospitalization and other health services to the AMA's about-face on the merits of such schemes (at least in comparison with national health insurance proposals). The heady growth in the commercial health insurance sector also stemmed from wartime tax policy changes that altered the terrain of workplace compensation for decades to come.

During World War II, the Roosevelt administration imposed strict wage and price controls as part of its overall effort to stop wartime inflation and keep manufacturing industries important to the war effort operating at top capacities. During this same period, Congress passed the Revenue Act of 1942, an anti–war profiteering bill that heavily taxed corporate earnings in excess of prewar levels. However, the Revenue Act contained a key provision: It excluded employer contributions to group health insurance (and pension) plans from taxable profits. One year later, on March 23, the National War Labor Board ruled that "to the extent that an insurance and pension benefit inuring to an employee is reasonable in amount, such benefit is not considered as salary."[22]

These developments gave employers and workers alike a clear path to improving their financial security and well-being without flouting the federal government's wage and price freezes, and they wasted no time in seizing it. "These rulings opened the flood-gates to health insurance and pension programs," wrote journalist Jill Quadagno. "In nonunionized firms employers purchased generous health insurance packages from commercial insurers, hoping to ward off unionization. In unionized firms employers began offering health benefits, without union input, to convince workers they had no need to join the union."[23] Union leaders were quick to recognize this threat, and they made health insurance and pensions central to their collective bargaining strategies with automakers, steel firms, and other titans of the American business world.

In 1948 only about 2.7 million workers were covered by negotiated health plans. Within two years, all of the nation's major automakers had negotiated health insurance plans with the United Auto Workers, and dozens of employer-union contracts containing insurance and pension guarantees were being announced in steel, textiles, and other industries on a monthly basis. A mere four years later, twelve million workers and seventeen million dependents were covered by health insurance garnered through collective bargaining.[24]

These arrangements were supplemented by innovative prepaid health insurance plans such as the one evolved by shipbuilding magnate Henry J. Kaiser and Dr. Sidney Garfield in California during World War II. An early forerunner of modern HMO (health maintenance organization) plans, the Kaiser Permanente program, which featured its own physicians, nurses, and facilities, was originally open only to Kaiser employees. After World War II, enrollment in the program was opened to the public. Medical societies and private practitioners in the region expressed hostility to the program's attractively priced fee-for-service structure, which threatened to lure patients away from their own practices, and condemned the idea of a health care program under lay control. But as historian Paul Starr noted, Kaiser's financial assets—and his willingness to use them to build, outfit, and staff health service facilities—enabled him to shrug off these blows. Acting with an "almost missionary zeal," Kaiser set out to show that "he could reorganize medical care on a self-sufficient basis, independent of government, to provide millions of Americans with prepaid and comprehensive services at prices they could afford. Ten years after the war,

Henry J. Kaiser (with arm over front seat), founder of Kaiser Permanente, a group-model health maintenance organization (HMO), accompanies President Franklin D. Roosevelt on a 1942 visit to Kaiser's shipyards. Since 1945, when Kaiser opened his company's health care plan to the public, the plan has grown to become one of the nation's largest nonprofit HMOs.

the Kaiser-Permanente health plan had a growing network of hospitals and clinics and a half million people enrolled."[25]

Overall, the surge in the development of private insurance plans brought about a truly startling transformation in the country's health care landscape from 1940 to 1950. At the beginning of that period, only 9 percent of American civilians had hospital insurance and only 4 percent were protected by insurance from surgical costs. That left more than 110 million Americans without private health insurance. By 1950, more than half of American civilians had gained hospitalization insurance, and 36 percent had obtained surgical insurance.[26] And as these policies emerged as important revenue streams for major commercial insurers such as Prudential, Aetna, and Metropolitan Life of New York, the insurance industry's interest in state and federal health insurance policies underwent a corresponding escalation.

MIXED FORTUNES FOR BLUE CROSS

The rapid midcentury growth of commercial health insurance came at the expense of Blue Cross, which only a few years earlier was being hailed by some observers as the magic bullet for America's health care woes. During the 1940s Blue Cross hospitalization insurance programs had proliferated across the country, in large measure because they enjoyed the general approbation of the medical community. As health care analyst Jonathan Cohn wrote, the doctors' stance was at first blush an odd one, given the fact that Blue Cross bore more than a passing resemblance to the social insurance schemes that their political adversaries had been pitching since the 1920s.

> Although the Blues were private entities, they pledged themselves to a public purpose: bringing health insurance to large numbers of people. They did so by basing their premiums on a "community rate"—every subscriber, regardless of age, sex, or medical condition, paid the same monthly amount (individuals paid higher rates than group members, because of the administrative overhead, but the difference was relatively modest). Many insurers also practiced some form of "guaranteed issue," giving coverage to anybody who agreed to pay their premiums. These two features made Blue Cross resemble social insurance—a protection scheme in which health people subsidized the costs of the sick, precisely as the Committee on the Cost of Medicine had recommended in 1932.[27]

Any queasiness with Blue Cross programs was eclipsed by the steady and significant financial revenue generated for Blue hospitals, as well as by the widespread recognition that the expansion of Blue Cross was undercutting calls for national health insurance. Or as one hospital administrator declared in 1950, "[The] brakes Blue Cross has applied to our swing towards socialization of medicine are perhaps the greatest benefits which we have all derived."[28]

In 1940 nationwide enrollment in Blue Cross programs stood at about six million subscribers spread across twenty-seven states. Three years later, the number of subscribers had more than doubled, to thirteen million, and in 1945 enrollment reached nineteen million. By the early 1950s more than forty million Americans were securing hospitalization insurance through Blue Cross programs, and a parallel program for payment of doctors' bills—dubbed Blue Shield—was up and running as well.[29]

The success of the nonprofit Blue Cross and Blue Shield programs convinced private insurers that had traditionally been extremely cautious about wading into the health insurance field to reconsider their positions. Their interest in the sector became even more intense in the mid-1940s, when health insurance became an integral component of employer-union collective bargaining agreements. Before long, major commercial insurers such as Prudential had figured out that writing health insurance policies could be profitable, provided they focused on groups of healthy subscribers instead of higher-risk groups (such as the elderly) who were more likely to require expensive medical care. "Under the Blue Cross 'community rate' scheme, [healthy] groups were, in effect, paying more to cover the expenses of less healthy beneficiaries," explained Cohn. "Commercial insurers offered to insure these people at rates that more closely reflected their own health status, then adjusted rates year after year according to how that status changed. This method of pricing insurance, known as experience rating, allowed commercial insurers to undercut the prices the Blues were offering."[30] Many of the Blues administrators were slow to recognize this threat, in part because the overall postwar jump in new policy-writing opportunities enabled both Blue Cross and Blue Shield to continue expanding in the 1950s. More perceptive Blue Cross and Blue Shield officials could see that their rates of growth were slowing when compared with those of the big commercial insurers.

INSURANCE REFORM FADES AS A POLITICAL ISSUE

The impressive growth of private health coverage in the late 1940s and early 1950s did not satisfy Truman, who remained an indefatigable champion of national health insurance. But his lame-duck status after the 1950 midterm elections reduced his political leverage, as did the rise to prominence of demagogic senator Joseph R. McCarthy in 1951. McCarthy's Red-baiting antics deepened anti-Communist hysteria across much of America, and the resulting political din made it nigh impossible for lawmakers, officials, and opinion-makers—whether conservative or liberal—who genuinely wanted to improve America's ongoing health care woes to make themselves heard.

Still, Truman pressed on. In 1951 he appointed the President's Commission on the Health Needs of the Nation to study the issue and deliver concrete recommendations for expanding access to health care to the indigent, the working poor, minorities, and other uninsured Americans. A year later, the commission, which was chaired by VA official (and Republican) Paul B. "Budd" Magnuson, who handpicked the other members from the ranks of labor, medicine, and industry, released a five-volume overview of the state of America's health care system.

The so-called Magnuson Commission report, *Building America's Health*, asserted that universal access to health care, which it termed a basic human right, could best be accomplished through increased federal support of voluntary insurance plans, expanded state and federal assistance to poor people who could not otherwise pay health insurance premiums, and increased investment in regionally organized group practices. The absence of any Truman-style compulsory national health insurance plan in the report was widely noted. *Time* magazine called the commission's recommendations a "middle way" between Truman's preferred model and the AMA's private payment–voluntary insurance hybrid.[31] But the commission's work was flatly rejected by AMA president John Cline and the rest of the organization's leadership. As historian Alan Derickson noted, they felt that unmet health care needs amounted to "an inevitable aspect of life in a free-enterprise society. AMA official George Cooley placed this interpretation directly before the presidential commission in a presentation later that year. 'Need, it seems to me, is a very poor term to use,' Cooley advised. 'All of us have unsatisfied needs and probably for a myriad of services and things. Usually when need is discussed at some detached faraway level, it becomes a subjective version of the rainbow's pot of gold.'"[32]

The Magnuson Commission's report never managed to gain any great traction in Washington. At that time, outgoing president Truman did not have any standing to push for implementation of the report's recommendations. Magnuson wrote in his memoirs that, although the report "didn't make much of a sensation," he "was informed by people at the White House that when Mr. Truman went out of office and had his desk cleared for his successor's use, the only thing he left for Mr. Eisenhower was our *Report on the Health Needs of the Nation* lying face up on the desk, right in front of the Presidential chair."[33]

Incoming Republican president Dwight D. Eisenhower shared the AMA's skepticism of the commission's findings. During the 1952 presidential campaign, he had made it clear that he viewed national health insurance as fundamentally unsound and fiscally irresponsible. He also argued that it was unnecessary over the long term, given the progress that private insurance was making in expanding coverage. This stance was echoed by Republican leaders who had reclaimed control of Congress in the 1952 election. Their preferred course of action was to refrain from interfering and let the free market do its work. As Eisenhower said in a speech to a group of medical professionals, "This is one profession [that] we don't want to get under the dead hand of bureaucracy."[34]

As politicians and interest groups settled in to see whether the private insurance sector could make acceptable headway in eliminating the problem of the uninsured, national health insurance temporarily faded as a political issue. But the experiment in voluntary insurance did not produce a decisive result, especially because progressives and conservatives measured "acceptable headway" through wildly different ideological prisms. Millions of Americans who had previously been uninsured did gain coverage during the 1950s. From 1940 to 1960, the percentage of Americans covered by private hospitalization insurance (whether from commercial insurers or nonprofits such as Blue Cross) jumped from 9 percent to 68 percent.[35] Similarly, physicians' services were increasingly covered by insurance policies. The percentage of such costs met by insurance rose from only 6 percent of total private expenditures in 1948 to 32 percent by 1960.[36] These trends led some free market disciples such as W. Glenn Campbell and Rita R. Campbell of the Hoover Institution to assert in 1960 that "private health insurance . . . is well on the way toward accomplishing what the 'experts' in the field of social security stated on innumerable occasions was impossible, namely, near universal coverage of the whole population."[37]

Liberals and even some longtime champions of the voluntary approach were underwhelmed by these results. In the late 1950s more than half of the population of elderly Americans (age sixty-five and over) remained uninsured and, thus, without any protection from fiscal catastrophe in the event of a serious or long-term illness. Millions of other high-risk individuals were similarly left without any protection for the simple reason that commercial insurers recognized that insuring people with disabilities or chronic health problems (such as heart disease, diabetes, and arthritis) was simply not a sound business practice from a fiscal standpoint. And as "experience rating" became more and more central to the business operations of commercial insurers, the burden of covering individuals who did not make the grade increasingly fell to the community-rated plans of the more traditionally altruistic Blue Cross. This shift in clientele quickly became a source of alarm to Blue Cross executives. "The logic of competition played itself out almost inexorably," wrote historian Paul Starr.

As the commercial insurers began to pick off the low-risk employee groups, they threatened to leave the high-cost population to the Blues. Had this process continued indefinitely, Blue Cross and Blue Shield would have been forced to raise their rates so high that even average-risk groups would have found it cheaper to buy commercial insurance. Eventually, the Blue plans would have become "dumping grounds" for the aged and the poor. This, however, was a function they preferred to leave to the government, and so, despite their reluctance, they, too, moved toward experience rating. By the end of the fifties, a majority of the [Blue Cross] plans were experience rating at least some employee groups.[38]

Eisenhower Touts "Reinsurance"

The ascendancy of experience rating as a central factor in health insurance underwriting greatly slowed the growth of private insurance. Millions of high-risk and poor Americans remained stranded without coverage, wholly dependent on a patchwork quilt of charitable organizations and public health services ill-equipped to treat serious or extended illnesses, diseases, and other complex health problems.

Liberal reformers and politicians loudly proclaimed that this state of affairs was a shameful one, given the country's overall level of wealth and the mighty arsenal of medical technology it had at its disposal. They also pointed out that the value of robust governmental intervention in health care matters was already proven, such as with its energetic promotion of polio vaccination. Reformers argued that the broad acceptance of federal public health actions such as polio vaccination **(See Document 6.10)** illustrated that the American people's reluctance to accept government involvement in health care dissipated when they realized that they personally benefited from such intervention. In addition, they noted accurately that the steadily rising costs of health care services were causing growing consternation among working-class and middle-class policyholders who were being hammered by continued high out-of-pocket expenses and rising insurance premiums.

Concerned that these rumblings constituted a possible bellwether of political peril for Republicans, the Eisenhower administration looked about with a growing sense of urgency for an initiative that would boost private health insurance's capacity—and will—to rein in costs and provide protection to the uninsured and, thus, assuage restive voters. In 1954 Eisenhower settled on a "reinsurance" scheme that had been suggested by Blue Cross officials in Philadelphia. Under this program, the federal government would subsidize commercial and nonprofit insurers that agreed to provide coverage to high-risk groups **(See Document 6.9)**. As expected, liberal supporters of national health insurance balked at the prospect of using taxpayer money to "subsidize the inadequacies of private insurance," in the words of scholar Antonia Maioni.[39] Members of the insurance, business, and medical lobbies also refused to lend their support, citing the usual concern that even this modest program constituted an unacceptable step toward the socialization of medicine. The only meaningful support that the administration was able to muster came from the American Hospital Association and the Blue Cross Commission, both of which stood to benefit from a program that subsidized the care of uninsured people.[40]

The intransigence of the AMA ultimately doomed Eisenhower's reinsurance proposal, which fell one vote short of passage in the Senate. Afterward, Eisenhower bitterly criticized the leadership of the organization as "just plain stupid" for failing to recognize that the limitations of private insurance, if left unaddressed, would resuscitate interest in national insurance. AMA officials, Eisenhower mournfully concluded, were "a little group of reactionary men dead set against any change."[41]

AID FOR THE AGED: THE FORAND BILL

Eisenhower was correct in his assessment of the political implications of reinsurance's downfall. As his second term progressed, calls for reform that had been faint and weak after his 1953 inauguration steadily increased in strength. One factor in this reversal was the 1956 elections, which returned Congress to the Democrats. Another was a strategic decision on the part of health care reformers to pursue incremental policy gains that, when strung together in multiple stages over time, would ultimately give them the fundamental reforms they desired.

Democratic lawmakers, liberal reform groups, and leaders of the labor movement ultimately decided that an amendment to the Social Security Act guaranteeing affordable hospitalization and other medical care for elderly Americans was a logical first step. "The Social Security Act had created an important clientele group of older Americans, whose lives were already greatly affected by state intervention. The aged represented the greatest high-risk group, both in medical and in economic terms, but at the same time they commanded public sympathy."[42] Moreover, arguments about self-help that resonated among some Americans when directed against poor, uninsured workers in their thirties and forties did not have the same affect when they were directed against the elderly. Finally, advocates of an increased federal role in health care pointed out that even Eisenhower's own Department of Health, Education, and Welfare (HEW) recognized that a severe problem existed. In 1959 the HEW publicly acknowledged that

> older persons have larger than average medical care needs. As a group they use about two-and-a-half times as much general hospital care as the average for persons under age 65, and they have special need for long-term institutional care. Their incomes are generally considerably lower than those of the rest of the population, and in many cases are either fixed or declining in amount. They have less opportunity than employed persons to spread the cost burden through health insurance. A larger proportion of the aged than of other persons must turn to public assistance for payment of their medical bills or rely on "free" care from hospitals and physicians. Because both the number and proportion of older persons in the population are increasing, a satisfactory solution to the problem of paying for adequate medical care for the aged will become more rather than less important.[43]

In 1958 a bill designed to rectify this situation by providing health insurance to Social Security beneficiaries was introduced in Congress. The bill had many architects, including Isidore Falk, University of Michigan professor Wilbur Cohen, SSA official Robert M. Ball, and Nelson Cruikshank, the AFL-CIO's point man on social welfare issues. But it quickly became known as the Forand bill in recognition of its chief sponsor, Democratic representative Aime Forand of New Jersey.

Highly publicized and contentious congressional hearings on the Forand bill were held in both 1958 and 1959, and a parallel war of words broke out in the nation's media outlets between representatives of the opposing camps. Those representing the AMA and the insurance industry assailed the proposed legislation as a dangerous and misguided expansion of the welfare state in their testimony, and they pointed out that many states and large counties already maintained programs of medical relief for the aged. Some local and state officials also questioned the need for federal intervention. "No ailing aged person goes uncared for in New York City," insisted New York City's commissioner of health in an interview with *Time.* "But the care isn't always available in the form people like. Middle-income people find it difficult to accept charity."[44] These detractors were countered by social welfare advocates and titans of labor such as Walter Reuther, who turned the spotlight again and again on the gaps in health care coverage that persisted in rural, poor, and minority communities. These spokespeople framed passage of the Forand bill as a moral imperative **(See Document 6.11)**.

By early 1960 the upcoming elections were casting a long shadow over the Forand bill debate. Sensing a winning political issue, leading Democratic presidential candidates proclaimed their support for the bill or touted similar versions. Nervous Republicans responded with their own means-tested plan to bestow federal matching grants on states to help them care for elderly residents earning less than three thousand dollars annually. In the end, neither side able was able to push its preferred bill across the legislative finish line. Instead, a compromise measure known as Medical Assistance for the Aged (MAA) emerged. This program was laid out in legislation drafted by House Ways and Means Committee chairman Wilbur Mills, a conservative Arkansas Democrat who had opposed the Forand bill, and Democratic senator Robert Kerr of Oklahoma. The Kerr-Mills Act, which was signed into law by Eisenhower on September 13, 1960, established a means-tested grant program that dispersed federal funds to states interested in providing financial assistance to qualified elderly individuals with high medical expenses **(See Document 6.12)**. "The Kerr-Mills approach," observed scholar Charlotte Twight, "was a preemptive effort by those who hoped that providing medical care for the aged poor would deflect broader efforts to inject government into the market for medical care. Their hope was misplaced."[45]

Notes

1. Quoted in Jaap Kooijman, . . . *And the Pursuit of National Health: The Incremental Strategy toward National Health Insurance in the United States of America* (Amsterdam, The Netherlands: Rodopi, 1999), 98.

2. "Medical Insurance," *Editorial Research Reports,* January 25, 1944.

3. Quoted in Alan Derickson, "Health for Three-Thirds of the Nation: Public Health Advocacy of Universal Access to Medical Care in the United States," *American Journal of Public Health* 92, no. 2 (February 2002): 180–90.

4. Social Security Board, *Eighth Annual Report to Congress* (Washington, DC: Government Printing Office, 1944), 28.

5. Samuel Lubell and Walter Everett, "Rehearsal for State Medicine," *Saturday Evening Post,* December 17, 1938, 23.

6. Michael R. Grey, *New Deal Medicine: The Rural Health Programs of the Farm Security Administration* (Baltimore: Johns Hopkins University Press, 1999), 109.

7. Antonia Maioni, *Parting at the Crossroads: The Emergence of Health Insurance in the United States and Canada* (Princeton, NJ: Princeton University Press, 1998), 81–82.

8. Theda Skocpol, *Social Policy in the United States: Future Possibilities in Historical Perspective* (Princeton, NJ: Princeton University Press, 1995).

9. Grey, *New Deal Medicine,* 161.

10. Quoted in Jill Quadagno, *One Nation Uninsured: Why the U.S. Has No National Health Insurance* (New York: Oxford University Press, 2005), 38.

11. Quadagno, *One Nation Uninsured,* 38.

12. Alan Derickson, *Health Security for All: Dreams of Universal Health Care in America* (Baltimore: Johns Hopkins University Press, 2005), 102.

13. William Shonick, *Government and Health Services: Government's Role in the Development of U.S. Health Services 1930–1980* (New York: Oxford University Press, 1995), 253.

14. Monte M. Poen, *Harry S. Truman versus the Medical Lobby: The Genesis of Medicare* (Columbia: University of Missouri Press, 1979), 80.

15. Grey, *New Deal Medicine,* 129–34.

16. Rosemary Stevens, *American Medicine and the Public Interest* (New Haven, CT: Yale University Press, 1971); rev. ed. (Berkeley: University of California Press, 1998), 273.

17. Quoted in Robert Justin Goldstein, "Prelude to McCarthyism: The Making of a Blacklist," *Prologue,* (Fall 2006), www.archives.gov/publications/prologue/2006/fall/agloso.html.

18. Quoted in Quadagno, *One Nation Uninsured,* 35.

19. Quoted in Quadagno, *One Nation Uninsured,* 34.

20. Quoted in Derickson, *Health Security for All,* 107.

21. Grey, *New Deal Medicine,* 167.

22. *Reports and Decisions of the National War Labor Board* (Washington, DC: Bureau of National Affairs, 1943), 4, LXIV.

23. Quadagno, *One Nation Uninsured,* 50–51.

24. Paul Starr, *The Social Transformation of American Medicine* (New York: Basic Books, 1982), 313.

25. Starr, *The Social Transformation of American Medicine,* 322.

26. Stevens, *American Medicine and the Public Interest,* 271.

27. Jonathan Cohn, *Sick: The Untold Story of America's Health Care Crisis—and the People Who Pay the Price* (New York: HarperCollins, 2007), 31.

28. Quoted in Cohn, *Sick,* 32.

29. O. Anderson, *Blue Cross since 1929: Accountability and the Public Trust* (Cambridge, MA: Ballinger, 1975), 45

30. Cohn, *Sick,* 32.

31. "Medicine: For the Nation's Health, *Time,* December 29, 1952, 32.

32. Derickson, *Health Security for All,* 119.

33. Paul B. Magnuson, *Ring the Night Bell: The Autobiography of a Surgeon* (Boston: Little, Brown, 1960), pp. 364–65.

34. Quoted in Poen, *Harry S. Truman versus the Medical Lobby,* 217.

35. Rosemary Stevens, *In Sickness and in Wealth: American Hospitals in the Twentieth Century* (New York: Basic Books, 1989), 259.

36. Louis Reed,"Private Medical Care Expenditures and Voluntary Health Insurance," *Social Security Bulletin* (December 24, 1961): 3.

37. Quoted in Derickson, *Health Security for All,* 101.

38. Starr, *The Social Transformation of American Medicine,* 330.

39. Maioni, *Parting at the Crossroads,* 107.

40. Maioni, *Parting at the Crossroads,* 107.

41. Quoted in Stephen Ambrose, *Eisenhower, the President* (New York: Simon and Schuster, 1984), 199.

42. Maioni, *Parting at the Crossroads,* 110.

43. Quoted in Peter Corning, "The Fourth Round: 1957 to 1965," in *The Evolution of Medicare . . . From Idea to Law* (Washington, DC: Social Security Administration, Office of Research and Statistics, 1969), www.ssa.gov/history/corningchap4.html.

44. "Pain, Pressure, and Politics Make Powerful Medicine," *Time*, May 9, 1960, www.time.com/time /magazine/article/0,9171,897447-1,00.html.

45. Charlotte Twight, "Medicare's Origin: The Economics and Politics of Dependency" *Cato Journal* 16, no. 3 (Fall 1997): 359–95.

DOCUMENT 6.1

A Progressive Call for an Expanded Governmental Role in All Phases of Health

"For All Our People to Enjoy a State of Buoyant Health and Vigor"

1943

After the United States entered World War II in December 1941, the conflict became the central focus of President Franklin D. Roosevelt and the nation as a whole. Existing New Deal programs took a backseat to wartime priorities, and efforts by reformers both inside and outside of government to further expand America's welfare state lost momentum. Not surprisingly, controversial proposals to increase federal involvement in the provision of health care services were among the campaigns that foundered during the war's early years, and health reform bills failed to get sufficient traction for passage in Congress. Nonetheless, many federal agencies continued to agitate for an expanded governmental role in ensuring that all citizens had access to affordable and competent health care. One of the agencies that helped keep this issue alive was the National Resources Planning Board (NRPB), which had been created in 1933 to help coordinate Great Depression–era public works projects. By the early 1940s the agency had emerged as an important proponent of social insurance programs in Washington, D.C., and in 1943 it published a massive three-volume report, excerpted here, arguing that increased government involvement in health care was necessary to ensure the nation's long-term vitality and security. (This report proved to be a last gasp of sorts for the board, which became a casualty of congressional-administration disputes over social welfare policymaking. In June 1943 Congress passed legislation terminating the NPRB, and by January of 1944 the agency was no more.)

Roosevelt refrained from committing political capital to specific health care legislation during his last years in office. But he continued to publicly defend the legitimacy of governmental involvement in health and other social welfare issues, most notably in his January 11, 1944, State of the Union message, in which he declared that every American had an "Economic Bill of Rights" that included the right to needed health care. Just as the NRPB had done, Roosevelt's speech asserted, in the words of biographer James MacGregor Burns, "that individual political liberty and collective welfare were not only compatible, but they were mutually fortifying."[1]

EQUAL ACCESS TO HEALTH

The health of the individual is the concern not only of the individual himself but of society as a whole. Disablement and loss of ability to participate in production is a waste of the Nation's most valuable resource. Every day lost because of illness, accident, or premature death is a day given to the enemy. Every dollar spent in maintaining in idleness, or institutions, those who are rendered incapable by reason of previous neglect is a dollar wasted. The state of the health of the Nation becomes a matter of acute national concern when the needs of war call for the most effective utilization of our man and woman power. But here, as elsewhere, war serves merely to throw into relief unpleasant facts which the less demanding ways of peace enabled us to disregard. This is especially true in regard to health. . . .

. . . In the last decade a great body of material has been accumulated, all of which points to the fact that if the health record of this country is, as often claimed, the best in the world, the level of health elsewhere must be low in the extreme. In 1938, the comprehensive report of the Technical Committee on Medical Care revealed an alarming amount of sickness and ill health. It was estimated, for example, that on an average day of the year over 4 million persons were disabled by illness. The general findings of this Committee as to the state of the Nation's health were confirmed by almost every participant in the National Health Conference which called together representative citizens and professional experts from all parts of the country.

Estimates by the United States Public Health Service indicate that on the basis of a peacetime labor force, some 400,000,000 man-days are lost annually from all types of disabilities. The economic cost amounts to 10 billion dollars. In 1940 this loss of working time was 50 times greater than that due to strikes and lockouts. More recently the U. S. Employment Service has reported that there are approximately 400,000 disabled persons registered at the public employment offices. . . .

Among the objectives of post-war planning, conservation and enhancement of the health of the people must occupy a prominent position. We must seek not merely to avoid the loss through ill health, accidents, and premature death of our most valuable national resource and to eliminate the unnecessary costs of maintaining those who are rendered incapable by reason of previous neglect, but we must also see that it is possible for all our people to enjoy a state of buoyant health and vigor. To achieve these objectives will call for action along many lines.

I. Elimination of All Preventable Diseases and Disabilities

The widespread prevalence in our country of preventable or controllable disease or disability is a sad commentary upon our national common sense. The very existence in our midst of malaria, hookworm, smallpox, and pellagra, and the prevalence of venereal disease and tuberculosis, in view of contemporary knowledge of techniques of control, is nothing less than a national disgrace. The loss of life due to preventable infant and maternal mortality and the prevalence in later life of physical and mental disabilities and constitutional impairments that could have been arrested [sic] by early diagnosis and treatment, the magnitude of our expenditures on institutions for the care of mental and tubercular cases, all testify to the failure of the Nation to appreciate the importance of preventive action. . . .

1. The Development of Adequate Public Health Services

Much of the improvement in the Nation's health which this century has witnessed can be credited to the development of public health services. Communicable disease control, immunization and innoculation services, sanitation measures, protection of food and drugs, the collection of essential health records and data, the operation of hospitals and institutions for the care of mental and tubercular cases have come to be accepted as the normal activities of the health department of a progressive community. Yet many cities and counties are still without some or all of these basic services. . . .

To exploit to the full existing knowledge of preventive health measures, two steps are therefore needed: The appropriation of adequate funds, and a broadened conception of the potentialities of public health services. Since 1936, Federal funds, under the Social Security Act and the later Venereal Diseases Control Act, have stimulated a great development of basic public-health services throughout the Nation. The number of full-time public-health departments increased from 540 to 976 in the 7 years following the passage of the Social Security Act, while expenditures by all levels of government for venereal-disease control increased threefold from 1938 to 1941. Appropriations are, however, still inadequate, . . .

2. Expansion of the Health Program for Mothers and Children

Medical science and the advancement of public health organization have contributed greatly to the health of mothers and children during the past decade. We know how to reduce illness and deaths of mothers in childbirth, how to prevent the deaths of infants, how to promote the sound growth and development of children and protect them against communicable disease. We know, too, that early medical care of children who develop physical defects or illness will be effective in most cases in restoring them to health and full physical activity. This knowledge has been utilized to begin the erection of a framework of maternal and child health services. A comprehensive program is needed to make available to mothers and children in every city and county the health supervision and promotion service that would foster the development of a healthy nation. It includes the provision of a full-time county or district health organization, public health nursing service, and medical service, usually from local practicing physicians, for the conduct of prenatal clinics, child health conferences, school medical examinations accompanied by adequate follow-up work, and hospital and clinic care of the sick. It must be confessed that as yet this program is far from fully developed in many parts of the country.

Since 1936 the Federal Government, through grants-in-aid, has been cooperating with the State health agencies in extending and improving maternal and child health services and with State crippled children's agencies in providing services for the physical restoration of crippled children. Yet the most recent figures reported by the State health officers show that in approximately one-fourth of our counties there is no public-health nursing service, in almost three-fourths of our counties prenatal clinics conducted monthly are not available, while in two-thirds of our counties there are no child health conferences held monthly. In only approximately one-fourth of our counties do we have all three of these types of service. The larger cities have well-developed maternal and child health programs, but many of the small cities and towns have very limited programs. Even where these programs are under way they are frequently too limited in personnel to undertake to reach all of the mothers and children who should benefit from the public program for the promotion of the health of mothers, preschool children, and school children. The war shortage of physicians and public health nurses has seriously curtailed even those programs that were under way when the United States entered the war. It is estimated that more than 50 percent of our children live in places of less than 10,000 population and yet only 2 percent of these places have out-patient clinics to which children can be taken for care; less than 2 percent have a pediatrician for local consultation. . . .

There is widespread professional and lay interest in the development of more adequate maternal and child health services throughout the Nation. But this interest has not yet been translated into a willingness to make available the appropriations necessary to attain the objectives sought. The effectiveness of Federal grants in stimulating action in the States and in calling forth State and local expenditures has been demonstrated since the passage of the Social Security Act. But these funds are still too limited. Larger appropriations for both maternal and child health services and services for crippled children should be made available under Title V of the Social Security Act. . . . And to secure the best results, maternal and child health clinics should be specifically authorized to provide treatment, where necessary, as well as diagnostic and advisory services. . . .

C. Protection of Factory and Farm Workers against Health Hazards

The risks to the health of the workers of the Nation arising out of industrial or occupational accidents or diseases suggest yet another area in which an investment in preventive programs would yield rich dividends. The United States Public Health Service has pointed out that the prompt adoption throughout industry of already known medical and engineering controls would immediately reduce by 10 percent the time lost due to sickness and accidents of an occupational character.

Yet recognition of the importance of industrial hygiene has been relatively slow. Basic legislation calling for minimum safeguards against the health hazards of production is still inadequate in certain States, and the small body of inspectors cannot bring to light all cases of noncompliance. By 1941 only 32 States and 4 large cities had industrial hygiene units; in many of these States such services as existed were meagre, and the units suffered from lack of personnel and equipment. Despite the assistance which the Federal Government has given to the States through assignment of personnel since the outbreak of the war, it has been impossible for the industrial hygiene units to contact more than about 2 million of the more than 50 million workers of the country. Moreover, the record shows that a substantial proportion of the suggestions offered are not acted upon. Industrial hygiene programs have been developed by many large corporations, but others still fail to appreciate their importance, while among the small firms they are the exception rather than the rule. . . .

II. Assurance of Proper Nutrition for All Our People

In the last two decades there have been great advances in the science of nutrition, but much still needs to be done if the Nation is to reap the full advantage of the scientific knowledge at its disposal. The growing recognition of the importance of proper nutrition to the welfare of the people led in 1941 to the convening of a National Nutrition Conference attended by some 900 delegates representing scientific workers and the medical profession, as well as agriculture, labor, industry, and consumer groups. The facts presented to the conference indicated that undernourishment is widespread among the people of this country and is serious enough to be a cause of acute concern among that third of the population living at or below the subsistence level. At the same time there was a wide measure of agreement as to the steps which should be taken to raise the nutritional standards of the Nation. Among the more important directions in which action is called for are the following:

1. Renewed efforts to assure to every family the minimum income necessary to purchase adequate diets. . . .

2. Continued support for public and private agencies engaged in the dissemination of sound nutritional practices and principles. . . .
3. More orderly and economical arrangements for the production and physical distribution of the basic foods essential to health. . . .
4. Encouragement of the production of foodstuffs for home use on the part of low-income or one-crop farmers. . . .

III. Assurance of Adequate Health and Medical Care for All

Adequate medical care, including measures for rehabilitation on a basis that is consistent with the self-respect of the recipient, is today impeded by inadequacy of facilities and financial restrictions. In 1941 there were in the United States 1,324,381 beds in 6,358 registered hospitals, distributed as follows: 603,872 beds in general and allied special hospitals; 638,144 in nervous and mental institutions; and 82,365 in tuberculosis sanatoria.

The 600,000 beds for general medical care represent a ratio of 4.6 beds per 1,000 population, a figure slightly above the generally-accepted standard for adequacy, 4.5 beds per 1,000 population. However, this over-all figure conceals a tremendous variation in facilities as between regions and States; in certain States the ratio is nearly 6 beds per 1,000 people, in others as low as 2. Within the States local variations are also great. Many of the Southern States are far below the mark in their hospital facilities. On the basis of a ratio of only 2 beds per 1,000 population, the United States Public Health Service estimated in 1940 that at least 270 new hospitals with a combined capacity of 15,500 beds would be required to provide minimal general hospital facilities for rural areas. The most recent careful estimates of the additional facilities required for adequate care of the tuberculous and mentally diseased, made by the Technical Committee on Medical Care in 1938, indicated that facilities for the tuberculous were deficient by 50,000 beds, and those for the mentally ill, by 130,000 beds.

The 1935 Business Census of Hospitals verified the fact that the existence of facilities depends in great measure upon the level of wealth, as measured by per capita income. It was found that, regardless of the type of hospital, the number of beds per unit of population was roughly proportionate to the income of the area. Bed facilities in general and allied special hospitals, for example, were almost two and a half times as numerous in the wealthiest quarter of our States as in the poorest quarter. The need for Federal aid is manifest if the problem is to be met in the less well-to-do areas.

There are also great disparities in the availability of medical personnel in various parts of the country. Before the rapid changes resulting from the war, the national ratio of physicians to population was about 1 to 800, ranging in individual States from 1 to 500, to 1 to 1,400. Similar variations exist in the distribution of dentists and nurses. . . .

Even with more nearly adequate facilities, adequate medical care for all will not be assured until the financial problem is solved. The vast majority of the population desire to contribute toward the cost of the medical care they receive. But the ability of many to do so is impeded by the low level of private incomes and the high and unpredictable costs of illness. Hitherto the problem has been tackled by adjustments between the individual physician and patient, by private insurance, and by free medical care for those who are destitute. All these measures have important shortcomings.

Individual adjustment between patient and physician is unsatisfactory to the patient, for it introduces an extraneous element into the relationship of patient and doctor and is so distasteful to many that they refrain from seeking the care they need. It is unsatisfactory to the doctor, who is not trained as a medical social worker. Furthermore, the incidence of this free or reduced-fee service does not fall on all doctors alike because many who practice in the poorer areas have little opportunity to compensate for these services by higher charges to richer patients. In the future this source of compensation may be even more drastically reduced as the higher income brackets feel the full force of heavier taxation.

Private insurance has made a real contribution and is growing in popularity, as the phenomenally rapid growth of hospitalization insurance has demonstrated. But as a solution of the basic problem it, too, has shortcomings. It has been applied only sparingly and with limited success to medical care, as apart from hospitalization. Insurance has also hitherto failed to appeal widely to the lower income groups, and it seems doubtful whether those who have difficulty in meeting the minimum necessities of decent maintenance can be expected voluntarily to budget for medical costs.

Public medical care for the needy varies widely in availability and quality in different parts of the country. There is need for better professional supervision, closer cooperation between the various agencies concerned, more rational administrative organization and procedures, and the allocation of more adequate funds to this public welfare service.

The problem presented by the financial obstacles to assurance of adequate medical care for all is one of the most important in the entire field of public health. Its solution will call for the closest cooperation between the medical profession and government. It will require, too, the courage to face economic realities and to explore not only the potentialities of expansion of publicly provided medical care but also the feasibility of methods such as social insurance which have successfully operated elsewhere.

Source: National Resources Planning Board. "Equal Access to Health." *National Resources Development Report for 1943: Part 1. Post-War Plan and Program.* Washington, DC: Government Printing Office, 1943, pp. 60–66.

NOTE

1. James MacGregor Burns, *Roosevelt: The Soldier of Freedom,* vol. 2 (New York: Harcourt Brace Jovanovich, 1970), 426.

DOCUMENT 6.2

California Medical Association Defeats State Health Insurance Legislation

"It Was the Foot in the Door, the Camel's Head in the Tent"

1945

In the mid-1940s California governor Earl Warren, a liberal Republican, proposed a state-administered health insurance plan to assist working Californians who were being swamped by rising health care costs. The state chapter of the American Medical Association (AMA), the California Medical Association (CMA), mounted a counteroffensive that effectively killed Warren's proposal. This was a bitter defeat to state legislators such as Byrl Salsman who actively supported Warren's proposal and tried to get it passed. As chair of the Senate Public Health Committee, Salsman had a ringside seat for the political battle that erupted between Warren and the CMA over his proposed health reforms. In 1970 Salsman recalled various aspects of that clash in an interview with Gabrielle Morris, excerpted here.

Reasons for Health Insurance

Morris: There seem to be conflicting points of view on Warren and the health legislation, depending on which source, it was either that he himself was personally concerned about health services for the people because of personal experiences of his own, or the other point of view was he was doing it to show what a good fellow he was for political expediency.

Salsman: I give you my view on that. I think Governor Warren proposed his health insurance plans because he recognized as every thinking person would have to recognize, that people of low and middle income have an extremely difficult time in meeting hospital and doctor bills and I think that's why he proposed it, I don't think he proposed it as a matter of political expediency, I don't think he proposed it because of his own personal experiences. Even today, suppose a middle income person has no health insurance protection at all, no voluntary policy, no insurance policy, and no public protection, a middle income person today would have a very difficult time paying his medical bills and his hospital bills and his drug bills. If he had an illness that lasted for thirty days, or if he had some hospitalization that lasted for thirty days, he would have a very difficult time doing that. And you must remember that in 1945, I believe the major source of protection for someone who wanted health insurance was the private insurance company.

Morris: And very few of those.

Salsman: Well, there were lots of them, but their coverage was inadequate. And if you got sick more than once you might find your policy cancelled. And if you examine, as I did, the reports of the health insurance people to the California Insurance Commissioner, you will find that they took in two dollars for every dollar they paid out. And this is simply too much.

Morris: Private companies?

Salsman: Yes, all private companies. This was just about the ratio. Two to one.

Morris: That's a statistic I haven't come across.

Salsman: Well, take a look at some of the old reports and you'll find that up till about 1947 that was about it, they took in two dollars in premiums for every dollar they paid out in benefits. And then of course, the policies had all kinds of loopholes. Limitations on the amount that could be drawn and limitations on the amount they would pay for this or pay for that. They still have those limitations, though they're greatly improved over what they used to be and I think Governor Warren proposed health insurance because he recognized first that the average man has a terrible time paying those bills and secondly he felt, and I felt at that time too, that private insurance simply did not do the job. It just didn't cover the field. Now, Warren's proposal, of course, was not all-encompassing. My recollection is that Warren's proposal really covered about the same field that unemployment insurance would cover.

Morris: This was what the proposals were, to cover again the working population.

Salsman: That's right. The wage earners and the middle income people.

Morris: And this would have been, according to the statistics I read, about four and a half million people.

Salsman: Well, it would have covered a large number.

Morris: But that was still only about half of the population in the state.

Salsman: That's right.

Morris: This is why, again looking back on it, it is surprising that the furor against it seems so large.

Organized Opposition to State Health Insurance

Salsman: No. It was the foot in the door, the camel's head under the tent. That's the way it was regarded by the medical people. And also by the insurance people. You see there were two vested interests here. First the doctors and secondly the insurance people. Now both had vested interests to protect. You have a third very large segment of opposition to this kind of thing and that is the business community and the business community simply doesn't want to bear the expense of it. First, they don't want to be called upon to pay any part of the tax and, secondly, they don't want all of the record keeping and all of the work involved to support this kind of a system. But the main vested interest, of course, is the doctors.

Fee Control a Major Issue

Morris: Now they seem to have done a very effective. . .

Salsman: They did a perfect job. You can't improve on it. And let me refine that, simplify it. This is its lowest common denominator. You know the real argument in this health insurance business, in spite of all of the things that the doctors say, the real argument is the control of the doctor's fee. That's the real guts of the thing. That's where the argument comes about. And in any public health insurance system, you must have control of the doctor's fee. That's all there is to it. . . .

. . . And if you don't do that, then, of course, the medical profession can bankrupt any system. And of course, in Warren's bill you had a board of administration and that board of administration was not controlled by the doctors. They were represented on the board, but they didn't control it. And so, while it was not expressed in the bill, it was implicit in Warren's legislative proposals that some kind of control over medical fees and costs would be forced upon the medical profession by the board of administration that was set up in the bill.

There's nothing new in this. This is as old as history. In the workmen's compensation system which we have in this state and which works so beautifully, in workmen's compensation, the administration of that system controls medical fees. Now, many doctors hate the workman's compensation system. But it's a fair system. The doctors are reasonably well paid and the system supports itself. And this was exactly what would have happened if Warren's bill had been enacted.

Morris: Well, looking at the legislative history, it seems like it was sort of a logical next step. . .

Salsman: Yes.

Proposed State Administration

Morris: And the first proposals were to combine it with workmen's compensation?

Salsman: Yes. But even considered as an independent system, it would have been run by the board of administration that Warren had proposed, there is no reason why it wouldn't have been self-supporting from the funds collected. There would have been a tax upon employees and a tax upon employers. Probably the deficit, if there had been a deficit, would have been met from funds taken from the General Fund of the state, but the funds from the tax should have paid all the hospital and medical bills.

But the medical bills would have been controlled. If you had a doctor reducing a fracture of the arm there would have been a fixed fee for it, just like there is in the workmen's compensation system. If someone has to have their hip set from a break in the hip or have a nail put in their hip, there would have been a fixed fee for that. Or if someone had to have a tumor removed, there would have been a fixed fee for that surgical procedure. And that fee would have hopefully been a fair fee as the fees are fair under the workmen's compensation system. If not fair, then the obvious answer would have been to raise the fee of the doctor. But that's really where the opposition comes from. . . .

. . . Let me say that I understand the doctor's objection to someone else fixing his fee. He's a professional man, and if he's an orthopedist, let's say, or if he's a thoracic surgeon, or if he's a neurosurgeon or something of that sort, he wants to fix his own fee, based upon his own skill, his own learning, his own time, the difficulty of the operation and all that sort of thing. He doesn't want some administrative board saying that for the reduction of a fracture of the hip he's entitled to two hundred dollars. He wants to fix his own fee. And I understand that. But we're talking now about something that's social, for the good of all, not for the good of one particular group. . . .

Morris: Not one special group. . . .

Opponents' Arguments Refuted

Salsman: That's right, and so while I understand it, I don't mean to say that I think the doctor's fees do not have to be controlled. I think they do in any system of this kind. Whether it's workmen's compensation or public health insurance. One of the arguments that the doctors used to advance against Warren's bill was that it was compulsory, that everybody had to join the system and you couldn't have a voluntary plan. That this was simply unAmerican because it was compulsory. . . .

. . . But we have so many examples in our society of things that are compulsory. In fact in organized society most things are compulsory. And then of course the doctors argued that the voluntary plans would do the job and they pointed to their own CPS [California Physicians' Service] as an example of a voluntary plan. Well, CPS, of course, in my opinion was started as a backfire to Olson's plans for compulsory health insurance [liberal Democrat Culbert Olson served as governor of California from 1939 to 1943]. And CPS didn't do the job and at the time Warren proposed his bills there were many medical organizations in this state that would not support their own CPS plan. The Alameda County Medical Society wouldn't do it. The San Diego County Medical Society would not do it. They wouldn't have anything to do with CPS which was their own baby. They disowned it.

So, the second argument that was advanced by the doctors and by those who supported their position was that voluntary plans would do the job. Now voluntary plans almost always envision insurance as a part of a voluntary plan and insurance meant insurance companies who have to do business on a profit basis in order to survive.

I've already mentioned the figures that you can verify from the Insurance Commissioner's office, that most health insurance policies in 1945 were cancellable, contained limited benefits, and the cost was high and as the records that I referred to will show, about two dollars in premium was collected for one dollar in benefits paid, and it never seemed to me that voluntary plans could do the job adequately and nothing has happened since 1945 to change my mind on that subject either.

The third argument that was advanced was that medical insurance would bankrupt the state. Well this, of course, is utterly and completely ridiculous. We have a system of workmen's compensation insurance now which carries not only the cost of medical and hospital care, but also carries wages with it. That doesn't bankrupt anybody. There is no reason why a plan that would cover only medical and hospital and drugs would bankrupt the state if extended to everyone, and if everyone was required to contribute to it, as Warren proposed.

In 1945, the same thing's pretty much true today, a workman could be standing on a ladder painting a wall for his employer, fall and break his leg. He would not only have his medical bills taken care of, his leg would be set by the doctor. He'd have his hospital bills paid, he would receive his wages or a proportion of his wages until he could return to work. But if at the end of his day's job, instead of falling off of a ladder while he was working painting the wall for his employer, he went home to paint a wall of his own house and fell off of the ladder, he'd get nothing.

Morris: Nothing.

Salsman: No medical coverage, no hospital coverage. Now why, if you can cover the former, can't you cover the latter? Why would it bankrupt the state? Of course, it would be more expensive. You'd have to add something for the additional coverage, but to say it would bankrupt the state is completely ridiculous.

And then, there was an argument that it would be government control of medicine. There is an element of truth in this, because the board of administration, as envisioned by Warren, would not have been controlled by doctors, so to this extent there would have been some control of the fees charged by doctors to individual patients, but I don't see how anyone can ever control the practice of medicine, except the doctors themselves.

So it would not have been the control of the practice of medicine. No lay administrative board can sensibly do that, but it might have been a control of costs.

Morris: There would have been doctors on each of the boards.

Salsman: Oh, yes, sure. But they would not have been a majority. I think Warren's board was a nine man board, I think it called for four doctors as I recall, I may be mistaken about that, but they would have been represented on the board, but they simply would not have been in the majority. They wouldn't have controlled it.

Then, of course, another argument that was often made which was really laughable, and that was that there was a sacred right on the part of the patient to choose his own doctor, and under the health insurance system as proposed by Warren, this would be completely eliminated. Well, so what. Under the workmen's Compensation Insurance Act no injured workman has a right to choose his own doctor. That right is vested by law in the employer, not in the injured workman, so there is nothing new in that. And secondly, the so-called sacred right doesn't exist anyway, because what does a patient know about his needs.

If a patient falls off the ladder and breaks his leg, he doesn't know whether he needs a neurologist or an orthodondist or whether he needs an orthopedist to look after him. His doctor tells him what doctor he's going to get.

The chances are that if he has an orthopedist reduce his fracture, the chances are he's never seen or heard of the man before the operation is performed, and probably will never see or hear from him again. There's simply nothing to that argument in my opinion.

There is another argument made which appealed purely to the emotions of people and that is that it was a socialistic scheme. It was a foreign scheme, it was of German origin perhaps and certainly at the very least, European and unAmerican. Well, perhaps it is socialistic in the sense that everyone draws together for mutual protection, but we have so many examples of that sort of thing that it just doesn't seem to me ever to have been a valid argument. Workmen's compensation also can be said to be socialistic, so can unemployment insurance, that was derived from the German experience.

Morris: Was "socialistic" more of a threat or more of an emotional appeal to . . .

Salsman: It was an emotional appeal.

Morris: Well, it keeps cropping up. . . .

Salsman: Because, you see those were the arguments that were advanced against President Roosevelt and many of the programs that he was advocating. They were called socialistic, and even worse.

Morris: I think the question I am asking is: was socialism more terrifying or did it make more of an emotional impact 25 years ago than it does now?

Salsman: I think it made more of an impact then, because there was more of a tendency to equate it with straight out and out authoritarian communism. In other words, when they said 'socialistic' they sort of went right through Germany to Russia and thought about Joseph Stalin.

Source: "Shepherding Health Insurance Bills through the California Legislature." Interview of Byrl R. Salsman by Gabrielle Morris. *Earl Warren Oral History Project: Earl Warren and Health Insurance, 1943–1949.* http://content.cdlib.org/view?docId=kt7s2005p0;NAAN=13030&doc.view=frames&chunk.id=Byrl%20R.%20Salsman&toc.id=0&brand=calisphere. Used with permission.

DOCUMENT 6.3

Truman Calls for National Health Insurance

"This Is Not Socialized Medicine"

1945

On November 19, 1945, President Harry S. Truman went before a joint session of Congress and delivered a bold address on U.S. health care policy. This speech, excerpted here, set the tone on the issue for the next seven years of his presidency. Truman's remarks contained requests for new investments in hospitals, public health services, disability care, and medical research—many of which were granted by Congress over the next few years. But the centerpiece of Truman's speech was a strongly worded appeal for legislation that would establish a national prepaid medical insurance program for all citizens. This plank of Truman's health program was excoriated by Republicans, conservative southern lawmakers in his own party, and the medical, insurance, and business lobbies as "socialized medicine." This alliance thwarted all subsequent attempts by Truman and his liberal allies to pass a national health insurance bill. Despite these setbacks, Truman's regular pronouncements about the benefits of national health insurance helped keep the issue alive throughout the late 1940s and early 1950s.

To the Congress of the United States:

In my message to the Congress of September 6, 1945, there were enumerated in a proposed Economic Bill of Rights certain rights which ought to be assured to every American citizen.

One of them was: "The right to adequate medical care and the opportunity to achieve and enjoy good health." Another was the "right to adequate protection from the economic fears of . . . sickness. . . ."

Millions of our citizens do not now have a full measure of opportunity to achieve and enjoy good health. Millions do not now have protection or security against the economic effects of sickness. The time has arrived for action to help them attain that opportunity and that protection. . . .

In the past, the benefits of modern medical science have not been enjoyed by our citizens with any degree of equality. Nor are they today. Nor will they be in the future—unless government is bold enough to do something about it.

People with low or moderate incomes do not get the same medical attention as those with high incomes. The poor have more sickness, but they get less medical care. People who live in rural areas do not get the same amount or quality of medical attention as those who live in our cities.

Our new Economic Bill of Rights should mean health security for all, regardless of residence, station, or race—everywhere in the United States.

We should resolve now that the health of this Nation is a national concern; that financial barriers in the way of attaining health shall be removed; that the health of all its citizens deserves the help of all the Nation.

There are five basic problems which we must attack vigorously if we would reach the health objectives of our Economic Bill of Rights.

1. The first has to do with the number and distribution of doctors and hospitals. One of the most important requirements for adequate health service is professional personnel—doctors, dentists, public health and hospital administrators, nurses and other experts.

The United States has been fortunate with respect to physicians. In proportion to population it has more than any large country in the world, and they are well trained for their calling. It is not enough, however, that we have them in sufficient numbers. They should be located where their services are needed. In this respect we are not so fortunate.

The distribution of physicians in the United States has been grossly uneven and unsatisfactory. Some communities have had enough or even too many; others have had too few. Year by year the number in our rural areas has been diminishing. Indeed, in 1940, there were 31 counties in the United States, each with more than a thousand inhabitants, in which there was not a single practicing physician. The situation with respect to dentists was even worse.

One important reason for this disparity is that in some communities there are no adequate facilities for the practice of medicine. Another reason—closely allied with the first—is that the earning capacity of the people in some communities makes it difficult if not impossible for doctors who practice there to make a living.

The demobilization of 60,000 doctors, and of the tens of thousands of other professional personnel in the Armed Forces is now proceeding on a large scale. Unfortunately, unless we act rapidly, we may expect to see them concentrate in the places with greater financial resources and avoid other places, making the inequalities even greater than before the war.

Demobilized doctors cannot be assigned. They must be attracted. In order to be attracted, they must be able to see ahead of them professional opportunities and economic assurances.

Inequalities in the distribution of medical personnel are matched by inequalities in hospitals and other health facilities. Moreover, there are just too few hospitals, clinics and health centers to take proper care of the people of the United States.

About 1,200 counties, 40 percent of the total in the country, with some 15,000,000 people, have either no local hospital, or none that meets even the minimum standards of national professional associations.

The deficiencies are especially severe in rural and semirural areas and in those cities where changes in population have placed great strains on community facilities.

I want to emphasize, however, that the basic problem in this field cannot be solved merely by building facilities. They have to be staffed; and the communities have to be able to pay for the services. Otherwise the new facilities will be little used.

2. The second basic problem is the need for development of public health services and maternal and child care. The Congress can be justifiably proud of its share in making recent accomplishments possible. Public health and maternal and child health programs already have made important contributions to national health. But large needs remain. Great areas of our country are still without these services. This is especially true among our rural areas; but it is true also in far too many urban communities.

Although local public health departments are now maintained by some 18,000 counties and other local units, many of these have only skeleton organizations, and approximately 40,000,000 citizens of the United States still live in communities lacking full-time local public health service. At the recent rate of progress in developing such service, it would take more than a hundred years to cover the whole Nation.

If we agree that the national health must be improved, our cities, towns and farming communities must be made healthful places in which to live through provision of safe water systems, sewage disposal plants and sanitary facilities. Our streams and rivers must be safeguarded against pollution. In addition to building a sanitary environment for ourselves and for our children, we must provide those services which prevent disease and promote health.

Services for expectant mothers and for infants, care of crippled or otherwise physically handicapped children and inoculation for the prevention of communicable diseases are accepted public health functions. So too are many kinds of personal services such as the diagnosis and treatment of widespread infections like tuberculosis and venereal disease. A large part of the population today lacks many or all of these services.

Our success in the traditional public health sphere is made plain by the conquest over many communicable diseases. Typhoid fever, smallpox, and diphtheria—diseases for which there are effective controls-have become comparatively rare. We must make the same gains in reducing our maternal and infant mortality, in controlling tuberculosis, venereal disease, malaria, and other major threats to life and health. We are only beginning to realize our potentialities in achieving physical well-being for all our people.

3. The third basic problem concerns medical research and professional education.

We have long recognized that we cannot be content with what is already known about health or disease. We must learn and understand more about health and how to prevent and cure disease.

Research—well directed and continuously supported—can do much to develop ways to reduce those diseases of body and mind which now cause most sickness, disability, and premature death—diseases of the heart, kidneys and arteries, rheumatism, cancer, diseases of childbirth, infancy and childhood, respiratory diseases and tuberculosis. And research can do much toward teaching us how to keep well and how to prolong healthy human life.

Cancer is among the leading causes of death. It is responsible for over 160,000 recorded deaths a year, and should receive special attention. Though we already have the National Cancer Institute of the Public Health Service, we need still more coordinated research on the cause, prevention and cure of this disease. We need more financial support for research and to establish special clinics and hospitals for diagnosis and treatment of the disease especially in its early stages. We need to train more physicians for the highly specialized services so essential for effective control of cancer.

There is also special need for research on mental diseases and abnormalities. We have done pitifully little about mental illnesses. Accurate statistics are lacking, but there is no doubt that there are at least two million persons in the United States who are mentally ill, and that as many as ten million will probably need hospitalization for mental illness for some period in the course of their lifetime. A great many of these persons would be helped by proper care. Mental cases occupy more than one-half of the hospital beds, at a cost of about 500 million dollars per year—practically all of it coming out of taxpayers' money. Each year there are 125,000 new mental cases admitted to institutions. We need more mental-disease hospitals, more out-patient clinics. We need more services for early diagnosis, and especially we need much more research to learn how to prevent mental breakdown. Also, we must have many more trained and qualified doctors in this field.

It is clear that we have not done enough in peace-time for medical research and education in view of our enormous resources and our national interest in health progress. The money invested in research pays enormous dividends. If any one doubts this, let him think of penicillin, plasma, DDT powder, and new rehabilitation techniques.

4. The fourth problem has to do with the high cost of individual medical care. The principal reason why people do not receive the care they need is that they cannot afford to pay for it on an individual basis at the time they need it. This is true not only for needy persons. It is also true for a large proportion of normally self-supporting persons.

In the aggregate, all health services—from public health agencies, physicians, hospitals, dentists, nurses and laboratories—absorb only about 4 percent of the national income. We can afford to spend more for health.

But four percent is only an average. It is cold comfort in individual cases. Individual families pay their individual costs, and not average costs. They may be hit by sickness that calls for many times the average cost—in extreme cases for more than their annual income. When this happens they may come face to face with economic disaster. Many families, fearful of expense, delay calling the doctor long beyond the time when medical care would do the most good.

For some persons with very low income or no income at all we now use taxpayers' money in the form of free services, free clinics, and public hospitals. Tax-supported, free medical care for needy persons, however, is insufficient in most of our cities and in nearly all of our rural areas. This deficiency cannot be met by private charity or the kindness of individual physicians.

Each of us knows doctors who work through endless days and nights, never expecting to be paid for their services because many of their patients are unable to pay. Often the physician spends not only his time and effort, but even part of the fees he has collected from patients able to pay, in order to buy medical supplies for those who cannot afford them. I am sure that there are thousands of such physicians throughout our country. They cannot, and should not, be expected to carry so heavy a load.

5. The fifth problem has to do with loss of earnings when sickness strikes. Sickness not only brings doctor bills; it also cuts off income.

On an average day, there are about 7 million persons so disabled by sickness or injury that they cannot go about their usual tasks. Of these, about 3 1/4 millions are persons who, if they were not disabled, would be working or seeking employment. More than one-half of these disabled workers have already been disabled for six months; many of them will continue to be disabled for years, and some for the remainder of their lives.

Every year, four or five hundred million working days are lost from productive employment because of illness and accident among those working or looking for work—about forty times the number of days lost because of strikes on the average during the ten years before the war. About nine-tenths of this enormous loss is due to illness and accident that is not directly connected with employment, and is therefore not covered by workmen's compensation laws.

These then are the five important problems which must be solved, if we hope to attain our objective of adequate medical care, good health, and protection from the economic fears of sickness and disability.

To meet these problems, I recommend that the Congress adopt a comprehensive and modern health program for the Nation, consisting of five major parts—each of which contributes to all the others.

First: Construction of Hospitals and Related Facilities

The Federal Government should provide financial and other assistance for the construction of needed hospitals, health centers and other medical, health, and rehabilitation facilities. With the help of Federal funds, it should be possible to meet deficiencies in hospital and health facilities so that modern services—for both prevention and cure—can be accessible to all the people. Federal financial aid should be available not only to build new facilities where needed, but also to enlarge or modernize those we now have.

In carrying out this program, there should be a clear division of responsibilities between the States and the Federal Government. The States, localities and the Federal Government should share in the financial responsibilities. The Federal Government should not construct or operate these hospitals. It should, however, lay down minimum national standards for construction and operation, and should make sure that Federal funds are allocated to those areas and projects where Federal aid is needed most. In approving state plans and individual projects, and in fixing the national standards, the Federal agency should have the help of a strictly advisory body that includes both public and professional members.

Adequate emphasis should be given to facilities that are particularly useful for prevention of diseases—mental as well as physical—and to the coordination of various kinds of facilities. It should be possible to go a long way toward knitting together facilities for prevention with facilities for cure, the large hospitals of medical centers with the smaller institutions of surrounding areas, the facilities for the civilian population with the facilities for veterans.

The general policy of Federal-State partnership which has done so much to provide the magnificent highways of the United States can be adapted to the construction of hospitals in the communities which need them.

SECOND: EXPANSION OF PUBLIC HEALTH, MATERNAL AND CHILD HEALTH SERVICES

Our programs for public health and related services should be enlarged and strengthened. The present Federal-State cooperative health programs deal with general public health work, tuberculosis and venereal disease control, maternal and child health services, and services for crippled children.

These programs were especially developed in the ten years before the war, and have been extended in some areas during the war. They have already made important contributions to national health, but they have not yet reached a large proportion of our rural areas, and, in many cities, they are only partially developed.

No area in the Nation should continue to be without the services of a full-time health officer and other essential personnel. No area should be without essential public health services or sanitation facilities. No area should be without community health services such as maternal and child health care.

Hospitals, clinics and health centers must be built to meet the needs of the total population, and must make adequate provision for the safe birth of every baby, and for the health protection of infants and children. . . .

THIRD: MEDICAL EDUCATION AND RESEARCH

The Federal Government should undertake a broad program to strengthen professional education in medical and related fields, and to encourage and support medical research.

Professional education should be strengthened where necessary through Federal grants-in-aid to public and to non-profit private institutions. Medical research, also, should be encouraged and supported in the Federal agencies and by grants-in-aid to public and non-profit private agencies. . . .

Federal aid to promote and support research in medicine, public health and allied fields is an essential part of a general research program to be administered by a central Federal research agency. Federal aid for medical research and education is also an essential part of any national health program, if it is to meet its responsibilities for high grade medical services and for continuing progress. Coordination of the two programs is obviously necessary to assure efficient use of Federal funds. Legislation covering medical research in a national health program should provide for such coordination.

FOURTH: PREPAYMENT OF MEDICAL COSTS

Everyone should have ready access to all necessary medical, hospital and related services.

I recommend solving the basic problem by distributing the costs through expansion of our existing compulsory social insurance system. This is not socialized medicine.

Everyone who carries fire insurance knows how the law of averages is made to work so as to spread the risk, and to benefit the insured who actually suffers the loss. If instead of the costs of sickness being paid only by those who get sick, all the people—sick and well—were required to pay premiums into an insurance fund, the pool of funds thus created would enable all who do fall sick to be adequately served without overburdening anyone. That is the principle upon which all forms of insurance are based.

During the past fifteen years, hospital insurance plans have taught many Americans this magic of averages. Voluntary health insurance plans have been expanding during recent years; but their rate of growth does not justify the belief that they will meet more than a fraction of our people's needs. Only about 3% or 4% of our population now have insurance providing comprehensive medical care.

A system of required prepayment would not only spread the costs of medical care, it would also prevent much serious disease. Since medical bills would be paid by the insurance fund, doctors would more often be consulted when the first signs of disease occur instead of when the disease has become serious. Modern hospital, specialist and laboratory services, as needed, would also become available to all, and would improve the quality and adequacy of care. Prepayment of medical care would go a long way toward furnishing insurance against disease itself, as well as against medical bills.

Such a system of prepayment should cover medical, hospital, nursing and laboratory services. It should also cover dental care—as fully and for as many of the population as the available professional personnel and the financial resources of the system permit.

The ability of our people to pay for adequate medical care will be increased if, while they are well, they pay regularly into a common health fund, instead of paying sporadically and unevenly when they are sick. This health fund should be built up nationally, in order to establish the broadest and most stable basis for spreading the costs of illness, and to assure adequate financial support for doctors and hospitals everywhere. If we were to rely on state-by-state action only, many years would elapse before we had any general coverage. Meanwhile health service would continue to be grossly uneven, and disease would continue to cross state boundary lines.

Medical services are personal. Therefore the nation-wide system must be highly decentralized in administration. The local administrative unit must be the keystone of the system so as to provide for local services and adaptation to local needs and conditions. Locally as well as nationally, policy and administration should be guided by advisory committees in which the public and the medical professions are represented.

Subject to national standards, methods and rates of paying doctors and hospitals should be adjusted locally. All such rates for doctors should be adequate, and should be appropriately adjusted upward for those who are qualified specialists.

People should remain free to choose their own physicians and hospitals. The removal of financial barriers between patient and doctor would enlarge the present freedom of choice. The legal requirement on the population to contribute involves no compulsion over the doctor's freedom to decide what services his patient needs. People will remain free to obtain and pay for medical service outside of the health insurance system if they desire, even though they are members of the system; just as they are free to send their children to private instead of to public schools, although they must pay taxes for public schools.

Likewise physicians should remain free to accept or reject patients. They must be allowed to decide for themselves whether they wish to participate in the health insurance system full time, part time, or not at all. A physician may have some patients who are in the system and some who are not. Physicians must be permitted to be represented through organizations of their own choosing, and to decide whether to carry on in individual practice or to join with other doctors in group practice in hospitals or in clinics.

Our voluntary hospitals and our city, county and state general hospitals, in the same way, must be free to participate in the system to whatever extent they wish. In any case they must continue to retain their administrative independence.

Voluntary organizations which provide health services that meet reasonable standards of quality should be entitled to furnish services under the insurance system and to be reimbursed for them. Voluntary cooperative organizations concerned with paying doctors, hospitals or others for health services, but not providing services directly, should be entitled to participate if they can contribute to the efficiency and economy of the system.

None of this is really new. The American people are the most insurance-minded people in the world. They will not be frightened off from health insurance because some people have misnamed it "socialized medicine".

I repeat—what I am recommending is not socialized medicine.

Socialized medicine means that all doctors work as employees of government. The American people want no such system. No such system is here proposed.

Under the plan I suggest, our people would continue to get medical and hospital services just as they do now—on the basis of their own voluntary decisions and choices. Our doctors and hospitals would continue to deal with disease with the same professional freedom as now. There would, however, be this all-important difference: whether or not patients get the services they need would not depend on how much they can afford to pay at the time.

I am in favor of the broadest possible coverage for this insurance system. I believe that all persons who work for a living and their dependents should be covered under such an insurance plan. This would include wage and salary earners, those in business for themselves, professional persons, farmers, agricultural labor, domestic employees, government employees and employees of non-profit institutions and their families.

In addition, needy persons and other groups should be covered through appropriate premiums paid for them by public agencies. Increased Federal funds should also be made available by the Congress under the public assistance programs to reimburse the States for part of such premiums, as well as for direct expenditures made by the States in paying for medical services provided by doctors, hospitals and other agencies to needy persons.

Premiums for present social insurance benefits are calculated on the first $3,000 of earnings in a year. It might be well to have all such premiums, including those for health, calculated on a somewhat higher amount such as $3,600.

A broad program of prepayment for medical care would need total amounts approximately equal to 4% of such earnings. The people of the United States have been spending, on the average, nearly this percentage of their incomes for sickness care. How much of the total fund should come from the insurance premiums and how much from general revenues is a matter for the Congress to decide.

The plan which I have suggested would be sufficient to pay most doctors more than the best they have received in peacetime years. The payments of the doctors' bills would be guaranteed, and the doctors would be spared the annoyance and uncertainty of collecting fees from individual patients. The same assurance would apply to hospitals, dentists and nurses for the services they render.

Federal aid in the construction of hospitals will be futile unless there is current purchasing power so that people can use these hospitals. Doctors cannot be drawn to sections which need them without some assurance that they can make a living. Only a nation-wide spreading of sickness costs can supply such sections with sure and sufficient purchasing power to maintain enough physicians and hospitals.

We are a rich nation and can afford many things. But ill-health which can be prevented or cured is one thing we cannot afford.

FIFTH: PROTECTION AGAINST LOSS OF WAGES FROM SICKNESS AND DISABILITY

What I have discussed heretofore has been a program for improving and spreading the health services and facilities of the Nation, and providing an efficient and less burdensome system of paying for them.

But no matter what we do, sickness will of course come to many. Sickness brings with it loss of wages.

Therefore, as a fifth element of a comprehensive health program, the workers of the Nation and their families should be protected against loss of earnings because of illness. A comprehensive health program must include the payment of benefits to replace at least part of the earnings that are lost during the period of sickness and long-term disability. This protection can be readily and conveniently provided through expansion of our present social insurance system, with appropriate adjustment of premiums.

Insurance against loss of wages from sickness and disability deals with cash benefits, rather than with services. It has to be coordinated with the other cash benefits under existing social insurance systems. Such coordination should be effected when other social security measures are reexamined. I shall bring this subject again to the attention of the Congress in a separate message on social security.

I strongly urge that the Congress give careful consideration to this program of health legislation now. . . .

Source: Truman, Harry S. Special Message to the Congress Recommending a Comprehensive Health Program. *Public Papers of the Presidents of the United States: Harry S. Truman, 1945.* Washington, DC: Government Printing Office, 1961, pp. 475–85.

DOCUMENT 6.4

National Mental Health Act

"The Problem of Mental Illness Is Finally Being Attacked in a Realistic Manner"

1946

During the early 1940s the deplorable condition of many of America's hospitals for people with mental disabilities came under increased scrutiny from health care reformers, muckraking journalists, and mental health professionals. Mental hospitals had long been the lynchpin of the country's care and treatment practices for the mentally disabled, but critics asserted that most of these modestly funded institutions, which had come under even greater financial duress during the Great Depression years, had no rehabilitative function and simply served as caretakers for sufferers of psychiatric illness. Reformers such

*as Leonard Edelstein and Harold Barton of the Civilian Public Service (CPS) and
journalists Albert Maisel and Albert Deutsch asserted that this constituted a tragic waste
of the nation's human resources, given the advances that were being made at the time in
biomedical science and psychiatric therapies, and they urged Washington, D.C., to act.*

*These appeals received a considerable lift in 1944 and 1945, when it became
abundantly clear that existing mental health counseling services were inadequate to meet
the needs of battle-scarred World War II veterans returning home. In fairly short order,
then, a mental health reform movement led by Robert H. Felix, head of the US Public
Health Service's department of mental hygiene services, was able to marshal considerable
support in Congress for a bill that came to be known as the National Mental Health Act.
This legislation, which was enacted in 1946, provided important new federal financial
support for research and treatment of mental illness, including grants to states to support
existing outpatient facilities and establish new community-based psychiatric counseling
clinics. Mental health professionals lauded this policy as one that would encourage early
identification and treatment of mental illness, as well as reduce the need for expensive
long-term hospitalization.[1] In addition, the law laid the groundwork for the April 1949
establishment of the National Institute of Mental Health, which became the country's
preeminent institution in the realms of psychiatric research and mental health
policymaking at the local, state, and federal levels.*

*The following speech was delivered by Robert H. Felix to a gathering of state and
territorial health officers in Washington on December 3, 1946, only five months after the
bill's passage. In his address, he accurately describes the National Mental Health Act as a
landmark event in the nation's approach to mental illness.*

This is indeed a significant occasion. For the first time in the history of the United States
Public Health Service, the State and Territorial health officers are meeting with the State
mental health authorities to discuss ways and means of jointly working toward improving
mental health. It means that the problem of mental illness is finally being attacked in a
realistic manner commensurate with its seriousness and extent—in short, as a public health
problem. When one considers the prevalence of mental illness and its cost to the community in terms of loss of productivity and the expense of care, let alone in terms of human
suffering, the need is clear for a public health approach to the problem of mental illness.

It has been conservatively estimated that more than 8 million persons in this country are suffering from some form of mental illness. Some 600,000 are now in mental
hospitals, occupying more than half the hospital beds in the United States; and every year
a quarter of a million new patients are admitted. The figures on hospital population by no
means represent the number in need of such care since in many States admissions are
determined by the availability of beds rather than by the need.

Until now, a concerted public attack upon the problem of mental illness has been
hindered by the same factors that held back an effective attack on syphilis—the stigma
attached by society, with the consequent reluctance to admit its presence and to seek
medical aid early. There is considerable evidence, however, of an improved attitude on
the part of the public toward mental illness, which will not only permit but demand an
effective program. Perhaps the most significant evidence of the public's concern is the
recent passage by Congress of the National Mental Health Act, thus giving open recognition to the seriousness of the problem and making possible, for the first time in our history, a comprehensive, long-range program for the improvement of the mental health of
the nation.

The National Mental Health Act amends the Public Health Service Act (Public Law 410, 79th Cong.) and follows generally the same legislative pattern in the field of mental health as do the provisions in the Public Health Service Act regarding other public health problems.

The act is aimed at bringing about direct action in three inter-related fields: Increased research in nervous and mental disorders, the training of mental health personnel, and the improvement and expansion of community mental health services. No funds are available for the construction of mental hospitals or for financing the institutional care of the mentally ill.

Research.—Under the National Mental Health Act, the United States Public Health Service is authorized to make grants-in-aid for research directly to universities, hospitals, laboratories, and other public and private institutions, and to qualified individuals. Research projects must first be approved by the National Advisory Mental Health Council, which is composed of six persons selected without regard to civil-service laws from the leading authorities in the field of mental health. This authorization should do much to stimulate research which otherwise might remain in the idea stage. . . .

Training.—The shortage of well-trained personnel in the mental health field is one of the most serious handicaps to the development of an adequate mental health program. To promote training in this field, the act authorizes the Public Health Service to make grants to public and other nonprofit institutions for developing and improving their training facilities. In this way, institutions that already provide training in mental health fields can expand to accommodate more students, and potential training centers—in hospitals, medical and other schools—can be developed. Grants may not be used, however, for the construction of buildings.

Training stipends will also be available to selected students in psychiatry, psychology, psychiatric social work, and psychiatric nursing. The number of trainees who may receive stipends is to be determined by the National Advisory Mental Health Council.

Grants-in-aid to States.—The third category of mental health activity which the act seeks to promote is the improvement of mental health services in local communities through grants-in-aid to States. It is this aspect of the national program in particular which is to be discussed in detail here. Under this legislation, the amount authorized annually for general health purposes is increased by $10,000,000 this sum to be made available to States for the development and expansion of mental health programs at the State and community level.

Of the total sum appropriated for this purpose, allocations will be made to the States on the basis of population, the extent of the mental health problem, and the financial need of each State.

Responsibility for the development and execution of the State plans in the field of mental health is vested in the State mental health authority, which functions in the mental health program as does the State health authority in other health programs. . . .

What types of activities should be included in the plans of the State mental health authority in order to develop an adequate program for each State, utilizing the Federal assistance now made available under the Mental Health Act?

Of course not all of the activities to be described here can become immediate realities in all States. Nor need they be adopted *in toto* by every State. Programs naturally will differ with the special needs of each State. A program which is best for one State may not prove useful to another. Plans should be based upon the particular needs in the State, and should be geared toward meeting those which are most pressing. They should be reasonably flexible, drawn with an eye toward future growth.

In general, there are four basic activities which State plans should include:

1. There should be an appraisal of the State's mental health needs and resources, on the basis of which immediate and long-range plans should be developed. Although the State should assume responsibility for initiating the appraisal, the United States Public Health Service stands ready to offer consultative service and assistance when desired.

2. Where needed, the staff in the central office should be enlarged to carry out the functions incumbent upon the State mental health authority. Most important of these functions are:

(a) The development, subsidy, or operation of psychiatric clinical services for adults and for children. . . .
(b) The licensure of mental hospitals.
(c) The development of State-wide records of the incidence of mental diseases and emotional disorders.
(d) The training of professional personnel—psychiatrists, psychologists, and psychiatric social workers—for staffing State and local mental health programs.
(e) The development of research in the field of mental diseases and emotional disorders.
(f) The education of other professional health workers, particularly public health nurses, in mental hygiene in order that they may contribute to mental health in the performance of their regular duties.
(g) The development of a well-rounded and practical program of mental health education of the public.
(h) Liaison or consultation with other agencies, such as education, welfare, penal, courts, civil service, etc.

3. As these operations are developed, new services in the central office can be established. For example, a section on training might be set up to stimulate and coordinate in-service and out-service training programs for nurses, attendants, staff physicians, and other mental health personnel.

In this connection, the importance of a program for the psychiatric education of general practitioners must be emphasized. In the past, too many physicians have felt that they knew little or nothing about mental diseases. This attitude, reflected in their practice, can be blamed to a great extent upon those responsible for the physicians' training. This situation has changed recently to some extent. The war has served to stimulate the interest of many physicians in the emotional aspects of illness. Many doctors who prior to the war were unacquainted with or resistant to psychiatric concepts were confronted in their combat experiences with undeniable evidence of the influence of emotional disturbance upon bodily function. As a result, many are now eager to learn more about psychosomatic medicine and methods of treatment which they as general practitioners might competently apply.

We must take advantage of this new and hopeful trend. Aside from the acute shortage of psychiatrists, the character and magnitude of the problem of mental illness makes it imperative that the general practitioner help meet it. In mental, as in other illnesses, he is the first line of defense. . . .

4. We turn now to what is perhaps the central core of the State's program—the establishment and expansion of community mental health clinics.

It has been estimated that in the entire country there are only about one-fifth the clinic services needed. Those which are available are for the most part concentrated in the larger population centers. Fifteen States are entirely without mental health clinics, and there are large areas in other States where no psychiatric facilities whatsoever are available.

The present goal of the Public Health Service in the grants-to-States program is the establishment by the States of at least one out-patient mental health clinic for each 100,000 of the population. Although this goal is not immediately attainable owing to the shortage of personnel, it may eventually prove to be quite conservative in terms of the need. . . .

According to best present estimates, a full-time all-purpose mental health clinic should be provided for each 100,000 of the population. It is preferable that this service be integrated with other health services in the community. The basic staff of the clinic should consist of one psychiatrist, one psychologist, two psychiatric social workers, and the necessary clerical assistance. One psychiatrically trained public health nurse may be substituted for one psychiatric social worker. The clinic should be available to all segments and all ages of the population.

The State mental health authority should take responsibility for furnishing sparsely settled and rural areas with centralized service in the form of traveling clinics, to provide mental health services otherwise not available to them. . . .

These clinics, whether mobile or stationary, should furnish three broad services: (1) A community clinic; (2) an auxiliary service to the mental hospital; and (3) an agency for community mental health education.

Such a clinic would serve the community by providing out-patient psychiatric treatment or psychological counseling for patients not in need of hospitalization and, most significant, for patients in the early stage of illness, when the prospect for cure is greatest. . . .

Although the establishment of an all-purpose clinic for each community should be the goal, special problems frequently make themselves felt in a community before the need for an all-purpose clinic is appreciated. For example, there may be a pressing need for a child guidance clinic, for psychiatric services in the court, for an industrial psychiatric clinic. In such a case, it would be logical to initiate the mental health program by first establishing those services most urgently needed in the particular area. However, the program should not be allowed to stop there. It should be logically and progressively expanded to include the provision of mental health services for the whole community.

In developing your program, you should take advantage of whatever clinic facilities are available at present. These should be carefully scrutinized, expanded if feasible, and fully utilized. In some communities, a private nonprofit organization may furnish some degree of psychiatric service. If it were possible to give such an organization assistance through the State mental health authority, its facilities could perhaps be more widely utilized. It is important, therefore, than an appraisal of psychiatric resources be made at once in order to determine what facilities, either public or private, can be built upon and expanded.

After a clinic has established itself and demonstrated its worth through successful treatment of behavior problems in children, relieving psychoneurotic patients, and

successfully supervising former hospital patients, it can expand into more truly preventive fields. These might include such programs as parent education, the promotion
of special classes for exceptional children, marriage counselling, therapeutic recreational activities, and cooperative projects with courts and other agencies.

Such expansion, however, can succeed only if the clinic has full community support
and approval. In this connection, close cooperation with other State and local lay and
professional organizations in building up a good mental health program is so important
that it cannot be too strongly emphasized. . . .

The establishment of a comprehensive mental health program need not wait until
all or even most of the enigmas of nervous and mental disease are solved. Troubled people
need help now, and we know enough to make our effort worth while. If community mental health services are set up, new techniques can be applied as they evolve. This has been
the pattern in the development of programs for the prevention and control of venereal
disease, tuberculosis, and other public health problems. The same principles can be
applied successfully to mental disorders.

Source: Felix, Robert H. "The Relation of the National Mental Health Act to State Health Authorities."
Public Health Reports 62, no. 2, January 10, 1947, pp. 41–49. www.ncbi.nlm.nih.gov/pmc/articles
/PMC1995243/.

NOTE

1. Gerald N. Grob, *From Asylum to Community: Mental Health Policy in Modern America* (Princeton,
   NJ: Princeton University Press, 1991).

DOCUMENT
6.5

Laying the Groundwork for the Hill-Burton Act

"I Think [Lister Hill] Would Consider It One of the Great Accomplishments of His Life"

1946

*During the mid-1940s, lawmakers on Capitol Hill expressed growing alarm with the
dearth of hospital facilities in many parts of the country. In 1945 fully 40 percent of U.S.
counties, with a total population of about fifteen million people, did not have a registered
hospital within their borders, and a total of 845 counties did not even have a public health
nurse. Most of these shortfalls were in rural areas, which did not have the wealth or
number of patients that attracted hospitals and physicians to more populated areas. "The
technological advances of scientific medicine were not being transmitted to the general
population," summarized scholar Rosemary Stevens. "The affluent family in a large city
had available to it an array of specialists and superspecialists with appropriate support
facilities in the specialized departments of a large hospital. Small towns and villages could
not support the services of specialists, even if they could lure specialists away from the*

intellectual attraction of the major urban centers. As a result, the difference between urban and rural health services, which had been a source of anxiety as early as the 1920s, became even more marked."[1]

The disparities between rural and urban health care became a key focus of the American Hospital Association (AHA). The AHA had an obvious financial interest in new hospital construction, but AHA study groups convened to document the inequities, such as the Commission on Hospital Care, turned in convincing evidence that decisive government action was genuinely needed. In 1945 President Harry S. Truman formally asked Congress to make public financing of new hospital construction a legislative priority, and lawmakers of both parties—and especially those from rural districts in the South and West who recognized that a new hospital would be greeted with acclaim by voting constituents— responded with alacrity. The Hill-Burton Act became law one year later, and it set off a frenzy of hospital building over the next quarter-century. From 1947 to 1971, 30 percent of all hospital projects were partly paid for by federal Hill-Burton funds. During this same period, the program directly accounted for about 10 percent of the annual cost of hospital construction, and it generated an additional $9 billion for hospital construction in the form of state and local matching funds.[2] (In 1954 the act was amended to permit grants to ambulatory care and nursing home facilities.)

George Bugbee was executive director of the AHA when the Hill-Burton Act was crafted and passed, and he has been widely described as a key figure in shaping the legislation and organizing political support for its passage. In the following 1984 interview with Lewis E. Weeks, Bugbee recalled some of the political machinations that went into the passage of the historic bill.

Jim Hamilton and I working with him—I think he was the primary leader although Graham Davis was high in the [American Hospital] Association's councils, and he was in charge of the hospital division of the W.K. Kellogg Foundation—were a part of an effort made to create a Commission on Hospital Care to plan for postwar, this was '43 and '44. It was hard going to raise the money. Kellogg pledged a certain amount, and we solicited many other people.

The Commission was chaired by Thomas Gates, the President of the University of Pennsylvania, a very public-spirited gent. . . .

Eventually we persuaded Dr. Arthur Bachmeyer, then Associate Dean of Biological Sciences at Chicago and Superintendent of the University Hospital and Clinics . . . to become the Director. He said he would do it, but he couldn't spend more than half time. It was then that we persuaded Maurice Norby, who was an employee of Rufus Rorem at the Blue Cross Commission located in the headquarters that the Association owned, to take the staff job. The orderliness of the Commission's report and its success was partly Art Bachmeyer, but a great deal Maurice Norby.

I won't go through much of it except one part. There's always been a question whether the Commission of Hospital Care and its findings and report led to the Hill-Burton Act. Well, having been there, I am inclined to think they are related, but hardly as direct a lead-in as later the Public Health Service said. . . .

Many of the states began by the governor appointing a postwar planning committee to think through their needs in the state. That became a powerful pressure for the passage of the Hill-Burton Act.

I am going on about the Bishop Resolution [a 1943 resolution passed by the House of Delegates of the AHA calling for increased government spending on hospital construction] and the need for aid for construction of hospitals. The establishment of the Commission on Hospital Care was only one expression of the intent of the Association to drive for legislation. One of the major issues in that legislation was whether nonprofit hospitals should be eligible for grants. There had been major work relief programs for years prior to the war, and only one of them permitting grants for nonprofit hospitals. Since nonprofit or voluntary hospitals were doing most of the short-term care, it seemed not right. Certainly the nonprofit group didn't like it.

So a planning committee was set up under the (AHA) Council on Government Relations—Postwar Planning Committee was its title. It met in Washington. It began trying to figure out what might be done to see that the nongovernment hospital was considered in any postwar building program, public work relief, because the assumptions then were that there would be a depression as there was after World War I.

On the Postwar Planning Committee was Dr. Vane Hoge. He was one of the early graduates (1936) of Art Bachmeyer's from the University of Chicago Program in Hospital Administration. He had been sent there by the Public Health Service as an officer. He was close to Art and he was close to the Commission. I think the action was due to Vane and his boss, Surgeon General Dr. Thomas Parran, who was one of the very strong Surgeons General.

Parran thought: Things are coming together. Let's draft legislation for aid for hospitals. He brought the draft to the Postwar Planning Committee. Graham Davis and Vane Hoge were on the Committee. The Committee said this was just what they had been looking for. The essential points were that each state have a plan, pick the neediest areas, and federal aid was to be varied between the states according to need. The aid was to go within the state to government and nonprofit hospitals by priority of need. This in a way is what Hill-Burton turned out to be with considerable embroidery, one way or the other. The bill required the first country-wide planning of hospitals.

The bill as first drafted by the Public Health Service seemed good. Then the question was: How to get it introduced? . . .

. . . When I went to Cleveland to succeed Jim Hamilton (at Cleveland City Hospital), I was appointed by the mayor, then Harold Burton. Harold Burton later became United States Senator, and after that a justice of the Supreme Court. At the time I am talking about, 1944, he was in the Senate. So I went to see Harold Burton, whom I knew fairly well from that (Cleveland) experience. He agreed to introduce the bill with one reservation, and that was if Senator Robert Taft, the other—the senior—Senator from Ohio agreed. I did see Taft, and he did agree. He was getting ready to run for the Presidency. He said, "I have a labor bill, and I have this and that—education bill—I need a health bill." He later rewrote the bill, because he said he was going to make it a model of federal grant-in-aid, and, perhaps did in his opinion and other people's too. The bill was introduced January 10, 1945.

Then there was the question of someone else to sponsor the bill. We wanted a bipartisan introduction. I asked Harold Burton. He suggested Lister Hill. That was the move that really led to success with Hill-Burton, because Lister Hill took it on. I think he would consider it one of the great accomplishments of his life. Certainly it was a great accomplishment for his state of Alabama because the bill ended up with a weighting toward the South that was tremendous, and still is in effect—and probably is currently excessive. . . .

Senator Hill spent a lot of time on the bill, and it was his time that was needed.

Things then fit together. I don't think I said this before, but we called on members of the Commission on Hospital Care for support. The representative of the Farm Bureau was terribly key in getting support in the House on the bill. With the labor man, Golden, we immediately went to Nelson Cruikshank, who was on the staff of the Health and Welfare Committee of the AFL-CIO [at the time Hill-Burton passed Cruikshank was a leader of the Congress of Industrial Organizations, which merged with the American Federation of Labor in 1955]. He was very supportive, and so was industry. So we had a good group.

Source: Weeks, Lewis E. "George Bugbee: A First-Person Profile (Part I)." *Health Services Research* 60, no. 3, pp. 343-349. Copyright (©) 1981 Hospital Research Educational Trust. Reproduced with permission of Blackwell Publishing Ltd.

NOTES

1. Rosemary Stevens, *American Medicine and the Public Interest* (New Haven, CT: Yale University Press, 1971); rev. ed. (Berkeley: University of California Press, 1998), 275.

2. U.S. Department of Health, Education, and Welfare, *Facts about the Hill-Burton Program, 1947–1971* (Washington, DC: Government Printing Office, 1971).

DOCUMENT 6.6

Modernizing the Hospitals and Clinics of the Veterans Administration

"I Recognize the Emergency Situation"

1946

When the Veterans Administration (VA) was established in 1930, fifty-four hospitals across the country were made VA facilities. By the late 1930s and early 1940s, the quality of health care being provided by these institution had become the subject of intense concern in Washington, D.C., and around the country. Proliferating reports of crumbling and indifferently maintained facilities, poorly trained and unmotivated doctors and nurses, and crushing levels of bureaucratic red tape badly damaged the reputation of VA hospitals, which increasingly came to be seen as a professional backwater. In response, President Harry S. Truman appointed General Omar Bradley, a well-known Army commander during World War II, to take the reins of the VA and clean house. Bradley promptly recruited Paul Hawley, the Army's chief surgeon in Europe during World War II, to help with his rehabilitation project. In fairly short order Hawley and his top deputy, Chicago surgeon Paul B. "Budd" Magnuson, crafted what scholar Mark Van Ells described as "a plan to minimize administrative red tape and transform VA hospitals from the nadir to the zenith of the medical profession in the United States."[1]

Over the next few years the VA made major new investments in prosthetics research and established a "hometown care" program that expanded the use of approved non-VA physicians to treat veterans in their local communities on a fee-for-service basis. By 1947 more than half of all VA-approved outpatient treatments were being performed by non-VA providers.[2] The most ambitious element of their revitalization plan was to infuse the medical ranks of the VA with fresh blood by creating a VA Department of Medicine and Surgery. According to their blueprint, this agency would establish formal ties with respected medical schools that could supply residents and interns to help staff VA facilities. The department would also be empowered to hire surgeons, nurses, and other medical personnel outside the civil service system, which would give the VA greater flexibility in offering attractive salary and advancement packages to top professionals.

By late 1945 a bill (H.R. 4717)establishing the Department of Medicine and Surgery had made its way through Congress, despite opposition from the Civil Service Commission and some long-standing VA bureaucrats who felt threatened by the proposed changes. In January 1946 Truman formally signed the bill, which became Public Law 79–293. Following is Truman's January 3 note to Bradley notifying him of that fact.

After Public Law 79–293 became a reality, the number of physicians in the VA system quickly soared, from twenty-three hundred in 1945 to more than four thousand by 1947, and VA facilities underwent several years of badly needed expansion and modernization. "Public Law 293 was our Magna Carta," Magnuson later wrote. "I saw people in the Medical Department throw out their chests and act like men. They saw for themselves how we cut down on their paperwork . . . so they could spend their time practicing medicine. They saw, above all, how the treatment of their patients improved, and that is all that is really necessary with any doctor who is worth his salt."[3]

Dear General [Omar N.] Bradley:

I have today given my approval to H.R. 4717, an enactment to establish a Department of Medicine and Surgery in the Veterans' Administration.

I recognize the emergency situation which confronts the Veterans' Administration at the present time in the recruiting of physicians, dentists and nurses.

It is my desire that, in carrying out the provisions of this law, you develop a system of recruitment and placement which will grant priority to qualified veterans and which will also provide against any possibility of discrimination because of race or creed.

I hope that this legislation will enable you and your associates to move forward in your determination to provide the veterans of this country with a progressive up-to-date Department of Medicine and Surgery. Much progress has been made in this direction, and I shall watch with real interest the additional steps which will be taken by you under this new law.

Very sincerely yours,
HARRY S. TRUMAN

Source: Truman, Harry S. Letter to General Bradley, January 3, 1946. *Public Papers of the Presidents of the United States: Harry S. Truman, 1946.* Washington, DC: Government Printing Office, 1961, p. 1.

NOTES

1. Mark D. Van Ells, *To Hear Only Thunder Again: America's World War II Veterans Come Home* (Lanham, MD: Lexington Books, 2001), 123–24.

2. Van Ells, *To Hear Only Thunder Again,* 123–24.

3. Paul B. Magnuson, *Ring the Night Bell: The Autobiography of a Surgeon* (New York: Little, Brown, 1960), 300.

Senator Taft Denounces Compulsory Insurance as Socialized Medicine

"We Are Going to Turn Over Our Destiny to a Bureaucracy of Self-Styled Experts"

1946

Democratic proposals for national health insurance were bitterly opposed by Republican lawmakers in Washington, D.C., who supported instead a system of voluntary private insurance supplemented by public welfare services for those who could not afford medical care. They believed that the universal compulsory insurance schemes propagated by President Harry S. Truman, the sponsors of the Wagner-Murray-Dingell (WMD) bills, and other health care reformers flouted basic American principles of capitalism, liberty, states' rights, and limited government. From their perspective, a federally organized system of compulsory health insurance amounted to a dangerous and ill-conceived experiment in socialism. Ohio senator Robert A. Taft was among the most prominent Republicans to express these concerns during Truman's first term, when WMD came up for congressional debate and scrutiny. Moreover, Taft's presidential ambitions led him to voice his objections in venues far beyond Ohio and Washington. The speech on "socialization of medicine" excerpted here, for example, was delivered on October 7, 1946, to the Wayne County Medical Society in Detroit, Michigan.

FEDERAL COMPULSORY HEALTH INSURANCE IS NOT INSURANCE BUT SOCIALIZATION OF MEDICINE

. . . Long hearings have been held on the so-called Wagner-Murray-Dingell bill providing a universal compulsory sickness insurance in the United States. Extensive propaganda is being carried on in favor of that bill. Undoubtedly it will presented to the next session and a determined effort made to secure its enactment. President Truman has officially endorsed it, so that it has become an Administrative measure.

The proponents of this bill are studiously attempting to create the impression that it is just a form of insurance similar to life insurance, or hospital insurance, or any of the other kinds of insurance with which people are familiar; and that it will not change the character of medical service. But the fact is that this is not insurance. It is a plan for government administration of all medical care, supported by a tax on pay rolls. There is no difference between a pay roll tax and any other tax. This can't be insurance if a man has no option except to pay for it. Even the International Labour Office, which is the principal international proponent of sickness insurance, admits that this so-called insurance is not really insurance, or will not remain so for long. In a recent volume entitled *"Approaches to Social Security,"* it says:

> "The fact is that once the whole employed population, wives and children included, is brought within the scope of compulsory sickness insurance, the great majority of doctors, dentists, nurses, and hospitals find themselves engaged in the insurance medical service, which squeezes

out most of the private practice on the one hand, and most of the medical care hitherto given by the public assistance authorities, on the other.
The next step to a single national medical service is a short one . . ."

Obviously, since the tax is based on a percentage of pay roll, it relates itself to the
income of the employee, and not to the service performed. The man with a low income
and a number of dependents pays much less for more service than the unmarried man
with higher income. This is a principle of taxation, not of insurance.

A compulsory levy of this kind is a tax, because it deprives the employee of his
freedom of choice in the spending of money which he earns. . . . Of course it encourages
applications for medical service every time a man has a cold, and undoubtedly will
increase the total work to be done by doctors which has the effect of decreasing the quality of service. In any event, it cannot possibly be called insurance.

It is, in reality, a plan for the nationalization of our medical service. From three to
five billion dollars will pour into Washington. The money will be used by a Federal
bureau, with branches in every city and town, to pay all the doctors in the United States
to render without charge the medical service required by all citizens. The government
will have to issue regulations determining circumstances under which men and women
are entitled to medical care, when it is to be given in hospitals, when it is to be given in
clinics, when it is to be given in the doctors' offices, and when it can be given in the
home. Regulations of many kinds are necessary, because obviously the government cannot spend unlimited amounts simply because the patient or the doctor or a combination
of the two ask for more care than is reasonable. Regulations must limit the prescription
of expensive medicine, X-ray services and the like. Regulations must prescribe whether
doctors are paid on a per capita basis or on a service basis, and how much they shall
receive. Regardless of form and the protestations of the authors, this bill proposes, first,
a socialization of medicine, and, second, a transfer of all control over health activities
from the States and local governments to a Washington bureau.

It does not necessarily damn a program to call it socialization. We have long socialized primary and secondary education in the United States. The Government provides all
education without cost to the student and supports the expense by taxation. Nearly a million teachers are on the public pay roll. The situation regarding education, however, is
very different. The service to be performed can be reasonably adequate in lower grades
even if it is practically uniform for all students. A primary education must be compulsory
for every boy and girl in the nation, and education through private schools cannot begin
to do the job, and never has attempted to do it.

The providing of free medical care presents much more difficult problems than
education. Every individual case requires special treatment, and I have pointed out that
every individual should have the choice of paying for more or less medical care. Furthermore, the fact that we socialize education—and postal service is another example—
cannot be used as a precedent for doing the same in every other field or we would soon
have a completely socialized economy. If we are going to give medical care free to all
people, why not provide them with free transportation, free food, free housing and clothing, all at the expense of the tax payer? Everyone connected with these services could be
made a government employee. After all, socialization is a question of degree, and we cannot move much farther in that direction unless we do wish a completely socialistic state.

Under the proposed Truman plan, practically all doctors would become in effect
employees of the federal government. They would be responsible to the government
which pays them and not to their patients who do not. You know better than I whether

that would improve medical service, make better doctors, and stimulate progress in medicine. I should think it would have an utterly deadening effect on medical practice.

MEDICAL CARE SHOULD NOT BE SOCIALIZED OR NATIONALIZED

. . . I am strongly opposed to any socialization, by State or nation, of medical care except medical care to those unable to pay for it because of their financial condition. But above all, I deplore the federalization of medicine. Medical care has always been a function of the State and local governments. Under our Constitution that is where it belongs, and not in Washington. If the people of a State desire to socialize medicine, that is their privilege. But what possible justification can there be for giving a Washington bureau power to employ all physicians throughout the nation? That has not even been done in education. Our people in each State and each school district have retained complete control over the education of their children and the employment of their teachers. In most States the system has been separated from political government as it could not be under the present organization of the Federal government.

Our experience is that any attempt to regulate the affairs of all the people, of the average citizen in forty-eight states, is usually both tyrannical and inefficient. Conditions in various sections of the country are completely different. No man, certainly no federal bureaucrat, knows enough to draw regulations which fit all those conditions. If they fit the part of the country he does know, they are likely to be awkward or nonsensical in other areas. Furthermore the average man has no voice in the operation of a Washington bureau. In his own City council or State House, he can make himself heard by appearing personally. He can write letters to the newspapers. He can run for office himself and present his program in an election. But in Washington he can't even find the bureau or the man supposed to handle his problems. One of the principal services which Congressmen perform is to save their constituents two or three days tramping through marble corridors. Then when the man is located, the citizen from Detroit, Michigan, is not likely to get any serious consideration for his problem. Washington is confident of its own superiority, and its general attitude is that the public is "too damned dumb" to understand. Administration by States and local government is generally democratic. Administration by Washington boards and bureaus is tyrannical. . . .

Today we have moved far towards a totalitarian state until there is serious danger that our people will utterly lose by measures here at home the liberty for which we have fought two great world wars. This is the underlying issue today in practically all the legislation which comes before Congress. We must determine within the next few years whether we are going to plan our progress along the lines which have made this country the greatest and most powerful nation in the world, according to American principles of liberty and equal justice, or whether we are going to turn over our destiny to a bureaucracy of self-styled experts. I cannot conceive of a measure which will more greatly extend the power of the State or move further in one jump towards an all-powerful central government, than federal compulsory health insurance.

INADEQUACIES IN MEDICAL CARE DO NOT JUSTIFY DISTRUST OF PRESENT SYSTEM

The justification for this measure lies in the claim that medical service today in the United States is inadequate, and particularly inadequate for the low-income and middle-income groups. Extensive evidence has been offered in the effort to show that such an inadequacy exists, but I am not a sufficient expert to judge the truth of these claims. Certain facts, however, stand out. The health of the United States as a whole is as good as any nation, and better than most. Providing of medical care for individuals is only one of the measures which have an effect on health. Probably more has been done and can be done by preventive measures and the extension of public health work in the elimination of disease and epidemics. Great progress has been made in that field, and I think all those interested are prepared to extend Federal aid so that no State, through financial poverty, shall be unable to carry out all the measures of public health work which can have a substantial effect in preventing illness.

A great deal has been made of the number of rejections in selective service. A careful examination of these causes of rejection, however, will show that very few of these causes would have been removed by the furnishing of free medical care in youth. For the most part, the condition resulted from congenital defects, mental deficiencies or other causes which would not have been affected by more medical care, or not substantially affected.

On the other hand we must all recognize that from an overall national standpoint medical care is not adequate. There are gaps in the service which is rendered. Great as is the charity offered, those unable to pay for medical care undoubtedly fail to get it in many cases where it would be of substantial benefit to them. In the second place there is, in some localities, a lack of hospital and clinic facilities and a serious lack of doctors. This last deficiency has been accentuated during the war, but even in peace time it is likely that many districts will be unable to secure a physician because of the inadequate return offered. In the third place there is a large number of people in the middle class group who may be able to pay the total cost of necessary health service if spread over the years evenly, but who avoid visits to doctors because of the expense when they should go and may find themselves unable to pay the cost of an exceptional illness. These gaps in medical service, however, do not justify remedy of nationalizing all medical service.

The problem of providing medical care for the poor is not an insurance problem. We have always recognized the obligation of a government to provide free medical care to those unable to pay for it themselves. Nearly all of our cities have general hospitals where such care is freely given. Many localities have public health doctors. All doctors do a large amount of charity work, and there are many charity hospitals. It is true, however, that the work is not systematically organized by all States and local governments and that a more complete system could be stimulated by Federal aid.

The lack of facilities and of doctors would not be directly affected by sickness insurance. It would be more adequately taken care of by Federal aid in the construction of hospitals, and in the subsidizing of doctors where medical practice will not support a decent livelihood.

Public Health work and prevention programs would not be enlarged by sickness insurance. I believe that public health work should be extended substantially and supplemented by a more complete inspection of the health of school children in all public and private schools at the expense of the State, so that illness may not result or increase solely from ignorance or neglect in childhood. Legislation should be adopted for federal aid in the removal of pollution from interstate rivers. Federal assistance to research would not be increased by any program of compulsory sickness insurance. It is already well established.

The need for insurance for middle-income groups has not been adequately met, and such insurance is still in an experimental stage. Great progress has been made in the extension of hospital insurance under the Blue Cross plan. Promising experiments in voluntary health insurance are now being promoted by doctors in many States throughout the Union, perhaps the best one being that here in Michigan. Certainly anything the government can do to stimulate the formation of such funds should be done. I think it is peculiarly the obligation of the doctors to see that they exist. I do not think it is the function of government to compel men to insure themselves against a possible uneven burden of illness, but I do think that such insurance should be available to those who desire to take it out.

All of the measures I have outlined to meet the real deficiencies in medical service which exist today are entirely feasible without nationalizing the entire medical profession or forcing all of our people to accept State medicine. The Murray-Wagner-Dingell bill is not an effort in good faith to make our medical service better, but to scrap the present system, and control all medicine and all doctors from Washington. . . .

Source: Taft, Robert A. Speech to the Wayne County Medical Society, October 7, 1946. *The Papers of Robert A. Taft. Volume 3: 1945–1948,* edited by Clarence E. Wunderlin Jr. Kent, OH: Kent State University Press, 1997, pp. 202–8.

DOCUMENT
6.8

Truman Again Calls on Congress to Address National "Health Needs"

"Voluntary Plans Have Proved Inadequate to Meet the Need"

1949

President Harry S. Truman's first term in office was marred by a frustrating lack of progress in his campaign to pass a national health insurance program that would improve medical access for poor and working-class Americans. Time after time, his administration was thwarted by the physicians' and insurance lobbies, conservative Republicans, and Southern Democrats whose clashes with the president over civil rights issues had begun spilling over into other policy areas. But Truman remained unbowed, and after his upset victory in the November 1948 presidential election, he returned to Capitol Hill and delivered another address, reprinted here, in which he made the case for a national program of medical care that would cover all citizens.

To the Congress of the United States:

In a special message to the Congress on November 19, 1945, and in a number of messages since that date, I have recommended the enactment of comprehensive legislation to improve the health of our people.

The issues involved in these recommendations have been debated all over the country—in Congressional hearings, in medical societies, and in public forums. Out of all this discussion has come a large measure of agreement. There has been increasing recognition of the need for positive, planned action to bring adequate health services within the reach of all our people. With respect to most of my recommendations, there is no longer any substantial difference of opinion.

Legislation has already been enacted which is helping substantially to provide better health services and medical care. For example, Federal funds are now being made available to help in building badly needed hospitals. The Federal Government's programs of medical research have expanded. Additional grants have been made available to the States to aid in establishing and maintaining public health services.

However, the action thus far taken falls far short of our goal of adequate medical care for all our citizens. If we are to deal with the problem realistically and in its true dimensions, action is required on a broader scale.

We are in an era of startling medical progress. The technical resources available to the physician are tremendously greater than a generation ago. But to make these resources effective, he must use much more complicated, more exact equipment. He must turn to specialized laboratories and technicians for help. He must apply new techniques and must secure more effective drugs and appliances.

As a Nation we have not yet succeeded in making the benefits of these scientific advances available to all those who need them. The best hospitals, the finest research laboratories, and the most skillful physicians are of no value to those who cannot obtain their services.

Now that we have the medical knowledge that can bring good health within our reach to a degree heretofore undreamed of, we must improve the means for putting that knowledge to practical use. Good health is the foundation of a nation's strength. It is also the foundation upon which a better standard of living can be built for individuals. To see that our people actually enjoy the good health that medical science knows how to provide is one of the great challenges to our democracy.

Our objective must be two-fold: to make available enough medical services to go around, and to see that everybody has a chance to obtain those services. We cannot attain one part of that objective unless we attain the other as well.

Our needs are plain. We are, and shall be for some time, short of physicians, dentists, nurses, medical technicians and public health workers. We need more hospitals and clinics. Medical personnel and facilities are unevenly located in relation to the need in different parts of the country—and are particularly deficient in rural areas. We need broader, better supported medical research. We need much more attention to preventive health care and more adequate public health services. Most of all, we need more widespread use of the modern method of paying for medical care through prepaid insurance.

There is, so far as I am aware, no longer any significant disagreement on these basic objectives. And there is general agreement that the financial problem is at the base of our difficulties.

My first recommendation is that the Congress enact legislation providing for a nationwide system of health insurance.

The traditional method of paying for medical care cannot meet the health needs of today. As medical education and practice have become better, they have become more specialized and at the same time more expensive. As treatment has become more expensive, families have found it more and more difficult to meet the extraordinary costs of accidents, serious illness or major surgery. Thus, at the same time that our knowledge of how to provide medical care is at its highest point, more and more people are unable to afford it. It is no longer just the poor who are unable to pay for all the medical care they need—such care is now beyond the means of all but the upper income groups.

This is an anomalous situation. It can and should be met through social insurance. Under such a system, regular contributions to the insurance fund will replace irregular, often overwhelming, family outlays for medical care.

Insurance against the costs of medical care has been growing rapidly in this country in recent years. This growth is proof that our people understand the advantages of health insurance and desire its extension.

Unfortunately, however, voluntary plans have proved inadequate to meet the need. Most voluntary plans give only very limited protection. While some fifty million people now have some form of health insurance, this insurance usually provides only limited protection so far as hospitalization is concerned and in most cases makes no provision at all for other medical services. Only three and one-half million of our people have insurance which provides anything approaching adequate health protection. Most serious of all, since rates in these voluntary plans are not adjusted to incomes, those who need protection most cannot afford to join.

The only fair and effective means to assure adequate medical care through insurance is to build on the pattern of our existing social insurance plans. As in the case of those plans, we should seek to include as many persons as possible within the health insurance system, so that more may benefit, and costs can be more widely shared.

Health insurance is a method of paying for medical care. It will not require doctors to become employees of the Government. It will not disturb the freedom of doctors and hospitals to determine the nature and extent of treatment to be given. It will not interfere with the personal relationship between doctor and patient. Under such a plan, patients will remain free to choose their own doctors, and doctors will remain free to accept or reject patients. Moreover, patients, doctors, and hospitals will remain free to make their own arrangements for care outside the insurance system if they so choose.

The administration of the program should, of course, be decentralized to the greatest possible extent. It is also of the utmost importance that the quality of medical care be adequately safeguarded. Both these objectives can be accomplished in large measure by having the administration of the program in each locality guided by a local group in which the skills and judgment of local medical personnel are fully represented. Furthermore, the fullest possible use should be made of the medical schools and their faculties.

Health insurance will mean that proper medical care will be economically accessible to everyone covered by it, in the country as well as in the city, as a right and not as a medical dole.

It will mean that more people will obtain the preventive care which is so important, and that more people will be able to have better medical care. Thus health insurance will provide an effective demand for the additional doctors, nurses and other medical personnel we need to improve our health. The provision of more doctors and medical personnel goes hand in hand with better arrangements for paying for their services.

My second recommendation, therefore, is that the Congress enact legislation to help medical schools expand. Special financial aid should be provided for the construction of teaching hospitals and other facilities and to help the schools cover the cost of larger enrollments. At the same time, scholarship aid should be provided for good students who might otherwise lack the means to undertake the long period of professional training.

Today we have about 190,000 active physicians, of whom 145,000 are in private practice. This is not enough. It represents only about 80 per cent of the physicians we require. Unless we take prompt action to expand the medical schools, we shall be no better off ten years from now. We face similar shortages with respect to dentists, nurses, and other professional medical personnel. Obviously, the facilities for professional education will have to be expanded if we are to provide adequate care for our growing population.

Health insurance will have another extremely important result so far as medical personnel are concerned. Since payment of doctors' and other fees will be assured by the insurance system, doctors will be able to practice where they are needed most, without sacrificing income—as too many doctors must now do in rural and low-income areas. Comprehensive health insurance will thus lead to a more equitable distribution of doctors over the country, and we will no longer have the situation where some counties have only one active physician for every three thousand persons, while other counties have five or six.

My third recommendation is that the Federal Government provide increased aid for the construction of hospitals and other medical facilities in communities where they are needed.

In many cases adequate medical treatment can be provided only in hospitals. Under present circumstances, hospitalization is often impossible, both because of the shortage of hospitals and because of inability of the patient to pay the costs of hospital care.

The enactment of health insurance will, of course, permit more of our people to obtain the hospital care they need. Thus health insurance will make it possible to support hospitals in communities where they could not now be supported. At the same time, it will make the present need for hospital construction even more urgent.

The present Federal Hospital Survey and Construction Act, enacted in 1946, represents an important step in a national program to provide more hospitals. Under this Act, expiring in 1951, some funds are provided for the Government to contribute one-third of the construction costs of public and other non-profit hospitals.

I recommend that the Congress extend the duration of this program, increase the funds to be made available, and modify the program so that the Government's share will take account of the varying financial resources of different States.

Furthermore, the program should be broadened to include aid for the establishment of community health centers, diagnostic clinics, and group practice clinics, all of which have proved in recent years to be very effective means of providing better medical care. This aid should be provided in the form of grants to help finance the construction and equipping of public and other non-profit health centers and clinics, and in the form of Government guarantees of loans for the establishment of private facilities, similar to the mortgage guarantees the Government provides for private housing.

Closely related to these measures to increase the availability of private medical care are certain actions we should take to improve the public health preventive and disease control services, which are now inadequate in most areas and totally lacking in many.

At present, the Government provides grants to assist State and local governments in preventing and controlling certain diseases, and to promote maternal and child health services, services for crippled children, and general public health activities.

My fourth recommendation is that the Congress increase the amount of the Federal grants for these activities, consolidate the existing separate grants insofar as possible, and provide for matching by the States adjusted to their differing financial resources.

Another essential step, if we are to continue to improve our medical care system, is to continue to improve our medical research as more facilities and scientific personnel become available. The Government is already contributing substantially to the advance of medical knowledge by conferring fellowships for research in many specialized fields, by providing grants for research by public and non-profit agencies, and through its own research activities. We must keep alert to every opportunity to add to the program of medical research through new scientific techniques, such as the use of the products of atomic energy, and through the wise and balanced expansion of research into diseases which have not so far been conquered.

These recommendations are interrelated parts of a comprehensive plan for improving the quality of medical care and making such care more completely available to our people. They present a sensible and realistic program of action, which complements my recommendations for extending and improving the social security system, including the provision of insurance against loss of workers' incomes during periods of sickness or disability.

We should lose no time in making a full-scale beginning on all parts of our health program. At the same time that we are putting health insurance into operation, we should be establishing the hospitals and clinics, and training the medical personnel, that the insurance system will enable us to afford. We cannot, of course, achieve our goals fully until the system has been in operation for some time. That fact emphasizes the need for early legislative action.

Many people are concerned about the cost of a national health program. The truth is that it will save a great deal more than it costs. We are already paying about four per cent of our national income for health care. More and better care can be obtained for this same amount of money under the program I am recommending. Furthermore, we can and should invest additional amounts in an adequate health program-for the additional investment will more than pay for itself.

The real cost of our present inadequate medical care is not measured merely by doctors' bills and hospital bills. The real cost to society is in unnecessary human suffering and the yearly loss of hundreds of millions of productive working days. To the individual the real costs are the shattering of family budgets, the disruption of family life, the suffering and disabilities, the permanent physical impairments left by crippling diseases, and the deaths each year of tens of thousands of persons who might have lived. This is the price we are now paying for inadequate medical care.

It is plain common sense that we should not permit these needless costs to continue when we have it within our power to reduce them with a practical health program. Where there are differences remaining as to the details of the program, we should not permit these differences to stand in the way of our going forward. They should be threshed out with honesty and tolerance, as is our democratic fashion. We should enact the best possible program and then all of us should get behind it to make it work.

We are striving in this country to see that the strength and flexibility of our political and economic institutions are used to bring the greatest possible good to our people. I consider this health program as part of that endeavor—to adjust to modern conditions without losing traditional values, to bring to the people of this country the full enjoyment of the benefits which our freedom makes possible.

Source: Truman, Harry S. Special Message to the Congress on the Nation's Health Needs, April 22, 1949. *Public Papers of the Presidents of the United States: Harry S. Truman, 1949.* Washington, DC: Government Printing Office, 1964, p. 226.

Eisenhower Unveils a Health Care "Reinsurance" Proposal

DOCUMENT
6.9

"To Offer Broader Health Protection to More Families"

1954

Dwight D. Eisenhower entered the White House in 1953 as a determined foe of national health insurance and other proposed health care reforms that would necessitate a larger federal role in provision of medical care to the American people. He argued that a combination of private voluntary insurance (for people above poverty level) and public relief programs (for the poor) was better suited to the nation's needs and traditions. Within a year of taking office, however, Eisenhower recognized that rising anxieties among voters about soaring health insurance premiums and other medical costs posed a growing political danger. In addition, the insurance industry's evident distaste for providing policies to high-risk citizens threatened to torpedo conservative assurances that voluntary insurance, in and of itself, had the capacity to solve the problem of uninsured Americans.

Mindful of these factors, in early 1954 Eisenhower proposed a "reinsurance" plan to boost voluntary insurance. Under his plan, which he announced in an address to Congress excerpted here, the federal government would subsidize commercial and nonprofit insurers who agreed to provide coverage to high-risk groups. But reaction to the proposal from both ends of the political spectrum was hostile. With conservatives assailing it as an unacceptable step toward government-run health care and liberals denouncing it as a giveaway to big insurance companies, the administration's efforts to marshal support for the bill from moderate Democrats and loyal members of Eisenhower's own Republican Party ended in failure.

To the Congress of the United States:

I submit herewith for the consideration of the Congress recommendations to improve the health of the American people.

Among the concerns of our government for the human problems of our citizens, the subject of health ranks high. For only as our citizens enjoy good physical and mental health can they win for themselves the satisfactions of a fully productive, useful life.

The Health Problem

The progress of our people toward better health has been rapid. Fifty years ago their average life span was 49 years; today it is 68 years. In 1900 there were 676 deaths from infectious diseases for every 100,000 of our people; now there are 66. Between 1916 and 1950, maternal deaths per 100,000 live births dropped from 622 to 83. In 1916, ten percent of the babies born in this country died before their first birthday; today, less than 3 percent die in their first year.

This rapid progress toward better health has been the result of many particular efforts, and of one general effort. The general effort is the partnership and teamwork of private physicians and dentists and of those engaged in public health, with research scientists, sanitary engineers, the nursing profession and the many auxiliary professions related to health protection and care in illness. To all these dedicated people, America owes most of its recent progress toward better health.

Yet, much remains to be done. Approximately 224,000 of our people died of cancer last year. This means that cancer will claim the lives of 15,000,000 of our 160,000,000 people unless the present cancer mortality rate is lowered. Diseases of the heart and blood vessels alone now take over 817,000 lives annually. Over seven million Americans are estimated to suffer from arthritis and rheumatic diseases. Twenty-two thousand lose their sight each year. Diabetes annually adds 100,000 to its roll of sufferers. Two million of our fellow citizens now handicapped by physical disabilities could be, but are not, rehabilitated to lead full and productive lives. Ten million among our people will at some time in their lives be hospitalized with mental illness.

There exist in our Nation the knowledge and skill to reduce these figures, to give us all still greater health protection and still longer life. But this knowledge and skill are not always available to all our people where and when they are needed. Two of the key problems in the field of health today are the distribution of medical facilities and the costs of medical care.

Not all Americans can enjoy the best in medical care—because not always are the requisite facilities and professional personnel so distributed as to be available to them, particularly in our poorer communities and rural sections. There are, for example, 159 practicing physicians for every 100,000 of the civilian population in the Northeast United States. This is to be contrasted with 126 physicians in the West, 116 in the North central area, and 92 in the South. There are, for another example, only 4 or 5 hospital beds for each 1,000 people in some States, as compared with 10 or 11 in others.

Even where the best in medical care is available, its costs are often a serious burden. Major, long-term illness can become a financial catastrophe for a normal American family. Ten percent of American families are spending today more than $500 a year for medical care. Of our people reporting incomes under $3000, about 6 percent spend almost a fifth of their gross income for medical and dental care. The total private medical bill of the nation now exceeds nine billion dollars a year—an average of nearly $200 a family—and it is rising. This illustrates the seriousness of the problem of medical costs.

We must, therefore, take further action on the problems of distribution of medical facilities and the costs of medical care, but we must be careful and farsighted in the action that we take. Freedom, consent, and individual responsibility are fundamental to our system. In the field of medical care, this means that the traditional relationship of the physician and his patient, and the right of the individual to elect freely the manner of his care in illness, must be preserved.

In adhering to this principle, and rejecting the socialization of medicine, we can still confidently commit ourselves to certain national health goals.

One such goal is that the means for achieving good health should be accessible to all. A person's location, occupation, age, race, creed, or financial status should not bar him from enjoying this access.

Second, the results of our vast scientific research, which is constantly advancing our knowledge of better health protection and better care in illness, should be broadly applied for the benefit of every citizen. . . .

The specific recommendations which follow are designed to bring us closer to these goals.

Continuation of Present Federal Programs

In my Budget Message appropriations will be requested to carry on during the coming fiscal year the health and related programs of the newly-established Department of Health, Education, and Welfare.

These programs should be continued because of their past success and their present and future usefulness. The Public Health Service, for example, has had a conspicuous share in the prevention of disease through its efforts to control health hazards on the farm, in industry and in the home. Thirty years ago, the Public Health Service first recommended a standard milk sanitation ordinance; by last year this ordinance had been voluntarily adopted by 1558 municipalities with a total population of 70 million people. Almost twenty years ago the Public Health Service first recommended restaurant sanitation ordinances; today 685 municipalities and 347 counties, with a total population of 90 million people, have such ordinances. The purification of drinking water and the pasteurization of milk have prevented countless epidemics and saved thousands of lives. These and similar field projects of the Public Health Service, such as technical assistance to the States, and industrial hygiene work, have great public value and should be maintained.

In addition, the Public Health Service should be strengthened in its research activities. Through its National Institutes of Health, it maintains a steady attack against cancer, mental illness, heart diseases, dental problems, arthritis and metabolic diseases, blindness, and problems in microbiology and neurology. The new sanitary engineering laboratory at Cincinnati, to be dedicated in April, will make possible a vigorous attack on health problems associated with the rapid technological advances in industry and agriculture. In such direct research programs and in Public Health Service research grants to State and local governments and to private research institutions lies the hope of solving many of today's perplexing health problems.

The activities of the Children's Bureau and its assistance to the States for maternal and child health services are also of vital importance. The programs for children with such crippling diseases as epilepsy, cerebral palsy, congenital heart disease, and rheumatic fever should receive continued support.

Meeting the Cost of Medical Care

The best way for most of our people to provide themselves the resources to obtain good medical care is to participate in voluntary health insurance plans. During the past decade, private and non-profit health insurance organizations have made striking progress in offering such plans. The most widely purchased type of health insurance, which is hospitalization insurance, already meets approximately 40 percent of all private expenditures for hospital care. This progress indicates that these voluntary organizations can reach many more people and provide better and broader benefits. They should be encouraged and helped to do so.

Better health insurance protection for more people can be provided.

The Government need not and should not go into the insurance business to furnish the protection which private and non-profit organizations do not now provide. But the Government can and should work with them to study and devise better insurance protection to meet the public need.

I recommend the establishment of a limited Federal reinsurance service to encourage private and non-profit health insurance organizations to offer broader health protection to more families. This service would reinsure the special additional risks involved in such broader protection. It can be launched with a capital fund of twenty-five million dollars provided by the Government, to be retired from reinsurance fees. . . .

Source: Eisenhower, Dwight D. Special Message to the Congress on the Health Needs of the American People, January 18, 1954. *Public Papers of the Presidents of the United States: Dwight D. Eisenhower, 1954.* Washington, DC: Government Printing Office, 1960, pp. 69–73.

DOCUMENT 6.10

Polio Vaccination Assistance Act

"To Provide Children and Expectant Mothers an Opportunity for Vaccination against Poliomyelitis"

1955

Poliomyelitis ranked among the most dreaded diseases in postwar America. Whereas many other once-feared diseases had been tamed in the late nineteenth and early twentieth centuries, incidences of polio had risen, and by the early 1950s it was killing or causing permanent disability to more children than any other infectious disease. In 1954, a vaccine developed by scientist Jonas Salk was tested in clinical trials across the United States and much of Canada. Millions of families participated in the trials, which were carried out under a carefully constructed double-blind system. On April 12, 1955, researchers announced triumphantly that they had documented an amazing downturn in polio cases within the vaccinated test groups. Parents and communities across North America rejoiced, for they recognized that the results meant that the scourge of polio had finally been defeated.

A small fringe of conspiracy-minded people warned against widespread polio vaccinations. Blinded by the McCarthyite tenor of the time, these far-right voices insisted that large-scale public health measures such as polio vaccination and fluoridation of public water (a measure to prevent tooth decay) were diabolical Communist plots that would weaken America, either by sapping its physical vitality or rendering it vulnerable to mind control. But the vast majority of Americans recognized that Salk's breakthrough was a banner moment in the nation's history, and they applauded when Congress authorized a big federal aid package to help state public health departments carry out sweeping vaccination programs for children and expectant mothers (the text of the bill is reprinted here). The Salk vaccine, and its subsequent supplantation by an orally administered live-virus polio vaccine developed by scientist Albert Sabin, also made the American public much more accepting of government investments in other medical research areas. "If polio could be prevented, Americans had reason to think that cancer *and heart disease and mental illness could be stopped, too," wrote historian Paul Starr. "Who knew how long human life might be extended? Medical research might offer passage to immortality. Between 1955 and 1960, unswerving congressional support pushed up the [National Institutes of Health] budget from $81 million to $400 million."*[1]

S. 2501

A BILL

To amend the Public Health Service Act to authorize grants to States for the purpose of assisting States to provide children and expectant mothers an opportunity for vaccination against poliomyelitis.

Be it enacted by the Senate and House of Representatives of the United States of America in Congress assembled, That section 314 of the Public Health Service Act, as amended (42 U.S.C. 246), is amended—

(a) by redesignating subsection (c) as subsection (c)(1) and by adding at the end of such subsection a new paragraph as follows:

"(2) To enable the Surgeon General to assist, through grants, the States to provide children (under the age of 20) and expectant mothers an opportunity for vaccination against poliomyelitis, there are herby authorized to be appropriated for the period beginning July 1, 1955, and ending December 31, 1956, such sums as may be necessary to carry out the purposes of this paragraph. At the request of any State the Surgeon General may use all or any portion of any monetary grant authorized to be made to such State under this paragraph for the purchase of poliomyelitis vaccine to be furnished to the State in lieu of such grant (or such portion thereof). Vaccine so furnished shall be subject to the same requirements as to use as vaccine purchased from monetary grants to States under this paragraph. The Surgeon General may, in his discretion and in accordance with regulations designed to assure the most effective and equitable distribution of available supplies of poliomyelitis vaccine, specify certain categories of children and expectant mothers to be accorded priority in receiving an opportunity for vaccination against poliomyelitis, and during any period in which any priority group has been so established and is in effect all vaccine acquired by any State through assistance provided pursuant to this paragraph shall be made available only to persons within any such group. As used in this paragraph, the term 'State' means a State or the District of Columbia, Hawaii, Alaska, Puerto Rico, the Virgin Islands, Guam, American Samoa, and the Canal Zone." . . .

Source: U.S. Senate. S. 2501. 84th Cong., 1st sess., July 13, 1955. www.eisenhower.archives.gov/research/digital_documents/salk/Salk_F.pdf.

NOTE

1. Paul Starr, *The Social Transformation of American Medicine* (New York: Basic Books, 1982), 347.

Big Labor Pushes for Government Health Care for the Elderly

"The Forand Bill Is a Well Considered [and] . . . Practical Proposal"

1959

In 1958 a group of progressive health care reformers devised a plan to extend the reach of Social Security to include coverage of hospitalization costs. When the proposal hit Congress in legislative form, it became known as the Forand bill, in recognition of its leading congressional sponsor, New Jersey representative Aime Forand (D). The ensuing congressional hearings on the bill were heated, as the measure would constitute a significant expansion of the American welfare state. Many liberal organizations and individuals testified in support of the legislation, but few drew as much attention as the representatives of the nation's big unions, which lobbied furiously on behalf of the bill. One of the labor leaders who appeared on Capitol Hill was Walter Reuther, head of the powerful United Auto Workers. His July 16, 1959, statement to the House Ways and Means Committee on the need for a program of aid for the aged is excerpted here.

. . . As stated in the [1959] HEW [Health, Education and Welfare] report, three-fifths of all Americans sixty-five and over are receiving cash income from all possible sources of a thousand dollars a year or less and fourth-fifths are receiving less than two thousand dollars. When three out of five older Americans have no greater income than one thousand dollars a year, it does not take a mass of statistics and it does not take a means test to demonstrate that we are dealing with a group in great need.

The basic problem is that this period of life is one in which people face a tremendous increase in their need for health care and at the same time a radical drop in income. This glaring discrepancy between needs and resources has become so great that we commonly accept the notion that a large group of our older people, accustomed to supporting themselves, become indigents immediately upon facing any substantial medical expense. . . .

Even so crucial a form of health care as admission to hospitals is also related to the means possessed by patients. The access of older people to the hospital is strongly influenced by whether or not they have hospitalization insurance. Those with insurance go to the hospital more often, are cared for earlier, and stay for shorter periods than the uninsured. The OASI study for 1957 shows, for example, that for every one hundred with insurance fourteen were hospitalized; among the uninsured fewer than nine were hospitalized. . . .

The fact that the number of older people still uncovered is substantially higher than those covered is hardly surprising. The enthusiasm of insurance companies for covering the aged is of very recent origin. Not before legislation of this type began to be seriously considered was there any significant effort on the part of insurance companies to make available to people of advanced years their individual accident and health policies. As late as 1957, a tally of insurance companies, showing the highest age at which they could issue individual policies, revealed that 90 per cent ordinarily do not sell insurance to persons past a stated age. A few have set the maximums at very high ages, but almost half still will not write such policies for applicants over sixty-five and some of them adhere to limits of fifty-five and sixty. While I know there has been some progress I question whether very many major carriers have unfrozen those age limits for most of their policies.

Within the age-limit provisions, moreover, coverage was effectively denied for people who were in need of protection by the requirement of insurability whereby the individual had to undergo a medical examination to establish his good health and testify to his previous good health by giving a medical history. If, perchance, he successfully ran this gantlet [sic], he became insured. And if he subsequently became ill and needed his insurance, he could be weeded out as a bad risk by refusal of the company to renew, or by outright cancellation.

As for group insurance, before acquiring their new-found zeal for covering the aged, the insurance companies were discouraging employers from providing health insurance for older people and often, in many situations, refusing outright to provide such coverage. The rate manual of one of the most prominent insurance companies stated: "In general, hospital, surgical, medical, diagnostic, and other special features may not be continued for retired or pensioned employees or their dependents." . . .

In [1953], our union began a concerted drive to get carriers and employers to agree to voluntary insurance for our retirees. The automobile companies agreed to open enrollment for retirees, but refused to bear any part of the cost, thus making it necessary for the retired workers, themselves, to pay the full cost of protection out of their pensions. A checkoff for this purpose was agreed to.

Blue Cross and Blue Shield plans, after some initial resistance, generally agreed to provide this coverage, although the rules were made very strict. The retired workers were offered a single lifetime opportunity to become enrolled. An employee who was not covered by Blue Cross and Blue Shield at the time of his retirement was unable to obtain group coverage. A retired worker who, for any reason, missed a month's or quarter's premium was permanently removed from coverage. If for any reason the employed group ceased to be enrolled by Blue Cross and Blue Shield, the retirees were stranded. Several groups have lost coverage when plants closed. Others have been continued under precarious arrangements at the sufferance of Blue Cross with the chance that they may be discontinued. And if this sounds restrictive, the Blue Cross and Blue Shield have been the more cooperative among carriers. The experience with commercial insurance has been far worse.

About four out of five UAW retirees have tried to hang on to their hospital-medical coverage. To do so, however, the average retiree has to spend about $6 a month if he is single, and about $15.50 a month if he is married. On the average, this means that elderly couples have to spend about one-fourth of their negotiated pensions for health inurance. For some, the amount spent for health insurance is more than half of the pension.

When retirees, living under limited income, have to allocate this kind of money for health insurance, it hurts. . . .

The cost of hospitalization leads all items on the Consumer Price Index. The cost of drugs and medicines has been going up and often reaches unmanageable levels for older people. The phenomenal inflation which has taken place in the cost of hospital and medical care over the past few years has hit the retired worker especially hard. A dramatic example of how inflation has eaten into retired worker income occurred just these past few months. In September of last year our union, after hard-fought negotiations, was able to secure an increase in pension benefits for UAW retirees. On January 1, 1959, there was a rate increase in Michigan Blue Cross-Blue Shield which at one stroke completely wiped out the entire average pension increase.

As you have seen from the parade of witnesses from organized medicine, a great many of the medical societies are fighting [the Forand] bill.

It is a regrettable truth that the American Medical Association resisted the early development of the voluntary health insurance system which they now claim they are defending. Organized medicine has spent millions of dollars to confuse the American people with such slogans as "socialized medicine." Over a 3 ½-year period, through Whittaker & Baxter, a highly paid public relations firm, they spent $4,678,000, pumping to the public millions of pieces of spurious propaganda about "socialized medicine," a term which, according to the current issue of *Harper's* magazine, Whittaker & Baxter have themselves "conversationally abandoned."

Only recently, the AMA opposed disability benefits under Social Security, a feature that was earlier incorporated into the social security system of practically every civilized country in the world.

We did not adopt disability benefits until 1956, and then only after the program had been delayed and resisted for years, and after the insurance companies and doctors had so long threatened the Congress with almost every kind of danger, that the late Senator [Walter F.] George rose in indignation and made an impassioned plea to the Congress to support the measure.

What is the AMA now proposing? The AMA is exhorting state and county medical societies to extend Blue Shield coverage to older people and to establish cut-rate fees for their care. The March 14, 1959, *Journal of the American Medical Association,* describing this program, claimed that: "Such arrangements would make it possible to provide the coverage at low rates and constitute a program that persons living on retirement income could easily afford."

If the doctors of America really were living up to their principle of charging according to ability to pay, the present campaign for reduced fees would be entirely unnecessary. . . .

The AMA proposal to cut fees for the aged is indeed quixotic. Even if its members should accept this proposal, which apparently is not entirely certain, and agree to provide service benefits at reasonable cost for the aged people, it would do nothing to assure them hospitalization—a cost that will not be reduced by any medical fiat, or by some sleight of hand. How will the aged meet the cost of hospital care and nursing home care, and how will they meet the substantial cost of programs even after fee reduction without employer contributions to help pay for the cost?

The political doctors of the AMA have come up with an unworkable scheme. I would seriously urge the doctors of America to consider on its merits the Forand proposal, which would relieve the older patients of financial stress in obtaining hospital care, nursing home care, and surgical care. No fee cutting will replace the necessity for a decent insurance program—it just won't work.

In their testimony on the Social Security Amendments of 1955, the National Association of Life Underwriters asserted that all this is socialistic. They said:

> It would seem that many of our lawmakers in Washington have dedicated themselves to the implementation of this socialistic philosophy and are determined to forge the OASI program into a compulsory system of cradle-to-grave benefits, so comprehensive and costly that the citizens of this country will find it both unnecessary and financially

impossible to fend for themselves. If it happened in France, let us in the life insurance business not delude ourselves into believing that it cannot happen here.

It is high time that the organized medical profession and the insurance companies and a few of the businessmen's organizations of this country stop ganging up on the country's vulnerable older citizens.

Apart from an entirely unfounded optimism that they will somehow catch up with this problem, what have the insurance companies offered as solutions of their own? To meet the threat of federal legislation, some insurance companies have agreed to recommend the discontinuance of such practices as cancellations and failures to renew insurance for older people.

This outburst of social responsibility, even under pressure, to stop shabby practices that should have been illegal years ago is welcome but what does the industry offer by way of constructive solution? A few companies have been spending a small fortune to advertise prominently a type of individual accident and health insurance designed for the older people of the country—the so-called sixty-five-plus contracts.

The few liberalizations in these policies expose the indefensibility of previous practices of these same insurance companies. At that, they were unable to part with some of their customary tricks and even under these new policies, the status of people with pre-existing conditions is compromised by a six-month period of denial for any illness or condition for which the policyholder received treatment or had been advised to receive treatment before the policy began.

Accordingly, the benefits are appallingly inadequate. Hospitalization benefits in one such policy, for example, are limited to ten dollars a day when room rates often run about twice as much. This policy provides a maximum of thirty-one days, although one-third the bed-days occur for people over sixty-five after the thirty-first day of hospitalization. The one hundred dollar maximum for other hospital expenses is obviously insufficient at a time when the therapeutic charges, which would be covered without cash limits under the Forand bill, are almost as expensive as room and board. The surgical benefits are mere indemnities and offer no assurance of their acceptance as full payment by physicians.

Moreover, the monthly premium of $6.50 per person—$13 for an elderly couple—are attractive only in comparison with the previous offerings of insurance companies. I question whether, without employer contributions to help defray the cost, many of the aged people of our country will be able to enroll for these expensive but still inadequate benefits. . . .

While the insurance companies have made a few gestures toward older people, their practice of experience rating has done more harm than any other single factor in keeping satisfactory health insurance out of their reach. Instead of trying to spread the cost of high risk groups over as large a portion of the population as possible, insurance companies have stressed a sales approach of paying dividends to so-called more favorable groups. Thus groups are discouraged from meeting their responsibilities toward older people and induced to cut their protection or to exclude them.

Broad risk sharing is an essential part of any serious proposal to deal with the aged. Experience rating is directly opposed to this necessary risk sharing. The direction of voluntary health insurance has been toward, rather than away from, experience rating. Under the pressure of competition from commercial insurance companies, even Blue Cross and Blue Shield plans, which earlier embraced community rating and broad risk sharing, have been increasingly moving toward experience rating.

The Forand bill does not even attempt to meet all of the health needs of those Social Security beneficiaries it proposes to cover—the aged, widows, fatherless children, and dependent parents of the insured population. A strong case should be made that this bill should go much further into the range of care provided and the duration of its benefits.

But in spite of these limitations, I wholeheartedly endorse Representative Forand's bill and I strongly urge its passage. It would put a stop to the neglect of a segment of our population too long ignored. The provision of fully paid hospital care for up to sixty days is probably the most important segment of all health care and it would be extended to people now largely without such protection. The nursing home benefits provided in conjunction with hospital care would greatly raise the standard of treatment. Surgical services would provide a valuable form of protection against some of the more serious medical hazards. Obviously, the Forand bill will not solve all of the problems that I have enumerated which now face its potential beneficiaries. No initial piece of legislation of this type was ever perfect at its inception. The Forand bill will establish an advisory council that could study the operation of the measure and its ultimate effects on health care.

We recognize that the new benefits will cost money, and we stand ready to meet the cost. Under the Forand bill, Social Security taxes would be increased by a quarter of 1 per cent of taxable payrolls, both for employees and employers.

The estimates made of the cost of the Forand bill appeared to be competently derived on the basis of the best available evidence—I accept these estimates and believe that they serve as a valid basis for legislation. The Social Security system as it now stands is sound. The chronic accusations against its solvency are phony. The additional benefits which would be provided under the Forand bill would be fully supported by increased contributions.

The Forand bill is a well considered, carefully thought out, practical proposal. It is essentially sound and we stand ready to join with other constructive forces in America to support this legislation. The time is now long past when there was any real doubt as to what has to be done. We have to act now.

Source: Reuther, Walter. "Medical Care for the Aged." Statement to the House Committee on Ways and Means, July 16, 1959. In *Walter P. Reuther: Selected Papers,* edited by Henry M. Christman. New York: Macmillan, 1961, pp. 283–84, 288–98.

DOCUMENT
6.12   Congress Passes the Kerr-Mills Act

"The Selection of the Elderly Social Security Beneficiaries Was Purely a Political Idea"

1960

As the 1960 election season progressed, it became clear in Washington, D.C., that the defeat of the Forand bill early in the year had failed to derail the liberal crusade for a government program of health insurance for elderly Americans. To the contrary, the highly publicized public debate over the legislation had engaged senior citizens in a way that previous debates over federal health care had failed to do. "The old folks lined up by the dozens everyplace we went," recalled one Senate staffer at the time. "And they didn't talk much about housing or recreational centers or part-time work. They talked about medical care."[1]

As the political pressure to act rose, Rep. Wilbur Mills (D-AR), the powerful chair of the House Ways and Means Committee, and Sen. Robert Kerr, a conservative Democrat from Oklahoma, became the lead sponsors of a grant-in-aid bill that they hoped would mollify older voters, reduce support for future Forand-type bills (or even more ambitious ones), and meet with the approval of Southern Democrats who were leery of potential federal interference with the racially segregated health care systems that were in place back home. The Kerr-Mills Act garnered support from Southern Democrats, but it was an utter failure in the other two respects. Conservatives who accepted the necessity of Kerr-Mills to forestall more radical health care schemes did not realize that the measure established the principle, widely held for the next half-century, that the federal government was obliged to secure medical care for senior citizens. The Kerr-Mills Act, which was enacted on September 13, 1960, as part of the Social Security Amendments of 1960, is today recognized as a forerunner of Medicaid.

The following interview is with Robert M. Ball, who served as commissioner of the Social Security Administration from 1962 to 1973 under three presidents. In this excerpt, Ball, who was an important player in the creation of both Medicaid and Medicare, gives his assessment of the political forces that led to the development and passage of the Kerr-Mills Act.

Ball: . . . Roosevelt himself never specifically endorsed any plan of national health insurance. Although he did generalize in ways that would have included national health insurance, like the Four Freedoms, which you would think would require government to act with a health insurance system. But these are broad and quite vague. He also claimed credit for the phrase, "insurance from the cradle to the grave," which would involve the major risk of health. But he never specifically had any bill that he supported in health insurance. Harry Truman was the first President to do that.

But all the time during the Roosevelt New Deal era, the Social Security Board felt completely free to advocate national health insurance. Roosevelt didn't disapprove of it, he just didn't put his own reputation on the line to get it. But the Board was very active in promoting it. I. S. Falk, whose was head of research for the Social Security Board, was in that job primarily because he was an expert in health insurance. And the Board had conferences and other ways of promoting health insurance that drew a lot of Congressional opposition, and opposition from the AMA of course, and it was a very controversial thing that the Board pushed. But the first time the Board was successful in getting Presidential backing for national health insurance was from Truman. When Truman was elected in his own right—you remember, he was just barely elected, and nobody had expected him to get re-elected except Truman himself—and Truman had very little influence with the Congress, but he was for it. But that didn't get you very far.

The only people who were really scared by Truman's backing of national health insurance was the AMA. They took it seriously. They put on a tremendous campaign to prevent something that was not going happen anyhow. We, within the Social Security Administration, started—almost as soon as Truman had made the recommendation—we started to back off of that in our own thinking and started saying, "Well, this isn't going to actually pass. What can we do that would have a chance? What kind of a first step within a national health insurance plan could we devise?" That's when the notion of health insurance for Social Security beneficiaries came up. We had, we thought, a built-in defined group of people who the public might see as uniquely needing government health insurance as against buying private insurance because they were already identified as old or widowed or orphans. So, we started to pursue that and that was quite early. That would have been still in the Truman Administration, toward the end of it. The Federal Security Administrator, who was anxious to be thought out for a Vice Presidential candidacy on the Democratic ticket the next time, took that on as his "attention getting" proposal.

Interviewer: Are you talking about Paul McNutt?

Ball: Not Paul McNutt. Oscar Ewing. Both Paul McNutt and Oscar Ewing were in this position, but at different times. It was Ewing who took on what later became called Medicare.

Interviewer: OK.

Ball: And [Arthur] Altmeyer was involved with him around this issue. The Bureau of Old Age and Survivor's Insurance, as distinct from the Commissioner's office itself, started to get involved in this issue too. The Commissioner's Office, and Research in the Commissioner's office with Falk, had been doing stuff on health insurance for a long time. But the Bureau of Old Age and Survivor's Insurance started to get involved when it became a question of a limited program of insurance for Social Security beneficiaries. In other words, Old Age and Survivor's Insurance beneficiaries. At one time I actually located a very early memorandum, I forget who even signed it now, but out of the Bureau, recommending this kind of a program. I was involved in that. But the Bureau didn't particularly take stands like that as a Bureau, but some of us who were working in the Bureau, as individuals, would also be involved in things like this.

Now that never got anywhere until the 1950s really. Then it gets picked up by Labor as the practical first step. It is, in some ways, a very peculiar thing that a country would undertake to cover first in a health insurance plan the most difficult group, that would be the most expensive, and for whom, in a very practical sense, you get the least for your money because they are not going to live very long, relatively. The place to put a limited amount of money in health insurance, from a rational standpoint, would be kids. So the selection of the elderly Social Security beneficiaries was purely a political idea. Because we thought that it could easily be made clear that private insurance couldn't cover the elderly because they had low incomes and yet they used—I forget now whether it was two-and-half or three times as much hospitalization—as the average among younger people. The way private insurance finances a program, is on a yearly, pay-as-you-go basis. So that people who are at risk are charged premiums related to that risk as they go along. So that there would be very high premiums for the elderly because they use so much hospitalization, and yet they had incomes about half of what other people had. So, as the group, you could make a very good case that they would not be taken care of by private insurance.

Interviewer: And, in fact, they weren't being taken care of.

Ball: Right, right.

Interviewer: They would have unmet social needs.

Ball: Right. And the plans that they were under, to the extent that they were under anything, were very limited—like ten days in the hospital, or something like that. Also, the elderly could be a good strong voting block and personally be in favor of it. So it was pushed pretty much on those grounds. And it went on for a long time. It was, I'd say, roughly ten years from the time we got serious about a Medicare program until it actually passed in 1965. And it had different degrees of intensity from time to time.

By the early '60s, it was a major push by the Democrats and by Labor. And the main obstacles were Wilbur Mills in the House, and Kerr in the Senate. It wasn't really a Democratic position. It was a *liberal* Democratic position. Mills was very concerned about what this might open up, and so was Kerr. That's the origin of the Kerr-Mills Bill, which was a precursor of Medicaid, and which was really designed to head-off a universal Medicare-type plan and substitute just a means-tested basic program.

Interviewer: You knew Mills very well, and had a lot of dealings with him over the years. Why was it that he resisted health insurance? Was it what you just said, that he was concerned about the financial cost? Or were there more dimensions to it than that?

Ball: Well, I presume it had more dimensions. Mills was a conservative, not just in social policy, but he was a cautious man. He did not want to be the sponsor of anything that would not pass the Congress. He would not have been in favor of a Medicare program until he thought it was feasible to get the Congress to vote for it. I think it was both conviction, that it was a risky thing to start down that road from a financial standpoint, and a feeling that he couldn't get the votes for it in those early days anyhow. But later on, he just became a plan barrier to it, even though with his support I think it could have gotten passed three or four years before it did.

In the Senate, it was equally touch and go. Kerr was the most influential person on the Senate Finance Committee, even when he wasn't the Chairman. Byrd was the Chairman. Old Senator Byrd was very much against the program, and Kerr was against the program. Kerr worked very closely with the doctors in Oklahoma, who were against it. Wilbur Cohen helped them set up the Kerr-Mills Bill, which was designed to prevent Medicare. Wilbur, of course, was really for Medicare. That got Wilbur into a lot of fuss with his usual allies in labor and liberal groups. They thought he was betraying the Medicare program. But I agreed with Wilbur. What history shows us, if you have a category of programs on a means-tested basis, it really helps you get social insurance later on, rather than be a final solution that people point to and say, "Well, you don't need social insurance because we already have a means tested program." It doesn't work that way. People are not satisfied with a means-tested program and they will want to reduce the assistance cost by social insurance. . . .

Source: Ball, Robert M. Interview with Larry DeWitt, April 3, 2001. "Oral History Collection—Robert M. Ball Interview #3." Social Security Online. www.ssa.gov/history/orals/ball3.html.

NOTE

1. Quoted in Paul Starr, *The Social Transformation of American Medicine* (New York: Basic Books, 1982), 368.

CHAPTER 7

Medicare Changes
the Health Care Landscape

1960–1980

Liberal political power reached its zenith in the early and mid-1960s, ushering in a host of Great Society social welfare programs. In the realm of health care, the most transformative expansions of state power during this period were Medicare and Medicaid, both of which arrived in 1965 as amendments to the Social Security Act. These sweeping entitlement programs extended access to basic health care services to millions of Americans, and they also greatly expanded federal spending on and involvement in medicine and health care. Moreover, the programs, ambitious as they were, still left millions of Americans uncovered. During the 1970s both conservatives and liberals pushed legislative measures to rein in soaring medical costs, streamline the health care system, and further extend coverage. But neither Republicans nor Democrats could muster the necessary political leverage to pass their respective prescriptions for change.

THE ADVENT OF A DEMOCRATIC DECADE

The mood of the American electorate was anxious and restless at the close of the 1950s. Bedeviled by Cold War fears and recurring recessions, American voters responded positively to Democratic candidate John F. Kennedy's promises during the 1960 presidential campaign to reinvigorate the nation. Kennedy's subsequent victory over Republican candidate Richard M. Nixon in November still came by the narrowest of margins, but it was enough to give Democrats control of the White House. They also retained the majority in both houses of Congress.

One of the Kennedy administration's top priorities upon setting up shop in Washington, D.C., was to address rising public unhappiness with health care costs and access. The White House was convinced that tackling the nation's vexing health care problems was vitally important to the new president's political future, for as a 1961 Brookings Institution study observed, Americans were "living in a veritable 'revolution of rising expectations' in regard to health and medical care."[1] Yet the Kennedy White House knew that passing health care legislation of any consequence would be daunting, given the political alliance that had evolved during the 1950s and 1960s between Southern white Democrats who feared federal dismantlement of their segregated institutions and culture (and who by virtue of seniority held important committee chairmanships) and Republicans who viewed "big government" programs as anathema to American individualism and free

356

market capitalism. Their collaboration made the Democrats' huge numerical advantages in Congress (63–37 in the Senate and 263–174 in the House) something of a mirage.

Nevertheless, the Kennedy administration, working with liberal Democrats and moderate Republicans in Congress, rolled out two ambitious proposals to reform major sectors of American medicine. The first proposal concerned an overhaul of the nation's mental health and mental retardation care and treatment policies, which had long been neglected by both parties. The second campaign was an all-out effort to secure a federal program of medical insurance—Medicare—for America's senior citizens.

A Revolution in Mental Retardation Policy

Kennedy's interest in mental health and mental retardation issues had an intensely personal aspect. His younger sister Rosemary had been born with intellectual disabilities, and in 1946 his famous parents, Joseph and Rose Kennedy, had established the Joseph P. Kennedy Jr. Foundation to carry out mental retardation research and advocacy for those suffering from intellectual disabilities. In 1957 his sister Eunice Kennedy Shriver became director of the foundation, where she became one of the nation's most prominent advocates for families dealing with mental retardation. She was one of a growing chorus of critics who described state and federal outlays for mental health and mental retardation services as shamefully inadequate. Disability advocates and medical professionals also issued calls for fundamental reform of state mental hospitals, which were crowded with patients who, they insisted, could be better served through nursing homes, local community psychiatry services, and prescriptions for tranquilizers such as Thorazine.

Kennedy signaled his intention to shine a light on mental health and mental retardation issues even before entering the White House. As president-elect, he established a task force to study developmental disabilities issues so that he could hit the ground running when he was inaugurated. The task force, which was chaired by Robert E. Cooke, the Kennedy family's pediatrician, returned in 1961 with a call for much greater investments into child development and developmental disability research. One year later, Congress

In the early 1960s, the McGrath sisters were poster girls for President John F. Kennedy's push for funds for retarded children. Kennedy had a personal connection to this issue because his sister Rosemary suffered from intellectual disabilities. Standing behind the children, from left to right, are Eunice Kennedy Shriver (another Kennedy sister), the McGrath sisters' mother, President's Panel on Mental Retardation chairman Dr. Leonard W. Mayo, and the president himself.

approved the creation of a National Institute of Child Health and Human Development within the National Institutes of Health to coordinate private and public research on mental retardation and maternal and child health.

In October 1961 Kennedy announced that he was appointing a presidential panel of distinguished scientists, physicians, and advocates "to prescribe a plan of action in the field of mental retardation." One year later the President's Panel on Mental Retardation, which was chaired by longtime advocate Leonard W. Mayo, returned with a report that emphasized the importance of increased investment in scientific and biomedical research, new programs for maternity and prenatal care, and a more community-oriented approach to the treatment and care of people with mental illness and mental retardation, with the ultimate goal of more fully integrating them into society (See Document 7.4). On February 5, 1963, Kennedy used the panel's report as the blueprint for a Special Message to Congress on Mental Illness and Mental Retardation.

Kennedy's call to action was answered by Congress, which passed two major pieces of legislation before the year was out. On October 24, 1963, Kennedy signed the Maternal and Child Health and Mental Retardation Planning Amendment to the Social Security Act, the nation's first major legislation specifically crafted to combat mental illness and retardation. One week later, the Mental Retardation Services and Facilities Construction Act was signed into law. This legislation provided major federal funding for the construction of university-based developmental disability research, treatment, and diagnostic centers that eventually became the foundation of a new, community-based service system.

SURVEYING THE HEALTH CARE LANDSCAPE

Kennedy's other major health care push was to establish a health insurance program for the elderly known as Medicare (a hybrid of "medical" and "care" coined by reformers in the 1950s). Upon taking up residence in the White House in early 1961, Kennedy acknowledged that voluntary insurance had made significant strides in meeting the health care expenses of the American people over the previous quarter-century. About three-fourths of the population were now covered by some form of hospitalization health insurance, and most of those insured were covered for surgery costs as well. Half of the population benefited from some kind of additional medical service benefit, including about forty-three million Americans who were insured for loss of income because of injury or illness.[2]

But even though by 1960 "health insecurity" had become "the exception rather than the rule," in the words of historian Alan Derickson, the Kennedy administration also recognized that the voluntarist approach to health insurance was almost entirely predicated on employment-based policies.[3] This state of affairs left the unemployed and the disabled and their dependents without coverage. It also excluded millions of retirees. As late as 1957 only four out of ten seniors had health insurance.

This situation improved somewhat in the late 1950s, when collective bargaining agreements increasingly provided for continuation of health insurance benefits to workers after they retired. In addition, commercial insurers frantically signed up seniors during those years in an effort to blunt support for the Forand bill and other proposed expansions of government regulation of health insurance. In 1957, for example, Continental Casualty created the first hospital insurance program for the aged, and one year later Prudential Insurance negotiated a group policy with the fledgling American Association of Retired Persons (AARP).[4] Many of the senior policies that came into existence during this period, however, were pocked with high copayments, coverage exclusions, and other loopholes that limited the insurers' liability. In 1961, health insurance policies were covering only about 7 percent of the total medical expenses of America's elderly population.[5]

This paltry figure stemmed to a great degree on the fact that the health care policies being crafted by the nation's nearly eight hundred commercial insurers and various Blue Cross/Blue Shield plans were failing to keep pace with soaring health costs. The price of hospital care had roughly doubled during the 1950s, fueled by increased reliance on complex surgical procedures, high-tech diagnostic tests, the involvement of a wide array of skilled medical personnel in patient care, and the transformation of many hospitals into centers of medical research. As the American Hospital Association noted in 1962, "A patient-day of care today is not the same as it was in 1946."[6] In many hospitals, less than half of the facility space was devoted to the treatment and care of hospitalized patients. "The rest," wrote rehabilitative medicine pioneer Howard A. Rusk, "is for all the modern technological equipment science needs on the firing line of therapy—the scientific ammunition which requires an army of workers categorized by 200 different job descriptions."[7]

Other factors were feeding escalating health care costs as well. New waves of wonder drugs that combated disease, reduced pain, and otherwise benefited patients were appearing each year. Although many of these new drugs were a godsend to suffering patients and their families, insurance policies generally did not cover prescription costs, which were extremely high in many cases. In addition, the rising expense of malpractice insurance for individual surgeons, hospital facilities, group practices, and other health care providers was frequently passed on to patients.

KENNEDY'S CAMPAIGN FOR MEDICARE

The Kennedy administration and its allies concluded, just as reformers of the 1950s had done, that the most strategically sound way to expand health care coverage was to focus on uncovered senior citizens. They knew that such a stance would be popular with the American public, which generally granted that needy seniors—whose ailments were typically a product of aging and whose earning power was greatly reduced—were deserving of assistance.

In addition, the administration recognized that the early returns on the 1960 Kerr-Mills Act had been disappointing. This compromise measure, which provided federal matching funds to states to help them cover the medical expenses of needy residents, had been strongly supported by a Congress that was not yet ready to approve more robust federal intervention in the health care industry. But some observers had predicted from the outset that the program was doomed to fail. "The blunt truth," declared Sen. Pat McNamara (D-MI), "is that it would be the miracle of the century if all the states—or even a sizable number—would be in a position to provide the matching funds to make the program more than just a plan on paper."[8] This prognostication proved accurate. Hamstrung by budgetary constraints in poor states and ideological opposition in more conservative states (which were also in many cases among the poorer states), Kerr-Mills failed in all but a handful of northern industrial states to make an appreciable impact on the problem of uninsured seniors.

After taking stock of the political terrain, Kennedy and key health strategists in his administration such as Wilbur Cohen decided to seize full advantage of the rising public sentiment for a Medicare program. Less than a month after his inauguration, on February 10, 1961, Kennedy delivered a special health message to Congress specifically calling for a federal health program for senior citizens. Three days later, Sen. Clinton Anderson (D-NM) and Rep. Cecil King (D-CA) introduced a Medicare health insurance bill in Congress. This bill sought to expand Social Security so that Old Age Security Income (OASI) beneficiaries would receive coverage of hospital and nursing home costs. King-Anderson, as the bill came to be known, would be financed by a small increase in Social Security taxes.

The architects of King-Anderson excluded physicians' fees from coverage in the hope that the sacrifice would mollify the American Medical Association (AMA), or at least keep the organization from mounting a full-scale assault on the legislation. But this proved to be an unrealistic goal, given the AMA's antipathy for any expansion of federal involvement in health care financing issues. The AMA responded to the introduction of King-Anderson with characteristic fierceness. It roused conservative lawmakers and newspaper editors to denounce the bill, sent legions of anti-Medicare lobbyists to Capitol Hill, and rolled out public relations campaigns such as Operation Coffee Cup, featuring Hollywood star and politician-in-waiting Ronald Reagan, to counter Kennedy's push for Medicare **(See Document 7.1)**.

Medicare proponents fought back in a variety of ways. Some advocates trumpeted government reports and academic studies that quantified the severe financial stress that still afflicted millions of elderly Americans struggling with health problems. Other supporters challenged the merits of the objections raised by conservative critics. They took issue with "Medicare equals socialism" rhetoric and ridiculed the notion that Kerr-Mills obviated the need for a more extensive Medicare program **(See Document 7.3)**. But their efforts failed to sway conservatives such as House Ways and Means chairman Wilbur Mills (D-AR), who opposed King-Anderson as a quixotic piece of legislation given the political paralysis on Capitol Hill. The measure subsequently died in committee without ever coming to a full House vote.

Undaunted, Kennedy continued to champion the idea of expanding Social Security to include a Medicare program, and King-Anderson was resurrected in 1962. The most spectacular manifestation of the administration's dogged approach came on May 20, 1962, when Kennedy delivered a health care speech to more than twenty thousand senior citizens at Madison Square Garden in New York City **(See Document 7.2)**. The impact of the carefully choreographed event was blunted by Kennedy's curious decision to discard a prepared speech and speak extemporaneously on the issue. The result, admitted Nelson Cruikshank of the AFL-CIO (American Federation of Labor and Congress of Industrial Organizations), was "probably . . . the poorest speech he ever made."[9] A few hours later, AMA representative (and future AMA president) Edward R. Annis used the empty, litter-strewn hall as the backdrop for a strong and effective rebuttal that was recorded by AMA and broadcast to millions of NBC viewers the following evening. According to Annis, the Kennedy-supported King-Anderson bill would "put the government smack into your hospitals, defining services, setting standards, establishing committees, calling for reports, deciding who gets in and who gets out, what they get and what they don't, even getting into the teaching of medicine and all the time imposing a federally administered financial budget on our houses of mercy and healing."[10]

Two months later, King-Anderson went down to defeat for a second time. With the bill once again bottled up in the House by obstructionists on the Ways and Means Committee, Medicare supporters hoped that Senate passage of the bill would generate sufficient political pressure for Mills to get behind the legislation. But despite public support from organizations ranging from the National Council of Churches to the American

Public Health Association, King-Anderson fell in the Senate by a 52–48 tally. This result was widely attributed to election-year politics. "At the beginning of the year," noted historian Peter A. Corning, "Senate passage had seemed assured; some observers estimated as many as 60 votes for the bill. But some potential Republican votes had been lost because the bill was brought to a vote in an election year and was thereby tinged with partisanship. . . . Others were reportedly dissuaded because the bill stood virtually no chance in the House. A Senate vote for the bill would merely have antagonized the medical profession back home without leading to enactment of Medicare."[11]

This vote constituted a bitter loss for Kennedy, who later that evening rebuked the AMA for its opposition to Medicare in a nationally televised address. He also described the vote as "a most serious defeat for every American family, for the 17 million Americans who are over 65, whose means of support, whose livelihood is certainly lessened over what it was in their working days, who are more inclined to be ill, who will more likely be in hospitals, who are less able to pay their bills."[12] Three years later, Kennedy adviser and friend Theodore C. Sorensen wrote that Kennedy ranked the 1962 Medicare vote as the "most discouraging" of all his political setbacks in the White House. According to Sorensen, Kennedy "never got over the disappointment of this defeat."[13]

1964 ELECTION RESULTS SEEN AS MANDATE

The political deadlock over Medicare remained unchanged in 1963, despite attempts by progressive strategists in Congress and the Kennedy administration to craft a version of King-Anderson that would be more palatable to the AMA, fiscal conservatives, and the health care and insurance industries. With each passing month, though, the impasse seemed more likely to eventually break in the favor of the pro-Medicare crowd. For one thing, the inadequacies of the three-year-old Kerr-Mills Act were becoming apparent to all but its most ardent defenders. By 1963, five heavily populated northern states were accounting for 90 percent of all the federal funds distributed through Kerr-Mills, while eighteen states remained without any kind of Kerr-Mills program at all.[14] Meanwhile, the National Council for Senior Citizens (NCSC) and other pro-Medicare organizations maintained steady political pressure with a combination of lobbying and grassroots efforts. As NCSC official William Hutton later said, "The AMA had all the money, and we had all the old people. . . . My job was to switch them from the bingo circuit to social action."[15] Week after week, wrote scholar Edward D. Berkowitz, this coalition of activists joined with liberal policymakers in "reassuring Congress and its constituents that Medicare was not 'socialized medicine,' something ugly and alien, but rather a desirable and straightforward extension of the trusted Social Security program."[16]

The most transformative event of 1963 was the assassination of Kennedy on November 22 in Dallas, Texas. His tragic death altered the political arc of the Medicare debate. When Kennedy's successor, Lyndon B. Johnson, vowed to carry out Kennedy's ambitious New Frontier agenda of socially progressive legislation, a stunned and mournful nation quickly signaled its support. Congress dutifully fell in line on several big pieces of legislation, including the 1964 Civil Rights Act. As Social Security Administration historian Larry DeWitt observed, "Lyndon Johnson got a good deal of political mileage out of sentimental appeals to pass legislation as a tribute to the slain President."[17] Moreover, this groundswell of support for civil rights and social insurance legislation was augmented by important court rulings such as *Simkins v. Moses H. Cone Memorial Hospital* (1962), which was a milestone in ending hospital segregation in the South **(See**

Document 7.5). These political advantages were put to maximum use by Johnson, who had always been a skilled legislative tactician and arm-twister.

In 1964 Johnson faced off in the presidential election against Republican nominee Barry Goldwater, a deeply conservative senator from Arizona. Armed with a prosperous economy that was widely credited to Democratic stewardship, Johnson's campaign barnstormed across the country with unmistakable confidence. At each and every stop the president assured enthusiastic crowds of supporters that he remained focused on fulfilling Kennedy's unrealized political goals, including a comprehensive Medicare program for elderly Americans. Goldwater, meanwhile, offered a clear philosophical alternative to Johnson's Great Society vision. Regarding Medicare proposals, for instance, the Arizona senator employed sarcasm to let voters know where he stood: "Having *given our pensioners their medical care in kind, why not food baskets, why not public housing accommodations, why not vacation resorts, why not a ration of cigarettes* for those who smoke and of beer for those who drink?"[18]

In the end, the Republicans' selection of Goldwater to oppose the formidable Johnson presidential campaign proved disastrous. Many Americans rejected Goldwater as a dangerous right-wing extremist (a view that was relentlessly nurtured by Democrats), and Johnson cruised to victory with 61 percent of the popular vote. The only states that ended up in Goldwater's column were his home state of Arizona and a half-dozen Deep South states, where white voters were angry and anxious about Johnson's pro–civil rights record. Even worse for the GOP, Johnson's long coattails in the November 1964 elections enabled the Democratic Party to attain an absolute stranglehold over both houses of Congress. Now that Johnson was armed with two-thirds majorities in the House of Representatives and the Senate, the administration and Republicans recognized that the next two years amounted to a gaping window of opportunity for Democrats to pass Medicare and other sweeping antipoverty and social welfare legislation that had long floated just out of reach **(See Document 7.7)**.

Passing Medicare and Medicaid

As soon as the Democrat-dominated Eighty-ninth Congress convened on January 4, 1965, congressional leaders moved to get the ball rolling on Medicare. Johnson had already instructed Wilbur Mills to enlarge the Ways and Means Committee by stocking it with Medicare supporters, and the first bills introduced in both houses of Congress for the session were Medicare measures. The first gauntlet in the House was Mills's Ways and Means Committee, where King-Anderson had time and again been dashed to pieces. This time, though, Mills was much more amenable to the legislation. Fully cognizant of the liberal tidal wave that had swept through American voting booths a few months earlier, Chairman Mills spoke as if passage of the bill was all but certain. This assessment was shared by Republicans, the insurance industry, and the AMA, all of whom recognized that Johnson was on a mission **(See Document 7.8)**. In a tacit admission that simple obstructionism to Medicare would no longer suffice, they hurriedly crafted alternative legislative proposals to give health care assistance to the elderly and the poor. The insurance industry's Bettercare proposal, which called for federal subsidies so that Social Security beneficiaries could purchase private policies, quickly garnered Republican support. The AMA's alternative, dubbed Eldercare, took a similar tack. It recommended a program of federal and state grants to subsidize senior citizens' purchase of private health insurance policies with broad benefits, including coverage of physicians' services, which Medicare did not cover.

Eldercare's physicians' services coverage caught the attention of Mills, who feared a growing disconnect between the public's expectations of Medicare and its actual coverage parameters. He subsequently incorporated the AMA idea of using government-subsidized private insurance to cover doctors' "customary" and "reasonable" fees into the Medicare legislation being debated in his committee **(See Document 7.9)**. This element became known as Medicare Part B, and the compulsory hospital insurance program long championed by the Democrats became Part A. Mills's inspired political move not only made Medicare a much more extensive program, but it also muffled some of the AMA and Republican criticism of the bill.

Medicare advocates in Congress and negotiators representing the Johnson administration (most notably Wilbur Cohen and Lawrence F. O'Brien) managed to neutralize another powerful interest group—hospitals—by shaping the legislation so that the administration of Medicare Part A would be managed by Blue Cross, which had close ties to the hospital industry, instead of the government itself. "The hospitals needed protection," recalled American Hospital Association executive Kenneth Williamson, who played an important role in developing this feature. "They needed somebody they trusted between themselves and the government."[19] Blue Cross Association president Walter J. McNerney agreed that this approach amounted to another political masterstroke. "It was a very good way of getting the cooperation of the American hospitals—giving them the right of some say over the intermediary."[20] Meanwhile, commercial insurers were somewhat mollified by assurances that Medicare would provide only limited coverage of key services such as hospitalization (coverage was limited to sixty days per admittance). These limitations guaranteed a continued market for private supplemental insurance, yet the protection had the salutary effect of easing demands that commercial insurers extend unprofitable health insurance policies to elderly people with serious medical conditions.[21]

The final major plank of the Medicare legislation that came out of Mills's committee was an enhanced Kerr-Mills program to cover the medical expenses of the poor, the indigent, and those with blindness and other permanent disabilities. This program—Medicaid—was also supported by the hospitals, which had for decades toiled under the burden of providing free charity care to impoverished patients. It extended health coverage to all welfare recipients, primarily single mothers and their dependent children, and placed the bulk of funding responsibility on the federal government, despite the fact that the states were appointed the program's primary administrators (albeit in accordance with national guidelines). "It was a remarkably ambitious reach," wrote health care scholar Jonathan Cohn, "made possible by one key political ingredient: stealth. Unlike Medicare, which had been crafted after literally many years of testimony, argument, and (eventually) negotiation among the many interested parties, Medicaid was slapped together in the final weeks of legislative haggling. And even then, Medicare itself was still attracting most of the attention, allowing Medicaid to escape the intense scrutiny of officials and interest groups that might have seen fit to tinker with it."[22]

In March the House version of Medicare was approved by Mills's Ways and Means Committee, and on April 8 it was passed by the full House. It then went to the Senate Finance Committee, where the AMA made a last-ditch, and unsuccessful, stand against Medicare in committee hearings. The bill only narrowly made it out of the Senate Finance Committee, but it easily passed a vote by the full Senate on July 9. The bill then went to reconciliation under the supervision of Mills. On July 28, 1965, Congress passed the reworked Medicare (Parts A and B) and Medicaid packages as two amendments to the Social Security Act by an overwhelming margin: 307–116 in

President Lyndon B. Johnson signs Medicare into law on July 30, 1965. Sitting to his left is former president Harry S. Truman, the first chief executive who attempted to create a national health insurance program.

the House and 70–24 in the Senate. Two days later, Johnson signed the bill in a triumphant ceremony held at the Harry S. Truman Library in Independence, Missouri **(See Document 7.10)**.

MIXED RESULTS BRING NEW CONTROVERSIES

The Democratic Party reaped significant political dividends from the passage of Medicare and Medicaid for the next several years. Millions of elderly Americans experienced dramatic improvements in their financial security, access to necessary medical services, and overall quality of life as a result of Medicare. In the meantime, Medicaid paved the way for a sharp increase in the use of medical services by poor Americans. According to one study, nonpoor Americans went to the doctor about 20 percent more frequently than the poor in 1964, the year before Medicaid became law. Eleven years later, the percentages had virtually reversed, with poor people visiting doctors 18 percent more often than nonpoor patients.[23] This trend was not due to Medicaid alone. The composition of the poverty population in America changed during this time, as a reduction in poverty among working families left a higher percentage of disabled and chronically ill Americans in the poorest sector of the population.[24] Still, the ability to have medical expenses paid through Medicaid was unquestionably the primary impetus for the surge in health care services provided to the poor.

The Democrats who had championed these new entitlement programs benefited from their passage, as senior citizens and poor Americans rewarded Democrats with their political allegiance. But it did not take long for public perceptions of the efficacy of the two programs to diverge—and for Democratic "ownership" of Medicaid in particular to become something of a double-edged sword. This parting in perceptions of Medicare and Medicaid stemmed to some degree from the fact that Medicare benefits went to senior citizens of all economic classes and races, including whites, who still constituted a significant majority of the overall population, whereas poor minorities accounted for a disproportionate share of Medicaid beneficiaries. It also was grounded in long-standing concerns that programs of public assistance to the needy such as Medicaid too often bred a culture of dependency among recipients. Not surprisingly, these complaints became more common during the late 1960s, a period of heightened racial tensions in America. Public perceptions of the two programs were also influenced by the attitudes of medical professionals whose views on health care policy were sought out in many communities.

Physicians quickly warmed up to Medicare, which allowed doctors and hospitals to ramp up fees for all manner of services. Medicaid had no such flexibility in its reimbursement provisions, and so participation among physicians was far more limited.[25]

Even as the reputations of the two programs began to diverge somewhat along socioeconomic lines, fiscal conservatives expressed mounting frustration with both programs, and for good reason: Almost immediately, the price tags for Medicare and Medicaid began spiraling far beyond the projections of their architects. Medicaid planners had originally estimated that the program would add less than $250 million to the total cost of the Social Security Amendments of 1965. But when that number was obliterated by the first dozen states that got their Medicaid programs up and running, Congress stepped in and tightened eligibility to qualified people below or near the poverty line. This action, however, did nothing to stop other health industry factors that continued to drive Medicaid's escalating costs. Because nursing home care was not covered under Medicare, for example, the Medicaid program became the primary payer of nursing home bills in the late 1960s and 1970s.

Medicare, meanwhile, had cost problems of its own. Its spiraling costs were partly due to continued advances in medical technology that ushered in an exciting but expensive new era of cancer and heart disease treatments, organ transplants, and joint replacements. Medicare's cost-plus reimbursement formula was an even bigger culprit. Under this payment system, hospitals received compensation for the costs claimed for providing individual services plus an additional fee that served as profit. As health care analyst Julie Rovner observed, the chief drawback of this system was that it "entice[d] providers to serve beneficiaries by paying hospitals, doctors, and other health care purveyors essentially whatever they charged. Between 1975 and 1994 Medicare spending per enrollee grew by an average of 17 percent per year."[26] The fee-for-service financing arrangements in both Medicare and Medicaid gave participating doctors and hospitals a clear incentive to pile on medical tests, office visits, and other billable services, all of which added to the inflationary spiral of medical care.

A HEALTH CARE SYSTEM IN TRANSITION

Even as the benefits and problems of Medicare and Medicaid began coming into focus, American health care was undergoing other massive, and at times bewildering, changes in structure and orientation. Some of these changes stemmed from the policy ripple effects of the Social Security Amendments of 1965, but many others were attributable to broader trends in American society.

One such trend was the emergence of the women's liberation movement, which brought reproductive rights to the forefront of national debate. Feminists denounced anti-abortion and anti–birth control laws across the country as violations of the Ninth Amendment. They contended that this amendment implied a right to privacy—and thus, to control over personal medical decisions—that the state was obligated to respect. Moreover, critics of abortion criminalization argued that state prohibitions and restrictions on abortion were evident failures. "It is estimated that between 200,000 and over a million illegal abortions are performed in this country each year, and at least 4 out of 5 of them on married women," claimed the National Organization for Women (NOW) in 1967. "Criminal abortion laws clearly have proven to be ineffectual in eliminating the use of abortion as a means of birth control, and have driven women to unskilled practitioners, handicapped doctors in practicing their profession, and have made a mockery of the law."[27] Several state legislatures responded to this pressure by relaxing or repealing anti-abortion and anti–birth control laws, but the main action took place in the courts. In 1965 the U.S. Supreme Court issued a 7–2 ruling in *Griswold v. Connecticut* legalizing the distribution and use of birth control materials by married couples (seven years later, the Court formally legalized the use of birth control by unmarried people in *Eisenstadt v. Baird*), and in 1973 the Supreme Court issued its famous and controversial *Roe v. Wade* decision, which legalized abortion across the United States **(See Document 7.14)**.

Another major factor in the changing complexion of U.S. health policy was the rise of the environmental movement. The emergence of environmentalism as a significant force in American politics resulted not only in the passage of laws to shield endangered species and wilderness areas, but also in the creation of sweeping laws and major regulatory agencies, including the Environmental Protection Agency (EPA) and Occupational Safety and Health Administration (OSHA), to protect the American public against dangerous pollutants **(See Document 7.13)**. Numerous pieces of landmark environmental legislation with significant public health components were passed with bipartisan support from the mid-1960s through 1980, including the Water Quality Act (1965), the National Environmental Policy Act (1969), the Clean Air Acts (1963, 1966, and 1970), the Federal Environmental Pesticide Control Act (1972), the Clean Water Act (1972), the Safe Drinking Water Act (1974), the Toxic Substances Control Act (1976), and the Comprehensive Environmental Response, Compensation, and Liability Act (CERCLA, 1980), better known as Superfund. All of these laws gave the federal government broad new powers to address threats to public health and the environment.

The activist orientation of the 1960s had a notable impact on other realms of medicine and public health, ranging from children's nutrition to cancer research and treatment. The federal government, for instance, launched its famous War on Cancer crusade of the 1970s only after Mary Lasker's Citizens' Committee for the Conquest of Cancer and other organizations exerted relentless political pressure on policymakers for increased funding for cancer research **(See Document 7.11)**. Similarly, the Rehabilitation Act of 1973, the forerunner of the 1990 Americans with Disabilities Act (1990), was passed in no small measure due to the vigorous lobbying and public relations efforts of disability activists **(See Document 7.15)**.

Finally, the liberal-dominated Congresses of the 1960s passed a host of other measures to expand and rationalize the country's health care delivery system. New investments were made in hospitals, medical research programs, and community health centers, and many of these allocations paid important and lasting dividends, such as the government's research into the health dangers of smoking **(See Document 7.6)**. Washington also supplemented Medicare and Medicaid with a host of other laws designed to address gaps in the fabric of U.S. health care. Persistent shortages of primary care physicians and dentists and other medical professionals in rural and inner-city areas, for example, convinced Congress to pass a veritable flotilla of laws, including the Health Professions Educational Assistance Act of 1963, the Health Training Improvement Act of 1970, the Comprehensive Health Manpower Training Act of 1971, the Health Service Corps Act of 1972, and the National Health Planning and Resource Development Act of 1973.

Despite the arrival of Medicare, Medicaid, and numerous other new health care programs, and despite the continued robust expansion of America's health care infrastructure, a consensus began to emerge across the political spectrum that the nation's health care system simply was not working as it should. Millions of non–senior citizens above the poverty line, that is, those in working-class families, remained unable to afford quality health insurance. Other Americans who did have health insurance shouldered higher premiums even as their benefits were reduced. Health care entitlement programs were eating up more of the U.S. Treasury with each passing year. Studies indicated that America remained a laggard in many key health indices when compared with countries in Europe. And many consumers of health care services increasingly came to feel as if they were navigating blindly through a bureaucratic maze composed of equal parts overzealous regulation and dehumanizing and greedy private enterprise. "Money aside," wrote analysts Barbara Ehrenreich and John Ehrenreich in 1970, "the consumer's major problem is finding his way about an increasingly impersonal, fragmented, irrationally arranged set of health services."[28] By the late 1960s and early 1970s, critics from both the left and the right were describing the U.S. health care system as broken and in need of massive rehabilitation (See Document 7.12). "The economic and moral problems of medicine displaced scientific progress at the center of public attention," summarized scholar Paul Starr. "The prevailing assumptions about the need to expand medical care were reversed: The need now was to curb its apparently insatiable appetite for resources. In a short time, American medicine seemed to pass from stubborn shortages to irrepressible excess, without ever having passed through happy sufficiency."[29]

NIXON'S PRESCRIPTION FOR AMERICA'S HEALTH CARE "CRISIS"

The pervasive feelings of dissatisfaction and frustration with American health care were recognized by President Richard M. Nixon, who assumed office on January 20, 1969. Within months of inauguration, Nixon and his administration were signaling the American public that they understood the need to act. "The nation is faced with a breakdown in the delivery of health care unless immediate concerted action is taken by government and the private sector," warned Department of Health, Education, and Welfare (HEW) secretary Robert Finch in an appearance before Congress.[30] Nixon echoed Finch at a July press conference, saying that "we face a massive crisis." He further stated that "unless action is taken within the next two or three years . . . we will have a breakdown in our medical system."[31] This assessment was embraced by congressional lawmakers of various ideological persuasions, and by 1970 further change clearly was in the air.

Nearly everyone in Washington acknowledged that pulling the plug on Medicare or Medicaid was not a realistic political option. The former program had from its very inception been immensely popular with seniors, who voted in higher numbers than any other age group. The latter program, though riddled with problems, still provided assistance to millions of impoverished Americans who would otherwise be financially defenseless against sickness and injury. As a result, reformers focused on placing constraints on the physicians, hospitals, and insurance companies that had garnered large profits from health care during the previous decade.

These cost control efforts took a variety of forms. In 1971 the Nixon administration's concerns about rampant inflation led to the imposition of an across-the-board wage-price freeze that paid particular attention to medical care by placing low ceilings on the annual fee increases of both hospitals and physicians. Those price controls remained in place even after Nixon lifted the wage-price freeze for most other industries in January 1973.[32] In 1972 Congress established Professional Standards Review Organizations (PSROs) to assess the legitimacy of Medicare payments, and two years later it established the first price controls on Medicare payments for hospitalization-related services.

Meanwhile, Democrats and Republicans in Washington coalesced around competing health care restructuring proposals. The Democratic Health Security Plan, championed most prominently by Sen. Edward M. Kennedy of Massachusetts and Rep. Martha W. Griffiths of Michigan, both Democrats, laid out a blueprint for a universal, federally administered health insurance system, financed through payroll taxes, that would replace existing private and public plans. This scheme contained incentives for the establishment of prepaid group practices and empowered federal authorities to set budgetary parameters on the national and regional levels. And while it did not nationalize medical facilities or make nurses, physicians, or surgeons members of the civil service, it did include provisions giving government agencies the authority to set prices charged by various purveyors of medical services.

The Democrats' national health insurance plan horrified the AMA, but by the early 1970s the organization's clout was clearly on the wane. Decades on the front lines of political warfare over health care policy had exposed the organization to charges that it was a typical interest group, that is, one exclusively concerned with its own well-being, not a selfless guardian of American health. Moreover, spiraling health care costs and frustration with the "medical-industrial complex" were generating unprecedented challenges to professional sovereignty in Congress and American living rooms alike. All of these changes had taken their toll on the AMA's reputation within the ranks of physicians. By 1971 less than half of the nation's doctors were members of the organization.

Fortunately for the AMA, Senator Kennedy's national health insurance plan was also anathema to the Nixon administration and congressional Republicans who, although still the minority party in both houses, were gaining fast on the Democrats as a result of a growing voter backlash against the Democrats' Great Society programs and their prosecution of the Vietnam War. Eager to find a more palatable alternative, the Nixon administration hitched its political star to a group health practice variation championed by Paul M. Ellwood, a prominent Minneapolis neurologist. Ellwood convinced the Nixon White House to support what he called health maintenance organizations, managed care cooperative enterprises structured along the lines of the Kaiser Permanente group practice plans that had sprouted out of post–World War II California and Minnesota's own Mayo Clinic. "Rather than have the government take over the insurance business, as liberals like Kennedy always talked about doing, government could simply induce the private sector to create group practices," wrote Cohn. "By providing superior care at lower cost, the group practices would lure beneficiaries away from traditional insurers and eventually compete among themselves, making medicine more affordable—and better—for everybody. The market, in other words, would save the American health care system from its own excesses. . . . This was the kind of initiative a Republican administration like Nixon's could get behind."[33]

In early 1971 Republicans launched a concerted political blitz in support of the idea of health maintenance organizations, or HMOs as they came to be called. Republicans joined with moderate Democrats in Congress to craft the necessary legislation, and Republican governors ranging from Ronald Reagan in California to Nelson Rockefeller in New York incorporated HMOs into their states' health care policies.[34] Pro–free market groups such as the U.S. Chamber of Commerce and the Committee for Economic Development chimed in with support as well. This cheerleading from the conservative precincts of American politics was a remarkable phenomenon, for, as Starr pointed out, prepaid group practice had historically been treated by conservatives as a "utopian, slightly subversive idea. . . . The socialized medicine of one era had become the corporate reform of the next."[35]

After months of haggling, maneuvering, and deal cutting, a broad coalition of Republicans and Democrats passed the Health Maintenance Organization Act in late 1973, and Nixon signed it into law on December 29 **(See Document 7.16)**. It quickly became clear that HMOs did not constitute any sort of magic bullet for health care. Hobbled by provisions that mandated generous benefits, large cash reserves (just as commercial insurers were required to have), high qualification standards, and additional operating restrictions that placed them at a competitive disadvantage against other health delivery systems, HMO development was also hindered by HEW's spectacular mismanagement of the rollout.[36] It was not until 1976 and 1978, when Congress passed laws to give HMOs greater operational flexibility, that they began to make their presence felt in the marketplace. By the end of 1979 nearly eight million Americans were covered by HMO plans, but this still constituted only about 4 percent of the nation's total population.[37]

A Democratic Political Calculation Goes Awry

Washington launched a variety of legislative initiatives to shore up other problematic aspects of American health care. One of the most far-reaching and influential of these efforts was the Employee Retirement Income Security Act (ERISA) of 1974, which created national standards for employee health care and other fringe benefit plans **(See Document 7.18)**. But ERISA and all other health care legislation was eclipsed by a remarkable proposal made by Nixon himself for a universal health insurance system that would combine existing employer-based insurance plans with government subsidies to small business and the self-employed.

This scheme, first unveiled in Nixon's January 30, 1974, State of the Union Address, placed the president on record as supporting an employer mandate, annual caps on annual out-of-pocket expenses for patients, and a complete restructuring of government-supported health insurance for the poor. A few days later he formally introduced his Comprehensive Health Insurance Plan (CHIP) **(See Document 7.17)** to Congress.

While CHIP was clearly structured around the private market and was deferential to the insurance industry, it did offer a path to universal coverage, the holy grail of health reformers for more than a half-century. But Democrats and their allies in labor rejected Nixon's proposal as one that would, in the words of United Auto Workers (UAW) president Leonard Woodcock, "make us all serfs of the insurance industry."[38] Mindful of public opinion polls showing strong support for a national insurance program, they stuck with their demands for a single-payer system, that is, a streamlined health care system in which the federal government would pay all medical bills of the populace. Such a system would be funded by tax increases, but advocates asserted that the added tax burden for most people would in most cases not be any greater than the insurance premiums and out-of-pocket expenses they were currently paying.

For a brief time in early 1974 the opposition of labor to Nixon and his CHIP was almost circumvented by Senator Kennedy and Representative Mills, who still chaired Ways and Means. The two veteran legislators entered into secret negotiations on a compromise bill with administration officials, and before long they had crafted a moderate national health insurance bill that featured elements of both Kennedy's Health Security Plan and CHIP. The big labor base of the Democratic Party refused to endorse it and actively lobbied against it. This uncompromising stance stemmed to a large degree from liberal readings of the stiff political headwinds that Watergate was creating for Nixon and the Republicans. With public disgust with Nixon growing by the day, labor leaders made a calculated gamble that they could outlast the Republicans and pass the single-payer system they wanted in 1975, after angry voters extracted their pound of political flesh from the GOP in the 1974 midterms. And if such a bill failed to pass in 1975, labor leaders in the AFL-CIO and the UAW reasoned that they could transform the quest for national health insurance into a political weapon in the 1976 presidential campaign.

As it turned out, their blueprint for passing a truly liberal, compromise-free national health insurance program quickly turned to ashes. Proliferating health care reform proposals from both sides of the aisle muddied the waters, and the Watergate scandal and its aftermath sucked up so much of Washington's political oxygen that little legislating of any kind got done. Then in late 1974 Mills's career went into a sudden, scandal-driven tailspin that made it impossible for him to maintain a leadership role on health care. Upon becoming president in August 1974 following Nixon's resignation, Gerald R. Ford briefly flirted with the idea of pursuing universal health insurance. Inflation and other issues soon assumed higher priority in his administration, however, and an early 1976 swine flu outbreak proved to be a debacle for public health authorities. This outbreak of H1N1 influenza virus was very limited, but it prompted a mass immunization campaign that cost more than $130 million. Even worse, a rare side effect from the vaccine reportedly caused hundreds of cases of Guillain-Barre syndrome, a paralyzing nerve disease.[39]

The last genuine opportunity for Democrats to pass a national health insurance bill came in the late 1970s, but once again intraparty conflict doomed the effort. During his successful campaign for the presidency in 1976, Georgia's Democratic governor Jimmy Carter frequently expressed his firm support for establishing a "mandatory and universal" health insurance system in America. He repeated this pledge after taking office, while also calling on Congress to restrain skyrocketing hospital care costs by placing new caps on hospital charges. The latter initiative was killed in the House of Representatives due to massive lobbying from the hospital industry and strong opposition from Republicans who saw the idea as a blatant regulatory overreach that effectively punished hospitals with efficient operations.

Carter's strategy for passing a national health insurance program expired in much slower and hazier fashion. Mindful of the political hazards of supporting a health reform

President Gerald R. Ford receives a swine flu vaccine from his White House physician in October 1976. Ford ordered a nationwide vaccination program in response to a swine flu outbreak, but the program was halted at the end of 1976 in response to reports of serious side effects and deaths from the vaccine.

platform that would be seen by the public as another expensive, Great Society–style expansion of the welfare state, Carter wanted to pursue a incremental strategy for reform that was strong on cost containment above all else. Over time, however, Kennedy and other liberal leaders in Congress came to question whether Carter's heart was really in it. "By the summer of 1978," Kennedy wrote in his memoirs, "I felt that the president was squandering a real opportunity to get something done. The Jimmy Carter who had declared that he wanted mandatory and universal coverage and had a plan that was nearly identical to mine had now been replaced by the President Carter who wanted to approach health insurance in incremental steps, over time, if certain cost containment benchmarks were met—and after the 1978 midterm elections."[40]

Kennedy and the Committee for National Health Insurance (CNHI), which was labor's primary voice on the issue, subsequently decided to strike out on their own with a new universal health care proposal that preserved a place for private prepaid plans (ranging from commercial insurance and Blue Cross to HMOs and other cooperatives) instead of a government-run public system, which had long been the usual foundation of liberal reform schemes. Under the new Kennedy plan, employers would be responsible for 65 percent of health insurance for workers, with the government picking up the tab for the rest, as well as for coverage for the poor. Insurers, meanwhile, would receive financial incentives to provide policies to all Americans, not just the young and healthy. Costs would be restrained through negotiated rates for services rendered by hospitals and physicians as well as by providing financial incentives (such as rebates) for consumers to enroll in the most cost-effective plans.[41]

Kennedy and CNHI viewed several elements of their joint proposal as painful and difficult compromises, but they swallowed hard and accepted them because they thought that the legislation still constituted a step in the direction of national health insurance and that it could attract sufficient political support for passage. Instead, the Carter administration dismissed the plan as a political nonstarter and offered a series of more modest alternative measures. These included expanded government assistance to the poor, another effort to rein in hospitalization costs, and tepid support for an employer mandate to provide health insurance for workers. "Ted Kennedy was shocked," wrote historian Timothy Stanley. "The administration made no commitment to comprehensive coverage and the cost-containment package was likely actually to raise the price of health care as doctors hiked other charges to cover any loss in revenues. Worse still, the administration insisted that any future program be run by private insurers: there would be no 'public option' for consumers to buy from the government. Ted Kennedy denounced the Carter proposal and support for it in Congress collapsed. In this sense, it is accurate to say that Kennedy killed the bill. But Kennedy had no choice but to denounce it—it didn't meet his own publicly stated conditions for reform."[42]

Kennedy's stance deeply angered Carter, who wrote in his White House diary that "Kennedy [was] continuing his irresponsible and abusive attitude, immediately condemning our health plan. He couldn't get five votes for his plan."[43] When efforts between the two camps to reach a rapprochement failed, it became clear that major health care reform was doomed for the rest of Carter's first term.

The clash over health care cemented Kennedy's decision to wage his unsuccessful—and politically damaging—crusade to unseat Carter for the Democratic presidential nomination in 1980. "Carter regarded my efforts as a platform to challenge him for the presidency," Kennedy later asserted. "If that's why he slowed things down, then he made a poor political calculation. If we had passed comprehensive national health insurance together, it would have been a huge victory for Carter. And it would have been much more difficult for me to have challenged him for the nomination."[44]

NOTES

1. Herman M. Somers and Anne R. Somers, *Doctors, Patients, and Health Insurance* (Washington, DC: Brookings Institution, 1961), 27.

2. "Health Care Plans and Medical Practice," *Editorial Research Reports,* June 20, 1962.

3. Alan Derickson, *Health Security for All: Dreams of Universal Health Care in America* (Baltimore: Johns Hopkins University Press, 2005), 129.

4. Jill Quadagno, *One Nation Uninsured: Why the U.S. Has No National Health Insurance* (New York: Oxford University Press, 2005), 61.

5. Somers and Somers, *Doctors, Patients, and Health Insurance,* 426–44.

6. American Hospital Association, "Hospital Statistics," *Hospitals* (August 1, 1962): 408.

7. Howard A. Rusk, *Public Health Reports* (October 1967): 916.

8. Quoted in Theodore R. Marmor, *The Politics of Medicare,* 2nd ed. (New York: Aldine De Gruyter, 2000), 36.

9. Quoted in Lewis E. Weeks and Howard J. Berman, *Shapers of American Health Care Policy: An Oral History* (Ann Arbor, MI: Health Administration Press, 1985), 85.

10. Quoted in George D. Lundberg, with James Stacey, *Severed Trust: Why American Medicine Hasn't Been Fixed* (New York: Basic Books, 2002), 61.

11. Peter Corning, "The Fourth Round: 1957 to 1965," in *The Evolution of Medicare . . . From Idea to Law* (Washington, DC: Social Security Administration, Office of Research and Statistics, 1969), www.ssa.gov/history/corning.html.

12. John F. Kennedy, "Statement by the President on the Defeat of the Medical Care Bill," *Public Papers of the Presidents: John F. Kennedy 1962* (Washington, DC: Government Printing Office, 1964), 560–61.

13. Theodore C. Sorensen, *Kennedy* (New York: Harper and Row, 1965), 342–344.

14. Colin Gordon, *Dead on Arrival: The Politics of Health Care in Twentieth-Century America* (Princeton, NJ: Princeton University Press, 2003), 26.

15. Quoted in Richard A. Harris, *A Sacred Trust: The Story of Organized Medicine's Multi-Million Dollar Fight against Public Health Legislation* (New York: Penguin, 1969), 137–38.

16. Edward D. Berkowitz, "Why We Have Social Insurance: History and Social Security Reform," in *Social Security and Medicare: Individual vs. Collective Risk and Responsibility,* ed. Sheila Burke, Eric Kingson, and Uwe Reinhardt (Washington, DC: National Academy of Social Insurance, 2000), 43.

17. Larry DeWitt, "The Medicare Program as a Capstone to the Great Society—Recent Revelations in the LBJ White House Tapes," May 2003, www.larrydewitt.net/Essays/MedicareDaddy.htm.

18. "Washington News," *Journal of the American Medical Association* 189, no. 13 (1964): 17–18.

19. Quoted in Weeks and Berman, *Shapers of American Health Care Policy,* 100.

20. Quoted in Weeks and Berman, *Shapers of American Health Care Policy,* 101.

21. Jonathan Cohn, *Sick: The Untold Story of America's Health Care Crisis—and the People Who Pay the Price* (New York: HarperCollins, 2007), 93.

22. Cohn, *Sick,* 120.

23. Karen Davis and Cathy Schoen, *Health and the War on Poverty* (Washington, DC: Brookings Institution, 1978), 41–48.

24. Paul Starr, *The Social Transformation of American Medicine* (New York: Basic Books, 1982), 374.

25. Starr, *The Social Transformation of American Medicine,* 370; and Harold S. Luft, *Poverty and Health: Economic Causes and Consequences of Health Problems* (Cambridge, MA: Ballinger, 1978), 4.

26.   Julie Rovner, "Medicare," *Health Care Policy and Politics A to Z*, 3rd ed. (Washington, DC: CQ Press, 2009), 149.

27.   National Organization for Women, "The Right of a Woman to Determine Her Own Reproductive Process," proposal from the National Organization for Women membership conference, Washington, DC, 1967; reprinted in Toni Carabillo, Judith Meuli, and June Bundy Csida, eds., *Feminist Chronicles, 1953–1993* (Los Angeles: Women's Graphic, 1993), 192.

28.   Barbara Ehrenreich and John Ehrenreich, "The Medical-Industrial Complex," *New York Review of Books*, December 17, 1970, 14.

29.   Starr, *The Social Transformation of American Medicine*, 379.

30.   Quoted in Jan Coombs, *The Rise and Fall of HMOs: An American Health Care Revolution* (Madison: University of Wisconsin Press, 2005), 40.

31.   Richard M. Nixon, "Remarks at a Briefing on the Nation's Health System," July 10, 1969, The American Presidency Project, www.presidency.ucsb.edu/ws/?pid=2121.

32.   Starr, *The Social Transformation of American Medicine*, 398–99.

33.   Cohn, *Sick*, 65.

34.   Starr, *The Social Transformation of American Medicine*, 396.

35.   Starr, *The Social Transformation of American Medicine*, 396.

36.   Coombs, *The Rise and Fall of HMOs*, 52.

37.   Starr, *The Social Transformation of American Medicine*, 415.

38.   Quoted in Gordon, *Dead on Arrival*, 35.

39.   Ebe Harrell, "How to Deal with Swine Flu: Heeding the Mistakes of 1976," *Time*, April 27, 2009, www.time.com/time/health/article/0,8599,1894129,00.html.

40.   Edward M. Kennedy, *True Compass: A Memoir* (New York: Twelve, 2009), 360.

41.   Starr, *The Social Transformation of American Medicine*, 413.

42.   Timothy Stanley, "Memo to Jimmy Carter: Ted Kennedy Didn't Sabotage Health Care Reform," *History News Network*, September 20, 2010, http://hnn.us/articles/131473.html.

43.   Jimmy Carter, *White House Diary* (New York: Farrar Straus Giroux, 2010), 325.

44.   Kennedy, *True Compass*, 360.

DOCUMENT 7.1

Ronald Reagan Urges Opposition to Medicare

"We Do Not Want Socialized Medicine"

1961

As progressive efforts to pass a comprehensive Medicare bill intensified in the late 1950s and early 1960s, the American Medical Association (AMA) launched a sustained public relations campaign to defeat it. One major element of the AMA pushback was Operation Coffee Cup, wherein doctors' wives organized coffee meetings as a vehicle to convince women's clubs and other groups in their communities to speak out against Medicare to their representatives in Washington, D.C. The focal point of many of these meetings was the playing of a record that actor (and future California governor and U.S. president) Ronald Reagan recorded for the AMA. In this recording, titled Ronald Reagan Speaks

Out against Socialized Medicine, *Reagan covered all of the major lines of argument advanced by the AMA and other conservative critics against the King-Anderson bill in particular and Medicare in general. As Social Security Administration historian Larry DeWitt stated, "Reagan insisted throughout his Operation Coffee Cup speech that if the nation adopted Medicare this would just be the opening gambit in a movement for government-sponsored universal health care coverage and—given the equation between this state of affairs and 'socialized medicine'—that Medicare would thus be the first step on the road to socialism."[1] The transcript of Reagan's Operation Coffee Cup speech is excerpted here.*

My name is Ronald Reagan. I have been asked to talk on several subjects that have to do with the problems of the day. . . .

Now back in 1927 an American socialist, Norman Thomas, six times candidate for president on the Socialist Party ticket, said the American people would never vote for socialism. But he said under the name of liberalism the American people would adopt every fragment of the socialist program.

There are many ways in which our government has invaded the precincts of private citizens, the method of earning a living. Our government is in business to the extent of owning more than 19,000 businesses covering 47 different lines of activity. This amounts to a fifth of the total industrial capacity of the United States.

But at the moment I'd like to talk about another way because this threat is with us and at the moment is more imminent. One of the traditional methods of imposing statism or socialism on a people has been by way of medicine. It's very easy to disguise a medical program as a humanitarian project. Most people are a little reluctant to oppose anything that suggests medical care for people who possibly can't afford it. Now, the American people, if you put it to them about socialized medicine and gave them a chance to choose, would unhesitatingly vote against it. We have an example of this. Under the Truman administration it was proposed that we have a compulsory health insurance program for all people in the United States, and, of course, the American people unhesitatingly rejected this.

So, with the American people on record as not wanting socialized medicine, Congressman [Aime] Forand introduced the Forand Bill. This was the idea that all people of social security age should be brought under a program of compulsory health insurance. Now, this would not only be our senior citizens, this would be the dependents and those who are disabled, this would be young people if they are dependents of someone eligible for social security. Now, Congressman Forand brought the program out on that idea of just for that particular group of people. But Congressman Forand was subscribing to this foot-in-the-door philosophy because he said, "If we can only break through and get our foot inside the door, then we can expand the program after that." Walter Reuther said, "It's no secret that the United Automobile Workers is officially on record as backing a program of national health insurance." And by national health insurance he meant socialized medicine for every American.

Well, let's see what the socialists themselves had to say about it. They say, "Once the Forand bill is passed this nation will be provided with a mechanism for socialized medicine capable of indefinite expansion in every direction until it includes the entire population." Well, we can't say we haven't been warned. Now Congressman Forand is no longer a congressman of the United States government. He has been replaced, not in his particular assignment, but in his backing of such a bill, by Congressman King of California. It is presented in the idea of a great emergency that millions of our senior citizens are unable to provide needed medical care. But this ignores the fact that in the last decade 127 million of our citizens, in just ten years, have come under the protection of some form of privately owned medical or hospital insurance.

Now, the advocates of this bill, when you try to oppose it, challenge you on an emotional basis. They say, "What would you do, throw these poor old people out to die with no medical attention?" That's ridiculous and of course no one has advocated it. As a matter of fact, in the last session of Congress a bill was adopted known as the Kerr-Mills bill. Now, without even allowing this bill to be tried to see if it works, they have introduced this King bill which is really the Forand bill. What is the Kerr-Mills bill? It is a frank recognition of the medical need or problem of our senior citizens that I have mentioned. And it is provided from the Federal Government money to the states and the local communities that can be used at the discretion of the state to help those people who need it.

Now what reason could the other people have for backing a bill which says we insist on compulsory health insurance for senior citizens on a basis of age alone regardless of whether they are worth millions of dollars, whether they have an income, whether they're protected by their own insurance, whether they have savings. I think we could be excused for believing that, as ex-Congressman Forand said, this was simply an excuse to bring about what they wanted all the time: Socialized medicine. James Madison, in 1788, speaking to the Virginia Convention, said: "Since the general civilization of mankind I believe there are more instances of the abridgment of the freedom of the people by gradual and silent encroachment of those in power than by violent and sudden usurpations."

They want to attach this bill to social security and they say, "Here is a great insurance program, now instituted, now working." Let's take a look at social security itself. Again, very few of us disagree with the original premise that there should be some form of saving that would keep destitution from following unemployment by reason of death, disability, or old age. And to this end social security was adopted. But it was never intended to supplant private savings, private insurance, pension programs of unions and industries. Now, in our country under our free enterprise system we have seen medicine reach the greatest heights that it has in any country in the world. Today the relationship between patient and doctor in this country is something to be envied any place. The privacy, the care that is given to a person, the right to choose a doctor, the right to go from one doctor to the other. But let's also look from the other side at the freedom the doctor loses. A doctor would be reluctant to say this. Well, like you, I'm only a patient so I can say it in his behalf. The doctor begins to lose freedoms. It's like telling a lie and one leads to another. First you decide that the doctor can have so many patients. They are equally divided among the various doctors by the government. But then the doctors aren't equally divided geographically. So a doctor decides he wants to practice in one town and the government has to say to him, "You can't live in that town. They already have enough doctors. You have to go someplace else." And from here it's only a short step to dictating where he will go. This is a freedom that I wonder whether any of us have the right to take from any human being. I know how I'd feel if you, my fellow citizens, decided that to be an actor I had to become a government employee and work in a national theater. Take it into your own occupation or that of your husband. All of us can see what happens once you establish the precedent that the government can determine a man's working place and his working methods, determine his employment. From here it's a short step to all the rest of socialism to determining his pay. And pretty soon your son won't decide when he's in school, where he will go or what he will do for a living. He will wait for the government to tell him where he will go to work and what he will do.

In this country of ours took place the greatest revolution that has ever taken place in world's history, the only true revolution. Every other revolution simply exchanged one set of rulers for another. But here for the first time in all the thousands of years of man's relation to man a little group of men, the Founding Fathers, for the first time established the idea that you and I had within ourselves the God-given right and ability to determine our own destiny. This freedom was built into our government with safeguards. We talk democracy today and, strangely, we let democracy begin to assume the aspect of majority rule is all that is needed. Well, majority rule is a fine aspect of democracy, provided there are guarantees written into our government concerning the rights of the individual and of the minorities. What can we do about this? Well, you and I can do a great deal. We can write to our congressmen, to our senators. We can say right now that we want no further encroachment on these individual liberties and freedoms. And at the moment the key issue is: We do not want socialized medicine. Now, you may think when I say write to the congressman or the senator that this is like writing fan mail to a television program. It isn't. In Washington today 40,000 letters, less than 100 per congressman, are evidence of a trend in public thinking. Representative Charles Halleck of Indiana has said, "When the American people want something from Congress, regardless of its political complexion, if they make their wants known, Congress does what the people want." So write. . . . And if this man writes back to you and tells you that he, too, is for free enterprise, but we have these great services, and so forth that must be performed by government, don't let him get away with it. Show that you have not been convinced. Write a letter right back and tell him that you believe in government economy and fiscal responsibility, that you know that governments don't tax to get the money they need, governments will always find a need for the money they get, and that you demand the continuation of our traditional free enterprise system.

You and I can do this. The only way we can do it is by writing to our congressman even if we believe that he's on our side to begin with. Write to strengthen his hand. Give him the ability to stand before his colleagues in Congress and say, I have heard from my constituents and this is what they want. Write those letters now, call your friends and tell them to write them. If you don't, this program, I promise you, will pass just as surely as the sun will come up tomorrow. And behind it will come other federal programs that will invade every area of freedom as we have known it in this country. Until one day, as Norman Thomas said, we will awake to find that we have socialism. And if you don't do this and if I don't do it, one of these days you and I are going to spend our sunset years telling our children and our children's children what it once was like in America when men were free.

Source: "Ronald Reagan speaks out against socialized medicine." Audio recording. Audio available online: http://texasbestgrok.mu.nu/sounds/OperationCoffeecupIntro.mp3; http://texasbestgrok.mu.nu/sounds/OperationCoffeecupA.mp3; http://texasbestgrok.mu.nu/sounds/OperationCoffeecupB.mp3

NOTE

1. Larry DeWitt, "Operation Coffee Cup: Ronald Reagan's Effort to Prevent the Enactment of Medicare," September 2004, www.larrydewitt.net/Essays/Reagan.htm.

President Kennedy Tries to Rally Public Support for Medicare

"All These Arguments Were Made against Social Security at the Time of Franklin Roosevelt"

1962

When President John F. Kennedy and his health care advisers decided to throw their support behind the King-Anderson Medicare bill in 1962, they focused to a great extent on building and maintaining public support for a government health care program for the aged. One of the most carefully choreographed elements of this public relations blitz was a speech that Kennedy delivered at Madison Square Garden on May 20 to thousands of senior supporters. But Kennedy's last-minute tinkering with the wording and his tepid on-stage delivery made it one of the most widely panned speeches of his entire career. The following is an excerpt from that historic but poorly received speech.

My old colleague in the House of Representatives and friend Aime Forand, Mr. Meany, ladies and gentlemen, and fellow Americans:

I am very proud to be here today at one of over 33 meetings which are being held across the United States. . . .

I come to New York because I believe the effort in which we are engaged is worth the time and effort of all of us. I come from Boston, Mass., near Faneuil Hall, where for a whole period of years meetings were held by interested citizens in order to lay down the groundwork for American independence. And while there may be some who say that the business of government is so important that it should be confined to those who govern, in this free society of ours the consent and may I say the support of the citizens of this country is essential if this or any other piece of progressive legislation is going to be passed. Make no mistake about it—make no mistake about it.

Now why are we here? What is the issue which divides and arouses so much concern? I will take a case which may be typical, a family which may be found in any part of the United States.

The husband has worked hard all his life and he is retired. He might have been a clerk or a salesman or on the road or worked in a factory, stores, or whatever. He's always wanted to pay his own way. He does not ask anyone to care for him; he wants to care for himself. He has raised his own family, he has educated them—his children are now on their own. He and his wife are drawing social security, it may run seventy-five dollars, a hundred, hundred and twenty-five in the higher brackets let's say it's a hundred. He has a pension from where he worked, the results of years of effort.

Now, therefore, his basic needs are taken care of. He owns his house. He has twenty-five hundred or three thousand dollars in the bank. And then his wife gets sick—and we're all going to be in a hospital, 9 out of 10 of us, before we finally pass away, and particularly when we're over 65—now she is sick, not just for a week but for a long time. First goes the twenty-five hundred dollars—that's gone. Next he mortgages his house, even though he may have some difficulty making the payments out of his social security. Then he goes to his children, who themselves are heavily burdened because they're paying for their houses and they are paying for their sicknesses, and they want to educate their children. Then their savings begin to go.

This is not a rare case. I talked to a Member of the Congress from my own State a week ago, who told me he was going to send his daughter away to school but because his father had been sick for 2 years, he could not do it. And Congressmen are paid $22,500 a year—and that's more than most people get.

So therefore now, what is he going to do? His savings are gone—his children's savings, they're contributing though they have responsibilities of their own—and he finally goes in and signs a petition saying he's broke and needs assistance.

Now what do we say? We say that during his working years he will contribute to social security, as he has in the case of his retirement, twelve or thirteen dollars a month. When he becomes ill, or she becomes ill over a long period of time, he first pays ninety dollars, so that people will not abuse him. But then let's say he has a bill of fifteen hundred dollars. This bill does not, that we're talking about—Mr. Anderson's bill and Mr. King's— solve everything. But let's say it's fifteen hundred dollars, of which a thousand dollars are hospital bills. This bill will pay that thousand dollars in hospital bills. And then I believe that he, and the effort that he makes and his family, can meet his other responsibilities.

Now that does not seem such an extraordinary piece of legislation, 25 years after Franklin Roosevelt passed the Social Security Act.

Well, let's hear what some people say. First, we read that the AMA is against it, and they are entitled to be against it. Though I do question how many of those who speak so violently about it have read it. But they are against it, and they are entitled to be against it if they wish.

In the first place, there isn't one person here who is not indebted to the doctors of this country. Children are not born on an 8-hour day. All of us have been the beneficiaries of their help. This is not a campaign against doctors, because doctors have joined with us. This is a campaign to help people meet their responsibilities.

There are doctors in New Jersey who say they will not treat any patient who receives it. Of course they will. They are engaged in an effort to stop the bill. It is as if I took out somebody's appendix.

The point of the matter is that the AMA is doing very well in its efforts to stop this bill. And the doctors of New Jersey and every other State may be opposed to it, but I know that not a single doctor—if this bill is passed—is going to refuse to treat any patient. No one would become a doctor just as a business enterprise. It's a long, laborious discipline. We need more of them. We want their help—and gradually we're getting it.

The problem, however, is more complicated because they do not comprehend what we are trying to do. We do not cover doctors' bills here. We do not affect the freedom of choice. You can go to any doctor you want. The doctor and you work out your arrangements with him. We talk about his hospital bill. And that's an entirely different matter. And I hope that one by one the doctors of the United States will take the extraordinary step of not merely reading the journals and the publications of the AMA, because I do not recognize the bill when I hear those descriptions, but instead to write Secretary Ribicoff in Washington, or to me—and you know where I live—or to Senator Anderson or to Congressman King, if you are a doctor or opposed to this bill, and get a concise explanation and the bill itself and read it.

All these arguments were made against social security at the time of Franklin Roosevelt. They are made today. The mail pours in. And at least half of the mail which I receive in the White House, on this issue and others, is wholly misinformed. Last week I got 1,500 letters on a revenue measure—1,494 opposed, and 6 for. And at least half of those letters were completely misinformed about the details of what they wrote.

And why is that so? Because there are so many busy men in Washington who write—some organizations have six, seven, and eight hundred people spreading mail across the country, asking doctors and others to write in and tell your Congressman you're opposed to it. The mail pours into the White House, into the Congress and Senators' offices—Congressmen and Senators feel people are opposed to it. Then they read a Gallup Poll which says 75 percent of the people are in favor of it, and they say, "What has happened to my mail?"

The point of the matter is that this meeting and the others indicates that the people of the United States recognize one by one, thousand by thousand, million by million, that this is a problem whose solution is long overdue. And this year I believe, or certainly as inevitably as the tide comes in next year, this bill is going to pass.

And then other people say, "Why doesn't the Government mind its own business?" What is the Government's business, is the question.

Harry Truman said that 14 million Americans had enough resources so that they could hire people in Washington to protect their interests, and the rest of them depended upon the President of the United States and others.

This bill serves the public interest. It involves the Government because it involves the public welfare. The Constitution of the United States did not make the President or the Congress powerless. It gave them definite responsibilities to advance the general welfare—and that is what we're attempting to do.

And then I read that this bill will sap the individual self-reliance of Americans. I can't imagine anything worse, or anything better, to sap someone's self-reliance, than to be sick, alone, broke—or to have saved for a lifetime and put it out in a week, two weeks, a month, two months.

I visited twice, yesterday and today, in the hospital, where doctors labor for a long time, to visit my father. It isn't easy—it isn't easy. He can pay his bills, but otherwise I would be. And I am not as well off as he is. But what happens to him and to others when they put their life savings in, in a short time? So I must say that I believe we stand about where—in good company today, in halls such as this, where your predecessors—where Dave Dubinsky himself actually stood, where another former President stood, and fought this issue out of Social Security against the same charges.

This argument that the Government should stay out, that it saps our pioneer stock—I used to hear that argument when we were talking about raising the minimum wage to a dollar and a quarter. I remember one day being asked to step out into the hall, and up the corridor came four distinguished-looking men, with straw hats on and canes. They told me that they had just flown in from a State in their private plane, and they wanted me to know that if we passed a bill providing for time and a half for service station attendants, who were then working about 55 to 60 hours of straight time, it would sap their self-reliance.

The fact of the matter is what saps anyone's self-reliance is working 60 hours at straight time, or working at 85 or 95 at a dollar an hour. Or depending upon filling out a pauper's oath and then going and getting it free.

Nobody in this hall is asking for it for nothing. They are willing to contribute during their working years. That is the important principle which has been lost sight of.

I understand that there is going to be a program this week against this bill, in which an English physician is going to come and talk about how bad their plans are. It may be, but he ought to talk about it in England, because his plans—because his plans and what they do in England are entirely different. In England the entire cost of medicine for people of all ages, all of it, doctors, choice of doctors, hospitals, from the time you're born till the time you die, is included in a Government program. But what we're talking about is entirely different. And I hope that while he's here, he and Doctor Spock and others who have joined us, will come to see what we are trying to do.

The fact of the matter is that what we are now talking about doing, most of the countries of Europe did years ago. The British did it 30 years ago. We are behind every country, pretty nearly, in Europe, in this matter of medical care for our citizens.

And then those who say that this should be left to private efforts. In those hospitals in New Jersey where the doctors said they wouldn't treat anyone who paid their hospital bills through social security, those hospitals and every other new hospital, the American people—all of us—contribute one-half, one or two thirds for every new hospital, the National Government. We pay 55 percent of all the research done. We help young men become doctors.

We are concerned with the progress of this country, and those who say that what we are now talking about spoils our great pioneer heritage should remember that the West was settled with two great actions by the National Government; one, in President Lincoln's administration, when he gave a homestead to everyone who went West, and in 1862 he set aside Government property to build our land grant colleges.

This cooperation between an alert and Progressive citizen and a progressive Government is what has made this country great—and we shall continue as long as we have the opportunity to do so.

This matter should not be left to a mail campaign where Senators are inundated, and Congressmen—twenty-five and thirty thousand letters—the instructions go out, "Write it in your own hand. Don't use the same words." The letters pour in 2 or 3 weeks, half of them misinformed. This meeting today, on a hot, good day when everyone could be doing something else, and the 32 other meetings, this indicates that the American people are determined to put an end to meeting a challenge which hits them at a time when they're least able to meet it.

And then finally, I had a letter last week saying, "You're going to take care of all the millionaires and they don't need it." I do not know how many millionaires we are talking about, but they won't mind contributing $12 a month to social security, and they may be among those who will apply for it when they go to the hospital. But what I will say is that the National Government, through the tax laws, already takes care of them, because over 65 they can deduct all their medical expenses.

What we are concerned about is not the person who has not got a cent but those who saved and worked and then get hit. Then there are those who say, "Well, what happens if you die before you are 65?" Well, there isn't—you really don't care, you have no guarantee. But what we are talking about is, our people are living a long time, their housing is inadequate, in many cases their rehabilitation is inadequate. We've got great unfinished business in this country, and while this bill does not solve our problems in this area, I do not believe it is a valid argument to say, "This bill isn't going to do the job." It will not, but it will do part of it.

Our housing bill last year for the elderly, that won't do the job. But it will begin. When we retrain workers, that won't take care of unemployment chronically in some areas, but it's a start. We aren't able overnight to solve all the problems that this country faces, but is that any good reason why we should say, "Let's not even try"?

That's what we are going to do today, we are trying. We are trying. And what we're talking about here is true in a variety of other ways. All the great revolutionary movements of the Franklin Roosevelt administration in the thirties we now take for granted. But I refuse to see us live on the accomplishments of another generation. I refuse to see this country, and all of us, shrink from these struggles which are our responsibility in our time. Because what we are now talking about, in our children's day will seem to be the ordinary business of government.

So I come here today as a citizen, asking you to exert the most basic power which is contained in the Constitution of the United States and the Declaration of Independence, the right of a citizen to petition his Government. And I ask your support in this effort. This effort will be successful, and it will be successful because it is soundly based to meet a great national crisis. And it is based on the effort of responsible citizens. So I want to commend you for being here. I think it is most appropriate that the President of the United States, whose business place is in Washington, should come to this city and participate in these rallies. Because the business of the Government is the business of the people—and the people are right here. . . .

Source: Kennedy, John F. Address at a New York Rally in Support of the President's Program of Medical Care for the Aged. May 20, 1962. *Public Papers of the Presidents: John F. Kennedy, 1962.* Washington, DC: Government Printing Office, 1964, pp. 416–20.

| DOCUMENT 7.3 | # A Cartoonist Lampoons the American Medical Association |

"It Beats Getting Wet"

1962

The titanic political clashes that were waged in America during the late 1950s and 1960s over Medicare and other federal health and social insurance programs inspired frequent commentary from political pundits. Newspaper and magazine columnists and editors occupied center stage in this regard, but political cartoonists had their say as well. The cartoon depicted here was the handiwork of William "Bill" Mauldin, a famous World War II cartoonist with Stars and Stripes, *who went on to produce decades of acerbic, trenchant, and unabashedly liberal political commentary as a cartoonist for the* St. Louis Post-Dispatch *and the* Chicago Sun-Times. *The cartoon ridicules the American Medical Association (represented by a rain-soaked man) for its insistence that the 1960 Kerr-Mills Act (the tattered umbrella) can shield the organization from the King-Anderson Medicare Bill (the rainstorm), which seemed to be gathering political strength with each passing week.*

Source: "It Beats Getting Wet." *St. Louis Post-Dispatch*, June 24, 1962. Courtesy of the State Historical Society of Missouri.

DOCUMENT
7.4

Kennedy's Presidential Panel on Mental Retardation

"Bring Them as Close to the Main Stream of Independence and 'Normalcy' as Possible"

1962

During the three-and-a-half year presidency of John F. Kennedy, American policies and attitudes toward mental retardation and mental health underwent a remarkable sea change. These issues had long been neglected by policymakers at both the state and national levels. But Kennedy was urged to pay greater attention to mental retardation and other disability issues by his sister Eunice Kennedy Shriver, an energetic advocate for people with disabilities, and after becoming president he paved the way for significant reforms. Nine months after his inauguration, on October 11, 1961, Kennedy announced the formation of a panel of distinguished scientists, doctors, and activists to develop a governmental blueprint for combating mental retardation.

This committee, known as the President's Panel on Mental Retardation, studied the issue for a year before presenting more than one hundred policy recommendations to Kennedy on October 16, 1962. Many of these recommendations emphasized the importance of bringing people with mental disabilities out of institutional isolation and into more community-oriented treatment programs. The report, which is excerpted here, also urged the president to "think and plan boldly." Kennedy followed the panel's advice, calling on Congress to craft and support legislation that would fulfill many of its recommendations. Democrats and Republicans lined up in support of this campaign, and on October 24, 1963, Kennedy signed the Maternal and Child Health and Mental Retardation Planning Amendment to the Social Security Act. Speaking at a special ceremony arranged to celebrate the landmark legislation, Kennedy noted: "It was said, in an earlier age, that the mind of a man is a far country which can neither be approached nor explored. But, today, under present conditions of scientific achievement, it will be possible for a nation as rich in human and material resources as ours to make the remote reaches of the mind accessible. The mentally ill and the mentally retarded need no longer be alien to our affections or beyond the help of our communities."[1]

The Prevention, Treatment, and Amelioration of Mental Retardation

From the available evidence on the prevalence and the causes of mental retardation, the Panel believes that the broad outlines and the directions in which action is needed can be determined with substantial assurance.

In the light of preceding discussion, a program of action must take account of the following facts: mental retardation is a complex phenomenon stemming from multiple causes. Many of the specific causes are known and can be prevented or their results can be treated. These are largely in the biomedical area.

For the great bulk of mental retardation cases, however, a specific cause cannot yet be ascribed with present knowledge. But epidemiological data from many reliable studies show a remarkably heavy correlation between the incidence of mental retardation, particularly in its milder manifestations, and the adverse social, economic, and cultural status of families and groups of our population. These are for the most part the low income groups—who often live in the slums and are frequently minority groups—where the mother and the children receive inadequate medical care, where family breakdown is common, where individuals are without motivation and opportunity and without adequate education. In short, the conditions which spawn many other health and social problems are to a large extent the same ones which generate the problem of mental retardation. To be successful in preventing mental retardation on a large scale, a broad attack on the fundamental adverse conditions will be necessary.

Another significant consideration in developing action programs is the lifelong character of mental retardation. Unlike other major afflictions, such as cancer or heart disease, which often come relatively late in life, mental retardation typically appears in childhood and always before adulthood. And once incurred, it is essentially a permanent handicap, at least at the present stage of biomedical knowledge. In this light prevention—always desirable where illness is concerned—assumes an even higher priority both in terms of the standpoint of general community measures and also of measures which the individual should take.

Still a third consideration looms large. Unfortunately we do not yet know the causes or the means of preventing but a fraction of mental retardation cases through biomedical means. Prevention of the great bulk of mental retardation cases will require measures to eliminate causative factors embedded in our social, economic, and cultural environment, and this will obviously take time. For many years we will still have the retarded with us and we will have to provide care and rehabilitation for them—care which must contain an increasing component of restorative services.

From these basic considerations the fundamental strategy of our battle against mental retardation takes shape. Because its causes are complex, our attack will have to be "broad spectrum" in character. We must act on many fronts, not only against the specific cause of mental retardation but against the root problems in the social, economic, and cultural environment which nourish the specific causes and seem to have a major and direct causative influence of their own.

Essentially this means that our society will have to allocate more resources to basic services to the youth of the land—for health, for education and training, for community reconstruction and renewal, and for improved employment and social services. In these efforts we must particularly strive to improve opportunities and services for distressed groups in the population.

Our campaign will be costly, but we cannot afford inaction. On economic grounds alone, the costs of caring for mentally retarded persons in institutions are 3 or 4 times the cost of rearing and educating normal children. Moreover, improvements in opportunities and services for our youth are likely to have beneficial effects for solving other pressing social problems. The same preventive measures which strike at the basic causes of mental retardation will also help to overcome other problems such as juvenile delinquency, mental illness, and general poor health and lack of fitness. For example, maternal health measures which avert the birth of mentally retarded children will also pay dividends in improving the general health of mothers and children. . . .

Many new social measures have been spurred by Government action and private initiative during this century. They include numerous diverse and useful actions, including minimum wage laws, public health measures, improved educational services, and social security insurance programs, which help to alleviate the economic burden of care for the dependent. Many of these measures have a preventive effect on the conditions which engender mental retardation, while others help provide the services or the financial support for which the mentally retarded benefit along with other people in the community. The continued existence of mental retardation on a vast scale, however, indicates that our society is still far from its goal of providing the essential conditions for normal healthy physical and intellectual development for this large segment of our children and youth. In this connection, it is significant that while Federal expenditures from budget and trust accounts for benefits and services for the aged are now on the order of $15 or $16 billion per year, the corresponding expenditures for children and youth are $4 or $5 billion.

The National Action Program to Combat Mental Retardation

The Panel therefore urges high-priority consideration of necessary measures to improve and strengthen the health, the educational, and the social and community services for the youth of our land, particularly in instances where large concentrations of economically and culturally deprived families live. This is a sound and necessary course of action, not just because such services would directly benefit the mentally retarded, but because this is the only way which holds reasonable promise of preventing a large part of mental retardation from arising in the first instance. . . .

To attack a problem as pervasive and intertwined with fundamental social conditions as mental retardation, we must think and plan boldly. If, as it is apparent, the inadequate medical services available to large segments of our population during pregnancy and childhood play an important role in causing mental retardation, then we must remedy the basic situation of inadequate medical care. At a time when the infant mortality of some countries is reaching a new low, the infant mortality rate in the United States has leveled off at a relatively high rate. For example, it is now two-thirds higher than that of Sweden.

Likewise, we must have enough classrooms and teachers for all our students in order to provide adequate educational services to the mentally retarded. Although we have made excellent progress in providing increases in special educational facilities for the retarded, the shortages of classrooms and of teachers which are evident in education generally are even more aggravated in this area.

In addition to taking vigorous national action to improve the general programs, we must recognize that the mentally retarded who are in our population represent a group with extraordinary needs. Society's special responsibility to persons with extraordinary needs including the retarded is (1) to permit and actually foster the development of their maximum capacity and thus bring them as close to the main stream of independence and "normalcy" as possible; and (2) to provide some accommodation or adjustment in our society for those disabilities which cannot be overcome.

In the first of these two categories are such services as health care, guidance, special education, vocational rehabilitation, and the like, directed to groups especially prone to mental retardation or who are afflicted by it. Nowhere in our society are there more opportunities for constructive and useful innovation than in the development of improved techniques, better services, and improved institutional arrangements for the effective integration of such handicapped individuals into a self-reliant, productive, and happy life in our society.

The second part of the task concerns the provision of adequate and improved facilities for the care of the retarded individuals who must be maintained in institutions. Here, too, a positive and hopeful emphasis is possible and necessary, because improved methods and effective techniques can contribute immensely not only to the welfare of retarded persons as individuals but also can help them become at least partially self-maintaining.

Underlying effective action on all these fronts as they relate to retardation, there is the need for increased and more exact knowledge regarding the causes of retardation and the methods of prevention and care. More research support and capacity is therefore necessary not only specifically with respect to the mentally retarded but in the basic areas of health, learning processes, and other fundamental human processes which will apply to all people alike. The gaining of new fundamental knowledge can benefit not only the U.S. citizenry but all of mankind.

Thus, considering the problem of the mentally retarded in its broadest aspects, the Panel has addressed itself to both sides of the equation: (1) the necessary improvement of basic services to all people, and (2) to improved specific services to the mentally retarded. The Panel recognizes that extreme shortages of trained personnel and of funds will not make it possible to increase services and facilities greatly overnight. We must plan our campaign to combat mental retardation not for just next month or next year, but for the next decade. And we must move ahead vigorously and imaginatively. In this context, the main recommendations of the report are directed to—

1. *Research* in the causes of retardation and in method of care, rehabilitation, and learning.

2. *Preventive health measures* including (a) a greatly strengthened program of maternal and infant care directed first at the centers of population where prematurity and the rate of "damaged" children are high; (b) protection against such known hazards to pregnancy as radiation and harmful drugs; and (c) extended diagnostic and screening services.

3. *Strengthened educational programs generally and extended and enriched programs of special education* in public and private schools closely coordinated with vocational guidance, vocational rehabilitation, and specific training and preparation for employment; education for the adult mentally retarded, and workshops geared to their needs.

4. *More comprehensive and improved clinical and social services.*

5. *Improved methods and facilities for care,* with emphasis on the home and the development of a wide range of local community facilities.

6. *A new legal, as well as social, concept of the retarded,* including protection of their civil rights; life guardianship provisions when needed; an enlightened attitude on the part of the law and the courts; and clarification of the theory of responsibility in criminal acts.

7. *Helping overcome the serious problems of manpower* as they affect the entire field of science and every type of service through extended programs of recruiting with fellowships, and increased opportunities for graduate students, and those preparing for the professions to observe and learn at firsthand about the phenomenon of retardation. Because there will never be a fully adequate supply of personnel in this field and for other cogent reasons, the Panel has emphasized the need for more volunteers in health, recreation, and welfare activities, and for a domestic Peace Corps to stimulate voluntary service.

8. *Programs of education and information to increase public awareness* of the problem of mental retardation.

In addition to a strong emphasis on *research* and *prevention,* the report recommends—

1. That programs for the retarded, including modern day care, recreation, residential services, and ample educational and vocational opportunities, be *comprehensive.*

2. That they operate in or close to the communities where the retarded live—that is, that they be *community centered.*

3. That services be so organized as to provide a central or fixed point for the guidance, assistance, and protection of retarded persons if and when needed, and to assure a sufficient array or *continuum* of services to meet different types of need.

4. That private agencies as well as public agencies at the local, State, and Federal level continue to provide resources and to increase them for this worthy purpose. While the Federal Government can assist, the principal responsibility for financing and improving services for the mentally retarded must continue to be borne by States and local communities.

One may well ask how these broad objectives for the retarded differ in kind or degree from desirable goals for others. They do not differ fundamentally, but the retarded do not presently receive either the attention or the services accorded to other groups with special needs. . . .

The Panel's Work and Its Report

. . . A report of this type must be regarded as only one step in a process. In this instance the "process" may be said to have started with a heightened activity within the American Association on Mental Deficiency dating from the close of World War II and the upsurge of interest among parents leading to the founding of the National Association for Retarded Children. The support of the Congress and the subsequent emphasis on development of programs for the retarded in the Department of Health, Education, and Welfare were additional steps of major importance.

In appointing the Panel on Mental Retardation, the President recognized the emergence of an idea "whose time had arrived" and gave impetus and visibility to a complex problem that had not yet been brought into the full view of the country. . . .

A *substantial number of problems discussed in the report* require further study and most of the recommendations call for a vigorous followup. Studies must be supported and a followup program set in motion but, in the meantime, we must go forward on the basis of past experience and with the tools at hand.

Robert Frost once defined wisdom as that quality which motivates man to act in spite of insufficient knowledge. We must move ahead in mental retardation, although we lack conclusive knowledge and all the tools we need; but we must continue to search, to learn, and to gain new insights if the decade ahead is to be one of steady progress and high achievement.

Source: President's Panel on Mental Retardation. *A Proposed Program for National Action to Combat Mental Retardation.* Washington, DC: Government Printing Office, October 1962, pp. 9–17. www .mnddc.org/parallels2/pdf/60s/62/62-NAC-PPM.pdf.

NOTE

1. John F. Kennedy, "Remarks upon Signing the Maternal and Child Health and Mental Retardation Planning Bill," *Public Papers of the Presidents: John F. Kennedy, 1963* (Washington, DC: Government Printing Office, 1964), www.arcmass.org/Portals/0/JFK%20signing%20speech.pdf.

DOCUMENT
7.5

American Courts Order Desegregation of Southern Hospitals

"This Is Not Merely a Controversy over a Sum of Money"

1963

At the same time that the United States moved to address hospital shortages and other health care problems in post–World War II America with the Hill-Burton Act, African American civil rights leaders made discrimination in hospital policies and practices a major priority. These efforts picked up additional steam after 1954, when the U.S. Supreme Court issued its unanimous Brown v. Board of Education *ruling that struck down segregation in public education. Civil rights activists recognized that the Court's rejection of the separate-but-equal fig leaf, which had long been used across the South to rationalize nakedly discriminatory treatment of its African American citizens, gave them an opening to hit segregated Southern hospital systems where it would hurt most: in their pocketbooks.*

The Hill-Burton Act had paid for a flood of new hospital construction in the South since its passage in 1946, in large part because it stated that hospitals that maintained "separate but equal facilities" were not engaging in discriminatory behavior. But after the Brown *decision came down, medical civil rights activists realized that if Southern communities did not integrate their hospitals and other health care facilities in the same way that school districts were (reluctantly) doing, the courts might well turn off the spigot of federal funding for hospitals that Hill-Burton had been providing for the past number of years. In February 1962 the activists finally got the case they had been looking for in* Simkins v. Moses H. Cone Memorial Hospital. *In this case, a group of African American doctors, dentists, and patients from Greensboro, North Carolina, filed a lawsuit to stop racially discriminatory practices at two voluntary hospitals that had received close to $3 million under the Hill-Burton Act. The district court ruled against the plaintiffs, but in November 1963 the Court of Appeals found in their favor. This decision became the law of the land when the U.S. Supreme Court refused to hear the case on appeal. The decision is excerpted here (legal citations not included).*

Initially, the Simkins *ruling applied only to those hospitals that received Hill-Burton funds. But a 1964 federal court decision,* Eaton v. Grubbs, *broadened the prohibitions against racial discrimination to include voluntary hospitals that did not receive such funds, and the Civil Rights Act of 1964 prohibited racial discrimination in any programs that received federal assistance. One year later, the creation of the federal Medicare and Medicaid programs obligated almost all U.S. hospitals to integrate their facilities.*

Although the District Judge earnestly faced and sought to make a reasoned analysis of the problems presented, it is our conclusion that the case was wrongly decided. In the first place we would formulate the initial question differently to avoid the erroneous view that for an otherwise private body to be subject to the antidiscrimination requirements of the Fifth and the Fourteenth Amendments it must actually be "render[ed an] instrumentalit[y] of government * * *." In our view the initial question is, rather, whether the state or the federal government, or both, have become so involved in the conduct of these otherwise private bodies that their activities are also the activities of these governments and performed under their aegis without the private body necessarily becoming either their instrumentality or their agent in a strict sense. As the Supreme Court recently said in *Burton v. Wilmington Parking Authority,* a case involving racial discrimination by a privately owned restaurant operating on government property:

> "The Civil Rights Cases 'embedded in our constitutional law' the principle 'that the action inhibited by the first section [Equal Protection Clause] of the Fourteenth Amendment is only such action as may fairly be said to be that of the States. That Amendment erects no shield against merely private conduct, however discriminatory or wrongful.' Chief Justice Vinson in *Shelley v. Kraemer,* (1948). It was language in the opinion in the Civil Rights Cases, supra, that phrased the broad test of state responsibility under the Fourteenth Amendment, predicating its consequence upon 'State action of every kind * * * which denies * * * the equal protection of the laws.' And only two Terms ago, some 75 years later, the same concept of state responsibility was interpreted as necessarily following upon 'state participation through any arrangement, management, funds or property.' *Cooper v. Aaron* (1958). It is clear, as it always has been since the Civil Rights Cases, supra, that 'Individual invasion of individual rights is not the subject-matter of the amendment,' and that private conduct abridging individual rights does no violence to the Equal Protection Clause *unless to some significant extent the State in any of its manifestations has been found to have become involved in it.* Because the virtue of the right to equal protection

of the laws could lie only in the breadth of its application, its constitutional assurance was reserved in terms whose imprecision was necessary if the right were to be enjoyed in the variety of individual-state relationships which the Amendment was designed to embrace. For the same reason, to fashion and apply a precise formula for recognition of state responsibility under the Equal Protection Clause is an 'impossible task' which 'This Court has never attempted.' *Only by sifting facts and weighing circumstances can the nonobvious involvement of the State in private conduct be attributed its true significance."*

Weighing the circumstances we are of the opinion that this case is controlled by Burton, where the Court held that the "activities, obligations and responsibilities of the [Parking] Authority, the benefits mutually conferred, together with the obvious fact that the restaurant is operated as an integral part of a public building devoted to a public parking service, indicates that degree of state participation and involvement in discriminatory action which it was the design of the Fourteenth Amendment to condemn."

Here the most significant contacts compel the conclusion that the necessary "degree of state [in the broad sense, including federal] participation and involvement" is present as a result of the participation by the defendants in the Hill-Burton program. The massive use of public funds and extensive state-federal sharing in the common plan are all relevant factors. We deal here with the appropriation of millions of dollars of public monies pursuant to comprehensive governmental plans. But we emphasize that this is not merely a controversy over a sum of money. Viewed from the plaintiffs' standpoint it is an effort by a group of citizens to escape the consequences of discrimination in a concern touching health and life itself. As the case affects the defendants it raises the question of whether they may escape constitutional responsibilities for the equal treatment of citizens, arising from participation in a joint federal and state program allocating aid to hospital facilities throughout the state.

Not every subvention by the federal or state government automatically involves the beneficiary in "state action," and it is not necessary or appropriate in this case to undertake a precise delineation of the legal rule as it may operate in circumstances not now before the court. Prudence and established judicial practice counsel against such an attempt at needlessly broad adjudication. Our concern is with the Hill-Burton program, and examination of its functioning leads to the conclusion that we have state action here. Just as the Court in the Parking Authority case attached major significance to "the obvious fact that the restaurant is operated as an integral part of a public building devoted to a public parking service," we find it significant here that the defendant hospitals operate as integral parts of comprehensive joint or intermeshing state and federal plans or programs designed to effect a proper allocation of available medical and hospital resources for the best possible promotion and maintenance of public health. Such involvement in discriminatory action "it was the design of the Fourteenth Amendment to condemn." . . .

This court does not overlook the hospitals' contention that they accepted government grants without warning that they would thereby subject themselves to restrictions on their racial policies. Indeed they are being required to do what the Government assured them they would not have to do. But in this regard the defendants, owners of publicly assisted facilities, can stand no better than the collective body of Southern voters who approved school bond issues before the Brown decision or the private enterpreneur [sic] who outfitted his restaurant business in the Wilmington Parking Garage before the

Burton decision. The voters might not have approved some of the bond issues if they had known that the schools would be compelled to abandon their historic practice of separation of the races, and the restaurateur might have been unwilling to venture his capital in a business on the premises of the Wilmington Parking Authority if he had anticipated the imposition of a requirement for desegregated service. What was said by the Supreme Court in Burton in regard to the leases there in question is pertinent here:

"[W]hen a State leases public property in the manner and for the purpose shown to have been the case here, the proscriptions of the Fourteenth Amendment must be complied with by the lessee as certainly as though they were *binding covenants written into the agreement itself.*"

We accord full weight to the argument of the defendants, but it cannot prevail. Not only does the Constitution stand in the way of the claimed immunity but there are powerful countervailing equities in favor of the plaintiffs. Racial discrimination by hospitals visits severe consequences upon Negro physicians and their patients.

Giving recognition to its responsibilities for public health, the state elected not to build publicly owned hospitals, which concededly could not have avoided a legal requirement against discrimination. Instead it adopted and the defendants participated in a plan for meeting those responsibilities by permitting its share of Hill-Burton funds to go to existing private institutions. The appropriation of such funds to the Cone and Long Hospitals effectively limits Hill-Burton funds available in the future to create non-segregated facilities in the Greensboro area. In these circumstances, the plaintiffs can have no effective remedy unless the constitutional discrimination complained of is forbidden.

The order of the District Court is reversed and the case is remanded for the entry of an order in conformity with the opinion of this court.

Source: *Simkins v. Moses H. Cone Memorial Hospital,* 323 F.2d 959 (4th Cir. 1963). http://openjurist .org/323/f2d/959/simkins-v-moses-h-cone-memorial-hospital-h-a-o#fn24.

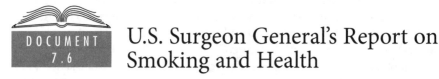

| DOCUMENT 7.6 | U.S. Surgeon General's Report on Smoking and Health |

"Cigarette Smoking Is Causally Related to Lung Cancer"

1964

During the 1940s and 1950s, a flurry of scientific studies documented alarming linkages between cigarette smoking and a variety of serious health problems, including lung cancer, coronary heart disease, bronchitis, and emphysema. By 1957 the growing body of medical evidence had convinced Surgeon General Leroy E. Burney of the U.S. Public Health Service to assert that a clear causal relationship existed between smoking and lung cancer. The tobacco industry and members of Congress from tobacco-growing states disputed this claim. They cited air pollution and other environmental contaminants as more likely culprits, and they said that their own internal studies indicated that smoking was not a health hazard.

As the debate over the health impact of smoking intensified, an alliance of private health organizations led by the American Cancer Society and the American Heart Association urged the Kennedy administration to conduct an official government study of smoking and its alleged health effects. Kennedy agreed, and in June 1962 Surgeon General Luther L. Terry announced that he was convening a panel of experts from medicine, pharmacology, statistics, and other relevant disciplines to conduct an exhaustive review of all scientific research on the issue. Eighteen months later, on January 11, 1964, the administration of Lyndon B. Johnson released the report. According to Terry, it "hit the country like a bombshell. It was front page news and a lead story on every radio and television station in the United States and many abroad."[1] The report's unambiguous declaration that smoking was a dangerous health hazard had an immediate impact oin private behavior, as smoking rates in virtually every demographic group declined over the next decade. It also led Congress to mandate health warning labels on all cigarette packaging (in 1965) and ban cigarette advertising on radio and television after September 1970.

THE EFFECTS OF SMOKING: PRINCIPAL FINDINGS

Cigarette smoking is associated with a 70 percent increase in the age-specific death rates of males, and to a lesser extent with increased death rates of females. The total number of excess deaths causally related to cigarette smoking in the U.S. population cannot be accurately estimated. In view of the continuing and mounting evidence from many sources, it is the judgment of the Committee that cigarette smoking contributes substantially to mortality from certain specific diseases and to the overall death rate.

Lung Cancer

Cigarette smoking is causally related to lung cancer in men; the magnitude of the effect of cigarette smoking far outweighs all other factors. The data for women, though less extensive, point in the same direction.

The risk of developing lung cancer increases with duration of smoking and the number of cigarettes smoked per day, and is diminished by discontinuing smoking. In comparison with non-smokers, average male smokers of cigarettes have approximately a 9- to 10-fold risk of developing lung cancer and heavy smokers at least a 20-fold risk.

The risk of developing cancer of the lung for the combined group of pipe smokers, cigar smokers, and pipe and cigar smokers is greater than for non-smokers, but much less than for cigarette smokers.

Cigarette smoking is much more important than occupational exposures in the causation of lung cancer in the general population.

Chronic Bronchitis and Emphysema

Cigarette smoking is the most important of the causes of chronic bronchitis in the United States, and increases the risk of dying from chronic bronchitis and emphysema. A relationship exists between cigarette smoking and emphysema but it has not been established that the relationship is causal. Studies demonstrate that fatalities from this disease are infrequent among non-smokers.

For the bulk of the population of the United States, the relative importance of cigarette smoking as a cause of chronic broncho-pulmonary disease is much greater than atmospheric pollution or occupational exposures.

Cardiovascular Diseases

It is established that male cigarette smokers have a higher death rate from coronary artery disease than non-smoking males. Although the causative role of cigarette smoking in deaths from coronary disease is not proven, the Committee considers it more prudent from the public health viewpoint to assume that the established association has causative meaning than to suspend judgment until no uncertainty remains.

Although a causal relationship has not been established, higher mortality of cigarette smokers is associated with many other cardiovascular diseases, including miscellaneous circulatory diseases, other heart diseases, hypertensive heart disease, and general arteriosclerosis.

Other Cancer Sites

Pipe smoking appears to be causally related to lip cancer. Cigarette smoking is a significant factor in the causation of cancer of the larynx. The evidence supports the belief that an association exists between tobacco use and cancer of the esophagus, and between cigarette smoking and cancer of the urinary bladder in men, but the data are not adequate to decide whether these relationships are causal. Data on an association between smoking and cancer of the stomach are contradictory and incomplete.

THE TOBACCO HABIT AND NICOTINE

The habitual use of tobacco is related primarily to psychological and social drives, reinforced and perpetuated by the pharmacological actions of nicotine.

Social stimulation appears to play a major role in a young person's early and first experiments with smoking. No scientific evidence supports the popular hypothesis that smoking among adolescents is an expression of rebellion against authority. Individual stress appears to be associated more with fluctuations in the amount of smoking than with the prevalence of smoking. The overwhelming evidence indicates that smoking—its beginning habituation, and occasional discontinuation—is to a very large extent psychologically and socially determined.

Nicotine is rapidly changed in the body to relatively inactive substances with low toxicity. The chronic toxicity of small doses of nicotine is low in experimental animals. These two facts, when taken in conjunction with the low mortality ratios of pipe and cigar smokers, indicate that the chronic toxicity of nicotine in quantities absorbed from smoking and other methods of tobacco use is very low and probably does not represent an important health hazard.

The significant beneficial effects of smoking occur primarily in the area of mental health, and the habit originates in a search for contentment. Since no means of measuring the quantity of these benefits is apparent, the Committee finds no basis for a judgment which would weigh benefits against hazards of smoking as it may apply to the general population.

THE COMMITTEE'S JUDGMENT IN BRIEF

On the basis of prolonged study and evaluation of many lines of converging evidence, the Committee makes the following judgment:

Cigarette smoking is a health hazard of sufficient importance in the United States to warrant appropriate remedial action.

Source: United States Surgeon General's Advisory Committee on Smoking and Health. *Smoking and Health.* Publication no. 1103. Washington, DC: U.S. Public Health Service, 1964, pp. 31–33. http://profiles .nlm.nih.gov/NN/B/B/M/T/_/nnbbmt.pdf.

Note

1. Quoted in *Reports of the Surgeon General: The 1964 Report on Smoking and Health,* Profiles in Science, National Institutes of Health, National Library of Medicine, http://profiles.nlm.nih.gov/NN /Views/Exhibit/narrative/smoking.html.

DOCUMENT
7.7

1964 Elections Break the Political Logjam on Medicare

"That Traditional House Roadblock Began to Disappear"

1965

During the late 1950s and early 1960s repeated attempts by liberal Democrats (and some moderate Republicans representing northern states) to pass a Medicare program of health insurance for the aged had been thwarted by a Republican–Southern Democrat coalition. The national election results of 1964, however, changed the political landscape for health care reform in significant ways. In this 1986 interview, Lawrence F. O'Brien, who directed Lyndon B. Johnson's successful 1964 presidential campaign and served as one of his top aides on health care, recalled how Johnson's landslide victory paved the way for the passage of Medicare one year later.

Gillette: Okay, why don't we begin [in] 1965? You talked briefly last time about the impact that the election had on the Congress and the large majorities.

    O'Brien: Yes. Well, of course, we struck it rich in terms of that election, and I think I had projected to the President that we would pick up seventeen, twenty or something House seats. We actually picked up double that, around thirty-eight, I guess, [and] picked up a couple of seats in the Senate. I projected two or three. The end result was we had two-to-one Democratic majorities in the House and Senate moving into the Eighty-Ninth Congress, the largest Democratic majority, I guess, in twenty, twenty-five years or more. So the stage was set and a lot of the problems that had existed over those early years perhaps would dissipate if we handled things properly. And in that context we felt that at long last we probably could finalize the break that we had been looking for in the southern Democrat-Republican coalition. That was a troublesome matter and had been for many Congresses.

    So, of course, the first item that you would focus on under those circumstances was Medicare. Medicare was pre-eminent in our efforts and had been from 1961. We had worked arduously to try to move Medicare in every way we could. We had a considerable amount of support from Clint Anderson and others on the Senate side. We couldn't budge Wilbur Mills. There had been strong opposition from the AMA and others over a period of years and it had been effective. But now it was conceivable that you could bring about a change in Wilbur Mills' view. Attempts to tack Medicare on in conference had failed. Other attempts to act on Medicare had failed and it was a very frustrating situation. We anticipated a very fruitful Eighty-Ninth Congress, the first session, particularly. Underscoring that the movement on Medicare, HR 1 and S 1, which started immediately and culminated in, at long last, victory.

Of course, it was not confined solely to Medicare. . . .

. . . We were going to finalize the New Frontier program and launch the Great Society program. And there were a lot of innovative programs that Lyndon Johnson had in mind that would be the focus for the Great Society. So we had a full plate. Our optimism was based on the election and that we had in place what we felt was an effective congressional relations program in which most of us involved, and certainly that applied to the President, had been through legislative struggles. We were not, as we had been in 1961, attempting to build a procedure. Spearheading all of this was the Medicare effort.

The fact is the first session of the Eighty-Ninth was [the] most productive in the history of the country. It brought comparisons with Roosevelt's first hundred days. It wasn't a valid comparison. The Supreme Court had knocked out most of the Roosevelt proposals that were enacted to attack a tremendous problem, the Depression, he had inherited as president. And with us, I think it was somewhat different. A commitment that had been made by the Democratic Party and by us in the Kennedy-Johnson period had not been fulfilled. . . . It seemed the switch of thirty-eight house seats in the 1964 election would give you just that additional elbowroom that could make the difference, and it did make the difference. It was a very productive session of Congress, it impacted on the vast majority of American people.

Medicare was pre-eminent in that regard. Of course you had voting rights, you had higher education, you had the whole field of medical research and—oh, you can name it. At the end of that session, of eighty-eight proposals that had been made to the Congress we had succeeded in eighty-four, which was just miraculous. It was unbelievable. Nothing like that had ever occurred in terms of depth and impact. . . .

Gillette: Was Congress itself changing, not in terms of the proportions you've already indicated?

O'Brien: Yes, it was changing in terms that I keep referring to—this so-called coalition in the House. It existed in the Senate, too, but in the House it had greater impact. It was an alliance, really, of southern Democrats and the Republicans who [had] effectively blocked, over many years, social legislation, civil rights. So the numerical advantage of the Democratic Party in the House was a phantom. It just wasn't there. In order for us to realistically count the House, we had to count perhaps ninety southern Democratic members along with the Republicans and say, "This is just about even. Anything you can accomplish, you're going to accomplish with a five- or six-vote margin or lose it by that." This had been an extremely effective procedure that went to the Democratic Party nationally. The difficulties in bridging the varying views in the Democratic Party had been in existence for some time. It became a matter of intense involvement with the advent of civil rights legislation. The Democratic Party platforms over a number of presidential elections advocated equal rights. It never faced reality, but you could mouth these platitudes.

A southern Democrat could recognize it for what it was. He would just maintain his historic position. Any time there was an effort congressionally, that effort was stymied, so the Democratic Party went on with this patchwork quilt, a supposed national party. If you analyze the House of Representatives—I don't intend to focus on the House exclusively; [it existed in] the Senate too, obviously, in filibusters—you had a two-party House. You had Democrats and then you had a southern Democrat-Republican side of the House. We had worked arduously to try to break that one on one, from the time that we went into the White House in 1961, and we had some degree of success. Sometimes it was success that was not really clear on the record. Some southern Democrats, to help Kennedy, or Johnson later, would do a little behind-the-scenes maneuvering, agree to move legislation they might oppose in a roll call, that sort of thing. That was breaking down.

We approached the 1964 election feeling that we had reduced the southern Democratic opposition to "liberal legislation" from ninety-plus to sixty or lower. There were some indications in roll calls we had cut it even further. That was primarily because of the intensive effort that was undertaken by the White House, by President Kennedy, Vice President Johnson, and later President Johnson. And it was really one on one. People like George Mahon and Al Thomas and Carl Vinson and any number of rather senior southern Democrats were anxious to be of some help if they could.

Now you have an unfinished agenda, the New Frontier; several New Frontier proposals had not been enacted. You have the advent of a broadly based Great Society program of President Johnson. Now you have a two-pronged objective.

But you have that elbowroom. Eighty-four out of eighty-eight legislative proposals made by the White House were enacted into law. I've tried to impress upon people in discussions the human element in all of this, that it isn't a cold statistic. This guy or gal has been elected to represent a district or state reflecting the attitude of his or her constituency. That person has no desire to embarrass or demean the president. Progress was made inch by inch or often was due to human relations. People wanted to be helpful with respect to the office of the presidency, rather than on the substance or merits of the legislative proposal. If it didn't have merit it wasn't going anywhere anyway. . . .

To stick with Medicare for a minute, [which was] a proposal of the Democratic Party platforms for decades. There had been advocacy on the part of Democratic presidents; Harry Truman was the first. It clearly was a commitment made by the party, and we all recognize the party platform probably isn't worth the reading most of the time, and I don't think many people ever read a party platform anyway after a convention.

So, with a two-to-one margin in the House, with evidence that you had succeeded in breaking down the coalition, you go for a program that was so broad in its elements that it spoke to every Democratic Party position leading with Medicare. In 1961 we avoided the conflict that would take place with little hope of success in civil rights in order to get some meaningful legislation without a complete war on the Hill at the beginning and eased into the major legislative commitments, civil rights, in due course down the road. The contrast is obvious in 1965. You could approach it by saying, "I'm going to propose legislation in every area of challenge that exists today and has existed over time—everything that I, the President of the United States, feel is in the national interest." And that's exactly what happened. There was one goal, 100 per cent success, not any ifs or maybes, just "we'll go for it." President Johnson, without hesitancy, made that decision and we went for it. And he was right. It worked. And you can't overlook the additional members in the House and the two additional seats in the Senate.

That traditional House roadblock began to disappear. The power of key Republicans and southern Democrats in terms of a coalition dissipated. And by the end of 1965 we weren't using the phrase "southern Democrat-Republican coalition," because it no longer existed. And that brought about a fantastic result. Everything that was occurring, every signing ceremony was impacting as we saw it, for good on the nation as a whole. It was fulfilling the role of the federal government.

We thought we might run out of pens to distribute at signing ceremonies. We had a heavy schedule of signing ceremonies and we weren't immediately focusing on the implementation of all of this. How could you assure proper implementation, administration, grassroots productivity in these programs? That came later, and certainly some of the adverse comment about some of these proposals that became law had to do with not the substance, not the purpose, not the goals, but the administrative aspects, which were faulty in many areas and still are to some extent. But that's beside the point in terms of what our objectives were then.

Source: Lawrence F. O'Brien Oral History Interview XI, July 24, 1986, by Michael L. Gillette. Transcript, pp. 1–6. Lyndon B. Johnson Library Oral History Collection. www.lbjlib.utexas.edu/johnson/archives .hom/oralhistory.hom/obrienl/OBRIEN11.PDF.

President Johnson Reflects on His Support for Medicare and Social Security

DOCUMENT
7.8

"By God You Can't Treat Grandma This Way"

1965

President Lyndon B. Johnson ardently supported the passage of Medicare legislation, and he and his administration were deeply involved in crafting and advancing the bill that ultimately received his signature on July 30, 1965. While Johnson's determination to pass a substantive Medicare bill was based in part on his certainty that it would pay enormous political dividends for himself and the Democratic Party, it was also based on a genuine belief in the moral rightness of the social welfare legislation for which they were fighting. This aspect of Johnson's White House tenure was evident in an Oval Office conversation he had with Press Secretary Bill Moyers on March 10, 1965. In this conversation, wrote historian Larry DeWitt, "Johnson permits himself to reflect almost philosophically on his support for a provision in a pending bill which would provide a retroactive increase in Social Security payments. Moyers is arguing that the President should support the retroactivity clause because it will provide a stimulus to the economy. Johnson supports the provision, but he makes clear to Moyers that he does not see programs like Social Security and Medicare as being about economics."[1]

Moyers: Has anyone talked to you about the consideration being given on the Hill not to make the Social Security benefits retroactive? There is a movement afoot, among some, to drop the retroactivity part of the Social Security benefit. . . . I and others feel that this would have a serious effect on the economic situation toward the end of the year, and we need to make a determined fight to keep that retroactive clause back to January 1 in the bill on Medicare and Social Security.

Johnson: My judgment is that it ought to be retroactive. . . . My reason though is not because of the economy. I think we use the economy too much to spend money. I think we—I'm just tired of these old clichés, [but] we just got to do it. . . .

My reason would be the same as I agreed to go $400 million on health. I've never seen an anti-trust suit lie against an old-age pensioner for monopoly or concentration of power or closely-held wealth. I've never seen it apply it to the average worker. And I've never seen one have too much health benefits. So when they come in to me and say we've got to have $400 million more so we can take care of some doctors bills, I'm for it on health. I'm pretty much for it on education. I'm for it anywhere it's practicable. . . .

My inclination would be, and the way that my judgment at this moment would be, [is] it ought to be retroactive as far back as you can get it, and I would guess January, because none of them ever get enough. And they are entitled to it, and that's an obligation of ours. It's just like your mother writing you and saying she wants $20, and I'd always sent mine a $100 when she did. I never did it because I thought it was going to be good for the economy of Austin. I always did it because I thought she was entitled to it. And I think that's a much better reason and a much better cause and I think it can be defended on a hell of a lot better basis. . . . We do know that it affects the economy, and I think we do think that on balance it helps us in that respect. But that's not the basis to go to the Hill, or the justification. We've just got to say that by God you can't treat grandma this way. She's entitled to it and we promised it to her. We held it up last year, and we're committed [now], and we're obligated."

Source: Johnson, Lyndon B. Conversation with Press Secretary Bill Moyers, March 10, 1965. Audiotape WH6503.05. Transcribed by the author. http://millercenter.org/scripps/archive/presidentialrecordings /johnson/1965/03_1965.

NOTE

1. Larry DeWitt, "The Medicare Program as a Capstone to the Great Society," May 2003, www. larrydewitt.net/Essays/MedicareDaddy.htm.

An Influential Member of Congress Recalls the Development of Medicare Part B

DOCUMENT 7.9

"We All Realized That the Time Had Come for It"

1965

The final months of legislative haggling over Medicare and Medicaid, which ultimately became law as part of the Social Security Amendments of 1965, featured a number of interesting political maneuvers. Most famously, Rep. Wilbur Mills (D-AR), the powerful chair of the House Ways and Means Committee, expanded Medicare to cover costs from doctors' visits and other physician services in addition to hospital costs. This idea, which had originated with the American Medical Association, came to be known as Medicare

Part B (the hospitalization portion of the bill was designated Part A). In the following excerpt from a 1986 interview with Michael L. Gillette, Mills provides his take on how Part B came to be included in the larger Medicare and Medicaid package and explains his shifting views on Medicare over time.

Gillette: Let's start, Chairman Mills, with Medicare in 1965.

Mills: Well, Medicare had been before us, you know, long before that. Aime Forand had introduced the bill. He was not the ranking Democrat to me, but well up toward the top of the [Ways and Means] Committee. The only people for it were labor unions, and he was the only one on the committee, apparently, that was for it. And then Johnson had his remarkable election in 1964, and that was a campaign issue. I thought then that the time had come to enact something, and he recommended that we take care of the hospital costs only of people over sixty-five under Social Security, in connection with Social Security.

And as we went into it and as it developed, we realized that that would take care of about 25 per cent of the total costs of the elderly, medical costs and things. So we knew that if we passed it—and I told him this—I said, "If we pass your program, Mr. President, and the American people find out that we're taking care of 25 per cent of them, we're going to be the laughingstock of the country. We've misled them, they'll think. And it'll react seriously on us." "Well, do what you want to do about it, then, and develop it as you want to develop it."

So we proceeded then, with the help of the developmental folks, to develop the whole thing, to take care of the out-of-hospital costs as well under Plan B, you remember. And I astutely got a Republican to offer that motion in the committee, so I got all the Republican votes for it. John Byrnes was not the usual Republican; he was from Wisconsin, and they were always a little bit more liberal in their thinking on things like that.

So we adopted the Plan B, and the President always thought that that was a great addition to it. He was always thanking me for that.

Gillette: Wilbur Cohen described that process as the greatest legislative maneuver that he'd ever witnessed.

Mills: (Laughter)

Gillette: Now, tell me where the idea of combining these—there were actually about three different proposals, weren't there, Eldercare—in a multiple-tiered piece of legislation?

Mills: Well, we had to put it somewhere, and I guess we came up with that idea; I don't remember the details of it. But I don't think it came from the Department [of Social Security]; I think it came from us on the committee. I don't remember just how, but I know that we had the three proposals. First of all, we had the Kerr-Mills thing in effect and had to replace that with Medicaid, and—I don't know; maybe I had the idea. I just don't remember. But it came from the committee, somewhere.

Gillette: But the supplemental aspect that Byrnes introduced was actually in concert with you?

Mills: Oh, I developed the whole thing in the committee. I mean, we did, with the help of the staff people, by my questions and other questions of other members we developed the idea and the program. Then I whispered in his ear, "John, I wish you'd offer a motion to include it." "I'd be glad to." (Laughter) He did.

Gillette: Cohen describes this almost with an element of amazement. Was it pieced together—?

Mills: No, it was planned.

Gillette: It was? You'd been working on it for some time.

Mills: We planned that, yes. Oh, yes. I'd developed some ideas on it, how we'd proceed to—I was always determined that whatever came out of the committee passed, you know. It was a waste of time to spend a month or two in the committee developing something that you couldn't pass, and I was always trying to get something I knew would appeal to a cross section of the membership. I got that idea from Sam Rayburn, of course.

Gillette: Historians are always, I guess, going to wonder about your own process of supporting the bill from I guess the time it was first introduced in 1961—

Mills: No, I wasn't for it then. I didn't think we could pass it.

Gillette: Let me ask you to describe what transformation, if any, in your own mind there was, and all of the elements: to what extent was it the ability to pass it? To what extent was it coming around to a different point of view on—?

Mills: Well, time had developed, I think, more support for it among the people. But then the election of the President in 1964 had the major impact, made the major difference. He had espoused it in his campaign, you know, and here he was elected by a 2 to 1 vote, which was a pretty strong endorsement of it, I thought. I thought the time had come to pass it. I don't think we could have passed it in 1961. I told Kennedy that, and he agreed, I guess. He never did really press me about it.

Gillette: Did LBJ press you before 1965?

Mills: Oh, no. No, not on that, he didn't. Actually, he talked to me I guess before he submitted it. He usually did, and I'm sure he did in that instance. But there was never any pressure on it. I was for it by then, in 1965.

Gillette: Was there anyone whose advice you may have sought during this period that may have also been instrumental in underscoring the popularity of it?

Mills: No, no, I could feel it, I think. I don't remember—the people that I talked to were doctors who were opposed to it, primarily, and we finally got some of them over to our point of view. And now, of course, they're living off of it.

Gillette: Let me ask you to describe the AMA's [American Medical Association] efforts to defeat the measure over the years, and to what extent they did put pressure on you.

Mills: Well, they put tremendous—or tried to put; I never did realize pressure was being put on me, I guess, but I knew the head of the AMA at the time. Was it Roth, Dr. Roth? What was his name, Dr. [James] Roth? I knew him quite well, and he visited me quite often about it, but I had pressure from my doctors down home, even, about it. And they didn't understand it: they were just reflecting what they were told to tell me. And I could always get around that by explaining a little bit about the problem and what I thought we ought to do. I said, "You ought to be for it. You're in the business of saving lives," and so on.

(Laughter)

They'd back off; they never really put too much pressure on me. I'm sure they thought they did, but I didn't think so. . . .

Source: Wilbur Mills Oral History Interview II, March 26, 1987, by Michael L. Gillette. Transcript, pp. 1–4. Lyndon B. Johnson Library Oral History Collection. www.lbjlib.utexas.edu/johnson/archives.hom/oralhistory.hom/Mills-w/mills2.pdf.

President Johnson Signs Medicare and Medicaid into Law

"No Longer Will Older Americans Be Denied the Healing Miracle of Modern Medicine"

1965

President Lyndon B. Johnson signed the Medicare and Medicaid packages into law as amendments to the Social Security Act on July 30, 1965, at a ceremony hosted by former president Harry S. Truman at the Harry S. Truman Library in Independence, Missouri. The locale chosen for the event was meant to honor Truman, who had helped lay the groundwork for the legislation during his own years in the White House. After the signing, Truman briefly spoke to the assembled crowd before introducing Johnson, who praised the legislation as a fulfillment of America's finest principles and traditions. Following are excerpts from Truman's and Johnson's remarks.

PRESIDENT TRUMAN: Mr. President, Mrs. Johnson, distinguished guests:

You have done me a great honor in coming here today, and you have made me a very, very happy man.

This is an important hour for the Nation, for those of our citizens who have completed their tour of duty and have moved to the sidelines. These are the days that we are trying to celebrate for them. These people are our prideful responsibility and they are entitled, among other benefits, to the best medical protection available.

Not one of these, our citizens, should ever be abandoned to the indignity of charity. Charity is indignity when you have to have it. But we don't want these people to have anything to do with charity and we don't want them to have any idea of hopeless despair.

Mr. President, I am glad to have lived this long and to witness today the signing of the Medicare bill which puts this Nation right where it needs to be, to be right. Your inspired leadership and a responsive forward-looking Congress have made it historically possible for this day to come about.

Thank all of you most highly for coming here. It is an honor I haven't had for, well, quite awhile, I'll say that to you, but here it is:

Ladies and gentlemen, the President of the United States.

PRESIDENT JOHNSON: President and Mrs. Truman, Secretary Celebrezze, Senator Mansfield, Senator Symington, Senator Long, Governor Hearnes, Senator Anderson and Congressman King of the Anderson-King team, Congressman Mills and Senator Long of the Mills-Long team, our beloved Vice President who worked in the vineyard many years to see this day come to pass, and all of my dear friends in the Congress—both Democrats and Republicans:

The people of the United States love and voted for Harry Truman, not because he gave them hell—but because he gave them hope.

I believe today that all America shares my joy that he is present now when the hope that he offered becomes a reality for millions of our fellow citizens.

I am so proud that this has come to pass in the Johnson administration. But it was really Harry Truman of Missouri who planted the seeds of compassion and duty which have today flowered into care for the sick, and serenity for the fearful.

Many men can make many proposals. Many men can draft many laws. But few have the piercing and humane eye which can see beyond the words to the people that they touch. Few can see past the speeches and the political battles to the doctor over there that is tending the infirm, and to the hospital that is receiving those in anguish, or feel in their heart painful wrath at the injustice which denies the miracle of healing to the old and to the poor. And fewer still have the courage to stake reputation, and position, and the effort of a lifetime upon such a cause when there are so few that share it.

But it is just such men who illuminate the life and the history of a nation. And so, President Harry Truman, it is in tribute not to you, but to the America that you represent, that we have come here to pay our love and our respects to you today. For a country can be known by the quality of the men it honors. By praising you, and by carrying forward your dreams, we really reaffirm the greatness of America.

It was a generation ago that Harry Truman said, and I quote him: "Millions of our citizens do not now have a full measure of opportunity to achieve and to enjoy good health. Millions do not now have protection or security against the economic effects of sickness. And the time has now arrived for action to help them attain that opportunity and to help them get that protection."

Well, today, Mr. President, and my fellow Americans, we are taking such action—20 years later. And we are doing that under the great leadership of men like John McCormack, our Speaker; Carl Albert, our majority leader; our very able and beloved majority leader of the Senate, Mike Mansfield; and distinguished Members of the Ways and Means and Finance Committees of the House and Senate—of both parties, Democratic and Republican.

Because the need for this action is plain; and it is so clear indeed that we marvel not simply at the passage of this bill, but what we marvel at is that it took so many years to pass it. And I am so glad that Aime Forand is here to see it finally passed and signed—one of the first authors.

There are more than 18 million Americans over the age of 65. Most of them have low incomes. Most of them are threatened by illness and medical expenses that they cannot afford.

And through this new law, Mr. President, every citizen will be able, in his productive years when he is earning, to insure himself against the ravages of illness in his old age.

This insurance will help pay for care in hospitals, in skilled nursing homes, or in the home. And under a separate plan it will help meet the fees of the doctors.

Now here is how the plan will affect you.

During your working years, the people of America—you—will contribute through the social security program a small amount each payday for hospital insurance protection. For example, the average worker in 1966 will contribute about $1.50 per month. The employer will contribute a similar amount. And this will provide the funds to pay up to 90 days of hospital care for each illness, plus diagnostic care, and up to 100 home health visits after you are 65. And beginning in 1967, you will also be covered for up to 100 days of care in a skilled nursing home after a period of hospital care.

And under a separate plan, when you are 65—that the Congress originated itself, in its own good judgment—you may be covered for medical and surgical fees whether you are in or out of the hospital. You will pay $3 per month after you are 65 and your Government will contribute an equal amount.

The benefits under the law are as varied and broad as the marvelous modern medicine itself. If it has a few defects—such as the method of payment of certain specialists—then I am confident those can be quickly remedied and I hope they will be.

No longer will older Americans be denied the healing miracle of modern medicine. No longer will illness crush and destroy the savings that they have so carefully put away over a lifetime so that they might enjoy dignity in their later years. No longer will young families see their own incomes, and their own hopes, eaten away simply because they are carrying out their deep moral obligations to their parents, and to their uncles, and their aunts.

And no longer will this Nation refuse the hand of justice to those who have given a lifetime of service and wisdom and labor to the progress of this progressive country.

And this bill, Mr. President, is even broader than that. It will increase social security benefits for all of our older Americans. It will improve a wide range of health and medical services for Americans of all ages.

In 1935 when the man that both of us loved so much, Franklin Delano Roosevelt, signed the Social Security Act, he said it was, and I quote him, "a cornerstone in a structure which is being built but it is by no means complete."

Well, perhaps no single act in the entire administration of the beloved Franklin D. Roosevelt really did more to win him the illustrious place in history that he has as did the laying of that cornerstone. And I am so happy that his oldest son Jimmy could be here to share with us the joy that is ours today. And those who share this day will also be remembered for making the most important addition to that structure, and you are making it in this bill, the most important addition that has been made in three decades.

History shapes men, but it is a necessary faith of leadership that men can help shape history. There are many who led us to this historic day. Not out of courtesy or deference, but from the gratitude and remembrance which is our country's debt, if I may be pardoned for taking a moment, I want to call a part of the honor roll: it is the able leadership in both Houses of the Congress.

Congressman Celler, Chairman of the Judiciary Committee, introduced the hospital insurance in 1952. Aime Forand from Rhode Island, then Congressman, introduced it in the House. Senator Clinton Anderson from New Mexico fought for Medicare through the years in the Senate. Congressman Cecil King of California carried on the battle in the House. The legislative genius of the Chairman of the Ways and Means Committee, Congressman Wilbur Mills, and the effective and able work of Senator Russell Long, together transformed this desire into victory.

And those devoted public servants, former Secretary, Senator Ribicoff; present Secretary, Tony Celebrezze; Under Secretary Wilbur Cohen; the Democratic whip of the House, Hale Boggs on the Ways and Means Committee; and really the White House's best legislator, Larry O'Brien, gave not just endless days and months and, yes, years of patience—but they gave their hearts—to passing this bill.

Let us also remember those who sadly cannot share this time for triumph. For it is their triumph too. It is the victory of great Members of Congress that are not with us, like John Dingell, Sr., and Robert Wagner, late a Member of the Senate, and James Murray of Montana.

And there is also John Fitzgerald Kennedy, who fought in the Senate and took his case to the people, and never yielded in pursuit, but was not spared to see the final concourse of the forces that he had helped to loose.

But it all started really with the man from Independence. And so, as it is fitting that we should, we have come back here to his home to complete what he began.

President Harry Truman, as any President must, made many decisions of great moment; although he always made them frankly and with a courage and a clarity that few men have ever shared. The immense and the intricate questions of freedom and survival were caught up many times in the web of Harry Truman's judgment. And this is in the tradition of leadership.

But there is another tradition that we share today. It calls upon us never to be indifferent toward despair. It commands us never to turn away from helplessness. It directs us never to ignore or to spurn those who suffer untended in a land that is bursting with abundance.

I said to Senator Smathers, the whip of the Democrats in the Senate, who worked with us in the Finance Committee on this legislation—I said, the highest traditions of the medical profession are really directed to the ends that we are trying to serve. And it was only yesterday, at the request of some of my friends, I met with the leaders of the American Medical Association to seek their assistance in advancing the cause of one of the greatest professions of all—the medical profession—in helping us to maintain and to improve the health of all Americans.

And this is not just our tradition—or the tradition of the Democratic Party—or even the tradition of the Nation. It is as old as the day it was first commanded: "Thou shalt open thine hand wide unto thy brother, to thy poor, to thy needy, in thy land."

And just think, Mr. President, because of this document—and the long years of struggle which so many have put into creating it—in this town, and a thousand other towns like it, there are men and women in pain who will now find ease. There are those, alone in suffering who will now hear the sound of some approaching footsteps coming to help. There are those fearing the terrible darkness of despairing poverty—despite their long years of labor and expectation—who will now look up to see the light of hope and realization.

There just can be no satisfaction, nor any act of leadership, that gives greater satisfaction than this.

And perhaps you alone, President Truman, perhaps you alone can fully know just how grateful I am for this day.

Source: Johnson, Lyndon B. Remarks with President Truman at the Signing in Independence of the Medicare Bill. *Papers of the Presidents of the United States: Lyndon B. Johnson, 1965.* Volume II, pp. 811–15. Washington, DC: Government Printing Office, 1966. www.lbjlib.utexas.edu/johnson/archives.hom/speeches.hom/650730.asp.

DOCUMENT
7.11

Launching the War on Cancer

"The Final Answer to Cancer Can Be Found"

1969

During the 1960s and 1970s direct federal involvement in medical research rose dramatically, lifting government laboratories and research institutions to the same status as universities, nonprofit institutes, and other private institutions that had previously been at the vanguard of medical research in the United States. This transformation owed much to the efforts of politically connected philanthropists such as Mary Lasker and Florence Mahoney, both of whom were convinced that the federal government had the capacity—if it applied itself—to eradicate dreaded diseases and other public health problems. The quest to reorganize and emphasize medical research was also aided by post–World War II economic prosperity, faith in science, and confidence in the state's ability to chart productive courses of research.

As a result, the annual budget of the National Institute of Health (NIH) jumped from $3 million in 1945 to $450 million by 1961, and to nearly $1 billion by the close of the 1960s. Many of these appropriations mandated the creation of distinct research arms within the NIH, such as the National Cancer Institute (NCI). This evolution of the National Institute of Health into the National Institutes of Health was not without controversy. "NIH scientists, although buoyed by the unprecedented resources and prestige they enjoyed in the postwar years, were wary of research funding by disease category through separate NIH institutes. They preferred allocations by scientific disciplines based on the process of peer review of research proposals initiated by investigators, not appropriations to individual NIH institutes for research on specific diseases selected by Congress, which some of them derisively called 'disease-of-the-month-club' legislation."[1]

Lasker and other supporters of expanded biomedical research shrugged off these complaints, and by the mid-1960s their crusade was increasingly focused on cancer research. Determined to force greater government expenditures in this realm, Lasker formed the Citizens' Committee for the Conquest of Cancer, which in late 1969 placed full-page advertisements in both the Washington Post *and the* New York Times *stating: "MR. NIXON: YOU CAN CURE CANCER" (the ad is reprinted here). The solution, according to Lasker and her allies, was to create a cancer research entity separate from the NIH that would report directly to the president. This demand was deeply unpopular with scientists and NIH officials who lambasted Lasker for politicizing medical research and unrealistically raising public expectations that cancer could be swiftly conquered.*

Two years later, Congress passed and Nixon signed a compromise measure known as the National Cancer Act of 1971. This legislation made an astounding $1.59 billion available for cancer research over a three-year period, and it separated the NCI budget from the wider NIH budget. "Like most of NIH I didn't like [the National Cancer Act]," admitted NIH official Vincent DeVita, who later became a director of the NCI. "I thought it was intrusion and so forth. When it was passed, though, it changed the mission not only of the NCI but of the NIH. The mandate of the Cancer Act was to support research and the application of the results of the research to reduce the incidence, morbidity and mortality from cancer. The NIH never had had a mission beyond supporting basic research. . . . Academia was against it, the NIH was against it, the [American Medical Association] was against it. So . . . it took a while for the changes to sink in but it changed immediately what the NIH was sort of expected to do and that was good in the end."[2]

Text of advertisement:

> If prayers are heard in Heaven, this prayer is heard the most:
>
> "Dear God, please. Not cancer."
>
> Still, more than 318,000 Americans died of cancer last year.
>
> This year, Mr. President, you have it in your power to begin to end this curse.
>
> As you agonize over the Budget, we beg you to remember the agony of those 318,000 American. And their families.

We urge you to remember also that we spend more each day on military matters than each *year* on cancer research. And, last year, more than 21 times as much on space research as on cancer research.

We ask a better perspective, a better way to allocate our money to save hundreds of thousands of lives each year.

America can do this. There is not a doubt in the minds of our top cancer researchers that the final answer to cancer can be found.

Already, 4 out of about 200 types of cancer can be cured with drugs. And 37 other drugs will cause temporary remission in 17 other types of cancer.

Dr. Sidney Farber, Past President of the American Cancer Society, believes: "We are so close to a cure for cancer. We lack only the will and the kind of money and comprehensive planning that went into putting a man on the moon."

Why don't we try to conquer cancer by America's 200th birthday?

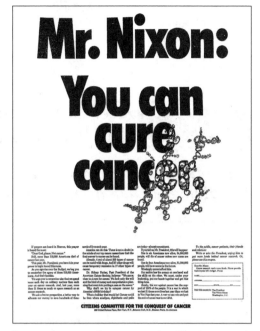

"1969 newspaper advertisement placed by the Citizens' Committee for the Conquest of Cancer advocating for increased federal research funding."

What a holiday that would be! Cancer could be then where smallpox, diphtheria and polio are today—almost nonexistent.

If you fail us, Mr. President, this will happen:

One in six Americans now alive, 34,000,000 people, will die of cancer unless new cures are found.

One in four Americans now alive, 51,000,000 people, will have cancer in the future. We simply cannot afford this.

Our Nation has the money on one hand and the skills on the other. We must, under your leadership, put our hands together and get this thing done.

Surely, the war against cancer has the support of 100% of the people. It is a war in which we lost 21 times more lives last year than we lost in Viet Nam last year. A war we can win and put the entire human race in our debt.

To the public, cancer patients, their friends and relatives:

Write or wire the President, urging him to put more funds behind cancer research. Or, please use this coupon.

Source: Citizens' Committee for the Conquest of Cancer. "Mr. Nixon: You Can Cure Cancer." *Washington Post.* December 9, 1969, p. C9. Mary Lasker Archives, National Library of Medicine. http://profiles.nlm .nih.gov/ps/retrieve/ResourceMetadata/TLBBBY.

Notes

1. "Mary Lasker and the Growth of the National Institutes of Health," Mary Lasker Papers, National Institutes of Health, U.S. National Library of Medicine, n.d., http://profiles.nlm.nih.gov/TL/Views /Exhibit/narrative/nih.html.

2. Vincent DeVita, interview on National Cancer Act of 1971, National Institutes of Health, National Cancer Institute, www.dtp.nci.nih.gov/timeline/videoclips/transcripts/M4_transcript.htm.

**DOCUMENT
7.12**

A Warning about America's Growing "Medical-Industrial Complex"

"Emerging Medical Empires Are No More Rational and Are Often Less Humane Than the Old System"

1970

In the late 1960s and early 1970s frustration with America's sprawling health care system was on the rise across much of the country. The specific complaints varied by geographic, demographic, and ideological subgroup, but widespread agreement existed that, when taken as a whole, U.S. health care was in crisis. This conviction sparked a flood of commentary on the issue from across the political spectrum. Most conservative observers identified "big government" bureaucracy as the chief culprit behind soaring health care costs and other health care problems. Liberals focused more of their fire on health industry "profiteers" and their ever-expanding business empires. These critics (joined by some conservatives) charged that many private sector institutions, fueled by incredible infusions of money from liberal government programs such as Medicare and Medicaid, had metastasized into growth-hungry entities that treated patients as a virtual afterthought.

One of the most influential and scathing assessments of American health care during this time was written by liberal social critics Barbara Ehrenreich and John Ehrenreich in the pages of the New York Review of Books. *The essay, which is excerpted here, begins by critiquing various health care policies and priorities of the Kennedy, Johnson, and Nixon administrations, then moves on to examine the various economic, political, and social factors that have combined to create what the authors termed America's "Medical-Industrial Complex." It then concludes with hopeful speculation that festering unhappiness with America's health care system might be laying the groundwork for massive restructuring and nationalization of health care services down the road.*

The American crisis over health has finally taken a place alongside the urban crisis, the ecological crisis, and the "youth crisis" as the subject for solemn Presidential announcements, TV documentaries, and special features of magazines ranging from *Fortune* to *Redbook*. But to the average consumer of pills, hospital care, and doctors' services, the crisis in health care is nothing new, except that the stakes—health, beauty, and life itself—get higher with each advance in medical technology, from miracle vaccines to organ transplants. The odds against the sick are high, and getting higher all the time.

Health care is, first of all, a scarce and expensive commodity. With the increasing centralization of medical manpower and modern equipment in a few big city medical centers, rural areas, small towns, and urban ghettos have been left empty of even the most rudimentary, old-fashioned services. Where services exist, their high cost is the most serious barrier to health care, not only for the very poor, but for growing numbers of working people as well. As the price of medical care mounts, health insurance has become a necessity; but insurance premiums are becoming more expensive too, while benefits dwindle as rapidly as the costs of medical treatment increase.

Money aside, the consumer's major problem is finding his way about an increasingly impersonal, fragmented, irrationally arranged set of health services. The patient, rich or poor, treks from specialist to subspecialist, from clinic to clinic, from doctor to laboratory, losing more money and time at each stop. No one is concerned with the general state of his health, as opposed to his immediate illness; fewer and fewer doctors are even concerned with the patient's whole body, sick or well. Long waiting times and brusque service are now almost as characteristic of private doctors' offices as they are of the hospital clinics used by the poor. And for the very poor, usually black and brown people, the price of care in a hospital's "charity" ward or clinic is often the humiliation of having his body used as "material" for research and the training of doctors. . . .

At the center of the health services industry is no longer the doctor, but the medical school or major teaching hospital with its "empire" of owned or affiliated institutions, and with a local monopoly on the production and distribution of advanced medical technology. New York City's medical scene, for example, is dominated by nine of these medical empires, which together control more than three-quarters of the city's hospital beds, more than half of its doctors, nurses, and other professionals, and the lion's share of public money for biomedical research and development. The majority of New York's doctors practice, full or part-time, in the empires' institutions. At least two million New Yorkers are wholly dependent, and another four million partly dependent on these medical empires for their health and strength.

For example, virtually all of the health resources in the Bronx are controlled by the coalition empire of Albert Einstein College of Medicine-Montefiore Hospital. The parent institutions control, directly or through affiliation contracts, three municipal hospitals, a Veterans' Administration hospital, a state mental hospital, two community mental health centers, two voluntary hospitals, and a community health center. They exert a lesser degree of control, through interlocking staff appointments, over the few remaining unaffiliated institutions in the Bronx. Similarly, Columbia-Presbyterian controls health resources in upper Manhattan, Downstate Medical Center in Brooklyn.

The physician in New York and other cities has lost his nineteenth-century entrepreneurial autonomy not to the encroachments of government, but to the exigencies of a technology controlled by the medical empires. The major medical centers have the advanced equipment, the hundreds of necessary paramedical workers, and the resources of scientific expertise. If the doctor wants to use them, he does so—and hence defines his practice—on terms set by the institution.

Liberals in the profession, as opposed to the conservatives of the AMA, have heralded this increasing centralization of medical resources into a few major institutions or multi-institutional networks as a step toward a more "rational," integrated health care system. But in their social effects the emerging medical empires are no more rational and are often less humane than the old system of private doctors they are replacing. As citadels of the most advanced medical technology, the major medical centers have emphasized esoteric, high technology treatment of hospitalized patients over preventive care or routine medical care, and they tend to emphasize medical research and education over human care of any kind. The middle-class patient runs the risk of costly—and sometimes harmful—medical overkill in the hands of the empire's scientist-practitioners. Poor patients, if they are medically "interesting," serve as the human material for research and teaching projects.

If they are uninteresting, they are processed hurriedly, or else "dumped" to a less prestigious institution.

The dominant medical institutions of this country are, for tax purposes, classified
as "nonprofit" corporations, but they have begun to display, over the last decade, the kind
of expansionist *élan* characteristic of frankly profit-making enterprises. Income in excess
of that required to meet expenses is plowed into real estate expansion, stockholdings, the
construction or acquisition of new subsidiary institutions, or the purchase of new,
research-oriented equipment.

Presbyterian Hospital, for example, the teaching hospital affiliated with Columbia
University College of Medicine, spends over $3 million a year on real estate and has
become a major slumlord in Washington Heights-West Harlem. Mount Sinai Hospital,
in East Harlem, recently sank $750 thousand into the construction of a hyperbaric
chamber—an asset of questionable value even in the treatment of the exotic diseases it
was designed for. Increasingly the funds for such ventures have come out of the public
treasury, either directly, through special grants, or indirectly, through inflated charges to
Medicaid and Medicare for "patient care." (In New York City, Medicare and Medicaid
contribute half of the hospitals' operating budgets.)

As the medical empires expand, relying more and more on government money to
nurture their development, they are themselves becoming essentially private "governments" of health, commanding medical and community resources on a city-wide or
borough-wide scale. They . . . are, in more and more American cities and suburbs, the
major force to be dealt with in creating a reasonable health care system.

While institutions have replaced physicians at the center of the health service industry, services themselves are no longer the only major product of the American health
industry. Health *goods*—drugs, hospital supplies, and equipment—have become increasingly essential elements of medical care, absorbing an ever larger share of national health
expenditures. Since 1960, sales of drugs have been growing at a rate of 9 percent a year;
sales of hospital supplies (linen, disposable syringes, etc.), by 11 percent a year. Sales of
medical electronic equipment alone hit $350 million in 1969. Profits throughout the
health industry increased even more rapidly. Attracted by the spectacular 1968/69 boom
in hospital supplies and equipment generated by Medicaid/Medicare, drug companies
such as Parke-Davis, Abbott Labs, and Warner-Lambert have diversified into supplies and
equipment. Conversely, supplies and equipment companies such as Baxter Labs, Becton-
Dickinson, and Johnson and Johnson have diversified into drugs—resulting in the emergence of a single, conglomerated "health products industry."

Economists have ignored the health products industry and its impact on the health
services industry. . . . Even to the most hardheaded economists, health services have an
aura of charity and voluntarism with which the exuberant profiteering of the health products industry contrasts distastefully. But, like it or not, the demand by the hospitals for
fancy, expensive equipment like cobalt radiation units, open-heart surgery equipment,
and computers often outweighs community health needs as a factor in hospital planning.
Mount Sinai's $750,000 hyperbaric chamber, for example, sits often unused in East Har-
lem, an area desperately in need of TB detection, lead poisoning screening, and addiction
programs. Within the hospitals, the rhythms and requirements of the major equipment,
rather than of the doctors or, of course, the patients, increasingly set the pace and style of
patient care. In the future, it is at least technically possible that computers, electronic
patient-monitoring devices, and mechanized, assembly-line diagnostic testing may

reduce the role of the doctor to that of a full-time technician, or hired consultant, to the hospital center.

The health services industry has not been an unwilling host to the growing health products industry. Executives of the health products companies sit on the boards of medical schools and medical centers and on prestigious commissions to study health policy. Research physicians consult eagerly and profitably for the health products industry. Health products industry executives are showing an increasing interest in expanding into the still largely nonprofit health care delivery system. Out of the growing rapport between the delivery and the products industry is emerging a single, American, Medical-Industrial Complex.

In turn, the health industry, taken as a whole, cannot be understood in isolation from the larger economy. Medical technology is the technology of plastics, chemicals, and electronics as much as it is the technology of human physiology. Drug companies, like Merck, make chemicals, and chemical companies, like Dow, make drugs. With the decline in spending on aerospace, giants like United Aircraft, North American, and TRW have been turning their engineering talents to the manufacture of heavy electronic equipment for hospitals. And, where there is no common technology to provide access to the health industry, the big firms move in through acquisitions and mergers. Conglomerates like American Home Products and Squibb-Beechnut have repertoires ranging from chewing gum and dog food to prescription drugs. More and more companies, in more and more sectors of American industry, look to health for a highly profitable, recession-proof, peace-proof sideline.

It was Medicaid and Medicare and, to a certain extent, Blue Cross which propelled the health industry from the remote periphery to a more central position in the national economy. All of these programs reimburse health care institutions essentially on the basis of the institution's total annual costs of providing care, multiplied by the fraction of the institution's total annual bed-days used by the "eligible population," e.g., by Medicare patients. The institutions are accountable to no one in determining what will go into the average "cost" per patient per day. Commonly listed as "administrative expenses" are salaries of $50,000 a year and up for administrators and physicians, public relations men to clean up the hospital's image in the community, and staffs of lawyers to fight worker attempts to unionize. Depreciation on a $40,000 piece of equipment is a legitimate charge to the cost of patient care even if a $20,000 machine would have done just as well, or even if the machine itself is of little medical or social utility.

With no limit to expenditures, so long as they could somehow be justified as "patient care," the hospitals went wild. "Medicare," exulted an electronics trade journal in 1969, "is the computer manufacturer's friend." It made no difference that Medicaid and Medicare did not lead to significant increases in the use of hospitals. It did lead to vast institutional and corporate growth, in which the individual (whatever his tastes, psychology, or effective "demand") is an increasingly incidental participant.

Thirty years ago, the independent doctor, with his AMA card in his wallet and all the mysteries of medicine in his black bag, was the major obstacle to change in the American medical system. Today he is not the only, and probably not the most able, profiteer in the health industry. To ask for an excellent and equitable health system for everyone is to ask our big city medical empires to turn their priorities from research, teaching, and institutional expansion to the care of sick people; it is to ask the health products industry to favor the consumer over the stockholder; it is to ask a growing sector of American industry to come into health as a public service, or not to come at all. . . . Fundamental improvements in health care can be achieved only through a head-on confrontation with our political and economic system. There can be no more damning indictment of capitalism.

As we have seen, Republican and Democratic strategies for reform differ sharply in style and scope, but both acquiesce unquestioningly in the constraints imposed by a private medical-industrial system. Nixon is justly skeptical of the experience of the inflated Johnson and Kennedy health programs, but his skepticism extends only to that narrow interface of the health system where patients encounter practitioners. The less visible heart of the system—the medical school-center empires, the health products companies and insurance companies—goes unchallenged. Meanwhile the health crisis, as experienced by the poor and by growing numbers of the middle class, has deepened. There are signs that disgust with the performance of the politicians and their expert consultants is producing a "movement" for radical change.

Students in medical and nursing schools are bringing the energy of the antiwar movement to the issue of health services. In Philadelphia and Boston, medical students have demanded open admissions—for third world students—to medical schools. In New York and other cities, students are challenging the priorities of their schools and teaching hospitals, demanding free, dignified care for the poor. Black and brown community health worker groups are bringing demands for community control into hospitals and health centers, in addition to escalating quantitative demands for more and more accessible health services.

In New York City, where agitation focuses on existing health institutions, sit-ins and police confrontations are becoming almost as common in health centers and hospitals as they are in the schools. In Chicago, where there are far fewer health institutions for the poor to attack, groups like the Young Lords, the Panthers, and the Young Patriots have set up free storefront clinics, staffed by students and radical young professionals. Finally, women, largely white women, are being to raise women's liberation issues in health institutions—demanding legal abortions, dignified obstetrical and gynecological care, as well as better, cheaper care in general.

What is now emerging is the outline, at least, of a common movement program: That health care should not be a commodity, to be bought by "consumers" and sold by "providers," but should be free at the point of delivery. (That is, the costs should be borne by the entire society, through an equitable tax system.) That medical empires should be decentralized, and be subject to community and worker control. That in all health institutions, priority should be put on patient care, with special emphasis on preventive health services. That the health products industry should be nationalized, and run as a nonprofit enterprise. That medical schools should open their doors to black, brown, and white women applicants and working-class youths, and should provide opportunities for professional training, up to the M.D. level, for all health care workers. That doctors everywhere should be salaried employees of community institutions, not private entrepreneurs.

In short, the health system should be re-created as a democratic enterprise, in which patients are participants (not customers or objects) and health workers, from physicians to aides, are all colleagues in a common undertaking.

Source: Ehrenreich, Barbara, and John Ehrenreich. "The Medical-Industrial Complex." *New York Review of Books.* December 17, 1970, pp. 14–21.

President Nixon Signs the Clean Air Act

"Emissions from Automobiles Which Pollute the Environment Will Be Reduced by 90 Percent"

1970

Rising concerns about environmental degradation and related negative impacts on human health brought about a massive wave of environmental legislation in the 1960s and early 1970s. Most of the landmark resource protection and antipollution legislation that the United States passed in the twentieth century came into being during this so-called golden age of environmentalism. These laws, whether designed to clean up the nation's air and water or preserve its dwindling open spaces from development, vastly expanded the authority and responsibilities of existing federal health and natural resource agencies. In addition, they created entirely new entities such as the Environmental Protection Agency (EPA) to enforce and monitor other newly minted public health and environmental regulations. Meanwhile, numerous states followed a similar path, creating new agencies or augmenting the powers of existing ones to clean up environmental problems and improve public health.

One of the most far-reaching environmental laws of this era was the Clean Air Act Amendments of 1970. A bold successor to the Clean Air Acts of 1955 and 1963, the Motor Vehicle Air Pollution Control Act of 1965, and the Air Quality Act of 1967, the 1970 legislation mandated the establishment of national air quality standards and empowered the EPA to regulate emissions from automobiles and a variety of industrial sources. Following are President Richard M. Nixon's remarks upon signing the Clean Air Act on New Year's Eve, 1970.

Ladies and gentlemen:

On the last day of the year 1970, I think it would be appropriate to make a very few remarks with regard to this piece of legislation that I will now be signing, the clean air act of 1970.

And I see in this room a few who were present in San Clemente on the first day of 1970 when I said that this would be the year of the environment, that it was now or never if we were to clean up the air and clean up the water in major parts of the United States and to provide the open spaces that are so important for the future generations in this country.

The year 1970 has been a year of great progress in this field. In February, you will recall that I submitted the most comprehensive message on the environment ever proposed by a President of the United States. During the year, there have been some administrative actions, some legislative actions.

Time, however, has been required for the Congress to consider the proposals of the administration and, finally, to agree on the legislation that will be sent to the President for signature.

This is the most important piece of legislation, in my opinion, dealing with the problem of clean air that we have this year and the most important in our history.

It provides, as you know, for provisions dealing with fuel emissions and also for air quality standards, and it provides for the additional enforcement procedures which are absolutely important in this particular area.

How did this come about? It came about by the President proposing. It came about by a bipartisan effort represented by the Senators and Congressmen, who are here today, in acting. Senator Randolph, Senator Cooper, and Congressman Springer represent both parties and both Houses of the Congress.

And I thank the Congress, and the country owes a debt to the Congress in its closing days, for acting in this particular field.

I would say, however, that as I sign this piece of legislation, it is only a beginning, because now comes the enforcement and that allows me to comment briefly upon how we in the administration are set up to handle the problems of the environment in the years ahead.

We have, first, the Environmental Quality Council under the chairmanship of Russell Train. That Council advises the President on the policies which should be recommended to the Congress and to the Nation. And consequently, as I submit new recommendations, and there will be very significant new recommendations submitted to the Congress early in the next session on the environment, those recommendations will be the result of the actions that the Council has taken and its studies and its proposals.

And then there is the Environmental Protection Agency, which has been established by the Congress, where Mr. Ruckelshaus is the man responsible. And that is the enforcement agency. He enforces those proposals that, first are recommended by the Council, submitted by the President to the Congress, enacted by the Congress, and then become law.

So, we have the enforcement agency on the one side. We have the policy agency on the other. We have the legislative branch of the Government, both parties represented here, and, of course, the President in the primary role of having to submit the legislation and then backing up those who have the responsibility for enforcing it.

If I can summarize briefly, I think that 1970 will be known as the year of the beginning, in which we really began to move on the problems of clean air and clean water and open spaces for the future generations of America.

I think 1971 will be known as the year of action. And as we look at action, I would suggest that this bill is an indication of what action can be, because if this bill is completely enforced, within 4 years it will mean that the emissions from automobiles which pollute the environment will be reduced by 90 percent.

And the problem of automobile pollution, as we know, is one that not only now plagues my native area of southern California but all the great cities of this Nation, particularly those which have heavy automobile traffic, and most of the great cities of the world have similar problems.

So, what we are doing here is, first, by signing this legislation, to provide the tools through which we can have action to avoid the dangers that continuing air pollution by automobiles and through other methods will be going forward.

So, it seems very appropriate that in this room, the Roosevelt Room, a room that is named for both Roosevelts, Franklin Roosevelt and Theodore Roosevelt, but particularly in view of the fact that Theodore Roosevelt, who was the man most remembered in American history for his interest in conservation, his interest in the environment, that this bill is being signed here; this, it seems to me, is most appropriate.

And I would only hope that as we go now from the year of the beginning, the year of proposing, the year 1970, to the year of action, 1971, that all of us, Democrats, Republicans, the House, the Senate, the executive branch, that all of us can look back upon this year as that time when we began to make a movement toward a goal that we all want, a goal that Theodore Roosevelt deeply believed in and a goal that he lived in his whole life. He loved the environment. He loved the clean air and the open spaces, and he loved the western part of the United States particularly, which will be greatly affected by this kind of action.

And if, as we sign this bill in this room, we can look back and say, in the Roosevelt Room on the last day of 1970, we signed a historic piece of legislation that put us far down the road toward a goal that Theodore Roosevelt, 70 years ago, spoke eloquently about: a goal of clean air, clean water, and open spaces for the future generations of America.

Source: Nixon, Richard M. Remarks on Signing the Clean Air Act Amendments of 1970, December 31, 1970. *Public Papers of the Presidents: Richard Nixon, 1970.* Washington, DC: Government Printing Office, 1971, pp. 65–67.

DOCUMENT
7.14

Justice Blackmun Delivers the Supreme Court Decision in *Roe v. Wade*

"The Right of Personal Privacy Includes the Abortion Decision"

1973

On January 22, 1973, the U.S. Supreme Court issued its famous Roe v. Wade *decision, which legalized abortion nationwide. The Court's 7–2 vote overturned state anti-abortion laws (including in Texas, where the* Roe v. Wade *case originated) and established the trimester formula for balancing the privacy rights of pregnant women with the state's interest in protecting the fetus. The ruling also made the abortion issue one of the most enduring hot-button issues of American politics. In the first three years after the* Roe *decision, more than four hundred bills restricting abortion were introduced in state legislatures across the country, and many of these were passed into law. At the national level, more than fifty bills limiting or banning abortion were introduced in the U.S. Congress during that same time span. Most of these measures failed to make any significant headway, but one—the so-called Hyde Amendment—banned all Medicaid-funded abortions. (Provisions allowing federal funds to be used for these procedures were later added in cases in which the pregnancy was a result of rape or incest or threatened the life of the pregnant woman.)*

In the years since Justice Harry A. Blackmun delivered the Court's opinion, excerpted here, in Roe v. Wade, *abortion rights has remained the single most emotional and divisive health issue in American politics. For many pro-life and pro-choice Americans, a politician's position on abortion is of greater importance than any other policy stance. Similarly, for advocates on both sides of the debate, the single greatest focus of every U.S. Supreme Court nomination made over the last four decades has been on whether the presence on the Court of the prospective justice strengthens or weakens the hand of the millions of Americans who would like to see* Roe v. Wade *overturned.*

[Case citations located in the original opinion have been removed.]

V

The principal thrust of appellant's [Roe's] attack on the Texas statutes is that they improperly invade a right, said to be possessed by the pregnant woman, to choose to terminate her pregnancy. Appellant would discover this right in the concept of personal "liberty" embodied in the Fourteenth Amendment's Due Process Clause; or in personal, marital, familial, and sexual privacy said to be protected by the Bill of Rights or its penumbras, or among those rights reserved to the people by the Ninth Amendment. Before addressing this claim, we feel it desirable briefly to survey, in several aspects, the history of abortion, for such insight as that history may afford us, and then to examine the state purposes and interests behind the criminal abortion laws.

VI

It perhaps is not generally appreciated that the restrictive criminal abortion laws in effect in a majority of States today are of relatively recent vintage. Those laws, generally proscribing abortion or its attempt at any time during pregnancy except when necessary to preserve the pregnant woman's life, are not of ancient or even of common law origin. Instead, they derive from statutory changes effected, for the most part, in the latter half of the 19th century. . . .

. . . In the past several years, however, a trend toward liberalization of abortion statutes has resulted in adoption, by about one-third of the States, of less stringent laws. . . .

It is thus apparent that, at common law, at the time of the adoption of our Constitution, and throughout the major portion of the 19th century, abortion was viewed with less disfavor than under most American statutes currently in effect. Phrasing it another way, a woman enjoyed a substantially broader right to terminate a pregnancy than she does in most States today. At least with respect to the early stage of pregnancy, and very possibly without such a limitation, the opportunity to make this choice was present in this country well into the 19th century. Even later, the law continued for some time to treat less punitively an abortion procured in early pregnancy. . . .

VII

Three reasons have been advanced to explain historically the enactment of criminal abortion laws in the 19th century and to justify their continued existence.

It has been argued occasionally that these laws were the product of a Victorian social concern to discourage illicit sexual conduct. Texas, however, does not advance this justification in the present case, and it appears that no court or commentator has taken the argument seriously. The appellants and *amici* ["friends of the court," or parties that filed amicus curiae briefs in the case] contend, moreover, that this is not a proper state purpose at all and suggest that, if it were, the Texas statutes are overbroad in protecting it, since the law fails to distinguish between married and unwed mothers.

A second reason is concerned with abortion as a medical procedure. When most criminal abortion laws were first enacted, the procedure was a hazardous one for the woman. This was particularly true prior to the development of antisepsis. Antiseptic techniques, of course, were based on discoveries by Lister, Pasteur, and others first announced in 1867, but were not generally accepted and employed until about the turn of the century. Abortion mortality was high. Even after 1900, and perhaps until as late as the development of antibiotics in the 1940's, standard modern techniques such as dilation and curettage were not nearly so safe as they are today. Thus, it has been argued that a State's real concern in enacting a criminal abortion law was to protect the pregnant woman, that is, to restrain her from submitting to a procedure that placed her life in serious jeopardy.

Modern medical techniques have altered this situation. Appellants and various *amici* refer to medical data indicating that abortion in early pregnancy, that is, prior to the end of the first trimester, although not without its risk, is now relatively safe. Mortality rates for women undergoing early abortions, where the procedure is legal, appear to be as low as or lower than the rates for normal childbirth. Consequently, any interest of the State in protecting the woman from an inherently hazardous procedure, except when it would be equally dangerous for her to forgo it, has largely disappeared. Of course, important state interests in the areas of health and medical standards do remain. The State has a legitimate interest in seeing to it that abortion, like any other medical procedure, is performed under circumstances that insure maximum safety for the patient. This interest obviously extends at least to the performing physician and his staff, to the facilities involved, to the availability of after-care, and to adequate provision for any complication or emergency that might arise. The prevalence of high mortality rates at illegal "abortion mills" strengthens, rather than weakens, the State's interest in regulating the conditions under which abortions are performed. Moreover, the risk to the woman increases as her pregnancy continues. Thus, the State retains a definite interest in protecting the woman's own health and safety when an abortion is proposed at a late stage of pregnancy.

The third reason is the State's interest—some phrase it in terms of duty—in protecting prenatal life. Some of the argument for this justification rests on the theory that a new human life is present from the moment of conception. The State's interest and general obligation to protect life then extends, it is argued, to prenatal life. Only when the life of the pregnant mother herself is at stake, balanced against the life she carries within her, should the interest of the embryo or fetus not prevail. Logically, of course, a legitimate state interest in this area need not stand or fall on acceptance of the belief that life begins at conception or at some other point prior to live birth. In assessing the State's interest, recognition may be given to the less rigid claim that as long as at least potential life is involved, the State may assert interests beyond the protection of the pregnant woman alone.

Parties challenging state abortion laws have sharply disputed in some courts the contention that a purpose of these laws, when enacted, was to protect prenatal life. Pointing to the absence of legislative history to support the contention, they claim that most state laws were designed solely to protect the woman. Because medical advances have lessened this concern, at least with respect to abortion in early pregnancy, they argue that with respect to such abortions the laws can no longer be justified by any state interest. There is some scholarly support for this view of original purpose. The few state courts called upon to interpret their laws in the late 19th and early 20th centuries did focus on the State's interest in protecting the woman's health rather than in preserving the embryo and fetus. Proponents of this view point out that in many States, including Texas, by statute or judicial interpretation, the pregnant woman herself could not be prosecuted for self-abortion or for cooperating in an abortion performed upon her by another. They claim that adoption of the "quickening" distinction through received common law and state statutes tacitly recognizes the greater health hazards inherent in late abortion and impliedly repudiates the theory that life begins at conception.

It is with these interests, and the weight to be attached to them, that this case is concerned.

VIII

The Constitution does not explicitly mention any right of privacy. In a line of decisions, however, going back perhaps as far as *Union Pacific Railroad Co. v. Botsford* (1891), the Court has recognized that a right of personal privacy, or a guarantee of certain areas or zones of privacy, does exist under the Constitution. In varying contexts, the Court or individual Justices have, indeed, found at least the roots of that right in the First Amendment; in the Fourth and Fifth Amendments; in the penumbras of the Bill of Rights; in the Ninth Amendment; or in the concept of liberty guaranteed by the first section of the Fourteenth Amendment. These decisions make it clear that only personal rights that can be deemed "fundamental" or "implicit in the concept of ordered liberty" . . . are included in this guarantee of personal privacy. They also make it clear that the right has some extension to activities relating to marriage; procreation; contraception; family relationships; and child rearing and education.

This right of privacy, whether it be founded in the Fourteenth Amendment's concept of personal liberty and restrictions upon state action, as we feel it is, or, as the District Court determined, in the Ninth Amendment's reservation of rights to the people, is broad enough to encompass a woman's decision whether or not to terminate her pregnancy. The detriment that the State would impose upon the pregnant woman by denying this choice altogether is apparent. Specific and direct harm medically diagnosable even in early pregnancy may be involved. Maternity, or additional offspring, may force upon the woman a distressful life and future. Psychological harm may be imminent. Mental and physical health may be taxed by child care. There is also the distress, for all concerned, associated with the unwanted child, and there is the problem of bringing a child into a family already unable, psychologically and otherwise, to care for it. In other cases, as in this one, the additional difficulties and continuing stigma of unwed motherhood may be involved. All these are factors the woman and her responsible physician necessarily will consider in consultation.

On the basis of elements such as these, appellant and some *amici* argue that the woman's right is absolute and that she is entitled to terminate her pregnancy at whatever time, in whatever way, and for whatever reason she alone chooses. With this we do not agree. Appellant's arguments that Texas either has no valid interest at all in regulating the abortion decision, or no interest strong enough to support any limitation upon the woman's sole determination, are unpersuasive. The Court's decisions recognizing a right of privacy also acknowledge that some state regulation in areas protected by that right is appropriate. As noted above, a State may properly assert important interests in safeguarding health, in maintaining medical standards, and in protecting potential life. At some point in pregnancy, these respective interests become sufficiently compelling to sustain regulation of the factors that govern the abortion decision. The privacy right involved, therefore, cannot be said to be absolute. In fact, it is not clear to us that the claim asserted by some *amici* that one has an unlimited right to do with one's body as one pleases bears a close relationship to the right of privacy previously articulated in the Court's decisions. The Court has refused to recognize an unlimited right of this kind in the past.

We, therefore, conclude that the right of personal privacy includes the abortion decision, but that this right is not unqualified and must be considered against important state interests in regulation. . . .

IX

. . . Texas urges that, apart from the Fourteenth Amendment, life begins at conception and is present throughout pregnancy, and that, therefore, the State has a compelling interest in protecting that life from and after conception. We need not resolve the difficult question of when life begins. When those trained in the respective disciplines of medicine, philosophy, and theology are unable to arrive at any consensus, the judiciary, at this point in the development of man's knowledge, is not in a position to speculate as to the answer. . . .

In areas other than criminal abortion, the law has been reluctant to endorse any theory that life, as we recognize it, begins before live birth, or to accord legal rights to the unborn except in narrowly defined situations and except when the rights are contingent upon live birth. For example, the traditional rule of tort law denied recovery for prenatal injuries even though the child was born alive. That rule has been changed in almost every jurisdiction. In most States, recovery is said to be permitted only if the fetus was viable, or at least quick, when the injuries were sustained, though few courts have squarely so held. In a recent development, generally opposed by the commentators, some States permit the parents of a stillborn child to maintain an action for wrongful death because of prenatal injuries. Such an action, however, would appear to be one to vindicate the parents' interest and is thus consistent with the view that the fetus, at most, represents only the potentiality of life. Similarly, unborn children have been recognized as acquiring rights or interests by way of inheritance or other devolution of property, and have been represented by guardians *ad litem*. Perfection of the interests involved, again, has generally been contingent upon live birth. In short, the unborn have never been recognized in the law as persons in the whole sense.

X

In view of all this, we do not agree that, by adopting one theory of life, Texas may override the rights of the pregnant woman that are at stake. We repeat, however, that the State does have an important and legitimate interest in preserving and protecting the health of the pregnant woman, whether she be a resident of the State or a nonresident who seeks medical consultation and treatment there, and that it has still *another* important and legitimate interest in protecting the potentiality of human life. These interests are separate and distinct. Each grows in substantiality as the woman approaches term and, at a point during pregnancy, each becomes "compelling."

With respect to the State's important and legitimate interest in the health of the mother, the "compelling" point, in the light of present medical knowledge, is at approximately the end of the first trimester. This is so because of the now-established medical fact . . . that, until the end of the first trimester mortality in abortion may be less than mortality in normal childbirth. It follows that, from and after this point, a State may regulate the abortion procedure to the extent that the regulation reasonably relates to the preservation and protection of maternal health. Examples of permissible state regulation in this area are requirements as to the qualifications of the person who is to perform the abortion; as to the licensure of that person; as to the facility in which the procedure is to be performed, that is, whether it must be a hospital or may be a clinic or some other place of less-than-hospital status; as to the licensing of the facility; and the like.

This means, on the other hand, that, for the period of pregnancy prior to this "compelling" point, the attending physician, in consultation with his patient, is free to determine, without regulation by the State, that, in his medical judgment, the patient's pregnancy should be terminated. If that decision is reached, the judgment may be effectuated by an abortion free of interference by the State.

With respect to the State's important and legitimate interest in potential life, the "compelling" point is at viability. This is so because the fetus then presumably has the capability of meaningful life outside the mother's womb. State regulation protective of fetal life after viability thus has both logical and biological justifications. If the State is interested in protecting fetal life after viability, it may go so far as to proscribe abortion during that period, except when it is necessary to preserve the life or health of the mother.

Measured against these standards, Art. 1196 of the Texas Penal Code, in restricting legal abortions to those "procured or attempted by medical advice for the purpose of saving the life of the mother," sweeps too broadly. The statute makes no distinction between abortions performed early in pregnancy and those performed later, and it limits to a single reason, "saving" the mother's life, the legal justification for the procedure. The statute, therefore, cannot survive the constitutional attack made upon it here.

This conclusion makes it unnecessary for us to consider the additional challenge to the Texas statute asserted on grounds of vagueness.

XI

To summarize and to repeat:

1. A state criminal abortion statute of the current Texas type, that excepts from criminality only a life-saving procedure on behalf of the mother, without regard to pregnancy stage and without recognition of the other interests involved, is violative of the Due Process Clause of the Fourteenth Amendment.

(a) For the stage prior to approximately the end of the first trimester, the abortion decision and its effectuation must be left to the medical judgment of the pregnant woman's attending physician.

(b) For the stage subsequent to approximately the end of the first trimester, the State, in promoting its interest in the health of the mother, may, if it chooses, regulate the abortion procedure in ways that are reasonably related to maternal health.

(c) For the stage subsequent to viability, the State in promoting its interest in the potentiality of human life may, if it chooses, regulate, and even proscribe, abortion except where it is necessary, in appropriate medical judgment, for the preservation of the life or health of the mother.

2. The State may define the term "physician," as it has been employed in the preceding paragraphs of this Part XI of this opinion, to mean only a physician currently licensed by the State, and may proscribe any abortion by a person who is not a physician as so defined.

In *Doe v. Bolton*, procedural requirements contained in one of the modern abortion statutes are considered. That opinion and this one, of course, are to be read together.

This holding, we feel, is consistent with the relative weights of the respective interests involved, with the lessons and examples of medical and legal history, with the lenity of the common law, and with the demands of the profound problems of the present day. The decision leaves the State free to place increasing restrictions on abortion as the period of pregnancy lengthens, so long as those restrictions are tailored to the recognized state interests. The decision vindicates the right of the physician to administer medical treatment according to his professional judgment up to the points where important state interests provide compelling justifications for intervention. Up to those points, the abortion decision in all its aspects is inherently, and primarily, a medical decision, and basic responsibility for it must rest with the physician. If an individual practitioner abuses the privilege of exercising proper medical judgment, the usual remedies, judicial and intra-professional, are available.

XII

Our conclusion that Art. 1196 is unconstitutional means, of course, that the Texas abortion statutes, as a unit, must fall. The exception of Art. 1196 cannot be struck down separately, for then the State would be left with a statute proscribing all abortion procedures no matter how medically urgent the case.

Although the District Court granted appellant Roe declaratory relief, it stopped short of issuing an injunction against enforcement of the Texas statutes. The Court has recognized that different considerations enter into a federal court's decision as to declaratory relief, on the one hand, and injunctive relief, on the other. We are not dealing with a statute that, on its face, appears to abridge free expression. . . .

We find it unnecessary to decide whether the District Court erred in withholding injunctive relief, for we assume the Texas prosecutorial authorities will give full credence to this decision that the present criminal abortion statutes of that State are unconstitutional.

The judgment of the District Court as to intervenor Hallford is reversed, and Dr. Hallford's complaint in intervention is dismissed. In all other respects, the judgment of the District Court is affirmed. Costs are allowed to the appellee.

It is so ordered.

Source: Blackmun, Harry A. Opinion of the Court, *Roe v. Wade,* 410 U.S. 113 (decided January 22, 1973). www.law.cornell.edu/supct/html/historics/USSC_CR_0410_0113_ZO.html.

DOCUMENT
7.15

Congress Passes the Rehabilitation Act

"To . . . Initiate and Expand Services to Groups of Handicapped Individuals"

1973

The Rehabilitation Act of 1973 was an ambitious law crafted with the goal of guaranteeing disabled people legal protection from discrimination. It replaced the Vocational Rehabilitation Act of 1920, which had created the first public rehabilitation programs for people with disabilities. Widely recognized as the predecessor to the 1990 Americans with Disabilities Act, the Rehabilitation Act's provisions were infused with a recognition that, as the bill itself stated, "disability is a natural part of the human experience and in no way diminishes the right of individuals to: a) live independently; b) enjoy self-determination; c) make choices; d) contribute to society; e) pursue meaningful careers; and f) enjoy full inclusion and integration in the economic, political, social, cultural, and educational mainstream of American society." The act, which was signed into law by President Richard M. Nixon on September 26, 1973, applied to programs conducted or funded by federal agencies (including colleges participating in federal student loan programs), federal employment, and employment practices of businesses with federal contracts. Following is an excerpt from the act's "Purpose" section.

An Act

To replace the Vocational Rehabilitation Act, to extend and revise the authorization of grants to States for vocational rehabilitation services, with special emphasis on services to those with the most severe handicaps, to expand special Federal responsibilities and research and training programs with respect to handicapped individuals, to establish special responsibilities in the Secretary of Health, Education, and Welfare for coordination of all programs with respect to handicapped individuals within the Department of Health, Education, and Welfare, and for other purposes.

Be it enacted by the Senate and House of Representatives of the United States of America in Congress assembled, That this Act, with the following table of contents, may be cited as the "Rehabilitation Act of 1973":

Declaration of Purpose

Sec. 2. The purpose of this Act is to provide a statutory basis for the Rehabilitation Services Administration, and to authorize programs to—

(1) develop and implement comprehensive and continuing State plans for meeting the current and future needs for providing vocational rehabilitation services to handicapped individuals and to provide such services for the benefit of such individuals, serving first those with the most severe handicaps, so that they may prepare for and engage in gainful employment;

(2) evaluate the rehabilitation potential of handicapped individuals;

(3) conduct a study to develop methods of providing rehabilitation services to meet the current and future needs of handicapped individuals for whom a vocational goal is not possible or feasible so that they may improve their ability to live with greater independence and self-sufficiency;

(4) assist in the construction and improvement of rehabilitation facilities;

(5) develop new and innovative methods of applying the most advanced medical technology, scientific achievement, and psychological and social knowledge to solve rehabilitation problems and develop new and innovative methods of providing rehabilitation services to handicapped individuals through research, special projects, and demonstration;

(6) initiate and expand services to groups of handicapped individuals (including those who are homebound or institutionalized) who have been underserved in the past;

(7) conduct various studies and experiments to focus on long neglected problem areas;

(8) promote and expand employment opportunities in the public and private sectors for handicapped individuals and to place such individuals in employment;

(9) establish client assistance pilot projects;

(10) provide assistance for the purpose of increasing the number of rehabilitation personnel and increasing their skills through training; and

(11) evaluate existing approaches to architectural and transportation barriers confronting handicapped individuals, develop new such approaches, enforce statutory and regulatory standards and requirements regarding barrier-free construction of public facilities and study and develop solutions to existing architectural and transportation barriers impeding handicapped individuals.

Source: Rehabilitation Act of 1973. H.R. 8070, Public Law 93–112, September 26, 1973. www.dotcr.ost .dot.gov/documents/ycr/REHABACT.HTM.

President Nixon Signs the Health Maintenance Organization Act

DOCUMENT
7.16

"Another Milestone in this Administration's National Health Strategy"

1973

By the time Richard M. Nixon entered the Oval Office in early 1969, politicians, policy analysts, and health care activists and executives were engaged in an increasingly acrimonious debate about how to contain spiraling health care costs, improve coverage and access to basic medical services, make delivery of health services and products more efficient, and bolster patient rights. In 1971 the Nixon administration announced its belief that a form of prepaid group practice known as a health maintenance organization or HMO had the capacity to address all of these shortcomings in the existing health care delivery system. Two years later, epic bouts of political horse-trading and intensive lobbying campaigns from various interest groups resulted in the Health Maintenance Organization Act of 1973. Nixon signed the legislation into law on December 29, 1973. His signing statement is below. The law struck down state laws that banned prepaid group practices, authorized $375 million in federal grants and loans to help businesses develop HMOs, and required private companies with at least twenty-five employees to provide their workforces with an HMO option. As it turned out, the HMO option developed much more slowly than its supporters anticipated, but subsequent amendments to the law made HMO operations much more profitable. By the mid-1990s about one out of four Americans were covered by HMO plans.

It is with great pleasure that I today sign into law S. 14, the Health Maintenance Organization Act of 1973. This legislation will enable the Federal Government to help demonstrate the feasibility of the HMO concept over the next 5 years.

Expanding the geographic distribution of health maintenance organizations is an integral part of the National Health Strategy that I first proposed nearly 3 years ago. S. 14

is somewhat broader than the Administration's proposal, but it nevertheless contains the essential concepts and principles that I support. It will provide initial Federal development assistance for a limited number of demonstration projects, with the intention that they become self-sufficient within fixed periods.

The national health insurance bill that I will be submitting to the next session of this Congress will allow patients to use such insurance to join HMO's. For that reason, it is particularly important that this demonstration effort get underway immediately and build upon the momentum which has already been achieved in this field.

Health maintenance organizations provide health care to their members on a prepaid basis with emphasis on essential preventive services. The establishment of HMO's will allow people to select for themselves either a prepaid system for obtaining health services or the more traditional approach which has served the American people so well over the years.

The Health Maintenance Organization Act makes Federal demonstration assistance available both to organized group practices and to medical foundations which provide prepaid care, further encouraging a diversified medical care system. HMO's which receive assistance under this act would agree to provide a comprehensive package of basic benefits, including essential preventive services, along with a list of supplemental benefits for which the enrollee could make an extra payment.

Under S. 14, the Government would provide financial assistance to help various groups determine the feasibility of developing an HMO in their area, as well as assistance for planning and initial development. HMO's would be required to operate competitively without Federal subsidies at the end of an initial period of Federal support.

S. 14 represents one response to the challenge of finding new and better ways to improve health care for the people of this country. It will build on the partnership that exists between the Federal and private sector by allowing both the provider and the consumer of health services to exercise the widest possible freedom of choice.

The signing of this act marks another milestone in this Administration's national health strategy. The major task of providing financial access to health services should be addressed in the next session of this Congress with the enactment of an appropriate and responsive national health insurance act.

Source: Nixon, Richard M. Statement on Signing the Health Maintenance Organization Act of 1973, December 29, 1973. *Public Papers of the Presidents: Richard Nixon, 1973.* Washington, DC: Government Printing Office, 1975. The American Presidency Project, www.presidency.ucsb.edu/ws/?pid=4092.

DOCUMENT
7.17

President Nixon Proposes a National Health Insurance Plan

"An Idea Whose Time Has Come in America"

1974

In January 1974 President Richard M. Nixon used the annual State of the Union Address to make a dramatic pitch for a national system of health insurance, declaring that "the time is at hand this year to bring comprehensive, high quality health care within the reach of every American."[1] *One week later, Nixon delivered another message to Congress (excerpted below) that provided more details about the administration's ambitious proposal. In the ensuing months, opposition from key Democratic constituencies—most notably the AFL-CIO (American Federation of Labor and Congress of Industrial Organizations), the United Auto Workers, and other big labor groups—scuttled the legislation. Many years later, liberal Democratic senator Edward M. Kennedy of Massachusetts described the decision not to pursue a deal with Nixon on his proposal as the biggest regret of his legislative career.*

Three years ago, I proposed a major health insurance program to the Congress, seeking to guarantee adequate financing of health care on a nationwide basis. That proposal generated widespread discussion and useful debate. But no legislation reached my desk.

Today the need is even more pressing because of the higher costs of medical care. Efforts to control medical costs under the New Economic Policy have been met with encouraging success, sharply reducing the rate of inflation for health care. Nevertheless, the overall cost of health care has still risen by more than 20 percent in the last two and one-half years, so that more and more Americans face staggering bills when they receive medical help today. . . .

For the average family, it is clear that without adequate insurance, even normal care can be a financial burden while a catastrophic illness can mean catastrophic debt.

Beyond the question of the prices of health care, our present system of health care insurance suffers from two major flaws:

First, even though more Americans carry health insurance than ever before, the 25 million Americans who remain uninsured often need it the most and are most unlikely to obtain it. They include many who work in seasonal or transient occupations, high-risk cases, and those who are ineligible for Medicaid despite low incomes.

Second, those Americans who do carry health insurance often lack coverage which is balanced, comprehensive and fully protective:

–Forty percent of those who are insured are not covered for visits to physicians on an out-patient basis, a gap that creates powerful incentives toward high cost care in hospitals;

–Few people have the option of selecting care through prepaid arrangements offered by Health Maintenance Organizations so the system at large does not benefit from the free choice and creative competition this would offer;

–Very few private policies cover preventive services;

–Most health plans do not contain built-in incentives to reduce waste and inefficiency. The extra costs of wasteful practices are passed on, of course, to consumers; and

–Fewer than half of our citizens under 65–and almost none over 65–have major medical coverage which pays for the cost of catastrophic illness.

These gaps in health protection can have tragic consequences. They can cause people to delay seeking medical attention until it is too late. Then a medical crisis ensues, followed by huge medical bills–or worse. Delays in treatment can end in death or lifelong disability.

Comprehensive Health Insurance Plan (Chip)

Early last year, I directed the Secretary of Health, Education, and Welfare to prepare a new and improved plan for comprehensive health insurance. That plan, as I indicated in my State of the Union message, has been developed and I am presenting it to the Congress today. I urge its enactment as soon as possible.

The plan is organized around seven principles:

First, it offers every American an opportunity to obtain a balanced, comprehensive range of health insurance benefits;

Second, it will cost no American more than he can afford to pay;

Third, it builds on the strength and diversity of our existing public and private systems of health financing and harmonizes them into an overall system;

Fourth, it uses public funds only where needed and requires no new Federal taxes;

Fifth, it would maintain freedom of choice by patients and ensure that doctors work for their patient, not for the Federal Government.

Sixth, it encourages more effective use of our health care resources;

And finally, it is organized so that all parties would have a direct stake in making the system work—consumer, provider, insurer, State governments and the Federal Government.

Broad and Balanced Protection for all Americans

Upon adoption of appropriate Federal and State legislation, the Comprehensive Health Insurance Plan would offer to every American the same broad and balanced health protection through one of three major programs:

-Employee Health Insurance, covering most Americans and offered at their place of employment, with the cost to be shared by the employer and employee on a basis which would prevent excessive burdens on either;

-Assisted Health Insurance, covering low-income persons, and persons who would be ineligible for the other two programs, with Federal and State government paying those costs beyond the means of the individual who is insured; and,

-An improved Medicare Plan, covering those 65 and over and offered through a Medicare system that is modified to include additional, needed benefits.

One of these three plans would be available to every American, but for everyone, participation in the program would be voluntary.

The benefits offered by the three plans would be identical for all Americans, regardless of age or income. Benefits would be provided for:

-hospital care;
-physicians' care in and out of the hospital;
-prescription and life-saving drugs;
-laboratory tests and X-rays;
-medical devices;
-ambulance services; and,
-other ancillary health care.

There would be no exclusions of coverage based on the nature of the illness. For example, a person with heart disease would qualify for benefits as would a person with kidney disease.

In addition, CHIP would cover treatment for mental illness, alcoholism and drug addiction, whether that treatment were provided in hospitals and physicians' offices or in community based settings.

Certain nursing home services and other convalescent services would also be covered. For example, home health services would be covered so that long and costly stays in nursing homes could be averted where possible.

The health needs of children would come in for special attention, since many conditions, if detected in childhood, can be prevented from causing lifelong disability and learning handicaps. Included in these services for children would be:

–preventive care up to age six;
–eye examinations;
–hearing examinations; and,
–regular dental care up to age 13.

Under the Comprehensive Health Insurance Plan, a doctor's decisions could be based on the health care needs of his patients, not on health insurance coverage. This difference is essential for quality care.

Every American participating in the program would be insured for catastrophic illnesses that can eat away savings and plunge individuals and families into hopeless debt for years. No family would ever have annual out-of-pocket expenses for covered health services in excess of $1,500, and low-income families would face substantially smaller expenses.

As part of this program, every American who participates in the program would receive a Healthcard when the plan goes into effect in his State. This card, similar to a credit card, would be honored by hospitals, nursing homes, emergency rooms, doctors, and clinics across the country. This card could also be used to identify information on blood type and sensitivity to particular drugs–information which might be important in an emergency.

Bills for the services paid for with the Healthcard would be sent to the insurance carrier who would reimburse the provider of the care for covered services, then bill the patient for his share, if any.

The entire program would become effective in 1976, assuming that the plan is promptly enacted by the Congress.

How Employee Health Insurance Would Work

Every employer would be required to offer all full-time employees the Comprehensive Health Insurance Plan. Additional benefits could then be added by mutual agreement. The insurance plan would be jointly financed, with employers paying 65 percent of the premium for the first three years of the plan, and 75 percent thereafter. Employees would pay the balance of the premiums. Temporary Federal subsidies would be used to ease the initial burden on employers who face significant cost increases.

Individuals covered by the plan would pay the first $150 in annual medical expenses. A separate $50 deductible provision would apply for out-patient drugs. There would be a maximum of three medical deductibles per family.

After satisfying this deductible limit, an enrollee would then pay for 25 percent of additional bills. However, $1,500 per year would be the absolute dollar limit on any family's medical expenses for covered services in any one year.

As an interim measure, the Medicaid program would be continued to meet certain needs, primarily long-term institutional care. I do not consider our current approach to long-term care desirable because it can lead to overemphasis on institutional as opposed to home care. The Secretary of Health, Education, and Welfare has undertaken a thorough study of the appropriate institutional services which should be included in health insurance and other programs and will report his findings to me.

Improving Medicare

The Medicare program now provides medical protection for over 23 million older Americans. Medicare, however, does not cover outpatient drugs, nor does it limit total out-of-pocket costs. It is still possible for an elderly person to be financially devastated by a lengthy illness even with Medicare coverage.

I therefore propose that Medicare's benefits be improved so that Medicare would provide the same benefits offered to other Americans under Employee Health Insurance and Assisted Health Insurance.

Any person 65 or over, eligible to receive Medicare payments, would ordinarily, under my modified Medicare plan, pay the first $100 for care received during a year, and the first $50 toward outpatient drugs. He or she would also pay 20 percent of any bills above the deductible limit. But in no case would any Medicare beneficiary have to pay more than $750 in out-of-pocket costs. The premiums and cost sharing for those with low incomes would be reduced, with public funds making up the difference.

The current program of Medicare for the disabled would be replaced. Those now in the Medicare for the disabled plan would be eligible for Assisted Health Insurance, which would provide better coverage for those with high medical costs and low incomes.

Premiums for most people under the new Medicare program would be roughly equal to that which is now payable under Part B of Medicare–the Supplementary Medical Insurance program.

How Assisted Health Insurance Would Work

The program of Assisted Health Insurance is designed to cover everyone not offered coverage under Employee Health Insurance or Medicare, including the unemployed, the disabled, the self-employed, and those with low incomes. In addition, persons with higher incomes could also obtain Assisted Health Insurance if they cannot otherwise get coverage at reasonable rates. Included in this latter group might be persons whose health status or type of work puts them in high-risk insurance categories.

Assisted Health Insurance would thus fill many of the gaps in our present health insurance system and would ensure that for the first time in our Nation's history, all Americans would have financial access to health protection regardless of income or circumstances.

A principal feature of Assisted Health Insurance is that it relates premiums and out-of-pocket expenses to the income of the person or family enrolled. Working families with incomes of up to $5,000, for instance, would pay no premiums at all. Deductibles, co-insurance, and maximum liability would all be pegged to income levels.

Assisted Health Insurance would replace State-run Medicaid for most services. Unlike Medicaid, where benefits vary in each State, this plan would establish uniform benefit and eligibility standards for all low-income persons. It would also eliminate artificial barriers to enrollment or access to health care.

Costs Of Comprehensive Health Insurance

When fully effective, the total new costs of CHIP to the Federal and State governments would be about $6.9 billion with an additional small amount for transitional assistance for small and low wage employers:

-The Federal Government would add about $5.9 billion over the cost of continuing existing programs to finance health care for low-income or high risk persons.
-State governments would add about $1.0 billion over existing Medicaid spending for the same purpose, though these added costs would be largely, if not wholly offset by reduced State and local budgets for direct provision of services.
-The Federal Government would provide assistance to small and low wage employers which would initially cost about $450 million but be phased out over five years.

For the average American family, what all of these figures reduce to is simply this:

-The national average family cost for health insurance premiums each year under Employee Health Insurance would be about $150; the employer would pay approximately $450 for each employee who participates in the plan.
-Additional family costs for medical care would vary according to need and use, but in no case would a family have to pay more than $1,500 in any one year for covered services.
-No additional taxes would be needed to pay for the cost of CHIP. The Federal funds needed to pay for this plan could all be drawn from revenues that would be generated by the present tax structure. I am opposed to any comprehensive health plan which requires new taxes.

Making The Health Care System Work Better

Any program to finance health care for the Nation must take close account of two critical and related problems–cost and quality.

When Medicare and Medicaid went into effect, medical prices jumped almost twice as fast as living costs in general in the next five years. These programs increased demand without increasing supply proportionately and higher costs resulted.

This escalation of medical prices must not recur when the Comprehensive Health Insurance Plan goes into effect. One way to prevent an escalation is to increase the supply of physicians, which is now taking place at a rapid rate. Since 1965, the number of first-year enrollments in medical schools has increased 55 percent. By 1980, the Nation should have over 440,000 physicians, or roughly one-third more than today. We are also taking steps to train persons in allied health occupations, who can extend the services of the physician.

With these and other efforts already underway, the Nation's health manpower supply will be able to meet the additional demands that will be placed on it.

Other measures have also been taken to contain medical prices. Under the New Economic Policy, hospital cost increases have been cut almost in half from their post-Medicare highs, and the rate of increase in physician fees has slowed substantially. It is extremely important that these successes be continued as we move toward our goal of comprehensive health insurance protection for all Americans. I will, therefore, recommend to the Congress that the Cost of Living Council's authority to control medical care costs be extended.

To contain medical costs effectively over the long-haul, however, basic reforms in the financing and delivery of care are also needed. We need a system with built-in incentives that operates more efficiently and reduces the losses from waste and duplication of effort. Everyone pays for this inefficiency through their health premiums and medical bills.

The measure I am recommending today therefore contains a number of proposals designed to contain costs, improve the efficiency of the system and assure quality health care. These proposals include:

1. HEALTH MAINTENANCE ORGANIZATIONS (HMO'S)

On December 29, 1973, I signed into law legislation designed to stimulate, through Federal aid, the establishment of prepaid comprehensive care organizations. HMO's have proved an effective means for delivering health care and the CHIP plan requires that they be offered as an option for the individual and the family as soon as they become available. This would encourage more freedom of choice for both patients and providers, while fostering diversity in our medical care delivery system.

2. PROFESSIONAL STANDARDS REVIEW ORGANIZATIONS (PSRO'S)

I also contemplate in my proposal a provision that would place health services provided under CHIP under the review of Professional Standards Review Organizations. These PSRO's would be charged with maintaining high standards of care and reducing needless hospitalization. Operated by groups of private physicians, professional review organizations can do much to ensure quality care while helping to bring about significant savings in health costs.

3. MORE BALANCED GROWTH IN HEALTH FACILITIES

Another provision of this legislation would call on the States to review building plans for hospitals, nursing homes and other health facilities. Existing health insurance has overemphasized the placement of patients in hospitals and nursing homes. Under this artificial stimulus, institutions have felt impelled to keep adding bed space. This has produced a growth of almost 75 percent in the number of hospital beds in the last twenty years, so that now we have a surplus of beds in many places and a poor mix of facilities in others. Under the legislation I am submitting, States can begin remedying this costly imbalance.

4. STATE ROLE

Another important provision of this legislation calls on the States to review the operation of health insurance carriers within their jurisdiction. The States would approve specific plans, oversee rates, ensure adequate disclosure, require an annual audit and take other appropriate measures. For health care providers, the States would assure fair reimbursement for physician services, drugs and institutional services, including a prospective reimbursement system for hospitals. . . .

Maintaining A Private Enterprise Approach

My proposed plan differs sharply with several of the other health insurance plans which have been prominently discussed. The primary difference is that my proposal would rely extensively on private insurers.

Any insurance company which could offer those benefits would be a potential supplier. Because private employers would have to provide certain basic benefits to their employees, they would have an incentive to seek out the best insurance company proposals and insurance companies would have an incentive to offer their plans at the lowest possible prices. If, on the other hand, the Government were to act as the insurer, there would be no competition and little incentive to hold down costs.

There is a huge reservoir of talent and skill in administering and designing health plans within the private sector. That pool of talent should be put to work.

It is also important to understand that the CHIP plan preserves basic freedoms for both the patient and doctor. The patient would continue to have a freedom of choice between doctors. The doctors would continue to work for their patients, not the Federal Government. By contrast, some of the national health plans that have been proposed in the Congress would place the entire health system under the heavy hand of the Federal Government, would add considerably to our tax burdens, and would threaten to destroy the entire system of medical care that has been so carefully built in America.

I firmly believe we should capitalize on the skills and facilities already in place, not replace them and start from scratch with a huge Federal bureaucracy to add to the ones we already have.

Comprehensive Health Insurance Plan—A Partnership Effort

No program will work unless people want it to work. Everyone must have a stake in the process.

This Comprehensive Health Insurance Plan has been designed so that everyone involved would have both a stake in making it work and a role to play in the process–consumer, provider, health insurance carrier, the States and the Federal Government. It is a partnership program in every sense.

By sharing costs, consumers would have a direct economic stake in choosing and using their community's health resources wisely and prudently. They would be assisted by requirements that physicians and other providers of care make available to patients full information on fees, hours of operation and other matters affecting the qualifications of providers. But they would not have to go it alone either: doctors, hospitals and other providers of care would also have a direct stake in making the Comprehensive Health Insurance Plan work. This program has been designed to relieve them of much of the red tape, confusion and delays in reimbursement that plague them under the bewildering assortment of public and private financing systems that now exist. Healthcards would relieve them of troublesome bookkeeping. Hospitals could be hospitals, not bill collecting agencies.

Conclusion

Comprehensive health insurance is an idea whose time has come in America.

There has long been a need to assure every American financial access to high quality health care. As medical costs go up, that need grows more pressing.

Now, for the first time, we have not just the need but the will to get this job done. There is widespread support in the Congress and in the Nation for some form of comprehensive health insurance.

Surely if we have the will, 1974 should also be the year that we find the way.

The plan that I am proposing today is, I believe, the very best way. Improvements can be made in it, of course, and the Administration stands ready to work with the Congress, the medical profession, and others in making those changes.

But let us not be led to an extreme program that would place the entire health care system under the dominion of social planners in Washington.

Let us continue to have doctors who work for their patients, not for the Federal Government. Let us build upon the strengths of the medical system we have now, not destroy it. Indeed, let us act sensibly. And let us act now–in 1974–to assure all Americans financial access to high quality medical care.

Source: Nixon, Richard M. Special Message to the Congress Proposing a Comprehensive Health Insurance Plan, February 6, 1974. *Public Papers of the Presidents: Richard Nixon, 1974.* Washington, DC: Government Printing Office, 1975, pp. 132–40.

Note

1. Richard M. Nixon, "Annual Message to the Congress on the State of the Union," *Public Papers of the Presidents: Richard Nixon, 1974* (Washington, DC: Government Printing Office, 1975), 26.

DOCUMENT
7.18

President Ford Signs the Employee Retirement Income Security Act

"A Brighter Future for Almost All the Men and Women of Our Labor Force"

1974

In the early 1970s representatives in Washington, D.C., acting at the behest of workers and employers, became intent on passing legislation that would prevent individual states from throwing regulatory monkey wrenches into the benefits packages offered by corporations operating in multiple states. Legislators from both parties worked together to craft the Employee Retirement Income Security Act (ERISA), which passed the House of Representatives by a 407-2 margin on August 20, 1974. Two days later it sailed through the Senate on an 85-0 vote. It was signed into law on September 2, 1974, by President Gerald R. Ford, who lavishly praised the legislation (see his signing statement below).

ERISA created national standards for employer fringe benefit plans, which gave corporations and workers much greater certainty in analyzing various benefit packages. A provision added late in the game exempted employer-provided fringe benefits, including health benefits, from state laws that would otherwise apply under the 1945 McCarran-Ferguson Act. This same provision exempted self-insured firms from paying taxes on premiums. This little-noticed language triggered an explosion in self-insured plans across corporate America. In 1975, the year after ERISA was signed into law, only 5 percent of employees were covered by self-insured plans. A mere ten years later, that figure had leaped to 42 percent.[1]

Dramatic growth in recent years has thrust private pension plans into a central role in determining how older Americans live in their retirement years.

From 1960 to 1970, private pension coverage increased from 21.2 million employees to approximately 30 million workers. During this same period, assets of these private plans increased from $52 billion to $138 billion. And they are now increasing at a rate of $12-15 billion a year. It will not be long before such assets become the largest source of capital in our economy.

Yet, this same growth in pension plans has brought with it a host of new problems. Many workers have ultimately lost their benefits—even after relatively long service—because when they left jobs, they thereby gave up rights to hard-earned pension benefits. Offers have sustained hardships because their companies folded with insufficient funds in the pension plan to pay promised pensions. In addition, some pension funds have been invested primarily for the benefit of the companies or plan administrators, not for the workers. It is essential to bring some order and humanity into this welter of different and sometimes inequitable retirement plans within private industry.

Today, with great pleasure, I am signing into law a landmark measure that may finally give the American worker solid protection in his pension plan.

Under this law, which is entitled the Employee Retirement Income Security Act of 1974, the men and women of our labor force will have much more clearly defined rights to pension funds and greater assurances that retirement dollars will be there when they are needed. Employees will also be given greater tax incentives to provide for their own retirement if a company plan is unavailable.

It is certainly appropriate that this law be signed on Labor Day, since this act marks a brighter future for almost all the men and women of our labor force. There are seven essential parts to this legislation:

- —first, it establishes major standards for employee participation in private retirement plans, standards which encourage earlier participation by workers, and longer periods over which benefits can be earned;
- —second, and perhaps most important to those already under private pension plans, the new law establishes equitable standards for the "vesting" of retirement benefits. The standards under this law will assure to the greatest possible extent that a worker who participates in a plan actually receives some benefits from that plan and does not lose them because of punishing forfeiture standards or inadequate pension fund resources;
- —third, the act requires that the fiduciaries who control the pension funds act as reasonable and prudent men, discharging their duties solely in the interests of protecting the beneficiaries of the fund;

—fourth, the law will impose a high standard upon the operation of plans by making mandatory full disclosure of all information concerning the operations of the employer's retirement plan;

—fifth, the tax laws will be revised to provide more nearly equal treatment to different kinds of plans. The new law will encourage the self-employed to provide for their retirement by raising the limits on the amount of their income which may be contributed on a deductible basis to a retirement fund. It will also allow the one-half of American employees not covered by private pension plans to enjoy equivalent tax advantages if they set up individual retirement accounts;

—sixth, as a final backstop to private pension plans, a federally sponsored, privately financed Pension Benefit Guaranty Corporation will be set up to pay an adequate retirement benefit to those whose private pension funds have foundered and are not adequate for the beneficiaries; and,

—seventh, the act will establish a limited form of portability of pension benefits by allowing workers to transfer some of their pension benefits to other plans or to their individual retirement accounts.

Together these seven points add up to a better deal for American workers than they have ever known before in private pension plans.

I believe this act is a model of what can be done by the Government to improve the lives of Americans within the private sector without harming the dynamics of our free enterprise system.

I also believe that its passage is a model of cooperation and hard work between the executive and the legislative branches.

The act has its genesis in a message to the Congress by President Nixon on December 8, 1971. The legislation was and is extraordinarily complicated. It was worked on relentlessly by four Congressional committees: House Ways and Means, House Education and Labor, Senate Labor and Public Welfare, and Senate Finance.

Individual members have devoted enormous effort to this bill. I believe we can all be proud that the Government has now taken action to make workers' lives more secure.

Source: Ford, Gerald R. Statement on the Employee Retirement Income Security Act, August 2, 1974. *Gerald R. Ford: Containing the Public Messages, Speeches, and Statements of the President.* Vol. 2. Washington, DC: Government Printing Office, 1977, p. 78. The American Presidency Project, www .presidency.ucsb.edu/ws/?pid=4679.

NOTE

1. Arnold Birenbaum, *Managed Care: Made in America* (Westport, CT: Praeger, 1997), 39.

CHAPTER 8

Restraining Health Care
Costs in the Age of Reagan

1980–1990

When Ronald Reagan assumed the presidency in 1981, the conservative Republican and his chief advisers immediately set about reining in the spiraling costs of Medicare and Medicaid. Reagan believed that his larger goals of reducing government spending and cutting taxes could not be met if these entitlement programs were not reformed. As time passed, however, the Reagan administration—which prided itself on its free market, antiregulatory orientation—determined that the best way to curtail Medicare costs was through a raft of new rules and regulations. Meanwhile, the administration, members of Congress, and the American public grappled with the political and policy implications of a succession of other changes to America's health care landscape in the 1980s, from the controversial ascendance of health maintenance organizations (HMOs) to the arrival of a mysterious and deadly new disease called acquired immune deficiency syndrome (AIDS).

Sensible Deficit Reduction or "Shifting the Shaft"?

Throughout his 1980 presidential campaign, Reagan had promised voters that, if elected, he would get America's fiscal house back in order and put the nation's sluggish economy back on the road to prosperity. Fast-rising costs related to Medicare, Medicaid, and other federal health programs thus became a particular focus of the Reagan administration from the outset.

The impact of this crusade to reduce spending and downsize the federal government was felt in many discretionary programs beginning in 1981, Reagan's first year in office. For example, the president in August signed the Omnibus Budget Reconciliation Act—which was passed by a coalition of Republicans and Southern Democrats in the House and by the GOP-led Senate—cutting $130 billion from food stamp, welfare, and various additional social programs, among other things. This same cost-cutting zeal extended to many federal programs and initiatives in the health sector. Within weeks of Reagan's inauguration, the administration announced that it was consolidating appropriations for nearly two dozen separate categorical health programs into four block grants. These block grants were organized in the broad areas of preventive health, mental health, primary care, and maternal and child health. By recasting the funding of the categorical health programs into a fistful of block grants to the states, the administration and

Ronald Reagan promised far-reaching reductions in federal spending on health care and other programs when he took occupancy of the Oval Office in 1981. Many of these proposed cuts elicited pushback from various constituencies. In 1984, for example, members of the National Council for Senior Citizens staged a protest in Philadelphia against cuts to federal programs.

Congress were able to disguise $200 million in cumulative cuts to various programs. In addition, "these reforms reversed nearly fifteen years of increasing federal involvement in the direct delivery of services and adopted a key Reagan administration concept that delivery of local health services should be a matter for state and local governments—not the federal government," observed Lynn Etheridge, a health policy analyst at the Office of Management and Budget during Reagan's first two years in office.[1]

Reagan's block grant scheme was harshly criticized by people such as Larry J. Gordon, president of the American Public Health Association. "Block Grants are only a first step in the abdication of federal support for public health" in such areas as family planning, mental health, migrant health, and community health, charged Gordon. "Block Grants are an entering wedge in a scheme to first reduce and eventually abolish federal aid for health services. Responsibilities are being transferred to the states and communities without a concurrent transfer of fiscal resources, with the states handing out the bad news. This has been termed 'shifting the shaft.'"[2]

The Reagan administration also moved swiftly to enact other cost-cutting measures in the realm of health care and public health and environmental protection. It worked with Congress to phase out some programs (such as the U.S. Public Health Service hospital system) and shrink funding for others. For instance, funding for the Professional Standards Review Organization (PSRO) program, which had been set up in 1972 to monitor the quality and efficiency of government health insurance programs, was shaved by Congress from $58 million in 1980 to $15 million in 1983 (PSROs were renamed Peer Review Organizations during this time).[3] The Reagan White House and its antiregulatory allies in Washington, D.C., also signaled their intention to cut funding for enforcement of various regulatory provisions in the Occupational Safety and Health Act, the Clean Air Act, the Safe Drinking Water Act, and other high-profile public health laws.

These moves elicited strong criticism from Democrats, environmental and health advocacy groups, and others who defended the need for a robust federal presence in public health matters. But the Reagan administration, conservatives on Capitol Hill, and business and industry groups with longtime ties to Republicans continued to insist that regulatory relief, a smaller federal bureaucracy, and a return to free market principles would reinvigorate the health care sector and other troubled elements of the U.S. economy.

Political Battles over Medicaid's Future

The Reagan administration's determination to curb federal spending on social programs made Medicaid an obvious focus of attention. The rising price tag of Medicaid was a major source of consternation to deficit hawks in both parties. Between 1977 and 1981 alone, a period in which the inflation rate averaged 8.4 percent, federal Medicaid expenditures had jumped by an annual average of 18 percent.[4] This increase occurred despite the fact that Medicaid coverage in many states remained unattainable to millions of the working poor. These households existed in a purgatorial realm in which they earned too much to qualify for Medicaid and other public assistance, but too little to afford private insurance premiums.

Reagan and his economic advisers explored several different strategies to cut Medicaid reimbursements to states in the early 1980s. (Under Medicaid, states pay hospitals and other health care providers for services rendered to enrollees, then get partial reimbursement—from 50 to 75 percent or more, depending on the relative wealth of the state—from the federal government.) A White House proposal to cap the growth of federal payments of Medicaid funds at 5 percent annually was quickly rejected by Democrats as unduly draconian and ill-timed, given that Medicaid enrollments typically expand and state tax revenues decrease during economic downturns (as was the case during parts of the 1980s).[5] Another proposal, to convert Medicaid into block grants to the states, ran aground on the shoals of liberal opposition on Capitol Hill. Opponents of the gambit argued that the ultimate objectives of shifting Medicaid expenditures to the states, which operated under balanced budget restrictions that the federal government did not face, was to gradually shrink down the plans until "welfare medicine" had been abolished as a basic "right."[6]

At one point, the Reagan administration's desire to reduce spending on entitlement programs led it to propose a deal wherein the federal government would take on all funding responsibilities for Medicaid, thus relieving states of this obligation, if state governments took sole funding responsibility for Aid to Families with Dependent Children (AFDC) and the food stamp program. This proposal ended up being a nonstarter with state legislatures and governors.[7]

Despite the Reagan administration's inability to make meaningful headway on reducing Medicaid costs at the federal level, the program nonetheless underwent significant changes in the early 1980s. The main architects and engineers of these changes were state-level policymakers engaged in a grim fight to keep their states' fiscal heads above water amid the recessionary conditions afflicting much of the country. In 1980 Congress had given states increased leverage to control Medicaid nursing home reimbursement rates, and in the next several years legislators and administrators moved decisively to extend these rate-setting powers to hospitals and other Medicaid service providers. By the mid-1980s almost every state had tightened up its Medicaid reimbursement formulas. These rate-setting schemes remained popular until the 1990s, when shifting political winds, improved economic conditions, the emergence of Medicaid managed care plans, and health industry complaints about the complexity of the formulas led to their gradual abandonment.

States tweaked their Medicaid programs in other ways as well, including tightening eligibility for Medicaid and reducing the number and amount of services covered. More than thirty states reduced Medicaid benefits or placed new limits on Medicaid eligibility in 1981 alone, according to one study conducted by the Intergovernmental Health Policy Project at George Washington University. A number of states also introduced copayment requirements for Medicaid enrollees. Supporters depicted the copayment requirement as a policy instrument that discouraged Medicaid recipients from frivolous use of health care services, but opponents decried even modest copayments as significant obstacles to poor people who needed medical care.

Meanwhile, Washington-based initiatives to expand health care coverage to the working poor and other uninsured Americans continued to flounder for the most part. Congress did manage to pass two meaningful augmentations to the health safety net during Reagan's second term. The 1986 Emergency Medical Treatment and Active Labor Act (EMTALA) was crafted in response to a surge in reports of hospitals that were refusing to treat poor people without health insurance or were transferring or prematurely discharging uninsured or underinsured poor people facing expensive medical care. EMTALA required U.S. hospitals participating in Medicare (the vast majority) to screen and treat all emergency room patients, regardless of their citizenship or ability to pay for treatment. That same year saw the introduction of COBRA (named after the larger bill in which it was included, the Consolidated Omnibus Budget Reconciliation Act of 1985), which guaranteed employees and their dependents the opportunity to temporarily retain health and life insurance coverage from former employers (See Document 8.7).

The Advent of Medicare's Prospective Payment System

Although the Reagan administration was stymied in its efforts to make fundamental changes to Medicaid, it had better luck with Medicare. The Reagan White House and leaders of the Republican-controlled Senate and Democrat-held House agreed that decisive steps needed to be taken to ensure Medicare's continued financial solvency. They also recognized that reining in Medicare costs, which were consuming an ever-larger chunk of the federal budget, was a politically explosive issue. Since its inception back in 1965, Medicare had become a vital part of the social welfare safety net for tens of millions of senior citizens and people with disabilities. In the process, these groups of enrollees had become formidable voting blocs that were hostile to any reforms that had the potential to diminish their benefits.

The solution arrived at by politicians in Washington was to squeeze Medicare savings out of hospitals, which, since Medicare's inception, had raked in enormous profits from the program. These profits were generated by a cost-plus payment system that financially rewarded hospitals for each medical service it provided to Medicare patients (and each day a Medicare patient occupied a hospital bed). "The traditional model of cost reimbursement was insanity," recalled Sheila Burke, who served as deputy staff director of the Senate Finance Committee in the early 1980s. "On the face of it, it encouraged people to do more; it paid them to do more and not in any particularly rational way."[8]

The first policy salvo against this retrospective cost-plus reimbursement system was the Tax Equity and Fiscal Responsibility Act (TEFRA) of 1982. Much of this law concerned revenue and taxation provisions unrelated to Medicare. TEFRA also included provisions that placed strict limits on the rate of increase in Medicare's per case payment rate to hospitals. Even more foreboding for the hospital industry, TEFRA mandated that the Department of Health and Human Services (HHS) secretary, at the time Richard S. Schweiker, and his agency develop and submit to Congress within five months a complete new Medicare payment system for hospitals.

Hospital executives, lobbyists, and even some free market conservatives balked at TEFRA, which they accurately framed as an expansion of government regulation of private industry. They expressed bewilderment and anger that Republicans were sanctioning such policies at a time when the party's leadership continued to tout the benefits of deregulation in other industries. These complaints, however, missed the central point—that concerns about the deficit had become great enough for Medicare policy to be subordinated to budgetary policy. "With Republicans in power, the onus fell squarely on them to find a way to avoid Medicare's approaching insolvency," wrote scholars Rick Mayes and Robert A. Berenson. "As a result, fiscal necessity overwhelmed political ideology. Republicans would have to increase the government's authority over medical providers, because the federal government needed budgetary savings immediately and the hospital industry had shown it was unable to reform itself."[9]

In addition, hospitals found themselves on the Medicare chopping block because, as a special interest group, they simply did not wield the same political clout as physicians in general and the American Medical Association (AMA) in particular. This essential reality did not escape policymakers in Washington. "We basically concluded that we had to fix the hospitals because there were fewer of them, they're less political, there's a lot of money there, and we thought we could beat them up a lot easier than three to four hundred thousand doctors," recalled Allen Dobson, who headed the Health Care Financing Administration (HCFA) Office of Research and Development in the early 1980s.[10]

The hospital industry's unhappiness with the TEFRA provisions was so great that when HHS unveiled a new Medicare payment system for hospitals in late 1982, administrators glumly accepted it as an improvement over TEFRA. This prospective payment system (PPS) was loosely modeled after a reimbursement system that recently had been launched in New Jersey. Crafted by Dobson and other HCFA officials in consultation with the White House and Congress, the cornerstone of PPS was an exhaustive index of medical conditions requiring hospitalization or treatment. These medical ailments and conditions were assigned to diagnosis-related groups, or DRGs, each of which was given a set reimbursement value by the federal government **(See Document 8.3)**.

Liberal support for PPS was understandable; the new system sought to put Medicare on a sounder financial footing through reductions of hospital payments instead of reductions of Medicare benefits. Support for PPS from the Reagan administration and conservatives in Congress seemed at first blush to be just as bizarre as their support for TEFRA. After all, PPS was a federally administered pricing system for hospital services, which under ordinary circumstances would be anathema to free market conservatives. But conservative defenders of the prospective payment system said that drastic measures were needed to shore up Medicare's solvency, and they further insisted that PPS would ultimately enhance and encourage free market values such as efficiency and competition in the industry.

Passage of PPS was also aided by the fact that its architects tucked it away in a corner of a much larger bill, the Social Security Amendments of 1983. Other elements in this bill, such as language that permitted limited taxation of Social Security benefits received by high-income seniors, attracted most of the political fire and media attention. As a result, PPS flew under the political radar. Formally introduced in early March, the legislation became law a mere six weeks later, when Reagan signed it on April 20, 1983. Years later, historians such as Jonathan Oberlander still marveled at this sequence of events. "The most consequential reform of Medicare regulation in program history," he wrote, "was enacted with hardly any political attention or public debate and, even more surprisingly, scarcely any opposition from the medical industry."[11]

DEBATING THE IMPACT OF PPS

As PPS advocates predicted, the introduction of the new system prompted a sea change in hospital operations. Under the old reimbursement system, hospitals had not been given any incentives to control costs or maximize their human, plant, or technological resources. With the advent of DRGs, they recognized that efficient, well-managed operations could reap big profits and that sloppy and wasteful performance would bring terrible financial losses. Over the first few years of PPS, most hospital administrators made a successful transition to the new regulatory landscape, and a number of institutions registered healthy profits from the new Medicare PPS. Hospitals also became adept at making up revenue lost to the reimbursement changes by increasing their profit margin on privately insured patients. These higher medical bills infuriated big employers who bore the brunt of the soaring costs, and this dynamic ended up being a big contributor to the corporate flight toward HMOs that took place in the latter half of the 1980s.

The advent of prospective payment also put the brakes on the runaway freight train of Medicare expenditures. Between 1982 and 1988, Medicare hospital days dropped by 20 percent, and the overall growth in Medicare hospital payments declined in spectacular fashion. Whereas Medicare hospital payments had risen by an annual average of 16.2 percent from 1980 to 1983, they dropped by an annual average of 6.5 percent from 1987 to 1990.[12]

The impact of these Medicare payment changes on patients was less clear. After the first full year of PPS implementation, the federal government reported that the average length of a hospital stay for Medicare enrollees had declined by over 15 percent. PPS supporters interpreted these shorter stays as clear evidence that prospective payment had removed the profit motive for hospitals to artificially extend the stays of Medicare patients. Some patient advocates and industry watchdog groups, though, argued that the drop showed that PPS was creating an environment that encouraged hospitals to push Medicare patients out the door more quickly to fill their beds with other revenue-generating patients (whether covered through Medicare or private insurance).

As this debate raged in health care circles, hospitals voiced increased apprehension about continued congressional tinkering with PPS. These adjustments had seemed minor at first, but hospital executives gradually realized that policymakers in Washington were getting increasingly comfortable with the idea of using PPS as a deficit reduction tool. By the midpoint of Reagan's second term, lawmakers and administration officials were manipulating Medicare payment rates for various DRGs to reap budgetary savings and subsidize selected members of the hospital industry, including politically connected rural, urban, and teaching hospitals. "As a result," observed Mayes and Berenson, "instead of becoming more simple and technocratic, Medicare payment policy became more complicated and political."[13] Further confirmation of the politicization of Medicare payments came a few years later, when political pressure from the American Hospital Association (AHA) convinced Congress to approve healthy increases in the DRG compensation rates.[14]

Tackling Medicare Physician Spending

The prospective payment system's effectiveness in reining in Medicare Part A (hospital) spending was widely noted. So when Medicare physician spending continued to grow unabated—Medicare spending on physician care rose by an average of 15–18 percent per year throughout the 1980s—public and private insurers relentlessly lobbied lawmakers to impose a standardized payment system for physicians' services as well.[15] As with hospitals, this regulatory move came only after years and years in which doctors and surgeons showed no willingness to voluntarily rein in their ever-rising financial demands.

This intransigence created what surgeon Atul Gawande described as "egregious distortions" in the health care sector.

> Fees for cataract surgery (which could reach six thousand dollars in 1985) had been set when the operation typically took two to three hours. When new technologies allowed ophthalmologists to do it in thirty minutes, the fees didn't change. Billings for this one operation grew to consume 4 percent of Medicare's budget. In general, payment for doing procedures had far outstripped payments for diagnoses. In the mid-eighties, doctors who spent an hour making a complex and lifesaving diagnosis were paid forty dollars; for spending an hour doing a colonoscopy and excising a polyp, they received more than six hundred dollars. . . . The system discouraged good primary care and corrupted specialty care. So the government determined that payments ought to be commensurate with the amount of work involved.[16]

Washington's resolve to rein in Medicare physician spending was backed by physicians and surgeons who were openly angry about the way that some of their peers had long been abusing the Medicare system. "Medical economics underwent a major metamorphosis when physicians' principal source of income shifted from the modest means of the average patient to the seemingly limitless insurance funds or tax dollars dispensed by an impersonal third-party bureaucracy," wrote physician Benson B. Roe in the *New England Journal of Medicine* in 1981. "The charges for medical services have escalated, with little or no restraint, to the point at which current fee levels in several medical and surgical specialties are simply indefensible and deserving of public censure."[17]

With the political winds firmly at its back, Congress subsequently crafted a bill containing a new index of physician reimbursement payments under Medicare Part B (outpatient care). This fee schedule, developed in large part by Harvard economist William Hsiao, was signed into law in 1989, and it went into full effect in 1992.

HMOs Remake the Health Care Landscape

The Reagan administration's willingness to use regulatory mechanisms to restrain Medicare spending did not preclude it from pushing for free market solutions to other problems in the health care sector. For example, the Reagan White House quickly became enamored with managed care's potential to remake the entire health care industry into a more competitive, productive, and free enterprise–oriented model. Reagan officials and allies in Congress described managed care systems (enterprises that integrated the financing and delivery of health care services) as a silver bullet capable of slaying all manner of budgetary ills and inefficiencies in health care.

The administration's first and most important step was to encourage heightened private investment in health maintenance organizations, in which subscribers pay a monthly premium for health services to a company that directly employs primary care physicians and other health care providers; preferred provider organizations (PPOs), in which employers and insurers contract with hospitals and physicians to serve their enrollees at discount rates; and other managed care organizations. It did so by cutting off the modest federal funding that had existed since 1973 for nonprofit HMOs, a move that effectively forced those organizations to turn to the private sector for money. In 1983 alone, five nonprofit HMOs with hundreds of thousands of enrollees converted to publicly owned corporations. The most notorious of these conversions came in suburban Philadelphia, where HMO of Pennsylvania became the first former nonprofit HMO to make an initial public offering of stock. Renamed U.S. Healthcare, this HMO became known across the country for tightfisted reimbursement practices, aggressive intervention in medical decisions, and financial rewards to doctors and hospitals that curbed their use of medical services.[18]

Simultaneously, the Reagan administration courted private investors, urging them to take a fresh look at the profit potential of managed care operations (**See Document 8.1**). Venture capitalists and existing health care corporations liked what they saw, in large part because they recognized that corporate America was desperate for relief from exploding employee and retiree health care costs. In the mid-1980s, for example, General Motors reported that it was paying twice as much for employee and pensioner health care as it was for steel for its automobiles.[19] Many small and midsize employers, meanwhile, were dropping health coverage or turning to extremely limited catastrophic coverage policies because of the spiraling rates.

The soaring expense of private insurance plans was not solely attributable to the insurers' appetite for profits. The problem was also exacerbated by state-level mandates for coverage of certain services (for people with physical or mental disabilities, for example), state taxes on insurance premiums, and other factors, all of which boosted the cost of policies.[20] In the final analysis, small and large employers alike were less interested in hearing policy wonks' explanations for their rising rates than in simply getting some relief from them.

That is where the HMOs came in. Major health care entities such as Blue Cross and Hospital Corporation of America (HCA) rushed to take advantage of this new business opportunity by unveiling new HMOs or swallowing up existing nonprofit managed care clinics and hospitals and converting them to for-profit enterprises. "This latest variant of HMO was a different breed from its predecessors," said historians Janet Firshein and Lewis G. Sandy. "Predominantly for-profit, the new HMO did not emerge out of the social ethos of earlier pioneers and was not anchored in a reform of the delivery system. Like many private sector innovations, it found a need and filled it—the need for employers to control their health care expenditures."[21]

Once these organizations began flexing their considerable marketing muscle, promising better care for enrollees at lower cost, employers large and small began a full-scale stampede toward the newly minted HMOs. "[We] no longer consider HMOs an experimental line of business," said Blue Cross executive Neil Hollander in 1982. "It's our bread and butter. It's our major growth in many parts of the country."[22] (In 1986

Congress removed the nonprofit tax exemption for Blue Cross, citing its increasingly commercial orientation.)

Patient Care in the Age of Free Market Medicine

From 1980 to 1990 total patient enrollment in HMOs jumped from 9.1 million to 33 million, and by 1995 it had soared to almost 51 million. During this same fifteen-year time span, the percentage of the U.S. population enrolled in HMO plans increased from 2.8 percent to 19.4 percent.[23] Clearly, so-called free market medicine was on the upswing. But in the midst of this meteoric rise, policymakers, medical professionals, and ordinary Americans became divided about the efficacy, quality, and even the morality of many managed care programs.

To some observers, the HMOs' emphasis on efficiency and value had a distinctly chilling quality. These critics, whether hailing from medical practices, congressional offices, op-ed pages, or American living rooms, asserted that the bottom-line orientation of managed care organizations exerted an unhealthy influence on the courses of medical treatment selected by physicians. In HMO after HMO, physician income was directly predicated on performance criteria "that, for the most part, considered how well the doctor had cut down on expenses, not how well he or she had treated patients. . . . Plans offered financial bonuses to doctors for ordering fewer tests, performing fewer procedures, and prescribing fewer drugs, while doctors who consistently ran up higher costs occasionally found themselves 'delisted'—industry parlance for a provider whose contract an insurance company has terminated."[24]

The dark clouds that built up over managed care's reputation during these years were fed to a great degree by horror stories about heartless and obtuse HMO bureaucrats who denied families desperately needed medical treatment so as to preserve profit margins and the sanctity of their HMO network of health care professionals. These stories ranged from deaths directly attributable to HMO denials or forced truncations of routine postoperative care to an episode in which a Tennessee town endured a bowel infection epidemic because state HMOs refused to cover the use of antibiotics that would have contained the outbreak. "The physicians knew what drug to prescribe," wrote reporter George Anders, "but—much like Peace Corps volunteers in a remote Third World village—they couldn't get it."[25]

The managed care industry and its supporters argued that incidents of HMO intransigence, ineptitude, and interference with doctors' decisions were the exception, not the rule. Statistical studies of HMO performance and anecdotal evidence supported many of these assertions, especially in the realm of preventive care, which lawmakers and health care experts of all political persuasions were increasingly identifying as essential to any effort to rein in U.S. health care costs. HMO enrollees were more likely to receive early diagnosis and treatment for a host of dreaded diseases, including breast cancer, cervical cancer, and colon cancer. The managed care industry also performed strongly in covering chronic diseases such as emphysema and diabetes and in bolstering prenatal care.

Some analysts have also defended HMOs from the charge that their greed was so great that they commonly refused to pay for life-saving treatments. Health care expert Jonathan Cohn, for instance, agrees that HMO abuses can be found but adds that "in other cases, the treatment an HMO refused to cover was very expensive and of questionable value to the patient. . . . Those were complicated questions, as much philosophical as medical, about which serious people could—and did—disagree."[26]

NEW POLICY PRESCRIPTIONS FOR THE PHARMACEUTICAL INDUSTRY

At the same time that lawmakers were overseeing dramatic changes in the public and private health insurance sectors, a number of important reforms were enacted related to medical drugs. The Orphan Drug Act, signed into law by Reagan in January 1983 (**See Document 8.2**), enjoyed broad bipartisan support and introduced a number of financial incentives for private drug makers to develop drugs and other treatments for people suffering from rare diseases and medical conditions. As Reagan himself stated, the Orphan Drug Act was an admission that there were instances in which the free market alone did not meet the needs of all Americans.

A 1983 U.S. Supreme Court ruling (*United States v. Generix Drug Corporation*) declaring that generic drugs needed to go through the same Food and Drug Administration (FDA) approval process as the brand-name drugs they were replicating prompted Congress to dive into pharmaceutical drug policymaking once again. The ruling, which was understandably condemned by generic drug manufacturers, came at a time when commercial drug companies were complaining about their own experiences with the FDA's review process. Specifically, they expressed enormous frustration with the regulatory agency's ponderous approval process. Drug makers complained that because they had only a limited number of years of patent exclusivity to make money off their pharmaceutical research, long approval delays were costing them millions of dollars on an annual basis.

Even some consumer and health care advocacy groups that supported the need for careful FDA review acknowledged that the regulatory process had become problematic. They opined that generic and brand-name manufacturers were recouping their FDA-related financial losses by jacking up the prices on drugs relied on by millions of Americans for everything from high blood pressure to pain management.

In 1983 Republican senator Orrin Hatch of Utah and Democratic representative Henry A. Waxman of California, both of whom had played important roles in shepherding the Orphan Drug Act into law, initiated an arduous but ultimately successful effort to craft legislation that would address these various concerns (**See Document 8.4**). The Drug Price Competition and Patent Term Restoration Act of 1984, better known as the Hatch-Waxman Act, streamlined the FDA approval process for generic copies of brand-name drugs and extended the patent life of innovator medicines created by drug research companies. Hatch-Waxman, as it turned out, was just one of several fruitful health-related collaborations between Hatch and Waxman. They worked together to pass a number of other health bills during the 1980s and 1990s, from the 1984 National Organ Transplant Act (**See Document 8.5**) to the Ryan White Comprehensive AIDS Resources Emergency (CARE) Act of 1990.

LAWYERS AND DOCTORS FACE OFF OVER MEDICAL MALPRACTICE

Another frequently cited factor in rising health care costs in the United States during the 1970s and 1980s was a sustained onslaught of medical malpractice litigation. Malpractice claims jumped by an average of 10 percent annually during the 1970s and experienced continued sharp growth in the 1980s.[27] Malpractice insurance carriers responded to this surge by issuing big premium hikes or withdrawing from some markets altogether. By 1984 malpractice premiums accounted for 9 percent of physician costs, up from 1 percent back in the 1950s.[28] According to the General Accounting Office, malpractice premiums rose by 45 percent nationwide just from 1982 to 1984. A number of medical specialties were particularly hard-hit by this trend. In some parts of the country, for example, obstetricians absorbed premium hikes of 300 percent or more in the space of only a few years.

Physicians, hospital administrators, therapists, and myriad other caregivers described the situation as a full-blown crisis that was forcing health care providers to pass on some of these "bloated" malpractice premium costs on to patients. Fears of malpractice suits were also blamed for an increase in the practice of defensive medicine, wherein physicians either ordered excessive amounts of diagnostic tests, drug prescriptions, and therapeutic measures to protect themselves from lawsuits or avoided high-risk procedures or patients altogether to minimize their exposure to legal action.

Not surprisingly, the health care industry spoke out against the litigation driving these trends. It demanded sweeping tort reform to get what it considered frivolous malpractice lawsuits under control and return a measure of stability to that aspect of medical practice (**See Document 8.8**). Some physicians also asked the nation to understand that human imperfections and frailties are a fact of life for even the most talented and dedicated physicians, surgeons, and nurses. As one North Carolina physician told a congressional subcommittee in 1986,

> I don't think that doctors can be held as supermen, as perfect people. We are not and we make mistakes. It is just unfortunate that the mistakes we make hurt people and that is the business we are in. We are in business to help people but every now and then when we make a mistake, someone is hurt. As medicine advances, we have so many more things that we can do to help people. We are doing things now that were unheard of 10 years ago. But these things are high-risk procedures and any high-risk procedure has to be—we have to accept the fact that some people are going to get hurt when this high-risk procedure doesn't turn out as well as we would want it to.[29]

The American Bar Association (ABA) took strong exception to the health care industry's characterization of the tort system (**See Document 8.9**). ABA spokesmen insisted that malpractice lawsuits—including punitive damages, which the health industry spoke out against with particular vigor—brought a measure of justice and financial security to individuals and families who had been victimized by the carelessness, incompetence, or venality of health care professionals and institutions. They also warned against wholesale experimentation with the American legal system just to mollify the health care industry. The ABA further argued that much of the "malpractice crisis" was a fiction propagated by price-gouging insurance companies and health care providers looking to cut their business expenses. Finally, lawyers and health care experts noted that the medical profession and state licensing boards were notorious for their negligent policing of the physicians' ranks.

The ABA membership benefited financially from big malpractice awards, as doctors were quick to point out. But the health care industry was less able to question the motives of patient advocacy groups, which sided with the lawyers in opposing caps on damages and other tort reform solutions offered by the health care lobby.

As this debate roared on, several states took the lead in passing tort reform measures. Some placed caps on the financial damages that could be awarded through malpractice lawsuits. Others shortened the statutes of limitations on malpractice filings, beefed up expert witness requirements, implemented sliding-scale attorney fees in malpractice cases, or established pretrial tribunals to weed out frivolous complaints. Many states, however, left their malpractice-related legal statutes largely intact.

At the federal level, the calls of the AMA went mostly unanswered. In 1987 a National Professional Liability Reform Act was introduced in Congress. This legislation would have introduced arbitration panels, caps on malpractice damages, and reduced statutes of limitations on malpractice claim filings, among other things. But this bill, like dozens of others tort reform measures that were introduced during the mid- and late 1980s, failed to win passage. Most of them, in fact, perished in committee without ever coming up for a formal vote. In 1986, Congress did pass the Health Care Quality Improvement Act, which contained provisions limiting the ability of physicians with histories of questionable performance to move their practices from state to state. It also established a national data bank of information about malpractice cases for use by licensing boards, hospitals, and other authorities.

THE AIDS EPIDEMIC

In 1981 the American people were profoundly shaken by the announcement from the Centers for Disease Control (CDC) that scientists had identified a terrible disease that was already laying waste to homosexual men. As incidences of this disease, which came to be known as acquired immune deficiency syndrome or AIDS, soared within the country's gay community (hemophiliacs and intravenous drug users were also affected as the disease spread), numerous scientists, researchers, and doctors warned that the nation faced a public health crisis of the highest order. Their calls to action were later amplified by advocacy groups such as the AIDS Coalition to Unleash Power (ACT UP), which organized rowdy protests and other direct actions of civil disobedience against drug manufacturers, Wall Street, the FDA, and other entities that were seen by the group's leadership as unresponsive to the crisis.

Congress and the White House were slow to boost funding for AIDS research, although scientists did devise an effective test for screening the nation's blood supply and identifying the presence of HIV (human immunodeficiency virus), the virus that causes AIDS. Reagan himself never even publicly addressed the subject in his first term. Scientists, AIDS activists, and many ordinary Americans attributed these stances to the influence of the Republican Party's strong links with the so-called Religious Right, which was hostile to homosexuality and trumpeted abstinence as the solution to the AIDS crisis. These religious conservatives roundly rejected calls from AIDS researchers for more scientific funding, sex education, testing programs, or free condom distribution in at-risk communities.

Reagan publicly discussed AIDS for the first time in September 1985, when he told reporters at a press conference that fighting AIDS was "a top priority" for the administration. His first speech devoted to the AIDS epidemic did not come for another twenty months, when he gave a controversial speech at the American Foundation for AIDS Research (AmFAR) Awards Dinner in Washington on May 31, 1987 **(See Document 8.10)**.

Throughout Reagan's second term, Congress approved higher levels of research funding for AIDS than the administration requested, then fended off White House attempts to reduce those research outlays. In each case, Reagan ultimately accepted the higher numbers from Congress, which was being relentlessly pushed for action by exceptionally well-organized and dedicated lobbying groups, and signed them into law.

In early 1986 Reagan also directed his surgeon general, C. Everett Koop, to prepare a major report on the AIDS crisis. Because Koop had to that point not spoken out on AIDS in any fashion, activists and researchers agreed that the report was unlikely to be of any import. They thus renewed their calls for higher research funding and the development and implementation of a national AIDS prevention program. In late 1986, for example, the prestigious Institute of Medicine of the National Academy of Sciences issued a report describing the Reagan administration's record on AIDS as "woefully inadequate." The authors also pointedly called for a greater level of "presidential leadership to bring together all elements of society to deal with the problem."[30]

Ultimately, and to the great surprise of activists, scientists, and physicians, the report that had the greatest impact on AIDS policy and public perceptions of the disease was Koop's report. Released in October 1986 without submitting it first to the White House for review or approval, the *Surgeon General's Report on Acquired Immune Deficiency Syndrome* was what historian Randy Shilts described as "a call to arms against the epidemic, complete with marching orders. For one of the first times, the problem of AIDS was addressed in purely public health terms, stripped of politics."[31] Koop's report ran afoul of virtually every policy position espoused by the Religious Right. It advocated condom use and early AIDS education in schools and emphasized that voluntary testing with strong safeguards guaranteeing confidentiality and nondiscrimination would be far more effective than any mandatory testing scheme.

Conservative policymakers and activists felt betrayed by Koop, but the surgeon general strongly defended the report, which seemed to spark a reassessment of the crisis from the American media and the public. From this point forward, AIDS policymaking became a much more high-profile issue. Congress took note as well, approving dramatically higher funding for AIDS education, testing, and research efforts and authorizing the formation of a national AIDS commission.

The most momentous event to arise out of Koop's bombshell report was the 1990 Ryan White Comprehensive AIDS Resources Emergency (CARE) Act. This watershed legislation created a federal program that bestowed desperately needed funding to urban hospitals and other health care institutions that were on the front lines of the battle against AIDS, and it greatly increased federal support for early intervention treatment and prevention programs **(See Document 8.15)**. Within a few years of its creation, the Ryan White program was firmly established as the main source of federal funding for initiatives to combat and treat AIDS and HIV. Despite the program's many successes as a facilitator of AIDS education, treatment, and primary care, HIV/AIDs remains a serious public health problem. The CDC estimated in July 2010 that more than one million people in the United States were HIV carriers and that more than 576,000 people in the United States had died of AIDS as of 2007.[32]

POLITICAL WRANGLING OVER WOMEN'S HEALTH RESEARCH

Political activism also played a major role in convincing federal officials to place medical research on women's health issues on a more equal footing with medical research on men. By the early 1980s, the women's movement that had risen to prominence a decade earlier had remade the world of American health care in many significant ways. "Advocates had

A man is arrested at the AIDS Coalition to Unleash Power (ACT UP) protest in New York City in March 1989. The response of the Reagan administration and public health officials to the arrival of acquired immune deficiency syndrome (AIDS) was widely condemned by public health advocates and gay activists in the 1980s.

When the federal government commenced the Understanding AIDS campaign, virtually every resident of the United States received notification, by mail, of this major health concern.

popularized natural childbirth, revived midwifery, and reclaimed labor and delivery as a family event," stated Suzanne G. Haynes of the HHS Office on Women's Health. "Women were allowed to more freely enroll in medical schools so that female enrollment had tripled. Advocates had effectively challenged the use of radical mastectomies and created an atmosphere where patients could become partners in selecting their treatment plans. Throughout this period, activists played a central role in the legalization and continued availability of abortion."[33]

The movement also was pressing for the medical establishment to stop giving short shrift to reproductive health issues and other areas of health that were of special interest and relevance to women. One special focus of these lobbying efforts was medical research studies, which commonly excluded women **(See Document 8.6)**. For years these research studies (almost always directed and conducted by male physicians and scientists) had excluded women from important research work. Sometimes they were omitted from studies because researchers harbored concerns that the reproductive cycle of women injected a note of uncertainty into test results or limited research trials. Oftentimes, however, they were not included because it was simply less expensive to conduct male-only studies, or because researchers chose to focus on diseases and treatments that applied only to boys or men. The end result of this pattern of exclusion was a paucity of information about the impact of various treatments on women and girls.

In the 1980s Congress began seriously exploring legislation that would promote the greater inclusion of women and women's health issues in biomedical research studies through a variety of means, including mandates for such coverage in any research studies funded by federal tax dollars. Women's health advocates undoubtedly played an important role in rousing Washington from its long slumber on this issue, but numerous other factors were at work, too. These elements included the increased prominence of women in medical practices, biomedical research, and academic medicine, as well as the growing percentage of women in the workforce. The latter development not only increased the economic and political clout of women, but it also heightened employer interest in the business ramifications of women's health care issues and policies.

Women activists and health professionals found a receptive audience for their cause among women lawmakers in Washington, who were also increasing in number. By the mid-1980s, women members of Congress had united to advance an ambitious legislative agenda for women's health research and other issues (the politically divisive issue of abortion was carefully avoided, however). These legislators, formally organized as the Congressional Caucus for Women's issues, were assisted in their efforts by Waxman and other sympathetic male members of Congress with strong health policy credentials.

In 1986, under prodding from caucus members, women's activists, and the media, the National Institutes of Health (NIH) amended its policies to require recipients of NIH research grants to include women in study populations. In 1990, however, a GAO audit of NIH operations revealed that little progress had been made in implementing that policy. Federally funded health research remained heavily slanted toward men-only trials, even in cases in which the medical condition affected both men and women (**See Document 8.16**). This revelation, widely reported in the press, forced the NIH to move more decisively to end gender bias in the health research that it was funding. It also led caucus leaders to introduce the 1990 Women's Health Equity Act (WHEA), which contained a wide range of provisions to bolster women's health research and services. Many of the research-oriented provisions of that legislation became law in 1993. Others were enacted with the 1998 passage of the Women's Health Research and Prevention Amendments, which expanded federal research into heart disease, strokes, and other cardiovascular diseases among women and provided funding for breast and cervical cancer screening programs for low-income women.

THE AMERICANS WITH DISABILITIES ACT

The Americans with Disabilities Act (ADA) of 1990 was another health policy milestone that owed its existence to political activism. In the 1960s and 1970s, the United States witnessed the birth of a disability rights movement that was determined to take full advantage of civil rights precedents established in the Civil Rights Act of 1964 and the Rehabilitation Act of 1973 to advance their cause. By the 1980s, America's disability community had forced itself into health care and civil rights policy discussions throughout Washington.

In 1984 the National Council on the Handicapped (NCH, later the National Council on Disability) was asked by Congress to review all federal policies and programs related to disability and study ways to boost the self-sufficiency and independence of people with disabilities. The organization subsequently submitted a report that called for a law guaranteeing the full equal rights of persons with disabilities. Working with the NCH's Bob Burgdorf and other leaders of the disability movement, Rep. Tony Coelho (D-CA) and Senators Lowell P. Weicker Jr. (R-CT) and Tom Harkin (D-IA) crafted a bill that would accomplish that fundamental goal. The Americans with Disabilities Act was then submitted to Congress for consideration in April 1988. Five months later, Reagan

President George H. W. Bush signs the Americans with Disabilities Act, which gave those with disabilities full and equal rights under the law. Surrounding the president are Rev. Harold Wilke, Equal Opportunity Employment Commission chair Evan Kemp, National Council on Disability chair Sandra Parrino, and President's Committee on the Employment of People with Disabilities chair Justin Dart.

signed into law the 1988 Fair Housing Amendments Act, which prohibited discrimination against people with disabilities in housing matters. The passage of that bill was a clear indication that the ADA was progressing through Congress with considerable political wind in its sails.

In 1989 public and political support for ADA continued to grow under the skillful direction of disability rights advocates. The bill's language underwent a number of changes to increase its chances for passage during this time, but the ADA's primary legislative shepherds—Harkin, Coelho, Hatch, Rep. Steny H. Hoyer (D-MD), and Sen. Edward M. Kennedy (D-MA)—kept its main provisions intact. The Senate passed the ADA by a 76–8 vote on September 7, 1989, but concerns about the ADA's financial impact on businesses prompted further reworking of the bill in the House, which passed the measure by a 403–20 vote on May 22, 1990. The bill then underwent fractious but ultimately successful negotiations between House and Senate conferees, and the two chambers cleared the ADA in its final form in July. President George H. W. Bush signed the ADA into law on July 26, 1990, to the great delight of disability activists who had worked for so many years for its passage **(See Document 8.17)**.

Today, the Americans with Disabilities Act remains one of the cornerstones of U.S. civil rights law. Millions of individuals and families affected by disabilities say that it fundamentally changed their lives forever. As the National Council on Disability stated a few years after the act became law,

> [t]he ADA is unique in the context of civil rights legislation because it requires that businesses and governments do more than just cease discriminatory actions. They must also take proactive steps to offer equal opportunity to persons with disabilities, commensurate with their economic resources. The ADA is distinctive in the context of disability legislation not for its individual provisions, most of which

were already established in some form by various state and local governments, but in its comprehensive nature and application to much of the private sector.[34]

Rising Costs Fuel Drive to Identify Best Practices

By the time Reagan administration rolled through its second term, assessments of its performance in the health sector were wildly divergent. Liberal opponents decried the administration's record on AIDS and asserted that steep Republican cuts to nutritional programs for poor children, child care services for low-income families, AFDC, and other social welfare programs jeopardized the health and well-being of the most vulnerable members of American society. Administration officials and their conservative supporters frequently sidestepped these charges by noting that it was the Reagan-supported Medicare prospective payment system that had helped shore up the financial solvency of one of the nation's foundational entitlement programs. They also pointed to the 1986 launch of the DSH (Disproportionate Share Hospital) program that boosted Medicare and Medicaid payment rates to safety net hospitals, that is, those that served large populations of uninsured or low-income patients.

The DSH program was enormously controversial. It had been designed to lend financial assistance to hospitals with large numbers of Medicaid cases. DSH payments were a financial lifeline to such hospitals, because the cost of treatment of Medicaid patients sometimes exceeded payment and hospital beds filled with uninsured people or Medicaid enrollees could not be used for privately insured patients who could be charged more for services provided. The DSH program, however, was manipulated by states in a variety of ways to fill their budgetary coffers, and DSH Medicaid payments soared from $1.3 billion in 1988 to $17 billion in 1992.

Lawmakers eventually passed new DSH restrictions that curbed the worst abuses. But overall federal expenditures on health care continued to escalate at rates that alarmed politicians, administrators, and health care professionals of all ideological stripes. By the late 1980s, complaints that the nation's health care system remained an essentially wasteful and inefficient one spawned a new focus for reform: identifying and implementing the most efficient and helpful forms of diagnosis and treatment, then encouraging their widespread adoption. "In a medical system in which doctors are paid only for doing *something*, and patients want something done, uncertainty over diagnosis and treatment makes for all kinds of unnecessary tests and treatments," wrote Joseph A. Califano Jr., a public health expert who served as Department of Health, Education, and Welfare secretary in the Carter administration. "I suggest we adopt a different attitude: unless the procedure has been proved effective, don't use it. . . . It's time for a rigorous effort to establish what procedures produce beneficial outcomes under what conditions—and to eliminate stark instances of 'overutilization' like those cited above. Physicians and hospital administrators should put establishing quality standards at the top of their agendas."[35]

This heightened interest in medical best practices—treatments that were both cost-effective and beneficial to patient health—led Congress in 1989 to amend the Public Health Service Act to create the Agency for Health Care Policy and Research (AHCPR). This agency was given a primary mission of conducting or commissioning studies that focus on the outcomes and effectiveness of various medical treatments (**See Document 8.14**).

This expansion in federal support for health services research—which had previously been as difficult to sell to Congress as "a dead fish wrapped in newspaper," in the words of one Washington insider—was attributable in part to the success of diagnosis-related groups in reining in Medicare expenditures.[36] Those results gave advocates a clear example of how careful study of health care practices could translate into budgetary savings. But it also stemmed from studies by the RAND Corporation and other research organizations revealing that common and expensive surgical procedures were being misused in many parts of the country. Capitol Hill and George H.W. Bush, who succeeded Reagan as president in 1989, thus became receptive to the capacity of effectiveness research to improve public health and stem both public and private health costs.

The legislation that created AHCPR moved funding for health care research to a whole new plane. Funding jumped from $53 million in 1989 (when health services research was conducted within another agency, the National Center for Health Services Research) to $97 million in 1990 and increased steadily in the early 1990s.[37] During the first few years of AHCPR's existence, its work in crafting and publicizing new practice guidelines was applauded by a wide range of important private sector health care players, including the American Medical Association, the American Hospital Association, the Health Insurance Association of America, the American Nurses Association, and the Association of American Medical Colleges. When the AHCPR's efforts became associated with President Bill Clinton's health care reform campaign in the mid-1990s, however, the bitter political gamesmanship that followed nearly wrecked the agency.

THE CATASTROPHIC COVERAGE DEBACLE

The Reagan administration's final attempt to leave its stamp on the U.S. health care system came in the form of the Medicare Catastrophic Coverage Act (MCCA) of 1988. The legislation, which was unveiled by HHS secretary Otis R. Bowen in 1986, sought to shore up the financial security of senior citizens facing big medical bills **(See Document 8.11)**. Bowen's proposal placed a $2,000 annual ceiling on out-of-pocket payments by Medicare beneficiaries for hospital (Part A) and physician (Part B) expenses. From that point on, Medicare would pay all deductibles and coinsurance. These new benefits would, at the administration's insistence, be financed entirely by the elderly, who would pay a flat monthly fee of $4.92 to cover the cost of the new program.

Bowen's proposed expansion of Medicare was strongly opposed by many administration officials. Key advisers ranging from Attorney General Edwin Meese III to Council of Economic Advisers chairman Beryl W. Sprinkel saw it as exactly the sort of "big government" intrusion into the marketplace that Reagan had spent much of his presidency railing against. But Reagan saw the legislation as a way to stanch the political damage he was suffering from Democrats, who relentlessly hammered his administration as one that was unconcerned about America's poor and needy (this message, in fact, helped Democrats reclaim the Senate in the 1986 midterm elections). In addition, Bowen proved an able defender of the potential social and political benefits of his plan. Democrats applauded the scheme as well, saying that it would reduce the need for seniors to purchase so-called Medigap policies, supplemental coverage from private insurers designed to cover areas where Medicare coverage was limited. Republicans, said Senator Kennedy, should "listen a little more" to Bowen and a "little less to the insurance industry."[38]

When Bowen's catastrophic coverage plan reached Capitol Hill, Democrats who now controlled both houses of Congress saw an opportunity to move the ball forward on a number of other health care priorities that previously had been stymied by the Reagan administration. Encouraged by health care advocates, they added numerous provisions and benefits to the bill, including coverage for prescription drugs, hospice care, home-based health care for the elderly and disabled, and mammography screening. "The bill became the vehicle for the deferred agenda in health care," summarized John Rother, who served as legislative director of the American Association of Retired Persons (AARP) at the time.[39]

As the Medicare Catastrophic Coverage Act moved through Congress, it became so festooned with additional programs and benefits that even Bowen spoke out against it. He voiced particular displeasure with the prescription drug benefit, which he saw as too expensive. The new features meant that additional financing had to be found. When Reagan remained insistent that the bill be financed entirely by those who would benefit—the elderly—Congress added a surtax for people over the age of sixty-five with incomes above $35,000.

The bill easily passed through both the House (by a 328–72 margin) and the Senate (86–11), and on July 1, 1988, Reagan signed the measure into law in a high-profile ceremony **(See Document 8.12)**. The atmosphere at the White House on that day was celebratory, and for good reason. The bill was seen as a political winner not only because of its presumed popularity with senior citizens, but also because many powerful lobbying constituencies had signaled their support. To be sure, the insurance industry had opposed it because companies stood to lose some Medigap policies. In addition, brand-name pharmaceutical manufacturers expressed concern that the prescription drug benefit might ultimately result in government-imposed price controls on medicine. But many other heavy hitters had lined up in support, including AARP, AHA, AMA, generic drug makers, and large corporations that would get long-sought relief from retiree health costs with the passage of MCCA.[40]

Within a matter of weeks, it became clear that the MCCA was not the crowd-pleaser that Congress thought it was. The legislation was of clear benefit to the 20 percent of American senior citizens who were not poor enough to qualify for Medicaid yet did not have the financial resources to purchase Medigap insurance. The legislation contained fewer benefits for financially secure seniors who already had strong coverage against catastrophic illness through Medigap policies or retirement pensions—and who were being asked to finance much of the law through those new surtaxes, which ran as high as $800 per individual and $1,600 per couple.

A popular revolt against the MCCA spread like a brushfire across the United States. Flames of discontent were first seen in affluent retirement communities in the South and West, then quickly spread to other parts of the country. A group called the National Committee to Preserve Social Security and Medicare (chaired by James Roosevelt, a son of Franklin D. Roosevelt) was particularly effective in fanning the discontent. Defenders of the legislation angrily denounced Roosevelt's group for its mass mailings, which were rife with distortions and overheated rhetoric, but to no avail.

By early 1989 members of the newly convened 101st Congress were being besieged by letters and telephone calls from angry seniors who demanded repeal of the MCCA. Conservative policymakers, pundits, and activists added their voices. The MCCA is "the ultimate in political immorality in a democratic republic," said Norman B. Ture of the Institute for Research on the Economics of Taxation. "It is . . . a tax-transfer scheme, requiring virtually all not-poor persons who are 65 or older to pay for the covered medical expenses of a small group of older persons who are not quite poor enough to qualify for Medicaid."[41]

In April the Senate Finance Committee opened formal hearings on MCCA. Proponents spent the next several weeks engaged in a belated, and somewhat frantic, campaign to educate the public about the act's many and varied benefits. But they were overwhelmed by conservative lawmakers and senior citizens who remained convinced that MCCA was a legislative monstrosity **(See Document 8.13)**. Committee member and MCCA supporter Bob Packwood, a moderate Republican from Oregon, became so exasperated by events that he lashed out in frustration against many of the witnesses: "I will tell you who we have heard from. They all live in Sun City [a wealthy Arizona retirement community] and they all have incomes of $30,000. I do not think it is unfair or unethical or immoral or wrong to ask those of us who are a little bit more privileged to give a little extra to take care of those who are a little less privileged."[42]

By summer, pro-MCCA forces were on the run, and talk of outright repeal was in the air. Opponents of the act kept the pressure on with letter-writing campaigns and political rallies and demonstrations. The emerging political Zeitgeist surrounding the MCCA was perfectly captured in mid-August, when national media outlets broadcast footage of Rep. Dan Rostenkowski (D-IL), the powerful chair of the House Ways and Means Committee, fleeing anti-MCCA demonstrators on foot after they confronted him on a Chicago street.

In October a thoroughly spooked House of Representatives voted 360–66 in favor of repealing the MCCA program. The Senate followed suit one month later, after last-ditch efforts to retain some of the legislation's long-term hospital benefits ended in failure. The Medicare Catastrophic Coverage Repeal Act (H.R. 3607) was ultimately passed by voice vote in both chambers, and President George H. W. Bush signed the measure on November 23, 1989. The whole episode was a potent reminder to Washington of the political power of American seniors in any discussion of health care policy.

Notes

1. Lynn Etheridge, "Reagan, Congress, and Health Spending," *Health Affairs* 2, no. 1 (January 1983): 14–24.

2. Larry J. Gordon, "The Impact of Reagan's Health Policies," paper presented at the annual meeting of the New Mexico Hospital Association, October 23, 1981, www.sanitarians.org/Gordon/Reagan_Health_Policies.pdf.

3. Etheridge, "Reagan, Congress, and Health Spending," 17.

4. John D. Klemm, "Medicaid Spending: A Brief History," *Health Care Financing Review* 22, no. 1 (Fall 2000): 105–12.

5. Laura Katz Olson, *The Politics of Medicaid* (New York: Columbia University Press, 2010), 57.

6. Olson, *The Politics of Medicaid*, 53.

7. Kant Patel and Mark E. Rushefsky, *Health Care Politics and Policy in America,* 2nd ed. (Armonk, NY: M.E. Sharpe, 1999), 43.

8. Quoted in Rick Mayes and Robert A. Berenson, *Medicare Prospective Payment and the Shaping of U.S. Health Care* (Baltimore: Johns Hopkins University Press, 2002), 32.

9. Mayes and Berenson, *Medicare Prospective Payment and the Shaping of U.S. Health Care,* 38.

10. Quoted in Mayes and Berenson, *Medicare Prospective Payment and the Shaping of U.S. Health Care,* 38.

11. Jonathan Oberlander *The Political Life of Medicare* (Chicago: University of Chicago Press, 2003), 124.

12. Robert Cunningham, "Prospective Payment: Medicare's Secret Success Story," *Health Affairs* 26, no. 3 (2007): 896.

13. Mayes and Berenson, *Medicare Prospective Payment and the Shaping of U.S. Health Care,* 12.

14. Jill Quadagno, *One Nation Uninsured: Why the U.S. Has No National Health Insurance* (New York: Oxford University Press, 2005), 136.

15. Julie Rovner, "Medicare: Cost Cutting Efforts," *Health Care Policy and Politics A to Z,* 3rd ed. (Washington, DC: CQ Press, 2009), 150.

16. Atul Gawande, *Better: A Surgeon's Notes on Performance,* (New York: Metropolitan, 2007), 114–115.

17. Benson B. Roe, "The UCR Boondoggle—A Death Knell for Private Practice?" *New England Journal of Medicine* (July 2, 1981): 41–45.

18. John Fairhall, "HMO Changes Medicine with Tough Bargaining," *Baltimore Sun,* October 9, 1994.

19. Susan Brink, Susan Nancy Shute, "Are HMOs the Right Prescription?" *U.S. News and World Report,* October 13, 1997, 60–64.

20. Quadagno, *One Nation Uninsured,* 141.

21. Janet Firshein and Lewis G. Sandy, "The Changing Approach to Managed Care," in *To Improve Health and Health Care, 2001,* ed. Stephen L. Isaacs and James R. Knickman (Princeton, NJ: Robert Wood Johnson Foundation, 2001), www.rwjf.org/files/publications/books/2001/chapter_04.html.

22. Quoted in K. Iglehart, "The Future of HMOs," *New England Journal of Medicine* (August 12, 1982): 453.

23. National Center for Health Statistics, *Health US, 1998* (Washington, DC: Government Printing Office, 1998), table 135, in Patel and Rushefsky, *Health Care Politics and Policy in America,* 305.

24. Jonathan Cohn, *Sick: The Untold Story of America's Health Care Crisis—and the People Who Pay the Price* (New York: HarperCollins, 2007), 68, 77.

25. George Anders, *Health against Wealth: HMOs and the Breakdown of Medical Trust* (Boston: Houghton Mifflin, 1996), 194.

26. Cohn, *Sick,* 75.

27. Patricia M. Danzon, "The Crisis in Medical Malpractice," *Law, Medicine, and Health Care* (Spring/Summer 1990): 48–58.

28. Patel and Rushefsky, *Health Care Politics and Policy in America,* 202.

29. Quoted in Bernard D. Reams, ed., *The Health Care Quality Improvement Act of 1986: A Legislative History of Pub. L. No. 99-660* (Buffalo, NY: Hein, 1990), 64.

30. Quoted in Randy Shilts, *And the Band Played On: Politics, People, and the AIDS Epidemic* (New York: St. Martin's Press, 1987), 586.

31. Shilts, *And the Band Played On,* 587.

32. Centers for Disease Control and Prevention, "HIV in the United States," July 2010, www.cdc.gov/hiv/resources/factsheets/PDF/us.pdf.

33. Suzanne G. Haynes, "The Role of Women in Health Care and Research," in *Women and Health,* ed. Marlene B. Goldman and Maureen Hatch (San Diego, CA: Academic Press, 2000), 30.

34. National Council on Disability, *Equality of Opportunity: The Making of the Americans with Disabilities Act* (Washington, DC: National Council on Disability, 1997), www.ncd.gov/newsroom/publications/1997/equality.htm.

35. Joseph Califano, "The Health-Care Chaos," *New York Times Magazine,* March 20, 1988, 44.

36. Quoted in Bradford H. Gray, Michal K. Gusmano, and Sara Collins, "AHCPR and the Changing Politics of Health Services Research," *Health Affairs* (2003), http://content.healthaffairs.org/content/early/2003/06/25/hlthaff.w3.283.

37. Gray, Gusmano, and Collins, "AHCPR and the Changing Politics of Health Services Research."

38. Quoted in Robert Englund, "The Catastrophic Health Care Blunder," *American Spectator,* November 1988, 28.

39. Quoted in Martin Tolchin, "Retreat in Congress: The Catastrophic Care Debacle—A Special Report; How the New Medicare Law Fell on Hard Times in a Hurry," *New York Times,* October 9, 1989, A1.

40. Quadagno, *One Nation Uninsured,* 153.

41. Norman B. Ture, "The Medicare Catastrophic Coverage Act: A Case for Repeal (Part II)," *IRET Policy Bulletin* (July 19, 1989): 1.

42. Quoted in Julie Rovner, "Catastrophic Coverage Law Narrowly Survives Test," *Congressional Quarterly Weekly Report,* June 10, 1989, 1402.

DOCUMENT 8.1

An Investor's Guide to Health Maintenance Organizations

"The Outlook for Continued Growth of HMO Enrollment Is Excellent"

1982

In 1981 the Reagan administration moved decisively on two fronts to change the fundamental structure of health maintenance organizations (HMOs). It ended federal subsidies for nonprofit HMOs, a move that effectively thrust the organizations into the unforgiving sink-or-swim world of the free market. At the same time, the administration actively promoted the profit potential of HMOs to the investment community. The Office of Health Maintenance Organizations (OHMO) took the lead in this regard, sponsoring conferences and publishing guidebooks that were explicitly designed to encourage Wall Street to think of HMOs as canny investments.

One such guidebook was the 1982 Investors Guide to Health Maintenance Organizations, *an OHMO offering prepared under contract by the accounting firm Touche Ross and Co. The guide presented a decidedly upbeat analysis of the HMO industry and the profit potential of managed care. The guide's introductory "executive summary" is excerpted here.*

PURPOSE OF THE GUIDE

The *Investors Guide to Health Maintenance Organizations* represents a unique effort on the part of the Federal government to inform private investors about investing in health maintenance organizations (HMOs).

The *Guide* is just one part of a broader promotional effort on the part of the Department of Health and Human Services (DHHS) to provide information to potential investors about HMO opportunities and to increase private funds available for new and expanding HMOs. This effort stems directly from the decision of the current administration to discontinue Federal grants and phase out loans to emerging HMOs in favor of greater support from the private sector.

Several types of investors are considered to be sources of HMO investment and users of this *Guide.* They are:

- Investment banking firms
- Venture capital firms

- Small business investment companies (SBICs)
- Physician/Administrator Partnerships
- Commercial Banks
- Major Health Insurance Companies
- HMO Management Companies
- Hospitals

These are considered potential investors because firms in each group at one time or another have considered or made recent investments in HMOs. Of course, these investors have had widely different objectives and employ different approaches. For example, investment banking firms may be interested in placing tax-exempt debt issues for large and mature non-profit HMOs. Venture capital firms and SBICs may be interested in recently established for-profit HMOs with high growth and profit potential. Physician/administrator partnerships may be interested in providing equity capital for start-up activities or the acquisition of health facilities for HMOs. Commercial banks may wish to help their HMO loan customers find sources of long-term financing.

Because the audience for this *Investors Guide* is assumed to be broad, our objective has been to provide as much information as possible about the operational, management, and financial aspects of HMOs and let the reader draw his or her own conclusions about specific objectives for investment in an HMO.

In the above context, the purpose of this *Guide* is to:

- Describe the current industry, enrollment trends, what HMOs are and how they work (Chapter II);
- Review the key factors that an investor must assess before making an investment in an HMO (Chapter III);
- Present industry financial and operating data compiled for the first time on a major segment of HMOs (Chapter III);
- Outline the capital needs of HMOs according to the stage of the organization's development (Chapter IV); and
- Present three case examples of recent, successful investment in HMOs (Chapter V).
- A summary of each of these topics follows. First, however, we will review why HMO investment should be profitable.

Should Investors be Interested in HMOs?

In considering HMOs for investment, it is important to understand that the HMO industry is still being established. Over half of the 243 operational prepaid health plans reported in the June 30, 1981 National HMO Census had been operational for less than five years. Only three HMOs currently have revenues of over $100 million although several others will reach this mark in the next five years. Well over half of the operational HMOs have revenues of less than $10 million and over a quarter have revenues of less than $5 million.

In an industry consisting primarily of small, recently established units, it should be expected that the technology of managing HMOs is still developing, that HMO growth and profitability varies widely, and that failures aren't uncommon. Given the above, why should investors be interested in HMOs? Are they good investments?

We believe the evidence is substantial and growing that effectively managed HMOs are good investments. Consider the following:

- *Industry leaders have established a proven track record.* The top 20 HMOs in terms of enrollment have been operational for a median period of almost 20 years, have demonstrated that they can provide quality health care at less cost than traditional health insurers, and have made reasonable returns on revenues and investment. For fiscal years ending in 1980, these HMOs had combined revenues of over $2.5 billion and a median return on equity of almost 13 percent.
- *The industry has grown at a real rate of over 12 percent annually.* HMO enrollment in the last ten years has increased an average of 12.4 percent annually. This represents a real growth in services that has been four to five times faster than our economy in general. When one assumes inflation of 8 to 10 percent annually during this same period, a 12.4 percent annual real growth translates into an annual revenue increase for the industry of well over 20 percent. Of course, numerous HMOs have fared much better than these averages—several HMOs in the "top 60" have increased their revenue 600 percent or more during the last four years.
- *Highly successful HMOs have earned a return on equity of over 20 percent.* The first quartile of the 39 HMOs in the "top 60" whose financial statements were analyzed for this *Investors Guide* earned a *minimum* of 20.6 percent on equity for fiscal years ending in 1980. Such returns are above average in any industry and, when coupled with rapid growth, demonstrate extraordinary investment opportunities.
- *Some investors have already recognized the opportunity in HMOs.* Since late 1980, investor activity in the HMO industry has been extraordinary. Major health insurers—Blue Cross/Blue Shield, Prudential, Insurance Company of North America, CNA, John Hancock—have undertaken aggressive acquisition and start-up programs. The venture capital firms of E.M. Warburg, Pincus & Co. and Warburg Paribas Becker, Inc. have invested in two plans. Group Health Cooperative of Puget Sound became the first HMO to go to the public tax-exempt bond market for funds. The issue raised $26.4 million and received an A+ rating from Standard and Poors. HMO management companies have been established with the goal of emulating similar organizations in the hospital field, and one has quickly entered into management contracts with and extended lines of credit to five plans representing almost 100,000 total enrollees.
- *Future market forces will continue to encourage HMO growth.* Rapidly rising health care costs will cause more employers and consumers to consider alternatives to their current health care coverage. Possible government legislation to promote more competition in health care coupled with escalating premiums of competing major health insurers will also favor the continued growth of HMOs.

In the remaining paragraphs below we will summarize the key points of each of the major sections of the *Investors Guide* and then return to a summary of the future outlook for HMOs.

Role and Growth of HMOs (Chapter II)

A health maintenance organization performs a unique role in American health care—it not only performs an insurance function, it also provides health care services to an organized, integrated system that holds down costs by changing the behavior of physicians and patients. Several studies have shown conclusively that medical care costs are lower for HMO enrollees than for comparable people with conventional health insurance while the quality of care is equivalent or better.

As a result of Federal legislation and of employer and consumer acceptance of HMOs as a legitimate alternative to traditional health care, national enrollment in the last ten years has tripled to 10.3 million enrollees in 1981 from 3 million in 1971. Market pentration [sic] is highest in the Pacific Coast states (e.g. 18 percent in California) but is over 10 percent in Minnesota and Wisconsin and 5 percent or above in several Western states, New York, and the District of Columbia. HMO services are now provided in 40 states and the District of Columbia. Enrollment growth has been greatest in areas of the upper Midwest, Northeast, and Southwest states.

What are the Key Elements of a Successful HMO? (Chapter III)

We have identified four key operational factors that an investor must assess to determine the desirability of HMO investment. They are (1) degree of the HMO's market acceptance, (2) effectiveness of its relationship with its physicians, (3) establishment of cost controls, and (4) capability of the HMO Board and top management. The first factor is mostly external to the HMO while the final three describe internal requirements. All four factors are critical to an HMO's long-term success. The *Guide* describes several activities that the investor can undertake to assess the potential performance of an HMO.

What are the Financial Characteristics of HMOs? (Chapter III)

The financial performance of the HMO industry has never been portrayed because no one organization currently collects financial data on all segments of the industry. For purposes of this *Guide,* we assembled and analyzed financial statements of 47 of the 60 largest HMOs for the two most recently completed fiscal years. These statements represented 74 percent of the industry's enrollment and 72 percent of the industry's total estimated revenue for fiscal years ending in 1980. From these statements we estimate that the HMO industry had revenues of approximately $4 billion in 1980.

Because the seven Kaiser Foundation Health Plans and their combined financial results represent such a large portion of the industry (39 percent of total enrollment and 43 percent of 1980 revenues), we excluded their results from the detailed analyses presented in this *Investors Guide* and summarized below. The results of the remaining 40 HMOs and their 39 financial statements were as follows:

- In 1980, 26 HMOs were profitable while 13 were not. Sixteen were profitable in both 1980 and 1979;
- In aggregate, the 39 HMOs had surpluses/profits of $13.3 million in 1980 on revenues of $1.18 billion for a profit margin of 1.1 percent. In 1979, surpluses/ profits were $16.3 million on revenues of $873 million, or a margin of 1.9 percent;
- Revenues in 1980 were 34.9 percent greater than in 1979. This increase was due to an increase in member months of 19.3 percent and an increase in revenue per member month of 13.1 percent;

- Investment income from the favorable cash flow experienced by HMOs was critically important to profitability; it contributed all of the profit in 1980 and 60 percent of 1979 surplus/profit;
- Combined assets in 1980 were $478 million, current liabilities $194 million, long-term liabilities and debt $153 million, and reserves/equity were $132 million. Assets per enrollee were $158;
- Return on equity was 10.2 percent for 1980, down from 14.6 percent in 1979. The return on invested capital (long-term liabilities and debt plus equity) was 7.7 percent in 1980 and 10.0 percent in 1979 while the return on total assets was 4.6 percent and 6.2 percent respectively for the two years.

As expected, these combined results mask considerable ranges in individual HMO financial performance which are analyzed in detail in Chapter III. . . .

Capital Needs (Chapter IV)

In reviewing the financial statements and discussing investment needs with several HMOs, we found that staff model HMOs required greater investment than other types because of longer periods of operation before reaching breakeven and higher initial outlays for buildings and equipment. For the other models (group, network, IPA) we could discern no significant differences for the HMOs in our survey.

The investment needs of older and more mature HMOs were primarily for facilities and equipment, while young HMOs required capital for start-up activities, operating deficits, and facilities. Other than these broad generalizations, factors such as the local market situation, nature of HMO sponsorship, and capability of management were important determinants in governing the timing and amount of investment needs.

The Future

We believe the outlook for continued growth of HMO enrollment is excellent. Most of this growth will be experienced by already established HMOs, since the rate of new HMO start-ups has diminished in recent years and will slow even further now that the Federal grant and loan program is being phased out. Previously mentioned market forces of high health care costs and rising competitive rates will continue to support HMO growth. The HMO "track record" will become more widely known and attract additional enrollment. Proposals in Congress to encourage more competition in health care are likely to give HMOs an additional boost in terms of public recognition and favorable marketing environment.

Not all the trends are positive, of course. HMOs face continued although weakening resistance to their development from the more conservative elements of the medical community. Financial failures of HMOs will continue and perhaps increase in the next few years as marginal plans exhaust their Federal loans without becoming profitable. The impact of these failures in terms of lost enrollment and revenues will be small, but the attendant publicity will magnify the impact and damage public acceptance of HMOs.

We remain firm, however, in our conviction that HMO investment can be highly attractive. Investors first need to understand the operating and financial aspects of HMOs and effectively assess management's performance—a need this document is intended to address.

Source: Touche Ross and Co. "Executive Summary." *Investors Guide to Health Maintenance Organizations.* Washington, DC: Government Printing Office, 1982, pp. 2–7.

President Reagan Signs the Orphan Drug Act

"This Legislation Exemplifies the Proper Role of Government"

1983

Congress passed the Orphan Drug Act (ODA) in an effort to stimulate private sector pharmaceutical manufacturers to develop drugs, medical devices, and biotechnology products for the treatment of rare diseases and medical conditions. Prior to the ODA, which was passed as an amendment to the Federal Food, Drug, and Cosmetic Act, pharmaceutical companies had shied away from developing these so-called orphan products for small patient populations. Pursuing such research simply did not make sense from a profitability standpoint. The ODA provided three incentives for drug makers to find treatments for hemophilia, Huntington's disease, ALS (amyotrophic lateral sclerosis or Lou Gehrig's disease), cystic fibrosis, muscular dystrophy, and other relatively rare conditions and diseases (a 1984 amendment to the ODA defined a rare disease as a condition affecting fewer than 200,000 people in the Untied States). These incentives were seven-year market exclusivity to sponsors of approved drugs or products, a 50 percent tax credit on expenses incurred conducting human clinical trials, and federal research grants for testing of new drugs, therapies, and diagnostic tools for rare diseases and conditions.

The ODA was signed into law by President Ronald Reagan on January 4, 1983. By that point in Reagan's first term, his administration had become well known for its efforts to deregulate American medicine and reshape it in accordance with free market principles. But Reagan declared in his ODA signing statement, reprinted here, that federal incentives for orphan drug development reflected the fact that in some cases "the free market alone can't do the job."

Since it became law, the ODA's effectiveness in spurring orphan drug research is unquestioned. In the ten years prior to its passage, only 10 orphan drugs were developed by the pharmaceutical industry. From 1983 to 2007, the Food and Drug Administration (FDA) granted marketing approval to 245 orphan products and bestowed orphan product status on more than 1,150 drugs, biotechnology products, and devices in the FDA approval pipeline.[1]

I am pleased to sign into law today the Orphan Drug Act.

Over the past century, the United States—largely through innovative pioneering by private industry and medical researchers in universities—has led the world in developing new drugs that have saved millions of lives. That is a gift to mankind we can be very proud of.

Yet the sad fact remains that many diseases still cripple or kill hundreds of thousands of Americans, as well as citizens of other countries, because no drugs have yet been developed. These diseases include cystic fibrosis, Wilson's disease, myoclonus, Tourette's syndrome, and certain neuromuscular disorders and cardiac arrhythmias. Statistically, they are rare; yet that is small comfort for those afflicted.

The cost of discovering and developing a new drug is often staggering. By definition, an orphan drug is one that treats a disease that affects 200,000 or fewer individuals—and, from an economic perspective, groups that small do not now justify the kind of research expenditures that companies must make.

The bill that I am signing today helps to cure that problem and consequently, we hope, some of the diseases as well. The bill provides incentives for the private sector to develop drugs to treat these rare diseases.

It should be pointed out that the Department of Health and Human Services has already made significant progress in this area. Secretary Schweiker established an Orphan Products Board in March 1982, with membership and functions similar to those in the bill. This bill will enhance the steps we have already taken to encourage the development of orphan drugs and ensure that our ongoing program will be permanent. This legislation exemplifies the proper role of government in helping meet legitimate needs in those cases where the free market alone can't do the job.

Source: Reagan, Ronald. Statement on Signing the Orphan Drug Act, January 4, 1983. *Public Papers of the Presidents: Ronald Reagan, 1983,* Book 2. Washington, DC: Government Printing Office, 1984. www .reagan.utexas.edu/archives/speeches/1983/83jan.htm.

NOTE

1. Julie Rovner, "Orphan Drugs," *Health Care Policy and Politics A to Z,* 3rd ed. (Washington, DC: CQ Press, 2009), 188.

DOCUMENT 8.3

Arrival of the Medicare Prospective Payment System

"Changing Hospital Behavior Is the Purpose of This Initiative"

1983

In the late 1970s and early 1980s Washington, D.C., became increasingly anxious about the solvency of Medicare, which was hemorrhaging prodigious amounts of money to hospitals on an annual basis. The Reagan administration and Republican and Democratic leaders in Congress responded in 1983 by replacing the unsustainable cost-based reimbursement system that had long held sway with a federally administered pricing system for Medicare payments to hospitals. The centerpiece of this prospective payment system (PPS) was an index of 468 diagnosis-related groups (DRGs) of medical conditions requiring hospitalization or treatment. Each DRG was given a set payment value by the federal government (adjusted according to geographic area, whether the hospital had a teaching program, and other considerations).

The seed for the Medicare prospective payment system was planted in the 1982 Tax Equity and Fiscal Responsibility Act (TEFRA). A little-noticed TEFRA provision instructed the Department of Health and Human Services (HHS) to present Congress with a

Medicare PPS plan for hospitals by the end of the year. This undertaking was spearheaded by Allen Dobson, head of the Office of Research and Development in the Health Care Financing Administration (HCFA). "I wrote the first draft in my kitchen," he recalled, "and then my colleagues . . . spent the next three months getting it right with all the details and complexity needed for the final report."[1]

The 1982 HHS Report to Congress: Hospital Prospective Payment for Medicare became the foundation for legislation that was folded into the much larger Social Security Amendments of 1983. The Social Security measure was described by Don Moran, Reagan's associate director for budget and legislation, as "the perfect vehicle for changing Medicare's Part A hospital program to a prospective payment system with DRGs. . . . Ideas like DRGs have an intellectual life of their own . . . but at some point these ideas hit their nexus to the real-world, tactical-political situation and they either do or do not adhere."[2]

Over the ensuing weeks virtually all of Washington's political energy was spent on other facets of the Social Security reform bill. Hospitals complained about the scheme, but otherwise the prospective payment system attracted little attention. As public policy scholar Paul Charles Light observed, Medicare's prospective payment program for hospitals "would have been a difficult fight on its own but [it] had a free ride on the Social Security bill."[3] The bill cleared Congress on March 24, and Reagan signed it into law on April 20. It was in this manner that, in the words of historians Rick Mayes and Robert A. Berenson, "the single biggest change to the American health care system since Medicare and Medicaid's passage in 1965 went largely unnoticed outside of a small group of hospital representatives and health policy leaders."[4]

A little more than a year after the Medicare prospective payment system was signed into law, Dobson delivered an address (excerpted here) in which he explained the problems that led to implementation of PPS, described how PPS worked, and surveyed various challenges to the system looming on the horizon. Since then, Dobson's faith in the system's cost-cutting capabilities has been borne out. It is true that PPS has been faulted for creating financial incentives for hospitals to release Medicare patients too early, but even its harshest critics acknowledge that the system accomplished its main goal—to rein in the alarming rate of growth of Medicare hospital costs.

DEFINING THE PROBLEM

American medicine is in the midst of a revolution—a revolution driven by public reaction to ever increasing expenditure for health care services. While the ultimate implications of the changes now taking place are as yet unclear, the roots of this revolt are more readily traceable. Increases in health care expenditures have been a persistent and growing problem for both the Medicare program and the general public for nearly two decades. In 1980 and 1981 alone, national health expenditures rose 15.8 percent and 15.1 percent, respectively. Not surprisingly, health care expenditures have been rising much more rapidly than has the Gross National Product (GNP). In 1982, for example, health care constituted 10.5 percent of the GNP, up from only 6.0 percent in 1965.

Of particular concern has been the significant impact of *hospital expenditures* on overall health care expenditure trends. During 1982, inflation in the hospital sector increased three times faster than the overall rate of inflation. Medicare expenditures for hospital care have increased 19 percent per year during the last three years. These rapid increases in the cost of hospital care and health care generally have raised serious concerns about the ability of the federal government to continue to meet Medicare beneficiary needs.

Current expenditure trends and the growing proportion of the U.S. population 65 and over have endangered the solvency of the Medicare trust fund. The rapid increases in expenditures have also constrained the ability of the federal government to fund remaining health and other social programs. For example, the annual increase in Medical expenditures is greater than the total budget of the National Institutes of Health. Opportunity costs in other policy areas are apparent as well: dollars invested in health care cannot be used to meet other needs such as more education, better housing, safer highways and bridges, and better energy sources.

At the same time that health care expenditures have become essentially uncontrollable, the political landscape has changed dramatically. On the one hand, it can be argued that there is no "correct" proportion of the GNP that health care resources should constitute, and that health care expenditures, after all, represent someone else's income. Clearly, the growth rates in health care expenditures would be considered a dramatic success story if they were non-health related corporate "sales." The predominance of government involvement in the health care sector, however, has made recent increases in health care expenditures all the more unacceptable. Even though the United States, by international comparison, is undertaxed relative to its overall demand for social goods, the current national mood calls for fewer taxes and less general involvement by government, not increased taxes to pay for health care. This conviction is made more firm by mounting public pressures surrounding budget deficits, concerns about an aging population, and a general erosion of confidence in our political and medical institutions. In summary, this country has rather rapidly moved from an era when health care was a clear right for all citizens to an era where cost considerations dominate considerations of access.

Unfortunately, health care cost containment is not a problem easily solved. It is perhaps a more difficult and complex task than addressing the issues confronting the Social Security program, for instance, because of the number of actors and the kinds of economic and social incentives embedded within the present system. The role of government in subsidizing costs, the inflation-oriented incentives of cost-based retrospective reimbursement, health insurance that insulates the consumer from costs, pressures favoring technology-intensive medicine, and the practice of defensive medicine are among a multitude of developing and interacting factors that have exerted continued upward pressure on health care expenditures.

ASSESSING POLICY ALTERNATIVES

Given the complexities of the health care system, and the emerging national consensus for change, a number of broad policy alternatives to control Medicare costs have been advanced in recent years. These alternatives include:

- increasing taxes
- cutting eligibility and/or benefits
- increasing cost-sharing (co-payments, deductibles, premiums)
- decreasing the quantity and quality of care provided to federal beneficiaries
- increasing regulatory apparatus (PSROs, Certificate-of-Need, etc.)
- altering reimbursement incentives
- increasing market efficiency

Analysis and debate surrounding these policy options have identified the potential political and economic consequences of each. For example, increasing taxes could be inefficient economically in its further diversion of resources to health care, as well as politically unwise. Greater use of market forces (through HMOs, preferred providers, and vouchers) could increase efficiency and moderate costs, but is a more long-range solution. Ten years of research, evaluation, and experimentation have clearly established the utility of prospective payment mechanisms. In 1983, recognizing its potential as a pragmatic yet immediate solution to spiralling [sic] costs, Congress enacted the Prospective Payment System (PPS) for most inpatient hospital services covered by Medicare. The PPS may be viewed as a first step in a series of policy decisions intended to increase market efficiency.

PPS: Objectives and Design Features

The PPS's primary purpose is to moderate the rate of growth of hospital expenditures for Medicare beneficiaries by changing the incentive structure in the health care industry. As stated in the Department of Health and Human Services, December 1982, *Report to Congress,* "When hospitals are paid in a different way, it is reasonable to expect that their behavior will change. Indeed, changing hospital behavior is the purpose of this initiative." Through the implementation of Diagnosis-Related Groups (DRGs), the Medicare program will move from using a retrospective payment system to using a payment-for-product system.

The primary motivating force behind the implementation of PPS is to base Medicare reimbursement upon a set, known price for a given product. Payments have thus been divorced from the inflationary concepts of retrospective cost-based reimbursement. Hospitals are changing their fundamental operating question from, "How much can be provided?" to "What will known hospital revenue support?" From this perspective, previous individual profit centers are now cost centers related to the overall profit center of the individual case. Hospitals are no longer able to do all things for all patients without regard to the constraints of fixed prices for their products.

The PPS went into effect for all hospitals beginning at the start of accounting years on or after October 1, 1983. The main elements of the PPS involve a three year transition into a national set of specific, predetermined prices for hospital care, based on 468 patient care categories (DRGs) that will be adjusted only for the hospital's area wage rate and its urban and rural location. All Medicare discharges are classified into one of the DRGs, and each DRG has a weight that is intended to reflect its relative resource consumption. The actual payment for each discharge is determined by multiplying an area's payment rate (mean) by the appropriate DRG weight.

The pricing system applies to all inpatient admissions except for a small number of cases with unusually long lengths of stay or unusually high costs. Additional payments will also be made for indirect costs of approved graduate medical education programs, and direct educational and capital costs are "passed through." Some hospitals are exempted, at least initially, and all hospitals in States with their own cost control systems are also exempted.

Any reimbursement system offers powerful behavioral incentives to the payer as well as the recipient. Such incentives clearly affected the hospital industry in the past, and will continue to do so in the future. But, the new rules are very different. The PPS legislation represents a revolutionary change in federally financed health care programs, and it can be expected that hospitals will respond to the PPS with both immediate and long-run adjustments. Immediate adjustments to hospital behavior are of six major types: 1) data building activities; 2) administration; 3) organization; 4) hospital-physician relationships;

5) volume; and 6) quality of care. Longer-run adjustments include: 1) setting objectives for long-term behavior; 2) capital investment strategies; 3) technological adjustments; 4) movement toward all-payer systems; 5) supply effects; and 6) ethical and legal issues.

RESPONSES TO PPS INCENTIVES: IMMEDIATE ADJUSTMENTS

Data Building Activities

The PPS is serving as an impetus for developing new data bases that can be used as administrative planning tools for controlling both production costs and quantities being provided. Because the medical record has now become the hospital bill, medical records are being linked to financial data, and medical records staff are being augmented to assure proper coding procedures. Hospital data generating processes will also likely move towards greater automation, with the eventuality of data base creation for tracking both intermediate and final production costs. A byproduct, then, of the PPS is improved data that can be used by both the hospital and others who are interested in hospital behavior.

These types of data building activities may ultimately be able to promote effective management of hospitals by providing more specific and more accurate individual hospital information as well as cross-hospital comparisons. Hospitals will be able to compare regional data on delivery of a product and hospital market share of DRG categories, both of which will contribute to long-term regional/area specialization.

Administration

Given more powerful data and altered incentives, hospital administration will surely change as a result of the PPS. At first, task forces of service departments might be formed for finding ways to reduce departmental costs. The task forces for the first time might integrate the abilities of hospital administrators, physicians, nurses, and medical records staff. Physicians will be encouraged to review standing orders and length of stay. This may involve elimination of automatic/routine tests. Medical educators may begin to emphasize more carefully the relevance of tests, as well as their comprehensiveness.

Administrators may cut back in certain areas as well, by eliminating supplementary services, such as patient education and social services. Engineering studies to determine least cost techniques will likely be conducted, and hospitals will certainly continue the trend toward formation of purchasing groups in attempts to buy in bulk and shop for the lowest prices.

Organization

Organizational changes within hospital corporate structures through horizontal and vertical integration are expected to be among the most immediate adjustments resulting from the PPS incentives. Increased consolidation of hospitals into for-profit chains and other forms of multi-hospital systems will increase service volume and purchasing power and reduce administrative overhead. In addition, hospitals are likely to offset less profitable services through vertical integration with home health agencies, skilled nursing facilities, clinics, etc.

Competition between hospitals will also undoubtedly increase. Shorter lengths of stay will mean that hospitals will have to compete for patients. This type of "defensive competition" will lead to attempts by hospitals to lock patients into their care system through such services as primary care networks, Preferred Provider Organizations (PPOs), and so on. This is a particularly interesting and somewhat ironic result of PPS; namely, that a system of regulations could ultimately foster predominantly competitive results.

Hospital-Physician Relationships

Hospital-physician relationships are changing as a result of PPS incentives, even though the PPS provides no direct incentives for physicians to reduce expenditures. Indeed, there may be a disincentive since reduced length-of-stay implies decreased physician incomes. However, hospital administrators are now using financial incentives as well as pressure on physicians to reduce length of patient stays and use of ancillaries due to the fixed price nature of the PPS.

Physicians are being invited to management committees to conduct expanded peer review, to deal with budgetary constraints, and to apply peer pressure or even sanctions to physicians who are overspending. Hospital administrators are also faced, many for the first time, with a sharply increasing physician supply. The corresponding increase in requests for staff privileges may alter the balance of power in the administrator's favor. The question of "who runs the Nation's hospitals?" is one that may have different answers as PPS incentives begin to take hold. The Health Care Financing Administration (HCFA) is also initiating studies to support eventual legislative proposals, which will bring physicians directly into the prospective payment era.

Volume

The PPS may alter the volume of patients admitted into a hospital. This is generally thought to be a key weakness of the PPS, because cases are the unit of payment. As the number of cases increases, the payment to hospitals increases. To counter the potential for dramatically increasing admissions, overall hospital volume will be monitored by HCFA and its agents, the Professional Review Organizations (PROs).

As PROs come on line, they will focus on volume control. PROs will eventually create admissions profiles by DRG, physician, hospital, and region. The PROs also will review hospital records for determining the necessity of admissions that appear unwarranted or are otherwise suspect. In addition, readmissions and patient transfers will be monitored.

Quality

The fear most frequently discussed about the PPS is that quality may be sacrificed. In fact, the incentives that have worked so well for maintaining quality in the past still remain. Physicians have long had established codes of professional ethics, and both physicians and hospitals will face malpractice suits if quality suffers. PROs will further ensure that medical care is being delivered properly.

The PPS system has been under development since 1970. HCFA demonstrations have indicated that prospective systems do not necessarily reduce quality. What might be reduced as a result of the PPS system is unnecessary care. Quality of care should, in fact, increase for certain highly technical procedures (e.g., open-heart surgery), where PPS-induced specialization will result in such procedures being offered only in facilities which can generate the appropriate volume to maintain efficiency, and the most effective care.

LONGER-RUN ADJUSTMENTS

Setting Objectives for Long-Term Behavior

The PPS provides hospitals with long-run incentives to provide cost-effective services.

This may involve making new long-term commitments to the community, the reevaluation of traditional "product lines," or a possible consolidation of services to ensure future survival. One way to face long-run changes in case-mix will be through staffing and capital investment patterns. To some extent, in the short run, the hospital's physical plant and labor mix controls case-mix, but over a longer time period, changes in staff and equipment mixes will allow for modification of services offered. Hospitals will "not only be doing things differently, but doing different things" under this new system.

Capital Investment Strategies

During the initial years of the PPS, there will be little direct incentive to reduce capital investments. Hospitals will continue to be reimbursed through a "pass-through" provision for legitimate capital costs. At first glance, it may appear that expanding expenditures in "pass-through" categories (especially capital) is typically advantageous to a hospital. However, there are indirect incentives appearing to limit this.

Whatever capital investments are made today will have operating expenses tomorrow. These operating expenses will be confronted with fixed PPS payment levels. Thus, capital expansion to some extent should be self-limiting—increasing operating costs and the uncertainty of future capital markets could very well lead to constrained capital spending in the near future. Congress has directed the Department of Health and Human Services to include capital payments into the PPS. Once accomplished, overall expenditures promise to be more consistent with the objectives of cost constraint.

Technological Adjustments

The PPS provides broad incentives to hospitals for implementing cost-reducing technologies. Those that are cost-increasing, for the most part, will be discouraged. For exceptional cases, such as newer pacemaker models that are more expensive but may improve overall quality of life, there is a forum for technology assessment involving a 15-member independent commission. As treatment improving technology emerges, the commission will review the price of technology and the quality. If the additional cost is seen as warranted, the commission will recommend its cost be incorporated into the DRG rate.

Under PPS, hospitals will likely become more prudent buyers of new technology. This may involve the sharing of expensive technologies between hospitals and result in the reduction of technology costs due to downward pressures of demand. Perhaps under PPS the hospital industry can become more like the computer/electronic industry, where technology both improves products and lowers prices over time.

Movement Towards All-Payer System

Remaining payers may want to adopt DRG reimbursement rates to avoid higher proportions of overall health care costs as a result of future Medicare payment levels. States already having all-payer systems (New York, Maryland, New Jersey, and Massachusetts) will be permitted to continue programs under the PPS, as long as their Medicare expenditures are no higher than they would be under the DRG program. In addition, States desiring to establish an alternative system may do so under the same restriction of maintaining expenditures at an amount equal to, or lower than those expected under the PPS. Pennsylvania and Ohio are among several States in the process of expanding some form of DRG system of payment to their Medicaid programs.

At present, a great amount of uncertainty surrounds States' attitudes toward implementing all-payer systems. States are waiting to see how other payers respond to the PPS implementation. Hopefully, too, individual hospital increases in efficiency will mitigate the need for, or perception of, extensive cost shifting. There also remains a question of who will absorb the cost of uncompensated care. As time passes, the impact of the PPS in these areas will be tested.

Supply Effects

In a broad sense, the cost containment incentive of the PPS is aimed at increasing hospital efficiency. However, there are hospitals that will experience fiscal problems due to PPS. In areas where a community desires the continuation of a service or entire hospital that is losing money, the hospital may have to renegotiate its mission statement and/or financial structure with the community in order to survive.

A three year phase-in of the PPS will provide hospitals with additional time to improve financial management. In the long-run, some adjustments to the PPS may be necessary to ensure survival of teaching hospitals, public hospitals, sole community providers, and others. In addition, there may be a need to provide adjustments for outliers and severity to ensure that hospitals will be able to continue admitting and treating such cases. However, a likely outcome of PPS is to force more care out of the hospital setting, and ultimately reduce the Nation's reliance on the hospital industry.

Ethical and Legal Issues

The PPS intensifies many existing ethical and legal questions and raises new ones. Malpractice suits may take new dimensions as patients attempt to determine who is responsible under the new rules. The PPS could also provide incentives to avoid admitting "unprofitable" patients, such as those with severe cases of an ailment. Will these patients be turned away? If admitted, will they receive less intensive treatment than they would have prior to PPS? And if so, will this be appropriate? Will there be rationing of expensive new technology to Medicare patients? Will the "plug be pulled" at an early stage to conserve resources? These are now and difficult questions to confront, but are ones that must be addressed.

To some extent, severity of illness cannot be completely determined at the time of admission. This, and the fact that higher DRG payments are made for more complex cases, should alleviate some of the problems of patients being turned away. Once admitted, inferior treatment or rationing of technologies will be countered by the spectre of costly malpractice suits against the physician or hospital. Finally, untimely termination of care would have to be ordered by the physician, who continues to have ethical, legal, and financial reasons to maintain high-quality standards of care. . . .

THE CHALLENGE OF PPS

The Medicare program has historically provided leadership for other hospital payment policies. With the new DRG system, the Medicare program promises to be a driving force in the current health care revolution. That's not to say that the PPS is "perfect"—or even permanent. The implementation of a national per-case payment system using DRGs, however, is a bold step toward improving the efficiency of the system.

The health care system in general and the hospital industry in particular have already begun to respond to the incentives created by the PPS. Challenges will continue for hospitals, physicians, and policymakers alike as the PPS evolves and matures. As lengths of stay decrease and occupancy rates fall, hospitals will face tough decisions about access, technologies, staffing and admission policies. Physicians will should greater responsibilities not only in containing costs, but in assuring quality patient care. Policymakers will uneasily attempt to balance fiscal burdens with the preservation of public health.

For better or for worse, the PPS has redirected the goals of the hospital care industry. But much remains to be done. Important refinements in the DRG system itself—such
as a severity adjustment—as well as reforms in other areas, await timely study and deliberation. Continued cost pressures will also demand consideration and development of
long-term strategies, such as capitation. The future, in short, will require both our good
technical expertise and our wise political judgment.

Source: Dobson, Allen. "The Medicare Prospective Payment System: Intent and Future Direction."
Proceedings of the Annual Symposium on Computer Applications in Medical Care, November 7, 1984,
pp. 497–501.

Notes

1. Quoted in Rick Mayes and Robert A. Berenson, *Medicare Prospective Payment and the Shaping of U.S.
   Health Care* (Baltimore: Johns Hopkins University Press, 2002), 42.

2. Quoted in Mayes and Berenson, *Medicare Prospective Payment and the Shaping of U.S. Health Care,*
   42, 43.

3. Paul Charles Light, *Artful Work: The Politics of Social Security Reform* (New York: Random House,
   1985), 189.

4. Mayes and Berenson, *Medicare Prospective Payment and the Shaping of U.S. Health Care,* 45.

DOCUMENT 8.4

Senator Hatch Recalls the Political Battle over the Hatch-Waxman Act

"No Matter How Often They Stormed Out in Anger, They Always Came Back"

1984

*The Drug Price Competition and Patent Term Restoration Act of 1984, also known as the
Hatch-Waxman Act, was the most important federal law governing drug regulation since
the 1962 Kefauver-Harris amendments to the Federal Food, Drug, and Cosmetic Act. The
1962 legislation, which had been created in response to a tragic wave of birth defects from
the drug thalidomide, required that drugs approved by the Food and Drug Administration
(FDA) be proven both safe and effective. By the early 1980s, the FDA's increasingly
cumbersome regulatory approval process was being cited as a culprit in spiraling
prescription drug prices. Drug manufacturers claimed that the lengthy FDA approval
process gave them little time to make a profit on their research investment before the drugs'
patent lives expired. Meanwhile, manufacturers of generic drugs complained that their
ability to provide low-cost alternatives to consumers was being torpedoed by the FDA,
which subjected generic drugs to the same review regimen as the brand-name drugs they
replicated. These complaints from generic drug makers intensified after March 22, 1983,
when the U.S. Supreme Court affirmed in* United States v. Generix Drug Corporation
that generic drugs were new drugs, subject to the full regulatory review process.

This state of affairs sparked a bipartisan response from Sen. Orrin Hatch, a conservative Republican from Utah, and Rep. Henry A. Waxman, a liberal Democratic from California. Working closely with drug industry representatives, Hatch and Waxman put together a bill designed to streamline the FDA regulatory approval process for generic drugs, bolster patent protections for creators of new brand-name (also known as "innovator") drugs, and curb the growth in prescription drug prices. President Reagan signed the bill into law on September 24, 1984.

Since its passage, Hatch-Waxman has been credited with lifting the generic drug industry to new prominence. From 1984 to 2010 low-cost generics soared from 19 percent to more than 70 percent of American prescriptions, in part because Hatch-Waxman greatly reduced the cost of post-patent generic entry into various pharmaceutical market niches. The legislation's impact on the research-based pharmaceutical industry, meanwhile, has been mixed. This industry sector has lost considerable overall market share to generics, but Hatch-Waxman did extend the patent life—and thus the revenue stream—of many commercially valuable innovator drugs.

In the following excerpts from his 2002 autobiography Square Peg: Confessions of a Citizen Senator, *Hatch provides his perspective on how the Hatch-Waxman Act came about. His remarks range from harsh criticism of the FDA's "bureaucratic morass" to a spirited defense of the drug industry's integral role in developing the legislation.*

In the early 1980s, major research companies were increasingly frustrated with spending hundreds of millions of dollars to develop a new product, only to see its patent life undercut by the staggering inefficiency of the Food and Drug Administration (FDA) in approving new drugs for marketing in the United States. Patents on other goods gave manufacturers as much as seventeen years of patent exclusivity.

Pharmaceutical companies, however, were looking at time frames of as little as four or five years, too short a period to recoup the cost of research, which today can run up to almost a billion dollars for a blockbuster drug. To protect against duplication, a drug has to be patented early in its evolution. Consequently, even under the best of circumstances, years of potential patent life are lost while a drug undergoes the years of testing necessary to win FDA approval. In fairness, why should a drug that saves lives have patent protection for only a fraction of the time given to protect a chainsaw or a toy?

The FDA was only compounding the problem. Congress has made the agency responsible for the safety and efficacy of pharmaceuticals, medical devices, food, nutritional supplements and other products consumed or used by Americans every second of every day. Every year, it seems that something new is added to the list. Today, more than 25 percent of all consumer products sold in the United States are either approved or regulated by this one agency.

The agency's mission would be impossible under the best of circumstances. Unfortunately, it has rarely operated under the best of circumstances. In 1984, the FDA was underfunded and understaffed, and dispersed throughout the Washington metropolitan area. It had neither the scientific equipment nor the personnel to keep pace with the rapid technological changes and improvements in the private sector.

It would be hard to conjure a scenario more likely to produce a bureaucratic morass, and the agency certainly did its part. Committee investigations revealed that important drug applications were lost. Others were ignored. One was simply stuck in a reviewer's drawer out of pique. The approval process had become a mess, ripe for abuse and misuse.

Already facing unrealistically limited time to recoup its investment, the pharmaceutical industry did not want competition from an aggressive generic industry, which could market copies of name-brand products once the patents expired. In the early 1980s, the brand pharmaceutical companies had little to worry about. The domestic generic pharmaceutical industry was realizing only a fraction of its potential. The handful of existing companies were struggling because they could not afford to replicate the same expensive and time-consuming safety and efficacy trials undertaken by the pioneer firms, as the FDA required them to do, and still sell the drug at a reduced price.

Important drugs were coming off patent, but generics were not being introduced. Moreover, in the few instances where generics were being developed, it routinely took years before the companies could win FDA approval to market their products.

In sum, the FDA's regulatory system was discouraging brand or innovator companies from investing in new research and development. At the same time, it was blocking the introduction of low-cost generic products. No one was benefiting, not the brand companies, not the generic firms and not consumers.

I had become Chairman of the Senate Labor Committee when the Republicans regained control of the body in 1980. Since the committee had jurisdiction over the FDA and the drug approval process, it would be my responsibility to decide whether this issue should become a priority.

It wasn't a hard decision. . . .

It took the better part of three years, but by the spring of 1984, I had succeeded in convincing both the Congress and the public that something needed to be done. Moreover, my staff and I finally understood the positions of the various interested parties and what they really needed, as opposed to what they demanded in public. The difficulty was finding a solution that would work and that could be supported by all sides. In addition, the end of the session was approaching.

Because 1984 was a presidential election year, the Senate was already beginning to slide into the traditional partisan bickering and posturing that dominates the months leading up to a major election. For legislation to pass, it would have to be seen as a real compromise both inside and outside Congress.

I found a willing ally in Representative Henry Waxman, the liberal Democrat from California and, at the time, the Chairman of the House Health Subcommittee. From the standpoint of political ideology, Henry is exactly what you might expect of a member of Congress whose district covers Hollywood and whose constituents include some of his party's largest contributors. He is an unabashed liberal, a skilled legislator and an effective inside player. Henry is also viewed as one of the most knowledgeable members of Congress on health issues, and he enjoys the confidence of consumer groups and a wide variety of public-interest organizations.

The year before, to the amazement of our respective colleagues, Henry and I had teamed up on the Orphan Drug Act of 1983, a bill that provides a series of economic incentives for companies to develop drugs that treat rare diseases and conditions. The potential patient pool for these drugs was too small for a company to recoup the cost of development. Because of the bill, 228 new drugs had been developed, which in turn have helped more than 11 million people who otherwise would have gone without treatment. We gave various incentives to the industry so that this turnaround could be accomplished.

Henry and I understood that the only way to fashion a compromise was to bring the brand companies and the generics together in an atmosphere that allowed them both to feel they had something to gain if they cooperated and, just as important, something to lose if they didn't. The meetings would have to be small and private, so that ideas could be discussed without fear of retribution or public posturing.

I invited a handful of industry leaders to meet with me personally. The brand companies were led by Joe Williams, the CEO of Warner-Lambert, one of the largest and most successful pharmaceutical companies at the time, and Jack Stafford, the CEO of American Home Products and a tough and shrewd negotiator. . . .

Taking the lead for the generics was Bill Haddad. A short, passionate, rumpled man, Bill looks exactly like the liberal political operative he used to be. . . . What Bill might have lacked in corporate experience he more than made up for with his knowledge of Congress and politics. . . .

We met in my office over several weeks. Not surprisingly, both sides were extremely skeptical of the other's intentions. Each thought the other's position not only illogical but avaricious.

Jack made clear that the brand companies wanted legislation completely restoring every day of patent life lost while their approvals were being processed by the FDA. They needed a greater period of market exclusivity to recover the high cost of their research.

Bill responded that these companies were already more than adequately compensated for their research. A drug company didn't need seventeen years to recoup its investment. A drug's patent life might be shorter than that for other products, but the prices that could be charged were so disproportionate to the cost of production that immense profits could be realized in short periods of time. One only had to look at the strength of pharmaceutical company stocks to understand that these firms were far more profitable.

Bill insisted that the generics needed to be able to bring a generic version of a drug to market immediately upon the expiration of the patent, without having to go through the extremely costly, time-consuming and unnecessarily repetitive exercise of re-proving that the drug was safe. . . .

Jack and Joe were more than skeptical of this assumption. Echoing a long-held conviction of the brand companies, they argued that generic firms were not real pharmaceutical companies. They were just copiers, they said, and not very good ones at that. They didn't have adequate personnel, laboratories or experience. They could not be trusted to make effective products on their own and they posed a real health risk to an unsuspecting public.

I gave them a copy of a draft bill my staff had prepared, and they proceeded to argue about every word, every punctuation mark, every inclusion and every omission. . . .

Jack would claim people would die if a generic drug company had only to prove bio-equivalence and not safety and efficacy. Bill would object, arguing that the issue wasn't safety. It was money. The brand companies simply wanted to protect their "ridiculous" profits. Jack would fire back that the brands created the products and the generics couldn't invent a drug if their lives depended on it. All they could do was leech off the brand's research. Bill would respond that the brands didn't want just a patent life. They wanted a permanent monopoly.

So it went, day after day, accusation and after accusation. . . .

Fortunately, no matter how often they stormed out in anger, they always came back, in part out of respect for my position as committee chairman and in part because both were worried that the legislation might be finalized in their absence. Over time, we narrowed the issues in contention, reaching agreement on a variety of secondary problems. Ultimately, the brand companies decided they had more to gain by passing legislation than by stopping it and agreed in principle to the concept of a rapid generic approval process at FDA. Once that occurred, everything else fell into place, and we quickly reached agreement.

Some might be surprised by the amount of industry involvement with legislation of this kind, but it was critical. Quite simply, only someone experienced with the industry could understand the nuances and consequences of legislative wording. Great care had to be taken because we were changing the rules for a process that was ongoing. While we were negotiating, innovator and generic drugs were working their way through the approval process. Without proper care, it would be easy to unintentionally eliminate an entire product line with language that would appear completely logical and legitimate on its face.

This is true in other areas. It is virtually impossible to draft many different kinds of legislation without the involvement of individuals who are expert in the problem or industry being addressed. Imagine writing a bill concerning nuclear reactors without an understanding of how they work, how they are constructed, what raw materials are needed or what is done with the waste. One of the realities of Congress is that despite the political benefits of bashing lobbyists, they can be invaluable in their role in providing the technical and practical information necessary to write bills that work. The difficulty, of course, is finding lobbyists who actually understand and can explain the interests they represent.

This time, each side had a vested economic interest in highlighting the inaccuracies or distortions made by the other. There was no shortage of criticism, constructive and personal.

When the deal was made public, a majority in Congress recognized the agreement for what it was: a balanced compromise that refocused federal regulatory drug policy on innovation and research while creating for the first time the real possibility of a vibrant generic industry that could save consumers billions of dollars.

Still, some were unhappy. A handful of brand companies objected, convinced they would do better in the next Congress. A few generic companies cried foul, believing they could force a more favorable compromise by holding out. Several public interest groups joined in, claiming that the bill was not sufficiently pro-consumer. Whatever the reason, they all began to lobby individual members in an attempt to amend or kill the legislation. . . .

Despite the initial concerns, the Drug Price Competition and Patent Term Restoration Act of 1984 is now considered to be one of the greatest pro-consumer bills of all time. It has been credited with revitalizing research and innovation in the pharmaceutical industry, enabling these businesses to become one of the most successful sectors in our economy. Generics benefited as well. Today, the generic industry provides the medicine that fills approximately 47 percent of all prescriptions issued in the United States, even though it accounts for less than 10 percent of the money spent annually on drugs.

The real beneficiaries, however, have been consumers and, since many drugs are purchased by federal and state health programs, taxpayers. Despite the dire predictions of Ralph Nader and others, according to the Congressional Budget Office, the legislation has saved Americans an average of more than $8 to $10 billion in pharmaceutical costs every year since its passage, a total in excess of more than $150 billion. It is true that after twenty years, creative lawyers have been able to take advantage of a few portions of the legislation, a problem that must be addressed. Nonetheless, more drugs are available today at far more reasonable prices than at any time in the history of our nation, and the predicted savings for the next ten years are even greater than the savings already seen.

DOCUMENT
8.5

Congress Passes the National Organ Transplant Act

"For the Establishment of an Organ Procurement and Transplantation Network"

1984

The National Organ Transplant Act was passed by Congress and signed by President Ronald Reagan in October 1984. Crafted in response to medical advances that had moved organ transplantation from the realm of science fiction into everyday reality, the act was the first major federal legislation regulating the practice of organ donation and transplantation in the United States.

Key elements of the act (excerpted here) included provisions that established a task force on organ donation and transplantation, set operational guidelines for organ procurement organizations, established a nonprofit Organ Procurement and Transplantation Network to oversee organ transplant activity, and made buying, selling, or trading organs for any form of compensation a criminal offense.

An Act to provide for the establishment of the Task Force on Organ Transplantation and the Organ Procurement and Transplantation Network, to authorize financial assistance for organ procurement organizations, and for other purposes.

Be it enacted by the Senate and House of Representatives of the United States of America in Congress assembled, That this Act may be cited as the "National Organ Transplant Act."

TITLE I—TASK FORCE ON ORGAN PROCUREMENT AND TRANSPLANTATION
Establishment and Duties of Task Force

Sec. 101. (a) Not later than ninety days after the date of the enactment of this Act, the Secretary of Health and Human Services (hereinafter in this title referred to as the "Secretary") shall establish a Task Force on Organ Transplantation (hereinafter in this title referred to as the "Task Force").

(b)(1) The Task Force shall—

    (A) conduct comprehensive examinations of the medical, legal, ethical, economic, and social issues presented by human organ procurement and transplantation,

    (B) prepare the assessment described in paragraph (2) and the report described in paragraph (3), and

    (C) advise the Secretary with respect to the development of regulations for grants under section 371 of the Public Health Service Act.

  (2) The Task Force shall make an assessment of immunosuppressive medications used to prevent organ rejection in transplant patients, including—

    (A) an analysis of the safety, effectiveness, and costs (including cost-savings from improved success rates of transplantation) of different modalities of treatment;

(B) an analysis of the extent of insurance reimbursement for long-term immu-nosuppressive drug therapy for organ transplant patients by private insur-ers and the public sector;

(C) an identification of problems that patients encounter in obtaining immu-nosuppressive medications; and

(D) an analysis of the comparative advantages of grants, coverage under exist-ing Federal programs, or other means to assure that individuals who need such medications can obtain them.

(3) The Task Force shall prepare a report which shall include—

(A) an assessment of public and private efforts to procure human organs for transplantation and an identification of factors that diminish the number of organs available for transplantation;

(B) an assessment of problems in coordinating the procurement of viable human organs including skin and bone;

(C) recommendations for the education and training of health professionals, including physicians, nurses, and hospital and emergency care personnel, with respect to organ procurement;

(D) recommendations for the education of the general public, the clergy, law enforcement officers, members of local fire departments, and other agencies and individuals that may be instrumental in effecting organ procurement;

(E) recommendations for assuring equitable access by patients to organ trans-plantation and for assuring the equitable allocation of donated organs among transplant centers and among patients medically qualified for an organ transplant;

(F) an identification of barriers to the donation of organs to patients (with special emphasis upon pediatric patients), including an assessment of—

(i) barriers to the improved identification of organ donors and their families and organ recipients;

(ii) the number of potential organ donors and their geographical distribution;

(iii) current health care services provided for patients who need organ transplantation and organ procurement procedures, systems, and programs which affect such patients;

(iv) cultural factors affecting the family with respect to the donation of the organs; and

(v) ethical and economic issues relating to organ transplantation needed by chronically ill patients.

(G) recommendations for the conduct and coordination of continuing research concerning all aspects of the transplantation of organs;

(H) an analysis of the factors involved in insurance reimbursement for trans-plant procedures by private insurers and the public sector;

(I) an analysis of the manner in which organ transplantation technology is dif-fused among and adopted by qualified medical centers, including a specifica-tion of the number and geographical distribution of qualified medical centers using such technology and an assessment of whether the number of centers using such technology is sufficient or excessive and of whether the public has sufficient access to medical procedures using such technology; and

(J) an assessment of the feasibility of establishing, and of the likely effectiveness of, a national registry of human organ donors. . . .

TITLE II—ORGAN PROCUREMENT ACTIVITIES

Sec. 201. Part H of title III of the Public Health Service Act is amended to read as follows:

Part H—Organ Transplants

Assistance for Organ Procurement Organizations

Sec. 371. (a)(1) The Secretary may make grants for the planning of qualified organ procurement organizations described in subsection (b).

(2) The Secretary may make grants for the establishment, initial operation, and expansion of qualified organ procurement organizations described in subsection (b). . . .

(b)(1) A qualified organ procurement organization for which grants may be made under subsection (a) is an organization which, as determined by the Secretary, will carry out the functions described in paragraph (2) and—

(A) is a nonprofit entity,

(B) has accounting and other fiscal procedures (as specified by the Secretary) necessary to assure the fiscal stability of the organization, . . .

(2) An organ procurement organization shall—

(A) have effective agreements, to identify potential organ donors, with a substantial majority of the hospitals and other health care entities in its service area which have facilities for organ donations,

(B) conduct and participate in systematic efforts, including professional education, to acquire all useable organs from potential donors,

(C) arrange for the acquisition and preservation of donated organs and provide quality standards for the acquisition of organs which are consistent with the standards adopted by the Organ Procurement and Transplantation Network . . . ,

(D) arrange for the appropriate tissue typing of donated organs,

(E) have a system to allocate donated organs among transplant centers and patients according to established medical criteria, . . .

ORGAN PROCUREMENT AND TRANSPLANTATION NETWORK

Sec. 372.(a) The Secretary shall by contract provide for the establishment and operation of an Organ Procurement and Transplantation Network which meets the requirements of subsection (b). The amount provided under such contract in any fiscal year may not exceed $2,000,000. Funds for such contracts shall be made available from funds available to the Public Health Service from appropriations for fiscal years beginning after fiscal year 1984. . . .

(b)(1) The Organ Procurement and Transplantation Network shall carry out the functions described in paragraph (2) and shall—

(A) be a private nonprofit entity which is not engaged in any activity unrelated to organ procurement, and

(B) have a board of directors which includes representatives of organ procurement organizations . . . transplant centers, voluntary health associations, and the general public.

(2)   The Organ Procurement and Transplantation Network shall—

    (A)   establish in one location or through regional centers—

        (i)   a national list of individuals who need organs, and

        (ii) a national system, through the use of computers and in accordance with established medical criteria, to match organs and individuals included in the list, especially individuals whose immune system makes it difficult for them to receive organs,

    (B)   maintain a twenty-four-hour telephone service to facilitate matching organs with individuals included in the list,

    (C)   assist organ procurement organizations in the distribution of organs which cannot be placed within the service areas of the organizations,

    (D)   adopt and use standards of quality for the acquisition and transportation of donated organs,

    (E)   prepare and distribute, on a regionalized basis, samples of blood sera from individuals who are included on the list and whose immune system makes it difficult for them to receive organs, in order to facilitate matching the compatibility of such individuals with organ donors,

    (F)   coordinate, as appropriate, the transportation of organs from organ procurement organizations to transplant centers,

    (G)   provide information to physicians and other health professionals regarding organ donation, and

    (H)   collect, analyze, and publish data concerning organ donation and transplants. . . .

TITLE III—PROHIBITION OF ORGAN PURCHASES

Sec. 301. (a) It shall be unlawful for any person to knowingly acquire, receive, or otherwise transfer any human organ for valuable consideration for use in human transplantation if the transfer affects interstate commerce.

(b) Any person who violates subsection (a) shall be fined not more than $50,000 or imprisoned not more than five years, or both. . . .

Source: National Organ Transplant Act. Public Law 98–507, October 19, 1984.

DOCUMENT
8.6

Women's Health Emerges as a Political Issue

"Economically Disadvantaged Women Are Medically Underserved"

1985

As women's health issues assumed new prominence in American society and politics, many federal agencies involved in health care responded with new studies, internal performance reviews, and other measures designed to get them up to speed on the evolving policy landscape. The first such effort of any consequence was undertaken in 1983 by the U.S. Public Health Service (PHS). The PHS commissioned a Task Force on Women's Health Issues to examine governmental and private sector policies and attitudes toward reproductive and other health issues of special import to women. Two years later, the task force returned with a report that took federal agencies, physicians, and health care institutions to task for their inattention to important women's health issues. This report, excerpted here, contributed greatly to the successful drive for reforms in women's health care practices and policies in the late 1980s and early 1990s.

The discussions at the regional sessions contributed insightful and often unique information about the many issues that directly or indirectly affect women's health.

The theme that seemed to dominate all of the sessions was that women's health is directly related to their access to sound information and quality medical care.

The participants agreed that, although there is a trend toward greater equity in the distribution of medical care in the United States, economically disadvantaged women are medically underserved. The participants identified specific populations of poor women who do not receive attention in the medical care system. These include minorities, the handicapped, the marginally poor, the elderly poor, migrants, female heads of households, rural women, homosexual women, the homeless, and the incarcerated.

Lack of health insurance and inability to qualify for Medicare, Medicaid, or Aid to Families with Dependent Children prevent many of these women from receiving medical care. Even among those who qualify for assistance under government programs, the attitudes and insensitivity of health care providers often discourage the needy from taking advantage of available help. Insensitivity of and stereotyping by physicians were seen as problems for women of all economic groups, not just the poor.

With regard to research, participants expressed interest in the initiation of studies that include women as well as men and asked that increased attention be focused on issues that relate specifically to women's health.

A number of significant issues were addressed at almost all the regional sessions. These included:

- the impact of social conditions on women's mental and physical health.
- the role of nutrition in women's health.
- female-intensive diseases, especially osteoporosis.
- stress, alcoholism, substance abuse, and suicide as growing problems, especially among younger women. (The mental health consequences of physical disease are often overlooked by physicians.)
- creative approaches to health care, particularly long-term care.
- the need of nurses, nurse practitioners, and midwives for sound information on specific diseases and health problems, so that they can serve as well-informed educators for their patients.
- the fragmentation of government efforts, despite an interest in women's health.

Participants made a number of recommendations for women themselves to implement. For example, several presenters suggested that women should intensify their networking and support group activities to foster self-awareness and encourage healthier female role modeling. Without these activities, participants pointed out, women will choose to continue their lifelong, traditional role of nurturing others while neglecting to obtain help for themselves.

Women were encouraged to participate fully in the sex education of their children, rather than leave this training entirely to the schools. They were also urged to educate themselves about the problems of physical abuse, incest, and sexual abuse and to seek professional help should they see these practices occurring in their homes.

A number of recommendations were also made pertaining to the need for expanding existing data and surveillance systems and information and educational programs.

Review of Reports and Recommendations

The full reports and the hundreds of recommendations that resulted from the regional sessions were discussed and reviewed at length both by this subcommittee and by the full Task Force. In its final assessment, the subcommittee singled out for presentation to the Task Force seven topical areas that seemed to encompass the most important concerns of participants in the regional sessions and formulated recommendations to address these concerns.

Health problems and issues of adolescent females. In reviewing the advances that have led to improvement in health care for women, participants in the regional sessions singled out adolescent females as a group that is frequently overlooked when medical needs are being assessed. They identified a number of general health problems, as well as issues specifically concerning reproduction, as meriting special consideration.

Though barely acknowledged as problems by some care givers, acne, excess weight or obesity, menstrual cramps, and mood swings confound the female teenager, lower her self-esteem, and interfere with her emotional and physical growth and maturation. These conditions can result from complex factors that are both physiological and psychological.

Another range of issues involves fostering early development by adolescents of habits conducive to health, including preventive dental care and good nutrition practices.

The emotional health of the female adolescent is important as well. Unfortunately, statistics indicate an increase in depression, suicide, and certain other mental or emotional illnesses among adolescent females. Eating disorders, such as anorexia nervosa and bulimia, are common in this group. Some forms of substance abuse by adolescents can also be categorized as symptomatic of emotional illness or distress.

In the past decade, an increasing number of teenagers have become sexually active, at an earlier age, with sometimes tragic consequences. Teenagers under 16 years have a higher incidence of pregnancy-induced hypertension and premature births. Many teenage mothers never finish school and are unable to find jobs. If they marry, all too often the marriages end in divorce. The infants born to these young women are at increased risk of adverse neonatal outcome, largely as a reflection of low birth weight, and the babies continue to be at increased risk of death or morbidity in the postneonatal period. The children who survive often become victims of abuse and neglect as a result of maternal inexperience and the socioeconomic disadvantages characteristic of many of these young mothers. Problems are most acute among economically disadvantaged groups whose access to prenatal care is limited or nonexistent until the time of delivery.

Research issues affecting women's health. Participants in the regional sessions identified gender bias in research as a detriment to obtaining accurate data on women's health, noting that data collected in studies that use only male subjects are often invalid for the female population. They urged that data both on gender and on women's changing role in society be collected and that these data be considered when health programs are developed and assessed.

Societal determinants of women's health. Participants in the regional sessions agreed that women's health is more than a medical issue. Cultural, social, and economic factors determine to a great extent the ease with which women can enter the health care system and receive proper treatment. Some of the factors influencing women's access to, and participation in, the health care system have been experienced by grandmother, mother, and daughter within a single family. Where women live and the attitudes of care givers also influence the accessibility and quality of the services and treatment women receive.

Access to health care and services was identified as being particularly limited for poor or marginally poor, elderly, and unemployed women. These groups include members of ethnic minorities, women who are geographically isolated, homosexual women, and incarcerated women, all of whom require special sensitivity of care as well as improved access to it. The participants noted that even when medical services are available, cultural and language differences often discourage women from using these services.

Training-sensitivity-care options. Participants in the regional sessions addressed the increased need for health services, the rising cost of institutional care, and the disproportionate impact these factors have on poor women, especially in the elderly and minority populations. Possible solutions offered to alleviate these problems emphasized (a) the need to train health care givers to educate women about how to stay well and (b) the responsibility of the health care establishment to eliminate conditions and attitudes that block women's access—at all stages of their lives—to adequate medical care and services.

Participants agreed that, as important as it is for women to stop smoking, drink only in moderation, eat well-balanced diets, exercise regularly, and get adequate rest, there are many times when the success of these [m]easures depends on help and encouragement from sensitive health care workers.

Women's responsibility for their own health. The need for women to become more deeply involved in their own health care and that of their families, especially in the area of prevention, was emphasized at the regional sessions. Participants identified a variety of preventive measures that women might adopt to safeguard their health. Participants recommended that women, in assuming greater responsibility for their own health, make full use of available information and support networks and become advocates for improvements in the health care system.

Women's role in the health care system. The consensus of participants in the 11 regional sessions was that if women played a greater role in making decisions related to health policy, they would be better able to address constructively the issues that were raised at the sessions. Concern was expressed that the recommendations resulting from the sessions would remain unimplemented until women like those present exerted more influence in the political, economic, informational, societal, and clinical decision arenas pertaining to women's health.

Specific health problems of women. The participants in the sessions reviewed a wide range of health problems that are prevalent among women and a number of issues that adversely affect women's mental and physical health. Osteoporosis, alcohol and drug abuse, stress, sexually transmitted diseases, genetic disorders, and family violence and sexual abuse were singled out for special attention.

Summary

As indicated by the enthusiastic response of invited participants to the regional meetings and the vehemence of the opinions expressed by the participants, there is little doubt that issues related to women's health are of special concern to American health care consumers and health care providers.

Although participants at a number of the regional meetings cited problems unique to particular areas (for instance, the problems of Appalachian women who feel geographically isolated from the mainstream of the American health care system; of poor black women in Mississippi who feel that childbirth is a time of special risk because of their lack of access to prenatal care; of homosexual women in New York City who feel insensitivity on the part of health care providers; and of American Indian women who feel that alcoholism is a special risk for them), the regional meetings were more similar than dissimilar. Common concerns were repeated at each meeting—concerns related to access to care, contraception for teenage girls, health problems of aging women, health problems of the reproductive system, cancer, family violence, and incest. In most cases, the concerns expressed seemed to indicate that American medical care is excellent, but that access to that care, sensitivity during its provision, and health information and education are overwhelming needs for American women.

The continuing need for biomedical research in certain areas of interest and concern American to women was stressed by many of the participants. However, the threads common to all the regional meetings seemed to be the more diffuse issues of access, sensitivity, information, and education.

Source: "Assessment of Women's Health Issues as Presented at Regional Meetings: Executive Summary." Report of the Public Health Service Task Force on Women's Health Issues. *Public Health Reports,* January–February 1985, vol. 100, no. 1, pp. 98–101. Copyright © 1985 Association of Schools of Public Health. Used with permission.

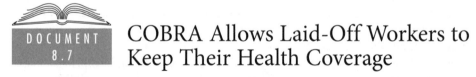

DOCUMENT
8.7

COBRA Allows Laid-Off Workers to Keep Their Health Coverage

"Each Qualified Beneficiary Is Entitled to Continuation Coverage"

1985

Recessionary conditions in the early 1980s exacerbated public concerns about a growing phenomenon: the loss of health insurance coverage as a result of layoff, divorce, or the retirement or death of a family policyholder. Congress responded with a piece of legislation that guaranteed employees and their dependents the opportunity to temporarily (up to thirty-six months) continue medical, dental, and life insurance coverage from employers even after layoffs, divorces, legal separations, and other "qualifying events," provided they paid the premiums themselves. This mandate to extend health coverage applied only to employers with twenty or more employees, but it did partially fill a significant gap in America's health care insurance system.

These continuation benefits quickly came to be known as COBRA because the provisions creating them (excerpted here) were contained within the much larger Consolidated Omnibus Budget Reconciliation Act of 1985. Since their formal introduction in 1986, COBRA provisions have been regularly tweaked and expanded by Congress. These changes have ranged from 1988 alterations to the penalties imposed on employers for COBRA noncompliance to 1989 legislation that expanded the eligibility period for disabled workers, enabling them to keep their COBRA coverage until they became protected by Social Security Disability Insurance.

Purpose

Sec. 601 [Sec. 1161]. (a) In general. The plan sponsor of each group health plan shall provide, in accordance with this part, that each qualified beneficiary who would lose coverage under the plan as a result of a qualifying event is entitled, under the plan, to elect, within the election period, continuation coverage under the plan.

(b) Exception for certain plans. Subsection (a) shall not apply to any group health plan for any calendar year if all employers maintaining such plan normally employed fewer than 20 employees on a typical business day during the preceding calendar year.

Continuation coverage

Sec. 602 [Sec. 1162]. For purposes of section 601, the term "continuation coverage" means coverage under the plan which meets the following requirements:

(1) Type of benefit coverage. The coverage must consist of coverage which, as of the time the coverage is being provided, is identical to the coverage provided under the plan to similarly situated beneficiaries under the plan with respect to whom a qualifying event has not occurred. If coverage is modified under the plan for any group of similarly situated beneficiaries, such coverage shall also be modified in the same manner for all individuals who are qualified beneficiaries under the plan pursuant to this part in connection with such group.

(2) Period of coverage. The coverage must extend for at least the period beginning on the date of the qualifying event and ending not earlier than the earliest of the following:

    (A) Maximum required period.

        (i) General rule for terminations and reduced hours. In the case of a qualifying event described in section 603(2), except as provided in clause (ii), the date which is 18 months after the date of the qualifying event.

        (ii) Special rule for multiple qualifying events. If a qualifying event (other than a qualifying event described in section 603(6)) occurs during the 18 months after the date of a qualifying event described in section 603(2), the date which is 36 months after the date of the qualifying event described in section 603(2).

       (iii) Special rule for certain bankruptcy proceedings. In the case of a qualifying event described in section 603(6) (relating to bankruptcy proceedings), the date of the death of the covered employee or qualified beneficiary (described in section 607(3)(C)(iii), or in the case of the surviving spouse or dependent children of the covered employee, 36 months after the date of the death of the covered employee.

(iv) General rule for other qualifying events. In the case of a qualifying event not described in section 603(2) or 603(6), the date which is 36 months after the date of the qualifying event. . . .

(B) End of plan. The date on which the employer ceases to provide any group health plan to any employee.

(C) Failure to pay premium. The date on which coverage ceases under the plan by reason of a failure to make timely payment of any premium required under the plan with respect to the qualified beneficiary. The payment of any premium . . . shall be considered to be timely if made within 30 days after the date due or within such longer period as applies to or under the plan.

(D) Group health plan coverage or medicare entitlement. The date on which the qualified beneficiary first becomes, after the date of the election—

(i) covered under any other group health plan (as an employee or otherwise) "which does not contain any exclusion or limitation with respect to any preexisting condition of such beneficiary" (other than such an exclusion or limitation which does not apply to (or is satisfied by) such beneficiary by reason of chapter 100 of Title 26, part 7 of this subtitle, or title XXVII of the Public Health Service Act . . . or

(ii) in the case of a qualified beneficiary other than a qualified beneficiary described in section 607(3)(C), entitled to benefits under title XVIII of the Social Security Act.

(3) Premium requirements. The plan may require payment of a premium for any period of continuation coverage, except that such premium—

(A) shall not exceed 102 percent of the applicable premium for such period, and

(B) may, at the election of the payor, be made in monthly installments.

In no event may the plan require the payment of any premium before the day which is 45 days after the day on which the qualified beneficiary made the initial election for continuation coverage. . . .

(4) No requirement of insurability. The coverage may not be conditioned upon, or discriminate on the basis of lack of, evidence of insurability.

(5) Conversion option. In the case of a qualified beneficiary whose period of continuation coverage expires under paragraph (2)(A), the plan must, during the 180-day period ending on such expiration date, provide to the qualified beneficiary the option of enrollment under a conversion health plan otherwise generally available under the plan.

Qualifying event

Sec. 603 [Sec. 1163]. For purposes of this part, the term "qualifying event" means, with respect to any covered employee, any of the following events which, but for the continuation coverage required under this part, would result in the loss of coverage of a qualified beneficiary:

(1) The death of the covered employee.

(2) The termination (other than by reason of such employee's gross misconduct), or reduction of hours, of the covered employee's employment.

(3) The divorce or legal separation of the covered employee from the employee's spouse.

(4) The covered employee becoming entitled to benefits under title XVIII of the Social Security Act.

(5) A dependent child ceasing to be a dependent child under the generally applicable requirements of the plan.

(6) A proceeding in a case under Title 11, United States Code, commencing on or after July 1, 1986, with respect to the employer from whose employment the covered employee retired at any time.

In the case of an event described in paragraph (6), a loss of coverage includes a substantial elimination of coverage with respect to a qualified beneficiary described in section 607(3)(C) within one year before or after the date of commencement of the proceeding. . . .

Definitions and special rules

Sec. 607 [Sec. 1167]. For purposes of this part—

(1) Group health plan. The term "group health plan" means an employee welfare benefit plan providing medical care (as defined in section 213(d) of the Internal Revenue Code of 1986) to participants or beneficiaries directly or through insurance, reimbursement, or otherwise.

(2) Covered employee. The term "covered employee" means an individual who is (or was) provided coverage under a group health plan by virtue of the performance of services by the individual for 1 or more persons maintaining the plan (including as an employee defined in section 401(c)(1) of the Internal Revenue Code of 1986).

(3) Qualified beneficiary.

    (A) In general. The term "qualified beneficiary" means, with respect to a covered employee under a group health plan, any other individual who, on the day before the qualifying event for that employee, is a beneficiary under the plan—

        (i) as the spouse of the covered employee, or

        (ii) as the dependent child of the employee

    (B) Special rule for terminations and reduced employment. In the case of a qualifying event described in section 603(2), the term "qualified beneficiary" includes the covered employee.

    (C) Special rule for retirees and widows. In the case of a qualifying event described in section 603(6), the term "qualified beneficiary" includes a covered employee who had retired on or before the date of substantial elimination of coverage and any other individual who, on the day before such qualifying event, is a beneficiary under the plan—

        (i)   as the spouse of the covered employee,

        (ii) as the dependent child of the employee, or

        (iii) as the surviving spouse of the covered employee . . . .

Source: Title X. Consolidated Omnibus Budget Reconciliation Act of 1985: Approved April 7, 1986. *U.S. Public Law 99–272 with Official Legislative History, Tables, and Index.* Eagan, MN: West, 1986.

AMA Calls for Relief from Medical Malpractice Lawsuits

DOCUMENT
8.8

"[America's Tort System] Has Become . . . Erratic, Expensive, and Unfair"

1986

During the 1970s and 1980s the U.S. health care system was roiled by a surge in medical malpractice lawsuits and claims. This wave of litigation prompted insurance companies to issue big hikes in medical malpractice premiums and, in some cases, to withdraw from that sector of the insurance business entirely. A number of states reported that the evolving crisis was making it impossible for physicians, midwives, and specialists such as neurosurgeons and obstetricians to practice medicine altogether, because licenses to practice were predicated on having malpractice insurance.

The rise in litigation was cited as a significant factor in the continuing upward spiral of health care costs in the United States. Critics inside and out of the health care community charged that physicians and other health care providers had no choice but to pass on at least some of their tort-related costs to consumers. They further asserted that the "broken" tort system was resulting in excessive reliance on so-called defensive medicine, that is, overprescription of diagnostic and treatment procedures to reduce caregiver vulnerability to malpractice lawsuits.

By the mid-1980s a number of congressional committees and subcommittees with jurisdiction over health care and legal issues were holding hearings to weigh the merits of these complaints and propose solutions. Representatives of the American Medical Association (AMA) often testified at these events, and they consistently urged Congress to pass legislation that would curb medical malpractice lawsuits. On March 18, 1986, for example, AMA senior deputy executive vice president James S. Todd testified on Capitol Hill about the need for tort reform. In his official statement, excerpted here, Todd recites a litany of alarming statistics about medical malpractice trends. He also calls on committee members to support the Federal Incentives for State Health Care Professional Liability Reform Act, a tort reform bill supported by the AMA. (The bill never came to a vote, but elements of it were later incorporated into the National Professional Liability Reform Act of 1987.)

. . . Although our testimony today will focus on the crisis facing the medical profession, we are acutely aware that medical professional liability represents only one part of an overall liability problem in this country. Our situation is unique, however, in that this is not the first time that medicine has had a professional liability crisis. Moreover, we have been experiencing an increasingly negative litigation climate for over a decade.

The problem, ironically in a sense, stems from our desire to care for injured persons and to see justice done. Those of us the profession of medicine, with its tradition of compassionate care for others, can readily identify with these motivations. The fundamental generosity and compassion of the American people have been reflected in recent years in a broadening of traditional negligence theory in an effort to compensate those injured even in cases where application of traditional negligence principles may not have resulted in damages.

Physicians are in favor of proper compensation and justice for those who are injured *due to the negligent or wrongful conduct of another.* This nation's civil tort system has been the channel through which justice and compensation have been obtained. We believe that the basic framework of our tort liability system has in the past worked reasonably well, it is *not* working well today. It has become an erratic, expensive, and unfair system.

The tort system has historically had its limits. It is not designed to compensate all maloccurrences. It requires that some named individual or entity be found responsible for the injury in order to justify compensation. "Acts of God" or injuries that are entirely the fault of the plaintiff are not intended to be compensable through the civil tort process. The system, clearly, is not intended to provide compensation for all injuries or maloccurrences.

In addition to the general expansion of negligence and other theories to provide greater degrees of injury compensation, the field of medicine has the added burden of meeting increasingly high expectations from patients and their families. No one can deny the astonishing progress we have made in this country in medical diagnosis and treatment with the concomitant decreases in infant mortality, increases in life expectancy and improvement in the quality of life of many through appropriate medical intervention. By every measure, the quality of medicine in this country has never been greater. However, an unfortunate side effect of these enormously beneficial developments is an increased level of unrealistic expectations by patients. Medicine is not an exact science and a desired outcome cannot always be obtained—even when everything is done appropriately. . . .

Physicians are on the cutting edge of the liability problem facing the nation. . . .

I would like to present this subcommittee with certain facts illustrating the gravity of the current medical professional liability crisis:

- The number of malpractice claims brought against physicians in 1983 is roughly double the number of claims brought in the mid-1970s.
- The size of the average award against physicians has increased dramatically resulting in an average verdict of $338,463 in 1984. The number of million dollar judgments per year has more than tripled since 1980.
- Premiums for physicians' professional liability insurance continue to rise dramatically. A few weeks ago in Massachusetts, physicians experienced an average 62% hike in their malpractice insurance rates. In Maryland, obstetricians saw their malpractice insurance rates increase by 130% last summer. For all physicians, premiums have increased by 44.8% in the last two years alone and by 236% in the last decade. Average premiums for New York physicians have risen by 312% since 1975. Neurosurgeons in New York face premiums of over $100,000 a year.
- Injured patients on average receive less than 30 cents of every premium dollar paid by physicians for professional liability insurance.
- Because of the increasing numbers of claims and higher premiums, physicians are reacting by:

  retiring early;
  discontinuing medical practice;
  restricting their practice to low-risk procedures;
  choosing lower risk specialties for practice;
  avoiding practice in localities where large numbers of medical professional liability suits are filed.

- A recent survey by the American College of Obstetricians and Gynecologists found that the economic pressures of malpractice suits have forced 12.3 percent of those surveyed to drop obstetrics practice. Those surveyed reported an *average* annual premium of more than $20,000. In Florida, obstetricians and gynecologists pay as much as $92,500 per year in malpractice premiums.
- The Florida Medical Association has estimated that from 25% to one-third of that state's approximately 850 obstetricians have stopped delivering babies because of the risk of lawsuits and the high cost of liability insurance. In Maryland, an estimated 12% of obstetricians have stopped delivering babies after the 130% hike in malpractice rates last summer.
- A 1984 American College of Surgeons survey found that concerns over potential medical professional liability suits have influenced 38% of responding surgeons (50% of orthopedic surgeons) to refer more cases or to refuse to accept cases.
- Physicians are also reacting to the professional liability crisis by practicing "defensive medicine," a practice which includes ordering additional tests and procedures primarily in anticipation of a possible lawsuit. Studies indicate that 70% of physicians surveyed practice some form of defensive medicine. While some "defensive medicine" is good, much of it is not, and it is expensive.
- In 1983, about half (45%) of persons 65 and over lived in seven states. California and New York had over two million each, and Florida, Illinois, Ohio, Pennsylvania and Texas each had over one million. The professional liability problems in these states have been well publicized in recent years. Hence, a large proportion of Medicare beneficiaries may already be feeling the impact of professional liability in terms of higher health care costs.

Costs of Professional Liability

The professional liability crisis not only is having a detrimental impact on physician practices and patient access to quality medical care, it also represents a significant and growing segment of the nation's health care bill. The costs of medical professional liability totaled an estimated *$11 to 13 billion in 1984*. These estimates suggest that costs generated by the current liability system were responsible for between 14.5% and 17.5% of the $75.4 billion spent on physicians' services in the United States in 1984.

It has been estimated that if the reforms advocated by the AMA were adopted, the potential annual savings would be $800 million to $1 billion in *premium costs alone*. Huge *additional* savings would be achieved through the reduction of the practice of defensive medicine. The federal government, which pays for nearly 30% of the nation's total health care bill, would realize major savings.

Federal Incentives for State Health Care Professional Liability Reform

An AMA Special Task Force on Professional Liability and Insurance last year gathered data about the professional liability crisis and met with medical, legal and insurance experts. The Task Force's report constituted an action plan containing a series of recommendations in the educational, medical, legal, and legislative fields. With regard to legislation, the Task Force recommended federal incentive legislation to encourage the states to adopt substantive reforms to the tort system in order to alleviate the professional liability pressures while at the same time encouraging greater physician responsibility. This approach is intended to allow states, within general directions provided at the federal level, to develop tort reform proposals designed to meet each state's unique characteristics and needs. Out of these recommendations, an AMA draft bill was developed which formed the basis for H.R. 3865, a bill sponsored by Congressman Lent and a number of other Representatives. A companion bill, S. 1804, is pending in the Senate.

H.R. 3865—The Federal Incentives for State Health Care Professional Liability Reform Act.

H.R. 3865 would provide federal incentives for states to adopt professional liability reforms. A state would be eligible to receive federal grants if the following tort reforms are adopted by the state and made applicable to cases involving health care malpractice:

1. Mandatory periodic payments for awards of future damages exceeding $100,000.
2. Reductions in awards for compensation received from other sources (eliminating collateral source rule).
3. Limiting awards for non-economic damages to $250,000.
4. Limiting attorneys' fees to 40% of first $50,000 of any award, 33.33% of next $50,000, 25% of next $100,000, and 10% of any further amounts in excess of $200,000.

These reforms are designed to attack the problem of windfalls and would leave the fault concepts and deterrence factors in the system.

In addition, to qualify for grants a state would have to adopt the following reforms:

1. Licensing fees from health care professionals would be allocated exclusively to the state agency responsible for disciplinary actions.
2. Hospitals would be required to have risk management systems.
3. Insurance companies would be required to make data concerning malpractice awards available to state disciplinary agencies.
4. State law would have to provide for expanded and protected peer review activities by state health professional societies in conjunction with their respective disciplinary boards.

Experience in states which have enacted reforms in their tort systems has shown that reforms such as those called for in H.R. 3865 can reduce unnecessary expenditures related to professional liability claims while providing more rapid compensation for individuals. . . .

Let us briefly examine each of the [tort] reforms.

Periodic Payments for Future Damages. Structured settlements with periodic payments for future damages over an injured claimant's lifetime, rather than a lump sum payment, should be required. Periodic payments are less expensive to finance and they assure that financial resources will be available to an injured person over time as needed.

H.R. 3865 also provides that payments should end if a patient dies, thus eliminating "windfall" payouts to persons other than the injured person. . . .

Elimination of Collateral Source Rule. The collateral source rule prohibits the introduction into evidence of any information about compensation a plaintiff may receive from sources other than the defendant. Therefore, plaintiffs may receive a double, triple or quadruple recovery for the same injury—one from an insurer or employer or other source, and one from the defendant. H.R. 3865 encourages states to eliminate this rule so that awards would be offset by the collateral source recovery. . . .

Limit on Non-Economic Damages. Pain and suffering, mental anguish, and loss of consortium are examples of non-economic damage. These damages are impossible to ascertain accurately, can be manipulated by emotion, and are inevitably subject to speculation. They are a primary cause of the grossly distorted awards in professional liability cases. Non-economic damages should be limited. H.R. 3865 would provide incentives for states to limit non-economic damages to $250,000 in health care malpractice cases. . . .

Restriction on Attorneys' Contingent Fees. The American Medical Association does not recommend abolition of the contingency fee system. However, a sliding scale for such fees should be established. Customarily, attorneys accept personal injury cases, as well as professional liability actions, on a contingent fee basis. The attorney may receive from 25% to 50% of any award eventually won. Injured patients on average receive less than 30 cents of every dollar paid by physicians for professional liability insurance. Moreover, two-thirds of claims are settled with no payment. . . . The disproportionate nature of the attorney's contingent fee is compounded by the fact that there is often no relationship between the size of such fee and the degree of complexity of the matter and amount of legal skill and time devoted to the case.

H.R. 3865 would encourage states to enact a sliding scale for such fees, with declining percentages paid to an attorney as the size of the award increases. This would help assure that the appropriate proportion—i.e., the bulk—of the award *goes as compensation to the injured party,* not to the lawyers. At the same time, because of the larger percentage at the lower end of the award scale, lawyers would still be encouraged to accept cases with lower anticipated judgments. This would not, as frequently charged, deny or restrict patient access to proper remedies.

The American Bar Association, in a report on a five-year study that was issued in August 1984, found that when lawyers reduce the amount of time spent working on a lawsuit, the savings are passed on to clients only if the clients are paying an hourly rate. When lawyers work on a contingent fee, "lawyers are benefitting," not clients, the report said. . . .

In closing, Mr. Chairman, I again commend you for your active interest in this critical issue as shown in your holding of this hearing.

The AMA strongly supports prompt passage of H.R. 3865. We believe that its enactment will assist in establishing a more rational professional liability compensation system that will achieve substantial savings to the health care system (including the federal and state governments) while maintaining patient access to high quality health care.

Source: Todd, James S. Statement of the American Medical Association re: The Crisis in Medical Professional Liability, to the House Committee on Energy and Commerce, Subcommittee on Health. March 18, 1986. Reprinted in Reams, Bernard D., ed. *The Health Care Quality Improvement Act of 1986: A Legislative History of Pub. L. No. 99–660.* Buffalo, NY: Hein, 1990, pp. 77–83, 88.

ABA Defends Medical Malpractice Laws in America's Tort System

"The Antiseptic Effect of the Tort System is a Major Protection for the Public"

1986

When medical malpractice lawsuits soared in number during the 1970s and 1980s, surgeons, physicians, hospitals, and other health care providers called on Washington, D.C., to intervene. They asserted that the tort system was out of control and that malpractice litigation was driving up health care prices, threatening the future of important medical specialties, and creating a trend toward counterproductive defensive medicine—excessive prescription of diagnostic and treatment procedures to reduce caregiver vulnerability to malpractice lawsuits. Lawyers' groups and many consumer advocates strongly opposed the calls for tort reform, however. They argued that seeking financial redress in cases of malpractice was an important and fundamental right and that calls for tort reform jeopardized that right.

Various congressional committees and subcommittees responded to this situation with hearings to study the issue. The American Bar Association (ABA) was a highly visible presence at these hearings. On October 8, 1986, for example, ABA president William A. Falsgraf testified on Capitol Hill about the importance of preserving the existing legal rights of health care consumers. His statement is excerpted here.

The American Bar Association recognizes the concerns being expressed about the issue of medical professional liability, and I personally view this issue as extremely important. It is for this reason that I appointed last summer the ABA Special Committee on Medical Professional Liability. . . . I charged this committee with studying current legislative initiatives in the medical malpractice area and developing ABA policy proposals for the Association's policy-making House of Delegates to consider. . . . The committee submitted its recommendations and report in December 1985, and in February of this year, the House of Delegates approved a number of measures at the recommendation of the committee. . . .

It is important to note that there are several measures in this newly-adopted ABA policy with which the medical profession should be able to agree. We call for rigorous enforcement of professional disciplinary code provisions which proscribe lawyers from filing frivolous lawsuits and defenses and for the imposition of sanctions when those provisions are violated. We endorse the American Medical Association's call for stronger medical licensing and disciplinary procedures and increased funding for state boards working in those areas. We also endorse efforts to implement effective risk management programs in the delivery of health care services. In the area of punitive damages, the Association has expressed opposition to requirements of disclosure of financial worth by a defendant in a tort action unless there is a showing by evidence in the record or proferred by the plaintiff that would provide a legal basis for recovery of punitive damages. In relation to the collateral source rule, we approved permitting third parties who have furnished monetary benefits to plaintiffs—generally plaintiffs' insureds—to seek reimbursement out of any recovery the plaintiffs receive; this would reduce the possibility of plaintiffs rerceiving what some perceive to be double recoveries in malpractice suits. As a way of assuring that medical malpractice suits are decided on the basis of an appropriate standard of care and that evidence is considered as clearly as possible, the Association urges trial courts to scrutinize carefully the qualifications of persons presented as experts to assure that only those persons are permitted to testify who, by knowledge, skill, experience, training or education, qualify as experts. Finally, the Association said that there is a need for the further collection and study of data on the cost and causes of professional liability claims.

This action by the House reflects the ABA's recognition that the issue is of vital importance not only to the legal profession but to the medical profession, the insurance industry, and, most of all, to the public.

It is, after all, the public's interest that is most at stake in this issue. Everyone has an interest in the quality and costs of health care services. And when any person suffers injury as a result of negligence by health care providers, he or she must have the right to seek recovery for the full measure of those damages. We believe that right is severely threatened by those who call for major changes in this country's tort law system, and particularly by those who propose that limits be placed on the amount of damages persons may seek in compensation for their injuries caused by the negligence, or worse, of health care providers.

We are particularly concerned with proposals to alter the system of medical malpractice compensation because we believe it is totally inappropriate to carve out exceptions in the tort law system for one group of potential defendants—in this case, doctors and other medical professionals. We are also vitally concerned that the AMA proposals would substantially alter the tort system in ways which would remove one of the principal virtues of the system—its significant deterrent effect on future negligence.

It is the ABA's belief that the rights of injured persons to recover fully for injuries caused by the wrongful acts of others must be protected. We are concerned that those who seek major changes in the way the tort law system deals with cases of medical malpractice show a willingness to trade away the rights of all individuals in the hope of easing a perceived burden on some. No single group in society should receive such special treatment under the law.

The ABA recognizes the widespread concern about liability insurance rates and, in some cases, availability. The insurance and liability problems that concern the medical profession are common to lawyers, too, who face claims for malpractice, as do architects, engineers and other professionals, manufacturers and government bodies. The resolution adopted by the ABA House of Delegates in February begins by stating that common problems should be addressed on a system-wide basis, not as they relate to any specific group. We are happy that organized medicine now appears to agree with our position that the issue should be addressed on a system-wide basis. . . .

We continue to believe that consideration of changes in the tort law system should proceed cautiously, especially when the rights of injured individuals are involved. The tort system under Anglo-American law took 400 to 500 years to develop, and during those years it has served society well. It should not be restructured overnight by frantic efforts to lessen the burden that some groups perceive it to be imposing on them. No substantial changes should be implemented without clear evidence that those changes will bring improvements to the system while protecting the rights of the injured. A rush to change this system without sufficient study would itself constitute negligence.

The tort system plays a role not only in compensating victims of negligence but also deterring future negligence. . . . Adequate deterrence, of course, requires other checks on potential negligence, including effective systems of licensing and discipline and risk management within the professions. But the tort system plays a highly effective role in this process. It brings to bear considerable pressure on misfeasants in the medical profession; the very force of its pressure is manifested in the extraordinary efforts which have been mounted by the medical profession to blunt its impact. We believe the antiseptic effect of the tort system is a major protection for the public, and we should not hasten to counteract its sting.

Let us now examine some of the specific issues raised in the current debate. Proposals to limit compensation to victims of medical malpractice have focused on awards for pain and suffering. Such limits are in effect in some states, although they have been declared unconstitutional in others. Illinois, New Hampshire, North Dakota, and others have ruled on equal protection grounds that such limits unreasonably discriminate against the most seriously injured victims of malpractice. The American Medical Association has proposed that caps on damages for pain and suffering be implemented in other states as well, and at least one bill pending in Congress calls for those other states to impose caps on those damages. (The bill, S.1804, the "Federal Incentives for State health Care Professional Liability Reform Act of 1985," based on AMA draft legislation, would provide federal incentives to states that adopt certain tort law changes, including a cap of $250,000 on damages for pain and suffering.). Proponents of these limits contend that because damages for pain and suffering compensate for "non-economic" damages, they somehow do not reflect real loss by injured persons.

We must disagree with that view. When a person loses the use of an arm or leg, or when a person is permanently disfigured, the actual costs of medical care may be relatively low and the amount of lost wages resulting from absence from work may be relatively small. But does recovery for those economic losses truly compensate injured persons for all their damages? Does it truly compensate them for the physical and emotional losses they suffer, often for the rest of their lives?

These questions are illustrated dramatically by the much-publicized case of Harry Jordan, the California man whose healthy kidney was mistakenly removed by physicians in 1982, leaving him with only the cancerous kidney that they were supposed to remove. What were Mr. Jordan's real damages? Just his medical expenses, lost wages, and perhaps some token amount for pain and suffering? Or were the real damages for his shortened life expectancy, and his lower quality of life for that shorter lifespan, much greater?

A person who is injured by the wrongful acts of others is, and should be, entitled under our legal system to seek recovery for the full measure of his or her damages, as decided by independent adjudicators.

We recognize that placing caps on those damages would not affect all medical malpractice plaintiffs; one study suggests that the median amount awarded in medical malpractice lawsuits is $200,000, far under the ceiling that is proposed for damages for pain and suffering alone. But caps on damages would deprive a great number of injured persons—usually those injured most seriously by medical malpractice—from recovering for the full measure of their losses. This infringement on the rights of those individuals is not in the public interest.

Some in organized medicine contend that only the quick adoption of the changes in the tort law system that have been proposed will sufficiently ease what has been termed the "crisis" in medical professional liability area. While there are problems in the medical professional liability area . . . the facts, as we understand them, do not justify a conclusion that such a crisis exists here.

> The costs of medical malpractice insurance and litigation are not significant elements of total health care costs in the United States. According to a study entitled "Medical Malpractice Insurance in Pennsylvania," prepared in 1985 under the co-sponsorship of several medical and legal organizations in that state (cited here as the "Pennsylvania study"), the nationwide cost of medical malpractice insurance, as of 1983, was $1.5 billion, less than one-half of one percent of the $355.4 billion the nation spent on total health care costs. . . .
>
> The amount of physicians' income consumed by malpractice insurance has not increased substantially in recent years. As of 1983, physicians overall were estimated to have spent only about 2.3 percent of their gross income on malpractice premiums. According to a study by Patricia M. Danzon, a professor in the Health Care Systems Department of the University of Pennsylvania in Philadelphia and a leading researcher in this field, the percentages ranged from one to two percent of gross income for general practitioners to as much as six percent for some high risk surgical specialties. Also, while malpractice premiums can total several thousand dollars, or even much more, the physicians paying them generally earn substantial incomes. . . . In its Feb. 24, 1986 issue, *Time* magazine cited figures indicating that while the average insurance premium paid by physicians had increased from $4,700 in 1976 to $8,400 in 1984, the percentage of income that physicians paid for malpractice insurance premiums actually decreased from 1976 to 1984, from 4.4 percent to 4.2 percent.
>
> States in which physicians have expressed great concern about medical malpractice insurance do not appear at this time to be experiencing shortages of medical practitioners. In New York, for example, *Newsday* reported in its Oct. 27 issue that, despite concerns about the state's high premiums, "physicians are not leaving the state in droves, as medical organizations have been predicting." Instead, the number of licensed physicians rose 24 percent between 1975 and 1983, a period during which the state's overall population remained stable. . . .

. . . The second question is whether the changes in the tort system being proposed by the medical profession would eliminate the perceived problems in medical professional liability insurance. Let us look at the record again.

When concerns over medical professional liability insurance rates and availability first arose in the mid-1970s, the medical profession called for changes in the tort law system similar to those now being sought, and legislatures in nearly every state responded by implementing at least some of those changes. Yet in its own reports prepared last year on this issue, the American Medical Association concluded that the effectiveness of these so-called tort "reforms" adopted by states in the mid-1970s is unclear at best. The AMA Special Task Force on Professional Liability and Insurance acknowledged in its second report that while the medical profession's efforts in the 1970s to change tort law succeeded in obtaining widespread legislative change, "in another sense, the campaign appears to have failed" because the hoped-for reductions in frequence [sic] and severity of claims have not occurred. The task force observed that the "impact of the wave of tort reforms of the late 1970s on medical liability costs is unclear. Yet it is undeniable that these reforms have not had the effect that their supporters hoped, or at least not yet." . . .

. . . Changes should not be made without strong evidence that they will accomplish the goals sought without sacrificing individual rights.

Observations by the Pennsylvania study ["Medical Malpractice Insurance in Pennsylvania," a 1985 study undertaken by several medical and legal organizations in Pennsylvania] on this point are worth noting:

> Many suggested modifications to the tort law system, e.g., caps on malpractice awards, reductions in the statute of limitations applicable to malpractice claims, or elimination of the collateral source rule, are merely cost shifting devices that partially shift the costs of medical malpractice from health care providers and their insurers to other forms of insurance, to state programs (taxpayers), and/or to malpractice victims themselves. They do not save money in the aggregate! In addition, such reforms diffuse the incentives to reduce malpractice incidence by reducing the cost impact of malpractice on health care providers. . . .

. . . More study should be made of how different approaches to rate-making might affect professional liability insurance rates overall. The Pennsylvania study suggests that, by relying on broad class ratings, insurers, at least in that state, are failing to take into account the effect that the claims experience of individual practitioners and hospitals has on overall rates. . . . There exists no comprehensive database containing the malpractice experience of individual health care providers. Because this data base is lacking, insurers rely on broad class ratings, which treat large groups of medical care providers from different fields and different rates of malpractice experience as though they were similar. . . .

The report concludes that:

> Experience rating as opposed to class or even specialty rating would not only permit reduced medical malpractice insurance premiums for quality physicians in terms of eliminating the problem of intra-class or intra-specialty subsidization, i.e., non or single offenders subsidizing multiple offenders of the same class, but would also provide economic incentive to reduce malpractice incidence overall. If physicians could expect prompt adjustment of their malpractice insurance premium rates based on their individual malpractice experience, it is evident that strong economic incentive could be brought to bear on the problem of malpractice. . . .

In conclusion, the American Bar Association recognizes that there are concerns about professional liability insurance. Those concerns are common to all areas of tort law and should be evaluated in the context of their broader implications for the tort system as a whole. We should not devise special solutions for particular groups of potential defendants, insulating them from the beneficial effects of the tort system. Those beneficial effects are principally twofold—first, the compensation of persons who are injured by the wrongful acts of others; and second, the deterrence of negligent and harmful acts against consumers of medical services. The protection of the public against negligence and misfeasance by those upon whom the public relies should be the standard against which all proposals to amend the tort system should be judged.

Source: Falsgraf, William W. Statement of October 8, 1986, before the House Committee on Energy and House Commerce Subcommittee on Health and the Environment. Reprinted in Reams, Bernard D., ed. *The Health Care Quality Improvement Act of 1986: A Legislative History of Pub. L. No. 99–660.* Buffalo, NY: Hein, 1990, pp. 91–107.

DOCUMENT
8.10

Reagan's First Major Speech on AIDS

"This is a Battle against Disease, Not against Our Fellow Americans"

1987

In 1987, six years after the first cases of acquired immune deficiency syndrome (AIDS) were diagnosed in the United States, President Ronald Reagan delivered his first major speech on the epidemic (his earlier comments on AIDS had been brief and limited). To many AIDS activists, public health experts, and lawmakers in Washington, D.C., the speech was long overdue. Many of them asserted that Reagan's years of silence reflected administration-wide indifference and lack of engagement on the AIDS issue.

As a consequence, Reagan's appearance on May 31, 1987, at the American Foundation for AIDS Research (AmFAR) Awards Dinner in Washington attracted huge levels of media attention. AmFAR was chaired by actress Elizabeth Taylor, an old friend of Reagan's from his Hollywood days who during the mid-1980s had emerged as one of the nation's most prominent advocates for increased AIDS research and education.

Reagan's speech was not well received by all audience members at the fund-raiser. The crowd responded warmly to his early remarks about the importance of compassion and his praise for volunteer groups that had helped HIV (human immunodeficiency virus, which causes AIDS) and AIDS sufferers. But the latter part of his address focused mostly on AIDS testing for immigrants and other groups, which was strongly opposed by activists in attendance. Afterward, some activists complained that Reagan never used the words "gay" or "homosexual" in his remarks, and they accused the president of avoiding statements about condom use or anything else that would arouse the anger of the so-called Religious Right, which had emerged as a key conservative constituency during his years in the White House. Defenders of the president insisted that his testing proposals were sensible and his expressions of compassion were genuine.

Given the level of anger that had built up during the mid-1980s among gays, AIDS activists, and some researchers toward the Reagan administration, it is little wonder that the president's carefully worded speech (excerpted here) did little to allay their distrust and hostility. By the time of the speech, more than twenty thousand Americans had already died from the disease. As biographer Lou Cannon later wrote, "if Reagan had delivered it two or three years earlier, it would have been seen as forward-looking and might have had significant impact. By mid-1987, however, Reagan was only repeating public knowledge when he declared that 'AIDS affects all of us.'"[1]

The President: . . . Fundraisers always remind me of one of my favorite but most well-worn stories. I've been telling it for years, so if you've heard it, please indulge me. A man had just been elected chairman of his community's annual charity drive. And he went over all the records, and he noticed something about one individual in town, a very wealthy man. And so, he paid a call on him, introduced himself as to what he was doing, and he said, "Our records show that you have never contributed anything to our charity." And the man said, "Well, do your records show that I also have a brother who, as the result of a disabling accident, is permanently disabled and cannot provide for himself?. Do your records show that I have an invalid mother and a widowed sister with several small children and no father to support them?" And the chairman, a little abashed and embarrassed, said, "Well, no, our records don't show that." The man said, "Well, I don't give anything to them. Why should I give something to you?" [Laughter]

Well, I do want to thank each of you for giving to the fight against AIDS. And I want to thank the American Foundation for AIDS Research and our award recipients for their contributions, as well. I'm especially pleased a member of the administration is one of tonight's recipients. Dr. [C. Everett] Koop is what every Surgeon General should be. He's an honest man, a good doctor, and an advocate for the public health. I also want to thank other doctors and researchers who aren't here tonight. Those individuals showed genuine courage in the early days of the disease when we didn't know how AIDS was spreading its death. They took personal risks for medical knowledge and for their patients' well-being, and that deserves our gratitude and recognition.

I want to talk tonight about the disease that has brought us all together. It has been talked about, and I'm going to continue. The poet W.H. Auden said that true men of action in our times are not the politicians and statesmen but the scientists. I believe that's especially true when it comes to the AIDS epidemic. Those of us in government can educate our citizens about the dangers. We can encourage safe behavior. We can test to determine how widespread the virus is. We can do any number of things. But only medical science can ever truly defeat AIDS. We've made remarkable progress, as you've heard, already. To think we didn't even know we had a disease until June of 1981, when five cases appeared in California. The AIDS virus itself was discovered in 1984. The blood test became available in 1985. A treatment drug, AZT, has been brought to market in record time, and others are coming. Work on a vaccine is now underway in many laboratories, as you've been told.

In addition to all the private and corporate research underway here at home and around the world, this fiscal year the Federal Government plans to spend $317 million on AIDS research and $766 million overall. Next year we intend to spend 30 percent more on research: $413 million out of $1 billion overall. Spending on AIDS has been one of the fastest growing parts of the budget, and, ladies and gentlemen, it deserves to be. We're also tearing down the regulatory barriers so as to move AIDS from the pharmaceutical laboratory to the marketplace as quickly as possible. It makes no sense, and in fact it's cruel, to keep the hope of new drugs from dying patients. And I don't blame those who are out marching and protesting to get AIDS drugs released before the I's were—or the T's were crossed and the I's were dotted. I sympathize with them, and we'll supply help and hope as quickly as we can.

Science is clearly capable of breathtaking advances, but it's not capable of miracles. Because of AIDS long incubation period, it'll take years to know if a vaccine works. These tests require time, and this is a problem money cannot overcome. We will not have a vaccine on the market until the mid-to late 1990's, at best. Since we don't have a cure for the disease and we don't have a vaccine against it, the question is how do we deal with it in the meantime. How do we protect the citizens of this nation, and where do we start? For one thing, it's absolutely essential that the American people understand the nature and the extent of the AIDS problem. And it's important that Federal and State Governments do the same.

I recently announced my intention to create a national commission on AIDS because of the consequences of this disease on our society. We need some comprehensive answers. What can we do to defend Americans not infected with the virus? How can we best care for those who are ill and dying? How do we deal with a disease that may swamp our health care system? The commission will help crystallize America's best ideas on how to deal with the AIDS crisis. We know some things already: the cold statistics. But I'm not going to read you gruesome facts on how many thousands have died or most certainly will die. I'm not going to break down the numbers and categories of those we've lost, because I don't want Americans to think AIDS simply affects only certain groups. AIDS affects all of us.

What our citizens must know is this: America faces a disease that is fatal and spreading. And this calls for urgency, not panic. It calls for compassion, not blame. And it calls for understanding, not ignorance. It's also important that America not reject those who have the disease, but care for them with dignity and kindness. Final judgment is up to God; our part is to ease the suffering and to find a cure. This is a battle against disease, not against our fellow Americans. We mustn't allow those with the AIDS virus to suffer discrimination. I agree with Secretary of Education Bennett: We must firmly oppose discrimination against those who have AIDS. We must prevent the persecution, through ignorance or malice, of our fellow citizens.

As dangerous and deadly as AIDS is, many of the fears surrounding it are unfounded. These fears are based on ignorance. I was told of a newspaper photo of a baby in a hospital crib with a sign that said, "AIDS—Do Not Touch." Fortunately, that photo was taken several years ago, and we now know there's no basis for this kind of fear. But similar incidents are still happening elsewhere in this country. I read of one man with AIDS who returned to work to find anonymous notes on his desk with such messages as, "Don't use our water fountain." I was told of a situation in Florida where 3 young brothers—ages 10, 9, and 7—were all hemophiliacs carrying the AIDS virus. The pastor asked the entire family not to come back to their church. Ladies and gentlemen, this is old-fashioned fear, and it has no place in the "home of the brave."

The Public Health Service has stated that there's no medical reason for barring a person with the virus from any routine school or work activity. There's no reason for those who carry the AIDS virus to wear a scarlet A. AIDS is not a casually contagious disease. We're still learning about how AIDS is transmitted, but experts tell us you don't get it from telephones or swimming pools or drinking fountains. You don't get it from shaking hands or sitting on a bus or anywhere else, for that matter. And most important, you don't get AIDS by donating blood. Education is critical to clearing up the fears. Education is also crucial to stopping the transmission of the disease. Since we don't yet have a cure or a vaccine, the only thing that can halt the spread of AIDS right now is a change in the behavior of those Americans who are at risk.

As I've said before, the Federal role is to provide scientific, factual information. Corporations can help get the information out, so can community and religious groups, and of course so can the schools, with guidance from the parents and with the commitment, I hope, that AIDS education or any aspect of sex education will not be value-neutral. A dean of St. Paul's Cathedral in London once said: "The aim of education is the knowledge not of facts, but of values." Well, that's not too far off. Education is knowing how to adapt, to grow, to understand ourselves and the world around us. And values are how we guide ourselves through the decisions of life. How we behave sexually is one of those decisions. As Surgeon General Koop has pointed out, if children are taught their own worth, we can expect them to treat themselves and others with greater respect. And wherever you have self-respect and mutual respect, you don't have drug abuse and sexual promiscuity, which of course are the two major causes of AIDS. Nancy, too, has found from her work that self-esteem is the best defense against drug abuse.

Now, we know there will be those who will go right ahead. So, yes, after there is a moral base, then you can discuss preventives and other scientific measures. And there's another aspect of teaching values that needs to be mentioned here. As individuals, we have a moral obligation not to endanger others, and that can mean endangering others with a gun, with a car, or with a virus. If a person has reason to believe that he or she may be a carrier, that person has a moral duty to be tested for AIDS; human decency requires it.

And the reason is very simple: Innocent people are being infected by this virus, and some of them are going to acquire AIDS and die.

Let me tell you a story about innocent, unknowing people. A doctor in a rural county in Kentucky treated a woman who caught the AIDS virus from her husband, who was an IV-drug user. They later got divorced, neither knowing that they were infected. They remarried other people, and now one of them has already transmitted the disease to her new husband. Just as most individuals don't know they carry the virus, no one knows to what extent the virus has infected our entire society. AIDS is surreptitiously spreading throughout our population, and yet we have no accurate measure of its scope. It's time we knew exactly what we were facing, and that's why I support some routine testing.

I've asked the Department of Health and Human Services to determine as soon as possible the extent to which the AIDS virus has penetrated our society and to predict its future dimensions. I've also asked HHS to add the AIDS virus to the list of contagious diseases for which immigrants and aliens seeking permanent residence in the United States can be denied entry.

Audience members. Boo!

The President. They are presently denied entry for other contagious diseases. I've asked the Department of Justice to plan for testing all Federal prisoners, as looking into ways to protect uninfected inmates and their families. In addition, I've asked for a review of other Federal responsibilities, such as veterans hospitals, to see if testing might be appropriate in those areas. This is in addition to the testing already underway in our military and foreign service.

Audience members. No! No!

The President. Now let me turn to what the States can do. Some are already at work. While recognizing the individual's choice, I encourage States to offer routine testing for those who seek marriage licenses and for those who visit sexually transmitted disease or drug abuse clinics. And I encourage States to require routine testing in State and local prisons. Not only will testing give us more information on which to make decisions, but in the case of marriage licenses, it might prevent at least some babies from being born with AIDS.

And anyone who knows how viciously AIDS attacks the body cannot object to this humane consideration. I should think that everyone getting married would want to be tested.

You know, it's been said that when the night is darkest, we see the stars. And there have been some shining moments throughout this horrible AIDS epidemic. I'm talking about all those volunteers across the country who've ministered to the sick and the helpless. For example, last year about 450 volunteers from the Shanti Project provided 130,000 hours of emotional and practical support for 87 percent of San Francisco's AIDS patients. That kind of compassion has been duplicated all over the country, and it symbolizes the best tradition of caring. And I encourage Americans to follow that example and volunteer to help their fellow citizens who have AIDS.

In closing, let me read to you something I saw in the paper that also embodies the American spirit. It's something that a young man with AIDS recently said. He said: "While I do accept death, I think the fight for life is important, and I'm going to fight the disease with every breath I have." Ladies and gentlemen, so must we. Thank you.

Source: Reagan, Ronald. Remarks at the American Foundation for AIDS Research Award Dinner, May 31, 1987. Ronald Reagan Presidential Library. www.reagan.utexas.edu/archives/speeches/1987/053187 a.htm.

NOTE

1. Lou Cannon, *Ronald Reagan: The Role of a Lifetime* (New York: Public Affairs, 1991), 734.

DOCUMENT 8.11

HHS Secretary Bowen Recalls the Creation of the Medicare Catastrophic Coverage Act

"They Did Everything They Could to Derail It Every Step of the Way"

1986–1988

The lead architect of the Medicare Catastrophic Coverage Act (MCCA) that President Ronald Reagan signed into law in 1988 was Otis Bowen, his Department of Health and Human Services (HHS) secretary. A former family doctor who had served as the Republican governor of Indiana from 1973 to 1981, Bowen was chairman of the Reagan administration's Social Security Advisory Council in the mid-1980s before becoming HHS secretary in late 1985.

When Bowen took the helm at HHS, his top priority was to address a problem that he had seen time and time again in private practice: the financial ruin of elderly Americans grappling with major health issues. In 1986 he spearheaded the creation of a Medicare catastrophic coverage plan designed to put an end to such stories. But the financial and political challenges of passing such a bill were formidable, as Bowen acknowledges in this 2001 interview with scholar James Sterling Young for the Miller Center of Public Affairs.

Bowen: The President's State of the Union message, my first year there, gave me marching orders to find out ways where the private and public sectors could work together to prevent the pauperization of senior citizens as a result of prolonged illnesses. So we started from there.

Young: Excuse me, how did that get in his message?

Bowen: Each department—whether it was Agriculture or Commerce, whatever—gave suggestions to the President on things that they'd like to see in the message, and that was the one that our department submitted.

Young: Were you there at the time?

Bowen: Yes, I was there.

Hult: So, in essence, that was your priority that went to the White House?

Bowen: Right.

Young: So, apparently that survived—that suggestion survived the battles and the vetting and what gets into the State of the Union.

Bowen: The President even said by name, "I am directing Secretary of Health and Human Services Bowen to do this. . . ." There were—I counted them up—69 different steps that we went through before the President signed the bill. I'm not going to read them all to you, but I've got a chronological order, meetings and things, before it became a bill.

The way it started out was, we developed an Executive Advisory Commission, composed of Tom Burke as a chairman, and then two or three others. Then I devised three separate groups—or task forces. One was to deal with the Medicare problems of those 65 and above, and then one for the 65 and below, and then on the long-term care such as nursing homes. The only one of the three that Congress was interested in was those above 65. They kind of sloughed off the others. Each of these task forces developed their recommendations. The President gave his address on February the 4th, 1986. Then on November the 19th, 1986, that was from February to November, we had our plan completed, because the President asked for the report by the first of December.

So we did three years' work [in] one, and got the plan to the President, and it wasn't until February the 24th, 1987—which was about four months after I delivered the plan to the President—that the President announced that he was preparing to send the plan to Congress.

Young: Wasn't there a lot of down-time during that period? He gave you marching orders that you yourself sort of wrote in the State of the Union message, and then there seemed to be a backsliding somewhere. Then it was on again, and then it was down again.

Bowen: The Domestic Policy Commission did that.

Young: Well, was the attempt made to get it off the agenda—how did you get it back on?

Bowen: I guess with dogged persistence.

Young: Did you ask to see the President at any time?

Bowen: No, I wanted to, but I wasn't able to, because the plan had to go before the Domestic Policy Commission, which [U.S. Attorney General and close Reagan advisor Edwin] Meese chaired, and Meese was adamantly opposed to anything like this.

Young: On what grounds?

Bowen: Expanding government, I guess, was the biggest complaint he had. Then, on June 24th—that was from February to June—the House of Representatives passed the bill, and sent it on to the Senate. Then, in October—from June to October—the Senate passed their version, and then December 9th, the conference committee was appointed to reconcile the differences between the House and the Senate. It wasn't until May the 31st—that's from December to May—that the conference committee reported a reconciled bill for final action. In June, the bill was approved by both Houses and sent to the President, and then June 1988—which was two-and-a-half years afterwards—it was signed by the President

Now, it took so long because the Domestic Policy Commission was, again, adamantly opposed, mainly because of Meese and [Council of Economic Advisors Chairman Beryl] Sprinkel and [Office of Management and Budget Director James C.] Miller and [Secretary of Interior Donald] Hodel . . . They did everything they could to derail it every step of the way—that's why there are so many time intervals in this. . . .

[*Bowen then discusses the pitch for the Medicare catastrophic coverage plan that convinced Reagan to approve it.*]

Bowen: I brought [to the interview] with me my remarks that I made to the President, and the entire Cabinet, when we were talking, trying to promote the bill. This was in the third meeting with the President—the final meeting, and just before he gave his okay. . . .

Young: Tell us who was in the room when you made this.

Bowen: This was a Cabinet meeting.

Young: Full Cabinet.

Bowen: Full Cabinet meeting, at which time the subject was the Catastrophic Medicare Insurance Bill. It was presented to the President and the Cabinet, and then after the President had agreed to send Congress the bill, he had a few remarks on that.

Young: Now, the Cabinet would have included Edwin Meese, who was then Attorney General.

Bowen: It included Sprinkel and Meese.

Young: Sprinkel was there, was he at the table?

Bowen: I think he was at the table.

Young: Really? And Jim Miller was there?

Bowen: They were all there.

Young: Okay.

Bowen: I said, "Mr. President, there is an honest difference of opinion on solutions that address the problem of catastrophic health care costs. The crucial challenge is to define the proper Federal role while the public is becoming increasingly concerned about the inadequacy of catastrophic health care coverage. It is an issue that has been smoldering for several years and is rapidly reaching a peak. This is a complex problem. There are many options floating around."

Incidentally, I had charts prepared that I would change with each little change in topic.

"Our report covered over 50 options and involved over 70 department staff; (1,600 pages of statistics and back-up information); several consultants; a private-public sector advisory committee, which was composed of consumers, employers, providers, insurers and elected officials; 8 nationwide hearings; and over 100 testifiers.

"After nine months of study, the result is a 117-page report and a 16-page executive summary which includes the options that we feel are the most practical. This in no way is meant to imply there are not other options. Before we did our study, I shared many of the concerns that are presently being voiced about our report. It does create a good starting point for further discussion and any needed modifications.

"I would be less than honest, however, if I did not say that I have a preference for what we have suggested in the executive summary and I will try to say why as I proceed.

"Permit me to say that in my 30-year political career I have a record as an opponent of expanding government, a proponent of the need for economy and common sense, a supporter of public-private sector partnerships and at the same time showing compassion for people. I'd match these conservative credentials and experience in public life against almost anyone's. This is the philosophy I followed in my eight years as Governor of the 13th most populous state [Indiana] and fourteen years in the legislature with six of those as Speaker of the House.

"By my seventh year as Governor, we cut every tax except sales and gasoline. By cutting the individual income tax, the corporate gross income tax, inheritance tax, intangibles tax, and the constantly growing and unpopular property tax, Indiana ranked 50th in the nation as to the percent of an individual's income it took to run state and local government. This long experience of dealing with the public and being on the problem solving end has enabled me to recognize issues that are not only important to but acceptable to the public. It is this conservative philosophy and public record that I applied while drafting my recommendations.

"Our senior citizens, especially, worry about two things—their health and their finances. They have an intense anxiety over which one will run out first. With the increase in longevity, the likelihood of a devastating illness is greater and thus the likelihood of losing one's entire life savings is also greater. They want 'peace of mind.' They know that they may not be able to do much to prevent their health from deteriorating with age. They do think something can be done to prevent them from becoming paupers as a result. Yet we estimate that 1.3 million elderly will face this catastrophic risk in 1987.

"There are 3 groups of people who must be considered if we are to grapple with the whole problem. Each has a different set of problems and no single policy approach is possible. But a combination of options can help reduce the financial risks for most.

"First is the Medicare age group, those primarily over 65, with acute illnesses. They have catastrophic costs when they require prolonged hospitalization for medical or surgical treatment.

Second is the Medicare age group with long term care needs. They have catastrophic costs when they require prolonged nursing home care.

Third is the general population below age 65.

"I will talk first about the acute care of the Medicare age group. There are about 30 million in this group. 65% have some form of Medigap insurance to cover some of the items Medicare does not pay for. It's unknown how many of these Medigap policies are really catastrophic in scope. After analyzing the nature of the Medigap market, the fact is that the private sector has not or cannot cover the majority of elderly who are at catastrophic risk. The average annual cost of a Medigap policy is $500 to $600." It is much more than that now. "The average payout for a Medigap policy is only 60 cents on the dollar."

That was a very telling thing, that the insurance really was pretty expensive.

"Many elderly have purchased multiple policies with duplicate coverage that do not cover catastrophic illnesses."

We found just thousands of people who had cancer insurance, diabetes insurance and single types.

"The health industry's estimate for private catastrophic coverage is $175. This amount on top of the cost of traditional Medigap makes it almost impossible for someone living on Social Security payments of $6-7,000 per year to afford. That's probably why 35 percent of all elderly have no Medigap insurance at all.

"The demographics of our nation point to an additional problem. The population is aging rapidly. Those over 85 are increasing the fastest, and will quadruple to 8 ½ million over the next years. Those over 85 are the frail elderly who are hospitalized more often than the rest, and require 1 ½ times as much medical care expense as one who is 65.

"Our recommendation to this serious problem is to restructure Medicare by covering all Medicare services over $2,000 a year. This amount of new coverage can be provided by an additional actuarially sound premium of only $4.92 a month. Both the $2,000 cap and the $4.92 premium would be indexed for future adjustments.

"One argument against this approach is that the Medigap insurance industry would be destroyed. I contend it will not destroy it, but in the long run—even in the short run—would stimulate the business. The most competitive part of the Medigap market would still be there, covering Medicare co-insurance and deductibles up to the $2,000 cap. Medigap would still be offered to cover non-Medicare services, such as drugs, eyeglasses, or dental care. In addition, existing policies could be combined with the developing market for long-term care insurance. This market is in its infancy.

"Therefore, because the present Medigap catastrophic coverage is only a small part of the Medigap market, and so few elderly have catastrophic coverage in their Medigap policies, we aren't replacing a private market with a public monopoly. This $4.92 will buy that peace of mind that I have been talking about, and for which senior citizens have been yearning.

"This, Mr. President, as I understand it is comparable to one of the proposals that you made when you were Governor in California. This plan is not a cost to the Federal government, it's a pay as you go plan. The people who get the benefits pay the cost."

And, I might add in the final version of it, it was on a graduated scale, those payments. I'll skip a bunch here.

"An editorial from the December 5th *New York Times* says"—and they paid a lot of attention to the *New York Times* in Washington—'Clearly an illness that requires prolonged hospitalization or drastic surgery could easily wipe out the savings of a lifetime. Only 1 in 35 of the 28 million covered by Medicare actually suffer potentially bankrupting illnesses each year. But all live in fear of it. That's why 65% of those on Medicare purchase 'Medigap' insurance. For premiums ranging up to more than $1,000 a year, these policies will cover some—though not all—of the costs that Medicare excludes. Yet the Medicare program remains marvelously amendable to adjustments. These 28 million beneficiaries are capable of sharing risks in ways that make them barely noticeable. That makes possible Dr. Bowen's calculation that increasing the premiums for Part B by only $4.92 a month, or $59.00 a year, could end the anxiety over catastrophic illness. . . . The catastrophic-care plan, however, stands out as practical, self-funding, and immediately responsive to a widely felt need.'"

That was the end of the *New York Times* article. . . .

"I will proceed to the second group—those in need of long-term care."

"The threat of catastrophic insurance is very real. I believe the time is right to forge a partnership between government and the private sector that will help provide coverage for catastrophic illness. I have personally been through it twice.

"My first wife died after a 3-year bout with cancer. In the first 2 years she was in and out of the hospital several times and in the last year was hospitalized several times, with the last time being over 3 months. My 86 year old mother, the wife of a school teacher and mother of 5 children has now been in a nursing home a little over two years. The hard earned savings of my deceased father are disappearing rapidly.

"There is intense interest in Congress by Republicans and Democrats. My guess is that they are going to act and act soon on some form of catastrophic care. I would like to see this administration get the credit for this needed, humane and compassionate people program. The problem will not disappear with time. Indeed, delay may make it harder to solve as the population ages.

"In closing, let me return to where I began. There is an honest difference of opinion on solutions that address the problem of catastrophic health care costs. After much study, I believe these recommendations are more advantageous than other options. This study has proved to be more time-consuming, complex, exciting, and at times frustrating, than I would have ever believed. But taken all together, I wish to express my heartfelt thanks to you, Mr. President, for this truly worthwhile endeavor."

That was the end of my remarks, and, of course, it came up for discussion and that's when—

Young: Did you get applause?

Bowen: No. . . . Now, at the end of my remarks, at the end of that Cabinet meeting, the President said he would think this over, and, in a few days, give his response. Then, about three days later, I was called to the White House and advised that he was giving his blessing to it, and was put immediately into a news conference concerning it—and that acted a little swifter than I would have liked, but it—

Young: Did you see him when you went to the White House?

Bowen: Did I see him? . . . No, that came through one of his aides, I think Ken Duberstein.

Young: You were in the press conference alone, not with him.

Bowen: Press conference alone. That was kind of interesting, because most of the media were with me on that, and I can well remember Sam Donaldson leading some of the cheers when he asked me good questions and was very complimentary.

Then the President, on February 12, 1987, said, "I will propose to Congress a comprehensive plan for providing health insurance for those who suffer a catastrophic illness. We all know family, friends, or neighbors, who have suffered a catastrophic illness. We all know family, friends, or neighbors, who have suffered a devastating illness that has destroyed their financial security. As medical science has given us longer lives, we must face the new challenges to ensure that the elderly have security in their old age.

"A catastrophic illness can be a short-term condition requiring intensive acute-care services, or a lingering illness requiring many years of care. It can affect anyone—the young, the middle-aged, the elderly. The single common denominator is financial. It can require personal sacrifices that haunt families for the rest of their lives.

"I am asking Congress to help give Americans that last full measure of security, to provide a health insurance plan that fights the fear of catastrophic illness.

"My plan would provide acute care for those over 65 by restructuring the Medicare program. Under my proposal, the elderly would receive the catastrophic health care coverage under Medicare while limiting out-of-pocket expenses to $2,000. This coverage will be made available for an additional monthly Medicare premium of $4.92. The plan also aims to improve protection for the general population and for the long-term care of the elderly.

"For too long, many of our senior citizens have been faced with making an intolerable choice—a choice between bankruptcy and death. This proposed legislation would go a long way to help solve that problem."

That ended a long—

Young: Then the gavel came down.

Bowen: Yes, the gave came down—

Young: On the Executive side.

Bowen: Then Meese and the rest of them—even though they were still not in favor of it—they had to act like they were, superficially. But behind the scenes, they were still doing everything they could in Congress to delay or postpone it or do it in.

Young: But they didn't succeed in that, did they? They didn't succeed in gutting the proposal.

Bowen: Oh no, they—

Young: In fact, Congress—

Bowen: No, the bill went way too far—

Young: It went the other way.

Bowen: They just hung too many, as I say, bells and whistles on it.

Source: Interview with Otis Bowen by Stephen Knott, Russell L. Riley, James Sterling Young, and Karen Hult, November 8–9, 2001, pp. 54–55, 76–82. Ronald Reagan Oral History Project. Miller Center of Public Affairs, Presidential Oral History Program. http://web1.millercenter.org/poh/transcripts/ohp_2001_1108_bowen.pdf. Reprinted with permission.

DOCUMENT 8.12

Reagan Signs the Medicare Catastrophic Coverage Act

"This Legislation Will [Replace] Worry and Fear with Peace of Mind"

1988

The July 1, 1988, signing ceremony in the White House Rose Garden for the Medicare Catastrophic Coverage Act (MCCA) was a celebratory occasion for Republicans and Democrats alike. The bill, which amounted to the largest expansion of Medicare since its inception in 1965, had enjoyed broad bipartisan support as it made its way through Congress. By the time it reached President Ronald Reagan's desk, it contained a host of provisions for American senior citizens, including caps on hospital and doctor bills, enhanced prescription drug coverage, and new financial protections for people with disabilities and elderly Americans in nursing homes and other assisted living settings.

In his remarks at the signing ceremony (reprinted here), Reagan praised the new law, which he had supported from the outset. He did sound one cautionary note, expressing determination to monitor the costs of these new benefits. As it turned out, the president's concerns that Congress underestimated the financial impact of the Medicare expansion were borne out. But it was another, unforeseen, development—a rowdy rebellion by senior citizens against the MCCA's financing mechanisms—that ultimately doomed the much-trumpeted legislation to a short life.

It was in my 1987 State of the Union Address—and by the way, one of the best parts of this job is that from time to time you get to quote yourself—[laughter]—but it was in my

State of the Union Address that I said, "Let us remove a financial specter facing our older Americans: the fear of an illness so expensive that it can result in having to make an intolerable choice between bankruptcy and death." Well, our administration, I went on to say, would soon submit legislation "to help free the elderly from the fear of catastrophic illness."

Well, that initiative has produced an historic piece of legislation, and in a moment, I will sign the Medicare Catastrophic Coverage Act of 1988. This legislation will help remove a terrible threat from the lives of elderly and disabled Americans, the threat of an illness requiring acute care, one so devastating that it could wipe out the savings of an entire lifetime. The scene is only too easy to picture. An elderly couple, perhaps one has a very long stay in the hospital; the other forced to empty the savings account, to skimp on groceries. And even for those never actually forced into this situation, there's the gnawing worry, the fear, that someday it might just happen. This legislation will change that, replacing worry and fear with peace of mind.

I'm proud to be able to note that the legislation follows the same premise as all sound insurance programs. It will be paid for by those who are covered by its services. Even so, I must add a word of caution. Every administration since the Medicare program was passed has worried about the seemingly uncontrollable cost increases in our government health care programs. Whoever the President in office, program costs have exceeded the best congressional budget estimates. Unless we're careful, it's possible that aspects of this legislation will do the same.

In particular, the legislation provides many new benefits, benefits like respite care and prescription drugs. Since these have never been covered by Medicare, we have no real way of knowing how much these services will cost. So, if future administrations and Congresses aren't diligent, these new benefits could contribute to a program we can't afford. This could be more than a budget problem; it could be a tragedy. The program, after all, is to be paid for by the elderly themselves. So, we must control the costs of these new benefits, or we'll harm the very people we're trying to help. And yet, if administered with prudence, this program can, as I said, provide countless Americans with peace of mind.

Many people share the credit for this achievement. In fact, I feel a little like an Academy Award winner back in my old profession: No matter how many I thank, I'm afraid I'll leave somebody out. There were the hundreds who testified at the regional meetings. There was the public-private working group consisting of many of the Nation's leading health experts. There were the Senators and Representatives of both parties, like Dan Rostenkowski, chairman of the House Ways and Means Committee; Lloyd Bentsen, chairman of the Senate Finance Committee; John Dingell, chairman of the House Energy and Commerce Committee; Bill Gradison; Pete Stark; and many others, some of whom are on the dais with me today, who toiled, compromised, and sacrificed. There were the elderly and their organizations who agreed to pay for this new benefit rather than have it placed on the backs of their children. And there was our Secretary of Health and Human Services, Dr. Otis Bowen, working tirelessly to bring this achievement about.

On behalf of a grateful nation, I thank you all. And now let me sign this historic legislation, the Medicare Catastrophic Coverage Act of 1988.

Source: Reagan, Ronald. Remarks on Signing the Medicare Catastrophic Care Act, July 1, 1988. Ronald Reagan Presidential Library. www.reagan.utexas.edu/archives/speeches/1988/070188d.htm.

DOCUMENT 8.13

Congress Repeals the Medicare Catastrophic Coverage Act

"We Should Take the . . . Time to Say, Look We Made a Mistake"

1989

In the early spring of 1989, months of sustained public protests against various elements of the Medicare Catastrophic Coverage Act (MCCA) convinced both the Senate and the House of Representatives to hold hearings on the issue. The hearings were seized on by various opponents of the MCCA, including affluent seniors—a significant voting bloc— who objected to the MCCA's special surtax on them, conservative opponents of the federal government's "intrusion" into private health insurance, and deficit hawks who saw the new law as fiscally irresponsible. As the hearings dragged on into the summer, architects and supporters of the MCCA found themselves perpetually on the defensive from witnesses, ranging from ordinary citizens to representatives of seniors organizations and other special interest groups, who lambasted them for their role in creating the "baleful, sinister, and deadly" surtax and engaging in "legislative fraud."[1] Supporters of the MCCA repeatedly tried to defuse the spiraling controversy, but their explanations of the act's benefits and their rationale for its funding structure were to no avail. Buffeted by months of adverse publicity, Congress voted to repeal the Medicare Catastrophic Coverage Act in November 1989, a mere sixteen months after its passage.

The following is an excerpt from one of the pressure-packed 1989 hearings on MCCA. In this particular hearing before the U.S. Senate Committee on Finance, Republican representative Harris W. Fawell of Illinois explains to committee chairman Lloyd Bentsen, a Democratic senator from Texas, and other committee members why he thinks the legislation sparked such a firestorm of outrage. During the course of his testimony, Fawell states his belief that outright repeal is unlikely, despite the furor. But Bentsen's remarks at the end of Fawell's appearance give a sense of just how shaken Congress had become by the negative public reaction to MCCA.

Congressman Fawell: First, I want to say thank you very much for once again opening your hearings. In regard to the possibility of funding estimates being altered and the voluntary aspect of this measure, I do appreciate that very much. I would like to read a statement by Joan Beck.

Perhaps if I can be of any help to the Committee at all it might be in regard to relating how the seniors feel. I agree with Senator [John] McCain, these are not selfish people who are not willing to give a lot, and indeed, they have done a great deal for this great nation of ours.

Joan Beck is a syndicated columnist with the Chicago Tribune and she recently said in testifying before our Task Force Committee on this bill that, "Thousands of senior citizens have tried very hard to change the Medicare Catastrophic Care Act—in all of the civics textbooks ways. They have written bags full of letters to members of Congress. They have formed coalitions, lobbied, held meetings. They have had surveys and polls taken. They persuaded sympathetic members of Congress to introduce bills to repeal or postpone or amend the law—and watched the proposals molder in committees, by and large."

Again, you are to be commended, Mr. Chairman, that this Committee is not one that allows things just to molder. You are trying to grapple with it, I know and I commend you for that.

I would express my feeling, and I think most seniors share my feeling, that there ought to be a repeal simply because we went in the wrong direction. We could not have done, I think—well, these are awfully strong words that I'm uttering here—but to utilize a special income tax for special people to try to finance this is something seniors are deeply frustrated about.

I think it is in the wrong direction because we have gone to expanding Medicare in the traditional areas of hospital and physician services. We have added prescription drugs and a number of other areas when seniors are deeply concerned about catastrophic care. Most American families are deeply concerned about this. It is mom and dad or grandma or grandpa, a favorite aunt or whoever it may be. All the blessings of living longer, of course, mean we can defer old age but we cannot set it off.

They are not selfish people. We asked them—it seems to me—and this is what they tell me—we ask them not only that they should self-finance but we also told them they are going to subsidize for a relatively large group of other people. Then we did not really sit down and say, what do you want, by the way, in terms of what you are going to have to self-finance?

Seniors recognize that as they look at long-term custodial nursing home care which is what they thought was in this bill that they do know they are going to have to share in the cost. I do not think that the Federal Government has to assume that burden all by itself. But we [in] other words told them they have got to self-finance. We told them they have to subsidize others with a special income tax on these special people and they are middle income people. The very rich can afford it—the very, very rich. The caps even protect them. The very poor have Medicaid.

Seventy percent—more than that probably—75 percent do have medigap or they have employer-provided insurance care which we are pushing in all other policies in this Federal Government that this is what ought to be done. They are coming in and saying, here you are elbowing out the private insurance industry completely and we think that if we are going to be called upon to participate—and because of the deficit problem I think they recognize that some participation of seniors is absolutely essential, they look to the private industry too, they look for the possibility of 2 or 3 years of co-insurance deductibles and things of this sort, so that the private insurance industry would have a chance to be able to participate, et cetera.

Then they say, you not only did all of this but you made it, you know, absolutely—it is not voluntary, the mere fact that I am eligible. I might be 67 years of age working for a corporation. I have employer-provided insurance. Bango! I am hit. Everybody is hit.

Their feeling is that that just was not fair. I tend to agree with them. They are also saying that when you come up with a tax on a tax and have the title, "Supplemental Premium" that that was not fair. That we have breached every promise we made in the Tax Reform Act when we said we took away a number of tax credits and deductions and income exclusions and we said we will not, as far as all of America is concerned, increase income taxes but we did it and for one group—the senior citizens who are proscribed and tied in their ability to earn because of the social security earnings test and for other reasons. They cannot go out and pick up a job as easily as many people can.

These are middle class seniors. It is an open-ended surtax—a tax on a tax which invites a double hit every time we redefine the definition of gross income, every time we alter those rates. We are always flirting with this and we know we are going to be doing it more, they get a double hit, with the increase in rate, the new definition of income and then they get a tax on the rate also.

That is what [my constituents] continuously bring out to me. That we have gone in the wrong direction and we have utilized one of the worst modes of financing. In regard to changing the estimates in reference to what the cost of this program, which was originally estimated at $31 billion to $35 billion over a 5-year phasein [sic] period only, I agree with what Senator McCain has indicated and what the Chairman has just indicated. That that probably is not a very good idea and, indeed, Congress has been notoriously always underestimating the cost of Medicare.

When Medicare first came into being in 1965 we said by 1990 it will cost $8.8 billion. Well we missed by close to $100 billion. We do it all the time and we are certainly not perfect here. HCFA has made it clear that in so far as the prescription drug program, absolutely, there is going to be a shortfall and there is an incentive to buy drugs. As Senator Pryor has pointed out, there is the greatest markup you will ever find and we are going to contribute a great deal to that.

I think that in my opinion that we really ought to repeal it. I do not think that is going to happen. I fully endorse the McCain amendment as the next best approach. It is a consensus of our Task Force over in the House—two of the Republican Task Forces studying this. We believe that, let us freeze what we have, but my goodness, let us hold back, let us review and let us think in terms of how we can after we talk to seniors move toward long-term custodial nursing home care. . . .

Let me conclude with just one final—and this is a harsh statement that Mrs. Beck made—I do not mean to imply this detrimentally to any member, least of all to the Chairman. But she said the letters senior citizens have written to her go along this line, "Their letters call the Medicare Catastrophic Coverage Act a hoax, a sham, a rip-off, a catastrophe itself, a nightmare, a clever ploy to soak retirees and shave the deficit, a sick joke, a swindle, 'elderly bashing,' and in the words of a veteran from Bessemer, Alabama, "a financial Pearl Harbor sneak attack."

Nobody in this Committee had any such intentions. We went so fast on this that we just kind—it grew a little topsy it seems and we came up with something that was the Catastrophic Coverage Act and AARP was for it and everybody thought it was a great thing. I voted against it. Maybe I was lucky.

But now we have and we should take the ought time to say, look we made a mistake. We are not perfect. Let us try to see what funds we have available from seniors. What may be available from government, how we can bring the private insurance industry into this and let us see if we can craft a program that everybody really wants— long-term custodial nursing home care. Again, not only seniors but just about every family in America because we all or will be facing this kind of a tussle and crisis in our family. . . .

Chairman: Mr. Fawell, thank you very much. I must tell you that this Committee labored long and hard on that, had all kinds of hearings, listened to all the interest groups, worked at it at length trying to develop a piece of legislation that met these concerns. I seriously doubt you will ever pass any major piece of legislation that satisfies everyone. There are no questions, but what there are some inequities in this. We are working to try to correct them.

We are going to devote some more attention to it, some more effort to it and that will be our objective. When we get all through not everyone will be happy.

Source: Senate Committee on Finance. Statement of Hon. Harris W. Fawell, a U.S. representative from Illinois. *Medicare Catastrophic Coverage: Hearing.* 101st Cong., 1st sess., July 11, 1989, 14–17.

NOTE

1. House Select Committee on Aging, Subcommittee on Retirement Income and Employment, Statement of Betty Dales, Grinnell, Iowa, *Hearing,* 101st Congress, 1st sess., March 6, 1989, 64; and Norman B. Ture, "The Medicare Catastrophic Coverage Act: A Case for Repeal (Part II)," *IRET Policy Bulletin* (July 19, 1989): 1.

DOCUMENT
8.14

Congress Agrees to Research Best Practices in Health Care

"To Enhance the Quality, Appropriateness, and Effectiveness of Health Care Services"

1989

In 1989 Congress created the Agency for Health Care Policy and Research (AHCPR) through an amendment to the Public Health Service Act. This amendment, which became law as part of the larger 1989 Omnibus Budget Reconciliation Act, signaled heightened interest in Washington, D.C., in identifying best practices that, if more widely practiced and distributed across the health care industry, could reduce America's health care costs and improve the public health. In addition, the law placed heavy emphasis on supporting research, demonstration, and evaluation activities of particular impact to rural areas that had historically been underserved by health care agencies and institutions. Excerpts of the authorizing legislation are here.

SEC. 6103. ESTABLISHMENT OF AGENCY FOR HEALTH CARE POLICY AND RESEARCH.

(a) IN GENERAL – The Public Health Service Act (42 U.S.C. 201 et. seq.) is amended by inserting after title VIII the following new title:

TITLE IX—AGENCY FOR HEALTH CARE POLICY AND RESEARCH

Part A—Establishment and General Duties

SEC. 901. ESTABLISHMENT.

(a) IN GENERAL – There is established within the Service an agency to be known as the Agency for Health Care Policy and Research.

(b) PURPOSE – The purpose of the agency is to enhance the quality, appropriateness, and effectiveness of health care services, and access to such services, through the establishment of a broad base of scientific research and through the promotion of improvements in clinical practice and in the organization, financing, and delivery of health care services. . . .

SEC. 902. GENERAL AUTHORITY AND DUTIES.

(a) IN GENERAL – In carrying out section 901(b), the Administrator shall conduct and support research, demonstration projects, evaluations, training, guideline development, and the dissemination of information, on health care services and on systems for
the delivery of such services, including activities with respect to—

    (1) the effectiveness, efficiency, and quality of health care services;

    (2) subject to subsection (d), the outcomes of health care services and procedures;

    (3) clinical practice, including primary care and practice-oriented research;

    (4) health care technologies, facilities, and equipment;

    (5) health care costs, productivity, and market forces;

    (6) health promotion and disease prevention;

    (7) health statistics and epidemiology; and

    (8) medical liability.

(b) REQUIREMENTS WITH RESPECT TO RURAL AREAS AND UNDERSERVED
POPULATIONS – In carrying out subsection (a), the Administrator shall undertake and
support research, demonstration projects, and evaluations with respect to—

    (1) the delivery of health care services in rural areas (including frontier areas);
      and

    (2) the health of low-income groups, minority groups, and the elderly.

(c) MULTIDISCIPLINARY CENTERS – The administrator may provide financial
assistance to public or nonprofit private entities for meeting the costs of planning and
establishing new centers, and operating existing and new centers, for multidisciplinary
health services research, demonstration projects, evaluations, training, policy analysis,
and demonstrations respecting the matters referred to in subsection (b). . . .

SEC. 904. HEALTH CARE TECHNOLOGY AND TECHNOLOGY ASSESSMENT.

(a) IN GENERAL – In carrying out section 901(b), the Administrator shall promote
the development and application of appropriate health care technology assessments—

    (1) by identifying needs in, and establishing priorities for, the assessment of
      specific health care technologies;

    (2) by developing and evaluating criteria and methodologies for health care
      technology assessment;

    (3) by conducting and supporting research on the development and diffusion
      of health care technology;

    (4) by conducting and supporting research on assessment methodologies; and

    (5) by promoting education, training, and technical assistance in the use of
      health care technology assessment methodologies and results.

(b) SPECIFIC ASSESSMENTS –

    (1) IN GENERAL – In carrying out section 901(b), the Administrator shall
      conduct and support specific assessments of health care technologies.

    (2) CONSIDERATION OF CERTAIN FACTORS – In carrying out paragraph
      (1), the Administrator shall consider the safety, efficacy, and effectiveness,
      and, as appropriate, the cost-effectiveness, legal, social, and ethical implica-
      tions, and appropriate uses of such technologies, including consideration of
      geographic factors. . . .

Source: Omnibus Budget Reconciliation Act of 1989. Establishment of Agency for Health Care Policy
and Research. P.L. 101–239, Sec. 6103, pp. 73–76.

Congress Throws Its Support behind the Ryan White CARE Act

"AIDS Is a Disaster as Severe as Any Earthquake, Hurricane, or Drought"

1990

In 1990 Congress passed and President George H. W. Bush signed the Ryan White Comprehensive AIDS Resources Emergency (CARE) Act. The act passed with broad bipartisan support. In the Senate, for example, the bill had sixty-six cosponsors and passed by a 95–4 vote, easily brushing off a filibuster threat from conservative Republican senator Jesse Helms of North Carolina. The law had been crafted to provide much-needed financial assistance to urban hospitals and other health care institutions that had been overwhelmed by the acquired immune deficiency syndrome (AIDS) crisis that had erupted across the United States during the 1980s. In addition, it provided more generous—and more reliable—funding streams for early intervention treatment and prevention programs, a move that significantly bolstered community-based AIDS programs that previously had been established through provisions of the 1988 Health Omnibus Programs Extension.

When the legislation first came up for consideration in Congress, it had simply been titled the Comprehensive AIDS Resources Emergency Act. But on May 15, 1990, the bill was retitled to honor Ryan White, an Indiana teen who had died of AIDS a little more than a month earlier, on April 8. White was a hemophiliac who had been infected with AIDS from a contaminated blood treatment, then expelled from school when administrators learned of his condition. White and his mother, Jennifer White Ginder, had responded with a public education campaign that had garnered national media attention and generated considerable public sympathy for people grappling with HIV (human immunodeficiency virus, which causes AIDS) and AIDS. "After he received that tainted blood transfusion, to the moment he drew his last breath here on Earth, he never condemned anyone," said Sen. Edward M. Kennedy (D-MA), who played a leading role in the bill's passage. "He was not looking for scapegoats. . . . What he was doing was reaching out in the true spirit of the American character to recognize that there were people who were suffering."[1]

Although the act easily passed both houses of Congress, differences between the two bills necessitated a conference to work out a final version. Following are excerpts from the August 4 remarks of several prominent Senate conferees—Kennedy, Frank R. Lautenberg (D-NJ), and Orrin Hatch (R-UT)—when they presented the final conference report to their colleagues for consideration. The Senate approved the report by voice vote later that day, clearing the way for Bush's signature.

Since the establishment of the Ryan White HIV/AIDS Program, funding to the Health Resources and Services Administration for fulfillment of its various provisions has steadily increased. In fiscal 1991, $220.6 million was appropriated for the program; by fiscal 2008, the figure had grown to $2.1 billion. The act has been reauthorized several times, most recently in 2009, when Congress passed the Ryan White HIV/AIDS Treatment Extension Act. This bill, signed by President Barack Obama on October 30, extended the Ryan White CARE Act for an additional four years.

Sen. Edward Kennedy: Mr. President, I am pleased to bring to the floor of the Senate the conference report on the Ryan White Comprehensive AIDS Resources Emergency Act of 1990. I am also proud to stand once again with my friend and colleague from Utah, Senator Hatch, who has made an extraordinary contribution to our Nation's battle against AIDS.

For 9 years, America has been grappling with the devastating effects of AIDS. Up to a million of our fellow citizens are already infected with the virus and are almost certain to face serious health problems as a result of HIV disease.

This critically important legislation provides emergency relief for the cities hit hardest by AIDS and funding for States to respond to the mounting need for AIDS health care, early intervention, and essential support services in both urban and rural areas.

In terms of pain, suffering and cost, AIDS is a disaster as severe as any earthquake, hurricane or drought. Because this tragedy continues to unfold, even now we cannot tally the full extent of devastation.

Health care institutions—and the vulnerable Americans who depend on these institutions—are in crisis.

AIDS by itself is certainly not the only cause of these problems. But it is adding to the stress that is leading toward a total breakdown of our health care system.

In passing this conference report, we respond to this emergency with financial assistance essential to the operation of effective and cost efficient alternatives for the delivery of health and support services to individuals and families with HIV disease.

This report is the product of months of consensus building and bipartisan cooperation. It consolidates the best efforts of both the Senate and the House in an effort to provide comprehensive care to hundreds of thousands of Americans in need.

The report contains essentially all of the components of the Senate bill which passed in late May by an overwhelming vote of 95 to 4. In addition, the Senate conferees have protected the integrity of all amendments that were added on the floor during consideration of the legislation.

The conference report also includes a State and a categorical HIV early intervention program and a pediatric AIDS research initiative which have been put forward by the House. These provisions had strong bipartisan support in that body and passed by a vote of 403 to 18.

Two successive, national commissions on AIDS have recommended Federal funding to develop the kind of care networks authorized in this report. Hundreds of national professional, business, labor, and religious organizations have helped to shape the Ryan White Act.

It is supported by the mayors, county executives, and Governors—and requires that all levels of government join together in providing services and maximizing resources in the battle against AIDS.

Until we take action to organize and integrate HIV health services, both costs and chaos will continue to increase—with devastating consequences for individuals and families throughout the United States.

This Nation can, and now will, do better.

America responded within days to the California earthquake last fall. We have pledged hundreds of billions of dollars to rescue the savings and loan industry. AIDS is a comparable disaster and we now begin to respond accordingly.

This conference report is about more than money. It is about caring and the American tradition of reaching out to people who are suffering and in desperate need of help.

As a nation, we pride ourselves on our ability to rally in the face of adversity. I am pleased that the Congress has affirmed its commitment to providing care and to showing compassion to people living with AIDS in communities throughout America.

I urge the Senate to approve the conference report.

Senator Frank Lautenberg: Mr. President, I rise in strong support of the conference report on the Ryan White Comprehensive AIDS Resources Emergency Act of 1990. I was an original cosponsor of this legislation which authorizes critical funds to help our cities, States, hospitals, and health care workers meet the needs of the ever-growing AIDS population.

The AIDS epidemic in this Nation has reached crisis proportions. To date, nearly 140,000 AIDS cases have been reported to the Centers For Disease Control. The Ryan White Comprehensive AIDS Resources Emergency Act of 1990 responds to the spiraling AIDS epidemic by authorizing critically needed funds for AIDS care programs.

In our cities and countries throughout the Nation, hospitals, clinics, and health care providers are struggling to provide services to people with AIDS and HIV disease. Many States and local governments lack the necessary resources to develop long-term strategies to combat the epidemic.

Public health systems are being pushed to the absolute limits as they struggle to fight the AIDS epidemic. Particularly our urban hospitals—already overburdened and under staffed—have described a `Calcutta-like' environment where patients spend weeks lying in the corridors waiting for hospital beds that are occupied. Rural areas have been reporting the most dramatic increases in AIDS cases over the past 3 years, and rural health care systems are having an increasingly difficult time meeting the challenges of AIDS care.

The Federal Government has spent money on AIDS research. However, 10 years into the AIDS epidemic, the Federal response to AIDS care has been minimal. Without Federal assistance this year, many health care professionals say that the AIDS crisis will result in the collapse of the public health system as we currently know it.

When Hurricane Hugo struck South Carolina, we responded immediately with assistance to help devastated cities and counties recover from the damage.

When an earthquake rocked northern California, we responded immediately with the assistance needed to rebuild roads and bridges.

When a drought threatened our farm States, we responded with assistance to avert a crisis in the agricultural community and to sustain the livelihood of our farmers.

The AIDS disaster is no different, and we must respond in the same way. We must provide relief to the areas where the AIDS epidemic is threatening public health systems and devastating entire communities. We must provide resources to help our States, cities, counties, and health care providers develop long-term plans to address the AIDS epidemic.

The Ryan White Comprehensive AIDS Resources Emergency Act of 1990 is a balanced bill that responds to the AIDS epidemic on a number of fronts. It authorizes $275 million in fiscal year 1991 for areas that have been hardest hit by the AIDS epidemic and are in desperate need of emergency relief. . . .

Mr. President, this bill goes well beyond providing emergency relief to hard-hit areas. It also authorizes dollars for States to assist additional impacted areas and to support comprehensive programs that respond to the devastating AIDS epidemic. For fiscal year 1991, it authorizes $275 million for these programs. These funds will be critical to my State of New Jersey. New Jersey has the fifth largest AIDS population nationwide, and through June 1989 the State had reported 9,143 AIDS cases to the Centers for Disease Control.

The bill authorizes $20 million in fiscal year 1991 for HIV health services research, including a Pediatric AIDS Research Demonstration Program. New Jersey has the third largest number of pediatric AIDS victims nationwide—237 reported cases. The University of Medicine and Dentistry of New Jersey in collaboration with Children's Hospital of Newark recently received a $1.3 million Federal grant for a Pediatric AIDS Resource

Center to help address this sad problem in New Jersey and elsewhere. The need to provide more Federal dollars for pediatric AIDS research and services to tackle the tragic pediatric AIDS problem in New Jersey and throughout the Nation is critical.

And, the bill authorizes $230 million in fiscal year 1991 for early intervention programs. . . .

Mr. President, our hospitals and cities and counties are in dire need of the help offered by the programs in the Ryan White Comprehensive AIDS Resources Emergency Act of 1990. Today, we are one step closer to providing them with the assistance they need and deserve. . . .

Senator Orrin Hatch: Mr. President, I urge my colleagues to join me in supporting the conference report on S. 2240. This legislation responds to the diverse treatment needs of those who have AIDS, including children, and provides relief for hospitals and other community programs straining under the economic burden to provide compassionate care.

Mr. President, most of us have heard the stories of family members whose loved ones are suffering from AIDS. We have seen babies with AIDS abandoned in hospital wards. And, we have seen both our rural and urban health care systems strained to the very limit.

The conference report responds to these cries for help. It will fill in the cracks in our health care system, and its sends a message of hope, care, and charity. It sends the message to families who have a child with HIV that they are not forgotten, that we want to help.

Source: Ryan White Comprehensive AIDS Resources Emergency Act—Conference Report. Congressional Record, 101st Cong., 2d sess., August 4, 1990. http://thomas.loc.gov/cgi-bin/query/D?r101:3:./temp /~r101hQzSl3::.

NOTE

1. *Congressional Record,* 101st Cong., 2d sess., May 15, 1990, S6198.

| DOCUMENT 8.16 | Government Report Takes the NIH to Task on Women's Health |

"NIH . . . Made Little Progress in Carrying Out Its 1987 Policy on Women"

1990

One of the leading sources of discontent within the women's health movement that emerged during the 1970s and 1980s was the second-class status of women's health issues in the medical research community. Activists, advocates within the scientific community, and women members of Congress worked together to rectify this inequity. They called for increased research into reproductive issues and other subjects (such as breast cancer and osteoporosis) of special importance to women. In addition, they demanded greater inclusion of women as research subjects in clinical studies on health issues. Leading figures in these efforts ranged from National Institutes of Health (NIH) scientist Florence

Haseltine, who played a leading role in the founding of the Society for the Advancement of Women's Health Research, to Representatives Patricia Schroeder (D-CO) and Olympia J. Snowe (R-ME), who cochaired the Congressional Caucus for Women's Issues.

In 1985 the efforts of women's health activists and proponents paid off with the publication of a U.S. Public Health Service report by a special Task Force on Women's Health Issues. The task force, helmed by Ruth Kirschstein, the only woman institute director at the NIH, called for increased federal funding for women's health research and emphasized the importance of including more women in clinical studies. The NIH responded to the report the following year with a new policy that promised, among other things, to include women in study populations from 1987 forward.

Over the next few years, however, women's health advocates complained that the new NIH policy existed mostly on paper and that federally funded research remained disproportionately slanted toward men's health issues. In late 1989 Schroeder and Snowe partnered with Rep. Henry A. Waxman (D-CA), chairman of the House Energy and Commerce Subcommittee on Health and the Environment and a caucus member, to issue a formal request that the General Accounting Office (GAO) evaluate the degree to which the 1987 NIH policy change had been implemented.

In June 1990 the GAO returned with a report, Problems in Implementing Policy on Women in Study Populations, *which was unveiled by Waxman's subcommittee with great fanfare. The GAO audit, authored by Mark V. Nadel, confirmed that the NIH had made virtually no effort to encourage greater inclusion of women in study populations. These findings prompted expressions of outrage from advocates such as Schroeder, who declared that "American women have been put at risk by medical practices that fail to include women in research studies. The health of American women will stay at risk until NIH fully implements its inclusion policy. American women deserve better treatment from the research community."*[1]

The damning GAO report gave women's health activists and advocates in Congress the ammunition they needed to press for measures to attack continued gender bias in the NIH and other sectors of the federal bureaucracy. Buoyed by extensive media coverage, Schroeder, Snowe, and Sen. Barbara A. Mikulski (D-MD) introduced the 1990 Women's Health Equity Act (WHEA), which contained a wide range of provisions to bolster women's health research and services. The research-oriented provisions of that legislation became law in 1993. Other WHEA proposals, such as federal funding for breast and cervical cancer screening programs, became law through other legislation.[2] *In 1998 many features of the initial WHEA were enacted with the passage of the Women's Health Research and Prevention Amendments.*

Meanwhile, the embarrassing revelations contained in the 1990 GAO report compelled the NIH to take more decisive steps to remove gender bias in the health research that it was funding. It also established an Office of Research on Women's Health at the NIH under the direction of Kirschstein.

The following document is an excerpt from Nadel's testimony before one of the many congressional committees that asked him to appear in the days and weeks after the release of the GAO report. His statement provides a solid overview of the various NIH shortcomings he documented in his GAO audit.

I am pleased to be here today to discuss our review of the progress the National Institutes of Health (NIH) has made in implementing its policy to encourage the inclusion of women in study populations and what effect the policy has had on the study populations of NIH-funded research. . . .

In brief, we found that NIH has not adequately implemented its policy. Although NIH announced its policy over 3 years ago, it has just begun to apply it systematically during the grant review process. NIH's various institutes have not consistently applied the policy, and NIH has no way to measure the policy's impact on the research it funds. Furthermore, the policy applies to extramural research only, and not to NIH's own intramural research projects. . . .

The 1985 Report of the Public Health Service Task Force on Women's Health Issues recommended increased research on health problems affecting women. In response, NIH promulgated a policy to ensure that women are included in study populations unless it would be scientifically inappropriate to do so. NIH has funded some projects that studied only men, even though the diseases being researched affect both men and women. According to NIH, the underrepresentation of women in such studies "has resulted in significant gaps in knowledge." In studies of some diseases and treatments, excluding women raises serious questions about whether the research results can be applied to women.

An example of the problem is a National Heart, Lung, and Blood Institute study of 22,000 male physicians begun in 1981. It found that men who took an aspirin every other day reduced their incidence of heart attacks. Institute officials told us women were not included in this study, because to do so would have increased the cost. However, we now have the dilemma of not knowing whether this preventive strategy would help women, harm them, or have no effect. . . .

Following publication of the 1985 Public Health Service Task Force report, the NIH Director established the NIH Advisory Committee on Women's Health Issues to monitor implementation of the Task Force's recommendations in NIH. The committee's work led to a policy that was first announced in October 1986 and restated in a January 1987 announcement. The 1987 announcement

- urged grant applicants to consider the inclusion of women in the study populations of all clinical research efforts;
- stated that if women were not to be included, applicants should provide a clear rationale for their exclusion; and
- said that researchers should note and evaluate gender differences.

The 1987 policy announcement urged rather than required attention to these issues. . . .

NIH Made Little Progress in Implementing Policy

The Office of the NIH Director has depended more on persuasion of NIH staff and outside scientists than on central direction to take action. At the time we began our work in January 1990, NIH had made little progress in carrying out its 1987 policy on women. Although some steps have been taken since January, several problems have characterized implementation:

- It has been very slow;
- The policy has not been well communicated or understood within NIH and in the scientific research community, and has been applied inconsistently among NIH components;

- Encouragement of gender analysis, a key part of the policy, has not been implemented; and
- It is impossible to determine the impact of the policy.

I will discuss each of these problems in turn.

Implementation Very Slow

Most of the responsibility for policy implementation was left to the individual institutes, which have responded with varying degrees of effort and speed. After publication of the policy in 1986 and 1987, some institutes began to inform their staff and researchers about the policy and some incorporated it in their grant review process. Others waited for further guidance. Because of the differences in implementation among the institutes and the lack of records, we cannot describe precisely the timing of each institute's actions. But of the four institutes we reviewed in depth, two began to apply the policy before NIH provided additional instructions and two began afterwards. The National Institute on Aging began to implement the policy in 1987.

It took NIH almost 3 years to issue detailed implementation guidelines to its staff. A comprehensive memorandum applying to all extramural research did not appear until July 1989. That memorandum strengthened implementation of the policy to include minorities in studies, as well as providing guidelines for the policy on women. . . .

The Division of Research Grants is responsible for the first level of review for most proposals received by NIH. In the Division, scientific reviewers did not begin to apply the policy until the February 1990 grant review cycle. Three of the four institutes we interviewed in depth including the National Institute on Aging, began to apply the policy by fall 1989, but in the National Institute of Allergy and Infectious Diseases, reviewers will first implement the policy this month. Because of these delays, many scientific review groups are just beginning to send to institute councils summary statements that highlight concerns about the exclusion of women from studies.

Policy Poorly Communicated, Inconsistently Applied

We found problems in the extent to which the policy is understood and applied by grant applicants, NIH staff, and scientific experts who review proposals for NIH funding.

The application booklet used by most NIH grant applicants—PHS Form 398—contains no reference to the policy to include women in study populations. This form is a primary source of instructions to investigators initiating their own proposals. A revised version of the form and its instructions will not appear until April 1991, over 4 years after the policy was first articulated.

As a result, NIH is still receiving many proposals that are not responsive to the policy. We reviewed about 50 recent grant applications, most proposing studies on conditions that affect both men and women. About twenty percent of the proposals provided no information on the sex of the study population. Over one-third indicated that both sexes would be included but did not say in what proportions. Some proposals for all-male studies provided no rationale for that design.

We found that some NIH staff were unaware of their responsibilities for implementing the policy. In addition, some reviewers demonstrated limited understanding of the policy. For example, a recent proposal to conduct an all-male study related to coronary artery disease was approved by the scientific review group with the comment that the exclusion of females was appropriate because the disease studied disproportionately affects men. While this observation may be true, it may be inadequate as a rationale for excluding women, because coronary artery disease is also a serious health problem in women. The institute council also approved this proposal for funding. . . .

No Policy on Women in Intramural Studies

NIH's intramural research program has no policy on the inclusion of women in study populations. In an August 1989 report, the Advisory Committee on Women's Health Issues recommended that NIH take steps to encourage inclusion of women in intramural as well as extramural studies. The Director of NIH has not formally transmitted that report to intramural officials or instructed them to develop a policy. In response to our review, the Human Research Review Panel of the NIH Clinical Center placed this issue on the agenda of its June meeting.

The National Institute on Aging (NIA) provides a good example of the problems that can arise from the lack of emphasis on including women in NIH's intramural research program. The Baltimore Longitudinal Study of Aging is part of NIA's intramural program. Its failure to recruit women as study subjects during its first twenty years has resulted in some research results than can be applced [sic] to men only. Research supported by other components of NIA's intramural program also has generated more information on men than on women.

Little Action Taken to Encourage Gender Analysis

Although the 1987 policy announcement also encouraged researchers to analyze study results by gender, NIH officials have taken little action to implement this element of the policy. The 1989 memorandum setting out guidelines for policy implementation calls for attention to issues of research design and sample size, but does not specify the need for gender analysis. NIH officials showed us solicitations that cited the importance of including women in study populations. We noted, however, that few suggested studies be designed to assess different results for men and women. NIH officials differ among themselves in their views on the types of studies for which gender analysis is appropriate.

Impossible to Determine Impact of Policy

You asked us to report on the extent to which the NIH policy has resulted in inclusion of women in clinical study populations. Because policy implementation began so late, it is too soon to determine what, if any, effect it is having on the demographic composition of study populations. Additionally, given the lack of data on previous study populations, analysis of the policy's impact is virtually impossible.

Steps could be taken, however, to maintain data that would be useful for future monitoring of the inclusion of women in studies. At present, no central NIH office collects the types of demographic data on study populations that you requested. Several years ago, NIH revived its Inventory of Clinical Trials and the current data collection form does ask for information about the gender composition planned for study populations. However, the gender question is not categorized specifically enough to provide complete information. As another means of monitoring inclusion of women in study populations, some institutes plan to begin collecting demographic data on studies they fund.

RECOMMENDATIONS

To ensure effective implementation of its policy to encourage the inclusion of women in study populations, the Director of NIH should take the following steps:

- Inform NIH staff, grant reviewers, and the community of researchers NIH supports of the reasons for the policy and how it should be carried out;
- Direct NIH institutes to maintain readily accessible data to allow assessment of the extent to which women are included in studies;
- Ensure that the planned revision of the grant application booklet (PHS Form 398) adds a section explaining the policy and instructing applicants to respond to the requirement to include women in study populations, or to justify their exclusion; and
- Instruct members of review groups always to determine whether the gender of the study population is an issue of scientific merit affecting the priority score, and to document their decisions in the summary statements.

Following our original testimony, the Acting Director of NIH said he would give serious consideration to these recommendations, and by law, federal agencies have 60 days to notify Congress on actions taken in response to GAO recommendations.

Source: Statement of Mark V. Nadel, associate director, National and Public Health Issues, Human Resources Division, before the House Select Committee on Aging, Subcommittee on Housing and Consumer Interests. *National Institutes of Health: Problems in Implementing Policy on Women in Study Populations.* Washington, DC: General Accounting Office, July 24, 1990.

NOTES

1. Quoted in Leslie Laurence and Beth Weinhouse, *Outrageous Practices: How Gender Bias Threatens Women's Health* (Piscataway, NJ: Rutgers University Press, 1997), 61.
2. Carol S. Weisman, *Women's Health Care: Activist Traditions and Institutional Change* (Baltimore: Johns Hopkins University Press, 1998), 81–85.

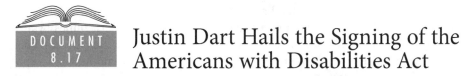

DOCUMENT
8.17

Justin Dart Hails the Signing of the Americans with Disabilities Act

"ADA Is a Landmark Commandment of Fundamental Human Morality"

1990

The passage of the Americans with Disabilities Act (ADA) marked the culmination of many years of tireless work by people with disabilities and the family members, friends, advocates, and lawmakers who supported their campaign for full civil rights. One of the most prominent figures in this crusade was Justin Dart, who became a wheelchair user after contracting polio in 1948. A tremendously successful businessman and prominent activist, Dart helped develop the ADA after being named a cochair of the Congressional Task Force on the Rights and Empowerment of Americans with Disabilities in 1988. (He served in this capacity for almost three years.) In 1989 Dart was appointed chair of the President's Committee on the Employment of People with Disabilities, where he continued his advocacy for full civil rights for people with disabilities.

In the following article, written shortly after the ADA became law, Dart explains what the legislation meant to him and millions of other Americans with disabilities.

President George Bush signed the Americans with Disabilities Act on July 26, 1990, a landmark date in the evolution of human culture.

Throughout all of reported history until recent decades, people perceived as having significant disabilities have been treated as sub-humans. At worst they were killed or left as beggar-outcasts to die, at best they were cared for through subsistence welfare, out of sight and mind in institutions and back rooms.

With the development of modern medicine and social responsibility, millions of 20th Century humans are surviving previously fatal conditions and living on with significant disabilities. These individuals have a great potential to be happy, productive members of their communities. However, our best efforts to fulfill this potential have been consistently limited by a massive residue of prejudice and paternalism. Our society is still infected by an insidious, now almost subconscious assumption that people with disabilities are less than fully human, and therefore are not fully eligible for the opportunities, services and support systems which are available to other people as a matter of right.

More than two decades ago many of us in the disability community concluded that Americans with disabilities would never achieve full, productive citizenship until this nation made a firm statement of law protecting their civil rights.

The Americans with Disabilities Act is such a law. It establishes "a clear and comprehensive prohibition of discrimination on the basis of disability." Taken in combination with previously existing disability rights law, it provides a sound legal framework for the practical implementation of the inalienable right of all people with disabilities to participate equally in the mainstream of society. It extends to people with disabilities the same protection of their rights that is already enjoyed by the members of all other minorities.

Most importantly, ADA is a landmark commandment of fundamental human morality. It is the world's first declaration of equality for people with disabilities by any nation. It will proclaim to America and to the world that people with disabilities are fully human; that paternalistic, discriminatory, segregationist attitudes are no longer acceptable; and that henceforth people with disabilities must be accorded the same personal respect and the same social and economic opportunities as other people.

ADA opens the doors of opportunity for millions of isolated, dependent Americans to become employees, taxpayers and welcome participants in the life of their communities. It prepares the way for the emancipation of more than half of a billion of the world's most oppressed people.

I am proud of America. I am proud of President Bush, Attorney General Thornburgh and Boyden Gray, and all the great Congressional and Administrative staff who authored and fought for the ADA, and thousands of other patriots who have struggled for long, hard years in a wilderness of prejudice and paternalism for the victory of ADA.

Once again America has passed the torch of liberty and productivity to the world.

All who love justice must unite in action to protect our hard won ADA rights, and to ensure that they are implemented through strong regulations, and enforced in every community.

We of the disability community must communicate to America that full compliance with ADA can be profitable for all citizens, and we must join in cooperative action with government and the private sector to ensure that all will profit.

But ADA is only the beginning. It is not a solution. Rather, it is an essential foundation on which solutions will be constructed.

We must undertake a courageous reallocation of our society's resources from paternalism to independence and productivity. We must invest in a continuum of new and strengthened programs to liberate people with disabilities from dependency, and empower them to be equal and productive participants in the mainstream: Productivity-oriented education for all citizens. Economic, technological, independent living, vocational rehabilitation, transitional, personal assistance and community based supports for productivity and quality of life. Prevention. Affordable insurance and health care for all. Incentives for productivity to replace disincentives. Accessible communications, transportation, housing, and completely new communities that are accessible as a whole.

A large agenda? Certainly! But no larger than that which faced our patriot forefathers at the successful conclusion of the revolutionary war.

Like then, we have accomplished much. Like them, we have a profound responsibility to make a bold declaration of equality real in the lives of hundreds of millions of people in future generations.

I believe that we will unite to fulfill that responsibility. Because I believe in you, the patriots of ADA. And I believe in you, the patriots to be.

Together we have overcome. Together we shall overcome.

Lead On!

Source: Dart, Justin. "ADA: Landmark Declaration of Equality." *Worklife.* Fall 1990. www.aapd.com /site/c.pvI1IkNWJqE/b.6098553/k.5303/ADA_Landmark_Declaration_of_Equality.htm.

CHAPTER 9

The Clinton Health Plan
and Scorched-Earth Politics

1990–2000

Health care politics and policymaking in the 1990s was dominated by President Bill Clinton's health reform efforts. The ultimate derailment of those efforts in 1994 by a united Republican Party constituted a crushing blow to the Clinton White House, and in the aftermath of that spectacular showdown the politicization of health care policymaking continued to escalate. Clinton managed to turn some of these showdowns to the political advantage of himself and his fellow Democrats, and occasionally the two parties were even able to find common ground on substantive health care issues, such as health insurance coverage for children. Most of the partisan sniping and brawling, however, produced policy deadlocks, and for much of the 1990s individual states, by default, took on an increasingly prominent role in health care policymaking.

UPSET VICTORY IN PENNSYLVANIA SEEN AS POLITICAL BELLWETHER

When Republican President George H. W. Bush and his staff began early preparations for his 1992 reelection campaign, it appeared that health care would not be a high-profile issue. The 1989 flameout of the Medicare Catastrophic Coverage Act had singed both parties and greatly dampened enthusiasm for health care reform in Washington, D.C. Moreover, pundits and political strategists confidently identified the explosive military situation in the Persian Gulf and the increasingly sluggish American economy as the issues that were most on voters' minds.

These observers failed to realize that, underneath the anxieties about job security and business profits, the nation's recessionary conditions were stirring renewed fears about health care security. Most Americans received their health insurance through their employers, and they worried, with good reason, that the recession meant higher copayments and premiums for those who kept their jobs and loss of coverage for the families of employees who fell victim to pink slips. Retirees from some of the nation's best-known companies were losing their benefits as their former employers scrambled to compete with foreign corporations with much lower business expenses. The number of uninsured Americans rose by several million from 1987 through the early 1990s. By 1992, nearly thirty-nine million Americans were uninsured (including nearly one out of five people under the age of sixty-five), a jump of more than four million from 1987, and another forty million Americans had only bare-bones policies that provided woefully inadequate protection in the event of a serious illness. Firmly yoked to the rising unemployment rate, the worrisome trend in coverage loss would have been even more severe had Medicaid eligibility not expanded during this same period.[1]

The submerged but intensely felt fears of voters about health care erupted to the political surface in spectacular fashion in 1991. Pennsylvania governor Robert P. Casey (D) had appointed Democrat Harris Wofford to fill the Senate seat left vacant by Republican John Heinz, who had died in an airplane crash, until a special election was held in November of that year. Casey had sought bigger names, but he was rebuffed by several Democrats who feared the prospect of tangling with Republican Dick Thornburgh, who had announced his intention to run for the seat. The formidable Thornburgh was not only a popular former governor of Pennsylvania, but he also had served as U.S. attorney general in the Reagan and Bush administrations.

Initially, the Wofford campaign appeared doomed. Private polling conducted by Wofford's strategists in July and August showed a stunning forty-plus point gap between their candidate and Thornburgh.[2] In September, however, Wofford began emphasizing national health insurance in his commercials, and the gap between the two candidates swiftly narrowed. On election day Wofford cruised to victory by ten points, a result that news media at the local, state, and national levels all attributed to his campaign's turn to the health care issue (**See Document 9.1**).

CLINTON PROMISES SWEEPING HEALTH CARE REFORM

The stunning outcome in Pennsylvania—and postelection polls indicating that one out of two voters in the state saw "national health insurance" as one of their top two voting issues—was a true wake-up call to lawmakers and officials in Washington. In the immediate aftermath of Wofford's victory, health care bills were introduced in Congress by the score, and think tanks and industry groups began examining reforms that would simultaneously mollify the public and advance their ideological or financial priorities. The paths offered by these disparate groups ranged mightily, from market-oriented reforms (favored by conservatives) to single-payer tax-financed plans (the preference of liberals) to play-or-pay proposals that would require employers to either cover employees (play) or subsidize governmental coverage of uninsured Americans (pay). All of these proposals shared the same stated goal of moving the United States toward a universal system that covered all Americans.

As Bush campaign strategists hurriedly floated incremental health reform proposals such as statewide health insurance purchasing pools for people with preexisting conditions, increased regulation of health insurers, and tax credits for low-income families seeking insurance, the crowded Democratic field of presidential candidates scrambled to gain the health care high ground. Candidates Bob Kerrey (sitting senator from Nebraska) and Paul E. Tsongas (former senator from Massachusetts) both labored mightily in this regard, but as analyst Jill Quadagno observed, "the candidate who came to own the issue . . . was Bill Clinton, the handsome, youthful, charismatic governor of Arkansas."[3]

Clinton stayed on equal footing with Kerrey and other Democrats on the health care issue during the primary campaign by touting a broad plan of managed competition that would use federal regulations and cost controls, and avoid new taxes, to achieve universal coverage. After securing the nomination, Clinton's vision for health care reform came into steadily clearer focus. In campaign stop after campaign stop, Clinton framed his plans for national health insurance as a centrist, cost-effective approach that preserved the existing "private health care system" while simultaneously extending new protections to middle-class America. In a special September 24, 1992, campaign speech devoted to health reform in New Jersey, Clinton summed up his plan as one that preserved "personal choice, private care, private insurance, [and] private management" even as it erected "a national system to put a lid on costs, to require insurance reforms, to facilitate partnerships between business, government, and health care providers." Clinton also pounded home his belief that health care reform was a major economic and budgetary priority for the nation. "If we can cover everybody and bring costs within inflation," he said, "we will save hundreds of billions of dollars per year by the end of the decade to the private sector— money which can be reinvested in growth, in productivity, in wages, in benefits, in making America a stronger country."[4] Finally, the candidate repeated an oft-stated promise to have a health care plan ready for Congress within one hundred days of his inauguration.

On November 3, 1992, Clinton won the presidency, defeating Bush and independent candidate H. Ross Perot. On January 15, 1993, five days before he was sworn in to office, he announced that he was creating a health care task force headed by his wife, Hillary Rodham Clinton, and Ira Magaziner, a business consultant and old Clinton friend. This task force would be responsible for crafting a health insurance reform package that would be acceptable to Congress. This approach was applauded by many health care experts and key leaders of Congress who agreed that Capitol Hill was better equipped to review (and modify as needed) a technically, economically, and politically viable health reform plan than to produce one itself.

Over the next several months, in a multitude of closed-door meetings, the President's Task Force on Health Care Reform toiled away on the complex task of remaking America's health care system. Using cluster teams and working groups that eventually included more than five hundred health policy experts and armies of congressional staffers and state officials, the task force dove into the intricacies of hundreds of health care issues related to hospitals, physicians and other caregivers, patients and their families, employers, health product manufacturers, and local, state, and federal health programs. "The scale of the project was astonishing even to some of us who had long advocated a comprehensive plan," recalled health care expert and historian Paul Starr, who participated in the effort.[5]

The task force kept industry at arm's length during this process. Insurance companies, hospitals and other health care providers, and employers were regularly consulted, but they did not have a hand in devising the plan. Unhappiness with this state of affairs became evident in February 1993, when three groups representing various sectors of the health care industry filed suit against the task force, arguing that Hillary Clinton's status as a private citizen meant that she did not have legal standing to chair, or even attend, the task force meetings. The lawsuit also demanded the release of task force memos and reports, as well as the names and affiliations of all task force participants. "It was a deft political move," Hillary Clinton later acknowledged in her memoirs. "Designed to disrupt our work . . . [it] foster[ed] an impression with the public and the news media that we were conducting 'secret' meetings."[6] The legal action soon convinced the administration to make a major dump of task force records, but foes found little that was of use to them.

Pushing Through Mounting Political Turbulence on Health Care Reform

The President's Task Force on Health Care Reform formally disbanded in May after four months of intensive labor, leaving the first lady, Magaziner, and a small core of experts and aides to put the finishing touches on what would become known as the Health Security

Act. A particular focus of task force leaders and White House officials at this time was making sure that the legislation's financial underpinnings would receive positive marks from the Congressional Budget Office (CBO). But delivery of the plan to Congress was delayed time and again through the summer of 1993 by a succession of political brush-fires. Partisan wrangling over the Clinton White House's budget proposal ate up considerable time and energy, as did debate over whether to allow gays to serve in the armed forces and how or whether to intervene in war-wracked Bosnia. In addition, the battle to get the North American Free Trade Agreement (NAFTA) through Congress occupied much of the administration's political energies and strained relations between the administration and anti-NAFTA labor unions. The labor movement had historically been an important proponent of national health insurance, but NAFTA made it enormously difficult for the Clintons and their allies to keep labor engaged on the health care front.

These delays and distractions gave opponents of the Health Security Act an opening, and they were swift to take advantage. Stakeholders in the existing system, including pharmaceutical manufacturers, hospitals, and insurance companies, launched battalions of lobbyists and negative advertisements against the White House's reform efforts. These attacks intensified in the late summer of 1993, when details of the plan began leaking. "The minute the Clinton plan officially appeared," wrote political historian Theda Skocpol, "all these groups could quickly decide how disappointed or angry they were with each relevant detail of the vast blueprint. Their leaders and staffs geared up to notify members across America about threatening features of the proposed legislation."[7]

Of the myriad groups that mobilized against Clinton's health care reform campaign, the one that assumed the highest profile was the Health Insurance Association of America (HIAA). Helmed by Bill Gradison, a politically connected former Republican member of the House of Representatives from Ohio, this association of small and midsize insurance companies displayed a genius for gumming up the reform drive. "We had lots of time to get geared up," Gradison later explained. "[The delays] gave us a lot more time to refine our message, raise our money, do internal staffing changes, and have training sessions with members of our association as to what they could do with their hometowns and their editorial boards."[8] The most famous HIAA contribution to the antireform effort was a series of television commercials starring "Harry" and "Louise," a fictitious middle-class white couple who warned viewers that the Clinton plan would be a bureaucratic nightmare and a fiscal boondoggle of the highest order.

In August 1993 Clinton finally put the fierce budget battle behind him by signing the Omnibus Budget Reconciliation Act, a deficit-reduction bill that was opposed by every Republican in Congress. The GOP voted en masse against the bill because its deficit-fighting measures included higher taxes on some businesses and the wealthiest 1.2 percent of taxpayers (the act's spending cuts and tax cuts for working-class families were less controversial). The Republicans' narrow defeat in this legislative showdown—Vice President Al Gore cast the deciding vote to carry it through a Senate that had deadlocked 50–50—further deepened the enmity that some in the party had come to feel toward the administration.

One month later the Clinton administration tried to regain the faltering political momentum for its health care reform plans through an elaborately staged formal rollout. The first step was a nationally televised prime-time address by the president on September 22. Clinton used the speech to remind viewers of the serious problems with the health care status quo, from spiraling medical costs to health insurance coverage that was out of reach to tens of millions of people. He assured his audience that the Health Security Act

*First lady Hillary Rodham
Clinton testifies before the
House Energy Committee
regarding the administration's
proposed Health Security Act.*

would take care of these problems in a fiscally responsible manner that also respected individual choice and freedoms (**See Document 9.2**).

Six days later, first lady Hillary Clinton made the first of several public appearances before powerful congressional committees to tout the benefits of the White House plan. Her testimony attracted huge amounts of press coverage. The heavy media attention was due in part to high public interest in health care reform. But it also stemmed from the fact that, by the fall of 1993, the first lady's unprecedented role as the lead architect of a major legislative initiative—and her bold and confident personality—had led both supporters and opponents to see her as a virtual personification of the Health Security Act.

By all accounts Clinton performed masterfully on Capitol Hill (**See Document 9.3**). "She was cool and poised as she sat alone, without notes, expressing herself clearly and convincingly hour after hour, easily fielding all questions," wrote journalists Haynes Johnson and David S. Broder. "Introducing herself in her opening words as 'a mother, a wife, a daughter, a sister, a woman,' she also consciously appealed to all women, seeking to undercut the tensions that exist between America's homemakers and its career women. It was a bravura performance."[9] In the wake of these appearances and the subsequent plaudits, supporters of the White House's national health insurance plan expressed optimism that, after the summer doldrums, wind was once again filling the sails of reform.

REPUBLICANS UNITE AGAINST THE HEALTH SECURITY ACT

Almost immediately, though, outside events once again undercut the administration's health care push. In early October, American television viewers were outraged by footage showing the bodies of American soldiers being dragged through the streets of Somalia. During this same period, conservative media outlets relentlessly flogged allegations of scandal surrounding the Clintons, such as the so-called Whitewater investigations of real estate transactions in which the couple were involved in the late 1970s and early 1980s.

Meanwhile, powerful stakeholder groups continued to level criticism at the proposed Health Security Act, and some of these efforts gradually found purchase in the public psyche. Almost imperceptibly at first, public support for Clinton's reforms began to sag under the weight of invective from small business owners (who opposed employer mandates), physicians (who opposed cost controls), insurance companies (which opposed caps on premiums and purchasing groups), pharmaceutical companies (which feared greater regulation of drug prices), and large manufacturers (which decided that managed care was a better antidote for their skyrocketing health care expenses). Most of these groups, it should be noted, favored the principle of comprehensive health care reform. They recognized that the American health care system was riddled with serious problems that badly needed attention. But these same stakeholders "strongly opposed any specifics that could step on their particular toes," said Skocpol. "Stakeholder groups tended to focus on attacking the exact provisions of the Health Security plan that each group liked least, while nobody ever mentioned in ads or public statements the parts they supposedly liked. . . . Stakeholders' public efforts and legislative maneuvers worked together to sow anxiety about virtually *all* the core public regulatory features of the Clinton plan: regional alliances, premium caps, employer mandates, and community rating rules."[10]

All of these factors convinced Republicans to undertake a careful reassessment of their assumptions about health care reform. Ever since Clinton's 1992 election victory, the GOP had behaved as if a substantive overhaul of the health care system was inevitable. Polls showed strong support for Clinton's proposed reforms for much of 1993, and many party leaders appreciated the administration's rejection of a single-payer plan and its focus on tough cost controls. In addition, the Democrats enjoyed healthy majorities in both houses of Congress, a political reality that further contributed to a mild sense of resignation and inevitability among Republicans regarding the health care issue. But when Republicans surveyed the political landscape in late 1993 and studied the cumulative impact of Somalia, Whitewater, NAFTA, the bruising budget battle, and the Harry and Louise advertisements on the Clinton White House, they realized that they had a fighting chance to torpedo the legislation. Some clear-eyed Democrats sensed the shifting dynamics as well. "Lots of good people are sitting around talking about how health reform's going to happen, arguing over the details," warned Sen. Jay D. Rockefeller IV (D-WV). "But nothing's happening in the American public except HIAA's out there bombing with nobody responding."[11]

As autumn ran its course and slipped into early winter, the oratory emanating from key Republican precincts toward the Health Security Act turned increasingly defiant. Moderate House minority leader Robert H. Michel (R-IL) echoed the rhetorical flourishes of right-wing voices such as Rush Limbaugh when he declared in late October that the GOP intended to resist Clinton's efforts to "embark on an uncharted course of government-run medicine."[12] Deeply conservative members of Congress such as Newt Gingrich of Georgia and Dick Armey of Texas inveighed against the plan on nightly news programs, mocking it as a bureaucratic monstrosity that was impossible for anyone to understand. And Republican strategists such as William Kristol framed the intensifying debate over "Hillarycare" as a potential watershed moment—a chance to cripple a Democratic presidency and pave the way for a new era of Republican governance (**See Document 9.4**).

REPUBLICAN CHARGES AGAINST HEALTH CARE REFORM GAIN TRACTION

On November 20, 1993, the Health Security Act was finally presented to Congress, but no action was taken on it before the holiday recess. When the 103rd Congress reconvened in January 1994, both Democrats and Republicans braced themselves for the upcoming battle over health care. The first major salvo was fired by Clinton in his January 24 State of the Union Address, in which he strongly defended the Health Security Act. He signaled his willingness to negotiate on various facets of the bill, stating that "I am open . . . to the best ideas of concerned members of both parties." But the president also vowed to the assembled members of Congress that "if you send me legislation that does not guarantee every American private health insurance that can never be taken away, you will force me to take this pen, veto the legislation, and we'll come right back here and start all over again."[13] Republicans were unmoved by this threat. Senate minority leader Bob Dole (R-KS) flatly told Americans that Clinton's plan to "put a mountain of bureaucrats between you and your doctor" was unsalvageable. He and other influential party spokesmen vowed to keep it from ever becoming law (**See Document 9.5**).

The criticisms leveled by Dole and other Republicans elicited a variety of reactions from historians and journalists. Some believed that "Dole was smart to couch his objections in antigovernment terms. In doing so, he caused people to think about health care reform in terms of how they felt about government. And, in 1994, those feelings were particularly negative. . . . Dole's statement was neither partisan, nor ideological. It was simply anti-Washington."[14] Journalist Bill Schneider indicated that Dole's central point was a valid one, declaring that the administration displayed "awesome political stupidity. . . . They came up with a 1,300-page document that could not have been better designed to scare the wits out of Americans. It was the living embodiment of Big Government—or Big Brother."[15] Others were more critical of the tactics employed by Dole and other Republicans. They acknowledged that "Dole's charge was certain to strike a responsive chord among a large segment of the population," but they asserted that the decision to exploit this fact "represented a cynical exercise in political deception, a misleading attempt at fear mongering designed to scare the public into opposing the president's program."[16]

In any case, the charge that the Health Security Act would plunge Americans into a scary and baffling "big government" health care maze was effective, in large measure because the legislation *did* have an extraordinary number of moving and interlocking parts. The act touched on virtually every aspect of health care and health insurance, and it introduced a multitude of new regulatory mechanisms. The act's architects believed that these changes would ultimately benefit the nation and its citizenry, and they emphasized that all the individual elements of the plan had been studied by policymakers for years. Several pillars of the plan, such as the individual mandate, had even attracted favorable reviews from conservatives in the past. Moreover, some defenders of the proposal took exception to the whole "too big" meme. "To say that the [administration's] package of proposals was 'too complex' is like saying that an airplane's blueprint is too complicated," wrote journalist James Fallows in 1995, after the plan had been defeated.

> The Medicare system is complex. So is every competing health care-reform plan. Most of the 1,342 pages of Clinton's Health Security Act (which I have read) are either pure legal boilerplate or amendments to existing law. Conventional wisdom now holds that the sheer bulk of the bill guaranteed its failure. The NAFTA bill was just as long. . . . If the health bill had been shorter and had not passed, everyone would know that any proposal so sketchy and incomplete never had a chance.[17]

In the final analysis, the scale of reengineering for which the Clinton administration was calling—and the plan's incomprehensibility to average Americans—proved to be a significant political weakness, for it lent itself to caricature and misrepresentation by those who opposed it. "We came up with such a big, fat, ugly bill that was such an easy target," lamented Clinton adviser and speechwriter Robert Boorstin. "We created a target the size of Philadelphia. I mean, Harry and Louise were good ads, but come on, they weren't that difficult to create. . . . Somebody should have gone to Ira and Hillary and said, 'This isn't a working document.'"[18]

AMERICAN NEWS MEDIA AND THE HEALTH SECURITY ACT

Bewilderment about the plan extended to the American news media. Millions of Americans turned to television news and print media in hopes of gaining a greater understanding of how Clinton's national health insurance plan would affect them and their families. These outlets obliged by unrolling numerous stories on health care reform. One authoritative survey indicated that during two periods (September 1 to November 30, 1993, and January 15 to November 13, 1994), America's five major television networks and its flagship newspapers provided fifty-six hundred stories on the issue.[19]

While the quantity of coverage was extensive, the quality of coverage was another matter. Some journalists who reported on the Health Security Act did not feel that they had an adequate understanding of the plan themselves. One veteran journalist with the *Los Angeles Times* admitted that she felt "swamped by the immensity of the policy stuff. . . . The plan was virtually unexplainable, and at first, [the architects of the plan] were just arrogant. They refused to confront hard questions. Then as it started to get in trouble, they realized it was out there and they couldn't move off of it, and they became defensive. When you questioned something, they lectured you on your inability to grasp their grand vision. Pretty soon, it was all being lost in confusion and fear."[20]

Some critics argued that most news outlets did not even attempt to process the Clinton health care plan, explain its most important features, or help the public gauge the veracity of claims—both pro and con—about the act and its likely impact on American life. Instead, news sources with clear ideological orientations offered a steady diet of slanted coverage, while the rest of the news media emphasized process over policy, running countless stories devoted to the political warfare being waged over reform instead of the nuts and bolts of the bills under consideration. "The journalist culture—both its professional mind-set and its commercial, competitive pressures—nudges the coverage strongly to emphasize conflict and dissent rather than clarification of alternatives and the search for consensus," according to one analysis. "That tendency showed in the speed and eagerness with which the press focus shifted from an explanation of the problem and the proposed solutions to an emphasis on what might be called the mugging of the Clinton plan. Health care reform became the prize in a classic power game, and the press was caught up quickly in gauging and guessing who would win, not in exploring what the consequences would be for the country."[21]

CLINTON'S HEALTH REFORM PLAN GOES DOWN TO DEFEAT

Clinton's health reform efforts continued to lose political steam throughout the first half of 1994. His own party became increasingly fractious on the issue, with some liberals grousing about their continued preference for a single-payer system at the same time that more conservative caucus members, most notably Jim Cooper of Tennessee, pressed for a "Clinton lite" package stripped of the individual mandate and other features. Republicans continued to pound away relentlessly at the Health Security Act using talking points (since discredited) taken from articles published in the conservative *Wall Street Journal* and liberal *New Republic*. Republicans also touted their own bill crafted by moderate senator John H. Chaffee (RI), the Health Equity and Access Reform Today Act. By March 1994, six health reform plans were circulating on Capitol Hill, each with devoted followings.[22] Meanwhile, stories about another alleged Clinton scandal from his days in Arkansas—"Troopergate"—dominated the evening news.

Despite the increasingly poisonous political atmosphere in Washington and polls showing growing disenchantment with the Clinton plan, most political analysts entered the summer of 1994 expecting that the Democrats would eventually coalesce around a compromise plan that they could tout to voters in the November elections. Republican pollster Bill McInturff recalled that "when Newt [Gingrich] asked me in May what I thought the likely outcome would be, I said that Bill Clinton's not going to get the package he wants, but he's going to get *something*. The Democrats are not going to be so dumb as to let nothing happen and go home. That's just so idiotic it couldn't possibly happen in my lifetime. Never in a million years."[23]

With each passing month, the prospects for passage of a reform bill dimmed. Frustrated by the divisions within the Democratic caucus, Rep. Richard A. Gephardt (MO) and Sen. George J. Mitchell (ME) cobbled together a new version of the act in August that received the welcome endorsement of the American Association of Retired Persons. Republicans delayed a vote on this bill by holding up a sweeping anticrime bill that sat ahead of it in the legislative queue. Meanwhile, last-ditch efforts by the self-styled Mainstream Group, a coalition of moderate senators (led by Chaffee, Kerrey, and Democrat John B. Breaux of Louisiana), to find a bipartisan solution to the impasse ended in failure. By the time the crime bill finally passed, lawmakers were desperate to return home and campaign for the fast-approaching midterm elections. As Washington emptied, leaders of both parties acknowledged that the Republicans' run-out-the-clock strategy had worked. With the public now polarized over health care reform and elections around the corner, the Democrats would never be able to gather the necessary votes for passage when they returned to the capital in September.

Following the recess, Democratic and Republican lawmakers engaged in a final spasm of recriminations about health care reform and the partisan warfare it inspired (**See Document 9.6 and Document 9.7**). But no health reform bill came up for a vote in the House, where Democrats held a 257–176 advantage, or the Senate, where Democrats knew that their fifty-six votes would not be enough to force cloture in the certain event of a Republican filibuster. On September 26, 1994, Senator Mitchell glumly announced that the long, exhausting drive to pass major health care reform in the 103rd Congress had come to an end (**See Document 9.8**).

States Move to Impose New Rules on HMOs

The battle royal over the Health Security Act left Washington with little appetite to tackle health care policy in any meaningful way. Democrats were dispirited by the whole affair, and Republicans, who had increasingly claimed that the health care system was decidedly not in crisis, had other policy priorities. So when public dissatisfaction with the managed care industry escalated in the mid-1990s, it was left to individual states to respond to the clamor.

By that time, health maintenance organizations (HMOs) and other forms of managed care had risen from their modest origins in the early 1970s to carve out a position of clear hegemony in medical care. As Lisa Belkin in the *New York Times Magazine* commented in 1996, "managed care is no longer a model proposed for the American health care system. It is the American health care system. Nearly 60 million people are enrolled in managed care insurance plans and three in four doctors participate in at least one managed care program."[24] Managed care organizations owed this rapid rise to prominence not only to corporations' desire to rein in the health care expenses of their employees and retirees and Reagan-era policies that encouraged investment in HMOs, but also to the public sector's desire to cut health care expenditures. Specifically, states had become increasingly anxious about the soaring expense of their Medicaid programs, which featured few stipulations or limitations on patients' options for medical service. In many states, Medicaid threatened to surpass public education in terms of total outlays. "When you've got a program growing 20 percent a year, that's a problem," said a former budget official in Tennessee. "When you've got a program that's one fifth of your budget growing 20 percent a year, that's a disaster."[25]

In the early 1990s numerous states submitted plans to Washington for shifting their Medicaid services to managed care plans, which they hoped would rein in program costs. These proposals were actively solicited by the Clinton administration, which saw Medicaid HMOs as a promising tool in its overall cost-cutting efforts. Administration officials believed that preventive medicine, a hallmark of managed care, could improve pregnancy, neonatal, and childhood care and reduce the number of high-priced emergency room visits and hospital stays that were responsible for so much of Medicaid's exploding costs. By the mid-1990s, a number of high-population states including Arizona, California, Florida, New York, Oregon, and Tennessee had moved at least a portion of their Medicaid programs into managed care plans.

During this same period, managed care assumed new heights of controversy. By almost every measure, HMOs and other managed care organizations were succeeding in reducing the rate of health care spending, and these accrued savings allowed many businesses to increase wages and otherwise boost the quickening U.S. economy. At the same time, consumer protection groups and physicians excoriated HMOs and other managed care entities for alleged abuses against patients. Some physicians claimed that the profit orientation of HMOs had so perverted medical care in America that they were moved to quit practicing medicine altogether. "The system of HMOs, managed care, restricted hospitals, and denial of needed medications has become so corrupt, so rotten, that I cannot stomach it any longer," said one doctor. "The system is controlled by for-profit HMOs with dividend-hungry shareholders and high-salaried administrators. I was beginning to feel the pressure and change my prescription habits from the best medicine I knew to the one that would look best on my profile and hating myself for it."[26]

The negative media attention swirling around HMOs convinced some managed care outfits to adjust their policies. More important, it prodded many state legislatures and governors to intervene by crafting new regulations designed to stop some of the more controversial practices of managed care operations (See Document 9.14). These regulations ranged from "any willing provider laws," which expanded the number of health professions that could participate in managed care plans, to minimum lengths of stay for maternity and mastectomy patients. Many states also passed laws against gag clauses, which were HMO regulations that prevented member physicians from telling patients about potentially effective but expensive treatment options. States also passed measures that gave managed care enrollees the right to appeal HMO coverage decisions to an independent commission or even sue managed care organizations for malpractice. The legality of many of these patients' rights laws was ultimately confirmed in the courts, but in 2004 the U.S. Supreme Court ruled in *Aetna Health Inc. v. Davila* that state laws allowing patients to sue their HMOs for malpractice violated provisions of the 1974 Employee Retirement Income Security Act (ERISA).[27]

Clinton Vetoes GOP Medicare and Medicaid Reform Proposals

In November 1994 the Republican Party won a smashing victory over President Clinton and the Democrats at the polls. The GOP traced its electoral success directly to its defeat of the Health Security Act, which had not only weakened the president but also given Republican a battle-tested thematic blueprint for attacking the White House and congressional Democrats. Republicans rode to majority status in the House of Representatives (their first majority in the House in forty years) campaigning on the Contract with America, which sought to retake the nation from "big government" Democrats and promote culturally conservative family values. The contract galvanized conservative voters, and Democrats were unable to get their own core constituencies to the polls in sufficient numbers to avoid an election-day debacle. All told, the GOP added fifty-six seats in the House. It also gained six seats in the Senate, bringing the total in the upper chamber to fifty-three, also a majority.

In the immediate aftermath of the midterms, speculation ran rampant across Washington that Clinton was destined to be a one-term president. With his approval ratings well under 50 percent and Congress now in the hands of conservative adversaries, including new Speaker of the House Newt Gingrich, such speculation was understandable. Clinton himself felt it necessary to plaintively insist to the Washington press corps, when asked, that he was still relevant.

Certainly, the Republicans viewed the 1994 election results as a mandate. Confident that they could roll Clinton and the Democrats in any political showdown, Gingrich, House majority leader Armey, Senate majority leader Dole, Senate majority whip Trent Lott (R-MS), and other Republican leaders moved forward decisively with an agenda that emphasized corporate deregulation (a move applauded by the business community and opposed by environmental, labor, and consumer protection organizations) and downsizing government through the slashing or outright elimination of funding for discretionary programs. This zeal for cutting the size of government extended to health care programs that for one reason or another had run afoul of Republicans **(See Document 9.9)**.

During 1995, however, it became clear that observers who had written Clinton's political obituary had been premature. His standing with the American public steadily rose during this period, and by early 1996 he was favored to win reelection. This turnaround stemmed from several factors, including an economy that roared into overdrive, the related success of the Democrats' 1993 budget legislation in reducing the deficit, and a perceived White House shift to more centrist positions on a variety of issues. Another important factor was a late 1995 showdown with Republicans over Medicare and Medicaid cuts that ended badly for the GOP.

In 1995 Republicans unveiled a fiscal plan to balance the budget and reduce the tax burden, especially on affluent Americans whose taxes had gone up during Clinton's first two years in office. These plans were predicated in large part on making massive reductions to the federal Medicare and Medicaid programs. Clinton and his fellow Democrats lined up against the Republican plan, which proposed taking more than $250 billion from Medicare and $175 billion from Medicaid and reducing the annual growth rates of both programs by more than one-third.

The Republicans argued that greater program efficiencies and innovative new health insurance proposals, such as medical savings accounts (MSAs), would cushion middle-class Americans against negative health or economic repercussions from these adjustments. Historians note that they were joined in this crusade by Republican governors who said that the Medicaid reforms in particular would free states of "hobbling federal regulation and of the obligation to keep pumping more and more of their own tax dollars into medical assistance for the needy."[28] Democrats charged that Republicans were engaging in an all-out assault on Medicare and Medicaid.

Clinton and other Democrats believed that the Republican plans to reengineer Medicaid would ultimately reduce or abolish health benefits for millions of the program's current beneficiaries, but they did not devote the bulk of their time to defending Medicaid. After all, as journalist George Anders observed, "middle-class voters wanted schools, roads, and police forces; they fumed at the fact that their state tax dollars were being consumed by Medicaid (particularly by unpopular items such as neonatal care for premature babies of drug-addicted mothers)."[29] Mindful of this fact, Democrats emphasized the alleged threat posed to the enormously popular Medicare program by Gingrich and his "radical" followers. Day after day, Democrats painted a picture of a GOP plan that would necessitate vastly higher copayments, force seniors to enroll in managed care plans with unfamiliar doctors, and visit assorted other cruelties on Medicare recipients, all so the wealthiest Americans could receive new tax breaks.

The GOP showed no inclination to negotiate, and in the fall of 1995 the Republican budget reconciliation plan passed both houses of Congress on votes that broke down along partisan lines. To the surprise of many Republicans, Clinton refused to go along and vetoed the measure. The bill's narrow voting margins indicated that no override was possible. Without an approved budget, federal operations for the new fiscal year (beginning on October 1) could be secured only through a continuing resolution authorizing funding until a new budget agreement was reached. When the continuing resolution expired on midnight of November 13 without any break in the impasse, all nonessential governmental operations ceased. This shutdown ended on November 19 with the passage of a temporary spending bill, but the struggle over the budget continued under the disbelieving gaze of an increasingly vexed American public.

With the political stakes rising with each passing day, neither congressional Republicans nor Clinton displayed any inclination to blink. In early December the GOP majority sent another budget reconciliation bill to the White House, but Clinton vetoed it on December 6, saying that it made the same draconian cuts to Medicare, Medicaid, education, and environmental protection that he had objected to weeks earlier (**See Document 9.10**). Clinton then counteroffered with a budget proposal of his own, but it was quickly dismissed by Gingrich, Dole, and other Republican leaders. The continued stalemate resulted in another government shutdown on December 16. During this second shutdown, polls consistently indicated that the dysfunction in Washington was doing far more damage to the Republican brand than to Clinton. Most Americans, it seemed, reached the conclusion that the GOP's inflexibility and hardball tactics were primarily to blame for the whole mess.

Chastened by growing indications that the government shutdowns loomed as a political fiasco for their party, Republican leaders began genuine negotiations with the White House. On January 6, 1996, the second shutdown ended when the battle-scarred combatants grimly reached a compromise. Clinton agreed to submit a seven-year balanced budget plan scored by the CBO, and Republicans agreed to accept smaller tax cuts and much more modest cuts to Medicare, Medicaid, and other domestic programs than they had previously demanded.

REACHING ACROSS THE POLITICAL DIVIDE

The budget battles of late 1995 and early 1996 took Democrat-Republican relations in Washington to a new nadir. But as 1996, a presidential election year, unfolded, the two camps managed to carve out fragile truces in a number of important policy areas. American health care, and Medicaid in particular, was materially impacted by several of these agreements.

On August 21, 1996, Clinton signed a bipartisan piece of legislation known as the Health Insurance Portability and Accountability ACT (HIPAA) into law. This measure, which came together after months of protracted legislative horse trading **(See Document 9.11)**, protected Americans from losing employer-based health insurance coverage when taking a new job by reducing the capacity of insurers to withhold coverage of new entrants because of preexisting conditions or family medical histories. (The bill, however, did nothing to keep insurers from charging outrageous premiums for that coverage.) The law also included antifraud provisions, new tax deductions for long-term care expenses, funding for a pilot MSA program, and provisions to increase the confidentiality of private medical information. Specifically, HIPAA ordered the Department of Health and Human Services to recommend penalties for wrongful disclosure of personal medical information and new processes for shoring up medical privacy.

One day after putting his signature on HIPAA, Clinton signed a historic welfare reform measure, the 1996 Personal Responsibility and Work Opportunity Reconciliation Act (PRWORA). Bucking liberal members of Congress who defended the old welfare system, Clinton worked with conservative Republicans to pass this legislation. The measure dramatically overhauled the nation's welfare system, replacing the federally based Aid to Families with Dependent Children (ADFC) program with a state-based Temporary Assistance to Needy Families (TANF) system that empowered states to place sweeping new restrictions on welfare eligibility and adjust TANF funding and programs as they saw fit. "As a result," wrote journalist Dan Froomkin, "assistance to the poor, which used to be pretty recognizable anywhere you went in the United States, now differs dramatically from state to state, from county to county, and even from caseworker to caseworker."[30]

PRWORA had a major impact on Medicaid, because Medicaid eligibility had traditionally been closely intertwined with AFDC. Under the new TANF arrangement, people who had previously been eligible for AFDC benefits remained eligible for Medicaid through a newly designated eligibility category known as Section 1931, but the law did not require that TANF-eligible people automatically be enrolled in Medicaid. These provisions made it easier for states to follow the pioneering lead of Oregon and Tennessee and place Medicaid services inside managed care plans (both states launched these ambitious efforts in 1994, before PRWORA was enacted). Finally, the law barred legal aliens who entered the United States on or after August 22, 1996 (the act's signing date), from receiving Medicaid or any other "federal means-tested public benefit" for five years from their date of entry (health and disability benefits for most legal immigrants were eventually restored as part of the 1997 Balanced Budget Act).[31]

In 1997 Clinton, who won reelection in November 1996 by a comfortable margin, and the Republican-controlled Congress made significant changes to both Medicaid and Medicare with a hard-fought budget deal. The 1997 Balanced Budget Act created

Medicare + Choice, also known as Medicare Part C, which greatly increased the role of private managed care organizations in senior health care. This experiment had mixed results. Many observers said that it improved preventive care for seniors and that it became a vital source of prescription drug coverage. But anticipated savings in Medicare costs never materialized, and the program failed to establish itself in rural parts of the country where managed care options were limited. And when Washington tried to reduce Medicare + Choice payments to HMOs and preferred provider organizations (PPOs), many managed care companies decided to reduce or suspend their involvement in the program. It thus became much less of a policy game-changer than either Democrats or Republicans had expected.

Another piece of legislation that had bipartisan support—and was a more evident success—was the State Children's Health Insurance Program (SCHIP), which expanded Medicaid eligibility to millions of children who had previously been uninsured. Established as part of the 1997 Balanced Budget Act, the SCHIP language provided $48 billion, mostly from new cigarette taxes, over a ten-year period to help states craft health insurance programs for the estimated ten million children in America who lacked coverage (See Document 9.12). Within a few years of its passage, nearly four million children, most of them from working poor families, were enrolled in SCHIP programs, and Republicans and Democrats were touting the bill as a stellar example of bipartisan cooperation.

Another bipartisan effort in the realm of health care came after the late 1999 release of a scathing study of U.S. hospitals carried out by the Institute of Medicine (See Document 9.16). The report, which estimated that between forty-four thousand and ninety-eight thousand patients died on an annual basis as a direct result of medical errors in U.S. hospitals, triggered such a swelling of public outrage that Democrats and Republicans set aside their usual squabbling and maneuvering and set to work on new laws and regulations that would improve patient safety.

Still, the bipartisanship that paved the way for SCHIP and a few other advances remained the exception rather than the rule in health care (as well as most other policy sectors) throughout Clinton's second term. Political hostilities between Democrats and Republicans remained at an extremely high level, and "red state" and "blue state" became entrenched in the political lexicon. Few areas of governance seemed untouched by political considerations. As a result, federal action on health care issues ranging from medical privacy to use of the RU486 abortion pill was limited to executive orders or agency-level policy directives that did not require support from the GOP (See Document 9.17 and Document 9.13). Other health policy changes stemmed from the courts, not Capitol Hill. In 1992, for example, the U.S. Supreme Court ruled in *Planned Parenthood of Southeastern Pennsylvania v. Casey* that the fundamental right to abortion stipulated in *Roe v. Wade* still held true. But the Court's opinion in this landmark case also made it easier for individual states to impose their own abortion restrictions, from twenty-four-hour waiting periods to mandatory counseling about adoption and other abortion alternatives.

The paralysis in Washington also hindered parties' efforts to intervene in several instances in which states passed health-related laws to which they objected. The most publicized example of this phenomenon took place when Oregon voters passed a Death with Dignity Act that permitted certain terminally ill individuals to request and receive lethal doses of medication from physicians willing to participate in the program (See Document 9.13). Urged on by the pro-life movement and other constituencies that were staunchly opposed to the law, Republicans repeatedly tried to overturn or otherwise neutralize the Death with Dignity Act, but to no avail.

Historic Tobacco Settlement Brings New Controversies

When SCHIP programs first came online in 1998, they received a big financial boost from the tobacco industry, of all places. This funding stemmed from a decision by Mississippi attorney general Mike Moore in May 1994 to file suit against Big Tobacco for the recovery of financial losses incurred by his state in treating lung cancer and other smoking-relating health problems of Medicaid enrollees. Moore's action came at a time when the Food and Drug Administration was already assessing its powers to regulate tobacco. Given the uncertainty about the outcome of that investigation, Moore took matters into his own hands with a lawsuit based on the state's financial injuries from smoking activity. "Because the state was the injured party under Moore's legal theory," explained an Institute of Medicine report, "he bypassed the industry's customary defense in suits filed by smokers that the smokers were responsible for their own injuries."[32] In moving against the tobacco industry, Moore also emphasized that the scale of the public health problems related to smoking was exacerbated by decades of deceit from tobacco companies related to the health risks associated with their products. "The lawsuit is premised on a simple notion," said Moore. "You caused the health crisis, you pay for it."[33]

Dozens of states followed Mississippi's lead, and forty-six states ultimately banded together in the legal fight against Big Tobacco (four states—Florida, Minnesota, Mississippi, and Texas—ultimately reached a separate settlement worth $40 billion). Initially, the cigarette makers adopted an unyielding stance. But when secret corporate documents that showed industry knowledge of smoking's health impact and a clear effort to attract underage customers were uncovered, the industry took a seat at the bargaining table. A tentative 1997 settlement fell apart in Congress, but this setback merely convinced the states to make an agreement that would not require congressional approval.

In November 1998, after four years of legal jousting, the nation's four major cigarette makers—Philip Morris, R. J. Reynolds, Brown & Williamson, and Lorillard—and the tobacco industry's trade associations and public relations agencies reached a settlement with the states **(See Document 9.15)**. This accord, dubbed the Tobacco Master Settlement

In early 1998, a settlement was reached between the state of Texas and the tobacco industry in a lawsuit over smoking-related health care costs. Texas attorney general Dan Morales holds up a "check" for $15.32 billion—the amount that tobacco companies agreed to pay the state over the next twenty-five years.

Agreement (MSA), placed major restrictions on tobacco advertising. It also required the tobacco industry to pay the states approximately $206 billion through the year 2025 to help them cover medical treatment for smoking-related illnesses and invest in antismoking initiatives targeted at young people and other health programs. In return, the agreement settled all lawsuits filed against the tobacco industry to that time, but it did not give the industry immunity from future lawsuits.

Numerous antismoking and health treatment programs were launched with tobacco settlement funds by the early 2000s. In addition, several states used the infusion of tobacco industry money to dramatically expand health insurance programs for residents. A number of traditionally progressive-minded states, such as Minnesota and Vermont, even managed to attain near-universal health care coverage.[34] Several states helmed by Republicans also used the settlement to expand their health insurance programs. New Jersey governor Christine Todd Whitman, for example, launched a highly successful FamilyCare health coverage program for low-income adults and children that received much of its funding from the state's share of tobacco settlement funds.

Programs paid for by tobacco settlement funds have been credited as an important factor in reducing rates of teen and adult smoking across much of America. Since the MSA's earliest days, however, the settlement has proven controversial on several scores. In the immediate aftermath of the MSA announcement, some critics asserted that the tobacco industry "got off easy," given the grim impact that their products have had on millions of American families over the decades. More recently, doctors, scientists, antismoking activists, and other public health advocates have expressed anger and disappointment with state legislatures that have gradually diverted ever-greater percentages of their tobacco settlement funds away from antismoking initiatives and other public health programs. These monies have increasingly gone to pay for other state programs unrelated to public health or to plug budgetary shortfalls. In 2010 a coalition of the nation's leading public health organizations reported that, for fiscal year 2011, states were expected to allocate only 2 percent of their revenue from tobacco settlement funds and tobacco taxes on programs to prevent smoking and help smokers quit. The report also found that only two states—Alaska and North Dakota—funded tobacco prevention programs at Centers for Disease Control and Prevention–recommended levels. Only five other states provided even half the recommended funding, while thirty-three states and the District of Columbia provided less than a quarter. Finally, three states—Nevada, New Hampshire, and Ohio—provided no state funds for tobacco prevention in 2010.[35]

Notes

1. Laura Summer and Isaac Shapiro, *Trends in Health Insurance Coverage, 1987 to 1993* (Washington, DC: Center on Budget and Policy Priorities, 1994), 4–6.

2. Theda Skocpal, *Boomerang: Clinton's Health Security Effort and the Turn against Government in U.S. Politics* (New York: Norton, 1996), 28.

3. Jill Quadagno, *One Nation Uninsured: Why the U.S. Has No National Health Insurance* (New York: Oxford University Press, 2005), 185.

4. Quoted in Skocpal, *Boomerang,* 45–46.

5. Paul Starr, *The Logic of Health Care Reform* (New York: Whittle/Penguin, 1994), xxix.

6. Hillary Rodham Clinton, *Living History* (New York: Simon and Schuster, 2003), 154.

7. Skocpol, *Boomerang,* 133–34.

8. Quoted in Darrell M. West and Burdette Loomis, *The Sound of Money: How Political Interests Get What They Want* (New York: W. W. Norton, 1999), 79.

9. Haynes Johnson and David S. Broder, *The System: The American Way of Politics at the Breaking Point* (Boston: Little, Brown, 1996), 183.

10. Skocpol, *Boomerang,* 142–43.

11. Quoted in Johnson and Broder, *The System,* 232.

12. Quoted in Johnson and Broder, *The System,* 191.

13. William J. Clinton, State of the Union Address, January 25, 1994, *Public Papers of the Presidents of the United States: William J. Clinton, 1994,* Vol. 1 (Washington, DC: Government Printing Office, 1995), 131.

14. Marc J. Hetherington, *Why Trust Matters: Declining Political Trust and the Demise of American Liberalism* (Princeton, NJ: Princeton University Press, 2005), 121.

15. William Schneider, "Why Health-Care Reform May Be Beyond Saving," *Los Angeles Times,* August 14, 1994, M1, M6.

16. Nicholas Laham, *A Lost Cause: Bill Clinton's Campaign for National Health Insurance* (Westport, CT: Praeger, 1996), 96.

17. James Fallows, "A Triumph of Misinformation," *The Atlantic,* January 1995, 26–37.

18. Quoted in Johnson and Broder, *The System,* 229.

19. Laham, *A Lost Cause,* 142.

20. Quoted in Johnson and Broder, *The System,* 230.

21. Johnson and Broder, *The System,* 634–35.

22. Steven Findlay, "Piecing Together the Plan: Congress Faces Some Tough Questions as It Puzzles over Six Plans," *Business and Health,* March 1994.

23. Quoted in Johnson and Broder, *The System,* 429.

24. Lisa Belkin, "The Ellwoods: But What about Quality?" *New York Times Magazine,* December 8, 1996, 68.

25. Quoted in George Anders, *Health against Wealth: HMOs and the Breakdown of Medical Trust* (Boston: Houghton Mifflin, 1996), 193.

26. Quoted in Jamie Court and Francis Smith, *Making a Killing: HMOs and the Threat to Your Health* (New York: Common Courage Press, 1999), 8.

27. Carol S. Weissert and William G. Wiessert, *Governing Health: The Politics of Health Policy,* 3rd ed. (Baltimore: Johns Hopkins University Press, 2006), 280.

28. Johnson and Broder, *The System,* 591.

29. Anders, *Health against Wealth,* 193.

30. Dan Froomkin, "Welfare's Changing Face," *Washington Post,* July 23, 1998, www.washingtonpost .com/wp-srv/politics/special/welfare/welfare.htm.

31. Julie Rovner, "Medicaid," *Health Care Policy and Politics A to Z,* 3rd ed. (Washington, DC: CQ Press, 2009), 133.

32. Institute of Medicine, *Ending the Tobacco Problem: A Blueprint for the Nation* (Washington, DC: National Academy Press, 2007), 122.

33. Quoted in Michael Janofsky, "Mississippi Seeks Damages from Tobacco Companies," *New York Times,* May 24, 1994, A12.

34. Jonathan Cohn, *Sick: The Untold Story of America's Health Care Crisis—and the People Who Pay the Price* (New York: HarperCollins, 2007), 133.

35. Campaign for Tobacco-Free Kids, *A Broken Promise to Our Children: The 1998 State Tobacco Settlement 12 Years Later* (Washington, DC: Campaign for Tobacco-Free Kids, American Heart Association, American Cancer Society Cancer Action Network, American Lung Association, and Robert Wood Johnson Foundation, November 17, 2010), www.rwjf.org/files/research/tobacco reportnovember2010.pdf.

Harris Wofford Rides Health Care to a Stunning Political Upset

"Maybe Pols Weren't Talking about It, but People Were"

1991

In November 1991 a special election was held in Pennsylvania to fill the seat of Democratic U.S. senator John Heinz, who had been killed in an April airplane crash. The Democratic candidate was Harris Wofford, who had been appointed by Pennsylvania governor Robert P. Casey to temporarily fill the seat after Heinz's death. He was opposed by Republican Dick Thornburgh, a popular former Pennsylvania governor who had also served as attorney general in the administrations of Ronald Reagan and George H. W. Bush.

For much of the campaign, Thornburgh looked as if he would cruise to victory. Polls consistently showed him far outpacing his Democratic opponent, in some polls by as much as forty points. In September, Wofford, with guidance from his chief political strategists Paul Begala and James Carville, began emphasizing health care issues in campaign speeches, debate appearances, and television ads. This new message was aptly symbolized in a September 6 Wofford-Thornburgh debate in which the Democrat held up a pocket copy of the U.S. Constitution and declared that "if the Constitution guarantees criminals the right to a lawyer, shouldn't it guarantee working Americans their right to a doctor as well?"

The shift in strategy struck a nerve with Pennsylvania citizens, who were clearly anxious about spiraling health care costs and diminishing access to quality health insurance. At first the Wofford campaign wondered if its improved poll results were a mirage, because health care reform had been a largely dormant issue on the national stage over the previous few years. But it soon became clear that health care remained an issue of deep resonance with voters, so as the campaign entered its final weeks the Wofford camp made national health insurance the centerpiece of its campaign. As Carville later stated, "reporters are like children in a school cafeteria. If you want them to eat spinach, don't put anything else on their plates."[1]

On election day, November 5, Wofford handily defeated Thornburgh, winning 55 percent of the vote. Health care's pivotal role in the upset victory did not escape the notice of Washington, D.C., which was suddenly deluged with new health care reform proposals. The Pennsylvania election also caught the eye of Arkansas governor Bill Clinton, who had decided to seek the Democrats' 1992 presidential nomination. Clinton added Begala and Carville to his campaign team, and within a matter of weeks the two political strategists made health care reform a central pillar of the governor's run for the presidency.

The following postelection analysis from the Philadelphia Daily News *summarizes how Wofford rode the health care issue to victory in Pennsylvania. (It subsequently published a correction acknowledging that Wofford did in fact mention health care in his June 1 Democratic Party nomination acceptance speech.)*

During Harris Wofford's 4 1/2 years as state labor secretary, he saw health care costs at the root of most labor disputes. What he didn't see was health care as his ticket to the U.S. Senate.

Most post-election noodlers and many pre-election polls say Wofford's call for national health insurance is the main reason he won.

It's an issue whose potency surprised observers and put Republicans on their heels. It seemed to come from nowhere.

When Wofford was named to succeed the late John Heinz on May 8, he never mentioned health care in his speech thanking Gov. Casey.

When he accepted the Democratic nomination for the post on June 1, he still didn't mention it. He said he'd run a campaign on "jobs and the economy." And when Wofford gave a far-ranging, hour-long interview in August, he said not one word about health insurance.

But on Sept. 9, there it was. Wofford's first TV campaign ad said criminals have a right to a lawyer but "millions of Americans aren't able to see a doctor . . . That's why I'm fighting for national health insurance."

Wofford's pollster, Dave Petts, found the issue was hot across Pennsylvania. Maybe pols [sic] weren't talking about it, but people were. And even when told the arguments against national health insurance—higher taxes, not being able to choose a doctor, a new government bureaucracy—they still wanted it.

"It was off the chart," said Wofford campaign manager Paul Begala.

Also, it had a life of its own, and carried a sort of political inoculation.

When Thornburgh fought back, correctly saying Wofford had no specific plan for health insurance, it didn't seem to matter. When Thornburgh charged the idea was "experimental" and "too costly," it sounded as if he didn't care about people.

That's what ongoing polls showed, so Wofford kept hammering the issue. He visited hospitals in every media market. He put up a second, then a third TV ad on health care. By the end of the race, every Wofford statement and TV ad mentioned health insurance—and that Thornburgh was against it.

When Thornburgh conceded last Tuesday night, he said, "Concerns and anxiety about the costs and coverage of health care obviously commanded much greater attention in this campaign than we anticipated."

The stunning success of health care as an issue was not lost on Republican Arlen Specter, who is up for re-election next year.

A day after Wofford's win, Specter joined with other Senate Republicans to introduce their own health care plan. The plan includes changes in the tax codes for small businesses and for individuals who are working but don't have health insurance.

Ironically, according to a Thornburgh confidant, Thornburgh himself raised the issue last summer. He told a pre-campaign gathering of aides that he and Republicans are "vulnerable" on health care, said the source, who added, "We all looked at him like he was crazy. I mean, we thought, who cares about health care?"

Also, ironically, Wofford never has laid out specific legislation to create national health insurance. His campaign first argued that the debate was about whether to have it or not, not its specific form.

Later, on Oct. 18, Wofford released a nine-page "practical plan for universal coverage."

But it's much more a general plan than specific. It calls for things like "reform" of health insurance practices; "a single, standard claims form" to cut administrative costs; "creation of a body" to oversee health-care costs; and a new, non-profit corporation to "deal directly with insurance companies and maximize economies of scale and minimize duplication, waste and red tape."

The "plan" concludes by saying national health care insurance is "a fundamental human right, not a privilege."

Source: Baer, John M. "Issue That Kept Wofford Healthy." *Philadelphia Daily News,* November 12, 1991, p. 5 (local). Used with permission.

NOTE

1. Quoted in "Campaign for United States Senate (1991)," *The Dick Thornburgh Papers,* University of Pittsburgh, www.library.pitt.edu/thornburgh/collection/series14.html.

DOCUMENT
9.2

Clinton Unveils His Health Care Plan to Congress

"With This Card, If You Lose Your Job or You Switch Jobs, You're Covered"

1993

On September 22, 1993, President Bill Clinton formally introduced his administration's plan for health care reform to a joint session of Congress and a national television audience. His address, excerpted here, emphasized the purported benefits of the White House proposal as well as the myriad problems afflicting the nation's current health care system.

My fellow Americans, tonight we come together to write a new chapter in the American story. Our forebears enshrined the American dream: life, liberty, the pursuit of happiness. Every generation of Americans has worked to strengthen that legacy, to make our country a place of freedom and opportunity, a place where people who work hard can rise to their full potential, a place where their children can have a better future.

From the settling of the frontier to the landing on the Moon, ours has been a continuous story of challenges defined, obstacles overcome, new horizons secured. That is what makes America what it is and Americans what we are. Now we are in a time of profound change and opportunity. The end of the cold war, the information age, the global economy have brought us both opportunity and hope and strife and uncertainty. Our purpose in this dynamic age must be to make change our friend and not our enemy.

To achieve that goal, we must face all our challenges with confidence, with faith, and with discipline, whether we're reducing the deficit, creating tomorrow's jobs and training our people to fill them, converting from a high-tech defense to a high-tech domestic economy, expanding trade, reinventing Government, making our streets safer, or rewarding work over idleness. All these challenges require us to change.

If Americans are to have the courage to change in a difficult time, we must first be secure in our most basic needs. Tonight I want to talk to you about the most critical thing we can do to build that security. This health care system of ours is badly broken, and it is time to fix it. Despite the dedication of literally millions of talented health care professionals, our health care is too uncertain and too expensive, too bureaucratic and too wasteful. It has too much fraud and too much greed.

At long last, after decades of false starts, we must make this our most urgent priority, giving every American health security, health care that can never be taken away, health care that is always there. That is what we must do tonight. . . .

So tonight I want to talk to you about the principles that I believe must embody our efforts to reform America's health care system: security, simplicity, savings, choice, quality, and responsibility.

When I launched our Nation on this journey to reform the health care system I knew we needed a talented navigator, someone with a rigorous mind, a steady compass, a caring heart. Luckily for me and for our Nation, I didn't have to look very far.

[At this point, audience members applauded Hillary Clinton, and she acknowledged them.]

Over the last 8 months, Hillary and those working with her have talked to literally thousands of Americans to understand the strengths and the frailties of this system of ours. They met with over 1,100 health care organizations. They talked with doctors and nurses, pharmacists and drug company representatives, hospital administrators, insurance company executives, and small and large businesses. They spoke with self-employed people. They talked with people who had insurance and people who didn't. They talked with union members and older Americans and advocates for our children. The First Lady also consulted, as all of you know, extensively with governmental leaders in both parties in the States of our Nation and especially here on Capitol Hill. Hillary and the task force received and read over 700,000 letters from ordinary citizens. What they wrote and the bravery with which they told their stories is really what calls us all here tonight.

Every one of us knows someone who's worked hard and played by the rules and still been hurt by this system that just doesn't work for too many people. But I'd like to tell you about just one. Kerry Kennedy owns a small furniture store that employs seven people in Titusville, Florida. Like most small business owners, he's poured his heart and soul, his sweat and blood into that business for years. But over the last several years, again like most small business owners, he's seen his health care premiums skyrocket, even in years when no claims were made. And last year, he painfully discovered he could no longer afford to provide coverage for all his workers because his insurance company told him that two of his workers had become high risks because of their advanced age. The problem was that those two people were his mother and father, the people who founded the business and still work in the store.

This story speaks for millions of others. And from them we have learned a powerful truth. We have to preserve and strengthen what is right with the health care system, but we have got to fix what is wrong with it. . . .

Millions of Americans are just a pink slip away from losing their health insurance and one serious illness away from losing all their savings. Millions more are locked into the jobs they have now just because they or someone in their family has once been sick and they have what is called the preexisting condition. And on any given day, over 37 million Americans, most of them working people and their little children, have no health insurance at all.

And in spite of all this, our medical bills are growing at over twice the rate of inflation, and the United States spends over a third more of its income on health care than any other nation on Earth. And the gap is growing, causing many of our companies in global competition severe disadvantage. There is no excuse for this kind of system. We know other people have done better. We know people in our own country are doing better. We have no excuse. My fellow Americans, we must fix this system, and it has to begin with congressional action.

I believe as strongly as I can say that we can reform the costliest and most wasteful system on the face of the Earth without enacting new broad-based taxes. I believe it because of the conversations I have had with thousands of health care professionals around the country, with people who are outside this city but are inside experts on the way this system works and wastes money. . . .

I want to say to all of you I have been deeply moved by the spirit of this debate, by the openness of all people to new ideas and argument and information. . . .

. . . Both [Democrats and Republicans], I think, understand the literal ethical imperative of doing something about the system we have now. Rising above these difficulties and our past differences to solve this problem will go a long way toward defining who we are and who we intend to be as a people in this difficult and challenging era. I believe we all understand that. And so tonight, let me ask all of you, every Member of the House, every Member of the Senate, each Republican and each Democrat, let us keep this spirit and let us keep this commitment until this job is done. We owe it to the American people. [Applause] . . .

Now, if I might, I would like to review the six principles I mentioned earlier and describe how we think we can best fulfill those principles.

First and most important, security. This principle speaks to the human misery, to the costs, to the anxiety we hear about every day, all of us, when people talk about their problems with the present system. Security means that those who do not now have health care coverage will have it, and for those who have it, it will never be taken away. We must achieve that security as soon as possible.

Under our plan, every American would receive a health care security card that will guarantee a comprehensive package of benefits over the course of an entire lifetime, roughly comparable to the benefit package offered by most Fortune 500 companies. This health care security card will offer this package of benefits in a way that can never be taken away. So let us agree on this: Whatever else we disagree on, before this Congress finishes its work next year, you will pass and I will sign legislation to guarantee this security to every citizen of this country.

With this card, if you lose your job or you switch jobs, you're covered. If you leave your job to start a small business, you're covered. If you're an early retiree, you're covered. If someone in your family has unfortunately had an illness that qualifies as a preexisting condition, you're still covered. If you get sick or a member of your family gets sick, even if it's a life-threatening illness, you're covered. And if an insurance company tries to drop you for any reason, you will still be covered, because that will be illegal. This card will give comprehensive coverage. It will cover people for hospital care, doctor visits, emergency and lab services, diagnostic services like Pap smears and mammograms and cholesterol tests, substance abuse, and mental health treatment.

And equally important, for both health care and economic reasons, this program for the first time would provide a broad range of preventive services including regular checkups and wellbaby visits. Now, it's just common sense. We know, any family doctor will tell you, that people will stay healthier and long-term costs of the health system will be lower if we have comprehensive preventive services. . . .

Health care security must also apply to older Americans. This is something I imagine all of us in this room feel very deeply about. The first thing I want to say about that is that we must maintain the Medicare program. It works to provide that kind of security. But this time and for the first time, I believe Medicare should provide coverage for the cost of prescription drugs.

Yes, it will cost some more in the beginning. But again, any physician who deals with the elderly will tell you that there are thousands of elderly people in every State who are not poor enough to be on Medicaid but just above that line and on Medicare, who desperately need medicine, who make decisions every week between medicine and food. Any doctor who deals with the elderly will tell you that there are many elderly people who don't get medicine, who get sicker and sicker and eventually go to the doctor and wind up spending more money and draining more money from the health care system than they would if they had regular treatment in the way that only adequate medicine can provide.

I also believe that over time, we should phase in long-term care for the disabled and the elderly on a comprehensive basis. As we proceed with this health care reform, we cannot forget that the most rapidly growing percentage of Americans are those over 80. We cannot break faith with them. We have to do better by them.

The second principle is simplicity. Our health care system must be simpler for the patients and simpler for those who actually deliver health care: our doctors, our nurses, our other medical professionals. Today we have more than 1,500 insurers, with hundreds and hundreds of different forms. No other nation has a system like this. These forms are time consuming for health care providers. They're expensive for health care consumers. They're exasperating for anyone who's ever tried to sit down around a table and wade through them and figure them out.

The medical care industry is literally drowning in paperwork. In recent years, the number of administrators in our hospitals has grown by 4 times the rate that the number of doctors has grown. A hospital ought to be a house of healing, not a monument to paperwork and bureaucracy. . . .

. . . I think we can save money in this system if we simplify it. And we can make the doctors and the nurses and the people that are giving their lives to help us all be healthier a whole lot happier, too, on their jobs.

Under our proposal there would be one standard insurance form, not hundreds of them. We will simplify also—and we must—the Government's rules and regulations, because they are a big part of this problem. This is one of those cases where the physician should heal thyself. We have to reinvent the way we relate to the health care system, along with reinventing Government. A doctor should not have to check with a bureaucrat in an office thousands of miles away before ordering a simple blood test. That's not right, and we can change it. And doctors, nurses, and consumers shouldn't have to worry about the fine print. If we have this one simple form, there won't be any fine print. People will know what it means.

The third principle is savings. Reform must produce savings in this health care system. It has to. We're spending over 14 percent of our income on health care. Canada's at 10. Nobody else is over 9. We're competing with all these people for the future. And the other major countries, they cover everybody, and they cover them with services as generous as the best company policies here in this country.

Rampant medical inflation is eating away at our wages, our savings, our investment capital, our ability to create new jobs in the private sector, and this public Treasury. You know the budget we just adopted had steep cuts in defense, a 5-year freeze on the discretionary spending, so critical to reeducating America and investing in jobs and helping us to convert from a defense to a domestic economy. But we passed a budget which has

Medicaid increases of between 16 and 11 percent a year over the next 5 years and Medicare increases of between 11 and 9 percent in an environment where we assume inflation will be at 4 percent or less. We cannot continue to do this. Our competitiveness, our whole economy, the integrity of the way the Government works, and ultimately, our living standards depend upon our ability to achieve savings without harming the quality of health care.

Unless we do this, our workers will lose $655 in income each year by the end of the decade. Small businesses will continue to face skyrocketing premiums. And a full third of small businesses now covering their employees say they will be forced to drop their insurance. Large corporations will bear bigger disadvantages in global competition. And health care costs will devour more and more and more of our budget. . . .

So how will we achieve these savings? Rather than looking at price control or looking away as the price spiral continues, rather than using the heavy hand of Government to try to control what's happening or continuing to ignore what's happening, we believe there is a third way to achieve these savings. First, to give groups of consumers and small businesses the same market bargaining power that large corporations and large groups of public employees now have, we want to let market forces enable plans to compete. We want to force these plans to compete on the basis of price and quality, not simply to allow them to continue making money by turning people away who are sick or old or performing mountains of unnecessary procedures. But we also believe we should back this system up with limits on how much plans can raise their premiums year-in and year-out, forcing people, again, to continue to pay more for the same health care, without regard to inflation or the rising population needs.

We want to create what has been missing in this system for too long and what every successful nation who has dealt with this problem has already had to do: to have a combination of private market forces and a sound public policy that will support that competition, but limit the rate at which prices can exceed the rate of inflation and population growth, if the competition doesn't work, especially in the early going.

The second thing I want to say is that unless everybody is covered—and this is a very important thing—unless everybody is covered, we will never be able to fully put the brakes on health care inflation. Why is that? Because when people don't have any health insurance, they still get health care, but they get it when it's too late, when it's too expensive, often from the most expensive place of all, the emergency room. Usually by the time they show up, their illnesses are more severe, and their mortality rates are much higher in our hospitals than those who have insurance. So they cost us more. And what else happens? Since they get the care but they don't pay, who does pay? All the rest of us.

We pay in higher hospital bills and higher insurance premiums. This cost shifting is a major problem.

The third thing we can do to save money is simply by simplifying the system, what we've already discussed. Freeing the health care providers from these costly and unnecessary paperwork and administrative decisions will save tens of billions of dollars. We spend twice as much as any other major country does on paperwork. . . .

We also have to crack down on fraud and abuse in the system. That drains billions of dollars a year. It is a very large figure, according to every health care expert I've ever spoken with. So I believe we can achieve large savings. And that large savings can be used to cover the unemployed uninsured and will be used for people who realize those savings in the private sector to increase their ability to invest and grow, to hire new workers or to give their workers pay raises, many of them for the first time in years. . . .

The fourth principle is choice. Americans believe they ought to be able to choose their own health care plan and keep their own doctors. And I think all of us agree. Under any plan we pass, they ought to have that right. But today, under our broken health care system, in spite of the rhetoric of choice, the fact is that that power is slipping away for more and more Americans. . . .

We propose to give every American a choice among high quality plans. You can stay with your current doctor, join a network of doctors and hospitals, or join a health maintenance organization. If you don't like your plan, every year you'll have the chance to choose a new one. The choice will be left to the American citizen, the worker, not the boss and certainly not some Government bureaucrat.

We also believe that doctors should have a choice as to what plans they practice in. Otherwise, citizens may have their own choices limited. . . .

The fifth principle is quality. If we reformed everything else in health care but failed to preserve and enhance the high quality of our medical care, we will have taken a step backward, not forward. Quality is something that we simply can't leave to chance. . . .

Our proposal will create report cards on health plans, so that consumers can choose the highest quality health care providers and reward them with their business. At the same time, our plan will track quality indicators, so that doctors can make better and smarter choices of the kind of care they provide. We have evidence that more efficient delivery of health care doesn't decrease quality. In fact, it may enhance it.

Let me just give you one example of one commonly performed procedure, the coronary bypass operation. Pennsylvania discovered that patients who were charged $21,000 for this surgery received as good or better care as patients who were charged $84,000 for the same procedure in the same State. High prices simply don't always equal good quality. . . .

The sixth and final principle is responsibility. We need to restore a sense that we're all in this together and that we all have a responsibility to be a part of the solution. Responsibility has to start with those who profit from the current system. Responsibility means insurance companies should no longer be allowed to cast people aside when they get sick. It should apply to laboratories that submit fraudulent bills, to lawyers who abuse malpractice claims, to doctors who order unnecessary procedures. It means drug companies should no longer charge 3 times more per prescription drugs, made in America here in the United States, than they charge for the same drugs overseas.

In short, responsibility should apply to anybody who abuses this system and drives up the cost for honest, hard-working citizens and undermines confidence in the honest, gifted health care providers we have. Responsibility also means changing some behaviors in this country that drive up our costs like crazy. And without changing it we'll never have the system we ought to have, we will never. . . .

. . . If we're going to produce a better health care system for every one of us, every one of us is going to have to do our part. There cannot be any such thing as a free ride. We have to pay for it. We have to pay for it.

Tonight I want to say plainly how I think we should do that. Most of the money will come, under my way of thinking, as it does today, from premiums paid by employers and individuals. That's the way it happens today. But under this health care security plan, every employer and every individual will be asked to contribute something to health care.

This concept was first conveyed to the Congress about 20 years ago by President Nixon.

And today, a lot of people agree with the concept of shared responsibility between employers and employees and that the best thing to do is to ask every employer and every employee to share that. The Chamber of Commerce has said that, and they're not in the business of hurting small business. The American Medical Association has said that.

Some call it an employer mandate, but I think it's the fairest way to achieve responsibility in the health care system. And it's the easiest for ordinary Americans to understand because it builds on what we already have and what already works for so many Americans. It is the reform that is not only easiest to understand but easiest to implement in a way that is fair to small business, because we can give a discount to help struggling small businesses meet the cost of covering their employees. . . .

. . . And we will impose new taxes on tobacco. I don't think that should be the only source of revenues. I believe we should also ask for a modest contribution from big employers who opt out of the system to make up for what those who are in the system pay for medical research, for health education centers, for all the subsidies to small business, for all the things that everyone else is contributing to. But between those two things, we believe we can pay for this package of benefits and universal coverage and a subsidy program that will help small business. . . .

Over the long run, we can all win. But some will have to pay more in the short run. Nevertheless, the vast majority of the Americans watching this tonight will pay the same or less for health care coverage that will be the same or better than the coverage they have tonight. That is the central reality.

If you currently get your health insurance through your job, under our plan you still will. And for the first time, everybody will get to choose from among at least three plans to belong to. If you're a small business owner who wants to provide health insurance to your family and your employees, but you can't afford it because the system is stacked against you, this plan will give you a discount that will finally make insurance affordable. If you're already providing insurance, your rates may well drop because we'll help you as a small business person join thousands of others to get the same benefits big corporations get at the same price they get those benefits. If you're self-employed, you'll pay less, and you will get to deduct from your taxes 100 percent of your health care premiums. If you're a large employer, your health care costs won't go up as fast, so that you will have more money to put into higher wages and new jobs and to put into the work of being competitive in this tough global economy. . . .

Over the coming months, you'll be bombarded with information from all kinds of sources. There will be some who will stoutly disagree with what I have proposed and with all other plans in the Congress, for that matter. And some of the arguments will be genuinely sincere and enlightening. Others may simply be scare tactics by those who are motivated by the self-interest they have in the waste the system now generates, because that waste is providing jobs, incomes, and money for some people. I ask you only to think of this when you hear all of these arguments: Ask yourself whether the cost of staying on this same course isn't greater than the cost of change. And ask yourself, when you hear the arguments, whether the arguments are in your interest or someone else's. This is something we have got to try to do together. . . .

I ask you to remember the kind of people I met over the last year and a half: the elderly couple in New Hampshire that broke down and cried because of their shame at having an empty refrigerator to pay for their drugs; a woman who lost a $50,000 job that she used to support her six children because her youngest child was so ill that she couldn't keep health insurance, and the only way to get care for the child was to get public assistance;

a young couple that had a sick child and could only get insurance from one of the parents' employers that was a nonprofit corporation with 20 employees, and so they had to face the question of whether to let this poor person with a sick child go or raise the premiums of every employee in the firm by $200; and on and on and on. . . .

Our history and our heritage tell us that we can meet this challenge. Everything about America's past tells us we will do it. So I say to you, let us write that new chapter in the American story. Let us guarantee every American comprehensive health benefits that can never be taken away. . . .

Source: Clinton, Bill. Address to a Joint Session of Congress on Health Care Reform, September 22, 1993. *Public Papers of the Presidents of the United States: William J. Clinton, 1993.* Vol. 2. Washington, DC: Government Printing Office, 1994, pp. 1556–1565.

DOCUMENT
9.3

Hillary Rodham Clinton Testifies in Support of Health Care Reform

"To Move This Health Care System to a Much More Efficient Level"

1993

In the days following first lady Hillary Rodham Clinton's September 1993 appearances on Capitol Hill, lawmakers and pundits of varying political persuasions agreed that her testimony in support of the administration's Health Security Act had been a tour de force. Bowled over by Clinton's poise and her clear command of the intricacies of health care policymaking, the New York Times *Week in Review declared that the first lady's "impressive testimony" had single-handedly raised hopes that "an issue that had stymied Congress for 50 years was now near solution."[1]*

Supporters of the act made no effort to hide their delight with Clinton's testimony. After she concluded a September 29 appearance before the Senate Committee on Labor and Human Resources, for example, Chairman Edward M. Kennedy (D-MA) offered a note of "personal congratulations" to the first lady and her husband for the "bipartisan momentum" for reform they had created. "Obviously, there will be adjustments and changes as the legislation moves along," stated Kennedy, "but I dare say that this has been really a perfect launch."[2]

The following is an excerpt from Clinton's triumphant appearance before Kennedy's committee. In this exchange, Clinton addresses concerns raised about the administration's plan by Daniel R. Coats, a conservative Republican from Indiana.

Senator Coats: Mrs. Clinton, thank you for appearing before us. I hope I am not the first dark cloud to appear on the horizon today for you. I hope what I say is not interpreted as being partisan politics because I do agree with every member on this committee and with you that there are inefficiencies and distortions in our health care system that are robbing people of care that they need. It is costing all of us more money than we ought to spend.

I think we all agree that reforms are needed and necessary. The question is not whether, but how we go about doing it.

I have joined some Senators in offering a proposal to deal with those reforms that is different than what you are advocating. It is primarily different because it is based on some different assumptions. I would like to just outline four of those assumptions and then ask the question as to whether or not you think those assumptions are valid or invalid and, if invalid, why and how we might address that.

The first assumption that we are operating under is that government, for all its good intentions, is less efficient than the private sector. My experience with government and my constituents' experience with government is that because it is not driven by a market system and does not have a profit motive, it is less efficient. I think anybody who stands 5 minutes in a post office and then goes and visits UPS sees the difference between a government-run operation and a private-run operation, if we look at the State level.

I just, in the last 2 days, have gone through the process of helping my 16-year-old son attain a driver's license. It has been a nightmare for my wife and I to go through the lines and the forms and delays just to get a driver's license.

The second assumption that we are operating under is that the political process often, almost always, overwhelms the marketplace. Outside my office every day that we are in session, there is a steady stream of people coming to try to influence the political process saying, include our program, include our benefits. Whether it is health care or any other aspect of what government does, it seems that the ultimate decision is not a marketplace decision, but a political decision.

Therefore, we are concerned that a health plan which basically says these are the benefits that will be available will simply invite many more saying, include us. Whether it makes economic sense or not, they will try to garner enough support from the political process to be included.

Third, it is my experience and our assumption that costs that government estimates for the costs of a program are always grossly, grossly underestimated. I went back and looked at the Congressional Record for when we enacted Medicare and the projections that were listed by Congress for expenditures under just Part A of Medicare for 19—they rose those out to 1990. They said by 1990, we would be spending $9 billion a year on Part A Medicare. The actual expenditure in 1990 was $67 billion, 7 ½ times the estimate.

So, we may estimate figures here today as associated with this health care plan. My experience is, like every other program government gets involved in, it grows partly because of this political process and the inefficiencies; it grows far beyond our estimates.

Our final assumption is that a great deal of health care expenditure is, as your husband pointed out in his speech to the Congress, caused by human behavior, choices that we as human beings make. Now, I appreciate your husband saying we must do much better than this, but my experience is that human beings react to incentives, positively to rewards and negatively to penalties.

It seems to me that any health care plan that is truly going to modify human behavior, and therefore help hold down health care costs, whether it is smoking, excessive drinking, unwarranted sexual practices that lead to disease, on and on, lack of exercise, overeating, et cetera—if we are going to affect that, we need a system of rewards or a system of penalties.

Why should someone who exercises behavior that results in lower health care costs be paying the same thing as someone who is disregarding that? Why shouldn't there be a differential?

Those are some basic assumptions on which we are basing our plan. I do not think I see those assumptions in your plan. Are my assumptions valid? If not, why are they invalid? How are we going to reconcile the differences? . . .

Mrs. Clinton: Let me start by stating that I do not know that any of your assumptions in general are wrong, but in particular, as applied to the health care system, I do not believe they are applicable. Let me run through them. In fact, what we are trying to do is create a system in which there truly is some kind of a market and some kind of competitive pressures that will enable us to move this health care system to a much more efficient level than it currently is operating on.

Your first assumption about government being less efficient than the private sector is not true in the health care system, as it is currently structured. I think that one of the Senators earlier referred to the fact that the administrative costs in Medicare are much less than they are in the private sector. The private sector has become much less efficient in health care delivery and health care pricing than you would think it should be, but it has done so because of the kinds of incentives currently in the market.

So, for example, the heavy administrative percentage that you will find in the private sector insurance market is due to a very clear decision, which is the more money we can spend making sure we do not insure people who might cost us money, the more money we will make. So, therefore, the kind of underwriting practices and the kind of selling practices that are aimed at insuring people are aimed in part at eliminating from coverage people who might be a cost on the insurance system. For example, it takes a lot of time, manpower, and resources to choose among everyone sitting in this room who is and who is not a good risk.

If you look at the way the current private sector operates, you will find an enormous amount of inefficiency, as Dr. [C. Everett] Koop has pointed out, not only on the insurance side, but on the medical decisionmaking side. Now, part of that is driven by decisions that are made in government as well as in the private sector. Government followed the private sector in deciding to reimburse for medical care based on procedure and on tests and on diagnosis, on the kind of fee-for-service model that we have grown up with in our country.

So in both the private sector and the government sector, with respect to health care, we do not have a real market. You will find a great deal of inefficiency in the private sector in the health care market.

Someone has pointed out recently that many of our industries have had to become more efficient in the last 20 years because of external competition. We are now producing high-quality cars in our country that are very productive and are really giving a good run for the money against our competitors. It took outside competition to come in and do that. We have to create a competitive marketplace. We do not currently have one.

The second point about the political process overwhelming the marketplace is also, in general, true and we have to be very careful about that in fashioning this health care reform. Senator [Nancy] Kassebaum and I have talked about this. In her bill, she puts the decision about what benefits will be covered at the level of the national board. She does this to take these difficult decisions out of politics, so you do not have people grabbing on you as you walk down the hallway saying, include this, include that, include my favorite, particular kind of treatment.

. . . We decided that, initially, we should have the benefits package approved by the Congress, so that individual citizens could know what was in it. Then any changes to it, any enhancements to it, should be moved to the national board, as the Kassebaum-Danforth

Bill had originally suggested. We do not want the political process overwhelming the marketplace and we agree with you that is something we have to guard against.

The third assumption about cost estimates by government being underestimated is absolutely right. In the health care system, cost estimates by the private sector have also been grossly underestimated. I think in large measure, you would see a parallel in the increase of government expenditures that is at least equal to, if not slightly below the increase in private sector expenditures in the health care system. Those two go hand in hand.

It is very difficult for you as a Senator to make projections about what Medicare or Medicaid will cost because what happens is you set a certain amount of money to be available in the budget. What the private sector does is to shift costs that they do not get from the budget out of your decisions onto the private sector. What the private sector consistently has done, both in employers buying insurance and insurers pricing insurance and doctors making decisions, is consistently underestimate what health care costs are or will be and, I would argue, what it should cost.

So this is an issue that is not just a government issue. This is a private sector issue. One of the reasons we want to have some market forces and some competition in this system is so that cost estimates can be made on the basis of delivering health care, not on a diagnosis-procedure basis, but on a per capita basis in which decisionmakers, insurers, doctors, hospitals and others have to make decisions so that costs will be kept down. We can no longer afford to write a blank check.

Finally, I think that there is no doubt that human choices drive health care costs, like it does in most other areas of our lives. What we are trying to do is to have a system in which everybody is part of that system because to leave some out who make bad choices is a cost to us whether we like it or not. Everyone who makes a bad choice who is uninsured drives our costs up. They will eventually cost us something either in more tax dollars or in higher insurance premiums.

If we have everybody covered and everybody in the system so that we finally can stop the cost-shifting, then I think health plans and individuals will be able to make cost-conscious choices that will reward us with the benefits of their decisionmaking. I think until we get everybody in the system, then the human choices that inevitably drive up health care costs will continue to be shifted onto the backs of those who have taken responsibility for their own insurance.

Chairman: Thanks very much.

Senator Dodd.

Senator Christopher Dodd: It is hard to follow that answer; that was so brilliant a response in my view. [Laughter.] ...

Source: Senate Committee on Labor and Human Services. *Examining the Administration's Proposed Health Security Act, To Establish Comprehensive Health Care for Every American: Hearings.* Part I. 103rd Cong., 1st sess., September 29, 1993, pp. 17–21.

Notes

1. Quoted in Haynes Johnson and David S. Broder, *The System: The American Way of Politics at the Breaking Point* (Boston: Little, Brown, 1996), 187.

2. Quoted in Senate Committee on Labor and Human Resources, *Examining the Administration's Proposed Health Security Act, To Establish Comprehensive Health Care for Every American: Hearings,* Part I, 103rd Cong., 1st sess., September 29, 1993, 49.

A Key Strategist Urges Republicans to Defeat Clinton's Health Reform Proposal

DOCUMENT 9.4

"Its Rejection by Congress and the Public Would Be a Monumental Setback for the President"

1993

When President Bill Clinton's political fortunes declined in late 1993, Republicans were quick to seize on the changed landscape in Washington, D.C. Specifically, many GOP politicians and strategists reassessed their stance toward Clinton's health care reform package. Only a few months before, passage of some version of Clinton's Health Security Act had seemed all but certain. But Clinton's accumulating political wounds convinced many Republicans that they could now express their objections to the White House's health care reforms without paying a severe political price. Moreover, some Republicans came to see the struggle over health care reform as a golden opportunity to rain further political damage on the president. This goal became particularly evident after conservative strategist William Kristol distributed a memo to Republican policymakers in December 1993 about the short- and long-term political benefits of derailing Clinton's health care plans. Kristol's memo (excerpted here), which was disseminated by the conservative advocacy group Project for a Republican Future, played a major role in uniting Republicans against the Clinton health reform plan.

December 2, 1993

TO: Republican Leaders

FROM: William Kristol

SUBJECT: Defeating President Clinton's Health Care Proposal

What follows is the first in what will be a series of political strategy memos prepared by The Project for the Republican Future. The topic of this memo is President Clinton's health care reform proposal, the single most ambitious item on the Administration's domestic policy agenda. . . .

Nothing in these pages is intended to supplant the many thoughtful analyses of the Clinton health are plan already produced by Republicans and others, analyses which have done much to expose both its glaring weaknesses and immediate dangers. In fact, this memo borrows heavily from articles and papers prepared by conservative public policy think tanks, the Republican National Committee, House and Senate Republicans, and the dozens of superb critiques that have appeared in newspapers and magazines. Nor is this an attempt to prescribe legislative tactics for defeating the Clinton bill; for that we defer to our Republican leaders in the Congress. Instead, it is an effort to assess the current political climate surrounding the health care debate and to provide a winning Republican strategy that will serve the best interests of the country. . . .

I. The Current Situation

Just after President Clinton introduced his health care plan in September, opinion polling reflected strong public support for it. That support has now sharply eroded. A late September Washington Post/ABC News poll, for example, had national respondents approving the plan by a 56 to 24 percent margin; the same poll in October had approval down to a 51 to 39 percent margin; and a mid-November Post/ABC poll now shows bare plurality support for the plan of 46 to 43 percent.

To some extent, these results follow a predictable pattern of Clinton Administration policy initiatives, which have tended to open well on the strength of the president's personal advocacy, and then to falter as revealed details make plain his attachment to traditional, big government, tax-and-spend liberalism. Faced with forceful objections in the past, the Administration has generally preferred to bargain and compromise with Congress so as to achieve any victory it can. But health care is not, in fact, just another Clinton domestic policy. And the conventional political strategies Republicans have used in the past are inadequate to the task of defeating the Clinton plan outright. That must be our goal.

Simple Criticism is Insufficient. Simple, green-eyeshades criticism of the plan—on the grounds that its numbers don't add up (they don't), or that it costs too much (it does), or that it will kill jobs and disrupt the economy (it will)—is fine so far as it goes. But in the current climate, such opposition only wins concessions, not surrender. The president will lobby intensively for his plan. It will surely be the central theme of his State of the Union Address in January. Health care reform remains popular in principle. And the Democratic Party has the votes. After all, the president's "tax fairness" budget, despite unanimous Republican opposition and rising public disapproval, did pass the Congress.

Any Republican urge to negotiate a "least bad" compromise with the Democrats, and thereby gain momentary public credit for helping the president "do something" about health care, should also be resisted. Passage of the Clinton health care plan, in any form, would guarantee and likely make permanent an unprecedented federal intrusion into and disruption of the American economy—and the establishment of the largest federal entitlement program since Social Security. Its success would signal a rebirth of centralized welfare-state policy at the very moment we have begun rolling back that idea in other areas. And, not least, it would destroy the present breadth and quality of the American health care system, still the world's finest. On grounds of national policy alone, the plan should not be amended; it should be erased.

But the Clinton proposal is also a serious political threat to the Republican Party. Republicans must therefore clearly understand the political strategy implicit in the Clinton plan—and then adopt an aggressive and uncompromising counterstrategy designed to delegitimize the proposal and defeat its partisan purpose.

II. The Clinton Strategy

"Health care will prove to be an enormously healthy project for Clinton . . . and for the Democratic Party." So predicts Stanley Greenberg, the president's strategist and pollster. If a Clinton health care plan succeeds without principled Republican opposition, Mr. Greenberg will be right. Because the initiative's inevitably destructive effect on American medical services will not be practically apparent for several years—no Carter-like gas lines, in other words—its passage in the short run will do nothing to hurt (and every-thing to help) Democratic electoral prospects in 1996. But the long-term political effects of a successful Clinton health care bill will be even worse—much worse. It will relegiti-mize middle-class dependence for "security" on government spending and regulation. It will revive the reputation of the party that spends and regulates, the Democrats, as the generous protector of middle-class interests. And it will at the same time strike a punish-ing blow against Republican claims to defend the middle class by restraining government.

The 80-80 Split. The president intends to convince the American middle class to buy into this new government dependency by overcoming their skepticism with fear. Poll numbers explain his tactics. A large majority of Americans consistently reports that it believes our country's health care system, writ large, to be dysfunctional; 79 percent of respondents to a Princeton Survey Research Associates/Newsweek poll in late September, for example, said the American health care system needed fundamental change or a com-plete rebuilding. Popular discomfort with American medicine as a "system" is Clinton's opportunity. But the same polls contain the key to Clinton's vulnerability, as well, The vast majority of Americans are pleased with the care this system now provides them person-ally; 80 percent of respondents to a late September Yankelovich/Time/CNN poll said they were "somewhat" or "very" satisfied with their own medical services.

So the president advances a promise of "universal" health care coverage as a solution to the problem of the uninsured, but his plan must win the approval of a middle class most members of which are generally happy with the health care they have. He cannot plausibly claim that his plan will make the middle class even happier with their present care. . . .

The Administration's only option, then, is singlemindedly to focus on the fears many middle-class Americans have about health care as an abstract "system" that might someday threaten them. The Administration's public pronouncements ignore all basic, practical questions about how their health plan will actually affect the quality and flexibil-ity of American medical care. And its spokesmen encourage the notion that radical change involving a sacrifice of quality and free choice is necessary for health "security."

III. A REPUBLICAN COUNTERSTRATEGY

The president makes his pitch to the 79 percent of Americans who are inclined to agree that "the system" isn't working, hoping to freeze health care debate on the level of grand generalization about structural defects. He is on the side of the angels rhetorically—denunciations of the status quo, easy moralism about his own alternative, rosy predictions of a utopian future in which security is absolutely guaranteed. Republicans can defeat him by shifting that debate toward specific, commonsense questions about the effect of Clin-ton's proposed reforms on individual American citizens and their families, the vast major-ity of whom, again, are content with the medical services they already enjoy.

Republicans should ask: what will Bill Clinton's health care plan do to the relation-ship most Americans now have with their family doctor or pediatrician. What will it do to the quality of care they receive? Such questions are the beginning of a genuine moral-political argument, based on human rather than bureaucratic needs. And they allow Republicans to trump Clinton's security strategy with an appeal to the enlightened self-interest of middle-class America.

The Republican counterstrategy involves pursuing three distinct tasks: 1) deflating the exaggerated fears of systemic health care collapse that Democrats have encouraged; 2) clarifying and publicizing how the Clinton reform plan would alter and damage the quality and choice of medical treatment most Americans now take for granted; and 3) pointing out that incremental and meaningful solutions to problems of health security—solutions that do not require scrapping the current structure of American medicine and experimenting with something invented in Washington—are already available and politically within reach.

Deflating Fear. Genuine, yet remediable problems do exist in the American system of medicine, but the rhetoric surrounding the president's health plan deliberately makes those problems sound apocalyptic. "Fear itself" does not trouble the New Dealers: Indeed, they welcome it as a powerful tool of political persuasion. Mrs. Clinton, in particular, routinely describes a nation of individual lives teetering on the brink, each only an illness or a job away from financial ruin. . . . It is a brazen political strategy of fear-mongering, conducted on a scale not seen since the Chicken Little energy crisis speeches of President Carter.

Fanning the flames of public unease is a purely political tactic for the Democrats, and it deserves to be exposed as such. For while public concern about health care is undoubtedly real, the president's deliberate campaign of fright seems designed less as a response to the public and more as a justification for his own far-reaching, grand reforms. . . . . Republicans should . . . remind the nation, point by point, that it currently enjoys the finest, most comprehensive, and most generous system of medical care in world history.

Raising Questions about Medical Quality and Choice. The most devastating indictment of the president's proposal is that it threatens to destroy virtually everything about American health care that's worth preserving. Under the plan's layers of regulation and oversight, even seeing a doctor whenever you like will be no easy matter: access to physicians will be carefully regulated by gatekeepers; referrals to specialists will be strongly discouraged; second opinions will be almost unheard of; and the availability of new drugs will be limited.

So while there are now countless valid criticisms of the Clinton plan's various aspects, the most politically effective ones focus on how the proposal would fundamentally change the quality and kind of medical service that Americans cherish and expect. This means an assault on the Clinton plan's two central tenets: mandatory, monopolistic health alliances and government price controls. Hand in hand, these two cornerstones of the president's plan will establish a system of rationed medical care.

Under Clinton's plan, the alliances will submit annual budgets to a national health board, thereby creating pressure to save money and trim service wherever possible. That means tightly regulated managed health care for most people, with an emphasis on efficiency over quality. Those who can afford huge premiums may be able to see a private fee-for-service doctor, though fee schedules will make it difficult for most independent physicians to stay in business. In time, the family doctor tradition will disappear. And avoiding this result by purchasing health insurance outside the alliances will be either impossible or criminal. The chief effect of price controls—the linchpin of the president's cost-containment theory—will be a rigid national system of pre-set budgets and medicine by accountants. There is no reason to believe that such a system won't follow the pattern that price controls have established in every other area: rationing, queueing, diminished innovation, black markets, and the creation of a government "health police" to enforce the rules.

Though the president and his surrogates deny all this, the basic building blocks of his proposal permit no other result. Republicans should insistently convey the message that mandatory health alliances and government price controls will destroy the character, quality, and inventiveness of American health care.

Advocating Security without Upheaval. The initial appeal of the president's proposal is its promise of lifelong, universal security, defined in standard Democratic terms as a federal entitlement benefit. But this promise can also be restated as the plan's most glaring weakness: it mistakes federal spending and regulation for individual security. In exchange for his government-program security, Americans must accept a massive uprooting of the entire U.S. health care system, with disruptive and deleterious consequences.

As both a political and policy matter, the best counter-strategy to Clinton's offer of security requires resisting the temptation to compete with the president in a contest of radical reforms. Allaying public concerns about health security can be achieved by addressing a few basic problems directly—and without unraveling the current system. The easiest way to do that is by pursuing the short list of reforms for which there is already a national consensus. Relatively simple changes to insurance regulation, for example, can eliminate the barriers to health insurance for people with pre-existing medical conditions. The unemployed or people whose employers do not provide health insurance should be able to deduct the full cost of their premiums. The federal government could target its health spending to provide clinics in rural areas and inner cities where access to health care remains a problem. Long-overdue reforms to medical malpractice law would help lower insurance rates across the board. And a simplified, uniform insurance form would reduce paperwork, another unnecessary irritant of the current system. All these small steps would make health insurance less costly and health care easier to obtain.

Even where national health budgeting is concerned, there exist opportunities for significant reform that do not involve Great Society-style upheaval. States might be permitted to operate Medicare and Medicaid programs through managed care, for example, rather than through now-mandated fee-for-service plans—and thereby realize huge cost savings in their own budgets. (The Democratic governor of Tennessee recently applied for, and received, the necessary waiver of federal regulations to pursue just such a reform.) In fact, there are all sorts of cumbersome and costly health care mandates and regulations now imposed on states: they should be lifted to allow governors to allocate their federal programs in the most efficient way. The potential savings from Medicare and Medicaid—the engine of our escalating federal deficit—are enormous.

These are hardly revolutionary or even visionary proposals. In fact, variations of these reforms have been floating around the Congress for some time. Their simplicity and their lack of big-government "sophistication" stand in stark contrast to the extensive controls, reorganizing, standardization, and rationing that are at the heart of president's Health Security Plan.

IV. Laying Groundwork for the Future

These may only be intermediate measures. A more ambitious agenda of free-market reforms remains open for the future: medical IRAs, tax credits and vouchers for insurance, and the like. But Republicans must recognize the policy and tactical risks involved in near-term advocacy of sweeping change, however "right" it might be in principle. The Clinton plan's radicalism depends almost entirely for its success on persuading the nation that American medicine is so broken that it must not just be fixed, but replaced—wholesale and immediately. And it would be a pity if the advancement of otherwise-worthy Republican proposals gave unintended support to the Democrats' sky-is-falling rationale.

The more modest Republican reforms discussed earlier would have the virtue of cooling the feverish atmosphere—fostered largely and deliberately by the Administration—in which health care is currently discussed. And they offer a potentially might larger benefit to the Republican Party as a model of future conservative public policy: a practical vision of principled incrementalism. The character of Republican opposition to the president's health care plan, properly pursued, has broad implications. The party's goal, in health care and in other policy areas, should be to make the case for limited government while avoiding either simple-minded bean-counting, on the one hand, or Democrat-like utopian overreach on the other. The target of Republican policy prescriptions must be the individual citizen, not some abstract "system" in need of ham-fisted government repair. If we can, in this way, provide a principled alternative to the paternalistic experimentalism that consistently underlies Democratic ideas of governance, Republicans will be poised to claim the moral high ground in this and future debates.

The first step in that process must be the unqualified political defeat of the Clinton health care proposal. Its rejection by Congress and the public would be a monumental setback for the president; and an incontestable piece of evidence that Democratic welfare-state liberalism remains firmly in retreat. Subsequent replacement of the Clinton scheme by a set of ever-more ambitious, free-market initiatives would make the coming year's health policy debate a watershed in the resurgence of a newly bold and principled Republican politics.

Source: Kristol, William. "Defeating President Clinton's Health Care Proposal." Project for the Republican Future, December 3, 1993. http://theplumline.whorunsgov.com/bill-kristols-1993-memo-calling-for-gop-to-block-health-care-reform/.

| DOCUMENT 9.5 | Senator Dole Lambastes the Clinton Health Care Plan |

"The President's Medicine [Is] a Massive Overdose of Government Control"

1994

On January 25, 1994, President Bill Clinton devoted much of his State of the Union address to pitch his vision for comprehensive reforms to America's health care system. He framed his proposed reforms as both a moral imperative and a financial necessity for the United States' long-term well-being, and he urged Republicans and Democrats to work in bipartisan fashion for the greater good of the country. The official Republican response to Clinton's message, made it clear that the GOP had no intention of relaxing its opposition to Clinton's proposed reforms, which seemed to be losing public support with each passing day. Senate minority leader Bob Dole (R-KS) used the nationally televised Republican response to criticize the White House's Health Security Act as a bureaucratic nightmare. Following are excerpts from Dole's remarks.

We know that America has the best health care system in the world, that people from every corner of the globe come here when they need the very best treatment, and that our goal should be to insure that every American has access to this system.

Of course, there are many Americans with a sick child or sick parent in real need, both in rural and urban America. Our country has health care problems, but not a health care crisis. But we will have a crisis if we take the President's medicine—a massive overdose of government control.

How massive? My colleague Senator Arlen Specter of Pennsylvania, has prepared a chart of what the health care bureaucracy would look like under the President's plan, and I'd like to show you this chart. It's a great, big chart. It contains 207 boxes. It would take a long time to fully explain it, and frankly, I have difficulty understanding it myself.

Let me point out of some of the new bureaucracies that the President's plan will create. Way up here is the National Health Board. Over here is the Advisory Commission on Regional Variations of Health Expenditures. And here's the National Institute for Health Care Workforce Development.

Now, you and I are way down here, way at the bottom. I don't know why we're not at the top, but we're at the bottom.

Now, the President's idea is to put a mountain of bureaucrats between you and your doctor. For example, if you are a family member and want to receive care from a specialist or a clinic outside your own state—let's say you live in Kansas and you want to go to Minnesota—then you probably can't do it without asking for approval. And under his plan, information about your health and your treatment can be sent to a national databank without your approval. And that's a compromise of privacy none of us should accept.

Now, these just are two examples, but there are many, many more. Clearly, the President is asking you to trust the Government more than you trust your doctor and yourselves with your lives and the lives of your loved ones. More cost, less choice, more taxes, less quality, more government control and less control for you and your family—that's what the President's Government-run plan is likely to give you.

Now, we can fix our most pressing problems without performing a triple bypass operation on our health care system. We can do it without the estimated $1 trillion gap—yes, $1 trillion gap—between the administration's own projections, their projections, of spending under the plan and the funds available to pay for it, and we can do it now. . . .

The President promised a middle-class tax cut, yet he and his party imposed the largest tax increase in American history. This $255 billion tax increase was opposed by every Republican in the House and in the Senate. We hope his higher taxes will not cut short the economic recovery and declining interest rates that he inherited. . . .

Now instead of stifling growth and expansion through higher taxes and increased government regulations, Republicans would take America in a different direction, and we can do that through alternatives that reward risk-taking and the creation of new jobs, and they give our small business men and women relief from the heavy hand of government.

Source: "State of the Union: Excerpts from the Republicans' Response to the President's Message." *New York Times,* January 26, 1994, p. A17.

DOCUMENT 9.6

A Democratic Senator Laments the Death of the Clinton Health Reform Plan

"This Congress Has Become Something That Our Forefathers Never Envisioned"

1994

By September 1994 the Clinton administration's campaign to pass sweeping changes to the nation's health care system clearly was headed for failure. Conservatives in Washington, D.C., rejoiced at this outcome, but liberal policymakers expressed anger and frustration at the demise of Clinton's plan, as well as several other compromise health care reform measures. The following speech, delivered by Sen. Tom Harkin (D-IA) on the floor of the Senate on September 22, is fairly representative of Democratic sentiments at that time. In this speech, Harkin asserts that the battles over health care reform exposed the Republicans as unprincipled opportunists willing to sacrifice the long-term health and security of the American people on the altar of short-term political gain.

Mr. HARKIN. Madam President, we have spent the better part of a year and three-quarters working together to try to find a solution to the health care crisis that we have in America. For the better part of that year and three-quarters, we have been intensely involved in trying to figure out and to work with one another to reach some kind of a consensus and compromise on this issue.

Certainly, not anyone in this country can say that they have not been involved in this debate. Mrs. Clinton opened the doors over a year ago. She opened the doors to let in everyone, whether it was insurance companies, providers, doctors, hospitals, no matter. Everyone had their input in this process. No one can say that they were left out.

Out of this process, the President and the administration fashioned a bill and sent it down to the Congress, as is their prerogative. It was a broad, comprehensive bill—very broad and very comprehensive. I supported that bill. I did not probably support every little bit of it. I would have supported some amendments to it to fashion it differently. But on the general concepts I supported it. After several months it looked as though that bill was not going to go anywhere.

Then our leader, Senator [George] Mitchell, introduced his bill, again after having worked with many people over long weeks and months of time on a scaled-down version, if you will, of the Clinton proposal. That bill was offered here on the Senate floor. We began debate on it in early August, before we recessed in August. It became clear that our friends on the other side of the aisle, the Republicans, decided that they were going to stretch this thing out, that we were not going to have any meaningful votes on Senator Mitchell's health care bill. That was the situation we found when we went up to the August recess.

Majority Leader Mitchell said he was going to keep us here until we had some action, until we got something done on health care. Well, it was obvious that after chewing up about 7 or 10 days of the August break that the Republicans simply were just going to talk it to death. They were going to offer amendments, talk on and on, and drag the whole process out and never reach any real, meaningful votes on Senator Mitchell's bill.

After the August break—we came back almost 2 weeks ago now—there was an effort by a group of Democrats and Republicans to put together a bill they fashioned as the mainstream or rump group, or whatever you want to call it. And now it appears that that, too, cannot fly. Again, perhaps it is a little bit too big and it covers too many things that are a little too contentious here.

So we now find ourselves, at this point in time, having started with the broad concept, the broad Clinton approach to health care reform, and that was not acceptable. Then we had the scaled-down majority leader's bill, and that was not acceptable. We now have a scaled-down version of the mainstream group, and that is not acceptable either. Recent reports indicate that we are about to pull the plug on health care reform for this year.

It is interesting what some Members on the other side are saying. I do not know precisely what some of those words are. I can only report them as were reported in the newspapers. The Senator from Oregon, Senator [Bob] Packwood is reported as saying, "Now that we have killed health care reform, we just cannot leave our fingerprints on it." I am only repeating what I read in the newspaper as a direct quote. The newspaper went on to say that when Mr. Packwood was asked about that later on, he said he did not remember what he said. He said, "I cannot remember from one day to the next what I said on it." That is just what I am reporting was said in the newspaper.

The leader of the Republican Campaign Committee, Senator Gramm, has said, "Do not blame us, blame them"—meaning the Democrats—"for killing health care reform." Now he is playing the blame game and saying, "Well, the Democrats are to blame, and Clinton is to blame because we do not have health care reform." That is a most disingenuous argument, if I have ever heard one in my life, when the facts are entirely the opposite. . . .

So the problems that were out there before are still there. The people that lacked coverage still lack coverage. But most important of all, Madam President, the most vulnerable in our society, who really needed this health care reform bill, who need something to give them coverage, and they have no voice, they have no vote, they have no money with which to try to influence campaigns, and we have forgotten about them, I am speaking about our children in America.

One-fourth of the Americans who do not have health care coverage are children. They are the most vulnerable in our society. They are the ones most apt—if they have an illness, or a disease, or injury—to have permanent disabilities, permanent repercussions from such illnesses or diseases, illnesses or diseases that may affect them for the remainder of their natural lives. Yet, we know that covering children is the cheapest thing we can do. We know it from an insurance standpoint. Insurance policies for children are cheaper than for adults. And whatever money is spent on insuring kids—and especially giving them preventive health care—is going to pay us back tenfold or one-hundredfold in the future.

We know these things.

That is why about a month and a half ago, I joined with other Senators in trying to devise yet another scaled-down package for health care reform this year. Forget about purchasing cooperatives. Forget about all of the so-called reforms. Forget about all of the things that are very contentious. Strip it down and let us cover our kids. We provided three things. We wanted to do three things for three of the most vulnerable in our society in terms of health care—first, cover kids; and, second, provide a capped, home and community-based, long-term care for the elderly and disabled; third, to provide 100 percent deductibility for the self-employed so they can buy health insurance and deduct it just like the big businesses can do.

That is not asking very much. It is very small, very scaled down, and it is the cheapest plan of all. It comes in at about $130 billion less than the so-called mainstream proposal. Yet, now I am told that we cannot even bring this out, that there would not be any support for that because the Republicans would filibuster that, they would hold that up, and that Mr. Gingrich has said they are going to stop any health care bill coming through.

So while I have refrained from thus far getting involved in the blame game and who is to blame, because I have always remained optimistic and hopeful that we can get something through—maybe not as much as we wanted, but at least something that would be a down payment on health care reform—I thought surely when you talked about just covering kids and about providing deductibility for the self-employed, and a small home and community-based long-term care program, that surely no one could object to this. It would be done through the private sector, so the insurance companies would not object. They would just have to come up with a separate kids' policy. That is no problem. Certainly the business sector could not object to 100 percent deductibility for the self-employed. We do not have employer mandates or anything like that in there. And certainly those who might be opposed in any way to opening up new entitlements could not be opposed to a capped program of long-term care for the elderly and sick. So we wanted to bring this out. . . .

. . . But now I am told the Republicans would not even let us vote on that. That is what we are now up against. We are up against the leader of the Republican Senate Campaign Committee, and Mr. Gramm of Texas who is saying, "Blame them, not us," After all they have done to slow down, stop, and stymie our efforts in health care reform. I ask could we have a meeting of the minds and we can all agree on one thing—let us cover our kids. If they will not even do that, then I think it is clear to the American people who has the keys to gridlock here in Washington; it is the Republicans who hold the keys to gridlock.

That lock is firmly on that door and behind that door is health care coverage for the children of America. Behind that locked door is 100 percent deductibility for self-employed. Behind that locked door is some long-term care for our elderly and disabled.

My friends on the other side of the aisle have the key to that padlock. They can choose to keep the lock on the door. And as I understand it, that is what they have chosen to do although I would wish and would hope with all of my heart that they would unlock that lock, that they would take that key and unlock it and open the door.

But they will not even do that. So now we go out of this Congress with no health care reform at all, without anything to help working Americans. And that is exactly what our bill is designed to do, to help working Americans. Obviously with Medicaid, if you are poor your kids are covered because you have Medicaid coverage. And obviously if you are well to do, or if you have a good job and you have a policy that your employer has for you, then your kids are probably covered. But if you are anywhere in between, if you are just above the poverty line, if you are working at a job that is just above the minimum wage, you are a single parent with a couple of children, you are trying to break out of welfare, you are trying to make it, you do not have any health care coverage for your kids.

Somewhere between 9 million and 11 million kids in this country do not have any health care coverage, and they are not children in poverty, they have Medicaid; they are not the children of Senators and Congressmen, we have full health care coverage.

It is the children of the working poor, people who are out there struggling day after day to make ends meet, they are the ones who do not have health care coverage for their kids. And that is who we are attempting to get covered, and the Republicans say no, we will not do that. We will not take the keys that we hold to gridlock and unlock that padlock and open the door and let these kids have some health care coverage. . . .

Madam President, I have served in the Congress now for 20 years. I have seen a lot of fights in the House and in the Senate, some pretty tough ones; I have seen some pretty tough debates and pretty tough issues. . . .

But in my 20 years in this Congress I have never seen anything like exists today. This attitude of gridlock, of stopping everything, the cynicism, the attitude that nothing can get through here because it might make President Clinton look good, that we have to stop things because perhaps the only way to take over is to tear it down. As Mr. Gingrich said some 15 years ago, the only way we are going to take over is to tear it down. I see a tearing down, a tearing down of the structure of Congress. . . .

I do not mean to get off on this, but something has to be done about these filibuster rules. If something is not done, then I am afraid this body, the Senate, of which I have been a Member now for 10 years, will just simply become irrelevant, will be a debating society. We get up and give fiery speeches like I am talking here, but nothing ever gets done. It might make us feel good and vent our frustrations perhaps. I am venting a few right now myself on a Friday afternoon with nobody else in the Chamber.

But this is not what our forefathers envisioned. They envisioned a legislative body that, yes, would debate and discuss and amend, but would do something and get something through. We now have a situation where the minority side will not permit that to happen.

So Madam President, I digressed a little bit, but the main point of what I wanted to say here today was that as this Congress draws to a close. . . . let us bring up a measure that will at least insure the children of America and give them the health care that they need. If we cannot even do that, then God help us all. . . .

. . . We tried to get a bigger package through, not acceptable. We tried to get a slimmed down package through, not acceptable. Now we are down to kids. If that is not even acceptable to the Republicans, then I think it is clear to the American people that it is the Republicans who will not let us have any measure of health care reform in this country.

Source: Harkin, Tom. The Health Care Debate. *Congressional Record,* 103rd Cong., 2d sess., September 22, 1994, p. S13262.

A Republican Senator Applauds the Demise of the Clinton Health Care Plan

"This Is What Democracy Is All About"

1994

When Republicans turned back the health care reform efforts of President Bill Clinton and congressional Democrats in the fall of 1994, many Democrats lashed out against the GOP, depicting their antireform stance as one of rank partisan obstructionism. Republicans asserted that their opposition stemmed from long-standing Republican principles of governance and increased public discomfort with the Clinton plan. And as the following remarks by Senate minority leader Bob Dole (R-NC) illustrate, the GOP contended that it was the administration that had refused to compromise during the health care negotiations.

Mr. DOLE. Mr. President, 1 year ago today the health care debate officially began when the President delivered his nationally televised address before a joint session of Congress.

There can be no doubt that over the past 12 months health care has been the most debated, discussed, and dissected issue, both on Capitol Hill and committee rooms and in living rooms and coffee shops all across America.

Immediately after the President's speech I stated that Republicans are ready to work with the President to achieve the right kind of reform that built upon the best health care delivery system in the world rather than reform that destroyed it. I asked the American people to keep four key issues in mind throughout the debate. Those issues were choice, quality, jobs, and cost.

After carefully studying President Clinton's health care plan for the better part of a year, the American people have reached a conclusion. Adopting the Clinton plan would mean less choice, less quality, fewer jobs, and greater cost.

Once this conclusion became apparent, the Democrat congressional leadership did what they had to do. They went down to the White House and told the President his plan was dead. In its place however, they introduced a proposal which may not have had the President's name on the top but had many of his proposals and ideas throughout. In fact, Senate Republicans and the American people soon concluded that they had far too much in common—too much complexity, too much cost, too much bureaucracy, too much Government, too many mandates.

And as the end of this session approaches the American people are telling us in overwhelming numbers—in my State a poll indicated that about 86 to 14 percent, 86 to 14 percent—that they want an opportunity to catch their breath. They do not want Congress to try to pass a massive health care reform plan in the final hours of the session, a plan that will have had no hearings, a plan no one had the time to read much less understand.

Some in the White House and some on Capitol Hill are wringing their hands and saying "What went wrong? What happened? What happened with health care reform?" Some will try to argue that Bob Dole and the Republicans killed health care reform, that we are not sensitive to those without insurance, that we are not sensitive to those with health care problems.

The fact of the matter is that throughout this debate—in fact, even before it began—Senate Republicans have offered solutions to help those in need. We worked to help those who cannot afford insurance. We have worked to help get those who cannot get insurance because of a preexisting condition, and we worked to help those who lose their insurance when they lose or want to change jobs. That is called portability.

We have had a number of initiatives on this side of the aisle. First, the initiative by Senator [Lincoln] Chafee and a number of Republicans, including this Republican; a proposal by Senator [Don] Nickles, which I also cosponsored; one by Senator [Phil] Gramm; and later we put together a plan which 40 of our Republicans either cosponsored or said they would support; 39 cosponsors and one additional Member who said they could support. And I think maybe at this point it has probably more votes than any other plan in the Congress; any other plan in the Congress.

No one claimed these plans were perfect. But they were substantive proposals to improve our health care system. But they were not allowed 1 minute of real consideration. Despite the fact they would have improved coverage for millions of Americans they were considered by some to be too minimalist to be serious.

One year ago today I said the Republicans were prepared to work with the President and our Democrat colleagues to give Americans the right reform. I meant it then, and I mean it now. The fact is, however, that from the first day of this debate the President locked all Republicans out of the process from the creation of the stealth task force to the introduction of his bill.

I am also disappointed that the President did not respond to the suggestion I made literally hundreds of times over the past year. That was to pass a reform bill—we could have done it 6 months ago, or 8 months ago. We could have done it a year ago today—which contains many of the provisions that were bipartisan which everyone in this Chamber probably agreed on: preexisting conditions, portability, malpractice reform, let small business go together; deductibility for the self-employed, for ranchers and farmers. And these provisions would have made our system more affordable and more accessible to millions of Americans today.

Some Democrats, including the distinguished chairman of the Senate Finance Committee, have suggested the same action. Unfortunately, at this late date I now find myself agreeing with the many who have suggested the time and the public's patience are too short for us to embark on this road.

So what is the bottom line? Did something go wrong as the White House insists? Was the past year a waste of time? Did Congress fail the American people? I think instead of wondering what went wrong, it went right. The American people looked at it. They studied it. They listened. They heard the debate. And in overwhelming numbers time after time, survey after survey, they said no. They said no.

That is what democracy is all about. If somebody has an idea, you go out and test it and test it and test it. And many of us I might add, including this Senator, have backed away from the positions I may have held a year ago on health care, and individual mandates. I thought it was a good idea. Nobody else did in the Senate Finance Committee, or at least only about four. And most of the American people did not like it either.

So there are a number of provisions that many of us thought were good. The American people said they were not as good as they should be or not good at all. So it seems to me that what we have is not gridlock that defeated a Government-run health care bill, as some would have you believe. It was not a parliamentary trick that Bob Dole had up his sleeve. And it was not the pressure tactics of so-called special interests. It was not the persuasiveness of "Harry and Louise." Anybody making those suggestions is guilty of political malpractice. It was a lot of other things.

What finally defeated the plan was the overwhelming consensus of the American people from all parts of the country, in both parties, regardless of where people lived, hardworking men and women who raise families, pay taxes, and create jobs. That is what happened. A consensus was reached after very careful study.

So we will be back with this. We are not finished with this. We know a great deal more about health care than we did a year ago. I think everybody has learned a lot, particularly those not on the Labor Committee or Finance Committee, where most of the action is. I think we have learned a lot, and in greater clarity, about what the American people believe we ought to do. We ought to fix the serious problems in health care. And it seems to me that we will have that opportunity next year. We meet every year. We will be back in January, and you can bet that health care will be near the top of the agenda, no matter which party controls the Congress. Americans can count on the fact that Republicans will continue to fight for reform that guarantees the choice and quality Americans have come to expect. I will continue to oppose any health care plan to turn our health care system over to the Federal Government.

Source: Dole, Robert. The Health Care Debate. *Congressional Record,* 103rd Cong., 2d sess., September 22, 1994, p. S13117.

DOCUMENT
9.8

Senator Mitchell Closes the Book on the Clinton Health Care Plan

"There Is now a Policy in Place . . . of Total Obstruction"

1994

At a press conference on September 26, 1994, Senate majority leader George J. Mitchell (D-ME) formally sounded the death knell for the Clinton administration's health reform efforts. During the course of a question-and-answer session with members of the Washington, D.C., press corps, Mitchell asserted that cynical Republican obstructionism and powerful special interest groups—most notably the insurance industry—were to blame for the defeat.

SEN. MITCHELL: . . . Most Americans like our health care system but they know the health insurance system is broken and needs fixing. Too many families have lost insurance because a child got cancer or a father lost his job. Too many families can't afford to pay $300 or $400 a month if the place they work doesn't provide health insurance. I believe that all Americans have a right to affordable, high-quality health care. Unfortunately, the overwhelming majority of our Republican colleagues in the Senate do not agree. Under the rules of the Senate, a minority can obstruct the majority. This is what happened to comprehensive health insurance reform.

Over the past few weeks I've had a number of productive meetings with senators in the so-called mainstream group to explore the possibility of a modified reform plan. We reached agreement on almost all issues. I believe we could have and would have come to final agreement on the substance of a bill, but that is not the only factor for a successful outcome. Any bill must command the votes necessary to pass. So we all agreed, all of the members of the mainstream group with whom I had these discussions, that it would serve no purpose to go forward unless we had the necessary votes.

I had hoped that agreement with the mainstream group would produce the 60 votes needed to defeat a Republican filibuster. Regrettably, very few Senate Republicans shared that view. The overwhelming majority opposed any health care legislation, even a modest bill to extend health insurance to children and reform some industry practices. Then last week the Republican leaders of the House and Senate said aloud wh[at] their colleagues had been saying privately: They will oppose any health care bill this year, modest or not, bipartisan or not. Even though Republicans are a minority in the Congress, in the Senate they're a minority with a veto. They have the ability to block legislation and they have done so on health care reform. Therefore, it is clear that health insurance reform cannot be enacted this year. . . .

Q: Senator, how about next year, what do you think the prospects are for passage of any legislation next year, the year after?

SEN. MITCHELL: I believe it inevitable that comprehensive health care reform will be enacted.

You will recall that it took 10 years or more to pass Medicare, and there was a great deal of opposition to it. It was not until after the decisive election of 1964 that it finally was enacted. And I believe that the same thing will happen inevitably on health care reform. I do not know and cannot say whether it will be next year or the year after. Obviously, many factors will contribute to that. But I believe, given the situation in the country today with respect to health insurance and health financing especially, that action is inevitable. . . .

Q: Has the acrimony in the final days of this session caused you, facetiously or not, to say that this is among the worst sessions you've seen and that's why you don't regret [not seeking reelection]?

SEN. MITCHELL: It's been a very difficult session, and the events of last week were unprecedented in the history of the Senate and the history of our nation. We've not had a situation, to the best of the knowledge of the Senate historian and the Senate parliamentarian and others of whom I've inquired, in which we had a filibuster on trying to take a bill to conference. And I think there is now a policy in place on the part of the Republicans of total obstruction—that is to say simply to block anything and everything no matter what. That is regrettable. I don't think it is helpful to the institution, nor do I think ultimately it would be helpful to either political party or to individual senators. . . .

Q: Can you go back a little bit over your own process in making this decision, and at what point you finally made the decision that this just was not doable. Was it over the weekend?

SEN. MITCHELL: I reached the decision in a preliminary way during the meeting at the White House last week when the Republican leaders of the House and Senate told President Clinton, in my presence, that they would oppose any type of health care legislation this year, and then went on to state that not only would they oppose any health care legislation, but that if an attempt was made to pass it they would try to kill other unrelated legislation which they otherwise might have supported. That clearly endangered every aspect of the legislative agenda and, in effect, placed other important measures in the position of being hostage to health care legislation. Since the prospects for passing health care legislation were not good in any event, I believe that I've made the appropriate decision.

I then discussed it further with members of the mainstream group, specifically Senator [John] Chafee and Senator [Dave] Durenberger on the Republican side, and Senator [John] Breaux and Senator [Bob] Kerrey of Nebraska on the Democratic side. I asked Senator Chafee to canvass his Republican colleagues who are part of the mainstream group to determine how many of them would support ending a filibuster on a compromise bill, were we able to reach compromise. And I also undertook to simultaneously consult with my Democratic colleagues. And following those discussions with the report I received from Senator Chafee, my conclusion—my tentative decision not to proceed was reinforced.

That is to say it became increasingly clear that it would not be possible, in any event, to get the 60 votes need to end the certain Republican filibuster against even a modified bill. . . .

Q: (Some Republicans have said?) that there were some miscalculations, that a deal could have been cut by you, perhaps by the president last winter with Republicans to get a bill through but that you weren't ready to deal, and in fact it was that sort of political miscalculation that brought us to where we are today.

SEN. MITCHELL: I do not believe that to be an accurate assessment. If you go back over time, you would see that late last year Senator Chafee introduced a bill which was co-sponsored by Senator [Bob] Dole and, I believe, a total of more than 20 Republican senators which proposed universal health care and a mandate to achieve universal health care, but over time, as the political circumstances changed, they abandoned their own legislation and moved away from it, and I do not believe that there was such a time or such an agreement possible. In fact, this is all, obviously, speculative, but I am very certain in my own mind that that was not possible. . . .

Q: What role do you see of any special interests playing in the outcome—(off mike)?

SEN. MITCHELL: I believe that special interests played a very large role in making it impossible to pass reform legislation this year. I've read newspaper accounts of the very large sums of money being spent in lobbying against the bill, and according to those accounts, it's by far a record, tens of millions of dollars being spent in lobbying activities against the bill, led by the insurance industry. And I must say a lot of the information about the bill was false. There was a substantial campaign of misinformation that raised questions in the minds of the American people, and I think the combination of the insurance industry on the outside and the majority of the Republicans on the inside proved too much to overcome. . . .

Source: News Conference with Senate Majority Leader George Mitchell. Transcript ID: 1112470. Senate Radio-TV Gallery. Washington, DC, September 26, 1994.

DOCUMENT
9.9

Appropriations Battles over Health Care Research

"We Can Fight for Total Elimination of This Agency"

1995

After Republicans won control of both houses of Congress in the November 1994 elections, clashes between the GOP and Democratic president Bill Clinton erupted in numerous policy areas. Long-standing differences between the parties on health care, reproductive rights, environmental protection, gun control, education policy, and other issues were cast in sharper relief than ever before. Many federal agencies became trapped in the intensifying political cross fire, including a number of agencies that had previously enjoyed bipartisan support and carried out their duties without controversy. One such agency was the Agency for Health Care Policy and Research (AHCPR), located within the Department of Health and Human Services.

When the AHCPR was established in 1989, lawmakers on both sides of the aisle were supportive. Republican president George H. W. Bush had requested the program in his fiscal 1990 budget thanks to prodding from White House health policy adviser William Roper, and the proposal was warmly received by progressive legislators. Liberals and conservatives could both find plenty to support in the agency's mandate, which was to improve the quality and cost-effectiveness of medical care by supporting medical effectiveness research and disseminating research findings and guidelines to health care providers, policymakers, and the public. "Serious concerns on Capitol Hill about health care costs and Medicare's financial viability," summarized one study, "created receptiveness to the suggestion that outcomes research, technology assessment, and the development and dissemination of practice guidelines would produce cost savings."[1] From fiscal 1991 to fiscal 1995, Congress boosted the AHCPR budget from $115 million to $159 million.

In 1994, the agency came under scrutiny from some Republicans who charged that it provided improper assistance to President Clinton's health care reform efforts. The agency also came under fire during this time from the North American Spine Society, an association of back surgeons angered by AHCPR clinical guidelines that questioned the efficacy of a certain type of back surgery. One year later, AHCPR became a focus of conservative Republicans eager to fulfill their Contract with America, a 1994 pledge to voters to dramatically reduce the size and influence of the federal government. The Republican-led House Budget Committee included the AHCPR on a hit list of 140 discretionary programs that it wanted to eliminate in the spring of 1995.

As the summer of 1995 wore on, the agency's future remained in doubt. In July the House Appropriations Committee approved $125 million for the agency's operations, but leading critic Rep. Sam Johnson (R-TX) proposed an amendment to completely defund the agency. This amendment failed to get the necessary traction, in part because of objections from influential House Republicans including Bill Thomas (CA) and John Edward Porter (IL) who thought the agency was doing good work. Undaunted, Johnson offered another amendment that stripped more than $65 million from the agency's budget, and this amendment was adopted. Over in the Senate, stalwart defenders of the program such as Minority Leader Tom Daschle (D-SD) managed to obtain an appropriation of more than $127 million for AHCPR, despite the vociferous objections of some Republican critics.[2]

The future of the agency remained in limbo during the government shutdowns of late 1995 and early 1996. Senate-House conferees finally agreed on an appropriation of $125 million for fiscal 1996, which was a 21 percent cut in AHCPR's budget from the previous year. The future of AHCPR remained shaky for the next few years, but political tensions surrounding the agency eased by the late 1990s, thanks in part to the diplomatic efforts of John Eisenberg, who assumed directorship of AHCPR in early 1997.[3] In 1999 the agency was renamed the Agency for Healthcare Research and Quality, and it remains the federal government's leading supporter of health services research today.

Following are two divergent assessments of the AHCPR that were offered on Capitol Hill in 1995. The first is Representative Johnson's comments upon introducing his amendment to strip $65 million from the AHCPR budget. The second is a defense of the AHCPR offered by Senator Daschle.

Representative Sam Johnson, Texas, August 3, 1995

Mr. Chairman, as you may or may not know, this is not the original amendment that I offered. My original amendment completely eliminated funding for the Agency for Health Care Policy and Research and used the savings for deficit reduction. However, it became necessary to make changes and offer the compromise that is before us today.

I have chosen to support this compromise amendment because it accomplishes two goals.

First, I believe that a cut of $60 million is an important first step toward the total elimination of this Agency. Next year, we can fight for total elimination of this Agency. We owe that to the taxpayers of this country.

The second, and most important part of this compromise, is the stipulation that AHCPR will not be able to continue to take $5.8 million each year from the Medicare trust fund as they have been doing since their creation in 1989.

Whether the Agency is eliminated or not, this house can not, in good conscience, take money from our Medicare system which will be broke by the year 2002. So, by supporting this amendment, you will be increasing the Medicare trust fund by $5.8 million.

I would like to share with you how AHCPR uses Medicare funds and its appropriated moneys. They are used to produce studies such as, and I quote, "Cardiologists Know More About New Heart Attack Treatments Than Primary Care Doctors"—and quote—the "Doctor-Patient Relationship Affects Whether Patients Sue for Malpractice".

Can you believe that a Government that has a $5 trillion debt take money from Medicare and spends millions on an agency that produces these types of reports and a host of others that are duplicative and useless.

The Office of Technology Assessment has concluded that AHCPR's guideline program is one of 1,500 such efforts performed by both the Federal Government and the private sector.

It is obvious that we do not need to fund this Agency that employs 270 bureaucrats and in 6 years has spent 778 million taxpayer dollars—$29.4 million of which has been siphoned off from the Medicare trust fund.

Let me reiterate this point. If we don't pass this amendment, $5.8 million will be taken out of Medicare next year and every year after that. In 7 years when Medicare goes broke, this agency will have stolen $80 million from our senior citizens.

The American people want a balanced budget. They want the Government to stop spending their money on things that we don't need and can't afford. And we don't need, nor can we afford, the Agency for Health Care Policy and Research. A better name for this Agency would be the Agency for High Cost Publications and Research.

I urge members to help lower the deficit, help save Medicare, and help protect taxpayers from having to fund a needless bureaucracy—help save Medicare—vote for this amendment.

Senator Tom Daschle, South Dakota, September 5, 1995

Mr. President, as the Congress considers its appropriations bills and strives to reduce the rate of growth of Federal programs, I would like to call attention to one very small, but important agency that policymakers and industry representatives alike have praised as responsible and cost-effective—the Agency for Health Care Policy and Research (AHCPR).

AHCPR, which is part of the Department of Health and Human Services, was established in 1989 with strong bipartisan support. Broadly stated, the agency's mission is to conduct impartial health services research and disseminate information that will complement public and private sector efforts to improve health care quality and contain costs.

AHCPR's charge is to find out what works and what does not work in the health care system, and the results of its research are being used voluntarily by the private sector to contain health care costs. The agency funds outcomes research projects that examine the efficacy of medical interventions in terms of how they affect patients. It also funds studies on the medical effectiveness of particular procedures and conducts assessments of health technologies utilized by HCFA and CHAMPUS to make coverage decisions. These projects have identified millions of dollars in potential savings to Medicare.

Finally, the agency convenes multidisciplinary panels of experts to develop clinical practice guidelines on such topics as low back pain, cataracts, sickle cell anemia, mammography, unstable angina, and cancer pain. These guidelines are disseminated to consumers, private and public sector health care policymakers, providers, and administrators for use as they see fit.

AHCPR is a true public/private partnership designed to improve the quality of health services and contain their cost. And it is working. Supporters of the agency include conservatives and liberals in both political parties and span the health care spectrum, from the insurance industry to providers to academia and other highly regarded public policy institutions. AHCPR has been called an "honest broker" because of the way it compiles and distributes health care cost and quality information among competing public and private sector interests.

It is very important to the health care system that AHCPR continue producing the kind of significant research it has developed in the past 5 years. To slash AHCPR's funding now would truly be penny-wise and pound-foolish: The current funding level for the agency amounts to a little more than a dollar per American. Yet potential savings from the use of its guidelines and research could save hundreds of millions, and by some estimate billions, of dollars.

AHCPR should continue to play a critical role as we struggle to control national health care costs, particularly in the Medicare and Medicaid programs. AHCPR-funded research has provided strong evidence that health care costs can be contained while improving the quality of services. It would be irresponsible to devastate funding to the only Government agency devoted to finding ways for us to improve quality and lower costs.

Source: Johnson, Sam. Amendment No. 130 Offered by Sam Johnson. *Congressional Record,* 104th Cong., 1st sess., August 3, 1995, p. H8413. Daschle, Tom. The Agency for Health Care Policy and Research: A Beacon for Policymakers. *Congressional Record,* 104th Cong., 1st sess., September 5, 1995, p. S12608.

NOTES

1. H. Gray Bradford, Michael K. Gusmano, and Sara Collins, "AHCPR and the Changing Politics of Health Services Research," *Health Affairs,* June 25, 2003, http://content/healthaffairs.org/content /early/2003/06/25/hithaff.w3.283.citation.

2. Bradford, Gusmano, and Collins, "AHCPR and the Changing Politics of Health Services Research."

3. Bradford, Gusmano, and Collins, "AHCPR and the Changing Politics of Health Services Research."

**DOCUMENT
9.10**

President Clinton Vetoes Cuts to Medicare and Medicaid

"This Bill Is Unacceptable"

1995

When budget disagreements between the Clinton administration and the Republican-led Congress produced two government shutdowns in late 1995 and early 1996, both sides jockeyed furiously to gain the political high ground with the American public. "'Protector of Medicare' is President Clinton's chosen role," observed political analyst Cokie Roberts. "Republicans are playing 'protectors of the purse,' but both sides are worried that voters will see them as game playing politicians."[1]

Led by Speaker Newt Gingrich and an army of conservative GOP freshmen who felt that the 1994 midterms had given them a mandate to cut taxes and reduce the deficit through major cuts to social programs, Republicans in Congress had pushed the president to accept their budget priorities or risk a shutdown of nonessential government operations. To the surprise of Republicans, Clinton did not knuckle under. Instead, he used the showdown to cast himself as the guardian of Medicare, Medicaid, and other established entitlement programs with significant middle-class constituencies. This stance resonated with the public, as evidenced by numerous polls indicating that Americans saw preservation of the social safety net as a higher priority than balancing the budget. By early 1996, when the GOP belatedly responded to the changing political landscape and relented in its budget demands, Clinton had dramatically improved his standing with American voters.

The following statement from Clinton was issued on December 6, 1995, a time when Washington, D.C., had just emerged from one shutdown and was bracing itself for a second one. This veto of budget reconciliation legislation passed by the Gingrich-led House features all of the themes that Clinton emphasized during this defining period of his presidency. Most notably, it relentlessly frames Republican efforts to reduce Medicare and Medicaid spending as dangerous and "extreme."

To the House of Representatives:

I am returning herewith without my approval H.R. 2491, the budget reconciliation bill adopted by the Republican majority, which seeks to make extreme cuts and other unacceptable changes in Medicare and Medicaid, and to raise taxes on millions of working Americans.

As I have repeatedly stressed, I want to find common ground with the Congress on a balanced budget plan that will best serve the American people. But, I have profound differences with the extreme approach that the Republican majority has adopted. It would hurt average Americans and help special interests.

My balanced budget plan reflects the values that Americans share—work and family, opportunity and responsibility. It would protect Medicare and retain Medicaid's guarantee of coverage; invest in education and training and other priorities; protect public health and the environment; and provide for a targeted tax cut to help middle-income

Americans raise their children, save for the future, and pay for postsecondary education. To reach balance, my plan would eliminate wasteful spending, streamline programs, and end unneeded subsidies; take the first, serious steps toward health care reform; and reform welfare to reward work.

By contrast, H.R. 2491 would cut deeply into Medicare, Medicaid, student loans, and nutrition programs; hurt the environment; raise taxes on millions of working men and women and their families by slashing the Earned Income Tax Credit (EITC); and provide a huge tax cut whose benefits would flow disproportionately to those who are already the most well-off.

Moreover, this bill creates new fiscal pressures. Revenue losses from the tax cuts grow rapidly after 2002, with costs exploding for provisions that primarily benefit upper-income taxpayers. Taken together, the revenue losses for the 3 years after 2002 for the individual retirement account (IRA), capital gains, and estate tax provisions exceed the losses for the preceding 6 years.

Title VIII would cut Medicare by $270 billion over 7 years—by far the largest cut in Medicare's 30-year history. While we need to slow the rate of growth in Medicare spending, I believe Medicare must keep pace with anticipated increases in the costs of medical services and the growing number of elderly Americans. This bill would fall woefully short and would hurt beneficiaries, over half of whom are women. In addition, the bill introduces untested, and highly questionable, Medicare "choices" that could increase risks and costs for the most vulnerable beneficiaries.

Title VII would cut Federal Medicaid payments to States by $163 billion over 7 years and convert the program into a block grant, eliminating guaranteed coverage to millions of Americans and putting States at risk during economic downturns. States would face untenable choices: cutting benefits, dropping coverage for millions of beneficiaries, or reducing provider payments to a level that would undermine quality service to children, people with disabilities, the elderly, pregnant women, and others who depend on Medicaid. I am also concerned that the bill has inadequate quality and income protections for nursing home residents, the developmentally disabled, and their families, and that it would eliminate a program that guarantees immunizations to many children. . . .

While making such devastating cuts in Medicare, Medicaid, and other vital programs, this bill would provide huge tax cuts for those who are already the most well-off. Over 47 percent of the tax benefits would go to families with incomes over $100,000—the top 12 percent. The bill would provide unwarranted benefits to corporations and new tax breaks for special interests. At the same time, it would raise taxes, on average, for the poorest one-fifth of all families. . . .

While cutting taxes for the well-off, this bill would cut the EITC for almost 13 million working families. It would repeal part of the scheduled 1996 increase for taxpayers with two or more children, and end the credit for workers who do not live with qualifying children. Even after accounting for other tax cuts in this bill, about eight million families would face a net tax increase.

The bill would threaten the retirement benefits of workers and increase the exposure of the Pension Benefit Guaranty Corporation by making it easy for companies to withdraw tax-favored pension assets for nonpension purposes. It also would raise Federal employee retirement contributions, unduly burdening Federal workers. Moreover, the bill would eliminate the low income housing tax credit and the community development corporation tax credit, which address critical housing needs and help rebuild communities. Finally, the bill would repeal the tax credit that encourages economic activity in Puerto

Rico. We must not ignore the real needs of our citizens in Puerto Rico, and any legislation must contain effective mechanisms to promote job creation in the islands.

Title XII includes many welfare provisions. I strongly support real welfare reform that strengthens families and encourages work and responsibility. But the provisions in this bill, when added to the EITC cuts, would cut low income programs too deeply. For welfare reform to succeed, savings should result from moving people from welfare to work, not from cutting people off and shifting costs to the States. The cost of excessive program cuts in human terms—to working families, single mothers with small children, abused and neglected children, low-income legal immigrants, and disabled children—would be grave. In addition, this bill threatens the national nutritional safety net by making unwarranted changes in child nutrition programs and the national food stamp program.

The agriculture provisions would eliminate the safety net that farm programs provide for U.S. agriculture. Title I would provide windfall payments to producers when prices are high, but not protect family farm income when prices are low. In addition, it would slash spending for agricultural export assistance and reduce the environmental benefits of the Conservation Reserve Program.

For all of these reasons, and for others detailed in the attachment, this bill is unacceptable.

Nevertheless, while I have major differences with the Congress, I want to work with Members to find a common path to balance the budget in a way that will honor our commitment to senior citizens, help working families, provide a better life for our children, and improve the standard of living of all Americans.

WILLIAM J. CLINTON

Source: Clinton, William J. Message to the House of Representatives Returning without Approval Budget Reconciliation Legislation, December 6, 1995. *Public Papers of the Presidents of the United States: William J. Clinton, 1995.* Vol. 2. Washington, DC: Government Printing Office, 1996, p. 1851.

NOTE

1. Quoted in "Government Shutdown Battle," transcript, *Nightline*, November 13, 1995, www.pbs.org /wgbh/pages/frontline/shows/clinton/etc/11131995.html.

Senator Kassebaum Touts the Health Insurance Portability and Accountability Act

DOCUMENT 9.11

"The Bill Will Help Millions of Americans with Preexisting Illnesses"

1996

After the demise of the Clinton health reform push of 1993–1994 and the epic political battles between the president and the GOP-led Congress of 1995, few political observers believed that lawmakers would revisit health care policy in any meaningful fashion in

1996. As the 1996 elections approached, however, Democrats and Republicans recognized the desirability of showing voters that they had done something in the realm of health care. Republican senator Nancy Landon Kassebaum (KS) and Democratic senator Edward M. Kennedy (MA) were able to seize on this atmosphere to pass the Health Insurance Portability and Accountability Act (HIPAA), which also came to be known as the Kassebaum-Kennedy Act. This bipartisan federal overhaul of private health insurance empowered millions of Americans to move from job to job without losing their health insurance coverage. It did so by forbidding insurers from rejecting individuals from coverage because of preexisting conditions or for other reasons. Advocates of the measure said that it would improve Americans' health care security and remove a long-standing obstacle to entrepreneurism. "Workers who want to change jobs must often give up the opportunity because it would mean losing their health insurance," said Kennedy. "A quarter of all workers say they are forced to stay in a job they otherwise would have left—because they are afraid of losing their health insurance."

HIPAA failed to include language that would prevent insurers from increasing policy prices for these individuals. In early 1998 the General Accounting Office reported that some insurers were charging premiums up to 600 percent of their standard rates to individuals covered by HIPAA. This practice greatly limited the practical usefulness of the law, for portability rights were of little use if one could not afford the premiums after switching jobs.

The following excerpt is from a floor speech that Kassebaum gave in support of the HIPAA legislation. On August 21, less than three weeks after Kassebaum delivered these remarks, President Bill Clinton signed the measure into law.

Mr. President, today, we stand on the threshold of passing long-overdue reforms to our Nation's health insurance system.

According to the General Accounting Office, the bipartisan conference agreement before us today will help at least 25 million Americans each year who now face discrimination and live in fear that their health insurance coverage will be canceled if they change jobs, lose their job, or become sick.

It was exactly 1 year ago today that the Senate Labor Committee passed the core provisions of this legislation by a unanimous vote. For many months prior to that time, Senator Kennedy and I worked together with insurance companies, consumers, Governors, State regulators, large employers, small employees, and other to forge a bipartisan consensus which would bring us to this day.

Mr. President, it has been a long, and sometimes bumpy, road. But the spirit of cooperation and bipartisanship that began this process 1 years [sic] ago has allowed us to overcome very difficult obstacles that threatened—but never derailed—our drive to pass common-sense health reforms that would provide real health security.

While there has been a great deal of debate and polemics over the last few months about extraneous provisions, Senator Kennedy and I have never lost sight of our primary goal. The heart and soul of the Kassebaum-Kennedy bill that passed the full Senate unanimously are firmly embedded in the conference agreement before us.

Mr. President, beginning July 1, 1997, every American who has played by the rules will be able to keep their health insurance coverage even if they change jobs, lose their job, or have a preexisting illness.

Last night, the House of Representatives passed the Health Insurance Portability and Accountability Act by an overwhelming vote of 421 to 2. Today, we will have the opportunity to do the same and to send this bill to President Clinton for his signature.

This is a dramatic victory for the American people—not only because the bill will help millions of Americans with preexisting illnesses, but also because—I believe—the process of compromise, negotiation, and bipartisanship that was the hallmark of this bill will go a long way toward restoring Americans' faith that their Government can work to address their most pressing concern.

Depending on who was speaking yesterday, one would think that health reform was entirely the province of one party. But as Senator Kennedy and I both know, this effort has been bipartisan from the start. . . . The majority and minority leaders, as well as Senator Dole, deserve much credit for breaking the gridlock over this bill.

In fact, Mr. President, I would just like to say a special word of appreciation to the majority leader. I think that Senator Lott has devoted a great deal of time and energy to making sure that we could reach this point this evening before we go out on our recess.

And there also has been significant bipartisan support in the House from Representatives Thomas, Bliley, Bilirakis, Waxman, Hyde, Dingell, and others. I especially want to recognize Representative Hastert of Illinois for his leadership in bringing together members of both parties to reach agreement on this very important bill.

I regret that we could not do more to help small employers. In an effort to avoid controversy that could have derailed the legislation, both the House and Senate small business pooling provisions were dropped from the conference agreement. Representative Fawell from Illinois is perhaps the greatest advocate of this reform, and Senator Jeffords, from Vermont, also has worked very diligently to help small employers enjoy the same economies of scale as large employers. My hope is that those Members and others will continue to show leadership in the future to find constructive bipartisan solutions in this area.

I also regret that this legislation does not include malpractice reforms that could significantly lower costs for consumers.

Finally, Mr. President, I know many of my colleagues are disappointed that the bill does not do more to help end discrimination against those with mental illnesses. I know that Senator Domenici and others will speak to that issue later. But I would just like to express my appreciation to Senator Domenici who has devoted his time and heartfelt efforts to achieving legislation to address parity in insurance coverage for those with mental illness.

We did not do enough in this bill, and I certainly can understand those who wish we could have done more. However, the bill does represent significant progress for those with mental illness and other chronic conditions. The bill expressly prohibits employers and insurers from denying coverage to individuals because of preexisting mental illnesses as well as physical illnesses, and people who suffer with mental illnesses will be able to change jobs without the fear of losing their health coverage. . . .

So, Mr. President, let us move forward. Let us cap this bipartisan effort with another strong vote today and send this historic legislation to the President's desk for his immediate signature.

There is no controversy about the central elements of the bill. There is no question that the President will sign the legislation. There is no question that—despite its long delay—the President, and members of both parties, in both the House and the Senate, can take credit for passing these sensible reforms.

And there is no question that the American people will be the real winners today. This bill will guarantee that those who need coverage the most are not shut out of the system. It is a small step forward, but it is a historic step. And it will mean the world to millions of Americans who will no longer live in fear that they will lose their health coverage when they change jobs or lose their job.

Source: Kassebaum, Nancy. Remarks in Health Insurance Portability and Accountability Act of 1996—Conference Report. *Congressional Record,* 104th Cong., 2d sess., August 2, 1996, p. S9501.

Senator Kennedy Urges Passage of Health Insurance Legislation for Children

DOCUMENT 9.12

"The Children's Health Care Crisis Is Real, and the Time to Address It Is Now"

1997

In 1997 lawmakers in Washington, D.C, passed the State Children's Health Insurance Program (SCHIP, also sometimes known as CHIP) as part of the larger Balanced Budget Act. This program, which was shepherded into existence by Senators Edward M. Kennedy (D-MA), Orrin Hatch (R-UT), and Jay D. Rockefeller IV (D-WV), constituted the biggest expansion of public health insurance coverage since the introduction of Medicaid and Medicare in 1965. The legislation extended health insurance coverage to four million to five million children of the working poor, those who were not poor enough to qualify for Medicaid but not financially secure enough to pay for insurance themselves.

When the measure was introduced by Hatch and Kennedy as the Child Health Insurance and Lower Deficit Act, many lawmakers and Washington watchers doubted that it would ever reach the president's desk for his signature. They acknowledged that helping needy American children obtain health care coverage was a worthy goal, but they expressed skepticism that any legislative formula could be found that would gain the necessary bipartisan support. As the SCHIP bill wound its way through Congress, Hatch and Kennedy managed to beat back criticisms from conservatives (who objected to SCHIP's cigarette tax, which was its main funding mechanism) and liberals (who wanted to make the bill even more wide-reaching). Hatch attributed this success to the fact that, while he and Kennedy took opposite sides on many policy issues, they occasionally were "able to find the common ground that is essential to passing legislation. This has been especially true on health issues, where the disagreements tend to be over how best to achieve a common objective and not over whether something needs to be done. Not surprisingly, once we are able to reach agreement on a bill, the legislation generally passes. If Kennedy and Hatch can agree, there's not much left uncovered on the political spectrum."[1]

*The following document is an excerpt from Kennedy's remarks of
April 8, 1997, when he and Hatch introduced the Child Health Insurance and Lower
Deficit Act—later renamed the State Children's Health Insurance Program—in the U.S.
Senate.*

. . . I am honored to join Senator HATCH in introducing the Child Health Insurance and Lower Deficit Act of 1997, which will be a major step toward making health insurance accessible and affordable for all of America's children. I am hopeful that the legislation we are introducing today will be approved by this Congress, and signed by President Clinton. It shows that Democrats and Republicans can work together to solve this national problem.

One of the most urgent needs of children is health insurance coverage. Insurance is the best possible ticket to adequate health care—and every child deserves such care.

Today, however, more than 10 million children have no health insurance—1 child in every 7—and the number has been increasing in recent years. Every day, 3,000 more children lose their private health insurance. If the total continues to rise at the current rate, 13 million children will have no insurance coverage by the year 2000.

Almost 90 percent of these uninsured children are members of working families. Two-thirds are in two-parent families. Most of these families have incomes above the Medicaid eligibility line, but well below the income level it takes to afford private health insurance today.

The children's health care crisis begins at the beginning—with inadequate prenatal care. Some 17 industrial countries have lower infant mortality rates than the United States. Every day, 636 infants are born to mothers in this country who did not have proper prenatal care; 56 die before they are 1 month old. And 110 die before the age of 1. Many more grow up with permanent disabilities that could have been avoided with prenatal care. Uninsured pregnant mothers have sicker babies, and these babies are at greater risk—low birth weight, miscarriage, and infant mortality.

Too many young children are not receiving the preventive medical care they need. Uninsured children are twice as likely to go without medical care for conditions such as asthma, sore throats, ear infections, and injuries. One child in four is not receiving basic childhood vaccines on a timely basis. Periodic physical examinations are out of reach for millions of children, even though such exams can identify and correct conditions before they cause a lifetime of pain and disability.

Preventive care is the key to a healthy childhood, and it also is a cost-effective investment for society. Every dollar invested in childhood immunizations saves $10 in later hospital and other treatment costs.

Some say there is no health care crisis for children. But I reply, tell that to the hard-working parents who cannot afford coverage for their families or whose employers won't provide it.

Tell it to the hospital emergency room physicians who are often the only family doctor these children know, and who have to treat them for heart-breaking conditions that could have been prevented or easily cured with timely care.

Tell it to school teachers struggling to teach children too sick to learn. Tell it to children's advocates across the country, who see children every day with health care needs neglected for too long. Between 30 and 40 percent of children in the child protective system suffer from significant health problems.

For all these reasons and many more—10 million more—the children's health care crisis is real, and the time to address it is now. Every child deserves a healthy start in life. No family should have to fear that the loss of a job, or an employer's decision to drop coverage or hike the insurance premium will leave their children without health care.

The current neglect is all the more unconscionable, because children and adolescents are so inexpensive to cover. That is why we can and must cover them this year—in this Congress. The cost is affordable—and the benefits for children are undeniable.

The legislation that Senator HATCH and I are introducing will make health insurance coverage more affordable for every working family with uninsured children. It does so without imposing new Government mandates. It encourages family responsibility, by offering parents the help they need to purchase affordable health insurance for their children.

Under our plan, $20 billion over the next 5 years will be available to expand health insurance coverage for children, and $10 billion will be available for deficit reduction. I share Senator HATCH's commitment to balancing the Federal budget by the year 2002. As our plan today suggests, we believe we can do it, and do it fairly.

When fully phased in, our legislation will provide direct financial assistance to approximately 5 million children annually. Every family with an uninsured child will have access to more affordable coverage. Combined with efforts to enroll more eligible children in Medicaid, this plan is a giant step toward the day when every American child has health insurance coverage. This bill is the most important single step the Congress can take this year to provide a better life for every American child.

States choosing to participate in the program will contract with private insurers to provide child-only private coverage. These subsidies will be available to help eligible families purchase coverage for their children, or participate in employment-based health plans. Coverage will be available for every child, including children in families not eligible for financial assistance. The program also allows States to allocate up to 5 percent of total program costs to provide preventive care and primary care to pregnant women. Participating States must contribute to the cost of the program, and must maintain their current levels of Medicaid coverage for children.

The basic principles of this proposal are neither novel nor untested. Fourteen States already have similar programs for children. In Massachusetts, an existing program was expanded last year, so that families up to 400 percent of the poverty level are now eligible for financial assistance to buy insurance. In 17 additional States, Blue Cross/Blue Shield offers children's-only coverage, with subsidies for low-income families. These State initiatives provide a solid base on which to build an effective Federal-State-private partnership to get the job done for all children.

Senator HATCH and I propose to pay for this program of children's health insurance and deficit reduction with an increase of 43 cents a pack in the Federal cigarette tax, from its current level of 24 cents. It makes sense to finance the coverage this way, because of the higher costs for health care and premature deaths caused by smoking.

Smoking is the leading preventable cause of death in the United States. It kills more than 400,000 Americans a year. It costs the Nation $50 billion a year in direct health costs, and another $50 billion in lost productivity. A cigarette pack sold for $1.80 costs the Nation $3.90 cents in smoking-related expenses.

Even with our proposed increase, cigarette taxes as a percent of the product price will still be lower than they were in 1965 and will be far below the levels in almost every other industrialized country.

A higher cigarette tax will have the added benefit of reducing smoking among teenagers. If we do nothing to reduce such smoking, 5 million deaths from smoking-related diseases will occur over the lifetime of the current generation of children.

Raising tobacco taxes to finance health insurance for children has the support of an overwhelming 73 percent of the public. If the tobacco tax is raised, an even higher 87 percent support using the revenue to expand health services for children.

I look forward to early action by Congress on this issue. Every day we delay means more children fail to get the healthy start in life they need. When we fail our children, we also fail our country and its future. . . .

Source: Kennedy, Edward M. Statements on Introduced Bills and Joint Resolutions. *Congressional Record*, 105th Cong., 1st sess., April 8, 1997, p. S2851.

NOTE

1. Orrin Hatch, *Square Peg: Confessions of a Citizen Senator* (New York: Basic Books, 2002), 112.

Tobacco Master Settlement Agreement

"To Counter the Use by Youth of Tobacco Products"

1998

In November 1998 the nation's four major cigarette makers—Philip Morris, R. J. Reynolds, Brown & Williamson, and Lorillard—and the tobacco industry's trade associations and public relations agencies reached a settlement with forty-six states that had filed suit against the tobacco industry for violating state antitrust and consumer protection laws. These lawsuits had been filed by state attorneys general who were seeking to recover billions of dollars in Medicaid and other public health program costs related to the treatment of smoking-related illnesses.

According to the terms of the Tobacco Master Settlement Agreement (MSA), the U.S. tobacco industry accepted major restrictions on its marketing operations, agreed to stand down against antitobacco legislation, and agreed to pay states approximately $206 billion through the year 2025 (with much of that money frontloaded) to help states cover medical treatment for smoking-related illnesses and launch major new antismoking campaigns aimed at America's youth.

The following excerpts from the MSA detail some of the advertising restrictions imposed on the tobacco industry, as well as the payment arrangement to bankroll the creation of a National Public Education Fund to coordinate antismoking efforts. The fund is perhaps best known for its contributions to the American Legacy Foundation, creator of the ongoing "truth" antismoking campaign.

This Master Settlement Agreement is made by the undersigned Settling State officials (on behalf of their respective Settling States) and the undersigned Participating Manufacturers to settle and resolve with finality all Released Claims against the Participating Manufacturers and related entities as set forth herein. This Agreement constitutes the documentation effecting this settlement with respect to each Settling State, and is intended to and shall be binding upon each Settling State and each Participating Manufacturer in accordance with the terms hereof.

I. Recitals

WHEREAS, more than 40 States have commenced litigation asserting various claims for monetary, equitable and injunctive relief against certain tobacco product manufacturers and others as defendants, and the States that have not filed suit can potentially assert similar claims;

WHEREAS, the Settling States that have commenced litigation have sought to obtain equitable relief and damages under state laws, including consumer protection and/ or antitrust laws, in order to further the Settling States' policies regarding public health, including policies adopted to achieve a significant reduction in smoking by Youth;

WHEREAS, defendants have denied each and every one of the Settling States' allegations of unlawful conduct or wrongdoing and have asserted a number of defenses to the Settling States' claims, which defenses have been contested by the Settling States;

WHEREAS, the Settling States and the Participating Manufacturers are committed to reducing underage tobacco use by discouraging such use and by preventing Youth access to Tobacco Products;

WHEREAS, the Participating Manufacturers recognize the concern of the tobacco grower community that it may be adversely affected by the potential reduction in tobacco consumption resulting from this settlement, reaffirm their commitment to work cooperatively to address concerns about the potential adverse economic impact on such community, and will, within 30 days after the MSA Execution Date, meet with the political leadership of States with grower communities to address these economic concerns;

WHEREAS, the undersigned Settling State officials believe that entry into this Agreement and uniform consent decrees with the tobacco industry is necessary in order to further the Settling States' policies designed to reduce Youth smoking, to promote the public health and to secure monetary payments to the Settling States; and

WHEREAS, the Settling States and the Participating Manufacturers wish to avoid the further expense, delay, inconvenience, burden and uncertainty of continued litigation (including appeals from any verdicts), and therefore, have agreed to settle their respective lawsuits and political claims pursuant to terms which will achieve for the Settling States and their citizens significant funding for the advancement of public health, the implementation of important tobacco-related public health measures, including the enforcements of the mandates and restrictions related to such measures, as well as funding for a national Foundation dedicated to significantly reducing the use of Tobacco Products by Youth;

NOW, THEREFORE, BE IT KNOWN THAT, in consideration of the implementation of tobacco-related health measures and the payments to be made by the Participating

Manufacturers, the release and discharge of all claims by the Settling States, and such other consideration as described herein, the sufficiency of which is hereby acknowledged, the Settling States and the Participating Manufacturers, acting by and through their authorized agents, memorialize and agree as follows. . . .

III. PERMANENT RELIEF

(a) <u>Prohibition on Youth Targeting.</u> No Participating Manufacturer may take any action, directly or indirectly, to target Youth within any Settling State in the advertising, promotion or marketing of Tobacco Products, or take any action the primary purpose of which is to initiate, maintain or increase the incidence of Youth smoking within any Settling State.

(b) <u>Ban on Use of Cartoons.</u> Beginning 180 days after the MSA Execution Date, no Participating Manufacturer may use or cause to be used any Cartoon in the advertising, promoting, packaging or labeling of Tobacco Products.

(c) Limitation of Tobacco Brand Name Sponsorships.

(1) <u>Prohibited Sponsorships.</u> After the MSA Execution Date, no Participating Manufacturer may engage in any Brand Name Sponsorship in any State consisting of:

    (A) concerts; or

    (B) events in which the intended audience is comprised of a significant percentage of Youth; or

    (C) events in which any paid participants or contestants are Youth; or

    (D) any athletic event between opposing teams in any football, basketball, baseball, soccer or hockey league.

(2) Limited Sponsorships.

    (A) No Participating Manufacturer may engage in more than one Brand Name Sponsorship in the States in any twelve-month period. . . .

(3) <u>Related Sponsorship Restrictions.</u> With respect to any Brand Name Sponsorship permitted under this subsection (c):

    (A) advertising of the Brand Name Sponsorship event shall not advertise any Tobacco Product (other than by using the Brand Name to identify such Brand Name Sponsorship event);

    (B) no Participating Manufacturer may refer to a Brand Name Sponsorship event or to a celebrity or other person in such an event in its advertising of a Tobacco Product. . . .

(4) <u>Corporate Name Sponsorships.</u> Nothing in this subsection (c) shall prevent a Participating Manufacturer from sponsoring or causing to be sponsored any athletic, musical, artistic, or other social or cultural event, or any entrant, participant or team in such event (or series of events) in the name of the corporation which manufactures Tobacco Products, provided that the corporate name does not include any Brand Name of domestic Tobacco Products.

(5) <u>Naming Rights Prohibition.</u> No Participating Manufacturer may enter into any agreement for the naming rights of any stadium or arena located within a Settling State using a Brand Name, and shall not otherwise cause a stadium or arena located within a Settling State to be named with a Brand Name.

(6) <u>Prohibition on Sponsoring Teams and Leagues.</u> No Participating Manufacturer may enter into any agreement pursuant to which payment is made (or other

consideration is provided) by such Participating Manufacturer to any football, basketball, baseball, soccer or hockey league (or any team involved in any such league) in exchange for use of a Brand Name.

(d) <u>Elimination of Outdoor Advertising and Transit Advertisements.</u> Each Participating Manufacturer shall discontinue Outdoor Advertising and Transit Advertisements advertising Tobacco Products within the Settling States as set forth herein.

(1) <u>Removal.</u> Except as otherwise provided in this section, each Participating Manufacturer shall remove from within the Settled States within 150 days after the MSA Execution Date all of its (A) billboards (to the extent that such billboards constitute Outdoor Advertising) advertising Tobacco Products; (B) signs and placards (to the extent that such signs and placards constitute Outdoor Advertising) advertising Tobacco Products in arenas, stadiums, shopping malls and Video Game Arcades; and (C) Transit Advertisements advertising Tobacco Products.

(2) <u>Prohibition on New Outdoor Advertising and Transit Advertisements.</u> No Participating Manufacturer may, after the MSA Execution Date, place or cause to be placed any new Outdoor Advertising advertising Tobacco Products or new Transit Advertisements advertising Tobacco Products within any Settling State.

(3) <u>Alternative Advertising.</u> With respect to those billboards required to be removed under subsection (1) that are leased (as opposed to owned) by any Participating Manufacturer, the Participating Manufacturer will allow the Attorney General of the Settling State within which such billboards are located to substitute, at the Settling State's option, alternative advertising intended to discourage the use of Tobacco Products by Youth and their exposure to second-hand smoke for the remaining term of the applicable contract (without regard to any renewal or option term that may be exercised by such Participating Manufacturer). The Participating Manufacturer will bear the cost of the lease through the end of such remaining term.

(4) <u>Ban on Agreements Inhibiting Anti-Tobacco Advertising.</u> Each Participating Manufacturer agrees that it will not enter into any agreement that prohibits a third party form selling, purchasing or displaying advertising discouraging the use of Tobacco Products or exposure to second-hand smoke. In the event and to the extent that any Participating Manufacturer has entered into an agreement containing any such prohibition, such Participating Manufacturer agrees to waive such prohibition in such agreement. . . .

(e) <u>Prohibition on Payments Related to Tobacco Products and Media.</u> No Participating Manufacturer may, beginning 30 days after the MSA Execution Date, make, or cause to be made, any payment or other consideration to any other person or entity to use, display, make reference to or use as a prop any Tobacco Product, Tobacco Product package, advertisement for a Tobacco Product, or any other item bearing a Brand name in any motion picture, television show, theatrical production or other live performance, live or recorded performance of music, commercial film or video, or video game ("Media"); provided, however, that the foregoing prohibition shall not apply to (1) Media where the audience or viewers are within an Adult-Only Facility (provided such Media are not visible to persons outside such Adult-Only Facility); (2) Media not intended for distribution or display to the public; or (3) instructional Media concerning non-conventional cigarettes viewed only by or provided only to smokers who are Adults.

(f) <u>Ban on Tobacco Brand Name Merchandise.</u> Beginning July 1, 1999, no Participating Manufacturer may, within any Settling State, market, distribute, offer, sell, license or cause to be marketed, distributed, offered, sold, or licensed (including, without limitation, by catalogue or direct mail), any apparel or other merchandise (other than Tobacco Products, items the sole function of which is to advertise Tobacco Products, or written or electronic publications) which bears a Brand Name. . . .

VI. Establishment of a National Foundation

(a) Foundation Purposes. The Settling States believe that a comprehensive, coordinated program of public education and study is important to further the remedial goals of this Agreement. Accordingly, as part of the settlement of claims described herein, the payments specified in subsections VI(b), VI(c), and IX(e) shall be made to a charitable foundation, trust or similar organization (the "Foundation") and/or to a program to be operated within the Foundation (the "National Public Education Fund"). The purposes of the Foundation will be to support (1) the study of and programs to reduce Youth Tobacco Product usage and Youth substance abuse in the States, and (2) the study of and education programs to prevent diseases associated with the use of Tobacco Products in the States.

(b) Base Foundation Payments. On March 31, 1999, and on March 31 of each subsequent year for a period of nine years thereafter, each Original Participating Manufacturer shall severally pay its Relative Market Share of $25,000,000 to fund the Foundation. The payments to be made by each of the Original Participating Manufacturers pursuant to this subsection (b) shall be subject to no adjustments, reductions, or offsets. . . .

(c) National Public Education Fund Payments.

(1) Each Original Participating Manufacturer shall severally pay its Relative Market Share of the following base amounts on the following dates to the Escrow Agent for the benefit of the Foundation's National Public Education Fund to be used for the purposes and described in subsections VI(f)(1), VI(g), and VI(h) below: $250,000,000 on March 31, 1999; $300,000,000 on March 31, 2000; $300,000,000 on March 31, 2001; $300,000,000 on March 31, 2002; and $300,000,000 on March 31, 2003. . . .

(f) Foundation Functions. The functions of the Foundation shall be:

(1) carrying out a nationwide sustained advertising and education program to (A) counter the use by Youth of Tobacco Products, and (B) educate consumers about the cause and prevention of diseases associated with the use of Tobacco Products;

(2) developing and disseminating model advertising and education programs to counter the use by Youth of substances that are unlawful for use or purchase by Youth, with an emphasis on reducing Youth smoking; monitoring and testing the effectiveness of such model programs; and, based on the information received from such monitoring and testing, continuing to develop and disseminate revised versions of such model programs, as appropriate;

(3) developing and disseminating model classroom education programs and curriculum ideas about smoking and substance abuse in the K-12 school system, including specific target programs for special at-risk populations; monitoring and testing the effectiveness of such model programs and ideas; and, based on the information received from such monitoring and testing, continuing to develop and disseminate revised versions of such model programs or ideas, as appropriate;

(4) developing and disseminating criteria for effective cessation programs; monitoring and testing the effectiveness of such criteria; and continuing to develop and disseminate revised versions of such criteria, as appropriate;

(5) commissioning studies, funding research, and publishing reports on factors that influence Youth smoking and substance abuse and developing strategies to address the conclusions of such studies and research;

(6) developing other innovative Youth smoking and substance abuse prevention programs;

(7) providing targeted training and information for parents;

(8) maintaining a library open to the public of Foundation-funded studies, reports and other publications related to the cause and prevention of Youth smoking and substance abuse;

(9) tracking and monitoring Youth smoking and substance abuse, with a focus on the reasons for any increases or failures to decrease Youth smoking and substance abuse and what actions can be taken to reduce Youth smoking and substance abuse;

(10) receiving, controlling, and managing contributions from other entities to further the purposes described in this Agreement;

(11) receiving, controlling, and managing such funds paid by the Participating Manufacturers pursuant to subsections VI(b) and VI(c) above. . . .

Source: Tobacco Master Settlement Agreement, November 23, 1998. http://ag.ca.gov/tobacco/pdf/1msa.pdf.

| DOCUMENT 9.14 | States Take Aim at Managed Care with New Consumer Protections |

"The Impact on Children"

1993–1997

As health maintenance organizations (HMOs) and other types of managed care rose to positions of dominance in the health care sector in the 1990s, state regulation of managed care entities increased. Passed in response to numerous news stories about HMO abuses of enrollees and intensive lobbying from consumer protection groups and physicians, the new state laws addressed many different aspects of managed care operations. Rhode Island and Virginia, for example, mandated independent reviews of HMO rejections of specialist referrals. New York passed a law requiring HMOs to reimburse patients for some types of care received from out-of-network health care professionals. Many states passed "any willing provider" laws, which opened HMO networks to a variety of health professions that had previously been excluded. Others outlawed the use of gag clauses by managed care organizations. These clauses had prevented physicians from informing patients about certain expensive treatment options for medical conditions. Other laws were passed forcing HMOs to accept longer hospital stays for mastectomy and maternity patients.

The map featured here illustrates the dramatic expansion of HMO regulations and reforms passed at the state level from 1993 to 1997, a five-year period of unprecedented managed care regulation across the United States.

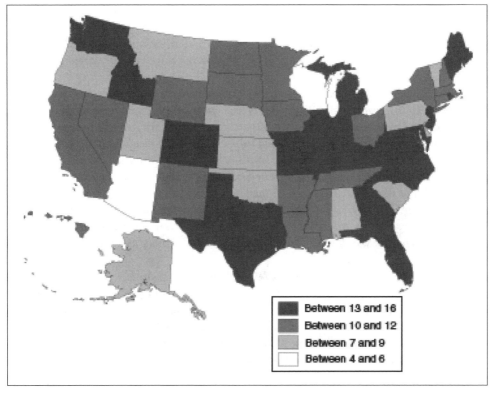

Source: Anderson, Gerard F. "State Regulation of Managed Care: The Impact on Children." *Children and Managed Health Care.* Summer/Fall 1998, p. 79. Used with permission.

DOCUMENT 9.15

Debating Oregon's Death with Dignity Law

"The Question Is whether This Law Is a Good One or Not"

1997

During the 1990s the already turbulent waters of American politics were further roiled by fierce and emotional debates about the practice of physician-assisted suicide. The epicenter of this issue was Oregon, which in 1994 became the first U.S. state to approve a law allowing for certain terminally ill individuals to request and receive lethal doses of medication from physicians willing to participate in the program.

    Oregon's Death with Dignity Act was approved by a 51–49 percent margin via a citizen's initiative, known as Measure 16, which appeared on the state's November 1994 ballot. Opponents filed an injunction that delayed implementation of the act until October 27, 1997. One month after that, Oregon residents were once again asked to weigh in on the issue by voting on Measure 51, a ballot initiative that would have repealed the Death with Dignity Act. As the date of the big vote drew near, the state of Oregon published a voting guide that included an explanation of Measure 51, as well as arguments for and against the measure. The explanatory statement is reprinted here, as well as three arguments for and against Measure 51.

The November 1997 election results amounted to a clear victory for Oregonians who wanted to keep the Death with Dignity Act on the books, as voters approved the act by a decisive 60–40 percent margin. Some conservative lawmakers tried to trump the Oregon law at the federal level. Their efforts ranged from claims to the Drug Enforcement Administration (DEA) that physician-assisted suicide violated provisions of the Controlled Substances Act to legislation championed by Sen. Don Nickles (R-OK) and Rep. Henry Hyde (R-IL) that would have overturned the law. United States attorney general Janet Reno subsequently ruled that the Controlled Substances Act did not authorize the DEA to intervene in Oregon, and attempts at a legislative solution were thwarted primarily by Democrats, including Sen. Ron Wyden (D-OR), and by the threat of a veto from President Bill Clinton.

In 2001, the newly installed George W. Bush administration took a variety of legal steps to stop physician-assisted suicide from being utilized in Oregon, but all of these efforts were eventually shot down by the courts, and the law remains in effect. The state of Oregon reported that, as of the end of 2009, 460 residents used the provisions of the Death with Dignity Act to end their lives. In November 2008 Washington became the second state to pass a Death with Dignity Act when voters passed Initiative 1000. That legislation formally became law on March 5, 2009.

Explanatory Statement

This measure repeals the Oregon Death With Dignity Act (Measure 16) passed by voters in 1994.

1994's Measure 16 allows a terminally ill patient the voluntary choice to obtain a physician's prescription for a lethal dose of medication to hasten the patient's death when the patient is judged to have less than six months to live. Measure 51, placed on the ballot by legislative referral, would repeal that law.

1994's Measure 16 allows a terminally ill patient who meets the conditions of the law to voluntarily request a prescription for a lethal dose of medication to end his or her life. The Act also allows a physician to legally prescribe the medication, and inform and advise the patient throughout the process, once the physician ensures the patient has met all of the conditions of the law. The physician and others may legally be present when the medication is self-administered by the patient. Lethal injection, mercy killing and active euthanasia are not permitted under 1994's Measure 16.

Under 1994's Measure 16, physicians and other health care providers may refuse to participate for any reason. If they choose to participate, a detailed process with listed safeguards must be followed before the patient can receive the prescription for medication. The procedure begins when the patient makes the request of his or her physician.

Under 1994's Measure 16, coercing or exerting undue influence on a patient to request medication, or altering or forging a request for medication, is punishable as a Class A felony. The State Health Division is required to review physician documentation and publish statistical reports that respect patient confidentiality.

If passed, Measure 51 would repeal Measure 16, the Oregon Death With Dignity Act.

In order *to repeal* 1994's Measure 16, the voter must *vote yes* on this measure.

In order *to keep* 1994's Measure 16, the voter must *vote no* on this measure.

ARGUMENT IN FAVOR

A Message to the People of Oregon from the Oregon Medical Association

In the next three months you will hear a great deal about Measure 51 which, if passed, will repeal Measure 16, Oregon's "Death With Dignity Act" which permits physician-assisted suicide for terminally ill patients.

The Oregon Medical Association (OMA) wants the voters of Oregon to know exactly where we stand on physician-assisted suicide, without interpretation by political coalitions who support or oppose Measure 51.

- OMA supports and advocates for compassionate and competent palliative (comfort) care at the end of life;
- OMA acknowledges that medical efforts to eliminate irreversible and extreme pain at the end of life are an appropriate medical response that may result in hastening the patient's death;
- OMA acknowledges patients' legitimate right to autonomy at the end of life, but does not accept the proposition that death with dignity may only be achieved through physician-assisted suicide;
- OMA specifically opposes Oregon's Death With Dignity Act as seriously flawed.

When the Death With Dignity Act passed in 1994, the OMA chose to stay neutral because our 5,500 physician members were narrowly divided on physician-assisted suicide, as were all Oregonians. Oregon physicians have had three years to study the law and we believe it has serious medical deficiencies that will negatively affect the care we provide to seriously ill patients.

While it is clear there continues to be a deep division of opinion on physician-assisted suicide, that won't be the issue when we vote in November.

The question is whether this law is a good one or not.

We don't think it is.

OMA urges you to vote Yes on Measure 51 in November to repeal Oregon's flawed physician-assisted suicide law.

(This information furnished by J. T. Hoggard, MD, President Elect, Oregon Medical Association.) . . .

ARGUMENT IN FAVOR

Oregon Association of Hospitals and Health Systems

Position Statement on:Ballot Measure 51

Oregon Association of Hospitals and Health Systems supports the repeal of Oregon's "Death With Dignity Act" and therefore supports a "YES" vote on ballot Measure 51. We are opposed to Oregon's Death With Dignity Act for the following reasons:

We do not believe the concept of "death with dignity" requires the use of physician-assisted suicide as called for in Oregon's "Death With Dignity Act." We support more appropriate alternatives for terminally ill patients, including:

- Active education and involvement of the patient and family in treatment and care decision-making at the end of life;
- Compassionate and competent comfort care at the end of life;
- Aggressive medical efforts to eliminate irreversible and extreme pain at the end of life, recognizing that such treatment may result in hastening the patient's death;
- Improved cooperative and coordinated efforts with Hospice to ensure timely referral;
- Improved education and knowledge for healthcare providers to be more consistent in use of compassionate pain management and anxiety control for patients near the end of life.

There are fundamental problems with the provisions of the Act including:

- Use of oral medications, as proscribed in the act, can be very ineffective and require massive dosages. As a result, the possibility of actually increasing the patient's physical and mental distress is significant.
- Use of oral prescriptions for drugs that are not intended to be lethal can, in a significant number of cases, result in a failed suicide attempt.
- There is no requirement for a psychiatric evaluation for patients requesting physician assisted suicide.
- There is no requirement to notify the patient's family when a potentially lethal prescription is written.
- Physicians are not able to accurately determine when a patient will die and, therefore, when a lethal prescription is appropriate.

The Oregon Association of Hospitals and Health Systems urges voters to vote Yes on Measure 51 to repeal Oregon's flawed and unneeded physician-assisted suicide law.

(This information furnished by Ken Rutledge, Oregon Association of Hospitals and Health Systems.) . . .

ARGUMENT IN FAVOR

Doctor/Patient Trust Essential

I have been a medical doctor in Oregon for most of 40 years. This great state has been good to me and my family. I am appalled at the prospect of Oregon becoming the main facilitator of an evil culture of disrespect and incivility at best, and violence and death at worst, all because of a very vocal few who have, I believe, a misguided concept of compassion.

As a physician, I was honored to attend, and not extend, the dying of many wonderful men and women. With God's help, I was never unable to help them to end their lives more easily and contentedly, mainly just through simply caring about them, being there, and meeting their medical needs.

Are we physicians now expected to ignore and deny our oath and ethical code of Hippocrates—"The regimen I adopt shall be for the benefit of my patients according to my ability and judgment, and not for their hurt or for any wrong. I will give no deadly drug to any, though it be asked of me, nor will I counsel such, and especially I will not aid a woman to procure abortion".

Can we really afford to ignore our pledge of allegiance "to one nation under God" and deny His dominion over us by again usurping His power of life and death? It continues to be our ultimate human arrogance to take what we cannot replace.

Do we really want to not be able to consistently trust our caregivers with our health and lives?

Are our individual rights more important than our responsibilities to each other and society as a whole?

Is not reverence for life from God the basis for all ethics, morality, civility, peace, and love—and disrespect for life the basis for their destruction?

Chesterton said, "Before you take down a wall, be sure you understand why it was put there in the first place". The Netherlands and the Nazi doctors are tragic examples.

I know I need not remind Oregonians that the worth of a nation (or state) is measured by how well it cares for its more vulnerable.

Please vote yes on Measure 51.

Joseph H. Eusterman, MD

(This information furnished by Joseph H. Eusterman, MD) . . .

ARGUMENT IN OPPOSITION

OMA MEMBERS URGE A NO VOTE ON MEASURE 51.

We are physicians and members of the Oregon Medical Association. We are opposed to the OMA's recent position on Measure 51, the effort to repeal Oregon's Death With Dignity law that was passed by voters in 1994.

The OMA wisely voted to remain neutral in 1994, allowing physicians to be guided by their personal convictions. As the OMA president said then, "Let the people of Oregon tell us what they want."

Unfortunately, a group of doctors, whose single goal is to advocate for the repeal of 1994's Measure 16, took over the House of Delegates in 1997, forcing through a resolution opposing Measure 16. **Most Oregon doctors do not support this position.**

In the past, organized medicine has frequently lagged behind the needs and desires of patients. The American Medical Association opposed such common medical practices as smallpox vaccinations, Advance Directives, blood banks and even group health insurance. The opposition of the OMA to Oregon's Death With Dignity law is just another example.

The OMA House of Delegates does not speak for the majority of Oregon physicians who support a law with well-defined safeguards giving patients' autonomy at the end of their lives.

Our patients have the right to hasten death under the limited circumstances outlined in Oregon's Death With Dignity Law.

We believe Oregon's Death With Dignity Act (1994's Measure 16), is a carefully crafted law.

We urge you to vote No on Measure 51 to keep Oregon's Death With Dignity Law.

Under Oregon's Death With Dignity law any physician or health care provider may refuse to participate. The numerous safeguards ensure that patients are fully informed and acting completely voluntarily.

Vote No on Measure 51.
Keep Oregon's Death With Dignity Law.
It's a good law.

Dr. Peter Rasmussen	Dr. Glenn Gordon, former OMA President	Dr. Joan Tanner
Dr. Calvin Collins	Dr. Bruce Johnson	Dr. Robert Hartog
Dr. R.W. Gerber	Dr. Peter Reagan	

(This information furnished by Dr. Joan Tanner, MD.) . . .

ARGUMENT IN OPPOSITION

Governor John Kitzhaber Says He'll Vote No on Measure 51.

As a physician, I can tell you there is a clear difference between prolonging someone's life and prolonging their death. One of the down sides of modern medicine is that often it prolongs people's deaths, which I am not sure is humane and I'm not sure is ethical.

I believe an individual should have control, should be able to make choices about the end of their life.

I don't think this issue is going to go away. We've got to get it out in the open . . . and come to terms with those implementation questions.

They [the legislature] didn't have the courage to repeal the measure. They didn't have the will to make it work. They just sent it back to voters.

We're talking about giving an individual access to a means to not prolong their death.

Governor John Kitzhaber
The Sunday *Oregonian*
August 2, 1997
(This information furnished by Margaret Tafoya Surguine, Oregon Right To Die.) . . .

ARGUMENT IN OPPOSITION

Now the opposition to Oregon's Death With Dignity law is crystal clear.

It's the OCA, back again to spread its divisive message of hate throughout Oregon.

The OCA Family Values PAC has registered with the Oregon Secretary of State to oppose Oregon's Death With Dignity law.

The OCA is joined by the Christian Coalition PAC and Oregon Right to Life as organizations working for the repeal of the law you passed in 1994.

We all knew the political arm of the Oregon Catholic Conference wanted to impose its religious beliefs on the rest of us.

Now you know — with the OCA at their side — that the threat of forcing their narrow views on the rest of us is much more dangerous.

While the majority of Catholics support a terminally ill patient's right to hasten death, the political arm of the Catholic Church has spent literally millions of dollars to try to convince voters they were wrong.

Now the Catholic Church is linked up with the OCA and the Christian Coalition, pledging to spend over $5 million to repeal Oregon's Death With Dignity Law.

Is it right for these groups to force their religious views on the rest of us?

Don't give them a victory at the ballot box.

The executive director of Oregon Right to Life, the state's biggest organization opposing personal liberty on death with dignity and other issues, had this to say on the day the Oregon Senate sent Measure 16 back to the ballot:

"That was the biggest victory the pro-life community has had in at least 20 years in the Oregon Legislature."

Gayle Atterberry

Salem *Statesman Journal*, June 16, 1997

Vote No on Measure 51.

It's Your Choice. . . Not Theirs.

(This information furnished by Kelli K. Watanabe, Oregon Right To Die.) . . .

Source: State of Oregon Election Guide, 1997. "Explanatory Statement." www.sos.state.or.us/elections/nov497/voters.guide/M51/M51ex.htm. "Arguments in Opposition." www.sos.state.or.us/elections/nov497/voters.guide/M51/M51ao.htm. "Arguments in Favor." www.sos.state.or.us/elections/nov497/voters.guide/M51/M51arf.htm.

DOCUMENT
9.16

Institute of Medicine Sounds an Alarm about Medical Errors in Hospitals

"Horrific Headlines That Make the Headlines Are Just the Tip of the Iceberg"

1999

Each year, federal and state agencies, think tanks, and issue advocacy groups publish thousands of studies and reports on various issues, trends, and events concerning different aspects of American life. Many of these reports find receptive audiences in policymaking circles and thus help shape public and private sector responses to various issues confronting the United States, but relatively few penetrate the consciousness of the wider American public. Occasionally, however, such a study does come along, and when it does, politicians and industry players rush to respond to the study's revelations before public outrage overtakes them.

One such study was a November 1999 Institute of Medicine report called To Err Is Human: Building a Better Health System *(the report's "Executive Summary" is excerpted here). The study, which was led by Linda T. Kohn, Janet M. Corrigan, and Molla S. Donaldson, estimated that between forty-four thousand and ninety-eight thousand patients died on an annual basis as a direct result of medical errors in U.S. hospitals. It also estimated that medical errors cost the nation $37.6 billion on an annual basis. The report, wrote health care analyst Julie Rovner, "hit the nation's health policy-making machinery like a ton of bricks. . . . The reported magnitude of the problem—that, even using the lower estimate, medical mistakes killed more Americans each year than highway accidents, breast cancer, or Acquired Immune Deficiency Syndrome (AIDS), according to* *the researchers—put the issue firmly on the nation's health agenda, with both the private sector and the policy makers vowing to act."[1]*

In 2001 Congress passed a measure that authorized the creation of a Center for Patient Safety within the Agency for Healthcare Research and Quality, and many hospitals introduced new operating processes to address concerns raised by the study. But the health care industry balked at the prospect of mandatory reporting of medical errors, one of the central recommendations of the study's authors. Efforts to pass medical reforms on Capitol Hill suffered as a result. With Democrats insisting on mandatory reporting systems and Republicans equally adamant that a voluntary reporting system was the way to go, no bill could gain the necessary support for passage. Most of the advancement in fighting medical errors thus came at the state level. Numerous states passed laws designed to reduce medical errors, and some, such as Pennsylvania, even established mandatory hospital error reporting systems.

The federal government finally moved on this issue in 2005, when Congress approved and President George W. Bush signed a compromise bill known as the Patient Safety and Quality Improvement Act. This measure required some mandatory reporting of medical errors but strictly limited access to this information by employers and lawyers.

Executive Summary

The knowledgeable health reporter for the *Boston Globe*, Betsy Lehman, died from an overdose during chemotherapy. Willie King had the wrong leg amputated. Ben Kolb was eight years old when he died during "minor" surgery due to a drug mix-up.[1]

These horrific cases that make the headlines are just the tip of the iceberg. Two large studies, one conducted in Colorado and Utah and the other in New York, found that adverse events occurred in 2.9 and 3.7 percent of hospitalizations, respectively.[2] In Colorado and Utah hospitals, 6.6 percent of adverse events led to death, as compared with 13.6 percent in New York hospitals. In both of these studies, over half of these adverse events resulted from medical errors and could have been prevented.

When extrapolated to the over 33.6 million admissions to U.S. hospitals in 1997, the results of the study in Colorado and Utah imply that at least 44,000 Americans die each year as a result of medical errors.[3] The results of the New York Study suggest the number may be as high as 98,000.[4] Even when using the lower estimate, deaths due to medical

---

[1]Cook, Richard; Woods, David; Miller, Charlotte, *A Tale of Two Stories: Contrasting Views of Patient Safety.* Chicago: National Patient Safety Foundation, 1998.

[2]Brennan, Troyen A.; Leape, Lucian L.; Laird, Nan M., et al. Incidence of adverse events and negligence in hospitalized patients: Results of the Harvard Medical Practice Study I. *N Engl J Med.* 324:370–376, 1991. See also: Leape, Lucian L.; Brennan, Troyen A.; Laird, Nan M., et al. The Nature of Adverse Events in Hospitalized Patients: Results of the Harvard Medical Practice Study II. *N Engl J Med.* 324(6):377–384, 1991. See also: Thomas, Eric J.; Studdert, David M.; Burstin, Helen R., et al. Incidence and Types of Adverse Events and Negligent Care in Utah and Colorado. *Med Care* forthcoming Spring 2000.

[3]American Hospital Association. Hospital Statistics. Chicago. 1999. See also: Thomas, Eric J.; Studdert, David M.; Burstin, Helen R., et al. Incidence and Types of Adverse Events and Negligent Care in Utah and Colorado. *Med Care* forthcoming Spring 2000. See also: Thomas, Eric J.; Studdert, David M.; Newhouse, Joseph P., et al. Costs of Medical Injuries in Utah and Colorado. *Inquiry.* 36:255–264, 1999.

[4]American Hospital Association. Hospital Statistics. Chicago. 1999. See also: Brennan, Troyen A.; Leape, Lucian L.; Laird, Nan M., et al. Incidence of adverse events and negligence in hospitalized patients: Results of the Harvard Medical Practice Study I. *N Engl J Med.* 324:370–376, 1991. See also: Leape, Lucian L.; Brennan, Troyen A.; Laird, Nan M., et al. The Nature of Adverse Events in Hospitalized Patients: Results of the Harvard Medical Practice Study II. *N Engl J Med.* 324(6):377–384, 1991.

errors exceed the number attributable to the 8th-leading cause of death.[5] More people die in a given year as a result of medical errors than from motor vehicle accidents (43,458), breast cancer (42,297), or AIDS (16,516).[6]

Total national costs (lost income, lost household production, disability and health care costs) of preventable adverse events (medical errors resulting in injury) are estimated to be between $17 billion and $29 billion, of which health care costs represent over one-half.[7]

In terms of lives lost, patient safety is as important an issue as worker safety. Every year, over 6,000 Americans die from workplace injuries.[8] Medication errors alone, occurring either in or out of the hospital, are estimated to account for over 7,000 deaths annually.[9]

Medication-related errors occur frequently in hospitals and although not all result in actual harm, those that do, are costly. One recent study conducted at two prestigious teaching hospitals, found that about two out of every 100 admissions experienced a preventable adverse drug event, resulting in average increased hospital costs of $4,700 per admission or about $2.8 million annually for a 700-bed teaching hospital.[10] If these findings are generalizable, the increased hospital costs alone of preventable adverse drug events affecting inpatients are about $2 billion for the nation as a whole.

These figures offer only a very modest estimate of the magnitude of the problem since hospital patients represent only a small proportion of the total population at risk, and direct hospital costs are only a fraction of total costs. More care and increasingly complex care is provided in ambulatory settings. Outpatient surgical centers, physician offices and clinics serve thousands of patients daily. Home care requires patients and their families to use complicated equipment and perform follow-up care. Retail pharmacies play a major role in filling prescriptions for patients and educating them about their use. Other institutional settings, such as nursing homes, provide a broad array of services to vulnerable populations. Although many of the available studies have focused on the hospital setting, medical errors present a problem in any setting, not just hospitals.

Errors are also costly in terms of opportunity costs. Dollars spent on having to repeat diagnostic tests or counteract adverse drug events are dollars unavailable for other purposes. Purchasers and patients pay for errors when insurance costs and copayments are inflated by services that would not have been necessary had proper care been provided. It is impossible for the nation to achieve the greatest value possible from the billions of dollars spent on medical care if the care contains errors.

---

[5]Centers for Disease Control and Prevention (National Center for Health Statistics). Deaths: Final Data for 1997. *National Vital Statistics Reports*. 47(19):27, 1999.

[6]Centers for Disease Control and Prevention (National Center for Health Statistics). Births and Deaths: Preliminary Data for 1998. *National Vital Statistics Reports*. 47(25):6, 1999.

[7]Thomas, Eric J.; Studdert, David M.; Newhouse, Joseph P., et al. Costs of Medical Injuries in Utah and Colorado. *Inquiry*. 36:255–264, 1999. See also: Johnson, W.G.; Brennan, Troyen A.; Newhouse, Joseph P., et al. The Economic Consequences of Medical Injuries. *JAMA*. 267:2487–2492, 1992.

[8]Occupational Safety and Health Administration. The New OSHA: Reinventing Worker Safety and Health [Web Page]. Dec. 16, 1998. www.osha.gov/oshinfo/reinvent.html.

[9]Phillips, David P.; Christenfeld, Nicholas; and Glynn, Laura M. Increase in US Medication-Error Deaths between 1983 and 1993. *The Lancet*. 351:643–644, 1998.

[10]Bates, David W.; Spell, Nathan; Cullen, David J., et al. The Costs of Adverse Drug Events in Hospitalized Patients. *JAMA*. 277:307–311, 1997.

But not all the costs can be directly measured. Errors are also costly in terms of loss of trust in the system by patients and diminished satisfaction by both patients and health professionals. Patients who experience a longer hospital stay or disability as a result of errors pay with physical and psychological discomfort. Health care professionals pay with loss of morale and frustration at not being able to provide the best care possible. Employers and society, in general, pay in terms of lost worker productivity, reduced school attendance by children, and lower levels of population health status.

Yet silence surrounds this issue. For the most part, consumers believe they are protected. Media coverage has been limited to reporting of anecdotal cases. Licensure and accreditation confer, in the eyes of the public, a "Good Housekeeping Seal of Approval." Yet, licensing and accreditation processes have focused only limited attention on the issue, and even these minimal efforts have confronted some resistance from health care organizations and providers. Providers also perceive the medical liability system as a serious impediment to systematic efforts to uncover and learn from errors.[11]

The decentralized and fragmented nature of the health care delivery system (some would say "nonsystem") also contributes to unsafe conditions for patients, and serves as an impediment to efforts to improve safety. Even within hospitals and large medical groups, there are rigidly-defined areas of specialization and influence. For example, when patients see multiple providers in different settings, none of whom have access to complete information, it is easier for something to go wrong than when care is better coordinated. At the same time, the provision of care to patients by a collection of loosely affiliated organizations and providers makes it difficult to implement improved clinical information systems capable of providing timely access to complete patient information. Unsafe care is one of the prices we pay for not having organized systems of care with clear lines of accountability.

Lastly, the context in which health care is purchased further exacerbates these problems. Group purchasers have made few demands for improvements in safety.[12] Most third party payment systems provide little incentive for a health care organization to improve safety, nor do they recognize and reward safety or quality.

The goal of this report is to break this cycle of inaction. The status quo is not acceptable and cannot be tolerated any longer. Despite the cost pressures, liability constraints, resistance to change and other seemingly insurmountable barriers, it is simply not acceptable for patients to be harmed by the same health care system that is supposed to offer healing and comfort. "First do no harm" is an often quoted term from Hippocrates.[13] Everyone working in health care is familiar with the term. At a very minimum, the health system needs to offer that assurance and security to the public. . . .

RECOMMENDATIONS

. . . In developing its recommendations, the committee seeks to strike a balance between regulatory and market-based initiatives, and between the roles of professionals

---

[11]Leape, Lucian; Brennan, Troyen; Laird, Nan; et al., The Nature of Adverse Events in Hospitalized Patients, Results of the Harvard Medical Practice Study II. *N EnglJ Med.* 324(6):377–384, 1991.

[12]Milstein, Arnold, presentation at "Developing a National Policy Agenda for Improving Patient Safety," meeting sponsored by National Patient Safety Foundation, Joint Commission on Accreditation of Health Care Organizations and American Hospital Association, July 15, 1999, Washington, D.C.

[13]Veatch, Robert M., Cross-Cultural Perspectives in Medical Ethics: Readings. Boston: Jones and Bartlett Publishers, 1989.

and organizations. No single action represents a complete answer, nor can any single group or sector offer a complete fix to the problem. However, different groups can, and should, make significant contributions to the solution. The committee recognizes that a number of groups are already working on improving patient safety, such as the National Patient Safety Foundation and the Anesthesia Patient Safety Foundation.

The recommendations contained in this report lay out a four-tiered approach:

- establishing a national focus to create leadership, research, tools and protocols to enhance the knowledge base about safety;
- identifying and learning from errors through immediate and strong mandatory reporting efforts, as well as the encouragement of voluntary efforts, both with the aim of making sure the system continues to be made safer for patients;
- raising standards and expectations for improvements in safety through the actions of oversight organizations, group purchasers, and professional groups; and
- creating safety systems inside health care organizations through the implementation of safe practices at the delivery level. This level is the ultimate target of all the recommendations. . . .

Source: Kohn, Linda T., Janet M. Corrigan, and Molla S. Donaldson, eds. "Executive Summary." *To Err Is Human: Building a Safer Health System.* Washington, DC: National Academy Press and Institute of Medicine, 2000, pp. 1–6. Copyright (©) 2000 National Academy of Sciences. Reprinted with permission.

Note

1   Julie Rovner, "Medical Errors," *Health Care Policy and Politics A to Z,* 3rd ed. (Washington, DC: CQ Press, 2009), 137.

<table>
<tr><td>DOCUMENT
9.17</td><td></td></tr>
</table>

President Clinton Extols New Rules to Ensure Medical Privacy

"To Protect the Sanctity of Individual Medical Records"

2000

During the course of the 1990s, the national health care system adopted many information storage and retrieval technologies for medical records. As President Bill Clinton noted in October 1999, this transition was beneficial in many ways, for "electronic records are not only cost effective; they can save lives by helping doctors to make quicker and better informed decisions, by helping to prevent dangerous drug interactions, by giving patients in rural areas the benefit of specialist care hundreds of miles away." But privacy advocates noted that computer automation of medical records also made confidentiality of personal information a growing concern.

As reports proliferated of employers and other third parties accessing private medical records, Congress considered a variety of measures to enhance personal privacy in this area. Many of these bills were based on medical privacy recommendations handed down to Congress in September 1997 by the Department of Health and Human Services. Partisan sniping and jockeying hindered passage of comprehensive federal legislation for the next few years, so the Clinton administration proposed its own medical privacy rules on December 20, 2000, only a few weeks before the president was leaving office. Clinton's remarks unveiling the Privacy Rule are reprinted here.

The Privacy Rule underwent several subsequent modifications at the behest of insurers, pharmaceutical manufacturers, and hospital systems during George W. Bush's first term in office, but many of the privacy safeguards first proposed by the Clinton administration remained intact. The revised version, the Medical Privacy Rule, took effect on April 14, 2003.

. . . In 1928 Justice Brandeis wrote his famous words saying that privacy was "the right most valued by civilized people," and he defined it simply as the right to be left alone.

Nothing is more private than someone's medical or psychiatric records. And therefore, if we are to make freedom fully meaningful in the information age, when most of our stuff is on some computer somewhere, we have to protect the privacy of individual health records.

The new rules we release today protect the medical records of virtually every American. They represent the most sweeping privacy protections ever written, and they are built on the foundation of the bipartisan Kennedy-Kassebaum legislation I signed 4 years ago.

This action is required by the great tides of technological and economic change that have swept through the medical profession over the last few years. In the past, medical records were kept on paper by doctors and stored in file cabinets by nurses; doctors and nurses, by and large, known to their patients. Seldom were those records shared with anyone outside the doctor's office.

Today, physicians increasingly store them electronically, and they are now obliged to share those records in paper or electronic form with insurance companies and other reviewers. To be sure, storing and transmitting medical records electronically is a remarkable application of information technology. They're cost-effective; they can save lives by helping doctors to make quicker and better-informed decisions.But it is quite a problem that, with a click of a mouse, your personal health information can be accessed without your consent by people you don't know, who aren't physicians, for reasons that have nothing to do with your health care. It doesn't take a doctor to understand that that is a prescription for abuse.

So, the rules that we release today have been carefully crafted for this new era, to make medical records easier to see for those who should see them and much harder to see for those who shouldn't. Employers, for instance, shouldn't see medical records, except for limited reasons, such as to process insurance claims. Yet, too often they do, as you just heard.

A recent survey showed that more than a third of all Fortune 500 companies check medical records before they hire or promote. One large employer in Pennsylvania had no trouble obtaining detailed information on the prescription drugs taken by its workers, easily discovering that one employee was HIV positive. That is wrong. Under the rules we released today, it will now be illegal.

There's something else that's really bothered me too, for years, and that is that private companies should not be able to get hold of the most sensitive medical information for marketing purposes. Yet, too often, that happens as well. Recently, expectant mothers who haven't even told their friends the good news are finding sales letters for baby products in their mailboxes. That's also wrong. And under these new rules, it will also be illegal.

Health insurance companies should not be able to share medical records with mortgage companies who might be able to use them to deny you a loan. That actually happens today, but under these rules, it will be illegal. Health insurance companies shouldn't be able to keep you from seeing your own medical records. Up to now, they could. Under these rules, they won't be able to do that anymore.

Under the rules being issued today, health plans and providers will have to tell you up front who will and won't be allowed to see your records. And under an Executive order I am issuing today, the Federal Government will no longer have free rein to launch criminal prosecutions based on information gleaned from routine audits of medical records.

With these actions today, I have done everything I can to protect the sanctity of individual medical records. But there are further protections our families need that only Congress can provide. For example, only new legislation from Congress can make these new protections fully enforceable and cover every entity which holds medical records. So I urge the new Congress to quickly act to provide these additional protections.

For 8 years now, I have worked to marry our enduring values to the stunning possibilities of the information age. In many ways, these new medical privacy rules exemplify what we have tried to do in this administration and how we have tried to do it. We can best meet the future if we take advantage of all these marvelous possibilities but we don't permit them to overwhelm our most fundamental values.

I hope that these privacy rules achieve that goal. And again, let me say, for this and so much more, I am profoundly grateful to the people who work here at HHS, the people who work with them at OMB and in the White House. In this action, you have done an enormous amount to reassure and improve the lives of your fellow Americans.

Thank you very much.

Source: Clinton, Bill. Remarks on the Issuance of Final Regulations on Protection of Medical Records Privacy. *Public Papers of the Presidents: William J. Clinton, 2000.* Vol. 3. Washington, DC: Government Printing Office, p. 2751.

DOCUMENT
9.18

RU486 Abortion Pill Adds Fuel to America's Political "Culture Wars"

"Tragic and Sad" or a "Giant Step Forward for Women"?

2000

In 2000 the Food and Drug Administration (FDA) approved the use of RU486 (formally known as mifepristone), a pill that can induce early abortion without surgery, for use in the United States. The announcement capped more than a decade of fierce political warfare over the introduction of RU486. The pill had first been introduced in France in 1988, but the pro-life administrations of Ronald Reagan and George H. W. Bush kept it away from American shores. Citing safety concerns, FDA administrators during the Reagan and Bush years issued instructions that called for the confiscation of any RU486 pills that entered the country. When President Bill Clinton took office in 1993, he immediately lifted this import restriction. This move was loudly applauded by the pro-choice movement, one of Clinton's key political constituencies.

The battle to gain FDA approval for RU486, however, was not over. The Religious Right lobbied fiercely against its introduction, and in the late 1990s conservatives in Congress nearly succeeded in passing legislation that would have barred the FDA from granting approval to any drug "for the inducement of abortion." On September 28, 2000, the FDA formally cleared the way for physicians to subscribe RU486 to patients in the United States. This announcement sparked starkly divergent reactions from the pro-life and pro-choice movements, as the following excerpt shows. This is the transcript of a debate between Laura Echevarria of the National Right to Life Committee and Gloria Feldt of Planned Parenthood that took place a few hours after the FDA announcement came down. The interviewer is Margaret Warner of PBS's Online NewsHour with Jim Lehrer.

The interview includes speculation that Republican presidential candidate George W. Bush, a conservative with strong pro-life credentials, might take action against RU486. Bush took the oath of office in 2001, but his administration was unable to reverse FDA approval for mifepristone without new clinical evidence that cast the drug's efficacy or safety into doubt. In the ten years since the drug's introduction, the FDA estimates that the RU486 abortion pill has been used by nearly 1.4 million women in America. The pill accounts for about one out of four abortions performed in the United States in the first nine weeks of pregnancy and about 15 percent of all abortions carried out in America. Opponents continue to characterize use of RU486 as immoral and dangerous to the health of women. Defenders of the pill's availability say that it is much safer than other forms of abortion or childbirth. As of 2010 mifepristone has been approved for use in thirty-five countries, mostly in the industrialized West.

[Ellipses in this interview denote pauses, not text omissions.]

Warner: For more we turn to Gloria Feldt, president of the Planned Parenthood Federation of America; and Laura Echevarria, the chief spokesperson for the National Right to Life Committee. Ms. Feldt, what is the significance of this medically for women?

Feldt: We applaud the FDA's decision today. It is a giant step forward for women, a quantum leap in reproductive health technology and an option that American women have wanted for many years, so that we can have the same option that our sisters in Europe have had during all this time. It's been an arduous process. The scientific process has been long and arduous. But quite frankly, the political process has been even more arduous and longer. And having to overcome those hurdles of the pressures of anti-choice hardliners who want to keep this very safe, early option from American women has been quite a battle. And we're very grateful that today the FDA has approved the early option.

Warner: All right, but let me just ask you about the medical side of this. For a woman who is seeking an abortion, how does this compare to the surgical alternative in terms of safety, risks, benefits?

Feldt: Well, since it is a very early option and the earlier in pregnancy that an abortion can be done, the safer it is, it is a very, very safe alternative. Also, the fact that it's done without surgery means that there are lower to virtually no risks of infection. Now, surgically abortion is also extremely safe, and in any case, either of those options is much safer than carrying a pregnancy to term and full term and in delivery. But it's very important for women to have the information and the counseling so that they can decide which one of these procedures best fits their personal needs.

Warner: All right, Ms. Echevarria, how do you see this decision today?

Echevarria: We see it as tragic and sad that American women are going to suffer because of the use of RU-486 in the United States. Certainly their child is going to die, and that's something that's tragic right then and there of itself. But we also see that, if RU-486 is administered to American women, that certainly tragedies can result as a result of that. We know that there are side effects associated with RU-486 that can be quite severe, including nausea and vomiting and excessive bleeding. We know that in the studies, 2 percent of the women who take RU-486 hemorrhage severely enough that they require surgical intervention. And so certainly we see this as a sad day for American women and certainly for unborn children.

Warner: And do you find . . . the FDA did add certain restrictions, as we just heard the commissioner describe. What do you think of those? Does that allay the safety issues, as far as you're concerned?

Echevarria: We don't think that they go far enough. They are minimal requirements, in order to protect American women. But certainly the chance of a woman dying as a result of taking RU-486 still exists. We know that during the trials, during controlled clinical trials, that one woman in Iowa almost died as a result of taking RU-486. And certainly if that can happen during U.S. drug trials, then it can happen if RU-486 is introduced at large to American women.

Warner: Ms. Feldt, what is your view on these extra restrictions and what that does in the safety area?

Feldt: Thank you. First, let me just say that Laura has greatly overstated and misrepresented the facts. But that should come as no surprise because, after all, she does represent an organization whose goal it is to make sure that women do not have the right to safe legal abortion, and we need to remember that. The . . .

Warner: The additional requirements, did you find them appropriate?

Feldt: Yes, actually, yeah, they really are by and large. I think that, as we use mifepristone, we may find that some of these requirements can go by the wayside. But I think, for example, it's entirely normal standard of practice for a physician to be able to either provide the surgical abortion or to be able to refer it to another doctor who can. That happens all the time when we go to our primary care physician and he or she doesn't have the specialty to be able to follow up on a medical problem that may be diagnosed. So I think by and large, they are appropriate, and that providers will be able to work within them very well.

Warner: Do you see, Ms. Echevarria, this drug being used for other purposes, for instance, as a preventive measure, to prevent pregnancy?

Echevarria: Well, the way it works, it blocks progesterone, and to prevent pregnancy, at this point in time, nothing has indicated that it could do that. Certainly we've never opposed its use to treat brain tumors or uterine fibroid tumors or cancers of any type. Certainly if it can provide life-saving solutions, then we would not oppose that. In this particular case, though, RU-486 has been introduced into the United States. It will be used in the United States and has been promoted for use in the United States only as an abortive agent.

Warner: Let me ask you about the examples in Europe. I gather . . . I understand that in France, for instance, it did not trigger any more abortions. Do you think it will trigger any more abortions here?

Echevarria: I don't think so. I think that what we're going to see is some women will choose RU-486 as opposed to surgical abortions. It is up in the air as to what result nationally we're going to have if we are going to see more abortions. But in all likelihood, we will find the same results that they have in France. I do think that, unfortunately, some women will end up suffering severe health consequences as a result of using RU-486. But certainly I don't see an increase in the number of abortions.

Warner: Ms. Feldt, do you think the fact that this drug and the way it's described, that it expels the embryo and it's not a fetus and it's not a baby, it's very early. Do you think that's going to change or does change the nature of the moral debate about abortion?

Feldt: Well, I know that many people have said and maybe want to believe that mifepristone will change the whole course of the abortion debate in this country. Because, frankly, I think people are tired of arguing about abortion and would prefer to spend more time, as Planned Parenthood does, trying to prevent the need for abortion through family planning and responsible sex education. But I'm not quite so sanguine about what I think mifepristone will do to the debate here in this country because those who oppose a woman's right to choose have the same opinion of mifepristone as they have of abortion in general. And I think they will continue fighting on the political front, and they will continue their attempts to harass and to vilify abortion providers. Now, that have been said, the promise of mifepristone is that more doctors will provide mifepristone than currently provide surgical abortion procedures, and that should make it more geographically accessible to women, and it should, over a long period of time, several years, make it more likely that it will be a more private decision and that women will be more likely to get mifepristone from their OB/GYN or their family practice doctor that they normally go to.

Warner: Ms. Echevarria, what's your view on how the earliness of this procedure and the fact that we're talking really about embryonic life here, whether that has any impact on the moral nature of the debate? Because there are many people who have moral, deep moral objections, as your organization represents, to abortion.

Echevarria: Right. No, it doesn't make a difference. You're still talking about an abortion, regardless of how it's done. The life of an unborn child is taken. And whether...

Warner: Though it isn't a child yet, that's correct?

Echevarria: We are talking about a child at this point in time when RU-486 is administered, by the time a woman realizes she's pregnant, the heart most likely already has begun to beat. That takes place between 18 and 22 days—days—after conception. So we're talking about an unborn child whose life is developing. On the outside end at seven weeks of pregnancy, that's about the time that brain waves can be detected. So most of the development of the child takes place in the early stages of pregnancy. The brain is developed, the heart is developed, the major organs are developed, fingers and toes. At the point when a child enters the fetal stage, that's when growth takes place, body fat is added; all of those things take place at later stages in the pregnancy. So you're talking about a developing human being genetically different from his or her parents whose life is taken as a result of RU-486.

Warner: So Ms. Feldt it sounds as if the moral and ethical debate isn't going to change.

Feldt: I think you're right about that, Margaret. I think the principle that a woman's life is a life first of all, that it's really a responsible thing to bring children into the world thoughtfully and carefully, and that women are capable moral decisionmakers, women can look at the options and, frankly, make better decisions for themselves morally and ethically, as well as medically, than the government or any other institution of society can make for them. This is such a personal decision, and I think no one really knows what their own personal moral and ethical decisions will be about it until they're faced with that situation.

Warner: Ms. Echevarria, you heard Gloria Feldt earlier predict that abortion opponents will continue to be active against abortion. Do you and your organization, and other groups have hopes of turning this around. For instance, if there were a new president, as there will be and George W. Bush opposes abortion, do you still hold out hope that you can reverse this?

Echevarria: Well, certainly we know that George W. Bush opposed RU-486. There is the hope that, under a different administration, one not so politically motivated to see RU-486 in the United States, that we may very well find the FDA will review RU-486, review the dangers associated with it, and possibly look into those dangers and a different decision would be made.

Warner: And Ms. Feldt, how about you? How final do you think this decision is?

Feldt: Well, I thank Laura for making that point. As president also of the Planned Parenthood Action Fund, Planned Parenthood's political arm, I think Laura's exactly right. A pro-choice president will make sure that women continue to have the right to choose, an anti-choice president, like George W. Bush, has already pledged to try to make abortion illegal. We can count an anti-choice president to make appointments to, for example, the head of the FDA or the head of the Department of Health and Human Services who would want to try to roll back access and perhaps even prevent access to mifepristone. And the person who signs or vetoes bills is the next president—the person who issues executive orders. There are many powers the president has, and it's important to have a pro-choice president if we're going to have the right to choose in the future.

Warner: All right, thanks Ms. Feldt and Ms. Echevarria, than you both very much.

Source: "Abortion Pill." Interview by Margaret Warner with Gloria Feldt of Planned Parenthood and Laura Echevarria of the National Right to Life Committee. The NewsHour with Jim Lehrer (air date: September 28, 2000. Copyright (©) 2000 MacNeil/Lehrer Productions. Reprinted with permission. Transcript available at www.pbs.org/newshour/bb/health/july-dec00/ru486_9-28.html.

CHAPTER 10

Controversial Policy Prescriptions
for American Health Care

2000–2010

During the first decade of the twenty-first century, the American people were whipsawed back and forth between two vastly different methodologies for addressing the nation's escalating health care crisis. Both Democrats and Republicans recognized the same grim trends: rapidly rising health care costs, growing numbers of uninsured people, and widespread evidence of waste and poor performance in health care sectors. And the two parties agreed that the impact of these trends—reduced investment in education and other public priorities, diminished competitiveness in global business sectors, and the risk of financial hardship or ruin for millions of families—made it imperative that Washington, D.C., take action. However, the divergent political ideologies and policy priorities of the two parties made it exceedingly difficult for them to find, or even seek out, common ground. The most spectacular evidence of this chasm came in 2009–2010, when President Barack Obama and Democratic majorities in Congress enacted the Patient Protection and Affordable Care Act without a single Republican vote.

George W. Bush Touts Pro-Life Policies

The decade began on a tense political note with the inauguration of Republican George W. Bush as the forty-third president of the United States. The former governor of Texas and eldest son of former president George H. W. Bush had narrowly won the 2000 presidential election over Democratic nominee Al Gore—despite losing the popular vote—after a controversial U.S. Supreme Court decision (*Bush v. Gore*) preserved the Republican's narrow edge in the electoral college. Although Democrats and their core constituencies were embittered by the election results, their leverage over the new president was limited. The Republicans managed to maintain control of the House and Senate in the November 2000 elections, albeit by narrow margins.

As expected by friend and foe, the Bush administration's stance on some health care issues was greatly influenced by the president's pro-life orientation. In one of his first acts as president, Bush reinstated a Ronald Reagan–era ban on federal aid to international family planning organizations that provide abortions or counsel women about the practice. He regularly commented on the need to add pro-life votes to the bench of the Supreme Court, and he spoke approvingly of the efforts of individual states to enact new limits on abortion. Bush also strongly supported the 2003 Partial-Birth Abortion Ban Act, the country's first federal ban on a specific abortion procedure. "The facts about partial-birth abortion are troubling and tragic, and no lawyer's brief can make them seem otherwise," said Bush at the signing of the legislation on November 5. "The bill I am about to sign protecting innocent new life from this practice reflects the compassion and humanity of America."[1]

The law was denounced by pro-choice advocates such as National Organization for Women (NOW) president Kim Gandy, who described it as "a dangerous piece of legislation that ultimately seeks to outlaw even the safest abortion procedures. The truth is that the term 'partial birth abortion' doesn't exist in the medical world—it's a fabrication of the anti-choice machine. The law doesn't even contain an exception to preserve a woman's health and future fertility."[2] NOW and other pro-choice groups tried to strike down the law in the courts, but the Bush administration and pro-life organizations mounted a vigorous legal defense. In 2007, after four years of legal battles, the Supreme Court ruled 5–4 in *Gonzales v. Carhart* in favor of the act, a judgment that elicited dramatically different reactions on Capitol Hill **(See Document 10.5)**.

Bush's pro-life views also shaped his administration's position on embryonic stem cell research. Scientists believed that such research could greatly advance organ regeneration and limb replacement therapies, as well as provide cures for diabetes and other diseases that afflict millions of Americans. But conservative religious and pro-life groups argued that extracting embryonic stem cells—a process that destroyed the embryo—was tantamount to murder. They urged Bush and Congress to limit federal funding to research that used only adult stem cells, even though scientists believed that embryonic stem cells might hold greater promise for medical breakthroughs.

The moral and ethical complexities of the issue were brought home by divisions within Bush's own Republican caucus. Some lawmakers with strong pro-life records such as Senators Bill Frist (R-TN), Orrin Hatch (R-UT), and Strom Thurmond (R-SC) threw their support behind embryonic stem cell research, which they viewed as an issue distinct from abortion. In mid-2001 Bush announced that his administration would permit federal funding of research on existing stem cell lines, but that it would not support research on any other embryos **(See Document 10.1)**. This position was generally interpreted as a victory for the so-called Religious Right, but a few conservative pro-life groups, such as the U.S. Catholic Conference, asserted that the administration should have taken an even harder line. Over the remainder of his presidency, Bush opposed all efforts to loosen these funding restrictions. On two occasions, he vetoed bipartisan bills that would have allowed funding of research on stem cells in embryos leftover from in-vitro fertilization that were destined to be destroyed anyway.

Bush's successor in the White House took very different positions on these issues. Within a week of his January 20, 2009, inauguration, President Barack Obama overturned the ban on federal aid to nongovernmental organizations that include abortion in their family planning services. Three months later, the Food and Drug Administration (FDA) overturned a controversial Bush-era regulation from 2006 that limited access to the over-the-counter Plan B "morning after" emergency contraception pill to adults. Acting in compliance with a federal judge's order, the FDA lowered the age for purchase of the drug without a doctor's prescription to seventeen.

In March 2009 Obama issued an executive order expanding federal funding for "responsible, scientifically worthy" human stem cell research, including human embryonic stem cell research, to the extent permitted by law. Under this order, researchers still needed to obtain embryonic stem cells via private monies and in accordance with strict guidelines, but they could henceforth use federal funding to conduct research on those stem cell lines. In mid-2010, however, a federal judge issued a ruling that blocked implementation of the executive order. The ruling, which cast a cloud of uncertainty over stem cell research at the National Institutes of Health and research institutions across the country, was swiftly appealed by the Obama administration.

Controversy Rages over the Medicare Modernization Act

Although Bush's pro-life policy positions received considerable attention from the media and the American public, the most far-reaching health policy initiative of his first term came in 2003, when he championed a major overhaul of Medicare. This Republican-led expansion of Medicare was an oddity at first glance, given the GOP's long-standing opposition to "big government," its hostility to Medicare at its inception, and its warnings about the dangers of ballooning entitlement programs. The legislation that wound its way through Congress that year had a distinctly free market and pro-industry stamp to it. The ambitious Medicare Prescription Drug, Improvement, and Modernization Act (also known as the Medicare Modernization Act) included a new prescription drug benefit funneled through private insurers; a revamped version of Medicare + Choice known as Medicare Advantage (MA), a private plan alternative to traditional Medicare; and the enactment of privately maintained, tax-exempt health savings accounts (HSAs) for the non-Medicare population.

Democrats' opposition to the legislation was fierce. They admitted that the idea of extending limited prescription drug coverage to an estimated forty-one million senior citizens was appealing. But they charged that the prescription drug benefit (which became known as Medicare Part D) was fiscally irresponsible, given that it was unfunded and that the Bush White House was already projecting the largest deficit in U.S. history to that point. Without exception, Democrats believed that the prescription drug benefit was rooted in a GOP political goal: to curry favor with senior voters prior to the 2004 elections. The Democrats further asserted that other aspects of the bill, such as Medicare Advantage and HSA initiatives, were steps in a larger plot to dismantle Medicare and shift its services to the private sector. These accusations were flatly rejected by the GOP. "[Democrats] are nervous about the government losing a monopoly and empowering people to make choices," said Karl Rove, Bush's chief political adviser. "Under the new law, seniors will be able to choose between traditional Medicare and plans administered by private companies. . . . We're going to use the market, choice, innovation, and empowerment of the individual and incentives for savings and for taking personal responsibility to try to achieve [quality senior health care]."[3]

Bush signed the Medicare Modernization Act in late 2003, but even some of its most steadfast supporters acknowledged that the process under which Congress passed the bill was an embarrassing spectacle. As the legislation was being debated, Democrats asked the chief actuary of Medicare, Rick Foster, to provide an estimate of the cost of the prescription drug benefit in its first ten years (the GOP's own budget bill authorized no more than $400 billion for the benefit, and the Congressional Budget Office (CBO) had previously estimated that it would cost $395 billion). When Foster put the price tag at $534 billion, the Bush administration suppressed his report out of fear that it would erode support for the bill among deficit hawks in the Republican caucus.

After Foster's report was buried, Republican House leaders brought the bill up for a final vote at 3:30 a.m. on November 22, 2003. To their great surprise, the bill seemed headed for certain defeat after a small group of Republicans joined the Democrats in opposing the measure as an expensive giveaway to the drug industry. In speech after speech, these critics accused House leaders of letting pharmaceutical lobbyists write the legislation. Instead of accepting the setback, the GOP leadership took the unprecedented step of holding open the vote for three hours. They spent that time roaming the House floor in search of rebellious Republicans, besieging them with demands and pleas that they change their vote to "yes." Republican representative Jo Ann Emerson of Missouri was reportedly so unnerved by the proceedings that she spent the time hiding in a crouch on the Democratic side of the floor. Rep. Nick Smith of Michigan later accused his fellow Republicans of engaging in blatant bribery and blackmail to get him to switch his vote **(See Document 10.2)**. Republican Walter B. Jones of North Carolina, who also opposed the bill, called it "the ugliest night I have ever seen in 22 years [of politics]."[4]

The political arm-twisting eventually paid off. Just before 6 a.m., a sufficient numbers of Republicans switched their vote to get the measure passed by a 220–215 tally (204 Republicans and 16 Democrats voted "yes"; 25 Republicans, 189 Democrats, and 1 independent voted "no"). The measure then went before the Senate, where it was passed over mostly Democratic opposition. Bush signed the bill into law on December 8. One year later, Republican representative Billy Tauzin (LA), who played a major role in steering the bill through the House, finished his term in office and became president of the Pharmaceutical Research and Manufacturers of America (PhRMA), the industry's most powerful trade group in Washington.

THE PROS AND CONS OF MEDICARE ADVANTAGE

Once the Medicare Modernization Act was enacted, senior citizens, policy analysts, lawmakers, insurers, and various other health sector players all set about preparing for the changes. As both supporters and detractors of Medicare Advantage anticipated, interest in the private plan alternative was high. For-profit insurers heavily publicized their MA offerings, secure in the knowledge that, under the legislation, the federal government would pay them 12 percent more per beneficiary than regular Medicare would spend to cover the same people. Insurance companies defended this deal as reasonable, given that their plans contained vision benefits, dental care, and other benefits not available through regular Medicare. But critics charged that some of the private MA plans being pitched to seniors contained payment caps and exclusions that would translate into higher copayments and out-of-pocket costs for some enrollees than if they remained with traditional Medicare.[5]

Despite these warnings, enrollment soared from 5.3 million (under the old Medicare + Choice scheme) in 2003 to 9 million by early 2008. This meant that about one of every five Medicare beneficiaries was enrolled in an MA plan. Many seniors—especially healthy ones—fared well under these plans, as the Bush administration was quick to note. "Medicare Advantage plans," said one official with the Centers for Medicare and Medicaid Services, "are offering an average of approximately $1,100 in additional annual value to beneficiaries in terms of cost savings and added benefits."[6]

As critics feared, however, some MA enrollees grappling with serious health issues suffered greater financial hardship under the program than if they had remained with traditional Medicare. The Congressional Budget Office reported in 2008 that 19 percent of MA enrollees faced higher cost-sharing for home health services, while 16 percent of MA beneficiaries were projected to experience higher cost-sharing for inpatient services. The CBO report also found that 29 percent of private MA policies equipped with out-of-pocket limits did not count certain cancer drugs toward the caps, while 21 percent of the private plans excluded home health care services from out-of-pocket limits.[7] Consumer advocates alleged that some MA enrollees were being tricked into joining by duplicitous sales agents. (This charge eventually led the seven largest MA insurers to temporarily suspend their marketing activities in 2007 and revise their practices to place a greater emphasis on beneficiary education.)

The other criticism of Medicare Advantage, which by March 2010 covered approximately 11.1 million seniors (nearly one in four Medicare beneficiaries), has focused on its expense. Defying the prognostications of its chief architects and supporters, MA plans have, from the very outset, cost the government more on a per beneficiary basis than traditional Medicare. As a result, Republicans and Democrats alike began exploring politically tenable ways to reduce MA payments to the private insurers.

MAKING SENSE OF THE MEDICARE PRESCRIPTION DRUG BENEFIT

The Medicare prescription drug benefit (Part D) contained in the Medicare Modernization Act received even more scrutiny, because it would impact the lives of tens of millions of American seniors as soon as it took effect on January 1, 2006. The provisions governing the drug benefit were extraordinarily complex, but in essence the law was crafted to provide Medicare enrollees with discounts for routine prescription drugs as well as catastrophic coverage that would enable them to purchase high-cost medicines used to fight serious diseases and conditions.[8] In the original rollout, enrollees in the program were responsible for a $250 annual deductible and a small monthly premium. Medicare covered 75 percent of prescription costs up to $2,250, after which the beneficiary paid the full cost. Once the beneficiary reached a catastrophic-level threshold of $3,600 in out-of-pocket expenses (not including premiums, drugs not covered in the plan, or prescriptions filled in pharmacies not in the patient's network), the government stepped back into the picture and absorbed 95 percent of all remaining prescription costs. The coverage gap between the initial coverage limit of $2,250 and the catastrophic coverage limit of $3,600 quickly came to be known as the donut hole.

Since 2007, all of the dollar amounts in the Medicare Part D formula have been adjusted annually to reflect rising drug costs.

Within those broad parameters, the Medicare Modernization Act empowered seniors to select the plan that made the most sense to them. But as the January 1, 2006, start date approached, it became clear that, in delivering Medicare Part D through private insurers instead of the government's Medicare program, Bush and his fellow Republicans in effect forced potential enrollees to sort through a blizzard of competing plans with differing deductibles and copay schemes. Moreover, the introduction of "commercial middlemen" into the drug program necessitated the creation of a complex new public-private processing infrastructure for claims, prescription fulfillment, and other recordkeeping.[9]

Many seniors expressed bafflement with the impending new system, and experts began predicting a calamitous rollout. It was not until mid-2005 that the administration seemed to recognize that the prescription drug benefit had the potential to metastasize from a clear political winner into a public relations disaster. At that point Washington belatedly mobilized to educate America's seniors about resources that could help guide them through the enrollment process, with Bush himself serving as the point man in these efforts (See Document 10.3).

The late scramble to get the system in order before January 1 fell short, and the program misfired badly coming out of the gate. In Maine, one of the most lightly populated states in the union, a hotline for confused seniors logged eighteen thousand calls in a single day.[10] By mid-January the *Washington Post* was reporting that as many as 6.4 million "of the nation's sickest and poorest elderly and disabled people are being turned away or overcharged at pharmacies," a state of affairs that prompted more than a dozen states—including heavily populated states such as Arkansas, California, Illinois, New Jersey, Ohio, and Pennsylvania—to declare health emergencies and pay for residents' life-saving prescriptions.[11]

Despite Medicare Part D's shaky beginnings, American seniors eventually found their footing in the program. By mid-2006 the vast majority of eligible seniors were enrolled in one plan or another, and pharmacists, insurers, and other important elements of the drug delivery pipeline had identified and fixed many of the glitches that had dogged the program earlier in the year. And as the political dust settled and the true scale of the program came into view, observers agreed that Bush had presided over a major milestone in the history of American health care. The Medicare prescription drug benefit, observed the *New York Times*, amounted to "the largest expansion of Medicare in decades and it dragged the program, at long last, into the modern medical era, in which drugs are a cornerstone of treatment."[12]

While Republicans and Democrats applauded the program's value to millions of seniors, the benefit's fiscal underpinnings remained a sore spot for people across the political spectrum. The Bush administration's insistence on funneling the benefit through private insurers, who did not have the authority to negotiate lower prices from drug makers, added tens of billions of dollars to the expense of Medicare Part D. Study after study showed that participants in the prescription drug program were charged much higher prices than enrollees in other federal programs empowered to negotiate with the pharmaceutical industry on price. The nonprofit health advocacy organization Families USA reported in 2007, for example, that Medicare patients were being charged nearly 60 percent more for twenty commonly prescribed drugs than veterans paid for the same drugs under a Veterans Health Administration (VHA) program. And for some of these drugs, the disparity was truly shocking. According to the Families USA study, the best Medicare price for a year's supply of the cholesterol drug Zocor was $1,485; the same drug cost only $127 a year under the VHA plan.[13]

Insurance industry profits were the other main driver of the high cost of Medicare Part D. Back in the 1990s, commercial insurers had made it clear with Medicare + Choice that they would walk away from any business that did not deliver solid streams of revenue. Because the Bush administration was determined to keep the prescription drug benefit machinery in the hands of the private sector as much as possible, it had thus felt obligated to include a variety of subsidies to insurance carriers when it crafted the Medicare Modernization Act.[14]

The Bush administration's generous treatment of the insurance and pharmaceutical industries reflected an abiding conviction that the free market's "inherent efficiencies" would produce cost savings over the long term. But as the months passed and the predicted savings failed to materialize, observers such as health care expert Jonathan Cohn wondered aloud about the long-term repercussions for the prescription drug program. "The more expensive the drug benefit became, the more insistent calls for reining it in were bound to become," he wrote. "Medicare had finally expanded to meet society's growing needs, as its original architects always hoped it would. But, at the behest of those who never really believed in the program, it had expanded in a way that undermined its effectiveness—and jeopardized its long-term survival."[15]

POLITICAL BRAWL OVER SCHIP OBSCURES AREAS OF CONSENSUS

In terms of health policy, President Bush's second term in office went much as his first one had—repeated clashes with Democrats, punctuated by an occasional flash of bipartisan comity. On the positive side of the ledger, the two sides agreed to increase U.S. financial support for international efforts to combat acquired immune deficiency syndrome (AIDS), malaria, and tuberculosis. Bush's creation of a President's Emergency Plan for AIDS Relief (PEPFAR) was a particularly signal accomplishment. In 2008 Congress approved $48 billion over five years for this program, which marked a new level of U.S. engagement with the global HIV (human immunodeficiency virus, which causes AIDS) and AIDS crisis. Bush also surprised and impressed Democrats with his vigorous and steady support for community health centers. In many isolated rural areas and inner-city neighborhoods, these centers stand as the only source for basic health services such as childhood immunizations, prenatal care, and screenings for cancer and sexually transmitted diseases. During his years in the White House, Bush doubled federal financing for these clinics, paving the way for the expansion or establishment of nearly thirteen hundred centers across the nation.

A broad consensus also existed in Washington in the wake of the September 11, 2001, terrorist attacks that national defenses against bioterrorism needed greater attention. In 2002 the Public Health Security and Bioterrorism Preparedness and Response Act was signed into law. This act provided for increased protection of national water, food, and drug supplies; enhanced control of dangerous toxins and biological agents; and new public emergency preparedness measures. In 2004 Congress followed up with the Project BioShield Act, which provided funding for the development of medical treatments and procedures in the event of an act of bioterrorism.

Another notable bipartisan triumph of Bush's second term was the Wellstone Mental Health Parity Act of 2008, which required insurers to provide equal benefits for mental and physical conditions **(See Document 10.7)**. Finally, Bush's push to increase

One of the major components of President George W. Bush's health agenda was reducing the spread of infectious disease, particularly human immunodeficiency virus (HIV, which causes acquired immune deficiency syndrome or AIDS), tuberculosis, and malaria, in Africa. Here, the president distributes mosquito netting to women at a health clinic in Arusha, Tanzania, in February 2008.

health system efficiency by encouraging health care providers to make new investments in information technology drew plaudits from Democrats and Republicans, although medical privacy considerations slowed progress toward this goal.

These bright spots in health care policymaking and politicking, however, were the exceptions. In most other areas, Republicans and Democrats could find little common ground. Abortion remained a contentious issue that regularly sparked partisan fireworks. Bush and Republicans repeatedly moved to enact medical malpractice reform laws that would have placed caps on punitive damages and economic damages, only to be blocked by Democrats. Similarly, conservative efforts to resurrect the idea of Medicaid block grants to states were stymied by liberal opposition. The two parties also remained at loggerheads over a wide assortment of public health and environmental protection laws. Eager to please their traditional business constituencies, Republicans said that they wanted to reform sclerotic laws so as to provide long-suffering businesses and industries with relief from onerous, innovation-stifling regulations. Democrats charged that these proposals, which were fiercely opposed by one of *their* core constituencies—environmental groups—would gut key consumer protections and endanger the health of Americans by increasing water and air pollution levels. Not surprisingly, the chasm between these two perspectives produced political paralysis.

The animosity between the president and Democrats in Congress on health issues was particularly evident in 2007, when the 1997 State Children's Health Insurance Program (SCHIP) came up for reauthorization. Democrats, who had gained majorities in both houses of Congress in the 2006 midterms, wanted to expand the popular program, which had greatly reduced the number of poor children in America without health insurance. This proposed expansion was supported by a number of Republicans as well. But the Bush administration opposed the proposed changes, saying that they put too much control in the hands of the federal government and added too much to the deficit. When Democrats and a coalition of Republicans went ahead and passed an SCHIP expansion bill anyway, Bush vetoed the measure. His veto sparked a storm of angry recriminations on Capitol Hill **(See Document 10.6)**. After absorbing this setback, Democrats and moderate Republicans tweaked the bill, passed it (though without meeting their goal of securing enough support for a veto override), and sent it to the White House. Once again, Bush vetoed the legislation. Ultimately, frustrated Democrats and their Republican allies on the issue were forced to settle for a temporary extension of SCHIP that kept its existing level of funding to the end of Bush's second term.

HEIGHTENED CALLS FOR SWEEPING HEALTH CARE REFORM

Amid this perpetual whirl of political jousting and posturing, economists and health care experts issued increasingly dire warnings about the fiscal health, accessibility, and quality of American health care. These blaring sirens emanated from liberal bastions of academia as well as conservative think tanks, and by the last year of Bush's presidency they had taken on such urgency that health care once again became a major issue in a presidential election, in this case, the 2008 race that pitted Republican senator John McCain (AZ) against Democratic senator Barack Obama (IL).

The problem that got the lion's share of attention in this period was the sheer runaway expense of the system. In 2005 total annual spending on health care in the United States had broken through the $2 trillion mark. Accounting for about 16 percent of the nation's gross domestic product, this spending averaged out to about $7,100 a person.

Medicare and Medicaid had expanded to the point that they accounted for 20 percent of total government spending. The result of this rapid growth, wrote health care critic David Goldhill in 2009, was that "the federal government spends eight times as much on health care as it does on education, 12 times what it spends on food aid to children and families, 30 times what it spends on law enforcement, 78 times what it spends on land management and conservation, 87 times the spending on water supply, and 830 times the spending on energy conservation. Education, public safety, environment, infrastructure—all other public priorities are being slowly devoured by the health-care beast."[16]

Worst of all, experts asserted that the rate of spending on health care was accelerating, threatening the long-term futures of Medicare and Medicaid. Actuaries with the Centers for Medicare and Medicaid Services predicted that annual health care costs would blow through the $4 trillion mark by 2016, to more than $12,300 per person. Economists warned that such growth, if unabated, would force cuts to Medicare and Medicaid programs and necessitate brutal spending cuts to education, transportation, public health, and other vital sectors. Moreover, it would act as an anchor on overall economic growth, because employers confronted with spiraling health care costs would continue to divert compensation that might once have gone to wages into their health benefit packages. Insurance premiums in the United States throughout the mid-2000s rose at a far greater pace than the rate of inflation. From 2001 to 2007, the Kaiser Family Foundation reported that health insurance premiums for family coverage jumped 78 percent. During that same time span, wages rose 19 percent and inflation went up 17 percent.[17]

These skyrocketing costs were made even more difficult to accept given that, as reflected in key performance indices such as child mortality and life expectancy, American health care lagged behind that of many other industrialized countries. "Something's wrong here when one of the richest countries in the world, the one that spends the most on health care, is not able to keep up with other countries," remarked health statistician Christopher Murray of the Institute for Health Metrics and Evaluation at the University of Washington in Seattle.

These results were shaped to a considerable extent by the fact that the United States continued to carry a much higher percentage of uninsured people than other industrialized countries. In 2005 some forty-five million Americans had no health insurance, a figure that virtually everyone expected to grow in the years ahead, as employers dropped health care from their benefits packages. And without health insurance, many sick people delay or forego treatment, with sometimes deadly results. According to a 2009 Institute of Medicine (IOM) report, uninsured adults in the United States were 25 percent more likely to die prematurely than insured adults. In the case of some serious conditions (such as cancer, diabetes, and heart disease), the IOM reported that the uninsured population's risk of premature death was up to 50 percent higher.[18] Other studies estimated that about twenty thousand Americans a year were dying because they lacked health insurance.[19]

TARGETING WASTE AND INEFFICIENCY IN THE HEALTH CARE SYSTEM

Many analysts asserted that much of the high cost of American health care could be traced to waste and inefficiencies that took a wide variety of forms. One frequently cited problem was high administrative overhead, a consequence of the health care system's extensive recordkeeping requirements and archaic paper-based recordkeeping systems. "We have 900 billing clerks [at a nine hundred–bed hospital in the Duke University Medical System]," testified health care economist Uwe Reinhardt at a 2008 Senate hearing.

"I'm not sure we have a nurse per bed, but we have a billing clerk per bed. . . . It's obscene."[20] Fraud and abuse in the Medicare and Medicaid programs, such as billing for tests and procedures not performed, have also been blamed for contributing to the spiraling costs of those programs. Another frequent criticism leveled at the U.S. health care system is that it invests too little in obesity mitigation, antismoking initiatives, and other preventive measures that could save billions of dollars in health care costs down the road. Meanwhile, a 2003 study published in the *New England Journal of Medicine* indicated that doctors and surgeons frequently failed to direct patients to recommended drugs, tests, and treatments for their medical conditions. Worse still, the study indicated that this phenomenon was especially problematic in hospitals that delivered the most intensive treatments.[21]

Experts also complained that American health care is riddled with sweetheart deals that insulate one constituency or another from competition, enabling various health care sectors to command artificially high prices for goods and services without penalty. One such example is the incestuous business relationship between hospital group purchasing organizations (GPOs) and big medical device suppliers. This relationship is founded on an obscure 1986 Medicare provision that perversely tied GPO revenues to the profits of the leading medical suppliers instead of the hospitals themselves. Because GPOs make most hospital supply purchasing decisions, this provision has made it enormously difficult for small medical suppliers to break into the market, even when armed with innovative life-saving devices or lower-cost supplies that are the equal of the high-priced wares offered by the medical supply giants.[22] Another example of shortsighted preferential treatment was Congress's decision to accede to hospital industry lobbying and include an eighteen-month ban on the opening of new specialty hospitals in the 2003 Medicare Modernization Act, despite the fact that these specialty hospitals often provide better medical treatment at lower cost than traditional hospitals.[23]

Health care analysts and economists asserted that the American health care system, as constituted in the mid-2000s, was bedeviled by excessive consumption of health care resources. "One estimate puts the number of death due to unnecessary care at thirty thousand Americans a year," wrote health policy expert Shannon Brownlee. "That's the equivalent of a 747 airliner crashing and killing everyone aboard at least once a week. . . . If overtreatment were a disease, there would be a patient advocacy group out there raising money for a cure."[24]

Experts agree that overtreatment is the direct result of financial incentives that have been baked into the health care cake over the decades. The practice of defensive medicine, in which doctors feel coerced to recommend extensive batteries of tests and treatments so as to inoculate themselves against malpractice suits, is one such example. But observers argue that overtreatment has a much more systemic basis. "Every time you walk into a doctor's office," wrote Goldhill, "it's implicit that someone else will be paying most or all of your bill; for most of us, that means we give less attention to prices for medical services than we do to prices for anything else. Most physicians, meanwhile, benefit financially from ordering diagnostic tests, doing procedures, and scheduling follow-up appointments. Combine these two features of the system with a third—the informational advantage that extensive training has given physicians over their patients, and the authority that advantage confers—and you have a system where physicians can, to some extent, generate demand at will."[25] Experts and health care professionals acknowledge that the continued hegemony of the fee-for-service payment system has altered how entire fields of medicine, ranging from dermatology to back surgery, now operate. "The specialties themselves have changed," wrote journalist Alix Spiegel, "bending like flowers to the sun, moving toward the source of heat."[26]

This view is supported by the experiences of people such as Atul Gawande, a surgeon and health care analyst who in early 2009 traveled to McAllen, Texas, to investigate why the city had become the second-most expensive health care market in the country per capita. (In 2006, for example, Medicare spent almost twice the national average in McAllen per enrollee.) At one point Gawande sat down with a half-dozen McAllen doctors and laid out the statistics for them. Upon being confronted with these data, the doctors initially pondered whether better service or defensive medicine could account for the findings, then finally acknowledged the true cause.

> "Come on," the general surgeon finally said. "We all know these arguments are bullshit. There is overutilization here, pure and simple." Doctors, he said, were racking up charges with extra tests, services, and procedures. . . .
>
> I gave the doctors around the table a scenario. A forty-year-old woman comes in with chest pain after a fight with her husband. An EKG is normal. The chest pain goes away. She has no family history of heart disease. What did McAllen doctors do fifteen years ago?
>
> Send her home, they said. Maybe get a stress test to confirm that there's no issue, but even that might be overkill.
>
> And today? Today, the cardiologist said, she would get a stress test, an echocardiogram, a mobile Holter moniter, and maybe even a cardiac catheterization.
>
> "Oh, she's *definitely* getting a cath," the internist said, laughing grimly."[27]

Experts, lawmakers, and patient advocates acknowledged that these regional disparities in health care costs would be easier to swallow if the higher prices brought better care. Prominent studies however, indicated that health outcomes in high-spending states were poorer than in states that spent less. These stark findings underscored that "more care" did not equal "better care."[28]

POLICY PRESCRIPTIONS FOR ADDRESSING THE HEALTH CARE CRISIS

In the mid-2000s, broad agreement existed among health care experts, health care professionals, policymakers, and many ordinary citizens that the American health care system had major structural defects. And they recognized that many of these structural defects would be difficult to change, because they were jealously defended by powerful insurance companies and key health care sectors. "Hospitals, nurses, specialists, and all of the industries that produce medical goods have a vested interest in maintaining the status quo; they don't want to see health care shrink," wrote Brownlee. "Drug companies don't want doctors to write fewer prescriptions, and latex glove manufacturers don't want cardiologists to perform fewer angioplasties."[29] In addition, reformers knew that the contrasting ideological orientations and political constituencies of the nation's two major parties posed yet another formidable hurdle to meaningful change.

Would-be reformers also acknowledged that much-vaunted health policy reforms of yesteryear had failed to become the game changers they were supposed to be. Instead, supposed saviors such as managed care had simply been assimilated into the "medical-industrial complex." In 2007, for example, the most common form of managed care, the health maintenance organization (HMO), covered 91 percent of all people in employer-provided health insurance plans. As scholar Bradford H. Gray noted, distinctions between most HMOs and other types of health care services had by that point become "increasingly difficult to discern." As Gray explained,

> "HMO" no longer necessarily referred to an organization; it could be, instead, one of several "products" offered by an organization. Customers of a single managed-care organization might choose from options ranging from a plan in which all services were provided by members of a network to a plan in which enrollees had broad freedom of choice. . . . As a new century began, HMOs had largely ceased to exist as distinctive organizations.[30]

While the task of simultaneously "bending the curve" (lowering the rate of growth) on health care spending and filling its gaping holes in coverage was universally recognized as a supremely daunting one, health care experts and civic-minded physicians, administrators, politicians, and political activists agreed that they had no choice but to make the attempt.

Fortunately for them, some reform proposals enjoyed robust support from conservatives, moderates, and liberals alike (though not necessarily from industry players). One idea that continued to receive bipartisan support was increased investment in health information technologies, which had the potential to both improve operational efficiency and bolster patient safety. The Bush administration had begun pushing for industry-wide adoption of electronic medical recordkeeping in 2004. By the end of his second term, both Republicans and Democrats were commonly citing digitization of medical histories and other records as a commonsense way to integrate the operations of fragmented institutions in ways that improve health care outcomes (by eliminating the need for nurses and pharmacists to accurately decipher doctors' handwriting, for example) and reduce medical expenses (such as by easing distribution of the results of a single test to multiple institutions, thus saving them—and the patient—the trouble of carrying out the same test multiple times).

Moreover, implementation of electronic medical recordkeeping was widely seen as a prerequisite to another popular reform idea: increased investment in comparative effectiveness research. Researchers asserted that if the effectiveness of various medical treatments was more closely monitored and distributed to doctors, surgeons, and other health care professionals, patients would receive better care at lower expense. These claims were not universally accepted. Critics said that the purported savings from comparative effectiveness research were highly speculative. Journalist Jonathan Alter pointed out that "the only potential savings in this area would come from *telling* doctors how to practice: withholding reimbursements for treatments that supposedly didn't work. Once doctors and patients got wind of this, it was bound to be wildly unpopular."[31] Despite complaints about the governmental paternalism inherent in such research, many analysts insisted that it was a smart way to weed out wasteful, outdated, and ineffective treatments. "Comparative effectiveness research," wrote health industry consultant Michael Millenson, "is a way to use the power of government to promote private sector efficiency."[32]

Beyond these limited reforms, health care experts and policymakers found it difficult to reach any consensus on how to proceed. For example, the Republican and conservative camp continued to support free market–oriented reform proposals that were viewed with skepticism or outright hostility by many Democrats. Republicans expressed particular enthusiasm for health savings accounts, the tax-exempt plans that Bush had launched in 2003, and other types of so-called consumer-directed health plans. Under the most sweeping of these proposals, ineffective government- and employer-based insurance regimes that have traditionally shielded patients from the true cost of their health care would give way to individual plans, purchasable from commercial insurers, that place health care decisions squarely in the hands of consumers and physicians. The role of the federal government would be limited to providing tax breaks (and subsidies for low-income families) so individuals can buy their own insurance and serving consumers as a broker, auditor, and distributor of information on the price and quality of insurance plans, hospitals, and clinic services. Such consumer-driven programs, according to Harvard professor Regina E. Herzlinger and other proponents, would improve the quality and efficiency of health care by removing hidebound and self-interested public and private bureaucracies from the picture, discouraging frivolous use of health care resources, and forcing greater fiscal transparency in health care transactions.[33]

Liberal Democrats and policy analysts continued to champion systemic reforms that were anathema to Republicans. Some progressives urged the adoption of a single-payer system similar to what Canada and France use. Under single-payer, the federal government would purchase health care services for all citizens, but it would neither employ the doctors or nurses providing that care nor own the hospitals, nursing homes, and rehabilitation facilities where that care takes place. Advocates say that, unlike private insurers, the government would not have to burn up money marketing its product, plying executives with fat salaries and bonuses, or satisfying stockholders. In addition to these overhead savings, the government would be able to marshal its enormous marketing clout to negotiate lower prices for all manner of medical goods and services. Proponents often summed up a single-payer system as "Medicare for all."

Most elected Democrats rejected single-payer as too radical and politically unrealistic, but many of them expressed considerable excitement about a more incremental approach to insurance reform called the public option, which had been developed by health care expert Jacob Hacker. Under this scheme, employer-based insurance would be preserved, but the government would give many people the option of enrolling in a public plan (uninsured Americans would also be covered by the public plan). Under this approach, the public insurer would be able to bargain down the prices of health services and products in the same manner as Medicare does. More significant, it would "apply competitive pressure to the rest of the insurance industry," explained *Washington Post* policy blogger Ezra Klein. "If the public plan is ruthlessly lowering its administrative costs and garnering a reputation for decent, good-faith service, it will take market share from the private insurers. The private insurers will have to respond in kind to retain their customers. If they fail to adapt, the system could become something resembling a single-payer structure."[34]

In addition to those policy prescriptions championed by the bases of the two parties, lawmakers and experts studied a multitude of other proposals that had advocates and detractors in both parties. Examples of such offerings included the individual mandate, which was designed to achieve universal coverage and lower costs by requiring all Americans to buy health insurance; bundling, which would change the compensation structure for health care providers from fee-for-service to fixed bulk payments; insurance exchanges, in which small businesses, individuals, and the uninsured could shop within a marketplace of plans offered by commercial insurers; and guaranteed issue, a proposed federal law that would require health insurers to cover all applicants and end deeply unpopular industry practices such as rescission (the practice of dropping patients from coverage for alleged misrepresentation of medical history) and turning down applicants on the basis of preexisting conditions.

Obama Lays Out His Plan for Passing Health Care Reform

By the time Barack Obama won the presidency in November 2008, all of these various reform ideas had been cobbled together in endless permutations. Assessing this tumultuous terrain, even the most optimistic members of the incoming Obama administration admitted that health care reform was going to be a tough nut to crack. But they genuinely believed that they could take the various reform proposals circulating in Washington and create a politically viable hybrid plan that met Obama's campaign pledge to achieve "affordable care for all Americans."

This confidence was fed by three big advantages held by Obama and his fellow Democrats in early 2009: (1) significant public goodwill surrounding the historic election of Obama, the first African American president of the United States; (2) sizable majorities in Congress, including a filibuster-proof sixty-vote majority in the Senate after Al Franken (MN) was sworn in on July 7; and (3) a resignation among commercial insurers, pharmaceutical companies, and other key health care players that some kind of reform was inevitable. This perspective had convinced many industry sectors to adopt a posture of damage-limiting cooperation instead of a hopeless stance of defiance that might result in more injurious or punitive legislation **(See Document 10.9)**.

Obama's political strategy for passing health care reform came into clear view during the first months of the new administration. In speeches and staged events such as a March 5 White House Forum on Health Reform that brought together leaders from both parties and representatives of various interest groups, Obama outlined broad cost-control and quality goals that he felt were essential to genuine reform. He also reiterated his belief that the time had come for universal coverage. But he emphasized his administration's flexibility on how it achieved those goals. He refused to frame the public option as a must-have, even though it was already becoming the linchpin of reform in the eyes of many liberals. In addition, Obama urged Republicans and the various interest groups to come to the table with their own ideas **(See Document 10.8)**. These statements undoubtedly were crafted in part to satisfy the American public's well-known desire that Washington solve the nation's problems in a bipartisan manner. But they also reflected the White House's pragmatic judgment that passage of a bill was more likely if it could get some measure of cooperation from Republicans and industry.

After laying out these broad parameters, the Obama administration told Congress—and in particular Speaker of the House Nancy Pelosi (D-CA) and Senate majority leader Harry Reid (D-NV)—to get to work fleshing out the legislative details of the plan. This amounted to a complete strategic reversal of the failed Clinton health care initiative of 1993–1994, in which reform plans had been hammered out almost exclusively in the executive branch. The decision to give Congress primary responsibility for moving the health reform ball forward reflected the fact that the Obama White House already had a full plate. Upon arriving in Washington, Obama had been greeted by two major wars (in

Iraq and Afghanistan) and an economic crisis that threatened to plummet the nation into another Great Depression. The administration knew that crafting, defending, and carrying out responses to these challenges, such as the much-debated American Recovery and Reinvestment Act (the economic stimulus bill), would demand a great deal of the White House's time and energy during Obama's first year in office.

LOOKING TO THE EXAMPLE OF MASSACHUSETTS

The stimulus bill, which Obama signed into law on February 17, 2009, got the ball rolling on a number of health reforms that had bipartisan support (though the stimulus itself did not get Republican support). For example, the act included $17 billion in incentives for physicians and hospitals to upgrade to electronic information systems. Lawmakers, lobbyists, political activists, and the news media knew, however, that the challenge of enacting a true overhaul of U.S. health care and health insurance still loomed on the horizon.

For much of the spring and early summer of 2009 the momentum for reform remained strong. Key industry groups (pharmaceuticals, physicians, and hospitals) remained cautiously supportive or neutral, and the insurance industry's main lobbying voice, America's Health Insurance Plans (AHIP), signaled support for community rating (wherein insurance companies provide health policies to all people within a given region at the same price, regardless of differences in health status), guaranteed issue, an individual mandate, and other reforms long favored by progressives.

During this same time, the broad contours of the health care legislation coming into focus on Capitol Hill bore more than a passing resemblance to a comprehensive reform package that had been signed into law at the state level three years earlier—and by a Republican governor at that. On April 12, 2006, Massachusetts governor Mitt Romney had signed legislation mandating that nearly all state residents obtain health insurance coverage or face a financial penalty **(See Document 10.4)**. This bid for universal coverage rested on a package of reforms that included an individual mandate, insurance exchanges, subsidies to help the poor secure insurance, guaranteed issue, and assorted other insurance regulations.

The Massachusetts plan, which was paid for through a combination of Medicaid adjustments, assessments on insurers, hospitals, and employers, and state funds, was described by Romney as a fundamental statement of personal responsibility that would end the "free ride" for people who could afford insurance but chose not to buy it: "They shouldn't be allowed to just show up at the hospital and say, somebody else should pay for me. So we said: No more free riders. It was like bringing 'workfare' to welfare. We said: If you can afford insurance, then either have the insurance or get a health savings account. Pay your own way, but no more free ride. That was what the mandate did."[35]

The Democratic motivation for crafting a national health insurance bill patterned in significant respects after the 2006 Massachusetts reforms was obvious. Party leaders believed that "a plan that a Republican governor could sign into law would be a plan that could attract Republican votes." But as Ezra Klein noted, this theory would prove to be an erroneous one. Democrats instead discovered that "an approach to universal coverage that represented 'health insurance for everyone without a government takeover' when it was signed by a Republican governor in Massachusetts was spun by congressional Republicans as the missing final chapter of 'The Communist Manifesto' when Democrats tried to scale it nationally."[36]

HEALTH REFORM HITS TEA PARTY TURBULENCE

Republican opposition to the Democrats' health care reform drive was significant from the outset. Some moderate Republicans were intrigued by the coalescing legislation and Obama's insistence that the final package of reforms remain deficit-neutral and bend the cost curve. Hundreds of individual amendments sponsored by Republicans were incorporated into the bills making their way through the House and Senate. But conservatives, who made up the great majority of the party's caucus, objected to further expansion of government's role in health care on philosophical grounds. Republican leadership on Capitol Hill, led by Senate minority leader Mitch McConnell (KY) and House minority leader John A. Boehner (OH), placed enormous pressure on moderate members of their party to oppose any Democratic plan. Only complete unity would enable the Republicans to defeat health care reform, which would in turn greatly improve GOP political prospects in the 2010 midterms, the 2012 presidential election, and beyond. As McConnell himself stated, "It was absolutely critical that everybody be together because if the proponents of the bill were able to say it was bipartisan, it tended to convey to the public that this is O.K., they must have figured it out."[37]

Still, most Republican statements of opposition were carefully calibrated for the first few months of Obama's tenure in light of the new president's popularity and polling indicating continued public support for reform. In the spring of 2009, the newly created Tea Party Movement began pushing the Republicans into a more publicly confrontational stance on the health care issue. Though somewhat amorphous in organization and structure, the Tea Partiers subscribed to an anti-incumbent and anti-"big government" philosophy that resonated with many Americans and especially with older white conservatives who had been left discouraged by the recession, Bush's overall second-term struggles, Obama's decisive victory over McCain, and passage of the stimulus package. The Tea Party Movement reenergized this vital Republican constituency in a big way, in no small part because it received extensive positive coverage from Fox News and other conservative media outlets.

During the summer of 2009 Tea Party protests against "Obamacare" became extremely fierce, and the U.S. Chamber of Commerce and other business interests that opposed health reform ramped up their opposition as well. Public support for health reform in general and Obama in particular began to slide, and some Republicans became so emboldened by the shifting momentum that they felt free to acknowledge that their opposition was predicated on the political stakes involved. "If we're able to stop Obama on this, it will be his Waterloo," predicted Sen. Jim DeMint (R-SC) in July. "It will break him."

The turmoil surrounding the Democrats' health care initiative deepened in August, when Congress went into recess. By this time Obama had hoped to have a comprehensive health reform bill on his desk. But the legislation had gotten bogged down on Capitol Hill, and especially in the Senate Finance Committee, where Chairman Max Baucus (D-MT) had spent weeks desperately, and fruitlessly, courting the support of Republican moderate Olympia J. Snowe (ME) with bouquets of amendments and language revisions.

When lawmakers returned home, opponents of health care took full advantage. Democratic members who were considering voting for health reform were excoriated at town hall meetings by Tea Partiers who decried the public option and other proposed provisions as unadulterated socialism. In the meantime, media coverage became increasingly fixated on the political messaging and legislative horse-trading surrounding the issue—"the process"—instead of on the merits or flaws of the policy ideas themselves. Taking stock of all of these developments, the insurance industry began reassessing its own stance on health care reform. Convinced for the first time that Obama's health care drive could be defeated, AHIP and other representatives of the industry stopped bargaining with the Democrats. By October it was running antireform television ads and releasing studies purporting to show that the administration's reforms would trigger huge increases in policy premiums.

Some of the charges leveled against the reform packages being considered in Congress were willful distortions or the product of right-wing hysteria. The most notorious example of this was the oft-stated accusation that an amendment providing end-of-life counseling (an amendment that was initially proposed by Republican Johnny Isakson of Georgia) would result in the creation of federal "death panels" empowered to euthanize elderly citizens. Other specious claims ranged from accusations that passage of the legislation would explode the deficit (the bills being crafted would actually reduce it) to assertions that the so-called doc fix should be calculated into the cost of the Democrats' proposals. (The doc fix issue dated back to 1997, when the Republican-led Congress enacted a poorly designed cut in Medicare reimbursements to doctors. When the cut ended up slashing reimbursements far more than intended, Congress responded by passing a one-year doc fix that kept the cuts from being enacted, even though they technically still existed. Each year thereafter, Congress passed doc fix legislation instead of repealing the provision, which would have required difficult offsets in spending or a surge in deficit estimates. The doc fix problem, in other words, predated Obama's health care push and would still exist even if it was defeated.)

Vexed and dispirited by the traction that these distortions were gaining in the public arena, defenders of health reform attributed the situation to a long-present strain of paranoia in conservative politics. "Liberal power of all sorts induces an organic and crazy-making panic in a considerable number of Americans, while people with no particularly susceptibility to existential terror—powerful elites—find reason to stoke and exploit that fear," asserted journalist Rick Perlstein. "My personal favorite? The federal government expanded mental health services in the Kennedy era, and one bill provided for a new facility in Alaska. One of the most widely listened-to right-wing programs in the country, hosted by a former FBI agent, had millions of Americans believing it was being built to intern political dissidents, just like in the Soviet Union."[38]

Other criticisms voiced in town halls, conservative blogs, and elsewhere were harder for the administration and Democrats in Congress to dismiss out of hand. The White House did carry out extensive private negotiations with major industry players. And the bargains they reached, though based on political pragmatism, not corrupt intent, did result in concessions to those interest groups. Moreover, features such as the individual mandate and the public option, which looked locked into the House plan and were still under consideration in the Senate, did represent a major expansion of federal involvement in American health care. Many conservatives felt that these provisions, whether well meant or not, were genuinely intrusive and threatening to America's long-term vitality and health. Regarding the individual mandate, for example, Michael D. Tanner of the libertarian Cato Institute wrote that the provision "crosses an important line: accepting the principle that it is the government's responsibility to ensure that every American has health insurance. In doing so, it opens the door to widespread regulation of the health care industry and political interference in personal health care decisions. The result will be a slow but steady spiral downward toward a government-run national health care system."[39]

Complaints that Obama's overhaul of health care would saddle the American people with an unresponsive and expensive bureaucracy also proved difficult to neutralize. Administration officials, Democratic lawmakers, and progressive reformers and opinion-makers sometimes tried to defuse this line of attack by pointing to the popular Medicare program, where spending growth had for many years trended well below that of private sector insurance. They also highlighted success stories such as the Veterans Health Administration, a federal agency with its own medical personnel that in the 1990s and 2000s drew plaudits within health policy circles for the outstanding and low-cost health care it was providing for veterans, a demographic group that is older and suffers from more health problems than the general population.[40] These comprehensive services included a strong slate of preventive care services; inpatient and outpatient medical, surgical, rehabilitation, and mental health services; provision of pharmaceutical and medical supplies; and emergency care. "The fact that [VHA health care is] actually better in many ways than the health care the rest of us receive violates everything we think we know," wrote Brownlee. "It's a government-run health care system—socialized medicine—that doesn't have long lines; doesn't ration care; isn't filled with lazy, poorly trained doctors; and costs less per capita than our private system."[41] But this line of reasoning failed to sway many Americans who had endured long lines at their local Department of Motor Vehicles or aggravating workplace encounters with state or federal agencies. Worst of all for Democrats, news media following the proceedings showed little interest in wading into this level of detail in their coverage. As a result, said Senator Franken, he and his fellow Democrats faced a real problem with messaging. "Their bumper sticker has one word: 'No.' Our bumper sticker has—it's just way too many words. And it says: 'Continued on next bumper sticker.'"[42]

Finally, conservatives expressed outrage at criticisms of Tea Partiers and others who had mobilized in opposition to the Democratic health care "agenda." "The liberal effort to discredit American citizens who are expressing their views on an issue of vital importance is completely without merit, but it is instructive," wrote Philip Klein, Washington correspondent for the *American Spectator*. "It tells us that liberals know that despite their tremendous advantages in terms of resources and power in Washington, they are losing the health care messaging war. It's becoming clear that Americans are not ready for a government takeover of the health care system, and they aren't going to sit by idly while Democrats ram it down their throats."[43]

DEMOCRATS PUSH TOWARD THE FINISH LINE ON HEALTH CARE

By September 2009, the campaign for national health care seemed increasingly on the ropes, despite the fact that Democrats still held the White House and their huge majorities in Congress. "Blue Dog" Democrats had been thoroughly spooked by the turmoil back in their home districts, the media narrative was increasingly negative, and McConnell and Senate Republicans were using the upper chamber's elaborate procedures and considerable minority powers to slow progress to a crawl.

Even the federal government's swine flu vaccination campaign was becoming a political drag on health care reform. This fall 2009 effort to ward off a potentially deadly pandemic of the swine or H1N1 flu had been hampered most visibly by widespread vaccine shortages, as well as by concerns about the vaccine's safety (overblown according to public health experts) and unfounded speculation that federal authorities might try to impose a policy of mandatory vaccination.

Surveying the deteriorating terrain, liberals in Congress and across the country urged Obama to end his above-the-fray stance, assume a greater leadership role in advancing health care legislation, fight for inclusion of a public option, and in general spell out exactly what he wanted in the bill. The president responded to these entreaties, but only to a degree. In August he had turned aside requests from close White House advisers to back off on comprehensive health reform and accept incremental, face-saving measures, and in September and October he issued a series of addresses that lambasted the insurance industry as greedy, chided Republicans as obstructionists, and reiterated that the Democratic reform package—which had not even been finalized yet—would improve American health care, extend coverage to everyone, and do so in a financially responsible manner. Obama emphasized that the Congressional Budget Office had scored both the House and Senate Democratic bills as significant deficit *reducers.* (Funding for the Democrats' reforms was based primarily on higher Medicare taxes for wealthy Americans, new fees on health care industries, and almost $500 billion (over the first decade) in reduced Medicare spending—mostly by reducing subsidies to the privately administered Medicare Advantage program.)

Obama refused to frame the public option as a must-have in the final bill. This stance triggered considerable vitriol and second-guessing on the left, but the president's reticence on the issue did not change. By this time Obama and his closest advisers harbored doubts that the public option had enough votes to get through both houses of Congress, but they worried that a public admission of this fact would so demoralize liberals that the entire health reform effort might collapse.

In early November Pelosi prepared to bring the House health reform bill, known in that body as the Affordable Health Care for America Act, to a formal vote. By this time, many Democrats from more conservative districts had dropped their support for the bill, and liberals had been forced to accept an extremely weak public option to keep the remaining moderate and conservative Democrats on board. In short, Pelosi's margin for error had become very slim, and just before the House bill reached the floor, Rep. Bart Stupak (D-MI) announced that he and several other pro-life Democrats would oppose the bill if it did not include an amendment banning abortion procedures in the commercial insurance exchanges that would be created by the legislation. Pro-choice Democrats fumed at Stupak's maneuver, which they viewed as political extortion. But they gritted their teeth and voted for the bill after accepting the assurances of Pelosi, one of Congress's most stalwart pro-choice voices, that the abortion language would be removed when the House and Senate got together in conference reconciliation to craft a final bill for Obama's signature. With the Stupak amendment in place, the bill passed by a 220–215 margin, with one Republican, Ahn "Joseph" Cao of Louisiana, joining 219 Democrats in the "yea" column.

The spotlight then turned to the Senate, where Reid had always had far less maneuvering room than Pelosi. Because the Democrats had been unable to attract Snowe or any other moderate Republicans, Reid knew that he needed all sixty votes at his usual disposal—the 58 Democratic senators and two independents that caucused with the Democrats—to repel attempted filibusters by the Republicans. Unfortunately for Reid, this arithmetic required him to, in the words of health policy experts Lawrence R. Jacobs and Theda Skocpol, "cater to the policy notions and personal whims of every single caucus member every day and every week and every month."[44]

Partisans on both sides were just as aware as Reid that turning one Democratic vote against the Senate bill, which was undergoing final revisions, could bring the whole universal health care campaign crashing down on Obama's head. Americans were thus treated to a fresh barrage of editorials, blog postings, and cable television debates about health care reform (**See Document 10.10**). A new round of well-attended Tea Party rallies against "Obamacare" also took place across the country. Although several of these events were marred by odious attacks on Obama and his fellow Democrats (such as placard-wielding attendees who compared them to Nazi perpetrators of the Holocaust), the well-attended rallies further fueled the impression that Americans had turned against health reform and, by extension, the Obama presidency.

This analysis extended well beyond conservative media outlets to mainstream news sources, especially after Sen. Joseph I. Lieberman of Connecticut single-handedly forced Reid to remove the public option from the Senate bill in mid-December. Defying virtually all prognostications, Reid had managed to retain a public health insurance option in the Senate bill. But Lieberman, a Democrat-turned-Independent whose relationship with liberals had become very strained in recent years, unexpectedly announced that he would join a Republican filibuster of any health reform bill that contained a public option (**See Document 10.11**). The ultimatum dismayed Reid and other supporters of the bill, especially considering Lieberman's previous statements of support for a public option. Ultimately, Reid was forced to bow to Lieberman's wishes and strip the public option out of the bill.

This dramatic turn of events triggered apoplexy among liberal groups and House Democrats. It also convinced a number of influential progressives to turn against a bill they had never loved in the first place. Well-known figures including former Vermont governor Howard Dean, MSNBC commentator Keith Olbermann, and Markos Moulitsas, the founder of the liberal newsblog Daily Kos, urged Democrats to abandon the Senate bill, which they now deemed a sellout to corporate interests. This development was understandably greeted with rejoicing from Republicans and other opponents of the bill. As conservative columnist Peggy Noonan told one Obama adviser on national television, "On the issue of health care, you are losing the left, you are losing the right, you are losing the center. That looks to me like a political disaster."[45]

The Obama White House, Democratic leaders, and other proponents of health care reform understood the frustration behind the liberal outcry, but they urged people on the left not to let "the perfect become the enemy of the good." They reminded disgruntled supporters that progressives had been fighting for universal health care since Theodore Roosevelt's day and that the House and Senate bills still realized this goal. Even Jacob Hacker, the intellectual father of the public option, urged liberals to buck up and support the Senate bill. "The public option was always a means to an end," he wrote.

> As weak as it is in numerous areas, the Senate bill contains three vital reforms. First, it creates a new framework, the "exchange," through which people who lack secure workplace coverage can obtain the same kind of group health insurance that workers in large companies take for granted. Second, it makes available hundreds of billions in federal help to allow people to buy coverage through the exchanges and through an expanded Medicaid program. Third, it places new regulations on private insurers that, if properly enforced, will reduce insurers' ability to discriminate against the sick and to undermine the health security of Americans. These are signal achievements, and they all would have been politically unthinkable just a few years ago.[46]

Reid forged ahead amid all of this clamor, but just as final preparations for a Senate vote on health care began, Democratic senator Ben Nelson of Nebraska informed Reid that he would oppose the bill unless language was inserted that permanently exempted his home state from paying the customary state share for the bill's expansion of Medicaid. Reid reluctantly agreed to the demand, whereupon a firestorm of criticism erupted over the deal, which came to be known pejoratively as the "cornhusker kickback." To many Americans, this eleventh-hour deal confirmed Republican charges that the Democrats' health reform bill was the product of corrupt backroom negotiations and Washington politics as usual.

As unseemly as the Nelson deal was, it did succeed in preserving Reid's filibuster-proof sixty-vote coalition. The bill, known as the Patient Protection and Affordable Care Act, was finally introduced in the Senate on December 21. Over the next four days it passed through attempted GOP filibusters on three different procedural votes. On Christmas Eve morning the bill finally came up for a vote. It passed by a 60–39 vote, with all sixty members of the Democratic caucus backing the measure.

The Senate vote seemed to bring an end to a political marathon that had left both supporters and opponents in a state of exhaustion. The only hurdle left was for the House and Senate to merge their respective bills into a single measure for Obama to sign, a task that was widely viewed as a formality. With the finish line seemingly in sight, Obama and weary but jubilant Democrats agreed to put off reconciliation until after New Years' Day.

Scott Brown's Victory Changes the Political Landscape

Congress returned to Washington in early January 2010, whereupon Democratic leaders organized a conference to reconcile the House and Senate health reform bills. Their negotiations were upended on January 19, however, when Massachusetts voters elected Republican Scott Brown to fill the Senate seat of the late Edward M. Kennedy, which had been temporarily held by Democrat Paul G. Kirk. As a result of this stunning upset, Republicans gained an all-important forty-first vote in the Senate **(See Document 10.12)**. With Brown in the fold, Minority Leader McConnell would be able to filibuster the Democratic health reform bill when it emerged from reconciliation, thus preventing it from ever coming up for a vote.

Republican leaders, Tea Party activists, and conservative voters reveled in this unexpected gift, while health reform advocates reacted with dazed disbelief. Two weeks of finger-pointing and second-guessing ensued among Democrats in Washington, leaving supporters of reform with a growing sense that a near-certain legislative triumph was slipping away. "As paralysis and interbranch distrust deepened, little happened beyond ritual declarations that health reform would not be dropped," wrote Jacobs and Skocpol. "This is how big undertakings die in Washington, D.C. Politicians always say they are not abandoning the important priority, but they stop doing things to move it along and allow even almost-completed legislation just to fade away. As of February, this looked like the fate of the health reform effort that had eaten up an entire year in Washington."[47]

In reality, after absorbing the titanic reversal of political fortunes in Massachusetts, Obama, Pelosi, and Reid took a deep breath and decided to make one more push for passage of health care reform legislation. Pelosi and Reid began reviewing legislative strategies that would allow the Democrats to sidestep Republican filibusters in the Senate. Obama, meanwhile, embarked on an ambitious and sustained effort to convince the public that (1) their health reform package was good for American families and (2) the fight was not yet over, despite claims from Republicans that health reform was "dead." "We're essentially on the five-yard line—for those who like football analogies," Obama said at a February 2 town hall meeting in Nashua, New Hampshire. "We've got to punch it through. What I've said is that both the House bill and the Senate bill were 90 percent there. Ten percent of each bill, people had some problems with, and legitimately so. So we were just about to clean those up, and then Massachusetts' election happened. Suddenly everybody says, oh, oh, it's over. Well, no, it's not over. We just have to make sure that we move methodically and that the American people understand exactly what's in the bill."[48]

THE DEMOCRATS FINALLY PASS HEALTH CARE REFORM

Almost imperceptibly, the Democrats began to regain some of their lost political momentum. Labor unions, the American Association of Retired Persons, the American Medical Association, and progressive groups stopped grousing about imperfections in the legislation and began touting its benefits. A strangely timed announcement by Anthem Blue Cross of California that it planned to increase health policy premiums by 39% gave reform proponents an unexpected boost as well. Finally, the White House placed Obama front and center in the final public relations blitz for health care reform. First, they managed to turn a January 29 House Republican retreat into a nationally televised question-and-answer session with Obama. The president's strong performance at the event, reported Politico.com, triggered a spate of "second-guessing . . . among Republicans, some of whom were embarrassed that the president had been able to walk into their event and leave with a victory."[49]

Four weeks later, the White House arranged a somewhat similar piece of political theatre—a February 25 Health Care Summit that Obama hosted at Blair House in Washington, D.C., featuring leaders of both parties. The nationally televised event did not result in any bipartisan breakthroughs, but it gave Obama another opportunity to make his case for health care reform to the American people **(See Document 10.13)**. "The session proved critical in putting health care back on the national agenda," asserted the *New York Times*.

President Barack Obama leans over to Speaker of the House Nancy Pelosi to discuss a point during the February 2010 bipartisan meeting on health insurance reform. The nationally televised meeting was held at Blair House in Washington, D.C.

> The event enabled Mr. Obama to claim the high ground on bipartisanship; after the Brown victory, he needed to be seen as reaching out to the other side. He also wanted to force Republicans to put their ideas on the table, so that the public would see the debate as a choice between two ways to attack a pressing problem, not just a referendum on what Republicans derisively called "ObamaCare." The meeting also gave the Democratic leadership the gift of time. While the spotlight shifted to Mr. Obama, Ms. Pelosi and Mr. Reid immersed themselves in figuring out their parliamentary options and, in Ms. Pelosi's case especially, soothing her members' jangled nerves."[50]

Pelosi and Reid ultimately negotiated a compromise, endorsed by the White House, that would enable Congress to pass health reform without running up against a Republican filibuster. They crafted a two-step reconciliation process that required the House to pass the already-approved Senate health bill—the Patient Protection and Affordable Care Act—in its entirety. Once the House approved that bill and sent it to Obama for his signature, the Senate would craft "sidecar" legislation that amended various tax and spending provisions in the act to satisfy House Democrats, including removal of the much-reviled cornhusker kickback. Because the sidecar bill was a fiscal bill subject to reconciliation rules, it could be passed by a simple majority in the Senate. Once the sidecar bill passed the Senate, Pelosi and House Democrats could then pass it as well and send it on for Obama's approval.

Republicans angrily denounced this plan and, especially, the use of budget reconciliation as an abuse of majority power and an affront to the will of the American people. Because Republicans and Democrats had frequently used reconciliation in the past to create COBRA (providing limited retention of insurance coverage by former employers) and SCHIP and to make major changes to other health care laws, the GOP complaints about its use in this instance did not gain much political traction beyond the Republican base.[51] The latter charge that Democrats were on the verge of passing a bill that America did not want resonated with a number of moderate Democrats in the House. They knew that public opinion on health care reform was at best sharply divided, and they worried that a "yes" vote would doom them in the 2010 elections. Meanwhile, several progressive members of Congress indicated that the final bill might not be liberal enough for them to support. Recognizing that they could ill-afford to lose any of these votes, Pelosi and Obama each arranged scores of one-on-one meetings with wavering members of Congress. In addition, Obama promised Stupak and other restless pro-life Democrats that he would issue an executive order immediately after the House vote to ensure that the health care reform package maintained the ban on public funding of abortions. Obama delivered a final speech to House Democrats about the importance of the pending legislation on March 20, the night before their vote on the Senate's version of the bill (See Document 10.14).

The following morning, Boehner and other House Republicans arrived at Capitol Hill with heavy hearts. They had come within a whisker of derailing the Democrats' health care drive, but they had no more political arrows to pull out of their quiver. Boehner and several other GOP members delivered forceful condemnations of the pending bill in the floor debate before the vote (See Document 10.15), but to no avail. The House passed the Senate's Patient Protection and Affordable Care Act by a 219–212 vote, with all Republicans voting against it. The bill then went to the White House, and on March 23 Obama signed it into law (See Document 10.17). Three days later, as Reid had promised, the Senate passed its sidecar legislation on health care via reconciliation by a 56–43 vote. The House then passed the reconciliation fixes by a 220–207 vote, and on March 30 Obama signed those final changes to the Patient Protection and Affordable Care Act into law.

DEMOCRATS CELEBRATE, REPUBLICANS VOW TO REPEAL

As expected, the dramatic passage of the national health insurance bill after more than a year of bitter political warfare and several near-death experiences elicited strong reactions from both the progressive and Democrat and the conservative and Republican camps.

Victory proved a soothing balm for many pro-reform constituencies that had chafed at the loss of the public option and other setbacks. Once Obama signed health care reform into law, many Democratic voters and other reform advocates adopted a much more positive attitude about the legislation. They voiced great satisfaction with numerous provisions in the law, which was designed to roll out in stages over a four-year period, with most changes enacted by 2014. They hailed its guaranteed issue provisions and other consumer protections against insurance industry abuses, its establishment of private sector state exchanges to give individuals and small businesses greater access to affordable coverage, its purported capacity to finally bend the cost curve on American health care costs, its closure of the "donut hole" in the Medicare prescription drug benefit, its expanded subsidies for poor people to purchase insurance, and its measure allowing parents to cover children eighteen to twenty-five on their own plans.

Progressive policy experts praised numerous aspects of the bill that got less media attention, such as financial incentives to increase the number of primary care doctors and nurses in underserved rural areas, increased investment in medical research, and modernization of the health care system in American Indian communities. The act included a 13 percent budget increase to the perpetually underfunded Indian Health Service, the main source of health care for 1.9 million American Indians and Alaska Natives. In addition, the legislation authorized public health programs to help American Indian communities reduce youth suicide rates, increase the retention of health care professionals, arrange long-term care services, and establish child sexual abuse prevention and domestic violence prevention programs.

Following his signing of the Patient Protection and Affordable Care Act, President Barack Obama embraces Health and Human Services secretary Kathleen Sebelius and Speaker of the House Nancy Pelosi in the East Room of the White House.

Opponents of Obama's health care reforms expressed tremendous disappointment and anger with the results. Some Republicans directed their frustration at members of their own party for pursuing flawed political strategies in the health care showdown. The prominent conservative commentator David Frum, for example, asserted that if the GOP leadership had exhibited a greater willingness to negotiate with Obama and the Democrats they might have crafted a far more acceptable bill than the big government "disaster" that eventually passed **(See Document 10.16)**. Many Republicans, Tea Party members, and conservative voters, however, trained most of their anger on Obama and his fellow Democrats. They believed that the Democrats had passed a law that was the gateway to a government takeover of health care services and had done so in brazen defiance of public opinion, to boot.

During the spring and summer of 2010, many Republican officials filed lawsuits urging the courts to strike down the Patient Protection and Affordable Care Act as unconstitutional. Numerous Republican congressional candidates affiliated with the Tea Party movement vowed to repeal or defund health care reform if elected. When Republicans easily reclaimed the House from Democrats in the November 2010 midterms, many observers (and not just conservatives) interpreted those results as, at least partially, a decision by voters to punish Democrats for their passage of the health care bill.

Political analysts say, however, that if the Republicans make good on their promise to attack "Obamacare" by repealing it or starving it of funds, they will be charting a potentially perilous political course. While the Affordable Care Act as a whole remains a polarizing document, many of its individual provisions are popular with the American public. Finally, any efforts to repeal or otherwise eviscerate the law will be complicated by the budgetary implications of such an action. In February 2011 the CBO estimated that repealing the act would explode the federal deficit by $210 billion over a ten-year period, a daunting number at a time when the national debt has been identified as a major concern of U.S. voters.

NOTES

1. George W. Bush,. Remarks on Signing the Partial-Birth Abortion Ban Act of 2003, *Public Papers of the Presidents of the United States: George W. Bush, 2003,* Vol. 2 (Washington, DC: Government Printing Office, 2004), 1466–67.

2. Kim Gandy, "Bush Takes Away Women's Reproductive Rights—Feminists Promise to Vote Him Out," press release, National Organization for Women, November 5, 2003, www.now.org/press/11-03/11-05.html.

3. Quoted in Ronald Kessler, *A Matter of Character: Inside the White House of George W. Bush* (New York: Sentinel, 2004), 268–69.

4. Quoted in "Under the Influence: Drug Lobbyists' Role in 2003 Medicare Modernization Act," transcript, *60 Minutes,* March 29, 2007.

5. Maggie Mahar and Niko Karvounis, "The High Cost of Medicare Advantage," blog, Health Beat by Maggie Mahar, April 11, 2008, www.healthbeatblog.com/2008/04/the-high-cost-o.html.

6. Quoted in Robert Pear, "Private Medicare Plans' Cost Questioned," *New York Times,* February 28, 2008, www.nytimes.com/2008/02/28/washington/28medicare.html.

7. Pear, "Private Medicare Plans' Cost Questioned."

8. Mary Agnes Carey, "Provisions of the Medicare Bill," *CQ Weekly,* January 24, 2004, 238–43.

9. Jane E. Brody, "Forge Your Way Through the Medicare Drug Maze," *New York Times,* April 25, 2006, www.nytimes.com/2006/04/25/health/25brod.html?pagewanted=all.

10. Ceci Connolly, "The States Step In as Medicare Falters," *Washington Post,* January 14, 2006, A1.

11. Connolly, "The States Step In as Medicare Falters," A1.

12. "Mr. Bush's Health Care Legacy," editorial, *New York Times,* January 2, 2009, www.nytimes .com/2009/01/03/opinion/03sat1.html.

13. "Under the Influence," *60 Minutes.*

14. Jonathan Cohn, *Sick: The Untold Story of America's Health Care Crisis—and the People Who Pay the Price* (New York: HarperCollins, 2007), 113.

15 Cohn, *Sick,* 114.

16. David Goldhill, "How American Health Care Killed My Father," *Atlantic,* September 2009, 41.

17. Kaiser Family Foundation and Health Research and Educational Trust, *2007 Employer Health Benefits Survey* (Washington, DC: Kaiser Family Foundation, 2007), 11.

18. Institute of Medicine, Board on Health Care Services, *America's Uninsured Crisis: Consequences for Health and Health Care* (Washington, DC: Institute of Medicine, 2009), 3.

19. Institute of Medicine, *Care without Coverage: Too Little, Too Late* (Washington, DC: Institute of Medicine, 2002); and Urban Institute, *Uninsured and Dying Because of It* (Washington, DC: Urban Institute, 2008).

20. Uwe Reinhardt, "Health Care Reform: An Economic Perspective," statement, Senate Committee on Finance, *Hearing,* 110th Cong., 2d sess., November 19, 2008.

21. Elizabeth McGlynn, S. M. Asch, J. Adams, J. Keesey, J. Hicks, A. DeCristofaro, and E. A. Kerr, "The Quality of Healthcare Delivered to Adults in the United States," *New England Journal of Medicine* 348, no. 26 (2003): 2635.

22. Mariah Blake, "Dirty Medicine," *Washington Monthly,* July/August 2010, www.washingtonmonthly .com/features/2010/1007.blake.html.

23. Regina E. Herzlinger, *Who Killed Health Care?* (New York: McGraw-Hill, 2007), 79.

24. Shannon Brownlee, *Overtreated: Why Too Much Medicine Is Making Us Sicker and Poorer* (New York: Bloomsbury, 2007), 6.

25. Goldhill, "How American Health Care Killed My Father," 42.

26. Alix Spiegel, "The Telltale Wombs of Lewiston, Maine," *NPR: All Things Considered,* October 8, 2009, www.npr.org/templates/story/story.php?storyId=113571111.

27. Atul Gawande, "The Cost Conundrum: What a Texas Town Can Teach Us about Health Care," *New Yorker,* June 1, 2009, www.newyorker.com/reporting/2009/06/01/090601fa_fact_gawande.

28. Elliott Fisher, David Goodman, Jonathan Skinner, and Kristen Bonner, "Health Care Spending, Quality, and Outcomes" (Lebanon, NH: Dartmouth Institute for Health Care and Quality Practice, February 27, 2009), www.dartmouthatlas.org/downloads/reports/Spending_Brief_022709.pdf.

29. Brownlee, *Overtreated,* 11.

30. Bradford H. Gray, "The Rise and Decline of the HMO: A Chapter in U.S. Health-Policy History," in *History and Health Policy in the United States: Putting the Past Back In,* ed. Rosemary A. Stevens, Charles E. Rosenberg, and Lawton R. Burns (New Brunswick, NJ: Rutgers University Press, 2006), 329–30.

31. Jonathan Alter, *The Promise: President Obama, Year One* (New York: Simon and Schuster, 2010), 248.

32. Michael Millenson, "The Health Reform That Scares Both Parties," *Kaiser Health News,* February 16, 2010, www.kaiserhealthnews.org/Columns/2010/February/021610Millenson.aspx.

33. Regina Herzlinger, *Market-Driven Health Care: Who Wins, Who Loses in the Transformation of America's Largest Service Industry* (New York: Basic Books, 1997); and Regina E. Herzlinger, *Who Killed Health Care?* (New York: McGraw-Hill, 2007).

34. Ezra Klein, "Health Care Reform for Beginners: The Many Flavors of the Public Plan," blog, *Washington Post,* June 8, 2009, http://voices.washingtonpost.com/ezra-klein/2009/06/health_care _reform_for_beginne_3.html.

35. Mitt Romney, "2008 Republican Debate at Reagan Library in Simi Valley, California, January 30, 2008," OnTheIssues.org, www.ontheissues.org/2008_GOP_Super_Tuesday.htm.

36. Ezra Klein, "A World with an Individual Mandate," blog, *Washington Post*, December 20, 2010, http://voices.washingtonpost.com/ezra-klein/2010/12/column_a_world_with_an_individ.html.

37. Quoted in Carl Hulse and Adam Nagourney, "Senate GOP Leader Finds Weapon in Unity," *New York Times*, March 16, 2010, www.nytimes.com/2010/03/17/us/politics/17mcconnell.html.

38. Rick Perlstein, "Birthers, Health Care Hecklers, and the Rise of Right-Wing Rage," *Washington Post*, August 16, 2009, www.washingtonpost.com/wp-dyn/content/article/2009/08/14/AR20090814014 95.html.

39. Michael D. Tanner, "Individual Mandates for Health Insurance: Slippery Slope to National health Care," Policy Analysis No. 565, Cato Institute, April 5, 2006.

40. Philip Longman, "The Best Care Anywhere," *Washington Monthly*, January/February 2005, www .washingtonmonthly.com/features/2007/0710.longman.html.

41. Brownlee, *Overtreated*, 271.

42. Quoted in Alter, *The Promise*, 420.

43. Philip Klein, "Durbin Accuses Citizens Opposed to Obamacare of Being Planted by Insurers," AmSpecBlog, *American Spectator*, August 3, 2009, http://spectator.org/blog/2009/08/03/durbin -accuses-citizens-oppose -.

44. Lawrence R. Jacobs and Theda Skocpol, *Health Care Reform and American Politics: What Everyone Needs to Know* (New York: Oxford University Press, 2010), 61.

45. Quoted in Mike Allen, "Left Rebels against Health Reform," Politico.com, December 17, 2009, www.politico.com/news/stories/1209/30737.html.

46. Jacob Hacker, "Why I Still Believe in This Bill," blog, *New Republic*, December 20, 2009, www.tnr .com/blog/the-treatment/why-i-still-believe-bill.

47. Jacobs and Skocpol, *Health Care Reform and American Politics*, 109.

48. "Obama: Reform in the 'Red Zone,' Time to 'Punch It Through,'" Politico.com, February 2, 2010, www.politico.com/livepulse/0210/Obama_Reform_in_the_red_zone_time_to_punch_it_through .html.

49. Patrick O'Connor and Mike Allen, "How the GOP Retreat Wound Up on TV," Politico.com, February 2, 2010, www.politico.com/news/stories/0210/32354.html.

50. Sheryl Gay Stolberg, Jeff Zeleny, and Carl Hulse, "Health Vote Caps a Journey Back from the Brink," *New York Times*, March 20, 2010, www.nytimes.com/2010/03/21/health/policy/21reconstruct.html.

51. Julie Rovner, "Health Care No Stranger to Reconciliation Process," *National Public Radio*, February 24, 2010.

DOCUMENT
10.1

President Bush Stakes Out His Position on Stem Cell Research

"We Must Proceed with Great Care"

2001

When President George W. Bush became president in 2001, he faced a controversy over stem cell research that had caught the attention of millions of Americans. Many members of the scientific and medical communities believed that stem cell research had the potential to help millions of Americans struggling under the burden of chronic, debilitating, and deadly diseases and medical conditions. These advocates expressed particular excitement about the inroads into medical treatment that could be made by using stem cells taken from human embryos. Their campaign to use stem cells from embryos, however, was fiercely opposed by pro-life groups and conservative religious organizations, both of which were important constituencies in Bush's political base. These opponents noted that because stem cell extraction destroys embryos, the process essentially destroys "human life."

Late in President Bill Clinton's term, the National Bioethics Advisory Commission had recommended federal funding for embryonic stem cell research, and the National Institutes of Health had even crafted preliminary guidelines for the bestowal of such funding. But the issue had still not been settled when Bush took office, and by August 2001 the matter had become grist for countless media stories.

After consulting with several high-profile pro-life Republicans who nonetheless supported limited embryonic stem cell research, including Department of Health and Human Services secretary Tommy G. Thompson and Senators Orrin Hatch (R-UT) and Bill Frist (R-TN), Bush gave a nationally televised address on the issue on August 9, 2001. The address is reprinted here. After emphasizing the profound moral complexity of the issue, Bush announced that he was approving federal funding of strictly regulated scientific research on sixty "genetically diverse stem cell lines" already in existence (the actual number of qualifying cell lines turned out to be twenty-one), but he would not support other embryonic stem cell research. Bush's announcement received mixed reviews from both supporters and opponents of embryonic stem cell research.

Political action on embryonic stem cell research subsided in Washington until the mid-2000s, even as a number of so-called "blue states" approved major new investments in embryonic stem cell research. In 2005, though, the House of Representatives passed a bill that would loosen some of the 2001 research restrictions on embryonic stem cells, and the Senate followed suit one year later. This bill enjoyed bipartisan support, but Bush vetoed the measure on July 19, 2006. One year later, Bush vetoed a similar measure that had been shepherded through Congress by the new Democratic leadership.

Good evening. I appreciate you giving me a few minutes of your time tonight so I can discuss with you a complex and difficult issue, an issue that is one of the most profound of our time.

The issue of research involving stem cells derived from human embryos is increasingly the subject of a national debate and dinner table discussions. The issue is confronted every day in laboratories as scientists ponder the ethical ramifications of their work. It is agonized over by parents and many couples as they try to have children or to save children already born. The issue is debated within the church, with people of different faiths, even many of the same faith, coming to different conclusions. Many people are finding that the more they know about stem cell research, the less certain they are about the right ethical and moral conclusions.

My administration must decide whether to allow Federal funds, your tax dollars, to be used for scientific research on stem cells derived from human embryos. A large number of these embryos already exist. They are the product of a process called in vitro fertilization, which helps so many couples conceive children. When doctors match sperm and egg to create life outside the womb, they usually produce more embryos than are implanted in the mother. Once a couple successfully has children, or if they are unsuccessful, the additional embryos remain frozen in laboratories. Some will not survive during long storage; others are destroyed. A number have been donated to science and used to create privately funded stem cell lines. And a few have been implanted in an adoptive mother and born and are today healthy children.

Based on preliminary work that has been privately funded, scientists believe further research using stem cells offers great promise that could help improve the lives of those who suffer from many terrible diseases, from juvenile diabetes to Alzheimer's, from Parkinson's to spinal cord injuries. And while scientists admit they are not yet certain, they believe stem cells derived from embryos have unique potential.

You should also know that stem cells can be derived from sources other than embryos: from adult cells, from umbilical cords that are discarded after babies are born, from human placentas. And many scientists feel research on these types of stem cells is also promising. Many patients suffering from a range of diseases are already being helped with treatments developed from adult stem cells. However, most scientists, at least today, believe that research on embryonic stem cells offer the most promise because these cells have the potential to develop in all of the tissues in the body.

Scientists further believe that rapid progress in this research will come only with Federal funds. Federal dollars help attract the best and brightest scientists. They ensure new discoveries are widely shared at the largest number of research facilities and that the research is directed toward the greatest public good.

The United States has a long and proud record of leading the world toward advances in science and medicine that improve human life. And the United States has a long and proud record of upholding the highest standards of ethics as we expand the limits of science and knowledge. Research on embryonic stem cells raises profound ethical questions, because extracting the stem cell destroys the embryo and thus destroys its potential for life. Like a snowflake, each of these embryos is unique, with the unique genetic potential of an individual human being.

As I thought through this issue, I kept returning to two fundamental questions: First, are these frozen embryos human life and, therefore, something precious to be protected? And second, if they're going to be destroyed anyway, shouldn't they be used for a greater good, for research that has the potential to save and improve other lives?

I've asked those questions and others of scientists, scholars, bioethicists, religious leaders, doctors, researchers, Members of Congress, my Cabinet, and my friends. I have read heartfelt letters from many Americans. I have given this issue a great deal of thought, prayer, and considerable reflection. And I have found widespread disagreement.

On the first issue, are these embryos human life? Well, one researcher told me he believes this 5-day-old cluster of cells is not an embryo, not yet an individual, but a pre-embryo. He argued that it has the potential for life, but it is not a life because it cannot develop on its own. An ethicist dismissed that as a callous attempt at rationalization. "Make no mistake," he told me, "that cluster of cells is the same way you and I and all the rest of us started our lives. One goes with a heavy heart if we use these," he said, "because we are dealing with the seeds of the next generation."

And to the other crucial question, if these are going to be destroyed anyway, why not use them for good purpose, I also found different answers. Many argue these embryos are byproducts of a process that helps create life, and we should allow couples to donate them to science so they can be used for good purpose instead of wasting their potential. Others will argue there's no such thing as excess life and the fact that a living being is going to die does not justify experimenting on it or exploiting it as a natural resource.

At its core, this issue forces us to confront fundamental questions about the beginnings of life and the ends of science. It lies at a difficult moral intersection, juxtaposing the need to protect life in all its phases with the prospect of saving and improving life in all its stages.

As the discoveries of modern science create tremendous hope, they also lay vast ethical minefields. As the genius of science extends the horizons of what we can do, we increasingly confront complex questions about what we should do. We have arrived at that brave new world that seemed so distant in 1932, when Aldous Huxley wrote about human beings created in test tubes in what he called a "hatchery." In recent weeks, we learned that scientists have created human embryos in test tubes solely to experiment on them. This is deeply troubling and a warning sign that should prompt all of us to think through these issues very carefully.

Embryonic stem cell research is at the leading edge of a series of moral hazards. The initial stem cell researcher was at first reluctant to begin his research, fearing it might be used for human cloning. Scientists have already cloned a sheep. Researchers are telling us the next step could be to clone human beings to create individual designer stem cells, essentially to grow another you, to be available in case you need another heart or lung or liver.

I strongly oppose human cloning, as do most Americans. We recoil at the idea of growing human beings for spare body parts or creating life for our convenience. And while we must devote enormous energy to conquering disease, it is equally important that we pay attention to the moral concerns raised by the new frontier of human embryo stem cell research. Even the most noble ends do not justify any means.

My position on these issues is shaped by deeply held beliefs. I'm a strong supporter of science and technology and believe they have the potential for incredible good, to improve lives, to save life, to conquer disease. Research offers hope that millions of our loved ones may be cured of a disease and rid of their suffering. I have friends whose children suffer from juvenile diabetes. Nancy Reagan has written me about President Reagan's struggle with Alzheimer's. My own family has confronted the tragedy of childhood leukemia. And like all Americans, I have great hope for cures.

I also believe human life is a sacred gift from our Creator. I worry about a culture that devalues life and believe as your President I have an important obligation to foster and encourage respect for life in America and throughout the world. And while we're all hopeful about the potential of this research, no one can be certain that the science will live up to the hope it has generated.

Eight years ago, scientists believed fetal tissue research offered great hope for cures and treatments, yet the progress to date has not lived up to its initial expectations. Embryonic stem cell research offers both great promise and great peril. So I have decided we must proceed with great care.

As a result of private research, more than 60 genetically diverse stem cell lines already exist. They were created from embryos that have already been destroyed, and they have the ability to regenerate themselves indefinitely, creating ongoing opportunities for research. I have concluded that we should allow Federal funds to be used for research on these existing stem cell lines, where the life and death decision has already been made.

Leading scientists tell me research on these 60 lines has great promise that could lead to breakthrough therapies and cures. This allows us to explore the promise and potential of stem cell research without crossing a fundamental moral line by providing taxpayer funding that would sanction or encourage further destruction of human embryos that have at least the potential for life.

I also believe that great scientific progress can be made through aggressive Federal funding of research on umbilical cord, placenta, adult, and animal stem cells which do not involve the same moral dilemma. This year, your Government will spend $250 million on this important research.

I will also name a President's council to monitor stem cell research, to recommend appropriate guidelines and regulations, and to consider all of the medical and ethical ramifications of biomedical innovation. This council will consist of leading scientists, doctors, ethicists, lawyers, theologians, and others and will be chaired by Dr. Leon Kass, a leading biomedical ethicist from the University of Chicago. This council will keep us apprised of new developments and give our Nation a forum to continue to discuss and evaluate these important issues.

As we go forward, I hope we will always be guided by both intellect and heart, by both our capabilities and our conscience. I have made this decision with great care, and I pray it is the right one.

Thank you for listening. Good night, and God bless America.

Source: Bush, George W. Address to the Nation on Stem Cell Research, August 9, 2001. *Public Papers of the Presidents of the United States: George W. Bush, 2001.* Vol. 2. Washington, DC: Government Printing Office, 2002, pp. 953–956.

Controversial Vote on the Medicare Prescription Drug Act

"Bribes and Special Deals Were Offered to Convince Members to Vote Yes"

2003

When the Republican leadership of the House of Representatives held its vote on the Medicare Prescription Drug, Improvement, and Modernization Act in the early morning hours of November 22, 2003, the proceedings degenerated into a sordid spectacle of political arm-twisting and intimidation. Of all such events that took place that morning, the one that attracted the most media attention was the political pressure brought by Republicans against six-term representative Nick Smith (R-MI), who bucked his party's leadership and voted against the bill because of concerns about its fiscal impact.

The day after the vote, Smith, who had already announced that he was retiring at the end of the term, posted a column on his official congressional website in which he complained that Republican leaders engaged in blatant "bribery and special deals" to "convince members to vote yes" on the measure. Smith specifically charged that lobbyists and fellow Republicans threatened to torpedo the political career of his son Brad, who was running for his father's seat, if he did not switch his vote on the bill to a "yes." Smith repeated these charges over the next several days. "I thought I knew 'arm-twisting' serving 16 years in the Michigan legislature and 11 years in the United States Congress," he said. "However, this was the most intense and strongest pressure to change my vote that I've ever experienced."[1]

Smith's remarks led the Justice Department to open an inquiry into the matter, and the House Committee on Standards of Official Conduct (ethics committee), chaired by Joel Hefley (R-CO), launched an investigation as well. In early December 2003, Smith unexpectedly recanted all the charges that he had previously made, and the Justice Department eventually dropped its inquiry. But the House ethics committee continued its work and, on September 30, 2004, released a report that formally admonished Smith, fellow Michigan representative Candice S. Miller (R), and Majority Leader Tom DeLay (R-TX) for their conduct during and after the vote. That report is excerpted here (footnotes removed).

In the 2004 Republican primary for Smith's seat, moderate Joe Schwarz defeated Smith's son Brad for the nomination, and Schwarz went on to win the general election in November 2004.

[Footnotes have been removed from the report.]

... B. Events on the House Floor During and Immediately Following the Vote

As noted, the vote on the Medicare legislation was called at 3:00 a.m. on Saturday, November 22 and was held open until approximately 5:51 a.m. Representative Smith recalls casting his "no" vote early on during the time that the vote was open. He considered voting and leaving the floor early as well but then he "decided if I was voting against the conference I should stay there and take my licks." Representative Smith also decided against staying in the company of other Republicans who had voted against the bill, as some of his fellow members of the RSC chose to do. Representative Smith told the Investigative Subcommittee that after he cast his vote he sat "approximately eight rows up in the northwest quadrant of the Republican area."

Representative Smith told the Investigative Subcommittee that during the time the vote was open, between 20 and 30 Members approached him or, those in close proximity to him, said things directed at him that were intended to persuade him to change his vote. All of these contacts occurred after Representative Smith had already cast his vote and all but one of the contacts occurred while the vote was open.

1. Representative Smith's Interaction with Speaker Hastert and Secretary Tommy Thompson ...

Representative Smith testified that he recalled speaking with Speaker [Dennis] Hastert and Secretary Tommy Thompson while the vote was open. In a written response to interrogatories provided voluntarily and under penalty of perjury, Secretary Thompson informed the Investigative Subcommittee that he was in the House cloakroom while the vote was open and had been asked to be available to answer questions from Members regarding the Medicare legislation. He stated that someone asked him to speak to Representative Smith "because he or she thought that Representative Smith could be convinced to change his mind and vote in favor" of the legislation. He does not recall who asked him to speak to Representative Smith. Secretary Thompson stated that he spoke briefly with Representative Smith on the House floor, "asking Representative Smith if he had any questions on the bill that I could answer, or if there was any information that I could provide to him. He said no." Secretary Thompson also asked Representative Smith "if there was any chance that he would vote for the bill. He said no." While the Secretary was "in the presence of Representative Smith," the Speaker joined them.

The Speaker told the Investigative Subcommittee that he prevailed on Representative Smith to vote in favor of the legislation based on the bill's merits. The Speaker testified that he spoke with Representative Smith for about ten minutes. He described their discussion as being "pretty much focused on policy," including discussion of cost-containment measures the Speaker said he knew would be of interest to Representative Smith. . . .

According to Representative Smith, neither the Speaker's comments nor those of Secretary Thompson formed any part of the basis for his subsequent allegations that "bribes and special deals" were offered to him in an effort to convince him to change his vote. . . .

3. Representative Smith's Interaction with Representative Candice Miller. . . .

Representative Miller told the Investigative Subcommittee that the first time she spoke to Representative Smith about his vote on the Medicare legislation was on the House floor while the vote was open, after Representative Smith had cast his vote. She estimated that she spoke with him during the first hour of the time that the vote was held open. Representative Miller saw Representative Smith's no vote on the board and she "didn't like the way that he voted." Representative Miller testified that, on her own initiative, she approached Representative Smith and said words to the effect of: "Is this how you're going to vote; or, This is how you're going to vote? And he said, Obviously."

Representative Miller recalled that she responded by saying words to the effect of: "Well, I hope your son doesn't come to Congress, or I'm not going to support your son, or something to that effect." Representative Smith then "rose up out of his seat and said, You get out of here." That was the end of the interaction between the two Members. . . .

. . . She [Miller] told the Investigative Subcommittee that Representative Smith was obviously angered by her remarks about his son. She testified that Representative Smith was "constantly asking [her] to support his son and help his son" because she had been a statewide officeholder in their home state of Michigan [as secretary of state] before she was elected to Congress and had been "the highest vote-getter in Michigan history." Representative Miller noted that she "probably could have some impact on his son's election." She told the Investigative Subcommittee that, even after the Medicare vote, Representative Smith invited her to a fundraiser for his son.

Representative Smith denied ever having asked Representative Miller for support for his son's campaign. He also denied inviting her to a fundraiser at any time after the Medicare vote. Representative Smith's recollection of his interaction with Representative Miller on the House floor while the Medicare vote was open was substantially similar to Representative Miller's recollection except in one respect. Representative Smith told that Investigative Subcommittee that Representative Miller specifically threatened to work against his son if he did not change his vote. Representative Smith's recollection was that Representative Miller "came up and said something like, I haven't been involved in this campaign before, but if you don't change your vote, I'll get involved, and I'll make sure Brad isn't elected." . . .

4. Representative Smith's Interaction with Representative James T. Walsh

. . . Representative James Walsh also approached Representative Smith. Representative Walsh told the Investigative Subcommittee that he had "worked very hard" on the Medicare bill and was "pretty invested in the success of [the] legislation" because it would have a "great impact on [his] community." Representative Walsh noted that his district "had already lost one hospital . . . [that] was in bankruptcy" and had another hospital "on the ropes." He believed that the Medicare legislation would improve the situation in his home district.

Most Members had already voted and Representative Walsh was feeling "frustrated" and "impatient" waiting for the outcome of the vote. These feelings led him to approach Representative Smith, knowing that Representative Smith had voted against the bill. Representative Walsh said that he made the decision to approach Representative Smith on his "own initiative." He asked Representative Smith "[C]an't you help us on this one?" Representative Smith said no and Representative Walsh responded by saying words to the effect of: "[W]ell . . . then, Nick, maybe you ought to think about sending me back that check that I sent to your son," referring to a campaign contribution Representative Walsh believed he had already made to Representative Smith son's campaign. . . .

Representative Walsh told the Investigative Subcommittee that he regretted making the statements to Representative Smith that he made during the Medicare vote. Representative Walsh said that he believed "it was a stupid thing to say" and that he had not planned to say it when he approached Representative Smith. Representative Walsh attributed his remarks to Representative Smith to "a combination of frustration and fatigue and a desire to get the bill passed." . . .

5. Representative Smith's Interaction with Representative Randy "Duke" Cunningham . . .

Representative Cunningham told the Investigative Subcommittee that the only reference to Representative Smith's son's campaign that he heard the morning of the Medicare vote was one that he himself made after the vote was closed. Representative Cunningham told the Investigative Subcommittee that after most Members had left the House floor, and as he was walking out past Representative Smith, he said words to the effect of: "[W]ell, if you son is as hard headed as you, I will be damned if I will vote for him or help him."

Representative Smith told the Investigative Subcommittee that after the vote was over and Members were leaving the floor, Representative Cunningham walked by him and waved what appeared to be a billfold at him while saying something to the effect of: "[W]e've got $10,000 already . . . to make sure your son doesn't get elected." When asked whether he waved a wallet or checkbook at Representative Smith while making such comments, Representative Cunningham said: "I don't remember if I waved the checkbook. I don't remember if I did or not. But I don't know. But I'm sure about that not supporting him." Representative Cunningham denied mentioning $10,000 or any other specific sum of money in connection with his remarks about not supporting Brad Smith's candidacy. . . .

Representative Cunningham and Representative Smith both testified that Representative Cunningham apologized for making remarks about Representative Smith's son the first time he saw Representative Smith after Congress was back in session.

6. Representative Smith's Contacts with Unidentified Members

Representative Smith told the Investigative Subcommittee that he could not recall every one of the 20 to 30 members who spoke to him on the House floor while the Medicare vote was open. He said, for example, that someone had said that if he changed his vote to support the legislation, three out of the five members of House leadership would be willing to go to his home district to campaign for his son. Representative Smith testified:

> A lot of it was fairly—look, Nick, help us if you can. Nick, this could— this could be important to you and your son. From the more subtle to the more aggressive, that, look, three of the five—it seems like I remem- ber somebody saying three of the five leadership would be willing to come to Michigan to campaign for your son. Somebody saying, look, you've got a pharmaceutical—you've got two pharmaceutical compa- nies in your district. There is [sic] important to them.

Representative Smith testified that he could not recall specifically who made those comments. Representative Smith further testified that there seemed "to be a constant stream of people coming by me to say, Nick, we really need your help on this one. Nick, this can be important to your future; and it can be important to your son's future. Nick— you know, just sort of a constant help us out on this one, and it can be important to you and your son." Various Members who appeared before the Investigative Subcommittee recalled seeing several people around Representative Smith at different points during the hours that the vote was open.

C. Representative Smith's Actions After the Vote and His Allegations of Wrongdoing

Representative Smith told the Investigative Subcommittee that after the vote was over, he felt "beat . . . tired, physically and mentally. And angry, as you might guess." Representa- tive Smith could not recall whether, after he left the House floor at the conclusion of the proceedings, he went home to his Washington apartment or if he went directly to his office in the Rayburn building to finish writing his weekly column. Representative Smith speculated that since he intended to finish the column, he probably went from the floor to his office without going to his home first.

Representative Smith told the Investigative Subcommittee that he and his Chief of Staff had written the bulk of the November 23, 2003 column prior to the actual vote on the Medicare legislation. After the vote, Representative Smith himself added the first two paragraphs of the column in which he expressed publicly for the first time his allegations of wrongdoing in connection with the Medicare vote.

As has been previously summarized, . . . in the first paragraph of the column, Rep- resentative Smith asserted that "bribes and special deals were offered to convince mem- bers to vote yes." In the second paragraph of the column, he asserted that he had been "targeted by lobbyists and the congressional leadership" and that "members and groups made offers of extensive financial campaign support and endorsements for my son Brad" if he voted yes. . . .

IV. Findings and Recommendations

A. Summary of Findings . . .

The Investigative Subcommittee finds that the late-night timing of the vote, the extended period of time for which the vote was held open, and the unusually lobbying pressure on Members (which included the appearance on the House floor by a member of the

President's Cabinet), exacerbated tensions on the House floor and contributed to an environment in which the usual traditions of civil discourse and decorum amongst Members were not always followed.

In addition, based on the record of evidence developed during its investigation, the Investigative Subcommittee reached the following conclusions regarding the public statements made by Representative Nick Smith:

The Investigative Subcommittee finds that no group, organization, business interest, or corporation of any kind, or any individual affiliated with any such entities, offered $100,000 or any other specific sum of money to support the congressional candidacy of Brad Smith in order to induce Representative Nick Smith to vote in favor of the Medicare Prescription Drug Act.

The Investigative Subcommittee finds that Representative Nick Smith was not offered an endorsement or financial support for his son's candidacy from the National Republican Congressional Committee in exchange for voting in favor of the Medicare Prescription Drug Act. There was no evidence adduced that any consideration or discussion of an endorsement was undertaken within the National Republican Congressional Committee with respect to the Republican primary election in the Seventh District of Michigan held on August 3, 2004. Any statements made by Representative Nick Smith in any setting related to an endorsement or other support for his son by the National Republican Congressional Committee appear to have been the result of speculation or exaggeration on the part of Representative Nick Smith and speculation on the part of Jason Roe, a former employee of Representative Smith.

The Investigative Subcommittee finds that Representative Randall "Duke" Cunningham, Representative James T. Walsh, and Representative Candice Miller, acting independently from each other, and not in coordination with any other person or organization, made statements to Representative Nick Smith on the House floor after learning of Representative Nick Smith's vote in opposition to the Medicare Prescription Drug Act. Each of these statements referenced the congressional candidacy of Representative Nick Smith's son. The statements made by Representative Walsh and Representative Miller were made before the vote on the Medicare Prescription Drug Act was closed. The statement made by Representative Cunningham was made after the vote on the Medicare Prescription Drug Act was concluded. All of the statements to Representative Nick Smith by these three Members were made after Representative Smith had cast his vote against the Medicare Prescription Drug Act.

The Investigative Subcommittee finds that Majority Leader Tom DeLay, prior to the vote on the Medicare legislation on November 22, 2003, and most likely during a vote held on the evening of November 21, 2003, offered to endorse Brad Smith in exchange for Representative Nick Smith's vote in favor of the Medicare Prescription Drug Act.

The Investigative Subcommittee finds that to the extent that other Members of the House or the Secretary of Health and Human Services attempted to persuade Representative Nick Smith to vote in favor of the Medicare Prescription Drug Act, such attempts did not involve any offers of improper "special deals." Rather, such individuals attempted to persuade Representative Smith to vote in favor of the bill on the basis of policy or party loyalty. . . .

The Investigative Subcommittee finds that while Representative Nick Smith's initial public announcement of his allegations on November 23, 2003 may have been fueled by emotion and ager stemming from certain statements made to him by other Members in connection with his vote on the Medicare Prescription Drug Act, he failed to exercise reasonable judgment and restraint under the circumstances. Moreover, no mitigating circumstance exists for Representative Smith's continued publication of his allegations in the days and weeks following November 23, 2003. . . .

Source: House Committee on Standards of Official Conduct. *Investigation of Certain Allegations Related to Voting on the Medicare Prescription Drug, Improvement, and Modernization Act of 2003.* 108th Cong., 2d sess., September 30, 2004, pp. 34–42, 45–53.

NOTE

1. Quoted in House Committee on Standards of Official Conduct, *Investigation of Certain Allegations Related to Voting on the Medicare Prescription Drug, Improvement, and Modernization Act of 2003,* 108th Cong., 2d sess., September 30, 2004, 4.

DOCUMENT
10.3

Bush Touts the Medicare Prescription Drug Benefit

"We're on a Massive Education Effort, Starting Today"

2005

When President George W. Bush and his fellow Republicans shepherded a major new Medicare prescription drug coverage bill into law in late 2003, they hailed it as the greatest advance in health care for seniors since Medicare itself came into being in 1965. This new benefit, which came to be known as Medicare Part D and would take effect on January 1, 2006, was channeled through private insurers, who prepared a plethora of different plans for seniors to choose from. But in 2005, as the enrollment deadline for the program drew near, news coverage of the impending rollout was dominated by stories of confused seniors who were paralyzed by the complexities of the competing insurance plans. Mindful that seniors' apparent confusion and apprehension about Medicare Part D had the potential to turn a popular benefit into a political nightmare, the Bush administration belatedly launched a public education campaign to encourage and guide seniors through the policy selection process. This outreach effort began in earnest on June 16, 2005, with a speech that Bush delivered at the Department of Health and Human Services in Washington, D.C. Bush's remarks are reprinted here.

I'm grateful to the men and women of this Department for their compassion and service. Thanks for serving our country. I want to thank you all for helping us launch a vital effort to bring greater peace of mind to America's seniors and people with disabilities. Over the next 11 months, we will spread important news to everyone receiving Medicare. This great and trusted program is about to become even better. Starting this November, every American on Medicare can sign up to get help paying for their prescription drugs. . . .

　　Forty years ago—think about that, 40 years ago this summer, President Lyndon Baines Johnson, from the great State of Texas—[laughter]—signed a law creating Medicare to guarantee health care for seniors and Americans with disabilities. In the decades since that historic act, Medicare has spared millions of our citizens from needless suffering and hardship. Medicare is a landmark achievement of a compassionate society. It is a basic trust that our Government will always honor.

Medicare has also faced challenges. For decades, medicine advanced rapidly and grew to include innovations like prescription drugs, but Medicare didn't keep pace. As a result, Medicare recipients were left with a program based on the medicine of the 1960s. For example, Medicare would pay $28,000 for ulcer surgery but not $500 for the prescription drugs that eliminate the cause of most ulcers. Medicare would pay more than $100,000 to treat the effects of a stroke but not $1,000 for blood-thinning drugs that could prevent strokes. That's an outdated system, and it made no sense for American seniors. It made no sense for Americans with disabilities, and it made no sense for American taxpayers.

Year after year, politicians pledged to reform Medicare, but the job never got done until 2003, when members of both political parties came together to deliver the greatest advance in health care for seniors since the founding of Medicare. This new law is bringing preventive medicine, better health care choices, and prescription drugs to every American receiving Medicare. The Medicare Modernization Act renewed the promise of Medicare for the 21st century, and I was honored and proud to sign that piece of legislation.

Over the past year, millions of Americans have started to benefit from the new Medicare program. Every senior entering Medicare is now eligible for a "Welcome to Medicare" physical. It's a fundamental improvement, and it makes a lot of sense. Medicare patients and doctors are now able to work together to diagnose health care and health concerns right away. And there's a simple reason: The sooner you diagnose a problem—you can treat problems before they become worse. Medicare now covers preventive screenings that can catch illness from diabetes to heart disease. Medicare is covering innovative programs to help seniors with chronic diseases like high blood pressure. I urge every senior to take advantage of these new benefits in Medicare.

In the 21st century, preventing and treating illness requires prescription drugs. Seniors know this. Yet because Medicare did not cover prescription drugs, many seniors had to make painful sacrifices to pay for medicine. In my travels around the country, I met seniors who faced the agonizing choice between buying prescription drugs and buying groceries. I met retirees who resorted to cutting pills in half. I met Americans who were forced to spend their retirement years working, just to pay for their prescriptions. These hardships undermine the basic promise of Medicare. And thanks to Medicare Modernization Act, those days are coming to an end.

To provide immediate help with drug costs, the new Medicare law created drug discount cards. Over the past year, millions of seniors have used these cards to save billions of dollars. In Missouri, I met a woman who used her discount card to buy $10 worth of drugs for $1.14. She was happy with the card. Another senior went to her pharmacy and spent under $30 for medicine that used to cost about four times as much. And here is what she said: "When he got out my medicine card . . . and told me what the savings was, I about dropped my false teeth." [Laughter]

The Medicare Modernization Act created a prescription drug benefit to replace drug discount cards and bring savings and peace of mind to all 42 million Medicare beneficiaries. The new benefit will help every senior as well as Americans with developmental and physical disabilities and mental illnesses and HIV/AIDS. Congress scheduled the prescription drug benefit to start in January of 2006. Thanks to the leadership of Secretary [of HHS Michael] Leavitt and Mark McClellan [administrator of the Centers for Medicare and Medicaid Services], we are on track to deliver prescription drug coverage on time to every American senior.

As Medicare's professional staff prepares to implement the prescription drug benefit, we also must ensure that seniors are ready to take full advantage of their new opportunities. And that's why I've come here today. It's important for everyone to understand that Medicare prescription drug coverage is voluntary. Seniors can choose to take advantage of the benefit, or they can choose not to. It's up to them.

And there's plenty of time to make the decision. Starting on October 1st, Medicare beneficiaries will begin getting information about the new prescription drug plans available. They will receive a handbook called "Medicare and You" that includes detailed information about their options. If they like what they see and choose to get prescription drug coverage, they can enroll any time between November 15th of this year and May 15th of next year. Beneficiaries should make their decisions as soon as they are ready, because enrolling before May will ensure that they pay the lowest possible premiums.

The Federal Government will work hard to ensure that Medicare beneficiaries understand their options. I've asked every agency that touches the lives of seniors or disabled Americans to devote resources to explaining the prescription drug benefit. And we need the help of people in the private sector as well. The only way to reach everyone on Medicare is to mobilize compassionate citizens in communities all over the country. And that's why we've come together this afternoon to kick off a nationwide outreach campaign.

Over the next 11 months, we will unite a wide range of Americans from doctors to nurses to pharmacists to State and local leaders to seniors groups to disability advocates to faith-based organizations. Together, we will work to ensure that every American on Medicare is ready to make a confident choice about prescription drug coverage, so they can finally receive the modern health care they deserve.

As we spread the word about the new opportunities in Medicare, we will make it clear that prescription drug coverage will provide greater peace of mind for beneficiaries in three key ways.

First, the new Medicare coverage will provide greater peace of mind by helping all seniors and Americans with disabilities pay for prescription drugs, no matter how they pay for medicine now. On average, Medicare beneficiaries will receive more than $1,300 in Federal assistance to pay for prescription drugs. Seniors with no drug coverage and average prescription expenses will see their drug bills reduced by half or more. The new Medicare benefits will also provide special help for seniors with the highest drug costs. Starting in January, Medicare will cover 95 percent of all prescription costs after a senior has spent $3,600 in a year. Seniors will never be able to predict what challenges life will bring, but thanks to Medicare, they can be certain they will never have their entire savings wiped out to pay for prescription drugs.

Second, the new Medicare coverage will provide greater peace of mind by offering beneficiaries better health care choices than they have ever had. Seniors will be able to choose any Medicare prescription drug plan that fits their needs and their medical history. Seniors who want to keep their Medicare the way it is will be able to do so. Seniors using Medicare Advantage to save money will be able to keep their plans and get better drug benefits. Seniors who receive drug coverage from a former employer or union can count on new support from Medicare to help them keep their good benefits. Every prescription drug plan will offer a broad choice of brand name drugs and generic drugs. Seniors will also have the choice to pick up their prescriptions at local pharmacies or to have the medicine delivered to their home.

These options might sound familiar to some of you here at the Department. It's got to sound familiar to Members of the United States Congress. After all, these health care choices, these kind of choices are available for people who work here in Washington. And if these choices are good enough for people who work here in Washington, they ought to be good enough for the seniors all across the country.

Third, the new Medicare coverage will provide greater peace of mind by extending extra help to low-income seniors and beneficiaries with disabilities. For years, beneficiaries on the tightest budgets received no help from Medicare to pay for prescription drugs. Because we acted, about a third of American seniors will be eligible for a Medicare drug benefit that includes little or no premiums, low deductibles, and no gaps in coverage. On average, Medicare will pick up the tab for more than 95 percent of prescription drug costs for low-income seniors. To receive this important assistance, low-income seniors have to fill out a straightforward, four-page application form with, at most, 16 questions. No financial documents or complicated records are required, and the forms are easy to obtain. In fact, millions of applications have already been mailed to low-income seniors. If you or a family member receives one of these, I urge you to fill it out and send it in. Some of the seniors groups that are here have a saying, "When in doubt, fill it out." [Laughter] By encouraging all low-income seniors to sign up for extra assistance, we will ensure that Medicare gives its greatest help to those with the greatest needs.

With all of these essential reforms, the Medicare Modernization Act created a new commitment to seniors and Americans with disabilities, and all of you are helping to make good on that commitment. By lending a hand to neighbors in need, you are strengthening your communities and showing the great compassion of our country. Many organizations have already launched innovative efforts to reach seniors. And I'll continue to call on people to put forth innovative strategies to reach our seniors.

For example, in Wisconsin and Indiana, more than 270 community leaders are coming together to find ways to get information to rural seniors. In Chicago, a food pantry, the Catholic Archdiocese, and a news publication are all working to get the word out about the new Medicare benefits. The Federal Department of Transportation, under the leadership of Norm Mineta, is working with local agencies to post Medicare information in buses and at highway rest stops. Thousands of pharmacies are working with Medicare to provide information for seniors. Countless other organizations are holding community events and connecting with seniors face to face, so Medicare recipients can get their questions answered and make informed choices about prescription drug coverage. In other words, we're on a massive education effort, starting today. And I'm asking for America's help.

You can help by making a call to your mother or father and tell them what's available. You can help by showing an older neighbor how to fill out a form. You can help by spending an afternoon at the local retirement home. And by the way, when you help somebody, you're really helping yourself. You can get information 24 hours a day calling 1-800-MEDICARE. It's pretty easy to remember, 1-800-MEDICARE. Or you can use the Internet to visit the official Medicare web site at medicare.gov. All you've got to do is type in medicare.gov, and you're going to find out what I'm talking about.

Remember that information about prescription drug plans will be available starting October 1st, and November 15th is the first day to sign up for the new coverage. You need to circle those dates on your calendar and tell the seniors in your life that modern medicine is on the way. This is a good deal, and people need to take advantage of it.

I think the passage of the Medicare Modernization Act is a good lesson for all of us who work in this city. You know, it wasn't all that long ago the leaders who talked about

Medicare reform faced a lot of name-calling—to say the least. When Congress finally rose above politics and fulfilled its duty to America's seniors, it showed what's possible in Washington, D.C. We need that same spirit—[applause]. I mean, this bill is proof that Americans really aren't interested in seeing one party win and another party lose. What Americans want to see is people coming together to solve problems. That's what they want to see.

We had a problem in Medicare. It wasn't working the way it should. It wasn't modern. It wasn't answering the needs of our seniors. And by coming together, we have done our job here in Washington. And as a result of working together, we have changed Medicare for the better. Medicare is now modern, reformed, and compassionate. And I urge all seniors—all seniors and those folks here in America who want to help seniors, look into this new prescription drug benefit; it will make your life better.

Thank you all for coming. God bless.

Source: Bush, George W. Remarks on Implementing the Medicare Modernization Act, June 16, 2005. *Public Papers of the Presidents of the United States: George W. Bush, 2005.* Vol. 1. Washington, DC: Government Printing Office, 2006, pp. 1001–1006.

DOCUMENT 10.4

Massachusetts Passes Major Health Insurance Reform

"Massachusetts Is Leading the Way with Health Insurance for Everyone"

2006

In 2006 Republican governor Mitt Romney of Massachusetts worked with the state's Democrat-dominated legislature to pass a universal health care coverage plan for Massachusetts residents, the first program of its kind in the nation. The overhaul featured subsidies for the poor, insurance exchanges, an individual mandate that levied financial penalties on residents who failed to obtain a state-regulated minimum level of coverage, and other elements designed to extend basic health insurance to all uninsured people in the state.

When Romney signed these reforms into law, he vetoed several provisions that the Democrats had written into the bill, including expansions of Medicaid, the State Children's Health Insurance Program, public health programs, and an employer assessment, an annual financial penalty on employers who failed to provide health coverage for their workers. But the Democratic-controlled legislature quickly overrode all eight of these section vetoes, so they became part of the law.

Romney expressed great satisfaction with the "Massachusetts plan" (as evidenced by his signing statement, excerpted here), and during his unsuccessful bid for the Republican presidential nomination in 2008, he often described it as his signature accomplishment as governor of the state. After the Obama administration cited the Massachusetts health insurance reforms as a model for its own health care reforms, however, Romney's

"Massachusetts plan" came under increased scrutiny from fellow Republicans. Because Obama's Patient Protection and Affordable Care Act was deeply unpopular with rank-and-file Republicans, Romney repeatedly rejected this politically damaging comparison. He argued that the Massachusetts plan was fundamentally different because it was enacted at the state level. Each state, Romney asserted, should be able "to create a solution to the uninsured in the way that [it thinks] best, that's the way the Constitution intended it. We are a federalist system. We don't need the federal government imposing a one-size-fits-all plan on the entire nation."[1]

Many policy analysts asserted however, that the basic policy underpinnings of the two pieces of legislation are strikingly similar. "Basically, it's the same thing," said Jonathan Gruber, a Massachusetts Institute of Technology economist who advised both the Romney and Obama administrations in their health reform efforts. "[Romney] is in many ways the intellectual father of national health reform."[2]

In any event, statistics indicate that the law Romney signed in 2006 has been effective in extending health insurance coverage to virtually all Massachusetts residents. In 2010, 98.1 percent of state residents had coverage (compared with a national average of 83.3 percent). The rate of coverage for children and seniors was even higher, at 99.8 percent and 99.6 percent, respectively.

To the Honorable Senate and House of Representatives:

Pursuant to the provisions of Section 5 of Article 63 of the Amendments to the Constitution, I am today signing House Bill No. 4479, "An Act Providing Access to Affordable, Quality, Accountable Health Care."

With the signing [of] this law today, every resident will have health insurance by 2009. An achievement like this comes around once in a generation, and it proves that government can work when people of both parties reach across the aisle for the common good. Today, Massachusetts is leading the way with health insurance for everyone, without a government takeover and without raising taxes.

By allowing insurers greater flexibility to design and offer more consumer responsive health insurance products and by remedying market breakdowns by merging the small group and non-group markets, this law will substantially reduce the average monthly premium for individuals and small businesses. In order to simplify the offer and purchase of insurance, especially by small businesses, the law creates a new independent authority call[ed] the insurance Commonwealth Care Health Insurance Connector Authority. The Connector will offer a choice of comprehensive, good value health insurance products to individuals and to small businesses for purchase on a pre-tax basis.

For those residents of the Commonwealth who do not qualify for Medicaid, but do not earn enough annual income to purchase health insurance on their own, this law will provide Commonwealth Care, a sliding scale premium assistance program for the purchase of private health insurance. With the Creation of Commonwealth Care, every resident of the Commonwealth will be able to buy health insurance according to their means.

Because this law will result in a greater availability of affordable health insurance products and subsidies will be provided to the working poor, it is fair to expect that all Massachusetts residents have health insurance by July 1, 2007. No longer can individuals free ride by seeking healthcare and expecting, [sic] society to bear the cost.

Lastly, but perhaps most critically, this bill takes bold steps to contain healthcare costs. By putting an end to cost-shifting from the uninsured and from the Medicaid program, businesses and individual[s] will no longer bear the cost of others' healthcare. This bill places critical healthcare cost and quality information in the hands of businesses and consumers. By creating cost and quality transparency, individuals will make more informed decisions about where and how to seek care.

In addition, I am vetoing in their entirety those sections of House 4479 itemized in Attachment A of this message, for the reasons set forth in that attachment.

The remainder of the bill I hereby approve.

Mitt Romney

Governor

Source: "Romney Signs Landmark Health Insurance Reform Bill." Press release. Commonwealth of Massachusetts, Executive Department, April 12, 2006.

NOTES

1. Mitt Romney, "Good Morning America," ABC, February 1, 2011, quoted in Carey Goldberg, "Mitt Romney on Mass. Health Reform: No Apologies, But Not for Everyone," *CommonHealth: Reform and Reality*, February 2, 2011, http://commonhealth.wbur.org/2011/02/mitt-romney-reform/.

2. Quoted in Sasha Issenberg, "Romney Defends Massachusetts Health Care Law," *Boston Globe*, March 30, 2010, www.boston.com/news/health/articles/2010/03/30/romney_defends_massachusetts_health _care_law/.

Washington Reacts to a Supreme Court Decision on "Partial-Birth" Abortion

DOCUMENT
10.5

"It Represents the Day That America Changed Direction"

2007

No issue symbolized the so-called culture wars that wracked US politics during the late 1980s through the first decade of the twenty-first century as much as abortion. This extraordinarily polarizing issue, freighted as it is with all sorts of moral, medical, and constitutional considerations, pitted the politically powerful and dedicated pro-life movement against the equally influential and determined pro-choice movement in a seemingly endless struggle for the hearts and minds of the American public. Inevitably, these tugs-of-war took on particularly urgency at times when important abortion-related laws or court decisions came to pass. Events such as the 1989 Supreme Court judgment in Webster v. Reproductive Health Services *restricting use of public funds and facilities in abortion procedures, the Food and Drug Administration's 2000 approval of the RU486 abortion pill, and various efforts by state legislatures to limit abortions all triggered firestorms of debate in media outlets and around American kitchen tables.*

Another landmark in the grueling battle over abortion rights in the United States came in 2003, when Congress passed and President George W. Bush signed the Partial-Birth Abortion Ban Act. (President Bill Clinton had twice vetoed similar legislation in the 1990s.) This legislation, the first-ever federal ban on a specific method of abortion, explicitly outlawed a rarely used abortion procedure used in the second trimester. The procedure, known medically as "intact dilation and extraction," requires removing the fetus in an intact condition. (About 85 to 90 percent of all abortions take place in the first trimester, when other abortion methods are available.)

The law was blocked for four years in the courts, but on April 18, 2007, the U.S. Supreme Court upheld the law by a 5–4 vote in Gonzales v. Carhart. *The key vote in affirming the law was registered by Samuel A. Alito Jr., who had joined the Court sixteen months earlier. Alito's predecessor, Justice Sandra Day O'Connor, had provided the decisive vote back in 2000, when the Supreme Court had struck down a state law outlawing the procedure by a 5–4 vote. Abortion supporters and opponents agreed that the change from O'Connor to Alito was a pivotal one.*

When the news of the Supreme Court decision reached Congress, reaction unfolded in predictable fashion. Well-known opponents of abortion such as Rep. Trent Franks (R-AZ) rushed to the House floor to hail the decision as an indication that the tide was finally turning against abortion rights in America. Meanwhile, supporters of abortion rights such as Rep. Dennis J. Kucinich (D-OH) framed the decision as a cataclysmic blow to women's rights. The remarks of both Franks and Kucinich are excerpted here.

Speech by Rep. Trent Franks (R-AZ) on the House Floor, April 18, 2007

Mr. FRANKS of Arizona. Mr. Speaker, today was a very important day. Today, the United States Supreme Court handed down a decision upholding the Federal law protecting unborn children from partial-birth abortion.

Mr. Speaker, perhaps it is important for those of us in this Chamber to first remind ourselves again of why we were really all put here. Thomas Jefferson said, "The care of human life and its happiness and not its destruction is the chief and only object of good government."

Mr. Speaker, protecting the lives of our innocent citizens and their constitutional rights is indeed why we are all here. The phrase in the 14th amendment capsulizes our entire Constitution. It says, "No State shall deprive any person of life, liberty or property without due process of law." The bedrock foundation of this Republic is the belief that all human beings are created equal and endowed by their Creator with the inalienable rights of life, liberty and the pursuit of happiness.

Every conflict and battle our Nation has ever faced can be traced to this core foundational belief on our part that every life, from the smallest child to the elderly widow, from the strongest and bravest soldiers on our front lines, to the weakest and most frail in our society, every human soul is of infinite worth and entitled by God to pursue liberty, prosperity and happiness.

But, Mr. Speaker, for 34 years, *Roe v. Wade* has been a desecration of that bedrock foundation upon which America stands, and *Roe v. Wade* sets itself apart from all of the other egregious decisions made by our courts in that its result is 45 million dead American children. . . .

. . . Mr. Speaker, we must not ever be so blind to the fact that each time an abortion takes place, a nameless little baby dies a lonely death; a mother is never quite the same, whether she realizes it or not; and all of the gifts that that child might have brought to humanity are lost forever.

It is often said, Mr. Speaker, that a society is measured by how it treats those in the dawn of life, those in the shadows of life, and those in the twilight of life. Because unborn children are hidden both in the dawn and in the shadows of life, we kill thousands of them every day in America, using sometimes methods like partial-birth abortion that cause so much agonizing pain that the child that is being killed, if they were an animal, it would be illegal under Federal law to do it the way we do it.

If we, as a human family in America, cannot find enough humanity within ourselves to change that, if this human rights atrocity of dismembering our own children alive is truly who we are, then the "invincible ignorance" Henry Hyde spoke of in this Chamber so long ago will indeed finally prevail, the patriots' dream will be lost, and those lying out in Arlington National Cemetery will have died in vain and twilight will have fallen upon us all.

Mr. Speaker, that day may come in America indeed. But, sir, that day has not come yet. It is not this day, because today, Mr. Speaker, the world changed. Today the United States Supreme Court upheld a law protecting unborn children from the barbaric, nightmarish procedure of partial-birth abortion. And with this ruling comes a brilliant, piercing ray of hope, because even though this ruling only upholds a law that protects a small number of late-term babies from this horrifying procedure called partial-birth abortion, it represents the day that America changed direction and turned her heart toward home.

I believe, Mr. Speaker, that this decision is part of a growing awareness on the part of all Americans of the simple truth that abortion takes the life of a child, and the United States of America is bigger than abortion on demand. We are beginning to look within ourselves and we are beginning to understand that the foundation of this Nation is within our own hearts.

Our Nation is beginning to understand that whether it is flying airplanes into buildings or blowing up buildings in Oklahoma City, or whether it is raping and pillaging in Bosnia, or whether it is violence in our streets or kidnapping little girls in broad daylight or murdering innocent unborn children, all of these have one inescapable common denominator, and that is the lack of respect for innocent human life. Americans are beginning to understand and realize that the reason crime is so rampant in this country is because we have taught our young people that it is all right to kill helpless unborn children. Should we then wonder why they kill each other on the school playground?

Americans are beginning to understand that the same mentality that allows a father to forsake his unborn child to an abortionist also allows him to forsake his born children to the welfare state.

Americans are beginning to understand that the abortion mentality is destroying families all over this country, and that if this epidemic of family disintegration continues, that we in this family will bankrupt this Nation in trying to deal with the results.

Americans are also trying to understand that there are better ways to help young mothers than killing their children for them.

And Americans are beginning to understand that if we, as a society, do not find or possess the courage and the will to protect innocent unborn children, that, in the final analysis, we may never find the will or the courage or the commitment to protect any kind of liberty for anyone of any kind. . . .

Speech by Rep. Dennis J. Kucinich (D-OH) on the House Floor, April 19, 2007

Mr. KUCINICH. Madam Speaker, yesterday's decision by the Supreme Court to uphold the Partial Birth Abortion Ban Act threatens a woman's right to make her own choices about abortion and consequently choices pertaining to her own body. By upholding the first ever federal abortion ban the Supreme Court has brought us dangerously close to allowing politicians to make decisions regarding the control a woman is allowed over her own body.

The Court has, for the first time since its original ruling in 1973 establishing a woman's right to an abortion, showed no consideration for the health and safety of a woman. The decision is contrary to that of six other federal courts throughout the country. This decision disallows exceptions to be made in instances where a woman's health is at risk. In circumstances where the banned procedure is the safest for the health of the female patient, doctors will be powerless, except under threat of a two year criminal penalty, to do the right thing for their patient. The American College of Obstetricians and Gynecologists, representing ninety percent of these medical officials, agrees that the ban causes interference in medical decision making and is detrimental to women's health.

The Court's decision forces us to look at where our society really is in respect to the rights and equality of women. How can we, in good conscience, tell the young women of today that they are equal and able to accomplish their dreams if at the same time society is seeking to control their actions and make decisions with regard to their own bodies? I empathize with the frustration that women around the country are feeling today; I realize the greater restrictive implications implied by the Court's ruling.

I imagine that a woman's decision to have an abortion, under any circumstances, must be one of the most difficult she will make in her life. It is a very private, very personal decision that is to be made by her and may include the support of family, friends and medical professionals. It is not a decision that is made lightly or without consequence. Today's decision has perilously hindered a woman's privacy and safety by allowing politics to interfere in medical decisions.

We must end the divisiveness that surrounds the issue of abortion so that we may begin the long overdue healing process. We must work to limit the need for abortions while at the same time ensuring safety. Access to prenatal and postnatal care through expanded Medicare coverage will be an important component as well as a living wage. I will maintain my support for social programs, and maternal and child nutrition programs to strengthen vulnerable families. I will continue to stand behind programs that teach sex education, domestic family planning and promote the use of contraception.

Source: Franks, Trent. The Scourge of Abortion in America. *Congressional Record.* 110th Cong., 1st sess., April 18, 2007, pp. H3552–H3553. Kucinich, Dennis J. Partial Birth Abortion Ban Act. *Congressional Record.* 110th Cong., 1st sess., April 19, 2007, p. E798.

DOCUMENT 10.6 Political Battle over SCHIP Reauthorization

"With This Veto, the President Is Playing Politics, Pure and Simple"

2007

In 2007 the Bush administration became locked in a bitter policy dispute with the Democrat-controlled Congress over reauthorization of the State Children's Health Insurance Program (SCHIP), a ten-year-old public health insurance program for needy children that had reduced by one-third the number of uninsured children in the country (and given cash-strapped states a welcome infusion of health care funding). Both Republicans and Democrats agreed that SCHIP was worthy of renewal, but mindful of the spiraling budget deficit, Bush and assorted deficit hawks in Congress wanted to approve only modest increases in the program's budget. Many Democrats, along with a good number of moderate and even conservative Republicans, rejected this stance and called for expansion of the program. They noted that if present rates of health care inflation remained steady, Bush's proposed investment in SCHIP would not even cover children already enrolled. And Democrats, who had reclaimed control of both the House and Senate in the fall 2006 midterms, were quick to point out that the deficit had been created in the first place by Bush policies, from big tax cuts for the wealthy and military operations in Iraq and Afghanistan to the new Medicare prescription drug benefit.

In early 2007 the Democratic leadership decided to fund its SCHIP expansion primarily through new tobacco taxes (which would have the salutary side effect of reducing smoking, a major public health problem). Mindful of the fact that Democrats had only a small majority in the Senate, House leaders who had passed a very ambitious SCHIP expansion bill grudgingly agreed to a more moderate measure that could get bipartisan support and thus evade a filibuster. In late September a bipartisan SCHIP reauthorization bill went to Bush for his signature, but the president vetoed it as an unacceptable expansion of health care into government hands. Bush's veto message, reprinted here, sparked strong recriminations of the president's stand, as well as spirited defenses of his action. This document features representative reactions from two critics, House majority leader Steny H. Hoyer (D-MD) and Rep. Frank Pallone Jr. (D-NJ), as well as a defense of the veto by Rep. Nathan Deal (R-GA).

In the aftermath of Bush's October 3 veto, Democrats and moderate Republicans who supported SCHIP expansion worked furiously for two months to craft a bill that could attract enough votes to override a second veto. Unable to do so, they nonetheless passed the bill by healthy margins and urged the president to sign it. Instead, Bush once again used his veto pen. Democrats subsequently agreed to a temporary extension of funding that effectively booted the question of SCHIP funding to Democrat Barack Obama, Bush's successor. The Democrat-controlled 111th Congress quickly sent SCHIP expansion legislation to the White House, and on February 4, 2009, Obama signed the Children's Health Insurance Reauthorization Act into law. This measure extended SCHIP eligibility to an additional four million children and pregnant women.

President Bush's Vetoes SCHIP Legislation

October 3, 2007

The Speaker pro tempore laid before the House the following veto message from the President of the United States:

To the House of Representatives:

I am returning herewith without my approval H.R. 976, the "Children's Health Insurance Program Reauthorization Act of 2007," because this legislation would move health care in this country in the wrong direction.

The original purpose of the State Children's Health Insurance Program (SCHIP) was to help children whose families cannot afford private health insurance, but do not qualify for Medicaid, to get the coverage they need. My Administration strongly supports reauthorization of SCHIP. That is why I proposed last February a 20 percent increase in funding for the program over 5 years.

This bill would shift SCHIP away from its original purpose and turn it into a program that would cover children from some families of four earning almost $83,000 a year. In addition, under this bill, government coverage would displace private health insurance for many children. If this bill were enacted, one out of every three children moving onto government coverage would be moving from private coverage. The bill also does not fully fund all its new spending, obscuring the true cost of the bill's expansion of SCHIP, and it raises taxes on working Americans.

Because the Congress has chosen to send me a bill that moves our health care system in the wrong direction, I must veto it. I hope we can now work together to produce a good bill that puts poorer children first, that moves adults out of a program meant for children, and that does not abandon the bipartisan tradition that marked the enactment of SCHIP. Our goal should be to move children who have no health insurance to private coverage, not to move children who already have private health insurance to government coverage.

George W. Bush.

The White House, October 3, 2007.

Post-veto remarks of House Majority Leader Steny Hoyer (D-MD), Representative Frank Pallone Jr. (D-NJ), and Representative Nathan Deal (R-GA)

October 3, 2007

Mr. Hoyer: Madam Speaker, earlier today, the President of the United States, in defiance of bipartisan majorities in the House and Senate, and in defiance of the will of a great majority of Americans, vetoed fiscally responsible legislation that would ensure that 10 million children in our Nation receive health insurance coverage. That's approximately 4 million more children than are covered under the highly successful Children's Health Insurance Program today.

I remind the Members of the House that that program was adopted in 1997 by a Republican-controlled Congress with strong Democratic support, a bipartisan program . Let us be clear, this is a defining moment for this Congress and for a President who has labeled himself a compassionate conservative.

The President's veto, my colleagues, must not stand. The President wrongly claims that this bipartisan legislation is fiscally irresponsible. But the truth is the Children's Health Insurance Program legislation, forged by Members on both sides of this aisle, is paid for. It does not add to the deficit or to the debt. Moreover, President Bush, whose policies over the last 6 years have instigated record budget deficits and spiraling debt, should not be lecturing anyone on the issue of fiscal discipline. This administration, I suggest to all of us, has pursued and enacted the most fiscally irresponsible policies perhaps in American history. In fact, even as the President vetoed this CHIP legislation, all of it paid for, he has asked Congress to approve another $190 billion to protect Baghdad and its environs. Mr. President, we need to protect the children of Bowie, of New York, of Peoria, of Miami, of California.

In fact, even as the President vetoed, as I said, this legislation, he sent to us a $190 billion request for more money for the war in Iraq, the civil war in Iraq, a place where, very frankly, it is far past time where the people of Iraq took the responsibility to defend and secure their country.

This legislation that the President has vetoed is about securing the health of America's children. With this veto, the President is playing politics, pure and simple.

After running up record deficits in debt, he is now trying to establish his fiscal bona fides with his conservative political base by denying health services to children.

Mr. President, it won't work. Mr. President, it shouldn't work. Mr. President, it is not compassionate, nor is it common sense.

Senator [Orrin] Hatch, no one's idea of a liberal or of a Democratic spinmeister, said on the Senate floor last week, and I quote, "It is unfortunate that the President has chosen to be on what, to me, is clearly the wrong side of the issue." That was Senator Hatch.

I hope all of us in this body, Republican and Democrat, decide, when this vote comes up, to determine whether or not the Congress should make policy or whether we will be subservient to the President's veto in protecting children.

I hope all of us, Republican and Democrat, liberal, moderate and conservative, will join together to respond to the children of this country and their families who agonize about not having the health insurance they need so that their children can be kept healthy.

Senator [Pat] Roberts of Kansas remarked, another leader in the Republican Party, "I am not for excessive spending and strongly oppose the federalization of health care. And if the administration's concerns with this bill were accurate, I would support a veto, but bluntly put," said Senator Roberts from Kansas, who served in this body, "the assertions of the President," he said, "are wrong." Technically, he said that the premises were inaccurate.

Madam Speaker, this legislation is not only supported by majorities in the House and Senate, it is supported by doctors, nurses, private insurers, children's advocates, 43 Governors. The list goes on and on and on. But most importantly, most importantly, it's supported by the parents of children who are working, working hard every day, playing by the rules. Perhaps both are working, if they're fortunate to have two parents in the home, or a single parent, mom or dad, working hard, but making too little to afford insurance and working for an employer who can't give them insurance. Most of all, that is the constituency, that is the voice we ought to hear, that is why we ought to override this veto.

According to an ABC News-Washington Post poll released just this week, 72 percent of Americans, including 61 percent of Republicans, support this legislation, 69 percent of independents. What is perhaps most stunning of all is that, with this veto, the President has violated his own pledge at the Republican National Convention in 2004. You've heard me say this before, but let me say it again: "In a new term we will lead an aggressive effort to enroll millions of children who are eligible but not signed up for government programs." "We will not allow," said the President, "a lack of attention or information to stand between these children and the health care they need." Mr. President, that is what you have done by this veto, stood between those children and the insurance they need.

I urge my colleagues, override this veto, support this motion, and on October 18 let us vote for the children.

Mr. Pallone: Madam Speaker, the Children's Health Insurance Program Reauthorization Act passed the House and the Senate with overwhelming bipartisan support. . . . Yet this is a bill that the President has been threatening to veto since this summer. I don't know what happened to the President's compassion or sense of social justice. I don't think he understands the negative impact his veto will have on the millions of children who would be denied regular visits to see the doctor because he refused to sign this bill into law.

Now, let's review who stands for what. Under the bipartisan bill that the President vetoed this morning, 4 million previously uninsured low-income children, many of whom are in working families, I know there was a reference to welfare from the gentleman from Louisiana. I don't think he was referencing these kids or their families because these are working families. But 4 million previously uninsured low-income children who are in working families would get health coverage under this bill. A total of 10 million children would have their health coverage secured.

Under the bipartisan bill, the vast majority of children covered are the lowest income children who are today uninsured. According to the CBO, under the bipartisan bill, about 84 percent of the uninsured children who would benefit live in families with incomes below $40,000 a year. In addition, 1.7 million uninsured children who are eligible for Medicaid but otherwise would be uninsured would gain coverage under the agreement. Most of these would likely be children living in families with incomes below $20,000 a year. Under the bipartisan bill, States would have new tools to conduct outreach and enrollments. States could use express-lane, one-stop-shopping at places like schools, community centers and hospitals to get children covered.

The President, while he recently put out a regulation that would actually block schools from helping to sign low-income, uninsured children up for coverage, he put out another regulation that would force children to go an entire year, that is one whole year, without insurance coverage before their parents could sign them up for CHIP. That is 1 year of earaches, strep throat, asthma, diabetes and toothaches that would be treated in emergency rooms rather than the doctor's office. The President talked about how kids can go to the emergency room. Well, has he been to an emergency room lately? I was at one in my district last weekend. It is not a great place for a kid to visit. It is a scene of trauma. People who have overdosed on alcohol and drugs. Most emergency rooms are overwhelmed with real emergencies and have few resources to treat people who need regular family care.

The President makes $400,000 a year. He is guaranteed health care for life. He has a government doctor that is at his immediate call. Yet today this President has denied millions of low-income children and working families the opportunity to get even basic health care. Working Americans understand the struggle families have to make ends meet and afford health care coverage for their children. But the President and very few, because I am not talking about all Republicans, but very few of my colleagues on the other side of the aisle appear to be the only people in America who do not understand the challenges these families face or the importance of securing affordable coverage for their children.

It is a sad day, Madam Speaker, for America that the President vetoed this bill. But there is an opportunity over the next 2 weeks, because I want everyone to support this motion, but in about a week or two, we are going to have a vote on the floor. I would urge all those on the other side of the aisle who did not vote for this bill to use that time to reconsider and think about these kids when they go and cast their vote and vote to override this veto by the President.

Mr. Deal: Madam Speaker, the State Children's Health Insurance Plan, there ought to be something that we can agree on. The first is that the program ought to be for children. And yet we are told that in the bill the President has rightfully vetoed, in 5 years there will be 780,000 adults still in a children's health program.

Secondly, this program ought to be, as its primary target was, for children below 200 percent of poverty. We know that in States that have gone above the 200 percent level, they have left behind up to a quarter of their children in their State that are below 200 percent of poverty, and there is nothing in this bill that requires them to go back and make sure that they enroll those children. In fact, this legislation repeals the outline that CMS had put out to require 95 percent saturation of children below 200 percent of poverty. So there is no effort to go back and do what the program was designed to do, and that is to help those between the 100 and 200 percent of poverty.

Madam Speaker, the third thing is that we all ought to agree that Medicaid and SCHIP ought to be for Americans, for American children. The change that this bill puts into place will allow people who are not qualified under our current law for Medicaid or SCHIP to become eligible. CBO says that the Federal cost of that alone is $3.7 billion.

I think the last thing we ought to agree on is that we should not take a major step toward socializing health care in this country. This bill does nothing to prevent States from having what is called "income disregards." That is, if a State says, well, we just won't count what it costs for housing, we won't count what it costs for food, we won't count what [it] costs for transportation in computing your percent of poverty eligibility, then you can go up to 800 percent of poverty. And that certainly distorts the program.

Madam Speaker, lastly, we want to talk about time and the use of time. We knew 10 years ago that this bill was going to expire at the end of last month. This was a 10-year authorization bill. We knew in 1997 when it was put in place that it was going to expire at the end of September of this year. We knew 9 months ago when this Congress went into session that unless something was done, the legislation was going to expire the end of September. And yet only at the last minute was legislation presented in this House, with no legislative hearing, and then asked to be voted on, and not a single House Republican participated in the conference committee report that we are now being asked to sustain and to agree to at this point.

Source: Children's Health Insurance Program Reauthorization Act of 2007—Veto Message from the President of the United States. *Congressional Record.* 110th Cong., 1st sess., October 3, 2007, pp. H11203–H11207.

DOCUMENT
10.7

Bipartisan Support for the Wellstone Mental Health Parity Act

"Diseases of the Brain Should Be Treated the Same as Diseases of the Body"

2008

In 1996 liberal senator Paul Wellstone (D-MN) and conservative senator Pete V. Domenici (R-NM) teamed up to win passage of a limited mental health parity law requiring that private insurers offer coverage for mental illness just as they did for physical ailments and conditions. But this law, like many state-level measures that passed in the 1990s and 2000s, had only a modest impact. The 1996 measure banned insurers from setting annual and lifetime spending limits for mental health treatments, but it did not regulate copayments or deductibles, which many insurers set at price levels that were beyond the reach of those who would have otherwise sought treatment. Most of the state plans, meanwhile, had big coverage gaps. Some excluded small employers, and others applied only to a limited set of mental health problems.

Wellstone and Domenici continued to work on mental health parity legislation, and President George W. Bush endorsed the concept. When Wellstone died in a 2002 plane crash, many supporters thought that the effort, which was opposed by the insurance lobby and big business, would come up short. But Domenici remained active on the issue, and several other legislators took up Wellstone's cause, most notably Rep. Jim Ramstad (R-MN), Rep. Patrick J. Kennedy (D-RI), Sen. Edward M. Kennedy (D-MA), Sen. Christopher J. Dodd (D-CT), and Sen. Michael B. Enzi (R-WY). In October 2008 Congress approved a beefed-up version of the 1996 law that banned insurers from differentiating between mental health (including substance abuse problems) and physical health in setting copayments, deductibles, and treatment limitations. The measure, which was folded into the Emergency Economic Stabilization Act of 2008, was signed into law by Bush on October 3.

The following remarks in support of the 2008 legislation, officially named the Paul Wellstone and Pete Domenici Mental Health Parity and Addiction Equity Act, were delivered in the House of Representatives by Representative Ramstad just before the historic vote on the measure.

Mr. Ramstad. Mr. Speaker, we would not be having the debate here today without the compassionate leadership of the late Senator Paul Wellstone.

I want to thank the Speaker and majority leader, as well as Chairmen RANGEL, STARK, GEORGE MILLER, DINGELL, PALLONE and ANDREWS, for their key support.

The issue before us today is not just another public policy issue. The issue today before us is a matter of life and death for 54 million Americans suffering the ravages of mental illness and 26 million Americans suffering from chemical addiction.

Last year alone, more than 30,000 Americans committed suicide from untreated depression and 150,000 Americans died as the direct result of chemical addiction. On top of the tragic loss of lives, untreated addiction and mental illness cost our economy $550 billion last year, according to the *Wall Street Journal*. In fact, the *Journal* cited $70 billion was lost from our economy because of untreated depression alone.

I am alive and sober today only because of the access that I had to treatment following my last alcoholic blackout on July 31, 1981. I woke up that day in a jail cell in Sioux Falls, South Dakota, and I am living proof that treatment works and recovery is possible.

But far too many people in our country don't have the same access to treatment that I and other Members of Congress, other Federal employees have.

A major barrier for thousands of Americans is insurance discrimination, plain and simple, against people in health plans who need treatment for mental illness or chemical addiction. The legislation my friend from Rhode Island (Mr. [Patrick] KENNEDY) and I have authored, H.R. 6983 before us today, would end this discrimination by prohibiting health insurers from placing discriminatory restrictions on treatment for people with mental illness or addiction.

No more inflated deductibles or copayments that don't exist for physical diseases. No more limited treatment stays that don't apply to physical ailments, no more discrimination against people with mental illness or chemical addiction.

I just want to say a word about the chief sponsor of this legislation, Mr. KENNEDY, who has worked tirelessly on this bill. We have worked together for many years now on this legislation since he first came to the House. I want to publicly acknowledge and thank Mr. KENNEDY, who has not only worked hard on this legislation, but has been an inspiration to literally hundreds of thousands of Americans as we traveled this country to 14 States, holding field hearings on this important legislation.

Simply stated, the Paul Wellstone and Pete Domenici Mental Health Parity and Addiction Equity Act, which has, by the way, 274 cosponsors from both sides of the aisle, simply stated, provides equal treatment for diseases of the brain with the body. Diseases of the brain should be treated the same as diseases of the body.

There is no government mandate. Nobody is mandated to insure anybody for treatment for mental illness or chemical addiction. There is no mandate in this bill. All it says is if your policy includes coverage for mental illness or addiction, then you cannot be discriminated against, that is, those ailments must be treated the same as physical ailments.

Providing treatment equity is not only the right thing to do, it's the cost-effective thing to do. Believe me, we have over the last 12 years assembled all the empirical data in the world, all the actuarial studies in the world, and they all showed the same thing, that equity for mental health and addiction treatment will save, not cost, but save, literally, billions of dollars nationally.

At the same time, treatment parity will not raise premiums more than two-tenths of 1 percent. That's according to the Congressional Budget Office. Let me repeat that. Premiums will not raise more than two-tenths of 1 percent.

So, in other words, for the price of a cheap cup of coffee per month, I am not talking about a fancy restaurant, I am talking about Pete's Diner, where many of us go, millions of people could receive treatment for chemical addiction and mental illness. In fact, 16 million people of the 26 million people in health plans could receive treatment under this bill.

When my friend from Rhode Island and I traveled this country holding field hearings on this legislation, we heard, literally, hundreds and hundreds of stories of human suffering that ripped your heart out, broken families, tragic deaths, ruined careers, shattered dreams, all because insurance companies would not provide access to treatment for mental illness and addiction for people who were in health plans. We could change that here today.

It's time to end the discrimination against people who need treatment for mental illness and addiction. It's time to prohibit health insurers from placing discriminatory barriers on treatment. It's time to join the coalition of insurance companies, yes, I said insurance companies. More than 10 of them now support this, as well as the major business groups who support parity. They know it's cost effective, they know parity saves health care dollars. It's time to make this bipartisan legislation the law of the land.

The people of America cannot wait any longer for Congress to act.

Source: Ramstad, Jim. Floor remarks on the Paul Wellstone and Pete Domenici Mental Health Parity and Addiction Equity Act of 2008. *Congressional Record.* 110th Cong., 2d sess., September 23, 2008, p. H8619.

DOCUMENT
10.8

White House Forum on Health Reform

"We Have to Keep What We Have Now Strong, and Make It Stronger"

2009

When the White House Forum on Health Reform was convened on March 5, 2009, a mere six weeks after President Barack Obama's inauguration, Democrats and Republicans sought to convey a sense of postpartisan comity throughout the proceedings. Occasionally, however, the simmering ideological and political tensions between the Democratic and Republican camps bubbled to the surface. This divergence was most evident in a somewhat contrived question-and-answer session between Obama and various lawmakers, industry representatives, and administration officials that capped the day. Amid the assurances of cooperation and good faith that dominated the session, a few discordant notes could be heard in Obama's exchanges with Republican Senate minority Leader Mitch McConnell of Kentucky and Republican senator Charles E. Grassley of Iowa. In the first exchange, which came at the very outset of the session, McConnell veered off the subject of health care reform to explore Obama's commitment to reining in the costs of entitlement programs. Political analyst Ezra Klein described these remarks, which included reference to a deficit reduction commission proposed by Senators Kent Conrad (D-ND) and Judd Gregg (R-NH), as a well-masked shot across Obama's bow. McConnell comments, wrote Klein, were "phrased in the delicate dialect of the Senate. An observer checking tone rather than words would consider it a courteous exchange. But it wasn't. Obama was looking for a show of bipartisan support for health reform and McConnell asked him to commit to Social Security cuts."[1]

The exchange between Obama and Grassley, the ranking Republican on the Senate Finance Committee, came immediately after the chair of that committee, Max Baucus (D-MT), praised the atmosphere of goodwill in Washington, D.C, about health care reform. Grassley expressed his anxiety about the public option, a health insurance reform enormously popular with liberal Democrats. Obama was noncommittal about the public option, a stance he maintained—to the great frustration of fellow Democrats—throughout the ensuing months.

SENATOR McCONNELL: First of all, Mr. President, thank you very much for having this session today. I think it's useful and it is significant, as Ted indicated, to have everybody in the room.

I'm also among those, as you and I have discussed before, interested in seeing us address entitlement reform—and admittedly, Medicare and Medicaid would be a part of that—but also Social Security. And particularly concerned about having a mechanism in place that guarantees you get a result. And I wonder where you see yourself and the administration now, for example, in supporting something like the Conrad-Gregg proposal, which would set in place a mechanism that could actually guarantee that we get a result—if not on Medicare and Medicaid, at least on Social Security.

THE PRESIDENT: Well, I appreciate the question, Mitch. As you know, we had a fiscal responsibility summit similar to the gathering that we've had here—although I have to say the attendance here is even greater—and what I said in that forum was that I was absolutely committed to making sure that we got entitlement reform done.

The mechanism by which we do it I think is going to have to be determined by you, Harry Reid, Nancy Pelosi and John Boehner and the members of Congress. We've got to make certain that the various committees are comfortable with how we move forward.

But the important point that I want to emphasize today is that on Medicare and Medicaid, in particular—which everybody here understands is the 800-pound gorilla—I don't see us being able to get an effective reform package around those entitlements without fixing the underlying problem of health care inflation. If we've got 6, 7, 8 percent health care inflation we could fix Medicare and Medicaid temporarily for a couple of years, but we would be back in the same fix 10 years from now. And so our most urgent task is to drive down costs both on the private side and on the public side, because Medicare and Medicaid costs have actually gone up fairly comparably to what's been happening in the private sector what businesses and families and others have been doing. That's why I think it's so important for us to focus on costs as part of this overall reform package.

With respect to Social Security, I actually think it's easier than Medicare and Medicaid, and as a consequence, I'm going to be interested in working with you. And I know that others like Senator [Dick] Durbin, Lindsay Graham have already begun discussions about what the best mechanisms would be. I remain committed to that task.

But if we don't tackle health care, then we're going to break the bank. I think that's true at the federal level, I think it's true at the state level. It's certainly true for businesses and it's certainly true for families, okay. . . .

Let me go to Max Baucus and then Chuck Grassley. I want to get a sense of the folks on the finance committee—they're going to have some influence on this process. (Laughter.) Just a little bit. (Laughter.) Max.

SENATOR BAUCUS: Thank you, Mr. President. First, we've got some real luminaries in this room—yourself. A few hours ago, you mentioned that President Roosevelt tried to accomplish health care reform. He's over there right there in the corner — (laughter) –

THE PRESIDENT: There's Teddy — the other Teddy. (Laughter.)

SENATOR BAUCUS: And the third luminary is sitting right to my right, right here. And I think in the spirit of all three of you, this is a terrific opportunity.

Second, the American public wants it. That's a no-brainer. We're at a time in American history when the American people want health care reform, for all the reasons that you mentioned. And it is, as you mentioned, a moral and physical imperative. There's no doubt about that. And you've started this process I think in very much the right way, namely, getting us all together, a tone and a culture and a feeling of cooperation in a constructive way, evidence-based—what's the science, what works/doesn't work, practically and pragmatically.

And the real key here is for us to continue that frame of mind, continue that attitude, keep everybody at the table. This is all-encompassing. There are tradeoffs everywhere. This is not a short-term, tactical exercise. This is a strategic, longer-term plan here.

There has to be a uniquely American solution. We're not Europe. We're not Canada. We're not Japan. We're not other countries. We're American, with public and private participation. And there's no doubt in my mind just tapping into the good old American can-do and entrepreneurial spirit that we are going to find a solution. And the key here really is to keep—for us to all stay at the table, keep an open mind, after we've seen how this works with that and so forth.

This is really not going to be easy, it has a fairly steep learning curve for an awful lot of people to get this done. But clearly the attitude is here, that is, the frame of mind is here, the desire is here to do this in a very cooperative way. And I can't thank you enough for your quiet leadership to help make all that happen. (Applause.)

THE PRESIDENT: Thank you, Max. Chuck.

SENATOR GRASSLEY: Mr. President, thank you very much for this opportunity.

From our breakout session you probably get the idea that it's pretty easy to get done. We know it's very difficult to get done. But without that sort of feeling starting out, nothing would get done. And I think you served with us in the Senate long enough to know that Max Baucus and I have a pretty good record of working out bipartisan things—neither one of us, or neither one of our parties get everything that they want, but we've had a pretty good record—I think only two bills in eight years that haven't been bipartisan.

And so we have a process in place that has hearings coming up, it has a process of getting roundtable discussions, getting stakeholders in, getting authorities in. And we expect to have—work on this in the committee in June. It maybe will sound a little ambitious, but if you are ambitious on a major problem like this that the country decides needs to be done, it will never get done.

So the only thing that I would throw out for your consideration—and please don't respond to this now, because I'm asking you just to think about it—there's a lot of us that feel that the public option that the government is an unfair competitor and that we're going to get an awful lot of crowd out, and we have to keep what we have now strong, and make it stronger.

THE PRESIDENT: Okay. Well, let me just—I'm not going to respond definitively. The thinking on the public option has been that it gives consumers more choices, and it helps give—keep the private sector honest, because there's some competition out there. That's been the thinking.

I recognize, though, the fear that if a public option is run through Washington, and there are incentives to try to tamp down costs and—or at least what shows up on the books, and you've got the ability in Washington, apparently, to print money—that private insurance plans might end up feeling overwhelmed. So I recognize that there's that concern. I think it's a serious one and a real one. And we'll make sure that it gets addressed, partly because I assume it will be very—be very hard to come out of committee unless we're thinking about it a little bit. And so we want to make sure that that's something that we pay attention to. . . .

Source: Town Hall Discussion. White House Forum on Health Reform, March 5, 2009. Transcript. Washington, DC: White House, March 30, 2009, pp. 33–34, 36–37. www.whitehouse.gov/assets /documents/White_House_Forum_on_Health_Reform_Report.pdf.

Note

1. Ezra Klein, "The Health Summit Q&A," blog, *American Prospect*, March 5, 2009, www.prospect.org /csnc/blogs/ezraklein_archive?month=03&year=2009&base_name=the_health_summit_qa#113501.

Major Stakeholders Signal Support for Obama's Health Reform Efforts

"We Applaud Your Strong Commitment"

2009

One of the keys to President Barack Obama's ultimate success in passing health care reform legislation was that his administration was able to keep most major players in the health care industry from actively opposing the effort during its formative months. The Obama White House managed to secure at least some level of cooperation in its health reform efforts from all major institutional stakeholders, including doctors (represented by the American Medical Association), medical device manufacturers (Advanced Medical Technology Association), insurers (America's Health Insurance Plans), hospitals (American Hospital Association), drug makers (Pharmaceutical Research and Manufacturers of America), and organized labor (Service Employees International Union). The following is a carefully worded letter from all of the above-mentioned organizations assuring Obama— and the American public—that they shared his desire to see that "all Americans . . . have access to affordable, high quality health care services."

May 11, 2009

The President
The White House
Washington, D.C. 20500
Dear Mr. President:

We believe that all Americans should have access to affordable, high quality health care services. Thus, we applaud your strong commitment to reforming our nation's health care system. The times demand and the nation expects that we, as health care leaders, work with you to reform the health care system.

The annual growth in national health expenditures—including public and private spending—is projected by government actuaries to average 6.2% through the next decade. At that rate, the percent of gross domestic product spent on health care would increase from 17.6% this year to 20.3% in 2018—higher than any country in the world.

We are determined to work together to provide quality, affordable coverage and access for every American. It is critical, however, that health reform also enhance quality, improve the overall health of the population, and reduce cost growth. We believe that the proper approach to achieve and sustain reduced cost growth is one that will: improve the population's health; continuously improve quality; encourage the advancement of medical treatments, approaches, and science; streamline administration; and encourage efficient care delivery based on evidence and best practice.

To achieve all of these goals, we have joined together in an unprecedented effort, as private sector stakeholders—physicians, hospitals, other health care workers, payors, suppliers, manufacturers, and organized labor—to offer concrete initiatives that will transform the health care system. As restructuring takes hold and the population's health improves over the coming decade, we will do our part to achieve your Administration's goal of decreasing by 1.5 percentage points the annual health care spending growth rate—saving $2 trillion or more. This represents more than a 20% reduction in the projected rate of growth. We believe this approach can be highly successful and can help the nation to achieve the reform goals we all share.

To respond to this challenge, we are developing consensus proposals to reduce the rate of increase in future health and insurance costs through changes made in all sectors of the health care system. We are committed to taking action in public-private partnership to create a more stable and sustainable health care system that will achieve billions in savings through:

- Implementing proposals in all sectors of the health care system, focusing on administrative simplification, standardization, and transparency that supports effective markets;
- Reducing over-use and under-use of health care by aligning quality and efficiency incentives among providers across the continuum of care so that physicians, hospitals, and other health care providers are encouraged and enabled to work together towards the highest standards of quality and efficiency;
- Encouraging coordinated care, both in the public and private sectors, and adherence to evidence-based best practices and therapies that reduce hospitalization, manage chronic disease more efficiently and effectively, and implement proven clinical prevention strategies; and
- Reducing the cost of doing business by addressing cost drivers in each sector and through common sense improvements in care delivery models, health information technology, workforce deployment and development, and regulatory reforms.

These and other reforms will make our health care system stronger and more sustainable. However, there are many important factors driving health care costs that are beyond the control of the delivery system alone. Billions in savings can be achieved through a large-scale national effort of health promotion and disease prevention to reduce the prevalence of chronic disease and poor health status, which leads to unnecessary sickness and higher health costs. Reform should include a specific focus on obesity prevention commensurate with the scale of the problem. These initiatives are crucial to transform health care in America and to achieve our goal of reducing the rate of growth in health costs.

We, as stakeholder representatives, are committed to doing our part to make reform a reality in order to make the system more affordable and effective for patients and purchasers. We stand ready to work with you to accomplish this goal.

Sincerely,
Stephen J. Ubl
President and CEO
Advanced Medical Technology Association

J. James Rohack, MD
President-elect
American Medical Association

Karen Ignagni
President and CEO
America's Health Insurance Plans

Billy Tauzin
President and CEO
Pharmaceutical Research and Manufacturers of America

Rich Umbdenstock
President and CEO
American Hospital Association

Dennis Rivera
Chair, SEIU Healthcare
Service Employees International Union

Source: Letter to the President, May 11, 2009. http://graphics8.nytimes.com/packages/pdf/politics
/20090511_HealthGroups_Letter.pdf.

DOCUMENT
10.10

An Obama Budget Official Defends Health Reform

"Ideological Partisans Wish to See the World as They Want, Not as It Is"

2009

As criticism of Democratic health care reform efforts intensified in the second half of 2009, the Obama administration devoted significant time and effort to debunking charges from the right that its reforms were fiscally irresponsible or constituted a government takeover of health care, as well as charges from the left that the proposed legislation had been fatally compromised by giveaways to various industry stakeholders. These rhetorical barricades were manned by a wide assortment of White House officials including Office of Management and Budget director Peter R. Orszag, who maintained an official blog throughout the battle over health care reform. In the following blog entry posted on December 14, 2009, Orszag responds to a Wall Street Journal *editorial that excoriated "Obamacare" for lacking realistic cost control features and chided Orszag and other White House "acolytes" for hawking a "political bill of goods."[1]*

We are closer than ever before to passing fiscally responsible health reform legislation. So it's not a surprise that the most reflexively and ideologically partisan commentators are lashing out. Today, it's the editorial board of the *Wall Street Journal*.

For an economist, the irony is rich. The editorial board that did more to bring supply-side economics—or in George H. W. Bush's immortal words, "voodoo economics"—to Washington is raising the specter of a fiscally irresponsible health reform bill in which efforts to rein in health care cost growth are an "illusion." But the ironies run richer, since an editorial that hurls accusations of overselling cost containment itself displays more impressive rhetoric than substantive content.

The *Journal* makes three fundamental claims. The first is that health reform represents a huge risk to the federal budget, and will end up exploding the deficit, because it relies on an array of speculative policies to control costs.

What the *Journal* misses is the crucial difference between this health reform effort and the flawed supply-side economics that drove the country into the deep deficits of the 1980s: we are insisting that the legislation be deficit neutral as scored by the Congressional Budget Office (CBO) in addition to including a variety of delivery system reform and other cost-containment measures for the long term. In other words, unlike supply-siders, we are not waiting for magic savings to appear. Instead, we are relying on hard, scoreable savings—not the long-term cost-control measures—to pay for the expansion of health care coverage. This "belt and suspenders" approach provides a crucial fiscal backstop, and it's the prudent, realistic, and wise thing to do. . . .

With regard to the delivery system reform and cost-containment component of this belt-and-suspenders approach, we have always been clear that we do not know with absolute certainty the changes that will most effectively improve quality and restrain health care cost growth over the long term. But research does suggest the most auspicious approaches, and we are pursuing those.

Indeed, economists have agreed upon the pillars of a fiscally responsible health reform. In a recent letter, 23 of America's leading health economists (including former CBO Directors Alice Rivlin and Robert Reischauer, and a Director of CMS during the Bush Administration, Mark McClellan, as well as other Republicans) identified those four pillars. The list includes:

- Deficit neutrality, using hard, scoreable savings as analyzed by the non-partisan CBO;
- An excise tax on the highest-cost insurance plans;
- An independent Medicare commission; and
- An array of delivery system reforms.

All of these components are in the health reform legislation being considered on the Senate floor (even if some of them are not quite as strong as the signers of the letter would like).

Which brings us to the *Journal*'s second argument: that Congress lacks the stomach for serious cost control or always undoes the savings later. This is an interesting argument for a newspaper like the *Journal* to make, when its closest allies on Capitol Hill spent the better part of last week opposing hundreds of billions of dollars in Medicare savings. Moreover, it is fundamentally an argument for hopelessness and inaction in the face of our nation's most serious long-term fiscal challenge: If Congress is institutionally incapable of ever reducing the rate of health cost growth because projected savings are always undone by future Congresses, why even try in the first place? Thankfully, the *Journal*'s fiscal nihilism is belied by the facts—Congress has both enacted and carried out substantial health expenditure reductions several times in the past. For example, according to a new report by two former CBO officials now working at the Center on Budget and Policy Priorities, "virtually all of the Medicare cuts enacted in 1990 and 1993, which accounted for a significant portion of the savings in those large deficit-reduction packages, were implemented, and *nearly four-fifths* of the savings enacted in 1997 other than the SGR cuts were implemented as well."

This brings us to the *Journal*'s third argument, which can be summed up in their warning, "Technocracy rarely, if ever, works as intended." Too often, ideological partisans wish to see the world as they want, not as it is. Recognizing the limits of what government can and cannot do is actually at the foundation of the health reform approach embodied in the legislation, a foundation which reflects a significant amount of policymaking humility.

We are not setting out a plan with every detail laid out for what the health care system of the future should look like. Thinking that we could lay out in full detail a perfect system today would show a foolish disregard for the dynamism of the health care sector—and of the American economy in general. Instead, we are putting in place processes by which what works and what doesn't can be rigorously tested, and then scaled up over time as they are reflected in the decisions of thousands upon thousands of hospitals, physicians, and other providers. Does the *Journal* have a better suggestion about how to approach policymaking in a dynamic world?

So what about the savings in the bill being considered by the Senate? The President's Council of Economic Advisers is releasing a new report today on that legislation. Based on CBO's own estimates and other evidence, CEA concludes that the health reform bill being considered in the Senate could reduce the growth of health care costs by 1 percentage point per year in Medicare and Medicaid and, also, in the private sector. Although one percentage point may sound small, it would represent a boon both to the federal budget and to Americans more generally. As a point of comparison, slowing the rate of cost growth in Medicare and Medicaid by just 0.15 percentage points per year would be the fiscal equivalent, over the long term, of eliminating the entire Social Security shortfall.

Can more work be done on health reform? Sure. And that is what is occurring through the legislative process as I write. Moreover, even after passage, we will need a continuous assessment of what works and what doesn't and rapid adjustments to a changing market—all of which can be done with the mechanisms laid out in this bill.

The bottom line is that continuing on the road we are on will overwhelm our economy and our federal budget. The health care plan being considered in the Senate now is built on the best available knowledge and most promising ideas from across the political spectrum. Critics may fear this change, but what we should fear more is doing nothing.

Source: Orszag, Peter R. "No Illusions." *Director's blog.* Office of Management and Budget. December 14, 2009. /www.whitehouse.gov/omb/blog/09/12/14/No-Illusions.

NOTE

1. "The 'Cost Control' Bill of Goods: How Peter Orszag and the White House Sold a Health-Care Illusion," editorial, *Wall Street Journal,* December 14, 2009, A24.

DOCUMENT 10.11

Senator Lieberman Turns against the Public Option

"I Hope There Will Be No Attempt to Reinsert a So-called Public Option"

2009

In early December 2009 President Barack Obama and Democratic leaders in Congress felt increasingly confident that passage of a major health care reform bill containing a public option was possible. Speaker of the House Nancy Pelosi (D-CA) had shepherded such a bill through the House in early November, and Senate majority leader Harry Reid (D-NV) was preparing a similar vote. Reid knew that his margin for error was nonexistent. He needed the votes of all fifty-eight Democrats and the body's two independents, Joseph I. Lieberman of Connecticut and Bernard Sanders of Vermont, to overcome a threatened Republican filibuster. Reid recognized that Lieberman and Sanders had long supported a public option, so when he convinced every Democrat to stand behind the bill, he thought victory was imminent. In mid-December, however, Lieberman stunned Reid, his fellow senators, the White House, and activists and pundits of all political persuasions by announcing that he would support a Republican filibuster of any health reform bill that contained provisions for a public option. He further indicated that he would support a filibuster of any legislation that included a so-called Medicare buy-in, a proposal to expand the Medicare system to cover Americans age fifty-five to sixty-four. Lieberman's stand forced the Democrats to strip both the public option and Medicare buy-in out of the bill.

The reversal of Lieberman, a former Democrat, delighted opponents of the public option, but it enraged activists on the left, many of whom had come to see the public option as essential. Numerous progressives characterized Lieberman's shift as a transparent bid to punish them for their turn against him in his 2006 senatorial campaign. (Lieberman lost the Democratic nomination that year to Ned Lamont but prevailed in Connecticut's general election as an Independent.) Progressive columnist Ezra Klein wrote that "at this point, Lieberman seems primarily motivated by torturing liberals."[1] Writer Jonathan Cohn told readers to "decide for yourself whether today's news" of Lieberman's demands "is the product of principle, pique, or both."[2] Lieberman rejected accusations that his stand was the by-product of a vendetta against liberals. He claimed in speeches such as the one excerpted below (delivered on the Senate floor on December 21, 2009) that he opposed the provisions because they would place an unacceptable strain on the nation's finances and threaten Medicare's viability.

MR. LIEBERMAN: Madam President, I rise to declare and explain my support for the Patient Protection and Affordable Care Act. First, I commend Senator REID and all those who worked so long and hard, including my friend and colleague from Connecticut, Senator DODD, for all they have achieved in this legislation. The truth is, no piece of legislation, as significant and complicated as this is, could possibly be totally satisfying to every one of us. In the end, each one of us has to ask ourselves: Do the positives in this legislation substantially outweigh the negatives? Are the things we like in the bill greater than the things that worry us? For me, the answer to both these questions is yes, because this bill makes real progress on the three important goals I have had, and I think most people have had, for health care reform.

First, most of us have wanted to stop the continuous increases in the cost of health care that burden every individual, family, business, our Government, and our economy. Second, we have wanted to regulate insurance companies to provide better protections for consumers and patients. Third, we have wanted to find a way to make it easier for millions of Americans who cannot afford health insurance today to be able to buy it tomorrow. I believe this bill makes real progress in achieving each of these three goals. Most importantly, it does so in a fiscally responsible way.

The Patient Protection and Affordable Care Act not only does not add to our national debt, through new health care delivery reforms it will help reduce the debt by $130 billion over the first 10 years, according to the independent Congressional Budget Office. That figure could multiply many times over during the second 10 years, thanks, in part, to the managers' amendment that incorporated stronger cost-containment proposals that several of us, across party lines, made to Senator REID.

In addition, it is very significant that, according to the Actuary at the Center for Medicare & Medicaid Services, this bill will extend the solvency of the Medicare trust fund for an additional 9 years. This act will also take substantial steps toward creating a health care delivery system that pays for the quality of the care patients receive rather than the quantity of care. I am proud to have worked with Members of both sides of the aisle to include amendments that would do that.

For instance, Senator [Susan] COLLINS and I introduced an amendment, parts of which were included in the managers' package, that will enhance transparency for consumers so they can make more informed decisions in choosing their health care providers and insurers. . . .

I also cosponsored an amendment introduced by Senator [Mark] WARNER and some other freshman Senators that will contain costs even more. This amendment creates prevention programs to help us understand how to effectively manage chronic diseases such as diabetes, and it requires prescription drug plans under Medicare Part D to offer medication therapy management services to beneficiaries so they can better adhere to their prescription treatments. All that is progress on the first goal that I and most others had, which is to reduce the cost of health care without compromising—in fact, improving—its quality.

The second goal. If this bill passes, insurance companies, as Senator KERRY said, will not only not be able to deny coverage if an individual has a preexisting condition, they will not be allowed to rescind coverage if you become sick, which is the outrageous reality today. Thanks to changes made by the managers' amendment, insurance companies will also be required to spend more of the premiums they collect on medical expenses for patients rather than on administrative costs and profits. . . .

As for the third goal, the fact is attested to by the CMS Actuary and CBO, 31 million more Americans will be able to have health insurance as a result of this legislation. We say that so often I think we forget the power of it—31 million people who do not have health insurance today will have it after this bill passes. . . .

Is there anything in the bill that worries me? Of course, there is. I would say, most of all, I worry that we, and future Congresses, will not have the discipline to keep many of the promises we have made in this bill to control costs by transforming the way health care is delivered because some of these reforms are controversial and they are going to be opposed by some health care providers and health care beneficiaries. Without the kind of discipline I have just mentioned, this bill will add to our national debt or increase taxes. Neither of those results is acceptable. If we stick to the contents of the bill, this bill will cut health care costs and it will reduce our national debt.

In my opinion, our exploding national debt is the biggest domestic threat to our country's future. That is why I have said this bill must reduce that debt, not increase it. . . .

We cannot bring the fiscal books of our Government back into balance by only making the health care system more cost efficient, but we will never control our national debt without doing so. Medicare is in a particularly perilous condition today. Without reform, the Medicare trust fund will be broke in 8 years—broke. With tens of millions of baby boomers reaching the age of eligibility, we simply must protect Medicare so it remains a viable program for both current and future generations.

This leads me to my firm opposition to the creation of a new government-run insurance program and to lowering the age of eligibility for Medicare to 55 years. That opposition was rooted in my very serious concerns about our long-term national debt and the fragile fiscal condition of Medicare. For any new government-run insurance program, including the Medicare extension-expansion idea, the moment premiums do not cover costs the Federal Government—that is Federal taxpayers, the American people—would have to pay the difference. That could easily put our Federal Government and the taxpayers on the hook for billions and billions of dollars in future liabilities and further jeopardize the solvency of Medicare.

Because of the insurance market reforms in this bill and other measures—the creation of a new system of tax credits and subsidies for people making up to 400 percent of poverty—the creation of a new government-run health care, the so-called public option or the expansion of Medicare to people under 65 is not necessary. Neither proposal would extend coverage to one person who will not be benefited by the new provisions of this bill, neither the public option nor the expansion of Medicare. Yet both proposals would, in my opinion, lead to higher premiums for the 180 million people who have insurance today and are struggling to afford the health insurance they have now because of cost shifting.

According to studies by the CBO, a new government-run insurance program, a public option, would actually likely charge higher premiums than competing private plans on the exchange, and expanding Medicare to cover people 55 years or older would lead to additional cost shifting.

I know the removal of the public option from the bill in the Senate disappointed and angered many Members of the Senate and the House, while I know it pleased and reassured others. I wish to say to those who were not happy about the removal of the public option from this bill that I believe President Obama never said a public option was essential to the reform goals he set out to achieve and that most of us have. When the President spoke earlier this year to the Joint Session of Congress, he said a public option is "an additional step we can take." An additional step, he said, but not an essential one. Then, he added, "The public option is only a means to that end." He concluded that we should remain "open to other ideas that accomplish our ultimate goal."

I am confident this bill accomplishes the goal the President and most of us set out to achieve without the creation of a brand-new government-run insurance company or the further weakening of Medicare. This bill, as it appears it will emerge from the Senate, is delicately balanced. I understand the normal inclination in a conference committee with our colleagues in the House is to split the difference. But splitting the difference on this bill runs a real risk of breaking the fragile 60-vote Senate consensus we have now and preventing us from adopting health care reform in this Congress.

That would be a very sad ending. Rather than splitting our differences, I hope the conferees will adopt our agreements so we can enact health care reform this year....

Each Member of the Senate will have to decide once again when this bill emerges from the conference whether he or she wants to be one of the 60 votes necessary to take up and pass the conference report. In this case my own sense of the Senate is the same as that expressed in the last few days by Senators CONRAD, NELSON, and others. If significant changes are made to the Senate bill in conference, it will be difficult to hold the 60 votes we now have. I have two priorities that will matter a lot to me. The first is to continue and maintain the health care reforms that will improve the cost-effectiveness of our health care system and help reduce the national debt. Second, I hope there will be no attempt to reinsert a so-called public option in any form in the conference report. That would mean I will not be able to support the report.

I want to support it. I believe I am not alone in that opinion among the 60 who supported the bill last night. Our exploding national debt is the biggest threat to our Nation's future. That means we must begin to make politically difficult decisions to reduce our debt. That means saying no to some groups and some ideas, including some we would otherwise support, because we simply cannot afford them.

A final hope about the conference report. Perhaps some will say it is naive. I hope the conferees will find a way to produce a report that can be supported by some Republican Members of the Senate and House. It is a sad commentary on this moment in our political history that so major a reform will be adopted with no bipartisan support. Hopefully the conference will find a way, difficult as I know it might be, to conclude this long legislative journey with a bill that is not only worth supporting, as I believe the Senate bill now surely is, but also engages the support of Members of both parties.

I yield the floor.

Source: Lieberman, Joseph I. Remarks on the Patient Protection and Affordable Care Act. *Congressional Record.* 111th Cong., 1st sess., December 21, 2009, pp. S13679–S13680.

NOTES

1. Ezra Klein, "Joe Lieberman: Let's Not Make a Deal," blog, *Washington Post*, December 14, 2009, http://voices.washingtonpost.com/ezra-klein/2009/12/joe_lieberman_lets_not_make_a.html.

2. Jonathan Cohn, "Did Lieberman Double-Cross Reid?," blog, *New Republic*, December 13, 2009, www.tnr.com/blog/the-treatment/did-lieberman-double-cross-reid.

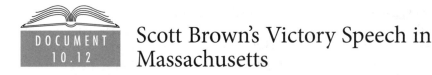

| DOCUMENT 10.12 | Scott Brown's Victory Speech in Massachusetts |

"Taking over Our Health Care . . . Is the Wrong Agenda"

2010

In early January 2010 the Obama White House and Democratic leaders in Congress were deep in negotiations, finalizing a compromise between the House and Senate health reform bills that could go back to the two chambers for final passage. In the second week of

January, however, Democratic pollsters privately warned that a special January 19 election in Massachusetts to fill the Senate seat of the late Ted Kennedy was likely going to go the Republicans' way. Democrats were initially incredulous at the news, given Massachusetts' reputation as the bluest of blue states. The pollsters explained, however, that Republican candidate and Tea Party favorite Scott Brown had waged a much stronger campaign than Democratic candidate Martha Coakley—and that his late surge stemmed at least in part from public uneasiness about "Obamacare," which Brown vowed to oppose.

Recognizing that a Brown victory would give Republicans a 41st vote in the Senate—just enough to carry out a filibuster of any health care bill—the White House frantically arranged a last-minute campaign trip to Boston by Obama to drum up support for Coakley. But the visit came too late to rescue Coakley's campaign, and on January 19, 2010 Brown became the first elected Republican Senator from Massachusetts in 38 years. Here are excerpts from Brown's victory speech:

Thank you very much . . . I bet they can hear this cheering all the way in Washington, D.C.!

And I hope they're paying close attention, because tonight the independent voice of Massachusetts has spoken.

From the Berkshires to Boston, from Springfield to Cape Cod, the voters of this Commonwealth defied the odds and the experts. Tonight the independent majority has delivered a great victory.

I thank the people of Massachusetts for electing me as your next United States senator.

And every day I hold this office, I will give all that is in me to serve you well and make you proud.

Most of all, I will remember that while the honor is mine, this Senate seat belongs to no one person, no one political party—and as I have said before, and you've heard it today and you'll hear it loud and clear, this is the people's seat. . . .

As you know, this special election came about because we lost someone very, very dear to Massachusetts, and to America. Senator Ted Kennedy was a tireless worker and a big-hearted public servant, and for most of his lifetime was a force like no other in this state. The first call I made was to his wife Vicki and I told her that his name will always command the affection and respect by the people of Massachusetts, and I said we feel the same about her. There's no replacing a man like that, but tonight I honor the memory, and I pledge to be the very best and try to be a worthy successor to the late Senator Kennedy.

I said at the very beginning, when I sat down at the dinner table with my family, that win or lose, we would run a race which would make all of us proud. I kept my word and we ran a clean, issues oriented, upbeat campaign—and I wouldn't trade that for anything.

And when I first started running, I asked for a lot of help, because I knew it was going to be me against the machine. I was wrong, it was all of us against the machine. And tonight we have shown everybody now that you are the machine. . . .

And I'm grateful for all those from across Massachusetts who came through for me even when I was a long shot. And I especially thank a very special friend whose encouragement from the beginning helped show me the way and show us the way to victory—former Governor Mitt Romney.

. . . I'll never forget the help of another man who took the time to meet with me—who told me that I could actually win, and gave me the confidence for the fight. It was all so characteristic of a great American and true hero, and tonight I thank my new colleague, Senator John McCain. . . .

We had the machine scared and scrambling, and for them it is just the beginning of an election year filled with many, many surprises—I can tell you that. They will be challenged again and again across this great land. And when there's trouble in Massachusetts, rest assured there's trouble everywhere—and they know it.

In every corner of our state, I met with people, looked them in the eye, shook their hand, and asked them for their vote. I didn't care about party affiliation, and they didn't worry about mine. It was simply a shared conviction that brought us all together and for that I'm very thankful.

One thing is very, very clear, as I traveled throughout the state, people do not want the trillion-dollar health care plan that is being forced on the American people.

And this bill is not being debated openly and fairly. It will raise taxes, it will hurt Medicare, it will destroy jobs, and run our nation deeper into debt . . . It's not in the interest of our state and our country—and we can do better. . . .

When I'm in Washington, I will work in the Senate with Democrats and Republicans to reform health care in an open and honest way. No more closed-door meetings, back room deals, with an out of touch party leadership. No more hiding costs, concealing taxes, collaborating with the special interests, and leaving more trillions in debt for our children to pay.

In health care, we need to start fresh, work together to do the job right. Once again, we can do better.

I will work in the Senate to put government back on the side of people who create jobs, and the millions of people who need jobs—and remember as President John F. Kennedy stated, that starts with an across the board tax cut for businesses and families that will create jobs, put more money in people's pockets, and stimulate the economy. It's that simple.

I will work with the Senators in the Senate to defend our nation's interests and to keep our military second to none. And as a lieutenant colonel and 30-year member of the Massachusetts Army National Guard, I will absolutely keep faith with all those who have served, and get our veterans all of the benefits they deserve. . . .

Raising taxes, taking over our health care, and giving new rights to terrorists is the wrong agenda for our country. What I've heard again and again on the campaign trail, is that our political leaders have grown aloof from the people, they're impatient with dissent, and comfortable in making back room deals, and we can do better.

You know the funny thing is they thought that you were all on board with all of their ambitions. Yes they did. They thought that they owned your vote. They thought that they couldn't lose. But tonight, you and you and you, you all set them straight. Thank you!

Across this country, we are united by basic convictions that only need to be clearly stated to win a majority. If anyone doubts that, in this next election season that's about to begin, we'll let them take a look at what happened in Massachusetts.

What happened here in Massachusetts can happen all over America. We are all witnesses, you and I, to the truth that ideals, hard work, strength of heart can overcome the political machine. And as you know we ran a campaign never to be forgotten, and led a cause that deserved and received all that we could give it.

And now, because of your independence, and your trust, I will hold for a time the seat once filled by patriots from John Quincy Adams to John F. Kennedy and his brother

Ted. And as I proudly take up the duty you have given me, I promise to do my very, very best for Massachusetts and America every time the roll is called. . . .

Source: Brown, Scott. "Scott Brown's Victory Speech." *New York Times,* January 19, 2010. http://www .nytimes.com/2010/01/20/us/politics/20text-brown.html.

DOCUMENT 10.13 President Obama and Senator Kyl Square Off at the Health Care Summit

"This Is Not a Government Takeover of Insurance"

2010

Fresh off President Barack Obama's triumphant appearance at the Republican House retreat in late January 2010, the White House decided to organize a nationally televised health care summit of Republican and Democratic leaders at the Blair House on February 25. Republicans were distinctly unenthused about participating in the event, which they knew would play to the president's oratorical strengths and command of policy. They recognized, however, that declining the invitation would be interpreted by many Americans as a sign of pettiness or weakness. Republicans thus accepted the invitation, then arrived at Blair House loaded with a wide assortment of arguments against the Democrats' health reform plans. During the course of the seven-hour session, Obama locked horns, albeit in civil tones, with numerous Republicans, including Senators Lamar Alexander (TN) and Tom Coburn (OK) on cost containment, Representatives Paul D. Ryan (WI) and Eric Cantor (VA) on regulatory concerns, Senator John McCain (AZ) on the bill-making process, and Senator Chuck E. Grassley (IA) on the bill's impact on Medicare. Obama also had a spirited exchange with Senator Jon Kyl (R-AZ) over the plan's cost, both to taxpayers and policyholders. Their discussion, excerpted here, is fairly representative of sparring that took place throughout the entire summit between Democrats and Republicans in attendance.

THE PRESIDENT: . . . We're going to go to Jon [Kyl], and then we're going to go to Jim Clyburn. And then I think we're going to take a break because we've run out of time.

So, Jon?

SENATOR KYLE: Thank you, Mr. President. I think you framed the issue very well just a moment ago, because there are some fundamental differences between us here that we cannot paper over. And, Mr. President, when you said that this is a philosophical debate and it's a legitimate debate, I agree with that. We do not agree about the fundamental question of who should be mostly in charge. And you identified this question as central: Do you trust the states, or do you trust Washington? Do you trust patients and doctors making the decision, or do you trust Washington?

Now, there is a mix of both, of course, in health care. But there is a big difference between our approaches. And there is so much in the bills that you've supported that puts control in Washington that we have a very difficult time supporting those provisions. And it's not a matter of just saying we all agree on the goal of reducing waste, fraud, and abuse. We all do, of course. It's how you do it.

Now, let me give you a couple of examples. Dave Camp, I think, pointed out the answer to the dispute that you and Lamar Alexander had a moment ago, and he was exactly right. Let me quote from the Congressional Budget Office letter — this is from Doug Elmendorf to Evan Bayh, November 30th, 2009: "CBO and Joint Tax Committee estimate that the average premium per person covered, including dependents for new non-group policies, would be about 10 percent to 13 percent higher in 2016 than the average premium for non-group coverage in the same year under current law." Oliver Wyman, a very respected third-party group says it's even more — about 54 percent; in my state of Arizona, 72 percent increase. Why is it so? For a variety of reasons, but one of which both you and Dave Camp agreed on. It is a richer benefit. How did it get that way? Because the federal government would mandate it under your legislation in the insurance exchanges. And as a result, there would be a higher cost. How does this happen?

There is an actuarial requirement of 60 percent actuarial value in the exchange for the least costly plan. But the average in the country today of a high deductible plan is 48 percent. The range today is 40 to 80 percent, and the average is between 55 and 60. So what the government is doing here is saying, we're going to mandate that the insurance cover more things than it does right now, and therefore the cost is going to go up.

Second example, you say, how can we help small businesses? Well, we know one way you don't help small businesses is by raising the payroll — the Medicare payroll tax on them, which is what this legislation does. Besides that, it's a job killer. Look at the taxes on beneficiaries as well — this is a third example. You don't cut costs when you raise taxes on medical devices that help us, when you raise taxes on pharmaceutical products, when you raise taxes on the insurance premiums themselves. "These fees on insurers, medical devices, and pharmaceuticals would increase costs for the affected firms, which would be passed on to purchasers and would ultimately raise insurance premiums by a corresponding amount"—[according to the] Congressional Budget Office.

So when you raise these taxes in all of the different fees that are in this legislation, it inevitably increases the costs on the consumer. And why do you have to raise all of this money? Because of the expenses of the legislation that underlie all of this. That's why Republicans would rather start not by having to raise a lot of money in order to pay the high cost of this bill, but to start a piece at a time, directing solutions to specific problems. That way, you don't incur all of the costs up front, which require you to raise the taxes.

The last quick point, one of the worst things about this is for people that have catastrophic medical expenses today after you've spent 7.5 percent of your adjusted gross income, you can deduct that. This bill would raise that to 10 percent. Who does that hurt? The very people you promised, Mr. President, that you wouldn't allow taxes to be raised on — average age, 45; average income, $69,000. These are not wealthy people. It's just another example of why because the bill has to raise so much money, it ends up hurting the very people that we want to help.

THE PRESIDENT: Okay, Jon. I'm going to go to you, Jim, but I — since as has tended to happen here, we end up talking about criticisms of the existing bill as opposed to where we might find agreement, I feel obliged just to go through a couple of the points that you raised.

Just to go back to the original argument that Lamar and I had and we've now chased around for quite some time. Look, if I'm a self-employed person who right now can't get coverage or can only buy the equivalent of Acme insurance that I had for my car — so I have some sort of high-deductible plan. It's basically not health insurance; it's house insurance. I'm going to — I'm buying that to protect me from some catastrophic situation; otherwise, I'm just paying out of pocket. I don't go to the doctor. I don't get preventive care. There are a whole bunch of things I just do without. But if I get hit by a truck, maybe I don't go bankrupt. All right, so that's what I'm purchasing right now.

What the Congressional Budget Office is saying is, is that if I now have the opportunity to actually buy a decent package inside the exchange that costs me about 10 to 13 percent more but is actually real insurance, then there are going to be a bunch of people who take advantage of that. So, yes, I'm paying 10 to 13 percent more, because instead of buying an apple, I'm getting an orange. They're two different things.

Now, you can still — you still have an option of — no, no, let me finish. The way that this bill is structured uses a high-cost pool, a catastrophic pool, for people who can't afford to buy that better insurance, but overall for a basic package — which, by the way, is a lot less generous than we give ourselves in Congress. So I'm amused when people say, let people have this not-so-good plan, let them have a high-deductible. But there would be a riot in Congress if we suddenly said, let's have Congress have a high-deductible plan, because we all think it's pretty important to provide coverage for our families. And the federal health insurance program has a minimum benefit that all of us take advantage of. And I haven't seen any Republicans — or Democrats — in Congress suddenly say, "You know what, we should have more choices and not have to have this minimum benefit."

So what we're basically saying is we're going to do the same thing for these other folks that we do for ourselves — on the taxpayers' dime, by the way.

Now, there is a legitimate philosophical difference around that, but I think it's just very important for us to remember that saying there's a baseline of coverage that people should be able to get if they're participating in this big pool is not some radical idea. And it's an idea that a lot of states — you know we were talking earlier about what states do — a lot of states already do it.

This, by the way, goes to the other difference that we have when it comes to interstate purchase of insurance. Actually, this is a Republican idea, been championed by the Republicans. We actually agree with the idea that maybe if you get more regional markets and national markets, as opposed to just state-by-state markets, you might get more choice and competition. People would be able to say, gosh, there's a great insurance company in Nevada and I live in New York and maybe I can purchase it. That's actually something that we find attractive.

So do you guys. But again, the one difference, as I understand it, and the reason you're not supporting the approach that we take, is what we say is there should be sort of a minimum baseline benefit, because if not, what ends up happening is you get a company set up in Nevada — let's assume there were no rules there, there are no protections for the woman who's got breast cancer; they go into New York, they offer pretty cheap insurance to everybody who's healthy; they don't offer the same insurance to people who aren't so healthy or have preexisting conditions. They drain from New York all the healthy people who are getting cheaper rates, but now suddenly everybody left in New York who doesn't qualify for that cheaper plan is in a pool that's sicker, older, and their premiums go up.

So what we've said is, well, if we can set a baseline, then you can have interstate competition, but it's not a race to the bottom; rather everybody has got some basic care.

Now, these are legitimate arguments to have. But I just want to point out that this issue of government regulation, which we're going to also be talking about with respect to insurance, is very different than the way this has been framed during the course of the debate over the last year, which is government takeover of insurance. This is not a government takeover of insurance. What it is, is saying let's set up some baselines and then use market principles, the private sector and pooling in order to make sure that people get a better deal.

So, Jim. And then what we're going to do is we're just going to move on to the next topic. But anybody who wants to pick up on what we've just talked about obviously can return to that as well. . . .

Source: Remarks of Senator Jon Kyl and President Barack Obama. "Transcript: White House Health Summit, Morning Session." *Kaiser Health News*, February 25, 2010. www.kaiserhealthnews.org/Stories /2010/February/25/health-care-reform-transcript.aspx. Video available at: http://www.whitehouse.gov /photos-and-video/video/bipartisan-meeting-health-reform-part-2

DOCUMENT 10.14

Obama Speaks to House Democrats on the Eve of the Health Reform Vote

"We Are Not Bound to Win, But We Are Bound to Be True"

2010

On March 20, 2010, President Barack Obama met with the House Democratic caucus one final time before the chamber's upcoming vote on the Patient Protection and Affordable Care Act. In his address to his fellow Democrats, excerpted here, Obama acknowledged that the political journey to that point had been an exhausting one. But he framed the bill that they would be voting on as both historic and vital to the nation's future prosperity.

To Leader Reid, to Steny Hoyer, John Larson, Xavier Becerra, Jim Clyburn, Chris Van Hollen, to an extraordinary leader and extraordinary Speaker of the House, Nancy Pelosi, and to all the members here today, thank you very much for having me. (Applause.) Thanks for having me and thanks for your tireless efforts waged on behalf of health insurance reform in this country.

I have the great pleasure of having a really nice library at the White House. And I was tooling through some of the writings of some previous Presidents and I came upon this quote by Abraham Lincoln: "I am not bound to win, but I'm bound to be true. I'm not bound to succeed, but I'm bound to live up to what light I have."

This debate has been a difficult debate. This process has been a difficult process. And this year has been a difficult year for the American people. When I was sworn in, we were in the midst of the worst recession since the Great Depression. Eight hundred thousand people per month were losing their jobs. Millions of people were losing their health insurance. And the financial system was on the verge of collapse.

And this body has taken on some of the toughest votes and some of the toughest decisions in the history of Congress. Not because you were bound to win, but because you were bound to be true. Because each and every one of you made a decision that at a moment of such urgency, it was less important to measure what the polls said than to measure what was right.

A year later, we're in different circumstances. Because of the actions that you've taken, the financial system has stabilized. The stock market has stabilized. Businesses are starting to invest again. The economy, instead of contracting, is now growing again. There are signs that people are going to start hiring again. There's still tremendous hardship all across the country, but there is a sense that we are making progress—because of you.

But even before this crisis, each and every one of us knew that there were millions of people across America who were living their own quiet crises. Maybe because they had a child who had a preexisting condition and no matter how desperate they were, no matter what insurance company they called, they couldn't get coverage for that child. Maybe it was somebody who had been forced into early retirement, in their 50s not yet eligible for Medicare, and they couldn't find a job and they couldn't find health insurance, despite the fact that they had some sort of chronic condition that had to be tended to.

Every single one of you at some point before you arrived in Congress and after you arrived in Congress have met constituents with heart-breaking stories. And you've looked them in the eye and you've said, we're going to do something about it—that's why I want to go to Congress.

And now, we're on the threshold of doing something about it. We're a day away. After a year of debate, after every argument has been made, by just about everybody, we're 24 hours away.

As some of you know, I'm not somebody who spends a lot of time surfing the cable channels, but I'm not completely in the bubble. I have a sense of what the coverage has been, and mostly it's an obsession with "What will this mean for the Democratic Party? What will this mean for the President's polls? How will this play out in November? Is this good or is this bad for the Democratic majority? What does it mean for those swing districts?"

And I noticed that there's been a lot of friendly advice offered all across town. (Laughter.) Mitch McConnell, John Boehner, Karl Rove—they're all warning you of the horrendous impact if you support this legislation. Now, it could be that they are suddenly having a change of heart and they are deeply concerned about their Democratic friends. (Laughter.) They are giving you the best possible advice in order to assure that Nancy Pelosi remains Speaker and Harry Reid remains Leader and that all of you keep your seats. That's a possibility. (Laughter.)

But it may also be possible that they realize after health reform passes and I sign that legislation into law, that it's going to be a little harder to mischaracterize what this effort has been all about.

Because this year, small businesses will start getting tax credits so that they can offer health insurance to employees who currently don't have it. (Applause.) Because this year, those same parents who are worried about getting coverage for their children with preexisting conditions now are assured that insurance companies have to give them coverage—this year. (Applause.)

Because this year, insurance companies won't suddenly be able to drop your coverage when you get sick — (applause) — or impose lifetime limits or restrictive limits on the coverage that you have. Maybe they know that this year, for the first time, young people will be able to stay on their parents' health insurance until they're 26 years old and they're thinking that just might be popular all across the country. (Applause.)

And what they also know is what won't happen. They know that after this legislation passes and after I sign this bill, lo and behold nobody is pulling the plug on Granny. (Laughter.) It turns out that in fact people who like their health insurance are going to be able to keep their health insurance; that there's no government takeover. People will discover that if they like their doctor, they'll be keeping their doctor. In fact, they're more likely to keep their doctor because of a stronger system.

It'll turn out that this piece of historic legislation is built on the private insurance system that we have now and runs straight down the center of American political thought. It turns out this is a bill that tracks the recommendations not just of Democrat Tom Daschle, but also Republicans Bob Dole and Howard Baker; that this is a middle-of-the-road bill that is designed to help the American people in an area of their lives where they urgently need help.

Now, there are some who wanted a single-payer government-run system. That's not this bill. The Republicans wanted what I called the "foxes guard the henhouse approach" in which we further deregulate the insurance companies and let them run wild, the notion being somehow that that was going to lower costs for the American people. I don't know a serious health care economist who buys that idea, but that was their concept. And we rejected that, because what we said was we want to create a system in which health care is working not for insurance companies but it's working for the American people, it's working for middle class families.

So what did we do? What is the essence of this legislation? Number one, this is the toughest insurance reforms in history. (Applause.) We are making sure that the system of private insurance works for ordinary families. A prescription—this is a patient's bill of rights on steroids. So many of you individually have worked on these insurance reforms—they are in this package—to make sure that families are getting a fair deal; that if they're paying a premium, that they're getting a good service in return; making sure that employers, if they are paying premiums for their employees, that their employees are getting the coverage that they expect; that insurance companies are not going to game the system with fine print and rescissions and dropping people when they need it most, but instead are going to have to abide by some basic rules of the road that exemplify a sense of fairness and good value. That's number one.

The second thing this does is it creates a pool, a marketplace, where individuals and small businesses, who right now are having a terrible time out there getting health insurance, are going to be able to purchase health insurance as part of a big group—just like federal employees, just like members of Congress. They are now going to be part of a pool that can negotiate for better rates, better quality, more competition.

And that's why the Congressional Budget Office says this will lower people's rates for comparable plans by 14 to 20 percent. That's not my numbers—that's the Congressional Budget Office's numbers. So that people will have choice and competition just like members of Congress have choice and competition.

Number three, if people still can't afford it we're going to provide them some tax credits—the biggest tax cut for small businesses and working families when it comes to health care in history. (Applause.)

And number four, this is the biggest reduction in our deficit since the Budget Balance Act—one of the biggest deficit reduction measures in history—over $1.3 trillion that will help put us on the path of fiscal responsibility. (Applause.)

And that's before we count all the game-changing measures that are going to assure, for example, that instead of having five tests when you go to the doctor you just get one; that the delivery system is working for patients, not just working for billings. And everybody who's looked at it says that every single good idea to bend the cost curve and start actually reducing health care costs are in this bill. . . .

And by the way, not only does it reduce the deficit—we pay for it responsibly in ways that the other side of the aisle that talks a lot about fiscal responsibility but doesn't seem to be able to walk the walk can't claim when it comes to their prescription drug bill. We are actually doing it. (Applause.) This is paid for and will not add a dime to the deficit—it will reduce the deficit. (Applause.)

Now, is this bill perfect? Of course not. Will this solve every single problem in our health care system right away? No. There are all kinds of ideas that many of you have that aren't included in this legislation. . . .

. . . There are some things I'd like to see that's not in this legislation. But is this the single most important step that we have taken on health care since Medicare? Absolutely. . . . I know this is a tough vote. I've talked to many of you individually. And I have to say that if you honestly believe in your heart of hearts, in your conscience, that this is not an improvement over the status quo; if despite all the information that's out there that says that without serious reform efforts like this one people's premiums are going to double over the next five or 10 years, that folks are going to keep on getting letters from their insurance companies saying that their premium just went up 40 or 50 percent; if you think that somehow it's okay that we have millions of hardworking Americans who can't get health care and that it's all right, it's acceptable, in the wealthiest nation on Earth that there are children with chronic illnesses that can't get the care that they need—if you think that the system is working for ordinary Americans rather than the insurance companies, then you should vote no on this bill. If you can honestly say that, then you shouldn't support it. You're here to represent your constituencies and if you think your constituencies honestly wouldn't be helped, you shouldn't vote for this.

But if you agree that the system is not working for ordinary families, if you've heard the same stories that I've heard everywhere, all across the country, then help us fix this system. Don't do it for me. Don't do it for Nancy Pelosi or Harry Reid. Do it for all those people out there who are struggling. . . .

Do it for people who are really scared right now through no fault of their own, who've played by the rules, who've done all the right things, and have suddenly found out that because of an accident, because of an ailment, they're about to lose their house; or they can't provide the help to their kids that they need; or they're a small business who up until now has always taken pride in providing care for their workers and it turns out that they just can't afford to do it anymore and they've having to make a decision about do I keep providing health insurance for my workers or do I just drop their coverage or do I not hire some people because I simply can't afford it—it's all being gobbled up by the insurance companies.

Don't do it for me. Don't do it for the Democratic Party. Do it for the American people. They're the ones who are looking for action right now. (Applause.). . . .

Now, I can't guarantee that this is good politics. Every one of you know your districts better than I do. You talk to folks. You're under enormous pressure. You're getting robocalls. You're getting e-mails that are tying up the communications system. I know the pressure you're under. I get a few comments made about me. I don't know if you've noticed. (Laughter.) I've been in your shoes. I know what it's like to take a tough vote.

But what did Lincoln say? "I am not bound to win, but I am bound to be true." Two generations ago, folks who were sitting in your position, they made a decision—we are going to make sure that seniors and the poor have health care coverage that they can count on. And they did the right thing.

And I'm sure at the time they were making that vote, they weren't sure how the politics were either, any more than the people who made the decision to make sure that Social Security was in place knew how the politics would play out, or folks who passed the civil rights acts knew how the politics were going to play out. They were not bound to win, but they were bound to be true.

And now we've got middle class Americans, don't have Medicare, don't have Medicaid, watching the employer-based system fray along the edges or being caught in terrible situations. And the question is, are we going to be true to them?

Sometimes I think about how I got involved in politics. I didn't think of myself as a potential politician when I get out of college. I went to work in neighborhoods, working with Catholic churches in poor neighborhoods in Chicago, trying to figure out how people could get a little bit of help. And I was skeptical about politics and politicians, just like a lot of Americans are skeptical about politics and politicians are right now. Because my working assumption was when push comes to shove, all too often folks in elected office, they're looking for themselves and not looking out for the folks who put them there; that there are too many compromises; that the special interests have too much power; they just got too much clout; there's too much big money washing around.

And I decided finally to get involved because I realized if I wasn't willing to step up and be true to the things I believe in, then the system wouldn't change. Every single one of you had that same kind of moment at the beginning of your careers. . . .

Something inspired you to get involved, and something inspired you to be a Democrat instead of running as a Republican. Because somewhere deep in your heart you said to yourself, I believe in an America in which we don't just look out for ourselves, that we don't just tell people you're on your own, that we are proud of our individualism, we are proud of our liberty, but we also have a sense of neighborliness and a sense of community — (applause) — and we are willing to look out for one another and help people who are vulnerable and help people who are down on their luck and give them a pathway to success and give them a ladder into the middle class. That's why you decided to run. (Applause.)

And now a lot of us have been here a while and everybody here has taken their lumps and their bruises. And it turns out people have had to make compromises, and you've been away from families for a long time and you've missed special events for your kids sometimes. And maybe there have been times where you asked yourself, why did I ever get involved in politics in the first place? And maybe things can't change after all. And when you do something courageous, it turns out sometimes you may be attacked. And sometimes the very people you thought you were trying to help may be angry at you and shout at you. And you say to yourself, maybe that thing that I started with has been lost.

But you know what? Every once in a while, every once in a while a moment comes where you have a chance to vindicate all those best hopes that you had about yourself, about this country, where you have a chance to make good on those promises that you made in all those town meetings and all those constituency breakfasts and all that traveling through the district, all those people who you looked in the eye and you said, you know what, you're right, the system is not working for you and I'm going to make it a little bit better.

And this is one of those moments. This is one of those times where you can honestly say to yourself, doggone it, this is exactly why I came here. This is why I got into politics. This is why I got into public service. This is why I've made those sacrifices. Because I believe so deeply in this country and I believe so deeply in this democracy and I'm willing to stand up even when it's hard, even when it's tough.

Every single one of you have made that promise not just to your constituents but to yourself. And this is the time to make true on that promise. We are not bound to win, but we are bound to be true. We are not bound to succeed, but we are bound to let whatever light we have shine. We have been debating health care for decades. It has now been debated for a year. It is in your hands. It is time to pass health care reform for America, and I am confident that you are going to do it tomorrow.

Thank you very much, House of Representatives. Let's get this done. (Applause.)

Source: Obama, Barack. Remarks by the President to the House Democratic Caucus, March 20, 2010. www.whitehouse.gov/the-press-office/remarks-president-house-democratic-congress.

DOCUMENT 10.15 Minority Leader Boehner Urges a Vote against the Affordable Care Act

"Shame on This Body"

2010

During the final House debate over health care reform prior to the decisive vote on the Patient Protection and Affordable Care Act, House minority leader John A. Boehner (R-OH) gave an impassioned speech against the legislation. He urged Democrats to reconsider their support for the bill, which he framed as fatally flawed and wrongheaded legislation that would "ruin" the country. Boehner's remarks, excerpted here, were to no avail. Relying exclusively on Democratic votes, the House cleared the bill by a 219–212 margin and sent it on to the president for his signature.

Mr. Boehner. Mr. Speaker and my colleagues, I rise tonight with a sad and heavy heart. Today we should be standing together reflecting on a year of bipartisanship and working to answer our country's call and their challenge to address the rising costs of health insurance in our country.

Today, this body, this institution, enshrined in the first article of the Constitution by our Founding Fathers as a sign of the importance they placed on this House, should be looking with pride on this legislation and our work.

But it is not so.

No, today we're standing here looking at a health care bill that no one in this body believes is satisfactory. Today we stand here amidst the wreckage of what was once the respect and honor that this House was held in by our fellow citizens. And we all know why it is so. We have failed to listen to America. And we have failed to reflect the will of our constituents. And when we fail to reflect that will, we fail ourselves, and we fail our country.

Look at this bill. Ask yourself, do you really believe that if you like the health plan that you have that you can keep it? No, you can't. You can't say that.

In this economy, with this unemployment, with our desperate need for jobs and economic growth, is this really the time to raise taxes, to create bureaucracies, and burden every job creator in our land? The answer is no.

Can you go home and tell your senior citizens that these cuts in Medicare will not limit their access to doctors or further weaken the program instead of strengthening it? No, you cannot.

Can you go home and tell your constituents with confidence that this bill respects the sanctity of all human life and that it won't allow for taxpayer funding of abortions for the first time in 30 years? No, you cannot.

And look at how this bill was written. Can you say it was done openly, with transparency and accountability? Without backroom deals and struck behind closed doors hidden from the people? Hell, no, you can't.

Have you read the bill? Have you read the reconciliation bill? Have you read the manager's amendment? Hell, no, you haven't.

Announcement by the Speaker Pro Tempore

The Speaker pro tempore. Both sides would do well to remember the dignity of the House.

Mr. Boehner. Mr. Speaker, in a few minutes we will cast some of the most consequential votes that any of us will ever cast in this Chamber. The decision we make will affect every man, woman, and child in this Nation for generations to come. If we're going to vote to defy the will of the American people, then we ought to have the courage to stand before them and announce our votes, one at a time.

I sent a letter to the Speaker this week asking that the "call of the roll" be ordered for this vote. Madam Speaker, I ask you, will you, in the interest of this institution, grant my request?

The Speaker pro tempore. Is the gentleman asking a rhetorical question?

Mr. Boehner. Mr. Speaker, will you grant my request that we have a call of the roll?

The Speaker pro tempore. Under clause 2(a) of rule XX, a record vote is conducted by electronic device unless the Speaker directs otherwise.

Mr. Boehner. And you, Mr. Speaker, will you grant that request?

The Speaker pro tempore. The Chair will decide at the time the question is ripe. This is not it.

Mr. Boehner. My colleagues, this is the People's House.

When we came here, we each swore an oath to uphold and abide by the Constitution as representatives of the people. But the process here is broken. The institution is broken. And as a result, this bill is not what the American people need nor what our constituents want.

Americans are out there making sacrifices and struggling to make a better future for their kids, and over the last year as the damn-the-torpedoes outline of this legislation became more clear, millions of Americans lifted their voices and many, for the first time, asking us to slow down, not to try to cram through more than this system could handle, not to spend money that we didn't have. In this time of recession, they wanted us to focus on jobs, not more spending, not more government, and certainly not more taxes.

But what they see today frightens them. They're frightened because they don't know what comes next. They're disgusted because what they see is one political party closing out the other from what should be a national solution. And they're angry. They're angry that no matter how they engage in this debate, this body moves forward against their will.

Shame on us. Shame on this body. Shame on each and every one of you who substitutes your will and your desires above those of your fellow countrymen.

Around this Chamber, looking upon us are the lawgivers from Moses, to Gaius, to Blackstone, to Thomas Jefferson. By our actions today, we disgrace their values. We break the ties of history in this Chamber. We break our trust with America.

When I handed the Speaker the gavel in 2007, I said this: "This is the People's House. And the moment a majority forgets it, it starts writing itself a ticket to minority status."

If we pass this bill, there will be no turning back. It will be the last straw for the American people. In a democracy, you can only ignore the will of the people for so long and get away with it. And if we defy the will of our fellow citizens and pass this bill, we're going to be held to account by those who have placed us in their trust. We will have shattered those bonds of trust.

I beg you, I beg each and every one of you on both sides of the aisle: do not further strike at the heart of this country and this institution with arrogance, for surely you will not strike with impunity.

I ask each of you to vow to never let this happen again—this process, this defiance of our citizens. It's not too late to begin to restore the bonds of trust with our Nation and return comity to this institution.

And so join me. Join me in voting against this bill so that we can come together, together anew and addressing the challenge of health care in a manner that brings credit to this body and brings credit to the ideals of this Nation, and most importantly, that reflects the will of the American people.

Source: Boehner, John A. Floor speech on the Affordable Care Act. *Congressional Record.* 111th Cong., 2d sess., March 21, 2010, p. H1895.

DOCUMENT 10.16

A Republican Pundit Laments a Conservative "Waterloo"

"It's Hard to Exaggerate the Magnitude of the Disaster"

2010

On the morning of March 21, 2010, Republican lawmakers, activists, pundits, and citizens were largely resigned to the likelihood that the House of Representatives would later that day pass President Barack Obama's health care reform legislation, paving the way for the bill to become law. While most conservative pundits and activists issued final broadsides against the measure and its Democratic architects in the hours before the fateful vote, the well-known conservative political commentator David Frum aimed his fire at fellow Republicans. Frum, a former speechwriter for President George W. Bush, wrote a blog post, titled "Waterloo," that harshly criticized Republicans in Washington, D.C., and conservative media outlets for their performances on health care reform. He asserted that in embracing obstructionism for short-term political advantage, Republicans wasted a golden opportunity to make the final law much more palatable.

Frum's post, which is reprinted here, quickly became the subject of intense debate in conservative political circles. Three days after his "Waterloo" post, the American Enterprise Institute (AEI), a prominent conservative think tank, yanked Frum's AEI fellowship. Many Republicans issued blistering rejoinders criticizing Frum for disloyalty or chiding him for his interpretation of events. For example, conservative writer Tunku Varadarajan stated that Frum's "argument that Republicans and Democrats were not that far apart just goes to show how naïve he is on this question. Health care, for anybody who has been paying attention, is becoming a referendum on bigger issues like the size of government, and personal freedom. The public option, the individual mandate, all the bill's taxes, the end of Medicare advantage, none of these were 'little' questions to negotiate over and move on."[1]

But other analysts defended Frum's post as a clear-eyed and candid appraisal of the policy fallout from Republican health care tactics. "David's clear and explicit goal is not to subvert the conservative movement, but to strengthen and modernize it," wrote conservative blogger John R. Guardiano.[2] And conservatives such as Bruce Bartlett, a former official in the Ronald Reagan and George W. Bush administrations whose own relationship with the GOP had become strained after he criticized Bush's fiscal record, asserted that Frum's dismissal from the AEI symbolized a troubling "closing of the conservative mind [in America]. Rigid conformity is being enforced [and] no dissent is allowed."[3]

Waterloo

Conservatives and Republicans today suffered their most crushing legislative defeat since the 1960s.

It's hard to exaggerate the magnitude of the disaster. Conservatives may cheer themselves that they'll compensate for today's expected vote with a big win in the November 2010 elections. But:

(1) It's a good bet that conservatives are over-optimistic about November—by then the economy will have improved and the immediate goodies in the healthcare bill will be reaching key voting blocs.

(2) So what? Legislative majorities come and go. This healthcare bill is forever. A win in November is very poor compensation for this debacle now.

So far, I think a lot of conservatives will agree with me. Now comes the hard lesson: A huge part of the blame for today's disaster attaches to conservatives and Republicans ourselves.

At the beginning of this process we made a strategic decision: unlike, say, Democrats in 2001 when President Bush proposed his first tax cut, we would make no deal with the administration. No negotiations, no compromise, nothing. We were going for all the marbles. This would be Obama's Waterloo—just as healthcare was Clinton's in 1994.

Only, the hardliners overlooked a few key facts: Obama was elected with 53% of the vote, not Clinton's 42%. The liberal block within the Democratic congressional caucus is bigger and stronger than it was in 1993-94. And of course the Democrats also remember their history, and also remember the consequences of their 1994 failure.

This time, when we went for all the marbles, we ended with none.

Could a deal have been reached? Who knows? But we do know that the gap between this plan and traditional Republican ideas is not very big. The Obama plan has a broad family resemblance to Mitt Romney's Massachusetts plan. It builds on ideas developed at the Heritage Foundation in the early 1990s that formed the basis for Republican counter-proposals to Clintoncare in 1993-1994.

Barack Obama badly wanted Republican votes for his plan. Could we have leveraged his desire to align the plan more closely with conservative views? To finance it without redistributive taxes on productive enterprise—without weighing so heavily on small business—without expanding Medicaid? Too late now. They are all the law.

No illusions please: This bill will not be repealed. Even if Republicans scored a 1994 style landslide in November, how many votes could we muster to re-open the "doughnut hole" and charge seniors more for prescription drugs? How many votes to re-allow insurers to rescind policies when they discover a pre-existing condition? How many votes to banish 25 year olds from their parents' insurance coverage? And even if the votes were there—would President Obama sign such a repeal?

We followed the most radical voices in the party and the movement, and they led us to abject and irreversible defeat.

There were leaders who knew better, who would have liked to deal. But they were trapped. Conservative talkers on Fox and talk radio had whipped the Republican voting base into such a frenzy that deal-making was rendered impossible. How do you negotiate with somebody who wants to murder your grandmother? Or—more exactly—with somebody whom your voters have been persuaded to believe wants to murder their grandmother?

I've been on a soapbox for months now about the harm that our overheated talk is doing to us. Yes it mobilizes supporters—but by mobilizing them with hysterical accusations and pseudo-information, overheated talk has made it impossible for representatives to represent and elected leaders to lead. The read leaders are on TV and radio, and they have very different imperatives from people in government. Talk radio thrives on confrontation and recrimination. When Rush Limbaugh said that he wanted President Obama to fail, he was intelligently explaining his own interests. What he omitted to say—but what is equally true—is that he also wants Republicans to fail. If Republicans succeed—if they govern successfully in office and negotiate attractive compromises out of office—Rush's listeners get less angry. And if they are less angry, they listen to the radio less, and hear fewer ads for Sleepnumber beds.

So today's defeat for free-market economics and Republican values is a huge win for the conservative entertainment industry. Their listeners and viewers will now be even more enraged, even more frustrated, even more disappointed in everybody except the responsibility-free talkers on television and radio. For them, its mission accomplished. For the cause they purport to represent, its Waterloo all right: ours.

Source: Frum, David. "Waterloo." FrumForum.com, March 21, 2010. www.frumforum.com/waterloo. Copyright © 2010 David Frum. Used with permission.

Notes

1. Tunku Varadarajan, "The Conservative the Right Loves to Hate," *Daily Beast,* March 23, 2010, www.thedailybeast.com/blogs-and-stories/2010-03-23/the-conservative-the-right-loves-to-hate/.

2. John R. Guardiano, "David Frum vs. the Right's Company Men," *NewsReal Blog,* March 28, 2010, www.newsrealblog.com/2010/03/28/david-frum-vs-the-rights-company-men/.

3. Bruce Bartlett, "David Frum and the Closing of the Conservative Mind," blog, March 25, 2010, http://capitalgainsandgames.com/blog/bruce-bartlett/1601/groupthink-right-would-make-stalin-proud.

Obama Signs the Health Care Reform Bill into Law

"Here, In This Country, We Shape Our Own Destiny"

2010

On March 23, 2010, President Obama signed the Patient Protection and Affordable Care Act into law in a festive ceremony at the White House that was attended by more than two hundred Democratic lawmakers. Obama's remarks upon signing the landmark bill are excerpted here.

The President: . . . Today, after almost a century of trying; today, after over a year of debate; today, after all the votes have been tallied—health insurance reform becomes law in the United States of America. (Applause.) Today.

It is fitting that Congress passed this historic legislation this week. For as we mark the turning of spring, we also mark a new season in America. In a few moments, when I sign this bill, all of the overheated rhetoric over reform will finally confront the reality of reform. (Applause.)

And while the Senate still has a last round of improvements to make on this historic legislation—and these are improvements I'm confident they will make swiftly— (applause)—the bill I'm signing will set in motion reforms that generations of Americans have fought for, and marched for, and hungered to see.

It will take four years to implement fully many of these reforms, because we need to implement them responsibly. We need to get this right. But a host of desperately needed reforms will take effect right away. (Applause.)

This year, we'll start offering tax credits to about 4 million small businessmen and women to help them cover the cost of insurance for their employees. (Applause.) That happens this year.

This year, tens of thousands of uninsured Americans with preexisting conditions, the parents of children who have a preexisting condition, will finally be able to purchase the coverage they need. That happens this year. (Applause.)

This year, insurance companies will no longer be able to drop people's coverage when they get sick. (Applause.) They won't be able to place lifetime limits or restrictive annual limits on the amount of care they can receive. (Applause.)

This year, all new insurance plans will be required to offer free preventive care. And this year, young adults will be able to stay on their parents' policies until they're 26 years old. That happens this year. (Applause.)

And this year, seniors who fall in the coverage gap known as the doughnut hole will start getting some help. They'll receive $250 to help pay for prescriptions, and that will, over time, fill in the doughnut hole. And I want seniors to know, despite what some have said, these reforms will not cut your guaranteed benefits. (Applause.) In fact, under this law, Americans on Medicare will receive free preventive care without co-payments or deductibles. That begins this year. (Applause.)

Once this reform is implemented, health insurance exchanges will be created, a competitive marketplace where uninsured people and small businesses will finally be able to purchase affordable, quality insurance. They will be able to be part of a big pool and get the same good deal that members of Congress get. That's what's going to happen under this reform. (Applause.) And when this exchange is up and running, millions of people will get tax breaks to help them afford coverage, which represents the largest middle-class tax cut for health care in history. That's what this reform is about. (Applause.)

This legislation will also lower costs for families and for businesses and for the federal government, reducing our deficit by over $1 trillion in the next two decades. It is paid for. It is fiscally responsible. And it will help lift a decades-long drag on our economy. That's part of what all of you together worked on and made happen. (Applause.)

That our generation is able to succeed in passing this reform is a testament to the persistence—and the character—of the American people, who championed this cause; who mobilized; who organized; who believed that people who love this country can change it.

It's also a testament to the historic leadership—and uncommon courage—of the men and women of the United States Congress, who've taken their lumps during this difficult debate. (Laughter.)

Audience member: Yes, we did. (Laughter.)

The President: You know, there are few tougher jobs in politics or government than leading one of our legislative chambers. In each chamber, there are men and women who come from different places and face different pressures, who reach different conclusions about the same things and feel deeply concerned about different things.

By necessity, leaders have to speak to those different concerns. It isn't always tidy; it is almost never easy. But perhaps the greatest—and most difficult—challenge is to cobble together out of those differences the sense of common interest and common purpose that's required to advance the dreams of all people—especially in a country as large and diverse as ours.

And we are blessed by leaders in each chamber who not only do their jobs very well but who never lost sight of that larger mission. They didn't play for the short term; they didn't play to the polls or to politics: One of the best speakers the House of Representatives has ever had, Speaker Nancy Pelosi. (Applause.)

Audience: Nancy! Nancy! Nancy! Nancy!

The President: One of the best majority leaders the Senate has ever had, Mr. Harry Reid. (Applause.)

To all of the terrific committee chairs, all the members of Congress who did what was difficult, but did what was right, and passed health care reform—not just this generation of Americans will thank you, but the next generation of Americans will thank you.

And of course, this victory was also made possible by the painstaking work of members of this administration, including our outstanding Secretary of Health and Human Services, Kathleen Sebelius—(applause)—and one of the unsung heroes of this effort, an extraordinary woman who led the reform effort from the White House, Nancy-Ann DeParle. Where's Nancy? (Applause.)

Today, I'm signing this reform bill into law on behalf of my mother, who argued with insurance companies even as she battled cancer in her final days.

I'm signing it for Ryan Smith, who's here today. He runs a small business with five employees. He's trying to do the right thing, paying half the cost of coverage for his workers. This bill will help him afford that coverage.

I'm signing it for 11-year-old Marcelas Owens, who's also here. (Applause.) Marcelas lost his mom to an illness. And she didn't have insurance and couldn't afford the care that she needed. So in her memory he has told her story across America so that no other children have to go through what his family has experienced. (Applause.)

I'm signing it for Natoma Canfield. Natoma had to give up her health coverage after her rates were jacked up by more than 40 percent. She was terrified that an illness would mean she'd lose the house that her parents built, so she gave up her insurance. Now she's lying in a hospital bed, as we speak, faced with just such an illness, praying that she can somehow afford to get well without insurance. Natoma's family is here today because Natoma can't be. And her sister Connie is here. Connie, stand up. (Applause.)

I'm signing this bill for all the leaders who took up this cause through the generations—from Teddy Roosevelt to Franklin Roosevelt, from Harry Truman, to Lyndon Johnson, from Bill and Hillary Clinton, to one of the deans who's been fighting this so long, John Dingell. (Applause.) To Senator Ted Kennedy. (Applause.) And it's fitting that Ted's widow, Vicki, is here; and his niece Caroline; his son Patrick, whose vote helped make this reform a reality. (Applause.)

I remember seeing Ted walk through that door in a summit in this room a year ago—one of his last public appearances. And it was hard for him to make it. But he was confident that we would do the right thing.

Our presence here today is remarkable and improbable. With all the punditry, all of the lobbying, all of the game-playing that passes for governing in Washington, it's been easy at times to doubt our ability to do such a big thing, such a complicated thing; to wonder if there are limits to what we, as a people, can still achieve. It's easy to succumb to the sense of cynicism about what's possible in this country.

But today, we are affirming that essential truth—a truth every generation is called to rediscover for itself—that we are not a nation that scales back its aspirations. (Applause.) We are not a nation that falls prey to doubt or mistrust. We don't fall prey to fear. We are not a nation that does what's easy. That's not who we are. That's not how we got here.

We are a nation that faces its challenges and accepts its responsibilities. We are a nation that does what is hard. What is necessary. What is right. Here, in this country, we shape our own destiny. That is what we do. That is who we are. That is what makes us the United States of America.

And we have now just enshrined, as soon as I sign this bill, the core principle that everybody should have some basic security when it comes to their health care. (Applause.) And it is an extraordinary achievement that has happened because of all of you and all the advocates all across the country.

So, thank you. Thank you. God bless you, and may God bless the United States. (Applause.) Thank you. Thank you.

All right, I would now like to call up to stage some of the members of Congress who helped make this day possible, and some of the Americans who will benefit from these reforms. And we're going to sign this bill.

This is going to take a little while. I've got to use every pen, so it's going to take a really long time. (Laughter.) I didn't practice. (Laughter.)

(The bill is signed.)

We are done. (Applause.)

Source: Remarks by the President and the Vice President at Signing of the Health Insurance Reform Bill, March 23, 2010. www.whitehouse.gov/the-press-office/remarks-president-and-vice-president-signing -health-insurance-reform-bill.

Chronology

1610	Virginia colonists approve the first public health law in the New World.
1700	Pennsylvania lawmakers pass the first quarantine act in the colonies.
1721	Boston is wracked by a deadly smallpox epidemic.
1765	The University of Pennsylvania establishes the colonies' first formal medical school.
1798	Congress passes An Act for the Relief of Sick and Disabled Seamen, which establishes the U.S. Marine Service.
1813	Congress passes the nation's first federal vaccination act.
1841	Reformer Dorothea Dix begins her crusade to improve conditions in U.S. mental institutions.
1847	The American Medical Association (AMA) is founded.
1850	Lemuel Shattuck releases his *Report of a General Plan for the Promotion of Public and Personal Health.*
1861–1865	The nation's public health care institutions undergo expansion to treat casualties of the Civil War.
1870	Congress passes the Marine Hospitals Services Act, paving the way for the establishment of the U.S. Public Health Service.
1879	Congress creates the National Board of Health (NBH).
1888	The U.S. Supreme Court sanctions state licensing of medical practice in *Dent v. West Virginia.*
1906	The Pure Food and Drug Act becomes law. The Committee of One Hundred on National Health is established.
1910	The muckraking Flexner Report excoriates medical education in the United States.
1912	Theodore Roosevelt and the Progressive Party call for universal health insurance.
1918–1919	A Spanish flu epidemic claims the lives of as many as 675,000 Americans.
1918–1920	Compulsory health insurance initiatives go down to defeat across the country.
1921	Congress passes the Sheppard-Towner Maternity and Infancy Protection Act.
1927	The Committee on the Costs of Medical Care (CCMC) is established.

1929   Onset of the Great Depression triggers renewed interest in national health insurance and other social welfare legislation.
Baylor University Hospital establishes a Blue Cross plan that becomes a national model.

1930   The Ramsdell Act establishes the National Institute (later Institutes) of Health.

1935   Franklin D. Roosevelt signs the Social Security Act into law.

1938   Congress passes the Food, Drug and Cosmetic Act.

1939   Sen. Robert Wagner (D-NY) introduces the first of several "national health bills" designed to provide universal health coverage.

1942   The influential Beveridge Report is released in Great Britain.

1943   National War Labor Board rules that employer health insurance plans are tax-exempt.

1944   Congress passes the Serviceman's Readjustment Act, popularly known as the GI Bill.

1945   Harry S. Truman declares his support for a program of national health insurance.

1946   Truman signs the Hospital Survey and Construction Act (or Hill-Burton Act) into law, ushering in a wave of new hospital construction.
Congress passes the National Mental Health Act.

1954   Dwight D. Eisenhower announces his support for "reinsurance" legislation.

1958   The Forand bill providing health insurance to Social Security beneficiaries is introduced in Congress.

1961   John F. Kennedy urges Congress to pass a federal health program for senior citizens.

1963   Kennedy signs the Maternal and Child Health and Mental Retardation Planning Amendment to the Social Security Act.
Kennedy signs the Mental Retardation Services and Facilities Construction Act into law.

1964   The U.S. surgeon general issues a landmark report about the health dangers of cigarette smoking.

1965   Lyndon B. Johnson signs legislation creating the federal Medicare and Medicaid programs.

1970   The Clean Air Act Amendments is enacted.
The Environmental Protection Agency (EPA) is created by the Nixon administration.

1972   The Clean Water Act becomes law.

1973	The U.S. Supreme Court hands down its famous *Roe v. Wade* decision legalizing abortion.
1974	The Employee Retirement Income Security Act (ERISA) creates national standards for employee health care and other benefit plans.
1980	The Superfund program (technically the Comprehensive Environmental Response, Compensation, and Liability Act) becomes law.
1981	The Reagan administration eliminates subsidies for nonprofit health maintenance organizations (HMOs) and encourages private investment in for-profit HMOs.
	The Centers for Disease Control (CDC) announces discovery of a deadly new disease that would become known as acquired immune deficiency syndrome (AIDS).
1983	A prospective payment system (PPS) for Medicare is introduced in an effort to reduce the expense of the program.
	Ronald Reagan signs the Orphan Drug Act into law.
1984	Congress passes the Drug Price Competition and Patent Term Restoration Act (Hatch-Waxman Act).
1989	Congress repeals the Medicare Catastrophic Coverage Act after passing the legislation only sixteen months earlier.
1990	George H. W. Bush signs into law the Ryan White Comprehensive AIDS Resources Emergency (CARE) Act.
	Congress passes the Americans with Disabilities Act (ADA).
1992	U.S. Supreme Court decision in *Planned Parenthood of Southeastern Pennsylvania v. Casey* empowers states to impose their own abortion restrictions.
1993	Bill Clinton announces the creation of a President's Task Force on Health Care Reform.
1994	Oregon voters pass the Death with Dignity Act.
1995	Republicans defeat the Clinton administration's proposed health care reforms.
1996	Clinton signs the Health Insurance Portability and Accountability ACT (HIPAA).
1997	Clinton and congressional Republicans unite to craft Medicare Part C, which increases the role of commercial managed care organizations in the Medicare program.
	The State Children's Health Insurance Program (SCHIP) is enacted.
1998	A Tobacco Master Settlement Agreement (MSA) is announced between the tobacco industry and forty-six states that had sued cigarette makers for smoking-related health care costs.

2003   George W. Bush signs the Partial-Birth Abortion Ban Act.

In a controversial vote, Congress passes the Medicare Prescription Drug, Improvement, and Modernization Act (Medicare Modernization Act), which extends prescription drug coverage to Medicare beneficiaries.

2006   Massachusetts governor Mitt Romney signs a universal health insurance bill with an individual mandate for state residents.

2008   The Paul Wellstone and Pete Domenici Mental Health Parity and Addiction Equity Act becomes law.

2010   Barack Obama signs the Patient Protection and Affordable Care Act into law.

Bibliography

Anders, George. *Health against Wealth: HMOs and the Breakdown of Medical Trust.* Boston: Houghton Mifflin, 1996.

Annis, Edward R. *Code Blue: Health Care in Crisis.* Washington, DC: Regnery Gateway, 1993.

Baker, Tom. *The Medical Malpractice Myth.* Chicago: University of Chicago Press, 2005.

Barlett, Donald L., and James B. Steele. *Critical Condition: How Health Care in America Became Big Business and Bad Medicine.* New York: Doubleday, 2004.

Bennett, James T., and Thomas J. DiLorenzo. *From Pathology to Politics: Public Health in America.* New Brunswick, NJ: Transaction Publishers, 2000.

Billi, John E., and Gail B. Agrawal, eds. *The Challenge of Regulating Managed Care.* Ann Arbor: University of Michigan Press, 2001.

Birenbaum, Arnold. *Managed Care: Made in America.* Westport, CT: Praeger, 1997.

Blevins, Sue A. *Medicare's Midlife Crisis.* Washington, DC: Cato Institute, 2001.

Brownlee, Shannon. *Overtreated: Why Too Much Medicine Is Making Us Sicker and Poorer.* New York: Bloomsbury, 2007.

Burrow, James Gordon. *The American Medical Association: Voice of American Medicine.* Baltimore: Johns Hopkins University Press, 1963.

Cayleff, Susan E. *Wash and Be Healed: The Water-Cure Movement and Women's Health.* Philadelphia, PA: Temple University Press, 1987.

Cohn, Jonathan. "How They Did It," five-part series, *New Republic,* May 20–May 26, 2010.

Cohn, Jonathan. *Sick: The Untold Story of America's Health Care Crisis—and the People Who Pay the Price.* New York: HarperCollins, 2007.

Coombs, Jan. *The Rise and Fall of HMOs: An American Health Care Revolution.* Madison: University of Wisconsin Press, 2005.

Corning, Peter A. *The Evolution of Medicare . . . From Idea to Law.* Washington, DC: Social Security Administration, Office of Research and Statistics, 1969. www.ssa.gov/history/corning.html.

Cunningham, Robert III, and Robert M. Cunningham Jr. *The Blues: History of the Blue Cross and Blue Shield System.* DeKalb: Northern Illinois University Press, 1997.

Derickson, Alan. "Health for Three-Thirds of the Nation: Public Health Advocacy of Universal Access to Medical Care in the United States." *American Journal of Public Health* 92, no. 2 (February 2002): 180–90.

Derickson, Alan. *Health Security for All: Dreams of Universal Health Care in America.* Baltimore: Johns Hopkins University Press, 2005.

Duffy, John. *Epidemics in Colonial America.* Port Washington, NY: Kennikat Press, 1972.

Duffy, John. *From Humors to Medical Science: A History of American Medicine.* 2nd ed. Urbana: University of Illinois Press, 1993.

Duffy, John. *The Sanitarians: A History of American Public Health.* Chicago: University of Illinois Press, 1992.

Enthoven, Alain. *Health Plan: The Practical Solution to the Soaring Cost of Medicare.* Reading, MA: Addison-Wesley, 1980.

Field, Robert I. *Health Care Regulation in America: Complexity, Confrontation, and Compromise.* New York: Oxford University Press, 2007.

Fox, Daniel M. *Power and Illness: The Failure and Future of American Health Policy.* Berkeley: University of California Press, 1993.

Furman, Bess. *Profile of the United States Public Health Service, 1798–1948.* Washington, DC: U.S. National Library of Medicine, 1973.

Ginzberg, Eli. *The Medical Triangle: Physicians, Politicians, and the Public.* Cambridge, MA: Harvard University Press, 1990.

Goldfield, Norbert Israel. *National Health Reform American Style: Lessons from the Past: A Twentieth-Century Journey.* Tampa, FL: American College of Physician Executives, 2000.

Gordon, Colin. *Dead on Arrival: The Politics of Health Care in Twentieth-Century America.* Princeton, NJ: Princeton University Press, 2003.

Grey, Michael R. *New Deal Medicine: The Rural Health Programs of the Farm Security Administration.* Baltimore: Johns Hopkins University Press, 1999.

Hacker, Jacob S. *Blurring the Boundaries: The Battle over Public and Private Social Benefits in the United States.* Cambridge, MA: Cambridge University Press, 2002.

Hacker, Jacob S. *The Road to Nowhere: The Genesis of President Clinton's Plan for Health Security.* Princeton, NJ: Princeton University Press, 1997.

Hadley, Jack, and John Holahan. *The Cost of Care for the Uninsured: What Do We Spend, Who Pays, and What Would Full Coverage Add to Medical Spending?* Washington, DC: Kaiser Commission on Medicaid and the Uninsured, May 2004.

Herzlinger, Regina E. *Market-Driven Health Care: Who Wins, Who Loses in the Transformation of America's Largest Service Industry.* New York: Basic Books, 1997.

Herzlinger, Regina E. *Who Killed Health Care?* New York: McGraw-Hill, 2007.

Himelfarb, Richard. *Catastrophic Politics: The Rise and Fall of the Medicare Catastrophic Coverage Act of 1988.* University Park, PA: Pennsylvania State University Press, 1995.

Hirshfield, Daniel S. *The Lost Reform: The Campaign for Compulsory Health Insurance in the United States from 1932–1943.* Cambridge, MA: Harvard University Press, 1970.

Hoffman, Beatrix. *The Wages of Sickness: The Politics of Health Insurance in Progressive America.* Chapel Hill: University of North Carolina Press, 2001.

Hofstadter, Richard. *The Age of Reform: Bryan to F.D.R.* New York: Knopf, 1955.

Jacobs, Lawrence R., and Theda Skocpol. *Health Care Reform and American Politics: What Everyone Needs to Know.* New York: Oxford University Press, 2010.

Johnson, Haynes, and David S. Broder. *The System: The American Way of Politics at the Breaking Point.* Boston: Little, Brown, 1996.

Keller, Morton. *Regulating a New Society: Public Policy and Social Change in America, 1900–1933.* Cambridge, MA: Harvard University Press, 1994.

Knowles, John H., ed. *Doing Better and Feeling Worse: Health in the United States.* New York: W. W. Norton, 1977.

Kooijman, Jaap. . . . *And the Pursuit of National Health: The Incremental Strategy toward National Health Insurance in the United States of America.* Amsterdam, The Netherlands: Rodopi, 1999.

Kronenfeld, Jennie Jacobs. *The Changing Federal Role in U.S. Health Care Policy.* Westport, CT: Praeger, 1997.

Kronenfeld, Jennie Jacobs. *Health Care Policy: Issues and Trends.* Westport, CT: Praeger, 2002.

Laham, Nicholas. *A Lost Cause: Bill Clinton's Campaign for National Health Insurance.* Westport, CT: Praeger, 1996.

Leavitt, Judith Walzer, and Ronald L. Numbers, eds. *Sickness and Health in America: Readings in the History of Medicine and Public Health.* 2nd ed., rev. Madison: University of Wisconsin Press, 1985.

Longman, Phillip. *Best Care Anywhere: Why VA Health Care Is Better Than Yours.* Sausalito, CA: PoliPointPress, 2007.

Ludmerer, Kenneth M. *Time to Heal: American Medical Education from the Turn of the Century to the Era of Managed Care.* New York: Oxford University Press, 1999.

Maioni, Antonia. *Parting at the Crossroads: The Emergence of Health Insurance in the United States and Canada.* Princeton, NJ: Princeton University Press, 1998.

Mann, Barbara Alice. *The Tainted Gift: The Disease Method of Frontier Expansion.* Santa Barbara, CA: Praeger/ABC-CLIO, 2009.

Markowitz, Gerald, and David Rosner. *Deceit and Denial: The Deadly Politics of Industrial Pollution.* Berkeley: University of California Press, 2003.

Marmor, Theodore R. *The Politics of Medicare.* 2nd ed. New York: Aldine De Gruyter, 2000.

Mason, Diana J., Judith Kline Leavitt, and Mary W. Chaffee. *Policy and Politics in Nursing and Health Care.* St. Louis, MO: Saunders Elsevier, 2007.

Maxwell, William Q. *Lincoln's Fifth Wheel: The Political History of the United States Sanitary Commission.* New York: Longman, Green, 1956.

Mayes, Rick, and Robert A. Berenson. *Medicare Prospective Payment and the Shaping of U.S. Health Care.* Baltimore: Johns Hopkins University Press, 2002.

Melosi, Martin, ed. *Pollution and Reform in American Cities, 1870–1930.* Austin: University of Texas Press, 1980.

Miller, Irwin. *American Health Care Blues: Blue Cross, HMOs, and Pragmatic Reform since 1960.* New Brunswick, NJ: Transaction Publishers, 1996.

Murray, John. *Origins of American Health Insurance: A History of Industrial Sickness Funds.* New Haven, CT: Yale University Press, 2007.

Novak, William J. *The People's Welfare: Law and Regulation in Nineteenth-Century America.* Chapel Hill: University of North Carolina Press, 1996.

Numbers, Ronald L. *Almost Persuaded: American Physicians and Compulsory Health Insurance, 1912–1920.* Baltimore: Johns Hopkins University Press, 1978.

Oberlander, Jonathan. *The Political Life of Medicare.* Chicago: University of Chicago Press, 2003.

Olson, Laura Katz. *The Politics of Medicaid.* New York: Columbia University Press, 2010.

Packard, Francis R. *History of Medicine in the United States.* New York: Hoeber, 1931.

Patel, Kant, and Mark E. Rushefsky. *Health Care Politics and Policy in America.* 2nd ed. Armonk, NY: M.E. Sharpe, 1999.

Poen, Monte M. *Harry S. Truman versus the Medical Lobby.* Columbia: University of Missouri Press, 1979.

Quadagno, Jill. *One Nation Uninsured: Why the U.S. Has No National Health Insurance.* New York: Oxford University Press, 2005.

Raffel, Marshall W., and Norma K. Raffel. *The U.S. Health System: Origins and Functions.* New York: Wiley, 1989.

Reiss, Oscar. *Medicine in Colonial America.* Lanham, MD: University Press of America, 2000.

Rodgers, Daniel T. *Atlantic Crossings: Social Politics in a Progressive Age.* Cambridge, MA: Harvard University Press, 1998.

Rosen, George. *The Structure of American Medical Practice, 1875–1941.* Edited by Charles E. Rosenberg. Philadelphia: University of Pennsylvania Press, 1983.

Rosenberg, Charles E. *The Care of Strangers: The Rise of America's Hospital System.* New York: Basic Books, 1987.

Rosner, David, and Gerald Markowitz, eds. *Dying for Work: Workers' Safety and Health in Twentieth-Century America.* Bloomington: Indian University Press, 1987.

Ross, Joseph S. "The Committee on the Costs of Medical Care and the History of Health Insurance in the United States." *Einstein Quarterly Journal of Biology and Medicine* 19 (2002): 129–34.

Rothstein, William G. *American Physicians in the Nineteenth Century: From Sects to Science.* Baltimore: Johns Hopkins University Press, 1985.

Rovner, Julie. *Health Care Policy and Politics A to Z.* 3rd ed. Washington, DC: CQ Press, 2009.

Sage, William M., and Rogan Kersh, eds. *Medical Malpractice and the United States Health Care System.* New York: Cambridge University Press, 2006.

Savitt, Todd L. *Race and Medicine in Nineteenth- and Early-Twentieth-Century America.* Kent, OH: Kent State University Press, 2007.

Shilts, Randy. *And the Band Played On: Politics, People, and the AIDS Epidemic.* New York: St. Martin's Press, 1987.

Shonick, William. *Government and Health Services: Government's Role in the Development of U.S. Health Services 1930–1980.* New York: Oxford University Press, 1995.

Shryock, Richard H. *Medical Licensing in America, 1650–1965*. Baltimore: Johns Hopkins University Press, 1967.

Shryrock, Richard H. *Medicine and Society in America, 1760–1860*. New York: New York University press, 1960.

Skidmore, Max J. *Social Security and Its Enemies: The Case for America's Most Efficient Insurance Program*. Boulder, CO: Westview Press, 1999.

Skocpal, Theda. *Boomerang: Clinton's Health Security Effort and the Turn against Government in U.S. Politics*. New York: W. W. Norton, 1996.

Smillie, Wilson George. *Public Health: Its Promise for the Future*. New York: Macmillan, 1955. Reprint: New York: Arno Press, 1976.

"Social Security History." Social Security Online. www.ssa.gov/history/index.html.

Starr, Paul. *The Social Transformation of American Medicine*. New York: Basic Books, 1982.

Stevens, Rosemary. *American Medicine and the Public Interest*. New Haven, CT: Yale University Press, 1971. Rev. ed.: Berkeley: University of California Press, 1998.

Stevens, Rosemary. *In Sickness and in Wealth: American Hospitals in the Twentieth Century*. New York: Basic Books, 1989.

Stradling, David. *Smokestacks and Progressives: Environmentalists, Engineers, and Air Quality in America, 1881–1951*. Baltimore: Johns Hopkins University Press, 1999.

Studdert, D. M., M. M. Mello, and T. A. Brennan. "Medical Malpractice." *New England Journal of Medicine* 350 (2004): 283–92.

Thurm, Richard H. *For the Relief of the Sick and Disabled: The U.S. Public Health Service at Boston, 1799–1969*. Washington, DC: Government Printing Office, 1972.

Twiss, John Russell. "Medical Practice in Colonial America." *Bulletin of the New York Academy of Medicine* 36, no. 8 (August 1960): 538–51.

U.S. Department of Health, Education, and Welfare, U.S. Public Health Service. *Health in America, 1776–1976*. Washington, DC: Government Printing Office, 1977.

Warner, John Harley, and Janet A. Tighe, eds. *Major Problems in the History of American Medicine and Public Health*. Boston: Houghton Mifflin, 2001.

Weeks, Lewis E., and Howard J. Berman. *Shapers of American Health Care Policy: An Oral History*. Ann Arbor, MI: Health Administration Press, 1985.

Weisman, Carol S. *Women's Health Care: Activist Traditions and Institutional Change*. Baltimore: Johns Hopkins University Press, 1998.

Weissert, Carol S., and William G. Wiessert. *Governing Health: The Politics of Health Policy*. 3rd ed. Baltimore: Johns Hopkins University Press, 2006.

Illustration Credits

1. Health Care and Medical Practice in the New World, 1600–1800

6 The Granger Collection, NYC — All rights reserved.

2. Health Care and Regulation in Antebellum America, 1800–1860

40 National Library of Medicine
41 (Top) National Library of Medicine
   (Bottom) Library of Congress
45 National Library of Medicine

3. The Professionalization of American Medicine, 1860–1890

85 National Library of Medicine
86 Library of Congress
87 National Library of Medicine
88 National Library of Medicine

4. Health Care in the Progressive Era, 1890–1920

134 Library of Congress
135 Library of Congress
136 Library of Congress
138 National Library of Medicine

5. The Struggle Over Health Insurance between the Wars, 1920–1940

229 Library of Congress
231 Library of Congress

6. Partisan Jousting Over Health Care in the Postwar Era, 1940–1960

290 Library of Congress
298 AP Photo/Kaiser Permanente

7. Medicare Changes the Health Care Landscape, 1960–1980

357 AP Photo
364 Lyndon Johnson Library
370 Gerald R. Ford Presidential Library

8. Restraining Health Care Costs in the Age of Reagan, 1980–1990

434 AP Photo/George Widman
445 Getty Images

446 Centers for Disease Control
448 AP Photo

9. The Clinton Health Plan and Scorched-Earth Politics, 1990–2000

526 AP Photo/Doug Mills
536 AP Photo/Harry Cabluck

10. Controversial Policy Prescriptions for American Health Care, 2000–2010

608 JIM YOUNG/Reuters /Landov
623 Official White House Photo by Lawrence Jackson
625 Official White House Photo by Pete Souza

Index